INTRODUCTION TO

JAVA®

PROGRAMMING

BRIEF VERSION

Tenth Edition

Y. Daniel Liang

Armstrong Atlantic State University

PEARSON

Boston Columbus Indianapolis New York San Francisco Upper Saddle River
Amsterdam Cape Town Dubai London Madrid Milan Munich Paris Montreal Toronto
Delhi Mexico City São Paulo Sydney Hong Kong Seoul Singapore Taipei Tokyo

To Samantha, Michael, and Michelle

Editorial Director, ECS: Marcia Horton
Executive Editor: Tracy Johnson (Dunkelberger)
Editorial Assistant: Jenah Blitz-Stoehr
Director of Marketing: Christy Lesko
Marketing Manager: Yez Alayan
Marketing Assistant: Jon Bryant
Director of Program Management: Erin Gregg
Program Management-Team Lead: Scott Disanno
Program Manager: Carole Snyder
Project Management-Team Lead: Laura Burgess
Project Manager: Robert Engelhardt

Procurement Specialist: Linda Sager
Cover Designer: Marta Samsel
Permissions Supervisor: Michael Joyce
Permissions Administrator: Jenell Forschler
Director, Image Asset Services: Annie Atherton
Manager, Visual Research: Karen Sanatar
Image Permission Coordinator:
Cover Art: © alexpixel / Getty Images
Media Project Manager: Renata Butera
Full-Service Project Management: Haseen Khan,
    Laserwords Pvt Ltd

Credits and acknowledgments borrowed from other sources and reproduced, with permission, in this textbook appear on the appropriate page within text.

Microsoft® and Windows® are registered trademarks of the Microsoft Corporation in the U.S.A. and other countries. Screen shots and icons reprinted with permission from the Microsoft Corporation. This book is not sponsored or endorsed by or affiliated with the Microsoft Corporation.

Many of the designations by manufacturers and sellers to distinguish their products are claimed as trademarks. Where those designations appear in this book, and the publisher was aware of a trademark claim, the designations have been printed in initial caps or all caps.

Library of Congress Cataloging-in-Publication Data available upon request.

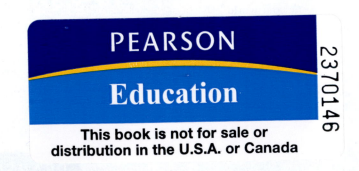

PEARSON

Education

This book is not for sale or distribution in the U.S.A. or Canada

2370146

Prentice Hall
is an imprint of

PEARSON

www.pearsonhighered.com

10 9 8 7 6 5 4 3 2 1

ISBN 10: 0-13-359220-0
ISBN 13: 978-0-13-359220-7

PREFACE

Dear Reader,

Many of you have provided feedback on earlier editions of this book, and your comments and suggestions have greatly improved the book. This edition has been substantially enhanced in presentation, organization, examples, exercises, and supplements. The new edition:

- Replaces Swing with JavaFX. JavaFX is a new framework for developing Java GUI programs. JavaFX greatly simplifies GUI programming and is easier to learn than Swing.

what is new?

- Introduces exception handling, abstract classes, and interfaces before GUI programming to enable the GUI chapters to be skipped completely if the instructor chooses not to cover GUI.

- Covers introductions to objects and strings earlier in Chapter 4 to enable students to use objects and strings to develop interesting programs early.

- Includes many new interesting examples and exercises to stimulate student interests. More than 100 additional programming exercises are provided to instructors only on the Companion Website.

Please visit www.pearsonhighered.com/liang for a complete list of new features as well as correlations to the previous edition.

The book is fundamentals first by introducing basic programming concepts and techniques before designing custom classes. The fundamental concepts and techniques of selection statements, loops, methods, and arrays are the foundation for programming. Building this strong foundation prepares students to learn object-oriented programming and advanced Java programming.

fundamentals-first

This book teaches programming in a problem-driven way that focuses on problem solving rather than syntax. We make introductory programming interesting by using thought-provoking problems in a broad context. The central thread of early chapters is on problem solving. Appropriate syntax and library are introduced to enable readers to write programs for solving the problems. To support the teaching of programming in a problem-driven way, the book provides a wide variety of problems at various levels of difficulty to motivate students. To appeal to students in all majors, the problems cover many application areas, including math, science, business, financial, gaming, animation, and multimedia.

problem-driven

The book is widely used in the introductory programming courses in the universities around the world. The book is a *brief version* of Introduction to Java Programming, *Comprehensive Version*, Tenth Edition. This version is designed for an introductory programming course, commonly known as CS1. It contains the first eighteen chapters in the comprehensive version and covers fundamentals of programming, object-oriented programming, GUI programming, exception handling, I/O, and recursion. The comprehensive version has additional twenty-four chapters that cover data structures, algorithms, concurrency, parallel programming, networking, internationalization, advanced GUI, database, and Web programming. The first thirteen chapters of this book are appropriate for preparing the AP Computer Science exam.

brief version
comprehensive version

AP Computer Science

The best way to teach programming is *by example*, and the only way to learn programming is *by doing*. Basic concepts are explained by example and a large number of exercises with various levels of difficulty are provided for students to practice. For our programming courses, we assign programming exercises after each lecture.

examples and exercises

Our goal is to produce a text that teaches problem solving and programming in a broad context using a wide variety of interesting examples. If you have any comments on and suggestions for improving the book, please email me.

Sincerely,

Y. Daniel Liang
y.daniel.liang@gmail.com
www.cs.armstrong.edu/liang
www.pearsonhighered.com/liang

ACM/IEEE Curricular 2013 and ABET Course Assessment

The new ACM/IEEE Computer Science Curricular 2013 defines the Body of Knowledge organized into 18 Knowledge Areas. To help instructors design the courses based on this book, we provide sample syllabi to identify the Knowledge Areas and Knowledge Units. The sample syllabi are for a three semester course sequence and serve as an example for institutional customization. The sample syllabi are available to instructors at www.pearsonhighered.com/liang.

Many of our users are from the ABET-accredited programs. A key component of the ABET accreditation is to identify the weakness through continuous course assessment against the course outcomes. We provide sample course outcomes for the courses and sample exams for measuring course outcomes on the instructor Website accessible from www.pearsonhighered.com/liang.

What's New in This Edition?

This edition is completely revised in every detail to enhance clarity, presentation, content, examples, and exercises. The major improvements are as follows:

■ Updated to Java 8.

■ Since Swing is replaced by JavaFX, all GUI examples and exercises are revised using JavaFX.

■ Lambda expressions are used to simplify coding in JavaFX and threads.

■ More than 100 additional programming exercises with solutions are provided to the instructor on the Companion Website. These exercises are not printed in the text.

■ Math methods are introduced earlier in Chapter 4 to enable students to write code using math functions.

■ Strings are introduced earlier in Chapter 4 to enable students to use objects and strings to develop interesting programs early.

■ The GUI chapters are moved to after abstract classes and interfaces so that these chapters can be easily skipped if the instructor chooses not to cover GUI.

■ Chapters 4, 14, 15, and 16 are brand new chapters.

Pedagogical Features

The book uses the following elements to help students get the most from the material:

- The **Objectives** at the beginning of each chapter list what students should learn from the chapter. This will help them determine whether they have met the objectives after completing the chapter.

- The **Introduction** opens the discussion with representative problems to give the reader an overview of what to expect from the chapter.

- **Key Points** highlight the important concepts covered in each section.

- **Check Points** provide review questions to help students track their progress as they read through the chapter and evaluate their learning.

- **Problems and Case Studies**, carefully chosen and presented in an easy-to-follow style, teach problem solving and programming concepts. The book uses many small, simple, and stimulating examples to demonstrate important ideas.

- The **Chapter Summary** reviews the important subjects that students should understand and remember. It helps them reinforce the key concepts they have learned in the chapter.

- **Quizzes** are accessible online, grouped by sections, for students to do self-test on programming concepts and techniques.

- **Programming Exercises** are grouped by sections to provide students with opportunities to apply the new skills they have learned on their own. The level of difficulty is rated as easy (no asterisk), moderate (*), hard (**), or challenging (***). The trick of learning programming is practice, practice, and practice. To that end, the book provides a great many exercises. Additionally, more than 100 programming exercises with solutions are provided to the instructors on the Companion Website. These exercises are not printed in the text.

- **Notes**, **Tips**, **Cautions**, and **Design Guides** are inserted throughout the text to offer valuable advice and insight on important aspects of program development.

Note
Provides additional information on the subject and reinforces important concepts.

Tip
Teaches good programming style and practice.

Caution
Helps students steer away from the pitfalls of programming errors.

Design Guide
Provides guidelines for designing programs.

Flexible Chapter Orderings

The book is designed to provide flexible chapter orderings to enable GUI, exception handling, and recursion to be covered earlier or later. The diagram on the next page shows the chapter dependencies.

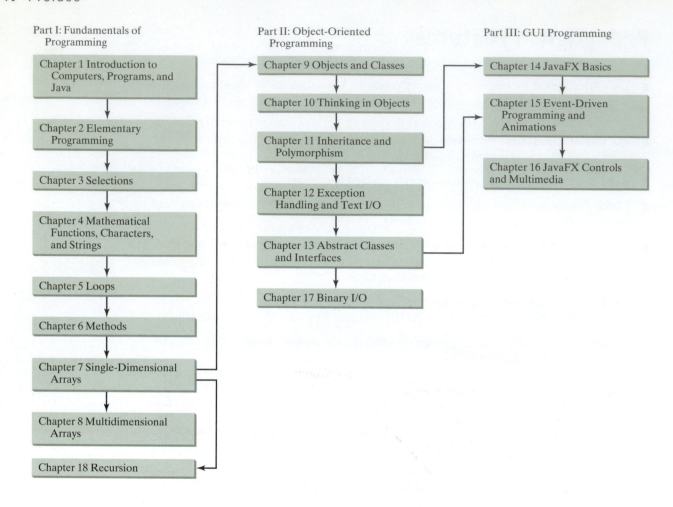

Part I: Fundamentals of Programming

- Chapter 1 Introduction to Computers, Programs, and Java
- Chapter 2 Elementary Programming
- Chapter 3 Selections
- Chapter 4 Mathematical Functions, Characters, and Strings
- Chapter 5 Loops
- Chapter 6 Methods
- Chapter 7 Single-Dimensional Arrays
- Chapter 8 Multidimensional Arrays
- Chapter 18 Recursion

Part II: Object-Oriented Programming

- Chapter 9 Objects and Classes
- Chapter 10 Thinking in Objects
- Chapter 11 Inheritance and Polymorphism
- Chapter 12 Exception Handling and Text I/O
- Chapter 13 Abstract Classes and Interfaces
- Chapter 17 Binary I/O

Part III: GUI Programming

- Chapter 14 JavaFX Basics
- Chapter 15 Event-Driven Programming and Animations
- Chapter 16 JavaFX Controls and Multimedia

Organization of the Book

The chapters in this brief version can be grouped into three parts that, taken together, form a solid introduction to Java programming. Because knowledge is cumulative, the early chapters provide the conceptual basis for understanding programming and guide students through simple examples and exercises; subsequent chapters progressively present Java programming in detail, culminating with the development of comprehensive Java applications. The appendixes contain a mixed bag of topics, including an introduction to number systems, bitwise operations, regular expressions, and enumerated types.

Part I: Fundamentals of Programming (Chapters 1–8, 18)

The first part of the book is a stepping stone, preparing you to embark on the journey of learning Java. You will begin to learn about Java (Chapter 1) and fundamental programming techniques with primitive data types, variables, constants, assignments, expressions, and operators (Chapter 2), selection statements (Chapter 3), mathematical functions, characters, and strings (Chapter 4), loops (Chapter 5), methods (Chapter 6), and arrays (Chapters 7–8). After Chapter 7, you can jump to Chapter 18 to learn how to write recursive methods for solving inherently recursive problems.

Part II: Object-Oriented Programming (Chapters 9–13, and 17)

This part introduces object-oriented programming. Java is an object-oriented programming language that uses abstraction, encapsulation, inheritance, and polymorphism to provide great flexibility, modularity, and reusability in developing software. You will learn programming with objects and classes (Chapters 9–10), class inheritance (Chapter 11), polymorphism

(Chapter 11), exception handling (Chapter 12), abstract classes (Chapter 13), and interfaces (Chapter 13). Text I/O is introduced in Chapter 12 and binary I/O is discussed in Chapter 17.

Part III: GUI Programming (Chapters 14–16)

JavaFX is a new framework for developing Java GUI programs. It is not only useful for developing GUI programs, but also an excellent pedagogical tool for learning object-oriented programming. This part introduces Java GUI programming using JavaFX in Chapters 14–16. Major topics include GUI basics (Chapter 14), container panes (Chapter 14), drawing shapes (Chapter 14), event-driven programming (Chapter 15), animations (Chapter 15), and GUI controls (Chapter 16), and playing audio and video (Chapter 16). You will learn the architecture of JavaFX GUI programming and use the controls, shapes, panes, image, and video to develop useful applications.

Appendixes

This part of the book covers a mixed bag of topics. Appendix A lists Java keywords. Appendix B gives tables of ASCII characters and their associated codes in decimal and in hex. Appendix C shows the operator precedence. Appendix D summarizes Java modifiers and their usage. Appendix E discusses special floating-point values. Appendix F introduces number systems and conversions among binary, decimal, and hex numbers. Finally, Appendix G introduces bitwise operations. Appendix H introduces regular expressions. Appendix I covers enumerated types.

Java Development Tools

You can use a text editor, such as the Windows Notepad or WordPad, to create Java programs and to compile and run the programs from the command window. You can also use a Java development tool, such as NetBeans or Eclipse. These tools support an integrated development environment (IDE) for developing Java programs quickly. Editing, compiling, building, executing, and debugging programs are integrated in one graphical user interface. Using these tools effectively can greatly increase your programming productivity. NetBeans and Eclipse are easy to use if you follow the tutorials. Tutorials on NetBeans and Eclipse can be found under Tutorials on the Student Companion Website at www.pearsonhighered.com/liang.

IDE tutorials

Student Resource Website

The Student Resource Website www.pearsonhighered.com/liang provides access to some of the following resources. Other resources are available using the student access code printed on the inside front cover of this book. (For students with a used copy of this book, you can purchase access to the premium student resources through www.pearsonhighered.com/liang.)

- Answers to review questions
- Solutions to even-numbered programming exercises
- Source code for the examples in the book
- Interactive quiz (organized by sections for each chapter)
- Supplements
- Debugging tips
- Algorithm animations
- Errata

Instructor Resource Website

The Instructor Resource Website, accessible from www.pearsonhighered.com/liang, provides access to the following resources:

- Microsoft PowerPoint slides with interactive buttons to view full-color, syntax-highlighted source code and to run programs without leaving the slides.

- Solutions to all programming exercises. Students will have access to the solutions of even-numbered programming exercises.

- More than 100 additional programming exercises organized by chapters. These exercises are available only to the instructors. Solutions to these exercises are provided.

- Web-based quiz generator. (Instructors can choose chapters to generate quizzes from a large database of more than two thousand questions.)

- Sample exams. Most exams have four parts:

  - Multiple-choice questions or short-answer questions

  - Correct programming errors

  - Trace programs

  - Write programs

- ACM/IEEE Curricula 2013. The new ACM/IEEE Computer Science Curricula 2013 defines the Body of Knowledge organized into 18 Knowledge Areas. To help instructors design the courses based on this book, we provide sample syllabi to identify the Knowledge Areas and Knowledge Units. The sample syllabi are for a three semester course sequence and serve as an example for institutional customization. Instructors can access the syllabi at www.pearsonhighered.com/liang.

- Sample exams with ABET course assessment.

- Projects. In general, each project gives a description and asks students to analyze, design, and implement the project.

Some readers have requested the materials from the Instructor Resource Website. Please understand that these are for instructors only. Such requests will not be answered.

MyProgrammingLab™

Online Practice and Assessment with MyProgrammingLab

MyProgrammingLab helps students fully grasp the logic, semantics, and syntax of programming. Through practice exercises and immediate, personalized feedback, MyProgrammingLab improves the programming competence of beginning students who often struggle with the basic concepts and paradigms of popular high-level programming languages.

A self-study and homework tool, a MyProgrammingLab course consists of hundreds of small practice problems organized around the structure of this textbook. For students, the system automatically detects errors in the logic and syntax of their code submissions and offers targeted hints that enable students to figure out what went wrong—and why. For instructors, a comprehensive gradebook tracks correct and incorrect answers and stores the code inputted by students for review.

MyProgrammingLab is offered to users of this book in partnership with Turing's Craft, the makers of the CodeLab interactive programming exercise system. For a full demonstration, to see feedback from instructors and students, or to get started using MyProgrammingLab in your course, visit www.myprogramminglab.com.

VideoNote

VideoNotes

We are excited about the new VideoNotes feature that is found in this new edition. These videos provide additional help by presenting examples of key topics and showing how to solve problems completely, from design through coding. VideoNotes are available from www.pearsonhighered.com/liang.

Algorithm Animations

Animation

We have provided numerous animations for algorithms. These are valuable pedagogical tools to demonstrate how algorithms work. Algorithm animations can be accessed from the Companion Website.

Acknowledgments

I would like to thank Armstrong Atlantic State University for enabling me to teach what I write and for supporting me in writing what I teach. Teaching is the source of inspiration for continuing to improve the book. I am grateful to the instructors and students who have offered comments, suggestions, bug reports, and praise.

This book has been greatly enhanced thanks to outstanding reviews for this and previous editions. The reviewers are: Elizabeth Adams (James Madison University), Syed Ahmed (North Georgia College and State University), Omar Aldawud (Illinois Institute of Technology), Stefan Andrei (Lamar University), Yang Ang (University of Wollongong, Australia), Kevin Bierre (Rochester Institute of Technology), David Champion (DeVry Institute), James Chegwidden (Tarrant County College), Anup Dargar (University of North Dakota), Charles Dierbach (Towson University), Frank Ducrest (University of Louisiana at Lafayette), Erica Eddy (University of Wisconsin at Parkside), Deena Engel (New York University), Henry A. Etlinger (Rochester Institute of Technology), James Ten Eyck (Marist College), Myers Foreman (Lamar University), Olac Fuentes (University of Texas at El Paso), Edward F. Gehringer (North Carolina State University), Harold Grossman (Clemson University), Barbara Guillot (Louisiana State University), Stuart Hansen (University of Wisconsin, Parkside), Dan Harvey (Southern Oregon University), Ron Hofman (Red River College, Canada), Stephen Hughes (Roanoke College), Vladan Jovanovic (Georgia Southern University), Edwin Kay (Lehigh University), Larry King (University of Texas at Dallas), Nana Kofi (Langara College, Canada), George Koutsogiannakis (Illinois Institute of Technology), Roger Kraft (Purdue University at Calumet), Norman Krumpe (Miami University), Hong Lin (DeVry Institute), Dan Lipsa (Armstrong Atlantic State University), James Madison (Rensselaer Polytechnic Institute), Frank Malinowski (Darton College), Tim Margush (University of Akron), Debbie Masada (Sun Microsystems), Blayne Mayfield (Oklahoma State University), John McGrath (J.P. McGrath Consulting), Hugh McGuire (Grand Valley State), Shyamal Mitra (University of Texas at Austin), Michel Mitri (James Madison University), Kenrick Mock (University of Alaska Anchorage), Frank Murgolo (California State University, Long Beach), Jun Ni (University of Iowa), Benjamin Nystuen (University of Colorado at Colorado Springs), Maureen Opkins (CA State University, Long Beach), Gavin Osborne (University of Saskatchewan), Kevin Parker (Idaho State University), Dale Parson (Kutztown University), Mark Pendergast (Florida Gulf Coast University), Richard Povinelli (Marquette University), Roger Priebe (University of Texas at Austin), Mary Ann Pumphrey (De Anza Junior College), Pat Roth (Southern Polytechnic State University), Amr Sabry (Indiana University), Ben Setzer (Kennesaw State University), Carolyn Schauble (Colorado State University), David Scuse (University of Manitoba), Ashraf Shirani (San Jose State University), Daniel Spiegel (Kutztown University), Joslyn A. Smith (Florida Atlantic University) , Lixin Tao (Pace University), Ronald F. Taylor (Wright State University), Russ Tront (Simon Fraser University), Deborah Trytten (University of Oklahoma), Michael Verdicchio (Citadel), Kent Vidrine (George Washington University), and Bahram Zartoshty (California State University at Northridge).

It is a great pleasure, honor, and privilege to work with Pearson. I would like to thank Tracy Johnson and her colleagues Marcia Horton, Yez Alayan, Carole Snyder, Scott Disanno, Bob Engelhardt, Haseen Khan, and their colleagues for organizing, producing, and promoting this project.

As always, I am indebted to my wife, Samantha, for her love, support, and encouragement.

BRIEF CONTENTS

1 Introduction to Computers, Programs, and Java   1
2 Elementary Programming   33
3 Selections   75
4 Mathematical Functions, Characters, and Strings   119
5 Loops   157
6 Methods   203
7 Single-Dimensional Arrays   245
8 Multidimensional Arrays   287
9 Objects and Classes   321
10 Object-Oriented Thinking   365
11 Inheritance and Polymorphism   409
12 Exception Handling and Text I/O   449
13 Abstract Classes and Interfaces   495
14 JavaFX Basics   535
15 Event-Driven Programming and Animations   585
16 JavaFX UI Controls and Multimedia   629
17 Binary I/O   677
18 Recursion   705

APPENDIXES

A Java Keywords   737
B The ASCII Character Set   740
C Operator Precedence Chart   742
D Java Modifiers   744
E Special Floating-Point Values   746
F Number Systems   747
G Bitwise Operatoirns   751
H Regular Expressions   752
I Enumerated Types   757

INDEX   763

CONTENTS

Chapter 1   **Introduction to Computers, Programs, and Java**   **1**

1.1	Introduction	2
1.2	What Is a Computer?	2
1.3	Programming Languages	7
1.4	Operating Systems	9
1.5	Java, the World Wide Web, and Beyond	10
1.6	The Java Language Specification, API, JDK, and IDE	11
1.7	A Simple Java Program	12
1.8	Creating, Compiling, and Executing a Java Program	15
1.9	Programming Style and Documentation	18
1.10	Programming Errors	20
1.11	Developing Java Programs Using NetBeans	23
1.12	Developing Java Programs Using Eclipse	25

Chapter 2   **Elementary Programming**   **33**

2.1	Introduction	34
2.2	Writing a Simple Program	34
2.3	Reading Input from the Console	37
2.4	Identifiers	39
2.5	Variables	40
2.6	Assignment Statements and Assignment Expressions	41
2.7	Named Constants	43
2.8	Naming Conventions	44
2.9	Numeric Data Types and Operations	44
2.10	Numeric Literals	48
2.11	Evaluating Expressions and Operator Precedence	50
2.12	Case Study: Displaying the Current Time	52
2.13	Augmented Assignment Operators	54
2.14	Increment and Decrement Operators	55
2.15	Numeric Type Conversions	56
2.16	Software Development Process	59
2.17	Case Study: Counting Monetary Units	63
2.18	Common Errors and Pitfalls	65

Chapter 3   **Selections**   **75**

3.1	Introduction	76
3.2	boolean Data Type	76
3.3	if Statements	78
3.4	Two-Way if-else Statements	80
3.5	Nested if and Multi-Way if-else Statements	81
3.6	Common Errors and Pitfalls	83
3.7	Generating Random Numbers	87
3.8	Case Study: Computing Body Mass Index	89
3.9	Case Study: Computing Taxes	90
3.10	Logical Operators	93
3.11	Case Study: Determining Leap Year	97
3.12	Case Study: Lottery	98
3.13	switch Statements	100
3.14	Conditional Expressions	103

xi

3.15 Operator Precedence and Associativity 104
3.16 Debugging 106

Chapter 4 Mathematical Functions, Characters, and Strings 119

4.1 Introduction 120
4.2 Common Mathematical Functions 120
4.3 Character Data Type and Operations 125
4.4 The String Type 130
4.5 Case Studies 139
4.6 Formatting Console Output 145

Chapter 5 Loops 157

5.1 Introduction 158
5.2 The while Loop 158
5.3 The do-while Loop 168
5.4 The for Loop 170
5.5 Which Loop to Use? 174
5.6 Nested Loops 176
5.7 Minimizing Numeric Errors 178
5.8 Case Studies 179
5.9 Keywords break and continue 184
5.10 Case Study: Checking Palindromes 187
5.11 Case Study: Displaying Prime Numbers 188

Chapter 6 Methods 203

6.1 Introduction 204
6.2 Defining a Method 204
6.3 Calling a Method 206
6.4 void Method Example 209
6.5 Passing Arguments by Values 212
6.6 Modularizing Code 215
6.7 Case Study: Converting Hexadecimals to Decimals 217
6.8 Overloading Methods 219
6.9 The Scope of Variables 222
6.10 Case Study: Generating Random Characters 223
6.11 Method Abstraction and Stepwise Refinement 225

Chapter 7 Single-Dimensional Arrays 245

7.1 Introduction 246
7.2 Array Basics 246
7.3 Case Study: Analyzing Numbers 253
7.4 Case Study: Deck of Cards 254
7.5 Copying Arrays 256
7.6 Passing Arrays to Methods 257
7.7 Returning an Array from a Method 260
7.8 Case Study: Counting the Occurrences of Each Letter 261
7.9 Variable-Length Argument Lists 264
7.10 Searching Arrays 265
7.11 Sorting Arrays 269
7.12 The Arrays Class 270
7.13 Command-Line Arguments 272

Chapter 8 Multidimensional Arrays 287

8.1 Introduction 288
8.2 Two-Dimensional Array Basics 288

8.3	Processing Two-Dimensional Arrays	291
8.4	Passing Two-Dimensional Arrays to Methods	293
8.5	Case Study: Grading a Multiple-Choice Test	294
8.6	Case Study: Finding the Closest Pair	296
8.7	Case Study: Sudoku	298
8.8	Multidimensional Arrays	301

Chapter 9 Objects and Classes 321

9.1	Introduction	322
9.2	Defining Classes for Objects	322
9.3	Example: Defining Classes and Creating Objects	324
9.4	Constructing Objects Using Constructors	329
9.5	Accessing Objects via Reference Variables	330
9.6	Using Classes from the Java Library	334
9.7	Static Variables, Constants, and Methods	337
9.8	Visibility Modifiers	342
9.9	Data Field Encapsulation	344
9.10	Passing Objects to Methods	347
9.11	Array of Objects	351
9.12	Immutable Objects and Classes	353
9.13	The Scope of Variables	355
9.14	The this Reference	356

Chapter 10 Object-Oriented Thinking 365

10.1	Introduction	366
10.2	Class Abstraction and Encapsulation	366
10.3	Thinking in Objects	370
10.4	Class Relationships	373
10.5	Case Study: Designing the Course Class	376
10.6	Case Study: Designing a Class for Stacks	378
10.7	Processing Primitive Data Type Values as Objects	380
10.8	Automatic Conversion between Primitive Types and Wrapper Class Types	383
10.9	The BigInteger and BigDecimal Classes	384
10.10	The String Class	386
10.11	The StringBuilder and StringBuffer Classes	392

Chapter 11 Inheritance and Polymorphism 409

11.1	Introduction	410
11.2	Superclasses and Subclasses	410
11.3	Using the super Keyword	416
11.4	Overriding Methods	419
11.5	Overriding vs. Overloading	420
11.6	The Object Class and Its toString() Method	422
11.7	Polymorphism	423
11.8	Dynamic Binding	424
11.9	Casting Objects and the instanceof Operator	427
11.10	The Object's equals Method	431
11.11	The ArrayList Class	432
11.12	Useful Methods for Lists	438
11.13	Case Study: A Custom Stack Class	439
11.14	The protected Data and Methods	440
11.15	Preventing Extending and Overriding	442

Chapter 12 Exception Handling and Text I/O 449

| 12.1 | Introduction | 450 |
| 12.2 | Exception-Handling Overview | 450 |

12.3	Exception Types	455
12.4	More on Exception Handling	458
12.5	The finally Clause	466
12.6	When to Use Exceptions	467
12.7	Rethrowing Exceptions	468
12.8	Chained Exceptions	469
12.9	Defining Custom Exception Classes	470
12.10	The File Class	473
12.11	File Input and Output	476
12.12	Reading Data from the Web	482
12.13	Case Study: Web Crawler	484

Chapter 13   Abstract Classes and Interfaces   495

13.1	Introduction	496
13.2	Abstract Classes	496
13.3	Case Study: the Abstract Number Class	501
13.4	Case Study: Calendar and GregorianCalendar	503
13.5	Interfaces	506
13.6	The Comparable Interface	509
13.7	The Cloneable Interface	513
13.8	Interfaces vs. Abstract Classes	517
13.9	Case Study: The Rational Class	520
13.10	Class Design Guidelines	525

Chapter 14   JavaFX Basics   535

14.1	Introduction	536
14.2	JavaFX vs Swing and AWT	536
14.3	The Basic Structure of a JavaFX Program	536
14.4	Panes, UI Controls, and Shapes	539
14.5	Property Binding	542
14.6	Common Properties and Methods for Nodes	545
14.7	The Color Class	546
14.8	The Font Class	547
14.9	The Image and ImageView Classes	549
14.10	Layout Panes	552
14.11	Shapes	560
14.12	Case Study: The ClockPane Class	572

Chapter 15   Event-Driven Programming and Animations   585

15.1	Introduction	586
15.2	Events and Event Sources	588
15.3	Registering Handlers and Handling Events	589
15.4	Inner Classes	593
15.5	Anonymous Inner Class Handlers	594
15.6	Simplifying Event Handling Using Lambda Expressions	597
15.7	Case Study: Loan Calculator	600
15.8	Mouse Events	602
15.9	Key Events	603
15.10	Listeners for Observable Objects	606
15.11	Animation	608
15.12	Case Study: Bouncing Ball	616

Chapter 16   JavaFX UI Controls and Multimedia   629

16.1	Introduction	630
16.2	Labeled and Label	630

16.3	Button	632
16.4	CheckBox	634
16.5	RadioButton	637
16.6	TextField	639
16.7	TextArea	641
16.8	ComboBox	644
16.9	ListView	647
16.10	ScrollBar	651
16.11	Slider	654
16.12	Case Study: Developing a Tic-Tac-Toe Game	657
16.13	Video and Audio	662
16.14	Case Study: National Flags and Anthems	665

Chapter 17 Binary I/O 677

17.1	Introduction	678
17.2	How Is Text I/O Handled in Java?	678
17.3	Text I/O vs. Binary I/O	679
17.4	Binary I/O Classes	680
17.5	Case Study: Copying Files	691
17.6	Object I/O	692
17.7	Random-Access Files	697

Chapter 18 Recursion 705

18.1	Introduction	706
18.2	Case Study: Computing Factorials	706
18.3	Case Study: Computing Fibonacci Numbers	709
18.4	Problem Solving Using Recursion	712
18.5	Recursive Helper Methods	714
18.6	Case Study: Finding the Directory Size	717
18.7	Case Study: Tower of Hanoi	719
18.8	Case Study: Fractals	722
18.9	Recursion vs. Iteration	726
18.10	Tail Recursion	727

APPENDIXES

Appendix A	Java Keywords	737
Appendix B	The ASCII Character Set	740
Appendix C	Operator Precedence Chart	742
Appendix D	Java Modifiers	744
Appendix E	Special Floating-Point Values	746
Appendix F	Number Systems	747
Appendix G	Bitwise Operations	751
Appendix H	Regular Expressions	752
Appendix I	Enumerated Types	757

INDEX 763

VideoNotes

Locations of **VideoNotes**

http://www.pearsonhighered.com/liang

VideoNote

Chapter 1	Introduction to Computers, Programs, and Java	1
	Your first Java program	12
	Compile and run a Java program	17
	NetBeans brief tutorial	23
	Eclipse brief tutorial	25

Chapter 2	Elementary Programming	33
	Obtain input	37
	Use operators / and %	52
	Software development process	59
	Compute loan payments	60
	Compute BMI	72

Chapter 3	Selections	75
	Program addition quiz	77
	Program subtraction quiz	87
	Use multi-way if-else statements	90
	Sort three integers	110
	Check point location	112

Chapter 4	Mathematical Functions, Characters, and Strings	119
	Introduce math functions	120
	Introduce strings and objects	130
	Convert hex to decimal	143
	Compute great circle distance	151
	Convert hex to binary	153

Chapter 5	Loops	157
	Guess a number	161
	Multiple subtraction quiz	164
	Minimize numeric errors	178
	Display loan schedule	194
	Sum a series	195

Chapter 6	Methods	203
	Define/invoke max method	206
	Use void method	209
	Modularize code	215
	Stepwise refinement	225
	Reverse an integer	234
	Estimate π	237

Chapter 7	Single-Dimensional Arrays	245
	Random shuffling	250
	Deck of cards	254
	Selection sort	269

	Command-line arguments	272
	Coupon collector's problem	281
	Consecutive four	283

Chapter 8	Multidimensional Arrays	287
	Find the row with the largest sum	292
	Grade multiple-choice test	294
	Sudoku	298
	Multiply two matrices	307
	Even number of 1s	314

Chapter 9	Objects and Classes	321
	Define classes and objects	322
	Use classes	334
	Static vs. instance	337
	Data field encapsulation	344
	The Fan class	362

Chapter 10	Object-Oriented Thinking	365
	The Loan class	367
	The BMI class	370
	The StackOfIntegers class	378
	Process large numbers	384
	The String class	386
	The MyPoint class	400

Chapter 11	Inheritance and Polymorphism	409
	Geometric class hierarchy	410
	Polymorphism and dynamic binding demo	424
	The ArrayList class	432
	The MyStack class	439
	New Account class	446

Chapter 12	Exception Handling and Text I/O	449
	Exception-handling advantages	450
	Create custom exception classes	470
	Write and read data	476
	HexFormatException	489

Chapter 13	Abstract Classes and Interfaces	495
	Abstract GeometricObject class	496
	Calendar and GregorianCalendar classes	503
	The concept of interface	506
	Redesign the Rectangle class	530

Chapter 14	JavaFX Basics	535
	Understand property binding	542
	Use Image and ImageView	549
	Use layout panes	552

Use shapes   560
Display a tictactoe board   578
Display a bar chart   580

Chapter 15 **Event-Driven Programming
            and Animations**   **585**
Handler and its registration   592
Anonymous handler   595
Move message using the mouse   602
Animate a rising flag   608
Flashing text   614
Simple calculator   621
Check mouse point location   622
Display a running fan   625

Chapter 16 **JavaFX UI Controls and Multimedia** **629**
Use ListView   647
Use Slider   654

TicTacToe   657
Use Media, MediaPlayer, and MediaView   662
Audio and image   666
Use radio buttons and text fields   669
Set fonts   671

Chapter 17 **Binary I/O**   **677**
Copy file   691
Object I/O   693
Split a large file   702

Chapter 18 **Recursion**   **705**
Binary search   716
Directory size   717
Fractal (Sierpinski triangle)   722
Search a string in a directory   733
Recursive tree   736

INTRODUCTION TO COMPUTERS, PROGRAMS, AND JAVA

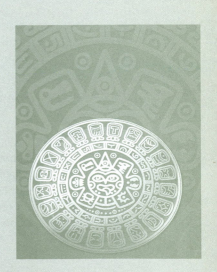

Objectives

- To understand computer basics, programs, and operating systems (§§1.2–1.4).

- To describe the relationship between Java and the World Wide Web (§1.5).

- To understand the meaning of Java language specification, API, JDK, and IDE (§1.6).

- To write a simple Java program (§1.7).

- To display output on the console (§1.7).

- To explain the basic syntax of a Java program (§1.7).

- To create, compile, and run Java programs (§1.8).

- To use sound Java programming style and document programs properly (§1.9).

- To explain the differences between syntax errors, runtime errors, and logic errors (§1.10).

- To develop Java programs using NetBeans (§1.11).

- To develop Java programs using Eclipse (§1.12).

1.1 Introduction

The central theme of this book is to learn how to solve problems by writing a program.

what is programming?
programming
program

This book is about programming. So, what is programming? The term *programming* means to create (or develop) software, which is also called a *program*. In basic terms, software contains the instructions that tell a computer—or a computerized device—what to do.

Software is all around you, even in devices that you might not think would need it. Of course, you expect to find and use software on a personal computer, but software also plays a role in running airplanes, cars, cell phones, and even toasters. On a personal computer, you use word processors to write documents, Web browsers to explore the Internet, and e-mail programs to send and receive messages. These programs are all examples of software. Software developers create software with the help of powerful tools called *programming languages.*

This book teaches you how to create programs by using the Java programming language. There are many programming languages, some of which are decades old. Each language was invented for a specific purpose—to build on the strengths of a previous language, for example, or to give the programmer a new and unique set of tools. Knowing that there are so many programming languages available, it would be natural for you to wonder which one is best. But, in truth, there is no "best" language. Each one has its own strengths and weaknesses. Experienced programmers know that one language might work well in some situations, whereas a different language may be more appropriate in other situations. For this reason, seasoned programmers try to master as many different programming languages as they can, giving them access to a vast arsenal of software-development tools.

If you learn to program using one language, you should find it easy to pick up other languages. The key is to learn how to solve problems using a programming approach. That is the main theme of this book.

You are about to begin an exciting journey: learning how to program. At the outset, it is helpful to review computer basics, programs, and operating systems. If you are already familiar with such terms as CPU, memory, disks, operating systems, and programming languages, you may skip Sections 1.2–1.4.

1.2 What Is a Computer?

A computer is an electronic device that stores and processes data.

hardware
software

A computer includes both *hardware* and *software.* In general, hardware comprises the visible, physical elements of the computer, and software provides the invisible instructions that control the hardware and make it perform specific tasks. Knowing computer hardware isn't essential to learning a programming language, but it can help you better understand the effects that a program's instructions have on the computer and its components. This section introduces computer hardware components and their functions.

A computer consists of the following major hardware components (Figure 1.1):

- A central processing unit (CPU)

- Memory (main memory)

- Storage devices (such as disks and CDs)

- Input devices (such as the mouse and keyboard)

- Output devices (such as monitors and printers)

- Communication devices (such as modems and network interface cards)

bus

A computer's components are interconnected by a subsystem called a *bus.* You can think of a bus as a sort of system of roads running among the computer's components; data and power travel along the bus from one part of the computer to another. In personal computers,

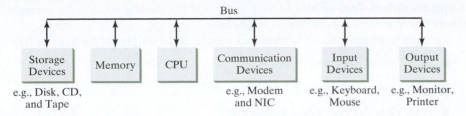

FIGURE 1.1 A computer consists of a CPU, memory, storage devices, input devices, output devices, and communication devices.

the bus is built into the computer's *motherboard*, which is a circuit case that connects all of the parts of a computer together.

motherboard

1.2.1 Central Processing Unit

The *central processing unit (CPU)* is the computer's brain. It retrieves instructions from memory and executes them. The CPU usually has two components: a *control unit* and an *arithmetic/logic unit.* The control unit controls and coordinates the actions of the other components. The arithmetic/logic unit performs numeric operations (addition, subtraction, multiplication, division) and logical operations (comparisons).

CPU

Today's CPUs are built on small silicon semiconductor chips that contain millions of tiny electric switches, called *transistors,* for processing information.

Every computer has an internal clock, which emits electronic pulses at a constant rate. These pulses are used to control and synchronize the pace of operations. A higher clock *speed* enables more instructions to be executed in a given period of time. The unit of measurement of clock speed is the *hertz (Hz),* with 1 hertz equaling 1 pulse per second. In the 1990s, computers measured clocked speed in *megahertz (MHz),* but CPU speed has been improving continuously; the clock speed of a computer is now usually stated in *gigahertz (GHz).* Intel's newest processors run at about 3 GHz.

speed

hertz

megahertz

gigahertz

CPUs were originally developed with only one core. The *core* is the part of the processor that performs the reading and executing of instructions. In order to increase CPU processing power, chip manufacturers are now producing CPUs that contain multiple cores. A multicore CPU is a single component with two or more independent cores. Today's consumer computers typically have two, three, and even four separate cores. Soon, CPUs with dozens or even hundreds of cores will be affordable.

core

1.2.2 Bits and Bytes

Before we discuss memory, let's look at how information (data and programs) are stored in a computer.

A computer is really nothing more than a series of switches. Each switch exists in two states: on or off. Storing information in a computer is simply a matter of setting a sequence of switches on or off. If the switch is on, its value is 1. If the switch is off, its value is 0. These 0s and 1s are interpreted as digits in the binary number system and are called *bits* (binary digits).

bits

The minimum storage unit in a computer is a *byte.* A byte is composed of eight bits. A small number such as 3 can be stored as a single byte. To store a number that cannot fit into a single byte, the computer uses several bytes.

byte

Data of various kinds, such as numbers and characters, are encoded as a series of bytes. As a programmer, you don't need to worry about the encoding and decoding of data, which the computer system performs automatically, based on the encoding scheme. An *encoding scheme* is a set of rules that govern how a computer translates characters, numbers, and symbols into data the computer can actually work with. Most schemes translate each character

encoding scheme

into a predetermined string of bits. In the popular ASCII encoding scheme, for example, the character **C** is represented as **01000011** in one byte.

A computer's storage capacity is measured in bytes and multiples of the byte, as follows:

kilobyte (KB)

- A *kilobyte (KB)* is about 1,000 bytes.

megabyte (MB)

- A *megabyte (MB)* is about 1 million bytes.

gigabyte (GB)

- A *gigabyte (GB)* is about 1 billion bytes.

terabyte (TB)

- A *terabyte (TB)* is about 1 trillion bytes.

A typical one-page word document might take 20 KB. Therefore, 1 MB can store 50 pages of documents and 1 GB can store 50,000 pages of documents. A typical two-hour high-resolution movie might take 8 GB, so it would require 160 GB to store 20 movies.

1.2.3   Memory

memory

A computer's *memory* consists of an ordered sequence of bytes for storing programs as well as data that the program is working with. You can think of memory as the computer's work area for executing a program. A program and its data must be moved into the computer's memory before they can be executed by the CPU.

unique address

Every byte in the memory has a *unique address*, as shown in Figure 1.2. The address is used to locate the byte for storing and retrieving the data. Since the bytes in the memory can

RAM

be accessed in any order, the memory is also referred to as *random-access memory (RAM)*.

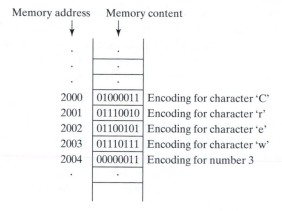

FIGURE 1.2   Memory stores data and program instructions in uniquely addressed memory locations.

Today's personal computers usually have at least 4 gigabyte of RAM, but they more commonly have 6 to 8 GB installed. Generally speaking, the more RAM a computer has, the faster it can operate, but there are limits to this simple rule of thumb.

A memory byte is never empty, but its initial content may be meaningless to your program. The current content of a memory byte is lost whenever new information is placed in it.

Like the CPU, memory is built on silicon semiconductor chips that have millions of transistors embedded on their surface. Compared to CPU chips, memory chips are less complicated, slower, and less expensive.

1.2.4   Storage Devices

A computer's memory (RAM) is a volatile form of data storage: any information that has been stored in memory (i.e., saved) is lost when the system's power is turned off. Programs

storage devices

and data are permanently stored on *storage devices* and are moved, when the computer actually uses them, to memory, which operates at much faster speeds than permanent storage devices can.

There are three main types of storage devices:

- Magnetic disk drives

- Optical disc drives (CD and DVD)

- USB flash drives

Drives are devices for operating a medium, such as disks and CDs. A storage medium physically stores data and program instructions. The drive reads data from the medium and writes data onto the medium.

drive

Disks

A computer usually has at least one hard disk drive. *Hard disks* are used for permanently storing data and programs. Newer computers have hard disks that can store from 500 gigabytes to 1 terabytes of data. Hard disk drives are usually encased inside the computer, but removable hard disks are also available.

hard disk

CDs and DVDs

CD stands for compact disc. There are two types of CD drives: CD-R and CD-RW. A *CD-R* is for read-only permanent storage; the user cannot modify its contents once they are recorded. A *CD-RW* can be used like a hard disk; that is, you can write data onto the disc, and then overwrite that data with new data. A single CD can hold up to 700 MB. Most new PCs are equipped with a CD-RW drive that can work with both CD-R and CD-RW discs.

CD-R

CD-RW

DVD stands for digital versatile disc or digital video disc. DVDs and CDs look alike, and you can use either to store data. A DVD can hold more information than a CD; a standard DVD's storage capacity is 4.7 GB. Like CDs, there are two types of DVDs: DVD-R (read-only) and DVD-RW (rewritable).

DVD

USB Flash Drives

Universal serial bus (USB) connectors allow the user to attach many kinds of peripheral devices to the computer. You can use a USB to connect a printer, digital camera, mouse, external hard disk drive, and other devices to the computer.

A USB *flash drive* is a device for storing and transporting data. A flash drive is small— about the size of a pack of gum. It acts like a portable hard drive that can be plugged into your computer's USB port. USB flash drives are currently available with up to 256 GB storage capacity.

1.2.5 Input and Output Devices

Input and output devices let the user communicate with the computer. The most common input devices are *keyboards* and *mice*. The most common output devices are *monitors* and *printers*.

The Keyboard

A keyboard is a device for entering input. Compact keyboards are available without a numeric keypad.

Function keys are located across the top of the keyboard and are prefaced with the letter *F*. Their functions depend on the software currently being used.

function key

A *modifier key* is a special key (such as the *Shift*, *Alt*, and *Ctrl* keys) that modifies the normal action of another key when the two are pressed simultaneously.

modifier key

The *numeric keypad*, located on the right side of most keyboards, is a separate set of keys styled like a calculator to use for entering numbers quickly.

numeric keypad

Arrow keys, located between the main keypad and the numeric keypad, are used to move the mouse pointer up, down, left, and right on the screen in many kinds of programs.

arrow keys

Insert key
Delete key
Page Up key
Page Down key

The *Insert*, *Delete*, *Page Up*, and *Page Down keys* are used in word processing and other programs for inserting text and objects, deleting text and objects, and moving up or down through a document one screen at a time.

The Mouse

A *mouse* is a pointing device. It is used to move a graphical pointer (usually in the shape of an arrow) called a *cursor* around the screen or to click on-screen objects (such as a button) to trigger them to perform an action.

The Monitor

The *monitor* displays information (text and graphics). The screen resolution and dot pitch determine the quality of the display.

screen resolution

pixels

The *screen resolution* specifies the number of pixels in horizontal and vertical dimensions of the display device. *Pixels* (short for "picture elements") are tiny dots that form an image on the screen. A common resolution for a 17-inch screen, for example, is 1,024 pixels wide and 768 pixels high. The resolution can be set manually. The higher the resolution, the sharper and clearer the image is.

dot pitch

The *dot pitch* is the amount of space between pixels, measured in millimeters. The smaller the dot pitch, the sharper the display.

1.2.6 Communication Devices

Computers can be networked through communication devices, such as a dial-up modem (*mo*dulator/*dem*odulator), a DSL or cable modem, a wired network interface card, or a wireless adapter.

dial-up modem

- A *dial-up modem* uses a phone line and can transfer data at a speed up to 56,000 bps (bits per second).

digital subscriber line (DSL)

- A *digital subscriber line (DSL)* connection also uses a standard phone line, but it can transfer data 20 times faster than a standard dial-up modem.

cable modem

- A *cable modem* uses the cable TV line maintained by the cable company and is generally faster than DSL.

network interface card (NIC)
local area network (LAN)
million bits per second (mbps)

- A *network interface card (NIC)* is a device that connects a computer to a *local area network (LAN)*. LANs are commonly used in universities, businesses, and government agencies. A high-speed NIC called *1000BaseT* can transfer data at 1,000 million bits per second (mbps).

- Wireless networking is now extremely popular in homes, businesses, and schools. Every laptop computer sold today is equipped with a wireless adapter that enables the computer to connect to a local area network and the Internet.

Note
Answers to checkpoint questions are on the Companion Website.

1.1 What are hardware and software?

1.2 List five major hardware components of a computer.

1.3 What does the acronym "CPU" stand for?

1.4 What unit is used to measure CPU speed?

1.5 What is a bit? What is a byte?

1.6 What is memory for? What does RAM stand for? Why is memory called RAM?

1.7 What unit is used to measure memory size?

1.8 What unit is used to measure disk size?

1.9 What is the primary difference between memory and a storage device?

1.3 Programming Languages

Computer programs, known as software, are instructions that tell a computer what to do.

Key Point

Computers do not understand human languages, so programs must be written in a language a computer can use. There are hundreds of programming languages, and they were developed to make the programming process easier for people. However, all programs must be converted into the instructions the computer can execute.

1.3.1 Machine Language

A computer's native language, which differs among different types of computers, is its *machine language*—a set of built-in primitive instructions. These instructions are in the form of binary code, so if you want to give a computer an instruction in its native language, you have to enter the instruction as binary code. For example, to add two numbers, you might have to write an instruction in binary code, like this:

machine language

```
1101101010011010
```

1.3.2 Assembly Language

Programming in machine language is a tedious process. Moreover, programs written in machine language are very difficult to read and modify. For this reason, *assembly language* was created in the early days of computing as an alternative to machine languages. Assembly language uses a short descriptive word, known as a *mnemonic*, to represent each of the machine-language instructions. For example, the mnemonic **add** typically means to add numbers and **sub** means to subtract numbers. To add the numbers **2** and **3** and get the result, you might write an instruction in assembly code like this:

assembly language

```
add 2, 3, result
```

Assembly languages were developed to make programming easier. However, because the computer cannot execute assembly language, another program—called an *assembler*—is used to translate assembly-language programs into machine code, as shown in Figure 1.3.

assembler

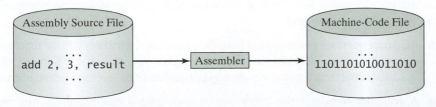

FIGURE 1.3 An assembler translates assembly-language instructions into machine code.

Writing code in assembly language is easier than in machine language. However, it is still tedious to write code in assembly language. An instruction in assembly language essentially corresponds to an instruction in machine code. Writing in assembly requires that you know how the CPU works. Assembly language is referred to as a *low-level language*, because assembly language is close in nature to machine language and is machine dependent.

low-level language

1.3.3   High-Level Language

high-level language

In the 1950s, a new generation of programming languages known as *high-level languages* emerged. They are platform independent, which means that you can write a program in a high-level language and run it in different types of machines. High-level languages are English-like and easy to learn and use. The instructions in a high-level programming language are called

statement

statements. Here, for example, is a high-level language statement that computes the area of a circle with a radius of **5**:

```
area = 5 * 5 * 3.14159;
```

There are many high-level programming languages, and each was designed for a specific purpose. Table 1.1 lists some popular ones.

TABLE I.I   Popular High-Level Programming Languages

Language	Description
Ada	Named for Ada Lovelace, who worked on mechanical general-purpose computers. The Ada language was developed for the Department of Defense and is used mainly in defense projects.
BASIC	Beginner's All-purpose Symbolic Instruction Code. It was designed to be learned and used easily by beginners.
C	Developed at Bell Laboratories. C combines the power of an assembly language with the ease of use and portability of a high-level language.
C++	C++ is an object-oriented language, based on C.
C#	Pronounced "C Sharp." It is a hybrid of Java and C++ and was developed by Microsoft.
COBOL	COmmon Business Oriented Language. Used for business applications.
FORTRAN	FORmula TRANslation. Popular for scientific and mathematical applications.
Java	Developed by Sun Microsystems, now part of Oracle. It is widely used for developing platform-independent Internet applications.
Pascal	Named for Blaise Pascal, who pioneered calculating machines in the seventeenth century. It is a simple, structured, general-purpose language primarily for teaching programming.
Python	A simple general-purpose scripting language good for writing short programs.
Visual Basic	Visual Basic was developed by Microsoft and it enables the programmers to rapidly develop graphical user interfaces.

source program
source code
interpreter
compiler

A program written in a high-level language is called a *source program* or *source code*. Because a computer cannot execute a source program, a source program must be translated into machine code for execution. The translation can be done using another programming tool called an *interpreter* or a *compiler*.

■ An interpreter reads one statement from the source code, translates it to the machine code or virtual machine code, and then executes it right away, as shown in Figure 1.4a. Note that a statement from the source code may be translated into several machine instructions.

■ A compiler translates the entire source code into a machine-code file, and the machine-code file is then executed, as shown in Figure 1.4b.

Check Point

1.10   What language does the CPU understand?

1.11   What is an assembly language?

1.12   What is an assembler?

1.13   What is a high-level programming language?

1.14   What is a source program?

1.15 What is an interpreter?

1.16 What is a compiler?

1.17 What is the difference between an interpreted language and a compiled language?

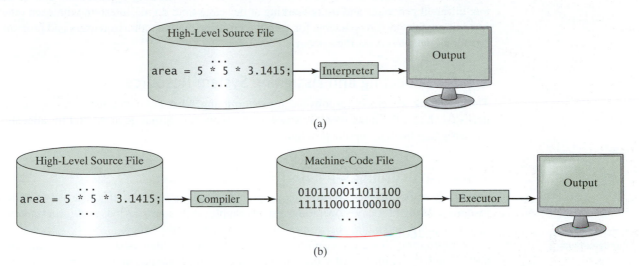

(a)

(b)

FIGURE 1.4 (a) An interpreter translates and executes a program one statement at a time. (b) A compiler translates the entire source program into a machine-language file for execution.

1.4 Operating Systems

The operating system (OS) *is the most important program that runs on a computer. The OS manages and controls a computer's activities.*

Key Point

operating system (OS)

The popular *operating systems* for general-purpose computers are Microsoft Windows, Mac OS, and Linux. Application programs, such as a Web browser or a word processor, cannot run unless an operating system is installed and running on the computer. Figure 1.5 shows the interrelationship of hardware, operating system, application software, and the user.

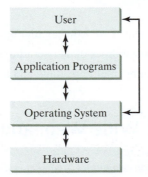

FIGURE 1.5 Users and applications access the computer's hardware via the operating system.

The major tasks of an operating system are as follows:

- Controlling and monitoring system activities

- Allocating and assigning system resources

- Scheduling operations

1.4.1 Controlling and Monitoring System Activities

Operating systems perform basic tasks, such as recognizing input from the keyboard, sending output to the monitor, keeping track of files and folders on storage devices, and controlling peripheral devices, such as disk drives and printers. An operating system must also ensure that different programs and users working at the same time do not interfere with each other. In addition, the OS is responsible for security, ensuring that unauthorized users and programs are not allowed to access the system.

1.4.2 Allocating and Assigning System Resources

The operating system is responsible for determining what computer resources a program needs (such as CPU time, memory space, disks, input and output devices) and for allocating and assigning them to run the program.

1.4.3 Scheduling Operations

The OS is responsible for scheduling programs' activities to make efficient use of system resources. Many of today's operating systems support techniques such as *multiprogramming*, *multithreading*, and *multiprocessing* to increase system performance.

multiprogramming

Multiprogramming allows multiple programs to run simultaneously by sharing the same CPU. The CPU is much faster than the computer's other components. As a result, it is idle most of the time—for example, while waiting for data to be transferred from a disk or waiting for other system resources to respond. A multiprogramming OS takes advantage of this situation by allowing multiple programs to use the CPU when it would otherwise be idle. For example, multiprogramming enables you to use a word processor to edit a file at the same time as your Web browser is downloading a file.

multithreading

Multithreading allows a single program to execute multiple tasks at the same time. For instance, a word-processing program allows users to simultaneously edit text and save it to a disk. In this example, editing and saving are two tasks within the same application. These two tasks may run concurrently.

multiprocessing

Multiprocessing, or *parallel processing*, uses two or more processors together to perform subtasks concurrently and then combine solutions of the subtasks to obtain a solution for the entire task. It is like a surgical operation where several doctors work together on one patient.

1.18 What is an operating system? List some popular operating systems.

1.19 What are the major responsibilities of an operating system?

1.20 What are multiprogramming, multithreading, and multiprocessing?

1.5 Java, the World Wide Web, and Beyond

Java is a powerful and versatile programming language for developing software running on mobile devices, desktop computers, and servers.

This book introduces Java programming. Java was developed by a team led by James Gosling at Sun Microsystems. Sun Microsystems was purchased by Oracle in 2010. Originally called *Oak*, Java was designed in 1991 for use in embedded chips in consumer electronic appliances. In 1995, renamed *Java*, it was redesigned for developing Web applications. For the history of Java, see www.java.com/en/javahistory/index.jsp.

Java has become enormously popular. Its rapid rise and wide acceptance can be traced to its design characteristics, particularly its promise that you can write a program once and run it anywhere. As stated by its designer, Java is *simple*, *object oriented*, *distributed*, *interpreted*, *robust*, *secure*, *architecture neutral*, *portable*, *high performance*, *multi-threaded*, and *dynamic*. For the anatomy of Java characteristics, see www.cs.armstrong.edu/liang/JavaCharacteristics.pdf.

Java is a full-featured, general-purpose programming language that can be used to develop robust mission-critical applications. Today, it is employed not only for Web programming but also for developing standalone applications across platforms on servers, desktop computers, and mobile devices. It was used to develop the code to communicate with and control the robotic rover on Mars. Many companies that once considered Java to be more hype than substance are now using it to create distributed applications accessed by customers and partners across the Internet. For every new project being developed today, companies are asking how they can use Java to make their work easier.

The World Wide Web is an electronic information repository that can be accessed on the Internet from anywhere in the world. The Internet, the Web's infrastructure, has been around for more than forty years. The colorful World Wide Web and sophisticated Web browsers are the major reason for the Internet's popularity.

Java initially became attractive because Java programs can be run from a Web browser. Such programs are called *applets*. Applets employ a modern graphical interface with buttons, text fields, text areas, radio buttons, and so on, to interact with users on the Web and process their requests. Applets make the Web responsive, interactive, and fun to use. Applets are embedded in an HTML file. *HTML (Hypertext Markup Language)* is a simple scripting language for laying out documents, linking documents on the Internet, and bringing images, sound, and video alive on the Web. Today, you can use Java to develop rich Internet applications. A rich Internet application (RIA) is a Web application designed to deliver the same features and functions normally associated with deskop applications.

Java is now very popular for developing applications on Web servers. These applications process data, perform computations, and generate dynamic Web pages. Many commercial Websites are developed using Java on the backend.

Java is a versatile programming language: you can use it to develop applications for desktop computers, servers, and small handheld devices. The software for Android cell phones is developed using Java.

1.21 Who invented Java? Which company owns Java now?

1.22 What is a Java applet?

1.23 What programming language does Android use?

1.6 The Java Language Specification, API, JDK, and IDE

Java syntax is defined in the Java language specification, and the Java library is defined in the Java API. The JDK is the software for developing and running Java programs. An IDE is an integrated development environment for rapidly developing programs.

Computer languages have strict rules of usage. If you do not follow the rules when writing a program, the computer will not be able to understand it. The Java language specification and the Java API define the Java standards.

The *Java language specification* is a technical definition of the Java programming language's syntax and semantics. You can find the complete Java language specification at http://docs.oracle.com/javase/specs/.

Java language specification

The *application program interface (API)*, also known as *library*, contains predefined classes and interfaces for developing Java programs. The API is still expanding. You can view and download the latest version of the Java API at http://download.java.net/jdk8/docs/api/.

API
library

Java is a full-fledged and powerful language that can be used in many ways. It comes in three editions:

Java SE, EE, and ME

- Java *Standard Edition (Java SE)* to develop client-side applications. The applications can run standalone or as applets running from a Web browser.

- *Java Enterprise Edition (Java EE)* to develop server-side applications, such as Java servlets, JavaServer Pages (JSP), and JavaServer Faces (JSF).

- *Java Micro Edition (Java ME)* to develop applications for mobile devices, such as cell phones.

This book uses Java SE to introduce Java programming. Java SE is the foundation upon which all other Java technology is based. There are many versions of Java SE. The latest, Java SE 8, is used in this book. Oracle releases each version with a *Java Development Toolkit (JDK)*. For Java SE 8, the Java Development Toolkit is called *JDK 1.8* (also known as *Java 8* or *JDK 8*).

Java Development
Toolkit (JDK)

JDK 1.8 = JDK 8

Integrated development
environment

The JDK consists of a set of separate programs, each invoked from a command line, for developing and testing Java programs. Instead of using the JDK, you can use a Java development tool (e.g., NetBeans, Eclipse, and TextPad)—software that provides an *integrated development environment (IDE)* for developing Java programs quickly. Editing, compiling, building, debugging, and online help are integrated in one graphical user interface. You simply enter source code in one window or open an existing file in a window, and then click a button or menu item or press a function key to compile and run the program.

Check Point

1.24 What is the Java language specification?

1.25 What does JDK stand for?

1.26 What does IDE stand for?

1.27 Are tools like NetBeans and Eclipse different languages from Java, or are they dialects or extensions of Java?

1.7 A Simple Java Program

Key Point

A Java program is executed from the **main** *method in the class.*

what is a console?
console input
console output

Let's begin with a simple Java program that displays the message **Welcome to Java!** on the console. (The word *console* is an old computer term that refers to the text entry and display device of a computer. *Console input* means to receive input from the keyboard, and *console output* means to display output on the monitor.) The program is shown in Listing 1.1.

LISTING I.I Welcome.java

class
main method
display message

```
1  public class Welcome {
2    public static void main(String[] args) {
3      // Display message Welcome to Java! on the console
4      System.out.println("Welcome to Java!");
5    }
6  }
```

VideoNote
Your first Java program

```
Welcome to Java!
```

line numbers

Note that the line numbers are for reference purposes only; they are not part of the program. So, don't type line numbers in your program.

Line 1 defines a class. Every Java program must have at least one class. Each class has a name. By convention, class names start with an uppercase letter. In this example, the class name is `Welcome`.

class name

Line 2 defines the `main` method. The program is executed from the `main` method. A class may contain several methods. The `main` method is the entry point where the program begins execution.

main method

A method is a construct that contains statements. The `main` method in this program contains the `System.out.println` statement. This statement displays the string `Welcome to Java!` on the console (line 4). *String* is a programming term meaning a sequence of characters. A string must be enclosed in double quotation marks. Every statement in Java ends with a semicolon (`;`), known as the *statement terminator*.

string

statement terminator

Reserved words, or *keywords*, have a specific meaning to the compiler and cannot be used for other purposes in the program. For example, when the compiler sees the word `class`, it understands that the word after `class` is the name for the class. Other reserved words in this program are `public`, `static`, and `void`.

reserved word

keyword

Line 3 is a *comment* that documents what the program is and how it is constructed. Comments help programmers to communicate and understand the program. They are not programming statements and thus are ignored by the compiler. In Java, comments are preceded by two slashes (`//`) on a line, called a *line comment,* or enclosed between `/*` and `*/` on one or several lines, called a *block comment* or *paragraph comment.* When the compiler sees `//`, it ignores all text after `//` on the same line. When it sees `/*`, it scans for the next `*/` and ignores any text between `/*` and `*/`. Here are examples of comments:

comment

line comment

block comment

```
// This application program displays Welcome to Java!
/* This application program displays Welcome to Java! */
/* This application program
   displays Welcome to Java! */
```

A pair of curly braces in a program forms a *block* that groups the program's components. In Java, each block begins with an opening brace (`{`) and ends with a closing brace (`}`). Every class has a *class block* that groups the data and methods of the class. Similarly, every method has a *method block* that groups the statements in the method. Blocks can be *nested*, meaning that one block can be placed within another, as shown in the following code.

block

```
public class Welcome {
    public static void main(String[] args) {            Class block
        System.out.println("Welcome to Java!");   Method block
    }
}
```

Tip

An opening brace must be matched by a closing brace. Whenever you type an opening brace, immediately type a closing brace to prevent the missing-brace error. Most Java IDEs automatically insert the closing brace for each opening brace.

match braces

Caution

Java source programs are case sensitive. It would be wrong, for example, to replace `main` in the program with `Main`.

case sensitive

You have seen several special characters (e.g., `{ }, //, ;`) in the program. They are used in almost every program. Table 1.2 summarizes their uses.

special characters

The most common errors you will make as you learn to program will be syntax errors. Like any programming language, Java has its own syntax, and you need to write code that

common errors

TABLE 1.2 Special Characters

Character	Name	Description
{}	Opening and closing braces	Denote a block to enclose statements.
()	Opening and closing parentheses	Used with methods.
[]	Opening and closing brackets	Denote an array.
//	Double slashes	Precede a comment line.
" "	Opening and closing quotation marks	Enclose a string (i.e., sequence of characters).
;	Semicolon	Mark the end of a statement.

syntax rules

conforms to the *syntax rules*. If your program violates a rule—for example, if the semicolon is missing, a brace is missing, a quotation mark is missing, or a word is misspelled—the Java compiler will report syntax errors. Try to compile the program with these errors and see what the compiler reports.

Note

You are probably wondering why the **main** method is defined this way and why **System.out.println(...)** is used to display a message on the console. For the time being, simply accept that this is how things are done. Your questions will be fully answered in subsequent chapters.

The program in Listing 1.1 displays one message. Once you understand the program, it is easy to extend it to display more messages. For example, you can rewrite the program to display three messages, as shown in Listing 1.2.

LISTING 1.2 WelcomeWithThreeMessages.java

class
main method
display message

```
1  public class WelcomeWithThreeMessages {
2    public static void main(String[] args) {
3      System.out.println("Programming is fun!");
4      System.out.println("Fundamentals First");
5      System.out.println("Problem Driven");
6    }
7  }
```

```
Programming is fun!
Fundamentals First
Problem Driven
```

Further, you can perform mathematical computations and display the result on the console. Listing 1.3 gives an example of evaluating $\frac{10.5 + 2 \times 3}{45 - 3.5}$.

LISTING 1.3 ComputeExpression.java

class
main method
compute expression

```
1  public class ComputeExpression {
2    public static void main(String[] args) {
3      System.out.println((10.5 + 2 * 3) / (45 - 3.5));
4    }
5  }
```

```
0.39759036144578314
```

The multiplication operator in Java is *. As you can see, it is a straightforward process to translate an arithmetic expression to a Java expression. We will discuss Java expressions further in Chapter 2.

1.28 What is a keyword? List some Java keywords.

1.29 Is Java case sensitive? What is the case for Java keywords?

1.30 What is a comment? Is the comment ignored by the compiler? How do you denote a comment line and a comment paragraph?

1.31 What is the statement to display a string on the console?

1.32 Show the output of the following code:

```java
public class Test {
  public static void main(String[] args) {
    System.out.println("3.5 * 4 / 2 - 2.5 is ");
    System.out.println(3.5 * 4 / 2 - 2.5);
  }
}
```

1.8 Creating, Compiling, and Executing a Java Program

You save a Java program in a .java file and compile it into a .class file. The .class file is executed by the Java Virtual Machine.

Key Point

You have to create your program and compile it before it can be executed. This process is repetitive, as shown in Figure 1.6. If your program has compile errors, you have to modify the program to fix them, and then recompile it. If your program has runtime errors or does not produce the correct result, you have to modify the program, recompile it, and execute it again.

You can use any text editor or IDE to create and edit a Java source-code file. This section demonstrates how to create, compile, and run Java programs from a command window. Sections 1.10 and 1.11 will introduce developing Java programs using NetBeans and Eclipse. From the command window, you can use a text editor such as Notepad to create the Java source-code file, as shown in Figure 1.7.

command window

Note

The source file must end with the extension .java and must have the same exact name as the public class name. For example, the file for the source code in Listing 1.1 should be named **Welcome.java**, since the public class name is Welcome.

file name Welcome.java,

A Java compiler translates a Java source file into a Java bytecode file. The following command compiles **Welcome.java**:

compile

```
javac Welcome.java
```

Note

You must first install and configure the JDK before you can compile and run programs. See Supplement I.B, Installing and Configuring JDK 8, for how to install the JDK and set up the environment to compile and run Java programs. If you have trouble compiling and running programs, see Supplement I.C, Compiling and Running Java from the Command Window. This supplement also explains how to use basic DOS commands and how to use Windows Notepad to create and edit files. All the supplements are accessible from the Companion Website at www.cs.armstrong.edu/liang/intro10e/supplement.html.

Supplement I.B

Supplement I.C

If there aren't any syntax errors, the *compiler* generates a bytecode file with a .class extension. Thus, the preceding command generates a file named **Welcome.class**, as shown

.class bytecode file

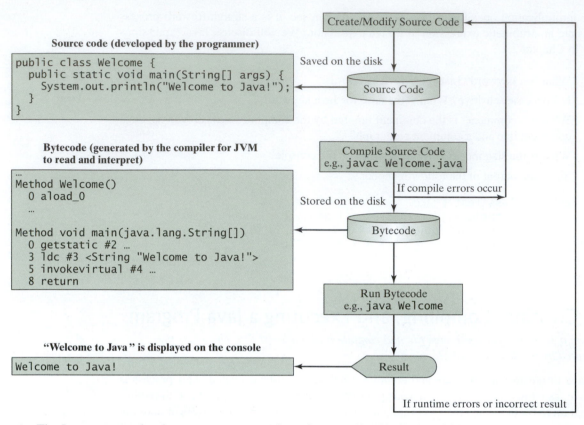

FIGURE 1.6 The Java program-development process consists of repeatedly creating/modifying source code, compiling, and executing programs.

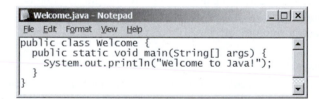

FIGURE 1.7 You can create a Java source file using Windows Notepad.

in Figure 1.8a. The Java language is a high-level language, but Java bytecode is a low-level language. The *bytecode* is similar to machine instructions but is architecture neutral and can run on any platform that has a *Java Virtual Machine (JVM)*, as shown in Figure 1.8b. Rather than a physical machine, the virtual machine is a program that interprets Java bytecode. This is one of Java's primary advantages: *Java bytecode can run on a variety of hardware platforms and operating systems*. Java source code is compiled into Java bytecode and Java bytecode is interpreted by the JVM. Your Java code may use the code in the Java library. The JVM executes your code along with the code in the library.

To execute a Java program is to run the program's bytecode. You can execute the bytecode on any platform with a JVM, which is an interpreter. It translates the individual instructions in the bytecode into the target machine language code one at a time rather than the whole program as a single unit. Each step is executed immediately after it is translated.

The following command runs the bytecode for Listing 1.1:

```
java Welcome
```

bytecode
Java Virtual Machine (JVM)

interpret bytecode

run

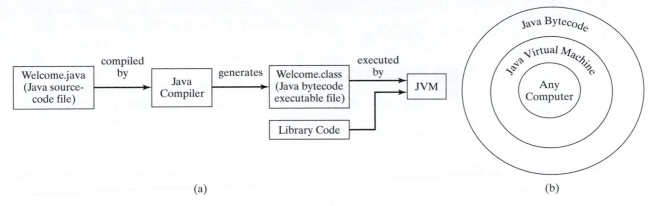

(a)   (b)

FIGURE 1.8 (a) Java source code is translated into bytecode. (b) Java bytecode can be executed on any computer with a Java Virtual Machine.

Figure 1.9 shows the **javac** command for compiling **Welcome.java**. The compiler generates the **Welcome.class** file, and this file is executed using the **java** command.

javac command

java command

Note
For simplicity and consistency, all source-code and class files used in this book are placed under **c:\book** unless specified otherwise.

c:\book

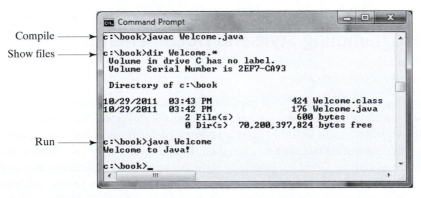

VideoNote
Compile and run a Java program

FIGURE 1.9 The output of Listing 1.1 displays the message "Welcome to Java!"

Caution
Do not use the extension **.class** in the command line when executing the program. Use **java ClassName** to run the program. If you use **java ClassName.class** in the command line, the system will attempt to fetch **ClassName.class.class**.

java ClassName

Tip
If you execute a class file that does not exist, a **NoClassDefFoundError** will occur. If you execute a class file that does not have a **main** method or you mistype the **main** method (e.g., by typing **Main** instead of **main**), a **NoSuchMethodError** will occur.

NoClassDefFoundError

NoSuchMethodError

Note
When executing a Java program, the JVM first loads the bytecode of the class to memory using a program called the *class loader*. If your program uses other classes, the class loader dynamically loads them just before they are needed. After a class is loaded, the JVM uses a program called the *bytecode verifier* to check the validity of the bytecode and

class loader

bytecode verifier

to ensure that the bytecode does not violate Java's security restrictions. Java enforces strict security to make sure that Java class files are not tampered with and do not harm your computer.

Pedagogical Note

use package

Your instructor may require you to use packages for organizing programs. For example, you may place all programs in this chapter in a package named *chapter1*. For instructions on how to use packages, see Supplement I.F, Using Packages to Organize the Classes in the Text.

Check
Point

1.33 What is the Java source filename extension, and what is the Java bytecode filename extension?

1.34 What are the input and output of a Java compiler?

1.35 What is the command to compile a Java program?

1.36 What is the command to run a Java program?

1.37 What is the JVM?

1.38 Can Java run on any machine? What is needed to run Java on a computer?

1.39 If a `NoClassDefFoundError` occurs when you run a program, what is the cause of the error?

1.40 If a `NoSuchMethodError` occurs when you run a program, what is the cause of the error?

1.9 Programming Style and Documentation

Key
Point

Good programming style and proper documentation make a program easy to read and help programmers prevent errors.

programming style

Programming style deals with what programs look like. A program can compile and run properly even if written on only one line, but writing it all on one line would be bad programming style because it would be hard to read. *Documentation* is the body of explanatory remarks and comments pertaining to a program. Programming style and documentation are as important as coding. Good programming style and appropriate documentation reduce the chance of errors and make programs easy to read. This section gives several guidelines. For more detailed guidelines, see Supplement I.D, Java Coding Style Guidelines, on the Companion Website.

documentation

1.9.1 Appropriate Comments and Comment Styles

Include a summary at the beginning of the program that explains what the program does, its key features, and any unique techniques it uses. In a long program, you should also include comments that introduce each major step and explain anything that is difficult to read. It is important to make comments concise so that they do not crowd the program or make it difficult to read.

javadoc comment

In addition to line comments (beginning with `//`) and block comments (beginning with `/*`), Java supports comments of a special type, referred to as *javadoc comments*. javadoc comments begin with `/**` and end with `*/`. They can be extracted into an HTML file using the JDK's `javadoc` command. For more information, see Supplement III.Y, javadoc Comments, on the companion Website.

Use javadoc comments (`/** ... */`) for commenting on an entire class or an entire method. These comments must precede the class or the method header in order to be extracted into a javadoc HTML file. For commenting on steps inside a method, use line comments (`//`).

To see an example of a javadoc HTML file, check out www.cs.armstrong.edu/liang/javadoc/ Exercise1.html. Its corresponding Java code is shown in www.cs.armstrong.edu/liang/javadoc/ Exercise1.java.

1.9.2 Proper Indentation and Spacing

A consistent indentation style makes programs clear and easy to read, debug, and maintain. *Indentation* is used to illustrate the structural relationships between a program's components or statements. Java can read the program even if all of the statements are on the same long line, but humans find it easier to read and maintain code that is aligned properly. Indent each subcomponent or statement at least *two* spaces more than the construct within which it is nested.

indent code

A single space should be added on both sides of a binary operator, as shown in the following statement:

```
System.out.println(3+4*4);          Bad style

System.out.println(3 + 4 * 4);      Good style
```

1.9.3 Block Styles

A *block* is a group of statements surrounded by braces. There are two popular styles, *next-line* style and *end-of-line* style, as shown below.

```
public class Test
{
  public static void main(String[] args)
  {
    System.out.println("Block Styles");
  }
}
```
Next-line style

```
public class Test {
  public static void main(String[] args) {
    System.out.println("Block Styles");
  }
}
```
End-of-line style

The next-line style aligns braces vertically and makes programs easy to read, whereas the end-of-line style saves space and may help avoid some subtle programming errors. Both are acceptable block styles. The choice depends on personal or organizational preference. You should use a block style consistently—mixing styles is not recommended. This book uses the *end-of-line* style to be consistent with the Java API source code.

1.41 Reformat the following program according to the programming style and documentation guidelines. Use the end-of-line brace style.

Check Point

```
public class Test
{
  // Main method
  public static void main(String[] args) {
  /** Display output */
  System.out.println("Welcome to Java");
  }
}
```

1.10 Programming Errors

Key Point

Programming errors can be categorized into three types: syntax errors, runtime errors, and logic errors.

1.10.1 Syntax Errors

syntax errors
compile errors

Errors that are detected by the compiler are called *syntax errors* or *compile errors*. Syntax errors result from errors in code construction, such as mistyping a keyword, omitting some necessary punctuation, or using an opening brace without a corresponding closing brace. These errors are usually easy to detect because the compiler tells you where they are and what caused them. For example, the program in Listing 1.4 has a syntax error, as shown in Figure 1.10.

LISTING 1.4 ShowSyntaxErrors.java

```
1  public class ShowSyntaxErrors {
2    public static main(String[] args) {
3      System.out.println("Welcome to Java);
4    }
5  }
```

Four errors are reported, but the program actually has two errors:

- The keyword **void** is missing before **main** in line 2.

- The string **Welcome to Java** should be closed with a closing quotation mark in line 3.

Since a single error will often display many lines of compile errors, it is a good practice to fix errors from the top line and work downward. Fixing errors that occur earlier in the program may also fix additional errors that occur later.

Compile →

```
c:\book>javac ShowSyntaxErrors.java
ShowSyntaxErrors.java:2: error: invalid method declaration; return type required

  public static main(String[] args) {
                ^
ShowSyntaxErrors.java:3: error: unclosed string literal
    System.out.println("Welcome to Java);
                       ^
ShowSyntaxErrors.java:3: error: ';' expected
    System.out.println("Welcome to Java);
                                        ^
ShowSyntaxErrors.java:5: error: reached end of file while parsing
}
 ^
4 errors

c:\book>
```

FIGURE 1.10 The compiler reports syntax errors.

Tip
If you don't know how to correct it, compare your program closely, character by character, with similar examples in the text. In the first few weeks of this course, you will probably spend a lot of time fixing syntax errors. Soon you will be familiar with Java syntax and can quickly fix syntax errors.

fix syntax errors

1.10.2 Runtime Errors

runtime errors

Runtime errors are errors that cause a program to terminate abnormally. They occur while a program is running if the environment detects an operation that is impossible to carry out. Input mistakes typically cause runtime errors. An *input error* occurs when the program is waiting for the user to enter a value, but the user enters a value that the program cannot handle. For instance, if the program expects to read in a number, but instead the user enters a string, this causes data-type errors to occur in the program.

Another example of runtime errors is division by zero. This happens when the divisor is zero for integer divisions. For instance, the program in Listing 1.5 would cause a runtime error, as shown in Figure 1.11.

LISTING 1.5 ShowRuntimeErrors.java

```
1  public class ShowRuntimeErrors {
2    public static void main(String[] args) {
3      System.out.println(1 / 0);                           runtime error
4    }
5  }
```

Run

FIGURE 1.11   The runtime error causes the program to terminate abnormally.

1.10.3 Logic Errors

Logic errors occur when a program does not perform the way it was intended to. Errors of   logic errors
this kind occur for many different reasons. For example, suppose you wrote the program in
Listing 1.6 to convert Celsius 35 degrees to a Fahrenheit degree:

LISTING 1.6 ShowLogicErrors.java

```
1  public class ShowLogicErrors {
2    public static void main(String[] args) {
3      System.out.println("Celsius 35 is Fahrenheit degree ");
4      System.out.println((9 / 5) * 35 + 32);
5    }
6  }
```

```
Celsius 35 is Fahrenheit degree
67
```

You will get Fahrenheit **67** degrees, which is wrong. It should be **95.0**. In Java, the division for integers is the quotient—the fractional part is truncated—so in Java **9 / 5** is **1**. To get the correct result, you need to use **9.0 / 5**, which results in **1.8**.

In general, syntax errors are easy to find and easy to correct because the compiler gives indications as to where the errors came from and why they are wrong. Runtime errors are not difficult to find, either, since the reasons and locations for the errors are displayed on the console when the program aborts. Finding logic errors, on the other hand, can be very challenging. In the upcoming chapters, you will learn the techniques of tracing programs and finding logic errors.

1.10.4 Common Errors

Missing a closing brace, missing a semicolon, missing quotation marks for strings, and misspelling names are common errors for new programmers.

Common Error 1: Missing Braces

The braces are used to denote a block in the program. Each opening brace must be matched by a closing brace. A common error is missing the closing brace. To avoid this error, type a closing brace whenever an opening brace is typed, as shown in the following example.

```
public class Welcome {

}  ← Type this closing brace right away to match the opening brace
```

If you use an IDE such as NetBeans and Eclipse, the IDE automatically inserts a closing brace for each opening brace typed.

Common Error 2: Missing Semicolons

Each statement ends with a statement terminator (;). Often, a new programmer forgets to place a statement terminator for the last statement in a block, as shown in the following example.

```
public static void main(String[] args) {
    System.out.println("Programming is fun!");
    System.out.println("Fundamentals First");
    System.out.println("Problem Driven")
}
                                      ↑
                        Missing a semicolon
```

Common Error 3: Missing Quotation Marks

A string must be placed inside the quotation marks. Often, a new programmer forgets to place a quotation mark at the end of a string, as shown in the following example.

```
System.out.println("Problem Driven );
                                  ↑
                    Missing a quotation mark
```

If you use an IDE such as NetBeans and Eclipse, the IDE automatically inserts a closing quotation mark for each opening quotation mark typed.

Common Error 4: Misspelling Names

Java is case sensitive. Misspelling names is a common error for new programmers. For example, the word **main** is misspelled as **Main** and **String** is misspelled as **string** in the following code.

```
1  public class Test {
2    public static void Main(string[] args) {
3      System.out.println((10.5 + 2 * 3) / (45 - 3.5));
4    }
5  }
```

Check Point

1.42 What are syntax errors (compile errors), runtime errors, and logic errors?

1.43 Give examples of syntax errors, runtime errors, and logic errors.

1.44 If you forget to put a closing quotation mark on a string, what kind error will be raised?

1.45 If your program needs to read integers, but the user entered strings, an error would occur when running this program. What kind of error is this?

1.46 Suppose you write a program for computing the perimeter of a rectangle and you mistakenly write your program so that it computes the area of a rectangle. What kind of error is this?

1.47 Identify and fix the errors in the following code:

```
1  public class Welcome {
2    public void Main(String[] args) {
3      System.out.println('Welcome to Java!);
4    }
5  }
```

1.11 Developing Java Programs Using NetBeans

You can edit, compile, run, and debug Java Programs using NetBeans.

Key Point

NetBeans and Eclipse are two free popular integrated development environments for developing Java programs. They are easy to learn if you follow simple instructions. We recommend that you use either one for developing Java programs. This section gives the essential instructions to guide new users to create a project, create a class, compile, and run a class in NetBeans. The use of Eclipse will be introduced in the next section. For instructions on downloading and installing latest version of NetBeans, see Supplement II.B.

VideoNote

NetBeans brief tutorial

1.11.1 Creating a Java Project

Before you can create Java programs, you need to first create a project. A project is like a folder to hold Java programs and all supporting files. You need to create a project only once. Here are the steps to create a Java project:

1. Choose *File*, *New Project* to display the New Project dialog box, as shown in Figure 1.12.

2. Select Java in the Categories section and Java Application in the Projects section and click *Next* to display the New Java Application dialog box, as shown in Figure 1.13.

3. Type `demo` in the Project Name field and `c:\michael` in Project Location field. Uncheck *Use Dedicated Folder for Storing Libraries* and uncheck *Create Main Class*.

4. Click *Finish* to create the project, as shown in Figure 1.14.

1.11.2 Creating a Java Class

After a project is created, you can create Java programs in the project using the following steps:

1. Right-click the demo node in the project pane to display a context menu. Choose *New*, *Java Class* to display the New Java Class dialog box, as shown in Figure 1.15.

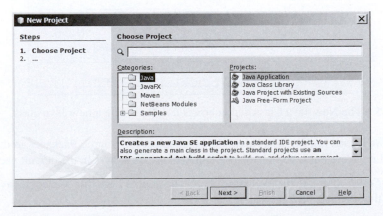

Figure 1.12 The New Project dialog is used to create a new project and specify a project type.

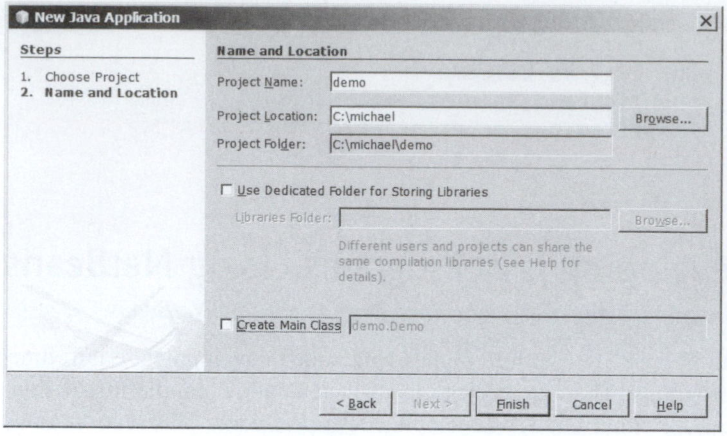

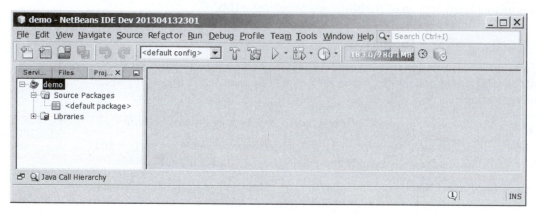

FIGURE 1.13 The New Java Application dialog is for specifying a project name and location.

FIGURE 1.14 A New Java project named demo is created.

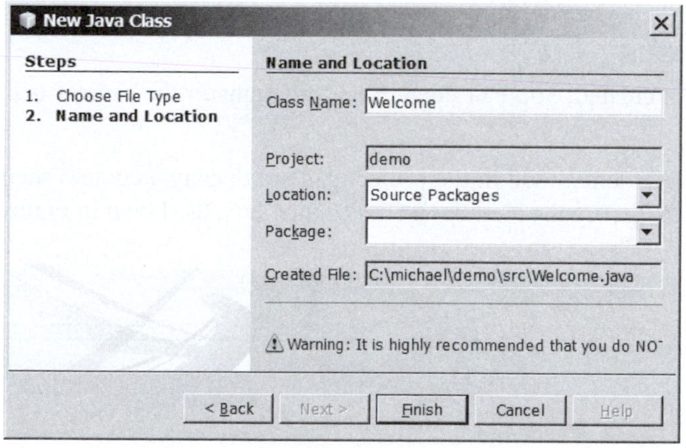

FIGURE 1.15 The New Java Class dialog box is used to create a new Java class.

2. Type `Welcome` in the Class Name field and select the Source Packages in the Location field. Leave the Package field blank. This will create a class in the default package.

3. Click *Finish* to create the Welcome class. The source code file Welcome.java is placed under the <default package> node.

4. Modify the code in the Welcome class to match Listing 1.1 in the text, as shown in Figure 1.16.

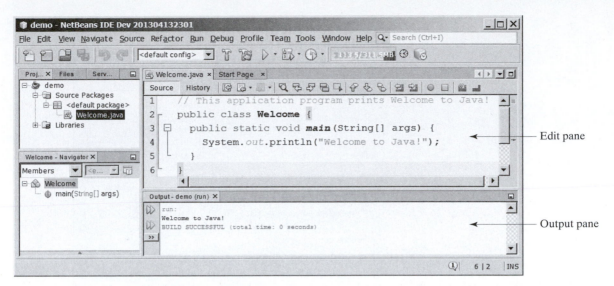

FIGURE 1.16 You can edit a program and run it in NetBeans.

1.11.3 Compiling and Running a Class

To run **Welcome.java**, right-click Welcome.java to display a context menu and choose *Run File*, or simply press Shift + F6. The output is displayed in the Output pane, as shown in Figure 1.16. The *Run File* command automatically compiles the program if the program has been changed.

1.12 Developing Java Programs Using Eclipse

You can edit, compile, run, and debug Java Programs using Eclipse.

Key Point

The preceding section introduced developing Java programs using NetBeans. You can also use Eclipse to develop Java programs. This section gives the essential instructions to guide new users to create a project, create a class, and compile/run a class in Eclipse. For instructions on downloading and installing latest version of Eclipse, see Supplement II.D.

1.12.1 Creating a Java Project

Before creating Java programs in Eclipse, you need to first create a project to hold all files.

VideoNote
Eclipse brief tutorial

Here are the steps to create a Java project in Eclipse:

1. Choose *File*, *New*, *Java Project* to display the New Project wizard, as shown in Figure 1.17.

2. Type **demo** in the Project name field. As you type, the Location field is automatically set by default. You may customize the location for your project.

3. Make sure that you selected the options *Use project folder as root for sources and class files* so that the .java and .class files are in the same folder for easy access.

4. Click *Finish* to create the project, as shown in Figure 1.18.

1.12.2 Creating a Java Class

After a project is created, you can create Java programs in the project using the following steps:

1. Choose *File*, *New*, *Class* to display the New Java Class wizard.

2. Type **Welcome** in the Name field.

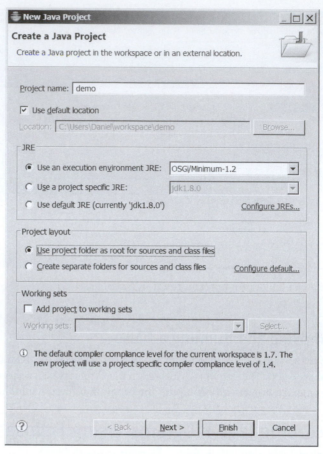

FIGURE 1.17 The New Java Project dialog is for specifying a project name and properties.

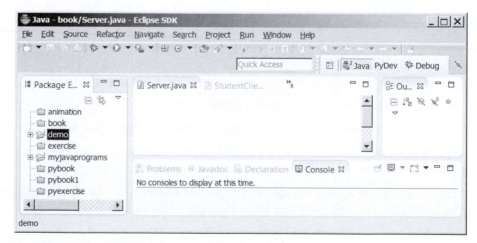

FIGURE 1.18 A New Java project named demo is created.

3. Check the option *public static void main(String[] args)*.

4. Click *Finish* to generate the template for the source code Welcome.java, as shown in Figure 1.19.

FIGURE 1.19 The New Java Class dialog box is used to create a new Java class.

1.12.3 Compiling and Running a Class

To run the program, right-click the class in the project to display a context menu. Choose *Run*, *Java Application* in the context menu to run the class. The output is displayed in the Console pane, as shown in Figure 1.20.

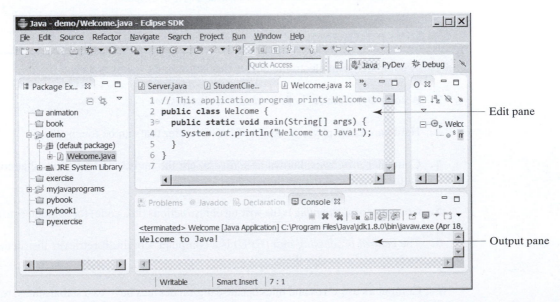

FIGURE 1.20 You can edit a program and run it in Eclipse.

KEY TERMS

Application Program Interface (API)   11
assembler   7
assembly language   7
bit   3
block   13
block comment   13
bus   2
byte   3
bytecode   16
bytecode verifier   17
cable modem   6
central processing unit (CPU)   3
class loader   17
comment   13
compiler   8
console   12
dot pitch   6
DSL (digital subscriber line)   6
encoding scheme   3
hardware   2
high-level language   8
integrated development environment
   (IDE)   12
interpreter   8
java command   17
Java Development Toolkit (JDK)   12
Java language specification   11

Java Virtual Machine (JVM)   16
javac command   17
keyword (or reserved word)   13
library   11
line comment   13
logic error   21
low-level language   7
machine language   7
main method   13
memory   4
modem   00
motherboard   3
network interface card (NIC)   6
operating system (OS)   9
pixel   6
program   2
programming   2
runtime error   20
screen resolution   6
software   2
source code   8
source program   8
statement   8
statement terminator   13
storage devices   4
syntax error   20

Note

The above terms are defined in this chapter. Supplement I.A, Glossary, lists all the key terms and descriptions in the book, organized by chapters.

CHAPTER SUMMARY

1. A computer is an electronic device that stores and processes data.

2. A computer includes both *hardware* and *software*.

3. Hardware is the physical aspect of the computer that can be touched.

4. Computer *programs*, known as *software*, are the invisible instructions that control the hardware and make it perform tasks.

5. Computer *programming* is the writing of instructions (i.e., code) for computers to perform.

6. The *central processing unit (CPU)* is a computer's brain. It retrieves instructions from *memory* and executes them.

7. Computers use zeros and ones because digital devices have two stable states, referred to by convention as zero and one.

8. A *bit* is a binary digit 0 or 1.

9. A *byte* is a sequence of 8 bits.

10. A kilobyte is about 1,000 bytes, a megabyte about 1 million bytes, a gigabyte about 1 billion bytes, and a terabyte about 1,000 gigabytes.

11. Memory stores data and program instructions for the CPU to execute.

12. A memory unit is an ordered sequence of bytes.

13. Memory is volatile, because information is lost when the power is turned off.

14. Programs and data are permanently stored on *storage devices* and are moved to memory when the computer actually uses them.

15. The *machine language* is a set of primitive instructions built into every computer.

16. *Assembly language* is a *low-level programming language* in which a mnemonic is used to represent each machine-language instruction.

17. *High-level languages* are English-like and easy to learn and program.

18. A program written in a high-level language is called a *source program*.

19. A *compiler* is a software program that translates the source program into a *machine-language program*.

20. The *operating system (OS)* is a program that manages and controls a computer's activities.

21. Java is platform independent, meaning that you can write a program once and run it on any computer.

22. Java programs can be embedded in HTML pages and downloaded by Web browsers to bring live animation and interaction to Web clients.

23. The Java source file name must match the public class name in the program. Java source code files must end with the `.java` extension.

24. Every class is compiled into a separate bytecode file that has the same name as the class and ends with the `.class` extension.

25. To compile a Java source-code file from the command line, use the **javac** command.

26. To run a Java class from the command line, use the **java** command.

27. Every Java program is a set of class definitions. The keyword `class` introduces a class definition. The contents of the class are included in a *block*.

28. A block begins with an opening brace ({) and ends with a closing brace (}).

29. Methods are contained in a class. To run a Java program, the program must have a `main` method. The `main` method is the entry point where the program starts when it is executed.

30. Every *statement* in Java ends with a semicolon (;), known as the *statement terminator*.

31. *Reserved words,* or *keywords,* have a specific meaning to the compiler and cannot be used for other purposes in the program.

32. In Java, comments are preceded by two slashes (//) on a line, called a *line comment,* or enclosed between /* and */ on one or several lines, called a *block comment* or *paragraph comment*. Comments are ignored by the compiler.

33. Java source programs are case sensitive.

34. Programming errors can be categorized into three types: *syntax errors*, *runtime errors*, and *logic errors*. Errors reported by a compiler are called syntax errors or *compile errors*. Runtime errors are errors that cause a program to terminate abnormally. Logic errors occur when a program does not perform the way it was intended to.

QUIZ

Answer the quiz for this chapter online at www.cs.armstrong.edu/liang/intro10e/quiz.html.

PROGRAMMING EXERCISES

MyProgrammingLab™

Note
Solutions to even-numbered programming exercises are on the Companion Website. Solutions to all programming exercises are on the Instructor Resource Website. Additional programming exercises with solutions are provided to the instructors on the Instructor Resource Website. The level of difficulty is rated easy (no star), moderate (*), hard (**), or challenging (***).

level of difficulty

1.1 (*Display three messages*) Write a program that displays `Welcome to Java`, `Welcome to Computer Science`, and `Programming is fun`.

1.2 (*Display five messages*) Write a program that displays `Welcome to Java` five times.

*__**1.3**__ (*Display a pattern*) Write a program that displays the following pattern:

```
    J     A     V     V     A
    J    A A    V     V    A A
J   J   AAAAA    V   V    AAAAA
 J J    A     A    V     A     A
```

1.4 (*Print a table*) Write a program that displays the following table:

```
a       a^2     a^3
1       1       1
2       4       8
3       9       27
4       16      64
```

1.5 (*Compute expressions*) Write a program that displays the result of

$$\frac{9.5 \times 4.5 - 2.5 \times 3}{45.5 - 3.5}.$$

1.6 (*Summation of a series*) Write a program that displays the result of

$$1 + 2 + 3 + 4 + 5 + 6 + 7 + 8 + 9.$$

1.7 (*Approximate* π) π can be computed using the following formula:

$$\pi = 4 \times \left(1 - \frac{1}{3} + \frac{1}{5} - \frac{1}{7} + \frac{1}{9} - \frac{1}{11} + \cdots \right)$$

Write a program that displays the result of $4 \times \left(1 - \frac{1}{3} + \frac{1}{5} - \frac{1}{7} + \frac{1}{9} - \frac{1}{11} \right)$
and $4 \times \left(1 - \frac{1}{3} + \frac{1}{5} - \frac{1}{7} + \frac{1}{9} - \frac{1}{11} + \frac{1}{13} \right)$. Use **1.0** instead of **1** in your program.

1.8 (*Area and perimeter of a circle*) Write a program that displays the area and perimeter of a circle that has a radius of **5.5** using the following formula:

$$perimeter = 2 \times radius \times \pi$$
$$area = radius \times radius \times \pi$$

1.9 (*Area and perimeter of a rectangle*) Write a program that displays the area and perimeter of a rectangle with the width of **4.5** and height of **7.9** using the following formula:

$$area = width \times height$$

1.10 (*Average speed in miles*) Assume a runner runs **14** kilometers in **45** minutes and **30** seconds. Write a program that displays the average speed in miles per hour. (Note that **1** mile is **1.6** kilometers.)

*∗**1.11** (*Population projection*) The U.S. Census Bureau projects population based on the following assumptions:

- One birth every 7 seconds
- One death every 13 seconds
- One new immigrant every 45 seconds

Write a program to display the population for each of the next five years. Assume the current population is 312,032,486 and one year has 365 days. *Hint*: In Java, if two integers perform division, the result is an integer. The fractional part is truncated. For example, **5 / 4** is **1** (not **1.25**) and **10 / 4** is **2** (not **2.5**). To get an accurate result with the fractional part, one of the values involved in the division must be a number with a decimal point. For example, **5.0 / 4** is **1.25** and **10 / 4.0** is **2.5**.

1.12 (*Average speed in kilometers*) Assume a runner runs **24** miles in **1** hour, **40** minutes, and **35** seconds. Write a program that displays the average speed in kilometers per hour. (Note that **1** mile is **1.6** kilometers.)

*∗**1.13** (*Algebra: solve 2 × 2 linear equations*) You can use Cramer's rule to solve the following 2 × 2 system of linear equation:

$$\begin{array}{ll} ax + by = e \\ cx + dy = f \end{array} \qquad x = \frac{ed - bf}{ad - bc} \qquad y = \frac{af - ec}{ad - bc}$$

Write a program that solves the following equation and displays the value for x and y:

$$3.4x + 50.2y = 44.5$$
$$2.1x + .55y = 5.9$$

ELEMENTARY PROGRAMMING

Objectives

- To write Java programs to perform simple computations (§2.2).
- To obtain input from the console using the `Scanner` class (§2.3).
- To use identifiers to name variables, constants, methods, and classes (§2.4).
- To use variables to store data (§§2.5–2.6).
- To program with assignment statements and assignment expressions (§2.6).
- To use constants to store permanent data (§2.7).
- To name classes, methods, variables, and constants by following their naming conventions (§2.8).
- To explore Java numeric primitive data types: `byte`, `short`, `int`, `long`, `float`, and `double` (§2.9.1).
- To read a `byte`, `short`, `int`, `long`, `float`, or `double` value from the keyboard (§2.9.2).
- To perform operations using operators +, -, *, /, and % (§2.9.3).
- To perform exponent operations using `Math.pow(a, b)` (§2.9.4).
- To write integer literals, floating-point literals, and literals in scientific notation (§2.10).
- To write and evaluate numeric expressions (§2.11).
- To obtain the current system time using `System.currentTimeMillis()` (§2.12).
- To use augmented assignment operators (§2.13).
- To distinguish between postincrement and preincrement and between postdecrement and predecrement (§2.14).
- To cast the value of one type to another type (§2.15).
- To describe the software development process and apply it to develop the loan payment program (§2.16).
- To write a program that converts a large amount of money into smaller units (§2.17).
- To avoid common errors and pitfalls in elementary programming (§2.18).

2.1 Introduction

Key Point

The focus of this chapter is on learning elementary programming techniques to solve problems.

In Chapter 1 you learned how to create, compile, and run very basic Java programs. Now you will learn how to solve problems by writing programs. Through these problems, you will learn elementary programming using primitive data types, variables, constants, operators, expressions, and input and output.

Suppose, for example, that you need to take out a student loan. Given the loan amount, loan term, and annual interest rate, can you write a program to compute the monthly payment and total payment? This chapter shows you how to write programs like this. Along the way, you learn the basic steps that go into analyzing a problem, designing a solution, and implementing the solution by creating a program.

2.2 Writing a Simple Program

Key Point

Writing a program involves designing a strategy for solving the problem and then using a programming language to implement that strategy.

problem

Let's first consider the simple problem of computing the area of a circle. How do we write a program for solving this problem?

algorithm

Writing a program involves designing algorithms and translating algorithms into programming instructions, or code. An *algorithm* describes how a problem is solved by listing the actions that need to be taken and the order of their execution. Algorithms can help the programmer plan a program before writing it in a programming language. Algorithms can be

pseudocode

described in natural languages or in *pseudocode* (natural language mixed with some programming code). The algorithm for calculating the area of a circle can be described as follows:

1. Read in the circle's radius.

2. Compute the area using the following formula:

$$area = radius \times radius \times \pi$$

3. Display the result.

Tip
It's always good practice to outline your program (or its underlying problem) in the form of an algorithm before you begin coding.

When you *code*—that is, when you write a program—you translate an algorithm into a program. You already know that every Java program begins with a class definition in which the keyword **class** is followed by the class name. Assume that you have chosen **ComputeArea** as the class name. The outline of the program would look like this:

```java
public class ComputeArea {
  // Details to be given later
}
```

As you know, every Java program must have a **main** method where program execution begins. The program is then expanded as follows:

```java
public class ComputeArea {
  public static void main(String[] args) {
    // Step 1: Read in radius

    // Step 2: Compute area
```

```
        // Step 3: Display the area
    }
}
```

The program needs to read the radius entered by the user from the keyboard. This raises two important issues:

- Reading the radius.

- Storing the radius in the program.

Let's address the second issue first. In order to store the radius, the program needs to declare a symbol called a *variable*. A variable represents a value stored in the computer's memory.

Rather than using **x** and **y** as variable names, choose descriptive names: in this case, **radius** for radius, and **area** for area. To let the compiler know what **radius** and **area** are, specify their data types. That is the kind of data stored in a variable, whether integer, real number, or something else. This is known as *declaring variables*. Java provides simple data types for representing integers, real numbers, characters, and Boolean types. These types are known as *primitive data types* or *fundamental types*.

Real numbers (i.e., numbers with a decimal point) are represented using a method known as *floating-point* in computers. So, the real numbers are also called *floating-point numbers*. In Java, you can use the keyword **double** to declare a floating-point variable. Declare **radius** and **area** as **double**. The program can be expanded as follows:

variable

descriptive names

data type
declare variables
primitive data types

floating-point number

```java
public class ComputeArea {
    public static void main(String[] args) {
        double radius;
        double area;

        // Step 1: Read in radius

        // Step 2: Compute area

        // Step 3: Display the area
    }
}
```

The program declares **radius** and **area** as variables. The reserved word **double** indicates that **radius** and **area** are floating-point values stored in the computer.

The first step is to prompt the user to designate the circle's **radius**. You will soon learn how to prompt the user for information. For now, to learn how variables work, you can assign a fixed value to **radius** in the program as you write the code; later, you'll modify the program to prompt the user for this value.

The second step is to compute **area** by assigning the result of the expression **radius * radius * 3.14159** to **area**.

In the final step, the program will display the value of **area** on the console by using the **System.out.println** method.

Listing 2.1 shows the complete program, and a sample run of the program is shown in Figure 2.1.

LISTING 2.1 ComputeArea.java

```java
1  public class ComputeArea {
2    public static void main(String[] args) {
3      double radius; // Declare radius
4      double area; // Declare area
5
6      // Assign a radius
```

```
 7    radius = 20; // radius is now 20
 8
 9    // Compute area
10    area = radius * radius * 3.14159;
11
12    // Display results
13    System.out.println("The area for the circle of radius " +
14       radius + " is " + area);
15  }
16 }
```

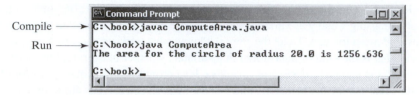

Compile ———►
Run ———►

FIGURE 2.1 The program displays the area of a circle.

declare variable
assign value

Variables such as **radius** and **area** correspond to memory locations. Every variable has a name, a type, a size, and a value. Line 3 declares that **radius** can store a **double** value. The value is not defined until you assign a value. Line 7 assigns **20** into variable **radius**. Similarly, line 4 declares variable **area**, and line 10 assigns a value into **area**. The following table shows the value in the memory for **area** and **radius** as the program is executed. Each row in the table shows the values of variables after the statement in the corresponding line in the program is executed. This method of reviewing how a program works is called *tracing a program*. Tracing programs are helpful for understanding how programs work, and they are useful tools for finding errors in programs.

tracing program

line#	radius	area
3	no value	
4		no value
7	20	
10		1256.636

concatenate strings

concatenate strings with numbers

The plus sign (+) has two meanings: one for addition and the other for concatenating (combining) strings. The plus sign (+) in lines 13–14 is called a *string concatenation operator*. It combines two strings into one. If a string is combined with a number, the number is converted into a string and concatenated with the other string. Therefore, the plus signs (+) in lines 13–14 concatenate strings into a longer string, which is then displayed in the output. Strings and string concatenation will be discussed further in Chapter 4.

Caution
A string cannot cross lines in the source code. Thus, the following statement would result in a compile error:

```
System.out.println("Introduction to Java Programming,
   by Y. Daniel Liang");
```

break a long string

To fix the error, break the string into separate substrings, and use the concatenation operator (+) to combine them:

```
System.out.println("Introduction to Java Programming, " +
   "by Y. Daniel Liang");
```

2.1   Identify and fix the errors in the following code:

Check
Point

```
 1  public class Test {
 2    public void main(string[] args) {
 3      double i = 50.0;
 4      double k = i + 50.0;
 5      double j = k + 1;
 6
 7      System.out.println("j is " + j + " and
 8        k is " + k);
 9    }
10  }
```

2.3 Reading Input from the Console

Reading input from the console enables the program to accept input from the user.

Key
Point

In Listing 2.1, the radius is fixed in the source code. To use a different radius, you have to modify the source code and recompile it. Obviously, this is not convenient, so instead you can use the **Scanner** class for console input.

VideoNote
Obtain input

Java uses **System.out** to refer to the standard output device and **System.in** to the standard input device. By default, the output device is the display monitor and the input device is the keyboard. To perform console output, you simply use the **println** method to display a primitive value or a string to the console. Console input is not directly supported in Java, but you can use the **Scanner** class to create an object to read input from **System.in**, as follows:

```
Scanner input = new Scanner(System.in);
```

The syntax **new Scanner(System.in)** creates an object of the **Scanner** type. The syntax **Scanner input** declares that **input** is a variable whose type is **Scanner**. The whole line **Scanner input = new Scanner(System.in)** creates a **Scanner** object and assigns its reference to the variable **input**. An object may invoke its methods. To invoke a method on an object is to ask the object to perform a task. You can invoke the **nextDouble()** method to read a **double** value as follows:

```
double radius = input.nextDouble();
```

This statement reads a number from the keyboard and assigns the number to **radius**. Listing 2.2 rewrites Listing 2.1 to prompt the user to enter a radius.

LISTING 2.2   ComputeAreaWithConsoleInput.java

```
 1  import java.util.Scanner; // Scanner is in the java.util package
 2
 3  public class ComputeAreaWithConsoleInput {
 4    public static void main(String[] args) {
 5      // Create a Scanner object
 6      Scanner input = new Scanner(System.in);
 7
 8      // Prompt the user to enter a radius
 9      System.out.print("Enter a number for radius: ");
10      double radius = input.nextDouble();
11
12      // Compute area
13      double area = radius * radius * 3.14159;
14
15      // Display results
```

import class

create a Scanner

read a double

```
16       System.out.println("The area for the circle of radius " +
17          radius + " is " + area);
18    }
19  }
```

```
Enter a number for radius:   2.5  ⏎Enter
The area for the circle of radius 2.5 is 19.6349375
```

```
Enter a number for radius:   23  ⏎Enter
The area for the circle of radius 23.0 is 1661.90111
```

prompt

Line 9 displays a string `"Enter a number for radius: "` to the console. This is known as a *prompt*, because it directs the user to enter an input. Your program should always tell the user what to enter when expecting input from the keyboard.

The `print` method in line 9

```
System.out.print("Enter a number for radius: ");
```

print vs. println

is identical to the `println` method except that `println` moves to the beginning of the next line after displaying the string, but `print` does not advance to the next line when completed.

Line 6 creates a `Scanner` object. The statement in line 10 reads input from the keyboard.

```
double radius = input.nextDouble();
```

After the user enters a number and presses the *Enter* key, the program reads the number and assigns it to `radius`.

More details on objects will be introduced in Chapter 9. For the time being, simply accept that this is how to obtain input from the console.

specific import

The `Scanner` class is in the `java.util` package. It is imported in line 1. There are two types of `import` statements: *specific import* and *wildcard import*. The *specific import* specifies a single class in the import statement. For example, the following statement imports `Scanner` from the package `java.util`.

```
import java.util.Scanner;
```

wildcard import

The *wildcard import* imports all the classes in a package by using the asterisk as the wildcard. For example, the following statement imports all the classes from the package `java.util`.

```
import java.uitl.*;
```

no performance difference

The information for the classes in an imported package is not read in at compile time or runtime unless the class is used in the program. The import statement simply tells the compiler where to locate the classes. There is no performance difference between a specific import and a wildcard import declaration.

Listing 2.3 gives an example of reading multiple input from the keyboard. The program reads three numbers and displays their average.

LISTING 2.3 ComputeAverage.java

import class

```
1  import java.util.Scanner; // Scanner is in the java.util package
2
3  public class ComputeAverage {
4    public static void main(String[] args) {
5      // Create a Scanner object
6      Scanner input = new Scanner(System.in);
7
```

create a Scanner

```
 8        // Prompt the user to enter three numbers
 9        System.out.print("Enter three numbers: ");
10        double number1 = input.nextDouble();
11        double number2 = input.nextDouble();
12        double number3 = input.nextDouble();
13
14        // Compute average
15        double average = (number1 + number2 + number3) / 3;
16
17        // Display results
18        System.out.println("The average of " + number1 + " " + number2
19          + " " + number3 + " is " + average);
20      }
21  }
```

read a double

```
Enter three numbers: 1 2 3 [↵Enter]
The average of 1.0 2.0 3.0 is 2.0
```

enter input in one line

```
Enter three numbers: 10.5 [↵Enter]
11 [↵Enter]
11.5 [↵Enter]
The average of 10.5 11.0 11.5 is 11.0
```

enter input in multiple lines

The code for importing the **Scanner** class (line 1) and creating a **Scanner** object (line 6) are the same as in the preceding example as well as in all new programs you will write for reading input from the keyboard.

Line 9 prompts the user to enter three numbers. The numbers are read in lines 10–12. You may enter three numbers separated by spaces, then press the *Enter* key, or enter each number followed by a press of the *Enter* key, as shown in the sample runs of this program.

If you entered an input other than a numeric value, a runtime error would occur. In Chapter 12, you will learn how to handle the exception so that the program can continue to run.

runtime error

> **Note**
> Most of the programs in the early chapters of this book perform three steps—input, process, and output—called *IPO*. Input is receiving input from the user; process is producing results using the input; and output is displaying the results.

IPO

2.2 How do you write a statement to let the user enter a double value from the keyboard? What happens if you entered **5a** when executing the following code?

```
double radius = input.nextDouble();
```

Check Point

2.3 Are there any performance differences between the following two **import** statements?

```
import java.util.Scanner;
import java.util.*;
```

2.4 Identifiers

Identifiers are the names that identify the elements such as classes, methods, and variables in a program.

Key Point

As you see in Listing 2.3, **ComputeAverage**, **main**, **input**, **number1**, **number2**, **number3**, and so on are the names of things that appear in the program. In programming terminology, such names are called *identifiers*. All identifiers must obey the following rules:

identifiers
identifier naming rules

■ An identifier is a sequence of characters that consists of letters, digits, underscores (_), and dollar signs ($).

- An identifier must start with a letter, an underscore (_), or a dollar sign ($). It cannot start with a digit.

- An identifier cannot be a reserved word. (See Appendix A for a list of reserved words.)

- An identifier cannot be **true**, **false**, or **null**.

- An identifier can be of any length.

For example, **$2**, **ComputeArea**, **area**, **radius**, and **print** are legal identifiers, whereas **2A** and **d+4** are not because they do not follow the rules. The Java compiler detects illegal identifiers and reports syntax errors.

case sensitive

Note

Since Java is case sensitive, **area**, **Area**, and **AREA** are all different identifiers.

Tip

descriptive names

Identifiers are for naming variables, methods, classes, and other items in a program. Descriptive identifiers make programs easy to read. Avoid using abbreviations for identifiers. Using complete words is more descriptive. For example, **numberOfStudents** is better than **numStuds**, **numOfStuds**, or **numOfStudents**. We use descriptive names for complete programs in the text. However, we will occasionally use variable names such as **i**, **j**, **k**, **x**, and **y** in the code snippets for brevity. These names also provide a generic tone to the code snippets.

Tip

the $ character

Do not name identifiers with the **$** character. By convention, the **$** character should be used only in mechanically generated source code.

2.4 Which of the following identifiers are valid? Which are Java keywords?

miles, **Test**, **a++**, **--a**, **4#R**, **$4**, **#44**, **apps**

class, **public**, **int**, **x**, **y**, **radius**

2.5 Variables

Variables are used to represent values that may be changed in the program.

why called variables?

As you see from the programs in the preceding sections, variables are used to store values to be used later in a program. They are called variables because their values can be changed. In the program in Listing 2.2, **radius** and **area** are variables of the **double** type. You can assign any numerical value to **radius** and **area**, and the values of **radius** and **area** can be reassigned. For example, in the following code, **radius** is initially **1.0** (line 2) and then changed to **2.0** (line 7), and area is set to **3.14159** (line 3) and then reset to **12.56636** (line 8).

```
1  // Compute the first area
2  radius = 1.0;                                              radius:  1.0
3  area = radius * radius * 3.14159;                            area:  3.14159
4  System.out.println("The area is " + area + " for radius " + radius);
5
6  // Compute the second area
7  radius = 2.0;                                              radius:  2.0
8  area = radius * radius * 3.14159;                            area:  12.56636
9  System.out.println("The area is " + area + " for radius " + radius);
```

Variables are for representing data of a certain type. To use a variable, you declare it by telling the compiler its name as well as what type of data it can store. The *variable declaration* tells the compiler to allocate appropriate memory space for the variable based on its data type. The syntax for declaring a variable is

```
datatype variableName;
```

Here are some examples of variable declarations:

declare variable

```
int count;        // Declare count to be an integer variable
double radius;    // Declare radius to be a double variable
double interestRate; // Declare interestRate to be a double variable
```

These examples use the data types **int** and **double**. Later you will be introduced to additional data types, such as **byte**, **short**, **long**, **float**, **char**, and **boolean**.

If variables are of the same type, they can be declared together, as follows:

```
datatype variable1, variable2, ..., variablen;
```

The variables are separated by commas. For example,

```
int i, j, k; // Declare i, j, and k as int variables
```

Variables often have initial values. You can declare a variable and initialize it in one step. Consider, for instance, the following code:

initialize variables

```
int count = 1;
```

This is equivalent to the next two statements:

```
int count;
count = 1;
```

You can also use a shorthand form to declare and initialize variables of the same type together. For example,

```
int i = 1, j = 2;
```

> **Tip**
> A variable must be declared before it can be assigned a value. A variable declared in a method must be assigned a value before it can be used.
>
> Whenever possible, declare a variable and assign its initial value in one step. This will make the program easy to read and avoid programming errors.

Every variable has a scope. The *scope of a variable* is the part of the program where the variable can be referenced. The rules that define the scope of a variable will be introduced gradually later in the book. For now, all you need to know is that a variable must be declared and initialized before it can be used.

2.5 Identify and fix the errors in the following code:

Check Point

```
1  public class Test {
2    public static void main(String[] args) {
3      int i = k + 2;
4      System.out.println(i);
5    }
6  }
```

2.6 Assignment Statements and Assignment Expressions

An assignment statement designates a value for a variable. An assignment statement can be used as an expression in Java.

Key Point

assignment statement
assignment operator

After a variable is declared, you can assign a value to it by using an *assignment statement*. In Java, the equal sign (=) is used as the *assignment operator*. The syntax for assignment statements is as follows:

```
variable = expression;
```

expression

An *expression* represents a computation involving values, variables, and operators that, taking them together, evaluates to a value. For example, consider the following code:

```
int y = 1;                    // Assign 1 to variable y
double radius = 1.0;          // Assign 1.0 to variable radius
int x = 5 * (3 / 2);          // Assign the value of the expression to x
x = y + 1;                    // Assign the addition of y and 1 to x
double area = radius * radius * 3.14159; // Compute area
```

You can use a variable in an expression. A variable can also be used in both sides of the = operator. For example,

```
x = x + 1;
```

In this assignment statement, the result of x + 1 is assigned to x. If x is 1 before the statement is executed, then it becomes 2 after the statement is executed.

To assign a value to a variable, you must place the variable name to the left of the assignment operator. Thus, the following statement is wrong:

```
1 = x;   // Wrong
```

Note

In mathematics, x = 2 * x + 1 denotes an equation. However, in Java, x = 2 * x + 1 is an assignment statement that evaluates the expression 2 * x + 1 and assigns the result to x.

In Java, an assignment statement is essentially an expression that evaluates to the value to be assigned to the variable on the left side of the assignment operator. For this reason, an assignment expression
assignment statement is also known as an *assignment expression*. For example, the following statement is correct:

```
System.out.println(x = 1);
```

which is equivalent to

```
x = 1;
System.out.println(x);
```

If a value is assigned to multiple variables, you can use this syntax:

```
i = j = k = 1;
```

which is equivalent to

```
k = 1;
j = k;
i = j;
```

Note

In an assignment statement, the data type of the variable on the left must be compatible with the data type of the value on the right. For example, int x = 1.0 would be illegal, because the data type of `x` is `int`. You cannot assign a **double** value (**1.0**) to an `int` variable without using type casting. Type casting is introduced in Section 2.15.

2.6 Identify and fix the errors in the following code:

Check
Point

```
1  public class Test {
2    public static void main(String[] args) {
3      int i = j = k = 2;
4      System.out.println(i + " " + j + " " + k);
5    }
6  }
```

2.7 Named Constants

A named constant is an identifier that represents a permanent value.

The value of a variable may change during the execution of a program, but a *named constant,* or simply *constant*, represents permanent data that never changes. In our **ComputeArea** program, π is a constant. If you use it frequently, you don't want to keep typing **3.14159**; instead, you can declare a constant for π. Here is the syntax for declaring a constant:

Key
Point

constant

```
final datatype CONSTANTNAME = value;
```

A constant must be declared and initialized in the same statement. The word **final** is a Java keyword for declaring a constant. For example, you can declare π as a constant and rewrite Listing 2.1 as in Listing 2.4.

final keyword

LISTING 2.4 ComputeAreaWithConstant.java

```
1  import java.util.Scanner; // Scanner is in the java.util package
2
3  public class ComputeAreaWithConstant {
4    public static void main(String[] args) {
5      final double PI = 3.14159; // Declare a constant
6
7      // Create a Scanner object
8      Scanner input = new Scanner(System.in);
9
10     // Prompt the user to enter a radius
11     System.out.print("Enter a number for radius: ");
12     double radius = input.nextDouble();
13
14     // Compute area
15     double area = radius * radius * PI;
16
17     // Display result
18     System.out.println("The area for the circle of radius " +
19       radius + " is " + area);
20   }
21 }
```

There are three benefits of using constants: (1) you don't have to repeatedly type the same value if it is used multiple times; (2) if you have to change the constant value (e.g., from **3.14** to **3.14159** for **PI**), you need to change it only in a single location in the source code; and (3) a descriptive name for a constant makes the program easy to read.

benefits of constants

2.8 Naming Conventions

Sticking with the Java naming conventions makes your programs easy to read and avoids errors.

Make sure that you choose descriptive names with straightforward meanings for the variables, constants, classes, and methods in your program. As mentioned earlier, names are case sensitive. Listed below are the conventions for naming variables, methods, and classes.

name variables and methods

- Use lowercase for variables and methods. If a name consists of several words, concatenate them into one, making the first word lowercase and capitalizing the first letter of each subsequent word—for example, the variables **radius** and **area** and the method **print**.

name classes

- Capitalize the first letter of each word in a class name—for example, the class names **ComputeArea** and **System**.

name constants

- Capitalize every letter in a constant, and use underscores between words—for example, the constants **PI** and **MAX_VALUE**.

It is important to follow the naming conventions to make your programs easy to read.

name classes

Caution

Do not choose class names that are already used in the Java library. For example, since the **System** class is defined in Java, you should not name your class **System**.

2.7 What are the benefits of using constants? Declare an **int** constant **SIZE** with value **20**.

2.8 What are the naming conventions for class names, method names, constants, and variables? Which of the following items can be a constant, a method, a variable, or a class according to the Java naming conventions?

MAX_VALUE, Test, read, readDouble

2.9 Translate the following algorithm into Java code:

Step 1: Declare a **double** variable named **miles** with initial value **100**.

Step 2: Declare a **double** constant named **KILOMETERS_PER_MILE** with value **1.609**.

Step 3: Declare a **double** variable named **kilometers**, multiply **miles** and **KILOMETERS_PER_MILE**, and assign the result to **kilometers**.

Step 4: Display **kilometers** to the console.

What is **kilometers** after Step 4?

2.9 Numeric Data Types and Operations

*Java has six numeric types for integers and floating-point numbers with operators +, -, *, /, and %.*

2.9.1 Numeric Types

Every data type has a range of values. The compiler allocates memory space for each variable or constant according to its data type. Java provides eight primitive data types for numeric values, characters, and Boolean values. This section introduces numeric data types and operators.

Table 2.1 lists the six numeric data types, their ranges, and their storage sizes.

TABLE 2.1 Numeric Data Types

Name	Range	Storage Size	
byte	-2^7 to $2^7 - 1$ (-128 to 127)	8-bit signed	byte type
short	-2^{15} to $2^{15} - 1$ (-32768 to 32767)	16-bit signed	short type
int	-2^{31} to $2^{31} - 1$ (-2147483648 to 2147483647)	32-bit signed	int type
long	-2^{63} to $2^{63} - 1$	64-bit signed	long type
	(i.e., -9223372036854775808 to 9223372036854775807)		
float	Negative range: $-3.4028235E + 38$ to $-1.4E - 45$	32-bit IEEE 754	float type
	Positive range: $1.4E - 45$ to $3.4028235E + 38$		
double	Negative range: $-1.7976931348623157E + 308$ to $-4.9E - 324$	64-bit IEEE 754	double type
	Positive range: $4.9E - 324$ to $1.7976931348623157E + 308$		

Note

IEEE 754 is a standard approved by the Institute of Electrical and Electronics Engineers for representing floating-point numbers on computers. The standard has been widely adopted. Java uses the 32-bit **IEEE 754** for the **float** type and the 64-bit **IEEE 754** for the **double** type. The **IEEE 754** standard also defines special floating-point values, which are listed in Appendix E.

Java uses four types for integers: **byte**, **short**, **int**, and **long**. Choose the type that is most appropriate for your variable. For example, if you know an integer stored in a variable is within a range of a byte, declare the variable as a **byte**. For simplicity and consistency, we will use **int** for integers most of the time in this book.

integer types

Java uses two types for floating-point numbers: **float** and **double**. The **double** type is twice as big as **float**, so the **double** is known as *double precision* and **float** as *single precision*. Normally, you should use the **double** type, because it is more accurate than the **float** type.

floating-point types

2.9.2 Reading Numbers from the Keyboard

You know how to use the **nextDouble()** method in the **Scanner** class to read a double value from the keyboard. You can also use the methods listed in Table 2.2 to read a number of the **byte**, **short**, **int**, **long**, and **float** type.

TABLE 2.2 Methods for **Scanner** Objects

Method	Description
nextByte()	reads an integer of the **byte** type.
nextShort()	reads an integer of the **short** type.
nextInt()	reads an integer of the **int** type.
nextLong()	reads an integer of the **long** type.
nextFloat()	reads a number of the **float** type.
nextDouble()	reads a number of the **double** type.

Here are examples for reading values of various types from the keyboard:

```
1  Scanner input = new Scanner(System.in);
2  System.out.print("Enter a byte value: ");
3  byte byteValue = input.nextByte();
4
5  System.out.print("Enter a short value: ");
6  short shortValue = input.nextShort();
7
8  System.out.print("Enter an int value: ");
9  int intValue = input.nextInt();
10
11  System.out.print("Enter a long value: ");
12  long longValue = input.nextLong();
13
14  System.out.print("Enter a float value: ");
15  float floatValue = input.nextFloat();
```

If you enter a value with an incorrect range or format, a runtime error would occur. For example, you enter a value **128** for line 3, an error would occur because **128** is out of range for a **byte** type integer.

2.9.3 Numeric Operators

operators +, -, *, /, %

operands

The operators for numeric data types include the standard arithmetic operators: addition (+), subtraction (−), multiplication (*), division (/), and remainder (%), as shown in Table 2.3. The *operands* are the values operated by an operator.

TABLE 2.3 Numeric Operators

Name	Meaning	Example	Result
+	Addition	34 + 1	35
−	Subtraction	34.0 − 0.1	33.9
*	Multiplication	300 * 30	9000
/	Division	1.0 / 2.0	0.5
%	Remainder	20 % 3	2

integer division

When both operands of a division are integers, the result of the division is the quotient and the fractional part is truncated. For example, **5 / 2** yields **2**, not **2.5**, and **−5 / 2** yields **-2**, not **-2.5**. To perform a float-point division, one of the operands must be a floating-point number. For example, **5.0 / 2** yields **2.5**.

The **%** operator, known as *remainder* or *modulo* operator, yields the remainder after division. The operand on the left is the dividend and the operand on the right is the divisor. Therefore, **7 % 3** yields **1**, **3 % 7** yields **3**, **12 % 4** yields **0**, **26 % 8** yields **2**, and **20 % 13** yields **7**.

```
      2          0          3          3                        1  ←—— Quotient
   3) 7       7) 3       4) 12      8) 26      Divisor ——→   13) 20  ←—— Dividend
      6          0         12         24                        13
    ─────      ─────      ─────      ─────                    ─────
      1          3          0          2                         7  ←—— Remainder
```

The **%** operator is often used for positive integers, but it can also be used with negative integers and floating-point values. The remainder is negative only if the dividend is negative. For example, **−7 % 3** yields **−1**, **−12 % 4** yields **0**, **−26 % −8** yields **−2**, and **20 % −13** yields **7**.

Remainder is very useful in programming. For example, an even number **%** **2** is always **0** and an odd number **%** **2** is always **1**. Thus, you can use this property to determine whether a number is even or odd. If today is Saturday, it will be Saturday again in 7 days. Suppose you and your friends are going to meet in 10 days. What day is in 10 days? You can find that the day is Tuesday using the following expression:

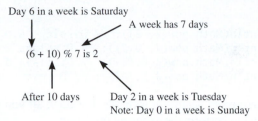

Day 6 in a week is Saturday

A week has 7 days

(6 + 10) % 7 is 2

After 10 days

Day 2 in a week is Tuesday
Note: Day 0 in a week is Sunday

The program in Listing 2.5 obtains minutes and remaining seconds from an amount of time in seconds. For example, **500** seconds contains **8** minutes and **20** seconds.

LISTING 2.5 DisplayTime.java

```
1  import java.util.Scanner;
2
3  public class DisplayTime {
4    public static void main(String[] args) {
5      Scanner input = new Scanner(System.in);
6      // Prompt the user for input
7      System.out.print("Enter an integer for seconds: ");
8      int seconds = input.nextInt();
9
10     int minutes = seconds / 60; // Find minutes in seconds
11     int remainingSeconds = seconds % 60; // Seconds remaining
12     System.out.println(seconds + " seconds is " + minutes +
13       " minutes and " + remainingSeconds + " seconds");
14   }
15 }
```

import Scanner

create a Scanner

read an integer

divide
remainder

```
Enter an integer for seconds: 500  ↵ Enter
500 seconds is 8 minutes and 20 seconds
```

line#	seconds	minutes	remainingSeconds
8	500		
10		8	
11			20

The **nextInt()** method (line 8) reads an integer for **seconds**. Line 10 obtains the minutes using **seconds** **/** **60**. Line 11 (**seconds** **%** **60**) obtains the remaining seconds after taking away the minutes.

The **+** and **-** operators can be both unary and binary. A *unary* operator has only one operand; a *binary* operator has two. For example, the **-** operator in **-5** is a unary operator to negate number **5**, whereas the **-** operator in **4** **-** **5** is a binary operator for subtracting **5** from **4**.

unary operator
binary operator

2.9.4 Exponent Operations

Math.pow(a, b) method

The `Math.pow(a, b)` method can be used to compute a^b. The **pow** method is defined in the **Math** class in the Java API. You invoke the method using the syntax `Math.pow(a, b)` (e.g., `Math.pow(2, 3)`), which returns the result of a^b (2^3). Here, **a** and **b** are parameters for the **pow** method and the numbers **2** and **3** are actual values used to invoke the method. For example,

```
System.out.println(Math.pow(2, 3)); // Displays 8.0
System.out.println(Math.pow(4, 0.5)); // Displays 2.0
System.out.println(Math.pow(2.5, 2)); // Displays 6.25
System.out.println(Math.pow(2.5, -2)); // Displays 0.16
```

Chapter 5 introduces more details on methods. For now, all you need to know is how to invoke the **pow** method to perform the exponent operation.

Check
Point

2.10   Find the largest and smallest **byte**, **short**, **int**, **long**, **float**, and **double**. Which of these data types requires the least amount of memory?

2.11   Show the result of the following remainders.

```
 56 %  6
 78 % -4
-34 %  5
-34 % -5
  5 %  1
  1 %  5
```

2.12   If today is Tuesday, what will be the day in 100 days?

2.13   What is the result of **25 / 4**? How would you rewrite the expression if you wished the result to be a floating-point number?

2.14   Show the result of the following code:

```
System.out.println(2 * (5 / 2 + 5 / 2));
System.out.println(2 * 5 / 2 + 2 * 5 / 2);
System.out.println(2 * (5 / 2));
System.out.println(2 * 5 / 2);
```

2.15   Are the following statements correct? If so, show the output.

```
System.out.println("25 / 4 is " + 25 / 4);
System.out.println("25 / 4.0 is " + 25 / 4.0);
System.out.println("3 * 2 / 4 is " + 3 * 2 / 4);
System.out.println("3.0 * 2 / 4 is " + 3.0 * 2 / 4);
```

2.16   Write a statement to display the result of $2^{3.5}$.

2.17   Suppose **m** and **r** are integers. Write a Java expression for mr^2 to obtain a floating-point result.

2.10 Numeric Literals

Key
Point

A literal is a constant value that appears directly in a program.

literal

For example, **34** and **0.305** are literals in the following statements:

```
int numberOfYears = 34;
double weight = 0.305;
```

2.10.1 Integer Literals

An integer literal can be assigned to an integer variable as long as it can fit into the variable. A compile error will occur if the literal is too large for the variable to hold. The statement **byte b = 128**, for example, will cause a compile error, because **128** cannot be stored in a variable of the **byte** type. (Note that the range for a byte value is from **-128** to **127**.)

An integer literal is assumed to be of the **int** type, whose value is between -2^{31} (-2147483648) and $2^{31} - 1$ (2147483647). To denote an integer literal of the **long** type, append the letter **L** or **l** to it. For example, to write integer **2147483648** in a Java program, you have to write it as **2147483648L** or **2147483648l**, because **2147483648** exceeds the range for the **int** value. **L** is preferred because **l** (lowercase L) can easily be confused with 1 (the digit one).

Note
By default, an integer literal is a decimal integer number. To denote a binary integer literal, use a leading *0b* or *0B* (zero B), to denote an octal integer literal, use a leading *0* (zero), and to denote a hexadecimal integer literal, use a leading *0x* or *0X* (zero X). For example,

binary, octal, and hex literals

```
System.out.println(0B1111); // Displays 15
System.out.println(07777); // Displays 4095
System.out.println(0XFFFF); // Displays 65535
```

Hexadecimal numbers, binary numbers, and octal numbers are introduced in Appendix F.

2.10.2 Floating-Point Literals

Floating-point literals are written with a decimal point. By default, a floating-point literal is treated as a **double** type value. For example, **5.0** is considered a **double** value, not a **float** value. You can make a number a **float** by appending the letter **f** or **F**, and you can make a number a **double** by appending the letter **d** or **D**. For example, you can use **100.2f** or **100.2F** for a **float** number, and **100.2d** or **100.2D** for a **double** number.

suffix f or F
suffix d or D

Note
The **double** type values are more accurate than the **float** type values. For example,

double vs. float

```
System.out.println("1.0 / 3.0 is " + 1.0 / 3.0);
```

displays **1.0 / 3.0 is 0.3333333333333333**

16 digits

```
System.out.println("1.0F / 3.0F is " + 1.0F / 3.0F);
```

displays **1.0F / 3.0F is 0.33333334**

8 digits

A float value has **7** to **8** number of significant digits and a double value has **15** to **17** number of significant digits.

2.10.3 Scientific Notation

Floating-point literals can be written in scientific notation in the form of $a \times 10^b$. For example, the scientific notation for 123.456 is 1.23456×10^2 and for 0.0123456 is 1.23456×10^{-2}. A special syntax is used to write scientific notation numbers. For example, 1.23456×10^2 is written as **1.23456E2** or **1.23456E+2** and 1.23456×10^{-2} as **1.23456E-2**. **E** (or **e**) represents an exponent and can be in either lowercase or uppercase.

why called floating-point?

Note
The **float** and **double** types are used to represent numbers with a decimal point. Why are they called *floating-point numbers*? These numbers are stored in scientific notation internally. When a number such as **50.534** is converted into scientific notation, such as **5.0534E+1**, its decimal point is moved (i.e., floated) to a new position.

Note
To improve readability, Java allows you to use underscores between two digits in a number literal. For example, the following literals are correct.

```
long ssn = 232_45_4519;
long creditCardNumber = 2324_4545_4519_3415L;
```

underscores in numbers

However, **45_** or **_45** is incorrect. The underscore must be placed between two digits.

Check
Point

2.18   How many accurate digits are stored in a **float** or **double** type variable?

2.19   Which of the following are correct literals for floating-point numbers?
12.3, **12.3e+2**, **23.4e-2**, **-334.4**, **20.5**, **39F**, **40D**

2.20   Which of the following are the same as **52.534**?
5.2534e+1, **0.52534e+2**, **525.34e-1**, **5.2534e+0**

2.21   Which of the following are correct literals?
5_2534e+1, **_2534**, **5_2**, **5_**

2.11 Evaluating Expressions and Operator Precedence

Key
Point

Java expressions are evaluated in the same way as arithmetic expressions.

Writing a numeric expression in Java involves a straightforward translation of an arithmetic expression using Java operators. For example, the arithmetic expression

$$\frac{3 + 4x}{5} - \frac{10(y - 5)(a + b + c)}{x} + 9\left(\frac{4}{x} + \frac{9 + x}{y}\right)$$

can be translated into a Java expression as:

```
(3 + 4 * x) / 5 - 10 * (y - 5) * (a + b + c) / x +
9 * (4 / x + (9 + x) / y)
```

evaluating an expression

Though Java has its own way to evaluate an expression behind the scene, the result of a Java expression and its corresponding arithmetic expression is the same. Therefore, you can safely apply the arithmetic rule for evaluating a Java expression. Operators contained within pairs of parentheses are evaluated first. Parentheses can be nested, in which case the expression in the inner parentheses is evaluated first. When more than one operator is used in an expression, the following operator precedence rule is used to determine the order of evaluation.

operator precedence rule

- Multiplication, division, and remainder operators are applied first. If an expression contains several multiplication, division, and remainder operators, they are applied from left to right.

- Addition and subtraction operators are applied last. If an expression contains several addition and subtraction operators, they are applied from left to right.

Here is an example of how an expression is evaluated:

```
3 + 4 * 4 + 5 * (4 + 3) - 1
                      ↑
                        ————————————— (1) inside parentheses first
3 + 4 * 4 + 5 * 7 - 1
      ↑
        ———————————————————————————— (2) multiplication
3 + 16 + 5 * 7 - 1
            ↑
              ———————————————————————— (3) multiplication
3 + 16 + 35 - 1
  ↑
    ——————————————————————————————————— (4) addition
19 + 35 - 1
  ↑
    ——————————————————————————————————— (5) addition
    54 - 1
      ↑
        ——————————————————————————————— (6) subtraction
    53
```

Listing 2.6 gives a program that converts a Fahrenheit degree to Celsius using the formula celsius $= (\frac{5}{9})$(fahrenheit $-$ 32).

LISTING 2.6 FahrenheitToCelsius.java

```java
1  import java.util.Scanner;
2
3  public class FahrenheitToCelsius {
4    public static void main(String[] args) {
5      Scanner input = new Scanner(System.in);
6
7      System.out.print("Enter a degree in Fahrenheit: ");
8      double fahrenheit = input.nextDouble();
9
10     // Convert Fahrenheit to Celsius
11     double celsius = (5.0 / 9) * (fahrenheit - 32);          divide
12     System.out.println("Fahrenheit " + fahrenheit + " is " +
13       celsius + " in Celsius");
14   }
15 }
```

```
Enter a degree in Fahrenheit: 100 ⏎ Enter
Fahrenheit 100.0 is 37.77777777777778 in Celsius
```

line#	fahrenheit	celsius
8	100	
11		37.77777777777778

Be careful when applying division. Division of two integers yields an integer in Java. $\frac{5}{9}$ is translated to **5.0 / 9** instead of **5 / 9** in line 11, because **5 / 9** yields **0** in Java.

integer vs. floating-point division

2.22 How would you write the following arithmetic expression in Java?

a. $\dfrac{4}{3(r + 34)} - 9(a + bc) + \dfrac{3 + d(2 + a)}{a + bd}$

b. $5.5 \times (r + 2.5)^{2.5+t}$

Check Point

2.12 Case Study: Displaying the Current Time

You can invoke `System.currentTimeMillis()` *to return the current time.*

VideoNote

Use operators / and %

currentTimeMillis
UNIX epoch

The problem is to develop a program that displays the current time in GMT (Greenwich Mean Time) in the format hour:minute:second, such as 13:19:8.

The `currentTimeMillis` method in the `System` class returns the current time in milliseconds elapsed since midnight, January 1, 1970 GMT, as shown in Figure 2.2. This time is known as the *UNIX epoch*. The epoch is the point when time starts, and **1970** was the year when the UNIX operating system was formally introduced.

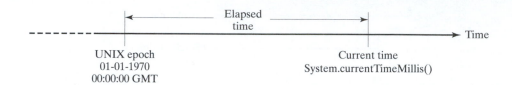

FIGURE 2.2 The `System.currentTimeMillis()` returns the number of milliseconds since the UNIX epoch.

You can use this method to obtain the current time, and then compute the current second, minute, and hour as follows.

1. Obtain the total milliseconds since midnight, January 1, 1970, in **totalMilliseconds** by invoking **System.currentTimeMillis()** (e.g., **1203183068328** milliseconds).

2. Obtain the total seconds **totalSeconds** by dividing **totalMilliseconds** by **1000** (e.g., **1203183068328** milliseconds / **1000** = **1203183068** seconds).

3. Compute the current second from **totalSeconds % 60** (e.g., **1203183068** seconds % **60** = **8**, which is the current second).

4. Obtain the total minutes **totalMinutes** by dividing **totalSeconds** by **60** (e.g., **1203183068** seconds / **60** = **20053051** minutes).

5. Compute the current minute from **totalMinutes % 60** (e.g., **20053051** minutes % **60** = **31**, which is the current minute).

6. Obtain the total hours **totalHours** by dividing **totalMinutes** by **60** (e.g., **20053051** minutes / **60** = **334217** hours).

7. Compute the current hour from **totalHours % 24** (e.g., **334217** hours % **24** = **17**, which is the current hour).

Listing 2.7 gives the complete program.

LISTING 2.7 ShowCurrentTime.java

```
 1  public class ShowCurrentTime {
 2    public static void main(String[] args) {
 3      // Obtain the total milliseconds since midnight, Jan 1, 1970
 4      long totalMilliseconds = System.currentTimeMillis();
 5
 6      // Obtain the total seconds since midnight, Jan 1, 1970
 7      long totalSeconds = totalMilliseconds / 1000;
 8
 9      // Compute the current second in the minute in the hour
10      long currentSecond = totalSeconds % 60;
```

totalMilliseconds

totalSeconds

currentSecond

```
11
12        // Obtain the total minutes                                    totalMinutes
13        long totalMinutes = totalSeconds / 60;
14
15        // Compute the current minute in the hour                      currentMinute
16        long currentMinute = totalMinutes % 60;
17
18        // Obtain the total hours                                      totalHours
19        long totalHours = totalMinutes / 60;
20
21        // Compute the current hour                                    currentHour
22        long currentHour = totalHours % 24;
23
24        // Display results                                             preparing output
25        System.out.println("Current time is " + currentHour + ":"
26            + currentMinute + ":" + currentSecond + " GMT");
27    }
28 }
```

```
Current time is 17:31:8 GMT
```

Line 4 invokes `System.currentTimeMillis()` to obtain the current time in milliseconds as a `long` value. Thus, all the variables are declared as the long type in this program. The seconds, minutes, and hours are extracted from the current time using the `/` and `%` operators (lines 6–22).

line# variables	4	7	10	13	16	19	22
totalMilliseconds	1203183068328						
totalSeconds		1203183068					
currentSecond			8				
totalMinutes				20053051			
currentMinute					31		
totalHours						334217	
currentHour							17

In the sample run, a single digit **8** is displayed for the second. The desirable output would be **08**. This can be fixed by using a method that formats a single digit with a prefix **0** (see Exercise 6.37).

2.23   How do you obtain the current second, minute, and hour?

Check Point

2.13 Augmented Assignment Operators

Key Point

The operators +, -, *, /, and % can be combined with the assignment operator to form augmented operators.

Very often the current value of a variable is used, modified, and then reassigned back to the same variable. For example, the following statement increases the variable **count** by **1**:

```
count = count + 1;
```

Java allows you to combine assignment and addition operators using an augmented (or compound) assignment operator. For example, the preceding statement can be written as

```
count += 1;
```

addition assignment operator

The **+=** is called the *addition assignment operator*. Table 2.4 shows other augmented assignment operators.

TABLE 2.4 Augmented Assignment Operators

Operator	Name	Example	Equivalent
+=	Addition assignment	i += 8	i = i + 8
-=	Subtraction assignment	i -= 8	i = i - 8
*=	Multiplication assignment	i *= 8	i = i * 8
/=	Division assignment	i /= 8	i = i / 8
%=	Remainder assignment	i %= 8	i = i % 8

The augmented assignment operator is performed last after all the other operators in the expression are evaluated. For example,

```
x /= 4 + 5.5 * 1.5;
```

is same as

```
x = x / (4 + 5.5 * 1.5);
```

Caution
There are no spaces in the augmented assignment operators. For example, + = should be +=.

Note
Like the assignment operator (=), the operators (+=, -=, *=, /=, %=) can be used to form an assignment statement as well as an expression. For example, in the following code, **x += 2** is a statement in the first line and an expression in the second line.

```
x += 2; // Statement
System.out.println(x += 2); // Expression
```

Check Point

2.24 Show the output of the following code:

```
double a = 6.5;
a += a + 1;
```

```
System.out.println(a);
a = 6;
a /= 2;
System.out.println(a);
```

2.14 Increment and Decrement Operators

The increment operator (++) and decrement operator (−−) are for incrementing and decrementing a variable by 1.

Key Point

The ++ and −− are two shorthand operators for incrementing and decrementing a variable by 1. These are handy because that's often how much the value needs to be changed in many programming tasks. For example, the following code increments i by 1 and decrements j by 1.

increment operator (++)
decrement operator (−−)

```
int i = 3, j = 3;
i++; // i becomes 4
j--; // j becomes 2
```

i++ is pronounced as i plus plus and i−− as i minus minus. These operators are known as *postfix increment* (or postincrement) and *postfix decrement* (or postdecrement), because the operators ++ and −− are placed after the variable. These operators can also be placed before the variable. For example,

postincrement
postdecrement

```
int i = 3, j = 3;
++i;  // i becomes 4
--j; // j becomes 2
```

++i increments i by 1 and −−j decrements j by 1. These operators are known as *prefix increment* (or preincrement) and *prefix decrement* (or predecrement).

preincrement
predecrement

As you see, the effect of i++ and ++i or i−− and −−i are the same in the preceding examples. However, their effects are different when they are used in statements that do more than just increment and decrement. Table 2.5 describes their differences and gives examples.

TABLE 2.5 Increment and Decrement Operators

Operator	Name	Description	Example (assume i = 1)
++var	preincrement	Increment var by 1, and use the new var value in the statement	`int j = ++i;` `// j is 2, i is 2`
var++	postincrement	Increment var by 1, but use the original var value in the statement	`int j = i++;` `// j is 1, i is 2`
−−var	predecrement	Decrement var by 1, and use the new var value in the statement	`int j = --i;` `// j is 0, i is 0`
var−−	postdecrement	Decrement var by 1, and use the original var value in the statement	`int j = i--;` `// j is 1, i is 0`

Here are additional examples to illustrate the differences between the prefix form of ++ (or −−) and the postfix form of ++ (or --). Consider the following code:

```
int i = 10;
int newNum = 10 * i++;
```
Same effect as →
```
int newNum = 10 * i;
i = i + 1;
```

```
System.out.print("i is " + i
    + ", newNum is " + newNum);
```

```
i is 11, newNum is 100
```

In this case, **i** is incremented by **1**, then the *old* value of **i** is used in the multiplication. So **newNum** becomes **100**. If **i++** is replaced by **++i** as follows,

```
int i = 10;
int newNum = 10 * (++i);
System.out.print("i is " + i
    + ", newNum is " + newNum);
```

Same effect as →

```
i = i + 1;
int newNum = 10 * i;
```

```
i is 11, newNum is 110
```

i is incremented by **1**, and the new value of **i** is used in the multiplication. Thus **newNum** becomes **110**.

Here is another example:

```
double x = 1.0;
double y = 5.0;
double z = x-- + (++y);
```

After all three lines are executed, **y** becomes **6.0**, **z** becomes **7.0**, and **x** becomes **0.0**.

Tip

Using increment and decrement operators makes expressions short, but it also makes them complex and difficult to read. Avoid using these operators in expressions that modify multiple variables or the same variable multiple times, such as this one: `int k = ++i + i`.

Check
Point

2.25 Which of these statements are true?

a. Any expression can be used as a statement.

b. The expression **x++** can be used as a statement.

c. The statement **x = x + 5** is also an expression.

d. The statement **x = y = x = 0** is illegal.

2.26 Show the output of the following code:

```
int a = 6;
int b = a++;
System.out.println(a);
System.out.println(b);
a = 6;
b = ++a;
System.out.println(a);
System.out.println(b);
```

2.15 Numeric Type Conversions

Key
Point

Floating-point numbers can be converted into integers using explicit casting.

Can you perform binary operations with two operands of different types? Yes. If an integer and a floating-point number are involved in a binary operation, Java automatically converts the integer to a floating-point value. So, **3 * 4.5** is same as **3.0 * 4.5**.

You can always assign a value to a numeric variable whose type supports a larger range of values; thus, for instance, you can assign a **long** value to a **float** variable. You cannot, however, assign a value to a variable of a type with a smaller range unless you use *type casting. Casting* is an operation that converts a value of one data type into a value of another data type. Casting a type with a small range to a type with a larger range is known as *widening a type.* Casting a type with a large range to a type with a smaller range is known as *narrowing a type.* Java will automatically widen a type, but you must narrow a type explicitly.

casting

widening a type

narrowing a type

The syntax for casting a type is to specify the target type in parentheses, followed by the variable's name or the value to be cast. For example, the following statement

```
System.out.println((int)1.7);
```

displays **1**. When a **double** value is cast into an **int** value, the fractional part is truncated. The following statement

```
System.out.println((double)1 / 2);
```

displays **0.5**, because **1** is cast to **1.0** first, then **1.0** is divided by **2**. However, the statement

```
System.out.println(1 / 2);
```

displays **0**, because **1** and **2** are both integers and the resulting value should also be an integer.

Caution

Casting is necessary if you are assigning a value to a variable of a smaller type range, such as assigning a **double** value to an **int** variable. A compile error will occur if casting is not used in situations of this kind. However, be careful when using casting, as loss of information might lead to inaccurate results.

possible loss of precision

Note

Casting does not change the variable being cast. For example, **d** is not changed after casting in the following code:

```
double d = 4.5;
int i = (int)d;   // i becomes 4, but d is still 4.5
```

Note

In Java, an augmented expression of the form **x1 op= x2** is implemented as **x1 = (T)(x1 op x2)**, where **T** is the type for **x1**. Therefore, the following code is correct.

casting in an augmented expression

```
int sum = 0;
sum += 4.5; // sum becomes 4 after this statement
```

sum += 4.5 is equivalent to **sum = (int)(sum + 4.5)**.

Note

To assign a variable of the **int** type to a variable of the **short** or **byte** type, explicit casting must be used. For example, the following statements have a compile error:

```
int i = 1;
byte b = i; // Error because explicit casting is required
```

However, so long as the integer literal is within the permissible range of the target variable, explicit casting is not needed to assign an integer literal to a variable of the **short** or **byte** type (see Section 2.10, Numeric Literals).

The program in Listing 2.8 displays the sales tax with two digits after the decimal point.

LISTING 2.8 SalesTax.java

```java
1  import java.util.Scanner;
2
3  public class SalesTax {
4    public static void main(String[] args) {
5      Scanner input = new Scanner(System.in);
6
7      System.out.print("Enter purchase amount: ");
8      double purchaseAmount = input.nextDouble();
9
10     double tax = purchaseAmount * 0.06;
11     System.out.println("Sales tax is $" + (int)(tax * 100) / 100.0);
12   }
13 }
```

casting

```
Enter purchase amount: 197.55  ⏎Enter
Sales tax is $11.85
```

line#	purchaseAmount	tax	output
8	197.55		
10		11.853	
11			11.85

formatting numbers

The variable **purchaseAmount** is **197.55** (line 8). The sales tax is **6%** of the purchase, so the **tax** is evaluated as **11.853** (line 10). Note that

```
tax * 100 is 1185.3
(int)(tax * 100) is 1185
(int)(tax * 100) / 100.0 is 11.85
```

So, the statement in line 11 displays the tax **11.85** with two digits after the decimal point.

Check Point

2.27 Can different types of numeric values be used together in a computation?

2.28 What does an explicit casting from a **double** to an **int** do with the fractional part of the **double** value? Does casting change the variable being cast?

2.29 Show the following output:

```java
float f = 12.5F;
int i = (int)f;
System.out.println("f is " + f);
System.out.println("i is " + i);
```

2.30 If you change **(int)(tax * 100) / 100.0** to **(int)(tax * 100) / 100** in line 11 in Listing 2.8, what will be the output for the input purchase amount of **197.55**?

2.31 Show the output of the following code:

```java
double amount = 5;
System.out.println(amount / 2);
System.out.println(5 / 2);
```

2.16 Software Development Process

The software development life cycle is a multistage process that includes requirements specification, analysis, design, implementation, testing, deployment, and maintenance.

Key Point

VideoNote
Software development process

Developing a software product is an engineering process. Software products, no matter how large or how small, have the same life cycle: requirements specification, analysis, design, implementation, testing, deployment, and maintenance, as shown in Figure 2.3.

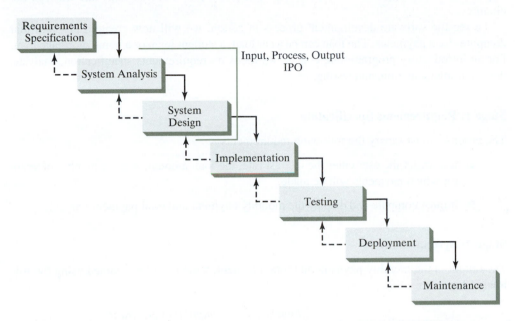

FIGURE 2.3 At any stage of the software development life cycle, it may be necessary to go back to a previous stage to correct errors or deal with other issues that might prevent the software from functioning as expected.

Requirements specification is a formal process that seeks to understand the problem that the software will address and to document in detail what the software system needs to do. This phase involves close interaction between users and developers. Most of the examples in this book are simple, and their requirements are clearly stated. In the real world, however, problems are not always well defined. Developers need to work closely with their customers (the individuals or organizations that will use the software) and study the problem carefully to identify what the software needs to do.

requirements specification

System analysis seeks to analyze the data flow and to identify the system's input and output. When you do analysis, it helps to identify what the output is first, and then figure out what input data you need in order to produce the output.

system analysis

System design is to design a process for obtaining the output from the input. This phase involves the use of many levels of abstraction to break down the problem into manageable components and design strategies for implementing each component. You can view each component as a subsystem that performs a specific function of the system. The essence of system analysis and design is input, process, and output (IPO).

system design

IPO

Implementation involves translating the system design into programs. Separate programs are written for each component and then integrated to work together. This phase requires the use of a programming language such as Java. The implementation involves coding, self-testing, and debugging (that is, finding errors, called *bugs,* in the code).

implementation

testing

deployment

maintenance

VideoNote

Compute loan payments

Testing ensures that the code meets the requirements specification and weeds out bugs. An independent team of software engineers not involved in the design and implementation of the product usually conducts such testing.

Deployment makes the software available for use. Depending on the type of software, it may be installed on each user's machine or installed on a server accessible on the Internet.

Maintenance is concerned with updating and improving the product. A software product must continue to perform and improve in an ever-evolving environment. This requires periodic upgrades of the product to fix newly discovered bugs and incorporate changes.

To see the software development process in action, we will now create a program that computes loan payments. The loan can be a car loan, a student loan, or a home mortgage loan. For an introductory programming course, we focus on requirements specification, analysis, design, implementation, and testing.

Stage 1: Requirements Specification

The program must satisfy the following requirements:

- It must let the user enter the interest rate, the loan amount, and the number of years for which payments will be made.

- It must compute and display the monthly payment and total payment amounts.

Stage 2: System Analysis

The output is the monthly payment and total payment, which can be obtained using the following formulas:

$$monthlyPayment = \frac{loanAmount \times monthlyInterestRate}{1 - \dfrac{1}{(1 + monthlyInterestRate)^{numberOfYears \times 12}}}$$

$$totalPayment = monthlyPayment \times numberOfYears \times 12$$

So, the input needed for the program is the monthly interest rate, the length of the loan in years, and the loan amount.

Note

The requirements specification says that the user must enter the annual interest rate, the loan amount, and the number of years for which payments will be made. During analysis, however, it is possible that you may discover that input is not sufficient or that some values are unnecessary for the output. If this happens, you can go back and modify the requirements specification.

Note

In the real world, you will work with customers from all walks of life. You may develop software for chemists, physicists, engineers, economists, and psychologists, and of course you will not have (or need) complete knowledge of all these fields. Therefore, you don't have to know how formulas are derived, but given the monthly interest rate, the number of years, and the loan amount, you can compute the monthly payment in this program. You will, however, need to communicate with customers and understand how a mathematical model works for the system.

Stage 3: System Design

During system design, you identify the steps in the program.

Step 1.   Prompt the user to enter the annual interest rate, the number of years, and the loan amount.

(The interest rate is commonly expressed as a percentage of the principal for a period of one year. This is known as the *annual interest rate*.)

Step 2.   The input for the annual interest rate is a number in percent format, such as 4.5%. The program needs to convert it into a decimal by dividing it by **100**. To obtain the monthly interest rate from the annual interest rate, divide it by **12**, since a year has 12 months. So, to obtain the monthly interest rate in decimal format, you need to divide the annual interest rate in percentage by **1200**. For example, if the annual interest rate is 4.5%, then the monthly interest rate is 4.5/1200 = 0.00375.

Step 3.   Compute the monthly payment using the preceding formula.

Step 4.   Compute the total payment, which is the monthly payment multiplied by **12** and multiplied by the number of years.

Step 5.   Display the monthly payment and total payment.

Stage 4: Implementation

Implementation is also known as *coding* (writing the code). In the formula, you have to compute $(1 + monthlyInterestRate)^{numberOfYears \times 12}$, which can be obtained using **Math.pow(1 + monthlyInterestRate, numberOfYears * 12)**.

Listing 2.9 gives the complete program.

Math.pow(a, b) method

LISTING 2.9   ComputeLoan.java

```
1   import java.util.Scanner;
2
3   public class ComputeLoan {
4     public static void main(String[] args) {
5       // Create a Scanner
6       Scanner input = new Scanner(System.in);
7
8       // Enter annual interest rate in percentage, e.g., 7.25%
9       System.out.print("Enter annual interest rate, e.g., 7.25%: ");
10      double annualInterestRate = input.nextDouble();
11
12      // Obtain monthly interest rate
13      double monthlyInterestRate = annualInterestRate / 1200;
14
15      // Enter number of years
16      System.out.print(
17        "Enter number of years as an integer, e.g., 5: ");
18      int numberOfYears = input.nextInt();
19
20      // Enter loan amount
21      System.out.print("Enter loan amount, e.g., 120000.95: ");
22      double loanAmount = input.nextDouble();
23
24      // Calculate payment
25      double monthlyPayment = loanAmount * monthlyInterestRate / (1
26        - 1 / Math.pow(1 + monthlyInterestRate, numberOfYears * 12));
```

import class

create a Scanner

enter interest rate

enter years

enter loan amount

monthlyPayment

totalPayment

```
27        double totalPayment = monthlyPayment * numberOfYears * 12;
28
29        // Display results
30        System.out.println("The monthly payment is $" +
31          (int)(monthlyPayment * 100) / 100.0);
32        System.out.println("The total payment is $" +
33          (int)(totalPayment * 100) / 100.0);
34    }
35  }
```

casting

casting

Enter annual interest rate, e.g., 5.75%: 5.75 ⏎Enter
Enter number of years as an integer, e.g., 5: 15 ⏎Enter
Enter loan amount, e.g., 120000.95: 250000 ⏎Enter
The monthly payment is $2076.02
The total payment is $373684.53

line#	10	13	18	22	25	27
variables						
annualInterestRate	5.75					
monthlyInterestRate		0.0047916666666				
numberOfYears			15			
loanAmount				250000		
monthlyPayment					2076.0252175	
totalPayment						373684.539

Line 10 reads the annual interest rate, which is converted into the monthly interest rate in line 13.

Choose the most appropriate data type for the variable. For example, **numberOfYears** is best declared as an **int** (line 18), although it could be declared as a **long**, **float**, or **double**. Note that **byte** might be the most appropriate for **numberOfYears**. For simplicity, however, the examples in this book will use **int** for integer and **double** for floating-point values.

The formula for computing the monthly payment is translated into Java code in lines 25–27.

Casting is used in lines 31 and 33 to obtain a new **monthlyPayment** and **totalPayment** with two digits after the decimal points.

java.lang package

The program uses the **Scanner** class, imported in line 1. The program also uses the **Math** class, and you might be wondering why that class isn't imported into the program. The **Math** class is in the **java.lang** package, and all classes in the **java.lang** package are implicitly imported. Therefore, you don't need to explicitly import the **Math** class.

Stage 5: Testing

After the program is implemented, test it with some sample input data and verify whether the output is correct. Some of the problems may involve many cases, as you will see in later chapters. For these types of problems, you need to design test data that cover all cases.

incremental code and test

Tip
The system design phase in this example identified several steps. It is a good approach to code and test these steps incrementally by adding them one at a time. This approach makes it much easier to pinpoint problems and debug the program.

2.32 How would you write the following arithmetic expression?

$$\frac{-b + \sqrt{b^2 - 4ac}}{2a}$$

2.17 Case Study: Counting Monetary Units

This section presents a program that breaks a large amount of money into smaller units.

Suppose you want to develop a program that changes a given amount of money into smaller monetary units. The program lets the user enter an amount as a **double** value representing a total in dollars and cents, and outputs a report listing the monetary equivalent in the maximum number of dollars, quarters, dimes, nickels, and pennies, in this order, to result in the minimum number of coins.

Here are the steps in developing the program:

1. Prompt the user to enter the amount as a decimal number, such as **11.56**.

2. Convert the amount (e.g., **11.56**) into cents (**1156**).

3. Divide the cents by **100** to find the number of dollars. Obtain the remaining cents using the cents remainder **100**.

4. Divide the remaining cents by **25** to find the number of quarters. Obtain the remaining cents using the remaining cents remainder **25**.

5. Divide the remaining cents by **10** to find the number of dimes. Obtain the remaining cents using the remaining cents remainder **10**.

6. Divide the remaining cents by **5** to find the number of nickels. Obtain the remaining cents using the remaining cents remainder **5**.

7. The remaining cents are the pennies.

8. Display the result.

The complete program is given in Listing 2.10.

LISTING 2.10 ComputeChange.java

```
1  import java.util.Scanner;                                                   import class
2
3  public class ComputeChange {
4    public static void main(String[] args) {
5      // Create a Scanner
6      Scanner input = new Scanner(System.in);
7
8      // Receive the amount
9      System.out.print(
10       "Enter an amount in double, for example 11.56: ");
11     double amount = input.nextDouble();                                      enter input
12
13     int remainingAmount = (int)(amount * 100);
14
15     // Find the number of one dollars
16     int numberOfOneDollars = remainingAmount / 100;                          dollars
17     remainingAmount = remainingAmount % 100;
18
19     // Find the number of quarters in the remaining amount
20     int numberOfQuarters = remainingAmount / 25;                             quarters
```

dimes

nickels

pennies

output

```
21          remainingAmount = remainingAmount % 25;
22
23          // Find the number of dimes in the remaining amount
24          int numberOfDimes = remainingAmount / 10;
25          remainingAmount = remainingAmount % 10;
26
27          // Find the number of nickels in the remaining amount
28          int numberOfNickels = remainingAmount / 5;
29          remainingAmount = remainingAmount % 5;
30
31          // Find the number of pennies in the remaining amount
32          int numberOfPennies = remainingAmount;
33
34          // Display results
35          System.out.println("Your amount " + amount + " consists of");
36          System.out.println("    " + numberOfOneDollars + " dollars");
37          System.out.println("    " + numberOfQuarters + " quarters ");
38          System.out.println("    " + numberOfDimes + " dimes");
39          System.out.println("    " + numberOfNickels + " nickels");
40          System.out.println("    " + numberOfPennies + " pennies");
41      }
42  }
```

```
Enter an amount, for example, 11.56: 11.56 ⏎Enter
Your amount 11.56 consists of
    11 dollars
    2 quarters
    0 dimes
    1 nickels
    1 pennies
```

variables \ line#	11	13	16	17	20	21	24	25	28	29	32
amount	11.56										
remainingAmount		1156		56		6		6		1	
numberOfOneDollars			11								
numberOfQuarters					2						
numberOfDimes							0				
numberOfNickels									1		
numberOfPennies											1

The variable **amount** stores the amount entered from the console (line 11). This variable is not changed, because the amount has to be used at the end of the program to display the results. The program introduces the variable **remainingAmount** (line 13) to store the changing remaining amount.

The variable **amount** is a **double** decimal representing dollars and cents. It is converted to an **int** variable **remainingAmount**, which represents all the cents. For instance, if **amount** is `11.56`, then the initial `remainingAmount` is `1156`. The division operator yields the integer part of the division, so `1156 / 100` is `11`. The remainder operator obtains the remainder of the division, so `1156 % 100` is `56`.

The program extracts the maximum number of singles from the remaining amount and obtains a new remaining amount in the variable `remainingAmount` (lines 16–17). It then extracts the maximum number of quarters from `remainingAmount` and obtains a new `remainingAmount` (lines 20–21). Continuing the same process, the program finds the maximum number of dimes, nickels, and pennies in the remaining amount.

One serious problem with this example is the possible loss of precision when casting a `double` amount to an `int remainingAmount`. This could lead to an inaccurate result. If you try to enter the amount `10.03`, `10.03 * 100` becomes `1002.9999999999999`. You will find that the program displays `10` dollars and `2` pennies. To fix the problem, enter the amount as an integer value representing cents (see Programming Exercise 2.22).

loss of precision

2.33 Show the output with the input value `1.99`.

Check Point

2.18 Common Errors and Pitfalls

Common elementary programming errors often involve undeclared variables, uninitialized variables, integer overflow, unintended integer division, and round-off errors.

Key Point

Common Error 1: Undeclared/Uninitialized Variables and Unused Variables

A variable must be declared with a type and assigned a value before using it. A common error is not declaring a variable or initializing a variable. Consider the following code:

```
double interestRate = 0.05;
double interest = interestrate * 45;
```

This code is wrong, because `interestRate` is assigned a value `0.05`; but `interestrate` has not been declared and initialized. Java is case sensitive, so it considers `interestRate` and `interestrate` to be two different variables.

If a variable is declared, but not used in the program, it might be a potential programming error. So, you should remove the unused variable from your program. For example, in the following code, `taxRate` is never used. It should be removed from the code.

```
double interestRate = 0.05;
double taxRate = 0.05;
double interest = interestRate * 45;
System.out.println("Interest is " + interest);
```

If you use an IDE such as Eclipse and NetBeans, you will receive a warning on unused variables.

Common Error 2: Integer Overflow

Numbers are stored with a limited numbers of digits. When a variable is assigned a value that is too large (*in size*) to be stored, it causes *overflow*. For example, executing the following statement causes overflow, because the largest value that can be stored in a variable of the `int` type is `2147483647`. `2147483648` will be too large for an `int` value.

what is overflow?

```
int value = 2147483647 + 1;
// value will actually be -2147483648
```

Likewise, executing the following statement causes overflow, because the smallest value that can be stored in a variable of the `int` type is `-2147483648`. `-2147483649` is too large in size to be stored in an `int` variable.

```
int value = -2147483648 - 1;
// value will actually be 2147483647
```

Java does not report warnings or errors on overflow, so be careful when working with numbers close to the maximum or minimum range of a given type.

what is underflow?

When a floating-point number is too small (i.e., too close to zero) to be stored, it causes *underflow*. Java approximates it to zero, so normally you don't need to be concerned about underflow.

Common Error 3: Round-off Errors

floating-point approximation

A *round-off error*, also called a *rounding error*, is the difference between the calculated approximation of a number and its exact mathematical value. For example, 1/3 is approximately 0.333 if you keep three decimal places, and is 0.3333333 if you keep seven decimal places. Since the number of digits that can be stored in a variable is limited, round-off errors are inevitable. Calculations involving floating-point numbers are approximated because these numbers are not stored with complete accuracy. For example,

```
System.out.println(1.0 - 0.1 - 0.1 - 0.1 - 0.1 - 0.1);
```

displays **0.5000000000000001**, not **0.5**, and

```
System.out.println(1.0 - 0.9);
```

displays **0.09999999999999998**, not **0.1**. Integers are stored precisely. Therefore, calculations with integers yield a precise integer result.

Common Error 4: Unintended Integer Division

Java uses the same divide operator, namely /, to perform both integer and floating-point division. When two operands are integers, the / operator performs an integer division. The result of the operation is an integer. The fractional part is truncated. To force two integers to perform a floating-point division, make one of the integers into a floating-point number. For example, the code in (a) displays that average is **1** and the code in (b) displays that average is **1.5**.

```
int number1 = 1;
int number2 = 2;
double average = (number1 + number2) / 2;
System.out.println(average);
```
(a)

```
int number1 = 1;
int number2 = 2;
double average = (number1 + number2) / 2.0;
System.out.println(average);
```
(b)

Common Pitfall 1: Redundant Input Objects

New programmers often write the code to create multiple input objects for each input. For example, the following code reads an integer and a double value.

```
Scanner input = new Scanner(System.in);
System.out.print("Enter an integer: ");
int v1 = input.nextInt();

Scanner input1 = new Scanner(System.in);        BAD CODE
System.out.print("Enter a double value: ");
double v2 = input1.nextDouble();
```

The code is not wrong, but inefficient. It creates two input objects unnecessarily and may lead to some subtle errors. You should rewrite the code as follows:

```
Scanner input = new Scanner(System.in);     GOOD CODE
System.out.print("Enter an integer: ");
int v1 = input.nextInt();
System.out.print("Enter a double value: ");
double v2 = input.nextDouble();
```

2.34 Can you declare a variable as `int` and later redeclare it as `double`?

2.35 What is an integer overflow? Can floating-point operations cause overflow?

2.36 Will overflow cause a runtime error?

2.37 What is a round-off error? Can integer operations cause round-off errors? Can floating-point operations cause round-off errors?

KEY TERMS

algorithm   34
assignment operator (=)   42
assignment statement   42
`byte` type   45
casting   57
constant   43
data type   35
declare variables   35
decrement operator (−−)   55
`double` type   45
expression   42
`final` keyword   43
`float` type   45
floating-point number   35
identifier   39
increment operator (++)   55
incremental code and testing   62
`int` type   45
IPO   39
literal   48
`long` type   45

narrowing (of types)   57
operands   46
operator   46
overflow   65
postdecrement   55
postincrement   55
predecrement   55
preincrement   55
primitive data type   35
pseudocode   34
requirements specification   59
scope of a variable   41
`short` type   45
specific import   38
system analysis   59
system design   59
underflow   66
UNIX epoch   52
variable   35
widening (of types)   57
wildcard import   00

CHAPTER SUMMARY

1. *Identifiers* are names for naming elements such as variables, constants, methods, classes, packages in a program.

2. An identifier is a sequence of characters that consists of letters, digits, underscores (_), and dollar signs ($). An identifier must start with a letter or an underscore. It cannot start with a digit. An identifier cannot be a reserved word. An identifier can be of any length.

3. *Variables* are used to store data in a program. To declare a variable is to tell the compiler what type of data a variable can hold.

4. There are two types of `import` statements: *specific import* and *wildcard import*. The specific import specifies a single class in the import statement; the wildcard import imports all the classes in a package.

5. In Java, the equal sign (=) is used as the *assignment operator*.

6. A variable declared in a method must be assigned a value before it can be used.

7. A *named constant* (or simply a *constant*) represents permanent data that never changes.

8. A named constant is declared by using the keyword `final`.

9. Java provides four integer types (`byte`, `short`, `int`, and `long`) that represent integers of four different sizes.

10. Java provides two *floating-point types* (`float` and `double`) that represent floating-point numbers of two different precisions.

11. Java provides *operators* that perform numeric operations: + (addition), – (subtraction), * (multiplication), / (division), and % (remainder).

12. Integer arithmetic (/) yields an integer result.

13. The numeric operators in a Java expression are applied the same way as in an arithmetic expression.

14. Java provides the augmented assignment operators += (addition assignment), –= (subtraction assignment), *= (multiplication assignment), /= (division assignment), and %= (remainder assignment).

15. The *increment operator* (++) and the *decrement operator* (−−) increment or decrement a variable by 1.

16. When evaluating an expression with values of mixed types, Java automatically converts the operands to appropriate types.

17. You can explicitly convert a value from one type to another using the `(type)value` notation.

18. *Casting* a variable of a type with a small range to a variable of a type with a larger range is known as *widening a type*.

19. Casting a variable of a type with a large range to a variable of a type with a smaller range is known as *narrowing a type*.

20. Widening a type can be performed automatically without explicit casting. Narrowing a type must be performed explicitly.

21. In computer science, midnight of January 1, 1970, is known as the *UNIX epoch*.

Quiz

Answer the quiz for this chapter online at www.cs.armstrong.edu/liang/intro10e/quiz.html.

PROGRAMMING EXERCISES

MyProgrammingLab™

Debugging TIP
The compiler usually gives a reason for a syntax error. If you don't know how to correct it, compare your program closely, character by character, with similar examples in the text.

learn from examples

Pedagogical Note
Instructors may ask you to document your analysis and design for selected exercises. Use your own words to analyze the problem, including the input, output, and what needs to be computed, and describe how to solve the problem in pseudocode.

document analysis and design

Sections 2.2–2.12

2.1 (*Convert Celsius to Fahrenheit*) Write a program that reads a Celsius degree in a **double** value from the console, then converts it to Fahrenheit and displays the result. The formula for the conversion is as follows:

fahrenheit = (9 / 5) * celsius + 32

Hint: In Java, **9 / 5** is **1**, but **9.0 / 5** is **1.8**.

Here is a sample run:

```
Enter a degree in Celsius: 43 ⏎Enter
43 Celsius is 109.4 Fahrenheit
```

2.2 (*Compute the volume of a cylinder*) Write a program that reads in the radius and length of a cylinder and computes the area and volume using the following formulas:

area = radius * radius * π
volume = area * length

Here is a sample run:

```
Enter the radius and length of a cylinder: 5.5 12 ⏎Enter
The area is 95.0331
The volume is 1140.4
```

2.3 (*Convert feet into meters*) Write a program that reads a number in feet, converts it to meters, and displays the result. One foot is **0.305** meter. Here is a sample run:

```
Enter a value for feet: 16.5 ⏎Enter
16.5 feet is 5.0325 meters
```

2.4 (*Convert pounds into kilograms*) Write a program that converts pounds into kilograms. The program prompts the user to enter a number in pounds, converts it to kilograms, and displays the result. One pound is **0.454** kilograms. Here is a sample run:

```
Enter a number in pounds: 55.5  ↵Enter
55.5 pounds is 25.197 kilograms
```

*2.5 (*Financial application: calculate tips*) Write a program that reads the subtotal and the gratuity rate, then computes the gratuity and total. For example, if the user enters **10** for subtotal and **15%** for gratuity rate, the program displays **$1.5** as gratuity and **$11.5** as total. Here is a sample run:

```
Enter the subtotal and a gratuity rate: 10 15  ↵Enter
The gratuity is $1.5 and total is $11.5
```

2.6 (*Sum the digits in an integer*) Write a program that reads an integer between **0 and **1000** and adds all the digits in the integer. For example, if an integer is **932**, the sum of all its digits is **14**.

Hint: Use the **%** operator to extract digits, and use the **/** operator to remove the extracted digit. For instance, **932 % 10 = 2** and **932 / 10 = 93**.

Here is a sample run:

```
Enter a number between 0 and 1000: 999  ↵Enter
The sum of the digits is 27
```

*2.7 (*Find the number of years*) Write a program that prompts the user to enter the minutes (e.g., 1 billion), and displays the number of years and days for the minutes. For simplicity, assume a year has **365** days. Here is a sample run:

```
Enter the number of minutes: 1000000000  ↵Enter
1000000000 minutes is approximately 1902 years and 214 days
```

*2.8 (*Current time*) Listing 2.7, ShowCurrentTime.java, gives a program that displays the current time in GMT. Revise the program so that it prompts the user to enter the time zone offset to GMT and displays the time in the specified time zone. Here is a sample run:

```
Enter the time zone offset to GMT: -5  ↵Enter
The current time is 4:50:34
```

2.9   (*Physics: acceleration*) Average acceleration is defined as the change of velocity divided by the time taken to make the change, as shown in the following formula:

$$a = \frac{v_1 - v_0}{t}$$

Write a program that prompts the user to enter the starting velocity v_0 in meters/second, the ending velocity v_1 in meters/second, and the time span t in seconds, and displays the average acceleration. Here is a sample run:

```
Enter v0, v1, and t: 5.5 50.9 4.5 ⏎Enter
The average acceleration is 10.0889
```

2.10   (*Science: calculating energy*) Write a program that calculates the energy needed to heat water from an initial temperature to a final temperature. Your program should prompt the user to enter the amount of water in kilograms and the initial and final temperatures of the water. The formula to compute the energy is

```
Q = M * (finalTemperature - initialTemperature) * 4184
```

where M is the weight of water in kilograms, temperatures are in degrees Celsius, and energy Q is measured in joules. Here is a sample run:

```
Enter the amount of water in kilograms: 55.5 ⏎Enter
Enter the initial temperature: 3.5 ⏎Enter
Enter the final temperature: 10.5 ⏎Enter
The energy needed is 1625484.0
```

2.11   (*Population projection*) Rewrite Programming Exercise 1.11 to prompt the user to enter the number of years and displays the population after the number of years. Use the hint in Programming Exercise 1.11 for this program. The population should be cast into an integer. Here is a sample run of the program:

```
Enter the number of years: 5 ⏎Enter
The population in 5 years is 325932970
```

2.12   (*Physics: finding runway length*) Given an airplane's acceleration a and take-off speed v, you can compute the minimum runway length needed for an airplane to take off using the following formula:

$$length = \frac{v^2}{2a}$$

Write a program that prompts the user to enter v in meters/second (m/s) and the acceleration a in meters/second squared (m/s²), and displays the minimum runway length. Here is a sample run:

```
Enter speed and acceleration: 60 3.5 ⏎Enter
The minimum runway length for this airplane is 514.286
```

2.13 (*Financial application: compound value*) Suppose you save **$100 *each* month into a savings account with the annual interest rate 5%. Thus, the monthly interest rate is 0.05/12 = 0.00417. After the first month, the value in the account becomes

```
100 * (1 + 0.00417) = 100.417
```

After the second month, the value in the account becomes

```
(100 + 100.417) * (1 + 0.00417) = 201.252
```

After the third month, the value in the account becomes

```
(100 + 201.252) * (1 + 0.00417) = 302.507
```

and so on.

Write a program that prompts the user to enter a monthly saving amount and displays the account value after the sixth month. (In Exercise 5.30, you will use a loop to simplify the code and display the account value for any month.)

```
Enter the monthly saving amount: 100 ↵Enter
After the sixth month, the account value is $608.81
```

VideoNote
Compute BMI

*2.14 (*Health application: computing BMI*) Body Mass Index (BMI) is a measure of health on weight. It can be calculated by taking your weight in kilograms and dividing by the square of your height in meters. Write a program that prompts the user to enter a weight in pounds and height in inches and displays the BMI. Note that one pound is **0.45359237** kilograms and one inch is **0.0254** meters. Here is a sample run:

```
Enter weight in pounds: 95.5 ↵Enter
Enter height in inches: 50 ↵Enter
BMI is 26.8573
```

2.15 (*Geometry: distance of two points*) Write a program that prompts the user to enter two points **(x1, y1)** and **(x2, y2)** and displays their distance between them. The formula for computing the distance is $\sqrt{(x_2 - x_1)^2 + (y_2 - y_1)^2}$. Note that you can use **Math.pow(a, 0.5)** to compute $\sqrt{a}$. Here is a sample run:

```
Enter x1 and y1: 1.5 -3.4 ↵Enter
Enter x2 and y2: 4 5 ↵Enter
The distance between the two points is 8.764131445842194
```

2.16 (*Geometry: area of a hexagon*) Write a program that prompts the user to enter the side of a hexagon and displays its area. The formula for computing the area of a hexagon is

$$\text{Area} = \frac{3\sqrt{3}}{2} s^2,$$

where *s* is the length of a side. Here is a sample run:

```
Enter the side: 5.5 ⏎Enter
The area of the hexagon is 78.5895
```

*2.17 (*Science: wind-chill temperature*) How cold is it outside? The temperature alone is not enough to provide the answer. Other factors including wind speed, relative humidity, and sunshine play important roles in determining coldness outside. In 2001, the National Weather Service (NWS) implemented the new wind-chill temperature to measure the coldness using temperature and wind speed. The formula is

$$t_{wc} = 35.74 + 0.6215t_a - 35.75v^{0.16} + 0.4275t_a v^{0.16}$$

where t_a is the outside temperature measured in degrees Fahrenheit and *v* is the speed measured in miles per hour. t_{wc} is the wind-chill temperature. The formula cannot be used for wind speeds below 2 mph or temperatures below $-58°F$ or above 41°F.

Write a program that prompts the user to enter a temperature between $-58°F$ and 41°F and a wind speed greater than or equal to 2 and displays the wind-chill temperature. Use **Math.pow(a, b)** to compute $v^{0.16}$. Here is a sample run:

```
Enter the temperature in Fahrenheit between -58°F and 41°F:
5.3 ⏎Enter
Enter the wind speed (>=2) in miles per hour: 6 ⏎Enter
The wind chill index is -5.56707
```

2.18 (*Print a table*) Write a program that displays the following table. Cast floating-point numbers into integers.

a	b	pow(a, b)
1	2	1
2	3	8
3	4	81
4	5	1024
5	6	15625

*2.19 (*Geometry: area of a triangle*) Write a program that prompts the user to enter three points **(x1, y1)**, **(x2, y2)**, **(x3, y3)** of a triangle and displays its area. The formula for computing the area of a triangle is

$$s = (side1 + side2 + side3)/2;$$

$$area = \sqrt{s(s - side1)(s - side2)(s - side3)}$$

Here is a sample run:

```
Enter three points for a triangle: 1.5 -3.4 4.6 5 9.5 -3.4 ⏎Enter
The area of the triangle is 33.6
```

Sections 2.13–2.17

*2.20 (*Financial application: calculate interest*) If you know the balance and the annual percentage interest rate, you can compute the interest on the next monthly payment using the following formula:

$$interest = balance \times (annualInterestRate/1200)$$

Write a program that reads the balance and the annual percentage interest rate and displays the interest for the next month. Here is a sample run:

```
Enter balance and interest rate (e.g., 3 for 3%): 1000 3.5  ↵Enter
The interest is 2.91667
```

*2.21 (*Financial application: calculate future investment value*) Write a program that reads in investment amount, annual interest rate, and number of years, and displays the future investment value using the following formula:

$$futureInvestmentValue =$$

$$investmentAmount \times (1 + monthlyInterestRate)^{numberOfYears*12}$$

For example, if you enter amount **1000**, annual interest rate **3.25%**, and number of years **1**, the future investment value is **1032.98**.

Here is a sample run:

```
Enter investment amount: 1000.56  ↵Enter
Enter annual interest rate in percentage: 4.25  ↵Enter
Enter number of years: 1  ↵Enter
Accumulated value is $1043.92
```

*2.22 (*Financial application: monetary units*) Rewrite Listing 2.10, ComputeChange .java, to fix the possible loss of accuracy when converting a **double** value to an **int** value. Enter the input as an integer whose last two digits represent the cents. For example, the input **1156** represents **11** dollars and **56** cents.

*2.23 (*Cost of driving*) Write a program that prompts the user to enter the distance to drive, the fuel efficiency of the car in miles per gallon, and the price per gallon, and displays the cost of the trip. Here is a sample run:

```
Enter the driving distance: 900.5  ↵Enter
Enter miles per gallon: 25.5  ↵Enter
Enter price per gallon: 3.55  ↵Enter
The cost of driving is $125.36
```

SELECTIONS

Objectives

- To declare `boolean` variables and write Boolean expressions using relational operators (§3.2).

- To implement selection control using one-way `if` statements (§3.3).

- To implement selection control using two-way `if-else` statements (§3.4).

- To implement selection control using nested `if` and multi-way `if` statements (§3.5).

- To avoid common errors and pitfalls in `if` statements (§3.6).

- To generate random numbers using the `Math.random()` method (§3.7).

- To program using selection statements for a variety of examples (`SubtractionQuiz`, `BMI`, `ComputeTax`) (§§3.7–3.9).

- To combine conditions using logical operators (`!`, `&&`, `||`, and `^`) (§3.10).

- To program using selection statements with combined conditions (`LeapYear`, `Lottery`) (§§3.11–3.12).

- To implement selection control using `switch` statements (§3.13).

- To write expressions using the conditional expression (§3.14).

- To examine the rules governing operator precedence and associativity (§3.15).

- To apply common techniques to debug errors (§3.16).

3.1 Introduction

problem

The program can decide which statements to execute based on a condition.

If you enter a negative value for **radius** in Listing 2.2, ComputeAreaWithConsoleInput.java, the program displays an invalid result. If the radius is negative, you don't want the program to compute the area. How can you deal with this situation?

selection statements

Like all high-level programming languages, Java provides *selection statements*: statements that let you choose actions with alternative courses. You can use the following selection statement to replace lines 12–17 in Listing 2.2:

```java
if (radius < 0) {
  System.out.println("Incorrect input");
}
else {
  area = radius * radius * 3.14159;
  System.out.println("Area is " + area);
}
```

Boolean expression
Boolean value

Selection statements use conditions that are Boolean expressions. A *Boolean expression* is an expression that evaluates to a *Boolean value*: **true** or **false**. We now introduce Boolean types and relational operators.

3.2 **boolean** Data Type

*The **boolean** data type declares a variable with the value either **true** or **false**.*

boolean data type
relational operators

How do you compare two values, such as whether a radius is greater than **0**, equal to **0**, or less than **0**? Java provides six *relational operators* (also known as *comparison operators*), shown in Table 3.1, which can be used to compare two values (assume radius is **5** in the table).

TABLE 3.1 Relational Operators

Java Operator	Mathematics Symbol	Name	Example (radius is 5)	Result
<	<	less than	radius < 0	false
<=	≤	less than or equal to	radius <= 0	false
>	>	greater than	radius > 0	true
>=	≥	greater than or equal to	radius >= 0	true
==	=	equal to	radius == 0	false
!=	≠	not equal to	radius != 0	true

Caution

== vs. =

The equality testing operator is two equal signs (==), not a single equal sign (=). The latter symbol is for assignment.

The result of the comparison is a Boolean value: **true** or **false**. For example, the following statement displays **true**:

```java
double radius = 1;
System.out.println(radius > 0);
```

Boolean variable

A variable that holds a Boolean value is known as a *Boolean variable*. The **boolean** data type is used to declare Boolean variables. A **boolean** variable can hold one of the two values: **true** or **false**. For example, the following statement assigns **true** to the variable **lightsOn**:

```
boolean lightsOn = true;
```

true and **false** are literals, just like a number such as **10**. They are treated as reserved words and cannot be used as identifiers in the program.

Suppose you want to develop a program to let a first-grader practice addition. The program randomly generates two single-digit integers, **number1** and **number2**, and displays to the student a question such as "What is 1 + 7?," as shown in the sample run in Listing 3.1. After the student types the answer, the program displays a message to indicate whether it is true or false.

There are several ways to generate random numbers. For now, generate the first integer using **System.currentTimeMillis() % 10** and the second using **System.current-TimeMillis() / 7 % 10**. Listing 3.1 gives the program. Lines 5–6 generate two numbers, **number1** and **number2**. Line 14 obtains an answer from the user. The answer is graded in line 18 using a Boolean expression **number1 + number2 == answer**.

Boolean literals

VideoNote

Program addition quiz

LISTING 3.1 AdditionQuiz.java

```
1  import java.util.Scanner;
2
3  public class AdditionQuiz {
4    public static void main(String[] args) {
5      int number1 = (int)(System.currentTimeMillis() % 10);
6      int number2 = (int)(System.currentTimeMillis() / 7 % 10);
7
8      // Create a Scanner
9      Scanner input = new Scanner(System.in);
10
11     System.out.print(
12       "What is " + number1 + " + " + number2 + "? ");
13
14     int number = input.nextInt();
15
16     System.out.println(
17       number1 + " + " + number2 + " = " + answer + " is " +
18       (number1 + number2 == answer));
19   }
20 }
```

generate number1
generate number2

show question

display result

```
What is 1 + 7? 8  ↵Enter
1 + 7 = 8 is true
```

```
What is 4 + 8? 9  ↵Enter
4 + 8 = 9 is false
```

line#	number1	number2	answer	output
5	4			
6		8		
14			9	
16				4 + 8 = 9 is false

3.1 List six relational operators.

3.2 Assuming that `x` is `1`, show the result of the following Boolean expressions:

```
(x > 0)
(x < 0)
(x != 0)
(x >= 0)
(x != 1)
```

3.3 Can the following conversions involving casting be allowed? Write a test program to verify your answer.

```java
boolean b = true;
i = (int)b;

int i = 1;
boolean b = (boolean)i;
```

3.3 `if` Statements

Key
Point

An `if` statement is a construct that enables a program to specify alternative paths of execution.

why `if` statement?

The preceding program displays a message such as "6 + 2 = 7 is false." If you wish the message to be "6 + 2 = 7 is incorrect," you have to use a selection statement to make this minor change.

Java has several types of selection statements: one-way `if` statements, two-way `if-else` statements, nested `if` statements, multi-way `if-else` statements, `switch` statements, and conditional expressions.

A one-way `if` statement executes an action if and only if the condition is `true`. The syntax for a one-way `if` statement is:

if statement

```java
if (boolean-expression) {
   statement(s);
}
```

flowchart

The flowchart in Figure 3.1a illustrates how Java executes the syntax of an `if` statement. A *flowchart* is a diagram that describes an algorithm or process, showing the steps as boxes of various kinds, and their order by connecting these with arrows. Process operations are represented in these boxes, and arrows connecting them represent the flow of control. A diamond box denotes a Boolean condition and a rectangle box represents statements.

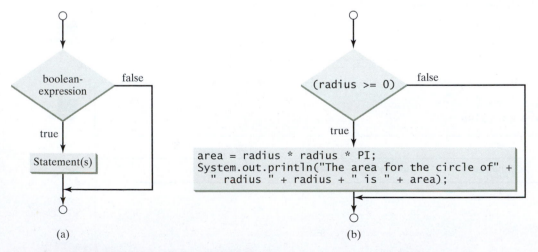

(a) (b)

FIGURE 3.1 An `if` statement executes statements if the **boolean-expression** evaluates to **true**.

If the `boolean-expression` evaluates to `true`, the statements in the block are executed. As an example, see the following code:

```java
if (radius >= 0) {
  area = radius * radius * PI;
  System.out.println("The area for the circle of radius " +
    radius + " is " + area);
}
```

The flowchart of the preceding statement is shown in Figure 3.1b. If the value of `radius` is greater than or equal to `0`, then the `area` is computed and the result is displayed; otherwise, the two statements in the block will not be executed.

The `boolean-expression` is enclosed in parentheses. For example, the code in (a) is wrong. It should be corrected, as shown in (b).

```java
if i > 0 {
  System.out.println("i is positive");
}
```
(a) Wrong

```java
if (i > 0) {
  System.out.println("i is positive");
}
```
(b) Correct

The block braces can be omitted if they enclose a single statement. For example, the following statements are equivalent.

```java
if (i > 0) {
  System.out.println("i is positive");
}
```
(a)

Equivalent

```java
if (i > 0)
  System.out.println("i is positive");
```
(b)

Note

Omitting braces makes the code shorter, but it is prone to errors. It is a common mistake to forget the braces when you go back to modify the code that omits the braces.

Omitting braces or not

Listing 3.2 gives a program that prompts the user to enter an integer. If the number is a multiple of `5`, the program displays `HiFive`. If the number is divisible by `2`, it displays `HiEven`.

LISTING 3.2 `SimpleIfDemo.java`

```java
1  import java.util.Scanner;
2
3  public class SimpleIfDemo {
4    public static void main(String[] args) {
5      Scanner input = new Scanner(System.in);
6      System.out.println("Enter an integer: ");
7      int number = input.nextInt();
8
9      if (number % 5 == 0)
10       System.out.println("HiFive");
11
12     if (number % 2 == 0)
13       System.out.println("HiEven");
14   }
15 }
```

enter input

check 5

check even

```
Enter an integer:  4  ⏎Enter
HiEven
```

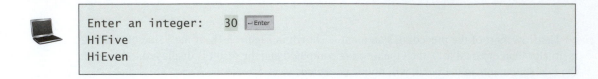

```
Enter an integer:  30  ⏎Enter
HiFive
HiEven
```

The program prompts the user to enter an integer (lines 6–7) and displays `HiFive` if it is divisible by **5** (lines 9–10) and `HiEven` if it is divisible by **2** (lines 12–13).

Check Point

3.4 Write an `if` statement that assigns **1** to **x** if **y** is greater than **0**.

3.5 Write an `if` statement that increases pay by 3% if **score** is greater than **90**.

3.4 Two-Way `if-else` Statements

Key Point

An `if-else` statement decides the execution path based on whether the condition is true or false.

A one-way `if` statement performs an action if the specified condition is `true`. If the condition is `false`, nothing is done. But what if you want to take alternative actions when the condition is `false`? You can use a two-way `if-else` statement. The actions that a two-way `if-else` statement specifies differ based on whether the condition is `true` or `false`.

Here is the syntax for a two-way `if-else` statement:

```
if (boolean-expression) {
  statement(s)-for-the-true-case;
}
else {
  statement(s)-for-the-false-case;
}
```

The flowchart of the statement is shown in Figure 3.2.

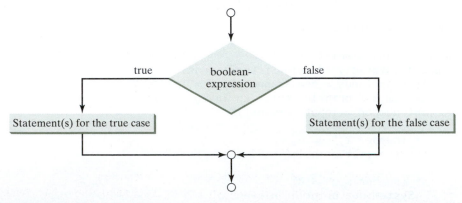

FIGURE 3.2 An `if-else` statement executes statements for the true case if the `Boolean-expression` evaluates to `true`; otherwise, statements for the false case are executed.

If the `boolean-expression` evaluates to `true`, the statement(s) for the true case are executed; otherwise, the statement(s) for the false case are executed. For example, consider the following code:

```
if (radius >= 0) {
  area = radius * radius * PI;
  System.out.println("The area for the circle of radius " +
    radius + " is " + area);
}
else {
  System.out.println("Negative input");
}
```

two-way `if-else` statement

If `radius >= 0` is `true`, `area` is computed and displayed; if it is `false`, the message `"Negative input"` is displayed.

As usual, the braces can be omitted if there is only one statement within them. The braces enclosing the `System.out.println("Negative input")` statement can therefore be omitted in the preceding example.

Here is another example of using the `if-else` statement. The example checks whether a number is even or odd, as follows:

```
if (number % 2 == 0)
  System.out.println(number + " is even.");
else
  System.out.println(number + " is odd.");
```

3.6 Write an `if` statement that increases `pay` by 3% if `score` is greater than `90`, otherwise increases `pay` by 1%.

3.7 What is the output of the code in (a) and (b) if `number` is `30`? What if `number` is `35`?

Check
Point

```
if (number % 2 == 0)
  System.out.println(number + " is even.");

System.out.println(number + " is odd.");
```
(a)

```
if (number % 2 == 0)
  System.out.println(number + " is even.");
else
  System.out.println(number + " is odd.");
```
(b)

3.5 Nested **if** and Multi-Way **if-else** Statements

An `if` statement can be inside another `if` statement to form a nested `if` statement.

Key
Point

The statement in an `if` or `if-else` statement can be any legal Java statement, including another `if` or `if-else` statement. The inner `if` statement is said to be *nested* inside the outer `if` statement. The inner `if` statement can contain another `if` statement; in fact, there is no limit to the depth of the nesting. For example, the following is a nested `if` statement:

nested `if` statement

```
if (i > k) {
  if (j > k)
    System.out.println("i and j are greater than k");
}
else
  System.out.println("i is less than or equal to k");
```

The `if (j > k)` statement is nested inside the `if (i > k)` statement.

The nested `if` statement can be used to implement multiple alternatives. The statement given in Figure 3.3a, for instance, prints a letter grade according to the score, with multiple alternatives.

```
if (score >= 90.0)
  System.out.print("A");
else
  if (score >= 80.0)
    System.out.print("B");
  else
    if (score >= 70.0)
      System.out.print("C");
    else
      if (score >= 60.0)
        System.out.print("D");
      else
        System.out.print("F");
```
(a)

Equivalent

This is better

```
if (score >= 90.0)
  System.out.print("A");
else if (score >= 80.0)
  System.out.print("B");
else if (score >= 70.0)
  System.out.print("C");
else if (score >= 60.0)
  System.out.print("D");
else
  System.out.print("F");
```
(b)

FIGURE 3.3 A preferred format for multiple alternatives is shown in (b) using a multi-way `if-else` statement.

The execution of this `if` statement proceeds as shown in Figure 3.4. The first condition (`score >= 90.0`) is tested. If it is **true**, the grade is **A**. If it is **false**, the second condition (`score >= 80.0`) is tested. If the second condition is **true**, the grade is **B**. If that condition is **false**, the third condition and the rest of the conditions (if necessary) are tested until a condition is met or all of the conditions prove to be **false**. If all of the conditions are **false**, the grade is **F**. Note that a condition is tested only when all of the conditions that come before it are **false**.

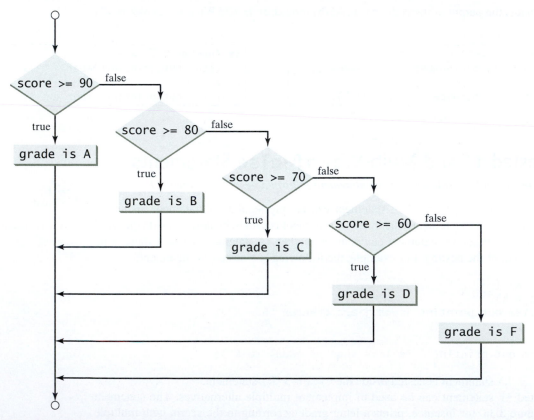

FIGURE 3.4 You can use a multi-way `if-else` statement to assign a grade.

The `if` statement in Figure 3.3a is equivalent to the `if` statement in Figure 3.3b. In fact, Figure 3.3b is the preferred coding style for multiple alternative `if` statements. This style, called *multi-way `if-else` statements*, avoids deep indentation and makes the program easy to read.

multi-way `if` statement

3.8 Suppose `x = 3` and `y = 2`; show the output, if any, of the following code. What is the output if `x = 3` and `y = 4`? What is the output if `x = 2` and `y = 2`? Draw a flowchart of the code.

Check Point

```
if (x > 2) {
  if (y > 2) {
    z = x + y;
    System.out.println("z is " + z);
  }
}
else
  System.out.println("x is " + x);
```

3.9 Suppose `x = 2` and `y = 3`. Show the output, if any, of the following code. What is the output if `x = 3` and `y = 2`? What is the output if `x = 3` and `y = 3`?

```
if (x > 2)
  if (y > 2) {
    int z = x + y;
    System.out.println("z is " + z);
  }
else
  System.out.println("x is " + x);
```

3.10 What is wrong in the following code?

```
if (score >= 60.0)
  System.out.println("D");
else if (score >= 70.0)
  System.out.println("C");
else if (score >= 80.0)
  System.out.println("B");
else if (score >= 90.0)
  System.out.println("A");
else
  System.out.println("F");
```

3.6 Common Errors and Pitfalls

*Forgetting necessary braces, ending an `if` statement in the wrong place, mistaking ==
for =, and dangling `else` clauses are common errors in selection statements.
Duplicated statements in `if-else` statements and testing equality of double values
are common pitfalls.*

Key Point

The following errors are common among new programmers.

Common Error 1: Forgetting Necessary Braces

The braces can be omitted if the block contains a single statement. However, forgetting the braces when they are needed for grouping multiple statements is a common programming error. If you modify the code by adding new statements in an `if` statement without braces, you will have to insert the braces. For example, the following code in (a) is wrong. It should be written with braces to group multiple statements, as shown in (b).

```
if (radius >= 0)
   area = radius * radius * PI;
   System.out.println("The area "
      + " is " + area);
```

```
if (radius >= 0) {
   area = radius * radius * PI;
   System.out.println("The area "
      + " is " + area);
}
```

(a) Wrong   (b) Correct

Common Error 2: Wrong Semicolon at the `if` Line

Adding a semicolon at the end of an `if` line, as shown in (a) below, is a common mistake.

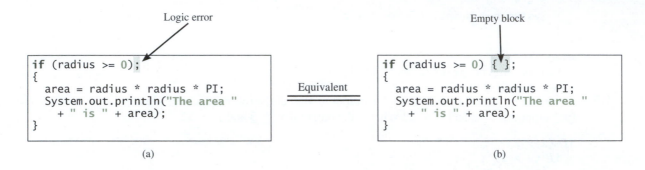

Logic error   Empty block

```
if (radius >= 0);
{
   area = radius * radius * PI;
   System.out.println("The area "
      + " is " + area);
}
```

Equivalent

```
if (radius >= 0) { };
{
   area = radius * radius * PI;
   System.out.println("The area "
      + " is " + area);
}
```

(a)   (b)

This mistake is hard to find, because it is neither a compile error nor a runtime error; it is a logic error. The code in (a) is equivalent to that in (b) with an empty block.

This error often occurs when you use the next-line block style. Using the end-of-line block style can help prevent this error.

Common Error 3: Redundant Testing of Boolean Values

To test whether a **boolean** variable is **true** or **false** in a test condition, it is redundant to use the equality testing operator like the code in (a):

```
if (even == true)
   System.out.println(
      "It is even.");
```

Equivalent

This is better

```
if (even)
   System.out.println(
      "It is even.");
```

(a)   (b)

Instead, it is better to test the **boolean** variable directly, as shown in (b). Another good reason for doing this is to avoid errors that are difficult to detect. Using the = operator instead of the == operator to compare the equality of two items in a test condition is a common error. It could lead to the following erroneous statement:

```
if (even = true)
   System.out.println("It is even.");
```

This statement does not have compile errors. It assigns **true** to **even**, so that **even** is always **true**.

Common Error 4: Dangling `else` Ambiguity

The code in (a) below has two `if` clauses and one `else` clause. Which `if` clause is matched by the `else` clause? The indentation indicates that the `else` clause matches the first `if` clause.

However, the `else` clause actually matches the second `if` clause. This situation is known as the *dangling else ambiguity*. The `else` clause always matches the most recent unmatched `if`   dangling else ambiguity
clause in the same block. So, the statement in (a) is equivalent to the code in (b).

```
int i = 1, j = 2, k = 3;

if (i > j)
  if (i > k)
    System.out.println("A");
else
    System.out.println("B");
```

(a)

Equivalent
——————————

This is better
with correct ——→
indentation

```
int i = 1, j = 2, k = 3;

if (i > j)
  if (i > k)
    System.out.println("A");
  else
    System.out.println("B");
```

(b)

Since `(i > j)` is false, nothing is displayed from the statements in (a) and (b). To force the `else` clause to match the first `if` clause, you must add a pair of braces:

```
int i = 1, j = 2, k = 3;

if (i > j) {
  if (i > k)
    System.out.println("A");
}
else
  System.out.println("B");
```

This statement displays **B**.

Common Error 5: Equality Test of Two Floating-Point Values

As discussed in Common Error 3 in Section 2.18, floating-point numbers have a limited precision and calculations; involving floating-point numbers can introduce round-off errors. So, equality test of two floating-point values is not reliable. For example, you expect the following code to display **true**, but surprisingly it displays **false**.

```
double x = 1.0 - 0.1 - 0.1 - 0.1 - 0.1 - 0.1;
System.out.println(x == 0.5);
```

Here, **x** is not exactly **0.5**, but is **0.5000000000000001**. You cannot reliably test equality of two floating-point values. However, you can compare whether they are close enough by testing whether the difference of the two numbers is less than some threshold. That is, two numbers x and y are very close if $|x-y| < \varepsilon$ for a very small value, ε. ε, a Greek letter pronounced epsilon, is commonly used to denote a very small value. Normally, you set ε to 10^{-14} for comparing two values of the **double** type and to 10^{-7} for comparing two values of the **float** type. For example, the following code

```
final double EPSILON = 1E-14;
double x = 1.0 - 0.1 - 0.1 - 0.1 - 0.1 - 0.1;
if (Math.abs(x - 0.5) < EPSILON)
  System.out.println(x + " is approximately 0.5");
```

will display that

```
0.5000000000000001 is approximately 0.5
```

The `Math.abs(a)` method can be used to return the absolute value of **a**.

Common Pitfall 1: Simplifying Boolean Variable Assignment

Often, new programmers write the code that assigns a test condition to a `boolean` variable like the code in (a):

```
if (number % 2 == 0)
   even = true;
else
   even = false;
```
Equivalent
This is shorter

```
boolean even
   = number % 2 == 0;
```

(a)   (b)

This is not an error, but it should be better written as shown in (b).

Common Pitfall 2: Avoiding Duplicate Code in Different Cases

Often, new programmers write the duplicate code in different cases that should be combined in one place. For example, the highlighted code in the following statement is duplicated.

```
if (inState) {
   tuition = 5000;
   System.out.println("The tuition is " + tuition);
}
else {
   tuition = 15000;
   System.out.println("The tuition is " + tuition);
}
```

This is not an error, but it should be better written as follows:

```
if (inState) {
   tuition = 5000;
}
else {
   tuition = 15000;
}
System.out.println("The tuition is " + tuition);
```

The new code removes the duplication and makes the code easy to maintain, because you only need to change in one place if the print statement is modified.

Check Point

3.11 Which of the following statements are equivalent? Which ones are correctly indented?

```
if (i > 0) if
(j > 0)
x = 0; else
if (k > 0) y = 0;
else z = 0;
```

(a)

```
if (i > 0) {
   if (j > 0)
      x = 0;
   else if (k > 0)
      y = 0;
}
else
   z = 0;
```

(b)

```
if (i > 0)
   if (j > 0)
      x = 0;
   else if (k > 0)
      y = 0;
   else
      z = 0;
```

(c)

```
if (i > 0)
   if (j > 0)
      x = 0;
   else if (k > 0)
      y = 0;
else
   z = 0;
```

(d)

3.12 Rewrite the following statement using a Boolean expression:

```
if (count % 10 == 0)
   newLine = true;
else
   newLine = false;
```

3.13 Are the following statements correct? Which one is better?

```
if (age < 16)
  System.out.println
    ("Cannot get a driver's license");
if (age >= 16)
  System.out.println
    ("Can get a driver's license");
```

(a)

```
if (age < 16)
  System.out.println
    ("Cannot get a driver's license");
else
  System.out.println
    ("Can get a driver's license");
```

(b)

3.14 What is the output of the following code if **number** is **14**, **15**, or **30**?

```
if (number % 2 == 0)
  System.out.println
    (number + " is even");
if (number % 5 == 0)
  System.out.println
    (number + " is multiple of 5");
```

(a)

```
if (number % 2 == 0)
  System.out.println
    (number + " is even");
else if (number % 5 == 0)
  System.out.println
    (number + " is multiple of 5");
```

(b)

3.7 Generating Random Numbers

You can use **Math.random()** *to obtain a random double value between* **0.0** *and* **1.0**, *excluding* **1.0**.

Key
Point

VideoNote
Program subtraction quiz

Suppose you want to develop a program for a first-grader to practice subtraction. The program randomly generates two single-digit integers, **number1** and **number2**, with **number1 >= number2**, and it displays to the student a question such as "What is 9 − 2?" After the student enters the answer, the program displays a message indicating whether it is correct.

The previous programs generate random numbers using **System.currentTimeMillis()**. A better approach is to use the **random()** method in the **Math** class. Invoking this method returns a random double value **d** such that 0.0 ≤ d < 1.0. Thus, **(int)(Math.random() * 10)** returns a random single-digit integer (i.e., a number between **0** and **9**).

random() method

The program can work as follows:

1. Generate two single-digit integers into **number1** and **number2**.

2. If **number1 < number2**, swap **number1** with **number2**.

3. Prompt the student to answer, **"What is number1 - number2?"**

4. Check the student's answer and display whether the answer is correct.

The complete program is shown in Listing 3.3.

LISTING 3.3 SubtractionQuiz.java

```
1  import java.util.Scanner;
2
3  public class SubtractionQuiz {
4    public static void main(String[] args) {
5      // 1. Generate two random single-digit integers
6      int number1 = (int)(Math.random() * 10);
7      int number2 = (int)(Math.random() * 10);
8
9      // 2. If number1 < number2, swap number1 with number2
10     if (number1 < number2) {
11       int temp = number1;
```

random number

```
12          number1 = number2;
13          number2 = temp;
14        }
15
16        // 3. Prompt the student to answer "What is number1 - number2?"
17        System.out.print
18          ("What is " + number1 + " - " + number2 + "? ");
19        Scanner input = new Scanner(System.in);
```

get answer

```
20        int answer = input.nextInt();
21
22        // 4. Grade the answer and display the result
```

check the answer

```
23        if (number1 - number2 == answer)
24          System.out.println("You are correct!");
25        else {
26          System.out.println("Your answer is wrong.");
27          System.out.println(number1 + " - " + number2 +
28            " should be " + (number1 - number2));
29        }
30      }
31    }
```

```
What is 6 - 6?  0  ↵Enter
You are correct!
```

```
What is 9 - 2?  5  ↵Enter
Your answer is wrong
9 - 2 is 7
```

line#	number1	number2	temp	answer	output
6	2				
7		9			
11			2		
12	9				
13		2			
20				5	
26					Your answer is wrong 9 - 2 should be 7

To swap two variables **number1** and **number2**, a temporary variable **temp** (line 11) is used to first hold the value in **number1**. The value in **number2** is assigned to **number1** (line 12), and the value in **temp** is assigned to **number2** (line 13).

Check Point

3.15 Which of the following is a possible output from invoking **Math.random()**?
323.4, 0.5, 34, 1.0, 0.0, 0.234

3.16 a. How do you generate a random integer **i** such that $0 \le i < 20$?

b. How do you generate a random integer **i** such that $10 \le i < 20$?

c. How do you generate a random integer **i** such that $10 \le i \le 50$?

d. Write an expression that returns **0** or **1** randomly.

3.8 Case Study: Computing Body Mass Index

You can use nested `if` *statements to write a program that interprets body mass index.*

Key Point

Body Mass Index (BMI) is a measure of health based on height and weight. It can be calculated by taking your weight in kilograms and dividing it by the square of your height in meters. The interpretation of BMI for people 20 years or older is as follows:

BMI	Interpretation
BMI < 18.5	Underweight
18.5 ≤ BMI < 25.0	Normal
25.0 ≤ BMI < 30.0	Overweight
30.0 ≤ BMI	Obese

Write a program that prompts the user to enter a weight in pounds and height in inches and displays the BMI. Note that one pound is `0.45359237` kilograms and one inch is `0.0254` meters. Listing 3.4 gives the program.

LISTING 3.4 `ComputeAndInterpretBMI.java`

```java
 1  import java.util.Scanner;
 2
 3  public class ComputeAndInterpretBMI {
 4    public static void main(String[] args) {
 5      Scanner input = new Scanner(System.in);
 6
 7      // Prompt the user to enter weight in pounds
 8      System.out.print("Enter weight in pounds: ");
 9      double weight = input.nextDouble();                    input weight
10
11      // Prompt the user to enter height in inches
12      System.out.print("Enter height in inches: ");
13      double height = input.nextDouble();                    input height
14
15      final double KILOGRAMS_PER_POUND = 0.45359237; // Constant
16      final double METERS_PER_INCH = 0.0254; // Constant
17
18      // Compute BMI
19      double weightInKilograms = weight * KILOGRAMS_PER_POUND;
20      double heightInMeters = height * METERS_PER_INCH;
21      double bmi = weightInKilograms /                       compute bmi
22        (heightInMeters * heightInMeters);
23
24      // Display result
25      System.out.println("BMI is " + bmi);                   display output
26      if (bmi < 18.5)
27        System.out.println("Underweight");
28      else if (bmi < 25)
29        System.out.println("Normal");
30      else if (bmi < 30)
31        System.out.println("Overweight");
32      else
33        System.out.println("Obese");
34    }
35  }
```

```
Enter weight in pounds:   146  ↵ Enter
Enter height in inches:   70   ↵ Enter
BMI is 20.948603801493316
Normal
```

line#	weight	height	weightInKilograms	heightInMeters	bmi	output
9	146					
13		70				
19			66.22448602			
20				1.778		
21					20.9486	
25						BMI is 20.95
31						Normal

The constants **KILOGRAMS_PER_POUND** and **METERS_PER_INCH** are defined in lines 15–16. Using constants here makes programs easy to read.

test all cases

You should test the input that covers all possible cases for BMI to ensure that the program works for all cases.

3.9 Case Study: Computing Taxes

Key Point

VideoNote

Use multi-way if-else statements

You can use nested **if** *statements to write a program for computing taxes.*

The United States federal personal income tax is calculated based on filing status and taxable income. There are four filing statuses: single filers, married filing jointly or qualified widow(er), married filing separately, and head of household. The tax rates vary every year. Table 3.2 shows the rates for 2009. If you are, say, single with a taxable income of $10,000, the first $8,350 is taxed at 10% and the other $1,650 is taxed at 15%, so, your total tax is $1,082.50.

TABLE 3.2 2009 U.S. Federal Personal Tax Rates

Marginal Tax Rate	Single	Married Filing Jointly or Qualifying Widow(er)	Married Filing Separately	Head of Household
10%	$0 – $8,350	$0 – $16,700	$0 – $8,350	$0 – $11,950
15%	$8,351 – $33,950	$16,701 – $67,900	$8,351 – $33,950	$11,951 – $45,500
25%	$33,951 – $82,250	$67,901 – $137,050	$33,951 – $68,525	$45,501 – $117,450
28%	$82,251 – $171,550	$137,051 – $208,850	$68,526 – $104,425	$117,451 – $190,200
33%	$171,551 – $372,950	$208,851 – $372,950	$104,426 – $186,475	$190,201 – $372,950
35%	$372,951+	$372,951+	$186,476+	$372,951+

You are to write a program to compute personal income tax. Your program should prompt the user to enter the filing status and taxable income and compute the tax. Enter **0** for single filers, **1** for married filing jointly or qualified widow(er), **2** for married filing separately, and **3** for head of household.

Your program computes the tax for the taxable income based on the filing status. The filing status can be determined using `if` statements outlined as follows:

```
if (status == 0) {
  // Compute tax for single filers
}
else if (status == 1) {
  // Compute tax for married filing jointly or qualifying widow(er)
}
else if (status == 2) {
  // Compute tax for married filing separately
}
else if (status == 3) {
  // Compute tax for head of household
}
else {
  // Display wrong status
}
```

For each filing status there are six tax rates. Each rate is applied to a certain amount of taxable income. For example, of a taxable income of \$400,000 for single filers, \$8,350 is taxed at 10%, (33,950 – 8,350) at 15%, (82,250 – 33,950) at 25%, (171,550 – 82,250) at 28%, (372,950 – 171,550) at 33%, and (400,000 – 372,950) at 35%.

Listing 3.5 gives the solution for computing taxes for single filers. The complete solution is left as an exercise.

LISTING 3.5 ComputeTax.java

```
import java.util.Scanner;

public class ComputeTax {
  public static void main(String[] args) {
    // Create a Scanner
    Scanner input = new Scanner(System.in);

    // Prompt the user to enter filing status
    System.out.print("(0-single filer, 1-married jointly or " +
      "qualifying widow(er), 2-married separately, 3-head of " +
      "household) Enter the filing status: ");

    int status = input.nextInt();

    // Prompt the user to enter taxable income
    System.out.print("Enter the taxable income: ");
    double income = input.nextDouble();

    // Compute tax
    double tax = 0;

    if (status == 0) { // Compute tax for single filers
      if (income <= 8350)
        tax = income * 0.10;
      else if (income <= 33950)
        tax = 8350 * 0.10 + (income - 8350) * 0.15;
      else if (income <= 82250)
        tax = 8350 * 0.10 + (33950 - 8350) * 0.15 +
          (income - 33950) * 0.25;
      else if (income <= 171550)
        tax = 8350 * 0.10 + (33950 - 8350) * 0.15 +
          (82250 - 33950) * 0.25 + (income - 82250) * 0.28;
```

input status

input income

compute tax

```
33        else if (income <= 372950)
34            tax = 8350 * 0.10 + (33950 - 8350) * 0.15 +
35                (82250 - 33950) * 0.25 + (171550 - 82250) * 0.28 +
36                (income - 171550) * 0.33;
37        else
38            tax = 8350 * 0.10 + (33950 - 8350) * 0.15 +
39                (82250 - 33950) * 0.25 + (171550 - 82250) * 0.28 +
40                (372950 - 171550) * 0.33 + (income - 372950) * 0.35;
41    }
42    else if (status == 1) { // Left as an exercise
43        // Compute tax for married file jointly or qualifying widow(er)
44    }
45    else if (status == 2) { // Compute tax for married separately
46        // Left as an exercise
47    }
48    else if (status == 3) { // Compute tax for head of household
49        // Left as an exercise
50    }
51    else {
52        System.out.println("Error: invalid status");
53        System.exit(1);
54    }
55
56    // Display the result
57    System.out.println("Tax is " + (int)(tax * 100) / 100.0);
58    }
59 }
```

exit program (line 53 label)

display output (line 57 label)

```
(0-single filer, 1-married jointly or qualifying widow(er),
2-married separately, 3-head of household)
Enter the filing status:   0  ↵Enter
Enter the taxable income:   400000  ↵Enter
Tax is 117683.5
```

line#	status	income	tax	output
13	0			
17		400000		
20			0	
38			117683.5	
57				Tax is 117683.5

The program receives the filing status and taxable income. The multi-way `if-else` statements (lines 22, 42, 45, 48, 51) check the filing status and compute the tax based on the filing status.

`System.exit(status)` (line 53) is defined in the `System` class. Invoking this method terminates the program. The status `0` indicates that the program is terminated normally. A nonzero status code indicates abnormal termination.

An initial value of `0` is assigned to `tax` (line 20). A compile error would occur if it had no initial value, because all of the other statements that assign values to `tax` are within the `if` statement. The compiler thinks that these statements may not be executed and therefore reports a compile error.

System.exit(status) (margin label)

To test a program, you should provide the input that covers all cases. For this program, your input should cover all statuses (**0, 1, 2, 3**). For each status, test the tax for each of the six brackets. So, there are a total of 24 cases.

test all cases

Tip

For all programs, you should write a small amount of code and test it before moving on to add more code. This is called *incremental development and testing*. This approach makes testing easier, because the errors are likely in the new code you just added.

incremental development and testing

3.17 Are the following two statements equivalent?

Check Point

```
if (income <= 10000)
  tax = income * 0.1;
else if (income <= 20000)
  tax = 1000 +
    (income - 10000) * 0.15;
```

```
if (income <= 10000)
  tax = income * 0.1;
else if (income > 10000 &&
        income <= 20000)
  tax = 1000 +
    (income - 10000) * 0.15;
```

3.10 Logical Operators

The logical operators !, &&, ||, and ^ can be used to create a compound Boolean expression.

Key Point

Sometimes, whether a statement is executed is determined by a combination of several conditions. You can use logical operators to combine these conditions to form a compound Boolean expression. *Logical operators*, also known as *Boolean operators*, operate on Boolean values to create a new Boolean value. Table 3.3 lists the Boolean operators. Table 3.4 defines the not (**!**) operator, which negates **true** to **false** and **false** to **true**. Table 3.5 defines the and (**&&**) operator. The and (**&&**) of two Boolean operands is **true** if and only if both operands are **true**. Table 3.6 defines the or (**||**) operator. The or (**||**) of two Boolean operands is **true** if at least one of the operands is **true**. Table 3.7 defines the exclusive or (**^**) operator. The exclusive or (**^**) of two Boolean operands is **true** if and only if the two operands have different Boolean values. Note that **p1 ^ p2** is the same as **p1 != p2**.

TABLE 3.3 Boolean Operators

Operator	Name	Description
!	not	logical negation
&&	and	logical conjunction
||	or	logical disjunction
^	exclusive or	logical exclusion

TABLE 3.4 Truth Table for Operator !

p	!p	Example (assume **age = 24**, **weight = 140**)
true	false	**!(age > 18)** is **false**, because **(age > 18)** is **true**.
false	true	**!(weight == 150)** is **true**, because **(weight == 150)** is **false**.

TABLE 3.5 Truth Table for Operator &&

p₁	p₂	p₁ && p₂	*Example (assume* **age = 24, weight = 140***)*
false	false	false	
false	true	false	(age > 28) && (weight <= 140) is true, because (age > 28) is false.
true	false	false	
true	true	true	(age > 18) && (weight >= 140) is true, because (age > 18) and (weight >= 140) are both true.

TABLE 3.6 Truth Table for Operator ||

p₁	p₂	p₁ || p₂	*Example (assume* **age = 24, weight = 140***)*
false	false	false	(age > 34) || (weight >= 150) is false, because (age > 34) and (weight >= 150) are both false.
false	true	true	
true	false	true	(age > 18) || (weight < 140) is true, because (age > 18) is true.
true	true	true	

TABLE 3.7 Truth Table for Operator ∧

p₁	p₂	p₁ ∧ p₂	*Example (assume* **age = 24, weight = 140***)*
false	false	false	(age > 34) ∧ (weight > 140) is false, because (age > 34) and (weight > 140) are both false.
false	true	true	(age > 34) ∧ (weight >= 140) is true, because (age > 34) is false but (weight >= 140) is true.
true	false	true	
true	true	false	

Listing 3.6 gives a program that checks whether a number is divisible by 2 and 3, by 2 or 3, and by 2 or 3 but not both:

LISTING 3.6 TestBooleanOperators.java

import class

```
1  import java.util.Scanner;
2
3  public class TestBooleanOperators {
4    public static void main(String[] args) {
5      // Create a Scanner
6      Scanner input = new Scanner(System.in);
7
8      // Receive an input
9      System.out.print("Enter an integer: ");
```
input
```
10     int number = input.nextInt();
11
```
and
```
12     if (number % 2 == 0 && number % 3 == 0)
13       System.out.println(number + " is divisible by 2 and 3.");
14
```

```
15      if (number % 2 == 0 || number % 3 == 0)                          or
16        System.out.println(number + " is divisible by 2 or 3.");
17
18      if (number % 2 == 0 ^ number % 3 == 0)                           exclusive or
19        System.out.println(number +
20          " is divisible by 2 or 3, but not both.");
21    }
22  }
```

```
Enter an integer: 4 ↵Enter
4 is divisible by 2 or 3.
4 is divisible by 2 or 3, but not both.
```

```
Enter an integer: 18 ↵Enter
18 is divisible by 2 and 3.
18 is divisible by 2 or 3.
```

(number % 2 == 0 && number % 3 == 0) (line 12) checks whether the number is divisible by both 2 and 3. (number % 2 == 0 || number % 3 == 0) (line 15) checks whether the number is divisible by 2 or by 3. (number % 2 == 0 ^ number % 3 == 0) (line 18) checks whether the number is divisible by 2 or 3, but not both.

Caution

In mathematics, the expression

```
1 <= numberOfDaysInAMonth <= 31
```

is correct. However, it is incorrect in Java, because 1 <= numberOfDaysInAMonth is   incompatible operands
evaluated to a boolean value, which cannot be compared with 31. Here, two operands
(a boolean value and a numeric value) are *incompatible*. The correct expression in
Java is

```
(1 <= numberOfDaysInAMonth) && (numberOfDaysInAMonth <= 31)
```

Note

De Morgan's law, named after Indian-born British mathematician and logician Augustus   De Morgan's law
De Morgan (1806–1871), can be used to simplify Boolean expressions. The law states:

```
!(condition1 && condition2) is the same as
  !condition1 || !condition2
!(condition1 || condition2) is the same as
  !condition1 && !condition2
```

For example,

```
! (number % 2 == 0 && number % 3 == 0)
```

can be simplified using an equivalent expression:

```
(number % 2 != 0 || number % 3 != 0)
```

As another example,

```
!(number == 2 || number == 3)
```

is better written as

```
number != 2 && number != 3
```

If one of the operands of an **&&** operator is **false**, the expression is **false**; if one of the operands of an **||** operator is **true**, the expression is **true**. Java uses these properties to improve the performance of these operators. When evaluating **p1 && p2**, Java first evaluates **p1** and then, if **p1** is **true**, evaluates **p2**; if **p1** is **false**, it does not evaluate **p2**. When evaluating **p1 || p2**, Java first evaluates **p1** and then, if **p1** is **false**, evaluates **p2**; if **p1** is **true**, it does not evaluate **p2**. In programming language terminology, **&&** and **||** are known as the *short-circuit* or *lazy* operators. Java also provides the unconditional AND (**&**) and OR (**|**) operators, which are covered in Supplement III.C for advanced readers.

short-circuit operator

lazy operator

Check Point

3.18 Assuming that **x** is **1**, show the result of the following Boolean expressions.

```
(true) && (3 > 4)
!(x > 0) && (x > 0)
(x > 0) || (x < 0)

(x != 0) || (x == 0)
(x >= 0) || (x < 0)
(x != 1) == !(x == 1)
```

3.19 (a) Write a Boolean expression that evaluates to **true** if a number stored in variable **num** is between **1** and **100**. (b) Write a Boolean expression that evaluates to **true** if a number stored in variable **num** is between **1** and **100** or the number is negative.

3.20 (a) Write a Boolean expression for $|x - 5| < 4.5$. (b) Write a Boolean expression for $|x - 5| > 4.5$.

3.21 Assume that **x** and **y** are **int** type. Which of the following are legal Java expressions?

```
x > y > 0
x = y && y
x /= y
x or y
x and y
(x != 0) || (x = 0)
```

3.22 Are the following two expressions the same?

```
a. x % 2 == 0 && x % 3 == 0
b. x % 6 == 0
```

3.23 What is the value of the expression **x >= 50 && x <= 100** if **x** is **45**, **67**, or **101**?

3.24 Suppose, when you run the following program, you enter the input **2 3 6** from the console. What is the output?

```java
public class Test {
  public static void main(String[] args) {
    java.util.Scanner input = new java.util.Scanner(System.in);
    double x = input.nextDouble();
    double y = input.nextDouble();
    double z = input.nextDouble();

    System.out.println("(x < y && y < z) is " + (x < y && y < z));
    System.out.println("(x < y || y < z) is " + (x < y || y < z));
    System.out.println("!(x < y) is " + !(x < y));
    System.out.println("(x + y < z) is " + (x + y < z));
    System.out.println("(x + y > z) is " + (x + y > z));
  }
}
```

3.25 Write a Boolean expression that evaluates to **true** if **age** is greater than **13** and less than **18**.

3.26 Write a Boolean expression that evaluates to `true` if `weight` is greater than `50` pounds or height is greater than `60` inches.

3.27 Write a Boolean expression that evaluates to `true` if `weight` is greater than `50` pounds and height is greater than `60` inches.

3.28 Write a Boolean expression that evaluates to `true` if either `weight` is greater than `50` pounds or height is greater than `60` inches, but not both.

3.11 Case Study: Determining Leap Year

A year is a leap year if it is divisible by 4 but not by 100, or if it is divisible by 400.

Key Point

You can use the following Boolean expressions to check whether a year is a leap year:

```
// A leap year is divisible by 4
boolean isLeapYear = (year % 4 == 0);

// A leap year is divisible by 4 but not by 100
isLeapYear = isLeapYear && (year % 100 != 0);

// A leap year is divisible by 4 but not by 100 or divisible by 400
isLeapYear = isLeapYear || (year % 400 == 0);
```

Or you can combine all these expressions into one like this:

```
isLeapYear = (year % 4 == 0 && year % 100 != 0) || (year % 400 == 0);
```

Listing 3.7 gives the program that lets the user enter a year and checks whether it is a leap year.

LISTING 3.7 `LeapYear.java`

```
 1  import java.util.Scanner;
 2
 3  public class LeapYear {
 4    public static void main(String[] args) {
 5      // Create a Scanner
 6      Scanner input = new Scanner(System.in);
 7      System.out.print("Enter a year: ");
 8      int year = input.nextInt();                                    input
 9
10      // Check if the year is a leap year
11      boolean isLeapYear =                                           leap year?
12        (year % 4 == 0 && year % 100 != 0) || (year % 400 == 0);
13
14      // Display the result
15      System.out.println(year + " is a leap year? " + isLeapYear);  display result
16    }
17  }
```

```
Enter a year: 2008 ⏎Enter
2008 is a leap year? true
```

```
Enter a year: 1900 ⏎Enter
1900 is a leap year? false
```

```
Enter a year:  2002 ⏎Enter
2002 is a leap year? false
```

3.12 Case Study: Lottery

Key Point

The lottery program involves generating random numbers, comparing digits, and using Boolean operators.

Suppose you want to develop a program to play lottery. The program randomly generates a lottery of a two-digit number, prompts the user to enter a two-digit number, and determines whether the user wins according to the following rules:

1. If the user input matches the lottery number in the exact order, the award is $10,000.

2. If all digits in the user input match all digits in the lottery number, the award is $3,000.

3. If one digit in the user input matches a digit in the lottery number, the award is $1,000.

Note that the digits of a two-digit number may be **0**. If a number is less than **10**, we assume the number is preceded by a **0** to form a two-digit number. For example, number **8** is treated as **08** and number **0** is treated as **00** in the program. Listing 3.8 gives the complete program.

LISTING 3.8 Lottery.java

```
1  import java.util.Scanner;
2
3  public class Lottery {
4    public static void main(String[] args) {
5      // Generate a lottery number
6      int lottery = (int)(Math.random() * 100);
7
8      // Prompt the user to enter a guess
9      Scanner input = new Scanner(System.in);
10     System.out.print("Enter your lottery pick (two digits): ");
11     int guess = input.nextInt();
12
13     // Get digits from lottery
14     int lotteryDigit1 = lottery / 10;
15     int lotteryDigit2 = lottery % 10;
16
17     // Get digits from guess
18     int guessDigit1 = guess / 10;
19     int guessDigit2 = guess % 10;
20
21     System.out.println("The lottery number is " + lottery);
22
23     // Check the guess
24     if (guess == lottery)
25       System.out.println("Exact match: you win $10,000");
26     else if (guessDigit2 == lotteryDigit1
27             && guessDigit1 == lotteryDigit2)
28       System.out.println("Match all digits: you win $3,000");
29     else if (guessDigit1 == lotteryDigit1
30             || guessDigit1 == lotteryDigit2
31             || guessDigit2 == lotteryDigit1
32             || guessDigit2 == lotteryDigit2)
33       System.out.println("Match one digit: you win $1,000");
```

generate a lottery number

enter a guess

exact match?

match all digits?

match one digit?

```
34      else
35          System.out.println("Sorry, no match");
36     }
37  }
```

```
Enter your lottery pick (two digits): 15 ↵Enter
The lottery number is 15
Exact match: you win $10,000
```

```
Enter your lottery pick (two digits): 45 ↵Enter
The lottery number is 54
Match all digits: you win $3,000
```

```
Enter your lottery pick:  23 ↵Enter
The lottery number is 34
Match one digit: you win $1,000
```

```
Enter your lottery pick: 23 ↵Enter
The lottery number is 14
Sorry: no match
```

line# variable	6	11	14	15	18	19	33
lottery	34						
guess		23					
lotteryDigit1			3				
lotteryDigit2				4			
guessDigit1					2		
guessDigit2						3	
Output							Match one digit: you win $1,000

The program generates a lottery using the **random()** method (line 6) and prompts the user to enter a guess (line 11). Note that **guess % 10** obtains the last digit from **guess** and **guess / 10** obtains the first digit from **guess**, since **guess** is a two-digit number (lines 18–19).

The program checks the guess against the lottery number in this order:

1. First, check whether the guess matches the lottery exactly (line 24).

2. If not, check whether the reversal of the guess matches the lottery (lines 26–27).

3. If not, check whether one digit is in the lottery (lines 29–32).

4. If not, nothing matches and display **"Sorry, no match"** (lines 34–35).

3.13 **switch** Statements

Key Point

A switch statement executes statements based on the value of a variable or an expression.

The **if** statement in Listing 3.5, ComputeTax.java, makes selections based on a single **true** or **false** condition. There are four cases for computing taxes, which depend on the value of **status**. To fully account for all the cases, nested **if** statements were used. Overuse of nested **if** statements makes a program difficult to read. Java provides a **switch** statement to simplify coding for multiple conditions. You can write the following **switch** statement to replace the nested **if** statement in Listing 3.5:

```java
switch (status) {
  case 0:   compute tax for single filers;
            break;
  case 1:   compute tax for married jointly or qualifying widow(er);
            break;
  case 2:   compute tax for married filing separately;
            break;
  case 3:   compute tax for head of household;
            break;
  default:  System.out.println("Error: invalid status");
            System.exit(1);
}
```

The flowchart of the preceding **switch** statement is shown in Figure 3.5.

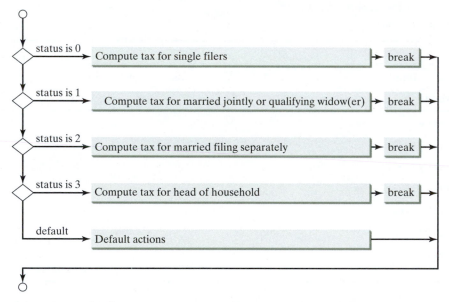

FIGURE 3.5 The **switch** statement checks all cases and executes the statements in the matched case.

This statement checks to see whether the status matches the value **0**, **1**, **2**, or **3**, in that order. If matched, the corresponding tax is computed; if not matched, a message is displayed. Here is the full syntax for the **switch** statement:

switch statement

```java
switch (switch-expression) {
  case value1: statement(s)1;
             break;
```

```
    case value2: statement(s)2;
                 break;
    ...
    case valueN: statement(s)N;
                 break;
    default:     statement(s)-for-default;
}
```

The **switch** statement observes the following rules:

- The **switch-expression** must yield a value of **char**, **byte**, **short**, **int**, or **String** type and must always be enclosed in parentheses. (The **char** and **String** types will be introduced in the next chapter.)

- The **value1**, . . ., and **valueN** must have the same data type as the value of the **switch-expression**. Note that **value1**, . . ., and **valueN** are constant expressions, meaning that they cannot contain variables, such as $1 + x$.

- When the value in a **case** statement matches the value of the **switch-expression**, the statements *starting from this case* are executed until either a **break** statement or the end of the **switch** statement is reached.

- The **default** case, which is optional, can be used to perform actions when none of the specified cases matches the **switch-expression**.

- The keyword **break** is optional. The **break** statement immediately ends the **switch** statement.

Caution

Do not forget to use a **break** statement when one is needed. Once a case is matched, the statements starting from the matched case are executed until a **break** statement or the end of the **switch** statement is reached. This is referred to as *fall-through* behavior. For example, the following code displays **Weekdays** for day of **1** to **5** and **Weekends** for day **0** and **6**.

without break

fall-through behavior

```
switch (day) {
  case 1:
  case 2:
  case 3:
  case 4:
  case 5: System.out.println("Weekday"); break;
  case 0:
  case 6: System.out.println("Weekend");
}
```

Tip

To avoid programming errors and improve code maintainability, it is a good idea to put a comment in a case clause if **break** is purposely omitted.

Now let us write a program to find out the Chinese Zodiac sign for a given year. The Chinese Zodiac is based on a twelve-year cycle, with each year represented by an animal—monkey, rooster, dog, pig, rat, ox, tiger, rabbit, dragon, snake, horse, or sheep—in this cycle, as shown in Figure 3.6.

Note that **year % 12** determines the Zodiac sign. 1900 is the year of the rat because **1900 % 12** is **4**. Listing 3.9 gives a program that prompts the user to enter a year and displays the animal for the year.

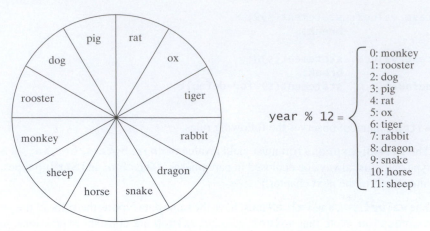

FIGURE 3.6 The Chinese Zodiac is based on a twelve-year cycle.

LISTING 3.9 ChineseZodiac.java

enter year

determine Zodiac sign

```java
 1  import java.util.Scanner;
 2
 3  public class ChineseZodiac {
 4    public static void main(String[] args) {
 5      Scanner input = new Scanner(System.in);
 6
 7      System.out.print("Enter a year: ");
 8      int year = input.nextInt();
 9
10      switch (year % 12) {
11        case 0: System.out.println("monkey"); break;
12        case 1: System.out.println("rooster"); break;
13        case 2: System.out.println("dog"); break;
14        case 3: System.out.println("pig"); break;
15        case 4: System.out.println("rat"); break;
16        case 5: System.out.println("ox"); break;
17        case 6: System.out.println("tiger"); break;
18        case 7: System.out.println("rabbit"); break;
19        case 8: System.out.println("dragon"); break;
20        case 9: System.out.println("snake"); break;
21        case 10: System.out.println("horse"); break;
22        case 11: System.out.println("sheep");
23      }
24    }
25  }
```

```
Enter a year:  1963  ↵Enter
rabbit
```

```
Enter a year:  1877  ↵Enter
ox
```

3.29 What data types are required for a **switch** variable? If the keyword **break** is not used after a case is processed, what is the next statement to be executed? Can you convert a **switch** statement to an equivalent **if** statement, or vice versa? What are the advantages of using a **switch** statement?

3.30   What is **y** after the following **switch** statement is executed? Rewrite the code using an **if-else** statement.

```
x = 3; y = 3;
switch (x + 3) {
  case 6:  y = 1;
  default: y += 1;
}
```

3.31   What is **x** after the following **if-else** statement is executed? Use a **switch** statement to rewrite it and draw the flowchart for the new **switch** statement.

```
int x = 1, a = 3;
if (a == 1)
  x += 5;
else if (a == 2)
  x += 10;
else if (a == 3)
  x += 16;
else if (a == 4)
  x += 34;
```

3.32   Write a **switch** statement that displays Sunday, Monday, Tuesday, Wednesday, Thursday, Friday, Saturday, if **day** is **0**, **1**, **2**, **3**, **4**, **5**, **6**, accordingly.

3.14 Conditional Expressions

A conditional expression evaluates an expression based on a condition.

Key Point

You might want to assign a value to a variable that is restricted by certain conditions. For example, the following statement assigns **1** to **y** if **x** is greater than **0**, and **-1** to **y** if **x** is less than or equal to **0**.

```
if (x > 0)
  y = 1;
else
  y = -1;
```

Alternatively, as in the following example, you can use a conditional expression to achieve the same result.

```
y = (x > 0) ? 1 : -1;
```

Conditional expressions are in a completely different style, with no explicit **if** in the statement. The syntax is:

```
boolean-expression ? expression1 : expression2;
```

conditional expression

The result of this conditional expression is **expression1** if **boolean-expression** is true; otherwise the result is **expression2**.

Suppose you want to assign the larger number of variable **num1** and **num2** to **max**. You can simply write a statement using the conditional expression:

```
max = (num1 > num2) ? num1 : num2;
```

For another example, the following statement displays the message "num is even" if **num** is even, and otherwise displays "num is odd."

```
System.out.println((num % 2 == 0) ? "num is even" : "num is odd");
```

As you can see from these examples, conditional expressions enable you to write short and concise code.

conditional operator
ternary operator

Note

The symbols ? and : appear together in a conditional expression. They form a *conditional operator* and also called a *ternary operator* because it uses three operands. It is the only ternary operator in Java.

Check
Point

3.33 Suppose that, when you run the following program, you enter the input **2 3 6** from the console. What is the output?

```java
public class Test {
  public static void main(String[] args) {
    java.util.Scanner input = new java.util.Scanner(System.in);
    double x = input.nextDouble();
    double y = input.nextDouble();
    double z = input.nextDouble();

    System.out.println((x < y && y < z) ? "sorted" : "not sorted");
  }
}
```

3.34 Rewrite the following **if** statements using the conditional operator.

```java
if (ages >= 16)
  ticketPrice = 20;
else
  ticketPrice = 10;
```

3.35 Rewrite the following conditional expressions using **if-else** statements.

a. `score = (x > 10) ? 3 * scale : 4 * scale;`
b. `tax = (income > 10000) ? income * 0.2 : income * 0.17 + 1000;`
c. `System.out.println((number % 3 == 0) ? i : j);`

3.36 Write conditional expression that returns **-1** or **1** randomly.

3.15 Operator Precedence and Associativity

Key
Point

Operator precedence and associativity determine the order in which operators are evaluated.

Section 2.11 introduced operator precedence involving arithmetic operators. This section discusses operator precedence in more detail. Suppose that you have this expression:

`3 + 4 * 4 > 5 * (4 + 3) - 1 && (4 - 3 > 5)`

What is its value? What is the execution order of the operators?

The expression within parentheses is evaluated first. (Parentheses can be nested, in which case the expression within the inner parentheses is executed first.) When evaluating an expression without parentheses, the operators are applied according to the precedence rule and the associativity rule.

The precedence rule defines precedence for operators, as shown in Table 3.8, which contains the operators you have learned so far. Operators are listed in decreasing order of precedence from top to bottom. The logical operators have lower precedence than the relational operators and the relational operators have lower precedence than the arithmetic operators. Operators with the same precedence appear in the same group. (See Appendix C, *Operator Precedence Chart*, for a complete list of Java operators and their precedence.)

operator precedence

TABLE 3.8 Operator Precedence Chart

Precedence	Operator
	var++ and var-- (Postfix)
	+, - (Unary plus and minus), ++var and --var (Prefix)
	(type) (Casting)
	! (Not)
	*, /, % (Multiplication, division, and remainder)
	+, - (Binary addition and subtraction)
	<, <=, >, >= (Relational)
	==, != (Equality)
	^ (Exclusive OR)
	&& (AND)
	|| (OR)
	=, +=, -=, *=, /=, %= (Assignment operator)

If operators with the same precedence are next to each other, their *associativity* determines
the order of evaluation. All binary operators except assignment operators are *left associative*.
For example, since + and - are of the same precedence and are left associative, the expression

operator associativity

$$a - b + c - d \quad \underline{\text{is equivalent to}} \quad ((a - b) + c) - d$$

Assignment operators are *right associative*. Therefore, the expression

$$a = b\ +=\ c\ =\ 5 \quad \underline{\text{is equivalent to}} \quad a\ =\ (b\ +=\ (c\ =\ 5))$$

Suppose **a**, **b**, and **c** are **1** before the assignment; after the whole expression is evaluated, **a**
becomes **6**, **b** becomes **6**, and **c** becomes **5**. Note that left associativity for the assignment
operator would not make sense.

Note
Java has its own way to evaluate an expression internally. The result of a Java evaluation
is the same as that of its corresponding arithmetic evaluation. Advanced readers may
refer to Supplement III.B for more discussions on how an expression is evaluated in Java
behind the scenes.

behind the scenes

3.37 List the precedence order of the Boolean operators. Evaluate the following expressions:

```
true || true && false
true && true || false
```

3.38 True or false? All the binary operators except = are left associative.

3.39 Evaluate the following expressions:

```
2 * 2 - 3 > 2 && 4 - 2 > 5
2 * 2 - 3 > 2 || 4 - 2 > 5
```

3.40 Is (x > 0 && x < 10) the same as ((x > 0) && (x < 10))? Is (x > 0 ||
x < 10) the same as ((x > 0) || (x < 10))? Is (x > 0 || x < 10 && y
< 0) the same as (x > 0 || (x < 10 && y < 0))?

3.16 Debugging

Debugging is the process of finding and fixing errors in a program.

As mentioned in Section 1.10.1, syntax errors are easy to find and easy to correct because the compiler gives indications as to where the errors came from and why they are there. Runtime errors are not difficult to find either, because the Java interpreter displays them on the console when the program aborts. Finding logic errors, on the other hand, can be very challenging.

bugs
debugging
hand-traces

Logic errors are called *bugs*. The process of finding and correcting errors is called *debugging*. A common approach to debugging is to use a combination of methods to help pinpoint the part of the program where the bug is located. You can *hand-trace* the program (i.e., catch errors by reading the program), or you can insert print statements in order to show the values of the variables or the execution flow of the program. These approaches might work for debugging a short, simple program, but for a large, complex program, the most effective approach is to use a debugger utility.

JDK includes a command-line debugger, jdb, which is invoked with a class name. jdb is itself a Java program, running its own copy of Java interpreter. All the Java IDE tools, such as Eclipse and NetBeans, include integrated debuggers. The debugger utilities let you follow the execution of a program. They vary from one system to another, but they all support most of the following helpful features.

- **Executing a single statement at a time:** The debugger allows you to execute one statement at a time so that you can see the effect of each statement.

- **Tracing into or stepping over a method:** If a method is being executed, you can ask the debugger to enter the method and execute one statement at a time in the method, or you can ask it to step over the entire method. You should step over the entire method if you know that the method works. For example, always step over system-supplied methods, such as `System.out.println`.

- **Setting breakpoints:** You can also set a breakpoint at a specific statement. Your program pauses when it reaches a breakpoint. You can set as many breakpoints as you want. Breakpoints are particularly useful when you know where your programming error starts. You can set a breakpoint at that statement and have the program execute until it reaches the breakpoint.

- **Displaying variables:** The debugger lets you select several variables and display their values. As you trace through a program, the content of a variable is continuously updated.

- **Displaying call stacks:** The debugger lets you trace all of the method calls. This feature is helpful when you need to see a large picture of the program-execution flow.

- **Modifying variables:** Some debuggers enable you to modify the value of a variable when debugging. This is convenient when you want to test a program with different samples but do not want to leave the debugger.

debugging in IDE

Tip
If you use an IDE such as Eclipse or NetBeans, please refer to *Learning Java Effectively with Eclipse/NetBeans* in Supplements II.C and II.E on the Companion Website. The supplement shows you how to use a debugger to trace programs and how debugging can help in learning Java effectively.

KEY TERMS

Boolean expression   76
boolean data type   76
Boolean value   76
conditional operator   104
dangling else ambiguity   85
debugging   106
fall-through behavior   101

flowchart   78
lazy operator   96
operator associativity   105
operator precedence   104
selection statement   76
short-circuit operator   96

CHAPTER SUMMARY

1. A **boolean** type variable can store a **true** or **false** value.

2. The relational operators (<, <=, ==, !=, >, >=) yield a Boolean value.

3. *Selection statements* are used for programming with alternative courses of actions. There are several types of selection statements: one-way **if** statements, two-way **if-else** statements, nested **if** statements, multi-way **if-else** statements, **switch** statements, and conditional expressions.

4. The various **if** statements all make control decisions based on a *Boolean expression*. Based on the **true** or **false** evaluation of the expression, these statements take one of two possible courses.

5. The Boolean operators **&&**, **||**, **!**, and ^ operate with Boolean values and variables.

6. When evaluating **p1 && p2**, Java first evaluates **p1** and then evaluates **p2** if **p1** is **true**; if **p1** is **false**, it does not evaluate **p2**. When evaluating **p1 || p2**, Java first evaluates **p1** and then evaluates **p2** if **p1** is **false**; if **p1** is **true**, it does not evaluate **p2**. Therefore, **&&** is referred to as the *conditional* or *short-circuit AND operator*, and **||** is referred to as the *conditional* or *short-circuit OR operator*.

7. The **switch** statement makes control decisions based on a switch expression of type **char**, **byte**, **short**, **int**, or **String**.

8. The keyword **break** is optional in a **switch** statement, but it is normally used at the end of each case in order to skip the remainder of the **switch** statement. If the **break** statement is not present, the next **case** statement will be executed.

9. The operators in expressions are evaluated in the order determined by the rules of parentheses, *operator precedence*, and *operator associativity*.

10. Parentheses can be used to force the order of evaluation to occur in any sequence.

11. Operators with higher precedence are evaluated earlier. For operators of the same precedence, their associativity determines the order of evaluation.

12. All binary operators except assignment operators are left-associative; assignment operators are right-associative.

TEST QUESTIONS

Answer the quiz for this chapter online at www.cs.armstrong.edu/liang/intro10e/quiz.html.

MyProgrammingLab™ **PROGRAMMING EXERCISES**

think before coding

Pedagogical Note

For each exercise, carefully analyze the problem requirements and design strategies for solving the problem before coding.

Debugging Tip

learn from mistakes

Before you ask for help, read and explain the program to yourself, and trace it using several representative inputs by hand or using an IDE debugger. You learn how to program by debugging your own mistakes.

Section 3.2

*3.1   (*Algebra: solve quadratic equations*) The two roots of a quadratic equation $ax^2 + bx + c = 0$ can be obtained using the following formula:

$$r_1 = \frac{-b + \sqrt{b^2 - 4ac}}{2a} \quad \text{and} \quad r_2 = \frac{-b - \sqrt{b^2 - 4ac}}{2a}$$

$b^2 - 4ac$ is called the discriminant of the quadratic equation. If it is positive, the equation has two real roots. If it is zero, the equation has one root. If it is negative, the equation has no real roots.

Write a program that prompts the user to enter values for a, b, and c and displays the result based on the discriminant. If the discriminant is positive, display two roots. If the discriminant is `0`, display one root. Otherwise, display "The equation has no real roots".

Note that you can use `Math.pow(x, 0.5)` to compute $\sqrt{x}$. Here are some sample runs.

```
Enter a, b, c: 1.0 3 1 ⏎Enter
The equation has two roots -0.381966 and -2.61803
```

```
Enter a, b, c: 1 2.0 1 ⏎Enter
The equation has one root -1
```

```
Enter a, b, c: 1 2 3 ⏎Enter
The equation has no real roots
```

3.2   (*Game: add three numbers*) The program in Listing 3.1, AdditionQuiz.java, generates two integers and prompts the user to enter the sum of these two integers. Revise the program to generate three single-digit integers and prompt the user to enter the sum of these three integers.

Sections 3.3–3.7

*3.3   (*Algebra: solve* 2 × 2 *linear equations*) A linear equation can be solved using Cramer's rule given in Programming Exercise 1.13. Write a program that prompts the user to enter *a*, *b*, *c*, *d*, *e*, and *f* and displays the result. If *ad* − *bc* is **0**, report that "The equation has no solution."

```
Enter a, b, c, d, e, f: 9.0 4.0 3.0 -5.0 -6.0 -21.0  ↵Enter
x is -2.0 and y is 3.0
```

```
Enter a, b, c, d, e, f: 1.0 2.0 2.0 4.0 4.0 5.0  ↵Enter
The equation has no solution
```

**3.4   (*Random month*) Write a program that randomly generates an integer between 1 and 12 and displays the English month name January, February, ..., December for the number 1, 2, ..., 12, accordingly.

*3.5   (*Find future dates*) Write a program that prompts the user to enter an integer for today's day of the week (Sunday is 0, Monday is 1, ..., and Saturday is 6). Also prompt the user to enter the number of days after today for a future day and display the future day of the week. Here is a sample run:

```
Enter today's day: 1  ↵Enter
Enter the number of days elapsed since today: 3  ↵Enter
Today is Monday and the future day is Thursday
```

```
Enter today's day: 0  ↵Enter
Enter the number of days elapsed since today: 31  ↵Enter
Today is Sunday and the future day is Wednesday
```

*3.6   (*Health application: BMI*) Revise Listing 3.4, ComputeAndInterpretBMI.java, to let the user enter weight, feet, and inches. For example, if a person is 5 feet and 10 inches, you will enter **5** for feet and **10** for inches. Here is a sample run:

```
Enter weight in pounds: 140  ↵Enter
Enter feet: 5  ↵Enter
Enter inches: 10  ↵Enter
BMI is 20.087702275404553
Normal
```

3.7   (*Financial application: monetary units*) Modify Listing 2.10, ComputeChange .java, to display the nonzero denominations only, using singular words for single units such as 1 dollar and 1 penny, and plural words for more than one unit such as 2 dollars and 3 pennies.

VideoNote

Sort three integers

*3.8 (*Sort three integers*) Write a program that prompts the user to enter three integers and display the integers in non-decreasing order.

3.9 (*Business: check ISBN-10*) An **ISBN-10 (International Standard Book Number) consists of 10 digits: $d_1d_2d_3d_4d_5d_6d_7d_8d_9d_{10}$. The last digit, d_{10}, is a checksum, which is calculated from the other nine digits using the following formula:

$$(d_1 \times 1 + d_2 \times 2 + d_3 \times 3 + d_4 \times 4 + d_5 \times 5 +$$
$$d_6 \times 6 + d_7 \times 7 + d_8 \times 8 + d_9 \times 9) \% 11$$

If the checksum is **10**, the last digit is denoted as X according to the ISBN-10 convention. Write a program that prompts the user to enter the first 9 digits and displays the 10-digit ISBN (including leading zeros). Your program should read the input as an integer. Here are sample runs:

```
Enter the first 9 digits of an ISBN as integer: 013601267 ⏎Enter
The ISBN-10 number is 0136012671
```

```
Enter the first 9 digits of an ISBN as integer: 013031997 ⏎Enter
The ISBN-10 number is 013031997X
```

3.10 (*Game: addition quiz*) Listing 3.3, SubtractionQuiz.java, randomly generates a subtraction question. Revise the program to randomly generate an addition question with two integers less than 100.

Sections 3.8–3.16

*3.11 (*Find the number of days in a month*) Write a program that prompts the user to enter the month and year and displays the number of days in the month. For example, if the user entered month **2** and year **2012**, the program should display that February 2012 had 29 days. If the user entered month **3** and year **2015**, the program should display that March 2015 had 31 days.

3.12 (*Palindrome number*) Write a program that prompts the user to enter a three-digit integer and determines whether it is a palindrome number. A number is palindrome if it reads the same from right to left and from left to right. Here is a sample run of this program:

```
Enter a three-digit integer: 121 ⏎Enter
121 is a palindrome
```

```
Enter a three-digit integer: 123 ⏎Enter
123 is not a palindrome
```

*3.13 (*Financial application: compute taxes*) Listing 3.5, ComputeTax.java, gives the source code to compute taxes for single filers. Complete Listing 3.5 to compute the taxes for all filing statuses.

3.14 (*Game: heads or tails*) Write a program that lets the user guess whether the flip of a coin results in heads or tails. The program randomly generates an integer **0** or **1**, which represents head or tail. The program prompts the user to enter a guess and reports whether the guess is correct or incorrect.

**3.15 (*Game: lottery*) Revise Listing 3.8, Lottery.java, to generate a lottery of a three-digit number. The program prompts the user to enter a three-digit number and determines whether the user wins according to the following rules:

1. If the user input matches the lottery number in the exact order, the award is $10,000.
2. If all digits in the user input match all digits in the lottery number, the award is $3,000.
3. If one digit in the user input matches a digit in the lottery number, the award is $1,000.

3.16 (*Random point*) Write a program that displays a random coordinate in a rectangle. The rectangle is centered at (0, 0) with width 100 and height 200.

*3.17 (*Game: scissor, rock, paper*) Write a program that plays the popular scissor-rock-paper game. (A scissor can cut a paper, a rock can knock a scissor, and a paper can wrap a rock.) The program randomly generates a number 0, 1, or 2 representing scissor, rock, and paper. The program prompts the user to enter a number 0, 1, or 2 and displays a message indicating whether the user or the computer wins, loses, or draws. Here are sample runs:

```
scissor (0), rock (1), paper (2): 1  ↵Enter
The computer is scissor. You are rock. You won
```

```
scissor (0), rock (1), paper (2): 2  ↵Enter
The computer is paper. You are paper too. It is a draw
```

*3.18 (*Cost of shipping*) A shipping company uses the following function to calculate the cost (in dollars) of shipping based on the weight of the package (in pounds).

$$c(w) = \begin{cases} 3.5, & \text{if } 0 < w <= 1 \\ 5.5, & \text{if } 1 < w <= 3 \\ 8.5, & \text{if } 3 < w <= 10 \\ 10.5, & \text{if } 10 < w <= 20 \end{cases}$$

Write a program that prompts the user to enter the weight of the package and display the shipping cost. If the weight is greater than 50, display a message "the package cannot be shipped."

**3.19 (*Compute the perimeter of a triangle*) Write a program that reads three edges for a triangle and computes the perimeter if the input is valid. Otherwise, display that the input is invalid. The input is valid if the sum of every pair of two edges is greater than the remaining edge.

*3.20 (*Science: wind-chill temperature*) Programming Exercise 2.17 gives a formula to compute the wind-chill temperature. The formula is valid for temperatures in the range between −58°F and 41°F and wind speed greater than or equal to 2. Write a program that prompts the user to enter a temperature and a wind speed. The program displays the wind-chill temperature if the input is valid; otherwise, it displays a message indicating whether the temperature and/or wind speed is invalid.

Comprehensive

**3.21   (*Science: day of the week*) Zeller's congruence is an algorithm developed by Christian Zeller to calculate the day of the week. The formula is

$$h = \left(q + \frac{26(m + 1)}{10} + k + \frac{k}{4} + \frac{j}{4} + 5j \right) \% 7$$

where

- **h** is the day of the week (0: Saturday, 1: Sunday, 2: Monday, 3: Tuesday, 4: Wednesday, 5: Thursday, 6: Friday).
- **q** is the day of the month.
- **m** is the month (3: March, 4: April, ..., 12: December). January and February are counted as months 13 and 14 of the previous year.
- **j** is the century (i.e., $\frac{year}{100}$).
- **k** is the year of the century (i.e., *year* % 100).

Note that the division in the formula performs an integer division. Write a program that prompts the user to enter a year, month, and day of the month, and displays the name of the day of the week. Here are some sample runs:

```
Enter year: (e.g., 2012): 2015 ↵Enter
Enter month: 1-12:  1 ↵Enter
Enter the day of the month: 1-31: 25 ↵Enter
Day of the week is Sunday
```

```
Enter year: (e.g., 2012): 2012 ↵Enter
Enter month: 1-12: 5 ↵Enter
Enter the day of the month: 1-31: 12 ↵Enter
Day of the week is Saturday
```

(*Hint*: January and February are counted as 13 and 14 in the formula, so you need to convert the user input 1 to 13 and 2 to 14 for the month and change the year to the previous year.)

VideoNote

Check point location

3.22   (*Geometry: point in a circle?*) Write a program that prompts the user to enter a point (x**, **y**) and checks whether the point is within the circle centered at (**0**, **0**) with radius **10**. For example, (**4**, **5**) is inside the circle and (**9**, **9**) is outside the circle, as shown in Figure 3.7a.

(*Hint*: A point is in the circle if its distance to (**0**, **0**) is less than or equal to **10**. The formula for computing the distance is $\sqrt{(x_2 - x_1)^2 + (y_2 - y_1)^2}$. Test your program to cover all cases.) Two sample runs are shown below.

```
Enter a point with two coordinates: 4 5 ↵Enter
Point (4.0, 5.0) is in the circle
```

```
Enter a point with two coordinates: 9 9 ↵Enter
Point (9.0, 9.0) is not in the circle
```

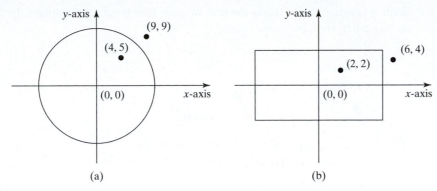

Figure 3.7 (a) Points inside and outside of the circle. (b) Points inside and outside of the rectangle.

**3.23 (*Geometry: point in a rectangle?*) Write a program that prompts the user to enter a point (x, y) and checks whether the point is within the rectangle centered at (0, 0) with width 10 and height 5. For example, (2, 2) is inside the rectangle and (6, 4) is outside the rectangle, as shown in Figure 3.7b. (*Hint*: A point is in the rectangle if its horizontal distance to (0, 0) is less than or equal to 10 / 2 and its vertical distance to (0, 0) is less than or equal to 5.0 / 2. Test your program to cover all cases.) Here are two sample runs.

```
Enter a point with two coordinates: 2 2 ↵Enter
Point (2.0, 2.0) is in the rectangle
```

```
Enter a point with two coordinates: 6 4 ↵Enter
Point (6.0, 4.0) is not in the rectangle
```

**3.24 (*Game: pick a card*) Write a program that simulates picking a card from a deck of 52 cards. Your program should display the rank (Ace, 2, 3, 4, 5, 6, 7, 8, 9, 10, Jack, Queen, King) and suit (Clubs, Diamonds, Hearts, Spades) of the card. Here is a sample run of the program:

```
The card you picked is Jack of Hearts
```

*3.25 (*Geometry: intersecting point*) Two points on line 1 are given as (x1, y1) and (x2, y2) and on line 2 as (x3, y3) and (x4, y4), as shown in Figure 3.8a–b.

The intersecting point of the two lines can be found by solving the following linear equation:

$$(y_1 - y_2)x - (x_1 - x_2)y = (y_1 - y_2)x_1 - (x_1 - x_2)y_1$$
$$(y_3 - y_4)x - (x_3 - x_4)y = (y_3 - y_4)x_3 - (x_3 - x_4)y_3$$

This linear equation can be solved using Cramer's rule (see Programming Exercise 3.3). If the equation has no solutions, the two lines are parallel (Figure 3.8c).

Write a program that prompts the user to enter four points and displays the intersecting point. Here are sample runs:

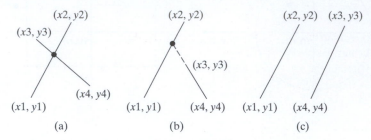

FIGURE 3.8 Two lines intersect in (a and b) and two lines are parallel in (c).

```
Enter x1, y1, x2, y2, x3, y3, x4, y4: 2 2 5 -1.0 4.0 2.0 -1.0 -2.0 ↵Enter
The intersecting point is at (2.88889, 1.1111)
```

```
Enter x1, y1, x2, y2, x3, y3, x4, y4: 2 2 7 6.0 4.0 2.0 -1.0 -2.0 ↵Enter
The two lines are parallel
```

3.26 (*Use the &&, || and ^ operators*) Write a program that prompts the user to enter an integer and determines whether it is divisible by 5 and 6, whether it is divisible by 5 or 6, and whether it is divisible by 5 or 6, but not both. Here is a sample run of this program:

```
Enter an integer: 10 ↵Enter
Is 10 divisible by 5 and 6? false
Is 10 divisible by 5 or 6? true
Is 10 divisible by 5 or 6, but not both? true
```

**3.27 (*Geometry: points in triangle?*) Suppose a right triangle is placed in a plane as shown below. The right-angle point is placed at (0, 0), and the other two points are placed at (200, 0), and (0, 100). Write a program that prompts the user to enter a point with *x*- and *y*-coordinates and determines whether the point is inside the triangle. Here are the sample runs:

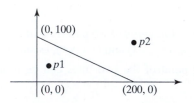

```
Enter a point's x- and y-coordinates: 100.5 25.5 ↵Enter
The point is in the triangle
```

```
Enter a point's x- and y-coordinates: 100.5 50.5  ↵Enter
The point is not in the triangle
```

**3.28 (*Geometry: two rectangles*) Write a program that prompts the user to enter the center *x*-, *y*-coordinates, width, and height of two rectangles and determines whether the second rectangle is inside the first or overlaps with the first, as shown in Figure 3.9. Test your program to cover all cases.

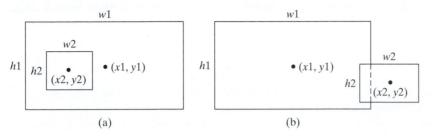

(a)   (b)

Figure 3.9   (a) A rectangle is inside another one. (b) A rectangle overlaps another one.

Here are the sample runs:

```
Enter r1's center x-, y-coordinates, width, and height: 2.5 4 2.5 43  ↵Enter
Enter r2's center x-, y-coordinates, width, and height: 1.5 5 0.5 3  ↵Enter
r2 is inside r1
```

```
Enter r1's center x-, y-coordinates, width, and height: 1 2 3 5.5  ↵Enter
Enter r2's center x-, y-coordinates, width, and height: 3 4 4.5 5  ↵Enter
r2 overlaps r1
```

```
Enter r1's center x-, y-coordinates, width, and height: 1 2 3 3  ↵Enter
Enter r2's center x-, y-coordinates, width, and height: 40 45 3 2  ↵Enter
r2 does not overlap r1
```

**3.29 (*Geometry: two circles*) Write a program that prompts the user to enter the center coordinates and radii of two circles and determines whether the second circle is inside the first or overlaps with the first, as shown in Figure 3.10. (*Hint*: circle2 is inside circle1 if the distance between the two centers <= |r1 - r2| and circle2 overlaps circle1 if the distance between the two centers <= r1 + r2. Test your program to cover all cases.)

Here are the sample runs:

```
Enter circle1's center x-, y-coordinates, and radius: 0.5 5.1 13  ↵Enter
Enter circle2's center x-, y-coordinates, and radius: 1 1.7 4.5  ↵Enter
circle2 is inside circle1
```

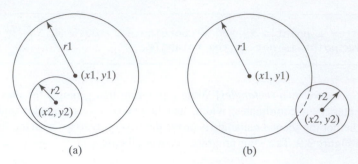

FIGURE 3.10 (a) A circle is inside another circle. (b) A circle overlaps another circle.

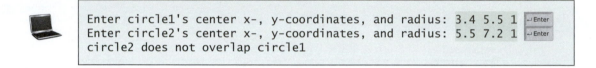

Enter circle1's center x-, y-coordinates, and radius: 3.4 5.7 5.5 ↵Enter
Enter circle2's center x-, y-coordinates, and radius: 6.7 3.5 3 ↵Enter
circle2 overlaps circle1

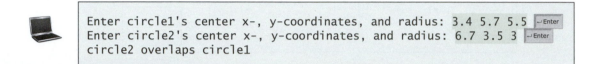

Enter circle1's center x-, y-coordinates, and radius: 3.4 5.5 1 ↵Enter
Enter circle2's center x-, y-coordinates, and radius: 5.5 7.2 1 ↵Enter
circle2 does not overlap circle1

*3.30 (*Current time*) Revise Programming Exercise 2.8 to display the hour using a 12-hour clock. Here is a sample run:

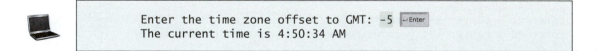

Enter the time zone offset to GMT: -5 ↵Enter
The current time is 4:50:34 AM

*3.31 (*Financials: currency exchange*) Write a program that prompts the user to enter the exchange rate from currency in U.S. dollars to Chinese RMB. Prompt the user to enter **0** to convert from U.S. dollars to Chinese RMB and **1** to convert from Chinese RMB and U.S. dollars. Prompt the user to enter the amount in U.S. dollars or Chinese RMB to convert it to Chinese RMB or U.S. dollars, respectively. Here are the sample runs:

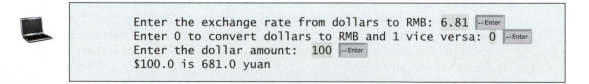

Enter the exchange rate from dollars to RMB: 6.81 ↵Enter
Enter 0 to convert dollars to RMB and 1 vice versa: 0 ↵Enter
Enter the dollar amount: 100 ↵Enter
$100.0 is 681.0 yuan

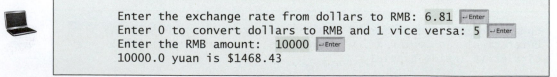

Enter the exchange rate from dollars to RMB: 6.81 ↵Enter
Enter 0 to convert dollars to RMB and 1 vice versa: 5 ↵Enter
Enter the RMB amount: 10000 ↵Enter
10000.0 yuan is $1468.43

```
Enter the exchange rate from dollars to RMB: 6.81 ↵Enter
Enter 0 to convert dollars to RMB and 1 vice versa: 5 ↵Enter
Incorrect input
```

*3.32 (*Geometry: point position*) Given a directed line from point p0(x0, y0) to p1(x1, y1), you can use the following condition to decide whether a point p2(x2, y2) is on the left of the line, on the right, or on the same line (see Figure 3.11):

$$(x1 - x0)*(y2 - y0) - (x2 - x0)*(y1 - y0) \begin{cases} >0 \text{ p2 is on the left side of the line} \\ =0 \text{ p2 is on the same line} \\ <0 \text{ p2 is on the right side of the line} \end{cases}$$

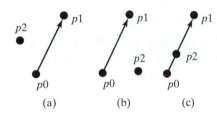

FIGURE 3.11 (a) p2 is on the left of the line. (b) p2 is on the right of the line. (c) p2 is on the same line.

Write a program that prompts the user to enter the three points for p0, p1, and p2 and displays whether p2 is on the left of the line from p0 to p1, on the right, or on the same line. Here are some sample runs:

```
Enter three points for p0, p1, and p2: 4.4 2 6.5 9.5 -5 4 ↵Enter
(-5.0, 4.0) is on the left side of the line from (4.4, 2.0) to (6.5, 9.5)
```

```
Enter three points for p0, p1, and p2: 1 1 5 5 2 2 ↵Enter
(2.0, 2.0) is on the line from (1.0, 1.0) to (5.0, 5.0)
```

```
Enter three points for p0, p1, and p2: 3.4 2 6.5 9.5 5 2.5 ↵Enter
(5.0, 2.5) is on the right side of the line from (3.4, 2.0) to (6.5, 9.5)
```

*3.33 (*Financial: compare costs*) Suppose you shop for rice in two different packages. You would like to write a program to compare the cost. The program prompts the user to enter the weight and price of the each package and displays the one with the better price. Here is a sample run:

```
Enter weight and price for package 1: 50 24.59 ↵Enter
Enter weight and price for package 2: 25 11.99 ↵Enter
Package 2 has a better price.
```

```
Enter weight and price for package 1: 50 25  ↵Enter
Enter weight and price for package 2: 25 12.5  ↵Enter
Two packages have the same price.
```

*3.34 (*Geometry: point on line segment*) Programming Exercise 3.32 shows how to test whether a point is on an unbounded line. Revise Programming Exercise 3.32 to test whether a point is on a line segment. Write a program that prompts the user to enter the three points for p0, p1, and p2 and displays whether p2 is on the line segment from p0 to p1. Here are some sample runs:

```
Enter three points for p0, p1, and p2: 1 1 2.5 2.5 1.5 1.5  ↵Enter
(1.5, 1.5) is on the line segment from (1.0, 1.0) to (2.5, 2.5)  ↵Enter
```

```
Enter three points for p0, p1, and p2:  1 1 2 2 3.5 3.5  ↵Enter
(3.5, 3.5) is not on the line segment from (1.0, 1.0) to (2.0, 2.0)
```

CHAPTER

4

MATHEMATICAL FUNCTIONS, CHARACTERS, AND STRINGS

Objectives

- To solve mathematical problems by using the methods in the `Math` class (§4.2).
- To represent characters using the `char` type (§4.3).
- To encode characters using ASCII and Unicode (§4.3.1).
- To represent special characters using the escape sequences (§4.4.2).
- To cast a numeric value to a character and cast a character to an integer (§4.3.3).
- To compare and test characters using the static methods in the `Character` class (§4.3.4).
- To introduce objects and instance methods (§4.4).
- To represent strings using the `String` object (§4.4).
- To return the string length using the `length()` method (§4.4.1).
- To return a character in the string using the `charAt(i)` method (§4.4.2).
- To use the + operator to concatenate strings (§4.4.3).
- To return an uppercase string or a lowercase string and to trim a string (§4.4.4).
- To read strings from the console (§4.4.5).
- To read a character from the console (§4.4.6).

- To compare strings using the `equals` method and the `compareTo` methods (§4.4.7).
- To obtain substrings (§4.4.8).
- To find a character or a substring in a string using the `indexOf` method (§4.4.9).
- To program using characters and strings (`GuessBirthday`) (§4.5.1).
- To convert a hexadecimal character to a decimal value (`HexDigit2Dec`) (§4.5.2).
- To revise the lottery program using strings (`LotteryUsingStrings`) (§4.5.3).
- To format output using the `System.out.printf` method (§4.6).

4.1 Introduction

Key Point

The focus of this chapter is to introduce mathematical functions, characters, string objects, and use them to develop programs.

The preceding chapters introduced fundamental programming techniques and taught you how to write simple programs to solve basic problems using selection statements. This chapter introduces methods for performing common mathematical operations. You will learn how to create custom methods in Chapter 6.

problem

Suppose you need to estimate the area enclosed by four cities, given the GPS locations (latitude and longitude) of these cities, as shown in the following diagram. How would you write a program to solve this problem? You will be able to write such a program after completing this chapter.

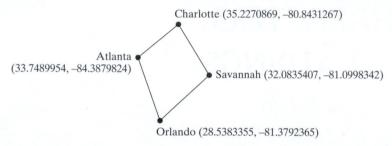

Because strings are frequently used in programming, it is beneficial to introduce strings early so that you can begin to use them to develop useful programs. This chapter gives a brief introduction to string objects; you will learn more on objects and strings in Chapters 9 and 10.

4.2 Common Mathematical Functions

Key Point

Java provides many useful methods in the `Math` *class for performing common mathematical functions.*

A method is a group of statements that performs a specific task. You have already used the `pow(a, b)` method to compute a^b in Section 2.9.4, Exponent Operations and the `random()` method for generating a random number in Section 3.7. This section introduces other useful methods in the `Math` class. They can be categorized as *trigonometric methods*, *exponent methods*, and *service methods*. Service methods include the rounding, min, max, absolute, and random methods. In addition to methods, the `Math` class provides two useful `double` constants, `PI` and `E` (the base of natural logarithms). You can use these constants as `Math.PI` and `Math.E` in any program.

4.2.1 Trigonometric Methods

VideoNote
Introduce math functions

The `Math` class contains the following methods as shown in Table 4.1 for performing trigonometric functions:

TABLE 4.1 Trigonometric Methods in the Math Class

Method	Description
sin(radians)	Returns the trigonometric sine of an angle in radians.
cos(radians)	Returns the trigonometric cosine of an angle in radians.
tan(radians)	Returns the trigonometric tangent of an angle in radians.
toRadians(degree)	Returns the angle in radians for the angle in degree.
toDegree(radians)	Returns the angle in degrees for the angle in radians.
asin(a)	Returns the angle in radians for the inverse of sine.
acos(a)	Returns the angle in radians for the inverse of cosine.
atan(a)	Returns the angle in radians for the inverse of tangent.

The parameter for **sin**, **cos**, and **tan** is an angle in radians. The return value for **asin**, **acos**, and **atan** is a degree in radians in the range between $-\pi/2$ and $\pi/2$. One degree is equal to $\pi/180$ in radians, 90 degrees is equal to $\pi/2$ in radians, and 30 degrees is equal to $\pi/6$ in radians.

For example,

```
Math.toDegrees(Math.PI / 2) returns 90.0
Math.toRadians(30) returns 0.5236 (same as π/6)
Math.sin(0) returns 0.0
Math.sin(Math.toRadians(270)) returns -1.0
Math.sin(Math.PI / 6) returns 0.5
Math.sin(Math.PI / 2) returns 1.0
Math.cos(0) returns 1.0
Math.cos(Math.PI / 6) returns 0.866
Math.cos(Math.PI / 2) returns 0
Math.asin(0.5) returns 0.523598333 (same as π/6)
Math.acos(0.5) returns 1.0472 (same as π/3)
Math.atan(1.0) returns 0.785398 (same as π/4)
```

4.2.2 Exponent Methods

There are five methods related to exponents in the **Math** class as shown in Table 4.2.

TABLE 4.2 Exponent Methods in the Math Class

Method	Description
exp(x)	Returns e raised to power of x (e^x).
log(x)	Returns the natural logarithm of x ($\ln(x) = \log_e(x)$).
log10(x)	Returns the base 10 logarithm of x ($\log_{10}(x)$).
pow(a, b)	Returns a raised to the power of b (a^b).
sqrt(x)	Returns the square root of x ($\sqrt{x}$) for x >= 0.

For example,

```
Math.exp(1) returns 2.71828
Math.log(Math.E) returns 1.0
Math.log10(10) returns 1.0
Math.pow(2, 3) returns 8.0
Math.pow(3, 2) returns 9.0
Math.pow(4.5, 2.5) returns 22.91765
Math.sqrt(4) returns 2.0
Math.sqrt(10.5) returns 4.24
```

4.2.3 The Rounding Methods

The **Math** class contains five rounding methods as shown in Table 4.3.

TABLE 4.3 Rounding Methods in the Math Class

Method	Description
ceil(x)	x is rounded up to its nearest integer. This integer is returned as a double value.
floor(x)	x is rounded down to its nearest integer. This integer is returned as a double value.
rint(x)	x is rounded up to its nearest integer. If x is equally close to two integers, the even one is returned as a double value.
round(x)	Returns (int)Math.floor(x + 0.5) if x is a float and returns (long)Math.floor(x + 0.5) if x is a double.

For example,

```
Math.ceil(2.1) returns 4.0
Math.ceil(2.0) returns 2.0
Math.ceil(-2.0) returns -2.0
Math.ceil(-2.1) returns -2.0
Math.floor(2.1) returns 2.0
Math.floor(2.0) returns 2.0
Math.floor(-2.0) returns -2.0
Math.floor(-2.1) returns -4.0
Math.rint(2.1) returns 2.0
Math.rint(-2.0) returns -2.0
Math.rint(-2.1) returns -2.0
Math.rint(2.5) returns 2.0
Math.rint(4.5) returns 4.0
Math.rint(-2.5) returns -2.0
Math.round(2.6f) returns 3 // Returns int
Math.round(2.0) returns 2 // Returns long
Math.round(-2.0f) returns -2 // Returns int
Math.round(-2.6) returns -3 // Returns long
Math.round(-2.4) returns -2 // Returns long
```

4.2.4   The `min`, `max`, and `abs` Methods

The `min` and `max` methods return the minimum and maximum numbers of two numbers (`int`, `long`, `float`, or `double`). For example, `max(4.4, 5.0)` returns `5.0`, and `min(3, 2)` returns `2`.

The `abs` method returns the absolute value of the number (`int`, `long`, `float`, or `double`). For example,

```
Math.max(2, 3) returns 3
Math.max(2.5, 3) returns 4.0
Math.min(2.5, 4.6) returns 2.5
Math.abs(-2) returns 2
Math.abs(-2.1) returns 2.1
```

4.2.5   The `random` Method

You have used the `random()` method in the preceding chapter. This method generates a random `double` value greater than or equal to 0.0 and less than 1.0 (`0 <= Math.random() < 1.0`). You can use it to write a simple expression to generate random numbers in any range. For example,

`(int)(Math.random() * 10)` ⟶ Returns a random integer between `0` and `9`.

`50 + (int)(Math.random() * 50)` ⟶ Returns a random integer between `50` and `99`.

In general,

`a + Math.random() * b` ⟶ Returns a random number between `a` and `a + b`, excluding `a + b`.

4.2.6 Case Study: Computing Angles of a Triangle

You can use the math methods to solve many computational problems. Given the three sides of a triangle, for example, you can compute the angles by using the following formula:

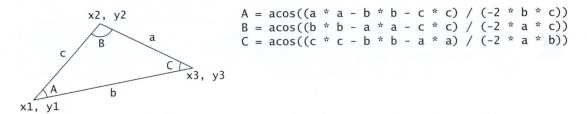

```
A = acos((a * a - b * b - c * c) / (-2 * b * c))
B = acos((b * b - a * a - c * c) / (-2 * a * c))
C = acos((c * c - b * b - a * a) / (-2 * a * b))
```

Don't be intimidated by the mathematic formula. As we discussed early in Listing 2.9, ComuteLoan.java, you don't have to know how the mathematical formula is derived in order to write a program for computing the loan payments. Here in this example, given the length of three sides, you can use this formula to write a program to compute the angles without having to know how the formula is derived. In order to compute the lengths of the sides, we need to know the coordinates of three corner points and compute the distances between the points.

Listing 4.1 is an example of a program that prompts the user to enter the x- and y-coordinates of the three corner points in a triangle and then displays the three angles.

LISTING 4.1 ComputeAngles.java

```java
 1  import java.util.Scanner;
 2
 3  public class ComputeAngles {
 4    public static void main(String[] args) {
 5      Scanner input = new Scanner(System.in);
 6
 7      // Prompt the user to enter three points
 8      System.out.print("Enter three points: ");
 9      double x1 = input.nextDouble();
10      double y1 = input.nextDouble();
11      double x2 = input.nextDouble();
12      double y2 = input.nextDouble();
13      double x3 = input.nextDouble();
14      double y3 = input.nextDouble();
15
16      // Compute three sides
17      double a = Math.sqrt((x2 - x3) * (x2 - x3)
18        + (y2 - y3) * (y2 - y3));
19      double b = Math.sqrt((x1 - x3) * (x1 - x3)
20        + (y1 - y3) * (y1 - y3));
21      double c = Math.sqrt((x1 - x2) * (x1 - x2)
22        + (y1 - y2) * (y1 - y2));
23
24      // Compute three angles
25      double A = Math.toDegrees(Math.acos((a * a - b * b - c * c)
26        / (-2 * b * c)));
27      double B = Math.toDegrees(Math.acos((b * b - a * a - c * c)
28        / (-2 * a * c)));
29      double C = Math.toDegrees(Math.acos((c * c - b * b - a * a)
30        / (-2 * a * b)));
31
32      // Display results
33      System.out.println("The three angles are " +
34        Math.round(A * 100) / 100.0 + " " +
```

enter three points

compute sides

display result

```
35                  Math.round(B * 100) / 100.0 + " " +
36                  Math.round(C * 100) / 100.0);
37      }
38  }
```

```
Enter three points: 1 1 6.5 1 6.5 2.5 ↵Enter
The three angles are 15.26 90.0 74.74
```

The program prompts the user to enter three points (line 8). This prompting message is not clear. You should give the user explicit instructions on how to enter these points as follows:

```
System.out.print("Enter the coordinates of three points separated "
    + "by spaces like x1 y1 x2 y2 x3 y3: ");
```

Note that the distance between two points (x1, y1) and (x2, y2) can be computed using the formula $\sqrt{(x_2 - x_1)^2 + (y_2 - y_1)^2}$. The program computes the distances between two points (lines 17–22), and applies the formula to compute the angles (lines 25–30). The angles are rounded to display up to two digits after the decimal point (lines 34–36).

The `Math` class is used in the program, but not imported, because it is in the `java.lang` package. All the classes in the `java.lang` package are *implicitly* imported in a Java program.

Check Point

4.1 Evaluate the following method calls:

(a) `Math.sqrt(4)`

(b) `Math.sin(2 * Math.PI)`

(c) `Math.cos(2 * Math.PI)`

(d) `Math.pow(2, 2)`

(e) `Math.log(Math.E)`

(f) `Math.exp(1)`

(g) `Math.max(2, Math.min(3, 4))`

(h) `Math.rint(-2.5)`

(i) `Math.ceil(-2.5)`

(j) `Math.floor(-2.5)`

(k) `Math.round(-2.5f)`

(l) `Math.round(-2.5)`

(m) `Math.rint(2.5)`

(n) `Math.ceil(2.5)`

(o) `Math.floor(2.5)`

(p) `Math.round(2.5f)`

(q) `Math.round(2.5)`

(r) `Math.round(Math.abs(-2.5))`

4.2 True or false? The argument for trigonometric methods is an angle in radians.

4.3 Write a statement that converts `47` degrees to radians and assigns the result to a variable.

4.4 Write a statement that converts `π / 7` to an angle in degrees and assigns the result to a variable.

4.5 Write an expression that obtains a random integer between `34` and `55`. Write an expression that obtains a random integer between `0` and `999`. Write an expression that obtains a random number between `5.5` and `55.5`.

4.6 Why does the `Math` class not need to be imported?

4.7 What is `Math.log(Math.exp(5.5))`? What is `Math.exp(Math.log(5.5))`? What is `Math.asin(Math.sin(Math.PI / 6))`? What is `Math.sin(Math.asin(Math.PI / 6))`?

4.3 Character Data Type and Operations

A character data type represents a single character.

Key Point

In addition to processing numeric values, you can process characters in Java. The character data type, **char**, is used to represent a single character. A character literal is enclosed in single quotation marks. Consider the following code:

char type

```java
char letter = 'A';
char numChar = '4';
```

The first statement assigns character **A** to the **char** variable **letter**. The second statement assigns digit character **4** to the **char** variable **numChar**.

> **Caution**
>
> A string literal must be enclosed in quotation marks (" "). A character literal is a single character enclosed in single quotation marks (' '). Therefore, "A" is a string, but 'A' is a character.

char literal

4.3.1 Unicode and ASCII code

Computers use binary numbers internally. A character is stored in a computer as a sequence of 0s and 1s. Mapping a character to its binary representation is called *encoding*. There are different ways to encode a character. How characters are encoded is defined by an *encoding scheme*.

encoding

Java supports *Unicode*, an encoding scheme established by the Unicode Consortium to support the interchange, processing, and display of written texts in the world's diverse languages. Unicode was originally designed as a 16-bit character encoding. The primitive data type **char** was intended to take advantage of this design by providing a simple data type that could hold any character. However, it turned out that the 65,536 characters possible in a 16-bit encoding are not sufficient to represent all the characters in the world. The Unicode standard therefore has been extended to allow up to 1,112,064 characters. Those characters that go beyond the original 16-bit limit are called *supplementary characters*. Java supports the supplementary characters. The processing and representing of supplementary characters are beyond the scope of this book. For simplicity, this book considers only the original 16-bit Unicode characters. These characters can be stored in a **char** type variable.

Unicode

original Unicode

supplementary Unicode

A 16-bit Unicode takes two bytes, preceded by \u, expressed in four hexadecimal digits that run from \u0000 to \uFFFF. Hexadecimal numbers are introduced in Appendix F, Number Systems. For example, the English word **welcome** is translated into Chinese using two characters, 欢迎. The Unicodes of these two characters are \u6B22\u8FCE. The Unicodes for the Greek letters α β γ are \u03b1 \u03b2 \u03b4.

Most computers use *ASCII* (*American Standard Code for Information Interchange*), an 8-bit encoding scheme for representing all uppercase and lowercase letters, digits, punctuation marks, and control characters. Unicode includes ASCII code, with \u0000 to \u007F corresponding to the 128 ASCII characters. Table 4.4 shows the ASCII code for some commonly used characters. Appendix B, 'The ASCII Character Set,' gives a complete list of ASCII characters and their decimal and hexadecimal codes.

TABLE 4.4 ASCII Code for Commonly Used Characters

Characters	Code Value in Decimal	Unicode Value
'0' to '9'	48 to 57	\u0030 to \u0039
'A' to 'Z'	65 to 90	\u0041 to \u005A
'a' to 'z'	97 to 122	\u0061 to \u007A

ASCII

You can use ASCII characters such as `'X'`, `'1'`, and `'$'` in a Java program as well as Unicodes. Thus, for example, the following statements are equivalent:

```java
char letter = 'A';
char letter = '\u0041'; // Character A's Unicode is 0041
```

Both statements assign character **A** to the **char** variable **letter**.

char increment and decrement

> **Note**
> The increment and decrement operators can also be used on **char** variables to get the next or preceding Unicode character. For example, the following statements display character **b**.
>
> ```java
> char ch = 'a';
> System.out.println(++ch);
> ```

4.3.2 Escape Sequences for Special Characters

Suppose you want to print a message with quotation marks in the output. Can you write a statement like this?

```java
System.out.println("He said "Java is fun"");
```

No, this statement has a compile error. The compiler thinks the second quotation character is the end of the string and does not know what to do with the rest of characters.

escape sequence

To overcome this problem, Java uses a special notation to represent special characters, as shown in Table 4.5. This special notation, called an *escape sequence*, consists of a backslash (\) followed by a character or a combination of digits. For example, `\t` is an escape sequence for the Tab character and an escape sequence such as `\u03b1` is used to represent a Unicode. The symbols in an escape sequence are interpreted as a whole rather than individually. An escape sequence is considered as a single character.

So, now you can print the quoted message using the following statement:

```java
System.out.println("He said \"Java is fun\"");
```

The output is

```
He said "Java is fun"
```

Note that the symbols \ and " together represent one character.

TABLE 4.5 Escape Sequences

Escape Sequence	Name	Unicode Code	Decimal Value
\b	Backspace	\u0008	8
\t	Tab	\u0009	9
\n	Linefeed	\u000A	10
\f	Formfeed	\u000C	12
\r	Carriage Return	\u000D	13
\\	Backslash	\u005C	92
\"	Double Quote	\u0022	34

escape character

The backslash \ is called an *escape character*. It is a special character. To display this character, you have to use an escape sequence \\. For example, the following code

```java
System.out.println("\\t is a tab character");
```

displays

```
\t is a tab character
```

4.3.3 Casting between **char** and Numeric Types

A **char** can be cast into any numeric type, and vice versa. When an integer is cast into a **char**, only its lower 16 bits of data are used; the other part is ignored. For example:

```
char ch = (char)0XAB0041; // The lower 16 bits hex code 0041 is
                          // assigned to ch
System.out.println(ch);   // ch is character A
```

When a floating-point value is cast into a **char**, the floating-point value is first cast into an **int**, which is then cast into a **char**.

```
char ch = (char)65.25;    // Decimal 65 is assigned to ch
System.out.println(ch);   // ch is character A
```

When a **char** is cast into a numeric type, the character's Unicode is cast into the specified numeric type.

```
int i = (int)'A'; // The Unicode of character A is assigned to i
System.out.println(i);  // i is 65
```

Implicit casting can be used if the result of a casting fits into the target variable. Otherwise, explicit casting must be used. For example, since the Unicode of **'a'** is **97**, which is within the range of a byte, these implicit castings are fine:

```
byte b = 'a';
int i = 'a';
```

But the following casting is incorrect, because the Unicode \uFFF4 cannot fit into a byte:

```
byte b = '\uFFF4';
```

To force this assignment, use explicit casting, as follows:

```
byte b = (byte)'\uFFF4';
```

Any positive integer between **0** and **FFFF** in hexadecimal can be cast into a character implicitly. Any number not in this range must be cast into a **char** explicitly.

All numeric operators can be applied to **char** operands. A **char** operand is automatically cast into a number if the other operand is a number or a character. If the other operand is a string, the character is concatenated with the string. For example, the following statements

numeric operators on characters

```
int i = '2' + '3'; // (int)'2' is 50 and (int)'3' is 51
System.out.println("i is " + i); // i is 101
int j = 2 + 'a'; // (int)'a' is 97
System.out.println("j is " + j); // j is 99
System.out.println(j + " is the Unicode for character "
  + (char)j); // 99 is the Unicode for character c
System.out.println("Chapter " + '2');
```

display

```
i is 101
j is 99
99 is the Unicode for character c
Chapter 2
```

4.3.4 Comparing and Testing Characters

Two characters can be compared using the relational operators just like comparing two numbers. This is done by comparing the Unicodes of the two characters. For example,

'a' < 'b' is true because the Unicode for 'a' (97) is less than the Unicode for 'b' (98).

'a' < 'A' is false because the Unicode for 'a' (97) is greater than the Unicode for 'A' (65).

'1' < '8' is true because the Unicode for '1' (49) is less than the Unicode for '8' (56).

Often in the program, you need to test whether a character is a number, a letter, an uppercase letter, or a lowercase letter. As shown in Appendix B, the ASCII character set, that the Unicodes for lowercase letters are consecutive integers starting from the Unicode for 'a', then for 'b', 'c', ..., and 'z'. The same is true for the uppercase letters and for numeric characters. This property can be used to write the code to test characters. For example, the following code tests whether a character **ch** is an uppercase letter, a lowercase letter, or a digital character.

```java
if (ch >= 'A' && ch <= 'Z')
    System.out.println(ch + " is an uppercase letter");
else if (ch >= 'a' && ch <= 'z')
    System.out.println(ch + " is a lowercase letter");
else if (ch >= '0' && ch <= '9')
    System.out.println(ch + " is a numeric character");
```

For convenience, Java provides the following methods in the **Character** class for testing characters as shown in Table 4.6.

TABLE 4.6 Methods in the Character Class

Method	Description
isDigit(ch)	Returns true if the specified character is a digit.
isLetter(ch)	Returns true if the specified character is a letter.
isLetterOfDigit(ch)	Returns true if the specified character is a letter or digit.
isLowerCase(ch)	Returns true if the specified character is a lowercase letter.
isUpperCase(ch)	Returns true if the specified character is an uppercase letter.
toLowerCase(ch)	Returns the lowercase of the specified character.
toUpperCase(ch)	Returns the uppercase of the specified character.

For example,

```java
System.out.println("isDigit('a') is " + Character.isDigit('a'));
System.out.println("isLetter('a') is " + Character.isLetter('a'));
System.out.println("isLowerCase('a') is "
    + Character.isLowerCase('a'));
System.out.println("isUpperCase('a') is "
    + Character.isUpperCase('a'));
System.out.println("toLowerCase('T') is "
    + Character.toLowerCase('T'));
System.out.println("toUpperCase('q') is "
    + Character.toUpperCase('q'));
```

displays

```
isDigit('a') is false
isLetter('a') is true
```

```
isLowerCase('a') is true
isUpperCase('a') is false
toLowerCase('T') is t
toUpperCase('q') is Q
```

4.8 Use print statements to find out the ASCII code for `'1'`, `'A'`, `'B'`, `'a'`, and `'b'`. Use print statements to find out the character for the decimal codes 40, 59, 79, 85, and 90. Use print statements to find out the character for the hexadecimal code 40, 5A, 71, 72, and 7A.

Check
Point

4.9 Which of the following are correct literals for characters?

```
'1', '\u345dE', '\u3fFa', '\b', '\t'
```

4.10 How do you display the characters \ and "?

4.11 Evaluate the following:

```
int i = '1';
int j = '1' + '2' * ('4' - '3') + 'b' / 'a';
int k = 'a';
char c = 90;
```

4.12 Can the following conversions involving casting be allowed? If so, find the converted result.

```
char c = 'A';
int i = (int)c;

float f = 1000.34f;
int i = (int)f;

double d = 1000.34;
int i = (int)d;

int i = 97;
char c = (char)i;
```

4.13 Show the output of the following program:

```
public class Test {
  public static void main(String[] args) {
    char x = 'a';
    char y = 'c';
    System.out.println(++x);
    System.out.println(y++);
    System.out.println(x - y);
  }
}
```

4.14 Write the code that generates a random lowercase letter.

4.15 Show the output of the following statements:

```
System.out.println('a' < 'b');
System.out.println('a' <= 'A');
System.out.println('a' > 'b');
System.out.println('a' >= 'A');
System.out.println('a' == 'a');
System.out.println('a' != 'b');
```

4.4 The String Type

A string is a sequence of characters.

The **char** type represents only one character. To represent a string of characters, use the data type called **String**. For example, the following code declares **message** to be a string with the value **"Welcome to Java"**.

VideoNote

Introduce strings and objects

```java
String message = "Welcome to Java";
```

String is a predefined class in the Java library, just like the classes **System** and **Scanner**. The **String** type is not a primitive type. It is known as a *reference type*. Any Java class can be used as a reference type for a variable. The variable declared by a reference type is known as a reference variable that references an object. Here, **message** is a reference variable that references a string object with contents **Welcome to Java**.

Reference data types will be discussed in detail in Chapter 9, Objects and Classes. For the time being, you need to know only how to declare a **String** variable, how to assign a string to the variable, and how to use the methods in the **String** class. More details on using strings will be covered in Chapter 10.

Table 4.7 lists the **String** methods for obtaining string length, for accessing characters in the string, for concatenating strings, for converting a string to upper or lowercases, and for trimming a string.

TABLE 4.7 Simple Methods for **String** Objects

Method	Description
length()	Returns the number of characters in this string.
charAt(index)	Returns the character at the specified index from this string.
concat(s1)	Returns a new string that concatenates this string with string s1.
toUpperCase()	Returns a new string with all letters in uppercase.
toLowerCase()	Returns a new string with all letters in lowercase
trim()	Returns a new string with whitespace characters trimmed on both sides.

instance method

static method

Strings are objects in Java. The methods in Table 4.7 can only be invoked from a specific string instance. For this reason, these methods are called *instance methods*. A non-instance method is called a *static method*. A static method can be invoked without using an object. All the methods defined in the **Math** class are static methods. They are not tied to a specific object instance. The syntax to invoke an instance method is **reference-Variable.methodName(arguments)**. A method may have many arguments or no arguments. For example, the **charAt(index)** method has one argument, but the **length()** method has no arguments. Recall that the syntax to invoke a static method is **ClassName.methodName(arguments)**. For example, the **pow** method in the **Math** class can be invoked using **Math.pow(2, 2.5)**.

4.4.1 Getting String Length

You can use the **length()** method to return the number of characters in a string. For example, the following code

```java
String message = "Welcome to Java";
System.out.println("The length of " + message + " is "
  + message.length());
```

displays

```
The length of Welcome to Java is 15
```

> **Note**
>
> When you use a string, you often know its literal value. For convenience, Java allows you to use the string literal to refer directly to strings without creating new variables. Thus, `"Welcome to Java".length()` is correct and returns `15`. Note that `""` denotes an *empty string* and `"".length()` is `0`.

string literal

empty string

4.4.2 Getting Characters from a String

The `s.charAt(index)` method can be used to retrieve a specific character in a string `s`, where the index is between `0` and `s.length()-1`. For example, `message.charAt(0)` returns the character `W`, as shown in Figure 4.1. Note that the index for the first character in the string is `0`.

`charAt(index)`

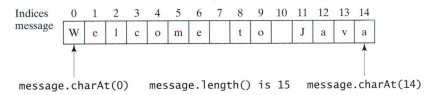

FIGURE 4.1 The characters in a `String` object can be accessed using its index.

> **Caution**
>
> Attempting to access characters in a string `s` out of bounds is a common programming error. To avoid it, make sure that you do not use an index beyond `s.length()` - `1`. For example, `s.charAt(s.length())` would cause a `StringIndexOutOfBoundsException`.

string index range

4.4.3 Concatenating Strings

You can use the `concat` method to concatenate two strings. The statement shown below, for example, concatenates strings `s1` and `s2` into `s3`:

```
String s3 = s1.concat(s2);
```

`s1.concat(s2)`

Because string concatenation is heavily used in programming, Java provides a convenient way to accomplish it. You can use the plus (+) operator to concatenate two strings, so the previous statement is equivalent to

```
String s3 = s1 + s2;
```

`s1 + s2`

The following code combines the strings `message`, `" and "`, and `"HTML"` into one string:

```
String myString = message + " and " + "HTML";
```

Recall that the + operator can also concatenate a number with a string. In this case, the number is converted into a string and then concatenated. Note that at least one of the operands must be a string in order for concatenation to take place. If one of the operands is a nonstring

concatenate strings and numbers

(e.g., a number), the nonstring value is converted into a string and concatenated with the other string. Here are some examples:

```
// Three strings are concatenated
String message = "Welcome " + "to " + "Java";

// String Chapter is concatenated with number 2
String s = "Chapter" + 2; // s becomes Chapter2

// String Supplement is concatenated with character B
String s1 = "Supplement" + 'B'; // s1 becomes SupplementB
```

If neither of the operands is a string, the plus sign (+) is the addition operator that adds two numbers.

The augmented += operator can also be used for string concatenation. For example, the following code appends the string **"and Java is fun"** with the string **"Welcome to Java"** in **message**.

```
message += " and Java is fun";
```

So the new **message** is **"Welcome to Java and Java is fun"**.
If i = 1 and j = 2, what is the output of the following statement?

```
System.out.println("i + j is " + i + j);
```

The output is **"i + j is 12"** because **"i + j is "** is concatenated with the value of i first. To force i + j to be executed first, enclose i + j in the parentheses, as follows:

```
System.out.println("i + j is " + (i + j));
```

4.4.4 Converting Strings

The **toLowerCase()** method returns a new string with all lowercase letters and the **toUpperCase()** method returns a new string with all uppercase letters. For example,

toLowerCase()
toUpperCase()

    "Welcome".toLowerCase() returns a new string **welcome**.
    "Welcome".toUpperCase() returns a new string **WELCOME**.

whitespace character

The **trim()** method returns a new string by eliminating whitespace characters from both ends of the string. The characters **' '**, **\t**, **\f**, **\r**, or **\n** are known as *whitespace characters*. For example,

trim()

    "\t Good Night \n".trim() returns a new string **Good Night**.

4.4.5 Reading a String from the Console

read strings

To read a string from the console, invoke the **next()** method on a **Scanner** object. For example, the following code reads three strings from the keyboard:

```
Scanner input = new Scanner(System.in);
System.out.print("Enter three words separated by spaces: ");
String s1 = input.next();
String s2 = input.next();
String s3 = input.next();
System.out.println("s1 is " + s1);
System.out.println("s2 is " + s2);
System.out.println("s3 is " + s3);
```

```
Enter three words separated by spaces: Welcome to Java ⏎Enter
s1 is Welcome
s2 is to
s3 is Java
```

The **next()** method reads a string that ends with a whitespace character. You can use *whitespace character* the **nextLine()** method to read an entire line of text. The **nextLine()** method reads a string that ends with the *Enter* key pressed. For example, the following statements read a line of text.

```
Scanner input = new Scanner(System.in);
System.out.println("Enter a line: ");
String s = input.nextLine();
System.out.println("The line entered is " + s);
```

```
Enter a line: Welcome to Java ⏎Enter
The line entered is Welcome to Java
```

Important Caution

To *avoid input errors*, do not use **nextLine()** after **nextByte()**, **nextShort()**, *avoid input errors* **nextInt()**, **nextLong()**, **nextFloat()**, **nextDouble()**, or **next()**. The reasons will be explained in Section 12.11.4, 'How Does **Scanner** Work?'

4.4.6 Reading a Character from the Console

To read a character from the console, use the **nextLine()** method to read a string and then invoke the **charAt(0)** method on the string to return a character. For example, the following code reads a character from the keyboard:

```
Scanner input = new Scanner(System.in);
System.out.print("Enter a character: ");
String s = input.nextLine();
char ch = s.charAt(0);
System.out.println("The character entered is " + ch);
```

4.4.7 Comparing Strings

The **String** class contains the methods as shown in Table 4.8 for comparing two strings.

TABLE 4.8 Comparison Methods for **String** Objects

Method	Description
equals(s1)	Returns true if this string is equal to string s1.
equalsIgnoreCase(s1)	Returns true if this string is equal to string s1; it is case insensitive.
compareTo(s1)	Returns an integer greater than 0, equal to 0, or less than 0 to indicate whether this string is greater than, equal to, or less than s1.
compareToIgnoreCase(s1)	Same as compareTo except that the comparison is case insensitive.
startsWith(prefix)	Returns true if this string starts with the specified prefix.
endsWith(suffix)	Returns true if this string ends with the specified suffix.
contains(s1)	Returns true if s1 is a substring in this string.

How do you compare the contents of two strings? You might attempt to use the == operator, as follows:

==

```
if (string1 == string2)
    System.out.println("string1 and string2 are the same object");
else
    System.out.println("string1 and string2 are different objects");
```

However, the == operator checks only whether **string1** and **string2** refer to the same object; it does not tell you whether they have the same contents. Therefore, you cannot use the == operator to find out whether two string variables have the same contents. Instead, you should use the **equals** method. The following code, for instance, can be used to compare two strings:

string1.equals(string2)

```
if (string1.equals(string2))
    System.out.println("string1 and string2 have the same contents");
else
    System.out.println("string1 and string2 are not equal");
```

For example, the following statements display **true** and then **false**.

```
String s1 = "Welcome to Java";
String s2 = "Welcome to Java";
String s3 = "Welcome to C++";
System.out.println(s1.equals(s2)); // true
System.out.println(s1.equals(s3)); // false
```

The **compareTo** method can also be used to compare two strings. For example, consider the following code:

s1.compareTo(s2)

```
s1.compareTo(s2)
```

The method returns the value **0** if **s1** is equal to **s2**, a value less than **0** if **s1** is lexicographically (i.e., in terms of Unicode ordering) less than **s2**, and a value greater than **0** if **s1** is lexicographically greater than **s2**.

The actual value returned from the **compareTo** method depends on the offset of the first two distinct characters in **s1** and **s2** from left to right. For example, suppose **s1** is **abc** and **s2** is **abg**, and **s1.compareTo(s2)** returns **-4**. The first two characters (**a** vs. **a**) from **s1** and **s2** are compared. Because they are equal, the second two characters (**b** vs. **b**) are compared. Because they are also equal, the third two characters (**c** vs. **g**) are compared. Since the character **c** is **4** less than **g**, the comparison returns **-4**.

Caution
Syntax errors will occur if you compare strings by using relational operators >, >=, <, or <=. Instead, you have to use **s1.compareTo(s2)**.

Note
The **equals** method returns **true** if two strings are equal and **false** if they are not. The **compareTo** method returns **0**, a positive integer, or a negative integer, depending on whether one string is equal to, greater than, or less than the other string.

The **String** class also provides the **equalsIgnoreCase** and **compareToIgnore-Case** methods for comparing strings. The **equalsIgnoreCase** and **compareToIgnore-Case** methods ignore the case of the letters when comparing two strings. You can also use **str.startsWith(prefix)** to check whether string **str** starts with a specified prefix, **str.endsWith(suffix)** to check whether string **str** ends with a specified suffix, and **str.contains(s1)** to check whether string **str** contains string **s1**. For example,

```
"Welcome to Java".startsWith("We") returns true.
"Welcome to Java".startsWith("we") returns false.
"Welcome to Java".endsWith("va") returns true.
```

```
"Welcome to Java".endsWith("v") returns false.
"Welcome to Java".contains("to") returns true.
"Welcome to Java".contains("To") returns false.
```

Listing 4.2 gives a program that prompts the user to enter two cities and displays them in alphabetical order.

LISTING 4.2 OrderTwoCities.java

```
1  import java.util.Scanner;
2
3  public class OrderTwoCities {
4    public static void main(String[] args) {
5      Scanner input = new Scanner(System.in);
6
7      // Prompt the user to enter two cities
8      System.out.print("Enter the first city: ");
9      String city1 = input.nextLine();                      input city1
10     System.out.print("Enter the second city: ");
11     String city2 = input.nextLine();                      input city2
12
13     if (city1.compareTo(city2) < 0)                        compare two cities
14       System.out.println("The cities in alphabetical order are " +
15         city1 + " " + city2);
16     else
17       System.out.println("The cities in alphabetical order are " +
18         city2 + " " + city1);
19   }
20 }
```

```
Enter the first city: New York  ↵Enter
Enter the second city: Boston  ↵Enter
The cities in alphabetical order are Boston New York
```

The program reads two strings for two cities (lines 9, 11). If `input.nextLine()` is replaced by `input.next()` (line 9), you cannot enter a string with spaces for `city1`. Since a city name may contain multiple words separated by spaces, the program uses the `nextLine` method to read a string (lines 9, 11). Invoking `city1.compareTo(city2)` compares two strings `city1` with `city2` (line 13). A negative return value indicates that `city1` is less than `city2`.

4.4.8 Obtaining Substrings

You can obtain a single character from a string using the `charAt` method. You can also obtain a substring from a string using the `substring` method in the `String` class, as shown in Table 4.9.

For example,

```
String message = "Welcome to Java";
String message = message.substring(0, 11) + "HTML";
```

The string `message` now becomes `Welcome to HTML`.

TABLE 4.9 The `String` class contains the methods for obtaining substrings.

Method	Description
substring(beginIndex)	Returns this string's substring that begins with the character at the specified beginIndex and extends to the end of the string, as shown in Figure 4.2.
substring(beginIndex, endIndex)	Returns this string's substring that begins at the specified beginIndex and extends to the character at index endIndex – 1, as shown in Figure 4.2. Note that the character at endIndex is not part of the substring.

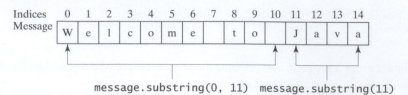

FIGURE 4.2 The substring method obtains a substring from a string.

> **Note**
>
> If **beginIndex** is **endIndex**, **substring(beginIndex, endIndex)** returns an empty string with length **0**. If **beginIndex > endIndex**, it would be a runtime error.

beginIndex <= endIndex

4.4.9 Finding a Character or a Substring in a String

The **String** class provides several versions of **indexOf** and **lastIndexOf** methods to find a character or a substring in a string, as shown in Table 4.10.

TABLE 4.10 The **String** class contains the methods for finding substrings.

Method	Description
index(ch)	Returns the index of the first occurrence of ch in the string. Returns –1 if not matched.
indexOf(ch, fromIndex)	Returns the index of the first occurrence of ch after fromIndex in the string. Returns –1 if not matched.
indexOf(s)	Returns the index of the first occurrence of string s in this string. Returns –1 if not matched.
indexOf(s, fromIndex)	Returns the index of the first occurrence of string s in this string after fromIndex. Returns –1 if not matched.
lastIndexOf(ch)	Returns the index of the last occurrence of ch in the string. Returns –1 if not matched.
lastIndexOf(ch, fromIndex)	Returns the index of the last occurrence of ch before fromIndex in this string. Returns –1 if not matched.
lastIndexOf(s)	Returns the index of the last occurrence of string s. Returns –1 if not matched.
lastIndexOf(s, fromIndex)	Returns the index of the last occurrence of string s before fromIndex. Returns –1 if not matched.

For example,

indexOf

```
"Welcome to Java".indexOf('W') returns 0.
"Welcome to Java".indexOf('o') returns 4.
"Welcome to Java".indexOf('o', 5) returns 9.
"Welcome to Java".indexOf("come") returns 3.
"Welcome to Java".indexOf("Java", 5) returns 11.
"Welcome to Java".indexOf("java", 5) returns -1.
```

lastIndexOf

```
"Welcome to Java".lastIndexOf('W') returns 0.
"Welcome to Java".lastIndexOf('o') returns 9.
"Welcome to Java".lastIndexOf('o', 5) returns 4.
"Welcome to Java".lastIndexOf("come") returns 3.
"Welcome to Java".lastIndexOf("Java", 5) returns -1.
"Welcome to Java".lastIndexOf("Java") returns 11.
```

Suppose a string **s** contains the first name and last name separated by a space. You can use the following code to extract the first name and last name from the string:

```
int k = s.indexOf(' ');
String firstName = s.substring(0, k);
String lastName = s.substring(k + 1);
```

For example, if **s** is **Kim Jones**, the following diagram illustrates how the first name and last name are extracted.

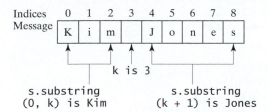

Indices   0   1   2   3   4   5   6   7   8
Message

| K | i | m | | J | o | n | e | s |

k is 3

s.substring
(0, k) is Kim

s.substring
(k + 1) is Jones

4.4.10 Conversion between Strings and Numbers

You can convert a numeric string into a number. To convert a string into an **int** value, use the **Integer.parseInt** method, as follows:

Integer.parseInt method

```
int intValue = Integer.parseInt(intString);
```

where **intString** is a numeric string such as **"123"**.

To convert a string into a **double** value, use the **Double.parseDouble** method, as follows:

Double.parseDouble method

```
double doubleValue = Double.parseDouble(doubleString);
```

where **doubleString** is a numeric string such as **"123.45"**.

If the string is not a numeric string, the conversion would cause a runtime error. The **Integer** and **Double** classes are both included in the **java.lang** package, and thus they are automatically imported.

You can convert a number into a string, simply use the string concatenating operator as follows:

```
String s = number + "";
```

number to string

4.16 Suppose that **s1**, **s2**, and **s3** are three strings, given as follows:

```
String s1 = "Welcome to Java";
String s2 = "Programming is fun";
String s3 = "Welcome to Java";
```

What are the results of the following expressions?

(a) s1 == s2

(b) s2 == s3

(c) s1.equals(s2)

(d) s1.equals(s3)

(e) s1.compareTo(s2)

(f) s2.compareTo(s3)

(g) s2.compareTo(s2)

(h) s1.charAt(0)

(i) s1.indexOf('j')

(j) s1.indexOf("to")

(k) s1.lastIndexOf('a')

(l) s1.lastIndexOf("o", 15)

(m) s1.length()

(n) s1.substring(5)

(o) s1.substring(5, 11)

(p) s1.startsWith("Wel")

(q) s1.endsWith("Java")

(r) s1.toLowerCase()

(s) s1.toUpperCase()

(t) s1.concat(s2)

(u) s1.contains(s2)

(v) "\t Wel \t".trim()

✓ Check Point

4.17 Suppose that `s1` and `s2` are two strings. Which of the following statements or expressions are incorrect?

```java
String s = "Welcome to Java";
String s3 = s1 + s2;
String s3 = s1 - s2;
s1 == s2;
s1 >= s2;
s1.compareTo(s2);
int i = s1.length();
char c = s1(0);
char c = s1.charAt(s1.length());
```

4.18 Show the output of the following statements (write a program to verify your results):

```java
System.out.println("1" + 1);
System.out.println('1' + 1);
System.out.println("1" + 1 + 1);
System.out.println("1" + (1 + 1));
System.out.println('1' + 1 + 1);
```

4.19 Evaluate the following expressions (write a program to verify your results):

```java
1 + "Welcome " + 1 + 1
1 + "Welcome " + (1 + 1)
1 + "Welcome " + ('\u0001' + 1)
1 + "Welcome " + 'a' + 1
```

4.20 Let `s1` be " Welcome " and `s2` be " welcome ". Write the code for the following statements:

(a) Check whether `s1` is equal to `s2` and assign the result to a Boolean variable `isEqual`.

(b) Check whether `s1` is equal to `s2`, ignoring case, and assign the result to a Boolean variable `isEqual`.

(c) Compare `s1` with `s2` and assign the result to an `int` variable `x`.

(d) Compare `s1` with `s2`, ignoring case, and assign the result to an `int` variable `x`.

(e) Check whether `s1` has the prefix `AAA` and assign the result to a Boolean variable `b`.

(f) Check whether `s1` has the suffix `AAA` and assign the result to a Boolean variable `b`.

(g) Assign the length of `s1` to an `int` variable `x`.

(h) Assign the first character of `s1` to a `char` variable `x`.

(i) Create a new string `s3` that combines `s1` with `s2`.

(j) Create a substring of `s1` starting from index `1`.

(k) Create a substring of `s1` from index `1` to index `4`.

(l) Create a new string `s3` that converts `s1` to lowercase.

(m) Create a new string `s3` that converts `s1` to uppercase.

(n) Create a new string `s3` that trims whitespace characters on both ends of `s1`.

    (o) Assign the index of the first occurrence of the character **e** in **s1** to an **int** variable **x**.

    (p) Assign the index of the last occurrence of the string **abc** in **s1** to an **int** variable **x**.

4.5 Case Studies

Strings are fundamental in programming. The ability to write programs using strings is essential in learning Java programming.

Key Point

You will frequently use strings to write useful programs. This section presents three examples of solving problems using strings.

4.5.1 Case Study: Guessing Birthdays

You can find out the date of the month when your friend was born by asking five questions. Each question asks whether the day is in one of the five sets of numbers.

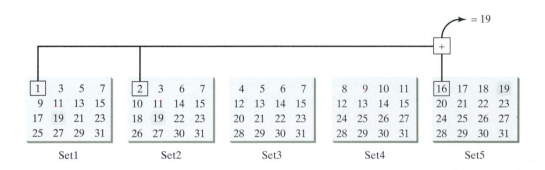

    The birthday is the sum of the first numbers in the sets where the day appears. For example, if the birthday is **19**, it appears in Set1, Set2, and Set5. The first numbers in these three sets are **1**, **2**, and **16**. Their sum is **19**.

    Listing 4.3 gives a program that prompts the user to answer whether the day is in Set1 (lines 41–44), in Set2 (lines 50–53), in Set3 (lines 59–62), in Set4 (lines 68–71), and in Set5 (lines 77–80). If the number is in the set, the program adds the first number in the set to **day** (lines 47, 56, 65, 74, 83).

LISTING 4.3 GuessBirthday.java

```java
 1  import java.util.Scanner;
 2
 3  public class GuessBirthday {
 4    public static void main(String[] args) {
 5      String set1 =
 6        " 1  3  5  7\n" +
 7        " 9 11 13 15\n" +
 8        "17 19 21 23\n" +
 9        "25 27 29 31";
10
11      String set2 =
12        " 2  3  6  7\n" +
```

```
13            "10 11 14 15\n" +
14            "18 19 22 23\n" +
15            "26 27 30 31";
16
17       String set3 =
18            "  4  5  6  7\n" +
19            "12 13 14 15\n" +
20            "20 21 22 23\n" +
21            "28 29 30 31";
22
23       String set4 =
24            "  8  9 10 11\n" +
25            "12 13 14 15\n" +
26            "24 25 26 27\n" +
27            "28 29 30 31";
28
29       String set5 =
30            "16 17 18 19\n" +
31            "20 21 22 23\n" +
32            "24 25 26 27\n" +
33            "28 29 30 31";
34
```
day to be determined
```
35       int day = 0;
36
37       // Create a Scanner
38       Scanner input = new Scanner(System.in);
39
40       // Prompt the user to answer questions
41       System.out.print("Is your birthday in Set1?\n");
42       System.out.print(set1);
43       System.out.print("\nEnter 0 for No and 1 for Yes: ");
44       int answer = input.nextInt();
45
```
in Set1?
```
46       if (answer == 1)
47         day += 1;
48
49       // Prompt the user to answer questions
50       System.out.print("\nIs your birthday in Set2?\n");
51       System.out.print(set2);
52       System.out.print("\nEnter 0 for No and 1 for Yes: ");
53       answer = input.nextInt();
54
```
in Set2?
```
55       if (answer == 1)
56         day += 2;
57
58       // Prompt the user to answer questions
59       System.out.print("Is your birthday in Set3?\n");
60       System.out.print(set3);
61       System.out.print("\nEnter 0 for No and 1 for Yes: ");
62       answer = input.nextInt();
63
```
in Set3?
```
64       if (answer == 1)
65         day += 4;
66
67       // Prompt the user to answer questions
68       System.out.print("\nIs your birthday in Set4?\n");
69       System.out.print(set4);
70       System.out.print("\nEnter 0 for No and 1 for Yes: ");
71       answer = input.nextInt();
72
```

```
73        if (answer == 1)
74          day += 8;
75
76          // Prompt the user to answer questions
77          System.out.print("\nIs your birthday in Set5?\n");
78          System.out.print(set5);
79          System.out.print("\nEnter 0 for No and 1 for Yes: ");
80          answer = input.nextInt();
81
82        if (answer == 1)
83          day += 16;
84
85          System.out.println("\nYour birthday is " + day + "!");
86      }
87  }
```

in Set4?

in Set5?

```
Is your birthday in Set1?
 1  3  5  7
 9 11 13 15
17 19 21 23
25 27 29 31
Enter 0 for No and 1 for Yes: 1 ↵Enter

Is your birthday in Set2?
 2  3  6  7
10 11 14 15
18 19 22 23
26 27 30 31
Enter 0 for No and 1 for Yes: 1 ↵Enter

Is your birthday in Set3?
 4  5  6  7
12 13 14 15
20 21 22 23
28 29 30 31
Enter 0 for No and 1 for Yes: 0 ↵Enter

Is your birthday in Set4?
 8  9 10 11
12 13 14 15
24 25 26 27
28 29 30 31
Enter 0 for No and 1 for Yes: 0 ↵Enter

Is your birthday in Set5?
16 17 18 19
20 21 22 23
24 25 26 27
28 29 30 31
Enter 0 for No and 1 for Yes: 1 ↵Enter
Your birthday is 19!
```

line#	day	answer	output
35	0		
44		1	
47	1		
53		1	
56	3		
62		0	
71		0	
80		1	
83	19		
85			Your birthday is 19!

mathematics behind the game

This game is easy to program. You may wonder how the game was created. The mathematics behind the game is actually quite simple. The numbers are not grouped together by accident—the way they are placed in the five sets is deliberate. The starting numbers in the five sets are **1**, **2**, **4**, **8**, and **16**, which correspond to **1**, **10**, **100**, **1000**, and **10000** in binary (binary numbers are introduced in Appendix F, Number Systems). A binary number for decimal integers between **1** and **31** has at most five digits, as shown in Figure 4.3a. Let it be $b_5b_4b_3b_2b_1$. Thus, $b_5b_4b_3b_2b_1 = b_50000 + b_4000 + b_300 + b_20 + b_1$, as shown in Figure 4.3b. If a day's binary number has a digit **1** in b_k, the number should appear in Set$k$. For example, number **19** is binary **10011**, so it appears in Set1, Set2, and Set5. It is binary **1** + **10** + **10000** = **10011** or decimal **1** + **2** + **16** = **19**. Number **31** is binary **11111**, so it appears in Set1, Set2, Set3, Set4, and Set5. It is binary **1** + **10** + **100** + **1000** + **10000** = **11111** or decimal **1** + **2** + **4** + **8** + **16** = **31**.

Decimal	Binary
1	00001
2	00010
3	00011
...	
19	10011
...	
31	11111

(a)

$$
\begin{array}{r}
b_5\,0\,0\,0\,0 \\
b_4\,0\,0\,0 \\
b_3\,0\,0 \\
b_2\,0 \\
+\quad b_1 \\
\hline
b_5\,b_4\,b_3\,b_2\,b_1
\end{array}
\qquad
\begin{array}{r}
10000 \\
10 \\
+\quad 1 \\
\hline
10011 \\
19
\end{array}
\qquad
\begin{array}{r}
10000 \\
1000 \\
100 \\
10 \\
+\quad 1 \\
\hline
11111 \\
31
\end{array}
$$

(b)

FIGURE 4.3 (a) A number between **1** and **31** can be represented using a five-digit binary number. (b) A five-digit binary number can be obtained by adding binary numbers **1**, **10**, **100**, **1000**, or **10000**.

Check Point

4.21 If you run Listing 4.3 GuessBirthday.java with input **1** for Set1, Set3, and Set4 and **0** for Set2 and Set5, what will be the birthday?

4.5.2 Case Study: Converting a Hexadecimal Digit to a Decimal Value

The hexadecimal number system has 16 digits: 0–9, A–F. The letters A, B, C, D, E, and F correspond to the decimal numbers 10, 11, 12, 13, 14, and 15. We now write a program that prompts the user to enter a hex digit and display its corresponding decimal value, as shown in Listing 4.4.

LISTING 4.4 `HexDigit2Dec.java`

```java
 1  import java.util.Scanner;
 2
 3  public class HexDigit2Dec {
 4    public static void main(String[] args) {
 5      Scanner input = new Scanner(System.in);
 6      System.out.print("Enter a hex digit: ");
 7      String hexString = input.nextLine();
 8
 9      // Check if the hex string has exactly one character
10      if (hexString.length() != 1) {
11        System.out.println("You must enter exactly one character");
12        System.exit(1);
13      }
14
15      // Display decimal value for the hex digit
16      char ch = hexString.charAt(0);
17      if (ch <= 'F' && ch >= 'A') {
18        int value = ch - 'A' + 10;
19        System.out.println("The decimal value for hex digit "
20          + ch + " is " + value);
21      }
22      else if (Character.isDigit(ch)) {
23        System.out.println("The decimal value for hex digit "
24          + ch + " is " + ch);
25      }
26      else {
27        System.out.println(ch + " is an invalid input");
28      }
29    }
30  }
```

VideoNote

Convert hex to decimal

input string

check length

is A-F?

is 0-9?

```
Enter a hex digit: AB7C  ↵ Enter
You must enter exactly one character
```

```
Enter a hex digit: B  ↵ Enter
The decimal value for hex digit B is 11
```

```
Enter a hex digit: 8  ↵ Enter
The decimal value for hex digit 8 is 8
```

```
Enter a hex digit: T  ↵ Enter
T is an invalid input
```

The program reads a string from the console (line 7) and checks if the string contains a single character (line 10). If not, report an error and exit the program (line 12).

The program invokes the **`Character.toUpperCase`** method to obtain the character **ch** as an uppercase letter (line 16). If **ch** is between **'A'** and **'F'** (line 17), the corresponding decimal value is **ch - 'A' + 10** (line 18). Note that **ch - 'A'** is **0** if **ch** is **'A'**, **ch - 'A'** is **1** if **ch** is **'B'**, and so on. When two characters perform a numerical operation, the characters' Unicodes are used in the computation.

The program invokes the **Character.isDigit(ch)** method to check if **ch** is between **'0'** and **'9'** (line 22). If so, the corresponding decimal digit is the same as **ch** (lines 23–24).

If **ch** is not between **'A'** and **'F'** nor a digit character, the program displays an error message (line 27).

4.5.3 Case Study: Revising the Lottery Program Using Strings

The lottery program in Listing 3.8, Lottery.java, generates a random two-digit number, prompts the user to enter a two-digit number, and determines whether the user wins according to the following rule:

1. If the user input matches the lottery number in the exact order, the award is $10,000.

2. If all the digits in the user input match all the digits in the lottery number, the award is $3,000.

3. If one digit in the user input matches a digit in the lottery number, the award is $1,000.

The program in Listing 3.8 uses an integer to store the number. Listing 4.5 gives a new program that generates a random two-digit string instead of a number and receives the user input as a string instead of a number.

LISTING 4.5 LotteryUsingStrings.java

```
1  import java.util.Scanner;
2
3  public class LotteryUsingStrings {
4    public static void main(String[] args) {
5      // Generate a lottery as a two-digit string
6      String lottery = "" + (int)(Math.random() * 10)
7        + (int)(Math.random() * 10);
8
9      // Prompt the user to enter a guess
10     Scanner input = new Scanner(System.in);
11     System.out.print("Enter your lottery pick (two digits): ");
12     String guess = input.nextLine();
13
14     // Get digits from lottery
15     char lotteryDigit1 = lottery.charAt(0);
16     char lotteryDigit2 = lottery.charAt(1);
17
18     // Get digits from guess
19     char guessDigit1 = guess.charAt(0);
20     char guessDigit2 = guess.charAt(1);
21
22     System.out.println("The lottery number is " + lottery);
23
24     // Check the guess
25     if (guess.equals(lottery))
26       System.out.println("Exact match: you win $10,000");
27     else if (guessDigit2 == lotteryDigit1
28              && guessDigit1 == lotteryDigit2)
29       System.out.println("Match all digits: you win $3,000");
30     else if (guessDigit1 == lotteryDigit1
31              || guessDigit1 == lotteryDigit2
32              || guessDigit2 == lotteryDigit1
33              || guessDigit2 == lotteryDigit2)
34       System.out.println("Match one digit: you win $1,000");
```

generate a lottery

enter a guess

exact match?

match all digits?

match one digit?

```
35       else
36           System.out.println("Sorry, no match");
37    }
38  }
```

```
Enter your lottery pick (two digits): 00 [↵Enter]
The lottery number is 00
Exact match: you win $10,000
```

```
Enter your lottery pick (two digits): 45 [↵Enter]
The lottery number is 54
Match all digits: you win $3,000
```

```
Enter your lottery pick: 23 [↵Enter]
The lottery number is 34
Match one digit: you win $1,000
```

```
Enter your lottery pick: 23 [↵Enter]
The lottery number is 14
Sorry: no match
```

The program generates two random digits and concatenates them into the string `lottery` (lines 6–7). After this, `lottery` contains two random digits.

The program prompts the user to enter a guess as a two-digit string (line 12) and checks the guess against the lottery number in this order:

- First check whether the guess matches the lottery exactly (line 25).

- If not, check whether the reversal of the guess matches the lottery (line 27).

- If not, check whether one digit is in the lottery (lines 30–33).

- If not, nothing matches and display "Sorry, no match" (line 36).

4.6 Formatting Console Output

You can use the `System.out.printf` method to display formatted output on the console.

🔑 **Key Point**

Often, it is desirable to display numbers in a certain format. For example, the following code computes interest, given the amount and the annual interest rate.

```
double amount = 12618.98;
double interestRate = 0.0013;
double interest = amount * interestRate;
System.out.println("Interest is $" + interest);
```

```
Interest is $16.404674
```

Because the interest amount is currency, it is desirable to display only two digits after the decimal point. To do this, you can write the code as follows:

```java
double amount = 12618.98;
double interestRate = 0.0013;
double interest = amount * interestRate;
System.out.println("Interest is $"
  + (int)(interest * 100) / 100.0);
```

```
Interest is $16.4
```

printf

However, the format is still not correct. There should be two digits after the decimal point: `16.40` rather than `16.4`. You can fix it by using the **printf** method, like this:

```java
double amount = 12618.98;
double interestRate = 0.0013;
double interest = amount * interestRate;
System.out.printf("Interest is $%4.2f",
  interest);
```

% 4 . 2 f ← format specifier
field width   conversion code
precision

```
Interest is $16.40
```

The syntax to invoke this method is

```java
System.out.printf(format, item1, item2, ..., itemk)
```

where **format** is a string that may consist of substrings and format specifiers.

format specifier

A *format specifier* specifies how an item should be displayed. An item may be a numeric value, a character, a Boolean value, or a string. A simple format specifier consists of a percent sign (%) followed by a conversion code. Table 4.11 lists some frequently used simple format specifiers.

TABLE 4.11 Frequently Used Format Specifiers

Format Specifier	Output	Example
%b	a Boolean value	true or false
%c	a character	'a'
%d	a decimal integer	200
%f	a floating-point number	45.460000
%e	a number in standard scientific notation	4.556000e+01
%s	a string	"Java is cool"

Here is an example:

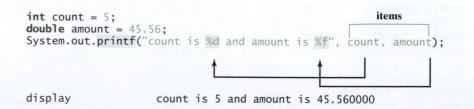

```java
int count = 5;
double amount = 45.56;
System.out.printf("count is %d and amount is %f", count, amount);
```
items

display   count is 5 and amount is 45.560000

Items must match the format specifiers in order, in number, and in exact type. For example, the format specifier for `count` is `%d` and for `amount` is `%f`. By default, a floating-point value is displayed with six digits after the decimal point. You can specify the width and precision in a format specifier, as shown in the examples in Table 4.12.

TABLE 4.12 Examples of Specifying Width and Precision

Example	Output
`%5c`	Output the character and add four spaces before the character item, because the width is 5.
`%6b`	Output the Boolean value and add one space before the false value and two spaces before the true value.
`%5d`	Output the integer item with width at least 5. If the number of digits in the item is < 5, add spaces before the number. If the number of digits in the item is > 5, the width is automatically increased.
`%10.2f`	Output the floating-point item with width at least 10 including a decimal point and two digits after the point. Thus, there are 7 digits allocated before the decimal point. If the number of digits before the decimal point in the item is < 7, add spaces before the number. If the number of digits before the decimal point in the item is > 7, the width is automatically increased.
`%10.2e`	Output the floating-point item with width at least 10 including a decimal point, two digits after the point and the exponent part. If the displayed number in scientific notation has width less than 10, add spaces before the number.
`%12s`	Output the string with width at least 12 characters. If the string item has fewer than 12 characters, add spaces before the string. If the string item has more than 12 characters, the width is automatically increased.

If an item requires more spaces than the specified width, the width is automatically increased. For example, the following code

```
System.out.printf("%3d#%2s#%4.2f\n", 1234, "Java", 51.6653);
```

displays

```
1234#Java#51.67
```

The specified width for `int` item `1234` is `3`, which is smaller than its actual size `4`. The width is automatically increased to `4`. The specified width for string item `Java` is `2`, which is smaller than its actual size `4`. The width is automatically increased to `4`. The specified width for `double` item `51.6653` is `4`, but it needs width 5 to display 51.67, so the width is automatically increased to `5`.

By default, the output is right justified. You can put the minus sign (–) in the format specifier to specify that the item is left justified in the output within the specified field. For example, the following statements

right justify
left justify

```
System.out.printf("%8d%8s%8.1f\n", 1234, "Java", 5.63);
System.out.printf("%-8d%-8s%-8.1f \n", 1234, "Java", 5.63);
```

display

```
|←— 8 —→|←— 8 —→|←— 8 —→|
□□□□1234□□□□Java□□□□□5.6
1234□□□□Java□□□□5.6□□□□□
```

where the square box (□) denotes a blank space.

Caution

The items must match the format specifiers in exact type. The item for the format specifier **%f** or **%e** must be a floating-point type value such as **40.0**, not **40**. Thus, an **int** variable cannot match **%f** or **%e**.

Tip

The **%** sign denotes a format specifier. To output a literal **%** in the format string, use **%%**.

Listing 4.6 gives a program that uses **printf** to display a table.

LISTING 4.6   FormatDemo.java

display table header

values for 30 degrees

values for 60 degrees

```java
 1  public class FormatDemo {
 2    public static void main(String[] args) {
 3      // Display the header of the table
 4      System.out.printf("%-10s%-10s%-10s%-10s%-10s\n", "Degrees",
 5        "Radians", "Sine", "Cosine", "Tangent");
 6
 7      // Display values for 30 degrees
 8      int degrees = 30;
 9      double radians = Math.toRadians(degrees);
10      System.out.printf("%-10d%-10.4f%-10.4f%-10.4f%-10.4f\n", degrees,
11        radians, Math.sin(radians), Math.cos(radians),
12        Math.tan(radians));
13
14      // Display values for 60 degrees
15      degrees = 60;
16      radians = Math.toRadians(degrees);
17      System.out.printf("%-10d%-10.4f%-10.4f%-10.4f%-10.4f\n", degrees,
18        radians, Math.sin(radians), Math.cos(radians),
19        Math.tan(radians));
20    }
21  }
```

Degrees	Radians	Sine	Cosine	Tangent
30	0.5236	0.5000	0.8660	0.5773
60	1.0472	0.8660	0.5000	1.7320

The statement in lines 4–5 displays the column names of the table. The column names are strings. Each string is displayed using the specifier **%-10s**, which left-justifies the string. The statement in lines 10–12 displays the degrees as an integer and four float values. The integer is displayed using the specifier **%-10d** and each float is displayed using the specifier **%-10.4f**, which specifies four digits after the decimal point.

4.22 What are the format specifiers for outputting a Boolean value, a character, a decimal integer, a floating-point number, and a string?

4.23 What is wrong in the following statements?

(a) `System.out.printf("%5d %d", 1, 2, 3);`

(b) `System.out.printf("%5d %f", 1);`

(c) `System.out.printf("%5d %f", 1, 2);`

4.24 Show the output of the following statements.

(a) `System.out.printf("amount is %f %e\n", 32.32, 32.32);`

(b) `System.out.printf("amount is %5.2%% %5.4e\n", 32.327, 32.32);`

(c) `System.out.printf("%6b\n", (1 > 2));`

(d) `System.out.printf("%6s\n", "Java");`

(e) `System.out.printf("%-6b%s\n", (1 > 2), "Java");`

(f) `System.out.printf("%6b%-8s\n", (1 > 2), "Java");`

KEY TERMS

char type   125
encoding   125
escape character   127
escape sequence   126
format specifier   146

instance method   130
static method   130
supplementary Unicode   125
Unicode   125
whitespace character   133

CHAPTER SUMMARY

1. Java provides the mathematical methods `sin`, `cos`, `tan`, `asin`, `acos`, `atan`, `toRadians`, `toDegree`, `exp`, `log`, `log10`, `pow`, `sqrt`, `cell`, `floor`, `rint`, `round`, `min`, `max`, `abs`, and `random` in the `Math` class for performing mathematical functions.

2. The character type `char` represents a single character.

3. An escape sequence consists of a backslash (\) followed by a character or a combination of digits.

4. The character \ is called the escape character.

5. The characters ' ', \t, \f, \r, and \n are known as the whitespace characters.

6. Characters can be compared based on their Unicode using the relational operators.

7. The `Character` class contains the methods `isDigit`, `isLetter`, `isLetterOrDigit`, `isLowerCase`, `isUpperCase` for testing whether a character is a digit, letter, lowercase, and uppercase. It also contains the `toLowerCase` and `toUpperCase` methods for returning a lowercase or uppercase letter.

8. A *string* is a sequence of characters. A string value is enclosed in matching double quotes ("). A character value is enclosed in matching single quotes (').

9. Strings are objects in Java. A method that can only be invoked from a specific object is called an *instance method*. A non-instance method is called a static method, which can be invoked without using an object.

10. You can get the length of a string by invoking its `length()` method, retrieve a character at the specified index in the string using the `charAt(index)` method, and use the `indexOf` and `lastIndexOf` methods to find a character or a substring in a string.

11. You can use the `concat` method to concatenate two strings, or the plus (+) operator to concatenate two or more strings.

12. You can use the `substring` method to obtain a substring from the string.

13. You can use the `equals` and `compareTo` methods to compare strings. The `equals` method returns `true` if two strings are equal, and `false` if they are not equal. The `compareTo` method returns `0`, a positive integer, or a negative integer, depending on whether one string is equal to, greater than, or less than the other string.

14. The `printf` method can be used to display a formatted output using format specifiers.

QUIZ

Answer the quiz for this chapter online at www.cs.armstrong.edu/liang/intro10e/quiz.html.

MyProgrammingLab™ **PROGRAMMING EXERCISES**

Section 4.2

4.1 (*Geometry: area of a pentagon*) Write a program that prompts the user to enter the length from the center of a pentagon to a vertex and computes the area of the pentagon, as shown in the following figure.

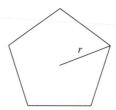

The formula for computing the area of a pentagon is $Area = \dfrac{5 \times s^2}{4 \times \tan\left(\dfrac{\pi}{5}\right)}$, where

s is the length of a side. The side can be computed using the formula $s = 2r \sin\dfrac{\pi}{5}$, where r is the length from the center of a pentagon to a vertex. Round up two digits after the decimal point. Here is a sample run:

```
Enter the length from the center to a vertex: 5.5  ↵Enter
The area of the pentagon is 71.92
```

*4.2 (*Geometry: great circle distance*) The great circle distance is the distance between two points on the surface of a sphere. Let $(x1, y1)$ and $(x2, y2)$ be the geographical latitude and longitude of two points. The great circle distance between the two points can be computed using the following formula:

$$d = radius \times \arccos(\sin(x_1) \times \sin(x_2) + \cos(x_1) \times \cos(x_2) \times \cos(y_1 - y_2))$$

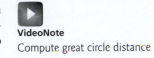

VideoNote

Compute great circle distance

Write a program that prompts the user to enter the latitude and longitude of two points on the earth in degrees and displays its great circle distance. The average earth radius is 6,371.01 km. Note that you need to convert the degrees into radians using the **Math.toRadians** method since the Java trigonometric methods use radians. The latitude and longitude degrees in the formula are for north and west. Use negative to indicate south and east degrees. Here is a sample run:

```
Enter point 1 (latitude and longitude) in degrees: 39.55, -116.25  ↵Enter
Enter point 2 (latitude and longitude) in degrees: 41.5, 87.37  ↵Enter
The distance between the two points is 10691.79183231593 km
```

*4.3 (*Geography: estimate areas*) Find the GPS locations for Atlanta, Georgia; Orlando, Florida; Savannah, Georgia; and Charlotte, North Carolina from www.gps-data-team.com/map/ and compute the estimated area enclosed by these four cities. (Hint: Use the formula in Programming Exercise 4.2 to compute the distance between two cities. Divide the polygon into two triangles and use the formula in Programming Exercise 2.19 to compute the area of a triangle.)

4.4 (*Geometry: area of a hexagon*) The area of a hexagon can be computed using the following formula (**s** is the length of a side):

$$Area = \frac{6 \times s^2}{4 \times \tan\left(\dfrac{\pi}{6}\right)}$$

Write a program that prompts the user to enter the side of a hexagon and displays its area. Here is a sample run:

```
Enter the side: 5.5  ↵Enter
The area of the hexagon is 78.59
```

*4.5 (*Geometry: area of a regular polygon*) A regular polygon is an *n*-sided polygon in which all sides are of the same length and all angles have the same degree (i.e., the polygon is both equilateral and equiangular). The formula for computing the area of a regular polygon is

$$Area = \frac{n \times s^2}{4 \times \tan\left(\dfrac{\pi}{n}\right)}$$

Here, s is the length of a side. Write a program that prompts the user to enter the number of sides and their length of a regular polygon and displays its area. Here is a sample run:

```
Enter the number of sides: 5  ↵Enter
Enter the side: 6.5  ↵Enter
The area of the polygon is 74.69017017488385
```

*4.6 (*Random points on a circle*) Write a program that generates three random points on a circle centered at (0, 0) with radius 40 and display three angles in a triangle formed by these three points, as shown in Figure 4.7a. (Hint: Generate a random angle α in radians between 0 and 2π, as shown in Figure 4.7b and the point determined by this angle is (r*cos(α), r*sin(α)).)

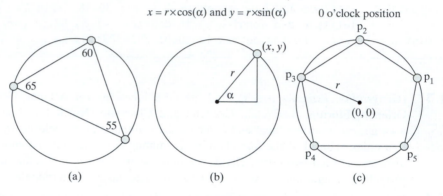

(a) (b) (c)

FIGURE 4.7 (a) A triangle is formed from three random points on the circle. (b) A random point on the circle can be generated using a random angle α. (c) A pentagon is centered at (0, 0) with one point at the 0 o'clock position.

*4.7 (*Corner point coordinates*) Suppose a pentagon is centered at (0, 0) with one point at the 0 o'clock position, as shown in Figure 4.7c. Write a program that prompts the user to enter the radius of the bounding circle of a pentagon and displays the coordinates of the five corner points on the pentagon. Here is a sample run:

```
Enter the radius of the bounding circle: 100  ↵Enter
The coordinates of five points on the pentagon are
(95.1057, 30.9017)
(0.000132679, 100)
(-95.1056, 30.9019)
(-58.7788, -80.9015)
(58.7782, -80.902)
```

Sections 4.3–4.6

*4.8 (*Find the character of an ASCII code*) Write a program that receives an ASCII code (an integer between 0 and 127) and displays its character. Here is a sample run:

```
Enter an ASCII code: 69  ↵Enter
The character for ASCII code 69 is E
```

*4.9 (*Find the Unicode of a character*) Write a program that receives a character and displays its Unicode. Here is a sample run:

```
Enter a character: E  ↵Enter
The Unicode for the character E is 69
```

*4.10 (*Guess birthday*) Rewrite Listing 4.3, GuessBirthday.java, to prompt the user to enter the character **Y** for Yes and **N** for No rather than entering **1** for Yes and **0** for No.

*4.11 (*Decimal to hex*) Write a program that prompts the user to enter an integer between **0** and **15** and displays its corresponding hex number. Here are some sample runs:

```
Enter a decimal value (0 to 15): 11  ↵Enter
The hex value is B
```

```
Enter a decimal value (0 to 15): 5  ↵Enter
The hex value is 5
```

```
Enter a decimal value (0 to 15): 31  ↵Enter
31 is an invalid input
```

4.12 (*Hex to binary*) Write a program that prompts the user to enter a hex digit and displays its corresponding binary number. Here is a sample run:

VideoNote
Convert hex to binary

```
Enter a hex digit: B  ↵Enter
The binary value is 1011
```

```
Enter a hex digit: G  ↵Enter
G is an invalid input
```

*4.13 (*Vowel or consonant?*) Write a program that prompts the user to enter a letter and check whether the letter is a vowel or consonant. Here is a sample run:

```
Enter a letter: B  ↵Enter
B is a consonant
```

```
Enter a letter grade: a  ↵Enter
a is a vowel
```

```
Enter a letter grade: #  ↵Enter
# is an invalid input
```

*4.14 (*Convert letter grade to number*) Write a program that prompts the user to enter a letter grade A, B, C, D, or F and displays its corresponding numeric value 4, 3, 2, 1, or 0. Here is a sample run:

```
Enter a letter grade: B  ↵Enter
The numeric value for grade B is 3
```

```
Enter a letter grade: T  ↵Enter
T is an invalid grade
```

*4.15 (*Phone key pads*) The international standard letter/number mapping found on the telephone is shown below:

Write a program that prompts the user to enter a letter and displays its corresponding number.

```
Enter a letter: A  ↵Enter
The corresponding number is 2
```

```
Enter a letter: a  ↵Enter
The corresponding number is 2
```

```
Enter a letter: +  ↵Enter
+ is an invalid input
```

4.16 (*Random character*) Write a program that displays a random uppercase letter using the `Math.random()` method.

*4.17 (*Days of a month*) Write a program that prompts the user to enter a year and the first three letters of a month name (with the first letter in uppercase) and displays the number of days in the month. Here is a sample run:

```
Enter a year: 2001  ↵Enter
Enter a month: Jan  ↵Enter
Jan 2001 has 31 days
```

```
Enter a year: 2016  ↵Enter
Enter a month: Feb  ↵Enter
Jan 2016 has 29 days
```

*4.18 (*Student major and status*) Write a program that prompts the user to enter two characters and displays the major and status represented in the characters. The first character indicates the major and the second is number character 1, 2, 3, 4, which indicates whether a student is a freshman, sophomore, junior, or senior. Suppose the following chracters are used to denote the majors:

   M: Mathematics
   C: Computer Science
   I: Information Technology

   Here is a sample run:

```
Enter two characters: M1  ↵Enter
Mathematics Freshman
```

```
Enter two characters: C3  ↵Enter
Computer Science Junior
```

```
Enter two characters: T3  ↵Enter
Invalid input
```

4.19 (*Business: check ISBN-10*) Rewrite the Programming Exercise 3.9 by entering the ISBN number as a string.

4.20 (*Process a string*) Write a program that prompts the user to enter a string and displays its length and its first character.

*4.21 (*Check SSN*) Write a program that prompts the user to enter a Social Security number in the format DDD-DD-DDDD, where D is a digit. Your program should check whether the input is valid. Here are sample runs:

```
Enter a SSN: 232-23-5435  ↵Enter
232-23-5435 is a valid social security number
```

```
Enter a SSN: 23-23-5435  ↵Enter
23-23-5435 is an invalid social security number
```

4.22 (*Check substring*) Write a program that prompts the user to enter two strings and reports whether the second string is a substring of the first string.

```
Enter string s1: ABCD  ↵Enter
Enter string s2: BC  ↵Enter
BC is a substring of ABCD
```

```
Enter string s1: ABCD  ↵Enter
Enter string s2: BDC  ↵Enter
BDC is not a substring of ABCD
```

*4.23 (*Financial application: payroll*) Write a program that reads the following information and prints a payroll statement:

> Employee's name (e.g., Smith)
> Number of hours worked in a week (e.g., 10)
> Hourly pay rate (e.g., 9.75)
> Federal tax withholding rate (e.g., 20%)
> State tax withholding rate (e.g., 9%)

A sample run is shown below:

```
Enter employee's name: Smith  ↵Enter
Enter number of hours worked in a week: 10  ↵Enter
Enter hourly pay rate: 9.75  ↵Enter
Enter federal tax withholding rate: 0.20  ↵Enter
Enter state tax withholding rate: 0.09  ↵Enter

Employee Name: Smith
Hours Worked: 10.0
Pay Rate: $9.75
Gross Pay: $97.5
Deductions:
   Federal Withholding (20.0%): $19.5
   State Withholding (9.0%): $8.77
   Total Deduction: $28.27
Net Pay: $69.22
```

*4.24 (*Order three cities*) Write a program that prompts the user to enter three cities and displays them in ascending order. Here is a sample run:

```
Enter the first city: Chicago  ↵Enter
Enter the second city: Los Angeles  ↵Enter
Enter the third city: Atlanta  ↵Enter
The three cities in alphabetical order are Atlanta Chicago Los Angeles
```

*4.25 (*Generate vehicle plate numbers*) Assume a vehicle plate number consists of three uppercase letters followed by four digits. Write a program to generate a plate number.

*4.26 (*Financial application: monetary units*) Rewrite Listing 2.10, ComputeChange. java, to fix the possible loss of accuracy when converting a float value to an **int** value. Read the input as a string such as **"11.56"**. Your program should extract the dollar amount before the decimal point and the cents after the decimal amount using the **indexOf** and **substring** methods.

LOOPS

Objectives

- To write programs for executing statements repeatedly using a `while` loop (§5.2).

- To follow the loop design strategy to develop loops (§§5.2.1–5.2.3).

- To control a loop with a sentinel value (§5.2.4).

- To obtain large input from a file using input redirection rather than typing from the keyboard (§5.2.5).

- To write loops using `do-while` statements (§5.3).

- To write loops using `for` statements (§5.4).

- To discover the similarities and differences of three types of loop statements (§5.5).

- To write nested loops (§5.6).

- To learn the techniques for minimizing numerical errors (§5.7).

- To learn loops from a variety of examples (`GCD`, `FutureTuition`, `Dec2Hex`) (§5.8).

- To implement program control with `break` and `continue` (§5.9).

- To process characters in a string using a loop in a case study for checking palindrome (§5.10).

- To write a program that displays prime numbers (§5.11).

5.1 Introduction

A loop can be used to tell a program to execute statements repeatedly.

problem

Suppose that you need to display a string (e.g., `Welcome to Java!`) a hundred times. It would be tedious to have to write the following statement a hundred times:

100 times
```
System.out.println("Welcome to Java!");
System.out.println("Welcome to Java!");
...
System.out.println("Welcome to Java!");
```

So, how do you solve this problem?

loop

Java provides a powerful construct called a *loop* that controls how many times an operation or a sequence of operations is performed in succession. Using a loop statement, you simply tell the computer to display a string a hundred times without having to code the print statement a hundred times, as follows:

```java
int count = 0;
while (count < 100) {
  System.out.println("Welcome to Java!");
  count++;
}
```

The variable `count` is initially `0`. The loop checks whether `count < 100` is `true`. If so, it executes the loop body to display the message `Welcome to Java!` and increments `count` by `1`. It repeatedly executes the loop body until `count < 100` becomes `false`. When `count < 100` is `false` (i.e., when `count` reaches `100`), the loop terminates and the next statement after the loop statement is executed.

Loops are constructs that control repeated executions of a block of statements. The concept of looping is fundamental to programming. Java provides three types of loop statements: `while` loops, `do-while` loops, and `for` loops.

5.2 The `while` Loop

Key Point

A `while` loop executes statements repeatedly while the condition is true.

The syntax for the `while` loop is:

while loop

```java
while (loop-continuation-condition) {
  // Loop body
  Statement(s);
}
```

loop body
iteration
loop-continuation-
  condition

Figure 5.1a shows the `while`-loop flowchart. The part of the loop that contains the statements to be repeated is called the *loop body*. A one-time execution of a loop body is referred to as an *iteration (or repetition) of the loop*. Each loop contains a *loop-continuation-condition*, a Boolean expression that controls the execution of the body. It is evaluated each time to determine if the loop body is executed. If its evaluation is `true`, the loop body is executed; if its evaluation is `false`, the entire loop terminates and the program control turns to the statement that follows the `while` loop.

The loop for displaying `Welcome to Java!` a hundred times introduced in the preceding section is an example of a `while` loop. Its flowchart is shown in Figure 5.1b. The

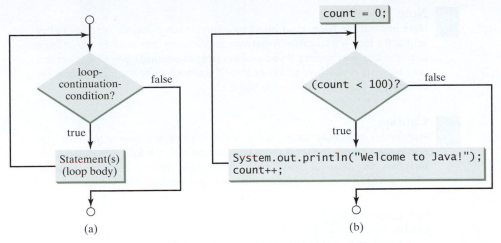

(a)   (b)

FIGURE 5.1 The **while** loop repeatedly executes the statements in the loop body when the **loop-continuation-condition** evaluates to **true**.

loop-continuation-condition is **count < 100** and the loop body contains the following two statements:

```
                              loop-continuation-condition
int count = 0;
while (count < 100)  {
  System.out.printIn("Welcome to Java!");     loop body
  count++;
}
```

In this example, you know exactly how many times the loop body needs to be executed because the control variable **count** is used to count the number of executions. This type of loop is known as a *counter-controlled loop*.

counter-controlled loop

 Note

The **loop-continuation-condition** must always appear inside the parentheses. The braces enclosing the loop body can be omitted only if the loop body contains one or no statement.

Here is another example to help understand how a loop works.

```
int sum = 0, i = 1;
while (i < 10) {
  sum = sum + i;
  i++;
}
System.out.println("sum is " + sum); // sum is 45
```

If **i < 10** is **true**, the program adds **i** to **sum**. Variable **i** is initially set to **1**, then is incremented to **2**, **3**, and up to **10**. When **i** is **10**, **i < 10** is **false**, so the loop exits. Therefore, the sum is **1 + 2 + 3 + ... + 9 = 45**.

What happens if the loop is mistakenly written as follows?

```
int sum = 0, i = 1;
while (i < 10) {
  sum = sum + i;
}
```

This loop is infinite, because **i** is always **1** and **i < 10** will always be **true**.

infinite loop

Note
Make sure that the `loop-continuation-condition` eventually becomes `false` so that the loop will terminate. A common programming error involves *infinite loops* (i. e., the loop runs forever). If your program takes an unusually long time to run and does not stop, it may have an infinite loop. If you are running the program from the command window, press *CTRL+C* to stop it.

off-by-one error

Caution
Programmers often make the mistake of executing a loop one more or less time. This is commonly known as the *off-by-one error*. For example, the following loop displays `Welcome to Java` 101 times rather than 100 times. The error lies in the condition, which should be `count < 100` rather than `count <= 100`.

```java
int count = 0;
while (count <= 100) {
  System.out.println("Welcome to Java!");
  count++;
}
```

Recall that Listing 3.1, AdditionQuiz.java, gives a program that prompts the user to enter an answer for a question on addition of two single digits. Using a loop, you can now rewrite the program to let the user repeatedly enter a new answer until it is correct, as shown in Listing 5.1.

LISTING 5.1 RepeatAdditionQuiz.java

```java
1  import java.util.Scanner;
2
3  public class RepeatAdditionQuiz {
4    public static void main(String[] args) {
5      int number1 = (int)(Math.random() * 10);
6      int number2 = (int)(Math.random() * 10);
7
8      // Create a Scanner
9      Scanner input = new Scanner(System.in);
10
11     System.out.print(
12       "What is " + number1 + " + " + number2 + "? ");
13     int answer = input.nextInt();
14
15     while (number1 + number2 != answer) {
16       System.out.print("Wrong answer. Try again. What is "
17         + number1 + " + " + number2 + "? ");
18       answer = input.nextInt();
19     }
20
21     System.out.println("You got it!");
22   }
23 }
```

generate number1 (line 5)
generate number2 (line 6)

show question (line 11)
get first answer (line 13)

check answer (line 15)

read an answer (line 18)

```
What is 5 + 9? 12 ↵Enter
Wrong answer. Try again. What is 5 + 9? 34 ↵Enter
Wrong answer. Try again. What is 5 + 9? 14 ↵Enter
You got it!
```

The loop in lines 15–19 repeatedly prompts the user to enter an **answer** when **number1** + **number2** != **answer** is **true**. Once **number1** + **number2** != **answer** is **false**, the loop exits.

5.2.1 Case Study: Guessing Numbers

VideoNote

Guess a number

The problem is to guess what number a computer has in mind. You will write a program that randomly generates an integer between **0** and **100**, inclusive. The program prompts the user to enter a number continuously until the number matches the randomly generated number. For each user input, the program tells the user whether the input is too low or too high, so the user can make the next guess intelligently. Here is a sample run:

```
Guess a magic number between 0 and 100
Enter your guess: 50  ↵Enter
Your guess is too high
Enter your guess: 25  ↵Enter
Your guess is too low
Enter your guess: 42  ↵Enter
Your guess is too high
Enter your guess: 39  ↵Enter
Yes, the number is 39
```

The magic number is between **0** and **100**. To minimize the number of guesses, enter **50** first. If your guess is too high, the magic number is between **0** and **49**. If your guess is too low, the magic number is between **51** and **100**. So, you can eliminate half of the numbers from further consideration after one guess.

intelligent guess

How do you write this program? Do you immediately begin coding? No. It is important to *think before coding*. Think how you would solve the problem without writing a program. You need first to generate a random number between **0** and **100**, inclusive, then to prompt the user to enter a guess, and then to compare the guess with the random number.

think before coding

It is a good practice to *code incrementally* one step at a time. For programs involving loops, if you don't know how to write a loop right away, you may first write the code for executing the loop one time, and then figure out how to repeatedly execute the code in a loop. For this program, you may create an initial draft, as shown in Listing 5.2.

code incrementally

LISTING 5.2 GuessNumberOneTime.java

```java
1  import java.util.Scanner;
2
3  public class GuessNumberOneTime {
4    public static void main(String[] args) {
5      // Generate a random number to be guessed
6      int number = (int)(Math.random() * 101);
7
8      Scanner input = new Scanner(System.in);
9      System.out.println("Guess a magic number between 0 and 100");
10
11     // Prompt the user to guess the number
12     System.out.print("\nEnter your guess: ");
13     int guess = input.nextInt();
14
15     if (guess == number)
16       System.out.println("Yes, the number is " + number);
```

generate a number

enter a guess

correct guess?

too high?

too low?

```
17          else if (guess > number)
18            System.out.println("Your guess is too high");
19          else
20            System.out.println("Your guess is too low");
21      }
22  }
```

When you run this program, it prompts the user to enter a guess only once. To let the user enter a guess repeatedly, you may wrap the code in lines 11–20 in a loop as follows:

```
while (true) {
  // Prompt the user to guess the number
  System.out.print("\nEnter your guess: ");
  guess = input.nextInt();

  if (guess == number)
    System.out.println("Yes, the number is " + number);
  else if (guess > number)
    System.out.println("Your guess is too high");
  else
    System.out.println("Your guess is too low");
} // End of loop
```

This loop repeatedly prompts the user to enter a guess. However, this loop is not correct, because it never terminates. When **guess** matches **number**, the loop should end. So, the loop can be revised as follows:

```
while (guess != number) {
  // Prompt the user to guess the number
  System.out.print("\nEnter your guess: ");
  guess = input.nextInt();

  if (guess == number)
    System.out.println("Yes, the number is " + number);
  else if (guess > number)
    System.out.println("Your guess is too high");
  else
    System.out.println("Your guess is too low");
} // End of loop
```

The complete code is given in Listing 5.3.

LISTING 5.3 GuessNumber.java

generate a number

```
 1  import java.util.Scanner;
 2
 3  public class GuessNumber {
 4    public static void main(String[] args) {
 5      // Generate a random number to be guessed
 6      int number = (int)(Math.random() * 101);
 7
 8      Scanner input = new Scanner(System.in);
 9      System.out.println("Guess a magic number between 0 and 100");
10
11      int guess = -1;
12      while (guess != number) {
13        // Prompt the user to guess the number
14        System.out.print("\nEnter your guess: ");
```

```
15          guess = input.nextInt();                                    enter a guess
16
17          if (guess == number)
18            System.out.println("Yes, the number is " + number);
19          else if (guess > number)
20            System.out.println("Your guess is too high");             too high?
21          else
22            System.out.println("Your guess is too low");              too low?
23      } // End of loop
24    }
25  }
```

	line#	number	guess	output
	6	39		
	11		−1	
iteration 1	15		50	
	20			Your guess is too high
iteration 2	15		25	
	22			Your guess is too low
iteration 3	15		42	
	20			Your guess is too high
iteration 4	15		39	
	18			Yes, the number is 39

The program generates the magic number in line 6 and prompts the user to enter a guess continuously in a loop (lines 12–23). For each guess, the program checks whether the guess is correct, too high, or too low (lines 17–22). When the guess is correct, the program exits the loop (line 12). Note that **guess** is initialized to **-1**. Initializing it to a value between **0** and **100** would be wrong, because that could be the number to be guessed.

5.2.2 Loop Design Strategies

Writing a correct loop is not an easy task for novice programmers. Consider three steps when writing a loop.

Step 1: Identify the statements that need to be repeated.

Step 2: Wrap these statements in a loop like this:

```
while (true) {
  Statements;
}
```

Step 3: Code the **loop-continuation-condition** and add appropriate statements for controlling the loop.

```
while (loop-continuation-condition) {
  Statements;
  Additional statements for controlling the loop;
}
```

VideoNote

Multiple subtraction quiz

5.2.3 Case Study: Multiple Subtraction Quiz

The Math subtraction learning tool program in Listing 3.3, SubtractionQuiz.java, generates just one question for each run. You can use a loop to generate questions repeatedly. How do you write the code to generate five questions? Follow the loop design strategy. First identify the statements that need to be repeated. These are the statements for obtaining two random numbers, prompting the user with a subtraction question, and grading the question. Second, wrap the statements in a loop. Third, add a loop control variable and the **loop-continuation-condition** to execute the loop five times.

Listing 5.4 gives a program that generates five questions and, after a student answers all five, reports the number of correct answers. The program also displays the time spent on the test and lists all the questions.

LISTING 5.4 SubtractionQuizLoop.java

```
1  import java.util.Scanner;
2
3  public class SubtractionQuizLoop {
4    public static void main(String[] args) {
5      final int NUMBER_OF_QUESTIONS = 5; // Number of questions
6      int correctCount = 0; // Count the number of correct answers
7      int count = 0; // Count the number of questions
8      long startTime = System.currentTimeMillis();
9      String output = " "; // output string is initially empty
10     Scanner input = new Scanner(System.in);
11
12     while (count < NUMBER_OF_QUESTIONS) {
13       // 1. Generate two random single-digit integers
14       int number1 = (int)(Math.random() * 10);
15       int number2 = (int)(Math.random() * 10);
16
17       // 2. If number1 < number2, swap number1 with number2
18       if (number1 < number2) {
19         int temp = number1;
20         number1 = number2;
21         number2 = temp;
22       }
23
24       // 3. Prompt the student to answer "What is number1 - number2?"
25       System.out.print(
26         "What is " + number1 + " - " + number2 + "? ");
27       int answer = input.nextInt();
28
29       // 4. Grade the answer and display the result
30       if (number1 - number2 == answer) {
31         System.out.println("You are correct!");
32         correctCount++; // Increase the correct answer count
33       }
34       else
35         System.out.println("Your answer is wrong.\n" + number1
36           + " - " + number2 + " should be " + (number1 - number2));
37
38       // Increase the question count
39       count++;
40
41       output += "\n" + number1 + "-" + number2 + "=" + answer +
42         ((number1 - number2 == answer) ? " correct" : " wrong");
```

get start time

loop

display a question

grade an answer

increase correct count

increase control variable

prepare output

```
43        }                                                       end loop
44
45        long endTime = System.currentTimeMillis();              get end time
46        long testTime = endTime - startTime;                    test time
47
48        System.out.println("Correct count is " + correctCount +  display result
49          "\nTest time is " + testTime / 1000 + " seconds\n" + output);
50    }
51 }
```

```
What is 9 – 2? 7 [↵Enter]
You are correct!

What is 3 – 0? 3 [↵Enter]
You are correct!

What is 3 – 2? 1 [↵Enter]
You are correct!

What is 7 – 4? 4 [↵Enter]
Your answer is wrong.
7 – 4 should be 3

What is 7 – 5? 4 [↵Enter]
Your answer is wrong.
7 – 5 should be 2

Correct count is 3
Test time is 1021 seconds

9–2=7 correct
3–0=3 correct
3–2=1 correct
7–4=4 wrong
7–5=4 wrong
```

The program uses the control variable `count` to control the execution of the loop. `count` is initially `0` (line 7) and is increased by `1` in each iteration (line 39). A subtraction question is displayed and processed in each iteration. The program obtains the time before the test starts in line 8 and the time after the test ends in line 45, and computes the test time in line 46. The test time is in milliseconds and is converted to seconds in line 49.

5.2.4 Controlling a Loop with a Sentinel Value

Another common technique for controlling a loop is to designate a special value when reading and processing a set of values. This special input value, known as a *sentinel value*, signifies the end of the input. A loop that uses a sentinel value to control its execution is called a *sentinel-controlled loop*.

sentinel value

sentinel-controlled loop

Listing 5.5 writes a program that reads and calculates the sum of an unspecified number of integers. The input `0` signifies the end of the input. Do you need to declare a new variable for each input value? No. Just use one variable named `data` (line 12) to store the input value and use a variable named `sum` (line 15) to store the total. Whenever a value is read, assign it to `data` and, if it is not zero, add it to `sum` (line 17).

LISTING 5.5 SentinelValue.java

```java
1   import java.util.Scanner;
2
3   public class SentinelValue {
4     /** Main method */
5     public static void main(String[] args) {
6       // Create a Scanner
7       Scanner input = new Scanner(System.in);
8
9       // Read an initial data
10      System.out.print(
11        "Enter an integer (the input ends if it is 0): ");
12      int data = input.nextInt();
13
14      // Keep reading data until the input is 0
15      int sum = 0;
16      while (data != 0) {
17        sum += data;
18
19        // Read the next data
20        System.out.print(
21          "Enter an integer (the input ends if it is 0): ");
22        data = input.nextInt();
23      }
24
25      System.out.println("The sum is " + sum);
26    }
27  }
```

input — line 12
loop — line 16
end of loop — line 23
display result — line 25

```
Enter an integer (the input ends if it is 0): 2  ⏎ Enter
Enter an integer (the input ends if it is 0): 3  ⏎ Enter
Enter an integer (the input ends if it is 0): 4  ⏎ Enter
Enter an integer (the input ends if it is 0): 0  ⏎ Enter
The sum is 9
```

	line#	Data	sum	output
	12	2		
	15		0	
iteration 1	17		2	
	22	3		
iteration 2	17		5	
	22	4		
iteration 3	17		9	
	22	0		
	25			The sum is 9

If **data** is not **0**, it is added to **sum** (line 17) and the next item of input data is read (lines 20–22). If **data** is **0**, the loop body is no longer executed and the **while** loop terminates. The input value **0** is the sentinel value for this loop. Note that if the first input read is **0**, the loop body never executes, and the resulting sum is **0**.

Caution

Don't use floating-point values for equality checking in a loop control. Because floating-point values are approximations for some values, using them could result in imprecise counter values and inaccurate results.

Consider the following code for computing $1 + 0.9 + 0.8 + ... + 0.1$:

```java
double item = 1; double sum = 0;
while (item != 0) { // No guarantee item will be 0
  sum += item;
  item -= 0.1;
}
System.out.println(sum);
```

Variable `item` starts with `1` and is reduced by `0.1` every time the loop body is executed. The loop should terminate when `item` becomes `0`. However, there is no guarantee that item will be exactly `0`, because the floating-point arithmetic is approximated. This loop seems okay on the surface, but it is actually an infinite loop.

numeric error

5.2.5 Input and Output Redirections

In the preceding example, if you have a large number of data to enter, it would be cumbersome to type from the keyboard. You can store the data separated by whitespaces in a text file, say **input.txt**, and run the program using the following command:

```
java SentinelValue < input.txt
```

This command is called *input redirection*. The program takes the input from the file **input .txt** rather than having the user type the data from the keyboard at runtime. Suppose the contents of the file are

input redirection

```
2 3 4 5 6 7 8 9 12 23 32
23 45 67 89 92 12 34 35 3 1 2 4 0
```

The program should get `sum` to be `518`.

Similarly, there is *output redirection*, which sends the output to a file rather than displaying it on the console. The command for output redirection is:

output redirection

```
java ClassName > output.txt
```

Input and output redirection can be used in the same command. For example, the following command gets input from **input.txt** and sends output to **output.txt**:

```
java SentinelValue  output.txt
```

Try running the program to see what contents are in **output.txt**.

5.1 Analyze the following code. Is `count < 100` always `true`, always `false`, or sometimes `true` or sometimes `false` at Point A, Point B, and Point C?

✓Check Point

```java
int count = 0;
while (count < 100) {
  // Point A
  System.out.println("Welcome to Java!");
  count++;
  // Point B
}
// Point C
```

5.2 What is wrong if **guess** is initialized to **0** in line 11 in Listing 5.3?

5.3 How many times are the following loop bodies repeated? What is the output of each loop?

```
int i = 1;
while (i < 10)
  if (i % 2 == 0)
    System.out.println(i);
```

(a)

```
int i = 1;
while (i < 10)
  if (i % 2 == 0)
    System.out.println(i++);
```

(b)

```
int i = 1;
while (i < 10)
  if ((i++) % 2 == 0)
    System.out.println(i);
```

(c)

5.4 Suppose the input is 2 3 4 5 0. What is the output of the following code?

```
import java.util.Scanner;

public class Test {
  public static void main(String[] args) {
    Scanner input = new Scanner(System.in);

    int number, max;
    number = input.nextInt();
    max = number;

    while (number != 0) {
      number = input.nextInt();
      if (number > max)
        max = number;
    }

    System.out.println("max is " + max);
    System.out.println("number " + number);
  }
}
```

5.5 What is the output of the following code? Explain the reason.

```
int x = 80000000;

while (x > 0)
  x++;

System.out.println("x is " + x);
```

5.3 The **do-while** Loop

Key Point

A do-while loop is the same as a while loop except that it executes the loop body first and then checks the loop continuation condition.

The **do-while** loop is a variation of the **while** loop. Its syntax is:

do-while loop

```
do {
  // Loop body;
  Statement(s);
} while (loop-continuation-condition);
```

Its execution flowchart is shown in Figure 5.2.

The loop body is executed first, and then the **loop-continuation-condition** is evaluated. If the evaluation is **true**, the loop body is executed again; if it is **false**, the **do-while**

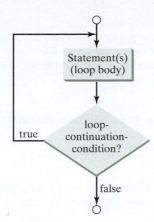

FIGURE 5.2 The **do-while** loop executes the loop body first, then checks the **loop-continuation-condition** to determine whether to continue or terminate the loop.

loop terminates. The difference between a **while** loop and a **do-while** loop is the order in which the **loop-continuation-condition** is evaluated and the loop body executed. You can write a loop using either the **while** loop or the **do-while** loop. Sometimes one is a more convenient choice than the other. For example, you can rewrite the **while** loop in Listing 5.5 using a **do-while** loop, as shown in Listing 5.6.

LISTING 5.6 TestDoWhile.java

```
1  import java.util.Scanner;
2
3  public class TestDoWhile {
4    /** Main method */
5    public static void main(String[] args) {
6      int data;
7      int sum = 0;
8
9      // Create a Scanner
10     Scanner input = new Scanner(System.in);
11
12     // Keep reading data until the input is 0
13     do {                                            loop
14       // Read the next data
15       System.out.print(
16         "Enter an integer (the input ends if it is 0): ");
17       data = input.nextInt();
18
19       sum += data;
20     } while (data != 0);                            end loop
21
22     System.out.println("The sum is " + sum);
23   }
24 }
```

```
Enter an integer (the input ends if it is 0): 3 ↵Enter
Enter an integer (the input ends if it is 0): 5 ↵Enter
Enter an integer (the input ends if it is 0): 6 ↵Enter
Enter an integer (the input ends if it is 0): 0 ↵Enter
The sum is 14
```

Tip

Use a `do-while` loop if you have statements inside the loop that must be executed *at least once*, as in the case of the `do-while` loop in the preceding `TestDoWhile` program. These statements must appear before the loop as well as inside it if you use a `while` loop.

5.6 Suppose the input is 2 3 4 5 0. What is the output of the following code?

```java
import java.util.Scanner;

public class Test {
  public static void main(String[] args) {
    Scanner input = new Scanner(System.in);

    int number, max;
    number = input.nextInt();
    max = number;

    do {
      number = input.nextInt();
      if (number > max)
        max = number;
    } while (number != 0);

    System.out.println("max is " + max);
    System.out.println("number " + number);
  }
}
```

5.7 What are the differences between a `while` loop and a `do-while` loop? Convert the following `while` loop into a `do-while` loop.

```java
Scanner input = new Scanner(System.in);
int sum = 0;
System.out.println("Enter an integer " +
  "(the input ends if it is 0)");
int number = input.nextInt();
while (number != 0) {
  sum += number;
  System.out.println("Enter an integer " +
    "(the input ends if it is 0)");
  number = input.nextInt();
}
```

5.4 The **for** Loop

*A **for** loop has a concise syntax for writing loops.*

Often you write a loop in the following common form:

```java
i = initialValue;  // Initialize loop control variable
while (i < endValue)
  // Loop body
  ...
  i++; // Adjust loop control variable
}
```

A **for** loop can be used to simplify the preceding loop as:

```
for (i = initialValue; i < endValue; i++)
  // Loop body
  ...
}
```

In general, the syntax of a **for** loop is:

```
for (initial-action; loop-continuation-condition;
     action-after-each-iteration) {
  // Loop body;
  Statement(s);
}
```

for loop

The flowchart of the **for** loop is shown in Figure 5.3a.

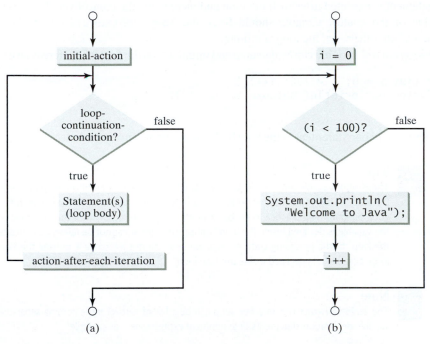

(a)   (b)

FIGURE 5.3   A **for** loop performs an initial action once, then repeatedly executes the statements in the loop body, and performs an action after an iteration when the `loop-continuation-condition` evaluates to **true**.

The **for** loop statement starts with the keyword **for**, followed by a pair of parentheses enclosing the control structure of the loop. This structure consists of `initial-action`, `loop-continuation-condition`, and `action-after-each-iteration`. The control structure is followed by the loop body enclosed inside braces. The `initial-action`, `loop-continuation-condition`, and `action-after-each-iteration` are separated by semicolons.

A **for** loop generally uses a variable to control how many times the loop body is executed and when the loop terminates. This variable is referred to as a *control variable*. The `initial-action` often initializes a control variable, the `action-after-each-iteration` usually increments or decrements the control variable, and the `loop-continuation-condition`

control variable

tests whether the control variable has reached a termination value. For example, the following **for** loop prints **Welcome to Java!** a hundred times:

```java
int i;
for (i = 0; i < 100; i++) {
  System.out.println("Welcome to Java!");
}
```

The flowchart of the statement is shown in Figure 5.3b. The **for** loop initializes **i** to **0**, then repeatedly executes the **println** statement and evaluates **i++** while **i** is less than **100**.

initial-action

The **initial-action, i = 0**, initializes the control variable, **i**. The **loop-continuation-condition, i < 100**, is a Boolean expression. The expression is evaluated right after the initialization and at the beginning of each iteration. If this condition is **true**, the loop body is executed. If it is **false**, the loop terminates and the program control turns to the line following the loop.

action-after-each-iteration

The **action-after-each-iteration, i++**, is a statement that adjusts the control variable. This statement is executed after each iteration and increments the control variable. Eventually, the value of the control variable should force the **loop-continuation-condition** to become **false**; otherwise, the loop is infinite.

The loop control variable can be declared and initialized in the **for** loop. Here is an example:

```java
for (int i = 0; i < 100; i++) {
  System.out.println("Welcome to Java!");
}
```

omitting braces

If there is only one statement in the loop body, as in this example, the braces can be omitted.

declare control variable

Tip

The control variable must be declared inside the control structure of the loop or before the loop. If the loop control variable is used only in the loop, and not elsewhere, it is a good programming practice to declare it in the **initial-action** of the **for** loop. If the variable is declared inside the loop control structure, it cannot be referenced outside the loop. In the preceding code, for example, you cannot reference **i** outside the **for** loop, because it is declared inside the **for** loop.

for loop variations

Note

The **initial-action** in a **for** loop can be a list of zero or more comma-separated variable declaration statements or assignment expressions. For example:

```java
for (int i = 0, j = 0; i + j < 10; i++, j++) {
  // Do something
}
```

The **action-after-each-iteration** in a **for** loop can be a list of zero or more comma-separated statements. For example:

```java
for (int i = 1; i < 100; System.out.println(i), i++);
```

This example is correct, but it is a bad example, because it makes the code difficult to read. Normally, you declare and initialize a control variable as an initial action and increment or decrement the control variable as an action after each iteration.

Note

If the **loop-continuation-condition** in a **for** loop is omitted, it is implicitly **true**. Thus the statement given below in (a), which is an infinite loop, is the same as in (b). To avoid confusion, though, it is better to use the equivalent loop in (c).

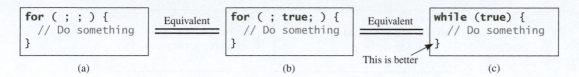

(a)   (b)   (c)

5.8 Do the following two loops result in the same value in **sum**?

Check
Point

```
for (int i = 0; i < 10; ++i) {
   sum += i;
}
```

```
for (int i = 0; i < 10; i++) {
   sum += i;
}
```

(a)   (b)

5.9 What are the three parts of a **for** loop control? Write a **for** loop that prints the numbers from **1** to **100**.

5.10 Suppose the input is **2 3 4 5 0**. What is the output of the following code?

```java
import java.util.Scanner;

public class Test {
  public static void main(String[] args) {
    Scanner input = new Scanner(System.in);

    int number, sum = 0, count;

    for (count = 0; count < 5; count++) {
      number = input.nextInt();
      sum += number;
    }

    System.out.println("sum is " + sum);
    System.out.println("count is " + count);
  }
}
```

5.11 What does the following statement do?

```java
for ( ; ; ) {
   // Do something
}
```

5.12 If a variable is declared in a **for** loop control, can it be used after the loop exits?

5.13 Convert the following **for** loop statement to a **while** loop and to a **do-while** loop:

```java
long sum = 0;
for (int i = 0; i <= 1000; i++)
   sum = sum + i;
```

5.14 Count the number of iterations in the following loops.

```java
int count = 0;
while (count < n) {
   count++;
}
```

```java
for (int count = 0;
   count <= n; count++) {
}
```

(a)   (b)

```
int count = 5;
while (count < n) {
    count++;
}
```

(c)

```
int count = 5;
while (count < n) {
    count = count + 3;
}
```

(d)

5.5 Which Loop to Use?

You can use a **for** *loop, a* **while** *loop, or a* **do-while** *loop, whichever is convenient.*

pretest loop
posttest loop

The **while** loop and **for** loop are called *pretest loops* because the continuation condition is checked before the loop body is executed. The **do-while** loop is called a *posttest loop* because the condition is checked after the loop body is executed. The three forms of loop statements—**while**, **do-while**, and **for**—are expressively equivalent; that is, you can write a loop in any of these three forms. For example, a **while** loop in (a) in the following figure can always be converted into the **for** loop in (b).

```
while (loop-continuation-condition) {
    // Loop body
}
```

Equivalent

```
for ( ; loop-continuation-condition; ) {
    // Loop body
}
```

(a)   (b)

A **for** loop in (a) in the next figure can generally be converted into the **while** loop in (b) except in certain special cases (see Checkpoint Question 5.25 for such a case).

```
for (initial-action;
     loop-continuation-condition;
     action-after-each-iteration) {
    // Loop body;
}
```

Equivalent

```
initial-action;
while (loop-continuation-condition) {
    // Loop body;
    action-after-each-iteration;
}
```

(a)   (b)

Use the loop statement that is most intuitive and comfortable for you. In general, a **for** loop may be used if the number of repetitions is known in advance, as, for example, when you need to display a message a hundred times. A **while** loop may be used if the number of repetitions is not fixed, as in the case of reading the numbers until the input is **0**. A **do-while** loop can be used to replace a **while** loop if the loop body has to be executed before the continuation condition is tested.

Caution

Adding a semicolon at the end of the **for** clause before the loop body is a common mistake, as shown below in (a). In (a), the semicolon signifies the end of the loop prematurely. The loop body is actually empty, as shown in (b). (a) and (b) are equivalent. Both are incorrect.

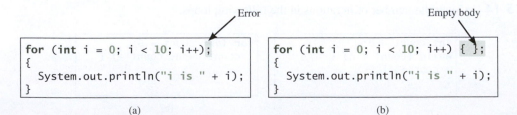

Error   Empty body

```
for (int i = 0; i < 10; i++);
{
    System.out.println("i is " + i);
}
```

```
for (int i = 0; i < 10; i++) { };
{
    System.out.println("i is " + i);
}
```

(a)   (b)

Similarly, the loop in (c) is also wrong. (c) is equivalent to (d). Both are incorrect.

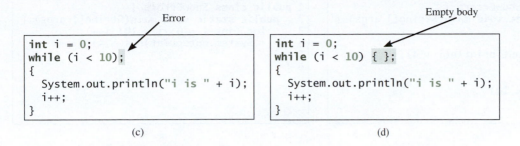

Error   Empty body

```java
int i = 0;
while (i < 10);
{
  System.out.println("i is " + i);
  i++;
}
```
(c)

```java
int i = 0;
while (i < 10) { };
{
  System.out.println("i is " + i);
  i++;
}
```
(d)

These errors often occur when you use the next-line block style. Using the end-of-line block style can avoid errors of this type.

In the case of the **do-while** loop, the semicolon is needed to end the loop.

```java
int i = 0;
do {
  System.out.println("i is " + i);
  i++;
} while (i < 10);
```

Correct

5.15 Can you convert a **for** loop to a **while** loop? List the advantages of using **for** loops.

5.16 Can you always convert a **while** loop into a **for** loop? Convert the following **while** loop into a **for** loop.

Check
Point

```java
int i = 1;
int sum = 0;
while (sum < 10000) {
  sum = sum + i;
  i++;
}
```

5.17 Identify and fix the errors in the following code:

```java
1  public class Test {
2    public void main(String[] args) {
3      for (int i = 0; i < 10; i++);
4        sum += i;
5
6      if (i < j);
7        System.out.println(i)
8      else
9        System.out.println(j);
10
11     while (j < 10);
12     {
13       j++;
14     }
15
16     do {
17       j++;
18     } while (j < 10)
19   }
20 }
```

5.18 What is wrong with the following programs?

```
1 public class ShowErrors {
2   public static void main(String[] args) {
3     int i = 0;
4     do {
5       System.out.println(i + 4);
6       i++;
7     }
8     while (i < 10)
9   }
10 }
```

(a)

```
1 public class ShowErrors {
2   public static void main(String[] args) {
3     for (int i = 0; i < 10; i++);
4       System.out.println(i + 4);
5   }
6 }
```

(b)

5.6 Nested Loops

Key Point

A loop can be nested inside another loop.

nested loop

Nested loops consist of an outer loop and one or more inner loops. Each time the outer loop is repeated, the inner loops are reentered, and started anew.

Listing 5.7 presents a program that uses nested **for** loops to display a multiplication table.

LISTING 5.7 MultiplicationTable.java

table title

outer loop

inner loop

```
1  public class MultiplicationTable {
2    /** Main method */
3    public static void main(String[] args) {
4      // Display the table heading
5      System.out.println("          Multiplication Table");
6
7      // Display the number title
8      System.out.print("    ");
9      for (int j = 1; j <= 9; j++)
10       System.out.print("   " + j);
11
12     System.out.println("\n---------------------------------------");
13
14     // Display table body
15     for (int i = 1; i <= 9; i++) {
16       System.out.print(i + " | ");
17       for (int j = 1; j <= 9; j++) {
18         // Display the product and align properly
19         System.out.printf("%4d", i * j);
20       }
21       System.out.println();
22     }
23   }
24 }
```

```
              Multiplication Table
        1    2    3    4    5    6    7    8    9
      ---------------------------------------------
    1 |   1    2    3    4    5    6    7    8    9
    2 |   2    4    6    8   10   12   14   16   18
    3 |   3    6    9   12   15   18   21   24   27
    4 |   4    8   12   16   20   24   28   32   36
    5 |   5   10   15   20   25   30   35   40   45
    6 |   6   12   18   24   30   36   42   48   54
    7 |   7   14   21   28   35   42   49   56   63
    8 |   8   16   24   32   40   48   56   64   72
    9 |   9   18   27   36   45   54   63   72   81
```

The program displays a title (line 5) on the first line in the output. The first **for** loop (lines 9–10) displays the numbers **1** through **9** on the second line. A dashed (-) line is displayed on the third line (line 12).

The next loop (lines 15–22) is a nested **for** loop with the control variable **i** in the outer loop and **j** in the inner loop. For each **i**, the product **i** * **j** is displayed on a line in the inner loop, with **j** being **1, 2, 3, ..., 9**.

> **Note**
>
> Be aware that a nested loop may take a long time to run. Consider the following loop nested in three levels:
>
> ```
> for (int i = 0; i < 10000; i++)
>   for (int j = 0; j < 10000; j++)
>     for (int k = 0; k < 10000; k++)
>       Perform an action
> ```
>
> The action is performed one trillion times. If it takes 1 microsecond to perform the action, the total time to run the loop would be more than 277 hours. Note that 1 microsecond is one millionth (10^{-6}) of a second.

5.19 How many times is the **println** statement executed?

```
for (int i = 0; i < 10; i++)
  for (int j = 0; j < i; j++)
    System.out.println(i * j)
```

5.20 Show the output of the following programs. (*Hint*: Draw a table and list the variables in the columns to trace these programs.)

```
public class Test {
  public static void main(String[] args) {
    for (int i = 1; i < 5; i++) {
      int j = 0;
      while (j < i) {
        System.out.print(j + " ");
        j++;
      }
    }
  }
}
```
(a)

```
public class Test {
  public static void main(String[] args) {
    int i = 0;
    while (i < 5) {
      for (int j = i; j > 1; j--)
        System.out.print(j + " ");
      System.out.println("****");
      i++;
    }
  }
}
```
(b)

```
public class Test {
  public static void main(String[] args) {
    int i = 5;
    while (i >= 1) {
      int num = 1;
      for (int j = 1; j <= i; j++) {
        System.out.print(num + "xxx");
        num *= 2;
      }

      System.out.println();
      i--;
    }
  }
}
```
(c)

```
public class Test {
  public static void main(String[] args) {
    int i = 1;
    do {
      int num = 1;
      for (int j = 1; j <= i; j++) {
        System.out.print(num + "G");
        num += 2;
      }

      System.out.println();
      i++;
    } while (i <= 5);
  }
}
```
(d)

5.7 Minimizing Numeric Errors

VideoNote

Minimize numeric errors

Using floating-point numbers in the loop continuation condition may cause numeric errors.

Numeric errors involving floating-point numbers are inevitable, because floating-point numbers are represented in approximation in computers by nature. This section discusses how to minimize such errors through an example.

Listing 5.8 presents an example summing a series that starts with **0.01** and ends with **1.0**. The numbers in the series will increment by **0.01**, as follows: **0.01 + 0.02 + 0.03**, and so on.

LISTING 5.8 TestSum.java

loop

```
 1  public class TestSum {
 2    public static void main(String[] args) {
 3      // Initialize sum
 4      float sum = 0;
 5
 6      // Add 0.01, 0.02, ..., 0.99, 1 to sum
 7      for (float i = 0.01f; i <= 1.0f; i = i + 0.01f)
 8        sum += i;
 9
10      // Display result
11      System.out.println("The sum is " + sum);
12    }
13  }
```

```
The sum is 50.499985
```

The **for** loop (lines 7–8) repeatedly adds the control variable **i** to **sum**. This variable, which begins with **0.01**, is incremented by **0.01** after each iteration. The loop terminates when **i** exceeds **1.0**.

The **for** loop initial action can be any statement, but it is often used to initialize a control variable. From this example, you can see that a control variable can be a **float** type. In fact, it can be any data type.

double precision

The exact **sum** should be **50.50**, but the answer is **50.499985**. The result is imprecise because computers use a fixed number of bits to represent floating-point numbers, and thus they cannot represent some floating-point numbers exactly. If you change **float** in the program to **double**, as follows, you should see a slight improvement in precision, because a **double** variable holds 64 bits, whereas a **float** variable holds 32 bits.

```
// Initialize sum
double sum = 0;

// Add 0.01, 0.02, ..., 0.99, 1 to sum
for (double i = 0.01; i <= 1.0; i = i + 0.01)
  sum += i;
```

numeric error

However, you will be stunned to see that the result is actually **49.50000000000003**. What went wrong? If you display **i** for each iteration in the loop, you will see that the last **i** is slightly larger than **1** (not exactly **1**). This causes the last **i** not to be added into **sum**. The fundamental problem is that the floating-point numbers are represented by approximation. To fix the problem, use an integer count to ensure that all the numbers are added to **sum**. Here is the new loop:

```
double currentValue = 0.01;

for (int count = 0; count < 100; count++) {
```

```
    sum += currentValue;
    currentValue += 0.01;
}
```

After this loop, **sum** is **50.50000000000003**. This loop adds the numbers from smallest to biggest. What happens if you add numbers from biggest to smallest (i.e., **1.0**, **0.99**, **0.98**, . . . , **0.02**, **0.01** in this order) as follows:

```
double currentValue = 1.0;

for (int count = 0; count < 100; count++) {
    sum += currentValue;
    currentValue -= 0.01;
}
```

After this loop, **sum** is **50.49999999999995**. Adding from biggest to smallest is less accurate than adding from smallest to biggest. This phenomenon is an artifact of the finite-precision arithmetic. Adding a very small number to a very big number can have no effect if the result requires more precision than the variable can store. For example, the inaccurate result of **100000000.0 + 0.000000001** is **100000000.0**. To obtain more accurate results, carefully select the order of computation. Adding smaller numbers before bigger numbers is one way to minimize errors.

avoiding numeric error

5.8 Case Studies

Loops are fundamental in programming. The ability to write loops is essential in learning Java programming.

Key Point

If you can write programs using loops, you know how to program! For this reason, this section presents four additional examples of solving problems using loops.

5.8.1 Case Study: Finding the Greatest Common Divisor

The greatest common divisor (gcd) of the two integers **4** and **2** is **2**. The greatest common divisor of the two integers **16** and **24** is **8**. How would you write this program to find the greatest common divisor? Would you immediately begin to write the code? No. It is important to *think before you code*. Thinking enables you to generate a logical solution for the problem without concern about how to write the code.

gcd

think before you code

Let the two input integers be **n1** and **n2**. You know that number **1** is a common divisor, but it may not be the greatest common divisor. So, you can check whether **k** (for **k** = **2**, **3**, **4**, and so on) is a common divisor for **n1** and **n2**, until **k** is greater than **n1** or **n2**. Store the common divisor in a variable named **gcd**. Initially, **gcd** is **1**. Whenever a new common divisor is found, it becomes the new gcd. When you have checked all the possible common divisors from **2** up to **n1** or **n2**, the value in variable **gcd** is the greatest common divisor. Once you have a logical solution, type the code to translate the solution into a Java program as follows:

logical solution

```
int gcd = 1; // Initial gcd is 1
int k = 2; // Possible gcd

while (k <= n1 && k <= n2) {
    if (n1 % k == 0 && n2 % k == 0)
        gcd = k; // Update gcd
    k++; // Next possible gcd
}

// After the loop, gcd is the greatest common divisor for n1 and n2
```

Listing 5.9 presents the program that prompts the user to enter two positive integers and finds their greatest common divisor.

LISTING 5.9   GreatestCommonDivisor.java

```java
 1  import java.util.Scanner;
 2
 3  public class GreatestCommonDivisor {
 4    /** Main method */
 5    public static void main(String[] args) {
 6      // Create a Scanner
 7      Scanner input = new Scanner(System.in);
 8
 9      // Prompt the user to enter two integers
10      System.out.print("Enter first integer: ");
11      int n1 = input.nextInt();
12      System.out.print("Enter second integer: ");
13      int n2 = input.nextInt();
14
15      int gcd = 1; // Initial gcd is 1
16      int k = 2; // Possible gcd
17      while (k <= n1 && k <= n2) {
18        if (n1 % k == 0 && n2 % k == 0)
19          gcd = k; // Update gcd
20        k++;
21      }
22
23      System.out.println("The greatest common divisor for " + n1 +
24        " and " + n2 + " is " + gcd);
25    }
26  }
```

input (line 11)
input (line 13)
gcd (line 15)
check divisor (line 18)
output (line 23)

```
Enter first integer: 125 ⏎Enter
Enter second integer: 2525 ⏎Enter
The greatest common divisor for 125 and 2525 is 25
```

Translating a logical solution to Java code is not unique. For example, you could use a **for** loop to rewrite the code as follows:

```java
for (int k = 2; k <= n1 && k <= n2; k++) {
  if (n1 % k == 0 && n2 % k == 0)
    gcd = k;
}
```

multiple solutions

A problem often has multiple solutions, and the gcd problem can be solved in many ways. Programming Exercise 5.14 suggests another solution. A more efficient solution is to use the classic Euclidean algorithm (see Section 22.6).

erroneous solutions

You might think that a divisor for a number **n1** cannot be greater than **n1 / 2** and would attempt to improve the program using the following loop:

```java
for (int k = 2; k <= n1 / 2 && k <= n2 / 2; k++) {
  if (n1 % k == 0 && n2 % k == 0)
    gcd = k;
}
```

This revision is wrong. Can you find the reason? See Checkpoint Question 5.21 for the answer.

5.8.2   Case Study: Predicting the Future Tuition

Suppose that the tuition for a university is **$10,000** this year and tuition increases **7%** every year. In how many years will the tuition be doubled?

Before you can write a program to solve this problem, first consider how to solve it by hand. The tuition for the second year is the tuition for the first year * **1.07**. The tuition for a future year is the tuition of its preceding year * **1.07**. Thus, the tuition for each year can be computed as follows:

think before you code

```
double tuition = 10000;    int year = 0;   // Year 0
tuition = tuition * 1.07; year++;          // Year 1
tuition = tuition * 1.07; year++;          // Year 2
tuition = tuition * 1.07; year++;          // Year 3
...
```

Keep computing the tuition for a new year until it is at least **20000**. By then you will know how many years it will take for the tuition to be doubled. You can now translate the logic into the following loop:

```
double tuition = 10000;    // Year 0
int year = 0;
while (tuition < 20000) {
  tuition = tuition * 1.07;
  year++;
}
```

The complete program is shown in Listing 5.10.

LISTING 5.10   FutureTuition.java

```
1  public class FutureTuition {
2    public static void main(String[] args) {
3      double tuition = 10000;    // Year 0
4      int year = 0;
5      while (tuition < 20000) {
6        tuition = tuition * 1.07;
7        year++;
8      }
9
10     System.out.println("Tuition will be doubled in "
11       + year + " years");
12     System.out.printf("Tuition will be $%.2f in %1d years",
13       tuition, year);
14   }
15 }
```

loop
next year's tuition

```
Tuition will be doubled in 11 years
Tuition will be $21048.52 in 11 years
```

The **while** loop (lines 5–8) is used to repeatedly compute the tuition for a new year. The loop terminates when the tuition is greater than or equal to **20000**.

5.8.3 Case Study: Converting Decimals to Hexadecimals

Hexadecimals are often used in computer systems programming (see Appendix F for an introduction to number systems). How do you convert a decimal number to a hexadecimal number? To convert a decimal number d to a hexadecimal number is to find the hexadecimal digits $h_n, h_{n-1}, h_{n-2}, \ldots, h_2, h_1$, and h_0 such that

$$d = h_n \times 16^n + h_{n-1} \times 16^{n-1} + h_{n-2} \times 16^{n-2} + \cdots$$
$$+ h_2 \times 16^2 + h_1 \times 16^1 + h_0 \times 16^0$$

These hexadecimal digits can be found by successively dividing d by 16 until the quotient is 0. The remainders are $h_0, h_1, h_2, \ldots, h_{n-2}, h_{n-1}$, and h_n. The hexadecimal digits include the decimal digits 0, 1, 2, 3, 4, 5, 6, 7, 8, and 9, plus A, which is the decimal value 10; B, which is the decimal value 11; C, which is 12; D, which is 13; E, which is 14; and F, which is 15.

For example, the decimal number **123** is **7B** in hexadecimal. The conversion is done as follows. Divide **123** by 16. The remainder is **11** (**B** in hexadecimal) and the quotient is **7**. Continue divide **7** by 16. The remainder is **7** and the quotient is **0**. Therefore **7B** is the hexadecimal number for **123**.

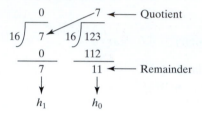

Listing 5.11 gives a program that prompts the user to enter a decimal number and converts it into a hex number as a string.

LISTING 5.11 Dec2Hex.java

input decimal

decimal to hex

```java
1   import java.util.Scanner;
2
3   public class Dec2Hex {
4     /** Main method */
5     public static void main(String[] args) {
6       // Create a Scanner
7       Scanner input = new Scanner(System.in);
8
9       // Prompt the user to enter a decimal integer
10      System.out.print("Enter a decimal number: ");
11      int decimal = input.nextInt();
12
13      // Convert decimal to hex
14      String hex = "";
15
16      while (decimal != 0) {
17        int hexValue = decimal % 16;
18
19        // Convert a decimal value to a hex digit
20        char hexDigit = (hexValue <= 9 && hexValue >= 0) ?
21          (char)(hexValue + '0') : (char)(hexValue - 10 + 'A');
22
23        hex = hexDigit + hex;
```

```
24          decimal = decimal / 16;
25      }
26
27      System.out.println("The hex number is " + hex);
28  }
29 }
```

get a hex char

get a letter

```
Enter a decimal number: 1234 ⏎Enter
The hex number is 4D2
```

	line#	decimal	hex	hexValue	hexDigit
	14	1234	""		
iteration 1	17			2	
	23		"2"		2
	24	77			
iteration 2	17			13	
	23		"D2"		D
	24	4			
iteration 3	17			4	
	23		"4D2"		4
	24	0			

The program prompts the user to enter a decimal integer (line 11), converts it to a hex number as a string (lines 14–25), and displays the result (line 27). To convert a decimal to a hex number, the program uses a loop to successively divide the decimal number by **16** and obtain its remainder (line 17). The remainder is converted into a hex character (lines 20–21). The character is then appended to the hex string (line 23). The hex string is initially empty (line 14). Divide the decimal number by **16** to remove a hex digit from the number (line 24). The loop ends when the remaining decimal number becomes **0**.

The program converts a **hexValue** between **0** and **15** into a hex character. If **hexValue** is between **0** and **9**, it is converted to **(char)(hexValue + '0')** (line 21). Recall that when adding a character with an integer, the character's Unicode is used in the evaluation. For example, if **hexValue** is **5**, **(char)(hexValue + '0')** returns **5**. Similarly, if **hexValue** is between **10** and **15**, it is converted to **(char)(hexValue - 10 + 'A')** (line 21). For instance, if **hexValue** is **11**, **(char)(hexValue - 10 + 'A')** returns **B**.

5.21 Will the program work if **n1** and **n2** are replaced by **n1 / 2** and **n2 / 2** in line 17 in Listing 5.9?

5.22 In Listing 5.11, why is it wrong if you change the code **(char)(hexValue + '0')** to **hexValue + '0'** in line 21?

5.23 In Listing 5.11, how many times the loop body is executed for a decimal number **245** and how many times the loop body is executed for a decimal number **3245**?

Check Point

5.9 Keywords *break* and *continue*

 Key Point

The break *and* continue *keywords provide additional controls in a loop.*

 Pedagogical Note

Two keywords, **break** and **continue**, can be used in loop statements to provide additional controls. Using **break** and **continue** can simplify programming in some cases. Overusing or improperly using them, however, can make programs difficult to read and debug. (*Note to instructors*: You may skip this section without affecting students' understanding of the rest of the book.)

break statement

You have used the keyword **break** in a **switch** statement. You can also use **break** in a loop to immediately terminate the loop. Listing 5.12 presents a program to demonstrate the effect of using **break** in a loop.

LISTING 5.12   TestBreak.java

```java
1   public class TestBreak {
2     public static void main(String[] args) {
3       int sum = 0;
4       int number = 0;
5
6       while (number < 20) {
7         number++;
8         sum += number;
9         if (sum >= 100)
10          break;
11      }
12
13      System.out.println("The number is " + number);
14      System.out.println("The sum is " + sum);
15    }
16  }
```

break

```
The number is 14
The sum is 105
```

The program in Listing 5.12 adds integers from **1** to **20** in this order to **sum** until **sum** is greater than or equal to **100**. Without the **if** statement (line 9), the program calculates the sum of the numbers from **1** to **20**. But with the **if** statement, the loop terminates when **sum** becomes greater than or equal to **100**. Without the **if** statement, the output would be:

```
The number is 20
The sum is 210
```

continue statement

You can also use the **continue** keyword in a loop. When it is encountered, it ends the current iteration and program control goes to the end of the loop body. In other words, **continue** breaks out of an iteration while the **break** keyword breaks out of a loop. Listing 5.13 presents a program to demonstrate the effect of using **continue** in a loop.

LISTING 5.13   TestContinue.java

```java
1   public class TestContinue {
2     public static void main(String[] args) {
3       int sum = 0;
```

```
 4        int number = 0;
 5
 6        while (number < 20) {
 7          number++;
 8          if (number ==10 || number == 11)
 9            continue;                                        continue
10          sum += number;
11        }
12
13        System.out.println("The sum is " + sum);
14      }
15    }
```

```
The sum is 189
```

The program in Listing 5.13 adds integers from 1 to 20 except 10 and 11 to sum. With the if statement in the program (line 8), the `continue` statement is executed when number becomes 10 or 11. The `continue` statement ends the current iteration so that the rest of the statement in the loop body is not executed; therefore, number is not added to sum when it is 10 or 11. Without the if statement in the program, the output would be as follows:

```
The sum is 210
```

In this case, all of the numbers are added to sum, even when number is 10 or 11. Therefore, the result is 210, which is 21 more than it was with the if statement.

Note

The `continue` statement is always inside a loop. In the `while` and `do-while` loops, the `loop-continuation-condition` is evaluated immediately after the `continue` statement. In the `for` loop, the `action-after-each-iteration` is performed, then the `loop-continuation-condition` is evaluated, immediately after the `continue` statement.

You can always write a program without using break or continue in a loop (see Checkpoint Question 5.26). In general, though, using break and continue is appropriate if it simplifies coding and makes programs easier to read.

Suppose you need to write a program to find the smallest factor other than 1 for an integer n (assume n >= 2). You can write a simple and intuitive code using the break statement as follows:

```
int factor = 2;
while (factor <= n) {
  if (n % factor == 0)
    break;
  factor++;
}
System.out.println("The smallest factor other than 1 for "
  + n + " is " + factor);
```

You may rewrite the code without using break as follows:

```
boolean found = false;
int factor = 2;
while (factor <= n && !found) {
  if (n % factor == 0)
```

```
      found = true;
   else
      factor++;
}
System.out.println("The smallest factor other than 1 for "
   + n + " is " + factor);
```

Obviously, the **break** statement makes this program simpler and easier to read in this case. However, you should use **break** and **continue** with caution. Too many **break** and **continue** statements will produce a loop with many exit points and make the program difficult to read.

goto

 Note

Some programming languages have a **goto** statement. The **goto** statement indiscriminately transfers control to any statement in the program and executes it. This makes your program vulnerable to errors. The **break** and **continue** statements in Java are different from **goto** statements. They operate only in a loop or a **switch** statement. The **break** statement breaks out of the loop, and the **continue** statement breaks out of the current iteration in the loop.

 Note

Programming is a creative endeavor. There are many different ways to write code. In fact, you can find a smallest factor using a rather simple code as follows:

```
int factor = 2;
while (factor <= n && n % factor != 0)
   factor++;
```

Check Point

5.24   What is the keyword **break** for? What is the keyword **continue** for? Will the following programs terminate? If so, give the output.

```
int balance = 10;
while (true) {
   if (balance < 9)
      break;
   balance = balance - 9;
}

System.out.println("Balance is "
   + balance);
```
(a)

```
int balance = 10;
while (true) {
   if (balance < 9)
      continue;
   balance = balance - 9;
}

System.out.println("Balance is "
   + balance);
```
(b)

5.25   The **for** loop on the left is converted into the **while** loop on the right. What is wrong? Correct it.

```
int sum = 0;
for (int i = 0; i < 4; i++) {
   if (i % 3 == 0) continue;
   sum += i;
}
```
Converted
Wrong conversion
```
int i = 0, sum = 0;
while (i < 4) {
   if (i % 3 == 0) continue;
   sum += i;
   i++;
}
```

5.26   Rewrite the programs **TestBreak** and **TestContinue** in Listings 5.12 and 5.13 without using **break** and **continue**.

5.27 After the **break** statement in (a) is executed in the following loop, which statement is executed? Show the output. After the **continue** statement in (b) is executed in the following loop, which statement is executed? Show the output.

```
for (int i = 1; i < 4; i++) {
  for (int j = 1; j < 4; j++) {
    if (i * j > 2)
      break;

    System.out.println(i * j);
  }

  System.out.println(i);
}
```
(a)

```
for (int i = 1; i < 4; i++) {
  for (int j = 1; j < 4; j++) {
    if (i * j > 2)
      continue;

    System.out.println(i * j);
  }

  System.out.println(i);
}
```
(b)

5.10 Case Study: Checking Palindromes

This section presents a program that checks whether a string is a palindrome.

Key Point

A string is a palindrome if it reads the same forward and backward. The words "mom," "dad," and "noon," for instance, are all palindromes.

The problem is to write a program that prompts the user to enter a string and reports whether the string is a palindrome. One solution is to check whether the first character in the string is the same as the last character. If so, check whether the second character is the same as the second-to-last character. This process continues until a mismatch is found or all the characters in the string are checked, except for the middle character if the string has an odd number of characters.

think before you code

Listing 5.14 gives the program.

LISTING 5.14 Palindrome.java

```
1  import java.util.Scanner;
2
3  public class Palindrome {
4    /** Main method */
5    public static void main(String[] args) {
6      // Create a Scanner
7      Scanner input = new Scanner(System.in);
8
9      // Prompt the user to enter a string
10     System.out.print("Enter a string: ");
11     String s = input.nextLine();                          input string
12
13     // The index of the first character in the string
14     int low = 0;                                          low index
15
16     // The index of the last character in the string
17     int high = s.length() - 1;                            high index
18
19     boolean isPalindrome = true;
20     while (low < high) {
21       if (s.charAt(low) != s.charAt(high)) {
22         isPalindrome = false;
23         break;
24       }
25
```

update indices

```
26          low++;
27          high--;
28        }
29
30        if (isPalindrome)
31          System.out.println(s + " is a palindrome");
32        else
33          System.out.println(s + " is not a palindrome");
34      }
35  }
```

```
Enter a string: noon  ↵Enter
noon is a palindrome
```

```
Enter a string: moon  ↵Enter
moon is not a palindrome
```

The program uses two variables, `low` and `high`, to denote the position of the two characters at the beginning and the end in a string `s` (lines 14, 17). Initially, `low` is `0` and `high` is `s.length() - 1`. If the two characters at these positions match, increment `low` by `1` and decrement `high` by `1` (lines 26–27). This process continues until (`low >= high`) or a mismatch is found (line 21).

The program uses a `boolean` variable `isPalindrome` to denote whether the string `s` is palindrome. Initially, it is set to `true` (line 19). When a mismatch is discovered (line 21), `isPalindrome` is to `false` (line 22) and the loop is terminated with a break statement (line 23).

5.11 Case Study: Displaying Prime Numbers

Key
Point

This section presents a program that displays the first fifty prime numbers in five lines, each containing ten numbers.

An integer greater than `1` is *prime* if its only positive divisor is `1` or itself. For example, `2`, `3`, `5`, and `7` are prime numbers, but `4`, `6`, `8`, and `9` are not.

The problem is to display the first 50 prime numbers in five lines, each of which contains ten numbers. The problem can be broken into the following tasks:

■ Determine whether a given number is prime.

■ For `number = 2, 3, 4, 5, 6, ...`, test whether it is prime.

■ Count the prime numbers.

■ Display each prime number, and display ten numbers per line.

Obviously, you need to write a loop and repeatedly test whether a new `number` is prime. If the `number` is prime, increase the count by `1`. The `count` is `0` initially. When it reaches `50`, the loop terminates.

Here is the algorithm for the problem:

```
Set the number of prime numbers to be printed as
  a constant NUMBER_OF_PRIMES;
Use count to track the number of prime numbers and
  set an initial count to 0;
Set an initial number to 2;
```

```
while (count < NUMBER_OF_PRIMES) {
  Test whether number is prime;

  if number is prime {
    Display the prime number and increase the count;
  }

  Increment number by 1;
}
```

To test whether a number is prime, check whether it is divisible by **2**, **3**, **4**, and so on up to **number/2**. If a divisor is found, the number is not a prime. The algorithm can be described as follows:

```
Use a boolean variable isPrime to denote whether
  the number is prime; Set isPrime to true initially;

for (int divisor = 2; divisor <= number / 2; divisor++) {
  if (number % divisor == 0) {
    Set isPrime to false
    Exit the loop;
  }
}
```

The complete program is given in Listing 5.15.

LISTING 5.15 PrimeNumber.java

```
1  public class PrimeNumber {
2    public static void main(String[] args) {
3      final int NUMBER_OF_PRIMES = 50; // Number of primes to display
4      final int NUMBER_OF_PRIMES_PER_LINE = 10; // Display 10 per line
5      int count = 0; // Count the number of prime numbers
6      int number = 2; // A number to be tested for primeness
7
8      System.out.println("The first 50 prime numbers are \n");
9
10     // Repeatedly find prime numbers
11     while (count < NUMBER_OF_PRIMES) {                              count prime numbers
12       // Assume the number is prime
13       boolean isPrime = true; // Is the current number prime?
14
15       // Test whether number is prime
16       for (int divisor = 2; divisor <= number / 2; divisor++) {    check primeness
17         if (number % divisor == 0) { // If true, number is not prime
18           isPrime = false; // Set isPrime to false
19           break; // Exit the for loop                              exit loop
20         }
21       }
22
23       // Display the prime number and increase the count
24       if (isPrime) {                                               display if prime
25         count++; // Increase the count
26
27         if (count % NUMBER_OF_PRIMES_PER_LINE == 0) {
28           // Display the number and advance to the new line
29           System.out.println(number);
30         }
31         else
32           System.out.print(number + " ");
```

```
33        }
34
35        // Check if the next number is prime
36        number++;
37      }
38    }
39  }
```

```
The first 50 prime numbers are
2 3 5 7 11 13 17 19 23 29
31 37 41 43 47 53 59 61 67 71
73 79 83 89 97 101 103 107 109 113
127 131 137 139 149 151 157 163 167 173
179 181 191 193 197 199 211 223 227 229
```

subproblem

This is a complex program for novice programmers. The key to developing a programmatic solution for this problem, and for many other problems, is to break it into subproblems and develop solutions for each of them in turn. Do not attempt to develop a complete solution in the first trial. Instead, begin by writing the code to determine whether a given number is prime, then expand the program to test whether other numbers are prime in a loop.

To determine whether a number is prime, check whether it is divisible by a number between 2 and **number/2** inclusive (lines 16–21). If so, it is not a prime number (line 18); otherwise, it is a prime number. For a prime number, display it. If the count is divisible by **10** (lines 27–30), advance to a new line. The program ends when the count reaches **50**.

The program uses the **break** statement in line 19 to exit the **for** loop as soon as the number is found to be a nonprime. You can rewrite the loop (lines 16–21) without using the **break** statement, as follows:

```
for (int divisor = 2; divisor <= number / 2 && isPrime;
     divisor++) {
  // If true, the number is not prime
  if (number % divisor == 0) {
    // Set isPrime to false, if the number is not prime
    isPrime = false;
  }
}
```

However, using the **break** statement makes the program simpler and easier to read in this case.

KEY TERMS

break statement 184	loop body 158
continue statement 184	nested loop 176
do-while loop 168	off-by-one error 160
for loop 171	output redirection 167
infinite loop 160	posttest loop 174
input redirection 167	pretest loop 174
iteration 158	sentinel value 165
loop 158	while loop 158

CHAPTER SUMMARY

1. There are three types of repetition statements: the `while` loop, the `do-while` loop, and the `for` loop.

2. The part of the loop that contains the statements to be repeated is called the *loop body*.

3. A one-time execution of a loop body is referred to as an *iteration of the loop*.

4. An *infinite loop* is a loop statement that executes infinitely.

5. In designing loops, you need to consider both the *loop control structure* and the loop body.

6. The `while` loop checks the `loop-continuation-condition` first. If the condition is `true`, the loop body is executed; if it is `false`, the loop terminates.

7. The `do-while` loop is similar to the `while` loop, except that the `do-while` loop executes the loop body first and then checks the `loop-continuation-condition` to decide whether to continue or to terminate.

8. The `while` loop and the `do-while` loop often are used when the number of repetitions is not predetermined.

9. A *sentinel value* is a special value that signifies the end of the loop.

10. The `for` loop generally is used to execute a loop body a fixed number of times.

11. The `for` loop control has three parts. The first part is an initial action that often initializes a control variable. The second part, the `loop-continuation-condition`, determines whether the loop body is to be executed. The third part is executed after each iteration and is often used to adjust the control variable. Usually, the loop control variables are initialized and changed in the control structure.

12. The `while` loop and `for` loop are called *pretest loops* because the continuation condition is checked before the loop body is executed.

13. The `do-while` loop is called a *posttest loop* because the condition is checked after the loop body is executed.

14. Two keywords, `break` and `continue`, can be used in a loop.

15. The `break` keyword immediately ends the innermost loop, which contains the break.

16. The `continue` keyword only ends the current iteration.

QUIZ

Answer the quiz for this chapter online at www.cs.armstrong.edu/liang/intro10e/quiz.html.

PROGRAMMING EXERCISES

MyProgrammingLab™

 Pedagogical Note

Read each problem several times until you understand it. Think how to solve the problem before starting to write code. Translate your logic into a program.

A problem often can be solved in many different ways. Students are encouraged to explore various solutions.

read and think before coding

explore solutions

Sections 5.2–5.7

*5.1 (*Count positive and negative numbers and compute the average of numbers*) Write a program that reads an unspecified number of integers, determines how many positive and negative values have been read, and computes the total and average of the input values (not counting zeros). Your program ends with the input **0**. Display the average as a floating-point number. Here is a sample run:

```
Enter an integer, the input ends if it is 0: 1 2 -1 3 0  ↵Enter
The number of positives is 3
The number of negatives is 1
The total is 5.0
The average is 1.25
```

```
Enter an integer, the input ends if it is 0: 0  ↵Enter
No numbers are entered except 0
```

5.2 (*Repeat additions*) Listing 5.4, SubtractionQuizLoop.java, generates five random subtraction questions. Revise the program to generate ten random addition questions for two integers between **1** and **15**. Display the correct count and test time.

5.3 (*Conversion from kilograms to pounds*) Write a program that displays the following table (note that **1** kilogram is **2.2** pounds):

```
Kilograms      Pounds
1                 2.2
3                 6.6
...
197             433.4
199             437.8
```

5.4 (*Conversion from miles to kilometers*) Write a program that displays the following table (note that 1 mile is 1.609 kilometers):

```
Miles       Kilometers
1           1.609
2           3.218
...
9           14.481
10          16.090
```

5.5 (*Conversion from kilograms to pounds and pounds to kilograms*) Write a program that displays the following two tables side by side:

```
Kilograms  Pounds    |    Pounds      Kilograms
1             2.2     |    20               9.09
3             6.6     |    25              11.36
...
197         433.4     |    510            231.82
199         437.8     |    515            234.09
```

5.6 (*Conversion from miles to kilometers*) Write a program that displays the following two tables side by side:

```
Miles       Kilometers  |  Kilometers    Miles
1           1.609       |  20            12.430
2           3.218       |  25            15.538
...
9           14.481      |  60            37.290
10          16.090      |  65            40.398
```

**5.7 (*Financial application: compute future tuition*) Suppose that the tuition for a university is $10,000 this year and increases 5% every year. In one year, the tuition will be $10,500. Write a program that computes the tuition in ten years and the total cost of four years' worth of tuition after the tenth year.

5.8 (*Find the highest score*) Write a program that prompts the user to enter the number of students and each student's name and score, and finally displays the name of the student with the highest score.

*5.9 (*Find the two highest scores*) Write a program that prompts the user to enter the number of students and each student's name and score, and finally displays the student with the highest score and the student with the second-highest score.

5.10 (*Find numbers divisible by 5 and 6*) Write a program that displays all the numbers from 100 to 1,000, ten per line, that are divisible by 5 and 6. Numbers are separated by exactly one space.

5.11 (*Find numbers divisible by 5 or 6, but not both*) Write a program that displays all the numbers from 100 to 200, ten per line, that are divisible by 5 or 6, but not both. Numbers are separated by exactly one space.

5.12 (*Find the smallest n such that $n^2 > 12,000$*) Use a `while` loop to find the smallest integer n such that n^2 is greater than 12,000.

5.13 (*Find the largest n such that $n^3 < 12,000$*) Use a `while` loop to find the largest integer n such that n^3 is less than 12,000.

Sections 5.8–5.10

*5.14 (*Compute the greatest common divisor*) Another solution for Listing 5.9 to find the greatest common divisor of two integers **n1** and **n2** is as follows: First find **d** to be the minimum of **n1** and **n2**, then check whether **d, d-1, d-2, …, 2**, or **1** is a divisor for both **n1** and **n2** in this order. The first such common divisor is the greatest common divisor for **n1** and **n2**. Write a program that prompts the user to enter two positive integers and displays the gcd.

*5.15 (*Display the ASCII character table*) Write a program that prints the characters in the ASCII character table from **!** to **~**. Display ten characters per line. The ASCII table is shown in Appendix B. Characters are separated by exactly one space.

*5.16 (*Find the factors of an integer*) Write a program that reads an integer and displays all its smallest factors in increasing order. For example, if the input integer is **120**, the output should be as follows: **2, 2, 2, 3, 5**.

5.17 (*Display pyramid*) Write a program that prompts the user to enter an integer from **1 to **15** and displays a pyramid, as shown in the following sample run:

```
Enter the number of lines: 7 ⏎Enter
                  1
                2 1 2
              3 2 1 2 3
            4 3 2 1 2 3 4
          5 4 3 2 1 2 3 4 5
        6 5 4 3 2 1 2 3 4 5 6
      7 6 5 4 3 2 1 2 3 4 5 6 7
```

*5.18 (*Display four patterns using loops*) Use nested loops that display the following patterns in four separate programs:

```
Pattern A          Pattern B          Pattern C          Pattern D
1                  1 2 3 4 5 6                    1       1 2 3 4 5 6
1 2                1 2 3 4 5                    2 1         1 2 3 4 5
1 2 3              1 2 3 4                    3 2 1           1 2 3 4
1 2 3 4            1 2 3                    4 3 2 1             1 2 3
1 2 3 4 5          1 2                    5 4 3 2 1               1 2
1 2 3 4 5 6        1                    6 5 4 3 2 1                 1
```

5.19 (*Display numbers in a pyramid pattern*) Write a nested **for loop that prints the following output:

```
                        1
                    1   2   1
                1   2   4   2   1
            1   2   4   8   4   2   1
        1   2   4   8  16   8   4   2   1
    1   2   4   8  16  32  16   8   4   2   1
  1   2   4   8  16  32  64  32  16   8   4   2   1
1   2   4   8  16  32  64 128  64  32  16   8   4   2   1
```

*5.20 (*Display prime numbers between 2 and 1,000*) Modify Listing 5.15 to display all the prime numbers between 2 and 1,000, inclusive. Display eight prime numbers per line. Numbers are separated by exactly one space.

Comprehensive

**5.21 (*Financial application: compare loans with various interest rates*) Write a program that lets the user enter the loan amount and loan period in number of years and displays the monthly and total payments for each interest rate starting from 5% to 8%, with an increment of 1/8. Here is a sample run:

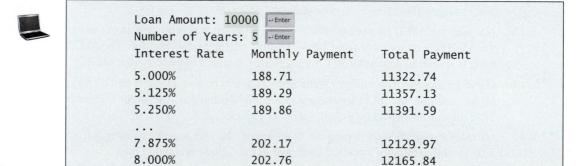

```
Loan Amount: 10000  ↵Enter
Number of Years: 5  ↵Enter
Interest Rate      Monthly Payment      Total Payment
5.000%             188.71               11322.74
5.125%             189.29               11357.13
5.250%             189.86               11391.59
...
7.875%             202.17               12129.97
8.000%             202.76               12165.84
```

For the formula to compute monthly payment, see Listing 2.9, ComputeLoan.java.

**5.22 (*Financial application: loan amortization schedule*) The monthly payment for a given loan pays the principal and the interest. The monthly interest is computed by multiplying the monthly interest rate and the balance (the remaining principal). The principal paid for the month is therefore the monthly payment minus the monthly interest. Write a program that lets the user enter the loan amount,

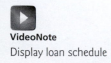

VideoNote

Display loan schedule

number of years, and interest rate and displays the amortization schedule for the loan. Here is a sample run:

```
Loan Amount: 10000  ⏎Enter
Number of Years: 1  ⏎Enter
Annual Interest Rate: 7  ⏎Enter

Monthly Payment: 865.26
Total Payment: 10383.21

Payment#        Interest        Principal       Balance
1               58.33           806.93          9193.07
2               53.62           811.64          8381.43
...
11              10.0            855.26          860.27
12              5.01            860.25          0.01
```

Note
The balance after the last payment may not be zero. If so, the last payment should be the normal monthly payment plus the final balance.

Hint: Write a loop to display the table. Since the monthly payment is the same for each month, it should be computed before the loop. The balance is initially the loan amount. For each iteration in the loop, compute the interest and principal, and update the balance. The loop may look like this:

```
for (i = 1; i <= numberOfYears * 12; i++) {
  interest = monthlyInterestRate * balance;
  principal = monthlyPayment - interest;
  balance = balance - principal;
  System.out.println(i + "\t\t" + interest
    + "\t\t" + principal + "\t\t" + balance);
}
```

*5.23 (*Demonstrate cancellation errors*) A cancellation error occurs when you are manipulating a very large number with a very small number. The large number may cancel out the smaller number. For example, the result of **100000000.0 + 0.000000001** is equal to **100000000.0**. To avoid cancellation errors and obtain more accurate results, carefully select the order of computation. For example, in computing the following series, you will obtain more accurate results by computing from right to left rather than from left to right:

$$1 + \frac{1}{2} + \frac{1}{3} + \ldots + \frac{1}{n}$$

Write a program that compares the results of the summation of the preceding series, computing from left to right and from right to left with **n = 50000**.

*5.24 (*Sum a series*) Write a program to sum the following series:

$$\frac{1}{3} + \frac{3}{5} + \frac{5}{7} + \frac{7}{9} + \frac{9}{11} + \frac{11}{13} + \ldots + \frac{95}{97} + \frac{97}{99}$$

VideoNote

Sum a series

**5.25 (*Compute* π) You can approximate π by using the following series:

$$\pi = 4\left(1 - \frac{1}{3} + \frac{1}{5} - \frac{1}{7} + \frac{1}{9} - \frac{1}{11} + \cdots + \frac{(-1)^{i+1}}{2i-1}\right)$$

Write a program that displays the π value for i = 10000, 20000, ..., and 100000.

**5.26 (*Compute* e) You can approximate e using the following series:

$$e = 1 + \frac{1}{1!} + \frac{1}{2!} + \frac{1}{3!} + \frac{1}{4!} + \cdots + \frac{1}{i!}$$

Write a program that displays the e value for i = 10000, 20000, ..., and 100000. (*Hint*: Because $i! = i \times (i - 1) \times \ldots \times 2 \times 1$, then

$$\frac{1}{i!} \text{ is } \frac{1}{i(i-1)!}$$

Initialize e and item to be 1 and keep adding a new item to e. The new item is the previous item divided by i for i = 2, 3, 4, ...)

**5.27 (*Display leap years*) Write a program that displays all the leap years, ten per line, from 101 to 2100, separated by exactly one space. Also display the number of leap years in this period.

**5.28 (*Display the first days of each month*) Write a program that prompts the user to enter the year and first day of the year, and displays the first day of each month in the year. For example, if the user entered the year 2013, and 2 for Tuesday, January 1, 2013, your program should display the following output:

```
January 1, 2013 is Tuesday
...
December 1, 2013 is Sunday
```

**5.29 (*Display calendars*) Write a program that prompts the user to enter the year and first day of the year and displays the calendar table for the year on the console. For example, if the user entered the year 2013, and 2 for Tuesday, January 1, 2013, your program should display the calendar for each month in the year, as follows:

January 2013

Sun	Mon	Tue	Wed	Thu	Fri	Sat
		1	2	3	4	5
6	7	8	9	10	11	12
13	14	15	16	17	18	19
20	21	22	23	24	25	26
27	28	29	30	31		

December 2013

Sun	Mon	Tue	Wed	Thu	Fri	Sat
1	2	3	4	5	6	7
8	9	10	11	12	13	14
15	16	17	18	19	20	21
22	23	24	25	26	27	28
29	30	31				

*5.30 (*Financial application: compound value*) Suppose you save $100 *each* month into a savings account with the annual interest rate 5%. So, the monthly interest rate is `0.05 / 12 = 0.00417`. After the first month, the value in the account becomes

$$100 * (1 + 0.00417) = 100.417$$

After the second month, the value in the account becomes

$$(100 + 100.417) * (1 + 0.00417) = 201.252$$

After the third month, the value in the account becomes

$$(100 + 201.252) * (1 + 0.00417) = 302.507$$

and so on.

Write a program that prompts the user to enter an amount (e.g., **100**), the annual interest rate (e.g., **5**), and the number of months (e.g., **6**) and displays the amount in the savings account after the given month.

*5.31 (*Financial application: compute CD value*) Suppose you put $10,000 into a CD with an annual percentage yield of 5.75%. After one month, the CD is worth

$$10000 + 10000 * 5.75 / 1200 = 10047.92$$

After two months, the CD is worth

$$10047.91 + 10047.91 * 5.75 / 1200 = 10096.06$$

After three months, the CD is worth

$$10096.06 + 10096.06 * 5.75 / 1200 = 10144.44$$

and so on.

Write a program that prompts the user to enter an amount (e.g., **10000**), the annual percentage yield (e.g., **5.75**), and the number of months (e.g., **18**) and displays a table as shown in the sample run.

```
Enter the initial deposit amount: 10000  ↵Enter
Enter annual percentage yield: 5.75  ↵Enter
Enter maturity period (number of months): 18  ↵Enter

Month   CD Value
1          10047.92
2          10096.06
...
17         10846.57
18         10898.54
```

**5.32 (*Game: lottery*) Revise Listing 3.8, Lottery.java, to generate a lottery of a two-digit number. The two digits in the number are distinct. (*Hint*: Generate the first digit. Use a loop to continuously generate the second digit until it is different from the first digit.)

**5.33 (*Perfect number*) A positive integer is called a *perfect number* if it is equal to the sum of all of its positive divisors, excluding itself. For example, 6 is the first perfect number because 6 = 3 + 2 + 1. The next is 28 = 14 + 7 + 4 + 2 + 1. There are four perfect numbers less than 10,000. Write a program to find all these four numbers.

***5.34 (*Game: scissor, rock, paper*) Programming Exercise 3.17 gives a program that plays the scissor-rock-paper game. Revise the program to let the user continuously play until either the user or the computer wins more than two times than its opponent.

*5.35 (*Summation*) Write a program to compute the following summation.

$$\frac{1}{1 + \sqrt{2}} + \frac{1}{\sqrt{2} + \sqrt{3}} + \frac{1}{\sqrt{3} + \sqrt{4}} + \ldots + \frac{1}{\sqrt{624} + \sqrt{625}}$$

**5.36 (*Business application: checking ISBN*) Use loops to simplify Programming Exercise 3.9.

**5.37 (*Decimal to binary*) Write a program that prompts the user to enter a decimal integer and displays its corresponding binary value. Don't use Java's `Integer.toBinaryString(int)` in this program.

**5.38 (*Decimal to octal*) Write a program that prompts the user to enter a decimal integer and displays its corresponding octal value. Don't use Java's `Integer.toOctalString(int)` in this program.

*5.39 (*Financial application: find the sales amount*) You have just started a sales job in a department store. Your pay consists of a base salary and a commission. The base salary is $5,000. The scheme shown below is used to determine the commission rate.

Sales Amount	Commission Rate
$0.01–$5,000	8 percent
$5,000.01–$10,000	10 percent
$10,000.01 and above	12 percent

Note that this is a graduated rate. The rate for the first $5,000 is at 8%, the next $5000 is at 10%, and the rest is at 12%. If the sales amount is 25,000, the commission is 5,000 * 8% + 5,000 * 10% + 15,000 * 12% = 2,700.

Your goal is to earn $30,000 a year. Write a program that finds the minimum sales you have to generate in order to make $30,000.

5.40 (*Simulation: heads or tails*) Write a program that simulates flipping a coin one million times and displays the number of heads and tails.

*5.41 (*Occurrence of max numbers*) Write a program that reads integers, finds the largest of them, and counts its occurrences. Assume that the input ends with number **0**. Suppose that you entered **3 5 2 5 5 5 0**; the program finds that the largest is **5** and the occurrence count for **5** is **4**.

(*Hint*: Maintain two variables, **max** and **count**. **max** stores the current max number, and **count** stores its occurrences. Initially, assign the first number to **max** and **1** to **count**. Compare each subsequent number with **max**. If the number is greater than **max**, assign it to **max** and reset **count** to **1**. If the number is equal to **max**, increment **count** by **1**.)

```
Enter numbers: 3 5 2 5 5 5 0  ↵Enter
The largest number is 5
The occurrence count of the largest number is 4
```

*5.42 (*Financial application: find the sales amount*) Rewrite Programming Exercise 5.39 as follows:

- Use a **for** loop instead of a **do-while** loop.
- Let the user enter **COMMISSION_SOUGHT** instead of fixing it as a constant.

*5.43 (*Math: combinations*) Write a program that displays all possible combinations for picking two numbers from integers **1** to **7**. Also display the total number of all combinations.

```
1 2
1 3
...
...

The total number of all combinations is 21
```

*5.44 (*Computer architecture: bit-level operations*) A **short** value is stored in **16** bits. Write a program that prompts the user to enter a short integer and displays the **16** bits for the integer. Here are sample runs:

```
Enter an integer: 5  ↵Enter
The bits are 0000000000000101
```

```
Enter an integer: -5  ↵Enter
The bits are 1111111111111011
```

(*Hint*: You need to use the bitwise right shift operator (**>>**) and the bitwise **AND** operator (**&**), which are covered in Appendix G, Bitwise Operations.)

**5.45 (*Statistics: compute mean and standard deviation*) In business applications, you are often asked to compute the mean and standard deviation of data. The mean is simply the average of the numbers. The standard deviation is a statistic that tells you how tightly all the various data are clustered around the mean in a set of data. For example, what is the average age of the students in a class? How close are the ages? If all the students are the same age, the deviation is 0.

Write a program that prompts the user to enter ten numbers, and displays the mean and standard deviations of these numbers using the following formula:

$$\text{mean} = \frac{\sum_{i=1}^{n} x_i}{n} = \frac{x_1 + x_2 + \cdots + x_n}{n} \qquad \text{deviation} = \sqrt{\frac{\sum_{i=1}^{n} x_i^2 - \frac{\left(\sum_{i=1}^{n} x_i\right)^2}{n}}{n-1}}$$

Here is a sample run:

```
Enter ten numbers: 1 2 3 4.5 5.6 6 7 8 9 10  ↵Enter
The mean is 5.61
The standard deviation is 2.99794
```

*5.46 (*Reverse a string*) Write a program that prompts the user to enter a string and displays the string in reverse order.

```
Enter a string: ABCD  ↵Enter
The reversed string is DCBA
```

*5.47 (*Business: check ISBN-13*) **ISBN-13** is a new standard for indentifying books. It uses 13 digits $d_1d_2d_3d_4d_5d_6d_7d_8d_9d_{10}d_{11}d_{12}d_{13}$. The last digit d_{13} is a checksum, which is calculated from the other digits using the following formula:

$$10 - (d_1 + 3d_2 + d_3 + 3d_4 + d_5 + 3d_6 + d_7 + 3d_8 + d_9 + 3d_{10} + d_{11} + 3d_{12})\%10$$

If the checksum is **10**, replace it with **0**. Your program should read the input as a string. Here are sample runs:

```
Enter the first 12 digits of an ISBN-13 as a string: 978013213080  ↵Enter
The ISBN-13 number is 9780132130806
```

```
Enter the first 12 digits of an ISBN-13 as a string: 978013213079  ↵Enter
The ISBN-13 number is 9780132130790
```

```
Enter the first 12 digits of an ISBN-13 as a string: 97801320  ↵Enter
97801320 is an invalid input
```

*5.48 (*Process string*) Write a program that prompts the user to enter a string and displays the characters at odd positions. Here is a sample run:

```
Enter a string: Beijing Chicago  ↵Enter
BiigCiao
```

*5.49   (*Count vowels and consonants*) Assume letters A, E, I, 0, and U as the vowels. Write a program that prompts the user to enter a string and displays the number of vowels and consonants in the string.

```
Enter a string: Programming is fun ⏎Enter
The number of vowels is 5
The number of consonants is 11
```

*5.50   (*Count uppercase letters*) Write a program that prompts the user to enter a string and displays the number of the uppercase letters in the string.

```
Enter a string: Welcome to Java ⏎Enter
The number of uppercase letters is 2
```

*5.51   (*Longest common prefix*) Write a program that prompts the user to enter two strings and displays the largest common prefix of the two strings. Here are some sample runs:

```
Enter the first string: Welcome to C++ ⏎Enter
Enter the second string: Welcome to programming ⏎Enter
The common prefix is Welcome to
```

```
Enter the first string: Atlanta ⏎Enter
Enter the second string: Macon ⏎Enter
Atlanta and Macon have no common prefix
```

CHAPTER

6

METHODS

Objectives

- To define methods with formal parameters (§6.2).

- To invoke methods with actual parameters (i.e., arguments) (§6.2).

- To define methods with a return value (§6.3).

- To define methods without a return value (§6.4).

- To pass arguments by value (§6.5).

- To develop reusable code that is modular, easy to read, easy to debug, and easy to maintain (§6.6).

- To write a method that converts hexadecimals to decimals (§6.7).

- To use method overloading and understand ambiguous overloading (§6.8).

- To determine the scope of variables (§6.9).

- To apply the concept of method abstraction in software development (§6.10).

- To design and implement methods using stepwise refinement (§6.10).

6.1 Introduction

Methods can be used to define reusable code and organize and simplify coding.

problem

Suppose that you need to find the sum of integers from **1** to **10**, from **20** to **37**, and from **35** to **49**, respectively. You may write the code as follows:

```
int sum = 0;
for (int i = 1; i <= 10; i++)
  sum += i;
System.out.println("Sum from 1 to 10 is " + sum);

sum = 0;
for (int i = 20; i <= 37; i++)
  sum += i;
System.out.println("Sum from 20 to 37 is " + sum);

sum = 0;
for (int i = 35; i <= 49; i++)
  sum += i;
System.out.println("Sum from 35 to 49 is " + sum);
```

You may have observed that computing these sums from **1** to **10**, from **20** to **37**, and from **35** to **49** are very similar except that the starting and ending integers are different. Wouldn't it be nice if we could write the common code once and reuse it? We can do so by defining a

why methods?

method and invoking it.

The preceding code can be simplified as follows:

define sum method

```
 1  public static int sum(int i1, int i2) {
 2    int result = 0;
 3    for (int i = i1; i <= i2; i++)
 4      result += i;
 5
 6    return result;
 7  }
 8
 9  public static void main(String[] args) {
10    System.out.println("Sum from 1 to 10 is " + sum(1, 10));
11    System.out.println("Sum from 20 to 37 is " + sum(20, 37));
12    System.out.println("Sum from 35 to 49 is " + sum(35, 49));
13  }
```

main method
invoke sum

Lines 1–7 define the method named **sum** with two parameters **i1** and **i2**. The statements in the **main** method invoke **sum(1, 10)** to compute the sum from **1** to **10**, **sum(20, 37)** to compute the sum from **20** to **37**, and **sum(35, 49)** to compute the sum from **35** to **49**.

method

A *method* is a collection of statements grouped together to perform an operation. In earlier chapters you have used predefined methods such as **System.out.println**, **System.exit**, **Math .pow**, and **Math.random**. These methods are defined in the Java library. In this chapter, you will learn how to define your own methods and apply method abstraction to solve complex problems.

6.2 Defining a Method

A method definition consists of its method name, parameters, return value type, and body.

The syntax for defining a method is as follows:

```
modifier returnValueType methodName(list of parameters) {
  // Method body;
}
```

Let's look at a method defined to find the larger between two integers. This method, named `max`, has two `int` parameters, `num1` and `num2`, the larger of which is returned by the method. Figure 6.1 illustrates the components of this method.

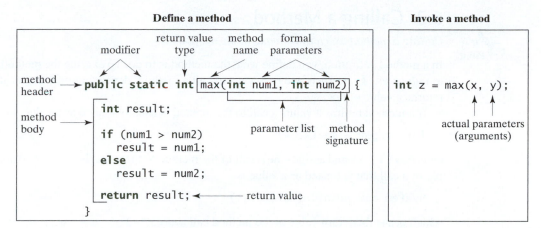

FIGURE 6.1 A method definition consists of a method header and a method body.

The *method header* specifies the *modifiers*, *return value type*, *method name*, and *parameters* of the method. The `static` modifier is used for all the methods in this chapter. The reason for using it will be discussed in Chapter 8, Objects and Classes.

method header

modifier

A method may return a value. The `returnValueType` is the data type of the value the method returns. Some methods perform desired operations without returning a value. In this case, the `returnValueType` is the keyword `void`. For example, the `returnValueType` is `void` in the `main` method, as well as in `System.exit`, and `System.out.println`. If a method returns a value, it is called a *value-returning method;* otherwise it is called a *void method*.

value-returning method

void method

The variables defined in the method header are known as *formal parameters* or simply *parameters*. A parameter is like a placeholder: when a method is invoked, you pass a value to the parameter. This value is referred to as an *actual parameter or argument*. The *parameter list* refers to the method's type, order, and number of the parameters. The method name and the parameter list together constitute the *method signature*. Parameters are optional; that is, a method may contain no parameters. For example, the `Math.random()` method has no parameters.

formal parameter

parameter

actual parameter

argument

parameter list

method signature

The method body contains a collection of statements that implement the method. The method body of the `max` method uses an `if` statement to determine which number is larger and return the value of that number. In order for a value-returning method to return a result, a return statement using the keyword `return` is *required*. The method terminates when a return statement is executed.

Note

Some programming languages refer to methods as *procedures* and *functions*. In those languages, a value-returning method is called a *function* and a void method is called a *procedure*.

Caution

In the method header, you need to declare each parameter separately. For instance, `max(int num1, int num2)` is correct, but `max(int num1, num2)` is wrong.

define vs. declare

Note

We say "*define* a method" and "*declare* a variable." We are making a subtle distinction here. A definition defines what the defined item is, but a declaration usually involves allocating memory to store data for the declared item.

6.3 Calling a Method

Key
Point

Calling a method executes the code in the method.

In a method definition, you define what the method is to do. To execute the method, you have to *call* or *invoke* it. There are two ways to call a method, depending on whether the method returns a value or not.

If a method returns a value, a call to the method is usually treated as a value. For example,

```java
int larger = max(3, 4);
```

calls `max(3, 4)` and assigns the result of the method to the variable `larger`. Another example of a call that is treated as a value is

```java
System.out.println(max(3, 4));
```

which prints the return value of the method call `max(3, 4)`.

If a method returns `void`, a call to the method must be a statement. For example, the method `println` returns `void`. The following call is a statement:

```java
System.out.println("Welcome to Java!");
```

Note

A value-returning method can also be invoked as a statement in Java. In this case, the caller simply ignores the return value. This is not often done, but it is permissible if the caller is not interested in the return value.

When a program calls a method, program control is transferred to the called method. A called method returns control to the caller when its return statement is executed or when its method-ending closing brace is reached.

Listing 6.1 shows a complete program that is used to test the `max` method.

LISTING 6.1 TestMax.java

VideoNote

Define/invoke `max` method

main method

invoke max

define method

```java
 1  public class TestMax {
 2    /** Main method */
 3    public static void main(String[] args) {
 4      int i = 5;
 5      int j = 2;
 6      int k = max(i, j);
 7      System.out.println("The maximum of " + i +
 8        " and " + j + " is " + k);
 9    }
10
11    /** Return the max of two numbers */
12    public static int max(int num1, int num2) {
13      int result;
14
15      if (num1 > num2)
16        result = num1;
17      else
18        result = num2;
19
20      return result;
21    }
22  }
```

```
The maximum of 5 and 2 is 5
```

	line#	i	j	k	num1	num2	result
	4	5					
	5		2				
Invoking max {	12				5	2	
	13						undefined
	16						5
	6			5			

This program contains the **main** method and the **max** method. The **main** method is just like any other method except that it is invoked by the JVM to start the program. main method

The **main** method's header is always the same. Like the one in this example, it includes the modifiers **public** and **static**, return value type **void**, method name **main**, and a parameter of the **String[]** type. **String[]** indicates that the parameter is an array of **String**, a subject addressed in Chapter 7.

The statements in **main** may invoke other methods that are defined in the class that contains the **main** method or in other classes. In this example, the **main** method invokes **max(i, j)**, which is defined in the same class with the **main** method.

When the **max** method is invoked (line 6), variable **i**'s value **5** is passed to **num1**, and variable **j**'s value **2** is passed to **num2** in the **max** method. The flow of control transfers to the **max** method, and the **max** method is executed. When the **return** statement in the **max** method is executed, the **max** method returns the control to its caller (in this case the caller is the **main** method). This process is illustrated in Figure 6.2. max method

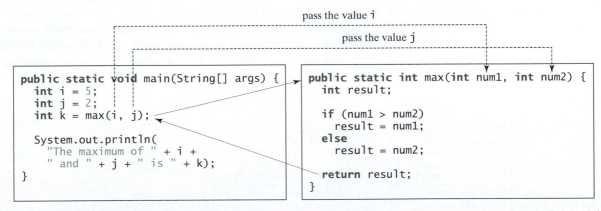

FIGURE 6.2 When the **max** method is invoked, the flow of control transfers to it. Once the **max** method is finished, it returns control back to the caller.

Caution

A **return** statement is required for a value-returning method. The method shown below in (a) is logically correct, but it has a compile error because the Java compiler thinks that this method might not return a value.

```
public static int sign(int n) {
  if (n > 0)
    return 1;
  else if (n == 0)
    return 0;
  else if (n < 0)
    return -1;
}
```
(a)

Should be →

```
public static int sign(int n) {
  if (n > 0)
    return 1;
  else if (n == 0)
    return 0;
  else
    return -1;
}
```
(b)

To fix this problem, delete **if (n < 0)** in (a), so the compiler will see a **return** statement to be reached regardless of how the **if** statement is evaluated.

Note

Methods enable code sharing and reuse. The **max** method can be invoked from any class, not just **TestMax**. If you create a new class, you can invoke the **max** method using **ClassName.methodName** (i.e., **TestMax.max**).

reusing method

activation record

call stack

Each time a method is invoked, the system creates an *activation record* (also called an *activation frame*) that stores parameters and variables for the method and places the activation record in an area of memory known as a *call stack*. A call stack is also known as an *execution stack*, *runtime stack*, or *machine stack*, and it is often shortened to just "the stack." When a method calls another method, the caller's activation record is kept intact, and a new activation record is created for the new method called. When a method finishes its work and returns to its caller, its activation record is removed from the call stack.

A call stack stores the activation records in a last-in, first-out fashion: The activation record for the method that is invoked last is removed first from the stack. For example, suppose method **m1** calls method **m2**, and **m2** calls method **m3**. The runtime system pushes **m1**'s activation record into the stack, then **m2**'s, and then **m3**'s. After **m3** is finished, its activation record is removed from the stack. After **m2** is finished, its activation record is removed from the stack. After **m1** is finished, its activation record is removed from the stack.

Understanding call stacks helps you to comprehend how methods are invoked. The variables defined in the **main** method in Listing 6.1 are **i**, **j**, and **k**. The variables defined in the **max** method are **num1**, **num2**, and **result**. The variables **num1** and **num2** are defined in the method signature and are parameters of the **max** method. Their values are passed through method invocation. Figure 6.3 illustrates the activation records for method calls in the stack.

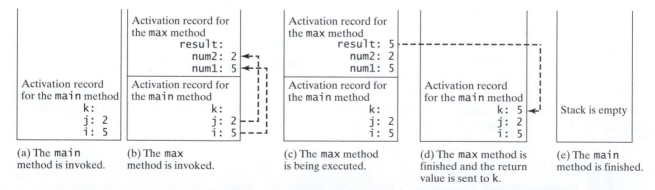

(a) The **main** method is invoked.

(b) The **max** method is invoked.

(c) The **max** method is being executed.

(d) The **max** method is finished and the return value is sent to k.

(e) The **main** method is finished.

FIGURE 6.3 When the **max** method is invoked, the flow of control transfers to the **max** method. Once the **max** method is finished, it returns control back to the caller.

6.4 **void** Method Example

*A **void** method does not return a value.*

The preceding section gives an example of a value-returning method. This section shows how to define and invoke a **void** method. Listing 6.2 gives a program that defines a method named **printGrade** and invokes it to print the grade for a given score.

VideoNote
Use void method

LISTING 6.2 TestVoidMethod.java

```java
1  public class TestVoidMethod {
2    public static void main(String[] args) {
3      System.out.print("The grade is ");
4      printGrade(78.5);
5
6      System.out.print("The grade is ");
7      printGrade(59.5);
8    }
9
10   public static void printGrade(double score) {
11     if (score >= 90.0) {
12       System.out.println('A');
13     }
14     else if (score >= 80.0) {
15       System.out.println('B');
16     }
17     else if (score >= 70.0) {
18       System.out.println('C');
19     }
20     else if (score >= 60.0) {
21       System.out.println('D');
22     }
23     else {
24       System.out.println('F');
25     }
26   }
27 }
```

main method

invoke printGrade

printGrade method

```
The grade is C
The grade is F
```

The **printGrade** method is a **void** method because it does not return any value. A call to a **void** method must be a statement. Therefore, it is invoked as a statement in line 4 in the **main** method. Like any Java statement, it is terminated with a semicolon.

invoke void method

To see the differences between a void and value-returning method, let's redesign the **printGrade** method to return a value. The new method, which we call **getGrade**, returns the grade as shown in Listing 6.3.

void vs. value-returned

LISTING 6.3 TestReturnGradeMethod.java

```java
1  public class TestReturnGradeMethod {
2    public static void main(String[] args) {
3      System.out.print("The grade is " + getGrade(78.5));
4      System.out.print("\nThe grade is " + getGrade(59.5));
5    }
6
```

main method

invoke getGrade

getGrade method

```
7   public static char getGrade(double score) {
8     if (score >= 90.0)
9       return 'A';
10    else if (score >= 80.0)
11      return 'B';
12    else if (score >= 70.0)
13      return 'C';
14    else if (score >= 60.0)
15      return 'D';
16    else
17      return 'F';
18  }
19 }
```

```
The grade is C
The grade is F
```

The **getGrade** method defined in lines 7–18 returns a character grade based on the numeric score value. The caller invokes this method in lines 3–4.

The **getGrade** method can be invoked by a caller wherever a character may appear. The **printGrade** method does not return any value, so it must be invoked as a statement.

return in void method

Note

A **return** statement is not needed for a **void** method, but it can be used for terminating the method and returning to the method's caller. The syntax is simply

```
return;
```

This is not often done, but sometimes it is useful for circumventing the normal flow of control in a **void** method. For example, the following code has a return statement to terminate the method when the score is invalid.

```
public static void printGrade(double score) {
  if (score < 0 || score > 100) {
    System.out.println("Invalid score");
    return;
  }

  if (score >= 90.0) {
    System.out.println('A');
  }
  else if (score >= 80.0) {
    System.out.println('B');
  }
  else if (score >= 70.0) {
    System.out.println('C');
  }
  else if (score >= 60.0) {
    System.out.println('D');
  }
  else {
    System.out.println('F');
  }
}
```

6.1 What are the benefits of using a method?

6.2 How do you define a method? How do you invoke a method?

6.3 How do you simplify the **max** method in Listing 6.1 using the conditional operator?

6.4 True or false? A call to a method with a **void** return type is always a statement itself, but a call to a value-returning method cannot be a statement by itself.

6.5 What is the **return** type of a **main** method?

6.6 What would be wrong with not writing a **return** statement in a value-returning method? Can you have a **return** statement in a **void** method? Does the **return** statement in the following method cause syntax errors?

```java
public static void xMethod(double x, double y) {
  System.out.println(x + y);
  return x + y;
}
```

6.7 Define the terms parameter, argument, and method signature.

6.8 Write method headers (not the bodies) for the following methods:

a. Return a sales commission, given the sales amount and the commission rate.

b. Display the calendar for a month, given the month and year.

c. Return a square root of a number.

d. Test whether a number is even, and returning **true** if it is.

e. Display a message a specified number of times.

f. Return the monthly payment, given the loan amount, number of years, and annual interest rate.

g. Return the corresponding uppercase letter, given a lowercase letter.

6.9 Identify and correct the errors in the following program:

```java
1  public class Test {
2    public static method1(int n, m) {
3      n += m;
4      method2(3.4);
5    }
6
7    public static int method2(int n) {
8      if (n > 0) return 1;
9      else if (n == 0) return 0;
10     else if (n < 0) return -1;
11   }
12 }
```

6.10 Reformat the following program according to the programming style and documentation guidelines proposed in Section 1.9, Programming Style and Documentation. Use the next-line brace style.

```java
public class Test {
  public static double method(double i, double j)
  {
  while (i < j) {
    j--;
  }

  return j;
  }
}
```

6.5 Passing Arguments by Values

Key Point

The arguments are passed by value to parameters when invoking a method.

The power of a method is its ability to work with parameters. You can use **println** to print any string and **max** to find the maximum of any two **int** values. When calling a method, you need to provide arguments, which must be given in the same order as their respective parameters in the method signature. This is known as *parameter order association*. For example, the following method prints a message **n** times:

parameter order association

```java
public static void nPrintln(String message, int n) {
  for (int i = 0; i < n; i++)
    System.out.println(message);
}
```

You can use **nPrintln("Hello", 3)** to print **Hello** three times. The **nPrintln("Hello", 3)** statement passes the actual string parameter **Hello** to the parameter **message**, passes **3** to **n**, and prints **Hello** three times. However, the statement **nPrintln(3, "Hello")** would be wrong. The data type of **3** does not match the data type for the first parameter, **message**, nor does the second argument, **Hello**, match the second parameter, **n**.

> **Caution**
>
> The arguments must match the parameters in *order, number,* and *compatible type,* as defined in the method signature. Compatible type means that you can pass an argument to a parameter without explicit casting, such as passing an **int** value argument to a **double** value parameter.

pass-by-value

When you invoke a method with an argument, the value of the argument is passed to the parameter. This is referred to as *pass-by-value*. If the argument is a variable rather than a literal value, the value of the variable is passed to the parameter. The variable is not affected, regardless of the changes made to the parameter inside the method. As shown in Listing 6.4, the value of **x (1)** is passed to the parameter **n** to invoke the **increment** method (line 5). The parameter **n** is incremented by **1** in the method (line 10), but **x** is not changed no matter what the method does.

LISTING 6.4 Increment.java

```java
 1  public class Increment {
 2    public static void main(String[] args) {
 3      int x = 1;
 4      System.out.println("Before the call, x is " + x);
 5      increment(x);
 6      System.out.println("After the call, x is " + x);
 7    }
 8
 9    public static void increment(int n) {
10      n++;
11      System.out.println("n inside the method is " + n);
12    }
13  }
```

invoke increment

increment n

```
Before the call, x is 1
n inside the method is 2
After the call, x is 1
```

Listing 6.5 gives another program that demonstrates the effect of passing by value. The program creates a method for swapping two variables. The **swap** method is invoked by passing two arguments. Interestingly, the values of the arguments are not changed after the method is invoked.

LISTING 6.5 TestPassByValue.java

```
 1  public class TestPassByValue {
 2    /** Main method */
 3    public static void main(String[] args) {
 4      // Declare and initialize variables
 5      int num1 = 1;
 6      int num2 = 2;
 7
 8      System.out.println("Before invoking the swap method, num1 is " +
 9        num1 + " and num2 is " + num2);
10
11      // Invoke the swap method to attempt to swap two variables
12      swap(num1, num2);                                                     false swap
13
14      System.out.println("After invoking the swap method, num1 is " +
15        num1 + " and num2 is " + num2);
16    }
17
18    /** Swap two variables */
19    public static void swap(int n1, int n2) {
20      System.out.println("\tInside the swap method");
21      System.out.println("\t\tBefore swapping, n1 is " + n1
22        + " and n2 is " + n2);
23
24      // Swap n1 with n2
25      int temp = n1;
26      n1 = n2;
27      n2 = temp;
28
29      System.out.println("\t\tAfter swapping, n1 is " + n1
30        + " and n2 is " + n2);
31    }
32  }
```

```
Before invoking the swap method, num1 is 1 and num2 is 2
  Inside the swap method
    Before swapping, n1 is 1 and n2 is 2
    After swapping, n1 is 2 and n2 is 1
After invoking the swap method, num1 is 1 and num2 is 2
```

Before the **swap** method is invoked (line 12), **num1** is **1** and **num2** is **2**. After the **swap** method is invoked, **num1** is still **1** and **num2** is still **2**. Their values have not been swapped. As shown in Figure 6.4, the values of the arguments **num1** and **num2** are passed to **n1** and **n2**, but **n1** and **n2** have their own memory locations independent of **num1** and **num2**. Therefore, changes in **n1** and **n2** do not affect the contents of **num1** and **num2**.

Another twist is to change the parameter name **n1** in **swap** to **num1**. What effect does this have? No change occurs, because it makes no difference whether the parameter and the argument have the same name. The parameter is a variable in the method with its own memory space. The variable is allocated when the method is invoked, and it disappears when the method is returned to its caller.

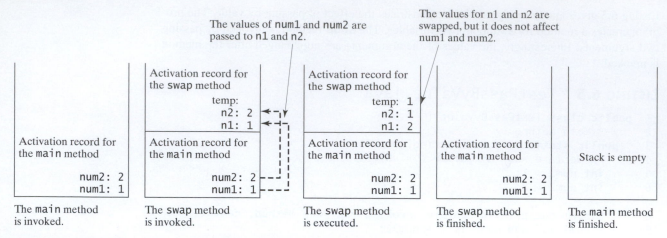

FIGURE 6.4 The values of the variables are passed to the method's parameters.

 Note

For simplicity, Java programmers often say *passing x to y*, which actually means *passing the value of argument x to parameter y*.

6.11 How is an argument passed to a method? Can the argument have the same name as its parameter?

6.12 Identify and correct the errors in the following program:

```
1   public class Test {
2     public static void main(String[] args) {
3       nPrintln(5, "Welcome to Java!");
4     }
5
6     public static void nPrintln(String message, int n) {
7       int n = 1;
8       for (int i = 0; i < n; i++)
9         System.out.println(message);
10    }
11  }
```

6.13 What is pass-by-value? Show the result of the following programs.

```
public class Test {
  public static void main(String[] args) {
    int max = 0;
    max(1, 2, max);
    System.out.println(max);
  }

  public static void max(
      int value1, int value2, int max) {
    if (value1 > value2)
      max = value1;
    else
      max = value2;
  }
}
```

(a)

```
public class Test {
  public static void main(String[] args) {
    int i = 1;
    while (i <= 6) {
      method1(i, 2);
      i++;
    }
  }

  public static void method1(
      int i, int num) {
    for (int j = 1; j <= i; j++) {
      System.out.print(num + " ");
      num *= 2;
    }

    System.out.println();
  }
}
```

(b)

```
public class Test {
  public static void main(String[] args) {
    // Initialize times
    int times = 3;
    System.out.println("Before the call,"
      + " variable times is " + times);

    // Invoke nPrintln and display times
    nPrintln("Welcome to Java!", times);
    System.out.println("After the call,"
      + " variable times is " + times);
  }

  // Print the message n times
  public static void nPrintln(
      String message, int n) {
    while (n > 0) {
      System.out.println("n = " + n);
      System.out.println(message);
      n--;
    }
  }
}
```

(c)

```
public class Test {
  public static void main(String[] args) {
    int i = 0;
    while (i <= 4) {
      method1(i);
      i++;
    }

    System.out.println("i is " + i);
  }

  public static void method1(int i) {
    do {
      if (i % 3 != 0)
        System.out.print(i + " ");
      i--;
    }
    while (i >= 1);

    System.out.println();
  }
}
```

(d)

6.14   For (a) in the preceding question, show the contents of the activation records in the call stack just before the method **max** is invoked, just as **max** is entered, just before **max** is returned, and right after **max** is returned.

6.6 Modularizing Code

Modularizing makes the code easy to maintain and debug and enables the code to be reused.

Key Point

Methods can be used to reduce redundant code and enable code reuse. Methods can also be used to modularize code and improve the quality of the program.

Listing 5.9 gives a program that prompts the user to enter two integers and displays their greatest common divisor. You can rewrite the program using a method, as shown in Listing 6.6.

VideoNote
Modularize code

LISTING 6.6   GreatestCommonDivisorMethod.java

```
1  import java.util.Scanner;
2
3  public class GreatestCommonDivisorMethod {
4    /** Main method */
5    public static void main(String[] args) {
6      // Create a Scanner
7      Scanner input = new Scanner(System.in);
8
9      // Prompt the user to enter two integers
10     System.out.print("Enter first integer: ");
11     int n1 = input.nextInt();
12     System.out.print("Enter second integer: ");
13     int n2 = input.nextInt();
14
```

invoke gcd

```
15      System.out.println("The greatest common divisor for " + n1 +
16        " and " + n2 + " is " + gcd(n1, n2));
17    }
18
19    /** Return the gcd of two integers */
20    public static int gcd(int n1, int n2) {
21      int gcd = 1; // Initial gcd is 1
22      int k = 2;   // Possible gcd
23
24      while (k <= n1 && k <= n2) {
25        if (n1 % k == 0 && n2 % k == 0)
26          gcd = k; // Update gcd
27        k++;
28      }
29
30      return gcd; // Return gcd
31    }
32  }
```

compute gcd (line 20)

return gcd (line 30)

```
Enter first integer: 45  ↵Enter
Enter second integer: 75  ↵Enter
The greatest common divisor for 45 and 75 is 15
```

By encapsulating the code for obtaining the gcd in a method, this program has several advantages:

1. It isolates the problem for computing the gcd from the rest of the code in the main method. Thus, the logic becomes clear and the program is easier to read.

2. The errors on computing the gcd are confined in the **gcd** method, which narrows the scope of debugging.

3. The **gcd** method now can be reused by other programs.

Listing 6.7 applies the concept of code modularization to improve Listing 5.15, PrimeNumber.java.

LISTING 6.7 PrimeNumberMethod.java

invoke printPrimeNumbers

printPrimeNumbers method

invoke isPrime

```
1  public class PrimeNumberMethod {
2    public static void main(String[] args) {
3      System.out.println("The first 50 prime numbers are \n");
4      printPrimeNumbers(50);
5    }
6
7    public static void printPrimeNumbers(int numberOfPrimes) {
8      final int NUMBER_OF_PRIMES_PER_LINE = 10; // Display 10 per line
9      int count = 0; // Count the number of prime numbers
10     int number = 2; // A number to be tested for primeness
11
12     // Repeatedly find prime numbers
13     while (count < numberOfPrimes) {
14       // Print the prime number and increase the count
15       if (isPrime(number)) {
16         count++; // Increase the count
17
```

```
18          if (count % NUMBER_OF_PRIMES_PER_LINE == 0) {
19              // Print the number and advance to the new line
20              System.out.printf("%-5s\n", number);
21          }
22          else
23              System.out.printf("%-5s", number);
24          }
25
26          // Check whether the next number is prime
27          number++;
28      }
29  }
30
31  /** Check whether number is prime */
32  public static boolean isPrime(int number) {
33      for (int divisor = 2; divisor <= number / 2; divisor++) {
34          if (number % divisor == 0) { // If true, number is not prime
35              return false; // Number is not a prime
36          }
37      }
38
39      return true; // Number is prime
40  }
41  }
```

isPrime method

```
The first 50 prime numbers are

2    3    5    7    11   13   17   19   23   29
31   37   41   43   47   53   59   61   67   71
73   79   83   89   97   101  103  107  109  113
127  131  137  139  149  151  157  163  167  173
179  181  191  193  197  199  211  223  227  229
```

We divided a large problem into two subproblems: determining whether a number is a prime and printing the prime numbers. As a result, the new program is easier to read and easier to debug. Moreover, the methods **printPrimeNumbers** and **isPrime** can be reused by other programs.

6.7 Case Study: Converting Hexadecimals to Decimals

This section presents a program that converts a hexadecimal number into a decimal number.

 Key Point

Listing 5.11, Dec2Hex.java, gives a program that converts a decimal to a hexadecimal. How would you convert a hex number into a decimal?

Given a hexadecimal number $h_n h_{n-1} h_{n-2} \ldots h_2 h_1 h_0$, the equivalent decimal value is

$$h_n \times 16^n + h_{n-1} \times 16^{n-1} + h_{n-2} \times 16^{n-2} + \ldots$$
$$+ h_2 \times 16^2 + h_1 \times 16^1 + h_0 \times 16^0$$

For example, the hex number **AB8C** is

$$10 \times 16^3 + 11 \times 16^2 + 8 \times 16^1 + 12 \times 16^0 = 43916$$

Our program will prompt the user to enter a hex number as a string and convert it into a decimal using the following method:

```
public static int hexToDecimal(String hex)
```

A brute-force approach is to convert each hex character into a decimal number, multiply it by 16^i for a hex digit at the i's position, and then add all the items together to obtain the equivalent decimal value for the hex number.

Note that

$$h_n \times 16^n + h_{n-1} \times 16^{n-1} + h_{n-2} \times 16^{n-2} + \ldots + h_1 \times 16^1 + h_0 \times 16^0$$
$$= (\ldots((h_n \times 16 + h_n - 1) \times 16 + h_n - 2) \times 16 + \ldots + h_1) \times 16 + h_0$$

This observation, known as the Horner's algorithm, leads to the following efficient code for converting a hex string to a decimal number:

```java
int decimalValue = 0;
for (int i = 0; i < hex.length(); i++) {
  char hexChar = hex.charAt(i);
  decimalValue = decimalValue * 16 + hexCharToDecimal(hexChar);
}
```

Here is a trace of the algorithm for hex number **AB8C**:

	i	hexChar	hexCharToDecimal (hexChar)	decimalValue
before the loop				0
after the 1st iteration	0	A	10	10
after the 2nd iteration	1	B	11	10 * 16 + 11
after the 3rd iteration	2	8	8	(10 * 16 + 11) * 16 + 8
after the 4th iteration	3	C	12	((10 * 16 + 11) * 16 + 8) * 16 + 12

Listing 6.8 gives the complete program.

LISTING 6.8 Hex2Dec.java

```java
 1  import java.util.Scanner;
 2
 3  public class Hex2Dec {
 4    /** Main method */
 5    public static void main(String[] args) {
 6      // Create a Scanner
 7      Scanner input = new Scanner(System.in);
 8
 9      // Prompt the user to enter a string
10      System.out.print("Enter a hex number: ");
11      String hex = input.nextLine();
12
13      System.out.println("The decimal value for hex number "
14        + hex + " is " + hexToDecimal(hex.toUpperCase()));
15    }
16
17    public static int hexToDecimal(String hex) {
18      int decimalValue = 0;
19      for (int i = 0; i < hex.length(); i++) {
20        char hexChar = hex.charAt(i);
21        decimalValue = decimalValue * 16 + hexCharToDecimal(hexChar);
```

input string

hex to decimal

```
22      }
23
24      return decimalValue;
25    }
26
27    public static int hexCharToDecimal(char ch) {
28      if (ch >= 'A' && ch <= 'F')
29        return 10 + ch - 'A';
30      else // ch is '0', '1', ..., or '9'
31        return ch - '0';
32    }
33  }
```

hex char to decimal
check uppercase

```
Enter a hex number: AB8C  ⏎Enter
The decimal value for hex number AB8C is 43916
```

```
Enter a hex number: af71  ⏎Enter
The decimal value for hex number af71 is 44913
```

The program reads a string from the console (line 11), and invokes the `hexToDecimal` method to convert a hex string to decimal number (line 14). The characters can be in either lowercase or uppercase. They are converted to uppercase before invoking the `hexToDecimal` method.

The `hexToDecimal` method is defined in lines 17–25 to return an integer. The length of the string is determined by invoking `hex.length()` in line 19.

The `hexCharToDecimal` method is defined in lines 27–32 to return a decimal value for a hex character. The character can be in either lowercase or uppercase. Recall that to subtract two characters is to subtract their Unicodes. For example, `'5' - '0'` is 5.

6.8 Overloading Methods

Overloading methods enables you to define the methods with the same name as long as their signatures are different.

Key Point

The `max` method that was used earlier works only with the `int` data type. But what if you need to determine which of two floating-point numbers has the maximum value? The solution is to create another method with the same name but different parameters, as shown in the following code:

```
public static double max(double num1, double num2) {
  if (num1 > num2)
    return num1;
  else
    return num2;
}
```

If you call `max` with `int` parameters, the `max` method that expects `int` parameters will be invoked; if you call `max` with `double` parameters, the `max` method that expects `double` parameters will be invoked. This is referred to as *method overloading*; that is, two methods have the same name but different parameter lists within one class. The Java compiler determines which method to use based on the method signature.

method overloading

Listing 6.9 is a program that creates three methods. The first finds the maximum integer, the second finds the maximum double, and the third finds the maximum among three double values. All three methods are named `max`.

LISTING 6.9 TestMethodOverloading.java

```
1  public class TestMethodOverloading {
2    /** Main method */
3    public static void main(String[] args) {
4      // Invoke the max method with int parameters
5      System.out.println("The maximum of 3 and 4 is "
6        + max(3, 4));
7
8      // Invoke the max method with the double parameters
9      System.out.println("The maximum of 3.0 and 5.4 is "
10       + max(3.0, 5.4));
11
12     // Invoke the max method with three double parameters
13     System.out.println("The maximum of 3.0, 5.4, and 10.14 is "
14       + max(3.0, 5.4, 10.14));
15   }
16
17   /** Return the max of two int values */
18   public static int max(int num1, int num2) {
19     if (num1 > num2)
20       return num1;
21     else
22       return num2;
23   }
24
25   /** Find the max of two double values */
26   public static double max(double num1, double num2) {
27     if (num1 > num2)
28       return num1;
29     else
30       return num2;
31   }
32
33   /** Return the max of three double values */
34   public static double max(double num1, double num2, double num3) {
35     return max(max(num1, num2), num3);
36   }
37 }
```

overloaded max (line 18)
overloaded max (line 26)
overloaded max (line 34)

```
The maximum of 3 and 4 is 4
The maximum of 3.0 and 5.4 is 5.4
The maximum of 3.0, 5.4, and 10.14 is 10.14
```

When calling `max(3, 4)` (line 6), the `max` method for finding the maximum of two integers is invoked. When calling `max(3.0, 5.4)` (line 10), the `max` method for finding the maximum of two doubles is invoked. When calling `max(3.0, 5.4, 10.14)` (line 14), the `max` method for finding the maximum of three double values is invoked.

Can you invoke the `max` method with an `int` value and a `double` value, such as `max(2, 2.5)`? If so, which of the `max` methods is invoked? The answer to the first question is yes. The answer to the second question is that the `max` method for finding the maximum of two `double` values is invoked. The argument value `2` is automatically converted into a `double` value and passed to this method.

You may be wondering why the method `max(double, double)` is not invoked for the call `max(3, 4)`. Both `max(double, double)` and `max(int, int)` are possible matches for `max(3, 4)`. The Java compiler finds the method that best matches a method invocation. Since the method `max(int, int)` is a better matches for `max(3, 4)` than `max(double, double)`, `max(int, int)` is used to invoke `max(3, 4)`.

Tip

Overloading methods can make programs clearer and more readable. Methods that perform the same function with different types of parameters should be given the same name.

Note

Overloaded methods must have different parameter lists. You cannot overload methods based on different modifiers or return types.

Note

Sometimes there are two or more possible matches for the invocation of a method, but the compiler cannot determine the best match. This is referred to as *ambiguous invocation*. Ambiguous invocation causes a compile error. Consider the following code:

ambiguous invocation

```
public class AmbiguousOverloading {
  public static void main(String[] args) {
    System.out.println(max(1, 2));
  }

  public static double max(int num1, double num2) {
    if (num1 > num2)
      return num1;
    else
      return num2;
  }

  public static double max(double num1, int num2) {
    if (num1 > num2)
      return num1;
    else
      return num2;
  }
}
```

Both `max(int, double)` and `max(double, int)` are possible candidates to match `max(1, 2)`. Because neither is better than the other, the invocation is ambiguous, resulting in a compile error.

6.15 What is method overloading? Is it permissible to define two methods that have the same name but different parameter types? Is it permissible to define two methods in a class that have identical method names and parameter lists but different return value types or different modifiers?

6.16 What is wrong in the following program?

```
public class Test {
  public static void method(int x) {
  }

  public static int method(int y) {
```

```
        return y;
      }
    }
```

6.17   Given two method definitions,

```java
public static double m(double x, double y)
```

```java
public static double m(int x, double y)
```

tell which of the two methods is invoked for:

a. **double** z = m(4, 5);

b. **double** z = m(4, 5.4);

c. **double** z = m(4.5, 5.4);

6.9 The Scope of Variables

Key Point

The scope of a variable is the part of the program where the variable can be referenced.

scope of variables

local variable

Section 2.5 introduced the scope of a variable. This section discusses the scope of variables in detail. A variable defined inside a method is referred to as a *local variable*. The scope of a local variable starts from its declaration and continues to the end of the block that contains the variable. A local variable must be declared and assigned a value before it can be used.

A parameter is actually a local variable. The scope of a method parameter covers the entire method. A variable declared in the initial-action part of a **for**-loop header has its scope in the entire loop. However, a variable declared inside a **for**-loop body has its scope limited in the loop body from its declaration to the end of the block that contains the variable, as shown in Figure 6.5.

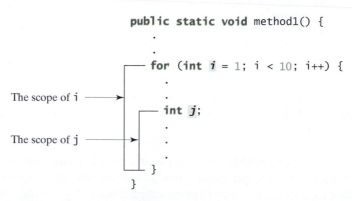

FIGURE 6.5   A variable declared in the initial action part of a **for**-loop header has its scope in the entire loop.

You can declare a local variable with the same name in different blocks in a method, but you cannot declare a local variable twice in the same block or in nested blocks, as shown in Figure 6.6.

It is fine to declare i in two nonnested blocks.

```
public static void method1() {
  int x = 1;
  int y = 1;

  for (int i = 1; i < 10; i++) {
    x += i;
  }

  for (int i = 1; i < 10; i++) {
    y += i;
  }
}
```

It is wrong to declare i in two nested blocks.

```
public static void method2() {

  int i = 1;
  int sum = 0;

  for (int i = 1; i < 10; i++)
    sum += i;

}
```

FIGURE 6.6 A variable can be declared multiple times in nonnested blocks, but only once in nested blocks.

Caution

Do not declare a variable inside a block and then attempt to use it outside the block. Here is an example of a common mistake:

```
for (int i = 0; i < 10; i++) {
}

System.out.println(i);
```

The last statement would cause a syntax error, because variable i is not defined outside of the **for** loop.

6.18 What is a local variable?

6.19 What is the scope of a local variable?

Check Point

6.10 Case Study: Generating Random Characters

A character is coded using an integer. Generating a random character is to generate an integer.

Key Point

Computer programs process numerical data and characters. You have seen many examples that involve numerical data. It is also important to understand characters and how to process them. This section presents an example of generating random characters.

As introduced in Section 4.3, every character has a unique Unicode between 0 and FFFF in hexadecimal (65535 in decimal). To generate a random character is to generate a random integer between 0 and 65535 using the following expression (note that since 0 <= Math.random() < 1.0, you have to add 1 to 65535):

```
(int)(Math.random() * (65535 + 1))
```

Now let's consider how to generate a random lowercase letter. The Unicodes for lowercase letters are consecutive integers starting from the Unicode for a, then that for b, c, . . . , and z. The Unicode for a is

```
(int)'a'
```

Thus, a random integer between `(int)'a'` and `(int)'z'` is

```
(int)((int)'a' + Math.random() * ((int)'z' - (int)'a' + 1))
```

As discussed in Section 4.3.3, all numeric operators can be applied to the **char** operands. The **char** operand is cast into a number if the other operand is a number or a character. Therefore, the preceding expression can be simplified as follows:

```
'a' + Math.random() * ('z' - 'a' + 1)
```

and a random lowercase letter is

```
(char)('a' + Math.random() * ('z' - 'a' + 1))
```

Hence, a random character between any two characters **ch1** and **ch2** with **ch1 < ch2** can be generated as follows:

```
(char)(ch1 + Math.random() * (ch2 - ch1 + 1))
```

This is a simple but useful discovery. Listing 6.10 defines a class named **RandomCharacter** with five overloaded methods to get a certain type of character randomly. You can use these methods in your future projects.

LISTING 6.10 RandomCharacter.java

getRandomCharacter

getRandomLower CaseLetter()

getRandomUpper CaseLetter()

getRandomDigit Character()

getRandomCharacter()

```java
 1  public class RandomCharacter {
 2    /** Generate a random character between ch1 and ch2 */
 3    public static char getRandomCharacter(char ch1, char ch2) {
 4      return (char)(ch1 + Math.random() * (ch2 - ch1 + 1));
 5    }
 6
 7    /** Generate a random lowercase letter */
 8    public static char getRandomLowerCaseLetter() {
 9      return getRandomCharacter('a', 'z');
10    }
11
12    /** Generate a random uppercase letter */
13    public static char getRandomUpperCaseLetter() {
14      return getRandomCharacter('A', 'Z');
15    }
16
17    /** Generate a random digit character */
18    public static char getRandomDigitCharacter() {
19      return getRandomCharacter('0', '9');
20    }
21
22    /** Generate a random character */
23    public static char getRandomCharacter() {
24      return getRandomCharacter('\u0000', '\uFFFF');
25    }
26  }
```

Listing 6.11 gives a test program that displays 175 random lowercase letters.

LISTING 6.11 TestRandomCharacter.java

constants

```java
 1  public class TestRandomCharacter {
 2    /** Main method */
 3    public static void main(String[] args) {
 4      final int NUMBER_OF_CHARS = 175;
 5      final int CHARS_PER_LINE = 25;
 6
 7      // Print random characters between 'a' and 'z', 25 chars per line
 8      for (int i = 0; i < NUMBER_OF_CHARS; i++) {
```

```
 9        char ch = RandomCharacter.getRandomLowerCaseLetter();
10        if ((i + 1) % CHARS_PER_LINE == 0)
11           System.out.println(ch);
12        else
13           System.out.print(ch);
14      }
15    }
16 }
```

lower-case letter

```
gmjsohezfkgtazqgmswfclrao
pnrunulnwmaztlfjedmpchcif
lalqdgivxkxpbzulrmqmbhikr
lbnrjlsopfxahssqhwuuljvbe
xbhdotzhpehbqmuwsfktwsoli
cbuwkzgxpmtzihgatdslvbwbz
bfesoklwbhnooygiigzdxuqni
```

Line 9 invokes **getRandomLowerCaseLetter()** defined in the **RandomCharacter** class. Note that **getRandomLowerCaseLetter()** does not have any parameters, but you still have to use the parentheses when defining and invoking the method.

parentheses required

6.11 Method Abstraction and Stepwise Refinement

The key to developing software is to apply the concept of abstraction.

Key Point

You will learn many levels of abstraction from this book. *Method abstraction* is achieved by separating the use of a method from its implementation. The client can use a method without knowing how it is implemented. The details of the implementation are encapsulated in the method and hidden from the client who invokes the method. This is also known as *information hiding* or *encapsulation*. If you decide to change the implementation, the client program will not be affected, provided that you do not change the method signature. The implementation of the method is hidden from the client in a "black box," as shown in Figure 6.7.

VideoNote

Stepwise refinement

method abstraction

information hiding

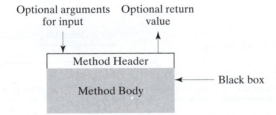

FIGURE 6.7 The method body can be thought of as a black box that contains the detailed implementation for the method.

You have already used the **System.out.print** method to display a string and the **max** method to find the maximum number. You know how to write the code to invoke these methods in your program, but as a user of these methods, you are not required to know how they are implemented.

The concept of method abstraction can be applied to the process of developing programs. When writing a large program, you can use the *divide-and-conquer* strategy, also known as *stepwise refinement*, to decompose it into subproblems. The subproblems can be further decomposed into smaller, more manageable problems.

divide and conquer

stepwise refinement

Suppose you write a program that displays the calendar for a given month of the year. The program prompts the user to enter the year and the month, then displays the entire calendar for the month, as shown in the following sample run.

```
Enter full year (e.g., 2012): 2012  ⏎Enter

Enter month as number between 1 and 12: 3  ⏎Enter

            March 2012
-----------------------------
 Sun Mon Tue Wed Thu Fri Sat
                   1   2   3
   4   5   6   7   8   9  10
  11  12  13  14  15  16  17
  18  19  20  21  22  23  24
  25  26  27  28  29  30
```

Let us use this example to demonstrate the divide-and-conquer approach.

6.11.1 Top-Down Design

How would you get started on such a program? Would you immediately start coding? Beginning programmers often start by trying to work out the solution to every detail. Although details are important in the final program, concern for detail in the early stages may block the problem-solving process. To make problem solving flow as smoothly as possible, this example begins by using method abstraction to isolate details from design and only later implements the details.

For this example, the problem is first broken into two subproblems: get input from the user and print the calendar for the month. At this stage, you should be concerned with what the subproblems will achieve, not with how to get input and print the calendar for the month. You can draw a structure chart to help visualize the decomposition of the problem (see Figure 6.8a).

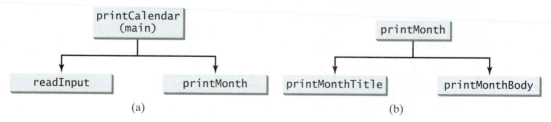

(a)　　　　　　　　　　　　　　　　(b)

FIGURE 6.8 The structure chart shows that the `printCalendar` problem is divided into two subproblems, `readInput` and `printMonth` in (a), and that `printMonth` is divided into two smaller subproblems, `printMonthTitle` and `printMonthBody` in (b).

You can use **Scanner** to read input for the year and the month. The problem of printing the calendar for a given month can be broken into two subproblems: print the month title and print the month body, as shown in Figure 6.8b. The month title consists of three lines: month and year, a dashed line, and the names of the seven days of the week. You need to get the month name (e.g., January) from the numeric month (e.g., 1). This is accomplished in **getMonthName** (see Figure 6.9a).

In order to print the month body, you need to know which day of the week is the first day of the month (**getStartDay**) and how many days the month has (**getNumberOfDaysInMonth**),

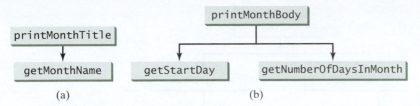

FIGURE 6.9 (a) To **printMonthTitle**, you need **getMonthName**. (b) The **printMonthBody** problem is refined into several smaller problems.

as shown in Figure 6.9b. For example, December 2013 has 31 days, and December 1, 2013, is a Sunday.

How would you get the start day for the first date in a month? There are several ways to do so. For now, we'll use an alternative approach. Assume you know that the start day for January 1, 1800, was a Wednesday (**START_DAY_FOR_JAN_1_1800 = 3**). You could compute the total number of days (**totalNumberOfDays**) between January 1, 1800, and the first date of the calendar month. The start day for the calendar month is **(totalNumberOfDays + START_DAY_FOR_JAN_1_1800) % 7**, since every week has seven days. Thus, the **getStartDay** problem can be further refined as **getTotalNumberOfDays**, as shown in Figure 6.10a.

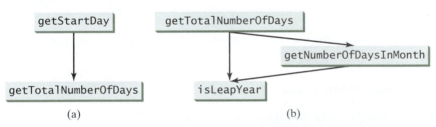

FIGURE 6.10 (a) To **getStartDay**, you need **getTotalNumberOfDays**. (b) The **getTotalNumberOfDays** problem is refined into two smaller problems.

To get the total number of days, you need to know whether the year is a leap year and the number of days in each month. Thus, **getTotalNumberOfDays** can be further refined into two subproblems: **isLeapYear** and **getNumberOfDaysInMonth**, as shown in Figure 6.10b. The complete structure chart is shown in Figure 6.11.

6.11.2 Top-Down and/or Bottom-Up Implementation

Now we turn our attention to implementation. In general, a subproblem corresponds to a method in the implementation, although some are so simple that this is unnecessary. You would need to decide which modules to implement as methods and which to combine with other methods. Decisions of this kind should be based on whether the overall program will be easier to read as a result of your choice. In this example, the subproblem **readInput** can be simply implemented in the **main** method.

You can use either a "top-down" or a "bottom-up" approach. The top-down approach implements one method in the structure chart at a time from the top to the bottom. *Stubs*— a simple but incomplete version of a method—can be used for the methods waiting to be implemented. The use of stubs enables you to quickly build the framework of the program. Implement the **main** method first, and then use a stub for the **printMonth** method. For example,

top-down approach

stub

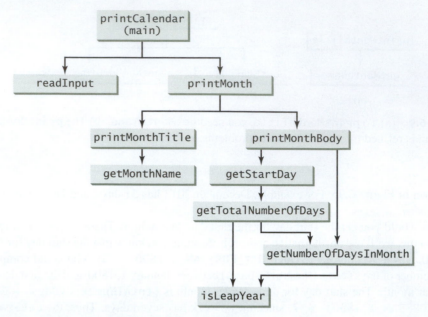

FIGURE 6.11 The structure chart shows the hierarchical relationship of the subproblems in the program.

let **printMonth** display the year and the month in the stub. Thus, your program may begin like this:

```java
public class PrintCalendar {
  /** Main method */
  public static void main(String[] args) {
    Scanner input = new Scanner(System.in);

    // Prompt the user to enter year
    System.out.print("Enter full year (e.g., 2012): ");
    int year = input.nextInt();

    // Prompt the user to enter month
    System.out.print("Enter month as a number between 1 and 12: ");
    int month = input.nextInt();

    // Print calendar for the month of the year
    printMonth(year, month);
  }

  /** A stub for printMonth may look like this */
  public static void printMonth(int year, int month){
    System.out.print(month + " " + year);
  }

  /** A stub for printMonthTitle may look like this */
  public static void printMonthTitle(int year, int month){
  }

  /** A stub for getMonthBody may look like this */
  public static void printMonthBody(int year, int month){
  }
```

```
/** A stub for getMonthName may look like this */
public static String getMonthName(int month) {
  return "January"; // A dummy value
}

/** A stub for getStartDay may look like this */
public static int getStartDay(int year, int month) {
  return 1; // A dummy value
}

/** A stub for getTotalNumberOfDays may look like this */
public static int getTotalNumberOfDays(int year, int month) {
  return 10000; // A dummy value
}

/** A stub for getNumberOfDaysInMonth may look like this */
public static int getNumberOfDaysInMonth(int year, int month) {
  return 31; // A dummy value
}

/** A stub for isLeapYear may look like this */
public static Boolean isLeapYear(int year) {
  return true; // A dummy value
}
}
```

Compile and test the program, and fix any errors. You can now implement the `printMonth` method. For methods invoked from the `printMonth` method, you can again use stubs.

The bottom-up approach implements one method in the structure chart at a time from the bottom to the top. For each method implemented, write a test program, known as the *driver*, to test it. The top-down and bottom-up approaches are equally good: Both approaches implement methods incrementally, help to isolate programming errors, and make debugging easy. They can be used together.

bottom-up approach

driver

6.11.3 Implementation Details

The `isLeapYear(int year)` method can be implemented using the following code from Section 3.11:

```
return year % 400 == 0 || (year % 4 == 0 && year % 100 != 0);
```

Use the following facts to implement `getTotalNumberOfDaysInMonth(int year, int month)`:

- January, March, May, July, August, October, and December have 31 days.

- April, June, September, and November have 30 days.

- February has 28 days during a regular year and 29 days during a leap year. A regular year, therefore, has 365 days, a leap year 366 days.

To implement `getTotalNumberOfDays(int year, int month)`, you need to compute the total number of days (`totalNumberOfDays`) between January 1, 1800, and the first day of the calendar month. You could find the total number of days between the year 1800 and the calendar year and then figure out the total number of days prior to the calendar month in the calendar year. The sum of these two totals is `totalNumberOfDays`.

To print a body, first pad some space before the start day and then print the lines for every week.

The complete program is given in Listing 6.12.

LISTING 6.12 PrintCalendar.java

```java
 1  import java.util.Scanner;
 2
 3  public class PrintCalendar {
 4    /** Main method */
 5    public static void main(String[] args) {
 6      Scanner input = new Scanner(System.in);
 7
 8      // Prompt the user to enter year
 9      System.out.print("Enter full year (e.g., 2012): ");
10      int year = input.nextInt();
11
12      // Prompt the user to enter month
13      System.out.print("Enter month as a number between 1 and 12: ");
14      int month = input.nextInt();
15
16      // Print calendar for the month of the year
17      printMonth(year, month);
18    }
19
20    /** Print the calendar for a month in a year */
21    public static void printMonth(int year, int month) {
22      // Print the headings of the calendar
23      printMonthTitle(year, month);
24
25      // Print the body of the calendar
26      printMonthBody(year, month);
27    }
28
29    /** Print the month title, e.g., March 2012 */
30    public static void printMonthTitle(int year, int month) {
31      System.out.println("            " + getMonthName(month)
32        + " " + year);
33      System.out.println("-----------------------------");
34      System.out.println(" Sun Mon Tue Wed Thu Fri Sat");
35    }
36
37    /** Get the English name for the month */
38    public static String getMonthName(int month) {
39      String monthName = "";
40      switch (month) {
41        case 1: monthName = "January"; break;
42        case 2: monthName = "February"; break;
43        case 3: monthName = "March"; break;
44        case 4: monthName = "April"; break;
45        case 5: monthName = "May"; break;
46        case 6: monthName = "June"; break;
47        case 7: monthName = "July"; break;
48        case 8: monthName = "August"; break;
49        case 9: monthName = "September"; break;
50        case 10: monthName = "October"; break;
51        case 11: monthName = "November"; break;
52        case 12: monthName = "December";
53      }
54
55      return monthName;
56    }
57
58    /** Print month body */
```

printMonth (line 21)

printMonthTitle (line 30)

getMonthName (line 38)

```
59  public static void printMonthBody(int year, int month) {            printMonthBody
60    // Get start day of the week for the first date in the month
61    int startDay = getStartDay(year, month)
62
63    // Get number of days in the month
64    int numberOfDaysInMonth = getNumberOfDaysInMonth(year, month);
65
66    // Pad space before the first day of the month
67    int i = 0;
68    for (i = 0; i < startDay; i++)
69      System.out.print("     ");
70
71    for (i = 1; i <= numberOfDaysInMonth; i++) {
72      System.out.printf("%4d", i);
73
74      if ((i + startDay) % 7 == 0)
75        System.out.println();
76    }
77
78    System.out.println();
79  }
80
81  /** Get the start day of month/1/year */
82  public static int getStartDay(int year, int month) {                getStartDay
83    final int START_DAY_FOR_JAN_1_1800 = 3;
84    // Get total number of days from 1/1/1800 to month/1/year
85    int totalNumberOfDays = getTotalNumberOfDays(year, month);
86
87    // Return the start day for month/1/year
88    return (totalNumberOfDays + START_DAY_FOR_JAN_1_1800) % 7;
89  }
90
91  /** Get the total number of days since January 1, 1800 */
92  public static int getTotalNumberOfDays(int year, int month) {       getTotalNumberOfDays
93    int total = 0;
94
95    // Get the total days from 1800 to 1/1/year
96    for (int i = 1800; i < year; i++)
97      if (isLeapYear(i))
98        total = total + 366;
99      else
100        total = total + 365;
101
102    // Add days from Jan to the month prior to the calendar month
103    for (int i = 1; i < month; i++)
104      total = total + getNumberOfDaysInMonth(year, i);
105
106    return total;
107  }
108
109  /** Get the number of days in a month */
110  public static int getNumberOfDaysInMonth(int year, int month) {     getNumberOfDaysInMonth
111    if (month == 1 || month == 3 || month == 5 || month == 7 ||
112      month == 8 || month == 10 || month == 12)
113      return 31;
114
115    if (month == 4 || month == 6 || month == 9 || month == 11)
116      return 30;
117
118    if (month == 2) return isLeapYear(year) ? 29 : 28;
```

```
119
120        return 0; // If month is incorrect
121    }
122
123    /** Determine if it is a leap year */
124    public static boolean isLeapYear(int year) {
125        return year % 400 == 0 || (year % 4 == 0 && year % 100 != 0);
126    }
127 }
```

isLeapYear

The program does not validate user input. For instance, if the user enters either a month not in the range between 1 and 12 or a year before 1800, the program displays an erroneous calendar. To avoid this error, add an **if** statement to check the input before printing the calendar.

This program prints calendars for a month but could easily be modified to print calendars for a whole year. Although it can print months only after January 1800, it could be modified to print months before 1800.

6.11.4 Benefits of Stepwise Refinement

Stepwise refinement breaks a large problem into smaller manageable subproblems. Each subproblem can be implemented using a method. This approach makes the program easier to write, reuse, debug, test, modify, and maintain.

Simpler Program

The print calendar program is long. Rather than writing a long sequence of statements in one method, stepwise refinement breaks it into smaller methods. This simplifies the program and makes the whole program easier to read and understand.

Reusing Methods

Stepwise refinement promotes code reuse within a program. The **isLeapYear** method is defined once and invoked from the **getTotalNumberOfDays** and **getNumberOfDayInMonth** methods. This reduces redundant code.

Easier Developing, Debugging, and Testing

Since each subproblem is solved in a method, a method can be developed, debugged, and tested individually. This isolates the errors and makes developing, debugging, and testing easier.

incremental development and testing

When implementing a large program, use the top-down and/or bottom-up approach. Do not write the entire program at once. Using these approaches seems to take more development time (because you repeatedly compile and run the program), but it actually saves time and makes debugging easier.

Better Facilitating Teamwork

When a large problem is divided into subprograms, subproblems can be assigned to different programmers. This makes it easier for programmers to work in teams.

KEY TERMS

actual parameter   205
ambiguous invocation   221
argument   205
divide and conquer   225
formal parameter (i.e., parameter)   205
information hiding   225
method   204
method abstraction   225

method overloading   219
method signature   205
modifier   205
parameter   205
pass-by-value   212
scope of a variable   222
stepwise refinement   225
stub   227

CHAPTER SUMMARY

1. Making programs modular and reusable is one of the central goals in software engineering. Java provides many powerful constructs that help to achieve this goal. *Methods* are one such construct.

2. The method header specifies the *modifiers*, *return value type*, *method name*, and *parameters* of the method. The `static` modifier is used for all the methods in this chapter.

3. A method may return a value. The `returnValueType` is the data type of the value the method returns. If the method does not return a value, the `returnValueType` is the keyword `void`.

4. The *parameter list* refers to the type, order, and number of a method's parameters. The method name and the parameter list together constitute the *method signature*. Parameters are optional; that is, a method doesn't need to contain any parameters.

5. A return statement can also be used in a `void` method for terminating the method and returning to the method's caller. This is useful occasionally for circumventing the normal flow of control in a method.

6. The arguments that are passed to a method should have the same number, type, and order as the parameters in the method signature.

7. When a program calls a method, program control is transferred to the called method. A called method returns control to the caller when its return statement is executed or when its method-ending closing brace is reached.

8. A value-returning method can also be invoked as a statement in Java. In this case, the caller simply ignores the return value.

9. A method can be overloaded. This means that two methods can have the same name, as long as their method parameter lists differ.

10. A variable declared in a method is called a local variable. The *scope of a local variable* starts from its declaration and continues to the end of the block that contains the variable. A local variable must be declared and initialized before it is used.

11. *Method abstraction* is achieved by separating the use of a method from its implementation. The client can use a method without knowing how it is implemented. The details of the implementation are encapsulated in the method and hidden from the client who invokes the method. This is known as *information hiding* or *encapsulation*.

12. Method abstraction modularizes programs in a neat, hierarchical manner. Programs written as collections of concise methods are easier to write, debug, maintain, and modify than would otherwise be the case. This writing style also promotes method reusability.

13. When implementing a large program, use the top-down and/or bottom-up coding approach. Do not write the entire program at once. This approach may seem to take more time for coding (because you are repeatedly compiling and running the program), but it actually saves time and makes debugging easier.

QUIZ

Answer the quiz for this chapter online at www.cs.armstrong.edu/liang/intro10e/quiz.html.

MyProgrammingLab™ **PROGRAMMING EXERCISES**

> **Note**
> A common error for the exercises in this chapter is that students don't implement the methods to meet the requirements even though the output from the main program is correct. For an example of this type of error see www.cs.armstrong.edu/liang/CommonMethodErrorJava.pdf.

Sections 6.2–6.9

6.1 (*Math: pentagonal numbers*) A pentagonal number is defined as $n(3n–1)/2$ for $n = 1, 2, \ldots$, and so on. Therefore, the first few numbers are 1, 5, 12, 22, ... Write a method with the following header that returns a pentagonal number:

```
public static int getPentagonalNumber(int n)
```

Write a test program that uses this method to display the first 100 pentagonal numbers with 10 numbers on each line.

*6.2 (*Sum the digits in an integer*) Write a method that computes the sum of the digits in an integer. Use the following method header:

```
public static int sumDigits(long n)
```

For example, **sumDigits(234)** returns **9** (2 + 3 + 4). (*Hint*: Use the **%** operator to extract digits, and the **/** operator to remove the extracted digit. For instance, to extract 4 from 234, use **234 % 10** (= 4). To remove 4 from 234, use **234 / 10** (= 23). Use a loop to repeatedly extract and remove the digit until all the digits are extracted. Write a test program that prompts the user to enter an integer and displays the sum of all its digits.

**6.3 (*Palindrome integer*) Write the methods with the following headers

```
// Return the reversal of an integer, i.e., reverse(456) returns 654
public static int reverse(int number)
```

```
// Return true if number is a palindrome
public static boolean isPalindrome(int number)
```

Use the **reverse** method to implement **isPalindrome**. A number is a palindrome if its reversal is the same as itself. Write a test program that prompts the user to enter an integer and reports whether the integer is a palindrome.

*6.4 (*Display an integer reversed*) Write a method with the following header to display an integer in reverse order:

```
public static void reverse(int number)
```

For example, **reverse(3456)** displays **6543**. Write a test program that prompts the user to enter an integer and displays its reversal.

*6.5 (*Sort three numbers*) Write a method with the following header to display three numbers in increasing order:

```
public static void displaySortedNumbers(
    double num1, double num2, double num3)
```

VideoNote

Reverse an integer

Write a test program that prompts the user to enter three numbers and invokes the method to display them in increasing order.

*6.6 (*Display patterns*) Write a method to display a pattern as follows:

```
        1
      2 1
    3 2 1
...
n n-1 ... 3 2 1
```

The method header is

```
public static void displayPattern(int n)
```

*6.7 (*Financial application: compute the future investment value*) Write a method that computes future investment value at a given interest rate for a specified number of years. The future investment is determined using the formula in Programming Exercise 2.21.

Use the following method header:

```
public static double futureInvestmentValue(
    double investmentAmount, double monthlyInterestRate, int years)
```

For example, `futureInvestmentValue(10000, 0.05/12, 5)` returns `12833.59`.

Write a test program that prompts the user to enter the investment amount (e.g., 1000) and the interest rate (e.g., 9%) and prints a table that displays future value for the years from 1 to 30, as shown below:

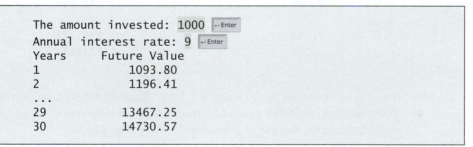

```
The amount invested: 1000  ⏎Enter
Annual interest rate: 9  ⏎Enter
Years      Future Value
1              1093.80
2              1196.41
...
29            13467.25
30            14730.57
```

6.8 (*Conversions between Celsius and Fahrenheit*) Write a class that contains the following two methods:

```
/** Convert from Celsius to Fahrenheit */
public static double celsiusToFahrenheit(double celsius)

/** Convert from Fahrenheit to Celsius */
public static double fahrenheitToCelsius(double fahrenheit)
```

The formula for the conversion is:

```
fahrenheit = (9.0 / 5) * celsius + 32
celsius = (5.0 / 9) * (fahrenheit - 32)
```

Write a test program that invokes these methods to display the following tables:

Celsius	Fahrenheit		Fahrenheit	Celsius
40.0	104.0		120.0	48.89
39.0	102.2		110.0	43.33
...				
32.0	89.6		40.0	4.44
31.0	87.8		30.0	-1.11

6.9 (*Conversions between feet and meters*) Write a class that contains the following two methods:

```
/** Convert from feet to meters */
public static double footToMeter(double foot)

/** Convert from meters to feet */
public static double meterToFoot(double meter)
```

The formula for the conversion is:

```
meter = 0.305 * foot
foot = 3.279 * meter
```

Write a test program that invokes these methods to display the following tables:

Feet	Meters		Meters	Feet
1.0	0.305		20.0	65.574
2.0	0.610		25.0	81.967
...				
9.0	2.745		60.0	196.721
10.0	3.050		65.0	213.115

6.10 (*Use the isPrime Method*) Listing 6.7, PrimeNumberMethod.java, provides the isPrime(int number) method for testing whether a number is prime. Use this method to find the number of prime numbers less than **10000**.

6.11 (*Financial application: compute commissions*) Write a method that computes the commission, using the scheme in Programming Exercise 5.39. The header of the method is as follows:

```
public static double computeCommission(double salesAmount)
```

Write a test program that displays the following table:

Sales Amount	Commission
10000	900.0
15000	1500.0
...	
95000	11100.0
100000	11700.0

6.12 (*Display characters*) Write a method that prints characters using the following header:

```
public static void printChars(char ch1, char ch2, int
  numberPerLine)
```

This method prints the characters between **ch1** and **ch2** with the specified numbers per line. Write a test program that prints ten characters per line from **1** to **Z**. Characters are separated by exactly one space.

*6.13 (*Sum series*) Write a method to compute the following series:

$$m(i) = \frac{1}{2} + \frac{2}{3} + \cdots + \frac{i}{i+1}$$

Write a test program that displays the following table:

i	m(i)
1	0.5000
2	1.1667
...	
19	16.4023
20	17.3546

*6.14 (*Estimate* π) π can be computed using the following series:

$$m(i) = 4\left(1 - \frac{1}{3} + \frac{1}{5} - \frac{1}{7} + \frac{1}{9} - \frac{1}{11} + \cdots + \frac{(-1)^{i+1}}{2i-1}\right)$$

VideoNote

Estimate π

Write a method that returns **m(i)** for a given **i** and write a test program that displays the following table:

i	m(i)
1	4.0000
101	3.1515
201	3.1466
301	3.1449
401	3.1441
501	3.1436
601	3.1433
701	3.1430
801	3.1428
901	3.1427

*6.15 (*Financial application: print a tax table*) Listing 3.5 gives a program to compute tax. Write a method for computing tax using the following header:

```
public static double computeTax(int status, double taxableIncome)
```

Use this method to write a program that prints a tax table for taxable income from $50,000 to $60,000 with intervals of $50 for all the following statuses:

Taxable Income	Single	Married Joint or Qualifying Widow(er)	Married Separate	Head of a House
50000	8688	6665	8688	7353
50050	8700	6673	8700	7365
. . .				
59950	11175	8158	11175	9840
60000	11188	8165	11188	9853

Hint: round the tax into integers using `Math.round` (i.e., `Math.round(computeTax(status, taxableIncome))`).

*6.16 (*Number of days in a year*) Write a method that returns the number of days in a year using the following header:

```
public static int numberOfDaysInAYear(int year)
```

Write a test program that displays the number of days in year from 2000 to 2020.

Sections 6.10–6.11

*6.17 (*Display matrix of 0s and 1s*) Write a method that displays an *n*-by-*n* matrix using the following header:

```
public static void printMatrix(int n)
```

Each element is 0 or 1, which is generated randomly. Write a test program that prompts the user to enter **n** and displays an *n*-by-*n* matrix. Here is a sample run:

```
Enter n: 3 ↵Enter
0 1 0
0 0 0
1 1 1
```

**6.18 (*Check password*) Some websites impose certain rules for passwords. Write a method that checks whether a string is a valid password. Suppose the password rules are as follows:

- A password must have at least eight characters.
- A password consists of only letters and digits.
- A password must contain at least two digits.

Write a program that prompts the user to enter a password and displays **Valid Password** if the rules are followed or **Invalid Password** otherwise.

*6.19 (*The* `MyTriangle` *class*) Create a class named `MyTriangle` that contains the following two methods:

```
/** Return true if the sum of any two sides is
 *  greater than the third side. */
public static boolean isValid(
  double side1, double side2, double side3)
```

```
/** Return the area of the triangle. */
public static double area(
   double side1, double side2, double side3)
```

Write a test program that reads three sides for a triangle and computes the area if the input is valid. Otherwise, it displays that the input is invalid. The formula for computing the area of a triangle is given in Programming Exercise 2.19.

*6.20 (*Count the letters in a string*) Write a method that counts the number of letters in a string using the following header:

```
public static int countLetters(String s)
```

Write a test program that prompts the user to enter a string and displays the number of letters in the string.

*6.21 (*Phone keypads*) The international standard letter/number mapping for telephones is shown in Programming Exercise 4.15. Write a method that returns a number, given an uppercase letter, as follows:

```
int getNumber(char uppercaseLetter)
```

Write a test program that prompts the user to enter a phone number as a string. The input number may contain letters. The program translates a letter (uppercase or lowercase) to a digit and leaves all other characters intact. Here is a sample run of the program:

```
Enter a string: 1-800-Flowers  ↵Enter
1-800-3569377
```

```
Enter a string: 1800flowers  ↵Enter
18003569377
```

6.22 (*Math: approximate the square root*) There are several techniques for implementing the **sqrt method in the **Math** class. One such technique is known as the *Babylonian method*. It approximates the square root of a number, **n**, by repeatedly performing a calculation using the following formula:

```
nextGuess = (lastGuess + n / lastGuess) / 2
```

When **nextGuess** and **lastGuess** are almost identical, **nextGuess** is the approximated square root. The initial guess can be any positive value (e.g., **1**). This value will be the starting value for **lastGuess**. If the difference between **nextGuess** and **lastGuess** is less than a very small number, such as **0.0001**, you can claim that **nextGuess** is the approximated square root of **n**. If not, **next-Guess** becomes **lastGuess** and the approximation process continues. Implement the following method that returns the square root of **n**.

```
public static double sqrt(long n)
```

*6.23 (*Occurrences of a specified character*) Write a method that finds the number of occurrences of a specified character in a string using the following header:

```
public static int count(String str, char a)
```

For example, `count("Welcome", 'e')` returns `2`. Write a test program that prompts the user to enter a string followed by a character and displays the number of occurrences of the character in the string.

Sections 6.10–6.12

**6.24 (*Display current date and time*) Listing 2.7, ShowCurrentTime.java, displays the current time. Improve this example to display the current date and time. The calendar example in Listing 6.12, PrintCalendar.java, should give you some ideas on how to find the year, month, and day.

**6.25 (*Convert milliseconds to hours, minutes, and seconds*) Write a method that converts milliseconds to hours, minutes, and seconds using the following header:

```java
public static String convertMillis(long millis)
```

The method returns a string as *hours:minutes:seconds*. For example, `convertMillis(5500)` returns a string `0:0:5`, `convertMillis(100000)` returns a string `0:1:40`, and `convertMillis(555550000)` returns a string `154:19:10`.

Comprehensive

**6.26 (*Palindromic prime*) A *palindromic prime* is a prime number and also palindromic. For example, 131 is a prime and also a palindromic prime, as are 313 and 757. Write a program that displays the first 100 palindromic prime numbers. Display 10 numbers per line, separated by exactly one space, as follows:

```
2  3  5  7  11  101  131  151  181  191
313  353  373  383  727  757  787  797  919  929
...
```

**6.27 (*Emirp*) An *emirp* (prime spelled backward) is a nonpalindromic prime number whose reversal is also a prime. For example, 17 is a prime and 71 is a prime, so 17 and 71 are emirps. Write a program that displays the first 100 emirps. Display 10 numbers per line, separated by exactly one space, as follows:

```
13  17  31  37  71  73  79  97  107  113
149  157  167  179  199  311  337  347  359  389
...
```

**6.28 (*Mersenne prime*) A prime number is called a *Mersenne prime* if it can be written in the form $2^p - 1$ for some positive integer p. Write a program that finds all Mersenne primes with $p \leq 31$ and displays the output as follows:

p	2^p – 1
2	3
3	7
5	31
...	

**6.29 (*Twin primes*) Twin primes are a pair of prime numbers that differ by 2. For example, 3 and 5 are twin primes, 5 and 7 are twin primes, and 11 and 13 are twin primes. Write a program to find all twin primes less than 1,000. Display the output as follows:

```
(3, 5)
(5, 7)
...
```

**6.30 (*Game: craps*) Craps is a popular dice game played in casinos. Write a program to play a variation of the game, as follows:

Roll two dice. Each die has six faces representing values 1, 2, …, and 6, respectively. Check the sum of the two dice. If the sum is 2, 3, or 12 (called *craps*), you lose; if the sum is 7 or 11 (called *natural*), you win; if the sum is another value (i.e., 4, 5, 6, 8, 9, or 10), a point is established. Continue to roll the dice until either a 7 or the same point value is rolled. If 7 is rolled, you lose. Otherwise, you win.

Your program acts as a single player. Here are some sample runs.

```
You rolled 5 + 6 = 11
You win
```

```
You rolled 1 + 2 = 3
You lose
```

```
You rolled 4 + 4 = 8
point is 8
You rolled 6 + 2 = 8
You win
```

```
You rolled 3 + 2 = 5
point is 5
You rolled 2 + 5 = 7
You lose
```

**6.31 (*Financial: credit card number validation*) Credit card numbers follow certain patterns. A credit card number must have between 13 and 16 digits. It must start with:

- 4 for Visa cards
- 5 for Master cards
- 37 for American Express cards
- 6 for Discover cards

In 1954, Hans Luhn of IBM proposed an algorithm for validating credit card numbers. The algorithm is useful to determine whether a card number is entered correctly or whether a credit card is scanned correctly by a scanner. Credit card numbers are generated following this validity check, commonly known as the *Luhn check* or the *Mod 10 check,* which can be described as follows (for illustration, consider the card number 4388576018402626):

1. Double every second digit from right to left. If doubling of a digit results in a two-digit number, add up the two digits to get a single-digit number.

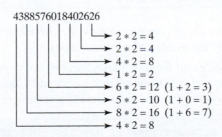

4388576018402626

$$2 * 2 = 4$$
$$2 * 2 = 4$$
$$4 * 2 = 8$$
$$1 * 2 = 2$$
$$6 * 2 = 12 \ (1 + 2 = 3)$$
$$5 * 2 = 10 \ (1 + 0 = 1)$$
$$8 * 2 = 16 \ (1 + 6 = 7)$$
$$4 * 2 = 8$$

2. Now add all single-digit numbers from Step 1.

$$4 + 4 + 8 + 2 + 3 + 1 + 7 + 8 = 37$$

3. Add all digits in the odd places from right to left in the card number.

$$6 + 6 + 0 + 8 + 0 + 7 + 8 + 3 = 38$$

4. Sum the results from Step 2 and Step 3.

$$37 + 38 = 75$$

5. If the result from Step 4 is divisible by 10, the card number is valid; otherwise, it is invalid. For example, the number 4388576018402626 is invalid, but the number 4388576018410707 is valid.

Write a program that prompts the user to enter a credit card number as a **long** integer. Display whether the number is valid or invalid. Design your program to use the following methods:

```
/** Return true if the card number is valid */
public static boolean isValid(long number)

/** Get the result from Step 2 */
public static int sumOfDoubleEvenPlace(long number)

/** Return this number if it is a single digit, otherwise,
 * return the sum of the two digits */
public static int getDigit(int number)

/** Return sum of odd-place digits in number */
public static int sumOfOddPlace(long number)

/** Return true if the digit d is a prefix for number */
public static boolean prefixMatched(long number, int d)

/** Return the number of digits in d */
public static int getSize(long d)

/** Return the first k number of digits from number. If the
 * number of digits in number is less than k, return number. */
public static long getPrefix(long number, int k)
```

Here are sample runs of the program: (You may also implement this program by reading the input as a string and processing the string to validate the credit card.)

```
Enter a credit card number as a long integer:
    4388576018410707  ↵Enter
4388576018410707 is valid
```

```
Enter a credit card number as a long integer:
    4388576018402626  ↵Enter
4388576018402626 is invalid
```

**6.32 (*Game: chance of winning at craps*) Revise Exercise 6.30 to run it 10,000 times and display the number of winning games.

6.33 (*Current date and time*) Invoking **System.currentTimeMillis() returns the elapsed time in milliseconds since midnight of January 1, 1970. Write a program that displays the date and time. Here is a sample run:

```
Current date and time is May 16, 2012 10:34:23
```

**6.34 (*Print calendar*) Programming Exercise 3.21 uses Zeller's congruence to calculate the day of the week. Simplify Listing 6.12, PrintCalendar.java, using Zeller's algorithm to get the start day of the month.

6.35 (*Geometry: area of a pentagon*) The area of a pentagon can be computed using the following formula:

$$Area = \frac{5 \times s^2}{4 \times \tan\left(\dfrac{\pi}{5}\right)}$$

Write a method that returns the area of a pentagon using the following header:

```
public static double area(double side)
```

Write a main method that prompts the user to enter the side of a pentagon and displays its area. Here is a sample run:

```
Enter the side: 5.5  Enter
The area of the pentagon is 52.04444136781625
```

*6.36 (*Geometry: area of a regular polygon*) A regular polygon is an *n*-sided polygon in which all sides are of the same length and all angles have the same degree (i.e., the polygon is both equilateral and equiangular). The formula for computing the area of a regular polygon is

$$Area = \frac{n \times s^2}{4 \times \tan\left(\dfrac{\pi}{n}\right)}$$

Write a method that returns the area of a regular polygon using the following header:

```
public static double area(int n, double side)
```

Write a main method that prompts the user to enter the number of sides and the side of a regular polygon and displays its area. Here is a sample run:

```
Enter the number of sides: 5  Enter
Enter the side: 6.5  Enter
The area of the polygon is 72.69017017488385
```

6.37 (*Format an integer*) Write a method with the following header to format the integer with the specified width.

```
public static String format(int number, int width)
```

The method returns a string for the number with one or more prefix 0s. The size of the string is the width. For example, **format(34, 4)** returns **0034** and **format(34, 5)** returns **00034**. If the number is longer than the width, the method returns the string representation for the number. For example, `format(34, 1)` returns `34`.

Write a test program that prompts the user to enter a number and its width and displays a string returned by invoking `format(number, width)`.

*6.38 (*Generate random characters*) Use the methods in **RandomCharacter** in Listing 6.10 to print 100 uppercase letters and then 100 single digits, printing ten per line.

6.39 (*Geometry: point position*) Programming Exercise 3.32 shows how to test whether a point is on the left side of a directed line, on the right, or on the same line. Write the methods with the following headers:

```
/** Return true if point (x2, y2) is on the left side of the
 *  directed line from (x0, y0) to (x1, y1) */
public static boolean leftOfTheLine(double x0, double y0,
  double x1, double y1, double x2, double y2)

/** Return true if point (x2, y2) is on the same
 *  line from (x0, y0) to (x1, y1) */
public static boolean onTheSameLine(double x0, double y0,
  double x1, double y1, double x2, double y2)

/** Return true if point (x2, y2) is on the
 *  line segment from (x0, y0) to (x1, y1) */
public static boolean onTheLineSegment(double x0, double y0,
  double x1, double y1, double x2, double y2)
```

Write a program that prompts the user to enter the three points for **p0**, **p1**, and **p2** and displays whether **p2** is on the left of the line from **p0** to **p1**, right, the same line, or on the line segment. Here are some sample runs:

```
Enter three points for p0, p1, and p2: 1 1 2 2 1.5 1.5  ↵Enter
(1.5, 1.5) is on the line segment from (1.0, 1.0) to (2.0, 2.0)
```

```
Enter three points for p0, p1, and p2: 1 1 2 2 3 3  ↵Enter
(3.0, 3.0) is on the same line from (1.0, 1.0) to (2.0, 2.0)
```

```
Enter three points for p0, p1, and p2: 1 1 2 2 1 1.5  ↵Enter
(1.0, 1.5) is on the left side of the line
  from (1.0, 1.0) to (2.0, 2.0)
```

```
Enter three points for p0, p1, and p2: 1 1 2 2 1 -1  ↵Enter
(1.0, -1.0) is on the right side of the line
  from (1.0, 1.0) to (2.0, 2.0)
```

SINGLE-DIMENSIONAL ARRAYS

Objectives

- To describe why arrays are necessary in programming (§7.1).

- To declare array reference variables and create arrays (§§7.2.1–7.2.2).

- To obtain array size using `arrayRefVar.length` and know default values in an array (§7.2.3).

- To access array elements using indexes (§7.2.4).

- To declare, create, and initialize an array using an array initializer (§7.2.5).

- To program common array operations (displaying arrays, summing all elements, finding the minimum and maximum elements, random shuffling, and shifting elements) (§7.2.6).

- To simplify programming using the for each loops (§7.2.7).

- To apply arrays in application development (`AnalyzeNumbers`, `DeckOfCards`) (§§7.3–7.4).

- To copy contents from one array to another (§7.5).

- To develop and invoke methods with array arguments and return values (§§7.6–7.8).

- To define a method with a variable-length argument list (§7.9).

- To search elements using the linear (§7.10.1) or binary (§7.10.2) search algorithm.

- To sort an array using the selection sort approach (§7.11).

- To use the methods in the `java.util.Arrays` class (§7.12).

- To pass arguments to the main method from the command line (§7.13).

7.1 Introduction

A single array variable can reference a large collection of data.

problem

why array?

Often you will have to store a large number of values during the execution of a program. Suppose, for instance, that you need to read 100 numbers, compute their average, and find out how many numbers are above the average. Your program first reads the numbers and computes their average, then compares each number with the average to determine whether it is above the average. In order to accomplish this task, the numbers must all be stored in variables. You have to declare 100 variables and repeatedly write almost identical code 100 times. Writing a program this way would be impractical. So, how do you solve this problem?

An efficient, organized approach is needed. Java and most other high-level languages provide a data structure, the *array*, which stores a fixed-size sequential collection of elements of the same type. In the present case, you can store all 100 numbers into an array and access them through a single array variable.

This chapter introduces single-dimensional arrays. The next chapter will introduce two-dimensional and multidimensional arrays.

7.2 Array Basics

Once an array is created, its size is fixed. An array reference variable is used to access the elements in an array using an index.

index

An array is used to store a collection of data, but often we find it more useful to think of an array as a collection of variables of the same type. Instead of declaring individual variables, such as **number0**, **number1**, . . . , and **number99**, you declare one array variable such as **numbers** and use **numbers[0]**, **numbers[1]**, . . . , and **numbers[99]** to represent individual variables. This section introduces how to declare array variables, create arrays, and process arrays using indexes.

7.2.1 Declaring Array Variables

To use an array in a program, you must declare a variable to reference the array and specify the array's *element type*. Here is the syntax for declaring an array variable:

element type

```
elementType[] arrayRefVar;
```

The **elementType** can be any data type, and all elements in the array will have the same data type. For example, the following code declares a variable **myList** that references an array of double elements.

```
double[] myList;
```

Note

You can also use **elementType arrayRefVar[]** to declare an array variable. This style comes from the C/C++ language and was adopted in Java to accommodate C/C++ programmers. The style **elementType[] arrayRefVar** is preferred.

preferred syntax

7.2.2 Creating Arrays

Unlike declarations for primitive data type variables, the declaration of an array variable does not allocate any space in memory for the array. It creates only a storage location for the reference to an array. If a variable does not contain a reference to an array, the value of the variable is **null**. You cannot assign elements to an array unless it has already been created. After an

null

array variable is declared, you can create an array by using the **new** operator and assign its reference to the variable with the following syntax:

```
arrayRefVar = new elementType[arraySize];
```

new operator

This statement does two things: (1) it creates an array using **new elementType[arraySize]**; (2) it assigns the reference of the newly created array to the variable **arrayRefVar**.

Declaring an array variable, creating an array, and assigning the reference of the array to the variable can be combined in one statement as:

```
elementType[] arrayRefVar = new elementType[arraySize];
```

or

```
elementType arrayRefVar[] = new elementType[arraySize];
```

Here is an example of such a statement:

```
double[] myList = new double[10];
```

This statement declares an array variable, **myList**, creates an array of ten elements of **double** type, and assigns its reference to **myList**. To assign values to the elements, use the syntax:

```
arrayRefVar[index] = value;
```

For example, the following code initializes the array.

```
myList[0] = 5.6;
myList[1] = 4.5;
myList[2] = 3.3;
myList[3] = 13.2;
myList[4] = 4.0;
myList[5] = 34.33;
myList[6] = 34.0;
myList[7] = 45.45;
myList[8] = 99.993;
myList[9] = 11123;
```

This array is illustrated in Figure 7.1.

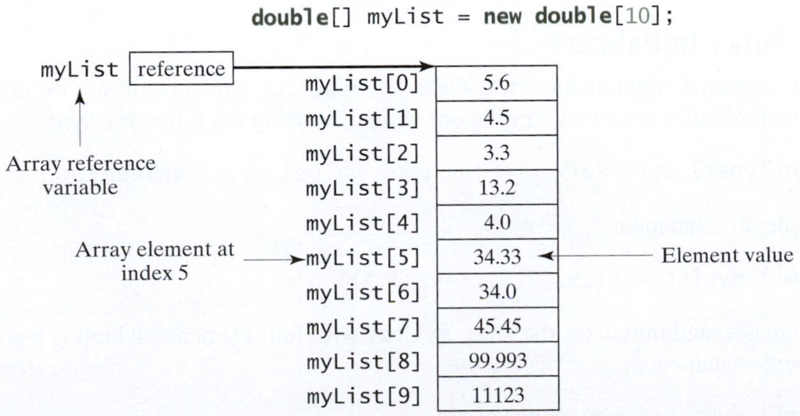

FIGURE 7.1 The array **myList** has ten elements of **double** type and **int** indices from **0** to **9**.

array vs. array variable

Note
An array variable that appears to hold an array actually contains a reference to that array. Strictly speaking, an array variable and an array are different, but most of the time the distinction can be ignored. Thus it is all right to say, for simplicity, that **myList** is an array, instead of stating, at greater length, that **myList** is a variable that contains a reference to an array of ten double elements.

7.2.3 Array Size and Default Values

array length

When space for an array is allocated, the array size must be given, specifying the number of elements that can be stored in it. The size of an array cannot be changed after the array is created. Size can be obtained using **arrayRefVar.length**. For example, **myList.length** is 10.

default values

When an array is created, its elements are assigned the default value of **0** for the numeric primitive data types, **\u0000** for **char** types, and **false** for **boolean** types.

7.2.4 Accessing Array Elements

0 based

The array elements are accessed through the index. Array indices are **0** based; that is, they range from **0** to **arrayRefVar.length-1**. In the example in Figure 7.1, **myList** holds ten **double** values, and the indices are from **0** to **9**.

indexed variable

Each element in the array is represented using the following syntax, known as an *indexed variable*:

```
arrayRefVar[index];
```

For example, **myList[9]** represents the last element in the array **myList**.

Caution
Some programming languages use parentheses to reference an array element, as in **myList(9)**, but Java uses brackets, as in **myList[9]**.

An indexed variable can be used in the same way as a regular variable. For example, the following code adds the values in **myList[0]** and **myList[1]** to **myList[2]**.

```
myList[2] = myList[0] + myList[1];
```

The following loop assigns 0 to **myList[0]**, 1 to **myList[1]**, . . . , and 9 to **myList[9]**:

```
for (int i = 0; i < myList.length; i++) {
  myList[i] = i;
}
```

7.2.5 Array Initializers

array initializer

Java has a shorthand notation, known as the *array initializer*, which combines the declaration, creation, and initialization of an array in one statement using the following syntax:

```
elementType[] arrayRefVar = {value0, value1, ..., valuek};
```

For example, the statement

```
double[] myList = {1.9, 2.9, 3.4, 3.5};
```

declares, creates, and initializes the array **myList** with four elements, which is equivalent to the following statements:

```
double[] myList = new double[4];
myList[0] = 1.9;
myList[1] = 2.9;
```

```
myList[2] = 3.4;
myList[3] = 3.5;
```

Caution

The **new** operator is not used in the array-initializer syntax. Using an array initializer, you have to declare, create, and initialize the array all in one statement. Splitting it would cause a syntax error. Thus, the next statement is wrong:

```
double[] myList;
myList = {1.9, 2.9, 3.4, 3.5};
```

7.2.6 Processing Arrays

When processing array elements, you will often use a **for** loop—for two reasons:

- All of the elements in an array are of the same type. They are evenly processed in the same fashion repeatedly using a loop.

- Since the size of the array is known, it is natural to use a **for** loop.

Assume the array is created as follows:

```
double[] myList = new double[10];
```

The following are some examples of processing arrays.

1. *Initializing arrays with input values:* The following loop initializes the array **myList** with user input values.

```
java.util.Scanner input = new java.util.Scanner(System.in);
System.out.print("Enter " + myList.length + " values: ");
for (int i = 0; i < myList.length; i++)
  myList[i] = input.nextDouble();
```

2. *Initializing arrays with random values:* The following loop initializes the array **myList** with random values between **0.0** and **100.0**, but less than **100.0**.

```
for (int i = 0; i < myList.length; i++) {
  myList[i] = Math.random() * 100;
}
```

3. *Displaying arrays:* To print an array, you have to print each element in the array using a loop like the following:

```
for (int i = 0; i < myList.length; i++) {
  System.out.print(myList[i] + " ");
}
```

Tip

For an array of the **char[]** type, it can be printed using one print statement. For example, the following code displays **Dallas**:

print character array

```
char[] city = {'D', 'a', 'l', 'l', 'a', 's'};
System.out.println(city);
```

4. *Summing all elements:* Use a variable named **total** to store the sum. Initially **total** is **0**. Add each element in the array to **total** using a loop like this:

```
double total = 0;
for (int i = 0; i < myList.length; i++) {
  total += myList[i];
}
```

5. *Finding the largest element:* Use a variable named **max** to store the largest element. Initially **max** is **myList[0]**. To find the largest element in the array **myList**, compare each element with **max**, and update **max** if the element is greater than **max**.

```java
double max = myList[0];
for (int i = 1; i < myList.length; i++) {
  if (myList[i] > max) max = myList[i];
}
```

6. *Finding the smallest index of the largest element:* Often you need to locate the largest element in an array. If an array has multiple elements with the same largest value, find the smallest index of such an element. Suppose the array **myList** is {1, 5, 3, 4, 5, 5}. The largest element is **5** and the smallest index for **5** is **1**. Use a variable named **max** to store the largest element and a variable named **indexOfMax** to denote the index of the largest element. Initially **max** is **myList[0]**, and **indexOfMax** is **0**. Compare each element in **myList** with **max**, and update **max** and **indexOfMax** if the element is greater than **max**.

```java
double max = myList[0];
int indexOfMax = 0;
for (int i = 1; i < myList.length; i++) {
  if (myList[i] > max) {
    max = myList[i];
    indexOfMax = i;
  }
}
```

Random shuffling

VideoNote

Random shuffling

7. *Random shuffling:* In many applications, you need to randomly reorder the elements in an array. This is called *shuffling*. To accomplish this, for each element **myList[i]**, randomly generate an index **j** and swap **myList[i]** with **myList[j]**, as follows:

```java
for (int i = myList.length - 1; i > 0; i--) {
  // Generate an index j randomly with 0 <= j <= i
  int j = (int)(Math.random()
    * (i + 1));

  // Swap myList[i] with myList[j]
  double temp = myList[i];
  myList[i] = myList[j];
  myList[j] = temp;
}
```

8. *Shifting elements:* Sometimes you need to shift the elements left or right. Here is an example of shifting the elements one position to the left and filling the last element with the first element:

```java
double temp = myList[0]; // Retain the first element

// Shift elements left
for (int i = 1; i < myList.length; i++) {
  myList[i - 1] = myList[i];
}

// Move the first element to fill in the last position
myList[myList.length - 1] = temp;
```

9. *Simplifying coding:* Arrays can be used to greatly simplify coding for certain tasks. For example, suppose you wish to obtain the English name of a given month by its number. If the month names are stored in an array, the month name for a given month can be

accessed simply via the index. The following code prompts the user to enter a month number and displays its month name:

```
String[] months = {"January", "February", ..., "December"};
System.out.print("Enter a month number (1 to 12): ");
int monthNumber = input.nextInt();
System.out.println("The month is " + months[monthNumber - 1]);
```

If you didn't use the **months** array, you would have to determine the month name using a lengthy multi-way **if-else** statement as follows:

```
if (monthNumber == 1)
  System.out.println("The month is January");
else if (monthNumber == 2)
  System.out.println("The month is February");
...
else
  System.out.println("The month is December");
```

7.2.7 Foreach Loops

Java supports a convenient **for** loop, known as a *foreach loop*, which enables you to traverse the array sequentially without using an index variable. For example, the following code displays all the elements in the array **myList**:

```
for (double e: myList) {
  System.out.println(e);
}
```

You can read the code as "for each element **e** in **myList**, do the following." Note that the variable, **e**, must be declared as the same type as the elements in **myList**.

In general, the syntax for a foreach loop is

```
for (elementType element: arrayRefVar) {
  // Process the element
}
```

You still have to use an index variable if you wish to traverse the array in a different order or change the elements in the array.

Caution

Accessing an array out of bounds is a common programming error that throws a runtime **ArrayIndexOutOfBoundsException**. To avoid it, make sure that you do not use an index beyond **arrayRefVar.length - 1**.

ArrayIndexOutOfBounds-
Exception

Programmers often mistakenly reference the first element in an array with index **1**, but it should be **0**. This is called the *off-by-one error*. Another common off-by-one error in a loop is using <= where < should be used. For example, the following loop is wrong.

off-by-one error

```
for (int i = 0; i <= list.length; i++)
  System.out.print(list[i] + " ");
```

The <= should be replaced by <.

7.1 How do you declare an array reference variable and how do you create an array?

7.2 When is the memory allocated for an array?

Check
Point

7.3   What is the output of the following code?

```
int x = 30;
int[] numbers = new int[x];
x = 60;
System.out.println("x is " + x);
System.out.println("The size of numbers is " + numbers.length);
```

7.4   Indicate **true** or **false** for the following statements:

- Every element in an array has the same type.

- The array size is fixed after an array reference variable is declared.

- The array size is fixed after it is created.

- The elements in an array must be a primitive data type.

7.5   Which of the following statements are valid?

```
int i = new int(30);
double d[] = new double[30];
char[] r = new char(1..30);
int i[] = (3, 4, 3, 2);
float f[] = {2.3, 4.5, 6.6};
char[] c = new char();
```

7.6   How do you access elements in an array?

7.7   What is the array index type? What is the lowest index? What is the representation of the third element in an array named **a**?

7.8   Write statements to do the following:

a.   Create an array to hold **10** double values.

b.   Assign the value **5.5** to the last element in the array.

c.   Display the sum of the first two elements.

d.   Write a loop that computes the sum of all elements in the array.

e.   Write a loop that finds the minimum element in the array.

f.   Randomly generate an index and display the element of this index in the array.

g.   Use an array initializer to create another array with the initial values **3.5**, **5.5**, **4.52**, and **5.6**.

7.9   What happens when your program attempts to access an array element with an invalid index?

7.10   Identify and fix the errors in the following code:

```
1  public class Test {
2    public static void main(String[] args) {
3      double[100] r;
4
5      for (int i = 0; i < r.length(); i++);
6        r(i) = Math.random * 100;
7    }
8  }
```

7.11   What is the output of the following code?

```
1  public class Test {
2    public static void main(String[] args) {
3      int list[] = {1, 2, 3, 4, 5, 6};
```

```
   4      for (int i = 1; i < list.length; i++)
   5        list[i] = list[i - 1];
   6
   7      for (int i = 0; i < list.length; i++)
   8        System.out.print(list[i] + " ");
   9    }
  10 }
```

7.3 Case Study: Analyzing Numbers

The problem is to write a program that finds the number of items above the average of all items.

**Key
Point**

Now you can write a program using arrays to solve the problem proposed at the beginning of this chapter. The problem is to read 100 numbers, get the average of these numbers, and find the number of the items greater than the average. To be flexible for handling any number of input, we will let the user enter the number of input, rather than fixing it to 100. Listing 7.1 gives a solution.

LISTING 7.1 AnalyzeNumbers.java

```
 1  public class AnalyzeNumbers {
 2    public static void main(String[] args) {
 3      java.util.Scanner input = new java.util.Scanner(System.in);
 4      System.out.print("Enter the number of items: ");
 5      int n = input.nextInt();
 6      double [] numbers = new double[n];
 7      double sum = 0;
 8
 9      System.out.print("Enter the numbers: ");
10      for (int i = 0; i < n; i++) {
11        numbers[i] = input.nextDouble();
12        sum += numbers[i];
13      }
14
15      double average = sum / n;
16
17      int count = 0; // The number of elements above average
18      for (int i = 0; i < n; i++)
19        if (numbers[i] > average)
20          count++;
21
22      System.out.println("Average is " + average);
23      System.out.println("Number of elements above the average is "
24        + count);
25    }
26  }
```

numbers[0]
numbers[1]:
numbers[2]:

.   create array

numbers[i]:   .

numbers[n - 3]:
numbers[n - 2]:   store number in array
numbers[n - 1]:

get average

above average?

```
Enter the number of items: 10 ↵Enter
Enter the numbers: 3.4 5 6 1 6.5 7.8 3.5 8.5 6.3 9.5 ↵Enter
Average is 5.75
Number of elements above the average is 6
```

The program prompts the user to enter the array size (line 5) and creates an array with the specified size (line 6). The program reads the input, stores numbers into the array (line 11), adds each number to **sum** in line 11, and obtains the average (line 15). It then compares each number in the array with the average to count the number of values above the average (lines 17–20).

7.4 Case Study: Deck of Cards

The problem is to create a program that will randomly select four cards from a deck of cards.

Say you want to write a program that will pick four cards at random from a deck of **52** cards. All the cards can be represented using an array named **deck**, filled with initial values **0** to **51**, as follows:

VideoNote

Deck of cards

```
int[] deck = new int[52];

// Initialize cards
for (int i = 0; i < deck.length; i++)
  deck[i] = i;
```

Card numbers **0** to **12**, **13** to **25**, **26** to **38**, and **39** to **51** represent 13 Spades, 13 Hearts, 13 Diamonds, and 13 Clubs, respectively, as shown in Figure 7.2. **cardNumber / 13** determines the suit of the card and **cardNumber % 13** determines the rank of the card, as shown in Figure 7.3. After shuffling the array **deck**, pick the first four cards from **deck**. The program displays the cards from these four card numbers.

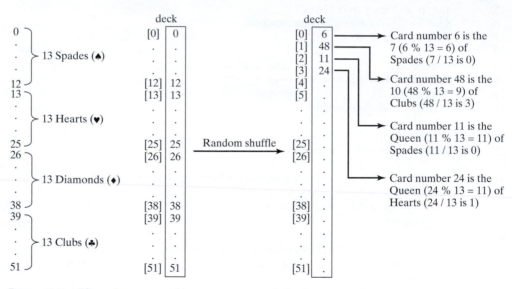

FIGURE 7.2 52 cards are stored in an array named **deck**.

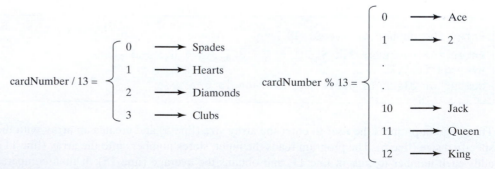

FIGURE 7.3 **CardNumber** identifies a card's suit and rank number.

Listing 7.2 gives the solution to the problem.

LISTING 7.2 DeckOfCards.java

```
1  public class DeckOfCards {
2    public static void main(String[] args) {
3      int[] deck = new int[52];                                    create array deck
4      String[] suits = {"Spades", "Hearts", "Diamonds", "Clubs"};  array of strings
5      String[] ranks = {"Ace", "2", "3", "4", "5", "6", "7", "8", "9",  array of strings
6        "10", "Jack", "Queen", "King"};
7
8      // Initialize the cards
9      for (int i = 0; i < deck.length; i++)                        initialize deck
10       deck[i] = i;
11
12     // Shuffle the cards
13     for (int i = 0; i < deck.length; i++) {                      shuffle deck
14       // Generate an index randomly
15       int index = (int)(Math.random() * deck.length);
16       int temp = deck[i];
17       deck[i] = deck[index];
18       deck[index] = temp;
19     }
20
21     // Display the first four cards
22     for (int i = 0; i < 4; i++) {
23       String suit = suits[deck[i] / 13];                         suit of a card
24       String rank = ranks[deck[i] % 13];                         rank of a card
25       System.out.println("Card number " + deck[i] + ": "
26         + rank + " of " + suit);
27     }
28   }
29 }
```

```
Card number 6: 7 of Spades
Card number 48: 10 of Clubs
Card number 11: Queen of Spades
Card number 24: Queen of Hearts
```

The program creates an array **suits** for four suits (line 4) and an array **ranks** for 13 cards in a suit (lines 5–6). Each element in these arrays is a string.

The program initializes **deck** with values **0** to **51** in lines 9–10. The **deck** value **0** represents the card Ace of Spades, **1** represents the card 2 of Spades, **13** represents the card Ace of Hearts, and **14** represents the card 2 of Hearts.

Lines 13–19 randomly shuffle the deck. After a deck is shuffled, **deck[i]** contains an arbitrary value. **deck[i] / 13** is **0, 1, 2,** or **3,** which determines the suit (line 23). **deck[i] % 13** is a value between **0** and **12,** which determines the rank (line 24). If the **suits** array is not defined, you would have to determine the suit using a lengthy multi-way **if-else** statement as follows:

```
if (deck[i] / 13 == 0)
  System.out.print("suit is Spades");
else if (deck[i] / 13 == 1)
  System.out.print("suit is Hearts");
else if (deck[i] / 13 == 2)
  System.out.print("suit is Diamonds");
else
  System.out.print("suit is Clubs");
```

With `suits = {"Spades", "Hearts", "Diamonds", "Clubs"}` created in an array, `suits[deck / 13]` gives the suit for the **deck**. Using arrays greatly simplifies the solution for this program.

7.12 Will the program pick four random cards if you replace lines 22–27 in Listing 7.2 DeckOfCards.java with the following code?

```java
for (int i = 0; i < 4; i++) {
  int cardNumber = (int)(Math.random() * deck.length);
  String suit = suits[cardNumber / 13];
  String rank = ranks[cardNumber % 13];
  System.out.println("Card number " + cardNumber + ": "
    + rank + " of " + suit);
}
```

7.5 Copying Arrays

To copy the contents of one array into another, you have to copy the array's individual elements into the other array.

Often, in a program, you need to duplicate an array or a part of an array. In such cases you could attempt to use the assignment statement (=), as follows:

```java
list2 = list1;
```

copy reference

garbage collection

However, this statement does not copy the contents of the array referenced by `list1` to `list2`, but instead merely copies the reference value from `list1` to `list2`. After this statement, `list1` and `list2` reference the same array, as shown in Figure 7.4. The array previously referenced by `list2` is no longer referenced; it becomes garbage, which will be automatically collected by the Java Virtual Machine (this process is called *garbage collection*).

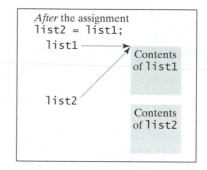

FIGURE 7.4 Before the assignment statement, `list1` and `list2` point to separate memory locations. After the assignment, the reference of the `list1` array is passed to `list2`.

In Java, you can use assignment statements to copy primitive data type variables, but not arrays. Assigning one array variable to another array variable actually copies one reference to another and makes both variables point to the same memory location.

There are three ways to copy arrays:

- Use a loop to copy individual elements one by one.

- Use the static **arraycopy** method in the **System** class.

- Use the **clone** method to copy arrays; this will be introduced in Chapter 13, Abstract Classes and Interfaces.

You can write a loop to copy every element from the source array to the corresponding element in the target array. The following code, for instance, copies **sourceArray** to **targetArray** using a **for** loop.

```java
int[] sourceArray = {2, 3, 1, 5, 10};
int[] targetArray = new int[sourceArray.length];
for (int i = 0; i < sourceArray.length; i++) {
  targetArray[i] = sourceArray[i];
}
```

Another approach is to use the **arraycopy** method in the **java.lang.System** class to copy arrays instead of using a loop. The syntax for **arraycopy** is:

arraycopy method

```java
arraycopy(sourceArray, srcPos, targetArray, tarPos, length);
```

The parameters **srcPos** and **tarPos** indicate the starting positions in **sourceArray** and **targetArray**, respectively. The number of elements copied from **sourceArray** to **targetArray** is indicated by **length**. For example, you can rewrite the loop using the following statement:

```java
System.arraycopy(sourceArray, 0, targetArray, 0, sourceArray.length);
```

The **arraycopy** method does not allocate memory space for the target array. The target array must have already been created with its memory space allocated. After the copying takes place, **targetArray** and **sourceArray** have the same content but independent memory locations.

> **Note**
> The **arraycopy** method violates the Java naming convention. By convention, this method should be named **arrayCopy** (i.e., with an uppercase C).

7.13 Use the **arraycopy** method to copy the following array to a target array **t**:

```java
int[] source = {3, 4, 5};
```

Check
Point

7.14 Once an array is created, its size cannot be changed. Does the following code resize the array?

```java
int[] myList;
myList = new int[10];
// Sometime later you want to assign a new array to myList
myList = new int[20];
```

7.6 Passing Arrays to Methods

When passing an array to a method, the reference of the array is passed to the method.

Key
Point

Just as you can pass primitive type values to methods, you can also pass arrays to methods. For example, the following method displays the elements in an **int** array:

```java
public static void printArray(int[] array) {
  for (int i = 0; i < array.length; i++) {
    System.out.print(array[i] + " ");
  }
}
```

You can invoke it by passing an array. For example, the following statement invokes the **printArray** method to display 3, 1, 2, 6, 4, and 2.

```java
printArray(new int[]{3, 1, 2, 6, 4, 2});
```

Note

The preceding statement creates an array using the following syntax:

new elementType[]{value0, value1, ..., value*k*};

anonymous array

There is no explicit reference variable for the array. Such array is called an *anonymous array*.

pass-by-value

Java uses *pass-by-value* to pass arguments to a method. There are important differences between passing the values of variables of primitive data types and passing arrays.

- For an argument of a primitive type, the argument's value is passed.

pass-by-sharing

- For an argument of an array type, the value of the argument is a reference to an array; this reference value is passed to the method. Semantically, it can be best described as *pass-by-sharing*, that is, the array in the method is the same as the array being passed. Thus, if you change the array in the method, you will see the change outside the method.

Take the following code, for example:

```java
public class Test {
  public static void main(String[] args) {
    int x = 1; // x represents an int value
    int[] y = new int[10]; // y represents an array of int values

    m(x, y); // Invoke m with arguments x and y

    System.out.println("x is " + x);
    System.out.println("y[0] is " + y[0]);
  }

  public static void m(int number, int[] numbers) {
    number = 1001; // Assign a new value to number
    numbers[0] = 5555; // Assign a new value to numbers[0]
  }
}
```

```
x is 1
y[0] is 5555
```

You may wonder why after **m** is invoked, **x** remains **1**, but **y[0]** become **5555**. This is because **y** and **numbers**, although they are independent variables, reference the same array, as illustrated in Figure 7.5. When **m(x, y)** is invoked, the values of **x** and **y** are passed to **number** and **numbers**. Since **y** contains the reference value to the array, **numbers** now contains the same reference value to the same array.

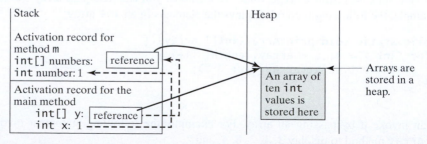

FIGURE 7.5 The primitive type value in **x** is passed to **number**, and the reference value in **y** is passed to **numbers**.

Note

Arrays are objects in Java (objects are introduced in Chapter 9). The JVM stores the objects in an area of memory called the *heap*, which is used for dynamic memory allocation.

heap

Listing 7.3 gives another program that shows the difference between passing a primitive data type value and an array reference variable to a method.

The program contains two methods for swapping elements in an array. The first method, named **swap**, fails to swap two **int** arguments. The second method, named **swapFirst-TwoInArray**, successfully swaps the first two elements in the array argument.

LISTING 7.3   TestPassArray.java

```java
 1  public class TestPassArray {
 2    /** Main method */
 3    public static void main(String[] args) {
 4      int[] a = {1, 2};
 5
 6      // Swap elements using the swap method
 7      System.out.println("Before invoking swap");
 8      System.out.println("array is {" + a[0] + ", " + a[1] + "}");
 9      swap(a[0], a[1]);
10      System.out.println("After invoking swap");
11      System.out.println("array is {" + a[0] + ", " + a[1] + "}");
12
13      // Swap elements using the swapFirstTwoInArray method
14      System.out.println("Before invoking swapFirstTwoInArray");
15      System.out.println("array is {" + a[0] + ", " + a[1] + "}");
16      swapFirstTwoInArray(a);
17      System.out.println("After invoking swapFirstTwoInArray");
18      System.out.println("array is {" + a[0] + ", " + a[1] + "}");
19    }
20
21    /** Swap two variables */
22    public static void swap(int n1, int n2) {
23      int temp = n1;
24      n1 = n2;
25      n2 = temp;
26    }
27
28    /** Swap the first two elements in the array */
29    public static void swapFirstTwoInArray(int[] array) {
30      int temp = array[0];
31      array[0] = array[1];
32      array[1] = temp;
33    }
34  }
```

false swap

swap array elements

```
Before invoking swap
array is {1, 2}
After invoking swap
array is {1, 2}
Before invoking swapFirstTwoInArray
array is {1, 2}
After invoking swapFirstTwoInArray
array is {2, 1}
```

As shown in Figure 7.6, the two elements are not swapped using the **swap** method. However, they are swapped using the **swapFirstTwoInArray** method. Since the parameters in the **swap** method are primitive type, the values of **a[0]** and **a[1]** are passed to **n1** and **n2** inside the method when invoking **swap(a[0], a[1])**. The memory locations for **n1** and **n2** are independent of the ones for **a[0]** and **a[1]**. The contents of the array are not affected by this call.

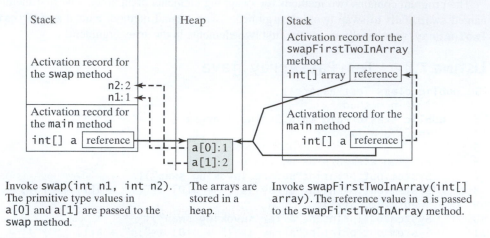

Invoke swap(int n1, int n2). The primitive type values in a[0] and a[1] are passed to the swap method.

The arrays are stored in a heap.

Invoke swapFirstTwoInArray(int[] array). The reference value in a is passed to the swapFirstTwoInArray method.

FIGURE 7.6 When passing an array to a method, the reference of the array is passed to the method.

The parameter in the **swapFirstTwoInArray** method is an array. As shown in Figure 7.6, the reference of the array is passed to the method. Thus the variables **a** (outside the method) and **array** (inside the method) both refer to the same array in the same memory location. Therefore, swapping **array[0]** with **array[1]** inside the method **swapFirstTwoInArray** is the same as swapping **a[0]** with **a[1]** outside of the method.

7.7 Returning an Array from a Method

When a method returns an array, the reference of the array is returned.

You can pass arrays when invoking a method. A method may also return an array. For example, the following method returns an array that is the reversal of another array.

create array

return array

```
 1  public static int[] reverse(int[] list) {
 2    int[] result = new int[list.length];
 3
 4    for (int i = 0, j = result.length - 1;
 5         i < list.length; i++, j--) {
 6      result[j] = list[i];
 7    }
 8
 9    return result;
10  }
```

Line 2 creates a new array **result**. Lines 4–7 copy elements from array **list** to array **result**. Line 9 returns the array. For example, the following statement returns a new array **list2** with elements **6, 5, 4, 3, 2, 1**.

```
int[] list1 = {1, 2, 3, 4, 5, 6};
int[] list2 = reverse(list1);
```

7.15 Suppose the following code is written to reverse the contents in an array, explain why it is wrong. How do you fix it?

```java
int[] list = {1, 2, 3, 5, 4};

for (int i = 0, j = list.length - 1; i < list.length; i++, j--) {
  // Swap list[i] with list[j]
  int temp = list[i];
  list[i] = list[j];
  list[j] = temp;
}
```

7.8 Case Study: Counting the Occurrences of Each Letter

This section presents a program to count the occurrences of each letter in an array of characters.

The program given in Listing 7.4 does the following:

1. Generates **100** lowercase letters randomly and assigns them to an array of characters, as shown in Figure 7.7a. You can obtain a random letter by using the **getRandomLower-CaseLetter()** method in the **RandomCharacter** class in Listing 6.10.

2. Count the occurrences of each letter in the array. To do so, create an array, say **counts**, of **26 int** values, each of which counts the occurrences of a letter, as shown in Figure 7.7b. That is, **counts[0]** counts the number of **a**'s, **counts[1]** counts the number of **b**'s, and so on.

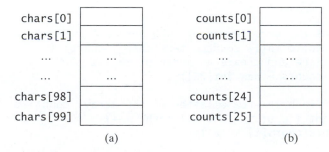

FIGURE 7.7 The **chars** array stores **100** characters, and the **counts** array stores **26** counts, each of which counts the occurrences of a letter.

LISTING 7.4 CountLettersInArray.java

```java
1  public class CountLettersInArray {
2    /** Main method */
3    public static void main(String[] args) {
4      // Declare and create an array
5      char[] chars = createArray();                            create array
6
7      // Display the array
8      System.out.println("The lowercase letters are:");
9      displayArray(chars);                                     pass array
10
```

return array

pass array

increase count

```
11       // Count the occurrences of each letter
12       int[] counts = countLetters(chars);
13
14       // Display counts
15       System.out.println();
16       System.out.println("The occurrences of each letter are:");
17       displayCounts(counts);
18    }
19
20    /** Create an array of characters */
21    public static char[] createArray() {
22       // Declare an array of characters and create it
23       char[] chars = new char[100];
24
25       // Create lowercase letters randomly and assign
26       // them to the array
27       for (int i = 0; i < chars.length; i++)
28          chars[i] = RandomCharacter.getRandomLowerCaseLetter();
29
30       // Return the array
31       return chars;
32    }
33
34    /** Display the array of characters */
35    public static void displayArray(char[] chars) {
36       // Display the characters in the array 20 on each line
37       for (int i = 0; i < chars.length; i++) {
38          if ((i + 1) % 20 == 0)
39             System.out.println(chars[i]);
40          else
41             System.out.print(chars[i] + " ");
42       }
43    }
44
45    /** Count the occurrences of each letter */
46    public static int[] countLetters(char[] chars) {
47       // Declare and create an array of 26 int
48       int[] counts = new int[26];
49
50       // For each lowercase letter in the array, count it
51       for (int i = 0; i < chars.length; i++)
52          counts[chars[i] - 'a']++;
53
54       return counts;
55    }
56
57    /** Display counts */
58    public static void displayCounts(int[] counts) {
59       for (int i = 0; i < counts.length; i++) {
60          if ((i + 1) % 10 == 0)
61             System.out.println(counts[i] + " " + (char)(i + 'a'));
62          else
63             System.out.print(counts[i] + " " + (char)(i + 'a') + " ");
64       }
65    }
66 }
```

```
The lowercase letters are:
e y l s r i b k j v j h a b z n w b t v
s c c k r d w a m p w v u n q a m p l o
a z g d e g f i n d x m z o u l o z j v
h w i w n t g x w c d o t x h y v z y z
q e a m f w p g u q t r e n n w f c r f

The occurrences of each letter are:
5 a 3 b 4 c 4 d 4 e 4 f 4 g 3 h 3 i 3 j
2 k 3 l 4 m 6 n 4 o 3 p 3 q 4 r 2 s 4 t
3 u 5 v 8 w 3 x 3 y 6 z
```

The **createArray** method (lines 21–32) generates an array of **100** random lowercase letters. Line 5 invokes the method and assigns the array to **chars**. What would be wrong if you rewrote the code as follows?

```
char[] chars = new char[100];
chars = createArray();
```

You would be creating two arrays. The first line would create an array by using **new char[100]**. The second line would create an array by invoking **createArray()** and assign the reference of the array to **chars**. The array created in the first line would be garbage because it is no longer referenced, and as mentioned earlier Java automatically collects garbage behind the scenes. Your program would compile and run correctly, but it would create an array unnecessarily.

Invoking **getRandomLowerCaseLetter()** (line 28) returns a random lowercase letter. This method is defined in the **RandomCharacter** class in Listing 6.10.

The **countLetters** method (lines 46–55) returns an array of **26 int** values, each of which stores the number of occurrences of a letter. The method processes each letter in the array and increases its count by one. A brute-force approach to count the occurrences of each letter might be as follows:

```
for (int i = 0; i < chars.length; i++)
  if (chars[i] == 'a')
    counts[0]++;
  else if (chars[i] == 'b')
    counts[1]++;
  ...
```

But a better solution is given in lines 51–52.

```
for (int i = 0; i < chars.length; i++)
  counts[chars[i] - 'a']++;
```

If the letter (**chars[i]**) is **a**, the corresponding count is **counts['a' - 'a']** (i.e., **counts[0]**). If the letter is **b**, the corresponding count is **counts['b' - 'a']** (i.e., **counts[1]**), since the Unicode of **b** is one more than that of **a**. If the letter is **z**, the corresponding count is **counts['z' - 'a']** (i.e., **counts[25]**), since the Unicode of **z** is **25** more than that of **a**.

Figure 7.8 shows the call stack and heap *during* and *after* executing **createArray**. See Checkpoint Question 7.18 to show the call stack and heap for other methods in the program.

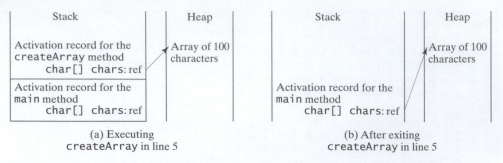

| Stack | Heap | Stack | Heap |

(a) Executing
createArray in line 5

(b) After exiting
createArray in line 5

FIGURE 7.8 (a) An array of 100 characters is created when executing **createArray**. (b) This array is returned and assigned to the variable **chars** in the **main** method.

Check Point

7.16 True or false? When an array is passed to a method, a new array is created and passed to the method.

7.17 Show the output of the following two programs:

```java
public class Test {
  public static void main(String[] args) {
    int number = 0;
    int[] numbers = new int[1];

    m(number, numbers);

    System.out.println("number is " + number
      + " and numbers[0] is " + numbers[0]);
  }

  public static void m(int x, int[] y) {
    x = 3;
    y[0] = 3;
  }
}
```

(a)

```java
public class Test {
  public static void main(String[] args) {
    int[] list = {1, 2, 3, 4, 5};
    reverse(list);
    for (int i = 0; i < list.length; i++)
      System.out.print(list[i] + " ");
  }

  public static void reverse(int[] list) {
    int[] newList = new int[list.length];

    for (int i = 0; i < list.length; i++)
      newList[i] = list[list.length - 1 - i];

    list = newList;
  }
}
```

(b)

7.18 Where are the arrays stored during execution? Show the contents of the stack and heap during and after executing **displayArray**, **countLetters**, **displayCounts** in Listing 7.4.

7.9 Variable-Length Argument Lists

Key Point

A variable number of arguments of the same type can be passed to a method and treated as an array.

You can pass a variable number of arguments of the same type to a method. The parameter in the method is declared as follows:

```
typeName... parameterName
```

In the method declaration, you specify the type followed by an ellipsis (...). Only one variable-length parameter may be specified in a method, and this parameter must be the last parameter. Any regular parameters must precede it.

Java treats a variable-length parameter as an array. You can pass an array or a variable number of arguments to a variable-length parameter. When invoking a method with a variable number of arguments, Java creates an array and passes the arguments to it. Listing 7.5 contains a method that prints the maximum value in a list of an unspecified number of values.

LISTING 7.5 VarArgsDemo.java

```java
 1  public class VarArgsDemo {
 2    public static void main(String[] args) {
 3      printMax(34, 3, 3, 2, 56.5);
 4      printMax(new double[]{1, 2, 3});
 5    }
 6
 7    public static void printMax(double... numbers) {
 8      if (numbers.length == 0) {
 9        System.out.println("No argument passed");
10        return;
11      }
12
13      double result = numbers[0];
14
15      for (int i = 1; i < numbers.length; i++)
16        if (numbers[i] > result)
17          result = numbers[i];
18
19      System.out.println("The max value is " + result);
20    }
21  }
```

pass variable-length arg list
pass an array arg

a variable-length arg
  parameter

Line 3 invokes the `printMax` method with a variable-length argument list passed to the array `numbers`. If no arguments are passed, the length of the array is `0` (line 8).

Line 4 invokes the `printMax` method with an array.

7.19 What is wrong in the following method header?

```java
public static void print(String... strings, double... numbers)
public static void print(double... numbers, String name)
public static double... print(double d1, double d2)
```

Check
Point

7.20 Can you invoke the `printMax` method in Listing 7.5 using the following statements?

```java
printMax(1, 2, 2, 1, 4);
printMax(new double[]{1, 2, 3});
printMax(new int[]{1, 2, 3});
```

7.10 Searching Arrays

If an array is sorted, binary search is more efficient than linear search for finding an element in the array.

Key
Point

Searching is the process of looking for a specific element in an array—for example, discovering whether a certain score is included in a list of scores. Searching is a common task in computer programming. Many algorithms and data structures are devoted to searching. This section discusses two commonly used approaches, *linear search* and *binary search*.

linear search
binary search

7.10.1 The Linear Search Approach

The linear search approach compares the key element **key** sequentially with each element in the array. It continues to do so until the key matches an element in the array or the array is exhausted without a match being found. If a match is made, the linear search returns the index

linear search animation on Companion Website

of the element in the array that matches the key. If no match is found, the search returns -1. The **linearSearch** method in Listing 7.6 gives the solution.

LISTING 7.6 **LinearSearch.java**

```java
1 public class LinearSearch {
2   /** The method for finding a key in the list */
3   public static int linearSearch(int[] list, int key) {
4     for (int i = 0; i < list.length; i++) {
5       if (key == list[i])
6         return i;
7     }
8     return -1;
9   }
10 }
```

```
                              [0] [1] [2] …
                         list ┌──┬──┬──┬─────┬──┐
                              └──┴──┴──┴─────┴──┘
                         key  Compare key with list[i] for i = 0, 1, …
```

To better understand this method, trace it with the following statements:

```java
1 int[] list = {1, 4, 4, 2, 5, -3, 6, 2};
2 int i = linearSearch(list, 4);   // Returns 1
3 int j = linearSearch(list, -4);  // Returns -1
4 int k = linearSearch(list, -3);  // Returns 5
```

The linear search method compares the key with each element in the array. The elements can be in any order. On average, the algorithm will have to examine half of the elements in an array before finding the key, if it exists. Since the execution time of a linear search increases linearly as the number of array elements increases, linear search is inefficient for a large array.

7.10.2 The Binary Search Approach

Binary search is the other common search approach for a list of values. For binary search to work, the elements in the array must already be ordered. Assume that the array is in ascending order. The binary search first compares the key with the element in the middle of the array. Consider the following three cases:

- If the key is less than the middle element, you need to continue to search for the key only in the first half of the array.

- If the key is equal to the middle element, the search ends with a match.

- If the key is greater than the middle element, you need to continue to search for the key only in the second half of the array.

Clearly, the binary search method eliminates at least half of the array after each comparison. Sometimes you eliminate half of the elements, and sometimes you eliminate half plus one. Suppose that the array has *n* elements. For convenience, let **n** be a power of **2**. After the first comparison, **n/2** elements are left for further search; after the second comparison, **(n/2)/2** elements are left. After the **k**th comparison, **n/2^k** elements are left for further search. When **k = log$_2$n**, only one element is left in the array, and you need only one more comparison. Therefore, in the worst case when using the binary search approach, you need **log$_2$n+1** comparisons to find an element in the sorted array. In the worst case for a list of **1024** (2^{10}) elements, binary search requires only **11** comparisons, whereas a linear search requires **1023** comparisons in the worst case.

binary search animation on Companion Website

The portion of the array being searched shrinks by half after each comparison. Let **low** and **high** denote, respectively, the first index and last index of the array that is currently being searched. Initially, **low** is **0** and **high** is **list.length−1**. Let **mid** denote the index of the middle element, so **mid** is **(low + high)/2**. Figure 7.9 shows how to find key **11** in the list {2, 4, 7, 10, 11, 45, 50, 59, 60, 66, 69, 70, 79} using binary search.

You now know how the binary search works. The next task is to implement it in Java. Don't rush to give a complete implementation. Implement it incrementally, one step at a time. You may start with the first iteration of the search, as shown in Figure 7.10a. It compares the key with the middle element in the list whose `low` index is `0` and `high` index is `list.length - 1`. If `key < list[mid]`, set the `high` index to `mid - 1`; if `key == list[mid]`, a match is found and return `mid`; if `key > list[mid]`, set the `low` index to `mid + 1`.

Next consider implementing the method to perform the search repeatedly by adding a loop, as shown in Figure 7.10b. The search ends if the key is found, or if the key is not found when `low > high`.

When the key is not found, `low` is the insertion point where a key would be inserted to maintain the order of the list. It is more useful to return the insertion point than `-1`. The method must return a negative value to indicate that the key is not in the list. Can it simply return `-low`? No. If the key is less than `list[0]`, `low` would be `0`. `-0` is `0`. This would indicate that the key matches `list[0]`. A good choice is to let the method return `-low - 1` if the key is not in the list. Returning `-low - 1` indicates not only that the key is not in the list, but also where the key would be inserted.

why not −1?

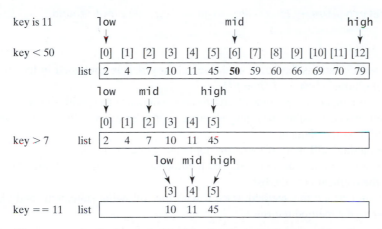

FIGURE 7.9 Binary search eliminates half of the list from further consideration after each comparison.

```java
public static int binarySearch(
    int[] list, int key) {
  int low = 0;
  int high = list.length - 1;


  int mid = (low + high) / 2;
  if (key < list[mid])
    high = mid - 1;
  else if (key == list[mid])
    return mid;
  else
    low = mid + 1;



}
```

(a) Version 1

```java
public static int binarySearch(
    int[] list, int key) {
  int low = 0;
  int high = list.length - 1;

  while (high >= low) {
    int mid = (low + high) / 2;
    if (key < list[mid])
      high = mid - 1;
    else if (key == list[mid])
      return mid;
    else
      low = mid + 1;
  }

  return -1; // Not found
}
```

(b) Version 2

FIGURE 7.10 Binary search is implemented incrementally.

The complete program is given in Listing 7.7.

LISTING 7.7 BinarySearch.java

```java
1  public class BinarySearch {
2    /** Use binary search to find the key in the list */
3    public static int binarySearch(int[] list, int key) {
4      int low = 0;
5      int high = list.length - 1;
6
7      while (high >= low) {
8        int mid = (low + high) / 2;
9        if (key < list[mid])
10         high = mid - 1;
11       else if (key == list[mid])
12         return mid;
13       else
14         low = mid + 1;
15     }
16
17     return -low - 1; // Now high < low, key not found
18   }
19 }
```

first half *(line 10)*

second half *(line 14)*

The binary search returns the index of the search key if it is contained in the list (line 12). Otherwise, it returns **-low - 1** (line 17).

What would happen if we replaced **(high >= low)** in line 7 with **(high > low)**? The search would miss a possible matching element. Consider a list with just one element. The search would miss the element.

Does the method still work if there are duplicate elements in the list? Yes, as long as the elements are sorted in increasing order. The method returns the index of one of the matching elements if the element is in the list.

To better understand this method, trace it with the following statements and identify **low** and **high** when the method returns.

```java
int[] list = {2, 4, 7, 10, 11, 45, 50, 59, 60, 66, 69, 70, 79};
int i = BinarySearch.binarySearch(list, 2); // Returns 0
int j = BinarySearch.binarySearch(list, 11); // Returns 4
int k = BinarySearch.binarySearch(list, 12); // Returns -6
int l = BinarySearch.binarySearch(list, 1); // Returns -1
int m = BinarySearch.binarySearch(list, 3); // Returns -2
```

Here is the table that lists the **low** and **high** values when the method exits and the value returned from invoking the method.

Method	Low	High	Value Returned
binarySearch(list, 2)	0	1	0
binarySearch(list, 11)	3	5	4
binarySearch(list, 12)	5	4	-6
binarySearch(list, 1)	0	-1	-1
binarySearch(list, 3)	1	0	-2

Note

Linear search is useful for finding an element in a small array or an unsorted array, but it is inefficient for large arrays. Binary search is more efficient, but it requires that the array be presorted.

binary search benefits

7.21 If **high** is a very large integer such as the maximum **int** value **2147483647**, **(low + high) / 2** may cause overflow. How do you fix it to avoid overflow?

7.22 Use Figure 7.9 as an example to show how to apply the binary search approach to a search for key **10** and key **12** in list {**2, 4, 7, 10, 11, 45, 50, 59, 60, 66, 69, 70, 79**}.

7.23 If the binary search method returns **-4**, is the key in the list? Where should the key be inserted if you wish to insert the key into the list?

7.11 Sorting Arrays

Sorting, like searching, is a common task in computer programming. Many different algorithms have been developed for sorting. This section introduces an intuitive sorting algorithm: selection sort.

Key Point

VideoNote

Selection sort

selection sort

Suppose that you want to sort a list in ascending order. Selection sort finds the smallest number in the list and swaps it with the first element. It then finds the smallest number remaining and swaps it with the second element, and so on, until only a single number remains. Figure 7.11 shows how to sort the list {**2, 9, 5, 4, 8, 1, 6**} using selection sort.

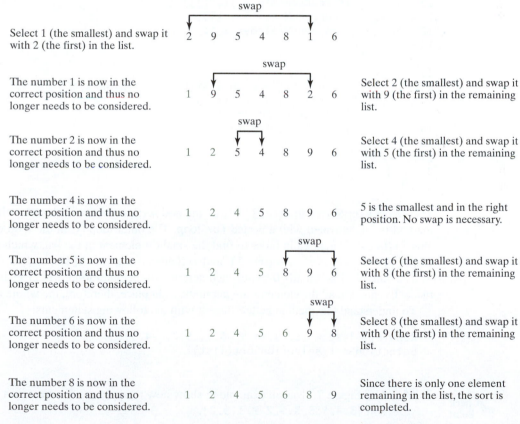

FIGURE 7.11 Selection sort repeatedly selects the smallest number and swaps it with the first number in the list.

You know how the selection-sort approach works. The task now is to implement it in Java. Beginners find it difficult to develop a complete solution on the first attempt. Start by writing the code for the first iteration to find the smallest element in the list and swap it with the first element, and then observe what would be different for the second iteration, the third, and so on. The insight this gives will enable you to write a loop that generalizes all the iterations.

selection sort animation on Companion Website

The solution can be described as follows:

```
for (int i = 0; i < list.length - 1; i++) {
  select the smallest element in list[i..list.length-1];
  swap the smallest with list[i], if necessary;
  // list[i] is in its correct position.
  // The next iteration applies on list[i+1..list.length-1]
}
```

Listing 7.8 implements the solution.

LISTING 7.8 SelectionSort.java

select

swap

```
 1  public class SelectionSort {
 2    /** The method for sorting the numbers */
 3    public static void selectionSort(double[] list) {
 4      for (int i = 0; i < list.length - 1; i++) {
 5        // Find the minimum in the list[i..list.length-1]
 6        double currentMin = list[i];
 7        int currentMinIndex = i;
 8
 9        for (int j = i + 1; j < list.length; j++) {
10          if (currentMin > list[j]) {
11            currentMin = list[j];
12            currentMinIndex = j;
13          }
14        }
15
16        // Swap list[i] with list[currentMinIndex] if necessary
17        if (currentMinIndex != i) {
18          list[currentMinIndex] = list[i];
19          list[i] = currentMin;
20        }
21      }
22    }
23  }
```

The **selectionSort(double[] list)** method sorts any array of **double** elements. The method is implemented with a nested **for** loop. The outer loop (with the loop control variable **i**) (line 4) is iterated in order to find the smallest element in the list, which ranges from **list[i]** to **list[list.length-1]**, and exchange it with **list[i]**.

The variable **i** is initially **0**. After each iteration of the outer loop, **list[i]** is in the right place. Eventually, all the elements are put in the right place; therefore, the whole list is sorted.

To understand this method better, trace it with the following statements:

```
double[] list = {1, 9, 4.5, 6.6, 5.7, -4.5};
SelectionSort.selectionSort(list);
```

7.24 Use Figure 7.11 as an example to show how to apply the selection-sort approach to sort {3.4, 5, 3, 3.5, 2.2, 1.9, 2}.

7.25 How do you modify the **selectionSort** method in Listing 7.8 to sort numbers in decreasing order?

7.12 The **Arrays** Class

*The **java.util.Arrays** class contains useful methods for common array operations such as sorting and searching.*

The `java.util.Arrays` class contains various static methods for sorting and searching arrays, comparing arrays, filling array elements, and returning a string representation of the array. These methods are overloaded for all primitive types.

You can use the **sort** or **parallelSort** method to sort a whole array or a partial array. For example, the following code sorts an array of numbers and an array of characters.

sort
parallelSort

```java
double[] numbers = {6.0, 4.4, 1.9, 2.9, 3.4, 3.5};
java.util.Arrays.sort(numbers); // Sort the whole array
java.util.Arrays.parallelSort(numbers); // Sort the whole array

char[] chars = {'a', 'A', '4', 'F', 'D', 'P'};
java.util.Arrays.sort(chars, 1, 3); // Sort part of the array
java.util.Arrays.parallelSort(chars, 1, 3); // Sort part of the array
```

Invoking **sort(numbers)** sorts the whole array **numbers**. Invoking **sort(chars, 1, 3)** sorts a partial array from **chars[1]** to **chars[3-1]**. **parallelSort** is more efficient if your computer has multiple processors.

You can use the **binarySearch** method to search for a key in an array. The array must be pre-sorted in increasing order. If the key is not in the array, the method returns -(**insertionIndex** + 1). For example, the following code searches the keys in an array of integers and an array of characters.

binarySearch

```java
int[] list = {2, 4, 7, 10, 11, 45, 50, 59, 60, 66, 69, 70, 79};
System.out.println("1. Index is " +
        java.util.Arrays.binarySearch(list, 11));
System.out.println("2. Index is " +
        java.util.Arrays.binarySearch(list, 12));

char[] chars = {'a', 'c', 'g', 'x', 'y', 'z'};
System.out.println("3. Index is " +
        java.util.Arrays.binarySearch(chars, 'a'));
System.out.println("4. Index is " +
        java.util.Arrays.binarySearch(chars, 't'));
```

The output of the preceding code is

1. Index is 4

2. Index is −6

3. Index is 0

4. Index is −4

You can use the **equals** method to check whether two arrays are strictly equal. Two arrays are strictly equal if their corresponding elements are the same. In the following code, **list1** and **list2** are equal, but **list2** and **list3** are not.

equals

```java
int[] list1 = {2, 4, 7, 10};
int[] list2 = {2, 4, 7, 10};
int[] list3 = {4, 2, 7, 10};
System.out.println(java.util.Arrays.equals(list1, list2)); // true
System.out.println(java.util.Arrays.equals(list2, list3)); // false
```

You can use the **fill** method to fill in all or part of the array. For example, the following code fills **list1** with **5** and fills **8** into elements **list2[1]** through **list2[5-1]**.

fill

```java
int[] list1 = {2, 4, 7, 10};
int[] list2 = {2, 4, 7, 7, 7, 10};
java.util.Arrays.fill(list1, 5); // Fill 5 to the whole array
java.util.Arrays.fill(list2, 1, 5, 8); // Fill 8 to a partial array
```

toString

You can also use the **toString** method to return a string that represents all elements in the array. This is a quick and simple way to display all elements in the array. For example, the following code

```java
int[] list = {2, 4, 7, 10};
System.out.println(Arrays.toString(list));
```

displays **[2, 4, 7, 10]**.

Check
Point

7.26 What types of array can be sorted using the **java.util.Arrays.sort** method? Does this **sort** method create a new array?

7.27 To apply **java.util.Arrays.binarySearch(array, key)**, should the array be sorted in increasing order, in decreasing order, or neither?

7.28 Show the output of the following code:

```java
int[] list1 = {2, 4, 7, 10};
java.util.Arrays.fill(list1, 7);
System.out.println(java.util.Arrays.toString(list1));

int[] list2 = {2, 4, 7, 10};
System.out.println(java.util.Arrays.toString(list2));
System.out.print(java.util.Arrays.equals(list1, list2));
```

7.13 Command-Line Arguments

Key
Point

*The **main** method can receive string arguments from the command line.*

VideoNote

Command-line arguments

Perhaps you have already noticed the unusual header for the **main** method, which has the parameter **args** of **String[]** type. It is clear that **args** is an array of strings. The **main** method is just like a regular method with a parameter. You can call a regular method by passing actual parameters. Can you pass arguments to **main**? Yes, of course you can. In the following examples, the **main** method in class **TestMain** is invoked by a method in **A**.

```java
public class A {
  public static void main(String[] args) {
    String[] strings = {"New York",
      "Boston", "Atlanta"};
    TestMain.main(strings);
  }
}
```

```java
public class TestMain {
  public static void main(String[] args) {
    for (int i = 0; i < args.length; i++)
      System.out.println(args[i]);
  }
}
```

A **main** method is just a regular method. Furthermore, you can pass arguments from the command line.

7.13.1 Passing Strings to the **main** Method

You can pass strings to a **main** method from the command line when you run the program. The following command line, for example, starts the program **TestMain** with three strings: **arg0**, **arg1**, and **arg2**:

```
java TestMain arg0 arg1 arg2
```

arg0, **arg1**, and **arg2** are strings, but they don't have to appear in double quotes on the command line. The strings are separated by a space. A string that contains a space must be enclosed in double quotes. Consider the following command line:

```
java TestMain "First num" alpha 53
```

It starts the program with three strings: `First num`, `alpha`, and `53`. Since `First num` is a string, it is enclosed in double quotes. Note that `53` is actually treated as a string. You can use `"53"` instead of `53` in the command line.

When the `main` method is invoked, the Java interpreter creates an array to hold the command-line arguments and pass the array reference to `args`. For example, if you invoke a program with `n` arguments, the Java interpreter creates an array like this one:

```java
args = new String[n];
```

The Java interpreter then passes `args` to invoke the `main` method.

> **Note**
> If you run the program with no strings passed, the array is created with `new String[0]`. In this case, the array is empty with length `0`. `args` references to this empty array. Therefore, `args` is not `null`, but `args.length` is `0`.

7.13.2 Case Study: Calculator

Suppose you are to develop a program that performs arithmetic operations on integers. The program receives an expression in one string argument. The expression consists of an integer followed by an operator and another integer. For example, to add two integers, use this command:

VideoNote
Command-line argument

```java
java Calculator 2 + 3
```

The program will display the following output:

```
2 + 3 = 5
```

Figure 7.12 shows sample runs of the program.

The strings passed to the main program are stored in `args`, which is an array of strings. The first string is stored in `args[0]`, and `args.length` is the number of strings passed.

Here are the steps in the program:

1. Use `args.length` to determine whether the expression has been provided as three arguments in the command line. If not, terminate the program using `System.exit(1)`.

2. Perform a binary arithmetic operation on the operands `args[0]` and `args[2]` using the operator in `args[1]`.

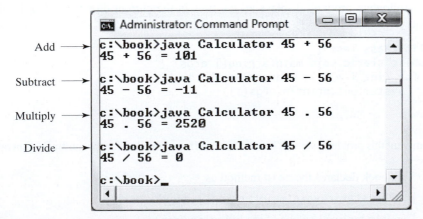

FIGURE 7.12 The program takes three arguments (`operand1 operator operand2`) from the command line and displays the expression and the result of the arithmetic operation.

The program is shown in Listing 7.9.

LISTING 7.9 Calculator.java

```java
1  public class Calculator {
2    /** Main method */
3    public static void main(String[] args) {
4      // Check number of strings passed
5      if (args.length != 3) {
6        System.out.println(
7          "Usage: java Calculator operand1 operator operand2");
8        System.exit(0);
9      }
10
11     // The result of the operation
12     int result = 0;
13
14     // Determine the operator
15     switch (args[1].charAt(0)) {
16       case '+': result = Integer.parseInt(args[0]) +
17                          Integer.parseInt(args[2]);
18               break;
19       case '-': result = Integer.parseInt(args[0]) -
20                          Integer.parseInt(args[2]);
21               break;
22       case '.': result = Integer.parseInt(args[0]) *
23                          Integer.parseInt(args[2]);
24               break;
25       case '/': result = Integer.parseInt(args[0]) /
26                          Integer.parseInt(args[2]);
27     }
28
29     // Display result
30     System.out.println(args[0] + ' ' + args[1] + ' ' + args[2]
31       + " = " + result);
32   }
33 }
```

check argument (line 5)

check operator (line 16)

`Integer.parseInt(args[0])` (line 16) converts a digital string into an integer. The string must consist of digits. If not, the program will terminate abnormally.

We used the `.` symbol for multiplication, not the common `*` symbol. The reason for this is that the `*` symbol refers to all the files in the current directory when it is used on a command line. The following program displays all the files in the current directory when issuing the command `java Test *`:

```java
public class Test {
  public static void main(String[] args) {
    for (int i = 0; i < args.length; i++)
      System.out.println(args[i]);
  }
}
```

To circumvent this problem, we will have to use a different symbol for the multiplication operator.

Check Point

7.29 This book declares the `main` method as

```java
public static void main(String[] args)
```

Can it be replaced by one of the following lines?

```java
public static void main(String args[])
public static void main(String[] x)
```

```
public static void main(String x[])
static void main(String x[])
```

7.30 Show the output of the following program when invoked using

1. **java Test I have a dream**

2. **java Test "1 2 3"**

3. **java Test**

```
public class Test {
  public static void main(String[] args) {
    System.out.println("Number of strings is " + args.length);
    for (int i = 0; i < args.length; i++)
      System.out.println(args[i]);
  }
}
```

KEY TERMS

anonymous array 258	index 246
array 246	indexed variable 248
array initializer 248	linear search 265
binary search 265	off-by-one error 251
garbage collection 256	selection sort 269

CHAPTER SUMMARY

1. A variable is declared as an *array* type using the syntax `elementType[] arrayRefVar` or `elementType arrayRefVar[]`. The style `elementType[] arrayRefVar` is preferred, although `elementType arrayRefVar[]` is legal.

2. Unlike declarations for primitive data type variables, the declaration of an array variable does not allocate any space in memory for the array. An array variable is not a primitive data type variable. An array variable contains a reference to an array.

3. You cannot assign elements to an array unless it has already been created. You can create an array by using the `new` operator with the following syntax: `new elementType[arraySize]`.

4. Each element in the array is represented using the syntax `arrayRefVar[index]`. An *index* must be an integer or an integer expression.

5. After an array is created, its size becomes permanent and can be obtained using `arrayRefVar.length`. Since the index of an array always begins with `0`, the last index is always `arrayRefVar.length - 1`. An out-of-bounds error will occur if you attempt to reference elements beyond the bounds of an array.

6. Programmers often mistakenly reference the first element in an array with index `1`, but it should be `0`. This is called the index *off-by-one error*.

7. When an array is created, its elements are assigned the default value of **0** for the numeric primitive data types, **\u0000** for char types, and **false** for **boolean** types.

8. Java has a shorthand notation, known as the *array initializer*, which combines declaring an array, creating an array, and initializing an array in one statement, using the syntax **elementType[] arrayRefVar = {value0, value1, ..., value*k*}**.

9. When you pass an array argument to a method, you are actually passing the reference of the array; that is, the called method can modify the elements in the caller's original array.

10. If an array is sorted, *binary search* is more efficient than *linear search* for finding an element in the array.

11. *Selection sort* finds the smallest number in the list and swaps it with the first element. It then finds the smallest number remaining and swaps it with the first element in the remaining list, and so on, until only a single number remains.

QUIZ

Answer the quiz for this chapter online at www.cs.armstrong.edu/liang/intro10e/quiz.html.

MyProgrammingLab™   **PROGRAMMING EXERCISES**

Sections 7.2–7.5

*7.1 (*Assign grades*) Write a program that reads student scores, gets the best score, and then assigns grades based on the following scheme:

Grade is A if score is ≥ best − 10

Grade is B if score is ≥ best − 20;

Grade is C if score is ≥ best − 30;

Grade is D if score is ≥ best − 40;

Grade is F otherwise.

The program prompts the user to enter the total number of students, then prompts the user to enter all of the scores, and concludes by displaying the grades. Here is a sample run:

```
Enter the number of students: 4  ↵Enter
Enter 4 scores: 40 55 70 58  ↵Enter
Student 0 score is 40 and grade is C
Student 1 score is 55 and grade is B
Student 2 score is 70 and grade is A
Student 3 score is 58 and grade is B
```

7.2 (*Reverse the numbers entered*) Write a program that reads ten integers and displays them in the reverse of the order in which they were read.

7.3 (*Count occurrence of numbers*) Write a program that reads the integers between 1 and 100 and counts the occurrences of each. Assume the input ends with **0. Here is a sample run of the program:

```
Enter the integers between 1 and 100: 2 5 6 5 4 3 23 43 2 0  ↵Enter
2 occurs 2 times
3 occurs 1 time
4 occurs 1 time
5 occurs 2 times
6 occurs 1 time
23 occurs 1 time
43 occurs 1 time
```

Note that if a number occurs more than one time, the plural word "times" is used in the output.

7.4 (*Analyze scores*) Write a program that reads an unspecified number of scores and determines how many scores are above or equal to the average and how many scores are below the average. Enter a negative number to signify the end of the input. Assume that the maximum number of scores is 100.

**7.5 (*Print distinct numbers*) Write a program that reads in ten numbers and displays the number of distinct numbers and the distinct numbers separated by exactly one space (i.e., if a number appears multiple times, it is displayed only once). (*Hint*: Read a number and store it to an array if it is new. If the number is already in the array, ignore it.) After the input, the array contains the distinct numbers. Here is the sample run of the program:

```
Enter ten numbers: 1 2 3 2 1 6 3 4 5 2  ↵Enter
The number of distinct number is 6
The distinct numbers are: 1 2 3 6 4 5
```

*7.6 (*Revise Listing 5.15, PrimeNumber.java*) Listing 5.15 determines whether a number **n** is prime by checking whether **2, 3, 4, 5, 6, ..., n/2** is a divisor. If a divisor is found, **n** is not prime. A more efficient approach is to check whether any of the prime numbers less than or equal to $\sqrt{n}$ can divide **n** evenly. If not, **n** is prime. Rewrite Listing 5.15 to display the first 50 prime numbers using this approach. You need to use an array to store the prime numbers and later use them to check whether they are possible divisors for **n**.

*7.7 (*Count single digits*) Write a program that generates 100 random integers between 0 and 9 and displays the count for each number. (*Hint*: Use an array of ten integers, say **counts**, to store the counts for the number of 0s, 1s, ..., 9s.)

Sections 7.6–7.8

7.8 (*Average an array*) Write two overloaded methods that return the average of an array with the following headers:

```
public static int average(int[] array)
public static double average(double[] array)
```

Write a test program that prompts the user to enter ten double values, invokes this method, and displays the average value.

7.9 (*Find the smallest element*) Write a method that finds the smallest element in an array of double values using the following header:

```
public static double min(double[] array)
```

Write a test program that prompts the user to enter ten numbers, invokes this method to return the minimum value, and displays the minimum value. Here is a sample run of the program:

```
Enter ten numbers: 1.9 2.5 3.7 2 1.5 6 3 4 5 2  ↵ Enter
The minimum number is: 1.5
```

7.10 (*Find the index of the smallest element*) Write a method that returns the index of the smallest element in an array of integers. If the number of such elements is greater than 1, return the smallest index. Use the following header:

```
public static int indexOfSmallestElement(double[] array)
```

Write a test program that prompts the user to enter ten numbers, invokes this method to return the index of the smallest element, and displays the index.

*7.11 (*Statistics: compute deviation*) Programming Exercise 5.45 computes the standard deviation of numbers. This exercise uses a different but equivalent formula to compute the standard deviation of **n** numbers.

$$mean = \frac{\sum_{i=1}^{n} x_i}{n} = \frac{x_1 + x_2 + \cdots + x_n}{n} \qquad deviation = \sqrt{\frac{\sum_{i=1}^{n} (x_i - mean)^2}{n - 1}}$$

To compute the standard deviation with this formula, you have to store the individual numbers using an array, so that they can be used after the mean is obtained. Your program should contain the following methods:

```
/** Compute the deviation of double values */
public static double deviation(double[] x)

/** Compute the mean of an array of double values */
public static double mean(double[] x)
```

Write a test program that prompts the user to enter ten numbers and displays the mean and standard deviation, as shown in the following sample run:

```
Enter ten numbers: 1.9 2.5 3.7 2 1 6 3 4 5 2  ↵ Enter
The mean is 3.11
The standard deviation is 1.55738
```

*7.12 (*Reverse an array*) The **reverse** method in Section 7.7 reverses an array by copying it to a new array. Rewrite the method that reverses the array passed in the argument and returns this array. Write a test program that prompts the user to enter ten numbers, invokes the method to reverse the numbers, and displays the numbers.

Section 7.9

*7.13   (*Random number chooser*) Write a method that returns a random number between 1 and 54, excluding the numbers passed in the argument. The method header is specified as follows:

```
public static int getRandom(int... numbers)
```

7.14   (*Computing gcd*) Write a method that returns the gcd of an unspecified number of integers. The method header is specified as follows:

```
public static int gcd(int... numbers)
```

Write a test program that prompts the user to enter five numbers, invokes the method to find the gcd of these numbers, and displays the gcd.

Sections 7.10–7.12

7.15   (*Eliminate duplicates*) Write a method that returns a new array by eliminating the duplicate values in the array using the following method header:

```
public static int[] eliminateDuplicates(int[] list)
```

Write a test program that reads in ten integers, invokes the method, and displays the result. Here is the sample run of the program:

```
Enter ten numbers: 1 2 3 2 1 6 3 4 5 2  ⏎Enter
The distinct numbers are: 1 2 3 6 4 5
```

7.16   (*Execution time*) Write a program that randomly generates an array of 100,000 integers and a key. Estimate the execution time of invoking the `linearSearch` method in Listing 7.6. Sort the array and estimate the execution time of invoking the `binarySearch` method in Listing 7.7. You can use the following code template to obtain the execution time:

```
long startTime = System.currentTimeMillis();
perform the task;
long endTime = System.currentTimeMillis();
long executionTime = endTime - startTime;
```

**7.17   (*Sort students*) Write a program that prompts the user to enter the number of students, the students' names, and their scores, and prints student names in decreasing order of their scores.

**7.18   (*Bubble sort*) Write a sort method that uses the bubble-sort algorithm. The bubble-sort algorithm makes several passes through the array. On each pass, successive neighboring pairs are compared. If a pair is not in order, its values are swapped; otherwise, the values remain unchanged. The technique is called a *bubble sort* or *sinking sort* because the smaller values gradually "bubble" their way to the top and the larger values "sink" to the bottom. Write a test program that reads in ten double numbers, invokes the method, and displays the sorted numbers.

**7.19 (*Sorted?*) Write the following method that returns true if the list is already sorted in increasing order.

```
public static boolean isSorted(int[] list)
```

Write a test program that prompts the user to enter a list and displays whether the list is sorted or not. Here is a sample run. Note that the first number in the input indicates the number of the elements in the list. This number is not part of the list.

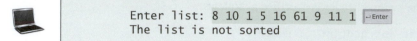

```
Enter list: 8 10 1 5 16 61 9 11 1  ↵Enter
The list is not sorted
```

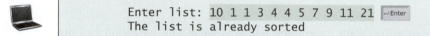

```
Enter list: 10 1 1 3 4 4 5 7 9 11 21  ↵Enter
The list is already sorted
```

*7.20 (*Revise selection sort*) In Section 7.11, you used selection sort to sort an array. The selection-sort method repeatedly finds the smallest number in the current array and swaps it with the first. Rewrite this program by finding the largest number and swapping it with the last. Write a test program that reads in ten double numbers, invokes the method, and displays the sorted numbers.

***7.21 (*Game: bean machine*) The bean machine, also known as a quincunx or the Galton box, is a device for statistics experiments named after English scientist Sir Francis Galton. It consists of an upright board with evenly spaced nails (or pegs) in a triangular form, as shown in Figure 7.13.

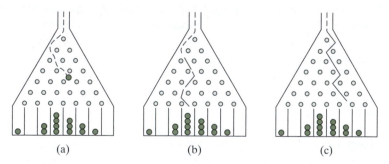

FIGURE 7.13 Each ball takes a random path and falls into a slot.

Balls are dropped from the opening of the board. Every time a ball hits a nail, it has a 50% chance of falling to the left or to the right. The piles of balls are accumulated in the slots at the bottom of the board.

Write a program that simulates the bean machine. Your program should prompt the user to enter the number of the balls and the number of the slots in the machine. Simulate the falling of each ball by printing its path. For example, the path for the ball in Figure 7.13b is LLRRLLR and the path for the ball in Figure 7.13c is

RLRRLRR. Display the final buildup of the balls in the slots in a histogram. Here is a sample run of the program:

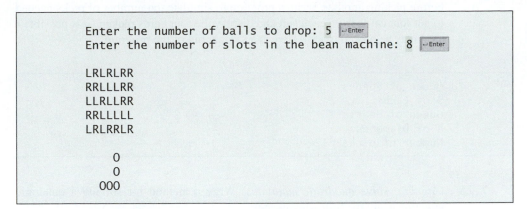

```
Enter the number of balls to drop: 5 ↵Enter
Enter the number of slots in the bean machine: 8 ↵Enter

LRLRLRR
RRLLLRR
LLRLLRR
RRLLLLL
LRLRRLR

          0
          0
        000
```

(*Hint*: Create an array named `slots`. Each element in `slots` stores the number of balls in a slot. Each ball falls into a slot via a path. The number of Rs in a path is the position of the slot where the ball falls. For example, for the path LRLRLRR, the ball falls into `slots[4]`, and for the path is RRLLLLL, the ball falls into `slots[2]`.)

***7.22 (*Game: Eight Queens*) The classic Eight Queens puzzle is to place eight queens on a chessboard such that no two queens can attack each other (i.e., no two queens are on the same row, same column, or same diagonal). There are many possible solutions. Write a program that displays one such solution. A sample output is shown below:

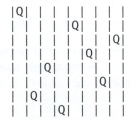

```
|Q| | | | | | | |
| | | | |Q| | | |
| | | | | | | |Q|
| | | | | |Q| | |
| | |Q| | | | | |
| | | | | | |Q| |
| |Q| | | | | | |
| | | |Q| | | | |
```

**7.23 (*Game: locker puzzle*) A school has 100 lockers and 100 students. All lockers are closed on the first day of school. As the students enter, the first student, denoted S1, opens every locker. Then the second student, S2, begins with the second locker, denoted L2, and closes every other locker. Student S3 begins with the third locker and changes every third locker (closes it if it was open, and opens it if it was closed). Student S4 begins with locker L4 and changes every fourth locker. Student S5 starts with L5 and changes every fifth locker, and so on, until student S100 changes L100.

After all the students have passed through the building and changed the lockers, which lockers are open? Write a program to find your answer and display all open locker numbers separated by exactly one space.

(*Hint*: Use an array of 100 Boolean elements, each of which indicates whether a locker is open (`true`) or closed (`false`). Initially, all lockers are closed.)

**7.24 (*Simulation: coupon collector's problem*) Coupon collector is a classic statistics problem with many practical applications. The problem is to pick objects from a set of objects repeatedly and find out how many picks are needed for all the

VideoNote

Coupon collector's problem

objects to be picked at least once. A variation of the problem is to pick cards from a shuffled deck of 52 cards repeatedly and find out how many picks are needed before you see one of each suit. Assume a picked card is placed back in the deck before picking another. Write a program to simulate the number of picks needed to get four cards from each suit and display the four cards picked (it is possible a card may be picked twice). Here is a sample run of the program:

```
Queen of Spades
5 of Clubs
Queen of Hearts
4 of Diamonds
Number of picks: 12
```

7.25 (*Algebra: solve quadratic equations*) Write a method for solving a quadratic equation using the following header:

public static int solveQuadratic(**double**[] eqn, **double**[] roots)

The coefficients of a quadratic equation $ax^2 + bx + c = 0$ are passed to the array **eqn** and the real roots are stored in roots. The method returns the number of real roots. See Programming Exercise 3.1 on how to solve a quadratic equation.

Write a program that prompts the user to enter values for *a*, *b*, and *c* and displays the number of real roots and all real roots.

7.26 (*Strictly identical arrays*) The arrays **list1** and **list2** are *strictly identical* if their corresponding elements are equal. Write a method that returns **true** if **list1** and **list2** are strictly identical, using the following header:

public static boolean equals(**int**[] list1, **int**[] list2)

Write a test program that prompts the user to enter two lists of integers and displays whether the two are strictly identical. Here are the sample runs. Note that the first number in the input indicates the number of the elements in the list. This number is not part of the list.

```
Enter list1: 5 2 5 6 1 6  ↵Enter
Enter list2: 5 2 5 6 1 6  ↵Enter
Two lists are strictly identical
```

```
Enter list1: 5 2 5 6 6 1  ↵Enter
Enter list2: 5 2 5 6 1 6  ↵Enter
Two lists are not strictly identical
```

7.27 (*Identical arrays*) The arrays **list1** and **list2** are *identical* if they have the same contents. Write a method that returns **true** if **list1** and **list2** are identical, using the following header:

public static boolean equals(**int**[] list1, **int**[] list2)

Write a test program that prompts the user to enter two lists of integers and displays whether the two are identical. Here are the sample runs. Note that the first number in the input indicates the number of the elements in the list. This number is not part of the list.

```
Enter list1: 5 2 5 6 6 1 ↵Enter
Enter list2: 5 5 2 6 1 6 ↵Enter
Two lists are identical
```

```
Enter list1: 5 5 5 6 6 1 ↵Enter
Enter list2: 5 2 5 6 1 6 ↵Enter
Two lists are not identical
```

*7.28 (*Math: combinations*) Write a program that prompts the user to enter 10 integers and displays all combinations of picking two numbers from the 10.

*7.29 (*Game: pick four cards*) Write a program that picks four cards from a deck of 52 cards and computes their sum. An Ace, King, Queen, and Jack represent 1, 13, 12, and 11, respectively. Your program should display the number of picks that yields the sum of 24.

*7.30 (*Pattern recognition: consecutive four equal numbers*) Write the following method that tests whether the array has four consecutive numbers with the same value.

VideoNote

Consecutive four

```java
public static boolean isConsecutiveFour(int[] values)
```

Write a test program that prompts the user to enter a series of integers and displays if the series contains four consecutive numbers with the same value. Your program should first prompt the user to enter the input size—i.e., the number of values in the series. Here are sample runs:

```
Enter the number of values: 8 ↵Enter
Enter the values: 3 4 5 5 5 5 4 5 ↵Enter
The list has consecutive fours
```

```
Enter the number of values: 9 ↵Enter
Enter the values: 3 4 5 5 6 5 5 4 5 ↵Enter
The list has no consecutive fours
```

**7.31 (*Merge two sorted lists*) Write the following method that merges two sorted lists into a new sorted list.

```java
public static int[] merge(int[] list1, int[] list2)
```

Implement the method in a way that takes at most `list1.length` + `list2.length` comparisons. Write a test program that prompts the user to enter two sorted lists and displays the merged list. Here is a sample run. Note that the first number in the input indicates the number of the elements in the list. This number is not part of the list.

```
Enter list1: 5 1 5 16 61 111  ⏎ Enter
Enter list2: 4 2 4 5 6  ⏎ Enter
The merged list is 1 2 4 5 5 6 16 61 111
```

**7.32 (*Partition of a list*) Write the following method that partitions the list using the first element, called a *pivot*.

```
public static int partition(int[] list)
```

After the partition, the elements in the list are rearranged so that all the elements before the pivot are less than or equal to the pivot and the elements after the pivot are greater than the pivot. The method returns the index where the pivot is located in the new list. For example, suppose the list is {5, 2, 9, 3, 6, 8}. After the partition, the list becomes {3, 2, 5, 9, 6, 8}. Implement the method in a way that takes at most `list.length` comparisons. Write a test program that prompts the user to enter a list and displays the list after the partition. Here is a sample run. Note that the first number in the input indicates the number of the elements in the list. This number is not part of the list.

```
Enter list: 8 10 1 5 16 61 9 11 1  ⏎ Enter
After the partition, the list is 9 1 5 1 10 61 11 16
```

*7.33 (*Culture: Chinese Zodiac*) Simplify Listing 3.9 using an array of strings to store the animal names.

**7.34 (*Sort characters in a string*) Write a method that returns a sorted string using the following header:

```
public static String sort(String s)
```

For example, `sort("acb")` returns `abc`.

Write a test program that prompts the user to enter a string and displays the sorted string.

***7.35 (*Game: hangman*) Write a hangman game that randomly generates a word and prompts the user to guess one letter at a time, as shown in the sample run. Each letter in the word is displayed as an asterisk. When the user makes a correct guess, the actual letter is then displayed. When the user finishes a word, display

the number of misses and ask the user whether to continue to play with another
word. Declare an array to store words, as follows:

```java
// Add any words you wish in this array
String[] words = {"write", "that", ...};
```

```
(Guess) Enter a letter in word ******* > p  ↵Enter
(Guess) Enter a letter in word p****** > r  ↵Enter
(Guess) Enter a letter in word pr**r** > p  ↵Enter
    p is already in the word
(Guess) Enter a letter in word pr**r** > o  ↵Enter
(Guess) Enter a letter in word pro*r** > g  ↵Enter
(Guess) Enter a letter in word progr** > n  ↵Enter
    n is not in the word
(Guess) Enter a letter in word progr** > m  ↵Enter
(Guess) Enter a letter in word progr*m > a  ↵Enter
The word is program. You missed 1 time
Do you want to guess another word? Enter y or n>
```

MULTIDIMENSIONAL ARRAYS

Objectives

- To give examples of representing data using two-dimensional arrays (§8.1).

- To declare variables for two-dimensional arrays, create arrays, and access array elements in a two-dimensional array using row and column indexes (§8.2).

- To program common operations for two-dimensional arrays (displaying arrays, summing all elements, finding the minimum and maximum elements, and random shuffling) (§8.3).

- To pass two-dimensional arrays to methods (§8.4).

- To write a program for grading multiple-choice questions using two-dimensional arrays (§8.5).

- To solve the closest-pair problem using two-dimensional arrays (§8.6).

- To check a Sudoku solution using two-dimensional arrays (§8.7).

- To use multidimensional arrays (§8.8).

8.1 Introduction

Data in a table or a matrix can be represented using a two-dimensional array.

The preceding chapter introduced how to use one-dimensional arrays to store linear collections of elements. You can use a two-dimensional array to store a matrix or a table. For example, the following table that lists the distances between cities can be stored using a two-dimensional array named `distances`.

problem

Distance Table (in miles)							
	Chicago	**Boston**	**New York**	**Atlanta**	**Miami**	**Dallas**	**Houston**
Chicago	0	983	787	714	1375	967	1087
Boston	983	0	214	1102	1763	1723	1842
New York	787	214	0	888	1549	1548	1627
Atlanta	714	1102	888	0	661	781	810
Miami	1375	1763	1549	661	0	1426	1187
Dallas	967	1723	1548	781	1426	0	239
Houston	1087	1842	1627	810	1187	239	0

```
double[][] distances = {
    {0, 983, 787, 714, 1375, 967, 1087},
    {983, 0, 214, 1102, 1763, 1723, 1842},
    {787, 214, 0, 888, 1549, 1548, 1627},
    {714, 1102, 888, 0, 661, 781, 810},
    {1375, 1763, 1549, 661, 0, 1426, 1187},
    {967, 1723, 1548, 781, 1426, 0, 239},
    {1087, 1842, 1627, 810, 1187, 239, 0},
};
```

8.2 Two-Dimensional Array Basics

An element in a two-dimensional array is accessed through a row and column index.

How do you declare a variable for two-dimensional arrays? How do you create a two-dimensional array? How do you access elements in a two-dimensional array? This section addresses these issues.

8.2.1 Declaring Variables of Two-Dimensional Arrays and Creating Two-Dimensional Arrays

The syntax for declaring a two-dimensional array is:

```
elementType[][] arrayRefVar;
```

or

```
elementType arrayRefVar[][]; // Allowed, but not preferred
```

As an example, here is how you would declare a two-dimensional array variable `matrix` of `int` values:

```
int[][] matrix;
```

or

```
int matrix[][]; // This style is allowed, but not preferred
```

You can create a two-dimensional array of 5-by-5 `int` values and assign it to `matrix` using this syntax:

```
matrix = new int[5][5];
```

Two subscripts are used in a two-dimensional array, one for the row and the other for the column. As in a one-dimensional array, the index for each subscript is of the `int` type and starts from `0`, as shown in Figure 8.1a.

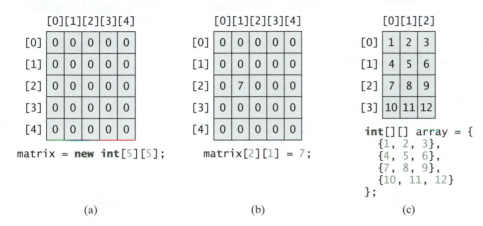

(a)   (b)   (c)

FIGURE 8.1 The index of each subscript of a two-dimensional array is an `int` value, starting from `0`.

To assign the value `7` to a specific element at row `2` and column `1`, as shown in Figure 8.1b, you can use the following syntax:

```
matrix[2][1] = 7;
```

Caution

It is a common mistake to use `matrix[2, 1]` to access the element at row `2` and column `1`. In Java, each subscript must be enclosed in a pair of square brackets.

You can also use an array initializer to declare, create, and initialize a two-dimensional array. For example, the following code in (a) creates an array with the specified initial values, as shown in Figure 8.1c. This is equivalent to the code in (b).

```
int[][] array = {
  {1, 2, 3},
  {4, 5, 6},
  {7, 8, 9},
  {10, 11, 12}
};
```

Equivalent

```
int[][] array = new int[4][3];
array[0][0] = 1; array[0][1] = 2; array[0][2] = 3;
array[1][0] = 4; array[1][1] = 5; array[1][2] = 6;
array[2][0] = 7; array[2][1] = 8; array[2][2] = 9;
array[3][0] = 10; array[3][1] = 11; array[3][2] = 12;
```

(a)   (b)

8.2.2 Obtaining the Lengths of Two-Dimensional Arrays

A two-dimensional array is actually an array in which each element is a one-dimensional array. The length of an array `x` is the number of elements in the array, which can be obtained using `x.length`. `x[0]`, `x[1]`, . . . , and `x[x.length-1]` are arrays. Their lengths can be obtained using `x[0].length`, `x[1].length`, . . . , and `x[x.length-1].length`.

For example, suppose `x = new int[3][4]`, `x[0]`, `x[1]`, and `x[2]` are one-dimensional arrays and each contains four elements, as shown in Figure 8.2. `x.length` is 3, and `x[0].length`, `x[1].length`, and `x[2].length` are 4.

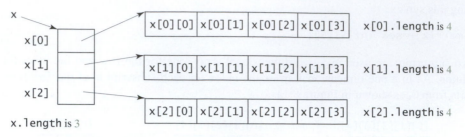

FIGURE 8.2 A two-dimensional array is a one-dimensional array in which each element is another one-dimensional array.

8.2.3 Ragged Arrays

ragged array

Each row in a two-dimensional array is itself an array. Thus, the rows can have different lengths. An array of this kind is known as a *ragged array*. Here is an example of creating a ragged array:

```
int[][] triangleArray = {
    {1, 2, 3, 4, 5},
    {2, 3, 4, 5},
    {3, 4, 5},
    {4, 5},
    {5}
};
```

As you can see, `triangleArray[0].length` is 5, `triangleArray[1].length` is 4, `triangleArray[2].length` is 3, `triangleArray[3].length` is 2, and `triangle-Array[4].length` is 1.

If you don't know the values in a ragged array in advance, but do know the sizes—say, the same as before—you can create a ragged array using the following syntax:

```
int[][] triangleArray = new int[5][];
triangleArray[0] = new int[5];
triangleArray[1] = new int[4];
triangleArray[2] = new int[3];
triangleArray[3] = new int[2];
triangleArray[4] = new int[1];
```

You can now assign values to the array. For example,

```
triangleArray[0][3] = 50;
triangleArray[4][0] = 45;
```

Note

The syntax `new int[5][]` for creating an array requires the first index to be specified. The syntax `new int[][]` would be wrong.

8.1 Declare an array reference variable for a two-dimensional array of **int** values, create a 4-by-5 **int** matrix, and assign it to the variable.

8.2 Can the rows in a two-dimensional array have different lengths?

8.3 What is the output of the following code?

```
int[][] array = new int[5][6];
int[] x = {1, 2};
array[0] = x;
System.out.println("array[0][1] is " + array[0][1]);
```

8.4 Which of the following statements are valid?

```
int[][] r = new int[2];
int[] x = new int[];
int[][] y = new int[3][];
int[][] z = {{1, 2}};
int[][] m = {{1, 2}, {2, 3}};
int[][] n = {{1, 2}, {2, 3}, };
```

8.3 Processing Two-Dimensional Arrays

Nested **for** *loops are often used to process a two-dimensional array.*

Suppose an array **matrix** is created as follows:

```
int[][] matrix = new int[10][10];
```

The following are some examples of processing two-dimensional arrays.

1. *Initializing arrays with input values.* The following loop initializes the array with user input values:

```
java.util.Scanner input = new Scanner(System.in);
System.out.println("Enter " + matrix.length + " rows and " +
  matrix[0].length + " columns: ");
for (int row = 0; row < matrix.length; row++) {
  for (int column = 0; column < matrix[row].length; column++) {
    matrix[row][column] = input.nextInt();
  }
}
```

2. *Initializing arrays with random values.* The following loop initializes the array with random values between **0** and **99**:

```
for (int row = 0; row < matrix.length; row++) {
  for (int column = 0; column < matrix[row].length; column++) {
    matrix[row][column] = (int)(Math.random() * 100);
  }
}
```

3. *Printing arrays.* To print a two-dimensional array, you have to print each element in the array using a loop like the following:

```
for (int row = 0; row < matrix.length; row++) {
  for (int column = 0; column < matrix[row].length; column++) {
    System.out.print(matrix[row][column] + " ");
  }

  System.out.println();
}
```

4. *Summing all elements.* Use a variable named `total` to store the sum. Initially `total` is `0`. Add each element in the array to `total` using a loop like this:

```
int total = 0;
for (int row = 0; row < matrix.length; row++) {
  for (int column = 0; column < matrix[row].length; column++) {
    total += matrix[row][column];
  }
}
```

5. *Summing elements by column.* For each column, use a variable named `total` to store its sum. Add each element in the column to `total` using a loop like this:

```
for (int column = 0; column < matrix[0].length; column++) {
  int total = 0;
  for (int row = 0; row < matrix.length; row++)
    total += matrix[row][column];
  System.out.println("Sum for column " + column + " is "
    + total);
}
```

6. *Which row has the largest sum?* Use variables `maxRow` and `indexOfMaxRow` to track the largest sum and index of the row. For each row, compute its sum and update `maxRow` and `indexOfMaxRow` if the new sum is greater.

```
int maxRow = 0;
int indexOfMaxRow = 0;

// Get sum of the first row in maxRow
for (int column = 0; column < matrix[0].length; column++) {
  maxRow += matrix[0][column];
}

for (int row = 1; row < matrix.length; row++) {
  int totalOfThisRow = 0;
  for (int column = 0; column < matrix[row].length; column++)
    totalOfThisRow += matrix[row][column];

  if (totalOfThisRow > maxRow) {
    maxRow = totalOfThisRow;
    indexOfMaxRow = row;
  }
}

System.out.println("Row " + indexOfMaxRow
  + " has the maximum sum of " + maxRow);
```

7. *Random shuffling.* Shuffling the elements in a one-dimensional array was introduced in Section 7.2.6. How do you shuffle all the elements in a two-dimensional array? To accomplish this, for each element `matrix[i][j]`, randomly generate indices `i1` and `j1` and swap `matrix[i][j]` with `matrix[i1][j1]`, as follows:

```
for (int i = 0; i < matrix.length; i++) {
  for (int j = 0; j < matrix[i].length; j++) {
    int i1 = (int)(Math.random() * matrix.length);
    int j1 = (int)(Math.random() * matrix[i].length);

    // Swap matrix[i][j] with matrix[i1][j1]
```

```
            int temp = matrix[i][j];
            matrix[i][j] = matrix[i1][j1];
            matrix[i1][j1] = temp;
        }
    }
```

8.5 Show the output of the following code:

Check
Point

```
int[][] array = {{1, 2}, {3, 4}, {5, 6}};
for (int i = array.length - 1; i >= 0; i--) {
  for (int j = array[i].length - 1; j >= 0; j--)
    System.out.print(array[i][j] + " ");
  System.out.println();
}
```

8.6 Show the output of the following code:

```
int[][] array = {{1, 2}, {3, 4}, {5, 6}};
int sum = 0;
for (int i = 0; i < array.length; i++)
  sum += array[i][0];
System.out.println(sum);
```

8.4 Passing Two-Dimensional Arrays to Methods

When passing a two-dimensional array to a method, the reference of the array is passed to the method.

Key
Point

You can pass a two-dimensional array to a method just as you pass a one-dimensional array. You can also return an array from a method. Listing 8.1 gives an example with two methods. The first method, **getArray()**, returns a two-dimensional array, and the second method, **sum(int[][] m)**, returns the sum of all the elements in a matrix.

LISTING 8.1 PassTwoDimensionalArray.java

```
 1  import java.util.Scanner;
 2
 3  public class PassTwoDimensionalArray {
 4    public static void main(String[] args) {
 5      int[][] m = getArray(); // Get an array                        get array
 6
 7      // Display sum of elements
 8      System.out.println("\nSum of all elements is " + sum(m));      pass array
 9    }
10
11    public static int[][] getArray() {                              getArray method
12      // Create a Scanner
13      Scanner input = new Scanner(System.in);
14
15      // Enter array values
16      int[][] m = new int[3][4];
17      System.out.println("Enter " + m.length + " rows and "
18        + m[0].length + " columns: ");
19      for (int i = 0; i < m.length; i++)
20        for (int j = 0; j < m[i].length; j++)
21          m[i][j] = input.nextInt();
22
```

return array

```
23          return m;
24      }
25
```

sum method

```
26      public static int sum(int[][] m) {
27          int total = 0;
28          for (int row = 0; row < m.length; row++) {
29              for (int column = 0; column < m[row].length; column++) {
30                  total += m[row][column];
31              }
32          }
33
34          return total;
35      }
36  }
```

```
Enter 3 rows and 4 columns:
1 2 3 4  ↵Enter
5 6 7 8  ↵Enter
9 10 11 12  ↵Enter

Sum of all elements is 78
```

The method **getArray** prompts the user to enter values for the array (lines 11–24) and returns the array (line 23).

The method **sum** (lines 26–35) has a two-dimensional array argument. You can obtain the number of rows using **m.length** (line 28) and the number of columns in a specified row using **m[row].length** (line 29).

Check Point

8.7   Show the output of the following code:

```
public class Test {
    public static void main(String[] args) {
        int[][] array = {{1, 2, 3, 4}, {5, 6, 7, 8}};
        System.out.println(m1(array)[0]);
        System.out.println(m1(array)[1]);
    }

    public static int[] m1(int[][] m) {
        int[] result = new int[2];
        result[0] = m.length;
        result[1] = m[0].length;
        return result;
    }
}
```

8.5 Case Study: Grading a Multiple-Choice Test

Key Point

The problem is to write a program that will grade multiple-choice tests.

VideoNote
Grade multiple-choice test

Suppose you need to write a program that grades multiple-choice tests. Assume there are eight students and ten questions, and the answers are stored in a two-dimensional array. Each row records a student's answers to the questions, as shown in the following array.

Students' Answers to the Questions:

```
            0 1 2 3 4 5 6 7 8 9
Student 0   A B A C C D E E A D
Student 1   D B A B C A E E A D
Student 2   E D D A C B E E A D
Student 3   C B A E D C E E A D
Student 4   A B D C C D E E A D
Student 5   B B E C C D E E A D
Student 6   B B A C C D E E A D
Student 7   E B E C C D E E A D
```

The key is stored in a one-dimensional array:

Key to the Questions:

```
      0 1 2 3 4 5 6 7 8 9
Key   D B D C C D A E A D
```

Your program grades the test and displays the result. It compares each student's answers with the key, counts the number of correct answers, and displays it. Listing 8.2 gives the program.

LISTING 8.2 GradeExam.java

```java
 1  public class GradeExam {
 2    /** Main method */
 3    public static void main(String[] args) {
 4      // Students' answers to the questions
 5      char[][] answers = {                                    2-D array
 6        {'A', 'B', 'A', 'C', 'C', 'D', 'E', 'E', 'A', 'D'},
 7        {'D', 'B', 'A', 'B', 'C', 'A', 'E', 'E', 'A', 'D'},
 8        {'E', 'D', 'D', 'A', 'C', 'B', 'E', 'E', 'A', 'D'},
 9        {'C', 'B', 'A', 'E', 'D', 'C', 'E', 'E', 'A', 'D'},
10        {'A', 'B', 'D', 'C', 'C', 'D', 'E', 'E', 'A', 'D'},
11        {'B', 'B', 'E', 'C', 'C', 'D', 'E', 'E', 'A', 'D'},
12        {'B', 'B', 'A', 'C', 'C', 'D', 'E', 'E', 'A', 'D'},
13        {'E', 'B', 'E', 'C', 'C', 'D', 'E', 'E', 'A', 'D'}};
14
15      // Key to the questions
16      char[] keys = {'D', 'B', 'D', 'C', 'C', 'D', 'A', 'E', 'A', 'D'};   1-D array
17
18      // Grade all answers
19      for (int i = 0; i < answers.length; i++) {
20        // Grade one student
21        int correctCount = 0;
22        for (int j = 0; j < answers[i].length; j++) {
23          if (answers[i][j] == keys[j])                       compare with key
24            correctCount++;
25        }
26
27        System.out.println("Student " + i + "'s correct count is " +
28          correctCount);
29      }
30    }
31  }
```

```
Student 0's correct count is 7
Student 1's correct count is 6
Student 2's correct count is 5
Student 3's correct count is 4
Student 4's correct count is 8
Student 5's correct count is 7
Student 6's correct count is 7
Student 7's correct count is 7
```

The statement in lines 5–13 declares, creates, and initializes a two-dimensional array of characters and assigns the reference to **answers** of the **char[][]** type.

The statement in line 16 declares, creates, and initializes an array of **char** values and assigns the reference to **keys** of the **char[]** type.

Each row in the array **answers** stores a student's answer, which is graded by comparing it with the key in the array **keys**. The result is displayed immediately after a student's answer is graded.

8.6 Case Study: Finding the Closest Pair

This section presents a geometric problem for finding the closest pair of points.

closest-pair animation on the Companion Website

Given a set of points, the closest-pair problem is to find the two points that are nearest to each other. In Figure 8.3, for example, points **(1, 1)** and **(2, 0.5)** are closest to each other. There are several ways to solve this problem. An intuitive approach is to compute the distances between all pairs of points and find the one with the minimum distance, as implemented in Listing 8.3.

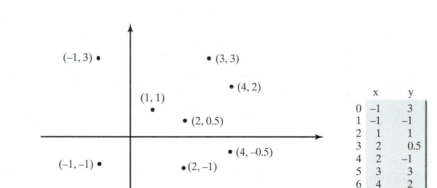

FIGURE 8.3 Points can be represented in a two-dimensional array.

LISTING 8.3 FindNearestPoints.java

```
1  import java.util.Scanner;
2
3  public class FindNearestPoints {
4    public static void main(String[] args) {
5      Scanner input = new Scanner(System.in);
6      System.out.print("Enter the number of points: ");
7      int numberOfPoints = input.nextInt();
8
9      // Create an array to store points
```

number of points

```
10        double[][] points = new double[numberOfPoints][2];              2-D array
11        System.out.print("Enter " + numberOfPoints + " points: ");
12        for (int i = 0; i < points.length; i++) {                       read points
13          points[i][0] = input.nextDouble();
14          points[i][1] = input.nextDouble();
15        }
16
17        // p1 and p2 are the indices in the points' array
18        int p1 = 0, p2 = 1; // Initial two points                       track two points
19        double shortestDistance = distance(points[p1][0], points[p1][1],  track shortestDistance
20          points[p2][0], points[p2][1]); // Initialize shortestDistance
21
22        // Compute distance for every two points
23        for (int i = 0; i < points.length; i++) {                       for each point i
24          for (int j = i + 1; j < points.length; j++) {                 for each point j
25            double distance = distance(points[i][0], points[i][1],      distance between i and j
26              points[j][0], points[j][1]); // Find distance             distance between two points
27
28            if (shortestDistance > distance) {
29              p1 = i; // Update p1
30              p2 = j; // Update p2
31              shortestDistance = distance; // Update shortestDistance    update shortestDistance
32            }
33          }
34        }
35
36        // Display result
37        System.out.println("The closest two points are " +
38          "(" + points[p1][0] + ", " + points[p1][1] + ") and (" +
39          points[p2][0] + ", " + points[p2][1] + ")");
40      }
41
42      /** Compute the distance between two points (x1, y1) and (x2, y2)*/
43      public static double distance(
44          double x1, double y1, double x2, double y2) {
45        return Math.sqrt((x2 - x1) * (x2 - x1) + (y2 - y1) * (y2 - y1));
46      }
47    }
```

```
Enter the number of points: 8  ↵Enter
Enter 8 points: -1 3  -1 -1  1 1  2 0.5  2 -1  3 3  4 2 4 -0.5  ↵Enter
The closest two points are (1, 1) and (2, 0.5)
```

The program prompts the user to enter the number of points (lines 6–7). The points are read from the console and stored in a two-dimensional array named **points** (lines 12–15). The program uses the variable **shortestDistance** (line 19) to store the distance between the two nearest points, and the indices of these two points in the **points** array are stored in **p1** and **p2** (line 18).

For each point at index **i**, the program computes the distance between **points[i]** and **points[j]** for all **j > i** (lines 23–34). Whenever a shorter distance is found, the variable **shortestDistance** and **p1** and **p2** are updated (lines 28–32).

The distance between two points **(x1, y1)** and **(x2, y2)** can be computed using the formula $\sqrt{(x_2 - x_1)^2 + (y_2 - y_1)^2}$ (lines 43–46).

The program assumes that the plane has at least two points. You can easily modify the program to handle the case if the plane has zero or one point.

multiple closest pairs

Note that there might be more than one closest pair of points with the same minimum distance. The program finds one such pair. You may modify the program to find all closest pairs in Programming Exercise 8.8.

input file

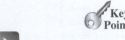

Tip
It is cumbersome to enter all points from the keyboard. You may store the input in a file, say **FindNearestPoints.txt**, and compile and run the program using the following command:

```
java FindNearestPoints < FindNearestPoints.txt
```

8.7 Case Study: Sudoku

The problem is to check whether a given Sudoku solution is correct.

This section presents an interesting problem of a sort that appears in the newspaper every day. It is a number-placement puzzle, commonly known as *Sudoku*. This is a very challenging problem. To make it accessible to the novice, this section presents a simplified version of the Sudoku problem, which is to verify whether a Sudoku solution is correct. The complete program for finding a Sudoku solution is presented in Supplement VI.A.

VideoNote

Sudoku

fixed cells
free cells

Sudoku is a 9 × 9 grid divided into smaller 3 × 3 boxes (also called *regions* or *blocks*), as shown in Figure 8.4a. Some cells, called *fixed cells*, are populated with numbers from **1** to **9**. The objective is to fill the empty cells, also called *free cells*, with the numbers **1** to **9** so that every row, every column, and every 3 × 3 box contains the numbers **1** to **9**, as shown in Figure 8.4b.

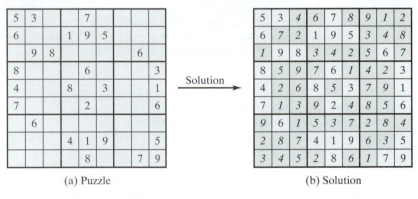

(a) Puzzle   (b) Solution

FIGURE 8.4 The Sudoku puzzle in (a) is solved in (b).

representing a grid

For convenience, we use value **0** to indicate a free cell, as shown in Figure 8.5a. The grid can be naturally represented using a two-dimensional array, as shown in Figure 8.5b.

5	3	0	0	7	0	0	0	0
6	0	0	1	9	5	0	0	0
0	9	8	0	0	0	0	6	0
8	0	0	0	6	0	0	0	3
4	0	0	8	0	3	0	0	1
7	0	0	0	2	0	0	0	6
0	6	0	0	0	0	2	8	0
0	0	0	4	1	9	0	0	5
0	0	0	0	8	0	0	7	9

```
int[][] grid =
 {{5, 3, 0, 0, 7, 0, 0, 0, 0},
  {6, 0, 0, 1, 9, 5, 0, 0, 0},
  {0, 9, 8, 0, 0, 0, 0, 6, 0},
  {8, 0, 0, 0, 6, 0, 0, 0, 3},
  {4, 0, 0, 8, 0, 3, 0, 0, 1},
  {7, 0, 0, 0, 2, 0, 0, 0, 6},
  {0, 6, 0, 0, 0, 0, 2, 8, 0},
  {0, 0, 0, 4, 1, 9, 0, 0, 5},
  {0, 0, 0, 0, 8, 0, 0, 7, 9}
};
```

(a)   (b)

FIGURE 8.5 A grid can be represented using a two-dimensional array.

To find a solution for the puzzle, we must replace each 0 in the grid with an appropriate number from 1 to 9. For the solution to the puzzle in Figure 8.5, the grid should be as shown in Figure 8.6.

Once a solution to a Sudoku puzzle is found, how do you verify that it is correct? Here are two approaches:

■ Check if every row has numbers from 1 to 9, every column has numbers from 1 to 9, and every small box has numbers from 1 to 9.

■ Check each cell. Each cell must be a number from 1 to 9 and the cell must be unique on every row, every column, and every small box.

```
A solution grid is
  {{5, 3, 4, 6, 7, 8, 9, 1, 2},
   {6, 7, 2, 1, 9, 5, 3, 4, 8},
   {1, 9, 8, 3, 4, 2, 5, 6, 7},
   {8, 5, 9, 7, 6, 1, 4, 2, 3},
   {4, 2, 6, 8, 5, 3, 7, 9, 1},
   {7, 1, 3, 9, 2, 4, 8, 5, 6},
   {9, 6, 1, 5, 3, 7, 2, 8, 4},
   {2, 8, 7, 4, 1, 9, 6, 3, 5},
   {3, 4, 5, 2, 8, 6, 1, 7, 9}
  };
```

FIGURE 8.6 A solution is stored in `grid`.

The program in Listing 8.4 prompts the user to enter a solution and reports whether it is valid. We use the second approach in the program to check whether the solution is correct.

LISTING 8.4 CheckSudokuSolution.java

```java
 1  import java.util.Scanner;
 2
 3  public class CheckSudokuSolution {
 4    public static void main(String[] args) {
 5      // Read a Sudoku solution
 6      int[][] grid = readASolution();                          read input
 7
 8      System.out.println(isValid(grid) ? "Valid solution" :    solution valid?
 9        "Invalid solution");
10    }
11
12    /** Read a Sudoku solution from the console */
13    public static int[][] readASolution() {                    read solution
14      // Create a Scanner
15      Scanner input = new Scanner(System.in);
16
17      System.out.println("Enter a Sudoku puzzle solution:");
18      int[][] grid = new int[9][9];
19      for (int i = 0; i < 9; i++)
20        for (int j = 0; j < 9; j++)
21          grid[i][j] = input.nextInt();
22
23      return grid;
24    }
25
26    /** Check whether a solution is valid */
27    public static boolean isValid(int[][] grid) {              check solution
```

```
28        for (int i = 0; i < 9; i++)
29          for (int j = 0; j < 9; j++)
30            if (grid[i][j] < 1 || grid[i][j] > 9
31                || !isValid(i, j, grid))
32              return false;
33        return true; // The solution is valid
34    }
35
36    /** Check whether grid[i][j] is valid in the grid */
37    public static boolean isValid(int i, int j, int[][] grid) {
38      // Check whether grid[i][j] is unique in i's row
39      for (int column = 0; column < 9; column++)
40        if (column != j && grid[i][column] == grid[i][j])
41          return false;
42
43      // Check whether grid[i][j] is unique in j's column
44      for (int row = 0; row < 9; row++)
45        if (row != i && grid[row][j] == grid[i][j])
46          return false;
47
48      // Check whether grid[i][j] is unique in the 3-by-3 box
49      for (int row = (i / 3) * 3; row < (i / 3) * 3 + 3; row++)
50        for (int col = (j / 3) * 3; col < (j / 3) * 3 + 3; col++)
51          if (row != i && col != j && grid[row][col] == grid[i][j])
52            return false;
53
54      return true; // The current value at grid[i][j] is valid
55    }
56  }
```

check rows (line 39)

check columns (line 44)

check small boxes (line 49)

```
Enter a Sudoku puzzle solution:
9 6 3 1 7 4 2 5 8  ↵Enter
1 7 8 3 2 5 6 4 9  ↵Enter
2 5 4 6 8 9 7 3 1  ↵Enter
8 2 1 4 3 7 5 9 6  ↵Enter
4 9 6 8 5 2 3 1 7  ↵Enter
7 3 5 9 6 1 8 2 4  ↵Enter
5 8 9 7 1 3 4 6 2  ↵Enter
3 1 7 2 4 6 9 8 5  ↵Enter
6 4 2 5 9 8 1 7 3  ↵Enter
Valid solution
```

The program invokes the **readASolution()** method (line 6) to read a Sudoku solution and return a two-dimensional array representing a Sudoku grid.

isValid method

The **isValid(grid)** method checks whether the values in the grid are valid by verifying that each value is between **1** and **9** and that each value is valid in the grid (lines 27–34).

overloaded isValid method

The **isValid(i, j, grid)** method checks whether the value at **grid[i][j]** is valid. It checks whether **grid[i][j]** appears more than once in row **i** (lines 39–41), in column **j** (lines 44–46), and in the 3 × 3 box (lines 49–52).

How do you locate all the cells in the same box? For any **grid[i][j]**, the starting cell of the 3 × 3 box that contains it is **grid[(i / 3) * 3][(j / 3) * 3]**, as illustrated in Figure 8.7.

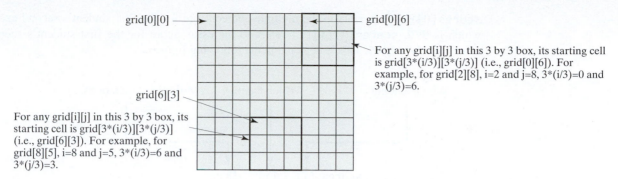

FIGURE 8.7   The location of the first cell in a 3 × 3 box determines the locations of other cells in the box.

With this observation, you can easily identify all the cells in the box. For instance, if `grid[r][c]` is the starting cell of a 3 × 3 box, the cells in the box can be traversed in a nested loop as follows:

```
// Get all cells in a 3-by-3 box starting at grid[r][c]
for (int row = r; row < r + 3; row++)
  for (int col = c; col < c + 3; col++)
    // grid[row][col] is in the box
```

It is cumbersome to enter 81 numbers from the console. When you test the program, you may store the input in a file, say **CheckSudokuSolution.txt** (see www.cs.armstrong.edu/liang/data/CheckSudokuSolution.txt), and run the program using the following command:

input file

```
java CheckSudokuSolution < CheckSudokuSolution.txt
```

8.8 Multidimensional Arrays

A two-dimensional array consists of an array of one-dimensional arrays and a three-dimensional array consists of an array of two-dimensional arrays.

Key Point

In the preceding section, you used a two-dimensional array to represent a matrix or a table. Occasionally, you will need to represent *n*-dimensional data structures. In Java, you can create *n*-dimensional arrays for any integer *n*.

The way to declare two-dimensional array variables and create two-dimensional arrays can be generalized to declare *n*-dimensional array variables and create *n*-dimensional arrays for *n* >= 3. For example, you may use a three-dimensional array to store exam scores for a class of six students with five exams, and each exam has two parts (multiple-choice and essay). The following syntax declares a three-dimensional array variable **scores**, creates an array, and assigns its reference to **scores**.

```
double[][][] scores = new double[6][5][2];
```

You can also use the short-hand notation to create and initialize the array as follows:

```
double[][][] scores = {
  {{7.5, 20.5}, {9.0, 22.5}, {15, 33.5}, {13, 21.5}, {15, 2.5}},
  {{4.5, 21.5}, {9.0, 22.5}, {15, 34.5}, {12, 20.5}, {14, 9.5}},
  {{6.5, 30.5}, {9.4, 10.5}, {11, 33.5}, {11, 23.5}, {10, 2.5}},
  {{6.5, 23.5}, {9.4, 32.5}, {13, 34.5}, {11, 20.5}, {16, 7.5}},
  {{8.5, 26.5}, {9.4, 52.5}, {13, 36.5}, {13, 24.5}, {16, 2.5}},
  {{9.5, 20.5}, {9.4, 42.5}, {13, 31.5}, {12, 20.5}, {16, 6.5}}};
```

`scores[0][1][0]` refers to the multiple-choice score for the first student's second exam, which is **9.0**. `scores[0][1][1]` refers to the essay score for the first student's second exam, which is **22.5**. This is depicted in the following figure:

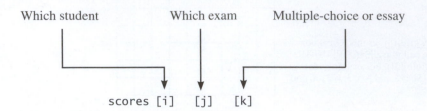

A multidimensional array is actually an array in which each element is another array. A three-dimensional array consists of an array of two-dimensional arrays. A two-dimensional array consists of an array of one-dimensional arrays. For example, suppose `x = new int[2][2][5]`, and `x[0]` and `x[1]` are two-dimensional arrays. `X[0][0]`, `x[0][1]`, `x[1][0]`, and `x[1][1]` are one-dimensional arrays and each contains five elements. `x.length` is **2**, `x[0].length` and `x[1].length` are **2**, and `X[0][0].length`, `x[0][1].length`, `x[1][0].length`, and `x[1][1].length` are **5**.

8.8.1 Case Study: Daily Temperature and Humidity

Suppose a meteorology station records the temperature and humidity every hour of every day and stores the data for the past ten days in a text file named **Weather.txt** (see www .cs.armstrong.edu/liang/data/Weather.txt). Each line of the file consists of four numbers that indicate the day, hour, temperature, and humidity. The contents of the file may look like the one in (a).

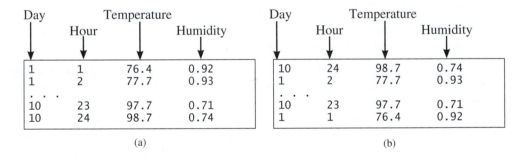

Day	Hour	Temperature	Humidity
1	1	76.4	0.92
1	2	77.7	0.93
. . .			
10	23	97.7	0.71
10	24	98.7	0.74

(a)

Day	Hour	Temperature	Humidity
10	24	98.7	0.74
1	2	77.7	0.93
. . .			
10	23	97.7	0.71
1	1	76.4	0.92

(b)

Note that the lines in the file are not necessarily in increasing order of day and hour. For example, the file may appear as shown in (b).

Your task is to write a program that calculates the average daily temperature and humidity for the **10** days. You can use the input redirection to read the file and store the data in a three-dimensional array named **data**. The first index of **data** ranges from **0** to **9** and represents **10** days, the second index ranges from **0** to **23** and represents **24** hours, and the third index ranges from **0** to **1** and represents temperature and humidity, as depicted in the following figure:

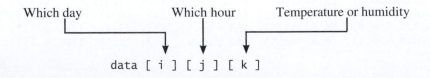

Note that the days are numbered from **1** to **10** and the hours from **1** to **24** in the file. Because the array index starts from **0**, **data[0][0][0]** stores the temperature in day **1** at hour **1** and **data[9][23][1]** stores the humidity in day **10** at hour **24**.

The program is given in Listing 8.5.

LISTING 8.5 Weather.java

```java
1  import java.util.Scanner;
2
3  public class Weather {
4    public static void main(String[] args) {
5      final int NUMBER_OF_DAYS = 10;
6      final int NUMBER_OF_HOURS = 24;
7      double[][][] data
8        = new double[NUMBER_OF_DAYS][NUMBER_OF_HOURS][2];      three-dimensional array
9
10     Scanner input = new Scanner(System.in);
11     // Read input using input redirection from a file
12     for (int k = 0; k < NUMBER_OF_DAYS * NUMBER_OF_HOURS; k++) {
13       int day = input.nextInt();
14       int hour = input.nextInt();
15       double temperature = input.nextDouble();
16       double humidity = input.nextDouble();
17       data[day - 1][hour - 1][0] = temperature;
18       data[day - 1][hour - 1][1] = humidity;
19     }
20
21     // Find the average daily temperature and humidity
22     for (int i = 0; i < NUMBER_OF_DAYS; i++) {
23       double dailyTemperatureTotal = 0, dailyHumidityTotal = 0;
24       for (int j = 0; j < NUMBER_OF_HOURS; j++) {
25         dailyTemperatureTotal += data[i][j][0];
26         dailyHumidityTotal += data[i][j][1];
27       }
28
29       // Display result
30       System.out.println("Day " + i + "'s average temperature is "
31         + dailyTemperatureTotal / NUMBER_OF_HOURS);
32       System.out.println("Day " + i + "'s average humidity is "
33         + dailyHumidityTotal / NUMBER_OF_HOURS);
34     }
35   }
36 }
```

```
Day 0's average temperature is 77.7708
Day 0's average humidity is 0.929583
Day 1's average temperature is 77.3125
Day 1's average humidity is 0.929583
. . .
Day 9's average temperature is 79.3542
Day 9's average humidity is 0.9125
```

You can use the following command to run the program:

```
java Weather < Weather.txt
```

A three-dimensional array for storing temperature and humidity is created in line 8. The loop in lines 12–19 reads the input to the array. You can enter the input from the keyboard, but doing so will be awkward. For convenience, we store the data in a file and use input redirection to read the data from the file. The loop in lines 24–27 adds all temperatures for each hour in a day to **dailyTemperatureTotal** and all humidity for each hour to **dailyHumidity-Total**. The average daily temperature and humidity are displayed in lines 30–33.

8.8.2 Case Study: Guessing Birthdays

Listing 3.3, GuessBirthday.java, gives a program that guesses a birthday. The program can be simplified by storing the numbers in five sets in a three-dimensional array, and it prompts the user for the answers using a loop, as shown in Listing 8.6. The sample run of the program can be the same as shown in Listing 4.3.

LISTING 8.6 GuessBirthdayUsingArray.java

```java
 1   import java.util.Scanner;
 2
 3   public class GuessBirthdayUsingArray {
 4     public static void main(String[] args) {
 5       int day = 0; // Day to be determined
 6       int answer;
 7
 8       int[][][] dates = {
 9         {{ 1,  3,  5,  7},
10          { 9, 11, 13, 15},
11          {17, 19, 21, 23},
12          {25, 27, 29, 31}},
13         {{ 2,  3,  6,  7},
14          {10, 11, 14, 15},
15          {18, 19, 22, 23},
16          {26, 27, 30, 31}},
17         {{ 4,  5,  6,  7},
18          {12, 13, 14, 15},
19          {20, 21, 22, 23},
20          {28, 29, 30, 31}},
21         {{ 8,  9, 10, 11},
22          {12, 13, 14, 15},
23          {24, 25, 26, 27},
24          {28, 29, 30, 31}},
25         {{16, 17, 18, 19},
26          {20, 21, 22, 23},
27          {24, 25, 26, 27},
28          {28, 29, 30, 31}}};
29
30       // Create a Scanner
31       Scanner input = new Scanner(System.in);
32
33       for (int i = 0; i < 5; i++) {
34         System.out.println("Is your birthday in Set" + (i + 1) + "?");
35         for (int j = 0; j < 4; j++) {
36           for (int k = 0; k < 4; k++)
37             System.out.printf("%4d", dates[i][j][k]);
38           System.out.println();
39         }
40
41         System.out.print("\nEnter 0 for No and 1 for Yes: ");
42         answer = input.nextInt();
43
44         if (answer == 1)
45           day += dates[i][0][0];
```

three-dimensional array

Set i

add to day

```
46      }
47
48      System.out.println("Your birthday is " + day);
49    }
50 }
```

A three-dimensional array `dates` is created in Lines 8–28. This array stores five sets of numbers. Each set is a 4-by-4 two-dimensional array.

The loop starting from line 33 displays the numbers in each set and prompts the user to answer whether the birthday is in the set (lines 41–42). If the day is in the set, the first number (`dates[i][0][0]`) in the set is added to variable `day` (line 45).

8.8 Declare an array variable for a three-dimensional array, create a 4 × 6 × 5 `int` array, and assign its reference to the variable.

Check Point

8.9 Assume `int[][][] x = new char[12][5][2]`, how many elements are in the array? What are `x.length`, `x[2].length`, and `x[0][0].length`?

8.10 Show the output of the following code:

```
int[][][] array = {{{1, 2}, {3, 4}}, {{5, 6},{7, 8}}};
System.out.println(array[0][0][0]);
System.out.println(array[1][1][1]);
```

CHAPTER SUMMARY

1. A two-dimensional array can be used to store a table.

2. A variable for two-dimensional arrays can be declared using the syntax: `elementType[][] arrayVar`.

3. A two-dimensional array can be created using the syntax: `new   elementType [ROW_SIZE][COLUMN_SIZE]`.

4. Each element in a two-dimensional array is represented using the syntax: `arrayVar[rowIndex][columnIndex]`.

5. You can create and initialize a two-dimensional array using an array initializer with the syntax: `elementType[][] arrayVar = {{row values}, . . . , {row values}}`.

6. You can use arrays of arrays to form multidimensional arrays. For example, a variable for three-dimensional arrays can be declared as `elementType[][][] arrayVar`, and a three-dimensional array can be created using `new elementType[size1][size2] [size3]`.

QUIZ

Answer the quiz for this chapter online at www.cs.armstrong.edu/liang/intro10e/quiz.html.

PROGRAMMING EXERCISES

MyProgrammingLab™

*8.1 (*Sum elements column by column*) Write a method that returns the sum of all the elements in a specified column in a matrix using the following header:

```
public static double sumColumn(double[][] m, int columnIndex)
```

Write a test program that reads a 3-by-4 matrix and displays the sum of each column. Here is a sample run:

```
Enter a 3-by-4 matrix row by row:
1.5 2 3 4 ↵Enter
5.5 6 7 8 ↵Enter
9.5 1 3 1 ↵Enter
Sum of the elements at column 0 is 16.5
Sum of the elements at column 1 is 9.0
Sum of the elements at column 2 is 13.0
Sum of the elements at column 3 is 13.0
```

*8.2 (*Sum the major diagonal in a matrix*) Write a method that sums all the numbers in the major diagonal in an $n \times n$ matrix of **double** values using the following header:

```
public static double sumMajorDiagonal(double[][] m)
```

Write a test program that reads a 4-by-4 matrix and displays the sum of all its elements on the major diagonal. Here is a sample run:

```
Enter a 4-by-4 matrix row by row:
1 2 3 4.0 ↵Enter
5 6.5 7 8 ↵Enter
9 10 11 12 ↵Enter
13 14 15 16 ↵Enter
Sum of the elements in the major diagonal is 34.5
```

*8.3 (*Sort students on grades*) Rewrite Listing 8.2, GradeExam.java, to display the students in increasing order of the number of correct answers.

**8.4 (*Compute the weekly hours for each employee*) Suppose the weekly hours for all employees are stored in a two-dimensional array. Each row records an employee's seven-day work hours with seven columns. For example, the following array stores the work hours for eight employees. Write a program that displays employees and their total hours in decreasing order of the total hours.

	Su	M	T	W	Th	F	Sa
Employee 0	2	4	3	4	5	8	8
Employee 1	7	3	4	3	3	4	4
Employee 2	3	3	4	3	3	2	2
Employee 3	9	3	4	7	3	4	1
Employee 4	3	5	4	3	6	3	8
Employee 5	3	4	4	6	3	4	4
Employee 6	3	7	4	8	3	8	4
Employee 7	6	3	5	9	2	7	9

8.5 (*Algebra: add two matrices*) Write a method to add two matrices. The header of the method is as follows:

```
public static double[][] addMatrix(double[][] a, double[][] b)
```

In order to be added, the two matrices must have the same dimensions and the same or compatible types of elements. Let **c** be the resulting matrix. Each element c_{ij} is $a_{ij} + b_{ij}$. For example, for two 3×3 matrices **a** and **b**, **c** is

$$
\begin{pmatrix} a_{11} & a_{12} & a_{13} \\ a_{21} & a_{22} & a_{23} \\ a_{31} & a_{32} & a_{33} \end{pmatrix}
+
\begin{pmatrix} b_{11} & b_{12} & b_{13} \\ b_{21} & b_{22} & b_{23} \\ b_{31} & b_{32} & b_{33} \end{pmatrix}
=
\begin{pmatrix} a_{11} + b_{11} & a_{12} + b_{12} & a_{13} + b_{13} \\ a_{21} + b_{21} & a_{22} + b_{22} & a_{23} + b_{23} \\ a_{31} + b_{31} & a_{32} + b_{32} & a_{33} + b_{33} \end{pmatrix}
$$

VideoNote

Multiply two matrices

Write a test program that prompts the user to enter two 3×3 matrices and displays their sum. Here is a sample run:

```
Enter matrix1: 1 2 3 4 5 6 7 8 9  ↵Enter
Enter matrix2: 0 2 4 1 4.5 2.2 1.1 4.3 5.2  ↵Enter
The matrices are added as follows
  1.0 2.0 3.0      0.0 2.0 4.0      1.0 4.0 7.0
  4.0 5.0 6.0  +   1.0 4.5 2.2  =   5.0 9.5 8.2
  7.0 8.0 9.0      1.1 4.3 5.2      8.1 12.3 14.2
```

**8.6 (*Algebra: multiply two matrices*) Write a method to multiply two matrices. The header of the method is:

```
public static double[][]
    multiplyMatrix(double[][] a, double[][] b)
```

To multiply matrix **a** by matrix **b**, the number of columns in **a** must be the same as the number of rows in **b**, and the two matrices must have elements of the same or compatible types. Let **c** be the result of the multiplication. Assume the column size of matrix a is **n**. Each element c_{ij} is $a_{i1} \times b_{1j} + a_{i2} \times b_{2j} + \ldots + a_{in} \times b_{nj}$. For example, for two 3×3 matrices **a** and **b**, **c** is

$$
\begin{pmatrix} a_{11} & a_{12} & a_{13} \\ a_{21} & a_{22} & a_{23} \\ a_{31} & a_{32} & a_{33} \end{pmatrix}
\times
\begin{pmatrix} b_{11} & b_{12} & b_{13} \\ b_{21} & b_{22} & b_{23} \\ b_{31} & b_{32} & b_{33} \end{pmatrix}
=
\begin{pmatrix} c_{11} & c_{12} & c_{13} \\ c_{21} & c_{22} & c_{23} \\ c_{31} & c_{32} & c_{33} \end{pmatrix}
$$

where $c_{ij} = a_{i1} \times b_{1j} + a_{i2} \times b_{2j} + a_{i3} \times b_{3j}$.

Write a test program that prompts the user to enter two 3×3 matrices and displays their product. Here is a sample run:

```
Enter matrix1: 1 2 3 4 5 6 7 8 9  ↵Enter
Enter matrix2: 0 2 4 1 4.5 2.2 1.1 4.3 5.2  ↵Enter
The multiplication of the matrices is
  1 2 3      0 2.0 4.0       5.3 23.9 24
  4 5 6  *   1 4.5 2.2   =   11.6 56.3 58.2
  7 8 9      1.1 4.3 5.2     17.9 88.7 92.4
```

*8.7 (*Points nearest to each other*) Listing 8.3 gives a program that finds two points in a two-dimensional space nearest to each other. Revise the program so that it finds two points in a three-dimensional space nearest to each other. Use a two-dimensional array to represent the points. Test the program using the following points:

```
double[][] points = {{-1, 0, 3}, {-1, -1, -1}, {4, 1, 1},
  {2, 0.5, 9}, {3.5, 2, -1}, {3, 1.5, 3}, {-1.5, 4, 2},
  {5.5, 4, -0.5}};
```

The formula for computing the distance between two points (x1, y1, z1) and (x2, y2, z2) is $\sqrt{(x_2 - x_1)^2 + (y_2 - y_1)^2 + (z_2 - z_1)^2}$.

**8.8 (*All closest pairs of points*) Revise Listing 8.3, FindNearestPoints.java, to display all closest pairs of points with the same minimum distance. Here is a sample run:

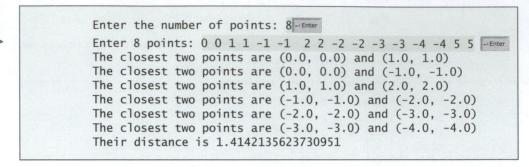

```
Enter the number of points: 8 ⏎Enter
Enter 8 points: 0 0 1 1 -1 -1  2 2 -2 -2 -3 -3 -4 -4 5 5 ⏎Enter
The closest two points are (0.0, 0.0) and (1.0, 1.0)
The closest two points are (0.0, 0.0) and (-1.0, -1.0)
The closest two points are (1.0, 1.0) and (2.0, 2.0)
The closest two points are (-1.0, -1.0) and (-2.0, -2.0)
The closest two points are (-2.0, -2.0) and (-3.0, -3.0)
The closest two points are (-3.0, -3.0) and (-4.0, -4.0)
Their distance is 1.4142135623730951
```

***8.9 (*Game: play a tic-tac-toe game*) In a game of tic-tac-toe, two players take turns marking an available cell in a 3 × 3 grid with their respective tokens (either X or O). When one player has placed three tokens in a horizontal, vertical, or diagonal row on the grid, the game is over and that player has won. A draw (no winner) occurs when all the cells on the grid have been filled with tokens and neither player has achieved a win. Create a program for playing tic-tac-toe.

The program prompts two players to enter an X token and O token alternately. Whenever a token is entered, the program redisplays the board on the console and determines the status of the game (win, draw, or continue). Here is a sample run:

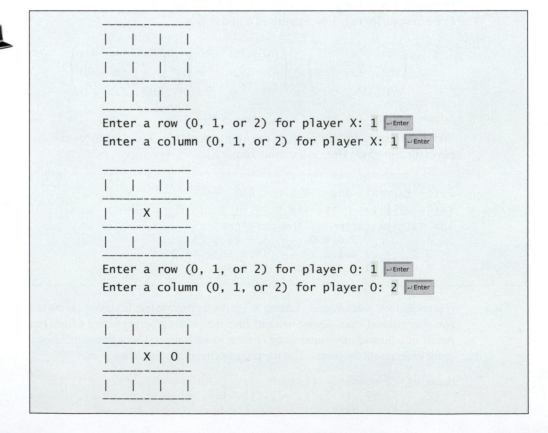

```
-------------
|   |   |   |
-------------
|   |   |   |
-------------
|   |   |   |
-------------
Enter a row (0, 1, or 2) for player X: 1 ⏎Enter
Enter a column (0, 1, or 2) for player X: 1 ⏎Enter

-------------
|   |   |   |
-------------
|   | X |   |
-------------
|   |   |   |
-------------
Enter a row (0, 1, or 2) for player O: 1 ⏎Enter
Enter a column (0, 1, or 2) for player O: 2 ⏎Enter

-------------
|   |   |   |
-------------
|   | X | O |
-------------
|   |   |   |
-------------
```

```
Enter a row (0, 1, or 2) for player X:

. . .

_____
| X |   |   |
_____
| O | X | O |
_____
|   |   | X |
_____
X player won
```

*8.10 (*Largest row and column*) Write a program that randomly fills in 0s and 1s into a 4-by-4 matrix, prints the matrix, and finds the first row and column with the most 1s. Here is a sample run of the program:

```
0011
0011
1101
1010
The largest row index: 2
The largest column index: 2
```

8.11 (*Game: nine heads and tails*) Nine coins are placed in a 3-by-3 matrix with some face up and some face down. You can represent the state of the coins using a 3-by-3 matrix with values **0 (heads) and **1** (tails). Here are some examples:

```
0 0 0     1 0 1     1 1 0     1 0 1     1 0 0
0 1 0     0 0 1     1 0 0     1 1 0     1 1 1
0 0 0     1 0 0     0 0 1     1 0 0     1 1 0
```

Each state can also be represented using a binary number. For example, the preceding matrices correspond to the numbers

000010000 101001100 110100001 101110100 100111110

There are a total of 512 possibilities, so you can use decimal numbers 0, 1, 2, 3, ..., and 511 to represent all states of the matrix. Write a program that prompts the user to enter a number between 0 and 511 and displays the corresponding matrix with the characters **H** and **T**. Here is a sample run:

```
Enter a number between 0 and 511: 7  ↵Enter
H H H
H H H
T T T
```

The user entered **7**, which corresponds to **000000111**. Since **0** stands for **H** and **1** for **T**, the output is correct.

**8.12 (*Financial application: compute tax*) Rewrite Listing 3.5, ComputeTax.java, using arrays. For each filing status, there are six tax rates. Each rate is applied to a certain amount of taxable income. For example, from the taxable income of $400,000 for a single filer, $8,350 is taxed at 10%, (33,950 − 8,350) at 15%,

(82,250 − 33,950) at 25%, (171,550 − 82,550) at 28%, (372,550 − 82,250) at 33%, and (400,000 − 372,950) at 36%. The six rates are the same for all filing statuses, which can be represented in the following array:

```
double[] rates = {0.10, 0.15, 0.25, 0.28, 0.33, 0.35};
```

The brackets for each rate for all the filing statuses can be represented in a two-dimensional array as follows:

```
int[][] brackets = {
  {8350, 33950, 82250, 171550, 372950},   // Single filer
  {16700, 67900, 137050, 20885, 372950},  // Married jointly
                                          // -or qualifying widow(er)
  {8350, 33950, 68525, 104425, 186475},   // Married separately
  {11950, 45500, 117450, 190200, 372950}  // Head of household
};
```

Suppose the taxable income is $400,000 for single filers. The tax can be computed as follows:

```
tax = brackets[0][0] * rates[0] +
    (brackets[0][1] - brackets[0][0]) * rates[1] +
    (brackets[0][2] - brackets[0][1]) * rates[2] +
    (brackets[0][3] - brackets[0][2]) * rates[3] +
    (brackets[0][4] - brackets[0][3]) * rates[4] +
    (400000 - brackets[0][4]) * rates[5]
```

*8.13 (*Locate the largest element*) Write the following method that returns the location of the largest element in a two-dimensional array.

```
public static int[] locateLargest(double[][] a)
```

The return value is a one-dimensional array that contains two elements. These two elements indicate the row and column indices of the largest element in the two-dimensional array. Write a test program that prompts the user to enter a two-dimensional array and displays the location of the largest element in the array. Here is a sample run:

```
Enter the number of rows and columns of the array: 3 4 ↵Enter
Enter the array:
23.5 35 2 10 ↵Enter
4.5 3 45 3.5 ↵Enter
35 44 5.5 9.6 ↵Enter
The location of the largest element is at (1, 2)
```

**8.14 (*Explore matrix*) Write a program that prompts the user to enter the length of a square matrix, randomly fills in 0s and 1s into the matrix, prints the matrix, and finds the rows, columns, and diagonals with all 0s or 1s. Here is a sample run of the program:

```
Enter the size for the matrix: 4 ↵Enter
0111
0000
0100
1111
All 0s on row 1
All 1s on row 3
No same numbers on a column
No same numbers on the major diagonal
No same numbers on the sub-diagonal
```

*8.15 (*Geometry: same line?*) Programming Exercise 6.39 gives a method for testing whether three points are on the same line.

Write the following method to test whether all the points in the array **points** are on the same line.

public static boolean sameLine(**double**[][] points)

Write a program that prompts the user to enter five points and displays whether they are on the same line. Here are sample runs:

```
Enter five points: 3.4 2 6.5 9.5 2.3 2.3 5.5 5 -5 4 ↵Enter
The five points are not on the same line
```

```
Enter five points: 1 1 2 2 3 3 4 4 5 5 ↵Enter
The five points are on the same line
```

*8.16 (*Sort two-dimensional array*) Write a method to sort a two-dimensional array using the following header:

public static void sort(**int** m[][])

The method performs a primary sort on rows and a secondary sort on columns. For example, the following array

{{4, 2},{1, 7},{4, 5},{1, 2},{1, 1},{4, 1}}

will be sorted to

{{1, 1},{1, 2},{1, 7},{4, 1},{4, 2},{4, 5}}.

***8.17 (*Financial tsunami*) Banks lend money to each other. In tough economic times, if a bank goes bankrupt, it may not be able to pay back the loan. A bank's total assets are its current balance plus its loans to other banks. The diagram in Figure 8.8 shows five banks. The banks' current balances are 25, 125, 175, 75, and 181 million dollars, respectively. The directed edge from node 1 to node 2 indicates that bank 1 lends 40 million dollars to bank 2.

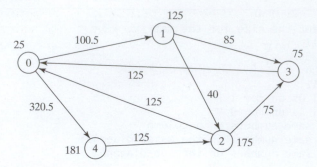

FIGURE 8.8 Banks lend money to each other.

If a bank's total assets are under a certain limit, the bank is unsafe. The money it borrowed cannot be returned to the lender, and the lender cannot count the loan in its total assets. Consequently, the lender may also be unsafe, if its total assets are under the limit. Write a program to find all the unsafe banks. Your program reads the input as follows. It first reads two integers n and limit, where n indicates the number of banks and limit is the minimum total assets for keeping a bank safe. It then reads n lines that describe the information for n banks with IDs from 0 to n-1.

The first number in the line is the bank's balance, the second number indicates the number of banks that borrowed money from the bank, and the rest are pairs of two numbers. Each pair describes a borrower. The first number in the pair is the borrower's ID and the second is the amount borrowed. For example, the input for the five banks in Figure 8.8 is as follows (note that the limit is 201):

```
5 201
25 2 1 100.5 4 320.5
125 2 2 40 3 85
175 2 0 125 3 75
75 1 0 125
181 1 2 125
```

The total assets of bank 3 are (75 + 125), which is under 201, so bank 3 is unsafe. After bank 3 becomes unsafe, the total assets of bank 1 fall below (125 + 40). Thus, bank 1 is also unsafe. The output of the program should be

```
Unsafe banks are 3 1
```

(*Hint*: Use a two-dimensional array **borrowers** to represent loans. **borrowers[i][j]** indicates the loan that bank j loans to bank j. Once bank j becomes unsafe, **borrowers[i][j]** should be set to 0.)

*8.18 (*Shuffle rows*) Write a method that shuffles the rows in a two-dimensional int array using the following header:

public static void shuffle(**int**[][] m)

Write a test program that shuffles the following matrix:

int[][] m = {{1, 2}, {3, 4}, {5, 6}, {7, 8}, {9, 10}};

**8.19 (*Pattern recognition: four consecutive equal numbers*) Write the following method that tests whether a two-dimensional array has four consecutive numbers of the same value, either horizontally, vertically, or diagonally.

public static boolean isConsecutiveFour(**int**[][] values)

Write a test program that prompts the user to enter the number of rows and columns of a two-dimensional array and then the values in the array and displays true if the array contains four consecutive numbers with the same value. Otherwise, display false. Here are some examples of the true cases:

0	1	0	3	1	6	1
0	1	6	8	6	0	1
5	6	2	1	8	2	9
6	5	6	1	1	9	1
1	3	6	1	4	0	7
3	3	3	3	4	0	7

0	1	0	3	1	6	1
0	1	6	8	6	0	1
5	5	2	1	8	2	9
6	5	6	1	1	9	1
1	5	6	1	4	0	7
3	5	3	3	4	0	7

0	1	0	3	1	6	1
0	1	6	8	6	0	1
5	6	2	1	6	2	9
6	5	6	6	1	9	1
1	3	6	1	4	0	7
3	6	3	3	4	0	7

0	1	0	3	1	6	1
0	1	6	8	6	0	1
9	6	2	1	8	2	9
6	9	6	1	1	9	1
1	3	9	1	4	0	7
3	3	3	9	4	0	7

***8.20** (*Game: connect four*) Connect four is a two-player board game in which the players alternately drop colored disks into a seven-column, six-row vertically suspended grid, as shown below.

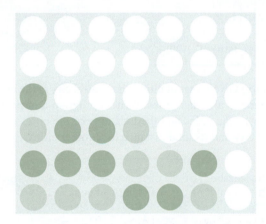

The objective of the game is to connect four same-colored disks in a row, a column, or a diagonal before your opponent can do likewise. The program prompts two players to drop a red or yellow disk alternately. In the preceding figure, the red disk is shown in a dark color and the yellow in a light color. Whenever a disk is dropped, the program redisplays the board on the console and determines the status of the game (win, draw, or continue). Here is a sample run:

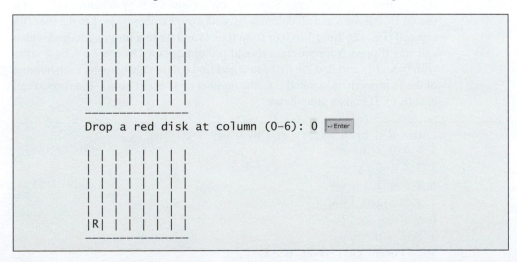

```
| | | | | | | |
| | | | | | | |
| | | | | | | |
| | | | | | | |
| | | | | | | |
| | | | | | | |
---------------
Drop a red disk at column (0-6): 0 ⏎Enter

| | | | | | | |
| | | | | | | |
| | | | | | | |
| | | | | | | |
| | | | | | | |
|R| | | | | | |
---------------
```

```
Drop a yellow disk at column (0-6): 3 ↵Enter
| | | | | | | |
| | | | | | | |
| | | | | | | |
| | | | | | | |
| | | | | | | |
|R| | |Y| | | |

 . . .
 . . .
 . . .

Drop a yellow disk at column (0-6): 6 ↵Enter
| | | | | | | |
| | | | | | | |
| | | |R| | | |
| | | |Y|R|Y| |
| | |R|Y|Y|Y|Y|
|R|Y|R|Y|R|R|R|
----------------
The yellow player won
```

*8.21 *(Central city)* Given a set of cities, the central city is the city that has the shortest total distance to all other cities. Write a program that prompts the user to enter the number of the cities and the locations of the cities (coordinates), and finds the central city and its total distance to all other cities.

```
Enter the number of cities: 5 ↵Enter
Enter the coordinates of the cities:
  2.5 5 5.1 3 1 9 5.4 54 5.5 2.1 ↵Enter
The central city is at (2.5, 5.0)
The total distance to all other cities is 60.81
```

*8.22 *(Even number of 1s)* Write a program that generates a 6-by-6 two-dimensional matrix filled with 0s and 1s, displays the matrix, and checks if every row and every column have an even number of 1s.

*8.23 *(Game: find the flipped cell)* Suppose you are given a 6-by-6 matrix filled with 0s and 1s. All rows and all columns have an even number of 1s. Let the user flip one cell (i.e., flip from 1 to 0 or from 0 to 1) and write a program to find which cell was flipped. Your program should prompt the user to enter a 6-by-6 array with 0s and 1s and find the first row r and first column c where the even number of the 1s property is violated (i.e., the number of 1s is not even). The flipped cell is at (r, c). Here is a sample run:

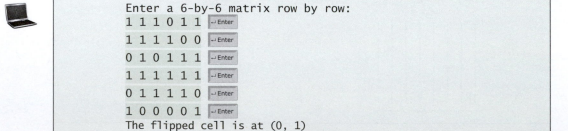

```
Enter a 6-by-6 matrix row by row:
1 1 1 0 1 1 ↵Enter
1 1 1 1 0 0 ↵Enter
0 1 0 1 1 1 ↵Enter
1 1 1 1 1 1 ↵Enter
0 1 1 1 1 0 ↵Enter
1 0 0 0 0 1 ↵Enter
The flipped cell is at (0, 1)
```

*8.24 (*Check Sudoku solution*) Listing 8.4 checks whether a solution is valid by checking whether every number is valid in the board. Rewrite the program by checking whether every row, every column, and every small box has the numbers 1 to 9.

*8.25 (*Markov matrix*) An $n \times n$ matrix is called a *positive Markov matrix* if each element is positive and the sum of the elements in each column is 1. Write the following method to check whether a matrix is a Markov matrix.

```
public static boolean isMarkovMatrix(double[][] m)
```

Write a test program that prompts the user to enter a 3×3 matrix of double values and tests whether it is a Markov matrix. Here are sample runs:

```
Enter a 3-by-3 matrix row by row:
0.15 0.875 0.375 ↵Enter
0.55 0.005 0.225 ↵Enter
0.30 0.12 0.4 ↵Enter
It is a Markov matrix
```

```
Enter a 3-by-3 matrix row by row:
0.95 -0.875 0.375 ↵Enter
0.65 0.005 0.225 ↵Enter
0.30 0.22 -0.4 ↵Enter
It is not a Markov matrix
```

*8.26 (*Row sorting*) Implement the following method to sort the rows in a two-dimensional array. A new array is returned and the original array is intact.

```
public static double[][] sortRows(double[][] m)
```

Write a test program that prompts the user to enter a 3×3 matrix of double values and displays a new row-sorted matrix. Here is a sample run:

```
Enter a 3-by-3 matrix row by row:
0.15 0.875 0.375 ↵Enter
0.55 0.005 0.225 ↵Enter
0.30 0.12 0.4 ↵Enter

The row-sorted array is
0.15 0.375 0.875
0.005 0.225 0.55
0.12 0.30 0.4
```

*8.27 (*Column sorting*) Implement the following method to sort the columns in a two-dimensional array. A new array is returned and the original array is intact.

```
public static double[][] sortColumns(double[][] m)
```

Write a test program that prompts the user to enter a 3 × 3 matrix of double values and displays a new column-sorted matrix. Here is a sample run:

```
Enter a 3-by-3 matrix row by row:
0.15 0.875 0.375 ⏎Enter
0.55 0.005 0.225 ⏎Enter
0.30 0.12 0.4 ⏎Enter

The column-sorted array is
0.15 0.0050 0.225
0.3  0.12   0.375
0.55 0.875  0.4
```

8.28   (*Strictly identical arrays*) The two-dimensional arrays `m1` and `m2` are *strictly identical* if their corresponding elements are equal. Write a method that returns `true` if `m1` and `m2` are strictly identical, using the following header:

public static boolean equals(**int**[][] m1, **int**[][] m2)

Write a test program that prompts the user to enter two 3 × 3 arrays of integers and displays whether the two are strictly identical. Here are the sample runs.

```
Enter list1: 51 22 25 6 1 4 24 54 6 ⏎Enter
Enter list2: 51 22 25 6 1 4 24 54 6 ⏎Enter
The two arrays are strictly identical
```

```
Enter list1: 51 25 22 6 1 4 24 54 6 ⏎Enter
Enter list2: 51 22 25 6 1 4 24 54 6 ⏎Enter
The two arrays are not strictly identical
```

8.29   (*Identical arrays*) The two-dimensional arrays `m1` and `m2` are *identical* if they have the same contents. Write a method that returns `true` if `m1` and `m2` are identical, using the following header:

public static boolean equals(**int**[][] m1, **int**[][] m2)

Write a test program that prompts the user to enter two 3 × 3 arrays of integers and displays whether the two are identical. Here are the sample runs.

```
Enter list1: 51 25 22 6 1 4 24 54 6 ⏎Enter
Enter list2: 51 22 25 6 1 4 24 54 6 ⏎Enter
The two arrays are identical
```

```
Enter list1: 51 5 22 6 1 4 24 54 6 ⏎Enter
Enter list2: 51 22 25 6 1 4 24 54 6 ⏎Enter
The two arrays are not identical
```

*8.30 (*Algebra: solve linear equations*) Write a method that solves the following 2×2 system of linear equations:

$$a_{00}x + a_{01}y = b_0 \qquad x = \frac{b_0a_{11} - b_1a_{01}}{a_{00}a_{11} - a_{01}a_{10}} \qquad y = \frac{b_1a_{00} - b_0a_{10}}{a_{00}a_{11} - a_{01}a_{10}}$$
$$a_{10}x + a_{11}y = b_1$$

The method header is

```
public static double[] linearEquation(double[][] a, double[] b)
```

The method returns **null** if $a_{00}a_{11} - a_{01}a_{10}$ is **0**. Write a test program that prompts the user to enter a_{00}, a_{01}, a_{10}, a_{11}, b_0, and b_1, and displays the result. If $a_{00}a_{11} - a_{01}a_{10}$ is **0**, report that "The equation has no solution." A sample run is similar to Programming Exercise 3.3.

*8.31 (*Geometry: intersecting point*) Write a method that returns the intersecting point of two lines. The intersecting point of the two lines can be found by using the formula shown in Programming Exercise 3.25. Assume that (**x1, y1**) and (**x2, y2**) are the two points on line 1 and (**x3, y3**) and (**x4, y4**) are on line 2. The method header is

```
public static double[] getIntersectingPoint(double[][] points)
```

The points are stored in a 4-by-2 two-dimensional array **points** with (**points[0][0], points[0][1]**) for (**x1, y1**). The method returns the intersecting point or **null** if the two lines are parallel. Write a program that prompts the user to enter four points and displays the intersecting point. See Programming Exercise 3.25 for a sample run.

*8.32 (*Geometry: area of a triangle*) Write a method that returns the area of a triangle using the following header:

```
public static double getTriangleArea(double[][] points)
```

The points are stored in a 3-by-2 two-dimensional array **points** with **points[0][0]** and **points[0][1]** for (**x1, y1**). The triangle area can be computed using the formula in Programming Exercise 2.19. The method returns **0** if the three points are on the same line. Write a program that prompts the user to enter three points of a triangle and displays the triangle's area. Here is a sample run of the program:

```
Enter x1, y1, x2, y2, x3, y3: 2.5 2 5 -1.0 4.0 2.0  ↵Enter
The area of the triangle is 2.25
```

```
Enter x1, y1, x2, y2, x3, y3: 2 2 4.5 4.5 6 6  ↵Enter
The three points are on the same line
```

*8.33 (*Geometry: polygon subareas*) A convex 4-vertex polygon is divided into four triangles, as shown in Figure 8.9.

Write a program that prompts the user to enter the coordinates of four vertices and displays the areas of the four triangles in increasing order. Here is a sample run:

```
Enter x1, y1, x2, y2, x3, y3, x4, y4:
  -2.5 2 4 4 3 -2 -2 -3.5  ↵Enter
The areas are 6.17 7.96 8.08 10.42
```

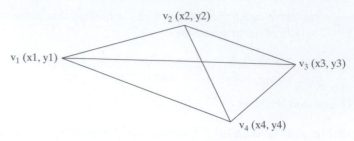

FIGURE 8.9   A 4-vertex polygon is defined by four vertices.

*8.34   (*Geometry: rightmost lowest point*) In computational geometry, often you need
          to find the rightmost lowest point in a set of points. Write the following method
          that returns the rightmost lowest point in a set of points.

```
public static double[]
        getRightmostLowestPoint(double[][] points)
```

Write a test program that prompts the user to enter the coordinates of six points
and displays the rightmost lowest point. Here is a sample run:

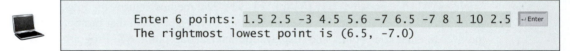

```
Enter 6 points: 1.5 2.5 -3 4.5 5.6 -7 6.5 -7 8 1 10 2.5  ↵Enter
The rightmost lowest point is (6.5, -7.0)
```

**8.35   (*Largest block*) Given a square matrix with the elements 0 or 1, write a program
          to find a maximum square submatrix whose elements are all 1s. Your program
          should prompt the user to enter the number of rows in the matrix. The program
          then displays the location of the first element in the maximum square submatrix
          and the number of the rows in the submatrix. Here is a sample run:

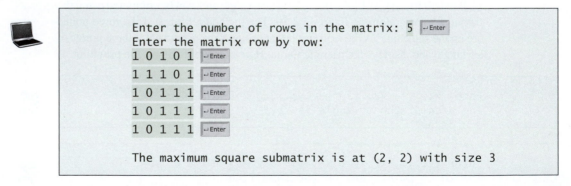

```
Enter the number of rows in the matrix: 5  ↵Enter
Enter the matrix row by row:
1 0 1 0 1  ↵Enter
1 1 1 0 1  ↵Enter
1 0 1 1 1  ↵Enter
1 0 1 1 1  ↵Enter
1 0 1 1 1  ↵Enter

The maximum square submatrix is at (2, 2) with size 3
```

Your program should implement and use the following method to find the maximum square submatrix:

```
public static int[] findLargestBlock(int[][] m)
```

The return value is an array that consists of three values. The first two values are
the row and column indices for the first element in the submatrix, and the third
value is the number of the rows in the submatrix.

8.36   (*Latin square*) A Latin square is an *n*-by-*n* array filled with **n different Latin let-
          ters, each occurring exactly once in each row and once in each column. Write a

program that prompts the user to enter the number **n** and the array of characters, as shown in the sample output, and checks if the input array is a Latin square. The characters are the first **n** characters starting from **A**.

```
Enter number n: 4 ↵Enter
Enter 4 rows of letters separated by spaces:
A B C D ↵Enter
B A D C ↵Enter
C D B A ↵Enter
D C A B ↵Enter
The input array is a Latin square
```

```
Enter number n: 3 ↵Enter
Enter 3 rows of letters separated by spaces:
A F D ↵Enter
Wrong input: the letters must be from A to C
```

8.37 (*Guess the capitals*) Write a program that repeatedly prompts the user to enter a capital for a state. Upon receiving the user input, the program reports whether the answer is correct. Assume that **50 states and their capitals are stored in a two-dimensional array, as shown in Figure 8.10. The program prompts the user to answer all states' capitals and displays the total correct count. The user's answer is not case-sensitive.

```
Alabama          Montgomery
Alaska           Juneau
Arizona          Phoenix
...              ...
...              ...
```

FIGURE 8.10   A two-dimensional array stores states and their capitals.

Here is a sample run:

```
What is the capital of Alabama? Montogomery ↵Enter
The correct answer should be Montgomery
What is the capital of Alaska? Juneau ↵Enter
Your answer is correct
What is the capital of Arizona? ...
...
The correct count is 35
```

OBJECTS AND CLASSES

Objectives

- To describe objects and classes, and use classes to model objects (§9.2).

- To use UML graphical notation to describe classes and objects (§9.2).

- To demonstrate how to define classes and create objects (§9.3).

- To create objects using constructors (§9.4).

- To access objects via object reference variables (§9.5).

- To define a reference variable using a reference type (§9.5.1).

- To access an object's data and methods using the object member access operator (.) (§9.5.2).

- To define data fields of reference types and assign default values for an object's data fields (§9.5.3).

- To distinguish between object reference variables and primitive data type variables (§9.5.4).

- To use the Java library classes **Date**, **Random**, and **Point2D** (§9.6).

- To distinguish between instance and static variables and methods (§9.7).

- To define private data fields with appropriate getter and setter methods (§9.8).

- To encapsulate data fields to make classes easy to maintain (§9.9).

- To develop methods with object arguments and differentiate between primitive-type arguments and object-type arguments (§9.10).

- To store and process objects in arrays (§9.11).

- To create immutable objects from immutable classes to protect the contents of objects (§9.12).

- To determine the scope of variables in the context of a class (§9.13).

- To use the keyword **this** to refer to the calling object itself (§9.14).

9.1 Introduction

Key Point

Object-oriented programming enables you to develop large-scale software and GUIs effectively.

Having learned the material in the preceding chapters, you are able to solve many programming problems using selections, loops, methods, and arrays. However, these Java features are not sufficient for developing graphical user interfaces and large-scale software systems. Suppose you want to develop a graphical user interface (GUI, pronounced *goo-ee*) as shown in Figure 9.1. How would you program it?

why OOP?

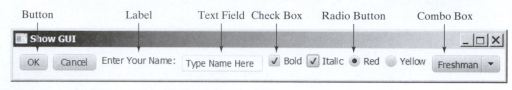

FIGURE 9.1 The GUI objects are created from classes.

This chapter introduces object-oriented programming, which you can use to develop GUI and large-scale software systems.

9.2 Defining Classes for Objects

Key Point

A class defines the properties and behaviors for objects.

VideoNote

Define classes and objects

object
state of an object
properties
attributes
data fields
behavior
actions

Object-oriented programming (OOP) involves programming using objects. An *object* represents an entity in the real world that can be distinctly identified. For example, a student, a desk, a circle, a button, and even a loan can all be viewed as objects. An object has a unique identity, state, and behavior.

- The *state* of an object (also known as its *properties* or *attributes*) is represented by *data fields* with their current values. A circle object, for example, has a data field **radius**, which is the property that characterizes a circle. A rectangle object has the data fields **width** and **height**, which are the properties that characterize a rectangle.

- The *behavior* of an object (also known as its *actions*) is defined by methods. To invoke a method on an object is to ask the object to perform an action. For example, you may define methods named **getArea()** and **getPerimeter()** for circle objects. A circle object may invoke **getArea()** to return its area and **getPerimeter()** to return its perimeter. You may also define the **setRadius(radius)** method. A circle object can invoke this method to change its radius.

class
contract

instantiation
instance

Objects of the same type are defined using a common class. A *class* is a template, blueprint, or *contract* that defines what an object's data fields and methods will be. An object is an instance of a class. You can create many instances of a class. Creating an instance is referred to as *instantiation*. The terms *object* and *instance* are often interchangeable. The relationship between classes and objects is analogous to that between an apple-pie recipe and apple pies: You can make as many apple pies as you want from a single recipe. Figure 9.2 shows a class named **Circle** and its three objects.

data field
method
constructors

A Java class uses variables to define data fields and methods to define actions. Additionally, a class provides methods of a special type, known as *constructors*, which are invoked to create a new object. A constructor can perform any action, but constructors are designed to perform initializing actions, such as initializing the data fields of objects. Figure 9.3 shows an example of defining the class for circle objects.

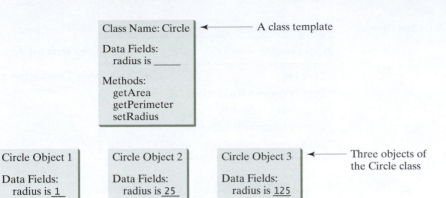

FIGURE 9.2 A class is a template for creating objects.

```
class Circle {
  /** The radius of this circle */
  double radius = 1;                         ←───────────── Data field

  /** Construct a circle object */─┐
  Circle() {
  }
                                              ←───────────── Constructors
  /** Construct a circle object */
  Circle(double newRadius) {
    radius = newRadius;
  }

  /** Return the area of this circle */
  double getArea() {
    return radius * radius * Math.PI;
  }

  /** Return the perimeter of this circle */
  double getPerimeter() {
    return 2 * radius * Math.PI;              ←───────────── Method
  }

  /** Set new radius for this circle */
  double setRadius(double newRadius) {
    radius = newRadius;
  }
}
```

FIGURE 9.3 A class is a construct that defines objects of the same type.

The `Circle` class is different from all of the other classes you have seen thus far. It does not have a `main` method and therefore cannot be run; it is merely a definition for circle objects. The class that contains the `main` method will be referred to in this book, for convenience, as the *main class*.

The illustration of class templates and objects in Figure 9.2 can be standardized using *Unified Modeling Language (UML)* notation. This notation, as shown in Figure 9.4, is called a *UML class diagram*, or simply a *class diagram*. In the class diagram, the data field is denoted as

main class

Unified Modeling Language (UML)

class diagram

```
dataFieldName: dataFieldType
```

The constructor is denoted as

```
ClassName(parameterName: parameterType)
```

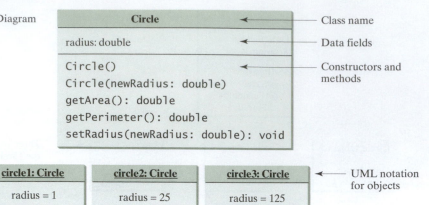

UML Class Diagram

Class name

Data fields

Constructors and methods

UML notation for objects

FIGURE 9.4 Classes and objects can be represented using UML notation.

The method is denoted as

```
methodName(parameterName: parameterType): returnType
```

9.3 Example: Defining Classes and Creating Objects

Classes are definitions for objects and objects are created from classes.

This section gives two examples of defining classes and uses the classes to create objects. Listing 9.1 is a program that defines the **Circle** class and uses it to create objects. The program constructs three circle objects with radius **1**, **25**, and **125** and displays the radius and area of each of the three circles. It then changes the radius of the second object to **100** and displays its new radius and area.

Note

To avoid a naming conflict with several enhanced versions of the **Circle** class introduced later in the chapter, the **Circle** class in this example is named **SimpleCircle**. For simplicity, we will still refer to the class in the text as **Circle**.

avoid naming conflicts

LISTING 9.1 TestSimpleCircle.java

main class

main method

create object

create object

create object

```java
1  public class TestSimpleCircle {
2    /** Main method */
3    public static void main(String[] args) {
4      // Create a circle with radius 1
5      SimpleCircle circle1 = new SimpleCircle();
6      System.out.println("The area of the circle of radius "
7        + circle1.radius + " is " + circle1.getArea());
8
9      // Create a circle with radius 25
10     SimpleCircle circle2 = new SimpleCircle(25);
11     System.out.println("The area of the circle of radius "
12       + circle2.radius + " is " + circle2.getArea());
13
14     // Create a circle with radius 125
15     SimpleCircle circle3 = new SimpleCircle(125);
16     System.out.println("The area of the circle of radius "
17       + circle3.radius + " is " + circle3.getArea());
18
19     // Modify circle radius
20     circle2.radius = 100; // or circle2.setRadius(100)
21     System.out.println("The area of the circle of radius "
22       + circle2.radius + " is " + circle2.getArea());
```

```
23    }
24  }
25
26  // Define the circle class with two constructors
27  class SimpleCircle {
28    double radius;
29
30    /** Construct a circle with radius 1 */
31    SimpleCircle() {
32      radius = 1;
33    }
34
35    /** Construct a circle with a specified radius */
36    SimpleCircle(double newRadius) {
37      radius = newRadius;
38    }
39
40    /** Return the area of this circle */
41    double getArea() {
42      return radius * radius * Math.PI;
43    }
44
45    /** Return the perimeter of this circle */
46    double getPerimeter() {
47      return 2 * radius * Math.PI;
48    }
49
50    /** Set a new radius for this circle */
51    void setRadius(double newRadius) {
52      radius = newRadius;
53    }
54  }
```

class SimpleCircle
data field

no-arg constructor

second constructor

getArea

getPerimeter

setRadius

```
The area of the circle of radius 1.0 is 3.141592653589793
The area of the circle of radius 25.0 is 1963.4954084936207
The area of the circle of radius 125.0 is 49087.385212340516
The area of the circle of radius 100.0 is 31415.926535897932
```

The program contains two classes. The first of these, `TestSimpleCircle`, is the main class. Its sole purpose is to test the second class, `SimpleCircle`. Such a program that uses the class is often referred to as a *client* of the class. When you run the program, the Java runtime system invokes the `main` method in the main class.

client

You can put the two classes into one file, but only one class in the file can be a *public class*. Furthermore, the public class must have the same name as the file name. Therefore, the file name is **TestSimpleCircle.java**, since `TestSimpleCircle` is public. Each class in the source code is compiled into a **.class** file. When you compile **TestSimpleCircle.java**, two class files **TestSimpleCircle.class** and **SimpleCircle.class** are generated, as shown in Figure 9.5.

public class

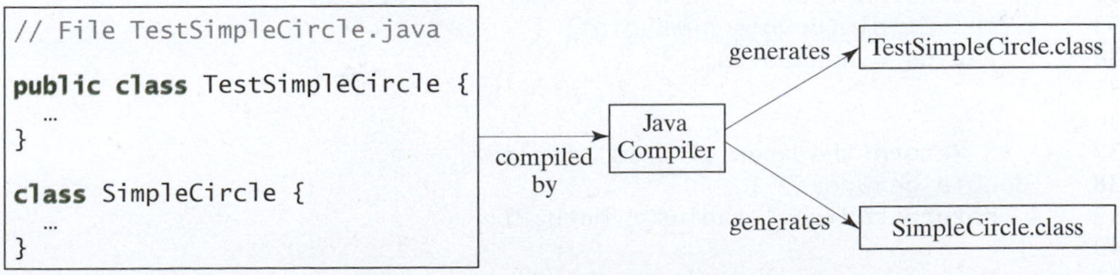

FIGURE 9.5 Each class in the source code file is compiled into a **.class** file.

The main class contains the `main` method (line 3) that creates three objects. As in creating an array, the `new` operator is used to create an object from the constructor: `new SimpleCircle()` creates an object with radius `1` (line 5), `new SimpleCircle(25)` creates an object with radius `25` (line 10), and `new SimpleCircle(125)` creates an object with radius `125` (line 15).

These three objects (referenced by `circle1`, `circle2`, and `circle3`) have different data but the same methods. Therefore, you can compute their respective areas by using the `getArea()` method. The data fields can be accessed via the reference of the object using `circle1.radius`, `circle2.radius`, and `circle3.radius`, respectively. The object can invoke its method via the reference of the object using `circle1.getArea()`, `circle2.getArea()`, and `circle3.getArea()`, respectively.

These three objects are independent. The radius of `circle2` is changed to `100` in line 20. The object's new radius and area are displayed in lines 21–22.

There are many ways to write Java programs. For instance, you can combine the two classes in the example into one, as shown in Listing 9.2.

LISTING 9.2 SimpleCircle.java

```
1  public class SimpleCircle {
2    /** Main method */
3    public static void main(String[] args) {
4      // Create a circle with radius 1
5      SimpleCircle circle1 = new SimpleCircle();
6      System.out.println("The area of the circle of radius "
7        + circle1.radius + " is " + circle1.getArea());
8
9      // Create a circle with radius 25
10     SimpleCircle circle2 = new SimpleCircle(25);
11     System.out.println("The area of the circle of radius "
12       + circle2.radius + " is " + circle2.getArea());
13
14     // Create a circle with radius 125
15     SimpleCircle circle3 = new SimpleCircle(125);
16     System.out.println("The area of the circle of radius "
17       + circle3.radius + " is " + circle3.getArea());
18
19     // Modify circle radius
20     circle2.radius = 100;
21     System.out.println("The area of the circle of radius "
22       + circle2.radius + " is " + circle2.getArea());
23   }
24
25   double radius;
26
27   /** Construct a circle with radius 1 */
28   SimpleCircle() {
29     radius = 1;
30   }
31
32   /** Construct a circle with a specified radius */
33   SimpleCircle(double newRadius) {
34     radius = newRadius;
35   }
36
37   /** Return the area of this circle */
38   double getArea() {
39     return radius * radius * Math.PI;
40   }
41
```

(margin notes) main method — data field — no-arg constructor — second constructor — method

```
42      /** Return the perimeter of this circle */
43      double getPerimeter() {
44        return 2 * radius * Math.PI;
45      }
46
47      /** Set a new radius for this circle */
48      void setRadius(double newRadius) {
49        radius = newRadius;
50      }
51    }
```

Since the combined class has a `main` method, it can be executed by the Java interpreter. The `main` method is the same as that in Listing 9.1. This demonstrates that you can test a class by simply adding a `main` method in the same class.

As another example, consider television sets. Each TV is an object with states (current channel, current volume level, power on or off) and behaviors (change channels, adjust volume, turn on/off). You can use a class to model TV sets. The UML diagram for the class is shown in Figure 9.6.

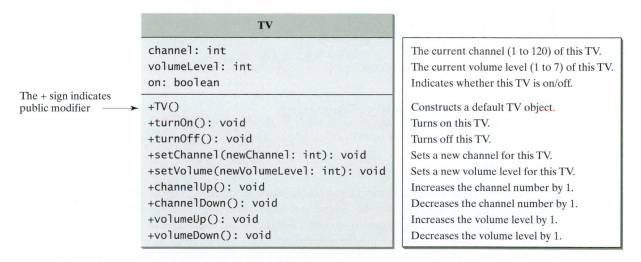

FIGURE 9.6 The TV class models TV sets.

Listing 9.3 gives a program that defines the **TV** class.

LISTING 9.3 TV.java

```
1   public class TV {
2     int channel = 1; // Default channel is 1                              data fields
3     int volumeLevel = 1; // Default volume level is 1
4     boolean on = false; // TV is off
5
6     public TV() {                                                          constructor
7     }
8
9     public void turnOn() {                                                 turn on TV
10      on = true;
11    }
12
13    public void turnOff() {                                                turn off TV
```

```
14        on = false;
15     }
16
17     public void setChannel(int newChannel) {
18         if (on && newChannel >= 1 && newChannel <= 120)
19             channel = newChannel;
20     }
21
22     public void setVolume(int newVolumeLevel) {
23         if (on && newVolumeLevel >= 1 && newVolumeLevel <= 7)
24             volumeLevel = newVolumeLevel;
25     }
26
27     public void channelUp() {
28         if (on && channel < 120)
29             channel++;
30     }
31
32     public void channelDown() {
33         if (on && channel > 1)
34             channel--;
35     }
36
37     public void volumeUp() {
38         if (on && volumeLevel < 7)
39             volumeLevel++;
40     }
41
42     public void volumeDown() {
43         if (on && volumeLevel > 1)
44             volumeLevel--;
45     }
46 }
```

set a new channel (17)
set a new volume (22)
increase channel (27)
decrease channel (32)
increase volume (37)
decrease volume (42)

The constructor and methods in the **TV** class are defined public so they can be accessed from other classes. Note that the channel and volume level are not changed if the TV is not on. Before either of these is changed, its current value is checked to ensure that it is within the correct range.

Listing 9.4 gives a program that uses the **TV** class to create two objects.

LISTING 9.4   TestTV.java

```
1  public class TestTV {
2    public static void main(String[] args) {
3      TV tv1 = new TV();
4      tv1.turnOn();
5      tv1.setChannel(30);
6      tv1.setVolume(3);
7
8      TV tv2 = new TV();
9      tv2.turnOn();
10     tv2.channelUp();
11     tv2.channelUp();
12     tv2.volumeUp();
13
14     System.out.println("tv1's channel is " + tv1.channel
15       + " and volume level is " + tv1.volumeLevel);
16     System.out.println("tv2's channel is " + tv2.channel
17       + " and volume level is " + tv2.volumeLevel);
18   }
19 }
```

main method (2)
create a TV (3)
turn on (4)
set a new channel (5)
set a new volume (6)
create a TV (8)
turn on (9)
increase channel (10)
increase volume (12)
display state (14)

```
tv1's channel is 30 and volume level is 3
tv2's channel is 3 and volume level is 2
```

The program creates two objects in lines 3 and 8 and invokes the methods on the objects to perform actions for setting channels and volume levels and for increasing channels and volumes. The program displays the state of the objects in lines 14–17. The methods are invoked using syntax such as `tv1.turnOn()` (line 4). The data fields are accessed using syntax such as `tv1.channel` (line 14).

These examples have given you a glimpse of classes and objects. You may have many questions regarding constructors, objects, reference variables, accessing data fields, and invoking object's methods. The sections that follow discuss these issues in detail.

9.1   Describe the relationship between an object and its defining class.

9.2   How do you define a class?

9.3   How do you declare an object's reference variable?

9.4   How do you create an object?

9.4 Constructing Objects Using Constructors

A constructor is invoked to create an object using the new operator.

Constructors are a special kind of method. They have three peculiarities:

- A constructor must have the same name as the class itself.

  constructor's name

- Constructors do not have a return type—not even `void`.

  no return type

- Constructors are invoked using the `new` operator when an object is created. Constructors play the role of initializing objects.

  new operator

The constructor has exactly the same name as its defining class. Like regular methods, constructors can be overloaded (i.e., multiple constructors can have the same name but different signatures), making it easy to construct objects with different initial data values.

overloaded constructors

It is a common mistake to put the `void` keyword in front of a constructor. For example,

```
public void Circle() {
}
```

no void

In this case, `Circle()` is a method, not a constructor.

Constructors are used to construct objects. To construct an object from a class, invoke a constructor of the class using the `new` operator, as follows:

constructing objects

```
new ClassName(arguments);
```

For example, `new Circle()` creates an object of the `Circle` class using the first constructor defined in the `Circle` class, and `new Circle(25)` creates an object using the second constructor defined in the `Circle` class.

A class normally provides a constructor without arguments (e.g., `Circle()`). Such a constructor is referred to as a *no-arg* or *no-argument constructor*.

no-arg constructor

A class may be defined without constructors. In this case, a public no-arg constructor with an empty body is implicitly defined in the class. This constructor, called a *default constructor*, is provided automatically *only if no constructors are explicitly defined in the class*.

default constructor

9.5   What are the differences between constructors and methods?

9.6   When will a class have a default constructor?

9.5 Accessing Objects via Reference Variables

Key Point

An object's data and methods can be accessed through the dot (.) operator via the object's reference variable.

Newly created objects are allocated in the memory. They can be accessed via reference variables.

9.5.1 Reference Variables and Reference Types

reference variable

Objects are accessed via the object's *reference variables*, which contain references to the objects. Such variables are declared using the following syntax:

```
ClassName objectRefVar;
```

reference type

A class is essentially a programmer-defined type. A class is a *reference type*, which means that a variable of the class type can reference an instance of the class. The following statement declares the variable **myCircle** to be of the **Circle** type:

```
Circle myCircle;
```

The variable **myCircle** can reference a **Circle** object. The next statement creates an object and assigns its reference to **myCircle**:

```
myCircle = new Circle();
```

You can write a single statement that combines the declaration of an object reference variable, the creation of an object, and the assigning of an object reference to the variable with the following syntax:

```
ClassName objectRefVar = new ClassName();
```

Here is an example:

```
Circle myCircle = new Circle();
```

The variable **myCircle** holds a reference to a **Circle** object.

object vs. object reference
variable

Note

An object reference variable that appears to hold an object actually contains a reference to that object. Strictly speaking, an object reference variable and an object are different, but most of the time the distinction can be ignored. Therefore, it is fine, for simplicity, to say that **myCircle** is a **Circle** object rather than use the longer-winded description that **myCircle** is a variable that contains a reference to a **Circle** object.

array object

Note

Arrays are treated as objects in Java. Arrays are created using the **new** operator. An array variable is actually a variable that contains a reference to an array.

9.5.2 Accessing an Object's Data and Methods

dot operator (.)

In OOP terminology, an object's member refers to its data fields and methods. After an object is created, its data can be accessed and its methods can be invoked using the *dot operator* (.), also known as the *object member access operator*:

- **objectRefVar.dataField** references a data field in the object.

- **objectRefVar.method(arguments)** invokes a method on the object.

For example, `myCircle.radius` references the radius in `myCircle`, and `myCircle` `.getArea()` invokes the `getArea` method on `myCircle`. Methods are invoked as operations on objects.

The data field `radius` is referred to as an *instance variable*, because it is dependent on a specific instance. For the same reason, the method `getArea` is referred to as an *instance method*, because you can invoke it only on a specific instance. The object on which an instance method is invoked is called a *calling object*.

instance variable

instance method

calling object

Caution

Recall that you use `Math.methodName(arguments)` (e.g., `Math.pow(3, 2.5)`) to invoke a method in the `Math` class. Can you invoke `getArea()` using `Circle.getArea()`? The answer is no. All the methods in the `Math` class are static methods, which are defined using the `static` keyword. However, `getArea()` is an instance method, and thus nonstatic. It must be invoked from an object using `objectRefVar.methodName(arguments)` (e.g., `myCircle.getArea()`). Further explanation is given in Section 9.7, Static Variables, Constants, and Methods.

invoking methods

Note

Usually you create an object and assign it to a variable, and then later you can use the variable to reference the object. Occasionally an object does not need to be referenced later. In this case, you can create an object without explicitly assigning it to a variable using the syntax:

```
new Circle();
```

or

```
System.out.println("Area is " + new Circle(5).getArea());
```

The former statement creates a `Circle` object. The latter creates a `Circle` object and invokes its `getArea` method to return its area. An object created in this way is known as an *anonymous object*.

anonymous object

9.5.3 Reference Data Fields and the `null` Value

The data fields can be of reference types. For example, the following `Student` class contains a data field `name` of the `String` type. `String` is a predefined Java class.

reference data fields

```
class Student {
  String name; // name has the default value null
  int age; // age has the default value 0
  boolean isScienceMajor; // isScienceMajor has default value false
  char gender; // gender has default value '\u0000'
}
```

If a data field of a reference type does not reference any object, the data field holds a special Java value, `null`. `null` is a literal just like `true` and `false`. While `true` and `false` are Boolean literals, `null` is a literal for a reference type.

null value

The default value of a data field is `null` for a reference type, `0` for a numeric type, `false` for a `boolean` type, and `\u0000` for a `char` type. However, Java assigns no default value to a local variable inside a method. The following code displays the default values of the data fields `name`, `age`, `isScienceMajor`, and `gender` for a `Student` object:

default field values

```
class Test {
  public static void main(String[] args) {
    Student student = new Student();
    System.out.println("name? " + student.name);
```

```
        System.out.println("age? " + student.age);
        System.out.println("isScienceMajor? " + student.isScienceMajor);
        System.out.println("gender? " + student.gender);
    }
}
```

The following code has a compile error, because the local variables x and y are not initialized:

```
class Test {
    public static void main(String[] args) {
        int x; // x has no default value
        String y; // y has no default value
        System.out.println("x is " + x);
        System.out.println("y is " + y);
    }
}
```

NullPointerException

Caution

NullPointerException is a common runtime error. It occurs when you invoke a method on a reference variable with a **null** value. Make sure you assign an object reference to the variable before invoking the method through the reference variable (See Checkpoint Question 9.11c).

9.5.4 Differences between Variables of Primitive Types and Reference Types

Every variable represents a memory location that holds a value. When you declare a variable, you are telling the compiler what type of value the variable can hold. For a variable of a primitive type, the value is of the primitive type. For a variable of a reference type, the value is a reference to where an object is located. For example, as shown in Figure 9.7, the value of **int** variable **i** is **int** value **1**, and the value of **Circle** object **c** holds a reference to where the contents of the **Circle** object are stored in memory.

When you assign one variable to another, the other variable is set to the same value. For a variable of a primitive type, the real value of one variable is assigned to the other variable. For a variable of a reference type, the reference of one variable is assigned to the other variable. As shown in Figure 9.8, the assignment statement **i = j** copies the contents of **j** into **i**

Created using new Circle()

Primitive type   int i = 1   i   [1]

Object type   Circle c   c   [reference] - - - - - - - → **c: Circle**
                                                            radius = 1

FIGURE 9.7 A variable of a primitive type holds a value of the primitive type, and a variable of a reference type holds a reference to where an object is stored in memory.

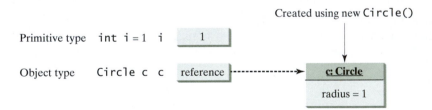

Primitive type assignment i = j

Before: After:

i   [1]   i   [2]

j   [2]   j   [2]

FIGURE 9.8 Primitive variable **j** is copied to variable **i**.

for primitive variables. As shown in Figure 9.9, the assignment statement **c1 = c2** copies the reference of **c2** into **c1** for reference variables. After the assignment, variables **c1** and **c2** refer to the same object.

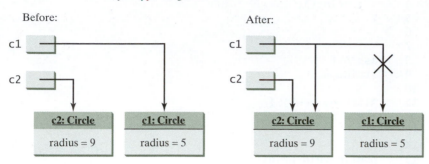

FIGURE 9.9 Reference variable **c2** is copied to variable **c1**.

Note

As illustrated in Figure 9.9, after the assignment statement **c1 = c2**, **c1** points to the same object referenced by **c2**. The object previously referenced by **c1** is no longer useful and therefore is now known as *garbage*. Garbage occupies memory space, so the Java runtime system detects garbage and automatically reclaims the space it occupies. This process is called *garbage collection*.

garbage

garbage collection

Tip

If you know that an object is no longer needed, you can explicitly assign **null** to a reference variable for the object. The JVM will automatically collect the space if the object is not referenced by any reference variable.

9.7 Which operator is used to access a data field or invoke a method from an object?

9.8 What is an anonymous object?

9.9 What is **NullPointerException**?

9.10 Is an array an object or a primitive type value? Can an array contain elements of an object type? Describe the default value for the elements of an array.

9.11 What is wrong with each of the following programs?

Check Point

```
1  public class ShowErrors {
2    public static void main(String[] args) {
3      ShowErrors t = new ShowErrors(5);
4    }
5  }
```
(a)

```
1  public class ShowErrors {
2    public static void main(String[] args) {
3      ShowErrors t = new ShowErrors();
4      t.x();
5    }
6  }
```
(b)

```
1  public class ShowErrors {
2    public void method1() {
3      Circle c;
4      System.out.println("What is radius "
5        + c.getRadius());
6      c = new Circle();
7    }
8  }
```
(c)

```
1  public class ShowErrors {
2    public static void main(String[] args) {
3      C c = new C(5.0);
4      System.out.println(c.value);
5    }
6  }
7
8  class C {
9    int value = 2;
10  }
```
(d)

9.12 What is wrong in the following code?

```
1  class Test {
2    public static void main(String[] args) {
3      A a = new A();
4      a.print();
5    }
6  }
7
8  class A {
9    String s;
10
11   A(String newS) {
12     s = newS;
13   }
14
15   public void print() {
16     System.out.print(s);
17   }
18 }
```

9.13 What is the output of the following code?

```
public class A {
  boolean x;

  public static void main(String[] args) {
    A a = new A();
    System.out.println(a.x);
  }
}
```

9.6 Using Classes from the Java Library

The Java API contains a rich set of classes for developing Java programs.

Listing 9.1 defined the **SimpleCircle** class and created objects from the class. You will frequently use the classes in the Java library to develop programs. This section gives some examples of the classes in the Java library.

9.6.1 The **Date** Class

In Listing 2.7, ShowCurrentTime.java, you learned how to obtain the current time using **System.currentTimeMillis()**. You used the division and remainder operators to extract the current second, minute, and hour. Java provides a system-independent encapsulation of date and time in the **java.util.Date** class, as shown in Figure 9.10.

VideoNote

Use classes

java.util.Date class

java.util.Date	
+Date()	Constructs a Date object for the current time.
+Date(elapseTime: long)	Constructs a Date object for a given time in milliseconds elapsed since January 1, 1970, GMT.
+toString(): String	Returns a string representing the date and time.
+getTime(): long	Returns the number of milliseconds since January 1, 1970, GMT.
+setTime(elapseTime: long): void	Sets a new elapse time in the object.

FIGURE 9.10 A **Date** object represents a specific date and time.

You can use the no-arg constructor in the **Date** class to create an instance for the current date and time, the **getTime()** method to return the elapsed time since January 1, 1970, GMT, and the **toString()** method to return the date and time as a string. For example, the following code

```
java.util.Date date = new java.util.Date();
System.out.println("The elapsed time since Jan 1, 1970 is " +
  date.getTime() + " milliseconds");
System.out.println(date.toString());
```

create object

get elapsed time
invoke toString

displays the output like this:

```
The elapsed time since Jan 1, 1970 is 1324903419651 milliseconds
Mon Dec 26 07:43:39 EST 2011
```

The **Date** class has another constructor, **Date(long elapseTime)**, which can be used to construct a **Date** object for a given time in milliseconds elapsed since January 1, 1970, GMT.

9.6.2 The **Random** Class

You have used **Math.random()** to obtain a random **double** value between **0.0** and **1.0** (excluding **1.0**). Another way to generate random numbers is to use the **java.util.Random** class, as shown in Figure 9.11, which can generate a random **int**, **long**, **double**, **float**, and **boolean** value.

java.util.Random	
+Random()	Constructs a Random object with the current time as its seed.
+Random(seed: long)	Constructs a Random object with a specified seed.
+nextInt(): int	Returns a random int value.
+nextInt(n: int): int	Returns a random int value between 0 and n (excluding n).
+nextLong(): long	Returns a random long value.
+nextDouble(): double	Returns a random double value between 0.0 and 1.0 (excluding 1.0).
+nextFloat(): float	Returns a random float value between 0.0F and 1.0F (excluding 1.0F).
+nextBoolean(): boolean	Returns a random boolean value.

FIGURE 9.11 A Random object can be used to generate random values.

When you create a **Random** object, you have to specify a seed or use the default seed. A seed is a number used to initialize a random number generator. The no-arg constructor creates a **Random** object using the current elapsed time as its seed. If two **Random** objects have the same seed, they will generate identical sequences of numbers. For example, the following code creates two **Random** objects with the same seed, **3**.

```
Random random1 = new Random(3);
System.out.print("From random1: ");
for (int i = 0; i < 10; i++)
  System.out.print(random1.nextInt(1000) + " ");

Random random2 = new Random(3);
System.out.print("\nFrom random2: ");
for (int i = 0; i < 10; i++)
  System.out.print(random2.nextInt(1000) + " ");
```

The code generates the same sequence of random **int** values:

```
From random1: 734 660 210 581 128 202 549 564 459 961
From random2: 734 660 210 581 128 202 549 564 459 961
```

same sequence

Note

The ability to generate the same sequence of random values is useful in software testing and many other applications. In software testing, often you need to reproduce the test cases from a fixed sequence of random numbers.

9.6.3 The **Point2D** Class

Java API has a conveninent **Point2D** class in the **javafx.geometry** package for representing a point in a two-dimensional plane. The UML diagram for the class is shown in Figure 9.12.

javafx.geometry.Point2D	
+Point2D(x: double, y: double)	Constructs a Point2D object with the specified *x*- and *y*-coordinates.
+distance(x: double, y: double): double	Returns the distance between this point and the specified point (*x*, *y*).
+distance(p: Point2D): double	Returns the distance between this point and the specified point p.
+getX(): double	Returns the *x*-coordinate from this point.
+getY(): double	Returns the *y*-coordinate from this point.
+toString(): String	Returns a string representation for the point.

FIGURE 9.12 A **Point2D** object represents a point with *x*- and *y*-coordinates.

You can create a **Point2D** object for a point with the specified *x*- and *y*-coordinates, use the **distance** method to compute the distance from this point to another point, and use the **toString()** method to return a string representation of the point. Lisitng 9.5 gives an example of using this class.

LISTING 9.5 TestPoint2D.java

```
1  import java.util.Scanner;
2  import javafx.geometry.Point2D;
3
4  public class TestPoint2D {
5    public static void main(String[] args) {
6      Scanner input = new Scanner(System.in);
7
8      System.out.print("Enter point1's x-, y-coordinates: ");
9      double x1 = input.nextDouble();
10     double y1 = input.nextDouble();
11     System.out.print("Enter point2's x-, y-coordinates: ");
12     double x2 = input.nextDouble();
13     double y2 = input.nextDouble();
14
15     Point2D p1 = new Point2D(x1, y1);
16     Point2D p2 = new Point2D(x2, y2);
17     System.out.println("p1 is " + p1.toString());
18     System.out.println("p2 is " + p2.toString());
19     System.out.println("The distance between p1 and p2 is " +
20       p1.distance(p2));
21   }
22 }
```

create an object

invoke toString()

get distance

```
Enter point1's x-, y-coordinates: 1.5 5.5  ↵Enter
Enter point2's x-, y-coordinates: -5.3 -4.4  ↵Enter
p1 is Point2D [x = 1.5, y = 5.5]
p2 is Point2D [x = -5.3, y = -4.4]
The distance between p1 and p2 is 12.010412149464313
```

This program creates two objects of the **Point2D** class (lines 15–16). The **toString()** method returns a string that describes the object (lines 17–18). Invoking **p1.distance(p2)** returns the distance between the two points (line 20).

9.14 How do you create a **Date** for the current time? How do you display the current time?

9.15 How do you create a **Point2D**? Suppose **p1** and **p2** are two instances of **Point2D**? How do you obtain the distance between the two points?

9.16 Which packages contain the classes **Date**, **Random**, **Point2D**, **System**, and **Math**?

Check Point

9.7 Static Variables, Constants, and Methods

A static variable is shared by all objects of the class. A static method cannot access instance members of the class.

Key Point

The data field **radius** in the circle class is known as an *instance variable*. An instance variable is tied to a specific instance of the class; it is not shared among objects of the same class. For example, suppose that you create the following objects:

Static vs. instance
instance variable

VideoNote
Static vs. instance

```
Circle circle1 = new Circle();
Circle circle2 = new Circle(5);
```

The **radius** in **circle1** is independent of the **radius** in **circle2** and is stored in a different memory location. Changes made to **circle1**'s **radius** do not affect **circle2**'s **radius**, and vice versa.

If you want all the instances of a class to share data, use *static variables*, also known as *class variables*. Static variables store values for the variables in a common memory location. Because of this common location, if one object changes the value of a static variable, all objects of the same class are affected. Java supports static methods as well as static variables. *Static methods* can be called without creating an instance of the class.

static variable

static method

Let's modify the **Circle** class by adding a static variable **numberOfObjects** to count the number of circle objects created. When the first object of this class is created, **numberOfObjects** is **1**. When the second object is created, **numberOfObjects** becomes **2**. The UML of the new circle class is shown in Figure 9.13. The **Circle** class defines the instance variable **radius** and the static variable **numberOfObjects**, the instance methods **getRadius**, **setRadius**, and **getArea**, and the static method **getNumberOfObjects**. (Note that static variables and methods are underlined in the UML class diagram.)

To declare a static variable or define a static method, put the modifier **static** in the variable or method declaration. The static variable **numberOfObjects** and the static method **getNumberOfObjects()** can be declared as follows:

```
static int numberOfObjects;
```

declare static variable

```
static int getNumberObjects() {
  return numberOfObjects;
}
```

define static method

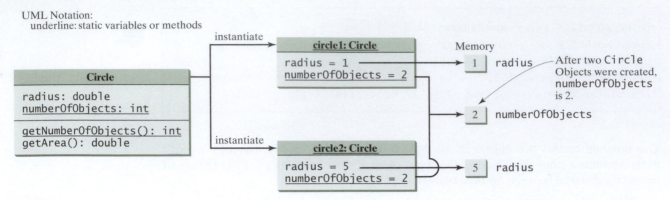

FIGURE 9.13 Instance variables belong to the instances and have memory storage independent of one another. Static variables are shared by all the instances of the same class.

declare constant

Constants in a class are shared by all objects of the class. Thus, constants should be declared as **final static**. For example, the constant **PI** in the **Math** class is defined as:

```
final static double PI = 3.14159265358979323846;
```

The new circle class, named **CircleWithStaticMembers**, is defined in Listing 9.6:

LISTING 9.6 CircleWithStaticMembers.java

```
1  public class CircleWithStaticMembers {
2    /** The radius of the circle */
3    double radius;
4
5    /** The number of objects created */
6    static int numberOfObjects = 0;
7
8    /** Construct a circle with radius 1 */
9    CircleWithStaticMembers() {
10     radius = 1;
11     numberOfObjects++;
12   }
13
14   /** Construct a circle with a specified radius */
15   CircleWithStaticMembers(double newRadius) {
16     radius = newRadius;
17     numberOfObjects++;
18   }
19
20   /** Return numberOfObjects */
21   static int getNumberOfObjects() {
22     return numberOfObjects;
23   }
24
25   /** Return the area of this circle */
26   double getArea() {
27     return radius * radius * Math.PI;
28   }
29 }
```

static variable

increase by 1

increase by 1

static method

Method **getNumberOfObjects()** in **CircleWithStaticMembers** is a static method. All the methods in the **Math** class are static. The **main** method is static, too.

Instance methods (e.g., **getArea()**) and instance data (e.g., **radius**) belong to instances and can be used only after the instances are created. They are accessed via a reference variable. Static methods (e.g., **getNumberOfObjects()**) and static data (e.g., **numberOfObjects**) can be accessed from a reference variable or from their class name.

The program in Listing 9.7 demonstrates how to use instance and static variables and methods and illustrates the effects of using them.

LISTING 9.7 TestCircleWithStaticMembers.java

```java
 1  public class TestCircleWithStaticMembers {
 2    /** Main method */
 3    public static void main(String[] args) {
 4      System.out.println("Before creating objects");
 5      System.out.println("The number of Circle objects is " +
 6        CircleWithStaticMembers.numberOfObjects);              // static variable
 7
 8      // Create c1
 9      CircleWithStaticMembers c1 = new CircleWithStaticMembers();
10
11      // Display c1 BEFORE c2 is created
12      System.out.println("\nAfter creating c1");
13      System.out.println("c1: radius (" + c1.radius +          // instance variable
14        ") and number of Circle objects (" +
15        c1.numberOfObjects + ")");                             // static variable
16
17      // Create c2
18      CircleWithStaticMembers c2 = new CircleWithStaticMembers(5);
19
20      // Modify c1
21      c1.radius = 9;                                           // instance variable
22
23      // Display c1 and c2 AFTER c2 was created
24      System.out.println("\nAfter creating c2 and modifying c1");
25      System.out.println("c1: radius (" + c1.radius +
26        ") and number of Circle objects (" +
27        c1.numberOfObjects + ")");                             // static variable
28      System.out.println("c2: radius (" + c2.radius +
29        ") and number of Circle objects (" +
30        c2.numberOfObjects + ")");                             // static variable
31    }
32  }
```

```
Before creating objects
The number of Circle objects is 0
After creating c1
c1: radius (1.0) and number of Circle objects (1)
After creating c2 and modifying c1
c1: radius (9.0) and number of Circle objects (2)
c2: radius (5.0) and number of Circle objects (2)
```

When you compile **TestCircleWithStaticMembers.java**, the Java compiler automatically compiles **CircleWithStaticMembers.java** if it has not been compiled since the last change.

Static variables and methods can be accessed without creating objects. Line 6 displays the number of objects, which is **0**, since no objects have been created.

The **main** method creates two circles, **c1** and **c2** (lines 9, 18). The instance variable **radius** in **c1** is modified to become **9** (line 21). This change does not affect the instance variable **radius** in **c2**, since these two instance variables are independent. The static variable **numberOfObjects** becomes **1** after **c1** is created (line 9), and it becomes **2** after **c2** is created (line 18).

Note that **PI** is a constant defined in **Math**, and **Math.PI** references the constant. **c1.numberOfObjects** (line 27) and **c2.numberOfObjects** (line 30) are better replaced by **CircleWithStaticMembers.numberOfObjects**. This improves readability, because other programmers can easily recognize the static variable. You can also replace **CircleWithStaticMembers.numberOfObjects** with **CircleWithStaticMembers.getNumberOfObjects()**.

Tip

Use **ClassName.methodName(arguments)** to invoke a static method and **ClassName.staticVariable** to access a static variable. This improves readability, because this makes the static method and data easy to spot.

An instance method can invoke an instance or static method and access an instance or static data field. A static method can invoke a static method and access a static data field. However, a static method cannot invoke an instance method or access an instance data field, since static methods and static data fields don't belong to a particular object. The relationship between static and instance members is summarized in the following diagram:

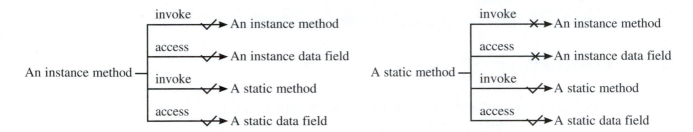

For example, the following code is wrong.

```
1  public class A {
2    int i = 5;
3    static int k = 2;
4
5    public static void main(String[] args) {
6      int j = i; // Wrong because i is an instance variable
7      m1(); // Wrong because m1() is an instance method
8    }
9
10   public void m1() {
11     // Correct since instance and static variables and methods
12     // can be used in an instance method
13     i = i + k + m2(i, k);
14   }
15
16   public static int m2(int i, int j) {
17     return (int)(Math.pow(i, j));
18   }
19 }
```

Note that if you replace the preceding code with the following new code, the program would be fine, because the instance data field `i` and method `m1` are now accessed from an object `a` (lines 7–8):

```
1  public class A {
2    int i = 5;
3    static int k = 2;
4
5    public static void main(String[] args) {
6      A a = new A();
7      int j = a.i; // OK, a.i accesses the object's instance variable
8      a.m1(); // OK. a.m1() invokes the object's instance method
9    }
10
11   public void m1() {
12     i = i + k + m2(i, k);
13   }
14
15   public static int m2(int i, int j) {
16     return (int)(Math.pow(i, j));
17   }
18 }
```

Design Guide

How do you decide whether a variable or a method should be an instance one or a static one? A variable or a method that is dependent on a specific instance of the class should be an instance variable or method. A variable or a method that is not dependent on a specific instance of the class should be a static variable or method. For example, every circle has its own radius, so the radius is dependent on a specific circle. Therefore, **radius** is an instance variable of the **Circle** class. Since the **getArea** method is dependent on a specific circle, it is an instance method. None of the methods in the **Math** class, such as **random**, **pow**, **sin**, and **cos**, is dependent on a specific instance. Therefore, these methods are static methods. The **main** method is static and can be invoked directly from a class.

instance or static?

Caution

It is a common design error to define an instance method that should have been defined as static. For example, the method **factorial(int n)** should be defined as static, as shown next, because it is independent of any specific instance.

common design error

```
public class Test {
  public int factorial(int n) {
    int result = 1;
    for (int i = 1; i <= n; i ++)
      result *= i;

    return result;
  }
}
```

(a) Wrong design

```
public class Test {
  public static int factorial(int n) {
    int result = 1;
    for (int i = 1; i <= n; i++)
      result *= i;

    return result;
  }
}
```

(b) Correct design

9.17 Suppose that the class **F** is defined in (a). Let **f** be an instance of **F**. Which of the statements in (b) are correct?

```
public class F {
  int i;
  static String s;

  void imethod() {
  }

  static void smethod() {
  }
}
```
(a)

```
System.out.println(f.i);
System.out.println(f.s);
f.imethod();
f.smethod();
System.out.println(F.i);
System.out.println(F.s);
F.imethod();
F.smethod();
```
(b)

9.18 Add the **static** keyword in the place of **?** if appropriate.

```
public class Test {
  int count;

  public ? void main(String[] args) {
    ...
  }

  public ? int getCount() {
    return count;
  }

  public ? int factorial(int n) {
    int result = 1;
    for (int i = 1; i <= n; i++)
      result *= i;

    return result;
  }
}
```

9.19 Can you invoke an instance method or reference an instance variable from a static method? Can you invoke a static method or reference a static variable from an instance method? What is wrong in the following code?

```
1  public class C {
2    public static void main(String[] args) {
3      method1();
4    }
5
6    public void method1() {
7      method2();
8    }
9
10   public static void method2() {
11     System.out.println("What is radius " + c.getRadius());
12   }
13
14   Circle c = new Circle();
15 }
```

9.8 Visibility Modifiers

Key Point

Visibility modifiers can be used to specify the visibility of a class and its members.

You can use the **public** visibility modifier for classes, methods, and data fields to denote that they can be accessed from any other classes. If no visibility modifier is used, then by default the classes, methods, and data fields are accessible by any class in the same package. This is known as *package-private* or *package-access*.

package-private (or
package-access)

Note

Packages can be used to organize classes. To do so, you need to add the following line as the first noncomment and nonblank statement in the program:

using packages

```
package packageName;
```

If a class is defined without the package statement, it is said to be placed in the *default package*.

Java recommends that you place classes into packages rather than using a default package. For simplicity, however, this book uses default packages. For more information on packages, see Supplement III.E, Packages.

In addition to the **public** and default visibility modifiers, Java provides the **private** and **protected** modifiers for class members. This section introduces the **private** modifier. The **protected** modifier will be introduced in Section 11.14, The **protected** Data and Methods.

The **private** modifier makes methods and data fields accessible only from within its own class. Figure 9.14 illustrates how a public, default, and private data field or method in class **C1** can be accessed from a class **C2** in the same package and from a class **C3** in a different package.

```
package p1;

public class C1 {
  public int x;
  int y;
  private int z;

  public void m1() {
  }
  void m2() {
  }
  private void m3() {
  }
}
```

```
package p1;

public class C2 {
  void aMethod() {
    C1 o = new C1();
    can access o.x;
    can access o.y;
    cannot access o.z;

    can invoke o.m1();
    can invoke o.m2();
    cannot invoke o.m3();
  }
}
```

```
package p2;

public class C3 {
  void aMethod() {
    C1 o = new C1();
    can access o.x;
    cannot access o.y;
    cannot access o.z;

    can invoke o.m1();
    cannot invoke o.m2();
    cannot invoke o.m3();
  }
}
```

FIGURE 9.14 The private modifier restricts access to its defining class, the default modifier restricts access to a package, and the public modifier enables unrestricted access.

If a class is not defined as public, it can be accessed only within the same package. As shown in Figure 9.15, **C1** can be accessed from **C2** but not from **C3**.

```
package p1;

class C1 {
  ...
}
```

```
package p1;

public class C2 {
  can access C1
}
```

```
package p2;

public class C3 {
  cannot access C1;
  can access C2;
}
```

FIGURE 9.15 A nonpublic class has package-access.

A visibility modifier specifies how data fields and methods in a class can be accessed from outside the class. There is no restriction on accessing data fields and methods from inside the class. As shown in Figure 9.16b, an object **c** of class **C** cannot access its private members, because **c** is in the **Test** class. As shown in Figure 9.16a, an object **c** of class **C** can access its private members, because **c** is defined inside its own class.

inside access

```java
public class C {
  private boolean x;

  public static void main(String[] args) {
    C c = new C();
    System.out.println(c.x);
    System.out.println(c.convert());
  }

  private int convert() {
    return x ? 1 : -1;
  }
}
```

(a) This is okay because object **c** is used inside the class **C**.

```java
public class Test {
  public static void main(String[] args) {
    C c = new C();
    System.out.println(c.x);
    System.out.println(c.convert());
  }
}
```

(b) This is wrong because **x** and **convert** are private in class **C**.

FIGURE 9.16 An object can access its private members if it is defined in its own class.

Caution

The **private** modifier applies only to the members of a class. The **public** modifier can apply to a class or members of a class. Using the modifiers **public** and **private** on local variables would cause a compile error.

Note

private constructor

In most cases, the constructor should be public. However, if you want to prohibit the user from creating an instance of a class, use a *private constructor*. For example, there is no reason to create an instance from the **Math** class, because all of its data fields and methods are static. To prevent the user from creating objects from the **Math** class, the constructor in **java.lang.Math** is defined as follows:

```java
private Math() {
}
```

9.9 Data Field Encapsulation

 Key Point

Making data fields private protects data and makes the class easy to maintain.

Data field encapsulation

VideoNote

Data field encapsulation

The data fields **radius** and **numberOfObjects** in the **CircleWithStaticMembers** class in Listing 9.6 can be modified directly (e.g., **c1.radius = 5** or **CircleWithStaticMembers .numberOfObjects = 10**). This is not a good practice—for two reasons:

- First, data may be tampered with. For example, **numberOfObjects** is to count the number of objects created, but it may be mistakenly set to an arbitrary value (e.g., **CircleWithStaticMembers.numberOfObjects = 10**).

- Second, the class becomes difficult to maintain and vulnerable to bugs. Suppose you want to modify the **CircleWithStaticMembers** class to ensure that the radius is nonnegative after other programs have already used the class. You have to change not only the **CircleWithStaticMembers** class but also the programs that use it, because the clients may have modified the radius directly (e.g., **c1.radius = -5**).

data field encapsulation

To prevent direct modifications of data fields, you should declare the data fields private, using the **private** modifier. This is known as *data field encapsulation*.

A private data field cannot be accessed by an object from outside the class that defines the private field. However, a client often needs to retrieve and modify a data field. To make a private data field accessible, provide a *getter* method to return its value. To enable a private data field to be updated, provide a *setter* method to set a new value. A getter method is also referred to as an *accessor* and a setter to a *mutator*.

getter (or accessor)
setter (or mutator)

A getter method has the following signature:

```
public returnType getPropertyName()
```

If the **returnType** is **boolean**, the getter method should be defined as follows by convention:

boolean accessor

```
public boolean isPropertyName()
```

A setter method has the following signature:

```
public void setPropertyName(dataType propertyValue)
```

Let's create a new circle class with a private data-field radius and its associated accessor and mutator methods. The class diagram is shown in Figure 9.17. The new circle class, named **CircleWithPrivateDataFields**, is defined in Listing 9.8:

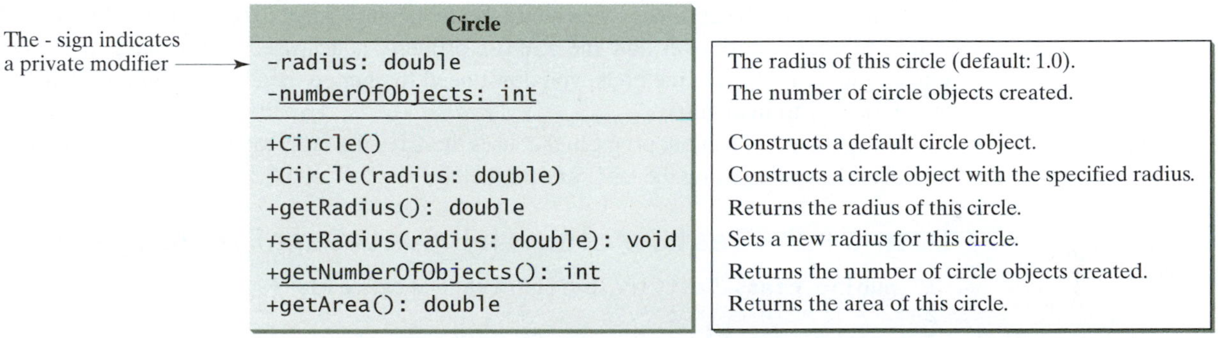

The - sign indicates a private modifier ⟶

Circle
-radius: double
-numberOfObjects: int
+Circle()
+Circle(radius: double)
+getRadius(): double
+setRadius(radius: double): void
+getNumberOfObjects(): int
+getArea(): double

The radius of this circle (default: 1.0).
The number of circle objects created.

Constructs a default circle object.
Constructs a circle object with the specified radius.
Returns the radius of this circle.
Sets a new radius for this circle.
Returns the number of circle objects created.
Returns the area of this circle.

FIGURE 9.17 The **Circle** class encapsulates circle properties and provides getter/setter and other methods.

LISTING 9.8 CircleWithPrivateDataFields.java

```
1  public class CircleWithPrivateDataFields {
2    /** The radius of the circle */
3    private double radius = 1;
4
5    /** The number of objects created */
6    private static int numberOfObjects = 0;
7
8    /** Construct a circle with radius 1 */
9    public CircleWithPrivateDataFields() {
10     numberOfObjects++;
11   }
12
13   /** Construct a circle with a specified radius */
14   public CircleWithPrivateDataFields(double newRadius) {
15     radius = newRadius;
16     numberOfObjects++;
```

encapsulate radius

encapsulate
  numberOfObjects

```
17    }
18
19    /** Return radius */
20    public double getRadius() {
21      return radius;
22    }
23
24    /** Set a new radius */
25    public void setRadius(double newRadius) {
26      radius = (newRadius >= 0) ? newRadius : 0;
27    }
28
29    /** Return numberOfObjects */
30    public static int getNumberOfObjects() {
31      return numberOfObjects;
32    }
33
34    /** Return the area of this circle */
35    public double getArea() {
36      return radius * radius * Math.PI;
37    }
38  }
```

accessor method (lines 20–22)
mutator method (lines 25)
accessor method (line 30)

The **getRadius()** method (lines 20–22) returns the radius, and the **setRadius(newRadius)** method (line 25–27) sets a new radius for the object. If the new radius is negative, **0** is set as the radius for the object. Since these methods are the only ways to read and modify the radius, you have total control over how the **radius** property is accessed. If you have to change the implementation of these methods, you don't need to change the client programs. This makes the class easy to maintain.

Listing 9.9 gives a client program that uses the **Circle** class to create a **Circle** object and modifies the radius using the **setRadius** method.

LISTING 9.9 TestCircleWithPrivateDataFields.java

```
1   public class TestCircleWithPrivateDataFields {
2     /** Main method */
3     public static void main(String[] args) {
4       // Create a circle with radius 5.0
5       CircleWithPrivateDataFields myCircle =
6         new CircleWithPrivateDataFields(5.0);
7       System.out.println("The area of the circle of radius "
8         + myCircle.getRadius() + " is " + myCircle.getArea());
9
10      // Increase myCircle's radius by 10%
11      myCircle.setRadius(myCircle.getRadius() * 1.1);
12      System.out.println("The area of the circle of radius "
13        + myCircle.getRadius() + " is " + myCircle.getArea());
14
15      System.out.println("The number of objects created is "
16        + CircleWithPrivateDataFields.getNumberOfObjects());
17    }
18  }
```

invoke public method (line 8)
invoke public method (line 13)
invoke public method (line 16)

The data field **radius** is declared private. Private data can be accessed only within their defining class, so you cannot use **myCircle.radius** in the client program. A compile error would occur if you attempted to access private data from a client.

Since **numberOfObjects** is private, it cannot be modified. This prevents tampering. For example, the user cannot set **numberOfObjects** to **100**. The only way to make it **100** is to create **100** objects of the **Circle** class.

Suppose you combined `TestCircleWithPrivateDataFields` and `Circle` into one class by moving the `main` method in `TestCircleWithPrivateDataFields` into `Circle`. Could you use `myCircle.radius` in the `main` method? See Checkpoint Question 9.22 for the answer.

Design Guide

To prevent data from being tampered with and to make the class easy to maintain, declare data fields private.

9.20 What is an accessor method? What is a mutator method? What are the naming conventions for accessor methods and mutator methods?

9.21 What are the benefits of data field encapsulation?

9.22 In the following code, `radius` is private in the `Circle` class, and `myCircle` is an object of the `Circle` class. Does the highlighted code cause any problems? If so, explain why.

```java
public class Circle {
  private double radius = 1;

  /** Find the area of this circle */
  public double getArea() {
    return radius * radius * Math.PI;
  }

  public static void main(String[] args) {
    Circle myCircle = new Circle();
    System.out.println("Radius is " + myCircle.radius);
  }
}
```

9.10 Passing Objects to Methods

Passing an object to a method is to pass the reference of the object.

Key
Point

You can pass objects to methods. Like passing an array, passing an object is actually passing the reference of the object. The following code passes the `myCircle` object as an argument to the `printCircle` method:

```java
1  public class Test {
2    public static void main(String[] args) {
3      // CircleWithPrivateDataFields is defined in Listing 9.8
4      CircleWithPrivateDataFields myCircle = new
5        CircleWithPrivateDataFields(5.0);
6      printCircle(myCircle);
7    }
8
9    public static void printCircle(CircleWithPrivateDataFields c) {
10      System.out.println("The area of the circle of radius "
11        + c.getRadius() + " is " + c.getArea());
12    }
13  }
```

pass an object

Java uses exactly one mode of passing arguments: pass-by-value. In the preceding code, the value of `myCircle` is passed to the `printCircle` method. This value is a reference to a `Circle` object.

pass-by-value

The program in Listing 9.10 demonstrates the difference between passing a primitive type value and passing a reference value.

LISTING 9.10 TestPassObject.java

```java
1  public class TestPassObject {
2    /** Main method */
3    public static void main(String[] args) {
4      // Create a Circle object with radius 1
5      CircleWithPrivateDataFields myCircle =
6        new CircleWithPrivateDataFields(1);
7
8      // Print areas for radius 1, 2, 3, 4, and 5.
9      int n = 5;
10     printAreas(myCircle, n);
11
12     // See myCircle.radius and times
13     System.out.println("\n" + "Radius is " + myCircle.getRadius());
14     System.out.println("n is " + n);
15   }
16
17   /** Print a table of areas for radius */
18   public static void printAreas(
19     CircleWithPrivateDataFields c, int times) {
20     System.out.println("Radius \t\tArea");
21     while (times >= 1) {
22       System.out.println(c.getRadius() + "\t\t" + c.getArea());
23       c.setRadius(c.getRadius() + 1);
24       times--;
25     }
26   }
27 }
```

pass object

object parameter

```
Radius        Area
1.0           3.141592653589793
2.0           12.566370614359172
3.0           29.274333882308138
4.0           50.26548245743669
5.0           79.53981633974483
Radius is 6.0
n is 5
```

The `CircleWithPrivateDataFields` class is defined in Listing 9.8. The program passes a `CircleWithPrivateDataFields` object `myCircle` and an integer value from `n` to invoke `printAreas(myCircle, n)` (line 10), which prints a table of areas for radii 1, 2, 3, 4, 5, as shown in the sample output.

Figure 9.18 shows the call stack for executing the methods in the program. Note that the objects are stored in a heap (see Section 7.6).

When passing an argument of a primitive data type, the value of the argument is passed. In this case, the value of `n` (5) is passed to `times`. Inside the `printAreas` method, the content of `times` is changed; this does not affect the content of `n`.

When passing an argument of a reference type, the reference of the object is passed. In this case, `c` contains a reference for the object that is also referenced via `myCircle`. Therefore, changing the properties of the object through `c` inside the `printAreas` method has the same effect as doing so outside the method through the variable `myCircle`. Pass-by-value on references can be best described semantically as *pass-by-sharing*; that is, the object referenced in the method is the same as the object being passed.

pass-by-sharing

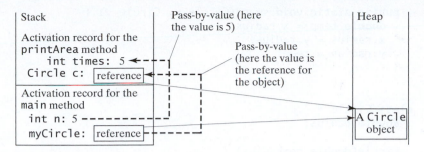

FIGURE 9.18   The value of **n** is passed to **times**, and the reference to **myCircle** is passed to **c** in the **printAreas** method.

9.23   Describe the difference between passing a parameter of a primitive type and passing a parameter of a reference type. Show the output of the following programs:

```java
public class Test {
  public static void main(String[] args) {
    Count myCount = new Count();
    int times = 0;

    for (int i = 0; i < 100; i++)
      increment(myCount, times);

    System.out.println("count is " + myCount.count);
    System.out.println("times is " + times);
  }

  public static void increment(Count c, int times) {
    c.count++;
    times++;
  }
}
```

```java
public class Count {
  public int count;

  public Count(int c) {
    count = c;
  }

  public Count() {
    count = 1;
  }
}
```

9.24   Show the output of the following program:

```java
public class Test {
  public static void main(String[] args) {
    Circle circle1 = new Circle(1);
    Circle circle2 = new Circle(2);

    swap1(circle1, circle2);
    System.out.println("After swap1: circle1 = " +
      circle1.radius + " circle2 = " + circle2.radius);

    swap2(circle1, circle2);
    System.out.println("After swap2: circle1 = " +
      circle1.radius + " circle2 = " + circle2.radius);
  }

  public static void swap1(Circle x, Circle y) {
    Circle temp = x;
    x = y;
    y = temp;
  }
```

```
            public static void swap2(Circle x, Circle y) {
              double temp = x.radius;
              x.radius = y.radius;
              y.radius = temp;
            }
          }

          class Circle {
            double radius;

            Circle(double newRadius) {
              radius = newRadius;
            }
          }
```

9.25 Show the output of the following code:

```
public class Test {
  public static void main(String[] args) {
    int[] a = {1, 2};
    swap(a[0], a[1]);
    System.out.println("a[0] = " + a[0]
      + " a[1] = " + a[1]);
  }

  public static void swap(int n1, int n2) {
    int temp = n1;
    n1 = n2;
    n2 = temp;
  }
}
```
(a)

```
public class Test {
  public static void main(String[] args) {
    int[] a = {1, 2};
    swap(a);
    System.out.println("a[0] = " + a[0]
      + " a[1] = " + a[1]);
  }

  public static void swap(int[] a) {
    int temp = a[0];
    a[0] = a[1];
    a[1] = temp;
  }
}
```
(b)

```
public class Test {
  public static void main(String[] args) {
    T t = new T();
    swap(t);
    System.out.println("e1 = " + t.e1
      + " e2 = " + t.e2);
  }

  public static void swap(T t) {
    int temp = t.e1;
    t.e1 = t.e2;
    t.e2 = temp;
  }
}

class T {
  int e1 = 1;
  int e2 = 2;
}
```
(c)

```
public class Test {
  public static void main(String[] args) {
    T t1 = new T();
    T t2 = new T();
    System.out.println("t1's i = " +
      t1.i + " and j = " + t1.j);
    System.out.println("t2's i = " +
      t2.i + " and j = " + t2.j);
  }
}

class T {
  static int i = 0;
  int j = 0;

  T() {
    i++;
    j = 1;
  }
}
```
(d)

9.26 What is the output of the following programs?

```java
import java.util.Date;

public class Test {
  public static void main(String[] args) {
    Date date = null;
    m1(date);
    System.out.println(date);
  }

  public static void m1(Date date) {
    date = new Date();
  }
}
```
(a)

```java
import java.util.Date;

public class Test {
  public static void main(String[] args) {
    Date date = new Date(1234567);
    m1(date);
    System.out.println(date.getTime());
  }

  public static void m1(Date date) {
    date = new Date(7654321);
  }
}
```
(b)

```java
import java.util.Date;

public class Test {
  public static void main(String[] args) {
    Date date = new Date(1234567);
    m1(date);
    System.out.println(date.getTime());
  }

  public static void m1(Date date) {
    date.setTime(7654321);
  }
}
```
(c)

```java
import java.util.Date;

public class Test {
  public static void main(String[] args) {
    Date date = new Date(1234567);
    m1(date);
    System.out.println(date.getTime());
  }

  public static void m1(Date date) {
    date = null;
  }
}
```
(d)

9.11 Array of Objects

An array can hold objects as well as primitive type values.

Key
Point

Chapter 7, Single-Dimensional Arrays, described how to create arrays of primitive type elements. You can also create arrays of objects. For example, the following statement declares and creates an array of ten `Circle` objects:

```java
Circle[] circleArray = new Circle[10];
```

To initialize `circleArray`, you can use a `for` loop like this one:

```java
for (int i = 0; i < circleArray.length; i++) {
  circleArray[i] = new Circle();
}
```

An array of objects is actually an *array of reference variables*. So, invoking `circleArray[1].getArea()` involves two levels of referencing, as shown in Figure 9.19. `circleArray` references the entire array; `circleArray[1]` references a `Circle` object.

Note
When an array of objects is created using the **new** operator, each element in the array is a reference variable with a default value of **null**.

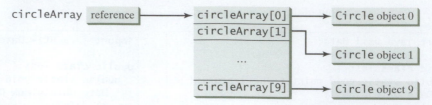

FIGURE 9.19 In an array of objects, an element of the array contains a reference to an object.

Listing 9.11 gives an example that demonstrates how to use an array of objects. The program summarizes the areas of an array of circles. The program creates **circleArray**, an array composed of five **Circle** objects; it then initializes circle radii with random values and displays the total area of the circles in the array.

LISTING 9.11 TotalArea.java

```java
 1  public class TotalArea {
 2    /** Main method */
 3    public static void main(String[] args) {
 4      // Declare circleArray
 5      CircleWithPrivateDataFields[] circleArray;
 6
 7      // Create circleArray
 8      circleArray = createCircleArray();
 9
10      // Print circleArray and total areas of the circles
11      printCircleArray(circleArray);
12    }
13
14    /** Create an array of Circle objects */
15    public static CircleWithPrivateDataFields[] createCircleArray() {
16      CircleWithPrivateDataFields[] circleArray =
17        new CircleWithPrivateDataFields[5];
18
19      for (int i = 0; i < circleArray.length; i++) {
20        circleArray[i] =
21          new CircleWithPrivateDataFields(Math.random() * 100);
22      }
23
24      // Return Circle array
25      return circleArray;
26    }
27
28    /** Print an array of circles and their total area */
29    public static void printCircleArray(
30        CircleWithPrivateDataFields[] circleArray) {
31      System.out.printf("%-30s%-15s\n", "Radius", "Area");
32      for (int i = 0; i < circleArray.length; i++) {
33        System.out.printf("%-30f%-15f\n", circleArray[i].getRadius(),
34          circleArray[i].getArea());
35      }
36
37      System.out.println("-------------------------------------------");
38
39      // Compute and display the result
40      System.out.printf("%-30s%-15f\n", "The total area of circles is",
41        sum(circleArray) );
42    }
```

array of objects

return array of objects

pass array of objects

```
43
44     /** Add circle areas */
45     public static double sum(CircleWithPrivateDataFields[] circleArray) {     pass array of objects
46       // Initialize sum
47       double sum = 0;
48
49       // Add areas to sum
50       for (int i = 0; i < circleArray.length; i++)
51         sum += circleArray[i].getArea();
52
53       return sum;
54     }
55   }
```

```
Radius                    Area
70.577708                 15649.941866
44.152266                 6124.291736
24.867853                 1942.792644
 5.680718                 101.380949
36.734246                 4239.280350

------------------------------------------------
The total area of circles is 28056.687544
```

The program invokes **createCircleArray()** (line 8) to create an array of five circle objects. Several circle classes were introduced in this chapter. This example uses the **CircleWithPrivateDataFields** class introduced in Section 9.9, Data Field Encapsulation.

The circle radii are randomly generated using the **Math.random()** method (line 21). The **createCircleArray** method returns an array of **CircleWithPrivateDataFields** objects (line 25). The array is passed to the **printCircleArray** method, which displays the radius and area of each circle and the total area of the circles.

The sum of the circle areas is computed by invoking the **sum** method (line 41), which takes the array of **CircleWithPrivateDataFields** objects as the argument and returns a **double** value for the total area.

9.27   What is wrong in the following code?

Check Point

```
1   public class Test {
2     public static void main(String[] args) {
3       java.util.Date[] dates = new java.util.Date[10];
4       System.out.println(dates[0]);
5       System.out.println(dates[0].toString());
6     }
7   }
```

9.12 Immutable Objects and Classes

You can define immutable classes to create immutable objects. The contents of immutable objects cannot be changed.

Key Point

Normally, you create an object and allow its contents to be changed later. However, occasionally it is desirable to create an object whose contents cannot be changed once the object has been created. We call such an object as *immutable object* and its class as *immutable class*. The **String** class, for example, is immutable. If you deleted the setter method in the **CircleWithPrivateDataFields** class in Listing 9.9, the class would be immutable, because radius is private and cannot be changed without a setter method.

immutable object
immutable class

If a class is immutable, then all its data fields must be private and it cannot contain public setter methods for any data fields. A class with all private data fields and no mutators is not necessarily immutable. For example, the following **Student** class has all private data fields and no setter methods, but it is not an immutable class.

Student class

```
1  public class Student {
2    private int id;
3    private String name;
4    private java.util.Date dateCreated;
5
6    public Student(int ssn, String newName) {
7      id = ssn;
8      name = newName;
9      dateCreated = new java.util.Date();
10   }
11
12   public int getId() {
13     return id;
14   }
15
16   public String getName() {
17     return name;
18   }
19
20   public java.util.Date getDateCreated() {
21     return dateCreated;
22   }
23 }
```

As shown in the following code, the data field **dateCreated** is returned using the **getDateCreated()** method. This is a reference to a **Date** object. Through this reference, the content for **dateCreated** can be changed.

```
public class Test {
  public static void main(String[] args) {
    Student student = new Student(111223333, "John");
    java.util.Date dateCreated = student.getDateCreated();
    dateCreated.setTime(200000); // Now dateCreated field is changed!
  }
}
```

For a class to be immutable, it must meet the following requirements:

- All data fields must be private.

- There can't be any mutator methods for data fields.

- No accessor methods can return a reference to a data field that is mutable.

Interested readers may refer to Supplement III.U for an extended discussion on immutable objects.

9.28 If a class contains only private data fields and no setter methods, is the class immutable?

9.29 If all the data fields in a class are private and of primitive types, and the class doesn't contain any setter methods, is the class immutable?

9.30 Is the following class immutable?

```
public class A {
  private int[] values;

  public int[] getValues() {
```

```
      return values;
    }
  }
```

9.13 The Scope of Variables

The scope of instance and static variables is the entire class, regardless of where the variables are declared.

Key Point

Section 6.9 discussed local variables and their scope rules. Local variables are declared and used inside a method locally. This section discusses the scope rules of all the variables in the context of a class.

Instance and static variables in a class are referred to as the *class's variables* or *data fields*. A variable defined inside a method is referred to as a *local variable*. The scope of a class's variables is the entire class, regardless of where the variables are declared. A class's variables and methods can appear in any order in the class, as shown in Figure 9.20a. The exception is when a data field is initialized based on a reference to another data field. In such cases, the other data field must be declared first, as shown in Figure 9.20b. For consistency, this book declares data fields at the beginning of the class.

class's variables

```
public class Circle {
  public double findArea() {
    return radius * radius * Math.PI;
  }

  private double radius = 1;
}
```

```
public class F {
  private int i ;
  private int j = i + 1;
}
```

(a) The variable **radius** and method **findArea()** can be declared in any order.

(b) **i** has to be declared before **j** because **j**'s initial value is dependent on **i**.

FIGURE 9.20 Members of a class can be declared in any order, with one exception.

You can declare a class's variable only once, but you can declare the same variable name in a method many times in different nonnesting blocks.

If a local variable has the same name as a class's variable, the local variable takes precedence and the class's variable with the same name is *hidden*. For example, in the following program, **x** is defined both as an instance variable and as a local variable in the method.

hidden variables

```
public class F {
  private int x = 0; // Instance variable
  private int y = 0;

  public F() {
  }

  public void p() {
    int x = 1; // Local variable
    System.out.println("x = " + x);
    System.out.println("y = " + y);
  }
}
```

What is the output for **f.p()**, where **f** is an instance of **F**? The output for **f.p()** is **1** for **x** and **0** for **y**. Here is why:

■ **x** is declared as a data field with the initial value of **0** in the class, but it is also declared in the method **p()** with an initial value of **1**. The latter **x** is referenced in the **System.out.println** statement.

■ **y** is declared outside the method **p()**, but **y** is accessible inside the method.

Tip
To avoid confusion and mistakes, do not use the names of instance or static variables as local variable names, except for method parameters.

9.31 What is the output of the following program?

```java
public class Test {
  private static int i = 0;
  private static int j = 0;

  public static void main(String[] args) {
    int i = 2;
    int k = 3;

    {
      int j = 3;
      System.out.println("i + j is " + i + j);
    }

    k = i + j;
    System.out.println("k is " + k);
    System.out.println("j is " + j);
  }
}
```

9.14 The **this** Reference

The keyword **this** *refers to the object itself. It can also be used inside a constructor to invoke another constructor of the same class.*

this keyword

The **this** *keyword* is the name of a reference that an object can use to refer to itself. You can use the **this** keyword to reference the object's instance members. For example, the following code in (a) uses **this** to reference the object's **radius** and invokes its **getArea()** method explicitly. The **this** reference is normally omitted, as shown in (b). However, the **this** reference is needed to reference hidden data fields or invoke an overloaded constructor.

```java
public class Circle {
  private double radius;

  ...

  public double getArea() {
  return this.radius * this.radius * Math.PI;
  }

  public String toString() {
    return "radius: " + this.radius
        + "area: " + this.getArea() ;
  }
}
```

(a)

Equivalent

```java
public class Circle {
  private double radius;

  ...

  public double getArea() {
    return radius * radius * Math.PI;
  }

  public String toString() {
    return "radius: " + radius
        + "area: " + getArea() ;
  }
}
```

(b)

9.14.1 Using **this** to Reference Hidden Data Fields

hidden data fields

The **this** keyword can be used to reference a class's *hidden data fields*. For example, a data-field name is often used as the parameter name in a setter method for the data field. In this case, the data field is hidden in the setter method. You need to reference the hidden data-field name in the method in order to set a new value to it. A hidden static variable can be accessed simply by using the `ClassName.staticVariable` reference. A hidden instance variable can be accessed by using the keyword `this`, as shown in Figure 9.21a.

```
public class F {
  private int i = 5;
  private static double k = 0;

  public void setI(int i) {
    this.i = i;
  }

  public static void setK(double k) {
    F.k = k;
  }

  // Other methods omitted
}
```
(a)

```
Suppose that f1 and f2 are two objects of F.

Invoking f1.setI(10) is to execute
    this.i = 10, where this refers f1

Invoking f2.setI(45) is to execute
    this.i = 45, where this refers f2

Invoking F.setK(33) is to execute
    F.k = 33. setK is a static method
```
(b)

FIGURE 9.21   The keyword `this` refers to the calling object that invokes the method.

The `this` keyword gives us a way to reference the object that invokes an instance method. To invoke `f1.setI(10)`, `this.i = i` is executed, which assigns the value of parameter `i` to the data field `i` of this calling object `f1`. The keyword `this` refers to the object that invokes the instance method `setI`, as shown in Figure 9.21b. The line `F.k = k` means that the value in parameter `k` is assigned to the static data field `k` of the class, which is shared by all the objects of the class.

9.14.2   Using **this** to Invoke a Constructor

The `this` keyword can be used to invoke another constructor of the same class. For example, you can rewrite the `Circle` class as follows:

```
public class Circle {
  private double radius;

  public Circle(double radius) {
    this.radius = radius;
  }                                    The this keyword is used to reference the hidden
                                       data field radius of the object being constructed.
  public Circle() {
    this(1.0);
  }                                    The this keyword is used to invoke another
                                       constructor.
  ...
}
```

The line `this(1.0)` in the second constructor invokes the first constructor with a `double` value argument.

Note

Java requires that the `this(arg-list)` statement appear first in the constructor before any other executable statements.

Tip

If a class has multiple constructors, it is better to implement them using `this(arg-list)` as much as possible. In general, a constructor with no or fewer arguments can invoke a constructor with more arguments using `this(arg-list)`. This syntax often simplifies coding and makes the class easier to read and to maintain.

9.32 Describe the role of the `this` keyword.

9.33 What is wrong in the following code?

```
1  public class C {
2    private int p;
3
4    public C() {
5      System.out.println("C's no-arg constructor invoked");
6      this(0);
7    }
8
9    public C(int p) {
10     p = p;
11   }
12
13   public void setP(int p) {
14     p = p;
15   }
16 }
```

9.34 What is wrong in the following code?

```
public class Test {
  private int id;

  public void m1() {
    this.id = 45;
  }

  public void m2() {
    Test.id = 45;
  }
}
```

KEY TERMS

action   322
anonymous object   331
attribute   322
behavior   322
class   322
class's variable   355
client   325
constructor   322
data field   322
data field encapsulation   344
default constructor   329
dot operator (.)   330
getter (or accessor)   345
instance   322
instance method   331
instance variable   331
instantiation   322
immutable class   353

immutable object   353
no-arg constructor   329
`null` value   331
object   322
object-oriented programming (OOP)   322
package-private (or package-access)   342
private constructor   344
property   322
public class   325
reference type   330
reference variable   330
setter (or mutator)   345
state   322
static method   337
static variable   337
`this` keyword   356
Unified Modeling Language (UML)   323

CHAPTER SUMMARY

1. A *class* is a template for *objects*. It defines the *properties* of objects and provides *constructors* for creating objects and methods for manipulating them.

2. A class is also a data type. You can use it to declare object *reference variables*. An object reference variable that appears to hold an object actually contains a reference to that object. Strictly speaking, an object reference variable and an object are different, but most of the time the distinction can be ignored.

3. An object is an *instance* of a class. You use the **new** operator to create an object, and the *dot operator* (**.**) to access members of that object through its reference variable.

4. An *instance variable* or *method* belongs to an instance of a class. Its use is associated with individual instances. A *static variable* is a variable shared by all instances of the same class. A *static method* is a method that can be invoked without using instances.

5. Every instance of a class can access the class's static variables and methods. For clarity, however, it is better to invoke static variables and methods using **ClassName.variable** and **ClassName.method**.

6. Visibility modifiers specify how the class, method, and data are accessed. A **public** class, method, or data is accessible to all clients. A **private** method or data is accessible only inside the class.

7. You can provide a getter (accessor) method or a setter (mutator) method to enable clients to see or modify the data.

8. A getter method has the signature **public returnType getPropertyName()**. If the **returnType** is **boolean**, the **get** method should be defined as **public boolean isPropertyName()**. A setter method has the signature **public void setPropertyName(dataType propertyValue)**.

9. All parameters are passed to methods using pass-by-value. For a parameter of a primitive type, the actual value is passed; for a parameter of a *reference type*, the reference for the object is passed.

10. A Java array is an object that can contain primitive type values or object type values. When an array of objects is created, its elements are assigned the default value of **null**.

11. Once it is created, an *immutable object* cannot be modified. To prevent users from modifying an object, you can define *immutable classes*.

12. The scope of instance and static variables is the entire class, regardless of where the variables are declared. Instance and static variables can be declared anywhere in the class. For consistency, they are declared at the beginning of the class in this book.

13. The keyword **this** can be used to refer to the calling object. It can also be used inside a constructor to invoke another constructor of the same class.

QUIZ

Answer the quiz for this chapter online at www.cs.armstrong.edu/liang/intro10e/quiz.html.

PROGRAMMING EXERCISES

three objectives

Pedagogical Note

The exercises in Chapters 9–13 help you achieve three objectives:

- Design classes and draw UML class diagrams.
- Implement classes from the UML.
- Use classes to develop applications.

Students can download solutions for the UML diagrams for the even-numbered exercises from the Companion Website, and instructors can download all solutions from the same site.

Sections 9.2–9.5

9.1 (*The Rectangle class*) Following the example of the `Circle` class in Section 9.2, design a class named `Rectangle` to represent a rectangle. The class contains:

- Two `double` data fields named `width` and `height` that specify the width and height of the rectangle. The default values are `1` for both `width` and `height`.
- A no-arg constructor that creates a default rectangle.
- A constructor that creates a rectangle with the specified `width` and `height`.
- A method named `getArea()` that returns the area of this rectangle.
- A method named `getPerimeter()` that returns the perimeter.

Draw the UML diagram for the class and then implement the class. Write a test program that creates two `Rectangle` objects—one with width `4` and height `40` and the other with width `3.5` and height `35.9`. Display the width, height, area, and perimeter of each rectangle in this order.

9.2 (*The Stock class*) Following the example of the `Circle` class in Section 9.2, design a class named `Stock` that contains:

- A string data field named `symbol` for the stock's symbol.
- A string data field named `name` for the stock's name.
- A `double` data field named `previousClosingPrice` that stores the stock price for the previous day.
- A `double` data field named `currentPrice` that stores the stock price for the current time.
- A constructor that creates a stock with the specified symbol and name.
- A method named `getChangePercent()` that returns the percentage changed from `previousClosingPrice` to `currentPrice`.

Draw the UML diagram for the class and then implement the class. Write a test program that creates a `Stock` object with the stock symbol `ORCL`, the name `Oracle Corporation`, and the previous closing price of `34.5`. Set a new current price to `34.35` and display the price-change percentage.

Section 9.6

*9.3 (*Use the Date class*) Write a program that creates a `Date` object, sets its elapsed time to `10000`, `100000`, `1000000`, `10000000`, `100000000`, `1000000000`, `10000000000`, and `100000000000`, and displays the date and time using the `toString()` method, respectively.

*9.4 (*Use the Random class*) Write a program that creates a `Random` object with seed `1000` and displays the first 50 random integers between `0` and `100` using the `nextInt(100)` method.

*9.5 (*Use the GregorianCalendar class*) Java API has the `GregorianCalendar` class in the `java.util` package, which you can use to obtain the year, month, and day of a date. The no-arg constructor constructs an instance for the current date, and the methods `get(GregorianCalendar.YEAR)`, `get(GregorianCalendar.MONTH)`, and `get(GregorianCalendar.DAY_OF_MONTH)` return the year, month, and day. Write a program to perform two tasks:

- Display the current year, month, and day.
- The `GregorianCalendar` class has the `setTimeInMillis(long)`, which can be used to set a specified elapsed time since January 1, 1970. Set the value to `1234567898765L` and display the year, month, and day.

Sections 9.7–9.9

*9.6 (*Stopwatch*) Design a class named `StopWatch`. The class contains:

- Private data fields `startTime` and `endTime` with getter methods.
- A no-arg constructor that initializes `startTime` with the current time.
- A method named `start()` that resets the `startTime` to the current time.
- A method named `stop()` that sets the `endTime` to the current time.
- A method named `getElapsedTime()` that returns the elapsed time for the stopwatch in milliseconds.

Draw the UML diagram for the class and then implement the class. Write a test program that measures the execution time of sorting 100,000 numbers using selection sort.

9.7 (*The Account class*) Design a class named `Account` that contains:

- A private `int` data field named `id` for the account (default `0`).
- A private `double` data field named `balance` for the account (default `0`).
- A private `double` data field named `annualInterestRate` that stores the current interest rate (default `0`). Assume all accounts have the same interest rate.
- A private `Date` data field named `dateCreated` that stores the date when the account was created.
- A no-arg constructor that creates a default account.
- A constructor that creates an account with the specified id and initial balance.
- The accessor and mutator methods for `id`, `balance`, and `annualInterestRate`.
- The accessor method for `dateCreated`.
- A method named `getMonthlyInterestRate()` that returns the monthly interest rate.
- A method named `getMonthlyInterest()` that returns the monthly interest.
- A method named `withdraw` that withdraws a specified amount from the account.
- A method named `deposit` that deposits a specified amount to the account.

Draw the UML diagram for the class and then implement the class. (*Hint*: The method `getMonthlyInterest()` is to return monthly interest, not the interest rate. Monthly interest is `balance * monthlyInterestRate`. `monthlyInterestRate` is `annualInterestRate / 12`. Note that `annualInterestRate` is a percentage, e.g., like 4.5%. You need to divide it by 100.)

Write a test program that creates an `Account` object with an account ID of 1122, a balance of $20,000, and an annual interest rate of 4.5%. Use the `withdraw` method to withdraw $2,500, use the `deposit` method to deposit $3,000, and print the balance, the monthly interest, and the date when this account was created.

VideoNote

The Fan class

9.8 (*The Fan class*) Design a class named **Fan** to represent a fan. The class contains:

- Three constants named **SLOW**, **MEDIUM**, and **FAST** with the values **1**, **2**, and **3** to denote the fan speed.
- A private **int** data field named **speed** that specifies the speed of the fan (the default is **SLOW**).
- A private **boolean** data field named **on** that specifies whether the fan is on (the default is **false**).
- A private **double** data field named **radius** that specifies the radius of the fan (the default is **5**).
- A string data field named **color** that specifies the color of the fan (the default is **blue**).
- The accessor and mutator methods for all four data fields.
- A no-arg constructor that creates a default fan.
- A method named **toString()** that returns a string description for the fan. If the fan is on, the method returns the fan speed, color, and radius in one combined string. If the fan is not on, the method returns the fan color and radius along with the string "fan is off" in one combined string.

Draw the UML diagram for the class and then implement the class. Write a test program that creates two **Fan** objects. Assign maximum speed, radius **10**, color **yellow**, and turn it on to the first object. Assign medium speed, radius **5**, color **blue**, and turn it off to the second object. Display the objects by invoking their **toString** method.

9.9 (*Geometry: n-sided regular polygon*) In an *n*-sided regular polygon, all sides have the same length and all angles have the same degree (i.e., the polygon is both equilateral and equiangular). Design a class named **RegularPolygon that contains:

- A private **int** data field named **n** that defines the number of sides in the polygon with default value **3**.
- A private **double** data field named **side** that stores the length of the side with default value **1**.
- A private **double** data field named **x** that defines the *x*-coordinate of the polygon's center with default value **0**.
- A private **double** data field named **y** that defines the *y*-coordinate of the polygon's center with default value **0**.
- A no-arg constructor that creates a regular polygon with default values.
- A constructor that creates a regular polygon with the specified number of sides and length of side, centered at (**0**, **0**).
- A constructor that creates a regular polygon with the specified number of sides, length of side, and *x*- and *y*-coordinates.
- The accessor and mutator methods for all data fields.
- The method **getPerimeter()** that returns the perimeter of the polygon.
- The method **getArea()** that returns the area of the polygon. The formula for computing the area of a regular polygon is $Area = \dfrac{n \times s^2}{4 \times \tan\left(\dfrac{\pi}{n}\right)}$.

Draw the UML diagram for the class and then implement the class. Write a test program that creates three **RegularPolygon** objects, created using the no-arg constructor, using **RegularPolygon(6, 4)**, and using **RegularPolygon(10, 4, 5.6, 7.8)**. For each object, display its perimeter and area.

*9.10 (*Algebra: quadratic equations*) Design a class named `QuadraticEquation` for a quadratic equation $ax^2 + bx + x = 0$. The class contains:

- Private data fields `a`, `b`, and `c` that represent three coefficients.
- A constructor for the arguments for `a`, `b`, and `c`.
- Three getter methods for `a`, `b`, and `c`.
- A method named `getDiscriminant()` that returns the discriminant, which is $b^2 - 4ac$.
- The methods named `getRoot1()` and `getRoot2()` for returning two roots of the equation

$$ r_1 = \frac{-b + \sqrt{b^2 - 4ac}}{2a} \quad \text{and} \quad r_2 = \frac{-b - \sqrt{b^2 - 4ac}}{2a} $$

These methods are useful only if the discriminant is nonnegative. Let these methods return `0` if the discriminant is negative.

Draw the UML diagram for the class and then implement the class. Write a test program that prompts the user to enter values for a, b, and c and displays the result based on the discriminant. If the discriminant is positive, display the two roots. If the discriminant is 0, display the one root. Otherwise, display "The equation has no roots." See Programming Exercise 3.1 for sample runs.

*9.11 (*Algebra: 2 × 2 linear equations*) Design a class named `LinearEquation` for a 2 × 2 system of linear equations:

$$ \begin{aligned} ax + by &= e \\ cx + dy &= f \end{aligned} \qquad x = \frac{ed - bf}{ad - bc} \qquad y = \frac{af - ec}{ad - bc} $$

The class contains:

- Private data fields `a`, `b`, `c`, `d`, `e`, and `f`.
- A constructor with the arguments for `a`, `b`, `c`, `d`, `e`, and `f`.
- Six getter methods for `a`, `b`, `c`, `d`, `e`, and `f`.
- A method named `isSolvable()` that returns true if $ad - bc$ is not 0.
- Methods `getX()` and `getY()` that return the solution for the equation.

Draw the UML diagram for the class and then implement the class. Write a test program that prompts the user to enter `a`, `b`, `c`, `d`, `e`, and `f` and displays the result. If $ad - bc$ is 0, report that "The equation has no solution." See Programming Exercise 3.3 for sample runs.

**9.12 (*Geometry: intersecting point*) Suppose two line segments intersect. The two endpoints for the first line segment are `(x1, y1)` and `(x2, y2)` and for the second line segment are `(x3, y3)` and `(x4, y4)`. Write a program that prompts the user to enter these four endpoints and displays the intersecting point. As discussed in Programming Exercise 3.25, the intersecting point can be found by solving a linear equation. Use the `LinearEquation` class in Programming Exercise 9.11 to solve this equation. See Programming Exercise 3.25 for sample runs.

**9.13 (*The `Location` class*) Design a class named `Location` for locating a maximal value and its location in a two-dimensional array. The class contains public data fields `row`, `column`, and `maxValue` that store the maximal value and its indices in a two-dimensional array with `row` and `column` as `int` types and `maxValue` as a `double` type.

Write the following method that returns the location of the largest element in a two-dimensional array:

```
public static Location locateLargest(double[][] a)
```

The return value is an instance of **Location**. Write a test program that prompts the user to enter a two-dimensional array and displays the location of the largest element in the array. Here is a sample run:

```
Enter the number of rows and columns in the array:  3 4  ⏎Enter
Enter the array:
23.5 35 2 10  ⏎Enter
4.5 3 45 3.5  ⏎Enter
35 44 5.5 9.6  ⏎Enter
The location of the largest element is 45 at (1, 2)
```

OBJECT-ORIENTED THINKING

Objectives

- To apply class abstraction to develop software (§10.2).

- To explore the differences between the procedural paradigm and object-oriented paradigm (§10.3).

- To discover the relationships between classes (§10.4).

- To design programs using the object-oriented paradigm (§§10.5–10.6).

- To create objects for primitive values using the wrapper classes (**Byte**, **Short**, **Integer**, **Long**, **Float**, **Double**, **Character**, and **Boolean**) (§10.7).

- To simplify programming using automatic conversion between primitive types and wrapper class types (§10.8).

- To use the **BigInteger** and **BigDecimal** classes for computing very large numbers with arbitrary precisions (§10.9).

- To use the **String** class to process immutable strings (§10.10).

- To use the **StringBuilder** and **StringBuffer** classes to process mutable strings (§10.11).

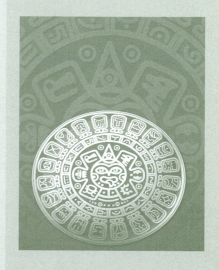

10.1 Introduction

The focus of this chapter is on class design and explores the differences between procedural programming and object-oriented programming.

The preceding chapter introduced objects and classes. You learned how to define classes, create objects, and use objects from several classes in the Java API (e.g., **Circle**, **Date**, **Random**, and **Point2D**). This book's approach is to teach problem solving and fundamental programming techniques before object-oriented programming. This chapter shows how procedural and object-oriented programming differ. You will see the benefits of object-oriented programming and learn to use it effectively.

Our focus here is on class design. We will use several examples to illustrate the advantages of the object-oriented approach. The examples involve designing new classes and using them in applications and introducing new classes in the Java API.

10.2 Class Abstraction and Encapsulation

Class abstraction is the separation of class implementation from the use of a class. The details of implementation are encapsulated and hidden from the user. This is known as class encapsulation.

class abstraction

class's contract

class encapsulation

abstract data type

In Chapter 6, you learned about method abstraction and used it in stepwise refinement. Java provides many levels of abstraction, and *class abstraction* separates class implementation from how the class is used. The creator of a class describes the functions of the class and lets the user know how the class can be used. The collection of methods and fields that are accessible from outside the class, together with the description of how these members are expected to behave, serves as the *class's contract*. As shown in Figure 10.1, the user of the class does not need to know how the class is implemented. The details of implementation are encapsulated and hidden from the user. This is called *class encapsulation*. For example, you can create a **Circle** object and find the area of the circle without knowing how the area is computed. For this reason, a class is also known as an *abstract data type* (ADT).

FIGURE 10.1 Class abstraction separates class implementation from the use of the class.

Class abstraction and encapsulation are two sides of the same coin. Many real-life examples illustrate the concept of class abstraction. Consider, for instance, building a computer system. Your personal computer has many components—a CPU, memory, disk, motherboard, fan, and so on. Each component can be viewed as an object that has properties and methods. To get the components to work together, you need know only how each component is used and how it interacts with the others. You don't need to know how the components work internally. The internal implementation is encapsulated and hidden from you. You can build a computer without knowing how a component is implemented.

The computer-system analogy precisely mirrors the object-oriented approach. Each component can be viewed as an object of the class for the component. For example, you might have a class that models all kinds of fans for use in a computer, with properties such as fan size and speed and methods such as start and stop. A specific fan is an instance of this class with specific property values.

As another example, consider getting a loan. A specific loan can be viewed as an object of a **Loan** class. The interest rate, loan amount, and loan period are its data properties, and computing the monthly payment and total payment are its methods. When you buy a car, a loan object is created by instantiating the class with your loan interest rate, loan amount, and loan period. You can then use the methods to find the monthly payment and total payment of your loan. As a user of the **Loan** class, you don't need to know how these methods are implemented.

VideoNote
The Loan class

Listing 2.9, ComputeLoan.java, presented a program for computing loan payments. That program cannot be reused in other programs because the code for computing the payments is in the **main** method. One way to fix this problem is to define static methods for computing the monthly payment and total payment. However, this solution has limitations. Suppose you wish to associate a date with the loan. There is no good way to tie a date with a loan without using objects. The traditional procedural programming paradigm is action-driven, and data are separated from actions. The object-oriented programming paradigm focuses on objects, and actions are defined along with the data in objects. To tie a date with a loan, you can define a loan class with a date along with the loan's other properties as data fields. A loan object now contains data and actions for manipulating and processing data, and the loan data and actions are integrated in one object. Figure 10.2 shows the UML class diagram for the **Loan** class.

Loan	
-annualInterestRate: double	The annual interest rate of the loan (default: 2.5).
-numberOfYears: int	The number of years for the loan (default: 1).
-loanAmount: double	The loan amount (default: 1000).
-loanDate: java.util.Date	The date this loan was created.
+Loan()	Constructs a default Loan object.
+Loan(annualInterestRate: double, numberOfYears: int,loanAmount: double)	Constructs a loan with specified interest rate, years, and loan amount.
+getAnnualInterestRate(): double	Returns the annual interest rate of this loan.
+getNumberOfYears(): int	Returns the number of the years of this loan.
+getLoanAmount(): double	Returns the amount of this loan.
+getLoanDate(): java.util.Date	Returns the date of the creation of this loan.
+setAnnualInterestRate(annualInterestRate: double): void	Sets a new annual interest rate for this loan.
+setNumberOfYears(numberOfYears: int): void	Sets a new number of years for this loan.
+setLoanAmount(loanAmount: double): void	Sets a new amount for this loan.
+getMonthlyPayment(): double	Returns the monthly payment for this loan.
+getTotalPayment(): double	Returns the total payment for this loan.

FIGURE 10.2 The Loan class models the properties and behaviors of loans.

The UML diagram in Figure 10.2 serves as the contract for the **Loan** class. Throughout this book, you will play the roles of both class user and class developer. Remember that a class user can use the class without knowing how the class is implemented.

Assume that the **Loan** class is available. The program in Listing 10.1 uses that class.

LISTING 10.1 TestLoanClass.java

```
1  import java.util.Scanner;
2
3  public class TestLoanClass {
4    /** Main method */
5    public static void main(String[] args) {
```

```
6      // Create a Scanner
7      Scanner input = new Scanner(System.in);
8
9      // Enter annual interest rate
10     System.out.print(
11       "Enter annual interest rate, for example, 8.25: ");
12     double annualInterestRate = input.nextDouble();
13
14     // Enter number of years
15     System.out.print("Enter number of years as an integer: ");
16     int numberOfYears = input.nextInt();
17
18     // Enter loan amount
19     System.out.print("Enter loan amount, for example, 120000.95: ");
20     double loanAmount = input.nextDouble();
21
22     // Create a Loan object
23     Loan loan =
24       new Loan(annualInterestRate, numberOfYears, loanAmount);
25
26     // Display loan date, monthly payment, and total payment
27     System.out.printf("The loan was created on %s\n" +
28       "The monthly payment is %.2f\nThe total payment is %.2f\n",
29       loan.getLoanDate().toString(), loan.getMonthlyPayment(),
30       loan.getTotalPayment());
31   }
32 }
```

create Loan object

invoke instance method
invoke instance method

```
Enter annual interest rate, for example, 8.25: 2.5  ↵Enter
Enter number of years as an integer: 5  ↵Enter
Enter loan amount, for example, 120000.95: 1000  ↵Enter
The loan was created on Sat Jun 16 21:12:50 EDT 2012
The monthly payment is 17.75
The total payment is 1064.84
```

The **main** method reads the interest rate, the payment period (in years), and the loan amount; creates a **Loan** object; and then obtains the monthly payment (line 29) and the total payment (line 30) using the instance methods in the **Loan** class.

The **Loan** class can be implemented as in Listing 10.2.

LISTING 10.2 Loan.java

```
1  public class Loan {
2    private double annualInterestRate;
3    private int numberOfYears;
4    private double loanAmount;
5    private java.util.Date loanDate;
6
7    /** Default constructor */
8    public Loan() {
9      this(2.5, 1, 1000);
10   }
11
12   /** Construct a loan with specified annual interest rate,
```

no-arg constructor

```
13        number of years, and loan amount
14     */
15    public Loan(double annualInterestRate, int numberOfYears,        constructor
16        double loanAmount) {
17      this.annualInterestRate = annualInterestRate;
18      this.numberOfYears = numberOfYears;
19      this.loanAmount = loanAmount;
20      loanDate = new java.util.Date();
21    }
22
23    /** Return annualInterestRate */
24    public double getAnnualInterestRate() {
25      return annualInterestRate;
26    }
27
28    /** Set a new annualInterestRate */
29    public void setAnnualInterestRate(double annualInterestRate) {
30      this.annualInterestRate = annualInterestRate;
31    }
32
33    /** Return numberOfYears */
34    public int getNumberOfYears() {
35      return numberOfYears;
36    }
37
38    /** Set a new numberOfYears */
39    public void setNumberOfYears(int numberOfYears) {
40      this.numberOfYears = numberOfYears;
41    }
42
43    /** Return loanAmount */
44    public double getLoanAmount() {
45      return loanAmount;
46    }
47
48    /** Set a new loanAmount */
49    public void setLoanAmount(double loanAmount) {
50      this.loanAmount = loanAmount;
51    }
52
53    /** Find monthly payment */
54    public double getMonthlyPayment() {
55      double monthlyInterestRate = annualInterestRate / 1200;
56      double monthlyPayment = loanAmount * monthlyInterestRate / (1 -
57        (1 / Math.pow(1 + monthlyInterestRate, numberOfYears * 12)));
58      return monthlyPayment;
59    }
60
61    /** Find total payment */
62    public double getTotalPayment() {
63      double totalPayment = getMonthlyPayment() * numberOfYears * 12;
64      return totalPayment;
65    }
66
67    /** Return loan date */
68    public java.util.Date getLoanDate() {
69      return loanDate;
70    }
71  }
```

From a class developer's perspective, a class is designed for use by many different customers. In order to be useful in a wide range of applications, a class should provide a variety of ways for customization through constructors, properties, and methods.

The **Loan** class contains two constructors, four getter methods, three setter methods, and the methods for finding the monthly payment and the total payment. You can construct a **Loan** object by using the no-arg constructor or the constructor with three parameters: annual interest rate, number of years, and loan amount. When a loan object is created, its date is stored in the **loanDate** field. The **getLoanDate** method returns the date. The methods—**getAnnualInterest**, **getNumberOfYears**, and **getLoanAmount**—return the annual interest rate, payment years, and loan amount, respectively. All the data properties and methods in this class are tied to a specific instance of the **Loan** class. Therefore, they are instance variables and methods.

Important Pedagogical Tip

Use the UML diagram for the **Loan** class shown in Figure 10.2 to write a test program that uses the **Loan** class even though you don't know how the **Loan** class is implemented. This has three benefits:

- It demonstrates that developing a class and using a class are two separate tasks.
- It enables you to skip the complex implementation of certain classes without interrupting the sequence of this book.
- It is easier to learn how to implement a class if you are familiar with it by using the class.

For all the class examples from now on, create an object from the class and try using its methods before turning your attention to its implementation.

10.1 If you redefine the **Loan** class in Listing 10.2 without setter methods, is the class immutable?

10.3 Thinking in Objects

The procedural paradigm focuses on designing methods. The object-oriented paradigm couples data and methods together into objects. Software design using the object-oriented paradigm focuses on objects and operations on objects.

Chapters 1–8 introduced fundamental programming techniques for problem solving using loops, methods, and arrays. Knowing these techniques lays a solid foundation for object-oriented programming. Classes provide more flexibility and modularity for building reusable software. This section improves the solution for a problem introduced in Chapter 3 using the object-oriented approach. From these improvements, you will gain insight into the differences between procedural and object-oriented programming and see the benefits of developing reusable code using objects and classes.

Listing 3.4, ComputeAndInterpretBMI.java, presented a program for computing body mass index. The code cannot be reused in other programs, because the code is in the **main** method. To make it reusable, define a static method to compute body mass index as follows:

```
public static double getBMI(double weight, double height)
```

This method is useful for computing body mass index for a specified weight and height. However, it has limitations. Suppose you need to associate the weight and height with a person's name and birth date. You could declare separate variables to store these values, but these values would not be tightly coupled. The ideal way to couple them is to create an object that contains them all. Since these values are tied to individual objects, they should be stored in instance data fields. You can define a class named **BMI** as shown in Figure 10.3.

VideoNote

The BMI class

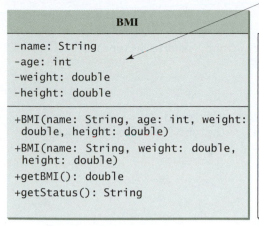

The getter methods for these data fields are provided in the class, but omitted in the UML diagram for brevity.

BMI
-name: String
-age: int
-weight: double
-height: double
+BMI(name: String, age: int, weight: double, height: double)
+BMI(name: String, weight: double, height: double)
+getBMI(): double
+getStatus(): String

The name of the person.
The age of the person.
The weight of the person in pounds.
The height of the person in inches.

Creates a BMI object with the specified name, age, weight, and height.
Creates a BMI object with the specified name, weight, height, and a default age 20.
Returns the BMI.
Returns the BMI status (e.g., normal, overweight, etc.).

FIGURE 10.3 The BMI class encapsulates BMI information.

Assume that the BMI class is available. Listing 10.3 gives a test program that uses this class.

LISTING 10.3 UseBMIClass.java

```
1  public class UseBMIClass {
2    public static void main(String[] args) {
3      BMI bmi1 = new BMI("Kim Yang", 18, 145, 70);          create an object
4      System.out.println("The BMI for " + bmi1.getName() + " is "   invoke instance method
5        + bmi1.getBMI() + " " + bmi1.getStatus());
6
7      BMI bmi2 = new BMI("Susan King", 215, 70);            create an object
8      System.out.println("The BMI for " + bmi2.getName() + " is "   invoke instance method
9        + bmi2.getBMI() + " " + bmi2.getStatus());
10   }
11 }
```

```
The BMI for Kim Yang is 20.81 Normal
The BMI for Susan King is 30.85 Obese
```

Line 3 creates the object **bmi1** for **Kim Yang** and line 7 creates the object **bmi2** for **Susan King**. You can use the instance methods **getName()**, **getBMI()**, and **getStatus()** to return the BMI information in a **BMI** object.

The BMI class can be implemented as in Listing 10.4.

LISTING 10.4 BMI.java

```
1  public class BMI {
2    private String name;
3    private int age;
4    private double weight; // in pounds
5    private double height; // in inches
6    public static final double KILOGRAMS_PER_POUND = 0.45359237;
7    public static final double METERS_PER_INCH = 0.0254;
8
9    public BMI(String name, int age, double weight, double height) {   constructor
10     this.name = name;
```

```
11        this.age = age;
12        this.weight = weight;
13        this.height = height;
14      }
15
16      public BMI(String name, double weight, double height) {
17        this(name, 20, weight, height);
18      }
19
20      public double getBMI() {
21        double bmi = weight * KILOGRAMS_PER_POUND /
22          ((height * METERS_PER_INCH) * (height * METERS_PER_INCH));
23        return Math.round(bmi * 100) / 100.0;
24      }
25
26      public String getStatus() {
27        double bmi = getBMI();
28        if (bmi < 18.5)
29          return "Underweight";
30        else if (bmi < 25)
31          return "Normal";
32        else if (bmi < 30)
33          return "Overweight";
34        else
35          return "Obese";
36      }
37
38      public String getName() {
39        return name;
40      }
41
42      public int getAge() {
43        return age;
44      }
45
46      public double getWeight() {
47        return weight;
48      }
49
50      public double getHeight() {
51        return height;
52      }
53    }
```

Margin labels: constructor (line 16); getBMI (line 20); getStatus (line 26)

The mathematical formula for computing the BMI using weight and height is given in Section 3.8. The instance method **getBMI()** returns the BMI. Since the weight and height are instance data fields in the object, the **getBMI()** method can use these properties to compute the BMI for the object.

The instance method **getStatus()** returns a string that interprets the BMI. The interpretation is also given in Section 3.8.

procedural vs. object-oriented paradigms

This example demonstrates the advantages of the object-oriented paradigm over the procedural paradigm. The procedural paradigm focuses on designing methods. The object-oriented paradigm couples data and methods together into objects. Software design using the object-oriented paradigm focuses on objects and operations on objects. The object-oriented approach combines the power of the procedural paradigm with an added dimension that integrates data with operations into objects.

In procedural programming, data and operations on the data are separate, and this methodology requires passing data to methods. Object-oriented programming places data and the operations that pertain to them in an object. This approach solves many of the problems inherent in procedural programming. The object-oriented programming approach organizes programs in a way that mirrors the real world, in which all objects are associated with both attributes and activities. Using objects improves software reusability and makes programs easier to develop and easier to maintain. Programming in Java involves thinking in terms of objects; a Java program can be viewed as a collection of cooperating objects.

10.2 Is the `BMI` class defined in Listing 10.4 immutable?

10.4 Class Relationships

To design classes, you need to explore the relationships among classes. The common relationships among classes are association, aggregation, composition, *and* inheritance.

This section explores association, aggregation, and composition. The inheritance relationship will be introduced in the next chapter.

10.4.1 Association

Association is a general binary relationship that describes an activity between two classes. For example, a student taking a course is an association between the `Student` class and the `Course` class, and a faculty member teaching a course is an association between the `Faculty` class and the `Course` class. These associations can be represented in UML graphical notation, as shown in Figure 10.4.

association

FIGURE 10.4 This UML diagram shows that a student may take any number of courses, a faculty member may teach at most three courses, a course may have from five to sixty students, and a course is taught by only one faculty member.

An association is illustrated by a solid line between two classes with an optional label that describes the relationship. In Figure 10.4, the labels are *Take* and *Teach*. Each relationship may have an optional small black triangle that indicates the direction of the relationship. In this figure, the direction indicates that a student takes a course (as opposed to a course taking a student).

Each class involved in the relationship may have a role name that describes the role it plays in the relationship. In Figure 10.4, *teacher* is the role name for `Faculty`.

Each class involved in an association may specify a *multiplicity*, which is placed at the side of the class to specify how many of the class's objects are involved in the relationship in UML. A multiplicity could be a number or an interval that specifies how many of the class's objects are involved in the relationship. The character * means an unlimited number of objects, and the interval `m..n` indicates that the number of objects is between `m` and `n`, inclusively. In Figure 10.4, each student may take any number of courses, and each course must have at least five and at most sixty students. Each course is taught by only one faculty member, and a faculty member may teach from zero to three courses per semester.

multiplicity

In Java code, you can implement associations by using data fields and methods. For example, the relationships in Figure 10.4 may be implemented using the classes in Figure 10.5. The relation "a student takes a course" is implemented using the **addCourse** method in the **Student** class and the **addStuent** method in the **Course** class. The relation "a faculty teaches a course" is implemented using the **addCourse** method in the **Faculty** class and the **set-Faculty** method in the **Course** class. The **Student** class may use a list to store the courses that the student is taking, the **Faculty** class may use a list to store the courses that the faculty is teaching, and the **Course** class may use a list to store students enrolled in the course and a data field to store the instructor who teaches the course.

```
public class Student {
  private Course[]
    courseList;

  public void addCourse(
    Course s) { ... }
}
```

```
public class Course {
  private Student[]
    classList;
  private Faculty faculty;

  public void addStudent(
    Student s) { ... }

  public void setFaculty(
    Faculty faculty) { ... }
}
```

```
public class Faculty {
  private Course[]
    courseList;

  public void addCourse(
    Course c) { ... }
}
```

FIGURE 10.5 The association relations are implemented using data fields and methods in classes.

many possible
  implementations

Note
There are many possible ways to implement relationships. For example, the student and faculty information in the **Course** class can be omitted, since they are already in the **Student** and **Faculty** class. Likewise, if you don't need to know the courses a student takes or a faculty member teaches, the data field **courseList** and the **add-Course** method in **Student** or **Faculty** can be omitted.

10.4.2 Aggregation and Composition

aggregation
aggregating object
aggregated object
aggregated class
aggregating class

composition

Aggregation is a special form of association that represents an ownership relationship between two objects. Aggregation models *has-a* relationships. The owner object is called an *aggregating object*, and its class is called an *aggregating class*. The subject object is called an *aggregated object*, and its class is called an *aggregated class*.

An object can be owned by several other aggregating objects. If an object is exclusively owned by an aggregating object, the relationship between the object and its aggregating object is referred to as a *composition*. For example, "a student has a name" is a composition relationship between the **Student** class and the **Name** class, whereas "a student has an address" is an aggregation relationship between the **Student** class and the **Address** class, since an address can be shared by several students. In UML, a filled diamond is attached to an aggregating class (in this case, **Student**) to denote the composition relationship with an aggregated class (**Name**), and an empty diamond is attached to an aggregating class (**Student**) to denote the aggregation relationship with an aggregated class (**Address**), as shown in Figure 10.6.

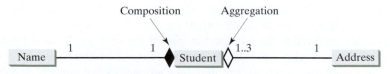

FIGURE 10.6 Each student has a name and an address.

In Figure 10.6, each student has only one multiplicity—address—and each address can be shared by up to **3** students. Each student has one name, and a name is unique for each student.

An aggregation relationship is usually represented as a data field in the aggregating class. For example, the relationships in Figure 10.6 may be implemented using the classes in Figure 10.7. The relation "a student has a name" and "a student has an address" are implemented in the data field **name** and **address** in the **Student** class.

```
public class Name {
   ...
}
```
Aggregated class

```
public class Student {
   private Name name;
   private Address address;
   ...
}
```
Aggregating class

```
public class Address {
   ...
}
```
Aggregated class

FIGURE 10.7 The composition relations are implemented using data fields in classes.

Aggregation may exist between objects of the same class. For example, a person may have a supervisor. This is illustrated in Figure 10.8.

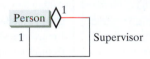

FIGURE 10.8 A person may have a supervisor.

In the relationship "a person has a supervisor," a supervisor can be represented as a data field in the **Person** class, as follows:

```
public class Person {
   // The type for the data is the class itself
   private Person supervisor;

   ...
}
```

If a person can have several supervisors, as shown in Figure 10.9a, you may use an array to store supervisors, as shown in Figure 10.9b.

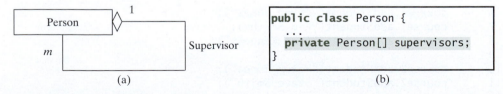

(a)

```
public class Person {
   ...
   private Person[] supervisors;
}
```
(b)

FIGURE 10.9 A person can have several supervisors.

Note

Since aggregation and composition relationships are represented using classes in the same way, we will not differentiate them and call both compositions for simplicity.

aggregation or composition

10.3 What are common relationships among classes?

10.4 What is association? What is aggregation? What is composition?

10.5 What is UML notation of aggregation and composition?

10.6 Why both aggregation and composition are together referred to as composition?

Check Point

10.5 Case Study: Designing the **Course** Class

Key Point

This section designs a class for modeling courses.

This book's philosophy is *teaching by example and learning by doing*. The book provides a wide variety of examples to demonstrate object-oriented programming. This section and the next offer additional examples on designing classes.

Suppose you need to process course information. Each course has a name and has students enrolled. You should be able to add/drop a student to/from the course. You can use a class to model the courses, as shown in Figure 10.10.

Course	
-courseName: String	The name of the course.
-students: String[]	An array to store the students for the course.
-numberOfStudents: int	The number of students (default: 0).
+Course(courseName: String)	Creates a course with the specified name.
+getCourseName(): String	Returns the course name.
+addStudent(student: String): void	Adds a new student to the course.
+dropStudent(student: String): void	Drops a student from the course.
+getStudents(): String[]	Returns the students for the course.
+getNumberOfStudents(): int	Returns the number of students for the course.

FIGURE 10.10 The **Course** class models the courses.

A **Course** object can be created using the constructor **Course(String name)** by passing a course name. You can add students to the course using the **addStudent(String student)** method, drop a student from the course using the **dropStudent(String student)** method, and return all the students in the course using the **getStudents()** method. Suppose the **Course** class is available; Listing 10.5 gives a test class that creates two courses and adds students to them.

LISTING 10.5 TestCourse.java

```
 1  public class TestCourse {
 2    public static void main(String[] args) {
 3      Course course1 = new Course("Data Structures");
 4      Course course2 = new Course("Database Systems");
 5
 6      course1.addStudent("Peter Jones");
 7      course1.addStudent("Kim Smith");
 8      course1.addStudent("Anne Kennedy");
 9
10      course2.addStudent("Peter Jones");
11      course2.addStudent("Steve Smith");
12
13      System.out.println("Number of students in course1: "
14        + course1.getNumberOfStudents());
15      String[] students = course1.getStudents();
16      for (int i = 0; i < course1.getNumberOfStudents(); i++)
17        System.out.print(students[i] + ", ");
18
19      System.out.println();
20      System.out.print("Number of students in course2: "
21        + course2.getNumberOfStudents());
22    }
23  }
```

create a course

add a student

number of students
return students

```
Number of students in course1: 3
Peter Jones, Kim Smith, Anne Kennedy,
Number of students in course2: 2
```

The **Course** class is implemented in Listing 10.6. It uses an array to store the students in the course. For simplicity, assume that the maximum course enrollment is **100**. The array is created using **new String[100]** in line 3. The **addStudent** method (line 10) adds a student to the array. Whenever a new student is added to the course, **numberOfStudents** is increased (line 12). The **getStudents** method returns the array. The **dropStudent** method (line 27) is left as an exercise.

LISTING 10.6 Course.java

```java
1  public class Course {
2    private String courseName;
3    private String[] students = new String[100];
4    private int numberOfStudents;
5
6    public Course(String courseName) {
7      this.courseName = courseName;
8    }
9
10   public void addStudent(String student) {
11     students[numberOfStudents] = student;
12     numberOfStudents++;
13   }
14
15   public String[] getStudents() {
16     return students;
17   }
18
19   public int getNumberOfStudents() {
20     return numberOfStudents;
21   }
22
23   public String getCourseName() {
24     return courseName;
25   }
26
27   public void dropStudent(String student) {
28     // Left as an exercise in Programming Exercise 10.9
29   }
30 }
```

create students

add a course

return students

number of students

The array size is fixed to be **100** (line 3), so you cannot have more than 100 students in the course. You can improve the class by automatically increasing the array size in Programming Exercise 10.9.

When you create a **Course** object, an array object is created. A **Course** object contains a reference to the array. For simplicity, you can say that the **Course** object contains the array.

The user can create a **Course** object and manipulate it through the public methods **addStudent**, **dropStudent**, **getNumberOfStudents**, and **getStudents**. However, the user doesn't need to know how these methods are implemented. The **Course** class encapsulates the internal implementation. This example uses an array to store students, but you could use a different data structure to store **students**. The program that uses **Course** does not need to change as long as the contract of the public methods remains unchanged.

10.6 Case Study: Designing a Class for Stacks

This section designs a class for modeling stacks.

Key Point

stack

Recall that a *stack* is a data structure that holds data in a last-in, first-out fashion, as shown in Figure 10.11.

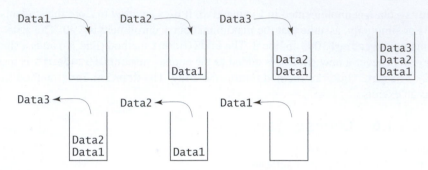

FIGURE 10.11 A stack holds data in a last-in, first-out fashion.

Stacks have many applications. For example, the compiler uses a stack to process method invocations. When a method is invoked, its parameters and local variables are pushed into a stack. When a method calls another method, the new method's parameters and local variables are pushed into the stack. When a method finishes its work and returns to its caller, its associated space is released from the stack.

VideoNote
The StackOfIntegers class

You can define a class to model stacks. For simplicity, assume the stack holds the **int** values. So name the stack class **StackOfIntegers**. The UML diagram for the class is shown in Figure 10.12.

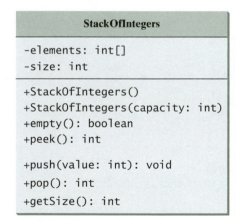

StackOfIntegers	
-elements: int[]	An array to store integers in the stack.
-size: int	The number of integers in the stack.
+StackOfIntegers()	Constructs an empty stack with a default capacity of 16.
+StackOfIntegers(capacity: int)	Constructs an empty stack with a specified capacity.
+empty(): boolean	Returns true if the stack is empty.
+peek(): int	Returns the integer at the top of the stack without removing it from the stack.
+push(value: int): void	Stores an integer into the top of the stack.
+pop(): int	Removes the integer at the top of the stack and returns it.
+getSize(): int	Returns the number of elements in the stack.

FIGURE 10.12 The **StackOfIntegers** class encapsulates the stack storage and provides the operations for manipulating the stack.

Suppose that the class is available. The test program in Listing 10.7 uses the class to create a stack (line 3), store ten integers **0, 1, 2, . . . ,** and **9** (line 6), and displays them in reverse order (line 9).

LISTING 10.7 TestStackOfIntegers.java

```
1  public class TestStackOfIntegers {
2    public static void main(String[] args) {
3      StackOfIntegers stack = new StackOfIntegers();
```

create a stack

```
4
5      for (int i = 0; i < 10; i++)
6        stack.push(i);                                          push to stack
7
8      while (!stack.empty())
9        System.out.print(stack.pop() + " ");                    pop from stack
10   }
11 }
```

```
9 8 7 6 5 4 3 2 1 0
```

How do you implement the **StackOfIntegers** class? The elements in the stack are stored in an array named **elements**. When you create a stack, the array is also created. The no-arg constructor creates an array with the default capacity of **16**. The variable **size** counts the number of elements in the stack, and **size** − 1 is the index of the element at the top of the stack, as shown in Figure 10.13. For an empty stack, **size** is **0**.

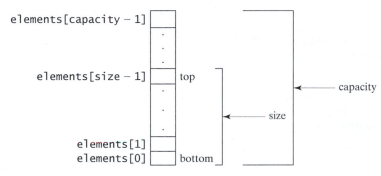

FIGURE 10.13 The **StackOfIntegers** class encapsulates the stack storage and provides the operations for manipulating the stack.

The **StackOfIntegers** class is implemented in Listing 10.8. The methods **empty()**, **peek()**, **pop()**, and **getSize()** are easy to implement. To implement **push(int value)**, assign **value** to **elements[size]** if **size** < **capacity** (line 24). If the stack is full (i.e., **size** >= **capacity**), create a new array of twice the current capacity (line 19), copy the contents of the current array to the new array (line 20), and assign the reference of the new array to the current array in the stack (line 21). Now you can add the new value to the array (line 24).

LISTING 10.8 StackOfIntegers.java

```
1  public class StackOfIntegers {
2    private int[] elements;
3    private int size;
4    public static final int DEFAULT_CAPACITY = 16;          max capacity 16
5
6    /** Construct a stack with the default capacity 16 */
7    public StackOfIntegers() {
8      this (DEFAULT_CAPACITY);
9    }
10
11   /** Construct a stack with the specified maximum capacity */
12   public StackOfIntegers(int capacity) {
13     elements = new int[capacity];
14   }
15
```

```
16    /** Push a new integer to the top of the stack */
17    public void push(int value) {
18      if (size >= elements.length) {
19        int[] temp = new int[elements.length * 2];
20        System.arraycopy(elements, 0, temp, 0, elements.length);
21        elements = temp;
22      }
23
24      elements[size++] = value;
25    }
26
27    /** Return and remove the top element from the stack */
28    public int pop() {
29      return elements[--size];
30    }
31
32    /** Return the top element from the stack */
33    public int peek() {
34      return elements[size - 1];
35    }
36
37    /** Test whether the stack is empty */
38    public boolean empty() {
39      return size == 0;
40    }
41
42    /** Return the number of elements in the stack */
43    public int getSize() {
44      return size;
45    }
46  }
```

double the capacity

add to stack

10.7 Processing Primitive Data Type Values as Objects

 Key Point

A primitive type value is not an object, but it can be wrapped in an object using a wrapper class in the Java API.

Owing to performance considerations, primitive data type values are not objects in Java. Because of the overhead of processing objects, the language's performance would be adversely affected if primitive data type values were treated as objects. However, many Java methods require the use of objects as arguments. Java offers a convenient way to incorporate, or wrap, a primitive data type into an object (e.g., wrapping `int` into the `Integer` class, wrapping `double` into the `Double` class, and wrapping `char` into the `Character` class,). By using a wrapper class, you can process primitive data type values as objects. Java provides `Boolean`, `Character`, `Double`, `Float`, `Byte`, `Short`, `Integer`, and `Long` wrapper classes in the `java.lang` package for primitive data types. The `Boolean` class wraps a Boolean value `true` or `false`. This section uses `Integer` and `Double` as examples to introduce the numeric wrapper classes.

why wrapper class?

naming convention

 Note

Most wrapper class names for a primitive type are the same as the primitive data type name with the first letter capitalized. The exceptions are `Integer` and `Character`.

Numeric wrapper classes are very similar to each other. Each contains the methods `doubleValue()`, `floatValue()`, `intValue()`, `longValue()`, `shortValue()`, and `byteValue()`. These methods "convert" objects into primitive type values. The key features of `Integer` and `Double` are shown in Figure 10.14.

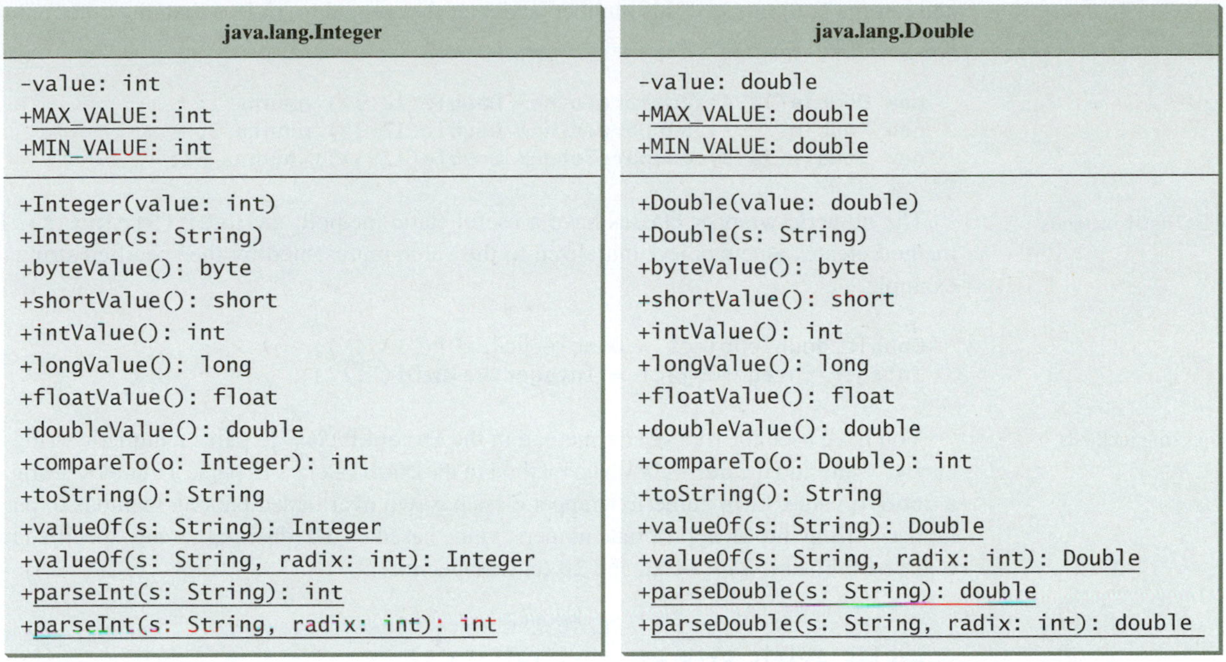

java.lang.Integer
-value: int
+MAX_VALUE: int
+MIN_VALUE: int
+Integer(value: int)
+Integer(s: String)
+byteValue(): byte
+shortValue(): short
+intValue(): int
+longValue(): long
+floatValue(): float
+doubleValue(): double
+compareTo(o: Integer): int
+toString(): String
+valueOf(s: String): Integer
+valueOf(s: String, radix: int): Integer
+parseInt(s: String): int
+parseInt(s: String, radix: int): int

java.lang.Double
-value: double
+MAX_VALUE: double
+MIN_VALUE: double
+Double(value: double)
+Double(s: String)
+byteValue(): byte
+shortValue(): short
+intValue(): int
+longValue(): long
+floatValue(): float
+doubleValue(): double
+compareTo(o: Double): int
+toString(): String
+valueOf(s: String): Double
+valueOf(s: String, radix: int): Double
+parseDouble(s: String): double
+parseDouble(s: String, radix: int): double

FIGURE 10.14 The wrapper classes provide constructors, constants, and conversion methods for manipulating various data types.

You can construct a wrapper object either from a primitive data type value or from a string representing the numeric value—for example, `new Double(5.0)`, `new Double("5.0")`, `new Integer(5)`, and `new Integer("5")`.

constructors

The wrapper classes do not have no-arg constructors. The instances of all wrapper classes are immutable; this means that, once the objects are created, their internal values cannot be changed.

no no-arg constructor
immutable

Each numeric wrapper class has the constants `MAX_VALUE` and `MIN_VALUE`. `MAX_VALUE` represents the maximum value of the corresponding primitive data type. For `Byte`, `Short`, `Integer`, and `Long`, `MIN_VALUE` represents the minimum `byte`, `short`, `int`, and `long` values. For `Float` and `Double`, `MIN_VALUE` represents the minimum *positive* `float` and `double` values. The following statements display the maximum integer (2,147,483,647), the minimum positive float (1.4E–45), and the maximum double floating-point number (1.79769313486231570e + 308d).

constants

```
System.out.println("The maximum integer is " + Integer.MAX_VALUE);
System.out.println("The minimum positive float is " +
  Float.MIN_VALUE);
System.out.println(
  "The maximum double-precision floating-point number is " +
  Double.MAX_VALUE);
```

Each numeric wrapper class contains the methods `doubleValue()`, `floatValue()`, `intValue()`, `longValue()`, and `shortValue()` for returning a `double`, `float`, `int`, `long`, or `short` value for the wrapper object. For example,

conversion methods

```
new Double(12.4).intValue() returns 12;
new Integer(12).doubleValue() returns 12.0;
```

Recall that the `String` class contains the `compareTo` method for comparing two strings. The numeric wrapper classes contain the `compareTo` method for comparing two numbers

compareTo method

and returns **1**, **0**, or **-1**, if this number is greater than, equal to, or less than the other number. For example,

```
new Double(12.4).compareTo(new Double(12.3)) returns 1;
new Double(12.3).compareTo(new Double(12.3)) returns 0;
new Double(12.3).compareTo(new Double(12.51)) returns -1;
```

static valueOf methods

The numeric wrapper classes have a useful static method, **valueOf (String s)**. This method creates a new object initialized to the value represented by the specified string. For example,

```
Double doubleObject = Double.valueOf("12.4");
Integer integerObject = Integer.valueOf("12");
```

static parsing methods

You have used the **parseInt** method in the **Integer** class to parse a numeric string into an **int** value and the **parseDouble** method in the **Double** class to parse a numeric string into a **double** value. Each numeric wrapper class has two overloaded parsing methods to parse a numeric string into an appropriate numeric value based on **10** (decimal) or any specified radix (e.g., **2** for binary, **8** for octal, and **16** for hexadecimal).

```
// These two methods are in the Byte class
public static byte parseByte(String s)
public static byte parseByte(String s, int radix)

// These two methods are in the Short class
public static short parseShort(String s)
public static short parseShort(String s, int radix)

// These two methods are in the Integer class
public static int parseInt(String s)
public static int parseInt(String s, int radix)

// These two methods are in the Long class
public static long parseLong(String s)
public static long parseLong(String s, int radix)

// These two methods are in the Float class
public static float parseFloat(String s)
public static float parseFloat(String s, int radix)

// These two methods are in the Double class
public static double parseDouble(String s)
public static double parseDouble(String s, int radix)
```

For example,

```
Integer.parseInt("11", 2) returns 3;
Integer.parseInt("12", 8) returns 10;
Integer.parseInt("13", 10) returns 13;
Integer.parseInt("1A", 16) returns 26;
```

Integer.parseInt("12", 2) would raise a runtime exception because **12** is not a binary number.

converting decimal to hex

Note that you can convert a decimal number into a hex number using the **format** method. For example,

```
String.format("%x", 26) returns 1A;
```

10.7 Describe primitive-type wrapper classes.

10.8 Can each of the following statements be compiled?

a. `Integer i = new Integer("23");`

b. `Integer i = new Integer(23);`

c. `Integer i = Integer.valueOf("23");`

d. `Integer i = Integer.parseInt("23", 8);`

e. `Double d = new Double();`

f. `Double d = Double.valueOf("23.45");`

g. `int i = (Integer.valueOf("23")).intValue();`

h. `double d = (Double.valueOf("23.4")).doubleValue();`

i. `int i = (Double.valueOf("23.4")).intValue();`

j. `String s = (Double.valueOf("23.4")).toString();`

10.9 How do you convert an integer into a string? How do you convert a numeric string into an integer? How do you convert a double number into a string? How do you convert a numeric string into a double value?

10.10 Show the output of the following code.

```java
public class Test {
  public static void main(String[] args) {
    Integer x = new Integer(3);
    System.out.println(x.intValue());
    System.out.println(x.compareTo(new Integer(4)));
  }
}
```

10.11 What is the output of the following code?

```java
public class Test {
  public static void main(String[] args) {
    System.out.println(Integer.parseInt("10"));
    System.out.println(Integer.parseInt("10", 10));
    System.out.println(Integer.parseInt("10", 16));
    System.out.println(Integer.parseInt("11"));
    System.out.println(Integer.parseInt("11", 10));
    System.out.println(Integer.parseInt("11", 16));
  }
}
```

10.8 Automatic Conversion between Primitive Types and Wrapper Class Types

A primitive type value can be automatically converted to an object using a wrapper class, and vice versa, depending on the context.

Converting a primitive value to a wrapper object is called *boxing*. The reverse conversion is called *unboxing*. Java allows primitive types and wrapper classes to be converted automatically. The compiler will automatically box a primitive value that appears in a context requiring an object, and will unbox an object that appears in a context requiring a primitive value. This is called *autoboxing* and *autounboxing*.

boxing
unboxing

autoboxing
autounboxing

For instance, the following statement in (a) can be simplified as in (b) due to autoboxing.

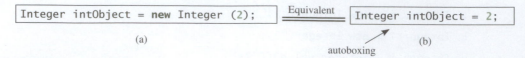

```
Integer intObject = new Integer (2);
```
(a)

Equivalent

```
Integer intObject = 2;
```
(b)

autoboxing

Consider the following example:

```
1  Integer[] intArray = {1, 2, 3};
2  System.out.println(intArray[0] + intArray[1] + intArray[2]);
```

In line 1, the primitive values **1**, **2**, and **3** are automatically boxed into objects **new Integer(1)**, **new Integer(2)**, and **new Integer(3)**. In line 2, the objects **intArray[0]**, **intArray[1]**, and **intArray[2]** are automatically unboxed into **int** values that are added together.

10.12 What are autoboxing and autounboxing? Are the following statements correct?

a. `Integer x = 3 + new Integer(5);`
b. `Integer x = 3;`
c. `Double x = 3;`
d. `Double x = 3.0;`
e. `int x = new Integer(3);`
f. `int x = new Integer(3) + new Integer(4);`

10.13 Show the output of the following code?

```java
public class Test {
  public static void main(String[] args) {
    Double x = 3.5;
    System.out.println(x.intValue());
    System.out.println(x.compareTo(4.5));
  }
}
```

10.9 The **BigInteger** and **BigDecimal** Classes

Key Point

*The **BigInteger** and **BigDecimal** classes can be used to represent integers or decimal numbers of any size and precision.*

If you need to compute with very large integers or high-precision floating-point values, you can use the **BigInteger** and **BigDecimal** classes in the **java.math** package. Both are *immutable*. The largest integer of the **long** type is **Long.MAX_VALUE** (i.e., **9223372036854775807**). An instance of **BigInteger** can represent an integer of any size. You can use **new BigInteger(String)** and **new BigDecimal(String)** to create an instance of **BigInteger** and **BigDecimal**, use the **add**, **subtract**, **multiply**, **divide**, and **remainder** methods to perform arithmetic operations, and use the **compareTo** method to compare two big numbers. For example, the following code creates two **BigInteger** objects and multiplies them.

immutable

VideoNote

Process large numbers

```java
BigInteger a = new BigInteger("9223372036854775807");
BigInteger b = new BigInteger("2");
BigInteger c = a.multiply(b); // 9223372036854775807 * 2
System.out.println(c);
```

The output is **18446744073709551614**.

There is no limit to the precision of a **BigDecimal** object. The **divide** method may throw an **ArithmeticException** if the result cannot be terminated. However, you can use the overloaded **divide(BigDecimal d, int scale, int roundingMode)** method to specify a scale and a rounding mode to avoid this exception, where **scale** is the maximum number of digits after the decimal point. For example, the following code creates two **BigDecimal** objects and performs division with scale **20** and rounding mode **BigDecimal.ROUND_UP**.

```
BigDecimal a = new BigDecimal(1.0);
BigDecimal b = new BigDecimal(3);
BigDecimal c = a.divide(b, 20, BigDecimal.ROUND_UP);
System.out.println(c);
```

The output is **0.33333333333333333334**.

Note that the factorial of an integer can be very large. Listing 10.9 gives a method that can return the factorial of any integer.

LISTING 10.9 LargeFactorial.java

```
 1  import java.math.*;
 2
 3  public class LargeFactorial {
 4    public static void main(String[] args) {
 5      System.out.println("50! is \n" + factorial(50));
 6    }
 7
 8    public static BigInteger factorial(long n) {
 9      BigInteger result = BigInteger.ONE;              constant
10      for (int i = 1; i <= n; i++)
11        result = result.multiply(new BigInteger(i + ""));   multiply
12
13      return result;
14    }
15  }
```

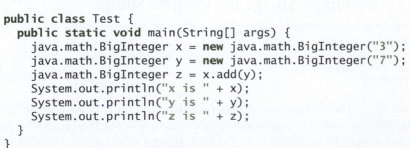

```
50! is
30414093201713378043612608166064768844377641568960512000000000000
```

BigInteger.ONE (line 9) is a constant defined in the **BigInteger** class. **BigInteger.ONE** is the same as **new BigInteger("1")**.

A new result is obtained by invoking the **multiply** method (line 11).

10.14 What is the output of the following code?

Check
Point

```
public class Test {
  public static void main(String[] args) {
    java.math.BigInteger x = new java.math.BigInteger("3");
    java.math.BigInteger y = new java.math.BigInteger("7");
    java.math.BigInteger z = x.add(y);
    System.out.println("x is " + x);
    System.out.println("y is " + y);
    System.out.println("z is " + z);
  }
}
```

10.10 The **String** Class

A **String** *object is immutable: Its content cannot be changed once the string is created.*

VideoNote

The **String** class

Strings were introduced in Section 4.4. You know strings are objects. You can invoke the **charAt(index)** method to obtain a character at the specified index from a string, the **length()** method to return the size of a string, the **substring** method to return a substring in a string, and the **indexOf** and **lastIndexOf** methods to return the first or last index of a matching character or a substring. We will take a closer look at strings in this section.

The **String** class has 13 constructors and more than 40 methods for manipulating strings. Not only is it very useful in programming, but it is also a good example for learning classes and objects.

10.10.1 Constructing a String

You can create a string object from a string literal or from an array of characters. To create a string from a string literal, use the syntax:

```
String newString = new String(stringLiteral);
```

The argument **stringLiteral** is a sequence of characters enclosed inside double quotes. The following statement creates a **String** object **message** for the string literal **"Welcome to Java"**:

```
String message = new String("Welcome to Java");
```

string literal object

Java treats a string literal as a **String** object. Thus, the following statement is valid:

```
String message = "Welcome to Java";
```

You can also create a string from an array of characters. For example, the following statements create the string **"Good Day"**:

```
char[] charArray = {'G', 'o', 'o', 'd', ' ', 'D', 'a', 'y'};
String message = new String(charArray);
```

> **Note**
>
> A **String** variable holds a reference to a **String** object that stores a string value. Strictly speaking, the terms ***String*** *variable,* ***String*** *object,* and *string value* are different, but most of the time the distinctions between them can be ignored. For simplicity, the term *string* will often be used to refer to **String** variable, **String** object, and string value.

String variable, String object, string value

10.10.2 Immutable Strings and Interned Strings

immutable

A **String** object is immutable; its contents cannot be changed. Does the following code change the contents of the string?

```
String s = "Java";
s = "HTML";
```

The answer is no. The first statement creates a **String** object with the content **"Java"** and assigns its reference to **s**. The second statement creates a new **String** object with the content **"HTML"** and assigns its reference to **s**. The first **String** object still exists after the assignment, but it can no longer be accessed, because variable **s** now points to the new object, as shown in Figure 10.15.

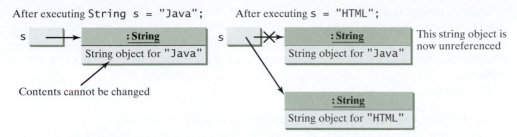

After executing `String s = "Java";`   After executing `s = "HTML";`

FIGURE 10.15   Strings are immutable; once created, their contents cannot be changed.

Because strings are immutable and are ubiquitous in programming, the JVM uses a unique instance for string literals with the same character sequence in order to improve efficiency and save memory. Such an instance is called an *interned string*. For example, the following statements:

interned string

```java
String s1 = "Welcome to Java";

String s2 = new String("Welcome to Java");

String s3 = "Welcome to Java";

System.out.println("s1 == s2 is " + (s1 == s2));
System.out.println("s1 == s3 is " + (s1 == s3));
```

display

```
s1 == s2 is false
s1 == s3 is true
```

In the preceding statements, **s1** and **s3** refer to the same interned string—**"Welcome to Java"**—so **s1 == s3** is **true**. However, **s1 == s2** is **false**, because **s1** and **s2** are two different string objects, even though they have the same contents.

10.10.3 Replacing and Splitting Strings

The **String** class provides the methods for replacing and splitting strings, as shown in Figure 10.16.

java.lang.String	
+replace(oldChar: char, newChar: char): String	Returns a new string that replaces all matching characters in this string with the new character.
+replaceFirst(oldString: String, newString: String): String	Returns a new string that replaces the first matching substring in this string with the new substring.
+replaceAll(oldString: String, newString: String): String	Returns a new string that replaces all matching substrings in this string with the new substring.
+split(delimiter: String): String[]	Returns an array of strings consisting of the substrings split by the delimiter.

FIGURE 10.16   The **String** class contains the methods for replacing and splitting strings.

Once a string is created, its contents cannot be changed. The methods **replace**, **replaceFirst**, and **replaceAll** return a new string derived from the original string (without changing the original string!). Several versions of the **replace** methods are provided to replace a character or a substring in the string with a new character or a new substring.

For example,

replace
replaceFirst
replace
replace

`"Welcome".replace('e', 'A')` returns a new string, WAlcomA.
`"Welcome".replaceFirst("e", "AB")` returns a new string, WABlcome.
`"Welcome".replace("e", "AB")` returns a new string, WABlcomAB.
`"Welcome".replace("el", "AB")` returns a new string, WABcome.

split

The **split** method can be used to extract tokens from a string with the specified delimiters. For example, the following code

```
String[] tokens = "Java#HTML#Perl".split("#");
for (int i = 0; i < tokens.length; i++)
  System.out.print(tokens[i] + " ");
```

displays

Java HTML Perl

10.10.4 Matching, Replacing and Splitting by Patterns

Often you will need to write code that validates user input, such as to check whether the input is a number, a string with all lowercase letters, or a Social Security number. How do you write this type of code? A simple and effective way to accomplish this task is to use the regular expression.

why regular expression?

regular expression
regex

A *regular expression* (abbreviated *regex*) is a string that describes a pattern for matching a set of strings. You can match, replace, or split a string by specifying a pattern. This is an extremely useful and powerful feature.

matches(regex)

Let us begin with the **matches** method in the **String** class. At first glance, the **matches** method is very similar to the **equals** method. For example, the following two statements both evaluate to **true**.

```
"Java".matches("Java");
"Java".equals("Java");
```

However, the **matches** method is more powerful. It can match not only a fixed string, but also a set of strings that follow a pattern. For example, the following statements all evaluate to **true**:

```
"Java is fun".matches("Java.*")
"Java is cool".matches("Java.*")
"Java is powerful".matches("Java.*")
```

Java.* in the preceding statements is a regular expression. It describes a string pattern that begins with Java followed by *any* zero or more characters. Here, the substring matches any zero or more characters.

The following statement evaluates to **true**.

```
"440-02-4534".matches("\\d{3}-\\d{2}-\\d{4}")
```

Here **\\d** represents a single digit, and **\\d{3}** represents three digits.

The **replaceAll**, **replaceFirst**, and **split** methods can be used with a regular expression. For example, the following statement returns a new string that replaces **$**, **+**, or **#** in **a+b$#c** with the string **NNN**.

```
String s = "a+b$#c".replaceAll("[$+#]", "NNN");
System.out.println(s);
```
replaceAll(regex)

Here the regular expression **[$+#]** specifies a pattern that matches **$**, **+**, or **#**. So, the output is **aNNNbNNNNNNc**.

The following statement splits the string into an array of strings delimited by punctuation marks.

```
String[] tokens = "Java,C?C#,C++".split("[.,:;?]");

for (int i = 0; i < tokens.length; i++)
  System.out.println(tokens[i]);
```
split(regex)

In this example, the regular expression **[.,:;?]** specifies a pattern that matches **.**, **,**, **:**, **;**, or **?**. Each of these characters is a delimiter for splitting the string. Thus, the string is split into **Java**, **C**, **C#**, and **C++**, which are stored in array **tokens**.

further studies

Regular expression patterns are complex for beginning students to understand. For this reason, simple patterns are introduced in this section. Please refer to Appendix H, Regular Expressions, to learn more about these patterns.

10.10.5 Conversion between Strings and Arrays

Strings are not arrays, but a string can be converted into an array, and vice versa. To convert a string into an array of characters, use the **toCharArray** method. For example, the following statement converts the string **Java** to an array.

toCharArray

```
char[] chars = "Java".toCharArray();
```

Thus, **chars[0]** is **J**, **chars[1]** is **a**, **chars[2]** is **v**, and **chars[3]** is **a**.

You can also use the **getChars(int srcBegin, int srcEnd, char[] dst, int dstBegin)** method to copy a substring of the string from index **srcBegin** to index **srcEnd-1** into a character array **dst** starting from index **dstBegin**. For example, the following code copies a substring **"3720"** in **"CS3720"** from index **2** to index **6-1** into the character array **dst** starting from index **4**.

```
char[] dst = {'J', 'A', 'V', 'A', '1', '3', '0', '1'};
"CS3720".getChars(2, 6, dst, 4);
```
getChars

Thus, **dst** becomes **{'J', 'A', 'V', 'A', '3', '7', '2', '0'}**.

To convert an array of characters into a string, use the **String(char[])** constructor or the **valueOf(char[])** method. For example, the following statement constructs a string from an array using the **String** constructor.

```
String str = new String(new char[]{'J', 'a', 'v', 'a'});
```

The next statement constructs a string from an array using the **valueOf** method.

valueOf

```
String str = String.valueOf(new char[]{'J', 'a', 'v', 'a'});
```

10.10.6 Converting Characters and Numeric Values to Strings

Recall that you can use **Double.parseDouble(str)** or **Integer.parseInt(str)** to convert a string to a **double** value or an **int** value and you can convert a character or a number into a string by using the string concatenating operator. Another way of converting a

overloaded valueOf

number into a string is to use the overloaded static **valueOf** method. This method can also be used to convert a character or an array of characters into a string, as shown in Figure 10.17.

java.lang.String	
+valueOf(c: char): String	Returns a string consisting of the character c.
+valueOf(data: char[]): String	Returns a string consisting of the characters in the array.
+valueOf(d: double): String	Returns a string representing the double value.
+valueOf(f: float): String	Returns a string representing the float value.
+valueOf(i: int): String	Returns a string representing the int value.
+valueOf(l: long): String	Returns a string representing the long value.
+valueOf(b: boolean): String	Returns a string representing the boolean value.

FIGURE 10.17 The **String** class contains the static methods for creating strings from primitive type values.

For example, to convert a **double** value **5.44** to a string, use **String.valueOf(5.44)**. The return value is a string consisting of the characters **'5'**, **'.'**, **'4'**, and **'4'**.

10.10.7 Formatting Strings

The **String** class contains the static **format** method to return a formatted string. The syntax to invoke this method is:

```
String.format(format, item1, item2, ..., itemk)
```

This method is similar to the **printf** method except that the **format** method returns a formatted string, whereas the **printf** method displays a formatted string. For example,

```
String s = String.format("%7.2f%6d%-4s", 45.556, 14, "AB");
System.out.println(s);
```

displays

```
  45.56    14AB
```

Note that

```
System.out.printf(format, item1, item2, ..., itemk);
```

is equivalent to

```
System.out.print(
   String.format(format, item1, item2, ..., itemk));
```

where the square box (□) denotes a blank space.

10.15 Suppose that **s1**, **s2**, **s3**, and **s4** are four strings, given as follows:

```
String s1 = "Welcome to Java";
String s2 = s1;
String s3 = new String("Welcome to Java");
String s4 = "Welcome to Java";
```

What are the results of the following expressions?

a. s1 == s2
b. s1 == s3

```
c. s1 == s4
d. s1.equals(s3)
e. s1.equals(s4)
f. "Welcome to Java".replace("Java", "HTML")
g. s1.replace('o', 'T')
h. s1.replaceAll("o", "T")
i. s1.replaceFirst("o", "T")
j. s1.toCharArray()
```

10.16 To create the string `Welcome to Java`, you may use a statement like this:

```
String s = "Welcome to Java";
```

or:

```
String s = new String("Welcome to Java");
```

Which one is better? Why?

10.17 What is the output of the following code?

```
String s1 = "Welcome to Java";
String s2 = s1.replace("o", "abc");
System.out.println(s1);
System.out.println(s2);
```

10.18 Let `s1` be `"Welcome"` and `s2` be `"welcome"`. Write the code for the following statements:

a. Replace all occurrences of the character `e` with `E` in `s1` and assign the new string to `s2`.

b. Split `Welcome to Java and HTML` into an array `tokens` delimited by a space and assign the first two tokens into `s1` and `s2`.

10.19 Does any method in the `String` class change the contents of the string?

10.20 Suppose string `s` is created using `new String()`; what is `s.length()`?

10.21 How do you convert a `char`, an array of characters, or a number to a string?

10.22 Why does the following code cause a `NullPointerException`?

```
1  public class Test {
2    private String text;
3
4    public Test(String s) {
5      String text  = s;
6    }
7
8    public static void main(String[] args) {
9      Test test = new Test("ABC");
10     System.out.println(test.text.toLowerCase());
11   }
12 }
```

10.23 What is wrong in the following program?

```
1  public class Test {
2    String text;
3
```

```
 4      public void Test(String s) {
 5        text = s;
 6      }
 7
 8      public static void main(String[] args) {
 9        Test test = new Test("ABC");
10        System.out.println(test);
11      }
12   }
```

10.24 Show the output of the following code.

```
public class Test {
  public static void main(String[] args) {
    System.out.println("Hi, ABC, good".matches("ABC "));
    System.out.println("Hi, ABC, good".matches(".*ABC.*"));
    System.out.println("A,B;C".replaceAll(",;", "#"));
    System.out.println("A,B;C".replaceAll("[,;]", "#"));

    String[] tokens = "A,B;C".split("[,;]");
    for (int i = 0; i < tokens.length; i++)
      System.out.print(tokens[i] +  " ");
  }
}
```

10.25 Show the output of the following code.

```
public class Test {
  public static void main(String[] args) {
    String s = "Hi, Good Morning";
    System.out.println(m(s));
  }

  public static int m(String s) {
    int count = 0;
    for (int i = 0; i < s.length(); i++)
      if (Character.isUpperCase(s.charAt(i)))
        count++;

    return count;
  }
}
```

10.11 The **StringBuilder** and **StringBuffer** Classes

Key Point

*The **StringBuilder** and **StringBuffer** classes are similar to the **String** class except that the **String** class is immutable.*

In general, the **StringBuilder** and **StringBuffer** classes can be used wherever a string is used. **StringBuilder** and **StringBuffer** are more flexible than **String**. You can add, insert, or append new contents into **StringBuilder** and **StringBuffer** objects, whereas the value of a **String** object is fixed once the string is created.

StringBuilder

The **StringBuilder** class is similar to **StringBuffer** except that the methods for modifying the buffer in **StringBuffer** are *synchronized*, which means that only one task is allowed to execute the methods. Use **StringBuffer** if the class might be accessed by multiple tasks concurrently, because synchronization is needed in this case to prevent corruptions to

StringBuffer. Concurrent programming will be introduced in Chapter 30. Using **String-Builder** is more efficient if it is accessed by just a single task, because no synchronization is needed in this case. The constructors and methods in **StringBuffer** and **StringBuilder** are almost the same. This section covers **StringBuilder**. You can replace **StringBuilder** in all occurrences in this section by **StringBuffer**. The program can compile and run without any other changes.

The **StringBuilder** class has three constructors and more than 30 methods for managing the builder and modifying strings in the builder. You can create an empty string builder or a string builder from a string using the constructors, as shown in Figure 10.18.

StringBuilder constructors

java.lang.StringBuilder	
+StringBuilder()	Constructs an empty string builder with capacity 16.
+StringBuilder(capacity: int)	Constructs a string builder with the specified capacity.
+StringBuilder(s: String)	Constructs a string builder with the specified string.

FIGURE 10.18 The **StringBuilder** class contains the constructors for creating instances of **StringBuilder**.

10.11.1 Modifying Strings in the **StringBuilder**

You can append new contents at the end of a string builder, insert new contents at a specified position in a string builder, and delete or replace characters in a string builder, using the methods listed in Figure 10.19.

java.lang.StringBuilder	
+append(data: char[]): StringBuilder	Appends a char array into this string builder.
+append(data: char[], offset: int, len: int): StringBuilder	Appends a subarray in data into this string builder.
+append(v: *aPrimitiveType*): StringBuilder	Appends a primitive type value as a string to this builder.
+append(s: String): StringBuilder	Appends a string to this string builder.
+delete(startIndex: int, endIndex: int): StringBuilder	Deletes characters from startIndex to endIndex-1.
+deleteCharAt(index: int): StringBuilder	Deletes a character at the specified index.
+insert(index: int, data: char[], offset: int, len: int): StringBuilder	Inserts a subarray of the data in the array into the builder at the specified index.
+insert(offset: int, data: char[]): StringBuilder	Inserts data into this builder at the position offset.
+insert(offset: int, b: *aPrimitiveType*): StringBuilder	Inserts a value converted to a string into this builder.
+insert(offset: int, s: String): StringBuilder	Inserts a string into this builder at the position offset.
+replace(startIndex: int, endIndex: int, s: String): StringBuilder	Replaces the characters in this builder from startIndex to endIndex-1 with the specified string.
+reverse(): StringBuilder	Reverses the characters in the builder.
+setCharAt(index: int, ch: char): void	Sets a new character at the specified index in this builder.

FIGURE 10.19 The **StringBuilder** class contains the methods for modifying string builders.

The **StringBuilder** class provides several overloaded methods to append **boolean**, **char**, **char[]**, **double**, **float**, **int**, **long**, and **String** into a string builder. For example, the following code appends strings and characters into **stringBuilder** to form a new string, **Welcome to Java**.

append

```
StringBuilder stringBuilder = new StringBuilder();
stringBuilder.append("Welcome");
stringBuilder.append(' ');
stringBuilder.append("to");
stringBuilder.append(' ');
stringBuilder.append("Java");
```

The **StringBuilder** class also contains overloaded methods to insert **boolean**, **char**, **char array**, **double**, **float**, **int**, **long**, and **String** into a string builder. Consider the following code:

insert

```
stringBuilder.insert(11, "HTML and ");
```

Suppose **stringBuilder** contains **Welcome to Java** before the **insert** method is applied. This code inserts **"HTML and "** at position 11 in **stringBuilder** (just before the **J**). The new **stringBuilder** is **Welcome to HTML and Java**.

You can also delete characters from a string in the builder using the two **delete** methods, reverse the string using the **reverse** method, replace characters using the **replace** method, or set a new character in a string using the **setCharAt** method.

For example, suppose **stringBuilder** contains **Welcome to Java** before each of the following methods is applied:

delete
deleteCharAt
reverse
replace
setCharAt

```
stringBuilder.delete(8, 11)  changes the builder to  Welcome Java.
stringBuilder.deleteCharAt(8)  changes the builder to  Welcome o Java.
stringBuilder.reverse()  changes the builder to  avaJ ot emocleW.
stringBuilder.replace(11, 15, "HTML")  changes the builder to  Welcome to HTML.
stringBuilder.setCharAt(0, 'w')  sets the builder to  welcome to Java.
```

All these modification methods except **setCharAt** do two things:

- Change the contents of the string builder

ignore return value

- Return the reference of the string builder

For example, the following statement

```
StringBuilder stringBuilder1 = stringBuilder.reverse();
```

reverses the string in the builder and assigns the builder's reference to **stringBuilder1**. Thus, **stringBuilder** and **stringBuilder1** both point to the same **StringBuilder** object. Recall that a value-returning method can be invoked as a statement, if you are not interested in the return value of the method. In this case, the return value is simply ignored. For example, in the following statement

```
stringBuilder.reverse();
```

the return value is ignored.

String or StringBuilder?

Tip

If a string does not require any change, use **String** rather than **StringBuilder**. Java can perform some optimizations for **String**, such as sharing interned strings.

10.11.2 The **toString**, **capacity**, **length**, **setLength**, and **charAt** Methods

The **StringBuilder** class provides the additional methods for manipulating a string builder and obtaining its properties, as shown in Figure 10.20.

java.lang.StringBuilder	
+toString(): String	Returns a string object from the string builder.
+capacity(): int	Returns the capacity of this string builder.
+charAt(index: int): char	Returns the character at the specified index.
+length(): int	Returns the number of characters in this builder.
+setLength(newLength: int): void	Sets a new length in this builder.
+substring(startIndex: int): String	Returns a substring starting at **startIndex**.
+substring(startIndex: int, endIndex: int): String	Returns a substring from **startIndex** to **endIndex-1**.
+trimToSize(): void	Reduces the storage size used for the string builder.

FIGURE 10.20 The **StringBuilder** class contains the methods for modifying string builders.

The **capacity()** method returns the current capacity of the string builder. The capacity is the number of characters the string builder is able to store without having to increase its size.

The **length()** method returns the number of characters actually stored in the string builder. The **setLength(newLength)** method sets the length of the string builder. If the **newLength** argument is less than the current length of the string builder, the string builder is truncated to contain exactly the number of characters given by the **newLength** argument. If the **newLength** argument is greater than or equal to the current length, sufficient null characters (**\u0000**) are appended to the string builder so that **length** becomes the **newLength** argument. The **newLength** argument must be greater than or equal to **0**.

The **charAt(index)** method returns the character at a specific **index** in the string builder. The index is **0** based. The first character of a string builder is at index **0**, the next at index **1**, and so on. The **index** argument must be greater than or equal to **0**, and less than the length of the string builder.

> **Note**
> The length of the string is always less than or equal to the capacity of the builder. The length is the actual size of the string stored in the builder, and the capacity is the current size of the builder. The builder's capacity is automatically increased if more characters are added to exceed its capacity. Internally, a string builder is an array of characters, so the builder's capacity is the size of the array. If the builder's capacity is exceeded, the array is replaced by a new array. The new array size is **2 * (the previous array size + 1)**.

> **Tip**
> You can use **new StringBuilder(initialCapacity)** to create a **String-Builder** with a specified initial capacity. By carefully choosing the initial capacity, you can make your program more efficient. If the capacity is always larger than the actual length of the builder, the JVM will never need to reallocate memory for the builder. On the other hand, if the capacity is too large, you will waste memory space. You can use the **trimToSize()** method to reduce the capacity to the actual size.

capacity()

length()
setLength(int)

charAt(int)

length and capacity

initial capacity

trimToSize()

10.11.3   Case Study: Ignoring Nonalphanumeric Characters When Checking Palindromes

Listing 5.14, Palindrome.java, considered all the characters in a string to check whether it is a palindrome. Write a new program that ignores nonalphanumeric characters in checking whether a string is a palindrome.

Here are the steps to solve the problem:

1. Filter the string by removing the nonalphanumeric characters. This can be done by creating an empty string builder, adding each alphanumeric character in the string to a string builder, and returning the string from the string builder. You can use the **isLetterOrDigit(ch)** method in the **Character** class to check whether character **ch** is a letter or a digit.

2. Obtain a new string that is the reversal of the filtered string. Compare the reversed string with the filtered string using the **equals** method.

The complete program is shown in Listing 10.10.

LISTING 10.10   PalindromeIgnoreNonAlphanumeric.java

```
 1  import java.util.Scanner;
 2
 3  public class PalindromeIgnoreNonAlphanumeric {
 4    /** Main method */
 5    public static void main(String[] args) {
 6      // Create a Scanner
 7      Scanner input = new Scanner(System.in);
 8
 9      // Prompt the user to enter a string
10      System.out.print("Enter a string: ");
11      String s = input.nextLine();
12
13      // Display result
14      System.out.println("Ignoring nonalphanumeric characters, \nis "
15        + s + " a palindrome? " + isPalindrome(s));
16    }
17
18    /** Return true if a string is a palindrome */
19    public static boolean isPalindrome(String s) {
20      // Create a new string by eliminating nonalphanumeric chars
21      String s1 = filter(s);
22
23      // Create a new string that is the reversal of s1
24      String s2 = reverse(s1);
25
26      // Check if the reversal is the same as the original string
27      return s2.equals(s1);
28    }
29
30    /** Create a new string by eliminating nonalphanumeric chars */
31    public static String filter(String s) {
32      // Create a string builder
33      StringBuilder stringBuilder = new StringBuilder();
34
35      // Examine each char in the string to skip alphanumeric char
36      for (int i = 0; i < s.length(); i++) {
37        if (Character.isLetterOrDigit(s.charAt(i))) {
38          stringBuilder.append(s.charAt(i));
39        }
```

check palindrome

add letter or digit

```
40        }
41
42        // Return a new filtered string
43        return stringBuilder.toString();
44    }
45
46    /** Create a new string by reversing a specified string */
47    public static String reverse(String s) {
48        StringBuilder stringBuilder = new StringBuilder(s);
49        stringBuilder.reverse(); // Invoke reverse in StringBuilder
50        return stringBuilder.toString();
51    }
52 }
```

```
Enter a string: ab<c>cb?a  ↵Enter
Ignoring nonalphanumeric characters,
is ab<c>cb?a a palindrome? true
```

```
Enter a string: abcc><?cab  ↵Enter
Ignoring nonalphanumeric characters,
is abcc><?cab a palindrome? false
```

The `filter(String s)` method (lines 31–44) examines each character in string **s** and copies it to a string builder if the character is a letter or a numeric character. The `filter` method returns the string in the builder. The `reverse(String s)` method (lines 47–51) creates a new string that reverses the specified string **s**. The `filter` and `reverse` methods both return a new string. The original string is not changed.

The program in Listing 5.14 checks whether a string is a palindrome by comparing pairs of characters from both ends of the string. Listing 10.10 uses the `reverse` method in the **StringBuilder** class to reverse the string, then compares whether the two strings are equal to determine whether the original string is a palindrome.

10.26 What is the difference between **StringBuilder** and **StringBuffer**?

10.27 How do you create a string builder from a string? How do you return a string from a string builder?

10.28 Write three statements to reverse a string **s** using the **reverse** method in the **StringBuilder** class.

10.29 Write three statements to delete a substring from a string **s** of **20** characters, starting at index **4** and ending with index **10**. Use the **delete** method in the **String-Builder** class.

10.30 What is the internal storage for characters in a string and a string builder?

10.31 Suppose that **s1** and **s2** are given as follows:

```
StringBuilder s1 = new StringBuilder("Java");
StringBuilder s2 = new StringBuilder("HTML");
```

Show the value of **s1** after each of the following statements. Assume that the statements are independent.

a. s1.append(" is fun");

b. s1.append(s2);

✓ **Check Point**

c. s1.insert(2, "is fun");

d. s1.insert(1, s2);

e. s1.charAt(2);

f. s1.length();

g. s1.deleteCharAt(3);

h. s1.delete(1, 3);

i. s1.reverse();

j. s1.replace(1, 3, "Computer");

k. s1.substring(1, 3);

l. s1.substring(2);

10.32 Show the output of the following program:

```java
public class Test {
  public static void main(String[] args) {
    String s = "Java";
    StringBuilder builder = new StringBuilder(s);
    change(s, builder);

    System.out.println(s);
    System.out.println(builder);
  }

  private static void change(String s, StringBuilder builder) {
    s = s + " and HTML";
    builder.append(" and HTML");
  }
}
```

KEY TERMS

abstract data type (ADT)   366
aggregation   374
boxing   383
class abstraction   366
class encapsulation   366
class's contract   366

composition   374
has-a relationship   374
multiplicity   373
stack   378
unboxing   383

CHAPTER SUMMARY

1. The procedural paradigm focuses on designing methods. The object-oriented paradigm couples data and methods together into objects. Software design using the object-oriented paradigm focuses on objects and operations on objects. The object-oriented approach combines the power of the procedural paradigm with an added dimension that integrates data with operations into objects.

2. Many Java methods require the use of objects as arguments. Java offers a convenient way to incorporate, or wrap, a primitive data type into an object (e.g., wrapping `int` into the `Integer` class, and wrapping `double` into the `Double` class).

3. Java can automatically convert a primitive type value to its corresponding wrapper object in the context and vice versa.

4. The **BigInteger** class is useful for computing and processing integers of any size. The **BigDecimal** class can be used to compute and process floating-point numbers with any arbitrary precision.

5. A **String** object is immutable; its contents cannot be changed. To improve efficiency and save memory, the JVM stores two literal strings that have the same character sequence in a unique object. This unique object is called an *interned string object*.

6. A *regular expression* (abbreviated *regex*) is a string that describes a pattern for matching a set of strings. You can match, replace, or split a string by specifying a pattern.

7. The **StringBuilder** and **StringBuffer** classes can be used to replace the **String** class. The **String** object is immutable, but you can add, insert, or append new contents into **StringBuilder** and **StringBuffer** objects. Use **String** if the string contents do not require any change, and use **StringBuilder** or **StringBuffer** if they might change.

QUIZ

Answer the quiz for this chapter online at www.cs.armstrong.edu/liang/intro10e/quiz.html.

PROGRAMMING EXERCISES

MyProgrammingLab™

Sections 10.2–10.3

*10.1 (*The Time class*) Design a class named **Time**. The class contains:

■ The data fields **hour**, **minute**, and **second** that represent a time.
■ A no-arg constructor that creates a **Time** object for the current time. (The values of the data fields will represent the current time.)
■ A constructor that constructs a **Time** object with a specified elapsed time since midnight, January 1, 1970, in milliseconds. (The values of the data fields will represent this time.)
■ A constructor that constructs a **Time** object with the specified hour, minute, and second.
■ Three getter methods for the data fields **hour**, **minute**, and **second**, respectively.
■ A method named **setTime(long elapseTime)** that sets a new time for the object using the elapsed time. For example, if the elapsed time is **555550000** milliseconds, the hour is **10**, the minute is **19**, and the second is **10**.

Draw the UML diagram for the class and then implement the class. Write a test program that creates two **Time** objects (using **new Time()** and **new Time(555550000)**) and displays their hour, minute, and second in the format hour:minute:second.

(*Hint*: The first two constructors will extract the hour, minute, and second from the elapsed time. For the no-arg constructor, the current time can be obtained using **System.currentTimeMillis()**, as shown in Listing 2.7, ShowCurrentTime.java.)

10.2   (*The BMI class*) Add the following new constructor in the BMI class:

```
/** Construct a BMI with the specified name, age, weight,
 * feet, and inches
 */
public BMI(String name, int age, double weight, double feet,
    double inches)
```

10.3   (*The MyInteger class*) Design a class named MyInteger. The class contains:

- An int data field named value that stores the int value represented by this object.
- A constructor that creates a MyInteger object for the specified int value.
- A getter method that returns the int value.
- The methods isEven(), isOdd(), and isPrime() that return true if the value in this object is even, odd, or prime, respectively.
- The static methods isEven(int), isOdd(int), and isPrime(int) that return true if the specified value is even, odd, or prime, respectively.
- The static methods isEven(MyInteger), isOdd(MyInteger), and isPrime(MyInteger) that return true if the specified value is even, odd, or prime, respectively.
- The methods equals(int) and equals(MyInteger) that return true if the value in this object is equal to the specified value.
- A static method parseInt(char[]) that converts an array of numeric characters to an int value.
- A static method parseInt(String) that converts a string into an int value.

Draw the UML diagram for the class and then implement the class. Write a client program that tests all methods in the class.

10.4   (*The MyPoint class*) Design a class named MyPoint to represent a point with x- and y-coordinates. The class contains:

- The data fields x and y that represent the coordinates with getter methods.
- A no-arg constructor that creates a point (0, 0).
- A constructor that constructs a point with specified coordinates.
- A method named distance that returns the distance from this point to a specified point of the MyPoint type.
- A method named distance that returns the distance from this point to another point with specified x- and y-coordinates.

Draw the UML diagram for the class and then implement the class. Write a test program that creates the two points (0, 0) and (10, 30.5) and displays the distance between them.

VideoNote

The MyPoint class

Sections 10.4–10.8

*10.5   (*Displaying the prime factors*) Write a program that prompts the user to enter a positive integer and displays all its smallest factors in decreasing order. For example, if the integer is 120, the smallest factors are displayed as 5, 3, 2, 2, 2. Use the StackOfIntegers class to store the factors (e.g., 2, 2, 2, 3, 5) and retrieve and display them in reverse order.

*10.6   (*Displaying the prime numbers*) Write a program that displays all the prime numbers less than 120 in decreasing order. Use the StackOfIntegers class to store the prime numbers (e.g., 2, 3, 5, . . .) and retrieve and display them in reverse order.

**10.7 (*Game: ATM machine*) Use the `Account` class created in Programming Exercise 9.7 to simulate an ATM machine. Create ten accounts in an array with id 0, 1, . . . , 9, and initial balance $100. The system prompts the user to enter an id. If the id is entered incorrectly, ask the user to enter a correct id. Once an id is accepted, the main menu is displayed as shown in the sample run. You can enter a choice 1 for viewing the current balance, 2 for withdrawing money, 3 for depositing money, and 4 for exiting the main menu. Once you exit, the system will prompt for an id again. Thus, once the system starts, it will not stop.

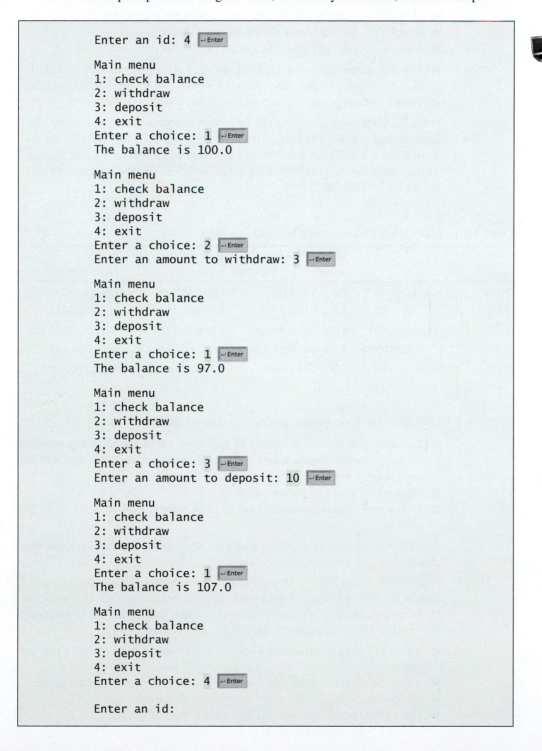

```
Enter an id: 4  ↵ Enter

Main menu
1: check balance
2: withdraw
3: deposit
4: exit
Enter a choice: 1  ↵ Enter
The balance is 100.0

Main menu
1: check balance
2: withdraw
3: deposit
4: exit
Enter a choice: 2  ↵ Enter
Enter an amount to withdraw: 3  ↵ Enter

Main menu
1: check balance
2: withdraw
3: deposit
4: exit
Enter a choice: 1  ↵ Enter
The balance is 97.0

Main menu
1: check balance
2: withdraw
3: deposit
4: exit
Enter a choice: 3  ↵ Enter
Enter an amount to deposit: 10  ↵ Enter

Main menu
1: check balance
2: withdraw
3: deposit
4: exit
Enter a choice: 1  ↵ Enter
The balance is 107.0

Main menu
1: check balance
2: withdraw
3: deposit
4: exit
Enter a choice: 4  ↵ Enter

Enter an id:
```

***10.8   (*Financial: the* Tax *class*) Programming Exercise 8.12 writes a program for computing taxes using arrays. Design a class named Tax to contain the following instance data fields:

- int filingStatus: One of the four tax-filing statuses: 0—single filer, 1—married filing jointly or qualifying widow(er), 2—married filing separately, and 3—head of household. Use the public static constants SINGLE_FILER (0), MARRIED_JOINTLY_OR_QUALIFYING_WIDOW(ER) (1), MARRIED_SEPARATELY (2), HEAD_OF_HOUSEHOLD (3) to represent the statuses.
- int[][] brackets: Stores the tax brackets for each filing status.
- double[] rates: Stores the tax rates for each bracket.
- double taxableIncome: Stores the taxable income.

Provide the getter and setter methods for each data field and the getTax() method that returns the tax. Also provide a no-arg constructor and the constructor Tax(filingStatus, brackets, rates, taxableIncome).

Draw the UML diagram for the class and then implement the class. Write a test program that uses the Tax class to print the 2001 and 2009 tax tables for taxable income from $50,000 to $60,000 with intervals of $1,000 for all four statuses. The tax rates for the year 2009 were given in Table 3.2. The tax rates for 2001 are shown in Table 10.1.

TABLE 10.1   2001 United States Federal Personal Tax Rates

Tax rate	Single filers	Married filing jointly or qualifying widow(er)	Married filing separately	Head of household
15%	Up to $27,050	Up to $45,200	Up to $22,600	Up to $36,250
27.5%	$27,051–$65,550	$45,201–$109,250	$22,601–$54,625	$36,251–$93,650
30.5%	$65,551–$136,750	$109,251–$166,500	$54,626–$83,250	$93,651–$151,650
35.5%	$136,751–$297,350	$166,501–$297,350	$83,251–$148,675	$151,651–$297,350
39.1%	$297,351 or more	$297,351 or more	$ 148,676 or more	$297,351 or more

**10.9   (*The* Course *class*) Revise the Course class as follows:

- The array size is fixed in Listing 10.6. Improve it to automatically increase the array size by creating a new larger array and copying the contents of the current array to it.
- Implement the dropStudent method.
- Add a new method named clear() that removes all students from the course.

Write a test program that creates a course, adds three students, removes one, and displays the students in the course.

*10.10   (*The* Queue *class*) Section 10.6 gives a class for Stack. Design a class named Queue for storing integers. Like a stack, a queue holds elements. In a stack, the elements are retrieved in a last-in first-out fashion. In a queue, the elements are retrieved in a first-in first-out fashion. The class contains:

- An int[] data field named elements that stores the int values in the queue.
- A data field named size that stores the number of elements in the queue.
- A constructor that creates a Queue object with default capacity 8.
- The method enqueue(int v) that adds v into the queue.

■ The method **dequeue()** that removes and returns the element from the queue.
■ The method **empty()** that returns true if the queue is empty.
■ The method **getSize()** that returns the size of the queue.

Draw an UML diagram for the class. Implement the class with the initial array size set to 8. The array size will be doubled once the number of the elements exceeds the size. After an element is removed from the beginning of the array, you need to shift all elements in the array one position the left. Write a test program that adds 20 numbers from 1 to 20 into the queue and removes these numbers and displays them.

*10.11   (*Geometry: the* **Circle2D** *class*) Define the **Circle2D** class that contains:

■ Two **double** data fields named **x** and **y** that specify the center of the circle with getter methods.
■ A data field **radius** with a getter method.
■ A no-arg constructor that creates a default circle with (**0**, **0**) for (**x**, **y**) and **1** for **radius**.
■ A constructor that creates a circle with the specified **x**, **y**, and **radius**.
■ A method **getArea()** that returns the area of the circle.
■ A method **getPerimeter()** that returns the perimeter of the circle.
■ A method **contains(double x, double y)** that returns **true** if the specified point (**x**, **y**) is inside this circle (see Figure 10.21a).
■ A method **contains(Circle2D circle)** that returns **true** if the specified circle is inside this circle (see Figure 10.21b).
■ A method **overlaps(Circle2D circle)** that returns **true** if the specified circle overlaps with this circle (see Figure 10.21c).

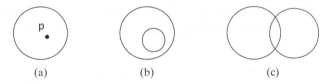

(a)   (b)   (c)

FIGURE 10.21   (a) A point is inside the circle. (b) A circle is inside another circle. (c) A circle overlaps another circle.

Draw the UML diagram for the class and then implement the class. Write a test program that creates a **Circle2D** object **c1** (**new Circle2D(2, 2, 5.5)**), displays its area and perimeter, and displays the result of **c1.contains(3, 3)**, **c1.contains(new Circle2D(4, 5, 10.5))**, and **c1.overlaps(new Circle2D(3, 5, 2.3))**.

***10.12   (*Geometry: the* **Triangle2D** *class*) Define the **Triangle2D** class that contains:

■ Three points named **p1**, **p2**, and **p3** of the type **MyPoint** with getter and setter methods. **MyPoint** is defined in Programming Exercise 10.4.
■ A no-arg constructor that creates a default triangle with the points (**0**, **0**), (**1**, **1**), and (**2**, **5**).
■ A constructor that creates a triangle with the specified points.
■ A method **getArea()** that returns the area of the triangle.
■ A method **getPerimeter()** that returns the perimeter of the triangle.
■ A method **contains(MyPoint p)** that returns **true** if the specified point **p** is inside this triangle (see Figure 10.22a).

■ A method **contains(Triangle2D t)** that returns **true** if the specified triangle is inside this triangle (see Figure 10.22b).

■ A method **overlaps(Triangle2D t)** that returns **true** if the specified triangle overlaps with this triangle (see Figure 10.22c).

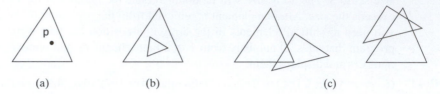

(a)   (b)   (c)

FIGURE 10.22 (a) A point is inside the triangle. (b) A triangle is inside another triangle. (c) A triangle overlaps another triangle.

Draw the UML diagram for the class and then implement the class. Write a test program that creates a **Triangle2D** objects **t1** using the constructor **new Triangle2D(new MyPoint(2.5, 2), new MyPoint(4.2, 3), new MyPoint(5, 3.5))**, displays its area and perimeter, and displays the result of **t1.contains(3, 3)**, **r1.contains(new Triangle2D(new MyPoint(2.9, 2), new MyPoint(4, 1), MyPoint(1, 3.4)))**, and **t1.overlaps(new Triangle2D(new MyPoint(2, 5.5), new MyPoint(4, -3), MyPoint(2, 6.5)))**.

(*Hint*: For the formula to compute the area of a triangle, see Programming Exercise 2.19. To detect whether a point is inside a triangle, draw three dashed lines, as shown in Figure 10.23. If the point is inside a triangle, each dashed line should intersect a side only once. If a dashed line intersects a side twice, then the point must be outside the triangle. For the algorithm of finding the intersecting point of two lines, see Programming Exercise 3.25.)

(a)   (b)

FIGURE 10.23 (a) A point is inside the triangle. (b) A point is outside the triangle.

*10.13 (*Geometry: the* **MyRectangle2D** *class*) Define the **MyRectangle2D** class that contains:

■ Two **double** data fields named **x** and **y** that specify the center of the rectangle with getter and setter methods. (Assume that the rectangle sides are parallel to **x-** or **y-** axes.)

■ The data fields **width** and **height** with getter and setter methods.

■ A no-arg constructor that creates a default rectangle with (**0, 0**) for (**x, y**) and **1** for both **width** and **height**.

■ A constructor that creates a rectangle with the specified **x, y, width**, and **height**.

- A method `getArea()` that returns the area of the rectangle.
- A method `getPerimeter()` that returns the perimeter of the rectangle.
- A method `contains(double x, double y)` that returns `true` if the specified point (x, y) is inside this rectangle (see Figure 10.24a).
- A method `contains(MyRectangle2D r)` that returns `true` if the specified rectangle is inside this rectangle (see Figure 10.24b).
- A method `overlaps(MyRectangle2D r)` that returns `true` if the specified rectangle overlaps with this rectangle (see Figure 10.24c).

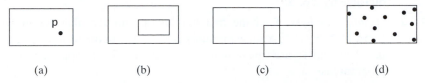

| (a) | (b) | (c) | (d) |

FIGURE 10.24 A point is inside the rectangle. (b) A rectangle is inside another rectangle. (c) A rectangle overlaps another rectangle. (d) Points are enclosed inside a rectangle.

Draw the UML diagram for the class and then implement the class. Write a test program that creates a `MyRectangle2D` object `r1` (`new MyRectangle2D(2, 2, 5.5, 4.9)`), displays its area and perimeter, and displays the result of `r1.contains(3, 3)`, `r1.contains(new MyRectangle2D(4, 5, 10.5, 3.2))`, and `r1.overlaps(new MyRectangle2D(3, 5, 2.3, 5.4))`.

*10.14 (*The* `MyDate` *class*) Design a class named `MyDate`. The class contains:

- The data fields `year`, `month`, and `day` that represent a date. `month` is 0-based, i.e., `0` is for January.
- A no-arg constructor that creates a `MyDate` object for the current date.
- A constructor that constructs a `MyDate` object with a specified elapsed time since midnight, January 1, 1970, in milliseconds.
- A constructor that constructs a `MyDate` object with the specified year, month, and day.
- Three getter methods for the data fields `year`, `month`, and `day`, respectively.
- A method named `setDate(long elapsedTime)` that sets a new date for the object using the elapsed time.

Draw the UML diagram for the class and then implement the class. Write a test program that creates two `MyDate` objects (using `new MyDate()` and `new MyDate(34355555133101L)`) and displays their year, month, and day.

(*Hint*: The first two constructors will extract the year, month, and day from the elapsed time. For example, if the elapsed time is `561555550000` milliseconds, the year is `1987`, the month is `9`, and the day is `18`. You may use the `GregorianCalendar` class discussed in Programming Exercise 9.5 to simplify coding.)

*10.15 (*Geometry: the bounding rectangle*) A bounding rectangle is the minimum rectangle that encloses a set of points in a two-dimensional plane, as shown in Figure 10.24d. Write a method that returns a bounding rectangle for a set of points in a two-dimensional plane, as follows:

public static MyRectangle2D getRectangle(**double**[][] points)

The `Rectangle2D` class is defined in Programming Exercise 10.13. Write a test program that prompts the user to enter five points and displays the bounding rectangle's center, width, and height. Here is a sample run:

```
Enter five points: 1.0 2.5 3 4 5 6 7 8 9 10 ↵Enter
The bounding rectangle's center (5.0, 6.25), width 8.0, height 7.5
```

Section 10.9

*10.16 (*Divisible by 2 or 3*) Find the first ten numbers with 50 decimal digits that are divisible by 2 or 3.

*10.17 (*Square numbers*) Find the first ten square numbers that are greater than `Long.MAX_VALUE`. A square number is a number in the form of n^2. For example, 4, 9, and 16 are square numbers. Find an efficient approach to run your program fast.

*10.18 (*Large prime numbers*) Write a program that finds five prime numbers larger than `Long.MAX_VALUE`.

*10.19 (*Mersenne prime*) A prime number is called a *Mersenne prime* if it can be written in the form $2^p - 1$ for some positive integer p. Write a program that finds all Mersenne primes with $p \le 100$ and displays the output as shown below. (*Hint*: You have to use `BigInteger` to store the number, because it is too big to be stored in `long`. Your program may take several hours to run.)

```
p          2^p - 1

2             3
3             7
5            31
...
```

*10.20 (*Approximate e*) Programming Exercise 5.26 approximates *e* using the following series:

$$e = 1 + \frac{1}{1!} + \frac{1}{2!} + \frac{1}{3!} + \frac{1}{4!} + \ldots + \frac{1}{i!}$$

In order to get better precision, use `BigDecimal` with 25 digits of precision in the computation. Write a program that displays the e value for i = 100, 200, ..., and 1000.

10.21 (*Divisible by 5 or 6*) Find the first ten numbers greater than `Long.MAX_VALUE` that are divisible by 5 or 6.

Sections 10.10–10.11

**10.22 (*Implement the String class*) The `String` class is provided in the Java library. Provide your own implementation for the following methods (name the new class `MyString1`):

```java
public MyString1(char[] chars);
public char charAt(int index);
public int length();
public MyString1 substring(int begin, int end);
public MyString1 toLowerCase();
public boolean equals(MyString1 s);
public static MyString1 valueOf(int i);
```

10.23 (*Implement the* ***String* *class*) The **String** class is provided in the Java library. Provide your own implementation for the following methods (name the new class **MyString2**):

```java
public MyString2(String s);
public int compare(String s);
public MyString2 substring(int begin);
public MyString2 toUpperCase();
public char[] toChars();
public static MyString2 valueOf(boolean b);
```

10.24 (*Implement the* ***Character*** *class*) The **Character** class is provided in the Java library. Provide your own implementation for this class. Name the new class **MyCharacter**.

10.25 (*New string* ***split* *method*) The **split** method in the **String** class returns an array of strings consisting of the substrings split by the delimiters. However, the delimiters are not returned. Implement the following new method that returns an array of strings consisting of the substrings split by the matching delimiters, including the matching delimiters.

```java
public static String[] split(String s, String regex)
```

For example, **split("ab#12#453", "#")** returns **ab**, **#**, **12**, **#**, **453** in an array of **String**, and **split("a?b?gf#e", "[?#]")** returns **a**, **b**, **?**, **b**, **gf**, **#**, and **e** in an array of **String**.

*10.26 (*Calculator*) Revise Listing 7.9, Calculator.java, to accept an expression as a string in which the operands and operator are separated by zero or more spaces. For example, **3+4** and **3 + 4** are acceptable expressions. Here is a sample run:

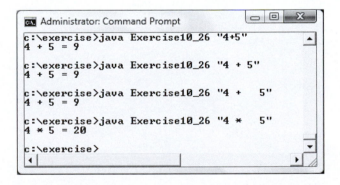

10.27 (*Implement the* ***StringBuilder* *class*) The **StringBuilder** class is provided in the Java library. Provide your own implementation for the following methods (name the new class **MyStringBuilder1**):

```java
public MyStringBuilder1(String s);
public MyStringBuilder1 append(MyStringBuilder1 s);
public MyStringBuilder1 append(int i);
public int length();
public char charAt(int index);
public MyStringBuilder1 toLowerCase();
public MyStringBuilder1 substring(int begin, int end);
public String toString();
```

10.28 (*Implement the StringBuilder class*) The **StringBuilder class is provided in the Java library. Provide your own implementation for the following methods (name the new class **MyStringBuilder2**):

```
public MyStringBuilder2();
public MyStringBuilder2(char[] chars);
public MyStringBuilder2(String s);
public MyStringBuilder2 insert(int offset, MyStringBuilder2 s);
public MyStringBuilder2 reverse();
public MyStringBuilder2 substring(int begin);
public MyStringBuilder2 toUpperCase();
```

INHERITANCE AND POLYMORPHISM

Objectives

- To define a subclass from a superclass through inheritance (§11.2).

- To invoke the superclass's constructors and methods using the **super** keyword (§11.3).

- To override instance methods in the subclass (§11.4).

- To distinguish differences between overriding and overloading (§11.5).

- To explore the **toString()** method in the **Object** class (§11.6).

- To discover polymorphism and dynamic binding (§§11.7–11.8).

- To describe casting and explain why explicit downcasting is necessary (§11.9).

- To explore the **equals** method in the **Object** class (§11.10).

- To store, retrieve, and manipulate objects in an **ArrayList** (§11.11).

- To construct an array list from an array, to sort and shuffle a list, and to obtain max and min element from a list (§11.12).

- To implement a **Stack** class using **ArrayList** (§11.13).

- To enable data and methods in a superclass accessible from subclasses using the **protected** visibility modifier (§11.14).

- To prevent class extending and method overriding using the **final** modifier (§11.15).

11.1 Introduction

Key Point

Object-oriented programming allows you to define new classes from existing classes. This is called inheritance.

inheritance

As discussed earlier in the book, the procedural paradigm focuses on designing methods and the object-oriented paradigm couples data and methods together into objects. Software design using the object-oriented paradigm focuses on objects and operations on objects. The object-oriented approach combines the power of the procedural paradigm with an added dimension that integrates data with operations into objects.

why inheritance?

Inheritance is an important and powerful feature for reusing software. Suppose you need to define classes to model circles, rectangles, and triangles. These classes have many common features. What is the best way to design these classes so as to avoid redundancy and make the system easy to comprehend and easy to maintain? The answer is to use inheritance.

11.2 Superclasses and Subclasses

Key Point

Inheritance enables you to define a general class (i.e., a superclass) and later extend it to more specialized classes (i.e., subclasses).

You use a class to model objects of the same type. Different classes may have some common properties and behaviors, which can be generalized in a class that can be shared by other classes. You can define a specialized class that extends the generalized class. The specialized classes inherit the properties and methods from the general class.

VideoNote

Geometric class hierarchy

Consider geometric objects. Suppose you want to design the classes to model geometric objects such as circles and rectangles. Geometric objects have many common properties and behaviors. They can be drawn in a certain color and be filled or unfilled. Thus a general class **GeometricObject** can be used to model all geometric objects. This class contains the properties **color** and **filled** and their appropriate getter and setter methods. Assume that this class also contains the **dateCreated** property and the **getDateCreated()** and **toString()** methods. The **toString()** method returns a string representation of the object. Since a circle is a special type of geometric object, it shares common properties and methods with other geometric objects. Thus it makes sense to define the **Circle** class that extends the **GeometricObject** class. Likewise, **Rectangle** can also be defined as a subclass of **GeometricObject**. Figure 11.1 shows the relationship among these classes. A triangular arrow pointing to the superclass is used to denote the inheritance relationship between the two classes involved.

subclass
superclass

In Java terminology, a class **C1** extended from another class **C2** is called a *subclass*, and **C2** is called a *superclass*. A superclass is also referred to as a *parent class* or a *base class*, and a subclass as a *child class*, an *extended class*, or a *derived class*. A subclass inherits accessible data fields and methods from its superclass and may also add new data fields and methods.

The **Circle** class inherits all accessible data fields and methods from the **GeometricObject** class. In addition, it has a new data field, **radius**, and its associated getter and setter methods. The **Circle** class also contains the **getArea()**, **getPerimeter()**, and **getDiameter()** methods for returning the area, perimeter, and diameter of the circle.

The **Rectangle** class inherits all accessible data fields and methods from the **GeometricObject** class. In addition, it has the data fields **width** and **height** and their associated getter and setter methods. It also contains the **getArea()** and **getPerimeter()** methods for returning the area and perimeter of the rectangle.

The **GeometricObject**, **Circle**, and **Rectangle** classes are shown in Listings 11.1, 11.2, and 11.3.

avoid naming conflicts

Note

To avoid a naming conflict with the improved **GeometricObject**, **Circle**, and **Rectangle** classes introduced in Chapter 13, we'll name these classes

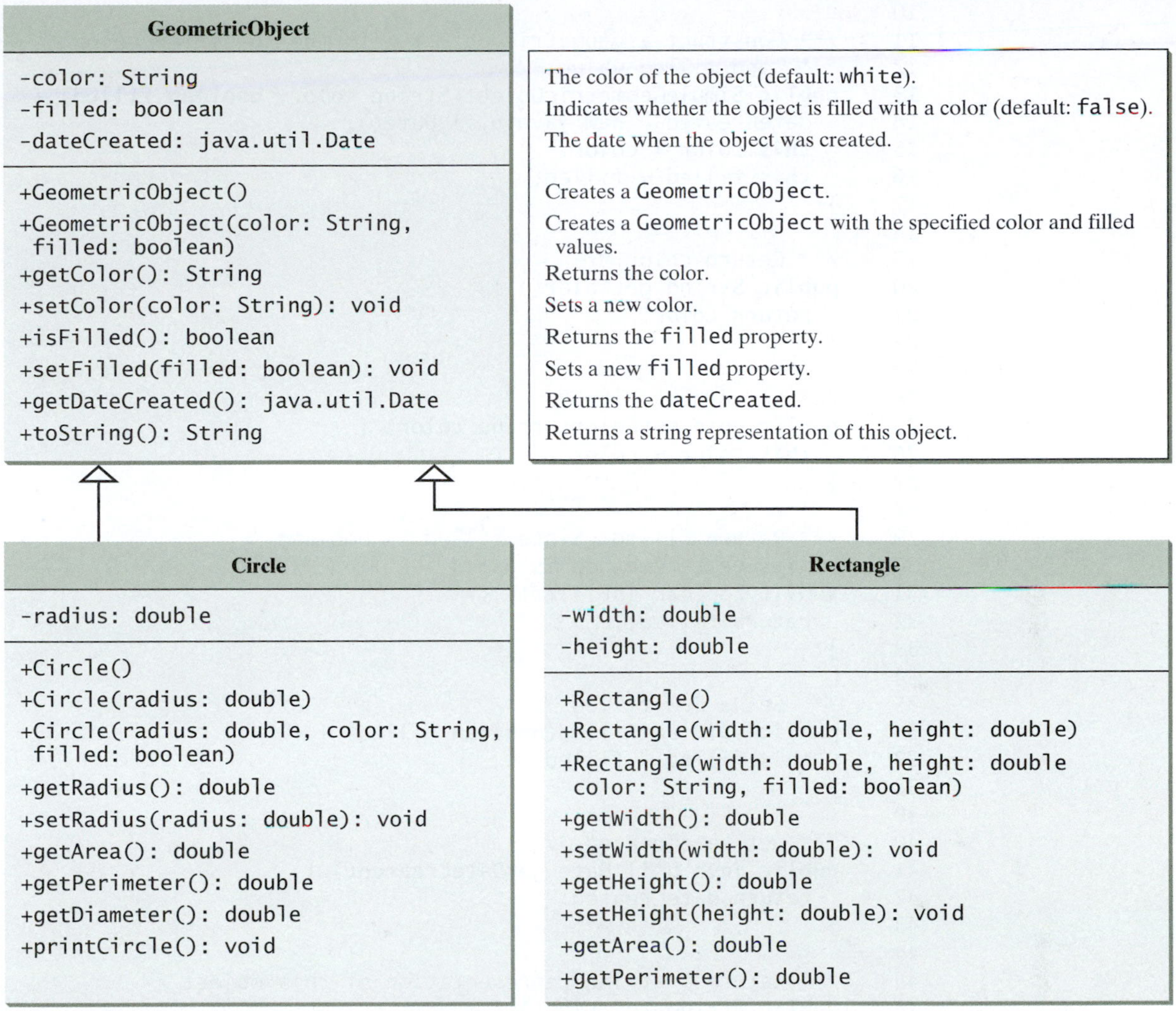

FIGURE 11.1 The `GeometricObject` class is the superclass for `Circle` and `Rectangle`.

`SimpleGeometricObject`, `CircleFromSimpleGeometricObject`, and `RectangleFromSimpleGeometricObject` in this chapter. For simplicity, we will still refer to them in the text as `GeometricObject`, `Circle`, and `Rectangle` classes. The best way to avoid naming conflicts is to place these classes in different packages. However, for simplicity and consistency, all classes in this book are placed in the default package.

LISTING 11.1 `SimpleGeometricObject.java`

```
 1  public class SimpleGeometricObject {
 2    private String color = "white";
 3    private boolean filled;
 4    private java.util.Date dateCreated;
 5
 6    /** Construct a default geometric object */
 7    public SimpleGeometricObject() {
 8      dateCreated = new java.util.Date();
 9    }
```

data fields

constructor
date constructed

```
10
11      /** Construct a geometric object with the specified color
12       *   and filled value */
13      public SimpleGeometricObject(String color, boolean filled) {
14        dateCreated = new java.util.Date();
15        this.color = color;
16        this.filled = filled;
17      }
18
19      /** Return color */
20      public String getColor() {
21        return color;
22      }
23
24      /** Set a new color */
25      public void setColor(String color) {
26        this.color = color;
27      }
28
29      /** Return filled. Since filled is boolean,
30         its getter method is named isFilled */
31      public boolean isFilled() {
32        return filled;
33      }
34
35      /** Set a new filled */
36      public void setFilled(boolean filled) {
37        this.filled = filled;
38      }
39
40      /** Get dateCreated */
41      public java.util.Date getDateCreated() {
42        return dateCreated;
43      }
44
45      /** Return a string representation of this object */
46      public String toString() {
47        return "created on " + dateCreated + "\ncolor: " + color +
48          " and filled: " + filled;
49      }
50    }
```

LISTING 11.2 CircleFromSimpleGeometricObject.java

```
1     public class CircleFromSimpleGeometricObject
2         extends SimpleGeometricObject {
3       private double radius;
4
5       public CircleFromSimpleGeometricObject() {
6       }
7
8       public CircleFromSimpleGeometricObject(double radius) {
9         this.radius = radius;
10      }
11
12      public CircleFromSimpleGeometricObject(double radius,
13          String color, boolean filled) {
14        this.radius = radius;
15        setColor(color);
16        setFilled(filled);
```

extends superclass
data fields

constructor

```
17      }
18
19      /** Return radius */
20      public double getRadius() {                                    methods
21        return radius;
22      }
23
24      /** Set a new radius */
25      public void setRadius(double radius) {
26        this.radius = radius;
27      }
28
29      /** Return area */
30      public double getArea() {
31        return radius * radius * Math.PI;
32      }
33
34      /** Return diameter */
35      public double getDiameter() {
36        return 2 * radius;
37      }
38
39      /** Return perimeter */
40      public double getPerimeter() {
41        return 2 * radius * Math.PI;
42      }
43
44      /** Print the circle info */
45      public void printCircle() {
46        System.out.println("The circle is created " + getDateCreated() +
47          " and the radius is " + radius);
48      }
49    }
```

The **Circle** class (Listing 11.2) extends the **GeometricObject** class (Listing 11.1) using the following syntax:

Subclass   Superclass

public class Circle **extends** GeometricObject

The keyword **extends** (lines 1–2) tells the compiler that the **Circle** class extends the **GeometricObject** class, thus inheriting the methods **getColor**, **setColor**, **isFilled**, **setFilled**, and **toString**.

The overloaded constructor **Circle(double radius, String color, boolean filled)** is implemented by invoking the **setColor** and **setFilled** methods to set the **color** and **filled** properties (lines 12–17). These two public methods are defined in the superclass **GeometricObject** and are inherited in **Circle**, so they can be used in the **Circle** class.

You might attempt to use the data fields **color** and **filled** directly in the constructor as   private member in superclass follows:

```
public CircleFromSimpleGeometricObject(
    double radius, String color, boolean filled) {
  this.radius = radius;
  this.color = color; // Illegal
  this.filled = filled; // Illegal
}
```

This is wrong, because the private data fields `color` and `filled` in the `GeometricObject` class cannot be accessed in any class other than in the `GeometricObject` class itself. The only way to read and modify `color` and `filled` is through their getter and setter methods.

The `Rectangle` class (Listing 11.3) extends the `GeometricObject` class (Listing 11.1) using the following syntax:

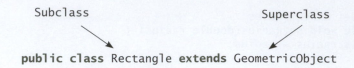

Subclass   Superclass

`public class Rectangle extends GeometricObject`

The keyword `extends` (lines 1–2) tells the compiler that the `Rectangle` class extends the `GeometricObject` class, thus inheriting the methods `getColor`, `setColor`, `isFilled`, `setFilled`, and `toString`.

LISTING 11.3 RectangleFromSimpleGeometricObject.java

```
 1  public class RectangleFromSimpleGeometricObject
 2      extends SimpleGeometricObject {
 3    private double width;
 4    private double height;
 5
 6    public RectangleFromSimpleGeometricObject() {
 7    }
 8
 9    public RectangleFromSimpleGeometricObject(
10        double width, double height) {
11      this.width = width;
12      this.height = height;
13    }
14
15    public RectangleFromSimpleGeometricObject(
16        double width, double height, String color, boolean filled) {
17      this.width = width;
18      this.height = height;
19      setColor(color);
20      setFilled(filled);
21    }
22
23    /** Return width */
24    public double getWidth() {
25      return width;
26    }
27
28    /** Set a new width */
29    public void setWidth(double width) {
30      this.width = width;
31    }
32
33    /** Return height */
34    public double getHeight() {
35      return height;
36    }
37
38    /** Set a new height */
39    public void setHeight(double height) {
40      this.height = height;
41    }
```

extends superclass
data fields

constructor

methods

```
42
43      /** Return area */
44      public double getArea() {
45        return width * height;
46      }
47
48      /** Return perimeter */
49      public double getPerimeter() {
50        return 2 * (width + height);
51      }
52    }
```

The code in Listing 11.4 creates objects of **Circle** and **Rectangle** and invokes the methods on these objects. The **toString()** method is inherited from the **GeometricObject** class and is invoked from a **Circle** object (line 5) and a **Rectangle** object (line 13).

LISTING 11.4 TestCircleRectangle.java

```
1   public class TestCircleRectangle {
2     public static void main(String[] args) {
3       CircleFromSimpleGeometricObject circle =
4         new CircleFromSimpleGeometricObject(1);
5       System.out.println("A circle " + circle.toString());
6       System.out.println("The color is " + circle.getColor());
7       System.out.println("The radius is " + circle.getRadius());
8       System.out.println("The area is " + circle.getArea());
9       System.out.println("The diameter is " + circle.getDiameter());
10
11      RectangleFromSimpleGeometricObject rectangle =
12        new RectangleFromSimpleGeometricObject(2, 4);
13      System.out.println("\nA rectangle " + rectangle.toString());
14      System.out.println("The area is " + rectangle.getArea());
15      System.out.println("The perimeter is " +
16        rectangle.getPerimeter());
17    }
18  }
```

*Circle object
invoke toString
invoke getColor*

*Rectangle object
invoke toString*

```
A circle created on Thu Feb 10 19:54:25 EST 2011
color: white and filled: false
The color is white
The radius is 1.0
The area is 3.141592653589793
The diameter is 2.0
A rectangle created on Thu Feb 10 19:54:25 EST 2011
color: white and filled: false
The area is 8.0
The perimeter is 12.0
```

Note the following points regarding inheritance:

- Contrary to the conventional interpretation, a subclass is not a subset of its superclass. In fact, a subclass usually contains more information and methods than its superclass.

more in subclass

- Private data fields in a superclass are not accessible outside the class. Therefore, they cannot be used directly in a subclass. They can, however, be accessed/mutated through public accessors/mutators if defined in the superclass.

private data fields

nonextensible is-a

- Not all is-a relationships should be modeled using inheritance. For example, a square is a rectangle, but you should not extend a **Square** class from a **Rectangle** class, because the **width** and **height** properties are not appropriate for a square. Instead, you should define a **Square** class to extend the **GeometricObject** class and define the **side** property for the side of a square.

no blind extension

- Inheritance is used to model the is-a relationship. Do not blindly extend a class just for the sake of reusing methods. For example, it makes no sense for a **Tree** class to extend a **Person** class, even though they share common properties such as height and weight. A subclass and its superclass must have the is-a relationship.

multiple inheritance

single inheritance

- Some programming languages allow you to derive a subclass from several classes. This capability is known as *multiple inheritance*. Java, however, does not allow multiple inheritance. A Java class may inherit directly from only one superclass. This restriction is known as *single inheritance*. If you use the **extends** keyword to define a subclass, it allows only one parent class. Nevertheless, multiple inheritance can be achieved through interfaces, which will be introduced in Section 13.4.

11.1 True or false? A subclass is a subset of a superclass.

11.2 What keyword do you use to define a subclass?

11.3 What is single inheritance? What is multiple inheritance? Does Java support multiple inheritance?

11.3 Using the **super** Keyword

*The keyword **super** refers to the superclass and can be used to invoke the superclass's methods and constructors.*

A subclass inherits accessible data fields and methods from its superclass. Does it inherit constructors? Can the superclass's constructors be invoked from a subclass? This section addresses these questions and their ramifications.

Section 9.14, The **this** Reference, introduced the use of the keyword **this** to reference the calling object. The keyword **super** refers to the superclass of the class in which **super** appears. It can be used in two ways:

- To call a superclass constructor.

- To call a superclass method.

11.3.1 Calling Superclass Constructors

A constructor is used to construct an instance of a class. Unlike properties and methods, the constructors of a superclass are not inherited by a subclass. They can only be invoked from the constructors of the subclasses using the keyword **super**.

The syntax to call a superclass's constructor is:

super(), or **super**(parameters);

The statement **super()** invokes the no-arg constructor of its superclass, and the statement **super(arguments)** invokes the superclass constructor that matches the **arguments**. The statement **super()** or **super(arguments)** must be the first statement of the subclass's constructor; this is the only way to explicitly invoke a superclass constructor. For example, the constructor in lines 12–17 in Listing 11.2 can be replaced by the following code:

```
public CircleFromSimpleGeometricObject(
    double radius, String color, boolean filled) {
```

```
      super(color, filled);
      this.radius = radius;
   }
```

 Caution

You must use the keyword **super** to call the superclass constructor, and the call must be the first statement in the constructor. Invoking a superclass constructor's name in a subclass causes a syntax error.

11.3.2 Constructor Chaining

A constructor may invoke an overloaded constructor or its superclass constructor. If neither is invoked explicitly, the compiler automatically puts **super()** as the first statement in the constructor. For example:

```
public ClassName() {
  // some statements
}
```
Equivalent
```
public ClassName() {
  super();
  // some statements
}
```

```
public ClassName(double d) {
  // some statements
}
```
Equivalent
```
public ClassName(double d) {
  super();
  // some statements
}
```

In any case, constructing an instance of a class invokes the constructors of all the superclasses along the inheritance chain. When constructing an object of a subclass, the subclass constructor first invokes its superclass constructor before performing its own tasks. If the superclass is derived from another class, the superclass constructor invokes its parent-class constructor before performing its own tasks. This process continues until the last constructor along the inheritance hierarchy is called. This is called *constructor chaining*.

constructor chaining

Consider the following code:

```
1   public class Faculty extends Employee {
2     public static void main(String[] args) {
3       new Faculty();
4     }
5
6     public Faculty() {
7       System.out.println("(4) Performs Faculty's tasks");
8     }
9   }
10
11  class Employee extends Person {
12    public Employee() {
13      this("(2) Invoke Employee's overloaded constructor");
14      System.out.println("(3) Performs Employee's tasks ");
15    }
16
17    public Employee(String s) {
18      System.out.println(s);
19    }
20  }
21
22  class Person {
```

invoke overloaded
constructor

```
23    public Person() {
24      System.out.println("(1) Performs Person's tasks");
25    }
26  }
```

```
(1) Performs Person's tasks
(2) Invoke Employee's overloaded constructor
(3) Performs Employee's tasks
(4) Performs Faculty's tasks
```

The program produces the preceding output. Why? Let us discuss the reason. In line 3, **new Faculty()** invokes **Faculty**'s no-arg constructor. Since **Faculty** is a subclass of **Employee**, **Employee**'s no-arg constructor is invoked before any statements in **Faculty**'s constructor are executed. **Employee**'s no-arg constructor invokes **Employee**'s second constructor (line 13). Since **Employee** is a subclass of **Person**, **Person**'s no-arg constructor is invoked before any statements in **Employee**'s second constructor are executed. This process is illustrated in the following figure.

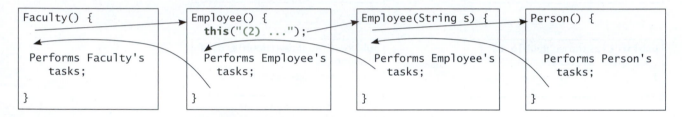

no-arg constructor

Caution

If a class is designed to be extended, it is better to provide a no-arg constructor to avoid programming errors. Consider the following code:

```
1  public class Apple extends Fruit {
2  }
3
4  class Fruit {
5    public Fruit(String name) {
6      System.out.println("Fruit's constructor is invoked");
7    }
8  }
```

Since no constructor is explicitly defined in **Apple**, **Apple**'s default no-arg constructor is defined implicitly. Since **Apple** is a subclass of **Fruit**, **Apple**'s default constructor automatically invokes **Fruit**'s no-arg constructor. However, **Fruit** does not have a no-arg constructor, because **Fruit** has an explicit constructor defined. Therefore, the program cannot be compiled.

Design Guide

no-arg constructor

If possible, you should provide a no-arg constructor for every class to make the class easy to extend and to avoid errors.

11.3.3 Calling Superclass Methods

The keyword **super** can also be used to reference a method other than the constructor in the superclass. The syntax is:

```
super.method(parameters);
```

You could rewrite the `printCircle()` method in the `Circle` class as follows:

```
public void printCircle() {
  System.out.println("The circle is created " +
    super.getDateCreated() + " and the radius is " + radius);
}
```

It is not necessary to put **super** before `getDateCreated()` in this case, however, because `getDateCreated` is a method in the `GeometricObject` class and is inherited by the `Circle` class. Nevertheless, in some cases, as shown in the next section, the keyword **super** is needed.

11.4 What is the output of running the class **C** in (a)? What problem arises in compiling the program in (b)?

Check Point

```
class A {
  public A() {
    System.out.println(
      "A's no-arg constructor is invoked");
  }
}

class B extends A {
}

public class C {
  public static void main(String[] args) {
    B b = new B();
  }
}
```
(a)

```
class A {
  public A(int x) {
  }
}

class B extends A {
  public B() {
  }
}

public class C {
  public static void main(String[] args) {
    B b = new B();
  }
}
```
(b)

11.5 How does a subclass invoke its superclass's constructor?

11.6 True or false? When invoking a constructor from a subclass, its superclass's no-arg constructor is always invoked.

11.4 Overriding Methods

To override a method, the method must be defined in the subclass using the same signature and the same return type as in its superclass.

Key Point

A subclass inherits methods from a superclass. Sometimes it is necessary for the subclass to modify the implementation of a method defined in the superclass. This is referred to as *method overriding*.

method overriding

The `toString` method in the `GeometricObject` class (lines 46–49 in Listing 11.1) returns the string representation of a geometric object. This method can be overridden to return the string representation of a circle. To override it, add the following new method in the `Circle` class in Listing 11.2.

```
1  public class CircleFromSimpleGeometricObject
2      extends SimpleGeometricObject {
3    // Other methods are omitted
4
5    // Override the toString method defined in the superclass
6    public String toString() {
7      return super.toString() + "\nradius is " + radius;
8    }
9  }
```

toString in superclass

The **toString()** method is defined in the **GeometricObject** class and modified in the **Circle** class. Both methods can be used in the **Circle** class. To invoke the **toString** method defined in the **GeometricObject** class from the **Circle** class, use **super.toString()** (line 7).

no super.super.methodName()

Can a subclass of **Circle** access the **toString** method defined in the **GeometricObject** class using syntax such as **super.super.toString()**? No. This is a syntax error.

Several points are worth noting:

override accessible instance method

- An instance method can be overridden only if it is accessible. Thus a private method cannot be overridden, because it is not accessible outside its own class. If a method defined in a subclass is private in its superclass, the two methods are completely unrelated.

cannot override static method

- Like an instance method, a static method can be inherited. However, a static method cannot be overridden. If a static method defined in the superclass is redefined in a subclass, the method defined in the superclass is hidden. The hidden static methods can be invoked using the syntax **SuperClassName.staticMethodName**.

11.7 True or false? You can override a private method defined in a superclass.

11.8 True or false? You can override a static method defined in a superclass.

11.9 How do you explicitly invoke a superclass's constructor from a subclass?

11.10 How do you invoke an overridden superclass method from a subclass?

11.5 Overriding vs. Overloading

Overloading means to define multiple methods with the same name but different signatures. Overriding means to provide a new implementation for a method in the subclass.

You learned about overloading methods in Section 6.8. To override a method, the method must be defined in the subclass using the same signature and the same return type.

Let us use an example to show the differences between overriding and overloading. In (a) below, the method **p(double i)** in class **A** overrides the same method defined in class **B**. In (b), however, the class **A** has two overloaded methods: **p(double i)** and **p(int i)**. The method **p(double i)** is inherited from **B**.

```java
public class Test {
  public static void main(String[] args) {
    A a = new A();
    a.p(10);
    a.p(10.0);
  }
}

class B {
  public void p(double i) {
    System.out.println(i * 2);
  }
}

class A extends B {
  // This method overrides the method in B
  public void p(double i) {
    System.out.println(i);
  }
}
```

(a)

```java
public class Test {
  public static void main(String[] args) {
    A a = new A();
    a.p(10);
    a.p(10.0);
  }
}

class B {
  public void p(double i) {
    System.out.println(i * 2);
  }
}

class A extends B {
  // This method overloads the method in B
  public void p(int i) {
    System.out.println(i);
  }
}
```

(b)

When you run the **Test** class in (a), both **a.p(10)** and **a.p(10.0)** invoke the **p(double i)** method defined in class **A** to display **10.0**. When you run the **Test** class in (b), **a.p(10)** invokes the **p(int i)** method defined in class **A** to display **10**, and **a.p(10.0)** invokes the **p(double i)** method defined in class **B** to display **20.0**.

Note the following:

- Overridden methods are in different classes related by inheritance; overloaded methods can be either in the same class or different classes related by inheritance.

- Overridden methods have the same signature and return type; overloaded methods have the same name but a different parameter list.

To avoid mistakes, you can use a special Java syntax, called *override annotation*, to place @**Override** before the method in the subclass. For example:

override annotation

```
1  public class CircleFromSimpleGeometricObject
2      extends SimpleGeometricObject {
3  // Other methods are omitted
4
5    @Override
6    public String toString() {
7      return super.toString() + "\nradius is " + radius;
8    }
9  }
```

toString in superclass

This annotation denotes that the annotated method is required to override a method in the superclass. If a method with this annotation does not override its superclass's method, the compiler will report an error. For example, if **toString** is mistyped as **tostring**, a compile error is reported. If the override annotation isn't used, the compile won't report an error. Using annotation avoids mistakes.

11.11 Identify the problems in the following code:

Check Point

```
1  public class Circle {
2    private double radius;
3
4    public Circle(double radius) {
5      radius = radius;
6    }
7
8    public double getRadius() {
9      return radius;
10   }
11
12   public double getArea() {
13     return radius * radius * Math.PI;
14   }
15 }
16
17 class B extends Circle {
18   private double length;
19
20   B(double radius, double length) {
21     Circle(radius);
22     length = length;
23   }
24
25   @Override
```

```
26      public double getArea() {
27        return getArea() * length;
28      }
29  }
```

11.12 Explain the difference between method overloading and method overriding.

11.13 If a method in a subclass has the same signature as a method in its superclass with the same return type, is the method overridden or overloaded?

11.14 If a method in a subclass has the same signature as a method in its superclass with a different return type, will this be a problem?

11.15 If a method in a subclass has the same name as a method in its superclass with different parameter types, is the method overridden or overloaded?

11.16 What is the benefit of using the `@Override` annotation?

11.6 The `Object` Class and Its `toString()` Method

Key Point

Every class in Java is descended from the `java.lang.Object` class.

If no inheritance is specified when a class is defined, the superclass of the class is `Object` by default. For example, the following two class definitions are the same:

```
public class ClassName {
    ...
}
```
Equivalent
```
public class ClassName extends Object {
    ...
}
```

Classes such as `String`, `StringBuilder`, `Loan`, and `GeometricObject` are implicitly subclasses of `Object` (as are all the main classes you have seen in this book so far). It is important to be familiar with the methods provided by the `Object` class so that you can use them in your classes. This section introduces the `toString` method in the `Object` class.

toString()

The signature of the `toString()` method is:

```
public String toString()
```

string representation

Invoking `toString()` on an object returns a string that describes the object. By default, it returns a string consisting of a class name of which the object is an instance, an at sign (@), and the object's memory address in hexadecimal. For example, consider the following code for the `Loan` class defined in Listing 10.2:

```
Loan loan = new Loan();
System.out.println(loan.toString());
```

The output for this code displays something like `Loan@15037e5`. This message is not very helpful or informative. Usually you should override the `toString` method so that it returns a descriptive string representation of the object. For example, the `toString` method in the `Object` class was overridden in the `GeometricObject` class in lines 46–49 in Listing 11.1 as follows:

```
public String toString() {
  return "created on " + dateCreated + "\ncolor: " + color +
      " and filled: " + filled;
}
```

Note

You can also pass an object to invoke `System.out.println(object)` or `System.out.print(object)`. This is equivalent to invoking `System.out.println(object.toString())` or `System.out.print(object.toString())`. Thus, you could replace `System.out.println(loan.toString())` with `System.out.println(loan)`.

print object

11.7 Polymorphism

Polymorphism means that a variable of a supertype can refer to a subtype object.

🔑 **Key Point**

The three pillars of object-oriented programming are encapsulation, inheritance, and polymorphism. You have already learned the first two. This section introduces polymorphism.

First, let us define two useful terms: subtype and supertype. A class defines a type. A type defined by a subclass is called a *subtype*, and a type defined by its superclass is called a *supertype*. Therefore, you can say that `Circle` is a subtype of `GeometricObject` and `GeometricObject` is a supertype for `Circle`.

subtype
supertype

The inheritance relationship enables a subclass to inherit features from its superclass with additional new features. A subclass is a specialization of its superclass; every instance of a subclass is also an instance of its superclass, but not vice versa. For example, every circle is a geometric object, but not every geometric object is a circle. Therefore, you can always pass an instance of a subclass to a parameter of its superclass type. Consider the code in Listing 11.5.

LISTING 11.5 PolymorphismDemo.java

```
1  public class PolymorphismDemo {
2    /** Main method */
3    public static void main(String[] args) {
4      // Display circle and rectangle properties
5      displayObject(new CircleFromSimpleGeometricObject
6              (1, "red", false));
7      displayObject(new RectangleFromSimpleGeometricObject
8              (1, 1, "black", true));
9    }
10
11   /** Display geometric object properties */
12   public static void displayObject(SimpleGeometricObject object) {
13     System.out.println("Created on " + object.getDateCreated() +
14       ". Color is " + object.getColor());
15   }
16 }
```

polymorphic call

polymorphic call

```
Created on Mon Mar 09 19:25:20 EDT 2011. Color is red
Created on Mon Mar 09 19:25:20 EDT 2011. Color is black
```

The method `displayObject` (line 12) takes a parameter of the `GeometricObject` type. You can invoke `displayObject` by passing any instance of `GeometricObject` (e.g., `new CircleFromSimpleGeometricObject(1, "red", false)` and `new RectangleFromSimpleGeometricObject(1, 1, "black", false)` in lines 5–8). An object of a subclass can be used wherever its superclass object is used. This is commonly known as *polymorphism* (from a Greek word meaning "many forms"). In simple terms, polymorphism means that a variable of a supertype can refer to a subtype object.

what is polymorphism?

11.8 Dynamic Binding

Key Point

A method can be implemented in several classes along the inheritance chain. The JVM decides which method is invoked at runtime.

A method can be defined in a superclass and overridden in its subclass. For example, the `toString()` method is defined in the `Object` class and overridden in `GeometricObject`. Consider the following code:

```
Object o = new GeometricObject();
System.out.println(o.toString());
```

Which `toString()` method is invoked by `o`? To answer this question, we first introduce two terms: declared type and actual type. A variable must be declared a type. The type that declares a variable is called the variable's *declared type*. Here `o`'s declared type is `Object`. A variable of a reference type can hold a `null` value or a reference to an instance of the declared type. The instance may be created using the constructor of the declared type or its subtype. The *actual type* of the variable is the actual class for the object referenced by the variable. Here `o`'s actual type is `GeometricObject`, because `o` references an object created using `new GeometricObject()`. Which `toString()` method is invoked by `o` is determined by `o`'s actual type. This is known as *dynamic binding*.

declared type

actual type

dynamic binding

Dynamic binding works as follows: Suppose an object `o` is an instance of classes $C_1, C_2, \ldots, C_{n-1}$, and C_n, where C_1 is a subclass of C_2, C_2 is a subclass of $C_3, \ldots,$ and C_{n-1} is a subclass of C_n, as shown in Figure 11.2. That is, C_n is the most general class, and C_1 is the most specific class. In Java, C_n is the `Object` class. If `o` invokes a method `p`, the JVM searches for the implementation of the method `p` in $C_1, C_2, \ldots, C_{n-1}$, and C_n, in this order, until it is found. Once an implementation is found, the search stops and the first-found implementation is invoked.

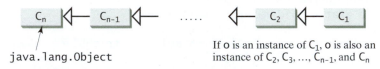

C_n ◁— C_{n-1} ◁— ..... ◁— C_2 ◁— C_1

java.lang.Object

If `o` is an instance of C_1, `o` is also an instance of $C_2, C_3, \ldots, C_{n-1}$, and C_n

FIGURE 11.2 The method to be invoked is dynamically bound at runtime.

VideoNote

Polymorphism and dynamic binding demo

Listing 11.6 gives an example to demonstrate dynamic binding.

LISTING 11.6 DynamicBindingDemo.java

polymorphic call

dynamic binding

override toString()

```java
 1  public class DynamicBindingDemo {
 2    public static void main(String[] args) {
 3      m(new GraduateStudent());
 4      m(new Student());
 5      m(new Person());
 6      m(new Object());
 7    }
 8
 9    public static void m(Object x) {
10      System.out.println(x.toString());
11    }
12  }
13
14  class GraduateStudent extends Student {
15  }
16
17  class Student extends Person {
18    @Override
19    public String toString() {
```

```
20        return "Student" ;
21      }
22    }
23
24    class Person extends Object {
25      @Override
26      public String toString() {
27        return "Person" ;
28      }
29    }
```

override toString()

```
Student
Student
Person
java.lang.Object@130c19b
```

Method **m** (line 9) takes a parameter of the **Object** type. You can invoke **m** with any object (e.g., **new GraduateStudent()**, **new Student()**, **new Person()**, and **new Object()**) in lines 3–6).

When the method **m(Object x)** is executed, the argument **x**'s **toString** method is invoked. **x** may be an instance of **GraduateStudent**, **Student**, **Person**, or **Object**. The classes **GraduateStudent**, **Student**, **Person**, and **Object** have their own implementations of the **toString** method. Which implementation is used will be determined by **x**'s actual type at runtime. Invoking **m(new GraduateStudent())** (line 3) causes the **toString** method defined in the **Student** class to be invoked.

Invoking **m(new Student())** (line 4) causes the **toString** method defined in the **Student** class to be invoked; invoking **m(new Person())** (line 5) causes the **toString** method defined in the **Person** class to be invoked; and invoking **m(new Object())** (line 6) causes the **toString** method defined in the **Object** class to be invoked.

Matching a method signature and binding a method implementation are two separate issues. The *declared type* of the reference variable decides which method to match at compile time. The compiler finds a matching method according to the parameter type, number of parameters, and order of the parameters at compile time. A method may be implemented in several classes along the inheritance chain. The JVM dynamically binds the implementation of the method at runtime, decided by the actual type of the variable.

matching vs. binding

11.17 What is polymorphism? What is dynamic binding?

11.18 Describe the difference between method matching and method binding.

11.19 Can you assign **new int[50]**, **new Integer[50]**, **new String[50]**, or **new Object[50]**, into a variable of **Object[]** type?

11.20 What is wrong in the following code?

Check
Point

```
1     public class Test {
2       public static void main(String[] args) {
3         Integer[] list1 = {12, 24, 55, 1};
4         Double[] list2 = {12.4, 24.0, 55.2, 1.0};
5         int[] list3 = {1, 2, 3};
6         printArray(list1);
7         printArray(list2);
8         printArray(list3);
9       }
10
11      public static void printArray(Object[] list) {
12        for (Object o: list)
```

```
13              System.out.print(o + " ");
14          System.out.println();
15      }
16  }
```

11.21 Show the output of the following code:

(a)
```
public class Test {
  public static void main(String[] args) {
    new Person().printPerson();
    new Student().printPerson();
  }
}

class Student extends Person {
  @Override
  public String getInfo() {
    return "Student";
  }
}

class Person {
  public String getInfo() {
    return "Person";
  }

  public void printPerson() {
    System.out.println(getInfo());
  }
}
```

(b)
```
public class Test {
  public static void main(String[] args) {
    new Person().printPerson();
    new Student().printPerson();
  }
}

class Student extends Person {
  private String getInfo() {
    return "Student";
  }
}

class Person {
  private String getInfo() {
    return "Person";
  }

  public void printPerson() {
    System.out.println(getInfo());
  }
}
```

11.22 Show the output of following program:

```
1  public class Test {
2    public static void main(String[] args) {
3      A a = new A(3);
4    }
5  }
6
7  class A extends B {
8    public A(int t) {
9      System.out.println("A's constructor is invoked");
10   }
11 }
12
13 class B {
14   public B() {
15     System.out.println("B's constructor is invoked");
16   }
17 }
```

Is the no-arg constructor of **Object** invoked when **new A(3)** is invoked?

11.23 Show the output of following program:

```
public class Test {
  public static void main(String[] args) {
    new A();
    new B();
  }
}
```

```
class A {
  int i = 7;

  public A() {
    setI(20);
    System.out.println("i from A is " + i);
  }

  public void setI(int i) {
    this.i = 2 * i;
  }
}

class B extends A {
  public B() {
    System.out.println("i from B is " + i);
  }

  public void setI(int i) {
    this.i = 3 * i;
  }
}
```

11.9 Casting Objects and the **instanceof** Operator

One object reference can be typecast into another object reference. This is called casting object.

Key Point

In the preceding section, the statement

casting object

```
m(new Student());
```

assigns the object **new Student()** to a parameter of the **Object** type. This statement is equivalent to

```
Object o = new Student(); // Implicit casting
m(o);
```

The statement **Object o = new Student()**, known as *implicit casting*, is legal because an instance of **Student** is an instance of **Object**.

implicit casting

Suppose you want to assign the object reference **o** to a variable of the **Student** type using the following statement:

```
Student b = o;
```

In this case a compile error would occur. Why does the statement **Object o = new Student()** work but **Student b = o** doesn't? The reason is that a **Student** object is always an instance of **Object**, but an **Object** is not necessarily an instance of **Student**. Even though you can see that **o** is really a **Student** object, the compiler is not clever enough to know it. To tell the compiler that **o** is a **Student** object, use *explicit casting*. The syntax is similar to the one used for casting among primitive data types. Enclose the target object type in parentheses and place it before the object to be cast, as follows:

explicit casting

```
Student b = (Student)o; // Explicit casting
```

It is always possible to cast an instance of a subclass to a variable of a superclass (known as *upcasting*), because an instance of a subclass is *always* an instance of its superclass. When casting an instance of a superclass to a variable of its subclass (known as *downcasting*), explicit

upcasting
downcasting

casting must be used to confirm your intention to the compiler with the **(SubclassName)** cast notation. For the casting to be successful, you must make sure that the object to be cast is an instance of the subclass. If the superclass object is not an instance of the subclass, a runtime ***ClassCastException*** occurs. For example, if an object is not an instance of **Student**, it cannot be cast into a variable of **Student**. It is a good practice, therefore, to ensure that the object is an instance of another object before attempting a casting. This can be accomplished by using the ***instanceof*** operator. Consider the following code:

ClassCastException

instanceof

```
Object myObject = new Circle();
... // Some lines of code
/** Perform casting if myObject is an instance of Circle */
if (myObject instanceof Circle) {
  System.out.println("The circle diameter is " +
    ((Circle)myObject).getDiameter());
  ...
}
```

You may be wondering why casting is necessary. The variable **myObject** is declared **Object**. The *declared type* decides which method to match at compile time. Using **myObject.getDiameter()** would cause a compile error, because the **Object** class does not have the **getDiameter** method. The compiler cannot find a match for **myObject.getDiameter()**. Therefore, it is necessary to cast **myObject** into the **Circle** type to tell the compiler that **myObject** is also an instance of **Circle**.

Why not define **myObject** as a **Circle** type in the first place? To enable generic programming, it is a good practice to define a variable with a supertype, which can accept an object of any subtype.

Note

lowercase keywords

instanceof is a Java keyword. Every letter in a Java keyword is in lowercase.

Tip

casting analogy

To help understand casting, you may also consider the analogy of fruit, apple, and orange, with the **Fruit** class as the superclass for **Apple** and **Orange**. An apple is a fruit, so you can always safely assign an instance of **Apple** to a variable for **Fruit**. However, a fruit is not necessarily an apple, so you have to use explicit casting to assign an instance of **Fruit** to a variable of **Apple**.

Listing 11.7 demonstrates polymorphism and casting. The program creates two objects (lines 5–6), a circle and a rectangle, and invokes the **displayObject** method to display them (lines 9–10). The **displayObject** method displays the area and diameter if the object is a circle (line 15), and the area if the object is a rectangle (lines 21–22).

LISTING 11.7 CastingDemo.java

```
 1  public class CastingDemo {
 2    /** Main method */
 3    public static void main(String[] args) {
 4      // Create and initialize two objects
 5      Object object1 = new CircleFromSimpleGeometricObject(1);
 6      Object object2 = new RectangleFromSimpleGeometricObject(1, 1);
 7
 8      // Display circle and rectangle
 9      displayObject(object1);
10      displayObject(object2);
11    }
12
```

```
13      /** A method for displaying an object */
14      public static void displayObject(Object object) {
15        if (object instanceof CircleFromSimpleGeometricObject) {
16          System.out.println("The circle area is " +
17            ((CircleFromSimpleGeometricObject)object).getArea());          polymorphic call
18          System.out.println("The circle diameter is " +
19            ((CircleFromSimpleGeometricObject)object).getDiameter());
20        }
21        else if (object instanceof
22                      RectangleFromSimpleGeometricObject) {
23          System.out.println("The rectangle area is " +
24            ((RectangleFromSimpleGeometricObject)object).getArea());        polymorphic call
25        }
26      }
27   }
```

```
The circle area is 3.141592653589793
The circle diameter is 2.0
The rectangle area is 1.0
```

The **displayObject(Object object)** method is an example of generic programming. It can be invoked by passing any instance of **Object**.

The program uses implicit casting to assign a **Circle** object to **object1** and a **Rectangle** object to **object2** (lines 5–6), then invokes the **displayObject** method to display the information on these objects (lines 9–10).

In the **displayObject** method (lines 14–26), explicit casting is used to cast the object to **Circle** if the object is an instance of **Circle**, and the methods **getArea** and **getDiameter** are used to display the area and diameter of the circle.

Casting can be done only when the source object is an instance of the target class. The program uses the **instanceof** operator to ensure that the source object is an instance of the target class before performing a casting (line 15).

Explicit casting to **Circle** (lines 17, 19) and to **Rectangle** (line 24) is necessary because the **getArea** and **getDiameter** methods are not available in the **Object** class.

Caution

The object member access operator (.) precedes the casting operator. Use parentheses   precedes casting
to ensure that casting is done before the . operator, as in

```
((Circle)object).getArea();
```

Casting a primitive type value is different from casting an object reference. Casting a primitive type value returns a new value. For example:

```
int age = 45;
byte newAge = (byte)age; // A new value is assigned to newAge
```

However, casting an object reference does not create a new object. For example:

```
Object o = new Circle();
Circle c = (Circle)o; // No new object is created
```

Now reference variables **o** and **c** point to the same object.

11.24 Indicate true or false for the following statements:

■ You can always successfully cast an instance of a subclass to a superclass.

■ You can always successfully cast an instance of a superclass to a subclass.

11.25 For the `GeometricObject` and `Circle` classes in Listings 11.1 and 11.2, answer the following questions:

a. Assume are `circle` and `object` created as follows:
```
Circle circle = new Circle(1);
GeometricObject object = new GeometricObject();
```

Are the following Boolean expressions true or false?
```
(circle instanceof GeometricObject)
(object instanceof GeometricObject)
(circle instanceof Circle)
(object instanceof Circle)
```

b. Can the following statements be compiled?
```
Circle circle = new Circle(5);
GeometricObject object = circle;
```

c. Can the following statements be compiled?
```
GeometricObject object = new GeometricObject();
Circle circle = (Circle)object;
```

11.26 Suppose that `Fruit`, `Apple`, `Orange`, `GoldenDelicious`, and `McIntosh` are defined in the following inheritance hierarchy:

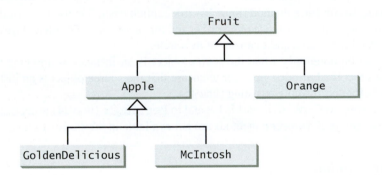

Assume that the following code is given:

```
Fruit fruit = new GoldenDelicious();
Orange orange = new Orange();
```

Answer the following questions:

a. Is `fruit instanceof Fruit`?

b. Is `fruit instanceof Orange`?

c. Is `fruit instanceof Apple`?

d. Is `fruit instanceof GoldenDelicious`?

e. Is `fruit instanceof McIntosh`?

f. Is `orange instanceof Orange`?

g. Is `orange instanceof Fruit`?

h. Is `orange instanceof Apple`?

i. Suppose the method `makeAppleCider` is defined in the `Apple` class. Can `fruit` invoke this method? Can `orange` invoke this method?

j. Suppose the method `makeOrangeJuice` is defined in the `Orange` class. Can `orange` invoke this method? Can `fruit` invoke this method?

k. Is the statement `Orange p = new Apple()` legal?

l. Is the statement `McIntosh p = new Apple()` legal?

m. Is the statement `Apple p = new McIntosh()` legal?

11.27 What is wrong in the following code?

```
1  public class Test {
2    public static void main(String[] args) {
3      Object fruit = new Fruit();
4      Object apple = (Apple)fruit;
5    }
6  }
7
8  class Apple extends Fruit {
9  }
10
11  class Fruit {
12  }
```

11.10 The **Object**'s **equals** Method

Like the `toString()` *method, the* `equals(Object)` *method is another useful method defined in the* `Object` *class.*

Key Point

Another method defined in the `Object` class that is often used is the `equals` method. Its signature is

`public boolean equals(Object o)`

This method tests whether two objects are equal. The syntax for invoking it is:

`object1.equals(object2);`

The default implementation of the `equals` method in the `Object` class is:

```
public boolean equals(Object obj) {
  return (this == obj);
}
```

This implementation checks whether two reference variables point to the same object using the `==` operator. You should override this method in your custom class to test whether two distinct objects have the same content.

The `equals` method is overridden in many classes in the Java API, such as `java.lang.String` and `java.util.Date`, to compare whether the contents of two objects are equal. You have already used the `equals` method to compare two strings in Section 4.4.7, The `String` Class. The `equals` method in the `String` class is inherited from the `Object` class and is overridden in the `String` class to test whether two strings are identical in content.

You can override the **equals** method in the **Circle** class to compare whether two circles are equal based on their radius as follows:

```
public boolean equals(Object o) {
  if (o instanceof Circle)
    return radius == ((Circle)o).radius;
  else
    return this == o;
}
```

== vs. equals

Note

The == comparison operator is used for comparing two primitive data type values or for determining whether two objects have the same references. The **equals** method is intended to test whether two objects have the same contents, provided that the method is overridden in the defining class of the objects. The == operator is stronger than the **equals** method, in that the == operator checks whether the two reference variables refer to the same object.

Caution

Using the signature **equals(SomeClassName obj)** (e.g., **equals(Circle c)**) to override the **equals** method in a subclass is a common mistake. You should use **equals(Object obj)**. See CheckPoint Question 11.29.

equals(Object)

11.28 Does every object have a **toString** method and an **equals** method? Where do they come from? How are they used? Is it appropriate to override these methods?

11.29 When overriding the **equals** method, a common mistake is mistyping its signature in the subclass. For example, the **equals** method is incorrectly written as **equals(Circle circle)**, as shown in (a) in following the code; instead, it should be **equals(Object circle)**, as shown in (b). Show the output of running class **Test** with the **Circle** class in (a) and in (b), respectively.

```
public class Test {
  public static void main(String[] args) {
    Object circle1 = new Circle();
    Object circle2 = new Circle();
    System.out.println(circle1.equals(circle2));
  }
}
```

```
class Circle {
  double radius;

  public boolean equals(Circle circle) {
    return this.radius == circle.radius;
  }
}
```

(a)

```
class Circle {
  double radius;

  public boolean equals(Object circle) {
    return this.radius ==
      ((Circle)circle).radius;
  }
}
```

(b)

If **Object** is replaced by **Circle** in the **Test** class, what would be the output to run **Test** using the **Circle** class in (a) and (b), respectively?

11.11 The **ArrayList** Class

*An **ArrayList** object can be used to store a list of objects.*

VideoNote

The ArrayList class

Now we are ready to introduce a very useful class for storing objects. You can create an array to store objects. But, once the array is created, its size is fixed. Java provides the **ArrayList** class, which can be used to store an unlimited number of objects. Figure 11.3 shows some methods in **ArrayList**.

java.util.ArrayList<E>	
+ArrayList()	Creates an empty list.
+add(o: E): void	Appends a new element o at the end of this list.
+add(index: int, o: E): void	Adds a new element o at the specified index in this list.
+clear(): void	Removes all the elements from this list.
+contains(o: Object): boolean	Returns true if this list contains the element o.
+get(index: int): E	Returns the element from this list at the specified index.
+indexOf(o: Object): int	Returns the index of the first matching element in this list.
+isEmpty(): boolean	Returns true if this list contains no elements.
+lastIndexOf(o: Object): int	Returns the index of the last matching element in this list.
+remove(o: Object): boolean	Removes the first element o from this list. Returns true if an element is removed.
+size(): int	Returns the number of elements in this list.
+remove(index: int): boolean	Removes the element at the specified index. Returns true if an element is removed.
+set(index: int, o: E): E	Sets the element at the specified index.

FIGURE 11.3   An **ArrayList** stores an unlimited number of objects.

ArrayList is known as a generic class with a generic type **E**. You can specify a concrete type to replace **E** when creating an **ArrayList**. For example, the following statement creates an **ArrayList** and assigns its reference to variable **cities**. This **ArrayList** object can be used to store strings.

```
ArrayList<String> cities = new ArrayList<String>();
```

The following statement creates an **ArrayList** and assigns its reference to variable **dates**. This **ArrayList** object can be used to store dates.

```
ArrayList<java.util.Date> dates = new ArrayList<java.util.Date> ();
```

Note

Since JDK 7, the statement

```
ArrayList<AConcreteType> list = new ArrayList<AConcreteType>();
```

can be simplified by

```
ArrayList<AConcreteType> list = new ArrayList<>();
```

The concrete type is no longer required in the constructor thanks to a feature called *type inference*. The compiler is able to infer the type from the variable declaration. More discussions on generics including how to define custom generic classes and methods will be introduced in Chapter 19, Generics.   type inference

Listing 11.8 gives an example of using **ArrayList** to store objects.

LISTING 11.8   TestArrayList.java

```
1  import java.util.ArrayList;
2
```

import ArrayList

```
 3  public class TestArrayList {
 4    public static void main(String[] args) {
 5      // Create a list to store cities
 6      ArrayList<String> cityList = new ArrayList<>();
 7
 8      // Add some cities in the list
 9      cityList.add("London");
10      // cityList now contains [London]
11      cityList.add("Denver");
12      // cityList now contains [London, Denver]
13      cityList.add("Paris");
14      // cityList now contains [London, Denver, Paris]
15      cityList.add("Miami");
16      // cityList now contains [London, Denver, Paris, Miami]
17      cityList.add("Seoul");
18      // Contains [London, Denver, Paris, Miami, Seoul]
19      cityList.add("Tokyo");
20      // Contains [London, Denver, Paris, Miami, Seoul, Tokyo]
21
22      System.out.println("List size? " + cityList.size());
23      System.out.println("Is Miami in the list? " +
24        cityList.contains("Miami"));
25      System.out.println("The location of Denver in the list? "
26        + cityList.indexOf("Denver"));
27      System.out.println("Is the list empty? " +
28        cityList.isEmpty()); // Print false
29
30      // Insert a new city at index 2
31      cityList.add(2, "Xian");
32      // Contains [London, Denver, Xian, Paris, Miami, Seoul, Tokyo]
33
34      // Remove a city from the list
35      cityList.remove("Miami");
36      // Contains [London, Denver, Xian, Paris, Seoul, Tokyo]
37
38      // Remove a city at index 1
39      cityList.remove(1);
40      // Contains [London, Xian, Paris, Seoul, Tokyo]
41
42      // Display the contents in the list
43      System.out.println(cityList.toString());
44
45      // Display the contents in the list in reverse order
46      for (int i = cityList.size() - 1; i >= 0; i--)
47        System.out.print(cityList.get(i) + " ");
48      System.out.println();
49
50      // Create a list to store two circles
51      ArrayList<CircleFromSimpleGeometricObject> list
52        = new ArrayList<>();
53
54      // Add two circles
55      list.add(new CircleFromSimpleGeometricObject(2));
56      list.add(new CircleFromSimpleGeometricObject(3));
57
58      // Display the area of the first circle in the list
59      System.out.println("The area of the circle? " +
60        list.get(0).getArea());
61    }
62  }
```

Margin notes:
- create ArrayList (line 6)
- add element (line 9)
- list size (line 22)
- contains element? (line 24)
- element index (line 26)
- is empty? (line 28)
- remove element (line 35)
- remove element (line 39)
- toString() (line 43)
- get element (line 47)
- create ArrayList (line 52)

```
List size? 6
Is Miami in the list? True
The location of Denver in the list? 1
Is the list empty? false
[London, Xian, Paris, Seoul, Tokyo]
Tokyo Seoul Paris Xian London
The area of the circle? 12.566370614359172
```

Since the **ArrayList** is in the **java.util** package, it is imported in line 1. The program creates an **ArrayList** of strings using its no-arg constructor and assigns the reference to **cityList** (line 6). The **add** method (lines 9–19) adds strings to the end of list. So, after **cityList.add("London")** (line 9), the list contains

add(Object)

    [London]

After **cityList.add("Denver")** (line 11), the list contains

    [London, Denver]

After adding **Paris**, **Miami**, **Seoul**, and **Tokyo** (lines 13–19), the list contains

    [London, Denver, Paris, Miami, Seoul, Tokyo]

Invoking **size()** (line 22) returns the size of the list, which is currently **6**. Invoking **contains("Miami")** (line 24) checks whether the object is in the list. In this case, it returns **true**, since **Miami** is in the list. Invoking **indexOf("Denver")** (line 26) returns the index of **Denver** in the list, which is **1**. If **Denver** were not in the list, it would return **-1**. The **isEmpty()** method (line 28) checks whether the list is empty. It returns **false**, since the list is not empty.

size()

    The statement **cityList.add(2, "Xian")** (line 31) inserts an object into the list at the specified index. After this statement, the list becomes

add(index, Object)

    [London, Denver, Xian, Paris, Miami, Seoul, Tokyo]

The statement **cityList.remove("Miami")** (line 35) removes the object from the list. After this statement, the list becomes

remove(Object)

    [London, Denver, Xian, Paris, Seoul, Tokyo]

The statement **cityList.remove(1)** (line 39) removes the object at the specified index from the list. After this statement, the list becomes

remove(index)

    [London, Xian, Paris, Seoul, Tokyo]

The statement in line 43 is same as

    System.out.println(cityList);

The **toString()** method returns a string representation of the list in the form of **[e0.toString(), e1.toString(), ..., ek.toString()]**, where **e0**, **e1**, ..., and **ek** are the elements in the list.

toString()

    The **get(index)** method (line 47) returns the object at the specified index.

get(index)

    ArrayList objects can be used like arrays, but there are many differences. Table 11.1 lists their similarities and differences.

array vs. ArrayList

    Once an array is created, its size is fixed. You can access an array element using the square-bracket notation (e.g., **a[index]**). When an **ArrayList** is created, its size is **0**.

TABLE 11.1 Differences and Similarities between Arrays and `ArrayList`

Operation	Array	ArrayList
Creating an array/ArrayList	`String[] a = new String[10]`	`ArrayList<String> list = new ArrayList<>();`
Accessing an element	`a[index]`	`list.get(index);`
Updating an element	`a[index] = "London";`	`list.set(index, "London");`
Returning size	`a.length`	`list.size();`
Adding a new element		`list.add("London");`
Inserting a new element		`list.add(index, "London");`
Removing an element		`list.remove(index);`
Removing an element		`list.remove(Object);`
Removing all elements		`list.clear();`

You cannot use the **get(index)** and **set(index, element)** methods if the element is not in the list. It is easy to add, insert, and remove elements in a list, but it is rather complex to add, insert, and remove elements in an array. You have to write code to manipulate the array in order to perform these operations. Note that you can sort an array using the **java.util.Arrays.sort(array)** method. To sort an array list, use the **java.util.Collections.sort(arraylist)** method.

Suppose you want to create an **ArrayList** for storing integers. Can you use the following code to create a list?

```
ArrayList<int> list = new ArrayList<>();
```

No. This will not work because the elements stored in an **ArrayList** must be of an object type. You cannot use a primitive data type such as **int** to replace a generic type. However, you can create an **ArrayList** for storing **Integer** objects as follows:

```
ArrayList<Integer> list = new ArrayList<>();
```

Listing 11.9 gives a program that prompts the user to enter a sequence of numbers and displays the distinct numbers in the sequence. Assume that the input ends with **0** and **0** is not counted as a number in the sequence.

LISTING 11.9 DistinctNumbers.java

```
1  import java.util.ArrayList;
2  import java.util.Scanner;
3
4  public class DistinctNumbers {
5    public static void main(String[] args) {
6      ArrayList<Integer> list = new ArrayList<>();
7
8      Scanner input = new Scanner(System.in);
9      System.out.print("Enter integers (input ends with 0): ");
10     int value;
11
12     do {
13       value = input.nextInt(); // Read a value from the input
14
15       if (!list.contains(value) && value != 0)
16         list.add(value); // Add the value if it is not in the list
17     } while (value != 0);
```

create an array list

contained in list?
add to list

```
18
19      // Display the distinct numbers
20      for (int i = 0; i < list.size(); i++)
21        System.out.print(list.get(i) + " ");
22  }
23  }
```

```
Enter numbers (input ends with 0): 1 2 3 2 1 6 3 4 5 4 5 1 2 3 0  ↵Enter
The distinct numbers are: 1 2 3 6 4 5
```

The program creates an **ArrayList** for **Integer** objects (line 6) and repeatedly reads a value in the loop (lines 12–17). For each value, if it is not in the list (line 15), add it to the list (line 16). You can rewrite this program using an array to store the elements rather than using an **ArrayList**. However, it is simpler to implement this program using an **ArrayList** for two reasons.

- First, the size of an **ArrayList** is flexible so you don't have to specify its size in advance. When creating an array, its size must be specified.

- Second, **ArrayList** contains many useful methods. For example, you can test whether an element is in the list using the **contains** method. If you use an array, you have to write additional code to implement this method.

You can traverse the elements in an array using a foreach loop. The elements in an array list can also be traversed using a foreach loop using the following syntax:

```
for (elementType element: arrayList) {
  // Process the element
}
```

For example, you can replace the code in lines 20-21 using the following code:

```
for (int number: list)
  System.out.print(number + " ");
```

11.30 How do you do the following?

a. Create an **ArrayList** for storing double values?

b. Append an object to a list?

c. Insert an object at the beginning of a list?

d. Find the number of objects in a list?

e. Remove a given object from a list?

f. Remove the last object from the list?

g. Check whether a given object is in a list?

h. Retrieve an object at a specified index from a list?

11.31 Identify the errors in the following code.

```
ArrayList<String> list = new ArrayList<>();
list.add("Denver");
list.add("Austin");
list.add(new java.util.Date());
String city = list.get(0);
list.set(3, "Dallas");
System.out.println(list.get(3));
```

11.32 Suppose the `ArrayList list` contains {`"Dallas"`, `"Dallas"`, `"Houston"`, `"Dallas"`}. What is the list after invoking `list.remove("Dallas")` one time? Does the following code correctly remove all elements with value `"Dallas"` from the list? If not, correct the code.

```
for (int i = 0; i < list.size(); i++)
  list.remove("Dallas");
```

11.33 Explain why the following code displays `[1, 3]` rather than `[2, 3]`.

```
ArrayList<Integer> list = new ArrayList<>();
list.add(1);
list.add(2);
list.add(3);
list.remove(1);
System.out.println(list);
```

11.34 Explain why the following code is wrong.

```
ArrayList<Double> list = new ArrayList<>();
list.add(1);
```

11.12 Useful Methods for Lists

Key Point

Java provides the methods for creating a list from an array, for sorting a list, and finding maximum and minimum element in a list, and for shuffling a list.

array to array list

Often you need to create an array list from an array of objects or vice versa. You can write the code using a loop to accomplish this, but an easy way is to use the methods in the Java API. Here is an example to create an array list from an array:

```
String[] array = {"red", "green", "blue"};
ArrayList<String> list = new ArrayList<>(Arrays.asList(array));
```

array list to array

The static method `asList` in the `Arrays` class returns a list that is passed to the `ArrayList` constructor for creating an `ArrayList`. Conversely, you can use the following code to create an array of objects from an array list.

```
String[] array1 = new String[list.size()];
list.toArray(array1);
```

Invoking `list.toArray(array1)` copies the contents from `list` to `array1`.

sort a list

If the elements in a list are comparable such as integers, double, or strings, you can use the static `sort` method in the `java.util.Collections` class to sort the elements. Here are examples:

```
Integer[] array = {3, 5, 95, 4, 15, 34, 3, 6, 5};
ArrayList<Integer> list = new ArrayList<>(Arrays.asList(array));
java.util.Collections.sort(list);
System.out.println(list);
```

max and min methods

You can use the static `max` and `min` in the `java.util.Collections` class to return the maximum and minimal element in a list. Here are examples:

```
Integer[] array = {3, 5, 95, 4, 15, 34, 3, 6, 5};
ArrayList<Integer> list = new ArrayList<>(Arrays.asList(array));
System.out.println(java.util.Collections.max(list));
System.out.println(java.util.Collections.min(list));
```

shuffle method

You can use the static **shuffle** method in the **java.util.Collections** class to perform a random shuffle for the elements in a list. Here are examples:

```
Integer[] array = {3, 5, 95, 4, 15, 34, 3, 6, 5};
ArrayList<Integer> list = new ArrayList<>(Arrays.asList(array));
java.util.Collections.shuffle(list);
System.out.println(list);
```

11.35 Correct errors in the following statements:

```
int[] array = {3, 5, 95, 4, 15, 34, 3, 6, 5};
ArrayList<Integer> list = new ArrayList<>(Arrays.asList(array));
```

Check
Point

11.36 Correct errors in the following statements:

```
int[] array = {3, 5, 95, 4, 15, 34, 3, 6, 5};
System.out.println(java.util.Collections.max(array));
```

11.13 Case Study: A Custom Stack Class

This section designs a stack class for holding objects.

Section 10.6 presented a stack class for storing **int** values. This section introduces a stack class to store objects. You can use an **ArrayList** to implement **Stack**, as shown in Listing 11.10. The UML diagram for the class is shown in Figure 11.4.

Key
Point

VideoNote
The MyStack class

MyStack	
-list: ArrayList<Object>	A list to store elements.
+isEmpty(): boolean	Returns true if this stack is empty.
+getSize(): int	Returns the number of elements in this stack.
+peek(): Object	Returns the top element in this stack without removing it.
+pop(): Object	Returns and removes the top element in this stack.
+push(o: Object): void	Adds a new element to the top of this stack.

FIGURE 11.4 The MyStack class encapsulates the stack storage and provides the operations for manipulating the stack.

LISTING 11.10 MyStack.java

```
1  import java.util.ArrayList;
2
3  public class MyStack {
4    private ArrayList<Object> list = new ArrayList<>();
5
6    public boolean isEmpty() {
7      return list.isEmpty();
8    }
9
10   public int getSize() {
11     return list.size();
12   }
13
14   public Object peek() {
15     return list.get(getSize() - 1);
16   }
```

array list

stack empty?

get stack size

peek stack

remove

```
17
18    public Object pop() {
19        Object o = list.get(getSize() - 1);
20        list.remove(getSize() - 1);
21        return o;
22    }
23
```

push

```
24    public void push(Object o) {
25        list.add(o);
26    }
27
28    @Override
29    public String toString() {
30        return "stack: " + list.toString();
31    }
32 }
```

An array list is created to store the elements in the stack (line 4). The **isEmpty()** method (lines 6–8) returns **list.isEmpty()**. The **getSize()** method (lines 10–12) returns **list.size()**. The **peek()** method (lines 14–16) retrieves the element at the top of the stack without removing it. The end of the list is the top of the stack. The **pop()** method (lines 18–22) removes the top element from the stack and returns it. The **push(Object element)** method (lines 24–26) adds the specified element to the stack. The **toString()** method (lines 28–31) defined in the **Object** class is overridden to display the contents of the stack by invoking **list.toString()**. The **toString()** method implemented in **ArrayList** returns a string representation of all the elements in an array list.

> **Design Guide**
>
> In Listing 11.10, **MyStack** contains **ArrayList**. The relationship between **MyStack** and **ArrayList** is *composition*. While inheritance models an *is-a* relationship, composition models a *has-a* relationship. You could also implement **MyStack** as a subclass of **ArrayList** (see Programming Exercise 11.10). Using composition is better, however, because it enables you to define a completely new stack class without inheriting the unnecessary and inappropriate methods from **ArrayList**.

composition
is-a
has-a

11.14 The **protected** Data and Methods

Key
Point

A protected member of a class can be accessed from a subclass.

So far you have used the **private** and **public** keywords to specify whether data fields and methods can be accessed from outside of the class. Private members can be accessed only from inside of the class, and public members can be accessed from any other classes.

Often it is desirable to allow subclasses to access data fields or methods defined in the superclass, but not to allow nonsubclasses to access these data fields and methods. To accomplish this, you can use the **protected** keyword. This way you can access protected data fields or methods in a superclass from its subclasses.

why protected?

The modifiers **private**, **protected**, and **public** are known as *visibility* or *accessibility modifiers* because they specify how classes and class members are accessed. The visibility of these modifiers increases in this order:

Visibility increases

$\longrightarrow$

private, default (no modifier), protected, public

Table 11.2 summarizes the accessibility of the members in a class. Figure 11.5 illustrates how a public, protected, default, and private datum or method in class **C1** can be accessed from a class **C2** in the same package, from a subclass **C3** in the same package, from a subclass **C4** in a different package, and from a class **C5** in a different package.

Use the `private` modifier to hide the members of the class completely so that they cannot be accessed directly from outside the class. Use no modifiers (the default) in order to allow the members of the class to be accessed directly from any class within the same package but not from other packages. Use the `protected` modifier to enable the members of the class to be accessed by the subclasses in any package or classes in the same package. Use the `public` modifier to enable the members of the class to be accessed by any class.

TABLE 11.2 Data and Methods Visibility

Modifier on members in a class	Accessed from the same class	Accessed from the same package	Accessed from a subclass in a different package	Accessed from a different package
public	✓	✓	✓	✓
protected	✓	✓	✓	–
default (no modifier)	✓	✓	–	–
private	✓	–	–	–

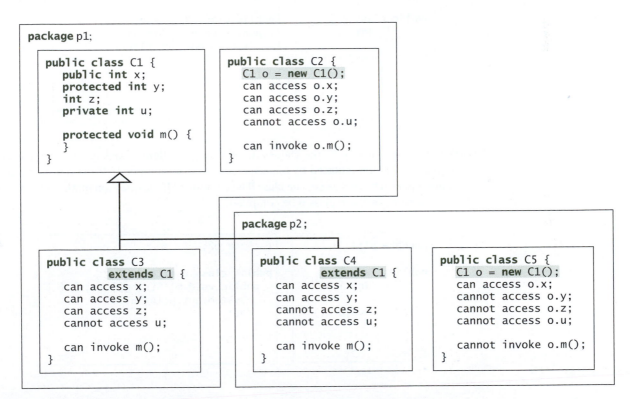

FIGURE 11.5 Visibility modifiers are used to control how data and methods are accessed.

Your class can be used in two ways: (1) for creating instances of the class and (2) for defining subclasses by extending the class. Make the members `private` if they are not intended for use from outside the class. Make the members `public` if they are intended for the users of the class. Make the fields or methods `protected` if they are intended for the extenders of the class but not for the users of the class.

The `private` and `protected` modifiers can be used only for members of the class. The `public` modifier and the default modifier (i.e., no modifier) can be used on members of the class as well as on the class. A class with no modifier (i.e., not a public class) is not accessible by classes from other packages.

change visibility

Note

A subclass may override a protected method defined in its superclass and change its visibility to public. However, a subclass cannot weaken the accessibility of a method defined in the superclass. For example, if a method is defined as public in the superclass, it must be defined as public in the subclass.

Check
Point

11.37 What modifier should you use on a class so that a class in the same package can access it, but a class in a different package cannot access it?

11.38 What modifier should you use so that a class in a different package cannot access the class, but its subclasses in any package can access it?

11.39 In the following code, the classes **A** and **B** are in the same package. If the question marks in (a) are replaced by blanks, can class **B** be compiled? If the question marks are replaced by **private**, can class **B** be compiled? If the question marks are replaced by **protected**, can class **B** be compiled?

```
package p1;

public class A {
    ?    int i;

    ?    void m() {
        ...
    }
}
```
(a)

```
package p1;

public class B extends A {
    public void m1(String[] args) {
        System.out.println(i);
        m();
    }
}
```
(b)

11.40 In the following code, the classes **A** and **B** are in different packages. If the question marks in (a) are replaced by blanks, can class **B** be compiled? If the question marks are replaced by **private**, can class **B** be compiled? If the question marks are replaced by **protected**, can class **B** be compiled?

```
package p1;

public class A {
    ?    int i;

    ?    void m() {
        ...
    }
}
```
(a)

```
package p2;

public class B extends A {
    public void m1(String[] args) {
        System.out.println(i);
        m();
    }
}
```
(b)

11.15 Preventing Extending and Overriding

Key
Point

Neither a final class nor a final method can be extended. A final data field is a constant.

You may occasionally want to prevent classes from being extended. In such cases, use the **final** modifier to indicate that a class is final and cannot be a parent class. The **Math** class is a final class. The **String**, **StringBuilder**, and **StringBuffer** classes are also final classes. For example, the following class **A** is final and cannot be extended:

```
public final class A {
    // Data fields, constructors, and methods omitted
}
```

You also can define a method to be final; a final method cannot be overridden by its subclasses.

For example, the following method `m` is final and cannot be overridden:

```java
public class Test {
  // Data fields, constructors, and methods omitted

  public final void m() {
    // Do something
  }
}
```

Note

The modifiers `public`, `protected`, `private`, `static`, `abstract`, and `final` are used on classes and class members (data and methods), except that the `final` modifier can also be used on local variables in a method. A `final` local variable is a constant inside a method.

11.41 How do you prevent a class from being extended? How do you prevent a method from being overridden?

Check Point

11.42 Indicate true or false for the following statements:

a. A protected datum or method can be accessed by any class in the same package.

b. A protected datum or method can be accessed by any class in different packages.

c. A protected datum or method can be accessed by its subclasses in any package.

d. A final class can have instances.

e. A final class can be extended.

f. A final method can be overridden.

KEY TERMS

actual type   424
casting objects   427
constructor chaining   417
declared type   424
dynamic binding   424
inheritance   410
`instanceof`   428
is-a relationship   440
method overriding   419
multiple inheritance   416
override   000
polymorphism   423
`protected`   440
single inheritance   416
subclass   410
subtype   423
superclass   410
supertype   423
type inference   433

CHAPTER SUMMARY

1. You can define a new class from an existing class. This is known as class *inheritance*. The new class is called a *subclass*, *child class*, or *extended class*. The existing class is called a *superclass*, *parent class*, or *base class*.

2. A constructor is used to construct an instance of a class. Unlike properties and methods, the constructors of a superclass are not inherited in the subclass. They can be invoked only from the constructors of the subclasses, using the keyword **super**.

3. A constructor may invoke an overloaded constructor or its superclass's constructor. The call must be the first statement in the constructor. If none of them is invoked explicitly, the compiler puts **super()** as the first statement in the constructor, which invokes the superclass's no-arg constructor.

4. To *override* a method, the method must be defined in the subclass using the same signature and the same return type as in its superclass.

5. An instance method can be overridden only if it is accessible. Thus, a private method cannot be overridden because it is not accessible outside its own class. If a method defined in a subclass is private in its superclass, the two methods are completely unrelated.

6. Like an instance method, a static method can be inherited. However, a static method cannot be overridden. If a static method defined in the superclass is redefined in a subclass, the method defined in the superclass is hidden.

7. Every class in Java is descended from the **java.lang.Object** class. If no superclass is specified when a class is defined, its superclass is **Object**.

8. If a method's parameter type is a superclass (e.g., **Object**), you may pass an object to this method of any of the parameter's subclasses (e.g., **Circle** or **String**). This is known as polymorphism.

9. It is always possible to cast an instance of a subclass to a variable of a superclass, because an instance of a subclass is *always* an instance of its superclass. When casting an instance of a superclass to a variable of its subclass, explicit casting must be used to confirm your intention to the compiler with the (**SubclassName**) cast notation.

10. A class defines a type. A type defined by a subclass is called a *subtype* and a type defined by its superclass is called a *supertype*.

11. When invoking an instance method from a reference variable, the *actual type of* the variable decides which implementation of the method is used *at runtime*. This is known as dynamic binding.

12. You can use **obj instanceof AClass** to test whether an object is an instance of a class.

13. You can use the **ArrayList** class to create an object to store a list of objects.

14. You can use the **protected** modifier to prevent the data and methods from being accessed by nonsubclasses from a different package.

15. You can use the **final** modifier to indicate that a class is final and cannot be extended and to indicate that a method is final and cannot be overridden.

QUIZ

Answer the quiz for this chapter online at www.cs.armstrong.edu/liang/intro10e/quiz.html.

PROGRAMMING EXERCISES

Sections 11.2–11.4

11.1 (*The* `Triangle` *class*) Design a class named `Triangle` that extends `GeometricObject`. The class contains:

- Three **double** data fields named `side1`, `side2`, and `side3` with default values `1.0` to denote three sides of the triangle.
- A no-arg constructor that creates a default triangle.
- A constructor that creates a triangle with the specified `side1`, `side2`, and `side3`.
- The accessor methods for all three data fields.
- A method named `getArea()` that returns the area of this triangle.
- A method named `getPerimeter()` that returns the perimeter of this triangle.
- A method named `toString()` that returns a string description for the triangle.

For the formula to compute the area of a triangle, see Programming Exercise 2.19. The `toString()` method is implemented as follows:

```
return "Triangle: side1 = " + side1 + " side2 = " + side2 +
  " side3 = " + side3;
```

Draw the UML diagrams for the classes `Triangle` and `GeometricObject` and implement the classes. Write a test program that prompts the user to enter three sides of the triangle, a color, and a Boolean value to indicate whether the triangle is filled. The program should create a `Triangle` object with these sides and set the `color` and `filled` properties using the input. The program should display the area, perimeter, color, and true or false to indicate whether it is filled or not.

Sections 11.5–11.14

11.2 (*The* `Person`, `Student`, `Employee`, `Faculty`, *and* `Staff` *classes*) Design a class named `Person` and its two subclasses named `Student` and `Employee`. Make `Faculty` and `Staff` subclasses of `Employee`. A person has a name, address, phone number, and email address. A student has a class status (freshman, sophomore, junior, or senior). Define the status as a constant. An employee has an office, salary, and date hired. Use the `MyDate` class defined in Programming Exercise 10.14 to create an object for date hired. A faculty member has office hours and a rank. A staff member has a title. Override the `toString` method in each class to display the class name and the person's name.

Draw the UML diagram for the classes and implement them. Write a test program that creates a `Person`, `Student`, `Employee`, `Faculty`, and `Staff`, and invokes their `toString()` methods.

11.3 (*Subclasses of* `Account`) In Programming Exercise 9.7, the `Account` class was defined to model a bank account. An account has the properties account number, balance, annual interest rate, and date created, and methods to deposit and withdraw funds. Create two subclasses for checking and saving accounts. A checking account has an overdraft limit, but a savings account cannot be overdrawn.

Draw the UML diagram for the classes and then implement them. Write a test program that creates objects of `Account`, `SavingsAccount`, and `CheckingAccount` and invokes their `toString()` methods.

11.4 (*Maximum element in* `ArrayList`) Write the following method that returns the maximum value in an `ArrayList` of integers. The method returns **null** if the list is **null** or the list size is `0`.

```
public static Integer max(ArrayList<Integer> list)
```

Write a test program that prompts the user to enter a sequence of numbers ending with **0**, and invokes this method to return the largest number in the input.

11.5 (*The Course class*) Rewrite the **Course** class in Listing 10.6. Use an **ArrayList** to replace an array to store students. Draw the new UML diagram for the class. You should not change the original contract of the **Course** class (i.e., the definition of the constructors and methods should not be changed, but the private members may be changed.)

11.6 (*Use ArrayList*) Write a program that creates an **ArrayList** and adds a **Loan** object, a **Date** object, a string, and a **Circle** object to the list, and use a loop to display all the elements in the list by invoking the object's **toString()** method.

11.7 (*Shuffle ArrayList*) Write the following method that shuffles the elements in an **ArrayList** of integers.

```
public static void shuffle(ArrayList<Integer> list)
```

VideoNote

New Account class

11.8 (*New Account class*) An **Account class was specified in Programming Exercise 9.7. Design a new **Account** class as follows:

■ Add a new data field **name** of the **String** type to store the name of the customer.

■ Add a new constructor that constructs an account with the specified name, id, and balance.

■ Add a new data field named **transactions** whose type is **ArrayList** that stores the transaction for the accounts. Each transaction is an instance of the **Transaction** class. The **Transaction** class is defined as shown in Figure 11.6.

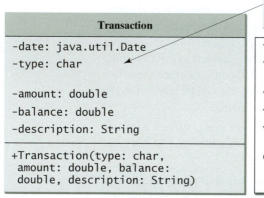

> The getter and setter methods for these data fields are provided in the class, but omitted in the UML diagram for brevity.

Transaction	
-date: java.util.Date	The date of this transaction.
-type: char	The type of the transaction, such as 'W' for withdrawal, 'D' for deposit.
-amount: double	The amount of the transaction.
-balance: double	The new balance after this transaction.
-description: String	The description of this transaction.
+Transaction(type: char, amount: double, balance: double, description: String)	Construct a Transaction with the specified date, type, balance, and description.

FIGURE 11.6 The **Transaction** class describes a transaction for a bank account.

■ Modify the **withdraw** and **deposit** methods to add a transaction to the **transactions** array list.

■ All other properties and methods are the same as in Programming Exercise 9.7.

Write a test program that creates an **Account** with annual interest rate **1.5%**, balance **1000**, id **1122**, and name **George**. Deposit $30, $40, and $50 to the account and withdraw $5, $4, and $2 from the account. Print an account summary that shows account holder name, interest rate, balance, and all transactions.

*11.9   (*Largest rows and columns*) Write a program that randomly fills in 0s and 1s into an n-by-n matrix, prints the matrix, and finds the rows and columns with the most 1s. (*Hint:* Use two **ArrayList**s to store the row and column indices with the most 1s.) Here is a sample run of the program:

```
Enter the array size n: 4 ⏎Enter
The random array is
0011
0011
1101
1010
The largest row index: 2
The largest column index: 2, 3
```

11.10   (*Implement MyStack using inheritance*) In Listing 11.10, **MyStack** is implemented using composition. Define a new stack class that extends **ArrayList**.

Draw the UML diagram for the classes and then implement **MyStack**. Write a test program that prompts the user to enter five strings and displays them in reverse order.

11.11   (*Sort ArrayList*) Write the following method that sorts an **ArrayList** of numbers:

public static void sort(ArrayList<Integer> list)

Write a test program that prompts the user to enter 5 numbers, stores them in an array list, and displays them in increasing order.

11.12   (*Sum ArrayList*) Write the following method that returns the sum of all numbers in an **ArrayList**:

public static double sum(ArrayList<Double> list)

Write a test program that prompts the user to enter 5 numbers, stores them in an array list, and displays their sum.

*11.13   (*Remove duplicates*) Write a method that removes the duplicate elements from an array list of integers using the following header:

public static void removeDuplicate(ArrayList<Integer> list)

Write a test program that prompts the user to enter 10 integers to a list and displays the distinct integers separated by exactly one space. Here is a sample run:

```
Enter ten integers: 34 5 3 5 6 4 33 2 2 4 ⏎Enter
The distinct integers are 34 5 3 6 4 33 2
```

11.14   (*Combine two lists*) Write a method that returns the union of two array lists of integers using the following header:

public static ArrayList<Integer> union(
    ArrayList<Integer> list1, ArrayList<Integer> list2)

For example, the union of two array lists {2, 3, 1, 5} and {3, 4, 6} is {2, 3, 1, 5, 3, 4, 6}. Write a test program that prompts the user to enter two lists, each with five integers, and displays their union. The numbers are separated by exactly one space in the output. Here is a sample run:

```
Enter five integers for list1: 3 5 45 4 3 ↵Enter
Enter five integers for list2: 33 51 5 4 13 ↵Enter
The combined list is 3 5 45 4 3 33 51 5 4 13
```

*11.15 (*Area of a convex polygon*) A polygon is convex if it contains any line segments that connects two points of the polygon. Write a program that prompts the user to enter the number of points in a convex polygon, then enter the points clockwise, and display the area of the polygon. Here is a sample run of the program:

```
Enter the number of the points: 7 ↵Enter
Enter the coordinates of the points:
 -12 0 -8.5 10 0 11.4 5.5 7.8 6 -5.5 0 -7 -3.5 -3.5 ↵Enter
The total area is 250.075
```

**11.16 (*Addition quiz*) Rewrite Listing 5.1 RepeatAdditionQuiz.java to alert the user if an answer is entered again. *Hint: use an array list to store answers.* Here is a sample run:

```
What is 5 + 9? 12 ↵Enter
Wrong answer. Try again. What is 5 + 9? 34 ↵Enter
Wrong answer. Try again. What is 5 + 9? 12 ↵Enter
You already entered 12
Wrong answer. Try again. What is 5 + 9? 14 ↵Enter
You got it!
```

**11.17 (*Algebra: perfect square*) Write a program that prompts the user to enter an integer m and find the smallest integer n such that m * n is a perfect square. (*Hint: Store all smallest factors of m into an array list. n is the product of the factors that appear an odd number of times in the array list. For example, consider m = 90, store the factors 2, 3, 3, 5 in an array list. 2 and 5 appear an odd number of times in the array list. So, n is 10.*) Here are sample runs:

```
Enter an integer m: 1500 ↵Enter
The smallest number n for m * n to be a perfect square is 15
m * n is 22500
```

```
Enter an integer m: 63 ↵Enter
The smalle
st number n for m * n to be a perfect square is 7
m * n is 441
```

Exception Handling and Text I/O

Objectives

- To get an overview of exceptions and exception handling (§12.2).

- To explore the advantages of using exception handling (§12.2).

- To distinguish exception types: **Error** (fatal) vs. **Exception** (nonfatal) and checked vs. unchecked (§12.3).

- To declare exceptions in a method header (§12.4.1).

- To throw exceptions in a method (§12.4.2).

- To write a **try-catch** block to handle exceptions (§12.4.3).

- To explain how an exception is propagated (§12.4.3).

- To obtain information from an exception object (§12.4.4).

- To develop applications with exception handling (§12.4.5).

- To use the **finally** clause in a **try-catch** block (§12.5).

- To use exceptions only for unexpected errors (§12.6).

- To rethrow exceptions in a **catch** block (§12.7).

- To create chained exceptions (§12.8).

- To define custom exception classes (§12.9).

- To discover file/directory properties, to delete and rename files/ directories, and to create directories using the **File** class (§12.10).

- To write data to a file using the **PrintWriter** class (§12.11.1).

- To use try-with-resources to ensure that the resources are closed automatically (§12.11.2).

- To read data from a file using the **Scanner** class (§12.11.3).

- To understand how data is read using a **Scanner** (§12.11.4).

- To develop a program that replaces text in a file (§12.11.5).

- To read data from the Web (§12.12).

- To develop a Web crawler (§12.13).

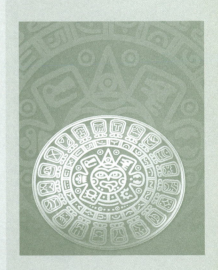

12.1 Introduction

Key Point

Exception handling enables a program to deal with exceptional situations and continue its normal execution.

Runtime errors occur while a program is running if the JVM detects an operation that is impossible to carry out. For example, if you access an array using an index that is out of bounds, you will get a runtime error with an **ArrayIndexOutOfBoundsException**. If you enter a **double** value when your program expects an integer, you will get a runtime error with an **InputMismatchException**.

exception

In Java, runtime errors are thrown as exceptions. An *exception* is an object that represents an error or a condition that prevents execution from proceeding normally. If the exception is not handled, the program will terminate abnormally. How can you handle the exception so that the program can continue to run or else terminate gracefully? This chapter introduces this subject and text input and output.

12.2 Exception-Handling Overview

Key Point

Exceptions are thrown from a method. The caller of the method can catch and handle the exception.

VideoNote

Exception-handling advantages

To demonstrate exception handling, including how an exception object is created and thrown, let's begin with the example in Listing 12.1, which reads in two integers and displays their quotient.

LISTING 12.1 Quotient.java

```java
1  import java.util.Scanner;
2
3  public class Quotient {
4    public static void main(String[] args) {
5      Scanner input = new Scanner(System.in);
6
7      // Prompt the user to enter two integers
8      System.out.print("Enter two integers: ");
9      int number1 = input.nextInt();
10     int number2 = input.nextInt();
11
12     System.out.println(number1 + " / " + number2 + " is " +
13       (number1 / number2));
14   }
15 }
```

read two integers

integer division

```
Enter two integers: 5 2 ↵Enter
5 / 2 is 2
```

```
Enter two integers: 3 0 ↵Enter
Exception in thread "main" java.lang.ArithmeticException: / by zero
    at Quotient.main(Quotient.java:11)
```

If you entered **0** for the second number, a runtime error would occur, because you cannot divide an integer by **0**. (*Note that a floating-point number divided by **0** does not raise an exception.*) A simple way to fix this error is to add an **if** statement to test the second number, as shown in Listing 12.2.

LISTING 12.2 QuotientWithIf.java

```java
 1  import java.util.Scanner;
 2
 3  public class QuotientWithIf {
 4    public static void main(String[] args) {
 5      Scanner input = new Scanner(System.in);
 6
 7      // Prompt the user to enter two integers
 8      System.out.print("Enter two integers: ");
 9      int number1 = input.nextInt();                          read two integers
10      int number2 = input.nextInt();
11
12      if (number2 != 0)                                       test number2
13        System.out.println(number1 + " / " + number2
14          + " is " + (number1 / number2));
15      else
16        System.out.println("Divisor cannot be zero ");
17    }
18  }
```

```
Enter two integers: 5 0  ↵Enter
Divisor cannot be zero
```

Before introducing exception handling, let us rewrite Listing 12.2 to compute a quotient using a method, as shown in Listing 12.3.

LISTING 12.3 QuotientWithMethod.java

```java
 1  import java.util.Scanner;
 2
 3  public class QuotientWithMethod {
 4    public static int quotient(int number1, int number2) {    quotient method
 5      if (number2 == 0) {
 6        System.out.println("Divisor cannot be zero");
 7        System.exit(1);                                       terminate the program
 8      }
 9
10      return number1 / number2;
11    }
12
13    public static void main(String[] args) {
14      Scanner input = new Scanner(System.in);
15
16      // Prompt the user to enter two integers
17      System.out.print("Enter two integers: ");
18      int number1 = input.nextInt();                          read two integers
19      int number2 = input.nextInt();
20
21      int result = quotient(number1, number2);                invoke method
22      System.out.println(number1 + " / " + number2 + " is "
23        + result);
24    }
25  }
```

```
Enter two integers: 5 3  ↵Enter
5 / 3 is 1
```

```
Enter two integers: 5 0  ↵Enter
Divisor cannot be zero
```

The method **quotient** (lines 4–11) returns the quotient of two integers. If **number2** is **0**, it cannot return a value, so the program is terminated in line 7. This is clearly a problem. You should not let the method terminate the program—the *caller* should decide whether to terminate the program.

How can a method notify its caller an exception has occurred? Java enables a method to throw an exception that can be caught and handled by the caller. Listing 12.3 can be rewritten, as shown in Listing 12.4.

LISTING 12.4 QuotientWithException.java

```java
 1  import java.util.Scanner;
 2
 3  public class QuotientWithException {
 4    public static int quotient(int number1, int number2) {
 5      if (number2 == 0)
 6        throw new ArithmeticException("Divisor cannot be zero");
 7
 8      return number1 / number2;
 9    }
10
11    public static void main(String[] args) {
12      Scanner input = new Scanner(System.in);
13
14      // Prompt the user to enter two integers
15      System.out.print("Enter two integers: ");
16      int number1 = input.nextInt();
17      int number2 = input.nextInt();
18
19      try {
20        int result = quotient(number1, number2);
21        System.out.println(number1 + " / " + number2 + " is "
22          + result);
23      }
24      catch (ArithmeticException ex) {
25        System.out.println("Exception: an integer " +
26          "cannot be divided by zero ");
27      }
28
29      System.out.println("Execution continues ...");
30    }
31  }
```

quotient method

throw exception

read two integers

try block
invoke method

If an ArithmeticException occurs

catch block

```
Enter two integers: 5 3  ↵Enter
5 / 3 is 1
Execution continues ...
```

```
Enter two integers: 5 0 ↵ Enter
Exception: an integer cannot be divided by zero
Execution continues ...
```

If **number2** is **0**, the method throws an exception (line 6) by executing

> **throw new** ArithmeticException("Divisor cannot be zero");

throw statement

The value thrown, in this case **new ArithmeticException("Divisor cannot be zero")**, is called an *exception*. The execution of a **throw** statement is called *throwing an exception*. The exception is an object created from an exception class. In this case, the exception class is **java.lang.ArithmeticException**. The constructor **ArithmeticException(str)** is invoked to construct an exception object, where **str** is a message that describes the exception.

exception

throw exception

When an exception is thrown, the normal execution flow is interrupted. As the name suggests, to "throw an exception" is to pass the exception from one place to another. The statement for invoking the method is contained in a **try** block and a **catch** block. The **try** block (lines 19–23) contains the code that is executed in normal circumstances. The exception is caught by the **catch** block. The code in the **catch** block is executed to *handle the exception*. Afterward, the statement (line 29) after the **catch** block is executed.

handle exception

The **throw** statement is analogous to a method call, but instead of calling a method, it calls a **catch** block. In this sense, a **catch** block is like a method definition with a parameter that matches the type of the value being thrown. Unlike a method, however, after the **catch** block is executed, the program control does not return to the **throw** statement; instead, it executes the next statement after the **catch** block.

The identifier **ex** in the **catch**–block header

> **catch** (ArithmeticException ex)

acts very much like a parameter in a method. Thus, this parameter is referred to as a **catch**–block parameter. The type (e.g., **ArithmeticException**) preceding **ex** specifies what kind of exception the **catch** block can catch. Once the exception is caught, you can access the thrown value from this parameter in the body of a **catch** block.

catch–block parameter

In summary, a template for a **try-throw-catch** block may look like this:

```
try {
  Code to run;
  A statement or a method that may throw an exception;
  More code to run;
}
catch (type ex) {
  Code to process the exception;
}
```

An exception may be thrown directly by using a **throw** statement in a **try** block, or by invoking a method that may throw an exception.

The main method invokes **quotient** (line 20). If the quotient method executes normally, it returns a value to the caller. If the **quotient** method encounters an exception, it throws the exception back to its caller. The caller's **catch** block handles the exception.

Now you can see the *advantage* of using exception handling: It enables a method to throw an exception to its caller, enabling the caller to handle the exception. Without this capability, the called method itself must handle the exception or terminate the program. Often the called method does not know what to do in case of error. This is typically the case for the library methods. The library method can detect the error, but only the caller knows what needs to be

advantage

done when an error occurs. The key benefit of exception handling is separating the detection of an error (done in a called method) from the handling of an error (done in the calling method).

Many library methods throw exceptions. Listing 12.5 gives an example that handles an `InputMismatchException` when reading an input.

LISTING 12.5 InputMismatchExceptionDemo.java

```
1   import java.util.*;
2
3   public class InputMismatchExceptionDemo {
4     public static void main(String[] args) {
5       Scanner input = new Scanner(System.in);
6       boolean continueInput = true;
7
8       do {
9         try {
10          System.out.print("Enter an integer: ");
11          int number = input.nextInt();
12
13          // Display the result
14          System.out.println(
15            "The number entered is " + number);
16
17          continueInput = false;
18        }
19        catch (InputMismatchException ex) {
20          System.out.println("Try again. (" +
21            "Incorrect input: an integer is required)");
22          input.nextLine(); // Discard input
23        }
24      } while (continueInput);
25    }
26  }
```

create a Scanner

try block

If an InputMismatch Exception occurs

catch block

```
Enter an integer: 3.5  ↵Enter
Try again. (Incorrect input: an integer is required)
Enter an integer: 4  ↵Enter
The number entered is 4
```

When executing **input.nextInt()** (line 11), an **InputMismatchException** occurs if the input entered is not an integer. Suppose **3.5** is entered. An **InputMismatchException** occurs and the control is transferred to the **catch** block. The statements in the **catch** block are now executed. The statement **input.nextLine()** in line 22 discards the current input line so that the user can enter a new line of input. The variable **continueInput** controls the loop. Its initial value is **true** (line 6), and it is changed to **false** (line 17) when a valid input is received. Once a valid input is received, there is no need to continue the input.

✓**Check Point**

12.1 What is the advantage of using exception handling?

12.2 Which of the following statements will throw an exception?

```
System.out.println(1 / 0);
System.out.println(1.0 / 0);
```

12.3 Point out the problem in the following code. Does the code throw any exceptions?

```
long value = Long.MAX_VALUE + 1;
System.out.println(value);
```

12.4 What does the JVM do when an exception occurs? How do you catch an exception?

12.5 What is the output of the following code?

```
public class Test {
  public static void main(String[] args) {
    try {
      int value = 30;
      if (value < 40)
        throw new Exception("value is too small");
    }
    catch (Exception ex) {
      System.out.println(ex.getMessage());
    }
    System.out.println("Continue after the catch block");
  }
}
```

What would be the output if the line

```
int value = 30;
```

were changed to

```
int value = 50;
```

12.6 Show the output of the following code.

```
public class Test {
  public static void main(String[] args) {
    for (int i = 0; i < 2; i++) {
      System.out.print(i + " ");
      try {
        System.out.println(1 / 0);
      }
      catch (Exception ex) {
      }
    }
  }
}
```
(a)

```
public class Test {
  public static void main(String[] args) {
    try {
      for (int i = 0; i < 2; i++) {
        System.out.print(i + " ");
        System.out.println(1 / 0);
      }
    }
    catch (Exception ex) {
    }
  }
}
```
(b)

12.3 Exception Types

Exceptions are objects, and objects are defined using classes. The root class for exceptions is `java.lang.Throwable`.

Key Point

The preceding section used the classes `ArithmeticException` and `InputMismatch-Exception`. Are there any other types of exceptions you can use? Can you define your own exception classes? Yes. There are many predefined exception classes in the Java API. Figure 12.1 shows some of them, and in Section 12.9 you will learn how to define your own exception classes.

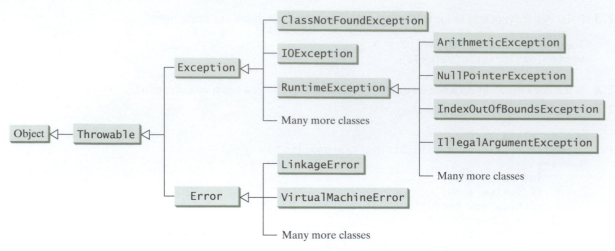

FIGURE 12.1 Exceptions thrown are instances of the classes shown in this diagram, or of subclasses of one of these classes.

 Note

The class names **Error**, **Exception**, and **RuntimeException** are somewhat confusing. All three of these classes are exceptions, and all of the errors occur at runtime.

The **Throwable** class is the root of exception classes. All Java exception classes inherit directly or indirectly from **Throwable**. You can create your own exception classes by extending **Exception** or a subclass of **Exception**.

The exception classes can be classified into three major types: system errors, exceptions, and runtime exceptions.

system error

■ *System errors* are thrown by the JVM and are represented in the **Error** class. The **Error** class describes internal system errors, though such errors rarely occur. If one does, there is little you can do beyond notifying the user and trying to terminate the program gracefully. Examples of subclasses of **Error** are listed in Table 12.1.

TABLE 12.1 Examples of Subclasses of **Error**

Class	Reasons for Exception
LinkageError	A class has some dependency on another class, but the latter class has changed incompatibly after the compilation of the former class.
VirtualMachineError	The JVM is broken or has run out of the resources it needs in order to continue operating.

exception

■ *Exceptions* are represented in the **Exception** class, which describes errors caused by your program and by external circumstances. These errors can be caught and handled by your program. Examples of subclasses of **Exception** are listed in Table 12.2.

TABLE 12.2 Examples of Subclasses of **Exception**

Class	Reasons for Exception
ClassNotFoundException	Attempt to use a class that does not exist. This exception would occur, for example, if you tried to run a nonexistent class using the **java** command, or if your program were composed of, say, three class files, only two of which could be found.
IOException	Related to input/output operations, such as invalid input, reading past the end of a file, and opening a nonexistent file. Examples of subclasses of **IOException** are **InterruptedIOException**, **EOFException** (EOF is short for End of File), and **FileNotFoundException**.

■ *Runtime exceptions* are represented in the `RuntimeException` class, which describes programming errors, such as bad casting, accessing an out-of-bounds array, and numeric errors. Runtime exceptions are generally thrown by the JVM. Examples of subclasses are listed in Table 12.3.

runtime exception

TABLE 12.3 Examples of Subclasses of `RuntimeException`

Class	Reasons for Exception
`ArithmeticException`	Dividing an integer by zero. Note that floating-point arithmetic does not throw exceptions (see Appendix E, Special Floating-Point Values).
`NullPointerException`	Attempt to access an object through a `null` reference variable.
`IndexOutOfBoundsException`	Index to an array is out of range.
`IllegalArgumentException`	A method is passed an argument that is illegal or inappropriate.

`RuntimeException`, `Error`, and their subclasses are known as *unchecked exceptions*. All other exceptions are known as *checked exceptions*, meaning that the compiler forces the programmer to check and deal with them in a `try-catch` block or declare it in the method header. Declaring an exception in the method header will be covered in Section 12.4.

unchecked exception

checked exception

In most cases, unchecked exceptions reflect programming logic errors that are unrecoverable. For example, a `NullPointerException` is thrown if you access an object through a reference variable before an object is assigned to it; an `IndexOutOfBoundsException` is thrown if you access an element in an array outside the bounds of the array. These are logic errors that should be corrected in the program. Unchecked exceptions can occur anywhere in a program. To avoid cumbersome overuse of `try-catch` blocks, Java does not mandate that you write code to catch or declare unchecked exceptions.

12.7 Describe the Java `Throwable` class, its subclasses, and the types of exceptions.

12.8 What `RuntimeException` will the following programs throw, if any?

Check
Point

```java
public class Test {
  public static void main(String[] args) {
    System.out.println(1 / 0);
  }
}
```
(a)

```java
public class Test {
  public static void main(String[] args) {
    int[] list = new int[5];
    System.out.println(list[5]);
  }
}
```
(b)

```java
public class Test {
  public static void main(String[] args) {
    String s = "abc";
    System.out.println(s.charAt(3));
  }
}
```
(c)

```java
public class Test {
  public static void main(String[] args) {
    Object o = new Object();
    String d = (String)o;
  }
}
```
(d)

```java
public class Test {
  public static void main(String[] args) {
    Object o = null;
    System.out.println(o.toString());
  }
}
```
(e)

```java
public class Test {
  public static void main(String[] args) {
    System.out.println(1.0 / 0);
  }
}
```
(f)

12.4 More on Exception Handling

A handler for an exception is found by propagating the exception backward through a chain of method calls, starting from the current method.

The preceding sections gave you an overview of exception handling and introduced several predefined exception types. This section provides an in-depth discussion of exception handling.

Java's exception-handling model is based on three operations: *declaring an exception*, *throwing an exception*, and *catching an exception*, as shown in Figure 12.2.

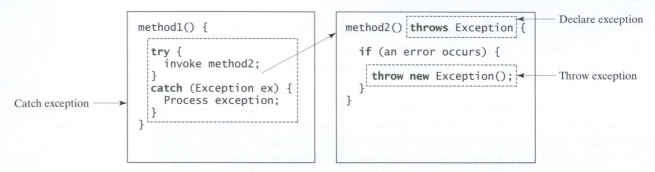

FIGURE 12.2 Exception handling in Java consists of declaring exceptions, throwing exceptions, and catching and processing exceptions.

12.4.1 Declaring Exceptions

declare exception

In Java, the statement currently being executed belongs to a method. The Java interpreter invokes the **main** method to start executing a program. Every method must state the types of checked exceptions it might throw. This is known as *declaring exceptions*. Because system errors and runtime errors can happen to any code, Java does not require that you declare **Error** and **RuntimeException** (unchecked exceptions) explicitly in the method. However, all other exceptions thrown by the method must be explicitly declared in the method header so that the caller of the method is informed of the exception.

To declare an exception in a method, use the **throws** keyword in the method header, as in this example:

```
public void myMethod() throws IOException
```

The **throws** keyword indicates that **myMethod** might throw an **IOException**. If the method might throw multiple exceptions, add a list of the exceptions, separated by commas, after **throws**:

```
public void myMethod()
    throws Exception1, Exception2, ..., ExceptionN
```

> **Note**
> If a method does not declare exceptions in the superclass, you cannot override it to declare exceptions in the subclass.

12.4.2 Throwing Exceptions

throw exception

A program that detects an error can create an instance of an appropriate exception type and throw it. This is known as *throwing an exception*. Here is an example: Suppose the program detects that an argument passed to the method violates the method contract (e.g., the argument must be nonnegative, but a negative argument is passed); the program can create an instance of `IllegalArgumentException` and throw it, as follows:

```
IllegalArgumentException ex =
  new IllegalArgumentException("Wrong Argument");
throw ex;
```

Or, if you prefer, you can use the following:

```
throw new IllegalArgumentException("Wrong Argument");
```

Note

`IllegalArgumentException` is an exception class in the Java API. In general, each exception class in the Java API has at least two constructors: a no-arg constructor, and a constructor with a `String` argument that describes the exception. This argument is called the *exception message*, which can be obtained using `getMessage()`.

exception message

Tip

The keyword to declare an exception is `throws`, and the keyword to throw an exception is `throw`.

throws vs. throw

12.4.3 Catching Exceptions

You now know how to declare an exception and how to throw an exception. When an exception is thrown, it can be caught and handled in a **try-catch** block, as follows:

catch exception

```
try {
  statements; // Statements that may throw exceptions
}
catch (Exception1 exVar1) {
  handler for exception1;
}
catch (Exception2 exVar2) {
  handler for exception2;
}
...
catch (ExceptionN exVarN) {
  handler for exceptionN;
}
```

If no exceptions arise during the execution of the **try** block, the **catch** blocks are skipped.

If one of the statements inside the **try** block throws an exception, Java skips the remaining statements in the **try** block and starts the process of finding the code to handle the exception. The code that handles the exception is called the *exception handler*; it is found by *propagating the exception* backward through a chain of method calls, starting from the current method. Each **catch** block is examined in turn, from first to last, to see whether the type of the exception object is an instance of the exception class in the **catch** block. If so, the exception object is assigned to the variable declared, and the code in the **catch** block is executed. If no handler is found, Java exits this method, passes the exception to the method that invoked the method, and continues the same process to find a handler. If no handler is found in the chain of methods being invoked, the program terminates and prints an error message on the console. The process of finding a handler is called *catching an exception*.

exception handler
exception propagation

Suppose the **main** method invokes **method1**, **method1** invokes **method2**, **method2** invokes **method3**, and **method3** throws an exception, as shown in Figure 12.3. Consider the following scenario:

- If the exception type is **Exception3**, it is caught by the **catch** block for handling exception **ex3** in **method2**. **statement5** is skipped, and **statement6** is executed.

- If the exception type is **Exception2**, **method2** is aborted, the control is returned to **method1**, and the exception is caught by the **catch** block for handling exception **ex2** in **method1**. **statement3** is skipped, and **statement4** is executed.

- If the exception type is **Exception1**, **method1** is aborted, the control is returned to the **main** method, and the exception is caught by the **catch** block for handling exception **ex1** in the **main** method. **statement1** is skipped, and **statement2** is executed.

- If the exception type is not caught in **method2**, **method1**, or **main**, the program terminates, and **statement1** and **statement2** are not executed.

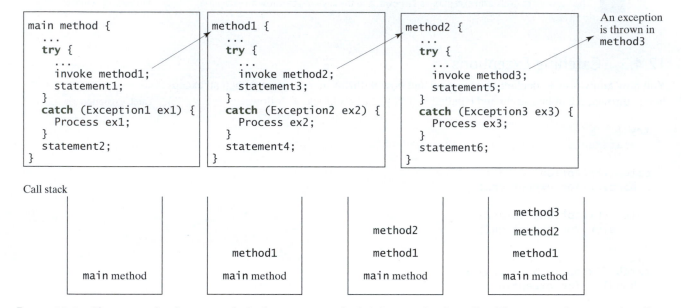

FIGURE 12.3 If an exception is not caught in the current method, it is passed to its caller. The process is repeated until the exception is caught or passed to the **main** method.

catch block

Note
Various exception classes can be derived from a common superclass. If a **catch** block catches exception objects of a superclass, it can catch all the exception objects of the subclasses of that superclass.

order of exception handlers

Note
The order in which exceptions are specified in **catch** blocks is important. A compile error will result if a catch block for a superclass type appears before a catch block for a subclass type. For example, the ordering in (a) on the next page is erroneous, because **RuntimeException** is a subclass of **Exception**. The correct ordering should be as shown in (b).

```
try {
   ...
}
catch (Exception ex) {
   ...
}
catch (RuntimeException ex) {
   ...
}
```

(a) Wrong order

```
try {
   ...
}
catch (RuntimeException ex) {
   ...
}
catch (Exception ex) {
   ...
}
```

(b) Correct order

> **Note**
>
> Java forces you to deal with checked exceptions. If a method declares a checked exception (i.e., an exception other than **Error** or **RuntimeException**), you must invoke it in a **try-catch** block or declare to throw the exception in the calling method. For example, suppose that method **p1** invokes method **p2**, and **p2** may throw a checked exception (e.g., **IOException**); you have to write the code as shown in (a) or (b) below.

catch or declare checked exceptions

```
void p1() {
   try {
      p2();
   }
   catch (IOException ex) {
      ...
   }
}
```

(a) Catch exception

```
void p1() throws IOException {

   p2();

}
```

(b) Throw exception

> **Note**
>
> You can use the new JDK 7 multi-catch feature to simplify coding for the exceptions with the same handling code. The syntax is:

JDK 7 multi-catch

```
catch (Exception1 | Exception2 | ... | Exceptionk ex) {
   // Same code for handling these exceptions
}
```

> Each exception type is separated from the next with a vertical bar (**|**). If one of the exceptions is caught, the handling code is executed.

12.4.4 Getting Information from Exceptions

An exception object contains valuable information about the exception. You may use the following instance methods in the **java.lang.Throwable** class to get information regarding the exception, as shown in Figure 12.4. The **printStackTrace()** method prints stack trace

methods in Throwable

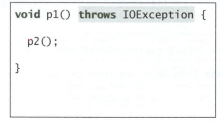

java.lang.Throwable	
+getMessage(): String	Returns the message that describes this exception object.
+toString(): String	Returns the concatenation of three strings: (1) the full name of the exception class; (2) ":" (a colon and a space); (3) the getMessage() method.
+printStackTrace(): void	Prints the Throwable object and its call stack trace information on the console.
+getStackTrace(): StackTraceElement[]	Returns an array of stack trace elements representing the stack trace pertaining to this exception object.

FIGURE 12.4 **Throwable** is the root class for all exception objects.

information on the console. The **getStackTrace()** method provides programmatic access to the stack trace information printed by **printStackTrace()**.

Listing 12.6 gives an example that uses the methods in **Throwable** to display exception information. Line 4 invokes the **sum** method to return the sum of all the elements in the array. There is an error in line 23 that causes the **ArrayIndexOutOfBoundsException**, a subclass of **IndexOutOfBoundsException**. This exception is caught in the **try-catch** block. Lines 7, 8, and 9 display the stack trace, exception message, and exception object and message using the **printStackTrace()**, **getMessage()**, and **toString()** methods, as shown in Figure 12.5. Line 12 brings stack trace elements into an array. Each element represents a method call. You can obtain the method (line 14), class name (line 15), and exception line number (line 16) for each element.

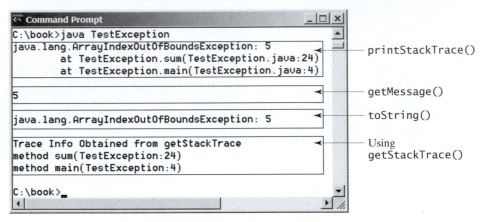

FIGURE 12.5 You can use the **printStackTrace()**, **getMessage()**, **toString()**, and **getStackTrace()** methods to obtain information from exception objects.

LISTING 12.6 TestException.java

```
1   public class TestException {
2     public static void main(String[] args) {
3       try {
4         System.out.println(sum(new int[] {1, 2, 3, 4, 5}));
5       }
6       catch (Exception ex) {
7         ex.printStackTrace();
8         System.out.println("\n" + ex.getMessage());
9         System.out.println("\n" + ex.toString());
10
11        System.out.println("\nTrace Info Obtained from getStackTrace");
12        StackTraceElement[] traceElements = ex.getStackTrace();
13        for (int i = 0; i < traceElements.length; i++) {
14          System.out.print("method " + traceElements[i].getMethodName());
15          System.out.print("(" + traceElements[i].getClassName() + ":");
16          System.out.println(traceElements[i].getLineNumber() + ")");
17        }
18      }
19    }
20
21    private static int sum(int[] list) {
22      int result = 0;
23      for (int i = 0; i <= list.length; i++)
```

invoke sum

printStackTrace()
getMessage()
toString()

getStackTrace()

cause an exception

```
24        result += list[i];
25      return result;
26    }
27  }
```

12.4.5 Example: Declaring, Throwing, and Catching Exceptions

This example demonstrates declaring, throwing, and catching exceptions by modifying the setRadius method in the **Circle** class in Listing 9.8, CircleWithPrivateDataFields.java. The new **setRadius** method throws an exception if the radius is negative.

Listing 12.7 defines a new circle class named **CircleWithException**, which is the same as **CircleWithPrivateDataFields** except that the **setRadius(double newRadius)** method throws an **IllegalArgumentException** if the argument **newRadius** is negative.

LISTING 12.7 CircleWithException.java

```
1  public class CircleWithException {
2    /** The radius of the circle */
3    private double radius;
4
5    /** The number of the objects created */
6    private static int numberOfObjects = 0;
7
8    /** Construct a circle with radius 1 */
9    public CircleWithException() {
10     this(1.0);
11   }
12
13   /** Construct a circle with a specified radius */
14   public CircleWithException(double newRadius) {
15     setRadius(newRadius);
16     numberOfObjects++;
17   }
18
19   /** Return radius */
20   public double getRadius() {
21     return radius;
22   }
23
24   /** Set a new radius */
25   public void setRadius(double newRadius)
26       throws IllegalArgumentException {          declare exception
27     if (newRadius >= 0)
28       radius = newRadius;
29     else
30       throw new IllegalArgumentException(        throw exception
31         "Radius cannot be negative");
32   }
33
34   /** Return numberOfObjects */
35   public static int getNumberOfObjects() {
36     return numberOfObjects;
37   }
38
39   /** Return the area of this circle */
40   public double findArea() {
41     return radius * radius * 3.14159;
42   }
43 }
```

A test program that uses the new `Circle` class is given in Listing 12.8.

LISTING 12.8 TestCircleWithException.java

try

catch

```java
1  public class TestCircleWithException {
2    public static void main(String[] args) {
3      try {
4        CircleWithException c1 = new CircleWithException(5);
5        CircleWithException c2 = new CircleWithException(-5);
6        CircleWithException c3 = new CircleWithException(0);
7      }
8      catch (IllegalArgumentException ex) {
9        System.out.println(ex);
10     }
11
12     System.out.println("Number of objects created: " +
13       CircleWithException.getNumberOfObjects());
14   }
15 }
```

```
java.lang.IllegalArgumentException: Radius cannot be negative
Number of objects created: 1
```

The original **Circle** class remains intact except that the class name is changed to **CircleWithException**, a new constructor **CircleWithException(newRadius)** is added, and the **setRadius** method now declares an exception and throws it if the radius is negative.

The **setRadius** method declares to throw **IllegalArgumentException** in the method header (lines 25–32 in CircleWithException.java). The **CircleWithException** class would still compile if the **throws IllegalArgumentException** clause (line 26) were removed from the method declaration, since it is a subclass of **RuntimeException** and every method can throw **RuntimeException** (an unchecked exception) regardless of whether it is declared in the method header.

The test program creates three **CircleWithException** objects—**c1**, **c2**, and **c3**—to test how to handle exceptions. Invoking **new CircleWithException(-5)** (line 5 in Listing 12.8) causes the **setRadius** method to be invoked, which throws an **IllegalArgumentException**, because the radius is negative. In the **catch** block, the type of the object **ex** is **IllegalArgumentException**, which matches the exception object thrown by the **setRadius** method, so this exception is caught by the **catch** block.

The exception handler prints a short message, **ex.toString()** (line 9 in Listing 12.8), about the exception, using **System.out.println(ex)**.

Note that the execution continues in the event of the exception. If the handlers had not caught the exception, the program would have abruptly terminated.

The test program would still compile if the **try** statement were not used, because the method throws an instance of **IllegalArgumentException**, a subclass of **RuntimeException** (an unchecked exception). If a method throws an exception other than **RuntimeException** or **Error**, the method must be invoked within a **try-catch** block.

12.9 What is the purpose of declaring exceptions? How do you declare an exception, and where? Can you declare multiple exceptions in a method header?

12.10 What is a checked exception, and what is an unchecked exception?

12.11 How do you throw an exception? Can you throw multiple exceptions in one **throw** statement?

12.12 What is the keyword **throw** used for? What is the keyword **throws** used for?

12.13 Suppose that `statement2` causes an exception in the following `try-catch` block:

```java
try {
  statement1;
  statement2;
  statement3;
}
catch (Exception1 ex1) {
}
catch (Exception2 ex2) {
}

statement4;
```

Answer the following questions:

- Will `statement3` be executed?
- If the exception is not caught, will `statement4` be executed?
- If the exception is caught in the `catch` block, will `statement4` be executed?

12.14 What is displayed when the following program is run?

```java
public class Test {
  public static void main(String[] args) {
    try {
      int[] list = new int[10];
      System.out.println("list[10] is " + list[10]);
    }
    catch (ArithmeticException ex) {
      System.out.println("ArithmeticException");
    }
    catch (RuntimeException ex) {
      System.out.println("RuntimeException");
    }
    catch (Exception ex) {
      System.out.println("Exception");
    }
  }
}
```

12.15 What is displayed when the following program is run?

```java
public class Test {
  public static void main(String[] args) {
    try {
      method();
      System.out.println("After the method call");
    }
    catch (ArithmeticException ex) {
      System.out.println("ArithmeticException");
    }
    catch (RuntimeException ex) {
      System.out.println("RuntimeException");
    }
    catch (Exception e) {
      System.out.println("Exception");
    }
  }

  static void method() throws Exception {
```

```
        System.out.println(1 / 0);
      }
    }
```

12.16 What is displayed when the following program is run?

```java
public class Test {
  public static void main(String[] args) {
    try {
      method();
      System.out.println("After the method call");
    }
    catch (RuntimeException ex) {
      System.out.println("RuntimeException in main");
    }
    catch (Exception ex) {
      System.out.println("Exception in main");
    }
  }

  static void method() throws Exception {
    try {
      String s = "abc";
      System.out.println(s.charAt(3));
    }
    catch (RuntimeException ex) {
      System.out.println("RuntimeException in method()");
    }
    catch (Exception ex) {
      System.out.println("Exception in method()");
    }
  }
}
```

12.17 What does the method `getMessage()` do?

12.18 What does the method `printStackTrace()` do?

12.19 Does the presence of a **try-catch** block impose overhead when no exception occurs?

12.20 Correct a compile error in the following code:

```java
public void m(int value) {
  if (value < 40)
    throw new Exception("value is too small");
}
```

12.5 The `finally` Clause

Key Point

The `finally` clause is always executed regardless whether an exception occurred or not.

Occasionally, you may want some code to be executed regardless of whether an exception occurs or is caught. Java has a `finally` clause that can be used to accomplish this objective. The syntax for the `finally` clause might look like this:

```java
try {
  statements;
}
catch (TheException ex) {
  handling ex;
}
```

```
finally {
  finalStatements;
}
```

The code in the **finally** block is executed under all circumstances, regardless of whether an exception occurs in the **try** block or is caught. Consider three possible cases:

- If no exception arises in the **try** block, **finalStatements** is executed, and the next statement after the **try** statement is executed.

- If a statement causes an exception in the **try** block that is caught in a **catch** block, the rest of the statements in the **try** block are skipped, the **catch** block is executed, and the **finally** clause is executed. The next statement after the **try** statement is executed.

- If one of the statements causes an exception that is not caught in any **catch** block, the other statements in the **try** block are skipped, the **finally** clause is executed, and the exception is passed to the caller of this method.

The **finally** block executes even if there is a **return** statement prior to reaching the **finally** block.

 Note
The **catch** block may be omitted when the **finally** clause is used.

omit catch block

12.21 Suppose that **statement2** causes an exception in the following statement:

```
try {
  statement1;
  statement2;
  statement3;
}
catch (Exception1 ex1) {
}
finally {
  statement4;
}
statement5;
```

Answer the following questions:

- If no exception occurs, will **statement4** be executed, and will **statement5** be executed?

- If the exception is of type **Exception1**, will **statement4** be executed, and will **statement5** be executed?

- If the exception is not of type **Exception1**, will **statement4** be executed, and will **statement5** be executed?

12.6 When to Use Exceptions

A method should throw an exception if the error needs to be handled by its caller.

The **try** block contains the code that is executed in normal circumstances. The **catch** block contains the code that is executed in exceptional circumstances. Exception handling separates error-handling code from normal programming tasks, thus making programs easier to read and to modify. Be aware, however, that exception handling usually requires more time and resources, because it requires instantiating a new exception object, rolling back the call stack, and propagating the exception through the chain of methods invoked to search for the handler.

An exception occurs in a method. If you want the exception to be processed by its caller, you should create an exception object and throw it. If you can handle the exception in the method where it occurs, there is no need to throw or use exceptions.

In general, common exceptions that may occur in multiple classes in a project are candidates for exception classes. Simple errors that may occur in individual methods are best handled without throwing exceptions. This can be done by using **if** statements to check for errors.

When should you use a **try-catch** block in the code? Use it when you have to deal with unexpected error conditions. Do not use a **try-catch** block to deal with simple, expected situations. For example, the following code

```
try {
  System.out.println(refVar.toString());
}
catch (NullPointerException ex) {
  System.out.println("refVar is null");
}
```

is better replaced by

```
if (refVar != null)
  System.out.println(refVar.toString());
else
  System.out.println("refVar is null");
```

Which situations are exceptional and which are expected is sometimes difficult to decide. The point is not to abuse exception handling as a way to deal with a simple logic test.

12.22 The following method checks whether a string is a numeric string:

```
public static boolean isNumeric(String token) {
  try {
    Double.parseDouble(token);
    return true;
  }
  catch (java.lang.NumberFormatException ex) {
    return false;
  }
}
```

Is it correct? Rewrite it without using exceptions.

12.7 Rethrowing Exceptions

Java allows an exception handler to rethrow the exception if the handler cannot process the exception or simply wants to let its caller be notified of the exception.

The syntax for rethrowing an exception may look like this:

```
try {
  statements;
}
catch (TheException ex) {
  perform operations before exits;
  throw ex;
}
```

The statement **throw ex** rethrows the exception to the caller so that other handlers in the caller get a chance to process the exception **ex**.

12.23 Suppose that `statement2` causes an exception in the following statement:

```
try {
  statement1;
  statement2;
  statement3;
}
catch (Exception1 ex1) {
}
catch (Exception2 ex2) {
  throw ex2;
}
finally {
  statement4;
}
statement5;
```

Answer the following questions:

- If no exception occurs, will `statement4` be executed, and will `statement5` be executed?
- If the exception is of type `Exception1`, will `statement4` be executed, and will `statement5` be executed?
- If the exception is of type `Exception2`, will `statement4` be executed, and will `statement5` be executed?
- If the exception is not `Exception1` nor `Exception2`, will `statement4` be executed, and will `statement5` be executed?

12.8 Chained Exceptions

Throwing an exception along with another exception forms a chained exception.

In the preceding section, the `catch` block rethrows the original exception. Sometimes, you may need to throw a new exception (with additional information) along with the original exception. This is called *chained exceptions*. Listing 12.9 illustrates how to create and throw chained exceptions.

chained exception

LISTING 12.9 `ChainedExceptionDemo.java`

```
1  public class ChainedExceptionDemo {
2    public static void main(String[] args) {
3      try {
4        method1();
5      }
6      catch (Exception ex) {
7        ex.printStackTrace();
8      }
9    }
10
11   public static void method1() throws Exception {
12     try {
13       method2();
14     }
15     catch (Exception ex) {
16       throw new Exception("New info from method1", ex);
17     }
18   }
```

stack trace

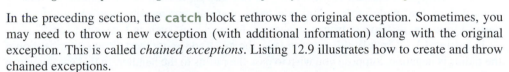

chained exception

```
19
20   public static void method2() throws Exception {
21     throw new Exception("New info from method2");
22   }
23 }
```

```
java.lang.Exception: New info from method1
  at ChainedExceptionDemo.method1(ChainedExceptionDemo.java:16)
  at ChainedExceptionDemo.main(ChainedExceptionDemo.java:4)
Caused by: java.lang.Exception: New info from method2
  at ChainedExceptionDemo.method2(ChainedExceptionDemo.java:21)
  at ChainedExceptionDemo.method1(ChainedExceptionDemo.java:13)
  ... 1 more
```

The **main** method invokes **method1** (line 4), **method1** invokes **method2** (line 13), and **method2** throws an exception (line 21). This exception is caught in the **catch** block in **method1** and is wrapped in a new exception in line 16. The new exception is thrown and caught in the catch block in the **main** method in line 6. The sample output shows the output from the **printStackTrace()** method in line 7. The new exception thrown from **method1** is displayed first, followed by the original exception thrown from **method2**.

12.24 What would be the output if line 16 is replaced by the following line?

```
throw new Exception("New info from method1");
```

12.9 Defining Custom Exception Classes

*You can define a custom exception class by extending the **java.lang.Exception** class.*

Java provides quite a few exception classes. Use them whenever possible instead of defining your own exception classes. However, if you run into a problem that cannot be adequately described by the predefined exception classes, you can create your own exception class, derived from **Exception** or from a subclass of **Exception**, such as **IOException**.

In Listing 12.7, CircleWithException.java, the **setRadius** method throws an exception if the radius is negative. Suppose you wish to pass the radius to the handler. In that case, you can define a custom exception class, as shown in Listing 12.10.

VideoNote
Create custom exception classes

LISTING 12.10 InvalidRadiusException.java

extends Exception

```
1  public class InvalidRadiusException extends Exception {
2    private double radius;
3
4    /** Construct an exception */
5    public InvalidRadiusException(double radius) {
6      super("Invalid radius " + radius);
7      this.radius = radius;
8    }
9
10   /** Return the radius */
11   public double getRadius() {
12     return radius;
13   }
14 }
```

This custom exception class extends **java.lang.Exception** (line 1). The **Exception** class extends **java.lang.Throwable**. All the methods (e.g., **getMessage()**, **toString()**, and `printStackTrace()`) in `Exception` are inherited from `Throwable`. The `Exception` class contains four constructors. Among them, the following two constructors are often used:

java.lang.Exception	
+Exception()	Constructs an exception with no message.
+Exception(message: String)	Constructs an exception with the specified message.

Line 6 invokes the superclass's constructor with a message. This message will be set in the exception object and can be obtained by invoking `getMessage()` on the object.

Tip

Most exception classes in the Java API contain two constructors: a no-arg constructor and a constructor with a message parameter.

To create an **InvalidRadiusException**, you have to pass a radius. Therefore, the **setRadius** method in Listing 12.7 can be modified as shown in Listing 12.11.

LISTING 12.11 `TestCircleWithCustomException.java`

```java
1  public class TestCircleWithCustomException {
2    public static void main(String[] args) {
3      try {
4        new CircleWithCustomException(5);
5        new CircleWithCustomException(-5);
6        new CircleWithCustomException(0);
7      }
8      catch (InvalidRadiusException ex) {
9        System.out.println(ex);
10     }
11
12     System.out.println("Number of objects created: " +
13       CircleWithCustomException.getNumberOfObjects());
14   }
15 }
16
17 class CircleWithCustomException {
18   /** The radius of the circle */
19   private double radius;
20
21   /** The number of objects created */
22   private static int numberOfObjects = 0;
23
24   /** Construct a circle with radius 1 */
25   public CircleWithCustomException() throws InvalidRadiusException {    declare exception
26     this(1.0);
27   }
28
29   /** Construct a circle with a specified radius */
30   public CircleWithCustomException(double newRadius)
31       throws InvalidRadiusException {
32     setRadius(newRadius);
33     numberOfObjects++;
34   }
35
36   /** Return radius */
37   public double getRadius() {
```

```
38       return radius;
39     }
40
41     /** Set a new radius */
42     public void setRadius(double newRadius)
43         throws InvalidRadiusException {
44       if (newRadius >= 0)
45         radius = newRadius;
46       else
47         throw new InvalidRadiusException(newRadius);
48     }
49
50     /** Return numberOfObjects */
51     public static int getNumberOfObjects() {
52       return numberOfObjects;
53     }
54
55     /** Return the area of this circle */
56     public double findArea() {
57       return radius * radius * 3.14159;
58     }
59   }
```

throw exception

```
InvalidRadiusException: Invalid radius -5.0
Number of objects created: 1
```

The **setRadius** method in **CircleWithCustomException** throws an **InvalidRadius-Exception** when radius is negative (line 47). Since **InvalidRadiusException** is a checked exception, the **setRadius** method must declare it in the method header (line 43). Since the constructors for **CircleWithCustomException** invoke the **setRadius** method to a set a new radius and it may throw an **InvalidRadiusException**, the constructors are declared to throw **InvalidRadiusException** (lines 25, 31).

Invoking **new CircleWithCustomException(-5)** (line 5) throws an **InvalidRadius-Exception**, which is caught by the handler. The handler displays the radius in the exception object **ex**.

checked custom exception

Tip

Can you define a custom exception class by extending **RuntimeException**? Yes, but it is not a good way to go, because it makes your custom exception unchecked. It is better to make a custom exception checked, so that the compiler can force these exceptions to be caught in your program.

12.25 How do you define a custom exception class?

12.26 Suppose the **setRadius** method throws the **InValidRadiusException** defined in Listing 12.10. What is displayed when the following program is run?

```
public class Test {
  public static void main(String[] args) {
    try {
      method();
      System.out.println("After the method call");
    }
    catch (RuntimeException ex) {
      System.out.println("RuntimeException in main");
    }
```

```
      catch (Exception ex) {
        System.out.println("Exception in main");
      }
    }

    static void method() throws Exception {
      try {
        Circle c1 = new Circle(1);
        c1.setRadius(-1);
        System.out.println(c1.getRadius());
      }
      catch (RuntimeException ex) {
        System.out.println("RuntimeException in method()");
      }
      catch (Exception ex) {
        System.out.println("Exception in method()");
        throw ex;
      }
    }
  }
```

12.10 The **File** Class

*The **File** class contains the methods for obtaining the properties of a file/directory and for renaming and deleting a file/directory.*

Key Point

Having learned exception handling, you are ready to step into file processing. Data stored in the program are temporary; they are lost when the program terminates. To permanently store the data created in a program, you need to save them in a file on a disk or other permanent storage device. The file can then be transported and read later by other programs. Since data are stored in files, this section introduces how to use the **File** class to obtain file/directory properties, to delete and rename files/directories, and to create directories. The next section introduces how to read/write data from/to text files.

why file?

Every file is placed in a directory in the file system. An *absolute file name* (or *full name*) contains a file name with its complete path and drive letter. For example, **c:\book\ Welcome.java** is the absolute file name for the file **Welcome.java** on the Windows operating system. Here **c:\book** is referred to as the *directory path* for the file. Absolute file names are machine dependent. On the UNIX platform, the absolute file name may be **/home/liang/book/Welcome.java**, where **/home/liang/book** is the directory path for the file **Welcome.java**.

absolute file name

directory path

A *relative file name* is in relation to the current working directory. The complete directory path for a relative file name is omitted. For example, **Welcome.java** is a relative file name. If the current working directory is **c:\book**, the absolute file name would be **c:\book\Welcome.java**.

relative file name

The **File** class is intended to provide an abstraction that deals with most of the machine-dependent complexities of files and path names in a machine-independent fashion. The **File** class contains the methods for obtaining file and directory properties and for renaming and deleting files and directories, as shown in Figure 12.6. However, *the **File** class does not contain the methods for reading and writing file contents.*

The file name is a string. The **File** class is a wrapper class for the file name and its directory path. For example, **new File("c:\\book")** creates a **File** object for the directory **c:\book**, and **new File("c:\\book\\test.dat")** creates a **File** object for the file **c:\book\test.dat**, both on Windows. You can use the **File** class's **isDirectory()** method to check whether the object represents a directory, and the **isFile()** method to check whether the object represents a file.

java.io.File	
+File(pathname: String)	Creates a File object for the specified path name. The path name may be a directory or a file.
+File(parent: String, child: String)	Creates a File object for the child under the directory parent. The child may be a file name or a subdirectory.
+File(parent: File, child: String)	Creates a File object for the child under the directory parent. The parent is a File object. In the preceding constructor, the parent is a string.
+exists(): boolean	Returns true if the file or the directory represented by the File object exists.
+canRead(): boolean	Returns true if the file represented by the File object exists and can be read.
+canWrite(): boolean	Returns true if the file represented by the File object exists and can be written.
+isDirectory(): boolean	Returns true if the File object represents a directory.
+isFile(): boolean	Returns true if the File object represents a file.
+isAbsolute(): boolean	Returns true if the File object is created using an absolute path name.
+isHidden(): boolean	Returns true if the file represented in the File object is hidden. The exact definition of *hidden* is system-dependent. On Windows, you can mark a file hidden in the File Properties dialog box. On Unix systems, a file is hidden if its name begins with a period(.) character.
+getAbsolutePath(): String	Returns the complete absolute file or directory name represented by the File object.
+getCanonicalPath(): String	Returns the same as getAbsolutePath() except that it removes redundant names, such as "." and "..", from the path name, resolves symbolic links (on Unix), and converts drive letters to standard uppercase (on Windows).
+getName(): String	Returns the last name of the complete directory and file name represented by the File object. For example, new File("c:\\book\\test.dat").getName() returns test.dat.
+getPath(): String	Returns the complete directory and file name represented by the File object. For example, new File("c:\\book\\test.dat").getPath() returns c:\book\test.dat.
+getParent(): String	Returns the complete parent directory of the current directory or the file represented by the File object. For example, new File("c:\\book\\test.dat").getParent() returns c:\book.
+lastModified(): long	Returns the time that the file was last modified.
+length(): long	Returns the size of the file, or 0 if it does not exist or if it is a directory.
+listFile(): File[]	Returns the files under the directory for a directory File object.
+delete(): boolean	Deletes the file or directory represented by this File object. The method returns true if the deletion succeeds.
+renameTo(dest: File): boolean	Renames the file or directory represented by this File object to the specified name represented in dest. The method returns true if the operation succeeds.
+mkdir(): boolean	Creates a directory represented in this File object. Returns true if the the directory is created successfully.
+mkdirs(): boolean	Same as mkdir() except that it creates directory along with its parent directories if the parent directories do not exist.

FIGURE 12.6 The File class can be used to obtain file and directory properties, to delete and rename files and directories, and to create directories.

\ in file names

Caution
The directory separator for Windows is a backslash (\). The backslash is a special character in Java and should be written as \\ in a string literal (see Table 4.5).

Note
Constructing a File instance does not create a file on the machine. You can create a File instance for any file name regardless whether it exists or not. You can invoke the **exists()** method on a File instance to check whether the file exists.

Do not use absolute file names in your program. If you use a file name such as **c:\\book\\Welcome.java**, it will work on Windows but not on other platforms. You should use a file name relative to the current directory. For example, you may create a File object using **new File("Welcome.java")** for the file **Welcome.java** in the current directory. You may create a File object using **new File("image/us.gif")** for the file **us.gif** under the **image** directory in the current directory. The forward slash (/) is the Java directory separator, which

relative file name

Java directory separator (/)

is the same as on UNIX. The statement `new File("image/us.gif")` works on Windows, UNIX, and any other platform.

Listing 12.12 demonstrates how to create a `File` object and use the methods in the `File` class to obtain its properties. The program creates a `File` object for the file **us.gif**. This file is stored under the **image** directory in the current directory.

LISTING 12.12 TestFileClass.java

```
 1  public class TestFileClass {
 2    public static void main(String[] args) {
 3      java.io.File file = new java.io.File("image/us.gif");            create a File
 4      System.out.println("Does it exist? " + file.exists());          exists()
 5      System.out.println("The file has " + file.length() + " bytes"); length()
 6      System.out.println("Can it be read? " + file.canRead());        canRead()
 7      System.out.println("Can it be written? " + file.canWrite());    canWrite()
 8      System.out.println("Is it a directory? " + file.isDirectory()); isDirectory()
 9      System.out.println("Is it a file? " + file.isFile());           isFile()
10      System.out.println("Is it absolute? " + file.isAbsolute());     isAbsolute()
11      System.out.println("Is it hidden? " + file.isHidden());         isHidden()
12      System.out.println("Absolute path is " +
13        file.getAbsolutePath());                                      getAbsolutePath()
14      System.out.println("Last modified on " +
15        new java.util.Date(file.lastModified()));                     lastModified()
16    }
17  }
```

The `lastModified()` method returns the date and time when the file was last modified, measured in milliseconds since the beginning of UNIX time (00:00:00 GMT, January 1, 1970). The `Date` class is used to display it in a readable format in lines 14–15.

Figure 12.7a shows a sample run of the program on Windows, and Figure 12.7b, a sample run on UNIX. As shown in the figures, the path-naming conventions on Windows are different from those on UNIX.

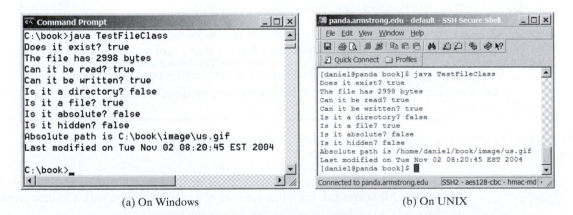

(a) On Windows   (b) On UNIX

FIGURE 12.7 The program creates a `File` object and displays file properties.

12.27 What is wrong about creating a `File` object using the following statement?

```
new File("c:\book\test.dat");
```

12.28 How do you check whether a file already exists? How do you delete a file? How do you rename a file? Can you find the file size (the number of bytes) using the `File` class? How do you create a directory?

12.29 Can you use the `File` class for I/O? Does creating a `File` object create a file on the disk?

12.11 File Input and Output

Key Point

Use the Scanner class for reading text data from a file and the PrintWriter class for writing text data to a file.

VideoNote

Write and read data

A **File** object encapsulates the properties of a file or a path, but it does not contain the methods for creating a file or for writing/reading data to/from a file (referred to as data *input* and *output*, or *I/O* for short). In order to perform I/O, you need to create objects using appropriate Java I/O classes. The objects contain the methods for reading/writing data from/to a file. There are two types of files: text and binary. Text files are essentially characters on disk. This section introduces how to read/write strings and numeric values from/to a text file using the **Scanner** and **PrintWriter** classes. Binary files will be introduced in Chapter 17.

12.11.1 Writing Data Using **PrintWriter**

The **java.io.PrintWriter** class can be used to create a file and write data to a text file. First, you have to create a **PrintWriter** object for a text file as follows:

```
PrintWriter output = new PrintWriter(filename);
```

Then, you can invoke the **print**, **println**, and **printf** methods on the **PrintWriter** object to write data to a file. Figure 12.8 summarizes frequently used methods in **PrintWriter**.

java.io.PrintWriter	
+PrintWriter(file: File)	Creates a PrintWriter object for the specified file object.
+PrintWriter(filename: String)	Creates a PrintWriter object for the specified file-name string.
+print(s: String): void	Writes a string to the file.
+print(c: char): void	Writes a character to the file.
+print(cArray: char[]): void	Writes an array of characters to the file.
+print(i: int): void	Writes an int value to the file.
+print(l: long): void	Writes a long value to the file.
+print(f: float): void	Writes a float value to the file.
+print(d: double): void	Writes a double value to the file.
+print(b: boolean): void	Writes a boolean value to the file.
Also contains the overloaded println methods.	A println method acts like a print method; additionally, it prints a line separator. The line-separator string is defined by the system. It is \r\n on Windows and \n on Unix.
Also contains the overloaded printf methods.	The printf method was introduced in §4.6, "Formatting Console Output."

FIGURE 12.8 The **PrintWriter** class contains the methods for writing data to a text file.

Listing 12.13 gives an example that creates an instance of **PrintWriter** and writes two lines to the file **scores.txt**. Each line consists of a first name (a string), a middle-name initial (a character), a last name (a string), and a score (an integer).

LISTING 12.13 WriteData.java

throws an exception
create File object
file exist?

```
1 public class WriteData {
2   public static void main(String[] args) throws IOException {
3     java.io.File file = new java.io.File("scores.txt");
4     if (file.exists()) {
5       System.out.println("File already exists");
6       System.exit(1);
7     }
8
```

```
 9      // Create a file
10      java.io.PrintWriter output = new java.io.PrintWriter(file);          create PrintWriter
11
12      // Write formatted output to the file
13      output.print("John T Smith ");                                        print data
14      output.println(90);
15      output.print("Eric K Jones ");
16      output.println(85);
17
18      // Close the file
19      output.close();                                                       close file
20    }
21 }
```

John T Smith 90   scores.txt
Eric K Jones 85

Lines 4–7 check whether the file scores.txt exists. If so, exit the program (line 6).

Invoking the constructor of **PrintWriter** will create a new file if the file does not exist. If the file already exists, the current content in the file will be discarded without verifying with the user.

Invoking the constructor of **PrintWriter** may throw an I/O exception. Java forces you to write the code to deal with this type of exception. For simplicity, we declare **throws IOException** in the main method header (line 2).

You have used the **System.out.print**, **System.out.println**, and **System.out.printf** methods to write text to the console. **System.out** is a standard Java object for the console output. You can create **PrintWriter** objects for writing text to any file using **print**, **println**, and **printf** (lines 13–16).

The **close()** method must be used to close the file (line 19). If this method is not invoked, the data may not be saved properly in the file.

12.11.2 Closing Resources Automatically Using try-with-resources

Programmers often forget to close the file. JDK 7 provides the followings new try-with-resources syntax that automatically closes the files.

```
try (declare and create resources) {
  Use the resource to process the file;
}
```

Using the try-with-resources syntax, we rewrite the code in Listing 12.13 in Listing 12.14.

LISTING 12.14 WriteDataWithAutoClose.java

```
 1 public class WriteDataWithAutoClose {
 2   public static void main(String[] args) throws Exception {
 3     java.io.File file = new java.io.File("scores.txt");
 4     if (file.exists()) {
 5       System.out.println("File already exists");
 6       System.exit(0);
 7     }
 8
 9     try (
10       // Create a file
11       java.io.PrintWriter output = new java.io.PrintWriter(file);          declare/create resource
12     ) {
13       // Write formatted output to the file
14       output.print("John T Smith ");                                        use the resouce
15       output.println(90);
16       output.print("Eric K Jones ");
17       output.println(85);
18     }
19   }
20 }
```

A resource is declared and created followed by the keyword **try**. Note that the resources are enclosed in the parentheses (lines 9–12). The resources must be a subtype of **AutoCloseable** such as a **PrinterWriter** that has the **close()** method. A resource must be declared and created in the same statement and multiple resources can be declared and created inside the parentheses. The statements in the block (lines 12–18) immediately following the resource declaration use the resource. After the block is finished, the resource's **close()** method is automatically invoked to close the resource. Using try-with-resources can not only avoid errors but also make the code simpler.

12.11.3 Reading Data Using **Scanner**

The **java.util.Scanner** class was used to read strings and primitive values from the console in Section 2.3, Reading Input from the Console. A **Scanner** breaks its input into tokens delimited by whitespace characters. To read from the keyboard, you create a **Scanner** for **System.in**, as follows:

```
Scanner input = new Scanner(System.in);
```

To read from a file, create a **Scanner** for a file, as follows:

```
Scanner input = new Scanner(new File(filename));
```

Figure 12.9 summarizes frequently used methods in **Scanner**.

java.util.Scanner	
+Scanner(source: File)	Creates a Scanner that scans tokens from the specified file.
+Scanner(source: String)	Creates a Scanner that scans tokens from the specified string.
+close()	Closes this scanner.
+hasNext(): boolean	Returns true if this scanner has more data to be read.
+next(): String	Returns next token as a string from this scanner.
+nextLine(): String	Returns a line ending with the line separator from this scanner.
+nextByte(): byte	Returns next token as a byte from this scanner.
+nextShort(): short	Returns next token as a short from this scanner.
+nextInt(): int	Returns next token as an int from this scanner.
+nextLong(): long	Returns next token as a long from this scanner.
+nextFloat(): float	Returns next token as a float from this scanner.
+nextDouble(): double	Returns next token as a double from this scanner.
+useDelimiter(pattern: String): Scanner	Sets this scanner's delimiting pattern and returns this scanner.

FIGURE 12.9   The **Scanner** class contains the methods for scanning data.

Listing 12.15 gives an example that creates an instance of **Scanner** and reads data from the file **scores.txt**.

LISTING 12.15   ReadData.java

```
 1  import java.util.Scanner;
 2
 3  public class ReadData {
 4    public static void main(String[] args) throws Exception {
 5      // Create a File instance
 6      java.io.File file = new java.io.File("scores.txt");
 7
 8      // Create a Scanner for the file
 9      Scanner input = new Scanner(file);
```

create a File

create a Scanner

```
10
11        // Read data from a file                          scores.txt
12        while (input.hasNext()) {                    John  T  Smith  90
13          String firstName = input.next();           Eric K Jones 85
14          String mi = input.next();
15          String lastName = input.next();
16          int score = input.nextInt();
17          System.out.println(
18            firstName + " " + mi + " " + lastName + " " + score);
19        }
20
21        // Close the file
22        input.close();
23      }
24    }
```

has next?
read items

close file

Note that **new Scanner(String)** creates a **Scanner** for a given string. To create a **Scanner** to read data from a file, you have to use the **java.io.File** class to create an instance of the **File** using the constructor **new File(filename)** (line 6), and use **new Scanner(File)** to create a **Scanner** for the file (line 9).

File class

Invoking the constructor **new Scanner(File)** may throw an I/O exception, so the **main** method declares **throws Exception** in line 4.

throws Exception

Each iteration in the **while** loop reads the first name, middle initial, last name, and score from the text file (lines 12–19). The file is closed in line 22.

It is not necessary to close the input file (line 22), but it is a good practice to do so to release the resources occupied by the file. You can rewrite this program using the try-with-resources syntax. See www.cs.armstrong.edu/liang/intro10e/html/ReadDataWithAutoClose.html.

close file

12.11.4 How Does **Scanner** Work?

The **nextByte()**, **nextShort()**, **nextInt()**, **nextLong()**, **nextFloat()**, **next-Double()**, and **next()** methods are known as *token-reading methods*, because they read tokens separated by delimiters. By default, the delimiters are whitespace characters. You can use the **useDelimiter(String regex)** method to set a new pattern for delimiters.

token-reading method
change delimiter

How does an input method work? A token-reading method first skips any delimiters (whitespace characters by default), then reads a token ending at a delimiter. The token is then automatically converted into a value of the **byte**, **short**, **int**, **long**, **float**, or **double** type for **nextByte()**, **nextShort()**, **nextInt()**, **nextLong()**, **nextFloat()**, and **nextDouble()**, respectively. For the **next()** method, no conversion is performed. If the token does not match the expected type, a runtime exception **java.util.InputMismatchException** will be thrown.

InputMismatchException

Both methods **next()** and **nextLine()** read a string. The **next()** method reads a string delimited by delimiters, and **nextLine()** reads a line ending with a line separator.

next() vs. nextLine()

Note

The line-separator string is defined by the system. It is **\r\n** on Windows and **\n** on UNIX. To get the line separator on a particular platform, use

line separator

```
String lineSeparator = System.getProperty("line.separator");
```

If you enter input from a keyboard, a line ends with the *Enter* key, which corresponds to the **\n** character.

The token-reading method does not read the delimiter after the token. If the **nextLine()** method is invoked after a token-reading method, this method reads characters that start from this delimiter and end with the line separator. The line separator is read, but it is not part of the string returned by **nextLine()**.

behavior of nextLine()

input from file

Suppose a text file named **test.txt** contains a line

```
34 567
```

After the following code is executed,

```
Scanner input = new Scanner(new File("test.txt"));
int intValue = input.nextInt();
String line = input.nextLine();
```

intValue contains **34** and **line** contains the characters ' ', **5**, **6**, and **7**.

input from keyboard

What happens if the input is *entered from the keyboard*? Suppose you enter **34**, press the *Enter* key, then enter **567** and press the *Enter* key for the following code:

```
Scanner input = new Scanner(System.in);
int intValue = input.nextInt();
String line = input.nextLine();
```

You will get **34** in **intValue** and an empty string in **line**. Why? Here is the reason. The token-reading method **nextInt()** reads in **34** and stops at the delimiter, which in this case is a line separator (the *Enter* key). The **nextLine()** method ends after reading the line separator and returns the string read before the line separator. Since there are no characters before the line separator, **line** is empty.

scan a string

You can read data from a file or from the keyboard using the **Scanner** class. You can also scan data from a string using the **Scanner** class. For example, the following code

```
Scanner input = new Scanner("13 14");
int sum = input.nextInt() + input.nextInt();
System.out.println("Sum is " + sum);
```

displays

```
The sum is 27
```

12.11.5 Case Study: Replacing Text

Suppose you are to write a program named **ReplaceText** that replaces all occurrences of a string in a text file with a new string. The file name and strings are passed as command-line arguments as follows:

```
java ReplaceText sourceFile targetFile oldString newString
```

For example, invoking

```
java ReplaceText FormatString.java t.txt StringBuilder StringBuffer
```

replaces all the occurrences of **StringBuilder** by **StringBuffer** in the file **FormatString .java** and saves the new file in **t.txt**.

Listing 12.16 gives the program. The program checks the number of arguments passed to the **main** method (lines 7–11), checks whether the source and target files exist (lines 14–25), creates a **Scanner** for the source file (line 29), creates a **PrintWriter** for the target file (line 30), and repeatedly reads a line from the source file (line 33), replaces the text (line 34), and writes a new line to the target file (line 35).

LISTING 12.16 ReplaceText.java

```
1  import java.io.*;
2  import java.util.*;
3
```

```
 4  public class ReplaceText {
 5    public static void main(String[] args) throws Exception {
 6      // Check command line parameter usage
 7      if (args.length != 4) {                                           check command usage
 8        System.out.println(
 9          "Usage: java ReplaceText sourceFile targetFile oldStr newStr");
10        System.exit(1);
11      }
12
13      // Check if source file exists
14      File sourceFile = new File(args[0]);
15      if (!sourceFile.exists()) {                                       source file exists?
16        System.out.println("Source file " + args[0] + " does not exist");
17        System.exit(2);
18      }
19
20      // Check if target file exists
21      File targetFile = new File(args[1]);
22      if (targetFile.exists()) {                                        target file exists?
23        System.out.println("Target file " + args[1] + " already exists");
24        System.exit(3);
25      }
26
27      try (                                                             try-with-resources
28        // Create input and output files
29        Scanner input = new Scanner(sourceFile);                        create a Scanner
30        PrintWriter output = new PrintWriter(targetFile);               create a PrintWriter
31      ) {
32        while (input.hasNext()) {                                       has next?
33          String s1 = input.nextLine();                                read a line
34          String s2 = s1.replaceAll(args[2], args[3]);
35          output.println(s2);
36        }
37      }
38    }
39  }
```

In a normal situation, the program is terminated after a file is copied. The program is terminated abnormally if the command-line arguments are not used properly (lines 7–11), if the source file does not exist (lines 14–18), or if the target file already exists (lines 22–25). The exit status code 1, 2, and 3 are used to indicate these abnormal terminations (lines 10, 17, 24).

12.30 How do you create a `PrintWriter` to write data to a file? What is the reason to declare `throws Exception` in the main method in Listing 12.13, WriteData.java? What would happen if the `close()` method were not invoked in Listing 12.13?

Check Point

12.31 Show the contents of the file **temp.txt** after the following program is executed.

```
public class Test {
  public static void main(String[] args) throws Exception {
    java.io.PrintWriter output = new
      java.io.PrintWriter("temp.txt");
    output.printf("amount is %f %e\r\n", 32.32, 32.32);
    output.printf("amount is %5.4f %5.4e\r\n", 32.32, 32.32);
    output.printf("%6b\r\n", (1 > 2));
    output.printf("%6s\r\n", "Java");
    output.close();
  }
}
```

12.32 Rewrite the code in the preceding question using a try-with-resources syntax.

12.33 How do you create a **Scanner** to read data from a file? What is the reason to define **throws Exception** in the main method in Listing 12.15, ReadData.java? What would happen if the **close()** method were not invoked in Listing 12.15?

12.34 What will happen if you attempt to create a **Scanner** for a nonexistent file? What will happen if you attempt to create a **PrintWriter** for an existing file?

12.35 Is the line separator the same on all platforms? What is the line separator on Windows?

12.36 Suppose you enter 45 57.8 789, then press the *Enter* key. Show the contents of the variables after the following code is executed.

```
Scanner input = new Scanner(System.in);
int intValue = input.nextInt();
double doubleValue = input.nextDouble();
String line = input.nextLine();
```

12.37 Suppose you enter 45, press the *Enter* key, 57.8, press the *Enter* key, 789, and press the *Enter* key. Show the contents of the variables after the following code is executed.

```
Scanner input = new Scanner(System.in);
int intValue = input.nextInt();
double doubleValue = input.nextDouble();
String line = input.nextLine();
```

12.12 Reading Data from the Web

Just like you can read data from a file on your computer, you can read data from a file on the Web.

In addition to reading data from a local file on a computer or file server, you can also access data from a file that is on the Web if you know the file's URL (Uniform Resource Locator—the unique address for a file on the Web). For example, www.google.com/index.html is the URL for the file **index.html** located on the Google Web server. When you enter the URL in a Web browser, the Web server sends the data to your browser, which renders the data graphically. Figure 12.10 illustrates how this process works.

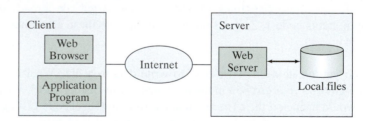

FIGURE 12.10 The client retrieves files from a Web server.

For an application program to read data from a URL, you first need to create a **URL** object using the **java.net.URL** class with this constructor:

    public URL(String spec) **throws** MalformedURLException

For example, the following statement creates a URL object for http://www.google.com/index.html.

```
1  try {
2    URL url = new URL("http://www.google.com/index.html");
3  }
```

```
 4   catch (MalformedURLException ex) {
 5     ex.printStackTrace();
 6   }
```

A `MalformedURLException` is thrown if the URL string has a syntax error. For example, the URL string "http:www.google.com/index.html" would cause a `MalformedURLException` runtime error because two slashes (`//`) are required after the colon (`:`). Note that the `http://` prefix is required for the `URL` class to recognize a valid URL. It would be wrong if you replace line 2 with the following code:

```
URL url = new URL("www.google.com/index.html");
```

After a `URL` object is created, you can use the `openStream()` method defined in the `URL` class to open an input stream and use this stream to create a `Scanner` object as follows:

```
Scanner input = new Scanner(url.openStream());
```

Now you can read the data from the input stream just like from a local file. The example in Listing 12.17 prompts the user to enter a URL and displays the size of the file.

Listing 12.17 ReadFileFromURL.java

```
 1   import java.util.Scanner;
 2
 3   public class ReadFileFromURL {
 4     public static void main(String[] args) {
 5       System.out.print("Enter a URL: ");
 6       String URLString = new Scanner(System.in).next();          enter a URL
 7
 8       try {
 9         java.net.URL url = new java.net.URL(URLString);           create a URL object
10         int count = 0;
11         Scanner input = new Scanner(url.openStream());           create a Scanner object
12         while (input.hasNext()) {                                 more to read?
13           String line = input.nextLine();                        read a line
14           count += line.length();
15         }
16
17         System.out.println("The file size is " + count + " characters");
18       }
19       catch (java.net.MalformedURLException ex) {                MalformedURLException
20         System.out.println("Invalid URL");
21       }
22       catch (java.io.IOException ex) {                           IOException
23         System.out.println("I/O Errors: no such file");
24       }
25     }
26   }
```

```
Enter a URL: http://cs.armstrong.edu/liang/data/Lincoln.txt  ↵Enter
The file size is 1469 characters
```

```
Enter a URL: http://www.yahoo.com  ↵Enter
The file size is 190006 characters
```

The program prompts the user to enter a URL string (line 6) and creates a **URL** object (line 9). The constructor will throw a **java.net.MalformedURLException** (line 19) if the URL isn't formed correctly.

The program creates a **Scanner** object from the input stream for the URL (line 11). If the URL is formed correctly but does not exist, an **IOException** will be thrown (line 22). For example, http://google.com/index1.html uses the appropriate form, but the URL itself does not exist. An **IOException** would be thrown if this URL was used for this program.

12.38 How do you create a **Scanner** object for reading text from a URL?

12.13 Case Study: Web Crawler

This case study develops a program that travels the Web by following hyperlinks.

Web crawler

The World Wide Web, abbreviated as WWW, W3, or Web, is a system of interlinked hypertext documents on the Internet. With a Web browser, you can view a document and follow the hyperlinks to view other documents. In this case study, we will develop a program that automatically traverses the documents on the Web by following the hyperlinks. This type of program is commonly known as a *Web crawler*. For simplicity, our program follows for the hyperlink that starts with **http://**. Figure 12.11 shows an example of traversing the Web. We start from a Web page that contains three URLs named **URL1**, **URL2**, and **URL3**. Following **URL1** leads to the page that contains three URLs named **URL11**, **URL12**, and **URL13**. Following **URL2** leads to the page that contains two URLs named **URL21** and **URL22**. Following **URL3** leads to the page that contains four URLs named **URL31**, **URL32**, and **URL33**, and **URL34**. Continue to traverse the Web following the new hyperlinks. As you see, this process may continue forever, but we will exit the program once we have traversed 100 pages.

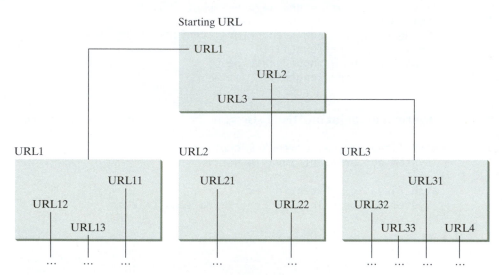

FIGURE 12.11 The client retrieves files from a Web server.

The program follows the URLs to traverse the Web. To ensure that each URL is traversed only once, the program maintains two lists of URLs. One list stores the URLs pending for traversing and the other stores the URLs that have already been traversed. The algorithm for this program can be described as follows:

```
Add the starting URL to a list named listOfPendingURLs;
while listOfPendingURLs is not empty and size of listOfTraversedURLs
<= 100 {
```

```
  Remove a URL from listOfPendingURLs;
  if this URL is not in listOfTraversedURLs {
    Add it to listOfTraversedURLs;
    Display this URL;
    Read the page from this URL and for each URL contained in the page {
      Add it to listOfPendingURLs if it is not in listOfTraversedURLs;
    }
  }
}
```

Listing 12.18 gives the program that implements this algorithm.

LISTING 12.18 WebCrawler.java

```
1  import java.util.Scanner;
2  import java.util.ArrayList;
3
4  public class WebCrawler {
5    public static void main(String[] args) {
6      java.util.Scanner input = new java.util.Scanner(System.in);
7      System.out.print("Enter a URL: ");
8      String url = input.nextLine();                              enter a URL
9      crawler(url); // Traverse the Web from the a starting url    craw from this URL
10   }
11
12   public static void crawler(String startingURL) {
13     ArrayList<String> listOfPendingURLs = new ArrayList<>();     list of pending URLs
14     ArrayList<String> listOfTraversedURLs = new ArrayList<>();   list of traversed URLs
15
16     listOfPendingURLs.add(startingURL);                         add starting URL
17     while (!listOfPendingURLs.isEmpty() &&
18         listOfTraversedURLs.size() <= 100) {
19       String urlString = listOfPendingURLs.remove(0);           get the first URL
20       if (!listOfTraversedURLs.contains(urlString)) {
21         listOfTraversedURLs.add(urlString);                     URL traversed
22         System.out.println("Craw " + urlString);
23
24         for (String s: getSubURLs(urlString)) {
25           if (!listOfTraversedURLs.contains(s))
26             listOfPendingURLs.add(s);                           add a new URL
27         }
28       }
29     }
30   }
31
32   public static ArrayList<String> getSubURLs(String urlString) {
33     ArrayList<String> list = new ArrayList<>();
34
35     try {
36       java.net.URL url = new java.net.URL(urlString);
37       Scanner input = new Scanner(url.openStream());
38       int current = 0;
39       while (input.hasNext()) {
40         String line = input.nextLine();                         read a line
41         current = line.indexOf("http:", current);               search for a URL
42         while (current > 0) {                                    end of a URL
43           int endIndex = line.indexOf("\"", current);
44           if (endIndex > 0) { // Ensure that a correct URL is found   URL ends with "
45             list.add(line.substring(current, endIndex));         extract a URL
46             current = line.indexOf("http:", endIndex);           search for next URL
47           }
```

```
48              else
49                 current = -1;
50            }
51         }
52      }
53      catch (Exception ex) {
54         System.out.println("Error: " + ex.getMessage());
55      }
56
57      return list;
58   }
59 }
```

return URLs

```
Enter a URL: http://cs.armstrong.edu/liang  ↵Enter
Enter a URL: http://www.cs.armstrong.edu/liang
Craw http://www.cs.armstrong.edu/liang
Craw http://www.cs.armstrong.edu
Craw http://www.armstrong.edu
Craw http://www.pearsonhighered.com/liang
...
```

The program prompts the user to enter a starting URL (lines 7–8) and invokes the `crawler(url)` method to traverse the web (line 9).

The `crawler(url)` method adds the starting url to `listOfPendingURLs` (line 16) and repeatedly processes each URL in `listOfPendingURLs` in a while loop (lines 17–29). It removes the first URL in the list (line 19) and processes the URL if it has not been processed (lines 20–28). To process each URL, the program first adds the URL to `listOfTraversedURLs` (line 21). This list stores all the URLs that have been processed. The `getSubURLs(url)` method returns a list of URLs in the Web page for the specified URL (line 24). The program uses a foreach loop to add each URL in the page into `listOfPendingURLs` if it is not in `listOfTraversedURLs` (lines 24–26).

The `getSubURLs(url)` method reads each line from the Web page (line 40) and searches for the URLs in the line (line 41). Note that a correct URL cannot contain line break characters. So it is sufficient to limit the search for a URL in one line of the text in a Web page. For simplicity, we assume that a URL ends with a quotation mark `"` (line 43). The method obtains a URL and adds it to a list (line 45). A line may contain multiple URLs. The method continues to search for the next URL (line 46). If no URL is found in the line, `current` is set to `-1` (line 49). The URLs contained in the page are returned in the form of a list (line 57).

The program terminates when the number of traversed URLs reaches to 100 (line 18).

This is a simple program to traverse the Web. Later you will learn the techniques to make the program more efficient and robust.

Check Point

12.39 Before a URL is added to `listOfPendingURLs`, line 25 checks whether it has been traversed. Is it possible that `listOfPendingURLs` contains duplicate URLs? If so, give an example.

KEY TERMS

absolute file name 473	exception 450
chained exception 469	exception propagation 459
checked exception 457	relative file name 473
declare exception 458	throw exception 452
directory path 473	unchecked exception 457

CHAPTER SUMMARY

1. Exception handling enables a method to throw an exception to its caller.

2. A Java *exception* is an instance of a class derived from `java.lang.Throwable`. Java provides a number of predefined exception classes, such as `Error`, `Exception`, `RuntimeException`, `ClassNotFoundException`, `NullPointerException`, and `ArithmeticException`. You can also define your own exception class by extending `Exception`.

3. Exceptions occur during the execution of a method. `RuntimeException` and `Error` are *unchecked exceptions*; all other exceptions are *checked*.

4. When *declaring a method*, you have to declare a checked exception if the method might throw it, thus telling the compiler what can go wrong.

5. The keyword for declaring an exception is `throws`, and the keyword for throwing an exception is `throw`.

6. To invoke the method that declares checked exceptions, enclose it in a `try` statement. When an exception occurs during the execution of the method, the `catch` block catches and handles the exception.

7. If an exception is not caught in the current method, it is passed to its caller. The process is repeated until the exception is caught or passed to the `main` method.

8. Various exception classes can be derived from a common superclass. If a `catch` block catches the exception objects of a superclass, it can also catch all the exception objects of the subclasses of that superclass.

9. The order in which exceptions are specified in a `catch` block is important. A compile error will result if you specify an exception object of a class after an exception object of the superclass of that class.

10. When an exception occurs in a method, the method exits immediately if it does not catch the exception. If the method is required to perform some task before exiting, you can catch the exception in the method and then rethrow it to its caller.

11. The code in the `finally` block is executed under all circumstances, regardless of whether an exception occurs in the `try` block or whether an exception is caught if it occurs.

12. Exception handling separates error-handling code from normal programming tasks, thus making programs easier to read and to modify.

13. Exception handling should not be used to replace simple tests. You should perform simple test using `if` statements whenever possible, and reserve exception handling for dealing with situations that cannot be handled with `if` statements.

14. The `File` class is used to obtain file properties and manipulate files. It does not contain the methods for creating a file or for reading/writing data from/to a file.

15. You can use `Scanner` to read string and primitive data values from a text file and use `PrintWriter` to create a file and write data to a text file.

16. You can read from a file on the Web using the `URL` class.

QUIZ

Answer the quiz for this chapter online at www.cs.armstrong.edu/liang/intro10e/quiz.html.

MyProgrammingLab™

PROGRAMMING EXERCISES

Sections 12.2–12.9

*12.1 (*NumberFormatException*) Listing 7.9, Calculator.java, is a simple command-line calculator. Note that the program terminates if any operand is nonnumeric. Write a program with an exception handler that deals with nonnumeric operands; then write another program without using an exception handler to achieve the same objective. Your program should display a message that informs the user of the wrong operand type before exiting (see Figure 12.12).

```
Command Prompt                                    _ □ ×
c:\exercise>java Exercise12_01 4 + 5
4 + 5 = 9

c:\exercise>java Exercise12_01 4 - 5
4 - 5 = -1

c:\exercise>java Exercise12_01 4x - 5
Wrong Input: 4x

c:\exercise>_
```

FIGURE 12.12 The program performs arithmetic operations and detects input errors.

*12.2 (*InputMismatchException*) Write a program that prompts the user to read two integers and displays their sum. Your program should prompt the user to read the number again if the input is incorrect.

*12.3 (*ArrayIndexOutOfBoundsException*) Write a program that meets the following requirements:

■ Creates an array with **100** randomly chosen integers.
■ Prompts the user to enter the index of the array, then displays the corresponding element value. If the specified index is out of bounds, display the message **Out of Bounds**.

*12.4 (*IllegalArgumentException*) Modify the **Loan** class in Listing 10.2 to throw **IllegalArgumentException** if the loan amount, interest rate, or number of years is less than or equal to zero.

*12.5 (*IllegalTriangleException*) Programming Exercise 11.1 defined the **Triangle** class with three sides. In a triangle, the sum of any two sides is greater than the other side. The **Triangle** class must adhere to this rule. Create the **IllegalTriangleException** class, and modify the constructor of the **Triangle** class to throw an **IllegalTriangleException** object if a triangle is created with sides that violate the rule, as follows:

```
/** Construct a triangle with the specified sides */
public Triangle(double side1, double side2, double side3)
  throws IllegalTriangleException {
  // Implement it
}
```

*12.6 (*NumberFormatException*) Listing 6.8 implements the **hex2Dec(String hexString)** method, which converts a hex string into a decimal number. Implement the **hex2Dec** method to throw a **NumberFormatException** if the string is not a hex string.

*12.7 (*NumberFormatException*) Write the **bin2Dec(String binaryString)** method to convert a binary string into a decimal number. Implement the **bin2Dec** method to throw a **NumberFormatException** if the string is not a binary string.

*12.8 (*HexFormatException*) Exercise 12.6 implements the **hex2Dec** method to throw a **NumberFormatException** if the string is not a hex string. Define a custom exception called **HexFormatException**. Implement the **hex2Dec** method to throw a **HexFormatException** if the string is not a hex string.

VideoNote

HexFormatException

*12.9 (*BinaryFormatException*) Exercise 12.7 implements the **bin2Dec** method to throw a **BinaryFormatException** if the string is not a binary string. Define a custom exception called **BinaryFormatException**. Implement the **bin2Dec** method to throw a **BinaryFormatException** if the string is not a binary string.

*12.10 (*OutOfMemoryError*) Write a program that causes the JVM to throw an **OutOfMemoryError** and catches and handles this error.

Sections 12.10–12.12

**12.11 (*Remove text*) Write a program that removes all the occurrences of a specified string from a text file. For example, invoking

```
java Exercise12_11 John filename
```

removes the string **John** from the specified file. Your program should get the arguments from the command line.

**12.12 (*Reformat Java source code*) Write a program that converts the Java source code from the next-line brace style to the end-of-line brace style. For example, the following Java source in (a) uses the next-line brace style. Your program converts it to the end-of-line brace style in (b).

```
public class Test
{
  public static void main(String[] args)
  {
    // Some statements
  }
}
```

```
public class Test {
  public static void main(String[] args) {
    // Some statements
  }
}
```

(a) Next-line brace style

(b) End-of-line brace style

Your program can be invoked from the command line with the Java source-code file as the argument. It converts the Java source code to a new format. For example, the following command converts the Java source-code file **Test.java** to the end-of-line brace style.

```
java Exercise12_12 Test.java
```

*12.13 (*Count characters, words, and lines in a file*) Write a program that will count the number of characters, words, and lines in a file. Words are separated by whitespace characters. The file name should be passed as a command-line argument, as shown in Figure 12.13.

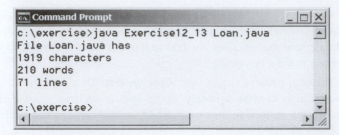

FIGURE 12.13 The program displays the number of characters, words, and lines in the given file.

*12.14 (*Process scores in a text file*) Suppose that a text file contains an unspecified number of scores separated by blanks. Write a program that prompts the user to enter the file, reads the scores from the file, and displays their total and average.

*12.15 (*Write/read data*) Write a program to create a file named **Exercise12_15.txt** if it does not exist. Write **100** integers created randomly into the file using text I/O. Integers are separated by spaces in the file. Read the data back from the file and display the data in increasing order.

**12.16 (*Replace text*) Listing 12.16, ReplaceText.java, gives a program that replaces text in a source file and saves the change into a new file. Revise the program to save the change into the original file. For example, invoking

```
java Exercise12_16 file oldString newString
```

replaces **oldString** in the source file with **newString**.

***12.17 (*Game: hangman*) Rewrite Programming Exercise 7.35. The program reads the words stored in a text file named **hangman.txt**. Words are delimited by spaces.

12.18 (*Add package statement*) Suppose you have Java source files under the directories **chapter1, **chapter2**, . . . , **chapter34**. Write a program to insert the statement **package chapteri;** as the first line for each Java source file under the directory **chapteri**. Suppose **chapter1**, **chapter2**, . . . , **chapter34** are under the root directory **srcRootDirectory**. The root directory and **chapteri** directory may contain other folders and files. Use the following command to run the program:

```
java Exercise12_18 srcRootDirectory
```

*12.19 (*Count words*) Write a program that counts the number of words in President Abraham Lincoln's Gettysburg address from http://cs.armstrong.edu/liang/data/Lincoln.txt.

12.20 (*Remove package statement*) Suppose you have Java source files under the directories **chapter1, **chapter2**, . . . , **chapter34**. Write a program to remove the statement **package chapteri;** in the first line for each Java source file under the directory **chapteri**. Suppose **chapter1**, **chapter2**, . . . , **chapter34** are under the root directory **srcRootDirectory**. The root directory and **chapteri** directory may contain other folders and files. Use the following command to run the program:

```
java Exercise12_20 srcRootDirectory
```

*12.21 (*Data sorted?*) Write a program that reads the strings from file **SortedStrings.txt** and reports whether the strings in the files are stored in increasing order.

If the strings are not sorted in the file, displays the first two strings that are out of the order.

**12.22 (*Replace text*) Revise Programming Exercise 12.16 to replace a string in a file with a new string for all files in the specified directory using the command:

```
java Exercise12_22 dir oldString newString
```

**12.23 (*Process scores in a text file on the Web*) Suppose that the text file on the Web http://cs.armstrong.edu/liang/data/Scores.txt contains an unspecified number of scores. Write a program that reads the scores from the file and displays their total and average. Scores are separated by blanks.

*12.24 (*Create large dataset*) Create a data file with 1,000 lines. Each line in the file consists of a faculty member's first name, last name, rank, and salary. The faculty member's first name and last name for the ith line are FirstName$i$ and LastName$i$. The rank is randomly generated as assistant, associate, and full. The salary is randomly generated as a number with two digits after the decimal point. The salary for an assistant professor should be in the range from 50,000 to 80,000, for associate professor from 60,000 to 110,000, and for full professor from 75,000 to 130,000. Save the file in **Salary.txt**. Here are some sample data:

FirstName1 LastName1 assistant 60055.95

FirstName2 LastName2 associate 81112.45

. . .

FirstName1000 LastName1000 full 92255.21

*12.25 (*Process large dataset*) A university posts its employees' salaries at http://cs.armstrong.edu/liang/data/Salary.txt. Each line in the file consists of a faculty member's first name, last name, rank, and salary (see Programming Exercise 12.24). Write a program to display the total salary for assistant professors, associate professors, full professors, and all faculty, respectively, and display the average salary for assistant professors, associate professors, full professors, and all faculty, respectively.

**12.26 (*Create a directory*) Write a program that prompts the user to enter a directory name and creates a directory using the `File`'s `mkdirs` method. The program displays the message "Directory created successfully" if a directory is created or "Directory already exists" if the directory already exists.

12.27 (*Replace words*) Suppose you have a lot of files in a directory that contain words **Exercise*i*_*j*, where i and j are digits. Write a program that pads a 0 before i if i is a single digit and 0 before j if j is a single digit. For example, the word **Exercise2_1** in a file will be replaced by **Exercise02_01**. In Java, when you pass the symbol * from the command line, it refers to all files in the directory (see Supplement III.V). Use the following command to run your program.

```
java Exercise12_27 *
```

12.28 (*Rename files*) Suppose you have a lot of files in a directory named **Exercise*i*_*j*, where i and j are digits. Write a program that pads a 0 before i if i is a single digit. For example, a file named **Exercise2_1** in a directory will be renamed to **Exercise02_1**. In Java, when you pass the symbol * from the command line, it refers to all files in the directory (see Supplement III.V). Use the following command to run your program.

```
java Exercise12_28 *
```

12.29 (*Rename files*) Suppose you have a lot of files in a directory named **Exercise*i_j*, where *i* and *j* are digits. Write a program that pads a 0 before *j* if *j* is a single digit. For example, a file named **Exercise2_1** in a directory will be renamed to **Exercise2_01**. In Java, when you pass the symbol * from the command line, it refers to all files in the directory (see Supplement III.V). Use the following command to run your program.

```
java Exercise12_29 *
```

**12.30 (*Occurrences of each letter*) Write a program that prompts the user to enter a file name and displays the occurrences of each letter in the file. Letters are case-insensitive. Here is a sample run:

```
Enter a filename: Lincoln.txt  ↵Enter
Number of A's: 56
Number of B's: 134
...
Number of Z's: 9
```

*12.31 (*Baby name popularity ranking*) The popularity ranking of baby names from years 2001 to 2010 is downloaded from www.ssa.gov/oact/babynames and stored in files named **babynameranking2001.txt, babynameranking2002.txt, . . . , babynameranking2010.txt**. Each file contains one thousand lines. Each line contains a ranking, a boy's name, number for the boy's name, a girl's name, and number for the girl's name. For example, the first two lines in the file **babynameranking2010.txt** are as follows:

1	Jacob	21,875	Isabella	22,731
2	Ethan	17,866	Sophia	20,477

So, the boy's name Jacob and girl's name Isabella are ranked #1 and the boy's name Ethan and girl's name Sophia are ranked #2. 21,875 boys are named Jacob and 22,731 girls are named Isabella. Write a program that prompts the user to enter the year, gender, and followed by a name, and displays the ranking of the name for the year. Here is a sample run:

```
Enter the year: 2010  ↵Enter
Enter the gender: M  ↵Enter
Enter the name: Javier  ↵Enter
Javier is ranked #190 in year 2010
```

```
Enter the year: 2010  ↵Enter
Enter the gender: F  ↵Enter
Enter the name: ABC  ↵Enter
The name ABC is not ranked in year 2010
```

*12.32   (*Ranking summary*) Write a program that uses the files described in Programming Exercise 12.31 and displays a ranking summary table for the first five girl's and boy's names as follows:

Year	Rank 1	Rank 2	Rank 3	Rank 4	Rank 5	Rank 1	Rank 2	Rank 3	Rank 4	Rank 5
2010	Isabella	Sophia	Emma	Olivia	Ava	Jacob	Ethan	Michael	Jayden	William
2009	Isabella	Emma	Olivia	Sophia	Ava	Jacob	Ethan	Michael	Alexander	William
...										
2001	Emily	Madison	Hannah	Ashley	Alexis	Jacob	Michael	Matthew	Joshua	Christopher

12.33   (*Search Web*) Modify Listing 12.18 WebCrawler.java to search for the word **Computer Programming starting from the URL http://cs.armstrong.edu/liang. Your program terminates once the word is found. Display the URL for the page that contains the word.

ABSTRACT CLASSES AND INTERFACES

Objectives

- To design and use abstract classes (§13.2).

- To generalize numeric wrapper classes, `BigInteger`, and `BigDecimal` using the abstract `Number` class (§13.3).

- To process a calendar using the `Calendar` and `GregorianCalendar` classes (§13.4).

- To specify common behavior for objects using interfaces (§13.5).

- To define interfaces and define classes that implement interfaces (§13.5).

- To define a natural order using the `Comparable` interface (§13.6).

- To make objects cloneable using the `Cloneable` interface (§13.7).

- To explore the similarities and differences among concrete classes, abstract classes, and interfaces (§13.8).

- To design the `Rational` class for processing rational numbers (§13.9).

- To design classes that follow the class-design guidelines (§13.10).

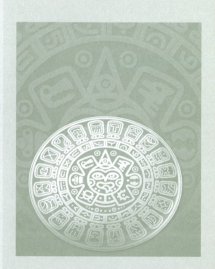

13.1 Introduction

A superclass defines common behavior for related subclasses. An interface can be used to define common behavior for classes (including unrelated classes).

problem
interface

You can use the `java.util.Arrays.sort` method to sort an array of numbers or strings. Can you apply the same `sort` method to sort an array of geometric objects? In order to write such code, you have to know about interfaces. An *interface* is for defining common behavior for classes (including unrelated classes). Before discussing interfaces, we introduce a closely related subject: abstract classes.

13.2 Abstract Classes

An abstract class cannot be used to create objects. An abstract class can contain abstract methods, which are implemented in concrete subclasses.

VideoNote

Abstract `GeometricObject`
class

abstract class

In the inheritance hierarchy, classes become more specific and concrete *with each new subclass*. If you move from a subclass back up to a superclass, the classes become more general and less specific. Class design should ensure that a superclass contains common features of its subclasses. Sometimes a superclass is so abstract that it cannot be used to create any specific instances. Such a class is referred to as an *abstract class*.

In Chapter 11, `GeometricObject` was defined as the superclass for `Circle` and `Rectangle`. `GeometricObject` models common features of geometric objects. Both `Circle` and `Rectangle` contain the `getArea()` and `getPerimeter()` methods for computing the area and perimeter of a circle and a rectangle. Since you can compute areas and perimeters for all geometric objects, it is better to define the `getArea()` and `getPerimeter()` methods in the `GeometricObject` class. However, these methods cannot be implemented in the `GeometricObject` class, because their implementation depends on the specific type of geometric object. Such methods are referred to as *abstract methods* and are denoted using the **abstract** modifier in the method header. After you define the methods in `GeometricObject`, it becomes an abstract class. Abstract classes are denoted using the **abstract** modifier in the class header. In UML graphic notation, the names of abstract classes and their abstract methods are italicized, as shown in Figure 13.1. Listing 13.1 gives the source code for the new `GeometricObject` class.

abstract method

abstract modifier

LISTING 13.1 GeometricObject.java

abstract class

```java
1  public abstract class GeometricObject {
2    private String color = "white";
3    private boolean filled;
4    private java.util.Date dateCreated;
5
6    /** Construct a default geometric object */
7    protected GeometricObject() {
8      dateCreated = new java.util.Date();
9    }
10
11   /** Construct a geometric object with color and filled value */
12   protected GeometricObject(String color, boolean filled) {
13     dateCreated = new java.util.Date();
14     this.color = color;
15     this.filled = filled;
16   }
17
18   /** Return color */
19   public String getColor() {
20     return color;
```

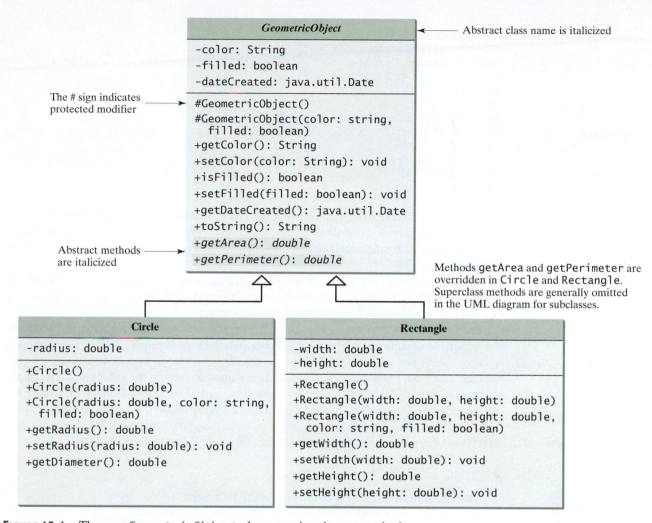

The # sign indicates protected modifier

Abstract class name is italicized

Abstract methods are italicized

Methods `getArea` and `getPerimeter` are overridden in `Circle` and `Rectangle`. Superclass methods are generally omitted in the UML diagram for subclasses.

FIGURE 13.1 The new `GeometricObject` class contains abstract methods.

```
21    }
22
23    /** Set a new color */
24    public void setColor(String color) {
25      this.color = color;
26    }
27
28    /** Return filled. Since filled is boolean,
29     *  the get method is named isFilled */
30    public boolean isFilled() {
31      return filled;
32    }
33
34    /** Set a new filled */
35    public void setFilled(boolean filled) {
36      this.filled = filled;
37    }
38
39    /** Get dateCreated */
40    public java.util.Date getDateCreated() {
41      return dateCreated;
42    }
```

```
43
44     @Override
45     public String toString() {
46       return "created on " + dateCreated + "\ncolor: " + color +
47         " and filled: " + filled;
48     }
49
50     /** Abstract method getArea */
51     public abstract double getArea();
52
53     /** Abstract method getPerimeter */
54     public abstract double getPerimeter();
55 }
```

abstract method *(line 51 margin note)*

abstract method *(line 54 margin note)*

Abstract classes are like regular classes, but you cannot create instances of abstract classes using the **new** operator. An abstract method is defined without implementation. Its implementation is provided by the subclasses. A class that contains abstract methods must be defined as abstract.

why protected constructor? *(margin note)*

The constructor in the abstract class is defined as protected, because it is used only by subclasses. When you create an instance of a concrete subclass, its superclass's constructor is invoked to initialize data fields defined in the superclass.

The **GeometricObject** abstract class defines the common features (data and methods) for geometric objects and provides appropriate constructors. Because you don't know how to compute areas and perimeters of geometric objects, **getArea()** and **getPerimeter()** are defined as abstract methods. These methods are implemented in the subclasses. The implementation of **Circle** and **Rectangle** is the same as in Listings 13.2 and 13.3, except that they extend the **GeometricObject** class defined in this chapter. You can see the complete code for these two programs from www.cs.armstrong.edu/liang/intro10e/html/Circle.html and www.cs.armstrong.edu/liang/intro10e/html/Rectangle.html, respectively.

implement Circle *(margin note)*
implement Rectangle *(margin note)*

LISTING 13.2 Circle.java

extends abstract GeometricObject *(margin note)*

```
1 public class Circle extends GeometricObject {
2    // Same as lines 3-48 in Listing 11.2, so omitted
3 }
```

LISTING 13.3 Rectangle.java

extends abstract GeometricObject *(margin note)*

```
1 public class Rectangle extends GeometricObject {
2    // Same as lines 3-51 in Listing 11.3, so omitted
3 }
```

13.2.1 Why Abstract Methods?

You may be wondering what advantage is gained by defining the methods **getArea()** and **getPerimeter()** as abstract in the **GeometricObject** class. The example in Listing 13.4 shows the benefits of defining them in the **GeometricObject** class. The program creates two geometric objects, a circle and a rectangle, invokes the **equalArea** method to check whether they have equal areas, and invokes the **displayGeometricObject** method to display them.

LISTING 13.4 TestGeometricObject.java

```
1 public class TestGeometricObject {
2    /** Main method */
3    public static void main(String[] args) {
4      // Create two geometric objects
5      GeometricObject geoObject1 = new Circle(5);
6      GeometricObject geoObject2 = new Rectangle(5, 3);
```

create a circle *(margin note)*
create a rectangle *(margin note)*

```
 7
 8       System.out.println("The two objects have the same area? " +
 9         equalArea(geoObject1, geoObject2));
10
11       // Display circle
12       displayGeometricObject(geoObject1);
13
14       // Display rectangle
15       displayGeometricObject(geoObject2);
16     }
17
18     /** A method for comparing the areas of two geometric objects */
19     public static boolean equalArea(GeometricObject object1,          equalArea
20        GeometricObject object2) {
21       return object1.getArea() == object2.getArea();
22     }
23
24     /** A method for displaying a geometric object */
25     public static void displayGeometricObject(GeometricObject object) {   displayGeometricObject
26       System.out.println();
27       System.out.println("The area is " + object.getArea());
28       System.out.println("The perimeter is " + object.getPerimeter());
29     }
30   }
```

```
The two objects have the same area? false

The area is 78.53981633974483
The perimeter is 31.41592653589793

The area is 13.0
The perimeter is 16.0
```

The methods **getArea()** and **getPerimeter()** defined in the **GeometricObject** class are overridden in the **Circle** class and the **Rectangle** class. The statements (lines 5–6)

```
GeometricObject geoObject1 = new Circle(5);
GeometricObject geoObject2 = new Rectangle(5, 3);
```

create a new circle and rectangle and assign them to the variables **geoObject1** and **geoObject2**. These two variables are of the **GeometricObject** type.

When invoking **equalArea(geoObject1, geoObject2)** (line 9), the **getArea()** method defined in the **Circle** class is used for **object1.getArea()**, since **geoObject1** is a circle, and the **getArea()** method defined in the **Rectangle** class is used for **object2.getArea()**, since **geoObject2** is a rectangle.

Similarly, when invoking **displayGeometricObject(geoObject1)** (line 12), the methods **getArea()** and **getPerimeter()** defined in the **Circle** class are used, and when invoking **displayGeometricObject(geoObject2)** (line 15), the methods **getArea** and **getPerimeter** defined in the **Rectangle** class are used. The JVM dynamically determines which of these methods to invoke at runtime, depending on the actual object that invokes the method.

Note that you could not define the **equalArea** method for comparing whether two geometric objects have the same area if the **getArea** method were not defined in **GeometricObject**. Now you have seen the benefits of defining the abstract methods in **GeometricObject**.   why abstract methods?

13.2.2 Interesting Points about Abstract Classes

The following points about abstract classes are worth noting:

abstract method in abstract class

■ An abstract method cannot be contained in a nonabstract class. If a subclass of an abstract superclass does not implement all the abstract methods, the subclass must be defined as abstract. In other words, in a nonabstract subclass extended from an abstract class, all the abstract methods must be implemented. Also note that abstract methods are nonstatic.

object cannot be created from abstract class

■ An abstract class cannot be instantiated using the **new** operator, but you can still define its constructors, which are invoked in the constructors of its subclasses. For instance, the constructors of **GeometricObject** are invoked in the **Circle** class and the **Rectangle** class.

abstract class without abstract method

■ A class that contains abstract methods must be abstract. However, it is possible to define an abstract class that doesn't contain any abstract methods. In this case, you cannot create instances of the class using the **new** operator. This class is used as a base class for defining subclasses.

concrete method overridden to be abstract

■ A subclass can override a method from its superclass to define it as abstract. This is *very unusual*, but it is useful when the implementation of the method in the superclass becomes invalid in the subclass. In this case, the subclass must be defined as abstract.

superclass of abstract class may be concrete

■ A subclass can be abstract even if its superclass is concrete. For example, the **Object** class is concrete, but its subclasses, such as **GeometricObject**, may be abstract.

abstract class as type

■ You cannot create an instance from an abstract class using the **new** operator, but an abstract class can be used as a data type. Therefore, the following statement, which creates an array whose elements are of the **GeometricObject** type, is correct.

```
GeometricObject[] objects = new GeometricObject[10];
```

You can then create an instance of **GeometricObject** and assign its reference to the array like this:

```
objects[0] = new Circle();
```

Check Point

13.1 Which of the following classes defines a legal abstract class?

```
class A {
  abstract void unfinished() {
  }
}
```
(a)

```
public class abstract A {
  abstract void unfinished();
}
```
(b)

```
class A {
  abstract void unfinished();
}
```
(c)

```
abstract class A {
  protected void unfinished();
}
```
(d)

```
abstract class A {
  abstract void unfinished();
}
```
(e)

```
abstract class A {
  abstract int unfinished();
}
```
(f)

13.2 The `getArea()` and `getPerimeter()` methods may be removed from the `GeometricObject` class. What are the benefits of defining `getArea()` and `getPerimeter()` as abstract methods in the `GeometricObject` class?

13.3 True or false?

    a. An abstract class can be used just like a nonabstract class except that you cannot use the **new** operator to create an instance from the abstract class.

    b. An abstract class can be extended.

    c. A subclass of a nonabstract superclass cannot be abstract.

    d. A subclass cannot override a concrete method in a superclass to define it as abstract.

    e. An abstract method must be nonstatic.

13.3 Case Study: the Abstract **Number** Class

Number is an abstract superclass for numeric wrapper classes, `BigInteger`, and `BigDecimal`.

Key Point

Section 10.7 introduced numeric wrapper classes and Section 10.9 introduced the `BigInteger` and `BigDecimal` classes. These classes have common methods `byteValue()`, `shortValue()`, `intValue()`, `longValue()`, `floatValue()`, and `doubleValue()` for returning a **byte**, **short**, **int**, **long**, **float**, and **double** value from an object of these classes. These common methods are actually defined in the **Number** class, which is a superclass for the numeric wrapper classes, `BigInteger`, and `BigDecimal`, as shown in Figure 13.2.

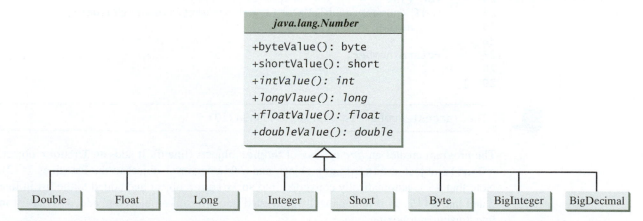

FIGURE 13.2 The **Number** class is an abstract superclass for **Double**, **Float**, **Long**, **Integer**, **Short**, **Byte**, `BigInteger` and `BigDecimal`.

Since the `intValue()`, `longValue()`, `floatValue()`, and `doubleValue()` methods cannot be implemented in the **Number** class, they are defined as abstract methods in the **Number** class. The **Number** class is therefore an abstract class. The `byteValue()` and `shortValue()` method are implemented from the `intValue()` method as follows:

```java
public byte byteValue() {
  return (byte)intValue();
}

public short shortValue() {
  return (short)intValue();
}
```

With **Number** defined as the superclass for the numeric classes, we can define methods to perform common operations for numbers. Listing 13.5 gives a program that finds the largest number in a list of **Number** objects.

LISTING 13.5 LargestNumbers.java

```
 1  import java.util.ArrayList;
 2  import java.math.*;
 3
 4  public class LargestNumbers {
 5    public static void main(String[] args) {
 6      ArrayList<Number> list = new ArrayList<>();
 7      list.add(45); // Add an integer
 8      list.add(3445.53); // Add a double
 9      // Add a BigInteger
10      list.add(new BigInteger("3432323234344343101"));
11      // Add a BigDecimal
12      list.add(new BigDecimal("2.0909090989091343433344343"));
13
14      System.out.println("The largest number is " +
15        getLargestNumber(list));
16    }
17
18    public static Number getLargestNumber(ArrayList<Number> list) {
19      if (list == null || list.size() == 0)
20        return null;
21
22      Number number = list.get(0);
23      for (int i = 1; i < list.size(); i++)
24        if (number.doubleValue() < list.get(i).doubleValue())
25          number = list.get(i);
26
27      return number;
28    }
29  }
```

create an array list
add number to list

invoke getLargestNumber

doubleValue

```
The largest number is 3432323234344343101
```

The program creates an **ArrayList** of **Number** objects (line 6). It adds an **Integer** object, a **Double** object, a **BigInteger** object, and a **BigDecimal** object to the list (lines 7–12). Note that **45** is automatically converted into an **Integer** object and added to the list in line 7 and that **3445.53** is automatically converted into a **Double** object and added to the list in line 8 using autoboxing.

Invoking the **getLargestNumber** method returns the largest number in the list (line 15). The **getLargestNumber** method returns **null** if the list is **null** or the list size is **0** (lines 19–20). To find the largest number in the list, the numbers are compared by invoking their **doubleValue()** method (line 24). The **doubleValue()** method is defined in the **Number** class and implemented in the concrete subclass of **Number**. If a number is an **Integer** object, the **Integer**'s **doubleValue()** is invoked. If a number is a **BigDecimal** object, the **BigDecimal**'s **doubleValue()** is invoked.

If the **doubleValue()** method were not defined in the **Number** class, you will not be able to find the largest number among different types of numbers using the **Number** class.

13.4 Why do the following two lines of code compile but cause a runtime error?

```
Number numberRef = new Integer(0);
Double doubleRef = (Double)numberRef;
```

13.5 Why do the following two lines of code compile but cause a runtime error?

```java
Number[] numberArray = new Integer[2];
numberArray[0] = new Double(1.5);
```

13.6 Show the output of the following code.

```java
public class Test {
  public static void main(String[] args) {
    Number x = 3;
    System.out.println(x.intValue());
    System.out.println(x.doubleValue());
  }
}
```

13.7 What is wrong in the following code? (Note that the **compareTo** method for the **Integer** and **Double** classes was introduced in Section 10.7.)

```java
public class Test {
  public static void main(String[] args) {
    Number x = new Integer(3);
    System.out.println(x.intValue());
    System.out.println(x.compareTo(new Integer(4)));
  }
}
```

13.8 What is wrong in the following code?

```java
public class Test {
  public static void main(String[] args) {
    Number x = new Integer(3);
    System.out.println(x.intValue());
    System.out.println(((Integer)x.compareTo(new Integer(4))));
  }
}
```

13.4 Case Study: **Calendar** and **GregorianCalendar**

*GregorianCalendar is a concrete subclass of the abstract class **Calendar**.*

An instance of **java.util.Date** represents a specific instant in time with millisecond precision. **java.util.Calendar** is an abstract base class for extracting detailed calendar information, such as the year, month, date, hour, minute, and second. Subclasses of **Calendar** can implement specific calendar systems, such as the Gregorian calendar, the lunar calendar, and the Jewish calendar. Currently, **java.util.GregorianCalendar** for the Gregorian calendar is supported in Java, as shown in Figure 13.3. The **add** method is abstract in the **Calendar** class, because its implementation is dependent on a concrete calendar system.

You can use **new GregorianCalendar()** to construct a default **GregorianCalendar** with the current time and **new GregorianCalendar(year, month, date)** to construct a **GregorianCalendar** with the specified **year**, **month**, and **date**. The **month** parameter is **0** based—that is, **0** is for January.

The **get(int field)** method defined in the **Calendar** class is useful for extracting the date and time information from a **Calendar** object. The fields are defined as constants, as shown in Table 13.1.

Listing 13.6 gives an example that displays the date and time information for the current time.

Key Point

VideoNote
Calendar and
GregorianCalendar classes

abstract add method

construct calendar

get(field)

java.util.Calendar	
#Calendar()	Constructs a default calendar.
+get(field: int): int	Returns the value of the given calendar field.
+set(field: int, value: int): void	Sets the given calendar to the specified value.
+set(year: int, month: int, dayOfMonth: int): void	Sets the calendar with the specified year, month, and date. The month parameter is 0-based; that is, 0 is for January.
+getActualMaximum(field: int): int	Returns the maximum value that the specified calendar field could have.
+*add(field: int, amount: int): void*	Adds or subtracts the specified amount of time to the given calendar field.
+getTime(): java.util.Date	Returns a Date object representing this calendar's time value (million second offset from the UNIX epoch).
+setTime(date: java.util.Date): void	Sets this calendar's time with the given Date object.

java.util.GregorianCalendar	
+GregorianCalendar()	Constructs a GregorianCalendar for the current time.
+GregorianCalendar(year: int, month: int, dayOfMonth: int)	Constructs a GregorianCalendar for the specified year, month, and date.
+GregorianCalendar(year: int, month: int, dayOfMonth: int, hour:int, minute: int, second: int)	Constructs a GregorianCalendar for the specified year, month, date, hour, minute, and second. The month parameter is 0-based, that is, 0 is for January.

FIGURE 13.3 The abstract Calendar class defines common features of various calendars.

TABLE 13.1 Field Constants in the Calendar Class

Constant	*Description*
YEAR	The year of the calendar.
MONTH	The month of the calendar, with 0 for January.
DATE	The day of the calendar.
HOUR	The hour of the calendar (12-hour notation).
HOUR_OF_DAY	The hour of the calendar (24-hour notation).
MINUTE	The minute of the calendar.
SECOND	The second of the calendar.
DAY_OF_WEEK	The day number within the week, with 1 for Sunday.
DAY_OF_MONTH	Same as DATE.
DAY_OF_YEAR	The day number in the year, with 1 for the first day of the year.
WEEK_OF_MONTH	The week number within the month, with 1 for the first week.
WEEK_OF_YEAR	The week number within the year, with 1 for the first week.
AM_PM	Indicator for AM or PM (0 for AM and 1 for PM).

LISTING 13.6 TestCalendar.java

```
1  import java.util.*;
2
3  public class TestCalendar {
4    public static void main(String[] args) {
5      // Construct a Gregorian calendar for the current date and time
6      Calendar calendar = new GregorianCalendar();
7      System.out.println("Current time is " + new Date());
8      System.out.println("YEAR: " + calendar.get(Calendar.YEAR));
```

calendar for current time

extract fields in calendar

```
 9        System.out.println("MONTH: " + calendar.get(Calendar.MONTH));
10        System.out.println("DATE: " + calendar.get(Calendar.DATE));
11        System.out.println("HOUR: " + calendar.get(Calendar.HOUR));
12        System.out.println("HOUR_OF_DAY: " +
13          calendar.get(Calendar.HOUR_OF_DAY));
14        System.out.println("MINUTE: " + calendar.get(Calendar.MINUTE));
15        System.out.println("SECOND: " + calendar.get(Calendar.SECOND));
16        System.out.println("DAY_OF_WEEK: " +
17          calendar.get(Calendar.DAY_OF_WEEK));
18        System.out.println("DAY_OF_MONTH: " +
19          calendar.get(Calendar.DAY_OF_MONTH));
20        System.out.println("DAY_OF_YEAR: " +
21          calendar.get(Calendar.DAY_OF_YEAR));
22        System.out.println("WEEK_OF_MONTH: " +
23          calendar.get(Calendar.WEEK_OF_MONTH));
24        System.out.println("WEEK_OF_YEAR: " +
25          calendar.get(Calendar.WEEK_OF_YEAR));
26        System.out.println("AM_PM: " + calendar.get(Calendar.AM_PM));
27
28        // Construct a calendar for September 11, 2001
29        Calendar calendar1 = new GregorianCalendar(2001, 8, 11);            create a calendar
30        String[] dayNameOfWeek = {"Sunday", "Monday", "Tuesday", "Wednesday",
31          "Thursday", "Friday", "Saturday"};
32        System.out.println("September 11, 2001 is a " +
33          dayNameOfWeek[calendar1.get(Calendar.DAY_OF_WEEK) - 1]);
34      }
35    }
```

```
Current time is Sun Nov 27 17:48:15 EST 2011
YEAR: 2011
MONTH: 10
DATE: 27
HOUR: 5
HOUR_OF_DAY: 17
MINUTE: 48
SECOND: 15
DAY_OF_WEEK: 1
DAY_OF_MONTH: 27
DAY_OF_YEAR: 331
WEEK_OF_MONTH: 5
WEEK_OF_YEAR: 49
AM_PM: 1
September 11, 2001 is a Tuesday
```

The **set(int field, value)** method defined in the **Calendar** class can be used to set a   set(field, value)
field. For example, you can use **calendar.set(Calendar.DAY_OF_MONTH, 1)** to set the
calendar to the first day of the month.

The **add(field, value)** method adds the specified amount to a given field. For exam-   add(field, amount)
ple, **add(Calendar.DAY_OF_MONTH, 5)** adds five days to the current time of the calendar. **add(Calendar.DAY_OF_MONTH, -5)** subtracts five days from the current time of the
calendar.

To obtain the number of days in a month, use **calendar.getActualMaximum(Calendar**   getActualMaximum(field)
.DAY_OF_MONTH). For example, if the **calendar** were for March, this method would
return **31**.

setTime(date)
getTime()

You can set a time represented in a `Date` object for the `calendar` by invoking `calendar.setTime(date)` and retrieve the time by invoking `calendar.getTime()`.

Check Point

13.9 Can you create a `Calendar` object using the `Calendar` class?

13.10 Which method in the `Calendar` class is abstract?

13.11 How do you create a `Calendar` object for the current time?

13.12 For a `Calendar` object `c`, how do you get its year, month, date, hour, minute, and second?

13.5 Interfaces

Key Point

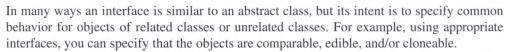
VideoNote

The concept of interface

An interface is a class-like construct that contains only constants and abstract methods.

In many ways an interface is similar to an abstract class, but its intent is to specify common behavior for objects of related classes or unrelated classes. For example, using appropriate interfaces, you can specify that the objects are comparable, edible, and/or cloneable.

To distinguish an interface from a class, Java uses the following syntax to define an interface:

```
modifier interface InterfaceName {
  /** Constant declarations */
  /** Abstract method signatures */
}
```

Here is an example of an interface:

```
public interface Edible {
  /** Describe how to eat */
  public abstract String howToEat();
}
```

An interface is treated like a special class in Java. Each interface is compiled into a separate bytecode file, just like a regular class. You can use an interface more or less the same way you use an abstract class. For example, you can use an interface as a data type for a reference variable, as the result of casting, and so on. As with an abstract class, you cannot create an instance from an interface using the **new** operator.

You can use the `Edible` interface to specify whether an object is edible. This is accomplished by letting the class for the object implement this interface using the **implements** keyword. For example, the classes `Chicken` and `Fruit` in Listing 13.7 (lines 20, 39) implement the `Edible` interface. The relationship between the class and the interface is known as *interface inheritance*. Since interface inheritance and class inheritance are essentially the same, we will simply refer to both as *inheritance*.

interface inheritance

LISTING 13.7 TestEdible.java

```
1  public class TestEdible {
2    public static void main(String[] args) {
3      Object[] objects = {new Tiger(), new Chicken(), new Apple()};
4      for (int i = 0; i < objects.length; i++) {
5        if (objects[i] instanceof Edible)
6          System.out.println(((Edible)objects[i]).howToEat());
7
8        if (objects[i] instanceof Animal) {
9          System.out.println(((Animal)objects[i]).sound());
10       }
11     }
12   }
13 }
```

```
14
15   abstract class Animal {                                          Animal class
16     /** Return animal sound */
17     public abstract String sound();
18   }
19
20   class Chicken extends Animal implements Edible {                  implements Edible
21     @Override
22     public String howToEat() {                                     howToEat()
23       return "Chicken: Fry it";
24     }
25
26     @Override
27     public String sound() {
28       return "Chicken: cock-a-doodle-doo";
29     }
30   }
31
32   class Tiger extends Animal {                                      Tiger class
33     @Override
34     public String sound() {
35       return "Tiger: RROOAARR";
36     }
37   }
38
39   abstract class Fruit implements Edible {                          implements Edible
40     // Data fields, constructors, and methods omitted here
41   }
42
43   class Apple extends Fruit {                                       Apple class
44     @Override
45     public String howToEat() {
46       return "Apple: Make apple cider";
47     }
48   }
49
50   class Orange extends Fruit {                                      Orange class
51     @Override
52     public String howToEat() {
53       return "Orange: Make orange juice";
54     }
55   }
```

```
Tiger: RROOAARR
Chicken: Fry it
Chicken: cock-a-doodle-doo
Apple: Make apple cider
```

This example uses several classes and interfaces. Their inheritance relationship is shown in Figure 13.4.

The `Animal` class defines the **sound** method (line 17). It is an abstract method and will be implemented by a concrete animal class.

The `Chicken` class implements `Edible` to specify that chickens are edible. When a class implements an interface, it implements all the methods defined in the interface with the exact signature and return type. The `Chicken` class implements the **howToEat** method (lines 22–24). `Chicken` also extends `Animal` to implement the **sound** method (lines 27–29).

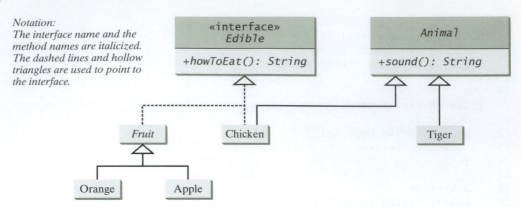

Notation:
The interface name and the
method names are italicized.
The dashed lines and hollow
triangles are used to point to
the interface.

FIGURE 13.4 `Edible` is a supertype for `Chicken` and `Fruit`. `Animal` is a supertype for `Chicken` and `Tiger`. `Fruit` is a supertype for `Orange` and `Apple`.

The `Fruit` class implements `Edible`. Since it does not implement the `howToEat` method, `Fruit` must be denoted as `abstract` (line 39). The concrete subclasses of `Fruit` must implement the `howToEat` method. The `Apple` and `Orange` classes implement the `howToEat` method (lines 45, 52).

The `main` method creates an array with three objects for `Tiger`, `Chicken`, and `Apple` (line 3), and invokes the `howToEat` method if the element is edible (line 6) and the `sound` method if the element is an animal (line 9).

common behavior

In essence, the `Edible` interface defines common behavior for edible objects. All edible objects have the `howToEat` method.

> **Note**
>
> omit modifiers
>
> Since all data fields are *public static final* and all methods are *public abstract* in an interface, Java allows these modifiers to be omitted. Therefore the following interface definitions are equivalent:

```
public interface T {
  public static final int K = 1;

  public abstract void p();
}
```
Equivalent
```
public interface T {
  int K = 1;

  void p();
}
```

13.13 Suppose `A` is an interface. Can you create an instance using `new A()`?

13.14 Suppose `A` is an interface. Can you declare a reference variable `x` with type `A` like this?

    `A x;`

13.15 Which of the following is a correct interface?

```
interface A {
  void print() { };
}
```
(a)

```
abstract interface A extends I1, I2 {
  abstract void print() { };
}
```
(b)

```
abstract interface A {
  print();
}
```
(c)

```
interface A {
  void print();
}
```
(d)

13.16 Show the error in the following code:

```java
interface A {
  void m1();
}

class B implements A {
  void m1() {
    System.out.println("m1");
  }
}
```

13.6 The **Comparable** Interface

The Comparable *interface defines the* compareTo *method for comparing objects.*

**Key
Point**

Suppose you want to design a generic method to find the larger of two objects of the same type, such as two students, two dates, two circles, two rectangles, or two squares. In order to accomplish this, the two objects must be comparable, so the common behavior for the objects must be comparable. Java provides the **Comparable** interface for this purpose. The interface is defined as follows:

```java
// Interface for comparing objects, defined in java.lang
package java.lang;

public interface Comparable<E> {
  public int compareTo(E o);
}
```

java.lang.Comparable

The **compareTo** method determines the order of this object with the specified object **o** and returns a negative integer, zero, or a positive integer if this object is less than, equal to, or greater than **o**.

The **Comparable** interface is a generic interface. The generic type **E** is replaced by a concrete type when implementing this interface. Many classes in the Java library implement **Comparable** to define a natural order for objects. The classes **Byte**, **Short**, **Integer**, **Long**, **Float**, **Double**, **Character**, **BigInteger**, **BigDecimal**, **Calendar**, **String**, and **Date** all implement the **Comparable** interface. For example, the **Integer**, **BigInteger**, **String**, and **Date** classes are defined as follows in the Java API:

```java
public class Integer extends Number
    implements Comparable<Integer> {
  // class body omitted

  @Override
  public int compareTo(Integer o) {
    // Implementation omitted
  }
}
```

```java
public class BigInteger extends Number
    implements Comparable<BigInteger> {
  // class body omitted

  @Override
  public int compareTo(BigInteger o) {
    // Implementation omitted
  }
}
```

```java
public class String extends Object
    implements Comparable<String> {
  // class body omitted

  @Override
  public int compareTo(String o) {
    // Implementation omitted
  }
}
```

```java
public class Date extends Object
    implements Comparable<Date> {
  // class body omitted

  @Override
  public int compareTo(Date o) {
    // Implementation omitted
  }
}
```

Thus, numbers are comparable, strings are comparable, and so are dates. You can use the **compareTo** method to compare two numbers, two strings, and two dates. For example, the following code

```
1  System.out.println(new Integer(3).compareTo(new Integer(5)));
2  System.out.println("ABC".compareTo("ABE"));
3  java.util.Date date1 = new java.util.Date(2013, 1, 1);
4  java.util.Date date2 = new java.util.Date(2012, 1, 1);
5  System.out.println(date1.compareTo(date2));
```

displays

```
-1
-2
 1
```

Line 1 displays a negative value since **3** is less than **5**. Line 2 displays a negative value since **ABC** is less than **ABE**. Line 5 displays a positive value since **date1** is greater than **date2**.

Let **n** be an **Integer** object, **s** be a **String** object, and **d** be a **Date** object. All the following expressions are **true**.

```
n instanceof Integer            s instanceof String            d instanceof java.util.Date
n instanceof Object             s instanceof Object            d instanceof Object
n instanceof Comparable         s instanceof Comparable        d instanceof Comparable
```

Since all **Comparable** objects have the **compareTo** method, the **java.util.Arrays .sort(Object[])** method in the Java API uses the **compareTo** method to compare and sorts the objects in an array, provided that the objects are instances of the **Comparable** interface. Listing 13.8 gives an example of sorting an array of strings and an array of **BigInteger** objects.

LISTING 13.8 SortComparableObjects.java

```
 1  import java.math.*;
 2
 3  public class SortComparableObjects {
 4    public static void main(String[] args) {
 5      String[] cities = {"Savannah", "Boston", "Atlanta", "Tampa"};
 6      java.util.Arrays.sort(cities);
 7      for (String city: cities)
 8        System.out.print(city + " ");
 9      System.out.println();
10
11      BigInteger[] hugeNumbers = {new BigInteger("2323231092923992"),
12        new BigInteger("432232323239292"),
13        new BigInteger("54623239292")};
14      java.util.Arrays.sort(hugeNumbers);
15      for (BigInteger number: hugeNumbers)
16        System.out.print(number + " ");
17    }
18  }
```

create an array (line 5)
sort the array (line 6)

create an array (line 11)

sort the array (line 14)

```
Atlanta Boston Savannah Tampa
54623239292 432232323239292 2323231092923992
```

The program creates an array of strings (line 5) and invokes the **sort** method to sort the strings (line 6). The program creates an array of **BigInteger** objects (lines 11–13) and invokes the **sort** method to sort the **BigInteger** objects (line 14).

You cannot use the **sort** method to sort an array of **Rectangle** objects, because **Rectangle** does not implement **Comparable**. However, you can define a new rectangle class that implements **Comparable**. The instances of this new class are comparable. Let this new class be named **ComparableRectangle**, as shown in Listing 13.9.

LISTING 13.9 ComparableRectangle.java

```
1  public class ComparableRectangle extends Rectangle
2       implements Comparable<ComparableRectangle> {              implements Comparable
3  /** Construct a ComparableRectangle with specified properties */
4    public ComparableRectangle(double width, double height) {
5      super(width, height);
6    }
7
8    @Override // Implement the compareTo method defined in Comparable
9    public int compareTo(ComparableRectangle o) {                implement compareTo
10     if (getArea() > o.getArea())
11       return 1;
12     else if (getArea() < o.getArea())
13       return -1;
14     else
15       return 0;
16   }
17
18   @Override // Implement the toString method in GeometricObject
19   public String toString() {                                   implement toString
20     return super.toString() + " Area: " + getArea();
21   }
22 }
```

ComparableRectangle extends **Rectangle** and implements **Comparable**, as shown in Figure 13.5. The keyword **implements** indicates that **ComparableRectangle** inherits all the constants from the **Comparable** interface and implements the methods in the interface. The **compareTo** method compares the areas of two rectangles. An instance of **ComparableRectangle** is also an instance of **Rectangle**, **GeometricObject**, **Object**, and **Comparable**.

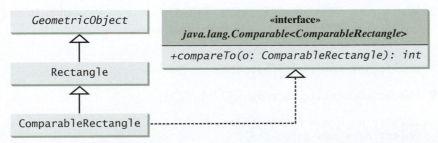

FIGURE 13.5 **ComparableRectangle** extends **Rectangle** and implements **Comparable**.

You can now use the **sort** method to sort an array of **ComparableRectangle** objects, as in Listing 13.10.

LISTING 13.10 SortRectangles.java

create an array

sort the array

```
1  public class SortRectangles {
2    public static void main(String[] args) {
3      ComparableRectangle[] rectangles = {
4        new ComparableRectangle(3.4, 5.4),
5        new ComparableRectangle(13.24, 55.4),
6        new ComparableRectangle(7.4, 35.4),
7        new ComparableRectangle(1.4, 25.4)};
8      java.util.Arrays.sort(rectangles);
9      for (Rectangle rectangle: rectangles) {
10       System.out.print(rectangle + " ");
11       System.out.println();
12     }
13   }
14 }
```

An interface provides another form of generic programming. It would be difficult to use a generic **sort** method to sort the objects without using an interface in this example, because

```
Width: 3.4 Height: 5.4 Area: 18.36
Width: 1.4 Height: 25.4 Area: 35.559999999999995
Width: 7.4 Height: 35.4 Area: 261.96
Width: 13.24 Height: 55.4 Area: 733.496
```

benefits of interface

multiple inheritance would be necessary to inherit **Comparable** and another class, such as **Rectangle**, at the same time.

The **Object** class contains the **equals** method, which is intended for the subclasses of the **Object** class to override in order to compare whether the contents of the objects are the same. Suppose that the **Object** class contains the **compareTo** method, as defined in the **Comparable** interface; the **sort** method can be used to compare a list of *any* objects. Whether a **compareTo** method should be included in the **Object** class is debatable. Since the **compareTo** method is not defined in the **Object** class, the **Comparable** interface is defined in Java to enable objects to be compared if they are instances of the **Comparable** interface. It is strongly recommended (though not required) that **compareTo** should be consistent with **equals**. That is, for two objects **o1** and **o2**, **o1.compareTo(o2) == 0** if and only if **o1.equals(o2)** is **true**.

Check Point

13.17 True or false? If a class implements **Comparable**, the object of the class can invoke the **compareTo** method.

13.18 Which of the following is the correct method header for the **compareTo** method in the **String** class?

```
public int compareTo(String o)
public int compareTo(Object o)
```

13.19 Can the following code be compiled? Why?

```
Integer n1 = new Integer(3);
Object n2 = new Integer(4);
System.out.println(n1.compareTo(n2));
```

13.20 You can define the **compareTo** method in a class without implementing the **Comparable** interface. What are the benefits of implementing the **Comparable** interface?

13.21 What is wrong in the following code?

```
public class Test {
  public static void main(String[] args) {
    Person[] persons = {new Person(3), new Person(4), new Person(1)};
    java.util.Arrays.sort(persons);
  }
}

class Person {
  private int id;

  Person(int id) {
    this.id = id;
  }
}
```

13.7 The **Cloneable** Interface

The **Cloneable** *interface specifies that an object can be cloned.*

**Key
Point**

Often it is desirable to create a copy of an object. To do this, you need to use the **clone** method and understand the **Cloneable** interface.

An interface contains constants and abstract methods, but the **Cloneable** interface is a special case. The **Cloneable** interface in the **java.lang** package is defined as follows:

```
package java.lang;

public interface Cloneable {
}
```

java.lang.Cloneable

This interface is empty. An interface with an empty body is referred to as a *marker interface*. A marker interface does not contain constants or methods. It is used to denote that a class possesses certain desirable properties. A class that implements the **Cloneable** interface is marked cloneable, and its objects can be cloned using the **clone()** method defined in the **Object** class.

marker interface

Many classes in the Java library (e.g., **Date**, **Calendar**, and **ArrayList**) implement **Cloneable**. Thus, the instances of these classes can be cloned. For example, the following code

```
1  Calendar calendar = new GregorianCalendar(2013, 2, 1);
2  Calendar calendar1 = calendar;
3  Calendar calendar2 = (Calendar)calendar.clone();
4  System.out.println("calendar == calendar1 is " +
5    (calendar == calendar1));
6  System.out.println("calendar == calendar2 is " +
7    (calendar == calendar2));
8  System.out.println("calendar.equals(calendar2) is " +
9    calendar.equals(calendar2));
```

displays

```
calendar == calendar1 is true
calendar == calendar2 is false
calendar.equals(calendar2) is true
```

In the preceding code, line 2 copies the reference of `calendar` to `calendar1`, so `calendar` and `calendar1` point to the same `Calendar` object. Line 3 creates a new object that is the clone of `calendar` and assigns the new object's reference to `calendar2`. `calendar2` and `calendar` are different objects with the same contents.

The following code

```
1   ArrayList<Double> list1 = new ArrayList<>();
2   list1.add(1.5);
3   list1.add(2.5);
4   list1.add(3.5);
5   ArrayList<Double> list2 = (ArrayList<Double>)list1.clone();
6   ArrayList<Double> list3 = list1;
7   list2.add(4.5);
8   list3.remove(1.5);
9   System.out.println("list1 is " + list1);
10  System.out.println("list2 is " + list2);
11  System.out.println("list3 is " + list3);
```

displays

```
list1 is [2.5, 3.5]
list2 is [1.5, 2.5, 3.5, 4.5]
list3 is [2.5, 3.5]
```

In the preceding code, line 5 creates a new object that is the clone of `list1` and assigns the new object's reference to `list2`. `list2` and `list1` are different objects with the same contents. Line 6 copies the reference of `list1` to `list3`, so `list1` and `list3` point to the same `ArrayList` object. Line 7 adds `4.5` into `list2`. Line 8 removes `1.5` from `list3`. Since `list1` and `list3` point to the same `ArrayList`, line 9 and 11 display the same content.

clone arrays

You can clone an array using the `clone` method. For example, the following code

```
1   int[] list1 = {1, 2};
2   int[] list2 = list1.clone();
3   list1[0] = 7;
4   list2[1] = 8;
5   System.out.println("list1 is " + list1[0] + ", " + list1[1]);
6   System.out.println("list2 is " + list2[0] + ", " + list2[1]);
```

displays

```
list1 is 7, 2
list2 is 1, 8
```

how to implement `Cloneable`

To define a custom class that implements the `Cloneable` interface, the class must override the `clone()` method in the `Object` class. Listing 13.11 defines a class named `House` that implements `Cloneable` and `Comparable`.

LISTING 13.11 House.java

```
1   public class House implements Cloneable, Comparable<House> {
2     private int id;
3     private double area;
4     private java.util.Date whenBuilt;
5
6     public House(int id, double area) {
7       this.id = id;
8       this.area = area;
9       whenBuilt = new java.util.Date();
10    }
```

```
11
12    public int getId() {
13      return id;
14    }
15
16    public double getArea() {
17      return area;
18    }
19
20    public java.util.Date getWhenBuilt() {
21      return whenBuilt;
22    }
23
24    @Override /** Override the protected clone method defined in
25      the Object class, and strengthen its accessibility */
26    public Object clone() throws CloneNotSupportedException {
27      return super.clone();
28    }
29
30    @Override // Implement the compareTo method defined in Comparable
31    public int compareTo(House o) {
32      if (area > o.area)
33        return 1;
34      else if (area < o.area)
35        return -1;
36      else
37        return 0;
38    }
39  }
```

This exception is thrown if House does not implement Cloneable

The **House** class implements the **clone** method (lines 26–28) defined in the **Object** class. The header is:

```
protected native Object clone() throws CloneNotSupportedException;
```

The keyword **native** indicates that this method is not written in Java but is implemented in the JVM for the native platform. The keyword **protected** restricts the method to be accessed in the same package or in a subclass. For this reason, the **House** class must override the method and change the visibility modifier to **public** so that the method can be used in any package. Since the **clone** method implemented for the native platform in the **Object** class performs the task of cloning objects, the **clone** method in the **House** class simply invokes **super.clone()**. The **clone** method defined in the **Object** class may throw **CloneNotSupportedException**.

CloneNotSupportedException

The **House** class implements the **compareTo** method (lines 31–38) defined in the **Comparable** interface. The method compares the areas of two houses.

You can now create an object of the **House** class and create an identical copy from it, as follows:

```
House house1 = new House(1, 1750.50);
House house2 = (House)house1.clone();
```

house1 and **house2** are two different objects with identical contents. The **clone** method in the **Object** class copies each field from the original object to the target object. If the field is of a primitive type, its value is copied. For example, the value of **area** (**double** type) is copied from **house1** to **house2**. If the field is of an object, the reference of the field is copied. For example, the field **whenBuilt** is of the **Date** class, so its reference is copied into **house2**, as shown in Figure 13.6. Therefore, **house1.whenBuilt == house2.whenBuilt** is true, although **house1 == house2** is false. This is referred to as a *shallow copy* rather than a

shallow copy

deep copy

deep copy, meaning that if the field is of an object type, the object's reference is copied rather than its contents.

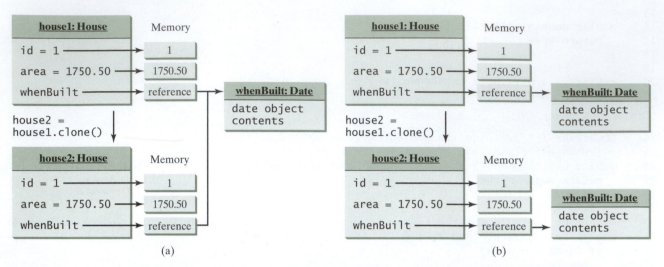

FIGURE 13.6 (a) The default **clone** method performs a shallow copy. (b) The custom **clone** method performs a deep copy.

deep copy

To perform a deep copy for a **House** object, replace the **clone()** method in lines 26–28 with the following code:

```
public Object clone() throws CloneNotSupportedException {
  // Perform a shallow copy
  House houseClone = (House)super.clone();
  // Deep copy on whenBuilt
  houseClone.whenBuilt = (java.util.Date)(whenBuilt.clone());
  return houseClone;
}
```

or

```
public Object clone() {
  try {
    // Perform a shallow copy
    House houseClone = (House)super.clone();
    // Deep copy on whenBuilt
    houseClone.whenBuilt = (java.util.Date)(whenBuilt.clone());
    return houseClone;
  }
  catch (CloneNotSupportedException ex) {
    return null;
  }
}
```

Now if you clone a **House** object in the following code:

```
House house1 = new House(1, 1750.50);
House house2 = (House)house1.clone();
```

house1.whenBuilt == house2.whenBuilt will be **false**. **house1** and **house2** contain two different **Date** objects, as shown in Figure 13.6b.

13.22 Can you invoke the `clone()` method to clone an object if the class for the object does not implement the `java.lang.Cloneable`? Does the `Date` class implement `Cloneable`?

13.23 What would happen if the **House** class (defined in Listing 13.11) did not override the `clone()` method or if **House** did not implement `java.lang.Cloneable`?

13.24 Show the output of the following code:

```java
java.util.Date date = new java.util.Date();
java.util.Date date1 = date;
java.util.Date date2 = (java.util.Date)(date.clone());
System.out.println(date == date1);
System.out.println(date == date2);
System.out.println(date.equals(date2));
```

13.25 Show the output of the following code:

```java
ArrayList<String> list = new ArrayList<>();
list.add("New York");
ArrayList<String> list1 = list;
ArrayList<String> list2 = (ArrayList<String>)(list.clone());
list.add("Atlanta");
System.out.println(list == list1);
System.out.println(list == list2);
System.out.println("list is " + list);
System.out.println("list1 is " + list1);
System.out.println("list2.get(0) is " + list2.get(0));
System.out.println("list2.size() is " + list2.size());
```

13.26 What is wrong in the following code?

```java
public class Test {
  public static void main(String[] args) {
    GeometricObject x = new Circle(3);
    GeometricObject y = x.clone();
    System.out.println(x == y);
  }
}
```

13.8 Interfaces vs. Abstract Classes

A class can implement multiple interfaces, but it can only extend one superclass.

An interface can be used more or less the same way as an abstract class, but defining an interface is different from defining an abstract class. Table 13.2 summarizes the differences.

TABLE 13.2 Interfaces vs. Abstract Classes

	Variables	*Constructors*	*Methods*
Abstract class	No restrictions.	Constructors are invoked by subclasses through constructor chaining. An abstract class cannot be instantiated using the new operator.	No restrictions.
Interface	All variables must be `public static final`.	No constructors. An interface cannot be instantiated using the new operator.	All methods must be public abstract instance methods

single inheritance
multiple inheritance

Java allows only *single inheritance* for class extension but allows *multiple extensions* for interfaces. For example,

```java
public class NewClass extends BaseClass
    implements Interface1, ..., InterfaceN {
  ...
}
```

subinterface

An interface can inherit other interfaces using the **extends** keyword. Such an interface is called a *subinterface*. For example, **NewInterface** in the following code is a subinterface of **Interface1,...,** and **InterfaceN**.

```java
public interface NewInterface extends Interface1, ... , InterfaceN {
  // constants and abstract methods
}
```

A class implementing **NewInterface** must implement the abstract methods defined in **NewInterface**, **Interface1,...,** and **InterfaceN**. An interface can extend other interfaces but not classes. A class can extend its superclass and implement multiple interfaces.

All classes share a single root, the **Object** class, but there is no single root for interfaces. Like a class, an interface also defines a type. A variable of an interface type can reference any instance of the class that implements the interface. If a class implements an interface, the interface is like a superclass for the class. You can use an interface as a data type and cast a variable of an interface type to its subclass, and vice versa. For example, suppose that **c** is an instance of **Class2** in Figure 13.7. **c** is also an instance of **Object**, **Class1**, **Interface1**, **Interface1_1**, **Interface1_2**, **Interface2_1**, and **Interface2_2**.

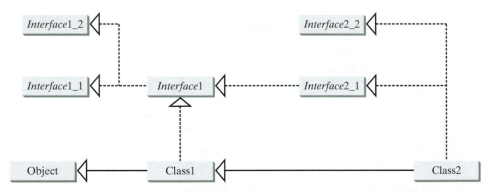

FIGURE 13.7 **Class1** implements **Interface1**; **Interface1** extends **Interface1_1** and **Interface1_2**. **Class2** extends **Class1** and implements **Interface2_1** and **Interface2_2**.

naming convention

Note
Class names are nouns. Interface names may be adjectives or nouns.

Design Guide
Abstract classes and interfaces can both be used to specify common behavior of objects. How do you decide whether to use an interface or a class? In general, a *strong is-a relationship* that clearly describes a parent-child relationship should be modeled using classes. For example, Gregorian calendar is a calendar, so the relationship between the class **java.util.GregorianCalendar** and **java.util.Calendar** is modeled

is-a relationship
is-kind-of relationship

using class inheritance. A *weak is-a relationship*, also known as an *is-kind-of relationship*, indicates that an object possesses a certain property. A weak is-a relationship can be modeled using interfaces. For example, all strings are comparable, so the **String** class implements the **Comparable** interface.

In general, interfaces are preferred over abstract classes because an interface can define a common supertype for unrelated classes. Interfaces are more flexible than classes. Consider the `Animal` class. Suppose the `howToEat` method is defined in the `Animal` class, as follows:

interface preferred

```
abstract class Animal {
  public abstract String howToEat();
}
```

Animal class

Two subclasses of `Animal` are defined as follows:

```
class Chicken extends Animal {
  @Override
  public String howToEat() {
    return "Fry it";
  }
}
```

Chicken class

```
class Duck extends Animal {
  @Override
  public String howToEat() {
    return "Roast it";
  }
}
```

Duck class

Given this inheritance hierarchy, polymorphism enables you to hold a reference to a `Chicken` object or a `Duck` object in a variable of type `Animal`, as in the following code:

```
public static void main(String[] args) {
  Animal animal = new Chicken();
  eat(animal);

  animal = new Duck();
  eat(animal);
}

public static void eat(Animal animal) {
  animal.howToEat();
}
```

The JVM dynamically decides which `howToEat` method to invoke based on the actual object that invokes the method.

You can define a subclass of `Animal`. However, there is a restriction: The subclass must be for another animal (e.g., `Turkey`).

Interfaces don't have this restriction. Interfaces give you more flexibility than classes, because you don't have to make everything fit into one type of class. You may define the `howToEat()` method in an interface and let it serve as a common supertype for other classes. For example,

```
public static void main(String[] args) {
  Edible stuff = new Chicken();
  eat(stuff);

  stuff = new Duck();
  eat(stuff);

  stuff = new Broccoli();
  eat(stuff);
}
```

```
                        public static void eat(Edible stuff) {
                          stuff.howToEat();
                        }
```

Edible interface
```
interface Edible {
  public String howToEat();
}
```

Chicken class
```
class Chicken implements Edible {
  @Override
  public String howToEat() {
    return "Fry it";
  }
}
```

Duck class
```
class Duck implements Edible {
  @Override
  public String howToEat() {
    return "Roast it";
  }
}
```

Broccoli class
```
class Broccoli implements Edible {
  @Override
  public String howToEat() {
    return "Stir-fry it";
  }
}
```

To define a class that represents edible objects, simply let the class implement the **Edible** interface. The class is now a subtype of the **Edible** type, and any **Edible** object can be passed to invoke the **howToEat** method.

13.27 Give an example to show why interfaces are preferred over abstract classes.

13.28 Define the terms abstract classes and interfaces. What are the similarities and differences between abstract classes and interfaces?

13.29 True or false?

   a. An interface is compiled into a separate bytecode file.

   b. An interface can have static methods.

   c. An interface can extend one or more interfaces.

   d. An interface can extend an abstract class.

   e. An abstract class can extend an interface.

13.9 Case Study: The **Rational** Class

*This section shows how to design the **Rational** class for representing and processing rational numbers.*

A rational number has a numerator and a denominator in the form **a/b**, where **a** is the numerator and **b** the denominator. For example, **1/3**, **3/4**, and **10/4** are rational numbers.

   A rational number cannot have a denominator of **0**, but a numerator of **0** is fine. Every integer **i** is equivalent to a rational number **i/1**. Rational numbers are used in exact computations involving fractions—for example, **1/3 = 0.33333. . . .** This number cannot be precisely represented in floating-point format using either the data type **double** or **float**. To obtain the exact result, we must use rational numbers.

Java provides data types for integers and floating-point numbers, but not for rational numbers. This section shows how to design a class to represent rational numbers.

Since rational numbers share many common features with integers and floating-point numbers, and **Number** is the root class for numeric wrapper classes, it is appropriate to define **Rational** as a subclass of **Number**. Since rational numbers are comparable, the **Rational** class should also implement the **Comparable** interface. Figure 13.8 illustrates the **Rational** class and its relationship to the **Number** class and the **Comparable** interface.

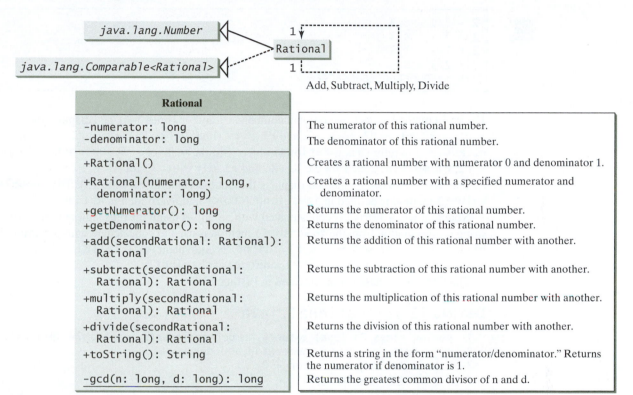

FIGURE 13.8 The properties, constructors, and methods of the **Rational** class are illustrated in UML.

A rational number consists of a numerator and a denominator. There are many equivalent rational numbers—for example, $1/3 = 2/6 = 3/9 = 4/12$. The numerator and the denominator of $1/3$ have no common divisor except 1, so $1/3$ is said to be in *lowest terms*.

To reduce a rational number to its lowest terms, you need to find the greatest common divisor (GCD) of the absolute values of its numerator and denominator, then divide both the numerator and denominator by this value. You can use the method for computing the GCD of two integers n and d, as suggested in Listing 5.9, GreatestCommonDivisor.java. The numerator and denominator in a **Rational** object are reduced to their lowest terms.

As usual, let us first write a test program to create two **Rational** objects and test its methods. Listing 13.12 is a test program.

LISTING 13.12 TestRationalClass.java

```
1  public class TestRationalClass {
2    /** Main method */
3    public static void main(String[] args) {
4      // Create and initialize two rational numbers r1 and r2
5      Rational r1 = new Rational(4, 2);
6      Rational r2 = new Rational(2, 3);
7
8      // Display results
```

create a Rational
create a Rational

add

```
9      System.out.println(r1 + " + " + r2 + " = " + r1.add(r2));
10     System.out.println(r1 + " - " + r2 + " = " + r1.subtract(r2));
11     System.out.println(r1 + " * " + r2 + " = " + r1.multiply(r2));
12     System.out.println(r1 + " / " + r2 + " = " + r1.divide(r2));
13     System.out.println(r2 + " is " + r2.doubleValue());
14   }
15 }
```

```
2 + 2/3 = 8/3
2 - 2/3 = 4/3
2 * 2/3 = 4/3
2 / 2/3 = 3
2/3 is 0.6666666666666666
```

The **main** method creates two rational numbers, **r1** and **r2** (lines 5–6), and displays the results of **r1 + r2**, **r1 - r2**, **r1 x r2**, and **r1 / r2** (lines 9–12). To perform **r1 + r2**, invoke **r1.add(r2)** to return a new **Rational** object. Similarly, invoke **r1.subtract(r2)** for **r1 - r2**, **r1.multiply(r2)** for **r1 x r2** , and **r1.divide(r2)** for **r1 / r2**.

The **doubleValue()** method displays the double value of **r2** (line 13). **The double-Value()** method is defined in **java.lang.Number** and overridden in **Rational**.

Note that when a string is concatenated with an object using the plus sign (+), the object's string representation from the **toString()** method is used to concatenate with the string. So **r1 + " + " + r2 + " = " + r1.add(r2)** is equivalent to **r1.toString() + " + " + r2.toString() + " = " + r1.add(r2).toString()**.

The **Rational** class is implemented in Listing 13.13.

LISTING 13.13 Rational.java

```
1  public class Rational extends Number implements Comparable<Rational> {
2    // Data fields for numerator and denominator
3    private long numerator = 0;
4    private long denominator = 1;
5
6    /** Construct a rational with default properties */
7    public Rational() {
8      this(0, 1);
9    }
10
11   /** Construct a rational with specified numerator and denominator */
12   public Rational(long numerator, long denominator) {
13     long gcd = gcd(numerator, denominator);
14     this.numerator = ((denominator > 0) ? 1 : -1) * numerator / gcd;
15     this.denominator = Math.abs(denominator) / gcd;
16   }
17
18   /** Find GCD of two numbers */
19   private static long gcd(long n, long d) {
20     long n1 = Math.abs(n);
21     long n2 = Math.abs(d);
22     int gcd = 1;
23
24     for (int k = 1; k <= n1 && k <= n2; k++) {
25       if (n1 % k == 0 && n2 % k == 0)
26         gcd = k;
27     }
28
29     return gcd;
```

```
30      }
31
32      /** Return numerator */
33      public long getNumerator() {
34        return numerator;
35      }
36
37      /** Return denominator */
38      public long getDenominator() {
39        return denominator;
40      }
41
42      /** Add a rational number to this rational */
43      public Rational add(Rational secondRational) {
44        long n = numerator * secondRational.getDenominator() +
45          denominator * secondRational.getNumerator();
46        long d = denominator * secondRational.getDenominator();
47        return new Rational(n, d);
48      }
49
50      /** Subtract a rational number from this rational */
51      public Rational subtract(Rational secondRational) {
52        long n = numerator * secondRational.getDenominator()
53          - denominator * secondRational.getNumerator();
54        long d = denominator * secondRational.getDenominator();
55        return new Rational(n, d);
56      }
57
58      /** Multiply a rational number by this rational */
59      public Rational multiply(Rational secondRational) {
60        long n = numerator * secondRational.getNumerator();
61        long d = denominator * secondRational.getDenominator();
62        return new Rational(n, d);
63      }
64
65      /** Divide a rational number by this rational */
66      public Rational divide(Rational secondRational) {
67        long n = numerator * secondRational.getDenominator();
68        long d = denominator * secondRational.numerator;
69        return new Rational(n, d);
70      }
71
72      @Override
73      public String toString() {
74        if (denominator == 1)
75          return numerator + "";
76        else
77          return numerator + "/" + denominator;
78      }
79
80      @Override // Override the equals method in the Object class
81      public boolean equals(Object other) {
82        if ((this.subtract((Rational)(other))).getNumerator() == 0)
83          return true;
84        else
85          return false;
86      }
87
88      @Override // Implement the abstract intValue method in Number
89      public int intValue() {
```

$$\frac{a}{b} + \frac{c}{d} = \frac{ad + bc}{bd}$$

$$\frac{a}{b} - \frac{c}{d} = \frac{ad - bc}{bd}$$

$$\frac{a}{b} \times \frac{c}{d} = \frac{ac}{bd}$$

$$\frac{a}{b} \div \frac{c}{d} = \frac{ad}{bc}$$

```
 90        return (int)doubleValue();
 91    }
 92
 93    @Override // Implement the abstract floatValue method in Number
 94    public float floatValue() {
 95        return (float)doubleValue();
 96    }
 97
 98    @Override // Implement the doubleValue method in Number
 99    public double doubleValue() {
100        return numerator * 1.0 / denominator;
101    }
102
103    @Override // Implement the abstract longValue method in Number
104    public long longValue() {
105        return (long)doubleValue();
106    }
107
108    @Override // Implement the compareTo method in Comparable
109    public int compareTo(Rational o) {
110        if (this.subtract(o).getNumerator() > 0)
111            return 1;
112        else if (this.subtract(o).getNumerator() < 0)
113            return -1;
114        else
115            return 0;
116    }
117 }
```

The rational number is encapsulated in a **Rational** object. Internally, a rational number is represented in its lowest terms (line 13), and the numerator determines its sign (line 14). The denominator is always positive (line 15).

The **gcd** method (lines 19–30 in the **Rational** class) is private; it is not intended for use by clients. The **gcd** method is only for internal use by the **Rational** class. The **gcd** method is also static, since it is not dependent on any particular **Rational** object.

The **abs(x)** method (lines 20–21 in the **Rational** class) is defined in the **Math** class and returns the absolute value of **x**.

Two **Rational** objects can interact with each other to perform add, subtract, multiply, and divide operations. These methods return a new **Rational** object (lines 43–70).

The methods **toString** and **equals** in the **Object** class are overridden in the **Rational** class (lines 72–86). The **toString()** method returns a string representation of a **Rational** object in the form **numerator/denominator**, or simply **numerator** if **denominator** is 1. The **equals(Object other)** method returns true if this rational number is equal to the other rational number.

The abstract methods **intValue**, **longValue**, **floatValue**, and **doubleValue** in the **Number** class are implemented in the **Rational** class (lines 88–106). These methods return the **int**, **long**, **float**, and **double** value for this rational number.

The **compareTo(Rational other)** method in the **Comparable** interface is implemented in the **Rational** class (lines 108–116) to compare this rational number to the other rational number.

Tip
The getter methods for the properties **numerator** and **denominator** are provided in the **Rational** class, but the setter methods are not provided, so, once a **Rational** object is created, its contents cannot be changed. The **Rational** class is immutable. The **String** class and the wrapper classes for primitive type values are also immutable.

immutable

Tip

The numerator and denominator are represented using two variables. It is possible to use an array of two integers to represent the numerator and denominator (see Programming Exercise 13.14). The signatures of the public methods in the **Rational** class are not changed, although the internal representation of a rational number is changed. This is a good example to illustrate the idea that the data fields of a class should be kept private so as to encapsulate the implementation of the class from the use of the class.

encapsulation

The **Rational** class has serious limitations and can easily overflow. For example, the following code will display an incorrect result, because the denominator is too large.

overflow

```java
public class Test {
  public static void main(String[] args) {
    Rational r1 = new Rational(1, 123456789);
    Rational r2 = new Rational(1, 123456789);
    Rational r3 = new Rational(1, 123456789);
    System.out.println("r1 * r2 * r3 is " +
      r1.multiply(r2.multiply(r3)));
  }
}
```

```
r1 * r2 * r3 is -1/2204193661661244627
```

To fix it, you can implement the **Rational** class using the **BigInteger** for numerator and denominator (see Programming Exercise 13.15).

13.30 Show the output of the following code?

Check Point

```java
Rational r1 = new Rational(-2, 6);
System.out.println(r1.getNumerator());
System.out.println(r1.getDenominator());
System.out.println(r1.intValue());
System.out.println(r1.doubleValue());
```

13.31 Why is the following code wrong?

```java
Rational r1 = new Rational(-2, 6);
Object r2 = new Rational(1, 45);
System.out.println(r2.compareTo(r1));
```

13.32 Why is the following code wrong?

```java
Object r1 = new Rational(-2, 6);
Rational r2 = new Rational(1, 45);
System.out.println(r2.compareTo(r1));
```

13.33 How do you simplify the code in lines 82–85 in Listing 13.13 Rational.java using one line of code without using the if statement?

13.34 Trace the program carefully and show the output of the following code.

```java
Rational r1 = new Rational(1, 2);
Rational r2 = new Rational(1, -2);
System.out.println(r1.add(r2));
```

13.10 Class Design Guidelines

Class design guidelines are helpful for designing sound classes.

Key Point

You have learned how to design classes from the preceding two examples and from many other examples in the preceding chapters. This section summarizes some of the guidelines.

13.10.1 Cohesion

coherent purpose

A class should describe a single entity, and all the class operations should logically fit together to support a coherent purpose. You can use a class for students, for example, but you should not combine students and staff in the same class, because students and staff are different entities.

separate responsibilities

A single entity with many responsibilities can be broken into several classes to separate the responsibilities. The classes **String**, **StringBuilder**, and **StringBuffer** all deal with strings, for example, but have different responsibilities. The **String** class deals with immutable strings, the **StringBuilder** class is for creating mutable strings, and the **StringBuffer** class is similar to **StringBuilder** except that **StringBuffer** contains synchronized methods for updating strings.

13.10.2 Consistency

naming conventions

Follow standard Java programming style and naming conventions. Choose informative names for classes, data fields, and methods. A popular style is to place the data declaration before the constructor and place constructors before methods.

naming consistency

Make the names consistent. It is not a good practice to choose different names for similar operations. For example, the **length()** method returns the size of a **String**, a **StringBuilder**, and a **StringBuffer**. It would be inconsistent if different names were used for this method in these classes.

no-arg constructor

In general, you should consistently provide a public no-arg constructor for constructing a default instance. If a class does not support a no-arg constructor, document the reason. If no constructors are defined explicitly, a public default no-arg constructor with an empty body is assumed.

If you want to prevent users from creating an object for a class, you can declare a private constructor in the class, as is the case for the **Math** class.

13.10.3 Encapsulation

encapsulate data fields

A class should use the **private** modifier to hide its data from direct access by clients. This makes the class easy to maintain.

Provide a getter method only if you want the data field to be readable, and provide a setter method only if you want the data field to be updateable. For example, the **Rational** class provides a getter method for **numerator** and **denominator**, but no setter method, because a **Rational** object is immutable.

13.10.4 Clarity

Cohesion, consistency, and encapsulation are good guidelines for achieving design clarity. Additionally, a class should have a clear contract that is easy to explain and easy to understand.

easy to explain

Users can incorporate classes in many different combinations, orders, and environments. Therefore, you should design a class that imposes no restrictions on how or when the user can use it, design the properties in a way that lets the user set them in any order and with any combination of values, and design methods that function independently of their order of occurrence.

independent methods

For example, the **Loan** class contains the properties **loanAmount**, **numberOfYears**, and **annualInterestRate**. The values of these properties can be set in any order.

intuitive meaning

Methods should be defined intuitively without causing confusion. For example, the **substring(int beginIndex, int endIndex)** method in the **String** class is somewhat confusing. The method returns a substring from **beginIndex** to **endIndex** − 1, rather than to **endIndex**. It would be more intuitive to return a substring from **beginIndex** to **endIndex**.

independent properties

You should not declare a data field that can be derived from other data fields. For example, the following **Person** class has two data fields: **birthDate** and **age**. Since **age** can be derived from **birthDate**, **age** should not be declared as a data field.

```java
public class Person {
    private java.util.Date birthDate;
```

```
   private int age;
   ...
}
```

13.10.5 Completeness

Classes are designed for use by many different customers. In order to be useful in a wide range of applications, a class should provide a variety of ways for customization through properties and methods. For example, the **String** class contains more than 40 methods that are useful for a variety of applications.

13.10.6 Instance vs. Static

A variable or method that is dependent on a specific instance of the class must be an instance variable or method. A variable that is shared by all the instances of a class should be declared static. For example, the variable **numberOfObjects** in **CircleWithPrivateDataFields** in Listing 9.8 is shared by all the objects of the **CircleWithPrivateDataFields** class and therefore is declared static. A method that is not dependent on a specific instance should be defined as a static method. For instance, the **getNumberOfObjects()** method in **CircleWithPrivateDataFields** is not tied to any specific instance and therefore is defined as a static method.

Always reference static variables and methods from a class name (rather than a reference variable) to improve readability and avoid errors.

Do not pass a parameter from a constructor to initialize a static data field. It is better to use a setter method to change the static data field. Thus, the following class in (a) is better replaced by (b).

```
public class SomeThing {
  private int t1;
  private static int t2;

  public SomeThing(int t1, int t2) {
    ...
  }
}
```

(a)

```
public class SomeThing {
  private int t1;
  private static int t2;

  public SomeThing(int t1) {
    ...
  }

  public static void setT2(int t2) {
    SomeThing.t2 = t2;
  }
}
```

(b)

Instance and static are integral parts of object-oriented programming. A data field or method is either instance or static. Do not mistakenly overlook static data fields or methods. It is a common design error to define an instance method that should have been static. For example, the **factorial(int n)** method for computing the factorial of **n** should be defined static, because it is independent of any specific instance.

common design error

A constructor is always instance, because it is used to create a specific instance. A static variable or method can be invoked from an instance method, but an instance variable or method cannot be invoked from a static method.

13.10.7 Inheritance vs. Aggregation

The difference between inheritance and aggregation is the difference between an is-a and a has-a relationship. For example, an apple is a fruit; thus, you would use inheritance to model the relationship between the classes **Apple** and **Fruit**. A person has a name; thus, you would use aggregation to model the relationship between the classes **Person** and **Name**.

13.10.8 Interfaces vs. Abstract Classes

Both interfaces and abstract classes can be used to specify common behavior for objects. How do you decide whether to use an interface or a class? In general, a strong is-a relationship that clearly describes a parent–child relationship should be modeled using classes. For example, since an orange is a fruit, their relationship should be modeled using class inheritance. A weak is-a relationship, also known as an is-kind-of relationship, indicates that an object possesses a certain property. A weak is-a relationship can be modeled using interfaces. For example, all strings are comparable, so the `String` class implements the `Comparable` interface. A circle or a rectangle is a geometric object, so `Circle` can be designed as a subclass of `GeometricObject`. Circles are different and comparable based on their radii, so `Circle` can implement the `Comparable` interface.

Interfaces are more flexible than abstract classes, because a subclass can extend only one superclass but can implement any number of interfaces. However, interfaces cannot contain concrete methods. The virtues of interfaces and abstract classes can be combined by creating an interface with an abstract class that implements it. Then you can use the interface or the abstract class, whichever is convenient. We will give examples of this type of design in Chapter 20, Lists, Stacks, Queues, and Priority Queues.

13.35 Describe class design guidelines.

KEY TERMS

abstract class 496
abstract method 496
deep copy 516
interface 496

marker interface 513
shallow copy 515
subinterface 518

CHAPTER SUMMARY

1. *Abstract classes* are like regular classes with data and methods, but you cannot create instances of abstract classes using the **new** operator.

2. An *abstract method* cannot be contained in a nonabstract class. If a subclass of an abstract superclass does not implement all the inherited abstract methods of the superclass, the subclass must be defined as abstract.

3. A class that contains abstract methods must be abstract. However, it is possible to define an abstract class that doesn't contain any abstract methods.

4. A subclass can be abstract even if its superclass is concrete.

5. An *interface* is a class-like construct that contains only constants and abstract methods. In many ways, an interface is similar to an abstract class, but an abstract class can contain constants and abstract methods as well as variables and concrete methods.

6. An interface is treated like a special class in Java. Each interface is compiled into a separate bytecode file, just like a regular class.

7. The `java.lang.Comparable` interface defines the `compareTo` method. Many classes in the Java library implement `Comparable`.

8. The `java.lang.Cloneable` interface is a *marker interface*. An object of the class that implements the `Cloneable` interface is cloneable.

9. A class can extend only one superclass but can implement one or more interfaces.

10. An interface can extend one or more interfaces.

QUIZ

Answer the quiz for this chapter online at www.cs.armstrong.edu/liang/intro10e/quiz.html.

PROGRAMMING EXERCISES

MyProgrammingLab™

Sections 13.2–13.3

**13.1 (*Triangle class*) Design a new `Triangle` class that extends the abstract `GeometricObject` class. Draw the UML diagram for the classes `Triangle` and `GeometricObject` and then implement the `Triangle` class. Write a test program that prompts the user to enter three sides of the triangle, a color, and a Boolean value to indicate whether the triangle is filled. The program should create a `Triangle` object with these sides and set the color and filled properties using the input. The program should display the area, perimeter, color, and true or false to indicate whether it is filled or not.

*13.2 (*Shuffle ArrayList*) Write the following method that shuffles an `ArrayList` of numbers:

```
public static void shuffle(ArrayList<Number> list)
```

*13.3 (*Sort ArrayList*) Write the following method that sorts an `ArrayList` of numbers.

```
public static void sort(ArrayList<Number> list)
```

**13.4 (*Display calendars*) Rewrite the `PrintCalendar` class in Listing 6.12 to display a calendar for a specified month using the `Calendar` and `GregorianCalendar` classes. Your program receives the month and year from the command line. For example:

```
java Exercise13_04 5 2016
```

This displays the calendar shown in Figure 13.9.

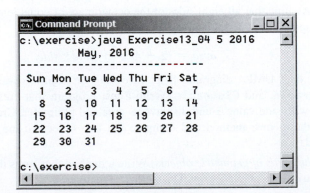

FIGURE 13.9 The program displays a calendar for May 2016.

You also can run the program without the year. In this case, the year is the current year. If you run the program without specifying a month and a year, the month is the current month.

Sections 13.4–13.8

*13.5 (*Enable GeometricObject comparable*) Modify the **GeometricObject** class to implement the **Comparable** interface, and define a static **max** method in the **GeometricObject** class for finding the larger of two **GeometricObject** objects. Draw the UML diagram and implement the new **GeometricObject** class. Write a test program that uses the **max** method to find the larger of two circles and the larger of two rectangles.

*13.6 (*The ComparableCircle class*) Define a class named **ComparableCircle** that extends **Circle** and implements **Comparable**. Draw the UML diagram and implement the **compareTo** method to compare the circles on the basis of area. Write a test class to find the larger of two instances of **ComparableCircle** objects.

*13.7 (*The Colorable interface*) Design an interface named **Colorable** with a **void** method named **howToColor()**. Every class of a colorable object must implement the **Colorable** interface. Design a class named **Square** that extends **GeometricObject** and implements **Colorable**. Implement **howToColor** to display the message **Color all four sides**.

Draw a UML diagram that involves **Colorable**, **Square**, and **GeometricObject**. Write a test program that creates an array of five **GeometricObjects**. For each object in the array, display its area and invoke its **howToColor** method if it is colorable.

*13.8 (*Revise the MyStack class*) Rewrite the **MyStack** class in Listing 11.10 to perform a deep copy of the **list** field.

*13.9 (*Enable Circle comparable*) Rewrite the **Circle** class in Listing 13.2 to extend **GeometricObject** and implement the **Comparable** interface. Override the **equals** method in the **Object** class. Two **Circle** objects are equal if their radii are the same. Draw the UML diagram that involves **Circle**, **GeometricObject**, and **Comparable**.

VideoNote
Redesign the **Rectangle** class

*13.10 (*Enable Rectangle comparable*) Rewrite the **Rectangle** class in Listing 13.3 to extend **GeometricObject** and implement the **Comparable** interface. Override the **equals** method in the **Object** class. Two **Rectangle** objects are equal if their areas are the same. Draw the UML diagram that involves **Rectangle**, **GeometricObject**, and **Comparable**.

*13.11 (*The Octagon class*) Write a class named **Octagon** that extends **GeometricObject** and implements the **Comparable** and **Cloneable** interfaces. Assume that all eight sides of the octagon are of equal length. The area can be computed using the following formula:

$$area = (2 + 4/\sqrt{2}) * side * side$$

Draw the UML diagram that involves **Octagon**, **GeometricObject**, **Comparable**, and **Cloneable**. Write a test program that creates an **Octagon** object with side value **5** and displays its area and perimeter. Create a new object using the **clone** method and compare the two objects using the **compareTo** method.

*13.12 (*Sum the areas of geometric objects*) Write a method that sums the areas of all the geometric objects in an array. The method signature is:

```
public static double sumArea(GeometricObject[] a)
```

Write a test program that creates an array of four objects (two circles and two rectangles) and computes their total area using the **sumArea** method.

*13.13 (*Enable the **Course** class cloneable*) Rewrite the **Course** class in Listing 10.6 to add a **clone** method to perform a deep copy on the **students** field.

Section 13.9

*13.14 (*Demonstrate the benefits of encapsulation*) Rewrite the **Rational** class in Listing 13.13 using a new internal representation for the numerator and denominator. Create an array of two integers as follows:

```
private long[] r = new long[2];
```

Use **r[0]** to represent the numerator and **r[1]** to represent the denominator. The signatures of the methods in the **Rational** class are not changed, so a client application that uses the previous **Rational** class can continue to use this new **Rational** class without being recompiled.

*13.15 (*Use **BigInteger** for the **Rational** class*) Redesign and implement the **Rational** class in Listing 13.13 using **BigInteger** for the numerator and denominator.

*13.16 (*Create a rational-number calculator*) Write a program similar to Listing 7.9, Calculator.java. Instead of using integers, use rationals, as shown in Figure 13.10a. You will need to use the **split** method in the **String** class, introduced in Section 10.10.3, Replacing and Splitting Strings, to retrieve the numerator string and denominator string, and convert strings into integers using the **Integer.parseInt** method.

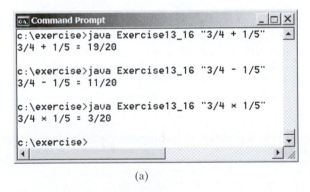

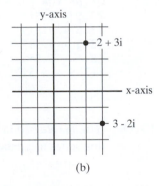

(a)   (b)

FIGURE 13.10 (a) The program takes three arguments (operand1, operator, and operand2) from the command line and displays the expression and the result of the arithmetic operation. (b) A complex number can be interpreted as a point in a plane.

*13.17 (*Math: The **Complex** class*) A complex number is a number in the form $a + bi$, where a and b are real numbers and i is $\sqrt{-1}$. The numbers **a** and **b** are known as the real part and imaginary part of the complex number, respectively. You can perform addition, subtraction, multiplication, and division for complex numbers using the following formulas:

$$a + bi + c + di = (a + c) + (b + d)i$$

$$a + bi - (c + di) = (a - c) + (b - d)i$$

$$(a + bi)*(c + di) = (ac - bd) + (bc + ad)i$$

$$(a + bi)/(c + di) = (ac + bd)/(c^2 + d^2) + (bc - ad)i/(c^2 + d^2)$$

You can also obtain the absolute value for a complex number using the following formula:

$$|a + bi| = \sqrt{a^2 + b^2}$$

(A complex number can be interpreted as a point on a plane by identifying the (a,b) values as the coordinates of the point. The absolute value of the complex number corresponds to the distance of the point to the origin, as shown in Figure 13.10b.)

Design a class named **Complex** for representing complex numbers and the methods **add**, **subtract**, **multiply**, **divide**, and **abs** for performing complex-number operations, and override **toString** method for returning a string representation for a complex number. The **toString** method returns **(a + bi)** as a string. If **b** is **0**, it simply returns **a**. Your **Complex** class should also implement the **Cloneable** interface.

Provide three constructors **Complex(a, b)**, **Complex(a)**, and **Complex()**. **Complex()** creates a **Complex** object for number **0** and **Complex(a)** creates a **Complex** object with **0** for **b**. Also provide the **getRealPart()** and **getImaginaryPart()** methods for returning the real and imaginary part of the complex number, respectively.

Write a test program that prompts the user to enter two complex numbers and displays the result of their addition, subtraction, multiplication, division, and absolute value. Here is a sample run:

```
Enter the first complex number:  3.5 5.5  ↵Enter
Enter the second complex number:  -3.5 1  ↵Enter
(3.5 + 5.5i) + (-3.5 + 1.0i) = 0.0 + 6.5i
(3.5 + 5.5i) - (-3.5 + 1.0i) = 7.0 + 4.5i
(3.5 + 5.5i) * (-3.5 + 1.0i) = -17.75 + -13.75i
(3.5 + 5.5i) / (-3.5 + 1.0i) = -0.5094 + -1.7i
|(3.5 + 5.5i)| = 6.519202405202649
```

13.18 (*Use the **Rational** class*) Write a program that computes the following summation series using the **Rational** class:

$$\frac{1}{2} + \frac{2}{3} + \frac{3}{4} + \ldots + \frac{98}{99} + \frac{99}{100}$$

You will discover that the output is incorrect because of integer overflow (too large). To fix this problem, see Programming Exercise 13.15.

13.19 (*Convert decimals to fractions*) Write a program that prompts the user to enter a decimal number and displays the number in a fraction. Hint: read the decimal number as a string, extract the integer part and fractional part from the string, and use the **BigInteger** implementation of the **Rational** class in Programming Exercise 13.15 to obtain a rational number for the decimal number. Here are some sample runs:

```
Enter a decimal number: 3.25  ↵Enter
The fraction number is 13/4
```

```
Enter a decimal number: -0.45452 ↵Enter
The fraction number is -11363/25000
```

13.20 (*Algebra: solve quadratic equations*) Rewrite Programming Exercise 3.1 to obtain imaginary roots if the determinant is less than 0 using the **Complex** class in Programming Exercise 13.17. Here are some sample runs.

```
Enter a, b, c: 1 3 1 ↵Enter
The roots are -0.381966 and -2.61803
```

```
Enter a, b, c: 1 2 1 ↵Enter
The root is -1
```

```
Enter a, b, c: 1 2 3 ↵Enter
The roots are -1.0 + 1.4142i and -1.0 + -1.4142i
```

13.21 (*Algebra: vertex form equations*) The equation of a parabola can be expressed in either standard form ($y = ax^2 + bx + c$) or vertex form ($y = a(x - h)^2 + k$). Write a program that prompts the user to enter a, b, and c as integers in standard form and displays h and k in the vertex form. Here are some sample runs.

```
Enter a, b, c: 1 3 1 ↵Enter
h is -3/2 k is -5/4
```

```
Enter a, b, c: 2 3 4 ↵Enter
h is -3/4 k is 23/8
```

JAVAFX BASICS

Objectives

- To distinguish between JavaFX, Swing, and AWT (§14.2).

- To write a simple JavaFX program and understand the relationship among stages, scenes, and nodes (§14.3).

- To create user interfaces using panes, UI controls, and shapes (§14.4).

- To update property values automatically through property binding (§14.5).

- To use the common properties **style** and **rotate** for nodes (§14.6).

- To create colors using the **Color** class (§14.7).

- To create fonts using the **Font** class (§14.8).

- To create images using the **Image** class and to create image views using the **ImageView** class (§14.9).

- To layout nodes using **Pane**, **StackPane**, **FlowPane**, **GridPane**, **BorderPane**, **HBox**, and **VBox** (§14.10).

- To display text using the **Text** class and create shapes using **Line**, **Circle**, **Rectangle**, **Ellipse**, **Arc**, **Polygon**, and **Polyline** (§14.11).

- To develop the reusable GUI component **ClockPane** for displaying an analog clock (§14.12).

14.1 Introduction

JavaFX is an excellent pedagogical tool for learning object-oriented programming.

JavaFX is a new framework for developing Java GUI programs. The JavaFX API is an excellent example of how the object-oriented principles are applied. This chapter serves two purposes. First, it presents the basics of JavaFX programming. Second, it uses JavaFX to demonstrate object-oriented design and programming. Specifically, this chapter introduces the framework of JavaFX and discusses JavaFX GUI components and their relationships. You will learn how to develop simple GUI programs using layout panes, buttons, labels, text fields, colors, fonts, images, image views, and shapes.

14.2 JavaFX vs Swing and AWT

Swing and AWT are replaced by the JavaFX platform for developing rich Internet applications.

AWT

Swing

JavaFX

When Java was introduced, the GUI classes were bundled in a library known as the *Abstract Windows Toolkit (AWT)*. AWT is fine for developing simple graphical user interfaces, but not for developing comprehensive GUI projects. In addition, AWT is prone to platform-specific bugs. The AWT user-interface components were replaced by a more robust, versatile, and flexible library known as *Swing components*. Swing components are painted directly on canvases using Java code. Swing components depend less on the target platform and use less of the native GUI resources. Swing is designed for developing desktop GUI applications. It is now replaced by a completely new GUI platform known as *JavaFX*. JavaFX incorporates modern GUI technologies to enable you to develop rich Internet applications. A rich Internet application (RIA) is a Web application designed to deliver the same features and functions normally associated with deskop applications. A JavaFX application can run seemlessly on a desktop and from a Web browser. Additionally, JavaFX provides a multi-touch support for touch-enabled devices such as tablets and smart phones. JavaFX has a built-in 2D, 3D, animation support, video and audio playback, and runs as a stand-alone application or from a browser.

why teaching JavaFX?

This book teaches Java GUI programming using JavaFX for two reasons. First, JavaFX is much simpler to learn and use for new Java programmers. Second, Swing is essentially dead, because it will not receive any further enhancement. JavaFX is the new GUI tool for developing cross-platform-rich Internet applications on desktop computers, on hand-held devices, and on the Web.

14.1 Explain the evolution of Java GUI technologies.

14.2 Explain why this book teaches Java GUI using JavaFX.

14.3 The Basic Structure of a JavaFX Program

The abstract `javafx.application.Application` class defines the essential framework for writing JavaFX programs.

We begin by writing a simple JavaFX program that illustrates the basic structure of a JavaFX program. Every JavaFX program is defined in a class that extends `javafx.application.Application`, as shown in Listing 14.1:

LISTING 14.1 MyJavaFX.java

```
1  import javafx.application.Application;
2  import javafx.scene.Scene;
3  import javafx.scene.control.Button;
4  import javafx.stage.Stage;
```

```
 5
 6  public class MyJavaFX extends Application {                        extend Application
 7    @Override // Override the start method in the Application class
 8    public void start(Stage primaryStage) {                         override start
 9      // Create a scene and place a button in the scene
10      Button btOK = new Button("OK");                               create a button
11      Scene scene = new Scene(btOK, 200, 250);                      create a scene
12      primaryStage.setTitle("MyJavaFX"); // Set the stage title     set stage title
13      primaryStage.setScene(scene); // Place the scene in the stage set a scene
14      primaryStage.show(); // Display the stage                     display stage
15    }
16
17    /**
18     * The main method is only needed for the IDE with limited
19     * JavaFX support. Not needed for running from the command line.
20     */
21    public static void main(String[] args) {                        main method
22      Application.launch(args);                                     launch application
23    }
24  }
```

You can test and run your program from a command window or from an IDE such as NetBeans or Eclipse. A sample run of the program is shown in Figure 14.1. Supplements II.F–H give the tips for running JavaFX programs from a command window, NetBeans, and Eclipse. A JavaFX program can run stand-alone or from a Web browser. For running a JavaFX program from a Web browser, see Supplement II.I.

JavaFX on NetBenas and Eclipse

FIGURE 14.1 A simple JavaFX displays a button in the window.

The **launch** method (line 22) is a static method defined in the **Application** class for launching a stand-alone JavaFX application. The **main** method (lines 21–23) is not needed if you run the program from the command line. It may be needed to launch a JavaFX program from an IDE with a limited JavaFX support. When you run a JavaFX application without a main method, JVM automatically invokes the **launch** method to run the application.

launch

The main class overrides the **start** method defined in **javafx.application.Application** (line 8). After a JavaFX application is launched, the JVM constructs an instance of the class using its **no-arg** constructor and invokes its **start** method. The **start** method normally places UI controls in a scene and displays the scene in a stage, as shown in Figure 14.2a.

construct application

start application

Line 10 creates a **Button** object and places it in a **Scene** object (line 11). A **Scene** object can be created using the constructor **Scene(node, width, height)**. This constructor specifies the width and height of the scene and places the node in the scene.

scene

A **Stage** object is a window. A **Stage** object called *primary stage* is automatically created by the JVM when the application is launched. Line 13 sets the scene to the primary stage and line 14 displays the primary stage. JavaFX names the **Stage** and **Scene** classes using the analogy from the theater. You may think stage as the platform to support scenes and nodes as actors to perform in the scenes.

primary stage

You can create additional stages if needed. The JavaFX program in Listing 14.2 displays two stages, as shown in Figure 14.2b.

FIGURE 14.2 (a) Stage is a window for displaying a scene that contains nodes. (b) Multiple stages can be displayed in a JavaFX program.

LISTING 14.2 MultipleStageDemo.java

```
1  import javafx.application.Application;
2  import javafx.scene.Scene;
3  import javafx.scene.control.Button;
4  import javafx.stage.Stage;
5
6  public class MultipleStageDemo extends Application {
7    @Override // Override the start method in the Application class
8    public void start(Stage primaryStage) {
9      // Create a scene and place a button in the scene
10     Scene scene = new Scene(new Button("OK"), 200, 250);
11     primaryStage.setTitle("MyJavaFX"); // Set the stage title
12     primaryStage.setScene(scene); // Place the scene in the stage
13     primaryStage.show(); // Display the stage
14
15     Stage stage = new Stage(); // Create a new stage
16     stage.setTitle("Second Stage"); // Set the stage title
17     // Set a scene with a button in the stage
18     stage.setScene(new Scene(new Button("New Stage"), 100, 100));
19     stage.show(); // Display the stage
20   }
21 }
```

primary stage in start

display primary stage

create second stage

display second stage

main method omitted

Note that the main method is omitted in the listing since it is identical for every JavaFX application. From now on, we will not list the **main** method in our JavaFX source code for brevity.

By default, the user can resize the stage. To prevent the user from resizing the stage, invoke **stage.setResizable(false)**.

prevent stage resizing

14.3 How do you define a JavaFX main class? What is the signature of the **start** method? What is a stage? What is a primary stage? Is a primary stage automatically created? How do you display a stage? Can you prevent the user from resizing the stage? Can you replace **Application.launch(args)** by **launch(args)** in line 22 in Listing 14.1?

14.4 Show the output of the following JavaFX program.

```
import javafx.application.Application;
import javafx.stage.Stage;

public class Test extends Application {
  public Test() {
    System.out.println("Test constructor is invoked");
  }
```

```
@Override // Override the start method in the Application class
public void start(Stage primaryStage) {
    System.out.println("start method is invoked");
}

public static void main(String[] args) {
    System.out.println("launch application");
    Application.launch(args);
}
```

14.4 Panes, UI Controls, and Shapes

Panes, UI controls, and shapes are subtypes of Node.

Key Point

When you run MyJavaFX in Listing 14.1, the window is displayed as shown in Figure 14.1. The button is always centered in the scene and occupies the entire window no matter how you resize it. You can fix the problem by setting the position and size properties of a button. However, a better approach is to use container classes, called *panes*, for automatically laying out the nodes in a desired location and size. You place nodes inside a pane and then place the pane into a scene. A *node* is a visual component such as a shape, an image view, a UI control, or a pane. A *shape* refers to a text, line, circle, ellipse, rectangle, arc, polygon, polyline, etc. A *UI control* refers to a label, button, check box, radio button, text field, text area, etc. A scene can be displayed in a stage, as shown in Figure 14.3a. The relationship among **Stage**, **Scene**, **Node**, **Control**, and **Pane** is illustrated in the UML diagram, as shown in Figure 14.3b. Note that a **Scene** can contain a **Control** or a **Pane**, but not a **Shape** or an **ImageView**. A **Pane** can contain any subtype of **Node**. You can create a **Scene** using the constructor **Scene(Parent, width, height)** or **Scene(Parent)**. The dimension of the scene is automatically decided in the latter constructor. Every subclass of **Node** has a no-arg constructor for creating a default node.

pane

node

shape

UI control

Listing 14.3 gives a program that places a button in a pane, as shown in Figure 14.4

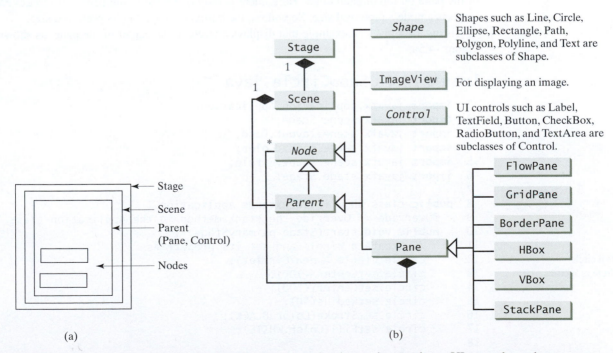

(a)　　　　　　　　　　　　　　　　(b)

FIGURE 14.3 (a) Panes are used to hold nodes. (b) Nodes can be shapes, image views, UI controls, and panes.

LISTING 14.3 ButtonInPane.java

```
 1  import javafx.application.Application;
 2  import javafx.scene.Scene;
 3  import javafx.scene.control.Button;
 4  import javafx.stage.Stage;
 5  import javafx.scene.layout.StackPane;
 6
 7  public class ButtonInPane extends Application {
 8    @Override // Override the start method in the Application class
 9    public void start(Stage primaryStage) {
10      // Create a scene and place a button in the scene
11      StackPane pane = new StackPane();
12      pane.getChildren().add(new Button("OK"));
13      Scene scene = new Scene(pane, 200, 50);
14      primaryStage.setTitle("Button in a pane"); // Set the stage title
15      primaryStage.setScene(scene); // Place the scene in the stage
16      primaryStage.show(); // Display the stage
17    }
18  }
```

create a pane — line 11
add a button — line 12
add pane to scene — line 13

display stage — line 16

main method omitted — line 18

FIGURE 14.4 A button is placed in the center of the pane.

The program creates a **StackPane** (line 11) and adds a button as a child of the pane (line 12). The **getChildren()** method returns an instance of **javafx.collections.ObservableList**. **ObservableList** behaves very much like an **ArrayList** for storing a collection of elements. Invoking **add(e)** adds an element to the list. The **StackPane** places the nodes in the center of the pane on top of each other. Here, there is only one node in the pane. The **StackPane** respects a node's preferred size. So you see the button displayed in its preferred size.

ObservableList

Listing 14.4 gives an example that displays a circle in the center of the pane, as shown in Figure 14.5a.

LISTING 14.4 ShowCircle.java

```
 1  import javafx.application.Application;
 2  import javafx.scene.Scene;
 3  import javafx.scene.layout.Pane;
 4  import javafx.scene.paint.Color;
 5  import javafx.scene.shape.Circle;
 6  import javafx.stage.Stage;
 7
 8  public class ShowCircle extends Application {
 9    @Override // Override the start method in the Application class
10    public void start(Stage primaryStage) {
11      // Create a circle and set its properties
12      Circle circle = new Circle();
13      circle.setCenterX(100);
14      circle.setCenterY(100);
15      circle.setRadius(50);
16      circle.setStroke(Color.BLACK);
17      circle.setFill(Color.WHITE);
18
19      // Create a pane to hold the circle
20      Pane pane = new Pane();
```

create a circle — line 12
set circle properties — line 13

create a pane — line 20

```
21        pane.getChildren().add(circle);                                     add circle to pane
22
23        // Create a scene and place it in the stage
24        Scene scene = new Scene(pane, 200, 200);                            add pane to scene
25        primaryStage.setTitle("ShowCircle"); // Set the stage title
26        primaryStage.setScene(scene); // Place the scene in the stage
27        primaryStage.show(); // Display the stage                           display stage
28    }
29 }                                                                          main method omitted
```

FIGURE 14.5 (a) A circle is displayed in the center of the scene. (b) The circle is not centered after the window is resized.

The program creates a **Circle** (line 12) and sets its center at (100, 100) (lines 13–14), which is also the center for the scene, since the scene is created with the width and height of 200 (line 24). The radius of the circle is set to 50 (line 15). Note that the measurement units for graphics in Java are all in *pixels*.

pixels

The stroke color (i.e., the color to draw the circle) is set to black (line 16). The fill color (i.e., the color to fill the circle) is set to white (line 17). You may set the color to **null** to specify that no color is set.

set color

The program creates a **Pane** (line 20) and places the circle in the pane (line 21). Note that the coordinates of the upper left corner of the pane is (**0, 0**) in the Java coordinate system, as shown in Figure 14.6a, as opposed to the conventional coordinate system where (0, 0) is at the center of the window, as shown in Figure 14.6b. The *x*-coordinate increases from left to right and the *y*-coordinate increases downward in the Java coordinate system.

The pane is placed in the scene (line 24) and the scene is set in the stage (line 26). The circle is displayed in the center of the stage, as shown in Figure 14.5a. However, if you resize the window, the circle is not centered, as shown in Figure 14.5b. In order to display the circle centered as the window resizes, the *x*- and *y*-coordinates of the circle center need to be reset to the center of the pane. This can be done by using property binding, introduced in the next section.

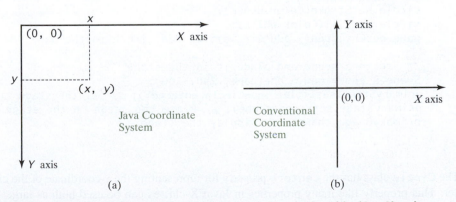

FIGURE 14.6 The Java coordinate system is measured in pixels, with (**0, 0**) at its upper-left corner.

Check Point

14.5 How do you create a `Scene` object? How do you set a scene in a stage? How do you place a circle into a scene?

14.6 What is a pane? What is a node? How do you place a node in a pane? Can you directly place a `Shape` or an `ImageView` into a `Scene`? Can you directly place a `Control` or a `Pane` into a `Scene`?

14.7 How do you create a `Circle`? How do you set its center location and radius? How do you set its stroke color and fill color?

14.5 Property Binding

Key Point

You can bind a target object to a source object. A change in the source object will be automatically reflected in the target object.

target object
source object
binding object
binding property
bindable object
observable object

JavaFX introduces a new concept called *property binding* that enables a *target object* to be bound to a *source object*. If the value in the source object changes, the target object is also changed automatically. The target object is called a *binding object* or a *binding property* and the source object is called a *bindable object* or *observable object*. As discussed in the preceding listing, the circle is not centered after the window is resized. In order to display the circle centered as the window resizes, the *x*- and *y*-coordinates of the circle center need to be reset to the center of the pane. This can be done by binding the `centerX` with pane's `width/2` and `centerY` with pane's `height/2`, as shown in Listing 14.5.

VideoNote

Understand property binding

LISTING 14.5 ShowCircleCentered.java

```
1  import javafx.application.Application;
2  import javafx.scene.Scene;
3  import javafx.scene.layout.Pane;
4  import javafx.scene.paint.Color;
5  import javafx.scene.shape.Circle;
6  import javafx.stage.Stage;
7
8  public class ShowCircleCentered extends Application {
9    @Override // Override the start method in the Application class
10   public void start(Stage primaryStage) {
11     // Create a pane to hold the circle
12     Pane pane = new Pane();
13
14     // Create a circle and set its properties
15     Circle circle = new Circle();
16     circle.centerXProperty().bind(pane.widthProperty().divide(2));
17     circle.centerYProperty().bind(pane.heightProperty().divide(2));
18     circle.setRadius(50);
19     circle.setStroke(Color.BLACK);
20     circle.setFill(Color.WHITE);
21     pane.getChildren().add(circle); // Add circle to the pane
22
23     // Create a scene and place it in the stage
24     Scene scene = new Scene(pane, 200, 200);
25     primaryStage.setTitle("ShowCircleCentered"); // Set the stage title
26     primaryStage.setScene(scene); // Place the scene in the stage
27     primaryStage.show(); // Display the stage
28   }
29 }
```

create a pane — line 12
create a circle — line 15
bind properties — lines 16–17
add circle to pane — line 21
add pane to scene — line 24
display stage — line 27

The `Circle` class has the `centerX` property for representing the *x*-coordinate of the circle center. This property like many properties in JavaFX classes can be used both as target and source in a property binding. A target listens to the changes in the source and automatically updates itself once a change is made in the source. A target binds with a source using the **bind** method as follows:

```
target.bind(source);
```

The **bind** method is defined in the **javafx.beans.property.Property** interface. A binding property is an instance of **javafx.beans.property.Property**. A source object is an instance of the **javafx.beans.value.ObservableValue** interface. An **ObservableValue** is an entity that wraps a value and allows to observe the value for changes.

JavaFX defines binding properties for primitive types and strings. For a **double**/**float**/**long**/**int**/**boolean** value, its binding property type is **DoubleProperty**/**FloatProperty**/**LongProperty**/**IntegerProperty**/**BooleanProperty**. For a string, its binding property type is **StringProperty**. These properties are also subtypes of **ObservableValue**. So they can also be used as source objects for binding properties.

By convention, each binding property (e.g., **centerX**) in a JavaFX class (e.g., **Circle**) has a getter (e.g., **getCenterX()**) and setter (e.g., **setCenterX(double)**) method for returning and setting the property's value. It also has a getter method for returning the property itself. The naming convention for this method is the property name followed by the word **Property**. For example, the property getter method for **centerX** is **centerXProperty()**. We call the **getCenterX()** method as the *value getter method*, the **setCenterX(double)** method as the *value setter method*, and **centerXProperty()** as the *property getter method*. Note that **getCenterX()** returns a **double** value and **centerXProperty()** returns an object of the **DoubleProperty** type. Figure 14.7a shows the convention for defining a binding property in a class and Figure 14.7b shows a concrete example in which **centerX** is a binding property of the type **DoubleProperty**.

the Property interface

the ObservableValue interface

common binding properties

common ObservableValue objects

value getter method
value setter method
property getter method

```java
public class SomeClassName {

  private PropertyType x;

  /** Value getter method */
  public propertyValueType getX() { ... }

  /** Value setter method */
  public void setX(propertyValueType value) { ... }

  /** Property getter method */
  public PropertyType
    xProperty() { ... }
}
```

(a) x is a binding property

```java
public class Circle {

  private DoubleProperty centerX;

  /** Value getter method */
  public double getCenterX() { ... }

  /** Value setter method */
  public void setCenterX(double value) { ... }

  /** Property getter method */
  public DoubleProperty centerXProperty() { ... }
}
```

(b) centerX is binding property

FIGURE 14.7 A binding property has a value getter method, setter method, and property getter method.

The program in Listing 14.5 is the same as in Listing 14.4 except that it binds **circle**'s **centerX** and **centerY** properties to half of **pane**'s width and height (lines 16–17). Note that **circle.centerXProperty()** returns **centerX** and **pane.widthProperty()** returns **width**. Both **centerX** and **width** are binding properties of the **DoubleProperty** type. The numeric binding property classes such as **DoubleProperty** and **IntegerProperty** contain the **add**, **subtract**, **multiply**, and **divide** methods for adding, subtracting, multiplying, and dividing a value in a binding property and returning a new observable property. So, **pane.widthProperty().divide(2)** returns a new observable property that represents half of the **pane**'s width. The statement

```
circle.centerXProperty().bind(pane.widthProperty().divide(2));
```

is same as

```
centerX.bind(width.divide(2));
```

Since `centerX` is bound to `width.divide(2)`, when `pane`'s width is changed, `centerX` automatically updates itself to match `pane`'s width / 2.

Listing 14.6 gives another example that demonstrates bindings.

LISTING 14.6 BindingDemo.java

```
 1  import javafx.beans.property.DoubleProperty;
 2  import javafx.beans.property.SimpleDoubleProperty;
 3
 4  public class BindingDemo {
 5    public static void main(String[] args) {
 6      DoubleProperty d1 = new SimpleDoubleProperty(1);
 7      DoubleProperty d2 = new SimpleDoubleProperty(2);
 8      d1.bind(d2);
 9      System.out.println("d1 is " + d1.getValue()
10        + " and d2 is " + d2.getValue());
11      d2.setValue(70.2);
12      System.out.println("d1 is " + d1.getValue()
13        + " and d2 is " + d2.getValue());
14    }
15  }
```

create a DoubleProperty
create a DoubleProperty
bind property

set a new source value

```
d1 is 2.0 and d2 is 2.0
d1 is 70.2 and d2 is 70.2
```

The program creates an instance of `DoubleProperty` using `SimpleDoubleProperty(1)` (line 6). Note that `DoubleProperty`, `FloatProperty`, `LongProperty`, `IntegerProperty`, and `BooleanProperty` are abstract classes. Their concrete subclasses `SimpleDoubleProperty`, `SimpleFloatProperty`, `SimpleLongProperty`, `SimpleIntegerProperty`, and `SimpleBooleanProperty` are used to create instances of these properties. These classes are very much like wrapper classes `Double`, `Float`, `Long`, `Integer`, and `Boolean` with additional features for binding to a source object.

The program binds `d1` with `d2` (line 8). Now the values in `d1` and `d2` are the same. After setting `d2` to `70.2` (line 11), `d1` also becomes `70.2` (line 13).

unidirectional binding

bidirectional binding

The binding demonstrated in this example is known as *unidirectional binding*. Occasionally, it is useful to synchronize two properties so that a change in one property is reflected in another object, and vice versa. This is called a *bidirectional binding*. If the target and source are both binding properties and observable properties, they can be bound bidirectionally using the `bindBidirectional` method.

✓ Check Point

14.8 What is a binding property? What interface defines a binding property? What interface defines a source object? What are the binding object types for `int`, `long`, `float`, `double`, and `boolean`? Are `Integer` and `Double` binding properties? Can `Integer` and `Double` be used as source objects in a binding?

14.9 Following the JavaFX binding property naming convention, for a binding property named `age` of the `IntegerProperty` type, what is its value getter method, value setter method, and property getter method?

14.10 Can you create an object of `IntegerProperty` using `new IntegerProperty(3)`? If not, what is the correct way to create it? What will the output if line 8 is replaced by `d1.bind(d2.multiply(2))` in Listing 14.6? What will the output if line 8 is replaced by `d1.bind(d2.add(2))` in Listing 14.6?

14.11 What is a unidirectional binding and what is bidirectional binding? Are all binding properties capable of bidirectional binding? Write a statement to bind property `d1` with property `d2` bidirectionally.

14.6 Common Properties and Methods for Nodes

*The abstract **Node** class defines many properties and methods that are common to all nodes.*

Key Point

Nodes share many common properties. This section introduces two such properties `style` and `rotate`.

JavaFX style properties are similar to cascading style sheets (CSS) used to specify the styles for HTML elements in a Web page. So, the style properties in JavaFX are called *JavaFX CSS*. In JavaFX, a style property is defined with a prefix `-fx-`. Each node has its own style properties. You can find these properties from http://docs.oracle.com/javafx/2/api/javafx/scene/doc-files/cssref.html. For information on HTML and CSS, see Supplements V.A and V.B. If you are not familiar with HTML and CSS, you can still use JavaFX CSS.

JavaFX CSS

The syntax for setting a style is `styleName:value`. Multiple style properties for a node can be set together separated by semicolon (`;`). For example, the following statement

```
circle.setStyle("-fx-stroke: black; -fx-fill: red;");
```

setStyle

sets two JavaFX CSS properties for a circle. This statement is equivalent to the following two statements.

```
circle.setStroke(Color.BLACK);
circle.setFill(Color.RED);
```

If an incorrect JavaFX CSS is used, your program will still compile and run, but the style is ignored.

The **rotate** property enables you to specify an angle in degrees for rotating the node from its center. If the degree is positive, the rotation is performed clockwise; otherwise, it is performed counterclockwise. For example, the following code rotates a button 80 degrees.

```
button.setRotate(80);
```

Listing 14.7 gives an example that creates a button, sets its style, and adds it to a pane. It then rotates the pane 45 degrees and set its style with border color red and background color light gray, as shown in Figure 14.8.

LISTING 14.7 NodeStyleRotateDemo.java

```
1  import javafx.application.Application;
2  import javafx.scene.Scene;
3  import javafx.scene.control.Button;
4  import javafx.stage.Stage;
5  import javafx.scene.layout.StackPane;
6
7  public class NodeStyleRotateDemo extends Application {
8    @Override // Override the start method in the Application class
9    public void start(Stage primaryStage) {
10     // Create a scene and place a button in the scene
11     StackPane pane = new StackPane();
12     Button btOK = new Button("OK");
13     btOK.setStyle("-fx-border-color: blue;");
14     pane.getChildren().add(btOK);
15
16     pane.setRotate(45);
17     pane.setStyle(
18       "-fx-border-color: red; -fx-background-color: lightgray;");
19
20     Scene scene = new Scene(pane, 200, 250);
21     primaryStage.setTitle("NodeStyleRotateDemo"); // Set the stage title
22     primaryStage.setScene(scene); // Place the scene in the stage
```

rotate the pane
set style for pane

```
23      primaryStage.show(); // Display the stage
24    }
25  }
```

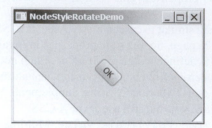

FIGURE 14.8 A pane's style is set and it is rotated 45 degrees.

As seen in Figure 14.8, the rotate on a pane causes all its containing nodes rotated too.

The **Node** class contains many useful methods that can be applied to all nodes. For example, you can use the **contains(double x, double y)** method to test where a point (*x*, *y*) is inside the boundary of a node.

contains method

 14.12 How do you set a style of a node with border color red? Modify the code to set the text color for the button to red.

14.13 Can you rotate a pane, a text, or a button? Modify the code to rotate the button 15 degrees counterclockwise?

14.7 The **Color** Class

*The **Color** class can be used to create colors.*

JavaFX defines the abstract **Paint** class for painting a node. The **javafx.scene.paint.Color** is a concrete subclass of **Paint**, which is used to encapsulate colors, as shown in Figure 14.9.

> The getter methods for property values are provided in the class, but omitted in the UML diagram for brevity.

javafx.scene.paint.Color	
-red: double	The red value of this Color (between 0.0 and 1.0).
-green: double	The green value of this Color (between 0.0 and 1.0).
-blue: double	The blue value of this Color (between 0.0 and 1.0).
-opacity: double	The opacity of this Color (between 0.0 and 1.0).
+Color(r: double, g: double, b: double, opacity: double)	Creates a Color with the specified red, green, blue, and opacity values.
+brighter(): Color	Creates a Color that is a brighter version of this Color.
+darker(): Color	Creates a Color that is a darker version of this Color.
+color(r: double, g: double, b: double): Color	Creates an opaque Color with the specified red, green, and blue values.
+color(r: double, g: double, b: double, opacity: double): Color	Creates a Color with the specified red, green, blue, and opacity values.
+rgb(r: int, g: int, b: int): Color	Creates a Color with the specified red, green, and blue values in the range from 0 to 255.
+rgb(r: int, g: int, b: int, opacity: double): Color	Creates a Color with the specified red, green, and blue values in the range from 0 to 255 and a given opacity.

FIGURE 14.9 **Color** encapsulates information about colors.

A color instance can be constructed using the following constructor:

```
public Color(double r, double g, double b, double opacity);
```

in which **r**, **g**, and **b** specify a color by its red, green, and blue components with values in the range from **0.0** (darkest shade) to **1.0** (lightest shade). The **opacity** value defines the transparency of a color within the range from **0.0** (completely transparent) to **1.0** (completely opaque). This is known as the RGBA model, where RGBA stands for red, green, blue, and alpha. The alpha value indicates the opacity. For example,

RBGA model

```
Color color = new Color(0.25, 0.14, 0.333, 0.51);
```

The **Color** class is immutable. Once a **Color** object is created, its properties cannot be changed. The **brighter()** method returns a new **Color** with a larger red, green, and blue values and the **darker()** method returns a new **Color** with a smaller red, green, and blue values. The **opacity** value is the same as in the original **Color** object.

You can also create a **Color** object using the static methods **color(r, g, b)**, **color(r, g, b, opacity)**, **rgb(r, g, b)**, and **rgb(r, g, b, opacity)**.

Alternatively, you can use one of the many standard colors such as **BEIGE**, **BLACK**, **BLUE**, **BROWN**, **CYAN**, **DARKGRAY**, **GOLD**, **GRAY**, **GREEN**, **LIGHTGRAY**, **MAGENTA**, **NAVY**, **ORANGE**, **PINK**, **RED**, **SILVER**, **WHITE**, and **YELLOW** defined as constants in the **Color** class. The following code, for instance, sets the fill color of a circle to red:

```
circle.setFill(Color.RED);
```

14.14 How do you create a color? What is wrong about creating a **Color** using **new Color(1.2, 2.3, 3.5, 4)**? Which of two colors is darker, **new Color(0, 0, 0, 1)** or **new Color(1, 1, 1, 1)**? Does invoking **c.darker()** change the color value in **c**?

Check Point

14.15 How do you create a **Color** object with a random color?

14.16 How do you set a circle object **c** with blue fill color using the **setFill** method and using the **setStyle** method?

14.8 The **Font** Class

*A **Font** describes font name, weight, and size.*

Key Point

You can set fonts for rendering the text. The **javafx.scene.text.Font** class is used to create fonts, as shown in Figure 14.10.

A **Font** instance can be constructed using its constructors or using its static methods. A **Font** is defined by its name, weight, posture, and size. Times, Courier, and Arial are the examples of the font names. You can obtain a list of available font family names by invoking the static **getFamilies()** method. **List** is an interface that defines common methods for a list. **ArrayList** is a concrete implementation of **List**. The font postures are two constants: **FontPosture.ITALIC** and **FontPosture.REGULAR**. For example, the following statements create two fonts.

```
Font font1 = new Font("SansSerif", 16);
Font font2 = Font.font("Times New Roman", FontWeight.BOLD,
  FontPosture.ITALIC, 12);
```

Listing 14.8 gives a program that displays a label using the font (Times New Roman, bold, italic, and size 20), as shown in Figure 14.11.

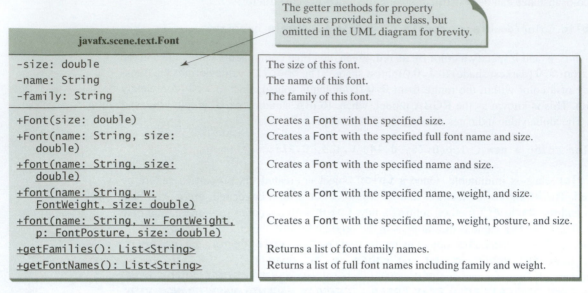

The getter methods for property values are provided in the class, but omitted in the UML diagram for brevity.

javafx.scene.text.Font	
-size: double	The size of this font.
-name: String	The name of this font.
-family: String	The family of this font.
+Font(size: double)	Creates a Font with the specified size.
+Font(name: String, size: double)	Creates a Font with the specified full font name and size.
+font(name: String, size: double)	Creates a Font with the specified name and size.
+font(name: String, w: FontWeight, size: double)	Creates a Font with the specified name, weight, and size.
+font(name: String, w: FontWeight, p: FontPosture, size: double)	Creates a Font with the specified name, weight, posture, and size.
+getFamilies(): List<String>	Returns a list of font family names.
+getFontNames(): List<String>	Returns a list of full font names including family and weight.

FIGURE 14.10 **Font** encapsulates information about fonts.

LISTING 14.8 FontDemo.java

```java
1   import javafx.application.Application;
2   import javafx.scene.Scene;
3   import javafx.scene.layout.*;
4   import javafx.scene.paint.Color;
5   import javafx.scene.shape.Circle;
6   import javafx.scene.text.*;
7   import javafx.scene.control.*;
8   import javafx.stage.Stage;
9
10  public class FontDemo extends Application {
11    @Override // Override the start method in the Application class
12    public void start(Stage primaryStage) {
13      // Create a pane to hold the circle
14      Pane pane = new StackPane();
15
16      // Create a circle and set its properties
17      Circle circle = new Circle();
18      circle.setRadius(50);
19      circle.setStroke(Color.BLACK);
20      circle.setFill(new Color(0.5, 0.5, 0.5, 0.1));
21      pane.getChildren().add(circle); // Add circle to the pane
22
23      // Create a label and set its properties
24      Label label = new Label("JavaFX");
25      label.setFont(Font.font("Times New Roman",
26        FontWeight.BOLD, FontPosture.ITALIC, 20));
27      pane.getChildren().add(label);
28
29      // Create a scene and place it in the stage
30      Scene scene = new Scene(pane);
31      primaryStage.setTitle("FontDemo"); // Set the stage title
32      primaryStage.setScene(scene); // Place the scene in the stage
```

create a StackPane — line 14
create a Circle — line 17
create a Color — line 20
add circle to the pane — line 21
create a label — line 24
create a font — line 25
add label to the pane — line 27

```
33        primaryStage.show(); // Display the stage
34    }
35 }
```

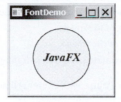

FIGURE 14.11 A label is on top of a circle displayed in the center of the scene.

The program creates a **StackPane** (line 14) and adds a circle and a label to it (lines 21, 27). These two statements can be combined using the following one statement:

```
pane.getChildren().addAll(circle, label);
```

A **StackPane** places the nodes in the center and nodes are placed on top of each other. A custom color is created and set as a fill color for the circle (line 20). The program creates a label and sets a font (line 25) so the text in the label is displayed in Times New Roman, bold, italic, and 20 pixels.

As you resize the window, the circle and label are displayed in the center of the window, because the circle and label are placed in the stack pane. Stack pane automatically places nodes in the center of the pane.

A **Font** object is immutable. Once a **Font** object is created, its properties cannot be changed.

14.17 How do you create a **Font** object with font name **Courier**, size **20**, and weight **bold**?

14.18 How do you find all available fonts on your system?

14.9 The **Image** and **ImageView** Classes

*The **Image** class represents a graphical image and the **ImageView** class can be used to display an image.*

The **javafx.scene.image.Image** class represents a graphical image and is used for loading an image from a specified filename or a URL. For example, **new Image("image/us.gif")** creates an **Image** object for the image file **us.gif** under the directory **image** in the Java class directory and **new Image("http://www.cs.armstrong.edu/liang/image/us.gif")** creates an **Image** object for the image file in the URL on the Web.

VideoNote

Use Image and ImageView

The **javafx.scene.image.ImageView** is a node for displaying an image. An **ImageView** can be created from an **Image** object. For example, the following code creates an **ImageView** from an image file:

```
Image image = new Image("image/us.gif");
ImageView imageView = new ImageView(image);
```

Alternatively, you can create an **ImageView** directly from a file or a URL as follows:

```
ImageView imageView = new ImageView("image/us.gif");
```

The UML diagrams for the **Image** and **ImageView** classes are illustrated in Figures 14.12 and 14.13.

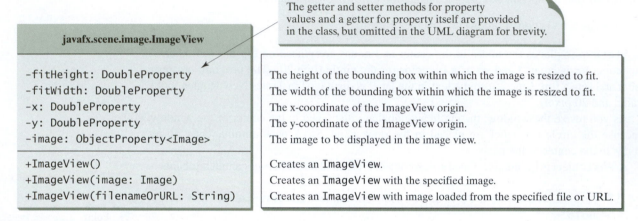

The getter methods for property values are provided in the class, but omitted in the UML diagram for brevity.

javafx.scene.image.Image

-error: ReadOnlyBooleanProperty

-height: ReadOnlyBooleanProperty

-width: ReadOnlyBooleanProperty

-progress: ReadOnlyBooleanProperty

+Image(filenameOrURL: String)

Indicates whether the image is loaded correctly?

The height of the image.

The width of the image.

The approximate percentage of image's loading that is completed.

Creates an **Image** with contents loaded from a file or a URL.

FIGURE 14.12 **Image** encapsulates information about images.

The getter and setter methods for property values and a getter for property itself are provided in the class, but omitted in the UML diagram for brevity.

javafx.scene.image.ImageView

-fitHeight: DoubleProperty

-fitWidth: DoubleProperty

-x: DoubleProperty

-y: DoubleProperty

-image: ObjectProperty<Image>

+ImageView()

+ImageView(image: Image)

+ImageView(filenameOrURL: String)

The height of the bounding box within which the image is resized to fit.

The width of the bounding box within which the image is resized to fit.

The x-coordinate of the ImageView origin.

The y-coordinate of the ImageView origin.

The image to be displayed in the image view.

Creates an **ImageView**.

Creates an **ImageView** with the specified image.

Creates an **ImageView** with image loaded from the specified file or URL.

FIGURE 14.13 **ImageView** is a node for displaying an image.

Listing 14.9 displays an image in three image views, as shown in Figure 14.14.

LISTING 14.9 ShowImage.java

```
1  import javafx.application.Application;
2  import javafx.scene.Scene;
3  import javafx.scene.layout.HBox;
4  import javafx.scene.layout.Pane;
5  import javafx.geometry.Insets;
6  import javafx.stage.Stage;
7  import javafx.scene.image.Image;
8  import javafx.scene.image.ImageView;
9
10 public class ShowImage extends Application {
11   @Override // Override the start method in the Application class
12   public void start(Stage primaryStage) {
13     // Create a pane to hold the image views
14     Pane pane = new HBox(10);
15     pane.setPadding(new Insets(5, 5, 5, 5));
16     Image image = new Image("image/us.gif");
17     pane.getChildren().add(new ImageView(image));
18
19     ImageView imageView2 = new ImageView(image);
20     imageView2.setFitHeight(100);
21     imageView2.setFitWidth(100);
```

create an HBox

create an image
add an image view to pane

create an image view
set image view properties

```
22        pane.getChildren().add(imageView2);                          add an image to pane
23
24        ImageView imageView3 = new ImageView(image);                 create an image view
25        imageView3.setRotate(90);                                    rotate an image view
26        pane.getChildren().add(imageView3);                          add an image to pane
27
28        // Create a scene and place it in the stage
29        Scene scene = new Scene(pane);
30        primaryStage.setTitle("ShowImage"); // Set the stage title
31        primaryStage.setScene(scene); // Place the scene in the stage
32        primaryStage.show(); // Display the stage
33      }
34  }
```

FIGURE 14.14 An image is displayed in three image views placed in a pane.

The program creates an **HBox** (line 14). An **HBox** is a pane that places all nodes horizontally in one row. The program creates an **Image**, and then an **ImageView** for displaying the iamge, and places the **ImageView** in the **HBox** (line 17).

The program creates the second **ImageView** (line 19), sets its **fitHeight** and **fitWidth** properties (lines 20–21) and places the **ImageView** into the **HBox** (line 22). The program creates the third **ImageView** (line 24), rotates it 90 degrees (line 25), and places it into the **HBox** (line 26). The **setRotate** method is defined in the **Node** class and can be used for any node. Note that an **Image** object can be shared by multiple nodes. In this case, it is shared by three **ImageView**. However, a node such as **ImageView** cannot be shared. You cannot place an **ImageView** multiple times into a pane or scene.

Note that you must place the image file in the same directory as the class file, as shown in the following figure.

```
Directory

    ├── ShowImage.class

    └── image

        └── us.gif
```

If you use the URL to locate the image file, the URL protocal http:// must be present. So the following code is wrong.

```
new Image("www.cs.armstrong.edu/liang/image/us.gif");
```

It must be replaced by

```
new Image("http://www.cs.armstrong.edu/liang/image/us.gif");
```

14.19 How do you create an **Image** from a URL or a filename?

14.20 How do you create an **ImageView** from an **Image**, or directly from a file or a URL?

14.21 Can you set an **Image** to multiple **ImageView**? Can you display the same **ImageView** multiple times?

14.10 Layout Panes

Key
Point

JavaFX provides many types of panes for automatically laying out nodes in a desired location and size.

JavaFX provides many types of panes for organizing nodes in a container, as shown in Table 14.1. You have used the layout panes **Pane**, **StackPane**, and **HBox** in the preceding sections for containing nodes. This section introduces the panes in more details.

VideoNote

Use layout panes

TABLE 14.1 Panes for Containing and Organizing Nodes

Class	Description
Pane	Base class for layout panes. It contains the **getChildren()** method for returning a list of nodes in the pane.
StackPane	Places the nodes on top of each other in the center of the pane.
FlowPane	Places the nodes row-by-row horizontally or column-by-column vertically.
GridPane	Places the nodes in the cells in a two-dimensional grid.
BorderPane	Places the nodes in the top, right, bottom, left, and center regions.
HBox	Places the nodes in a single row.
VBox	Places the nodes in a single column.

You have used the **Pane** in Listing 14.4, ShowCircle.java. A **Pane** is usually used as a canvas for displaying shapes. **Pane** is the base class for all specialized panes. You have used a specialized pane **StackPane** in Listing 14.3, ButtonInPane.java. Nodes are placed in the center of a **StackPane**. Each pane contains a list for holding nodes in the pane. This list is an instance of **ObservableList**, which can be obtained using pane's **getChildren()** method. You can use the **add(node)** method to add an element to the list, use **addAll(node1, node2, ...)** to add a variable number of nodes to the pane.

ObservableList
getChildren()

14.10.1 FlowPane

FlowPane arranges the nodes in the pane horizontally from left to right or vertically from top to bottom in the order in which they were added. When one row or one column is filled, a new row or column is started. You can specify the way the nodes are placed horizontally or vertically using one of two constants: **Orientation.HORIZONTAL** or **Orientation.VERTICAL**. You can also specify the gap between the nodes in pixels. The class diagram for **FlowPane** is shown in Figure 14.15.

Data fields **alignment**, **orientation**, **hgap**, and **vgap** are binding properties. Each binding property in JavaFX has a getter method (e.g., **getHgap()**) that returns its value, a setter method (e.g., **sethGap(double)**) for setting a value, and a getter method that returns the property itself (e.g., **hGapProperty()**). For a data field of **ObjectProperty<T>** type, the value getter method returns a value of type **T** and the property getter method returns a property value of type **ObjectProperty<T>**.

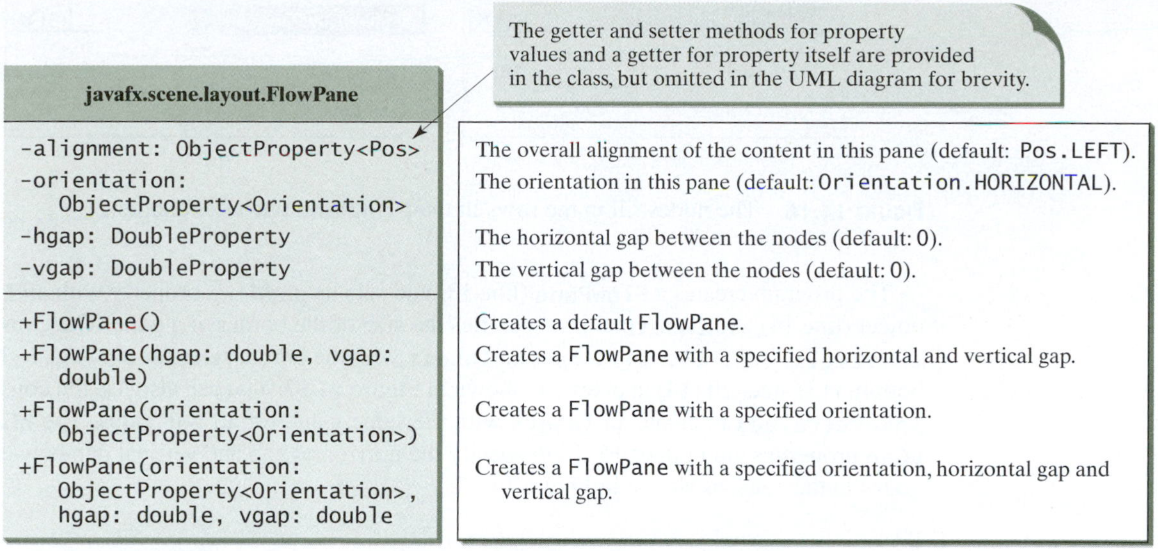

The getter and setter methods for property values and a getter for property itself are provided in the class, but omitted in the UML diagram for brevity.

javafx.scene.layout.FlowPane	
-alignment: ObjectProperty<Pos>	The overall alignment of the content in this pane (default: Pos.LEFT).
-orientation: ObjectProperty<Orientation>	The orientation in this pane (default: Orientation.HORIZONTAL).
-hgap: DoubleProperty	The horizontal gap between the nodes (default: 0).
-vgap: DoubleProperty	The vertical gap between the nodes (default: 0).
+FlowPane()	Creates a default FlowPane.
+FlowPane(hgap: double, vgap: double)	Creates a FlowPane with a specified horizontal and vertical gap.
+FlowPane(orientation: ObjectProperty<Orientation>)	Creates a FlowPane with a specified orientation.
+FlowPane(orientation: ObjectProperty<Orientation>, hgap: double, vgap: double	Creates a FlowPane with a specified orientation, horizontal gap and vertical gap.

FIGURE 14.15 FlowPane lays out nodes row by row horizontally or column by column vertically.

Listing 14.10 gives a program that demonstrates FlowPane. The program adds labels and text fields to a FlowPane, as shown in Figure 14.16.

LISTING 14.10 ShowFlowPane.java

```
1  import javafx.application.Application;
2  import javafx.geometry.Insets;
3  import javafx.scene.Scene;
4  import javafx.scene.control.Label;
5  import javafx.scene.control.TextField;
6  import javafx.scene.layout.FlowPane;
7  import javafx.stage.Stage;
8
9  public class ShowFlowPane extends Application {          extend Application
10   @Override // Override the start method in the Application class
11   public void start(Stage primaryStage) {
12     // Create a pane and set its properties
13     FlowPane pane = new FlowPane();                      create FlowPane
14     pane.setPadding(new Insets(11, 12, 13, 14));
15     pane.setHgap(5);
16     pane.setVgap(5);
17
18     // Place nodes in the pane
19     pane.getChildren().addAll(new Label("First Name:"),  add UI controls to pane
20       new TextField(), new Label("MI:"));
21     TextField tfMi = new TextField();
22     tfMi.setPrefColumnCount(1);
23     pane.getChildren().addAll(tfMi, new Label("Last Name:"),
24       new TextField());
25
26     // Create a scene and place it in the stage
27     Scene scene = new Scene(pane, 200, 250);             add pane to scene
28     primaryStage.setTitle("ShowFlowPane"); // Set the stage title
29     primaryStage.setScene(scene); // Place the scene in the stage   place scene to stage
30     primaryStage.show(); // Display the stage            display stage
31   }
32 }
```

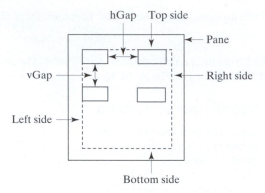

FIGURE 14.16 The nodes fill in the rows in the **FlowPane** one after another.

The program creates a **FlowPane** (line 13) and sets its **padding** property with an **Insets** object (line 14). An **Insets** object specifies the size of the border of a pane. The constructor **Insets(11, 12, 13, 14)** creates an **Insets** with the border sizes for top (11), right (12), bottom (13), and left (14) in pixels, as shown in Figure 14.17. You can also use the constructor **Insets(value)** to create an **Insets** with the same value for all four sides. The **hGap** and **vGap** properties are in lines 15–16 to specify the horizontal gap and vertical gap between two nodes in the pane, as shown in Figure 14.17.

FIGURE 14.17 You can specify **hGap** and **vGap** between the nodes in a **FlowLPane**.

Each **FlowPane** contains an object of **ObservableList** for holding the nodes. This list can be obtained using the **getChildren()** method (line 19). To add a node into a **FlowPane** is to add it to this list using the **add(node)** or **addAll(node1, node2, ...)** method. You can also remove a node from the list using the **remove(node)** method or use the **removeAll()** method to remove all nodes from the pane. The program adds the labels and text fields into the pane (lines 19–24). Invoking **tfMi.setPrefColumnCount(1)** sets the preferred column count to **1** for the MI text field (line 22). The program declares an explicit reference **tfMi** for a **TextField** object for MI. The explicit reference is necessary, because we need to reference the object directly to set its **prefColumnCount** property.

The program adds the pane to the scene (line 27), sets the scene in the stage (line 29), and displays the stage (line 30). Note that if you resize the window, the nodes are automatically rearranged to fit in the pane. In Figure 14.16a, the first row has three nodes, but in Figure 14.16b, the first row has four nodes, because the width has been increased.

Suppose you wish to add the object **tfMi** to a pane ten times; will ten text fields appear in the pane? No, a node such as a text field can be added to only one pane and once. Adding a node to a pane multiple times or to different panes will cause a runtime error.

Note
A node can be placed only in one pane. Therefore, the relationship between a pane and a node is the composition denoted by a filled diamond, as shown in Figure 14.3b.

14.10.2 **GridPane**

A **GridPane** arranges nodes in a grid (matrix) formation. The nodes are placed in the specified column and row indices. The class diagram for **GridPane** is shown in Figure 14.18.

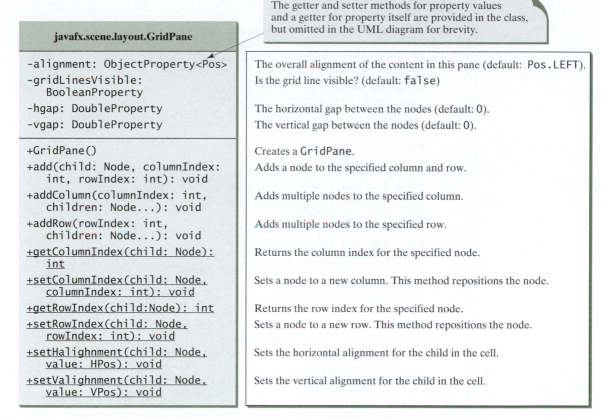

> The getter and setter methods for property values and a getter for property itself are provided in the class, but omitted in the UML diagram for brevity.

javafx.scene.layout.GridPane	
-alignment: ObjectProperty<Pos>	The overall alignment of the content in this pane (default: Pos.LEFT).
-gridLinesVisible: BooleanProperty	Is the grid line visible? (default: false)
-hgap: DoubleProperty	The horizontal gap between the nodes (default: 0).
-vgap: DoubleProperty	The vertical gap between the nodes (default: 0).
+GridPane()	Creates a GridPane.
+add(child: Node, columnIndex: int, rowIndex: int): void	Adds a node to the specified column and row.
+addColumn(columnIndex: int, children: Node...): void	Adds multiple nodes to the specified column.
+addRow(rowIndex: int, children: Node...): void	Adds multiple nodes to the specified row.
+getColumnIndex(child: Node): int	Returns the column index for the specified node.
+setColumnIndex(child: Node, columnIndex: int): void	Sets a node to a new column. This method repositions the node.
+getRowIndex(child:Node): int	Returns the row index for the specified node.
+setRowIndex(child: Node, rowIndex: int): void	Sets a node to a new row. This method repositions the node.
+setHalighnment(child: Node, value: HPos): void	Sets the horizontal alignment for the child in the cell.
+setValighnment(child: Node, value: VPos): void	Sets the vertical alignment for the child in the cell.

FIGURE 14.18   **GridPane** lays out nodes in the specified cell in a grid.

Listing 14.11 gives a program that demonstrates **GridPane**. The program is similar to the one in Listing 14.10, except that it adds three labels and three text fields, and a button to the specified location in a grid, as shown in Figure 14.19.

FIGURE 14.19   The **GridPane** places the nodes in a grid with a specified column and row indices.

LISTING 14.11 ShowGridPane.java

```
1  import javafx.application.Application;
2  import javafx.geometry.HPos;
3  import javafx.geometry.Insets;
```

```
 4  import javafx.geometry.Pos;
 5  import javafx.scene.Scene;
 6  import javafx.scene.control.Button;
 7  import javafx.scene.control.Label;
 8  import javafx.scene.control.TextField;
 9  import javafx.scene.layout.GridPane;
10  import javafx.stage.Stage;
11
12  public class ShowGridPane extends Application {
13    @Override // Override the start method in the Application class
14    public void start(Stage primaryStage) {
15      // Create a pane and set its properties
16      GridPane pane = new GridPane();
17      pane.setAlignment(Pos.CENTER);
18      pane.setPadding(new Insets(11.5, 12.5, 13.5, 14.5));
19      pane.setHgap(5.5);
20      pane.setVgap(5.5);
21
22      // Place nodes in the pane
23      pane.add(new Label("First Name:"), 0, 0);
24      pane.add(new TextField(), 1, 0);
25      pane.add(new Label("MI:"), 0, 1);
26      pane.add(new TextField(), 1, 1);
27      pane.add(new Label("Last Name:"), 0, 2);
28      pane.add(new TextField(), 1, 2);
29      Button btAdd = new Button("Add Name");
30      pane.add(btAdd, 1, 3);
31      GridPane.setHalignment(btAdd, HPos.RIGHT);
32
33      // Create a scene and place it in the stage
34      Scene scene = new Scene(pane);
35      primaryStage.setTitle("ShowGridPane"); // Set the stage title
36      primaryStage.setScene(scene); // Place the scene in the stage
37      primaryStage.show(); // Display the stage
38    }
39  }
```

Margin notes:
create a grid pane
set properties
add label
add text field
add button
align button right
create a scene
display stage
remove nodes

The program creates a **GridPane** (line 16) and sets its properties (line 17–20). The alignment is set to the center position (line 17), which causes the nodes to be placed in the center of the grid pane. If you resize the window, you will see the nodes remains in the center of the grid pane.

The program adds the label in column **0** and row **0** (line 23). The column and row index starts from **0**. The **add** method places a node in the specified column and row. Not every cell in the grid needs to be filled. A button is placed in column 1 and row 3 (line 30), but there are no nodes placed in column 0 and row 3. To remove a node from a **GridPane**, use **pane.getChildren().remove(node)**. To remove all nodes, use **pane.getChildren().removeAll()**.

The program invokes the static **setHalignment** method to align the button right in the cell (line 31).

Note that the scene size is not set (line 34). In this case, the scene size is automatically computed according to the sizes of the nodes placed inside the scene.

14.10.3 BorderPane

A **BorderPane** can place nodes in five regions: top, bottom, left, right, and center, using the **setTop(node)**, **setBottom(node)**, **setLeft(node)**, **setRight(node)**, and **setCenter(node)** methods. The class diagram for **GridPane** is shown in Figure 14.20.

The getter and setter methods for property values and a getter for property itself are provided in the class, but omitted in the UML diagram for brevity.

javafx.scene.layout.BorderPane
-top: ObjectProperty<Node> -right: ObjectProperty<Node> -bottom: ObjectProperty<Node> -left: ObjectProperty<Node> -center: ObjectProperty<Node>
+BorderPane() +setAlignment(child: Node, pos: Pos)

The node placed in the top region (default: null).
The node placed in the right region (default: null).
The node placed in the bottom region (default: null).
The node placed in the left region (default: null).
The node placed in the center region (default: null).

Creates a BorderPane.
Sets the alignment of the node in the BorderPane.

FIGURE 14.20 BorderPane places the nodes in top, bottom, left, right, and center regions.

Listing 14.12 gives a program that demonstrates BorderPane. The program places five buttons in the five regions of the pane, as shown in Figure 14.21.

LISTING 14.12 ShowBorderPane.java

```java
1  import javafx.application.Application;
2  import javafx.geometry.Insets;
3  import javafx.scene.Scene;
4  import javafx.scene.control.Label;
5  import javafx.scene.layout.BorderPane;
6  import javafx.scene.layout.StackPane;
7  import javafx.stage.Stage;
8
9  public class ShowBorderPane extends Application {
10   @Override // Override the start method in the Application class
11   public void start(Stage primaryStage) {
12     // Create a border pane
13     BorderPane pane = new BorderPane();                        create a border pane
14
15     // Place nodes in the pane
16     pane.setTop(new CustomPane("Top"));                        add to top
17     pane.setRight(new CustomPane("Right"));                    add to right
18     pane.setBottom(new CustomPane("Bottom"));                  add to bottom
19     pane.setLeft(new CustomPane("Left"));                      add to left
20     pane.setCenter(new CustomPane("Center"));                  add to center
21
22     // Create a scene and place it in the stage
23     Scene scene = new Scene(pane);
24     primaryStage.setTitle("ShowBorderPane"); // Set the stage title
25     primaryStage.setScene(scene); // Place the scene in the stage
26     primaryStage.show(); // Display the stage
27   }
28 }
29
30 // Define a custom pane to hold a label in the center of the pane
31 class CustomPane extends StackPane {                           define a custom pane
32   public CustomPane(String title) {
33     getChildren().add(new Label(title));                       add a label to pane
34     setStyle("-fx-border-color: red");                         set style
35     setPadding(new Insets(11.5, 12.5, 13.5, 14.5));            set padding
36   }
37 }
```

FIGURE 14.21 The BorderPane places the nodes in five regions of the pane.

The program defines **CustomPane** that extends **StackPane** (line 31). The constructor of **CustomPane** adds a label with the specified title (line 33), sets a style for the border color, and sets a padding using insets (line 35).

The program creates a **BorderPane** (line 13) and places five instances of **CustomPane** into five regions of the border pane (lines 16–20). Note that a pane is a node. So a pane can be added into another pane. To remove a node from the top region, invoke **setTop(null)**. If a region is not occupied, no space will be allocated for this region.

14.10.4 **HBox** and **VBox**

An **HBox** lays out its children in a single horizontal row. A **VBox** lays out its children in a single vertical column. Recall that a **FlowPane** can lay out its children in multiple rows or multiple columns, but an **HBox** or a **VBox** can lay out children only in one row or one column. The class diagrams for **HBox** and **VBox** are shown in Figures 14.22 and 14.23.

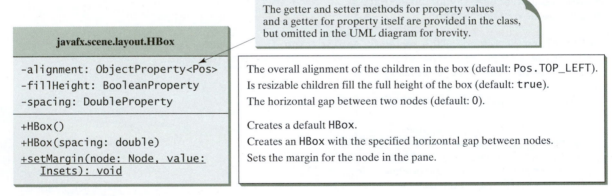

FIGURE 14.22 HBox places the nodes in one row.

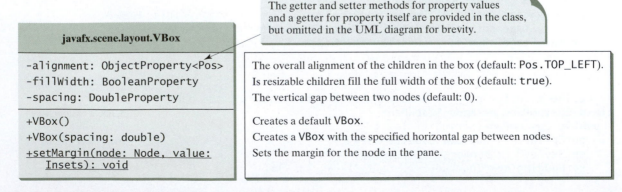

FIGURE 14.23 VBox places the nodes in one column.

Listing 14.12 gives a program that demonstrates **HBox** and **VBox**. The program places two buttons in an **HBox** and five labels in a **VBox**, as shown in Figure 14.24.

LISTING 14.13   ShowHBoxVBox.java

```
 1  import javafx.application.Application;
 2  import javafx.geometry.Insets;
 3  import javafx.scene.Scene;
 4  import javafx.scene.control.Button;
 5  import javafx.scene.control.Label;
 6  import javafx.scene.layout.BorderPane;
 7  import javafx.scene.layout.HBox;
 8  import javafx.scene.layout.VBox;
 9  import javafx.stage.Stage;
10  import javafx.scene.image.Image;
11  import javafx.scene.image.ImageView;
12
13  public class ShowHBoxVBox extends Application {
14    @Override // Override the start method in the Application class
15    public void start(Stage primaryStage) {
16      // Create a border pane
17      BorderPane pane = new BorderPane();                          create a border pane
18
19      // Place nodes in the pane
20      pane.setTop(getHBox());                                      add an HBox to top
21      pane.setLeft(getVBox());                                     add a VBox to left
22
23      // Create a scene and place it in the stage
24      Scene scene = new Scene(pane);                               create a scene
25      primaryStage.setTitle("ShowHBoxVBox"); // Set the stage title
26      primaryStage.setScene(scene); // Place the scene in the stage
27      primaryStage.show(); // Display the stage                    display stage
28    }
29
30    private HBox getHBox() {                                        getHBox
31      HBox hBox = new HBox(15);
32      hBox.setPadding(new Insets(15, 15, 15, 15));
33      hBox.setStyle("-fx-background-color: gold");
34      hBox.getChildren().add(new Button("Computer Science"));       add buttons to HBox
35      hBox.getChildren().add(new Button("Chemistry"));
36      ImageView imageView = new ImageView(new Image("image/us.gif"));
37      hBox.getChildren().add(imageView);
38      return hBox;                                                  return an HBox
39    }
40
41    private VBox getVBox() {                                        getVBox
42      VBox vBox = new VBox(15);
43      vBox.setPadding(new Insets(15, 5, 5, 5));
44      vBox.getChildren().add(new Label("Courses"));                add a label
45
46      Label[] courses = {new Label("CSCI 1301"), new Label("CSCI 1302"),
47          new Label("CSCI 2410"), new Label("CSCI 3720")};
48
49      for (Label course: courses) {
50        VBox.setMargin(course, new Insets(0, 0, 0, 15));           set margin
51        vBox.getChildren().add(course);                            add a label
52      }
53
54      return vBox;                                                 return vBox
55    }
56  }
```

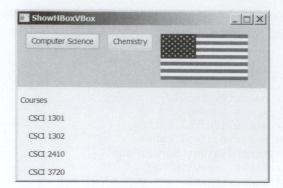

Figure 14.24 The **HBox** places the nodes in one row and the **VBox** places the nodes in one column.

The program defines the **getHBox()** method. This method returns an **HBox** that contains two buttons and an image view (lines 30–39). The background color of the **HBox** is set to gold using Java CSS (line 33). The program defines the **getVBox()** method. This method returns a **VBox** that contains five labels (lines 41–55). The first label is added to the **VBox** in line 44 and the other four are added in line 51. The **setMargin** method is used to set a node's margin when placed inside the **VBox** (line 50).

Check
Point

14.22 How do you add a node to a **Pane**, **StackPane**, **FlowPane**, **GridPane**, **BorderPane**, **HBox**, and **VBox**? How do you remove a node from these panes?

14.23 How do you set the alignment to right for nodes in a **FlowPane**, **GridPane**, **HBox**, and **VBox**?

14.24 How do you set the horizontal gap and vertical hap between nodes in 8 pixels in a **FlowPane** and **GridPane** and set spacing in 8 pixels in an **HBox** and **VBox**?

14.25 How do you get the column and row index of a node in a **GridPane**? How do you reposition a node in a **GridPane**?

14.26 What are the differences between a **FlowPane** and an **HBox** or a **VBox**?

14.11 Shapes

Key
Point

JavaFX provides many shape classes for drawing texts, lines, circles, rectangles, ellipses, arcs, polygons, and polylines.

The **Shape** class is the abstract base class that defines the common properties for all shapes. Among them are the **fill**, **stroke**, and **strokeWidth** properties. The **fill** property specifies a color that fills the interior of a shape. The **stroke** property specifies a color that is used to draw the outline of a shape. The **strokeWidth** property specifies the width of the outline of a shape. This section introduces the classes **Text**, **Line**, **Rectangle**, **Circle**, **Ellipse**, **Arc**, **Polygon**, and **Polyline** for drawing texts and simple shapes. All these are subclasses of **Shape**, as shown in Figure 14.25.

VideoNote
Use shapes

14.11.1 Text

The **Text** class defines a node that displays a string at a starting point (**x**, **y**), as shown in Figure 14.27a. A **Text** object is usually placed in a pane. The pane's upper-left corner point is (**0**, **0**) and the bottom-right point is (**pane.getWidth()**, **pane.getHeight()**). A string may be displayed in multiple lines separated by **\n**. The UML diagram for the **Text** class is shown in Figure 14.26. Listing 14.13 gives an example that demonstrates text, as shown in Figure 14.27b.

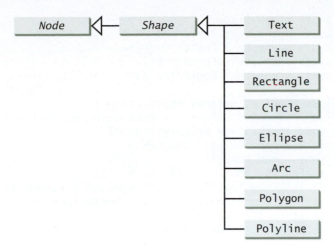

FIGURE 14.25 A shape is a node. The **Shape** class is the root of all shape classes.

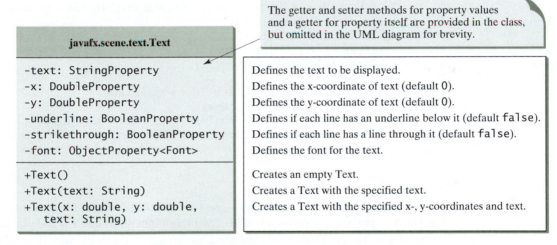

> The getter and setter methods for property values and a getter for property itself are provided in the class, but omitted in the UML diagram for brevity.

javafx.scene.text.Text	
-text: StringProperty	Defines the text to be displayed.
-x: DoubleProperty	Defines the x-coordinate of text (default 0).
-y: DoubleProperty	Defines the y-coordinate of text (default 0).
-underline: BooleanProperty	Defines if each line has an underline below it (default **false**).
-strikethrough: BooleanProperty	Defines if each line has a line through it (default **false**).
-font: ObjectProperty<Font>	Defines the font for the text.
+Text()	Creates an empty Text.
+Text(text: String)	Creates a Text with the specified text.
+Text(x: double, y: double, text: String)	Creates a Text with the specified x-, y-coordinates and text.

FIGURE 14.26 **Text** defines a node for displaying a text.

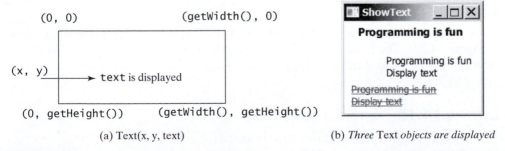

(a) Text(x, y, text)

(b) *Three* Text *objects are displayed*

FIGURE 14.27 A **Text** object is created to display a text.

LISTING 14.14 ShowText.java

```
1  import javafx.application.Application;
2  import javafx.scene.Scene;
3  import javafx.scene.layout.Pane;
4  import javafx.scene.paint.Color;
5  import javafx.geometry.Insets;
```

```
 6   import javafx.stage.Stage;
 7   import javafx.scene.text.Text;
 8   import javafx.scene.text.Font;
 9   import javafx.scene.text.FontWeight;
10   import javafx.scene.text.FontPosture;
11
12   public class ShowText extends Application {
13     @Override // Override the start method in the Application class
14     public void start(Stage primaryStage) {
15       // Create a pane to hold the texts
16       Pane pane = new Pane();
17       pane.setPadding(new Insets(5, 5, 5, 5));
18       Text text1 = new Text(20, 20, "Programming is fun");
19       text1.setFont(Font.font("Courier", FontWeight.BOLD,
20         FontPosture.ITALIC, 15));
21       pane.getChildren().add(text1);
22
23       Text text2 = new Text(60, 60, "Programming is fun\nDisplay text");
24       pane.getChildren().add(text2);
25
26       Text text3 = new Text(10, 100, "Programming is fun\nDisplay text");
27       text3.setFill(Color.RED);
28       text3.setUnderline(true);
29       text3.setStrikethrough(true);
30       pane.getChildren().add(text3);
31
32       // Create a scene and place it in the stage
33       Scene scene = new Scene(pane);
34       primaryStage.setTitle("ShowText"); // Set the stage title
35       primaryStage.setScene(scene); // Place the scene in the stage
36       primaryStage.show(); // Display the stage
37     }
38   }
```

Margin notes, top to bottom:
create a pane (line 16)
create a text / set text font (lines 18–19)
add text to pane (line 21)
create a two-line text / add text to pane (lines 23–24)
create a text / set text color / set underline / set strike line / add text to pane (lines 26–30)

The program creates a **Text** (line 18), sets its font (line 19), and places it to the pane (line 21). The program creates another **Text** with multiple lines (line 23) and places it to the pane (line 24). The program creates the third **Text** (line 26), sets its color (line 27), sets an underline and a strike through line (lines 28–29), and places it to the pane (line 30).

14.11.2 Line

A line connects two points with four parameters **startX**, **startY**, **endX**, and **endY**, as shown in Figure 14.29a. The **Line** class defines a line. The UML diagram for the **Line** class is shown in Figure 14.28. Listing 14.15 gives an example that demonstrates text, as shown in Figure 14.29b.

LISTING 14.15   ShowLine.java

```
 1   import javafx.application.Application;
 2   import javafx.scene.Scene;
 3   import javafx.scene.layout.Pane;
 4   import javafx.scene.paint.Color;
 5   import javafx.stage.Stage;
 6   import javafx.scene.shape.Line;
 7
 8   public class ShowLine extends Application {
 9     @Override // Override the start method in the Application class
10     public void start(Stage primaryStage) {
11       // Create a scene and place it in the stage
```

```
12        Scene scene = new Scene(new LinePane(), 200, 200);           create a pane in scene
13        primaryStage.setTitle("ShowLine"); // Set the stage title
14        primaryStage.setScene(scene); // Place the scene in the stage
15        primaryStage.show(); // Display the stage
16      }
17    }
18
19    class LinePane extends Pane {                                    define a custom pane
20      public LinePane() {
21        Line line1 = new Line(10, 10, 10, 10);                       create a line
22        line1.endXProperty().bind(widthProperty().subtract(10));
23        line1.endYProperty().bind(heightProperty().subtract(10));
24        line1.setStrokeWidth(5);                                     set stroke width
25        line1.setStroke(Color.GREEN);                                set stroke
26        getChildren().add(line1);                                    add line to pane
27
28        Line line2 = new Line(10, 10, 10, 10);                       create a line
29        line2.startXProperty().bind(widthProperty().subtract(10));
30        line2.endYProperty().bind(heightProperty().subtract(10));
31        line2.setStrokeWidth(5);
32        line2.setStroke(Color.GREEN);
33        getChildren().add(line2);                                    add line to pane
34      }
35    }
```

> The getter and setter methods for property values and a getter for property itself are provided in the class, but omitted in the UML diagram for brevity.

javafx.scene.shape.Line
-startX: DoubleProperty
-startY: DoubleProperty
-endX: DoubleProperty
-endY: DoubleProperty
+Line()
+Line(startX: double, startY: double, endX: double, endY: double)

The x-coordinate of the start point.
The y-coordinate of the start point.
The x-coordinate of the end point.
The y-coordinate of the end point.

Creates an empty Line.
Creates a Line with the specified starting and ending points.

FIGURE 14.28 The **Line** class defines a line.

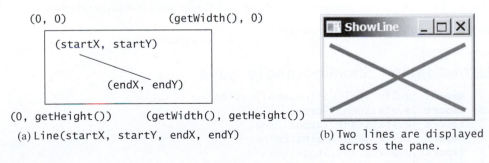

(a) Line(startX, startY, endX, endY)

(b) Two lines are displayed across the pane.

FIGURE 14.29 A **Line** object is created to display a line.

The program defines a custom pane class named **LinePane** (line 19). The custom pane class creates two lines and binds the starting and ending points of the line with the width and height of the pane (lines 22–23, 29–30) so that the two points of the lines are changed as the pane is resized.

14.11.3 **Rectangle**

A rectangle is defined by the parameters x, y, **width**, **height**, **arcWidth**, and **arcHeight**, as shown in Figure 14.31a. The rectangle's upper-left corner point is at (x, y) and parameter **aw** (**arcWidth**) is the horizontal diameter of the arcs at the corner, and **ah** (**arcHeight**) is the vertical diameter of the arcs at the corner.

The **Rectangle** class defines a rectangle. The UML diagram for the **Rectangle** class is shown in Figure 14.30. Listing 14.15 gives an example that demonstrates rectangles, as shown in Figure 14.31b.

> The getter and setter methods for property values and a getter for property itself are provided in the class, but omitted in the UML diagram for brevity.

javafx.scene.shape.Rectangle	
-x: DoubleProperty	The x-coordinate of the upper-left corner of the rectangle (default 0).
-y:DoubleProperty	The y-coordinate of the upper-left corner of the rectangle (default 0).
-width: DoubleProperty	The width of the rectangle (default: 0).
-height: DoubleProperty	The height of the rectangle (default: 0).
-arcWidth: DoubleProperty	The arcWidth of the rectangle (default: 0). arcWidth is the horizontal diameter of the arcs at the corner (see Figure 14.31a).
-arcHeight: DoubleProperty	The arcHeight of the rectangle (default: 0). arcHeight is the vertical diameter of the arcs at the corner (see Figure 14.31a).
+Rectangle()	Creates an empty Rectangle.
+Rectanlge(x: double, y: double, width: double, height: double)	Creates a Rectangle with the specified upper-left corner point, width, and height.

FIGURE 14.30 The **Rectangle** class defines a rectangle.

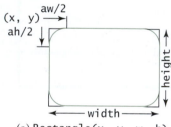 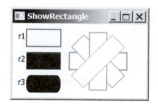 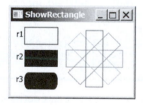

(a) Rectangle(x, y, w, h)   (b) Multiple rectangles are displayed   (c) Transparent rectangles are displayed

FIGURE 14.31 A **Rectangle** object is created to display a rectangle.

LISTING 14.16 ShowRectangle.java

```
1  import javafx.application.Application;
2  import javafx.scene.Scene;
3  import javafx.scene.layout.Pane;
4  import javafx.scene.paint.Color;
5  import javafx.stage.Stage;
6  import javafx.scene.text.Text;
7  import javafx.scene.shape.Rectangle;
8
9  public class ShowRectangle extends Application {
10    @Override // Override the start method in the Application class
11    public void start(Stage primaryStage) {
12      // Create a pane
```

```
13        Pane pane = new Pane();                                      create a pane
14
15        // Create rectangles and add to pane
16        Rectangle r1 = new Rectangle(25, 10, 60, 30);                create a rectangle r1
17        r1.setStroke(Color.BLACK);                                   set r1's properties
18        r1.setFill(Color.WHITE);
19        pane.getChildren().add(new Text(10, 27, "r1"));
20        pane.getChildren().add(r1);                                  add r1 to pane
21
22        Rectangle r2 = new Rectangle(25, 50, 60, 30);                create rectangle r2
23        pane.getChildren().add(new Text(10, 67, "r2"));
24        pane.getChildren().add(r2);                                  add r2 to pane
25
26        Rectangle r3 = new Rectangle(25, 90, 60, 30);                create rectangle r3
27        r3.setArcWidth(15);                                          set r3's arc width
28        r3.setArcHeight(25);                                         set r3's arc height
29        pane.getChildren().add(new Text(10, 107, "r3"));
30        pane.getChildren().add(r3);
31
32        for (int i = 0; i < 4; i++) {
33          Rectangle r = new Rectangle(100, 50, 100, 30);             create a rectangle
34          r.setRotate(i * 360 / 8);                                  rotate a rectangle
35          r.setStroke(Color.color(Math.random(), Math.random(),
36            Math.random()));
37          r.setFill(Color.WHITE);
38          pane.getChildren().add(r);                                 add rectangle to pane
39        }
40
41        // Create a scene and place it in the stage
42        Scene scene = new Scene(pane, 250, 150);
43        primaryStage.setTitle("ShowRectangle"); // Set the stage title
44        primaryStage.setScene(scene); // Place the scene in the stage
45        primaryStage.show(); // Display the stage
46      }
47    }
```

The program creates multiple rectangles. By default, the fill color is black. So a rectangle is filled with black color. The stroke color is white by default. Line 17 sets stroke color of rectangle **r1** to black. The program creates rectangle **r3** (line 26) and sets its arc width and arc height (lines 27–28). So **r3** is displayed as a rounded rectangle.

The program repeatedly creates a rectangle (line 33), rotates it (line 34), sets a random stroke color (lines 35–36), its fill color to white (line 37), and adds the rectangle to the pane (line 38).

If line 37 is replaced by the following line

```
r.setFill(null);
```

the rectangle is not filled with a color. So they are displayed as shown in Figure 14.31c.

14.11.4 `Circle` and `Ellipse`

You have used circles in several examples early in this chapter. A circle is defined by its parameters **centerX**, **centerY**, and **radius**. The **Circle** class defines a circle. The UML diagram for the **Circle** class is shown in Figure 14.32.

An ellipse is defined by its parameters **centerX**, **centerY**, **radiusX**, and **radiusY**, as shown in Figure 14.34a. The **Ellipse** class defines an ellipse. The UML diagram for the **Ellipse** class is shown in Figure 14.33. Listing 14.17 gives an example that demonstrates ellipses, as shown in Figure 14.34b.

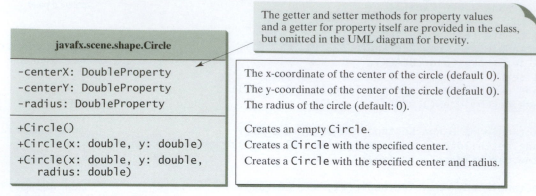

FIGURE 14.32 The `Circle` class defines circles.

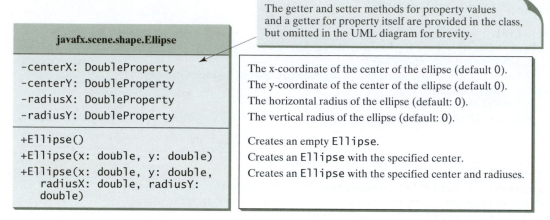

FIGURE 14.33 The `Ellipse` class defines ellipses.

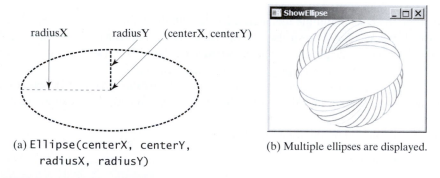

(a) `Ellipse(centerX, centerY, radiusX, radiusY)`

(b) Multiple ellipses are displayed.

FIGURE 14.34 An `Ellipse` object is created to display an ellipse.

LISTING 14.17 ShowEllipse.java

```
1  import javafx.application.Application;
2  import javafx.scene.Scene;
3  import javafx.scene.layout.Pane;
4  import javafx.scene.paint.Color;
5  import javafx.stage.Stage;
6  import javafx.scene.shape.Ellipse;
7
8  public class ShowEllipse extends Application {
9    @Override // Override the start method in the Application class
```

```
10    public void start(Stage primaryStage) {
11      // Create a pane
12      Pane pane = new Pane();                                    create a pane
13
14      for (int i = 0; i < 16; i++) {
15        // Create an ellipse and add it to pane
16        Ellipse e1 = new Ellipse(150, 100, 100, 50);            create an ellipse
17        e1.setStroke(Color.color(Math.random(), Math.random(),  set random color for stroke
18          Math.random()));
19        e1.setFill(Color.WHITE);                                 set fill color
20        e1.setRotate(i * 180 / 16);                              rotate ellipse
21        pane.getChildren().add(e1);                              add ellipse to pane
22      }
23
24      // Create a scene and place it in the stage
25      Scene scene = new Scene(pane, 300, 200);
26      primaryStage.setTitle("ShowEllipse"); // Set the stage title
27      primaryStage.setScene(scene); // Place the scene in the stage
28      primaryStage.show(); // Display the stage
29    }
30  }
```

The program repeatedly creates an ellipse (line 16), sets a random stroke color (lines 17–18), sets its fill color to white (line 19), rotates it (line 20), and adds the rectangle to the pane (line 21).

14.11.5 Arc

An arc is conceived as part of an ellipse, defined by the parameters **centerX**, **centerY**, **radiusX**, **radiusY**, **startAngle**, **length**, and an arc type (ArcType.OPEN, ArcType .CHORD, or ArcType.ROUND). The parameter **startAngle** is the starting angle; and **length** is the spanning angle (i.e., the angle covered by the arc). Angles are measured in degrees and follow the usual mathematical conventions (i.e., 0 degrees is in the easterly direction, and positive angles indicate counterclockwise rotation from the easterly direction), as shown in Figure 14.36a.

The **Arc** class defines an arc. The UML diagram for the **Arc** class is shown in Figure 14.35. Listing 14.18 gives an example that demonstrates ellipses, as shown in Figure 14.36b.

The getter and setter methods for property values and a getter for property itself are provided in the class, but omitted in the UML diagram for brevity.

javafx.scene.shape.Arc	
-centerX: DoubleProperty	The x-coordinate of the center of the ellipse (default 0).
-centerY: DoubleProperty	The y-coordinate of the center of the ellipse (default 0).
-radiusX: DoubleProperty	The horizontal radius of the ellipse (default: 0).
-radiusY: DoubleProperty	The vertical radius of the ellipse (default: 0).
-startAngle: DoubleProperty	The start angle of the arc in degrees.
-length: DoubleProperty	The angular extent of the arc in degrees.
-type: ObjectProperty<ArcType>	The closure type of the arc (ArcType.OPEN, ArcType.CHORD, ArcType.ROUND).
+Arc()	Creates an empty Arc.
+Arc(x: double, y: double, radiusX: double, radiusY: double, startAngle: double, length: double)	Creates an Arc with the specified arguments.

FIGURE 14.35 The **Arc** class defines an arc.

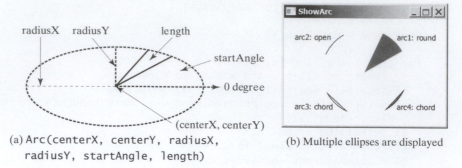

(a) `Arc(centerX, centerY, radiusX, radiusY, startAngle, length)`

(b) Multiple ellipses are displayed

FIGURE 14.36 An `Arc` object is created to display an arc.

LISTING 14.18 ShowArc.java

```
1  import javafx.application.Application;
2  import javafx.scene.Scene;
3  import javafx.scene.layout.Pane;
4  import javafx.scene.paint.Color;
5  import javafx.stage.Stage;
6  import javafx.scene.shape.Arc;
7  import javafx.scene.shape.ArcType;
8  import javafx.scene.text.Text;
9
10 public class ShowArc extends Application {
11   @Override // Override the start method in the Application class
12   public void start(Stage primaryStage) {
13     // Create a pane
14     Pane pane = new Pane();
15
16     Arc arc1 = new Arc(150, 100, 80, 80, 30, 35); // Create an arc
17     arc1.setFill(Color.RED); // Set fill color
18     arc1.setType(ArcType.ROUND); // Set arc type
19     pane.getChildren().add(new Text(210, 40, "arc1: round"));
20     pane.getChildren().add(arc1); // Add arc to pane
21
22     Arc arc2 = new Arc(150, 100, 80, 80, 30 + 90, 35);
23     arc2.setFill(Color.WHITE);
24     arc2.setType(ArcType.OPEN);
25     arc2.setStroke(Color.BLACK);
26     pane.getChildren().add(new Text(20, 40, "arc2: open"));
27     pane.getChildren().add(arc2);
28
29     Arc arc3 = new Arc(150, 100, 80, 80, 30 + 180, 35);
30     arc3.setFill(Color.WHITE);
31     arc3.setType(ArcType.CHORD);
32     arc3.setStroke(Color.BLACK);
33     pane.getChildren().add(new Text(20, 170, "arc3: chord"));
34     pane.getChildren().add(arc3);
35
36     Arc arc4 = new Arc(150, 100, 80, 80, 30 + 270, 35);
37     arc4.setFill(Color.GREEN);
38     arc4.setType(ArcType.CHORD);
```

create a pane

create arc1
set fill color for arc1
set arc1 as round arc

add arc1 to pane

create arc2
set fill color for arc2
set arc2 as round arc

add arc2 to pane

create arc3
set fill color for arc3
set arc3 as chord arc

add arc3 to pane

create arc4

```
39        arc4.setStroke(Color.BLACK);
40        pane.getChildren().add(new Text(210, 170, "arc4: chord"));
41        pane.getChildren().add(arc4);                                    add arc4 to pane
42
43        // Create a scene and place it in the stage
44        Scene scene = new Scene(pane, 300, 200);
45        primaryStage.setTitle("ShowArc"); // Set the stage title
46        primaryStage.setScene(scene); // Place the scene in the stage
47        primaryStage.show(); // Display the stage
48      }
49 }
```

The program creates an arc **arc1** centered at (**150, 100**) with **radiusX 80** and **radiusY 80**. The starting angle is **30** with **length 35** (line 15). **arc1**'s arc type is set to **ArcType.ROUND** (line 18). Since **arc1**'s fill color is red, **arc1** is displayed filled with red round.

The program creates an arc **arc3** centered at (**150, 100**) with **radiusX 80** and **radiusY 80**. The starting angle is **30+180** with **length 35** (line 29). Arc3's arc type is set to **ArcType. CHORD** (line 31). Since **arc3**'s fill color is white and stroke color is black, **arc3** is displayed with black outline as a chord.

Angles may be negative. A negative starting angle sweeps clockwise from the easterly direction, as shown in Figure 14.37. A negative spanning angle sweeps clockwise from the starting angle. The following two statements define the same arc:

negative degrees

```
new Arc(x, y, radiusX, radiusY, -30, -20);
new Arc(x, y, radiusX, radiusY, -50, 20);
```

The first statement uses negative starting angle **-30** and negative spanning angle **-20**, as shown in Figure 14.37a. The second statement uses negative starting angle **-50** and positive spanning angle **20**, as shown in Figure 14.37b.

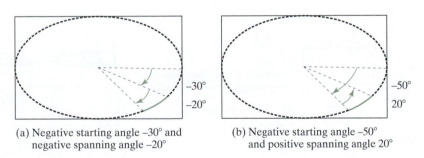

(a) Negative starting angle –30° and
negative spanning angle –20°

(b) Negative starting angle –50°
and positive spanning angle 20°

FIGURE 14.37 Angles may be negative.

Note that the trigonometric methods in the **Math** class use the angles in radians, but the angles in the **Arc** class are in degrees.

14.11.6 **Polygon** and **Polyline**

The **Polygon** class defines a polygon that connects a sequence of points, as shown in Figure 14.38a. The **Polyline** class is similar to the **Polygon** class except that the **Polyline** class is not automatically closed, as shown in Figure 14.38b.

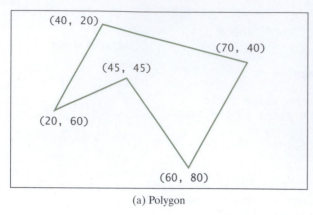

(a) Polygon

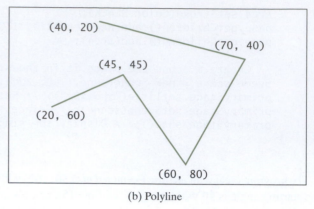

(b) Polyline

FIGURE 14.38 **Polygon** is closed and **Polyline** is not closed.

The UML diagram for the **Polygon** class is shown in Figure 14.39. Listing 14.19 gives an example that creates a hexagon, as shown in Figure 14.40.

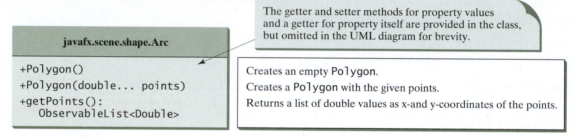

FIGURE 14.39 **Polygon** defines a polygon.

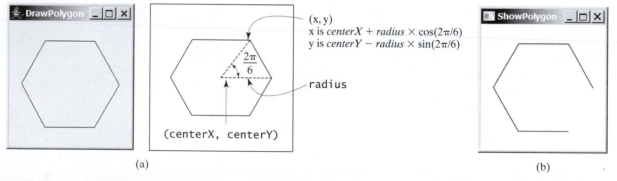

(a)

(b)

FIGURE 14.40 (a) A **Polygon** is displayed. (b) A **Polyline** is displayed.

LISTING 14.19 ShowPolygon.java

```
1  import javafx.application.Application;
2  import javafx.collections.ObservableList;
3  import javafx.scene.Scene;
4  import javafx.scene.layout.Pane;
5  import javafx.scene.paint.Color;
6  import javafx.stage.Stage;
7  import javafx.scene.shape.Polygon;
```

```
 8
 9  public class ShowPolygon extends Application {
10    @Override // Override the start method in the Application class
11    public void start(Stage primaryStage) {
12      // Create a pane, a polygon, and place polygon to pane
13      Pane pane = new Pane();                              create a pane
14      Polygon polygon = new Polygon();                     create a polygon
15      pane.getChildren().add(polygon);                     add polygon to pane
16      polygon.setFill(Color.WHITE);
17      polygon.setStroke(Color.BLACK);
18      ObservableList<Double> list = polygon.getPoints();   get a list of points
19
20      final double WIDTH = 200, HEIGHT = 200;
21      double centerX = WIDTH / 2, centerY = HEIGHT / 2;
22      double radius = Math.min(WIDTH, HEIGHT) * 0.4;
23
24      // Add points to the polygon list
25      for (int i = 0; i < 6; i++) {
26        list.add(centerX + radius * Math.cos(2 * i * Math.PI / 6));   add x-coordinate of a point
27        list.add(centerY - radius * Math.sin(2 * i * Math.PI / 6));   add y-coordinate of a point
28      }
29
30      // Create a scene and place it in the stage
31      Scene scene = new Scene(pane, WIDTH, HEIGHT);        add pane to scene
32      primaryStage.setTitle("ShowPolygon"); // Set the stage title
33      primaryStage.setScene(scene); // Place the scene in the stage
34      primaryStage.show(); // Display the stage
35    }
36  }
```

The program creates a polygon (line 14) and adds it to a pane (line 15). The **polygon .getPoints()** method returns an **ObservableList<Double>** (line 18), which contains the **add** method for adding an element to the list (lines 26–27). Note that the value passed to **add(value)** must be a **double** value. If an **int** value is passed, the **int** value would be automatically boxed into an **Integer**. This would cause an error because the **ObservableList<Double>** consists of **Double** elements.

The loop adds six points to the polygon (lines 25–28). Each point is represented by its *x*- and *y*-coordinates. For each point, its *x*-coordinate is added to the polygon's list (line 26) and then its *y*-coordinate is added to the list (line 27). The formula for computing the *x*- and *y*-coordinates for a point in the hexagon is illustrated in Figure 14.40a.

If you replace **Polygon** by **Polyline**, the program displays a polyline as shown in Figure 14.40b. The **Polyline** class is used in the same way as **Polygon** except that the starting and ending point are not connected in **Polyline**.

14.27 How do you display a text, line, rectangle, circle, ellipse, arc, polygon, and polyline?

Check Point

14.28 Write code fragments to display a string rotated 45 degrees in the center of the pane.

14.29 Write code fragments to display a thick line of **10** pixels from (**10**, **10**) to (**70**, **30**).

14.30 Write code fragments to fill red color in a rectangle of width **100** and height **50** with the upper-left corner at (**10**, **10**).

14.31 Write code fragments to display a round-cornered rectangle with width **100**, height **200** with the upper-left corner at (**10**, **10**), corner horizontal diameter **40**, and corner vertical diameter **20**.

14.32 Write code fragments to display an ellipse with horizontal radius **50** and vertical radius **100**.

14.33 Write code fragments to display the outline of the upper half of a circle with radius **50**.

14.34 Write code fragments to display the lower half of a circle with radius **50** filled with the red color.

14.35 Write code fragments to display a polygon connecting the following points: (**20**, **40**), (**30**, **50**), (**40**, **90**), (**90**, **10**), (**10**, **30**), and fill the polygon with green color.

14.36 Write code fragments to display a polyline connecting the following points: (**20**, **40**), (**30**, **50**), (**40**, **90**), (**90**, **10**), (**10**, **30**).

14.12 Case Study: The `ClockPane` Class

Key Point

This case study develops a class that displays a clock on a pane.

The contract of the `ClockPane` class is shown in Figure 14.41.

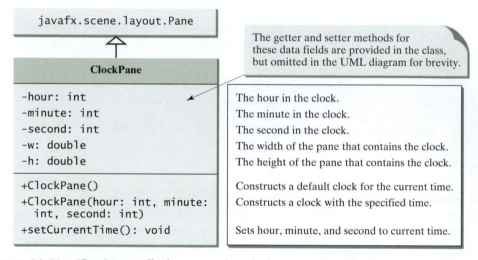

FIGURE 14.41 `ClockPane` displays an analog clock.

Assume `ClockPane` is available; we write a test program in Listing 14.20 to display an analog clock and use a label to display the hour, minute, and second, as shown in Figure 14.42.

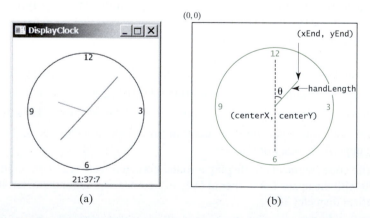

FIGURE 14.42 (a) The `DisplayClock` program displays a clock that shows the current time. (b) The endpoint of a clock hand can be determined, given the spanning angle, the hand length, and the center point.

LISTING 14.20   `DisplayClock.java`

```
 1  import javafx.application.Application;
 2  import javafx.geometry.Pos;
 3  import javafx.stage.Stage;
 4  import javafx.scene.Scene;
 5  import javafx.scene.control.Label;
 6  import javafx.scene.layout.BorderPane;
 7
 8  public class DisplayClock extends Application {
 9    @Override // Override the start method in the Application class
10    public void start(Stage primaryStage) {
11      // Create a clock and a label
12      ClockPane clock = new ClockPane();
13      String timeString = clock.getHour() + ":" + clock.getMinute()
14        + ":" + clock.getSecond();
15      Label lblCurrentTime = new Label(timeString);
16
17      // Place clock and label in border pane
18      BorderPane pane = new BorderPane();
19      pane.setCenter(clock);
20      pane.setBottom(lblCurrentTime);
21      BorderPane.setAlignment(lblCurrentTime, Pos.TOP_CENTER);
22
23      // Create a scene and place it in the stage
24      Scene scene = new Scene(pane, 250, 250);
25      primaryStage.setTitle("DisplayClock"); // Set the stage title
26      primaryStage.setScene(scene); // Place the scene in the stage
27      primaryStage.show(); // Display the stage
28    }
29  }
```

create a clock

create a label

add a clock
add a label

The rest of this section explains how to implement the **ClockPane** class. Since you can use the class without knowing how it is implemented, you may skip the implementation if you wish.

skip implementation?
implementation

To draw a clock, you need to draw a circle and three hands for the second, minute, and hour. To draw a hand, you need to specify the two ends of the line. As shown in Figure 14.42b, one end is the center of the clock at **(centerX, centerY)**; the other end, at **(endX, endY)**, is determined by the following formula:

```
endX = centerX + handLength × sin(θ)
endY = centerY - handLength × cos(θ)
```

Since there are 60 seconds in one minute, the angle for the second hand is

```
second × (2π/60)
```

The position of the minute hand is determined by the minute and second. The exact minute value combined with seconds is **minute + second/60**. For example, if the time is 3 minutes and 30 seconds, the total minutes are 3.5. Since there are 60 minutes in one hour, the angle for the minute hand is

```
(minute + second/60) × (2π/60)
```

Since one circle is divided into 12 hours, the angle for the hour hand is

```
(hour + minute/60 + second/(60 × 60)) × (2π/12)
```

For simplicity in computing the angles of the minute hand and hour hand, you can omit the seconds, because they are negligibly small. Therefore, the endpoints for the second hand, minute hand, and hour hand can be computed as:

$$secondX = centerX + secondHandLength \times \sin(second \times (2\pi/60))$$
$$secondY = centerY - secondHandLength \times \cos(second \times (2\pi/60))$$
$$minuteX = centerX + minuteHandLength \times \sin(minute \times (2\pi/60))$$
$$minuteY = centerY - minuteHandLength \times \cos(minute \times (2\pi/60))$$
$$hourX = centerX + hourHandLength \times \sin((hour + minute/60) \times (2\pi/12))$$
$$hourY = centerY - hourHandLength \times \cos((hour + minute/60) \times (2\pi/12))$$

The **ClockPane** class is implemented in Listing 14.21.

LISTING 14.21 ClockPane.java

```java
 1  import java.util.Calendar;
 2  import java.util.GregorianCalendar;
 3  import javafx.scene.layout.Pane;
 4  import javafx.scene.paint.Color;
 5  import javafx.scene.shape.Circle;
 6  import javafx.scene.shape.Line;
 7  import javafx.scene.text.Text;
 8
 9  public class ClockPane extends Pane {
10    private int hour;
11    private int minute;
12    private int second;
13
14    // Clock pane's width and height
15    private double w = 250, h = 250;
16
17    /** Construct a default clock with the current time*/
18    public ClockPane() {
19      setCurrentTime();
20    }
21
22    /** Construct a clock with specified hour, minute, and second */
23    public ClockPane(int hour, int minute, int second) {
24      this.hour = hour;
25      this.minute = minute;
26      this.second = second;
27      paintClock();
28    }
29
30    /** Return hour */
31    public int getHour() {
32      return hour;
33    }
34
35    /** Set a new hour */
36    public void setHour(int hour) {
37      this.hour = hour;
38      paintClock();
39    }
40
41    /** Return minute */
42    public int getMinute() {
43      return minute;
44    }
45
```

clock properties

no-arg constructor

constructor

set a new hour

paint clock

```
46      /** Set a new minute */
47      public void setMinute(int minute) {
48        this.minute = minute;
49        paintClock();
50      }
51
52      /** Return second */
53      public int getSecond() {
54        return second;
55      }
56
57      /** Set a new second */
58      public void setSecond(int second) {
59        this.second = second;
60        paintClock();
61      }
62
63      /** Return clock pane's width */
64      public double getW() {
65        return w;
66      }
67
68      /** Set clock pane's width */
69      public void setW(double w) {
70        this.w = w;
71        paintClock();
72      }
73
74      /** Return clock pane's height */
75      public double getH() {
76        return h;
77      }
78
79      /** Set clock pane's height */
80      public void setH(double h) {
81        this.h = h;
82        paintClock();
83      }
84
85      /* Set the current time for the clock */
86      public void setCurrentTime() {
87        // Construct a calendar for the current date and time
88        Calendar calendar = new GregorianCalendar();
89
90        // Set current hour, minute and second
91        this.hour = calendar.get(Calendar.HOUR_OF_DAY);
92        this.minute = calendar.get(Calendar.MINUTE);
93        this.second = calendar.get(Calendar.SECOND);
94
95        paintClock(); // Repaint the clock
96      }
97
98      /** Paint the clock */
99      protected void paintClock() {
100       // Initialize clock parameters
101       double clockRadius = Math.min(w, h) * 0.8 * 0.5;
102       double centerX = w / 2;
103       double centerY = h / 2;
104
105       // Draw circle
```

set a new minute

paint clock

set a new second

paint clock

set a new width

paint clock

set a new height

paint clock

set current time

paint clock

paint clock

get radius
set center

create a circle

create texts

create second hand

create minute hand

create hour hand

clear pane
add to pane

```
106    Circle circle = new Circle(centerX, centerY, clockRadius);
107    circle.setFill(Color.WHITE);
108    circle.setStroke(Color.BLACK);
109    Text t1 = new Text(centerX - 5, centerY - clockRadius + 12, "12");
110    Text t2 = new Text(centerX - clockRadius + 3, centerY + 5, "9");
111    Text t3 = new Text(centerX + clockRadius - 10, centerY + 3, "3");
112    Text t4 = new Text(centerX - 3, centerY + clockRadius - 3, "6");
113
114    // Draw second hand
115    double sLength = clockRadius * 0.8;
116    double secondX = centerX + sLength *
117      Math.sin(second * (2 * Math.PI / 60));
118    double secondY = centerY - sLength *
119      Math.cos(second * (2 * Math.PI / 60));
120    Line sLine = new Line(centerX, centerY, secondX, secondY);
121    sLine.setStroke(Color.RED);
122
123    // Draw minute hand
124    double mLength = clockRadius * 0.65;
125    double xMinute = centerX + mLength *
126      Math.sin(minute * (2 * Math.PI / 60));
127    double minuteY = centerY - mLength *
128      Math.cos(minute * (2 * Math.PI / 60));
129    Line mLine = new Line(centerX, centerY, xMinute, minuteY);
130    mLine.setStroke(Color.BLUE);
131
132    // Draw hour hand
133    double hLength = clockRadius * 0.5;
134    double hourX = centerX + hLength *
135      Math.sin((hour % 12 + minute / 60.0) * (2 * Math.PI / 12));
136    double hourY = centerY - hLength *
137      Math.cos((hour % 12 + minute / 60.0) * (2 * Math.PI / 12));
138    Line hLine = new Line(centerX, centerY, hourX, hourY);
139    hLine.setStroke(Color.GREEN);
140
141    getChildren().clear();
142    getChildren().addAll(circle, t1, t2, t3, t4, sLine, mLine, hLine);
143  }
144 }
```

The program displays a clock for the current time using the no-arg constructor (lines 18–20) and displays a clock for the specified hour, minute, and second using the other constructor (lines 23–28). The current hour, minute, and second is obtained by using the **GregorianCalendar** class (lines 86–96). The **GregorianCalendar** class in the Java API enables you to create a **Calendar** instance for the current time using its no-arg constructor. You can then use its methods **get(Calendar.HOUR)**, **get(Calendar .MINUTE)**, and **get(Calendar.SECOND)** to return the hour, minute, and second from a **Calendar** object.

The class defines the properties **hour**, **minute**, and **second** to store the time represented in the clock (lines 10–12) and uses the **w** and **h** properties to represent the width and height of the clock pane (line 15). The initial values of **w** and **h** are set to 250. The **w** and **h** values can be reset using the **setW** and **setH** methods (lines 69, 80). These values are used to draw a clock in the pane in the **paintClock()** method.

The **paintClock()** method paints the clock (lines 99–143). The clock radius is proportional to the width and height of the pane (line 101). A circle for the clock is created at the center of the pane (line 106). The text for showing the hours 12, 3, 6, 9 are created in lines 109–112.

The second hand, minute hand, and hour hand are the lines created in lines 114–139. The **paintClock()** method places all these shapes in the pane using the **addAll** method in a list (line 142). Because the **paintClock()** method is invoked whenever a new property (**hour**, **minute**, **second**, **w**, and **h**) is set (lines 27, 38, 49, 60, 71, 82, 95), before adding new contents into the pane, the old contents are cleared from the pane (line 141).

KEY TERMS

AWT   536
bidirectional binding   544
bindable object   542
binding object   542
binding property   542
JavaFX   536
node   539
observable object   542
pane   539

property getter method   543
primary stage   537
shape   539
Swing   536
value getter method   543
value setter method   543
UI control   539
unidirectional binding   544

CHAPTER SUMMARY

1. JavaFX is the new framework for developing rich Internet applications. JavaFX completely replaces Swing and AWT.

2. A main JavaFX class must extend **javafx.application.Application** and implement the **start** method. The primary stage is automatically created by the JVM and passed to the **start** method.

3. A stage is a window for displaying a scene. You can add nodes to a scene. Panes, controls, and shapes are nodes. Panes can be used as the containers for nodes.

4. A binding property can be bound to an observable source object. A change in the source object will be automatically reflected in the binding property. A binding property has a value getter method, value setter method, and property getter method.

5. The **Node** class defines many properties that are common to all nodes. You can apply these properties to panes, controls, and shapes.

6. You can create a **Color** object with the specified red, green, blue components, and opacity value.

7. You can create a **Font** object and set its name, size, weight, and posture.

8. The **javafx.scene.image.Image** class can be used to load an image and this image can be displayed in an **ImageView** object.

9. JavaFX provides many types of panes for automatically laying out nodes in a desired location and size. The **Pane** is the base class for all panes. It contains the **getChildren()** method to return an **ObservableList**. You can use **ObservableList**'s **add(node)** and **addAll(node1, node2, ...)** methods for adding nodes into a pane.

10. A **FlowPane** arranges the nodes in the pane horizontally from left to right or vertically from top to bottom in the order in which they were added. A **GridPane** arranges nodes in a grid (matrix) formation. The nodes are placed in the specified column and row indices. A **BorderPane** can place nodes in five regions: top, bottom, left, right, and center. An **HBox** lays out its children in a single horizontal row. A **VBox** lays out its children in a single vertical column.

11. JavaFX provides many shape classes for drawing texts, lines, circles, rectangles, ellipses, arcs, polygons, and polylines.

QUIZ

Answer the quiz for this chapter online at www.cs.armstrong.edu/liang/intro10e/quiz.html.

MyProgrammingLab™ **PROGRAMMING EXERCISES**

download image files

 Note
The image files used in the exercises can be obtained from www.cs.armstrong.edu/liang/intro10e/book.zip under the image folder.

Sections 14.2–14.9

14.1 (*Display images*) Write a program that displays four images in a grid pane, as shown in Figure 14.43a.

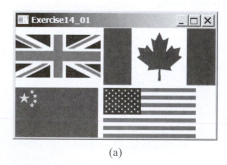 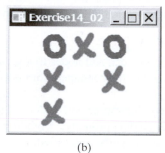 

(a)   (b)   (c)

FIGURE 14.43 (a) Exercise 14.1 displays four images. (b) Exercise 14.2 displays a tic-tac-toe board with images. (c) Three cards are randomly selected.

VideoNote
Display a tictactoe board

*14.2 (*Tic-tac-toe board*) Write a program that displays a tic-tac-toe board, as shown in Figure 14.43b. A cell may be X, O, or empty. What to display at each cell is randomly decided. The X and O are images in the files **x.gif** and **o.gif**.

*14.3 (*Display three cards*) Write a program that displays three cards randomly selected from a deck of 52, as shown in Figure 14.43c. The card image files are named **1.png**, **2.png**, …, **52.png** and stored in the **image/card** directory. All three cards are distinct and selected randomly. Hint: You can select random cards by storing the numbers 1–52 to an array list, perform a random shuffle introduced in Section 11.12, and use the first three numbers in the array list as the file names for the image.

14.4 (*Color and font*) Write a program that displays five texts vertically, as shown in Figure 14.44a. Set a random color and opacity for each text and set the font of each text to Times Roman, bold, italic, and 22 pixels.

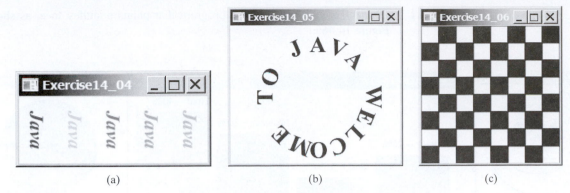

FIGURE 14.44 (a) Five texts are displayed with a random color and a specified font. (b) A string is displayed around the circle. (c) A checkerboard is displayed using rectangles.

14.5 (*Characters around circle*) Write a program that displays a string Welcome to Java around the circle, as shown in Figure 14.44b. Hint: You need to display each character in the right location with appropriate rotation using a loop.

*14.6 (*Game: display a checkerboard*) Write a program that displays a checkerboard in which each white and black cell is a **Rectangle** with a fill color black or white, as shown in Figure 14.44c.

Sections 14.10–14.11

*14.7 (*Display random 0 or 1*) Write a program that displays a 10-by-10 square matrix, as shown in Figure 14.45a. Each element in the matrix is **0** or **1**, randomly generated. Display each number centered in a text field. Use **TextField**'s **setText** method to set value **0** or **1** as a string.

Display a random matrix

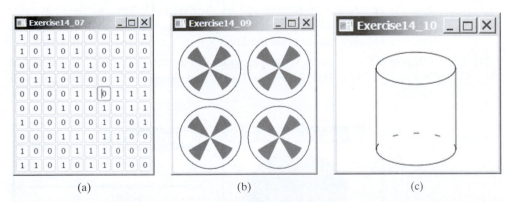

FIGURE 14.45 (a) The program randomly generates 0s and 1s. (b) Exercise 14.9 draws four fans. (c) Exercise 14.10 draws a cylinder.

14.8 (*Display 54 cards*) Expand Exercise 14.3 to display all 54 cards (including two jokers), nine per row. The image files are jokers and are named 53.jpg and 54.jpg.

*14.9 (*Create four fans*) Write a program that places four fans in a **GridPane** with two rows and two columns, as shown in Figure 14.45b.

*14.10 (*Display a cylinder*) Write a program that draws a cylinder, as shown in Figure 14.45b. You can use the following method to set the dashed stroke for an arc:

```
arc.getStrokeDashArray().addAll(6.0, 21.0);
```

*14.11 (*Paint a smiley face*) Write a program that paints a smiley face, as shown in Figure 14.46a.

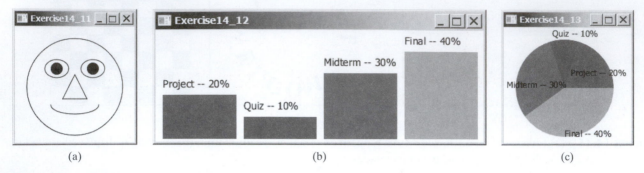

(a)   (b)   (c)

FIGURE 14.46 (a) Exercise 14.11 paints a smiley face. (b) Exercise 14.12 paints a bar chart. (c) Exercise 14.13 paints a pie chart.

VideoNote

Display a bar chart

14.12 (*Display a bar chart*) Write a program that uses a bar chart to display the percentages of the overall grade represented by projects, quizzes, midterm exams, and the final exam, as shown in Figure 14.46b. Suppose that projects take **20 percent and are displayed in red, quizzes take **10** percent and are displayed in blue, midterm exams take **30** percent and are displayed in green, and the final exam takes **40** percent and is displayed in orange. Use the **Rectangle** class to display the bars. Interested readers may explore the JavaFX **BarChart** class for further study.

14.13 (*Display a pie chart*) Write a program that uses a pie chart to display the percentages of the overall grade represented by projects, quizzes, midterm exams, and the final exam, as shown in Figure 14.46c. Suppose that projects take **20 percent and are displayed in red, quizzes take **10** percent and are displayed in blue, midterm exams take **30** percent and are displayed in green, and the final exam takes **40** percent and is displayed in orange. Use the **Arc** class to display the pies. Interested readers may explore the JavaFX **PieChart** class for further study.

14.14 (*Display a rectanguloid*) Write a program that displays a rectanguloid, as shown in Figure 14.47a. The cube should grow and shrink as the window grows or shrinks.

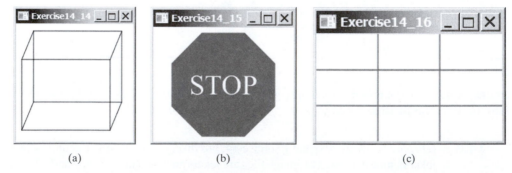

(a)   (b)   (c)

FIGURE 14.47 (a) Exercise 14.14 paints a rectanguloid. (b) Exercise 14.15 paints a STOP sign. (c) Exercise 14.13 paints a grid.

*14.15 (*Display a STOP sign*) Write a program that displays a STOP sign, as shown in Figure 14.47b. The octagon is in red and the sign is in white. (*Hint*: Place an octagon and a text in a stack pane.)

*14.16 (*Display a 3 × 3 grid*) Write a program that displays a 3 × 3 grid, as shown in Figure 14.47c. Use red color for vertical lines and blue for horizontals. The lines are automatically resized when the window is resized.

14.17 (*Game: hangman*) Write a program that displays a drawing for the popular hangman game, as shown in Figure 14.48a.

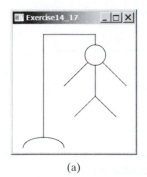 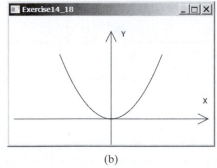 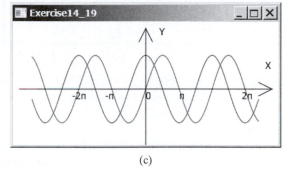

(a)   (b)   (c)

FIGURE 14.48 (a) Exercise 14.17 draws a sketch for the hangman game. (c) Exercise 14.18 plots the quadratic function. (c) Exercise 14.19 plots the sine/cosine functions.

*14.18 (*Plot the square function*) Write a program that draws a diagram for the function $f(x) = x^2$ (see Figure 14.48b).

Hint: Add points to a polyline using the following code:

```
Polyline polyline = new Polyline();
ObservableList<Double> list = polyline.getPoints();
double scaleFactor = 0.0125;
for (int x = -100; x <= 100; x++) {
  list.add(x + 200.0);
  list.add(scaleFactor * x * x);
}
```

**14.19 (*Plot the sine and cosine functions*) Write a program that plots the sine function in red and cosine in blue, as shown in Figure 14.48c.

Hint: The Unicode for π is \u03c0. To display -2π, use Text(x, y, "-2\u03c0"). For a trigonometric function like sin(x), x is in radians. Use the following loop to add the points to a polyline:

```
Polyline polyline = new Polyline();
ObservableList<Double> list = polyline.getPoints();
double scaleFactor = 50;
for (int x = -170; x <= 170; x++) {
  list.add(x + 200.0);
  list.add(100 - 50 * Math.sin((x / 100.0) * 2 * Math.PI));
}
```

**14.20 (*Draw an arrow line*) Write a static method that draws an arrow line from a starting point to an ending point in a pane using the following method header:

```
public static void drawArrowLine(double startX, double startY,
  double endX, double endY, Pane pane)
```

Write a test program that randomly draws an arrow line, as shown in Figure 14.49a.

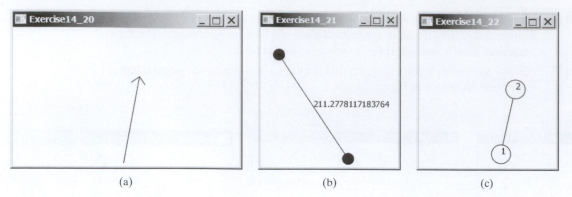

(a)   (b)   (c)

FIGURE 14.49 (a) The program displays an arrow line. (b) Exercise14.21 connects the centers of two filled circles. (c) Exercise14.22 connects two circles from their perimeter.

*14.21 (*Two circles and their distance*) Write a program that draws two filled circles with radius **15** pixels, centered at random locations, with a line connecting the two circles. The distance between the two centers is displayed on the line, as shown in Figure 14.49b.

*14.22 (*Connect two circles*) Write a program that draws two circles with radius **15** pixels, centered at random locations, with a line connecting the two circles. The line should not cross inside the circles, as shown in Figure 14.49c.

*14.23 (*Geometry: two rectangles*) Write a program that prompts the user to enter the center coordinates, width, and height of two rectangles from the command line. The program displays the rectangles and a text indicating whether the two are overlapping, whether one is contained in the other, or whether they don't overlap, as shown in Figure 14.50. See Programming Exercise 10.13 for checking the relationship between two rectangles.

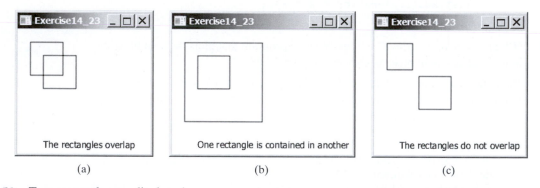

(a)   (b)   (c)

FIGURE 14.50 Two rectangles are displayed.

*14.24 (*Geometry: Inside a polygon?*) Write a program that prompts the user to enter the coordinates of five points from the command line. The first four points form a polygon, and the program displays the polygon and a text that indicates whether the fifth point is inside the polygon, as shown in Figure 14.51a. Hint: Use the **Node**'s **contains** method to test whether a point is inside a node.

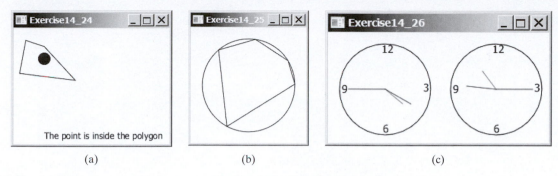

FIGURE 14.51 (a) The polygon and a point are displayed. (b) Exercise14.25 connects five random points on a circle. (c) Exercise 14.26 displays two clocks.

*14.25 (*Random points on a circle*) Modify Programming Exercise 4.6 to create five random points on a circle, form a polygon by connecting the points clockwise, and display the circle and the polygon, as shown in Figure 14.51b.

Section 14.12

14.26 (*Use the ClockPane class*) Write a program that displays two clocks. The hour, minute, and second values are **4**, **20**, **45** for the first clock and **22**, **46**, **15** for the second clock, as shown in Figure 14.51c.

*14.27 (*Draw a detailed clock*) Modify the **ClockPane** class in Section 14.12 to draw the clock with more details on the hours and minutes, as shown in Figure 14.52a.

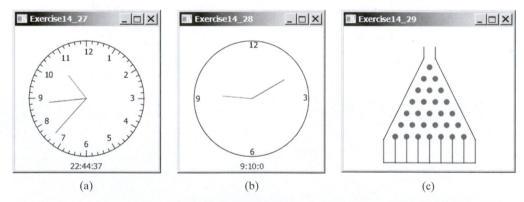

FIGURE 14.52 (a) Exercise 14.27 displays a detailed clock. (b) Exercise 14.28 displays a clock with random hour and minute values. (c) Exercise 14.29 displays a bean machine.

*14.28 (*Random time*) Modify the **ClockPane** class with three new Boolean properties— **hourHandVisible**, **minuteHandVisible**, and **secondHandVisible**—and their associated accessor and mutator methods. You can use the **set** methods to make a hand visible or invisible. Write a test program that displays only the hour and minute hands. The hour and minute values are randomly generated. The hour is between **0** and **11**, and the minute is either **0** or **30**, as shown in Figure 14.52b.

**14.29 (*Game: bean machine*) Write a program that displays a bean machine introduced in Programming Exercise 7.21, as shown in Figure 14.52c.

EVENT-DRIVEN PROGRAMMING AND ANIMATIONS

Objectives

- To get a taste of event-driven programming (§15.1).

- To describe events, event sources, and event classes (§15.2).

- To define handler classes, register handler objects with the source object, and write the code to handle events (§15.3).

- To define handler classes using inner classes (§15.4).

- To define handler classes using anonymous inner classes (§15.5).

- To simplify event handling using lambda expressions (§15.6).

- To develop a GUI application for a loan calculator (§15.7).

- To write programs to deal with **MouseEvent**s (§15.8).

- To write programs to deal with **KeyEvent**s (§15.9).

- To create listeners for processing a value change in an observable object (§15.10).

- To use the **Animation**, **PathTransition**, **FadeTransition**, and **Timeline** classes to develop animations (§15.11).

- To develop an animation for simulating a bouncing ball (§15.12).

15.1 Introduction

Key Point

You can write code to process events such as a button click, mouse movement, and keystrokes.

problem

Suppose you wish to write a GUI program that lets the user enter a loan amount, annual interest rate, and number of years and click the *Calculate* button to obtain the monthly payment and total payment, as shown in Figure 15.1. How do you accomplish the task? You have to use *event-driven programming* to write the code to respond to the button-clicking event.

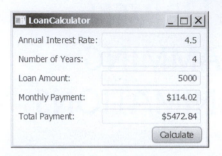

FIGURE 15.1 The program computes loan payments.

problem

Before delving into event-driven programming, it is helpful to get a taste using a simple example. The example displays two buttons in a pane, as shown in Figure 15.2.

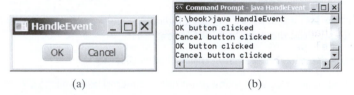

(a) (b)

FIGURE 15.2 (a) The program displays two buttons. (b) A message is displayed in the console when a button is clicked.

To respond to a button click, you need to write the code to process the button-clicking action. The button is an *event source object*—where the action originates. You need to create an object capable of handling the action event on a button. This object is called an *event handler*, as shown in Figure 15.3.

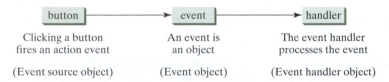

FIGURE 15.3 An event handler processes the event fired from the source object.

Not all objects can be handlers for an action event. To be a handler of an action event, two requirements must be met:

EventHandler interface

1. The object must be an instance of the **EventHandler<T extends Event>** interface. This interface defines the common behavior for all handlers. **<T extends Event>** denotes that **T** is a generic type that is a subtype of **Event**.

2. The **EventHandler** object **handler** must be registered with the event source object using the method **source.setOnAction(handler)**.

setOnAction(handler)

The `EventHandler<ActionEvent>` interface contains the `handle(ActionEvent)` method for processing the action event. Your handler class must override this method to respond to the event. Listing 15.1 gives the code that processes the `ActionEvent` on the two buttons. When you click the *OK* button, the message "OK button clicked" is displayed. When you click the *Cancel* button, the message "Cancel button clicked" is displayed, as shown in Figure 15.2.

LISTING 15.1 HandleEvent.java

```java
1  import javafx.application.Application;
2  import javafx.geometry.Pos;
3  import javafx.scene.Scene;
4  import javafx.scene.control.Button;
5  import javafx.scene.layout.HBox;
6  import javafx.stage.Stage;
7  import javafx.event.ActionEvent;
8  import javafx.event.EventHandler;
9
10 public class HandleEvent extends Application {
11   @Override // Override the start method in the Application class
12   public void start(Stage primaryStage) {
13     // Create a pane and set its properties
14     HBox pane = new HBox(10);
15     pane.setAlignment(Pos.CENTER);
16     Button btOK = new Button("OK");
17     Button btCancel = new Button("Cancel");
18     OKHandlerClass handler1 = new OKHandlerClass();          // create handler
19     btOK.setOnAction(handler1);                              // register handler
20     CancelHandlerClass handler2 = new CancelHandlerClass();  // create handler
21     btCancel.setOnAction(handler2);                          // register handler
22     pane.getChildren().addAll(btOK, btCancel);
23
24     // Create a scene and place it in the stage
25     Scene scene = new Scene(pane);
26     primaryStage.setTitle("HandleEvent"); // Set the stage title
27     primaryStage.setScene(scene); // Place the scene in the stage
28     primaryStage.show(); // Display the stage
29   }
30 }
31
32 class OKHandlerClass implements EventHandler<ActionEvent> {   // handler class
33   @Override
34   public void handle(ActionEvent e) {                        // handle event
35     System.out.println("OK button clicked");
36   }
37 }
38
39 class CancelHandlerClass implements EventHandler<ActionEvent> {  // handler class
40   @Override
41   public void handle(ActionEvent e) {                           // handle event
42     System.out.println("Cancel button clicked");
43   }
44 }
```

Two handler classes are defined in lines 32–44. Each handler class implements `EventHandler<ActionEvent>` to process `ActionEvent`. The object `handler1` is an instance of `OKHandlerClass` (line 18), which is registered with the button `btOK` (line 19). When the *OK* button is clicked, the `handle(ActionEvent)` method (line 34) in

OKHandlerClass is invoked to process the event. The object handler2 is an instance of CancelHandlerClass (line 20), which is registered with the button btCancel in line 21. When the *Cancel* button is clicked, the handle(ActionEvent) method (line 41) in CancelHandlerClass is invoked to process the event.

You now have seen a glimpse of event-driven programming in JavaFX. You probably have many questions, such as why a handler class is defined to implement the EventHandler<ActionEvent>. The following sections will give you all the answers.

15.2 Events and Event Sources

Key Point

An event is an object created from an event source. Firing an event means to create an event and delegate the handler to handle the event.

event-driven programming

event

When you run a Java GUI program, the program interacts with the user, and the events drive its execution. This is called *event-driven programming.* An *event* can be defined as a signal to the program that something has happened. Events are triggered by external user actions, such as mouse movements, mouse clicks, and keystrokes. The program can choose to respond to or ignore an event. The example in the preceding section gave you a taste of event-driven programming.

fire event

event source object

source object

The component that creates an event and fires it is called the *event source object*, or simply *source object* or *source component*. For example, a button is the source object for a button-clicking action event. An event is an instance of an event class. The root class of the Java event classes is java.util.EventObject. The root class of the JavaFX event classes is javafx.event.Event. The hierarchical relationships of some event classes are shown in Figure 15.4.

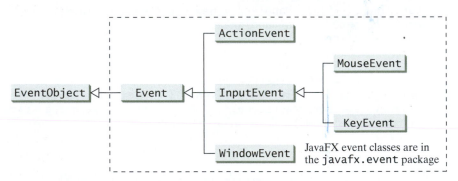

FIGURE 15.4 An event in JavaFX is an object of the javafx.event.Event class.

event object

getSource()

An *event object* contains whatever properties are pertinent to the event. You can identify the source object of an event using the getSource() instance method in the EventObject class. The subclasses of EventObject deal with specific types of events, such as action events, window events, mouse events, and key events. The first three columns in Table 15.1 list some external user actions, source objects, and event types fired. For example, when clicking a button, the button creates and fires an ActionEvent, as indicated in the first line of this table. Here, the button is an event source object, and an ActionEvent is the event object fired by the source object, as shown in Figure 15.3.

Note
If a component can fire an event, any subclass of the component can fire the same type of event. For example, every JavaFX shape, layout pane, and control can fire MouseEvent and KeyEvent since Node is the superclass for shapes, layout panes, and controls.

TABLE 15.1 User Action, Source Object, Event Type, Handler Interface, and Handler

User Action	Source Object	Event Type Fired	Event Registration Method
Click a button	`Button`	`ActionEvent`	`setOnAction(EventHandler<ActionEvent>)`
Press Enter in a text field	`TextField`	`ActionEvent`	`setOnAction(EventHandler<ActionEvent>)`
Check or uncheck	`RadioButton`	`ActionEvent`	`setOnAction(EventHandler<ActionEvent>)`
Check or uncheck	`CheckBox`	`ActionEvent`	`setOnAction(EventHandler<ActionEvent>)`
Select a new item	`ComboBox`	`ActionEvent`	`setOnAction(EventHandler<ActionEvent>)`
Mouse pressed	`Node, Scene`	`MouseEvent`	`setOnMousePressed(EventHandler<MouseEvent>)`
Mouse released			`setOnMouseReleased(EventHandler<MouseEvent>)`
Mouse clicked			`setOnMouseClicked(EventHandler<MouseEvent>)`
Mouse entered			`setOnMouseEntered(EventHandler<MouseEvent>)`
Mouse exited			`setOnMouseExited(EventHandler<MouseEvent>)`
Mouse moved			`setOnMouseMoved(EventHandler<MouseEvent>)`
Mouse dragged			`setOnMouseDragged(EventHandler<MouseEvent>)`
Key pressed	`Node, Scene`	`KeyEvent`	`setOnKeyPressed(EventHandler<KeyEvent>)`
Key released			`setOnKeyReleased(EventHandler<KeyEvent>)`
Key typed			`setOnKeyTyped(EventHandler<KeyEvent>)`

15.1 What is an event source object? What is an event object? Describe the relationship between an event source object and an event object.

15.2 Can a button fire a `MouseEvent`? Can a button fire a `KeyEvent`? Can a button fire an `ActionEvent`?

Check Point

15.3 Registering Handlers and Handling Events

A handler is an object that must be registered with an event source object, and it must be an instance of an appropriate event-handling interface.

Key Point

Java uses a delegation-based model for event handling: a source object fires an event, and an object interested in the event handles it. The latter object is called an *event handler* or an event *listener*. For an object to be a handler for an event on a source object, two things are needed, as shown in Figure 15.5.

event delegation
event handler

1. *The handler object must be an instance of the corresponding event-handler interface* to ensure that the handler has the correct method for processing the event. JavaFX defines a unified handler interface `EventHandler<T extends Event>` for an event `T`. The handler interface contains the `handle(T e)` method for processing the event. For example, the handler interface for `ActionEvent` is `EventHandler<ActionEvent>`; each handler for `ActionEvent` should implement the `handle(ActionEvent e)` method for processing an `ActionEvent`.

event-handler interface

`EventHandler<T extends Event>`

event handler

2. *The handler object must be registered by the source object.* Registration methods depend on the event type. For `ActionEvent`, the method is `setOnAction`. For a mouse pressed event, the method is `setOnMousePressed`. For a key pressed event, the method is `setOnKeyPressed`.

register handler

Let's revisit Listing 15.1, HandleEvent.java. Since a `Button` object fires `ActionEvent`, a handler object for `ActionEvent` must be an instance of `EventHandler<ActionEvent>`, so

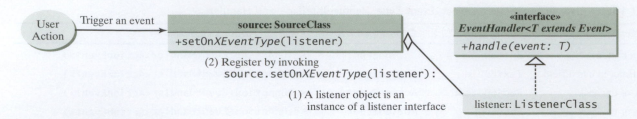

(a) A generic source object with a generic event T

(b) A `Button` source object with an `ActionEvent`

FIGURE 15.5 A listener must be an instance of a listener interface and must be registered with a source object.

the handler class implements **EventHandler<ActionEvent>** in line 34. The source object invokes **setOnAction(handler)** to register a handler, as follows:

create source object
create handler object
register handler

```
Button btOK = new Button("OK"); // Line 16 in Listing 15.1
OKHandlerClass handler1 = new OKHandlerClass(); // Line 18 in Listing 15.1
btOK.setOnAction(handler1); // Line 19 in Listing 15.1
```

When you click the button, the **Button** object fires an **ActionEvent** and passes it to invoke the handler's **handle(ActionEvent)** method to handle the event. The event object contains information pertinent to the event, which can be obtained using the methods. For example, you can use **e.getSource()** to obtain the source object that fired the event.

first version

We now write a program that uses two buttons to control the size of a circle, as shown in Figure 15.6. We will develop this program incrementally. First, we write the program in Listing 15.2 that displays the user interface with a circle in the center (lines 15-19) and two buttons on the bottom (lines 21-27).

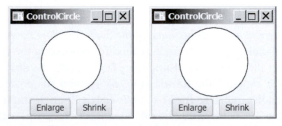

FIGURE 15.6 The user clicks the *Enlarge* and *Shrink* buttons to enlarge and shrink the size of the circle.

LISTING 15.2 ControlCircleWithoutEventHandling.java

```
1  import javafx.application.Application;
2  import javafx.geometry.Pos;
3  import javafx.scene.Scene;
4  import javafx.scene.control.Button;
```

```
 5  import javafx.scene.layout.StackPane;
 6  import javafx.scene.layout.HBox;
 7  import javafx.scene.layout.BorderPane;
 8  import javafx.scene.paint.Color;
 9  import javafx.scene.shape.Circle;
10  import javafx.stage.Stage;
11
12  public class ControlCircleWithoutEventHandling extends Application {
13    @Override // Override the start method in the Application class
14    public void start(Stage primaryStage) {
15      StackPane pane = new StackPane();
16      Circle circle = new Circle(50);                                    circle
17      circle.setStroke(Color.BLACK);
18      circle.setFill(Color.WHITE);
19      pane.getChildren().add(circle);
20
21      HBox hBox = new HBox();
22      hBox.setSpacing(10);
23      hBox.setAlignment(Pos.CENTER);
24      Button btEnlarge = new Button("Enlarge");                          buttons
25      Button btShrink = new Button("Shrink");
26      hBox.getChildren().add(btEnlarge);
27      hBox.getChildren().add(btShrink);
28
29      BorderPane borderPane = new BorderPane();
30      borderPane.setCenter(pane);
31      borderPane.setBottom(hBox);
32      BorderPane.setAlignment(hBox, Pos.CENTER);
33
34      // Create a scene and place it in the stage
35      Scene scene = new Scene(borderPane, 200, 150);
36      primaryStage.setTitle("ControlCircle"); // Set the stage title
37      primaryStage.setScene(scene); // Place the scene in the stage
38      primaryStage.show(); // Display the stage
39    }
49  }
```

How do you use the buttons to enlarge or shrink the circle? When the *Enlarge* button is clicked, you want the circle to be repainted with a larger radius. How can you accomplish this? You can expand and modify the program in Listing 15.2 into Listing 15.3 with the following features: *second version*

1. Define a new class named **CirclePane** for displaying the circle in a pane (lines 51–68). This new class displays a circle and provides the **enlarge** and **shrink** methods for increasing and decreasing the radius of the circle (lines 60–62, 64–67). It is a good strategy to design a class to model a circle pane with supporting methods so that these related methods along with the circle are coupled in one object.

2. Create a **CirclePane** object and declare **circlePane** as a data field to reference this object (line 15) in the **ControlCircle** class. The methods in the **ControlCircle** class can now access the **CirclePane** object through this data field.

3. Define a handler class named **EnlargeHandler** that implements **EventHandler<ActionEvent>** (lines 43–48). To make the reference variable **circlePane** accessible from the **handle** method, define **EnlargeHandler** as an *inner class* inner class of the **ControlCircle** class. (*Inner classes* are defined inside another class. We use an inner class here and will introduce it fully in the next section.)

4. Register the handler for the *Enlarge* button (line 29) and implement the **handle** method in **EnlargeHandler** to invoke **circlePane.enlarge()** (line 46).

VideoNote

Handler and its registration

LISTING 15.3 ControlCircle.java

```java
 1  import javafx.application.Application;
 2  import javafx.event.ActionEvent;
 3  import javafx.event.EventHandler;
 4  import javafx.geometry.Pos;
 5  import javafx.scene.Scene;
 6  import javafx.scene.control.Button;
 7  import javafx.scene.layout.StackPane;
 8  import javafx.scene.layout.HBox;
 9  import javafx.scene.layout.BorderPane;
10  import javafx.scene.paint.Color;
11  import javafx.scene.shape.Circle;
12  import javafx.stage.Stage;
13
14  public class ControlCircle extends Application {
15    private CirclePane circlePane = new CirclePane();
16
17    @Override // Override the start method in the Application class
18    public void start(Stage primaryStage) {
19      // Hold two buttons in an HBox
20      HBox hBox = new HBox();
21      hBox.setSpacing(10);
22      hBox.setAlignment(Pos.CENTER);
23      Button btEnlarge = new Button("Enlarge");
24      Button btShrink = new Button("Shrink");
25      hBox.getChildren().add(btEnlarge);
26      hBox.getChildren().add(btShrink);
27
28      // Create and register the handler
29      btEnlarge.setOnAction(new EnlargeHandler());
30
31      BorderPane borderPane = new BorderPane();
32      borderPane.setCenter(circlePane);
33      borderPane.setBottom(hBox);
34      BorderPane.setAlignment(hBox, Pos.CENTER);
35
36      // Create a scene and place it in the stage
37      Scene scene = new Scene(borderPane, 200, 150);
38      primaryStage.setTitle("ControlCircle"); // Set the stage title
39      primaryStage.setScene(scene); // Place the scene in the stage
40      primaryStage.show(); // Display the stage
41    }
42
43    class EnlargeHandler implements EventHandler<ActionEvent> {
44      @Override // Override the handle method
45      public void handle(ActionEvent e) {
46        circlePane.enlarge();
47      }
48    }
49  }
50
51  class CirclePane extends StackPane {
52    private Circle circle = new Circle(50);
53
54    public CirclePane() {
55      getChildren().add(circle);
56      circle.setStroke(Color.BLACK);
57      circle.setFill(Color.WHITE);
58    }
```

create/register handler

handler class

CirclePane class

```
59
60    public void enlarge() {                                      enlarge method
61      circle.setRadius(circle.getRadius() + 2);
62    }
63
64    public void shrink() {
65      circle.setRadius(circle.getRadius() > 2 ?
66        circle.getRadius() - 2 : circle.getRadius());
67    }
68  }
```

As an exercise, add the code for handling the *Shrink* button to display a smaller circle when   the *Shrink* button
the *Shrink* button is clicked.

15.3 Why must a handler be an instance of an appropriate handler interface?

15.4 Explain how to register a handler object and how to implement a handler interface.

15.5 What is the handler method for the **EventHandler<ActionEvent>** interface?

15.6 What is the registration method for a button to register an **ActionEvent** handler?

15.4 Inner Classes

An inner class, or nested class, is a class defined within the scope of another class.
Inner classes are useful for defining handler classes.

Inner classes are used in the preceding section. This section introduces inner classes in detail.
First, let us see the code in Figure 15.7. The code in Figure 15.7a defines two separate classes,
Test and **A**. The code in Figure 15.7b defines **A** as an inner class in **Test**.

```
public class Test {
  ...
}

public class A {
  ...
}
```
(a)

```
public class Test {
  ...

  // Inner class
  public class A {
    ...
  }
}
```
(b)

```
// OuterClass.java: inner class demo
public class OuterClass {
  private int data;

  /** A method in the outer class */
  public void m() {
    // Do something
  }

  // An inner class
  class InnerClass {
    /** A method in the inner class */
    public void mi() {
      // Directly reference data and method
      // defined in its outer class
      data++;
      m();
    }
  }
}
```
(c)

FIGURE 15.7 Inner classes combine dependent classes into the primary class.

The class **InnerClass** defined inside **OuterClass** in Figure 15.7c is another example
of an inner class. An inner class may be used just like a regular class. Normally, you define

a class as an inner class if it is used only by its outer class. An inner class has the following features:

- An inner class is compiled into a class named `OuterClassName$InnerClassName.class`. For example, the inner class `A` in `Test` is compiled into `Test$A.class` in Figure 15.7b.

- An inner class can reference the data and the methods defined in the outer class in which it nests, so you need not pass the reference of an object of the outer class to the constructor of the inner class. For this reason, inner classes can make programs simple and concise. For example, `circlePane` is defined in `ControlCircle` in Listing 15.3 (line 15). It can be referenced in the inner class `EnlargeHandler` in line 46.

- An inner class can be defined with a visibility modifier subject to the same visibility rules applied to a member of the class.

- An inner class can be defined as `static`. A `static` inner class can be accessed using the outer class name. A `static` inner class cannot access nonstatic members of the outer class.

- Objects of an inner class are often created in the outer class. But you can also create an object of an inner class from another class. If the inner class is nonstatic, you must first create an instance of the outer class, then use the following syntax to create an object for the inner class:

  ```
  OuterClass.InnerClass innerObject = outerObject.new InnerClass();
  ```

- If the inner class is static, use the following syntax to create an object for it:

  ```
  OuterClass.InnerClass innerObject = new OuterClass.InnerClass();
  ```

A simple use of inner classes is to combine dependent classes into a primary class. This reduces the number of source files. It also makes class files easy to organize since they are all named with the primary class as the prefix. For example, rather than creating the two source files **Test.java** and **A.java** as shown in Figure 15.7a, you can merge class `A` into class `Test` and create just one source file, **Test.java** as shown in Figure 15.7b. The resulting class files are **Test.class** and **Test$A.class**.

Another practical use of inner classes is to avoid class-naming conflicts. Two versions of `CirclePane` are defined in Listings 15.2 and 15.3. You can define them as inner classes to avoid a conflict.

A handler class is designed specifically to create a handler object for a GUI component (e.g., a button). The handler class will not be shared by other applications and therefore is appropriate to be defined inside the main class as an inner class.

15.7 Can an inner class be used in a class other than the class in which it nests?

15.8 Can the modifiers `public`, `protected`, `private`, and `static` be used for inner classes?

15.5 Anonymous Inner Class Handlers

An anonymous inner class is an inner class without a name. It combines defining an inner class and creating an instance of the class into one step.

anonymous inner class

Inner-class handlers can be shortened using *anonymous inner classes*. The inner class in Listing 15.3 can be replaced by an anonymous inner class as shown below.

```
public void start(Stage primaryStage) {
  // Omitted

  btEnlarge.setOnAction(
    new EnlargeHandler());
}

class EnlargeHandler
    implements EventHandler<ActionEvent> {
  public void handle(ActionEvent e) {
    circlePane.enlarge();
  }
}
```

```
public void start(Stage primaryStage) {
  // Omitted

  btEnlarge.setOnAction(
    new class EnlargeHandlner
      implements EventHandler<ActionEvent>() {
      public void handle(ActionEvent e) {
        circlePane.enlarge();
      }
    });
}
```

(a) Inner class `EnlargeListener`   (b) Anonymous inner class

The syntax for an anonymous inner class is shown below

```
new SuperClassName/InterfaceName() {
  // Implement or override methods in superclass or interface

  // Other methods if necessary
}
```

Since an anonymous inner class is a special kind of inner class, it is treated like an inner class with the following features:

- An anonymous inner class must always extend a superclass or implement an interface, but it cannot have an explicit **extends** or **implements** clause.

- An anonymous inner class must implement all the abstract methods in the superclass or in the interface.

- An anonymous inner class always uses the no-arg constructor from its superclass to create an instance. If an anonymous inner class implements an interface, the constructor is **Object()**.

- An anonymous inner class is compiled into a class named **OuterClassName$n.class**. For example, if the outer class **Test** has two anonymous inner classes, they are compiled into **Test$1.class** and **Test$2.class**.

Listing 15.4 gives an example that handles the events from four buttons, as shown in Figure 15.8.

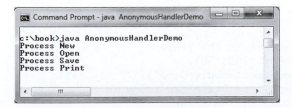
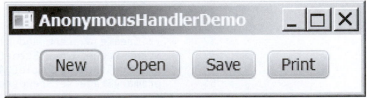

FIGURE 15.8   The program handles the events from four buttons.

LISTING 15.4 AnonymousHandlerDemo.java

```
1  import javafx.application.Application;
2  import javafx.event.ActionEvent;
3  import javafx.event.EventHandler;
4  import javafx.geometry.Pos;
5  import javafx.scene.Scene;
```

VideoNote

Anonymous handler

```
 6  import javafx.scene.control.Button;
 7  import javafx.scene.layout.HBox;
 8  import javafx.stage.Stage;
 9
10  public class AnonymousHandlerDemo extends Application {
11    @Override // Override the start method in the Application class
12    public void start(Stage primaryStage) {
13      // Hold two buttons in an HBox
14      HBox hBox = new HBox();
15      hBox.setSpacing(10);
16      hBox.setAlignment(Pos.CENTER);
17      Button btNew = new Button("New");
18      Button btOpen = new Button("Open");
19      Button btSave = new Button("Save");
20      Button btPrint = new Button("Print");
21      hBox.getChildren().addAll(btNew, btOpen, btSave, btPrint);
22
23      // Create and register the handler
24      btNew.setOnAction(new EventHandler<ActionEvent>() {
25        @Override // Override the handle method
26        public void handle(ActionEvent e) {
27          System.out.println("Process New");
28        }
29      });
30
31      btOpen.setOnAction(new EventHandler<ActionEvent>() {
32        @Override // Override the handle method
33        public void handle(ActionEvent e) {
34          System.out.println("Process Open");
35        }
36      });
37
38      btSave.setOnAction(new EventHandler<ActionEvent>() {
39        @Override // Override the handle method
40        public void handle(ActionEvent e) {
41          System.out.println("Process Save");
42        }
43      });
44
45      btPrint.setOnAction(new EventHandler<ActionEvent>() {
46        @Override // Override the handle method
47        public void handle(ActionEvent e) {
48          System.out.println("Process Print");
49        }
50      });
51
52      // Create a scene and place it in the stage
53      Scene scene = new Scene(hBox, 300, 50);
54      primaryStage.setTitle("AnonymousHandlerDemo"); // Set title
55      primaryStage.setScene(scene); // Place the scene in the stage
56      primaryStage.show(); // Display the stage
57    }
58  }
```

anonymous handler

handle event

The program creates four handlers using anonymous inner classes (lines 24–50). Without using anonymous inner classes, you would have to create four separate classes. An anonymous handler works the same way as that of an inner class handler. The program is condensed using an anonymous inner class.

The anonymous inner classes in this example are compiled into `AnonymousHandlerDemo$1.class`, `AnonymousHandlerDemo$2.class`, `AnonymousHandlerDemo$3.class`, and `AnonymousHandlerDemo$4.class`.

15.9 If class **A** is an inner class in class **B**, what is the .class file for **A**? If class **B** contains two anonymous inner classes, what are the .class file names for these two classes?

Check
Point

15.10 What is wrong in the following code?

```
public class Test extends Application {
  public void start(Stage stage) {
    Button btOK = new Button("OK");
  }

  private class Handler implements
      EventHandler<ActionEvent> {
    public void handle(Action e) {
      System.out.println(e.getSource());
    }
  }
}
```

(a)

```
public class Test extends Application {
  public void start(Stage stage) {
    Button btOK = new Button("OK");

    btOK.setOnAction(
      new EventHandler<ActionEvent> {
        public void handle
          (ActionEvent e) {
          System.out.println
            (e.getSource());
        }
    } // Something missing here
  }
}
```

(b)

15.6 Simplifying Event Handling Using Lambda Expressions

Lambda expressions can be used to greatly simplify coding for event handling.

Key
Point

Lambda expression is a new feature in Java 8. Lambda expressions can be viewed as an anonymous class with a concise syntax. For example, the following code in (a) can be greatly simplified using a lambda expression in (b) in three lines.

lambda expression

```
btEnlarge.setOnAction(
  new EventHandler<ActionEvent>() {
    @Override
    public void handle(ActionEvent e) {
      // Code for processing event e
    }
  }
});
```

(a) Anonymous inner class event handler

```
btEnlarge.setOnAction(e -> {
  // Code for processing event e
});
```

(b) Lambda expression event handler

The basic syntax for a lambda expression is either

```
(type1 param1, type2 param2, ...) -> expression
```

or

```
(type1 param1, type2 param2, ...) -> { statements; }
```

The data type for a parameter may be explicitly declared or implicitly inferred by the compiler. The parentheses can be omitted if there is only one parameter without an explicit data type. In the preceding example, the lambda expression is as follows

```
e -> {
  // Code for processing event e
}
```

The compiler treats a lambda expression as if it is an object created from an anonymous inner class. In this case, the compiler understands that the object must be an instance of **EventHandler<ActionEvent>**. Since the **EventHandler** interface defines the **handle** method with a parameter of the **ActionEvent** type, the compiler automatically recognizes that **e** is a parameter of the **ActionEvent** type, and the statements are for the body of the **handle** method. The **EventHandler** interface contains just one method. The statements in the lambda expression are all for that method. If it contains multiple methods, the compiler will not be able to compile the lambda expression. So, for the compiler to understand lambda expressions, the interface must contain exactly one abstract method. Such an interface is known as a *functional interface* or a *Single Abstract Method* (SAM) interface.

Listing 15.4 can be simplified using lambda expressions as shown in Listing 15.5.

functional interface

SAM interface

LISTING 15.5 LambdaHandlerDemo.java

```
 1  import javafx.application.Application;
 2  import javafx.event.ActionEvent;
 3  import javafx.geometry.Pos;
 4  import javafx.scene.Scene;
 5  import javafx.scene.control.Button;
 6  import javafx.scene.layout.HBox;
 7  import javafx.stage.Stage;
 8
 9  public class LambdaHandlerDemo extends Application {
10    @Override // Override the start method in the Application class
11    public void start(Stage primaryStage) {
12      // Hold two buttons in an HBox
13      HBox hBox = new HBox();
14      hBox.setSpacing(10);
15      hBox.setAlignment(Pos.CENTER);
16      Button btNew = new Button("New");
17      Button btOpen = new Button("Open");
18      Button btSave = new Button("Save");
19      Button btPrint = new Button("Print");
20      hBox.getChildren().addAll(btNew, btOpen, btSave, btPrint);
21
22      // Create and register the handler
23      btNew.setOnAction((ActionEvent e) -> {
24        System.out.println("Process New");
25      });
26
27      btOpen.setOnAction((e) -> {
28        System.out.println("Process Open");
29      });
30
31      btSave.setOnAction(e -> {
32        System.out.println("Process Save");
33      });
34
35      btPrint.setOnAction(e -> System.out.println("Process Print"));
```

lambda handler

lambda handler

lambda handler

lambda handler

```
36
37       // Create a scene and place it in the stage
38       Scene scene = new Scene(hBox, 300, 50);
39       primaryStage.setTitle("LambdaHandlerDemo"); // Set title
40       primaryStage.setScene(scene); // Place the scene in the stage
41       primaryStage.show(); // Display the stage
42     }
43   }
```

The program creates four handlers using lambda expressions (lines 23–35). Using lambda expressions, the code is shorter and cleaner. As seen in this example, lambda expressions may have many variations. Line 23 uses a declared type. Line 27 uses an inferred type since the type can be determined by the compiler. Line 31 omits the parentheses for a single inferred type. Line 35 omits the braces for a single statement in the body.

You can handle events by defining handler classes using inner classes, anonymous inner classes, or lambda expressions. We recommend that you use lambda expressions because it produces a shorter, clearer, and cleaner code.

inner class, anonymous class, or Lambda?

Check Point

15.11 What is a lambda expression? What is the benefit of using lambda expressions for event handling? What is the syntax of a lambda expression?

15.12 What is a functional interface? Why is a functional interface required for a lambda expression?

15.13 Show the output of the following code:

```java
public class Test {
  public static void main(String[] args) {
    Test test = new Test();
    test.setAction1(() -> System.out.print("Action 1! "));
    test.setAction2(e -> System.out.print(e + " "));
    System.out.println(test.setAction3(e -> e * 2));
  }

  public void setAction1(T1 t) {
    t.m();
  }

  public void setAction2(T2 t) {
    t.m(4.5);
  }

  public double setAction3(T3 t) {
    return t.m(5.5);
  }
}

interface T1 {
  public void m();
}

interface T2 {
  public void m(Double d);
}

interface T3 {
  public double m(Double d);
}
```

15.7 Case Study: Loan Calculator

Key Point

This case study develops a loan calculator using event-driven programming with GUI controls.

Now, we will write the program for the loan-calculator problem presented at the beginning of this chapter. Here are the major steps in the program:

1. Create the user interface, as shown in Figure 15.9.

   a. Create a **GridPane**. Add labels, text fields, and button to the pane.

   b. Set the alignment of the button to the right.

2. Process the event.

   Create and register the handler for processing the button-clicking action event. The handler obtains the user input on the loan amount, interest rate, and number of years, computes the monthly and total payments, and displays the values in the text fields.

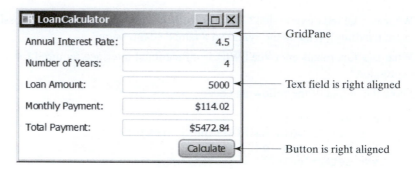

FIGURE 15.9 The program computes loan payments.

The complete program is given in Listing 15.6.

LISTING 15.6 LoanCalculator.java

```
1  import javafx.application.Application;
2  import javafx.geometry.Pos;
3  import javafx.geometry.HPos;
4  import javafx.scene.Scene;
5  import javafx.scene.control.Button;
6  import javafx.scene.control.Label;
7  import javafx.scene.control.TextField;
8  import javafx.scene.layout.GridPane;
9  import javafx.stage.Stage;
10
11 public class LoanCalculator extends Application {
12   private TextField tfAnnualInterestRate = new TextField();
13   private TextField tfNumberOfYears = new TextField();
14   private TextField tfLoanAmount = new TextField();
15   private TextField tfMonthlyPayment = new TextField();
16   private TextField tfTotalPayment = new TextField();
17   private Button btCalculate = new Button("Calculate");
18
19   @Override // Override the start method in the Application class
20   public void start(Stage primaryStage) {
21     // Create UI
22     GridPane gridPane = new GridPane();
```

text fields

button

create a grid pane

```
23        gridPane.setHgap(5);
24        gridPane.setVgap(5);
25        gridPane.add(new Label("Annual Interest Rate:"), 0, 0);        add to grid pane
26        gridPane.add(tfAnnualInterestRate, 1, 0);
27        gridPane.add(new Label("Number of Years:"), 0, 1);
28        gridPane.add(tfNumberOfYears, 1, 1);
29        gridPane.add(new Label("Loan Amount:"), 0, 2);
30        gridPane.add(tfLoanAmount, 1, 2);
31        gridPane.add(new Label("Monthly Payment:"), 0, 3);
32        gridPane.add(tfMonthlyPayment, 1, 3);
33        gridPane.add(new Label("Total Payment:"), 0, 4);
34        gridPane.add(tfTotalPayment, 1, 4);
35        gridPane.add(btCalculate, 1, 5);
36
37        // Set properties for UI
38        gridPane.setAlignment(Pos.CENTER);
39        tfAnnualInterestRate.setAlignment(Pos.BOTTOM_RIGHT);
40        tfNumberOfYears.setAlignment(Pos.BOTTOM_RIGHT);
41        tfLoanAmount.setAlignment(Pos.BOTTOM_RIGHT);
42        tfMonthlyPayment.setAlignment(Pos.BOTTOM_RIGHT);
43        tfTotalPayment.setAlignment(Pos.BOTTOM_RIGHT);
44        tfMonthlyPayment.setEditable(false);
45        tfTotalPayment.setEditable(false);
46        GridPane.setHalignment(btCalculate, HPos.RIGHT);
47
48        // Process events
49        btCalculate.setOnAction(e -> calculateLoanPayment());        register handler
50
51        // Create a scene and place it in the stage
52        Scene scene = new Scene(gridPane, 400, 250);
53        primaryStage.setTitle("LoanCalculator"); // Set title
54        primaryStage.setScene(scene); // Place the scene in the stage
55        primaryStage.show(); // Display the stage
56    }
57
58    private void calculateLoanPayment() {
59        // Get values from text fields
60        double interest =
61            Double.parseDouble(tfAnnualInterestRate.getText());        get input
62        int year = Integer.parseInt(tfNumberOfYears.getText());
63        double loanAmount =
64            Double.parseDouble(tfLoanAmount.getText());
65
66        // Create a loan object. Loan defined in Listing 10.2
67        Loan loan = new Loan(interest, year, loanAmount);        create loan
68
69        // Display monthly payment and total payment
70        tfMonthlyPayment.setText(String.format("$%.2f",        set result
71            loan.getMonthlyPayment()));
72        tfTotalPayment.setText(String.format("$%.2f",
73            loan.getTotalPayment()));
74    }
75 }
```

The user interface is created in the **start** method (lines 22–46). The button is the source of the event. A handler is created and registered with the button (line 49). The button handler invokes the **calculateLoanPayment()** method to get the interest rate (line 60), number of years (line 62), and loan amount (line 64). Invoking **tfAnnualInterestRate.getText()** returns the string text in the **tfAnnualInterestRate** text field. The **Loan** class is used for computing the loan payments. This class was introduced in Listing 10.2, Loan.java. Invoking **loan.getMonthlyPayment()** returns the monthly payment for the loan (line 71). The **String.format** method, introduced in Section 10.10.7, is used to format a number into a desirable format and returns it as a string (lines 70, 72). Invoking the **setText** method on a text field sets a string value in the text field.

15.8 Mouse Events

Key Point

*A **MouseEvent** is fired whenever a mouse button is pressed, released, clicked, moved, or dragged on a node or a scene.*

The **MouseEvent** object captures the event, such as the number of clicks associated with it, the location (the *x*- and *y*-coordinates) of the mouse, or which mouse button was pressed, as shown in Figure 15.10.

javafx.scene.input.MouseEvent	
+getButton(): MouseButton	Indicates which mouse button has been clicked.
+getClickCount(): int	Returns the number of mouse clicks associated with this event.
+getX(): double	Returns the *x*-coordinate of the mouse point in the event source node.
+getY(): double	Returns the *y*-coordinate of the mouse point in the event source node.
+getSceneX(): double	Returns the *x*-coordinate of the mouse point in the scene.
+getSceneY(): double	Returns the *y*-coordinate of the mouse point in the scene.
+getScreenX(): double	Returns the *x*-coordinate of the mouse point in the screen.
+getScreenY(): double	Returns the *y*-coordinate of the mouse point in the screen.
+isAltDown(): boolean	Returns true if the Alt key is pressed on this event.
+isControlDown(): boolean	Returns true if the Control key is pressed on this event.
+isMetaDown(): boolean	Returns true if the mouse Meta button is pressed on this event.
+isShiftDown(): boolean	Returns true if the Shift key is pressed on this event.

FIGURE 15.10 The **MouseEvent** class encapsulates information for mouse events.

Four constants—**PRIMARY**, **SECONDARY**, **MIDDLE**, and **NONE**—are defined in **MouseButton** to indicate the left, right, middle, and none mouse buttons. You can use the **getButton()** method to detect which button is pressed. For example, **getButton() == MouseButton.SECONDARY** indicates that the right button was pressed.

detect mouse buttons

The mouse events are listed in Table 15.1. To demonstrate using mouse events, we give an example that displays a message in a pane and enables the message to be moved using a mouse. The message moves as the mouse is dragged, and it is always displayed at the mouse point. Listing 15.7 gives the program. A sample run of the program is shown in Figure 15.11.

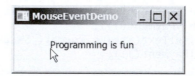

FIGURE 15.11 You can move the message by dragging the mouse.

LISTING 15.7 MouseEventDemo.java

VideoNote

Move message using the mouse

```java
1  import javafx.application.Application;
2  import javafx.scene.Scene;
3  import javafx.scene.layout.Pane;
```

```
 4   import javafx.scene.text.Text;
 5   import javafx.stage.Stage;
 6
 7   public class MouseEventDemo extends Application {
 8     @Override // Override the start method in the Application class
 9     public void start(Stage primaryStage) {
10       // Create a pane and set its properties
11       Pane pane = new Pane();                                        create a pane
12       Text text = new Text(20, 20, "Programming is fun");            create a text
13       pane.getChildren().addAll(text);                              add text to a pane
14       text.setOnMouseDragged(e -> {                                 lambda handler
15         text.setX(e.getX());                                       reset text position
16         text.setY(e.getY());
17       });
18
19       // Create a scene and place it in the stage
20       Scene scene = new Scene(pane, 300, 100);
21       primaryStage.setTitle("MouseEventDemo"); // Set the stage title
22       primaryStage.setScene(scene); // Place the scene in the stage
23       primaryStage.show(); // Display the stage
24     }
25   }
```

Each node or scene can fire mouse events. The program creates a **Text** (line 12) and registers a handler to handle move dragged event (line 14). Whenever a mouse is dragged, the text's *x*- and *y*-coordinates are set to the mouse position (lines 15 and 16).

15.14 What method do you use to get the mouse-point position for a mouse event?

15.15 What methods do you use to register a handler for a mouse pressed, released, clicked, entered, exited, moved and dragged event?

Check Point

15.9 Key Events

A KeyEvent is fired whenever a key is pressed, released, or typed on a node or a scene.

Key Point

Key events enable the use of the keys to control and perform actions or get input from the keyboard. The **KeyEvent** object describes the nature of the event (namely, that a key has been pressed, released, or typed) and the value of the key, as shown in Figure 15.12.

javafx.scene.input.KeyEvent	
+getCharacter(): String	Returns the character associated with the key in this event.
+getCode(): KeyCode	Returns the key code associated with the key in this event.
+getText(): String	Returns a string describing the key code.
+isAltDown(): boolean	Returns true if the Alt key is pressed on this event.
+isControlDown(): boolean	Returns true if the Control key is pressed on this event.
+isMetaDown(): boolean	Returns true if the mouse Meta button is pressed on this event.
+isShiftDown(): boolean	Returns true if the Shift key is pressed on this event.

FIGURE 15.12 The **KeyEvent** class encapsulates information about key events.

Every key event has an associated code that is returned by the **getCode()** method in **KeyEvent**. The *key codes* are constants defined in **KeyCode**. Table 15.2 lists some constants. **KeyCode** is an **enum** type. For use of **enum** types, see Appendix I. For the key-pressed and key code

key-released events, **getCode()** returns the value as defined in the table, **getText()** returns a string that describes the key code, and **getCharacter()** returns an empty string. For the key-typed event, **getCode()** returns **UNDEFINED** and **getCharacter()** returns the Unicode character or a sequence of characters associated with the key-typed event.

TABLE 15.2 KeyCode Constants

Constant	Description	Constant	Description
HOME	The Home key	CONTROL	The Control key
END	The End key	SHIFT	The Shift key
PAGE_UP	The Page Up key	BACK_SPACE	The Backspace key
PAGE_DOWN	The Page Down key	CAPS	The Caps Lock key
UP	The up-arrow key	NUM_LOCK	The Num Lock key
DOWN	The down-arrow key	ENTER	The Enter key
LEFT	The left-arrow key	UNDEFINED	The **keyCode** unknown
RIGHT	The right-arrow key	F1 to F12	The function keys from F1 to F12
ESCAPE	The Esc key	0 to 9	The number keys from 0 to 9
TAB	The Tab key	A to Z	The letter keys from A to Z

The program in Listing 15.8 displays a user-input character. The user can move the character up, down, left, and right, using the up, down, left, and right arrow keys. Figure 15.13 contains a sample run of the program.

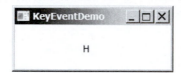

FIGURE 15.13 The program responds to key events by displaying a character and moving it up, down, left, or right.

LISTING 15.8 KeyEventDemo.java

```java
1  import javafx.application.Application;
2  import javafx.scene.Scene;
3  import javafx.scene.layout.Pane;
4  import javafx.scene.text.Text;
5  import javafx.stage.Stage;
6
7  public class KeyEventDemo extends Application {
8    @Override // Override the start method in the Application class
9    public void start(Stage primaryStage) {
10     // Create a pane and set its properties
11     Pane pane = new Pane();
12     Text text = new Text(20, 20, "A");
13
14     pane.getChildren().add(text);
15     text.setOnKeyPressed(e -> {
16       switch (e.getCode()) {
17         case DOWN: text.setY(text.getY() + 10); break;
18         case UP:  text.setY(text.getY() - 10); break;
19         case LEFT: text.setX(text.getX() - 10); break;
20         case RIGHT: text.setX(text.getX() + 10); break;
```

create a pane

register handler
get the key pressed
move a character

```
21             default:
22               if (Character.isLetterOrDigit(e.getText().charAt(0)))
23                 text.setText(e.getText());                              set a new character
24         }
25       });
26
27       // Create a scene and place it in the stage
28       Scene scene = new Scene(pane);
29       primaryStage.setTitle("KeyEventDemo"); // Set the stage title
30       primaryStage.setScene(scene); // Place the scene in the stage
31       primaryStage.show(); // Display the stage
32
33       text.requestFocus(); // text is focused to receive key input      request focus on text
34     }
35   }
```

The program creates a pane (line 11), creates a text (line 12), and places the text into the pane (line 14). The text registers the handler for the key-pressed event in lines 15–25. When a key is pressed, the handler is invoked. The program uses **e.getCode()** (line 16) to obtain the key code and **e.getText()** (line 23) to get the character for the key. When a nonarrow key is pressed, the character is displayed (lines 22 and 23). When an arrow key is pressed, the character moves in the direction indicated by the arrow key (lines 17–20). Note that in a switch statement for an enum type value, the cases are for the enum constants (lines 16–24). The constants are unqualified. For example, using **KeyCode.DOWN** in the case clause would be wrong (see Appendix I).

Only a focused node can receive **KeyEvent**. Invoking **requestFocus()** on **text** enables   requestFocus()
text to receive key input (line 33). This method must be invoked after the stage is displayed.

We can now add more control for our **ControlCircle** example in Listing 15.3 to increase/decrease the circle radius by clicking the left/right mouse button or by pressing the U and D keys. The new program is given in Listing 15.9.

LISTING 15.9 ControlCircleWithMouseAndKey.java

```
1   import javafx.application.Application;
2   import javafx.geometry.Pos;
3   import javafx.scene.Scene;
4   import javafx.scene.control.Button;
5   import javafx.scene.input.KeyCode;
6   import javafx.scene.input.MouseButton;
7   import javafx.scene.layout.HBox;
8   import javafx.scene.layout.BorderPane;
9   import javafx.stage.Stage;
10
11  public class ControlCircleWithMouseAndKey extends Application {
12    private CirclePane circlePane = new CirclePane();
13
14    @Override // Override the start method in the Application class
15    public void start(Stage primaryStage) {
16      // Hold two buttons in an HBox
17      HBox hBox = new HBox();
18      hBox.setSpacing(10);
19      hBox.setAlignment(Pos.CENTER);
20      Button btEnlarge = new Button("Enlarge");
21      Button btShrink = new Button("Shrink");
22      hBox.getChildren().add(btEnlarge);
23      hBox.getChildren().add(btShrink);
24
25      // Create and register the handler
26      btEnlarge.setOnAction(e -> circlePane.enlarge());          button handler
27      btShrink.setOnAction(e -> circlePane.shrink());
```

```
28
29      circlePane.setOnMouseClicked(e -> {
30        if (e.getButton() == MouseButton.PRIMARY) {
31          circlePane.enlarge();
32        }
33        else if (e.getButton() == MouseButton.SECONDARY) {
34          circlePane.shrink();
35        }
36      });
37
38      circlePane.setOnKeyPressed(e -> {
39        if (e.getCode() == KeyCode.U) {
40          circlePane.enlarge();
41        }
42        else if (e.getCode() == KeyCode.D) {
43          circlePane.shrink();
44        }
45      });
46
47      BorderPane borderPane = new BorderPane();
48      borderPane.setCenter(circlePane);
49      borderPane.setBottom(hBox);
50      BorderPane.setAlignment(hBox, Pos.CENTER);
51
52      // Create a scene and place it in the stage
53      Scene scene = new Scene(borderPane, 200, 150);
54      primaryStage.setTitle("ControlCircle"); // Set the stage title
55      primaryStage.setScene(scene); // Place the scene in the stage
56      primaryStage.show(); // Display the stage
57
58      circlePane.requestFocus(); // Request focus on circlePane
59    }
60  }
```

mouse-click handler

key-pressed handler
U key pressed

D key pressed

request focus

The **CirclePane** class (line 12) is already defined in Listing 15.3 and can be reused in this program.

A handler for mouse clicked events is created in lines 29–36. If the left mouse button is clicked, the circle is enlarged (lines 30–32); if the right mouse button is clicked, the circle is shrunk (lines 33–35).

mouse clicked event

A handler for key pressed events is created in lines 38–45. If the U key is pressed, the circle is enlarged (lines 39–41); if the D key is pressed, the circle is shrunk (lines 42–44).

key pressed event

Invoking **requestFocus()** on **circlePane** (line 58) makes **circlePane** to receive key events. Note that after you click a button, **circlePane** is no longer focused. To fix the problem, invoke **reuquestFocus()** on **circlePane** again after each button is clicked.

requestFocus()

15.16 What methods do you use to register handlers for key pressed, key released, and key typed events? In which classes are these methods defined? (See Table 15.1)

15.17 What method do you use to get the key character for a key-typed event? What method do you use to get the key code for a key-pressed or key-released event?

15.18 How do you set focus on a node so it can listen for key events?

15.10 Listeners for Observable Objects

You can add a listener to process a value change in an observable object.

Key Point

An instance of **Observable** is known as an *observable object*, which contains the **addListener(InvalidationListener listener)** method for adding a listener. The listener class must implement the **InvalidationListener** interface to override the **invalidated(Observable o)** method for handling the value change. Once the value is changed in the **Observable** object, the listener is notified by invoking its **invalidated(Observable o)** method. Every binding property is an instance of **Observable**. Listing 15.10 gives an example of observing and handling a change in a **DoubleProperty** object **balance**.

observable object

LISTING 15.10 ObservablePropertyDemo.java

```
1  import javafx.beans.InvalidationListener;
2  import javafx.beans.Observable;
3  import javafx.beans.property.DoubleProperty;
4  import javafx.beans.property.SimpleDoubleProperty;
5
6  public class ObservablePropertyDemo {
7    public static void main(String[] args) {
8      DoubleProperty balance = new SimpleDoubleProperty();
9      balance.addListener(new InvalidationListener() {
10       public void invalidated(Observable ov) {
11         System.out.println("The new value is " +
12           balance.doubleValue());
13       }
14     });
15
16     balance.set(4.5);
17   }
18 }
```

observable property
add listener
handle change

```
The new value is 4.5
```

When line 16 is executed, it causes a change in balance, which notifies the listener by invoking the listener's **invalidated** method.

Note that the anonymous inner class in lines 9–14 can be simplified using a lambda expression as follows:

```
balance.addListener(ov -> {
  System.out.println("The new value is " +
    balance.doubleValue());
});
```

Recall that in Listing 14.20 DisplayClock.java, the clock pane size is not changed when you resize the window. The problem can be fixed by adding a listener to change the clock pane size and register the listener to the window's width and height properties, as shown in Listing 15.11.

LISTING 15.11 DisplayResizableClock.java

```
1  import javafx.application.Application;
2  import javafx.geometry.Pos;
3  import javafx.stage.Stage;
4  import javafx.scene.Scene;
5  import javafx.scene.control.Label;
6  import javafx.scene.layout.BorderPane;
7
8  public class DisplayResizableClock extends Application {
9    @Override // Override the start method in the Application class
10   public void start(Stage primaryStage) {
11     // Create a clock and a label
12     ClockPane clock = new ClockPane();
13     String timeString = clock.getHour() + ":" + clock.getMinute()
14       + ":" + clock.getSecond();
```

```
15        Label lblCurrentTime = new Label(timeString);
16
17        // Place clock and label in border pane
18        BorderPane pane = new BorderPane();
19        pane.setCenter(clock);
20        pane.setBottom(lblCurrentTime);
21        BorderPane.setAlignment(lblCurrentTime, Pos.TOP_CENTER);
22
23        // Create a scene and place it in the stage
24        Scene scene = new Scene(pane, 250, 250);
25        primaryStage.setTitle("DisplayClock"); // Set the stage title
26        primaryStage.setScene(scene); // Place the scene in the stage
27        primaryStage.show(); // Display the stage
28
```

create a listener
set a new width for clock

```
29        pane.widthProperty().addListener(ov ->
30          clock.setW(pane.getWidth())
31        );
32
```

create a listener
set a new height for clock

```
33        pane.heightProperty().addListener(ov ->
34          clock.setH(pane.getHeight())
35        );
36    }
37 }
```

The program is identical to Listing 14.19 except that you added the code in lines 29–35 to register listeners for resizing the clock pane upon a change of the width or height of the scene. The code ensures that the clock pane size is synchronized with the scene size.

15.19 What would happen if you replace **pane** with **scene** or **primaryStage** in lines 29 and 33?

15.11 Animation

*JavaFX provides the **Animation** class with the core functionality for all animations.*

Suppose you want to write a program that animates a rising flag, as shown in Figure 15.14. How do you accomplish the task? There are several ways to program this. An effective one is to use the subclasses of the JavaFX **Animation** class, which is the subject of this section.

VideoNote
Animate a rising flag

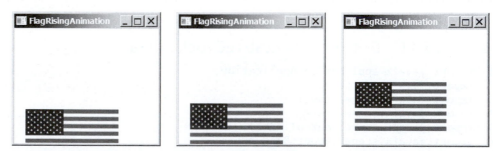

FIGURE 15.14 The animation simulates a flag rising.

The abstract **Animation** class provides the core functionalities for animations in JavaFX, as shown in Figure 15.15. Many concrete subclasses of **Animation** are provided in JavaFX. This section introduces **PathTransition**, **FadeTransition** and **Timeline**.

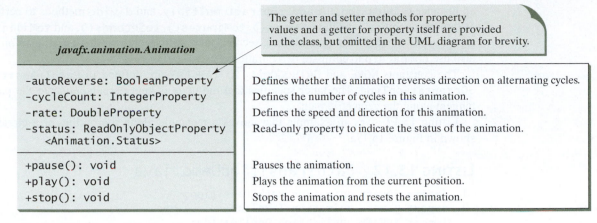

FIGURE 15.15 The abstract **Animation** class is the root class for JavaFX animations.

The **autoReverse** is a Boolean property that indicates whether an animation will reverse its direction on the next cycle. The **cycleCount** indicates the number of the cycles for the animation. You can use the constant **Timeline.INDEFINTE** to indicate an indefinite number of cycles. The **rate** defines the speed of the animation. A negative rate value indicates the opposite direction for the animation. The **status** is a read-only property that indicates the status of the animation (**Animation.Status.PAUSED**, **Animation.Status.RUNNING**, and **Animation.Status.STOPPED**). The methods **pause()**, **play()**, and **stop()** pauses, plays, and stops an animation.

15.11.1 PathTransition

The **PathTransition** class animates the the moves of a node along a path from one end to the other over a given time. **PathTransition** is a subtype of **Animation**. The UML class diagram for the class is shown in Figure 15.16.

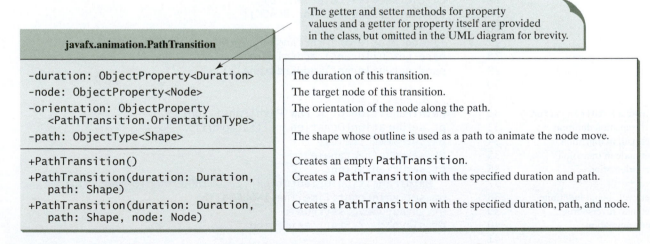

FIGURE 15.16 The **PathTransition** class defines an animation for a node along a path.

The **Duration** class defines a duration of time. It is an immutable class. The class defines constants **INDEFINTE**, **ONE**, **UNKNOWN**, and **ZERO** to represent an indefinite duration, 1 milliseconds, unknow, and 0 duration. You can use **new Duration(double millis)** to create an instance of **Duration**, the **add**, **subtract**, **multiply**, and **divide** methods to perform arithmetic operations, and the **toHours()**, **toMinutes()**, **toSeconds()**, and **toMillis()** to return the number of hours, minutes, seconds, and milliseconds in this duration. You can also use **compareTo** to compare two durations.

The constants **NONE** and **ORTHOGONAL_TO_TANGENT** are defined in **PathTransition .OrientationType**. The latter specifies that the node is kept perpendicular to the path's tangent along the geometric path.

Listing 15.12 gives an example that moves a rectangle along the outline of a circle, as shown in Figure 15.17a.

LISTING 15.12 PathTransitionDemo.java

```java
1   import javafx.animation.PathTransition;
2   import javafx.animation.Timeline;
3   import javafx.application.Application;
4   import javafx.scene.Scene;
5   import javafx.scene.layout.Pane;
6   import javafx.scene.paint.Color;
7   import javafx.scene.shape.Rectangle;
8   import javafx.scene.shape.Circle;
9   import javafx.stage.Stage;
10  import javafx.util.Duration;
11
12  public class PathTransitionDemo extends Application {
13    @Override // Override the start method in the Application class
14    public void start(Stage primaryStage) {
15      // Create a pane
16      Pane pane = new Pane();
17
18      // Create a rectangle
19      Rectangle rectangle = new Rectangle (0, 0, 25, 50);
20      rectangle.setFill(Color.ORANGE);
21
22      // Create a circle
23      Circle circle = new Circle(125, 100, 50);
24      circle.setFill(Color.WHITE);
25      circle.setStroke(Color.BLACK);
26
27      // Add circle and rectangle to the pane
28      pane.getChildren().add(circle);
29      pane.getChildren().add(rectangle);
30
31      // Create a path transition
32      PathTransition pt = new PathTransition();
33      pt.setDuration(Duration.millis(4000));
34      pt.setPath(circle);
35      pt.setNode(rectangle);
36      pt.setOrientation(
37        PathTransition.OrientationType.ORTHOGONAL_TO_TANGENT);
38      pt.setCycleCount(Timeline.INDEFINITE);
39      pt.setAutoReverse(true);
40      pt.play(); // Start animation
41
42      circle.setOnMousePressed(e -> pt.pause());
43      circle.setOnMouseReleased(e -> pt.play());
44
45      // Create a scene and place it in the stage
46      Scene scene = new Scene(pane, 250, 200);
47      primaryStage.setTitle("PathTransitionDemo"); // Set the stage title
```

Margin notes:
create a pane (16)
create a rectangle (19)
create a circle (23)
add circle to pane (28)
add rectangle to pane (29)
create a PathTransition (32)
set transition duration (33)
set path in transition (34)
set node in transition (35)
set orientation (36)
set cycle count indefinite (38)
set auto reverse true (39)
play animation (40)
pause animation (42)
resume animation (43)

```
48      primaryStage.setScene(scene); // Place the scene in the stage
49      primaryStage.show(); // Display the stage
50    }
51  }
```

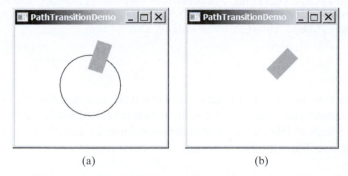

(a)   (b)

FIGURE 15.17 The `PathTransition` animates a rectangle moving along the circle.

The program creates a pane (line 16), a rectangle (line 19), and a circle (line 23). The circle and rectangle are placed in the pane (lines 28 and 29). If the circle was not placed in the pane, you will see the screen shot as shown in Figure 15.17b.

The program creates a path transition (line 32), sets its duration to 4 seconds for one cycle of animation (line 33), sets circle as the path (line 34), sets rectangle as the node (line 35), and sets the orientation to orthogonal to tangent (line 36).

The cycle count is set to indefinite (line 38) so the animation continues forever. The auto reverse is set to true (line 39) so that the direction of the move is reversed in the alternating cycle. The program starts animation by invoking the `play()` method (line 40).

If the `pause()` method is replaced by the `stop()` method in line 42, the animation will start over from the beginning when it restarts.

Listing 15.13 gives the program that animates a flag rising, as shown in Figure 15.14.

LISTING 15.13 FlagRisingAnimation.java

```
1   import javafx.animation.PathTransition;
2   import javafx.application.Application;
3   import javafx.scene.Scene;
4   import javafx.scene.image.ImageView;
5   import javafx.scene.layout.Pane;
6   import javafx.scene.shape.Line;
7   import javafx.stage.Stage;
8   import javafx.util.Duration;
9
10  public class FlagRisingAnimation extends Application {
11    @Override // Override the start method in the Application class
12    public void start(Stage primaryStage) {
13      // Create a pane
14      Pane pane = new Pane();                                          create a pane
15
16      // Add an image view and add it to pane
17      ImageView imageView = new ImageView("image/us.gif");            create an image view
18      pane.getChildren().add(imageView);                              add image view to pane
19
20      // Create a path transition
21      PathTransition pt = new PathTransition(Duration.millis(10000),  create a path transition
```

```
set cycle count     22              new Line(100, 200, 100, 0), imageView);
play animation      23          pt.setCycleCount(5);
                    24          pt.play(); // Start animation
                    25
                    26          // Create a scene and place it in the stage
                    27          Scene scene = new Scene(pane, 250, 200);
                    28          primaryStage.setTitle("FlagRisingAnimation"); // Set the stage title
                    29          primaryStage.setScene(scene); // Place the scene in the stage
                    30          primaryStage.show(); // Display the stage
                    31      }
                    32  }
```

The program creates a pane (line 14), an image view from an image file (line 17), and places the image view to the page (line 18). A path transition is created with duration of 10 seconds using a line as a path and the image view as the node (lines 21 and 22). The image view will move along the line. Since the line is not placed in the scene, you will not see the line in the window.

The cycle count is set to 5 (line 23) so that the animation is repeated five times.

15.11.2 FadeTransition

The **FadeTransition** class animates the change of the opacity in a node over a given time. **FadeTransition** is a subtype of **Animation**. The UML class diagram for the class is shown in Figure 15.18.

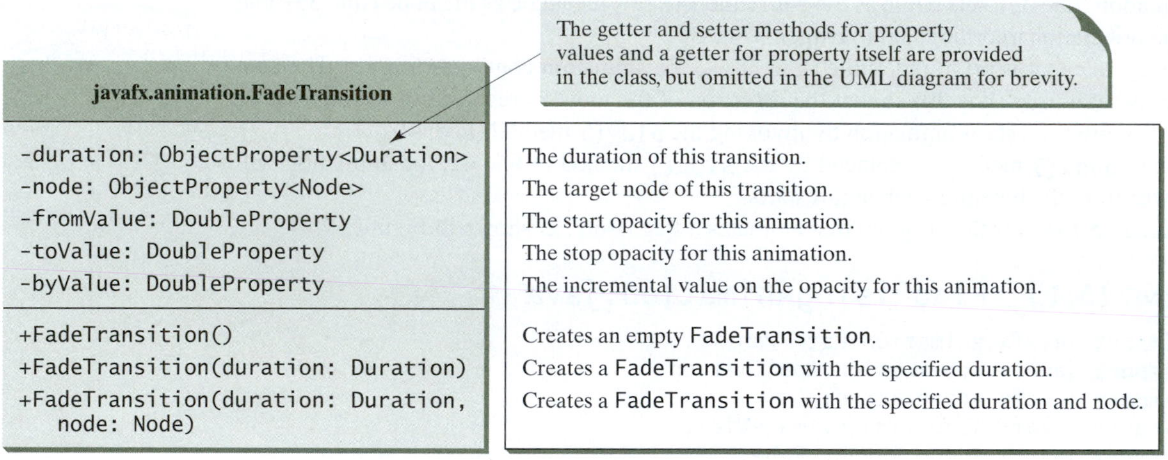

The getter and setter methods for property values and a getter for property itself are provided in the class, but omitted in the UML diagram for brevity.

javafx.animation.FadeTransition

-duration: ObjectProperty<Duration>
-node: ObjectProperty<Node>
-fromValue: DoubleProperty
-toValue: DoubleProperty
-byValue: DoubleProperty

+FadeTransition()
+FadeTransition(duration: Duration)
+FadeTransition(duration: Duration, node: Node)

The duration of this transition.
The target node of this transition.
The start opacity for this animation.
The stop opacity for this animation.
The incremental value on the opacity for this animation.

Creates an empty FadeTransition.
Creates a FadeTransition with the specified duration.
Creates a FadeTransition with the specified duration and node.

FIGURE 15.18 The **FadeTransition** class defines an animation for the change of opacity in a node.

Listing 15.14 gives an example that applies a fade transition to the filled color in an ellipse, as shown in Figure 15.19.

LISTING 15.14 FadeTransitionDemo.java

```
1  import javafx.animation.FadeTransition;
2  import javafx.animation.Timeline;
3  import javafx.application.Application;
4  import javafx.scene.Scene;
5  import javafx.scene.layout.Pane;
6  import javafx.scene.paint.Color;
7  import javafx.scene.shape.Ellipse;
8  import javafx.stage.Stage;
```

```
 9  import javafx.util.Duration;
10
11  public class FadeTransitionDemo extends Application {
12    @Override // Override the start method in the Application class
13    public void start(Stage primaryStage) {
14      // Place an ellipse to the pane
15      Pane pane = new Pane();                                           create a pane
16      Ellipse ellipse = new Ellipse(10, 10, 100, 50);                   create an ellipse
17      ellipse.setFill(Color.RED);                                       set ellipse fill color
18      ellipse.setStroke(Color.BLACK);                                   set ellipse stroke color
19      ellipse.centerXProperty().bind(pane.widthProperty().divide(2));   bind ellipse properties
20      ellipse.centerYProperty().bind(pane.heightProperty().divide(2));
21      ellipse.radiusXProperty().bind(
22        pane.widthProperty().multiply(0.4));
23      ellipse.radiusYProperty().bind(
24        pane.heightProperty().multiply(0.4));
25      pane.getChildren().add(ellipse);                                  add ellipse to pane
26
27      // Apply a fade transition to ellipse
28      FadeTransition ft =                                               create a FadeTransition
29        new FadeTransition(Duration.millis(3000), ellipse);
30      ft.setFromValue(1.0);                                             set start opaque value
31      ft.setToValue(0.1);                                               set end opaque value
32      ft.setCycleCount(Timeline.INDEFINITE);                            set cycle count
33      ft.setAutoReverse(true);                                          set auto reverse true
34      ft.play(); // Start animation                                     play animation
35
36      // Control animation
37      ellipse.setOnMousePressed(e -> ft.pause());                       pause animation
38      ellipse.setOnMouseReleased(e -> ft.play());                       resume animation
39
40      // Create a scene and place it in the stage
41      Scene scene = new Scene(pane, 200, 150);
42      primaryStage.setTitle("FadeTransitionDemo"); // Set the stage title
43      primaryStage.setScene(scene); // Place the scene in the stage
44      primaryStage.show(); // Display the stage
45    }
46  }
```

FIGURE 15.19   The `FadeTransition` animates the change of opacity in the ellipse.

The program creates a pane (line 15) and an ellipse (line 16) and places the ellipse into the pane (line 25). The ellipse's `centerX`, `centerY`, `radiusX`, and `radiusY` properties are bound to the pane's size (lines 19–24).

A fade transition is created with a duration of 3 seconds for the ellipse (line 29). It sets the start opaque to 1.0 (line 30) and the stop opaque 0.1 (line 31). The cycle count is set to infinite so the animation is repeated indefinitely (line 32). When the mouse is pressed, the animation is paused (line 37). When the mouse is released, the animation resumes from where it was paused (line 38).

15.11.3 **Timeline**

PathTransition and **FadeTransition** define specialized animations. The **Timeline** class can be used to program any animation using one or more **KeyFrame**s. Each **KeyFrame** is executed sequentially at a specified time interval. **Timeline** inherits from **Animation**. You can construct a **Timeline** using the constructor **new Timeline(KeyFrame... keyframes)**. A **KeyFrame** can be constructed using

```
new KeyFrame(Duration duration, EventHandler<ActionEvent> onFinished)
```

The handler **onFinished** is called when the duration for the key frame is elapsed.

Listing 15.15 gives an example that displays a flashing text, as shown in Figure 15.20. The text is on and off alternating to animate flashing.

VideoNote

Flashing text

LISTING 15.15 TimelineDemo.java

```java
 1  import javafx.animation.Animation;
 2  import javafx.application.Application;
 3  import javafx.stage.Stage;
 4  import javafx.animation.KeyFrame;
 5  import javafx.animation.Timeline;
 6  import javafx.event.ActionEvent;
 7  import javafx.event.EventHandler;
 8  import javafx.scene.Scene;
 9  import javafx.scene.layout.StackPane;
10  import javafx.scene.paint.Color;
11  import javafx.scene.text.Text;
12  import javafx.util.Duration;
13
14  public class TimelineDemo extends Application {
15    @Override // Override the start method in the Application class
16    public void start(Stage primaryStage) {
17      StackPane pane = new StackPane();
18      Text text = new Text(20, 50, "Programming is fun");
19      text.setFill(Color.RED);
20      pane.getChildren().add(text); // Place text into the stack pane
21
22      // Create a handler for changing text
23      EventHandler<ActionEvent> eventHandler = e -> {
24        if (text.getText().length() != 0) {
25          text.setText("");
26        }
27        else {
28          text.setText("Programming is fun");
29        }
30      };
31
32      // Create an animation for alternating text
33      Timeline animation = new Timeline(
34        new KeyFrame(Duration.millis(500), eventHandler));
35      animation.setCycleCount(Timeline.INDEFINITE);
36      animation.play(); // Start animation
37
38      // Pause and resume animation
39      text.setOnMouseClicked(e -> {
40        if (animation.getStatus() == Animation.Status.PAUSED) {
41          animation.play();
42        }
43        else {
44          animation.pause();
```

Margin notes:
create a stack pane (17)
create a text (18)
add text to pane (20)
handler for changing text (23)
set text empty (25)
set text (28)
create a Timeline (33)
create a KeyFrame for handler (34)
set cycle count indefinite (35)
play animation (36)
resume animation (41)
pause animation (44)

```
45         }
46       });
47
48       // Create a scene and place it in the stage
49       Scene scene = new Scene(pane, 250, 250);
50       primaryStage.setTitle("TimelineDemo"); // Set the stage title
51       primaryStage.setScene(scene); // Place the scene in the stage
52       primaryStage.show(); // Display the stage
53     }
54 }
```

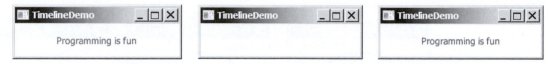

FIGURE 15.20   The handler is called to set the text to Programming is fun or empty in turn.

The program creates a stack pane (line 17) and a text (line 18) and places the text into the pane (line 20). A handler is created to change the text to empty (lines 24–26) if it is not empty or to **Progrmming is fun** if it is empty (lines 27–29). A **KeyFrame** is created to run an action event in every half second (line 34). A **Timeline** animation is created to contain a key frame (lines 33 and 34). The animation is set to run indefinitely (line 35).

The mouse clicked event is set for the text (lines 39–46). A mouse click on the text resumes the animation if the animation is paused (lines 40–42), and a mouse click on the text pauses the animation if the animation is running (lines 43–45).

In Section 14.12, Case Study: The **ClockPane** Class, you drew a clock to show the current time. The clock does not tick after it is displayed. What can you do to make the clock display a new current time every second? The key to making the clock tick is to repaint it every second with a new current time. You can use a **Timeline** to control the repainting of the clock with the code in Listing 15.16. The sample run of the program is shown in Figure 15.21.

LISTING 15.16   ClockAnimation.java

```
1  import javafx.application.Application;
2  import javafx.stage.Stage;
3  import javafx.animation.KeyFrame;
4  import javafx.animation.Timeline;
5  import javafx.event.ActionEvent;
6  import javafx.event.EventHandler;
7  import javafx.scene.Scene;
8  import javafx.util.Duration;
9
10 public class ClockAnimation extends Application {
11   @Override // Override the start method in the Application class
12   public void start(Stage primaryStage) {
13     ClockPane clock = new ClockPane(); // Create a clock          create a clock
14
15     // Create a handler for animation
16     EventHandler<ActionEvent> eventHandler = e -> {               create a handler
17       clock.setCurrentTime(); // Set a new clock time
18     };
19
20     // Create an animation for a running clock
21     Timeline animation = new Timeline(                            create a time line
```

create a key frame
set cycle count indefinite
play animation

```
22              new KeyFrame(Duration.millis(1000), eventHandler));
23          animation.setCycleCount(Timeline.INDEFINITE);
24          animation.play(); // Start animation
25
26          // Create a scene and place it in the stage
27          Scene scene = new Scene(clock, 250, 50);
28          primaryStage.setTitle("ClockAnimation"); // Set the stage title
29          primaryStage.setScene(scene); // Place the scene in the stage
30          primaryStage.show(); // Display the stage
31      }
32  }
```

FIGURE 15.21 A live clock is displayed in the window.

The program creates an instance **clock** of **ClockPane** for displaying a clock (line 13). The **ClockPane** class is defined in Listing 14.21. The clock is placed in the scene in line 27. An event handler is created for setting the current time in the clock (lines 16–18). This handler is called every second in the key frame in the time line animation (lines 21–24). So the clock time is updated every second in the animation.

15.20 How do you set the cycle count of an animation to infinite? How do you auto reverse an animation? How do you start, pause, and stop an animation?

15.21 Are **PathTransition**, **FadeTransition**, and **Timeline** a subtype of **Animation**?

15.22 How do you create a **PathTransition**? How do you create a **FadeTransition**? How do you create a **Timeline**?

15.23 How do you create a **KeyFrame**?

15.12 Case Study: Bouncing Ball

This section presents an animation that displays a ball bouncing in a pane.

The program uses **Timeline** to animation ball bouncing, as shown in Figure 15.22.

FIGURE 15.22 A ball is bouncing in a pane.

Here are the major steps to write this program:

1. Define a subclass of **Pane** named **BallPane** to display a ball bouncing, as shown in Listing 15.17.

2. Define a subclass of **Application** named **BounceBallControl** to control the bouncing ball with mouse actions, as shown in Listing 15.18. The animation pauses when the mouse is pressed and resumes when the mouse is released. Pressing the UP and DOWN arrow keys increases/decreases animation speed.

The relationship among these classes is shown in Figure 15.23.

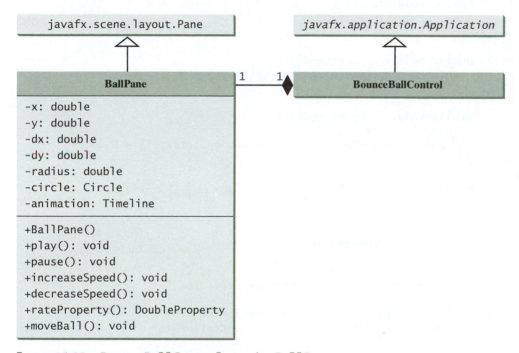

FIGURE 15.23 **BounceBallControl** contains **BallPane**.

LISTING 15.17 BallPane.java

```
1  import javafx.animation.KeyFrame;
2  import javafx.animation.Timeline;
3  import javafx.beans.property.DoubleProperty;
4  import javafx.scene.layout.Pane;
5  import javafx.scene.paint.Color;
6  import javafx.scene.shape.Circle;
7  import javafx.util.Duration;
8
9  public class BallPane extends Pane {
10     public final double radius = 20;
11     private double x = radius, y = radius;
12     private double dx = 1, dy = 1;
13     private Circle circle = new Circle(x, y, radius);
14     private Timeline animation;
15
16     public BallPane() {
17        circle.setFill(Color.GREEN); // Set ball color
18        getChildren().add(circle); // Place a ball into this pane
```

```
19
20      // Create an animation for moving the ball
21      animation = new Timeline(
22        new KeyFrame(Duration.millis(50), e -> moveBall()));
23      animation.setCycleCount(Timeline.INDEFINITE);
24      animation.play(); // Start animation
25    }
26
27    public void play() {
28      animation.play();
29    }
30
31    public void pause() {
32      animation.pause();
33    }
34
35    public void increaseSpeed() {
36      animation.setRate(animation.getRate() + 0.1);
37    }
38
39    public void decreaseSpeed() {
40      animation.setRate(
41        animation.getRate() > 0 ? animation.getRate() - 0.1 : 0);
42    }
43
44    public DoubleProperty rateProperty() {
45      return animation.rateProperty();
46    }
47
48    protected void moveBall() {
49      // Check boundaries
50      if (x < radius || x > getWidth() - radius) {
51        dx *= -1; // Change ball move direction
52      }
53      if (y < radius || y > getHeight() - radius) {
54        dy *= -1; // Change ball move direction
55      }
56
57      // Adjust ball position
58      x += dx;
59      y += dy;
60      circle.setCenterX(x);
61      circle.setCenterY(y);
62    }
63  }
```

create animation (line 21)
keep animation running (line 23)
start animation (line 24)
play animation (lines 27–29)
pause animation (lines 31–33)
increase animation rate (line 36)
decrease animation rate (lines 40–41)
change horizontal direction (line 51)
change verticaal direction (line 54)
set new ball position (lines 58–59)

BallPane extends **Pane** to display a moving ball (line 9). An instance of **Timeline** is created to control animation (lines 21 and 22). This instance contains a **KeyFrame** object that invokes the **moveBall()** method at a fixed rate. The **moveBall()** method moves the ball to simulate animation. The center of the ball is at (**x, y**), which changes to (**x + dx, y + dy**) on the next move (lines 58–61). When the ball is out of the horizontal boundary, the sign of **dx** is changed (from positive to negative or vice versa) (lines 50–52). This causes the ball to change its horizontal movement direction. When the ball is out of the vertical boundary, the sign of **dy** is changed (from positive to negative or vice versa) (lines 53–55). This causes the ball to change its vertical movement direction. The **pause** and **play** methods (lines 27–33) can be used to pause and resume the animation. The **increaseSpeed()** and **decreaseSpeed()** methods (lines 35–42) can be used to increase and decrease animation speed. The **rateProperty()**

method (lines 44–46) returns a binding property value for rate. This binding property is useful for binding the rate in future applications in the next chapter.

LISTING 15.18 BounceBallControl.java

```
1  import javafx.application.Application;
2  import javafx.stage.Stage;
3  import javafx.scene.Scene;
4  import javafx.scene.input.KeyCode;
5
6  public class BounceBallControl extends Application {
7    @Override // Override the start method in the Application class
8    public void start(Stage primaryStage) {
9      BallPane ballPane = new BallPane(); // Create a ball pane
10
11     // Pause and resume animation
12     ballPane.setOnMousePressed(e -> ballPane.pause());
13     ballPane.setOnMouseReleased(e -> ballPane.play());
14
15     // Increase and decrease animation
16     ballPane.setOnKeyPressed(e -> {
17       if (e.getCode() == KeyCode.UP) {
18         ballPane.increaseSpeed();
19       }
20       else if (e.getCode() == KeyCode.DOWN) {
21         ballPane.decreaseSpeed();
22       }
23     });
24
25     // Create a scene and place it in the stage
26     Scene scene = new Scene(ballPane, 250, 150);
27     primaryStage.setTitle("BounceBallControl"); // Set the stage title
28     primaryStage.setScene(scene); // Place the scene in the stage
29     primaryStage.show(); // Display the stage
30
31     // Must request focus after the primary stage is displayed
32     ballPane.requestFocus();
33   }
34 }
```

create a ball pane

pause animation
resume animation

increase speed

decrease speed

request focus on pane

The **BounceBallControl** class is the main JavaFX class that extends **Applicaiton** to display the ball pane with control functions. The mouse-pressed and mouse-released handlers are implemented for the ball pane to pause the animation and resume the animation (lines 12 and 13). When the UP arrow key is pressed, the ball pane's **increaseSpeed()** method is invoked to increase the ball's movement (line 18). When the DOWN arror key is pressed, the ball pane's **decreaseSpeed()** method is invoked to reduce the ball's movement (line 21).

Invoking **ballPane.requestFocus()** in line 32 sets the input focus to **ballPane**.

15.24 How does the program make the ball moving?

15.25 How does the code in Listing 15.17 BallPane.java change the direction of the ball movement?

15.26 What does the program do when the mouse is pressed on the ball pane? What does the program do when the mouse is released on the ball pane?

15.27 If line 32 in Listing 15.18 BounceBallControl.java is not in the program, what would happen when you press the UP or the DOWN arrow key?

15.28 If line 23 is not in Listing 15.17, what would happen?

Check
Point

KEY TERMS

anonymous inner class   594
event   588
event-driven programming   588
event handler   589
event-handler interface   589
event object   588
event source object   588

functional interface   598
lambda expression   597
inner class   591
key code   604
observable object   607
single abstract method interface   598

CHAPTER SUMMARY

1. The root class of the JavaFX event classes is **javafx.event.Event**, which is a sub-class of **java.util.EventObject**. The subclasses of **Event** deal with special types of events, such as action events, window events, mouse events, and key events. If a node can fire an event, any subclass of the node can fire the same type of event.

2. The handler object's class must implement the corresponding *event-handler interface*. JavaFX provides a handler interface **EventHandler<T extends Event>** for every event class **T**. The handler interface contains the **handle(T e)** method for handling event **e**.

3. The handler object must be registered by the *source object*. Registration methods depend on the event type. For an action event, the method is **setOnAction**. For a mouse-pressed event, the method is **setOnMousePressed**. For a key-pressed event, the method is **setOnKeyPressed**.

4. An *inner class*, or *nested class*, is defined within the scope of another class. An inner class can reference the data and methods defined in the outer class in which it nests, so you need not pass the reference of the outer class to the constructor of the inner class.

5. An anonymous inner class can be used to shorten the code for event handling. Furthermore, a lambda expression can be used to greatly simplify the event-handling code for functional interface handlers.

6. A *functional interface* is an interface with exactly one abstract method. This is also known as a single abstract method (SAM) interface.

7. A **MouseEvent** is fired whenever a mouse button is pressed, released, clicked, moved, or dragged on a node or a scene. The **getButton()** method can be used to detect which mouse button is pressed for the event.

8. A **KeyEvent** is fired whenever a key is pressed, released, or typed on a node or a scene. The **getCode()** method can be used to return the code value for the key.

9. An instance of **Observable** is known as an observable object, which contains the **addListener(InvalidationListener listener)** method for adding a listener. Once the value is changed in the property, a listener is notified. The listener class should implement the **InvalidationListener** interface, which uses the **invalidated** method to handle the property value change.

10. The abstract **Animation** class provides the core functionalities for animations in JavaFX. **PathTransition**, **FadeTransition**, and **Timeline** are specialized classes for implementing animations.

QUIZ

Answer the quiz for this chapter online at **www.cs.armstrong.edu/liang/intro10e/quiz.html**.

PROGRAMMING EXERCISES

MyProgrammingLab™

Sections 15.2–15.7

*15.1 (*Pick four cards*) Write a program that lets the user click the *Refresh* button to display four cards from a deck of 52 cards, as shown in Figure 15.24a. (See the hint in Programming Exercise 14.3 on how to obtain four random cards.)

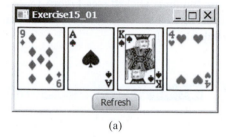
(a)

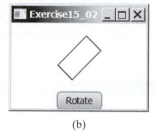
(b)

(c)

FIGURE 15.24 (a) Exercise 15.1 displays four cards randomly. (b) Exercise 15.2 rotates the rectangle. (c) Exercise 15.3 uses the buttons to move the ball.

15.2 (*Rotate a rectangle*) Write a program that rotates a rectangle 15 degrees right when the *Rotate* button is clicked, as shown in Figure 15.24b.

*15.3 (*Move the ball*) Write a program that moves the ball in a pane. You should define a pane class for displaying the ball and provide the methods for moving the ball left, right, up, and down, as shown in Figure 15.24c. Check the boundary to prevent the ball from moving out of sight completely.

*15.4 (*Create a simple calculator*) Write a program to perform addition, subtraction, multiplication, and division, as shown in Figure 15.25a.

VideoNote
Simple calculator

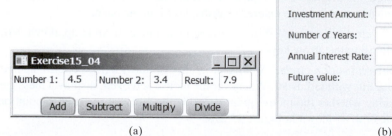

(a)   (b)

FIGURE 15.25 (a) Exercise 15.4 performs addition, subtraction, multiplication, and division on double numbers. (b) The user enters the investment amount, years, and interest rate to compute future value.

*15.5 (*Create an investment-value calculator*) Write a program that calculates the future value of an investment at a given interest rate for a specified number of years. The formula for the calculation is:

```
futureValue = investmentAmount * (1 + monthlyInterestRate)^(years*12)
```

Use text fields for the investment amount, number of years, and annual interest rate. Display the future amount in a text field when the user clicks the *Calculate* button, as shown in Figure 15.25b.

Sections 15.8 and 15.9

**15.6 (*Alternate two messages*) Write a program to display the text `Java is fun` and `Java is powerful` alternately with a mouse click.

*15.7 (*Change color using a mouse*) Write a program that displays the color of a circle as black when the mouse button is pressed and as white when the mouse button is released.

*15.8 (*Display the mouse position*) Write two programs, such that one displays the mouse position when the mouse button is clicked (see Figure 15.26a) and the other displays the mouse position when the mouse button is pressed and ceases to display it when the mouse button is released.

(a)   (b)

FIGURE 15.26 (a) Exercise 15.8 displays the mouse position. (b) Exercise 15.9 uses the arrow keys to draw the lines.

*15.9 (*Draw lines using the arrow keys*) Write a program that draws line segments using the arrow keys. The line starts from the center of the pane and draws toward east, north, west, or south when the right-arrow key, up-arrow key, left-arrow key, or down-arrow key is pressed, as shown in Figure 15.26b.

**15.10 (*Enter and display a string*) Write a program that receives a string from the keyboard and displays it on a pane. The *Enter* key signals the end of a string. Whenever a new string is entered, it is displayed on the pane.

*15.11 (*Move a circle using keys*) Write a program that moves a circle up, down, left, or right using the arrow keys.

15.12 (*Geometry: inside a circle?*) Write a program that draws a fixed circle centered at (100**, **60**) with radius **50**. Whenever the mouse is moved, display a message indicating whether the mouse point is inside the circle at the mouse point or outside of it, as shown in Figure 15.27a.

VideoNote

Check mouse point location

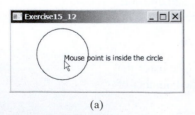

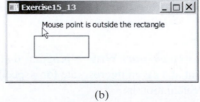

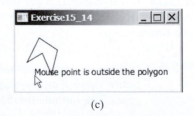

(a)   (b)   (c)

FIGURE 15.27 Detect whether a point is inside a circle, a rectangle, or a polygon.

15.13 (*Geometry: inside a rectangle?*) Write a program that draws a fixed rectangle centered at (100**, **60**) with width **100** and height **40**. Whenever the mouse is moved, display a message indicating whether the mouse point is inside the rectangle at the mouse point or outside of it, as shown in Figure 15.27b. To detect whether a point is inside a polygon, use the **contains** method defined in the **Node** class.

15.14 (*Geometry: inside a polygon?*) Write a program that draws a fixed polygon with points at (40**, **20**), (**70**, **40**), (**60**, **80**), (**45**, **45**), and (**20**, **60**). Whenever the mouse is moved, display a message indicating whether the mouse point is inside the polygon at the mouse point or outside of it, as shown in Figure 15.27c. To detect whether a point is inside a polygon, use the **contains** method defined in the **Node** class.

**15.15 (*Geometry: add and remove points*) Write a program that lets the user click on a pane to dynamically create and remove points (see Figure 15.28a). When the user left-clicks the mouse (primary button), a point is created and displayed at the mouse point. The user can remove a point by pointing to it and right-clicking the mouse (secondary button).

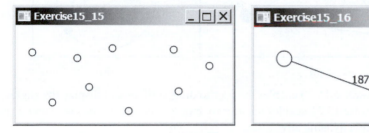

FIGURE 15.28 (a) Exercise 15.15 allows the user to create/remove points dynamically. (b) Exercise 15.16 displays two vertices and a connecting edge.

*15.16 (*Two movable vertices and their distances*) Write a program that displays two circles with radius **10** at location (**40**, **40**) and (**120**, **150**) with a line connecting the two circles, as shown in Figure 15.28b. The distance between the circles is displayed along the line. The user can drag a circle. When that happens, the circle and its line are moved and the distance between the circles is updated.

15.17 (*Geometry: find the bounding rectangle*) Write a program that enables the user to add and remove points in a two-dimensional plane dynamically, as shown in Figure 15.29a. A minimum bounding rectangle is updated as the points are added and removed. Assume that the radius of each point is **10 pixels.

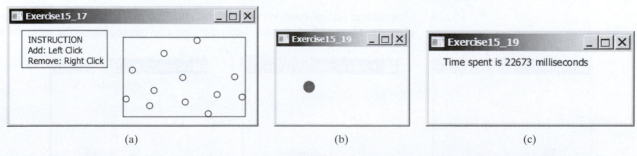

FIGURE 15.29 (a) Exercise 15.17 enables the user to add/remove points dynamically and displays the bounding rectangle. (b) When you click a circle, a new circle is displayed at a random location. (c) After 20 circles are clicked, the time spent is displayed in the pane.

**15.18 (*Move a rectangle using mouse*) Write a program that displays a rectangle. You can point the mouse inside the rectangle and drag (i.e., move with mouse pressed) the rectangle wherever the mouse goes. The mouse point becomes the center of the rectangle.

**15.19 (*Game: eye-hand coordination*) Write a program that displays a circle of radius 10 pixels filled with a random color at a random location on a pane, as shown in Figure 15.29b. When you click the circle, it disappears and a new random-color circle is displayed at another random location. After twenty circles are clicked, display the time spent in the pane, as shown in Figure 15.29c.

**15.20 (*Geometry: display angles*) Write a program that enables the user to drag the vertices of a triangle and displays the angles dynamically as the triangle shape changes, as shown in Figure 15.30a. The formula to compute angles is given in Listing 4.1.

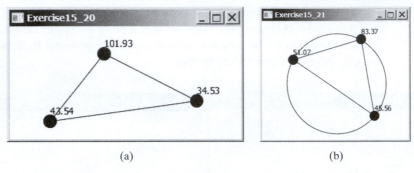

(a)   (b)

FIGURE 15.30 (a) Exercise 15.20 enables the user to drag vertices and display the angles dynamically. (b) Exercise 15.21 enables the user to drag vertices along the circle and display the angles in the triangle dynamically.

*15.21 (*Drag points*) Draw a circle with three random points on the circle. Connect the points to form a triangle. Display the angles in the triangle. Use the mouse to drag a point along the perimeter of the circle. As you drag it, the triangle and angles are redisplayed dynamically, as shown in Figure 15.30b. For computing angles in a triangle, see Listing 4.1.

Section 15.10

*15.22 (*Auto resize cylinder*) Rewrite Programming Exercise 14.10 so that the cylinder's width and height are automatically resized when the window is resized.

*15.23 (*Auto resize stop sign*) Rewrite Programming Exercise 14.15 so that the stop sign's width and height are automatically resized when the window is resized.

Section 15.11

**15.24 (*Animation: palindrome*) Write a program that animates a palindrome swing as shown in Figure 15.31. Press/release the mouse to pause/resume the animation.

  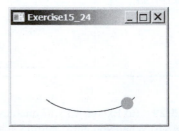

FIGURE 15.31 The program animates a palindrome swing.

**15.25 (*Animation: ball on curve*) Write a program that animates a ball moving along a sine curve, as shown in Figure 15.32. When the ball gets to the right border, it starts over from the left. Enable the user to resume/pause the animation with a click on the left/right mouse button.

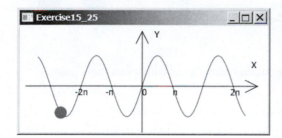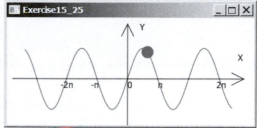

FIGURE 15.32   The program animates a ball traveling along a sine curve.

*15.26 (*Change opacity*) Rewrite Programming Exercise 15.24 so that the ball's opacity is changed as it swings.

*15.27 (*Control a moving text*) Write a program that displays a moving text, as shown in Figure 15.33a and b. The text moves from left to right circularly. When it disappears in the right, it reappears from the left. The text freezes when the mouse is pressed and moves again when the button is released.

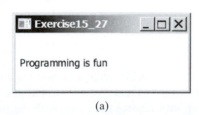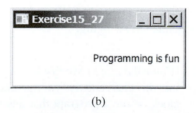

(a)	(b)	(c)

FIGURE 15.33   (a and b) A text is moving from left to right circularly. (c) The program simulates a fan running.

**15.28 (*Display a running fan*) Write a program that displays a running fan, as shown in Figure 15.33c. Use the *Pause*, *Resume*, *Reverse* buttons to pause, resume, and reverse fan running.

VideoNote

Display a running fan

**15.29 (*Racing car*) Write a program that simulates car racing, as shown in Figure 15.34a. The car moves from left to right. When it hits the right end, it restarts from the left and continues the same process. You can use a timer to control animation. Redraw the car with a new base coordinates (x, y), as shown in Figure 15.34b. Also let the user pause/resume the animation with a button press/release and increase/decrease the car speed by pressing the UP and DOWN arrow keys.

15.30 (*Slide show*) Twenty-five slides are stored as image files (slide0.jpg**, **slide1 .jpg**, . . . , **slide24.jpg**) in the **image** directory downloadable along with the source code in the book. The size of each image is 800×600. Write a program that automatically displays the slides repeatedly. Each slide is shown for

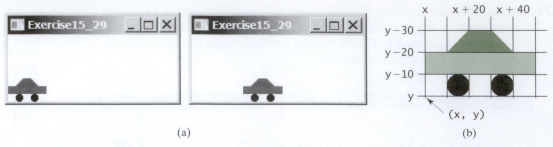

(a)

(b)

FIGURE 15.34 (a) The program displays a moving car. (b) You can redraw a car with a new base point.

two seconds. The slides are displayed in order. When the last slide finishes, the first slide is redisplayed, and so on. Click to pause if the animation is currently playing. Click to resume if the animation is currently paused.

**15.31 (*Geometry: pendulum*) Write a program that animates a pendulum swinging, as shown in Figure 15.35. Press the UP arrow key to increase the speed and the DOWN key to decrease it. Press the *S* key to stop animation and the *R* key to resume it.

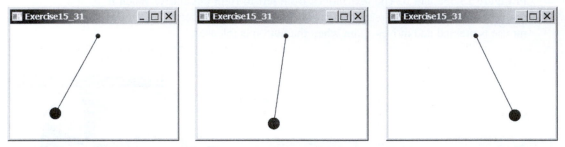

FIGURE 15.35 Exercise 15.31 animates a pendulum swinging.

*15.32 (*Control a clock*) Modify Listing 14.21, ClockPane.java, to add the animation into this class and add two methods **start()** and **stop()** to start and stop the clock. Write a program that lets the user control the clock with the *Start* and *Stop* buttons, as shown in Figure 15.36a.

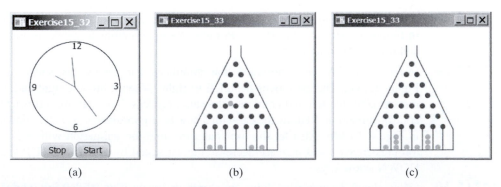

(a)   (b)   (c)

FIGURE 15.36 (a) Exercise 15.32 allows the user to start and stop a clock. (b and c) The balls are dropped into the bean machine.

***15.33   (*Game: bean-machine animation*) Write a program that animates the bean machine introduced in Programming Exercise 7.21. The animation terminates after ten balls are dropped, as shown in Figure 15.36b and c.

***15.34   (*Simulation: self-avoiding random walk*) A self-avoiding walk in a lattice is a path from one point to another that does not visit the same point twice. Self-avoiding walks have applications in physics, chemistry, and mathematics. They can be used to model chain-like entities such as solvents and polymers. Write a program that displays a random path that starts from the center and ends at a point on the boundary, as shown in Figure 15.37a or ends at a dead-end point (i.e., surrounded by four points that have already been visited), as shown in Figure 15.37b. Assume the size of the lattice is **16** by **16**.

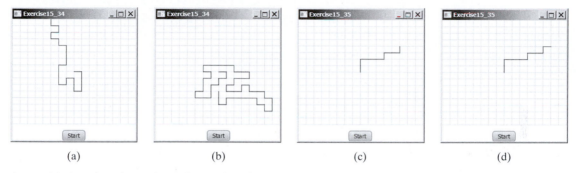

Figure 15.37   (a) A path ends at a boundary point. (b) A path ends at dead-end point. (c and d) Animation shows the progress of a path step by step.

***15.35   (*Animation: self-avoiding random walk*) Revise the preceding exercise to display the walk step by step in an animation, as shown in Figure 15.37c and d.

**15.36   (*Simulation: self-avoiding random walk*) Write a simulation program to show that the chance of getting dead-end paths increases as the grid size increases. Your program simulates lattices with size from 10 to 80. For each lattice size, simulate a self-avoiding random walk 10,000 times and display the probability of the dead-end paths, as shown in the following sample output:

```
For a lattice of size 10, the probability of dead-end paths is 10.6%
For a lattice of size 11, the probability of dead-end paths is 14.0%
...
For a lattice of size 80, the probability of dead-end paths is 99.5%
```

CHAPTER

16

JavaFX UI Controls and Multimedia

Objectives

- To create graphical user interfaces with various user-interface controls (§§16.2–16.11).

- To create a label with text and graphic using the `Label` class and explore properties in the abstract `Labeled` class (§16.2).

- To create a button with text and graphic using the `Button` class and set a handler using the `setOnAction` method in the abstract `ButtonBase` class (§16.3).

- To create a check box using the `CheckBox` class (§16.4).

- To create a radio button using the `RadioButton` class and group radio buttons using a `ToggleGroup` (§16.5).

- To enter data using the `TextField` class and password using the `PasswordField` class (§16.6).

- To enter data in multiple lines using the `TextArea` class (§16.7).

- To select a single item using `ComboBox` (§16.8).

- To select a single or multiple items using `ListView` (§16.9).

- To select a range of values using `ScrollBar` (§16.10).

- To select a range of values using `Slider` and explore differences between `ScrollBar` and `Slider` (§16.11).

- To develop a tic-tac-toe game (§16.12).

- To view and play video and audio using the `Media`, `MediaPlayer`, and `MediaView` (§16.13).

- To develop a case study for showing the national flag and playing anthem (§16.14).

16.1 Introduction

Key Point

JavaFX provides many UI controls for developing a comprehensive user interface.

GUI

A graphical user interface (GUI) makes a system user-friendly and easy to use. Creating a GUI requires creativity and knowledge of how UI controls work. Since the UI controls in JavaFX are very flexible and versatile, you can create a wide assortment of useful user interfaces for rich Internet applications.

Oracle provides tools for visually designing and developing GUIs. This enables the programmer to rapidly assemble the elements of a GUI with minimum coding. Tools, however, cannot do everything. You have to modify the programs they produce. Consequently, before you begin to use the visual tools, you must understand the basic concepts of JavaFX GUI programming.

Previous chapters used UI controls such as `Button`, `Label`, and `TextField`. This chapter introduces the frequently used UI controls in detail (see Figure 16.1).

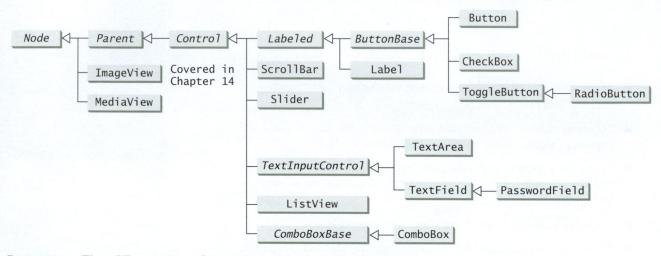

FIGURE 16.1 These UI controls are frequently used to create user interfaces.

Note

naming convention for controls

Throughout this book, the prefixes `lbl`, `bt`, `chk`, `rb`, `tf`, `pf`, `ta`, `cbo`, `lv`, `scb`, `sld`, and `mp` are used to name reference variables for `Label`, `Button`, `CheckBox`, `RadioButton`, `TextField`, `PasswordField`, `TextArea`, `ComboBox`, `ListView`, `ScrollBar`, `Slider`, and `MediaPlayer`.

16.2 Labeled and Label

A *label* is a display area for a short text, a node, or both. It is often used to label other controls (usually text fields). Labels and buttons share many common properties. These common properties are defined in the `Labeled` class, as shown in Figure 16.2.

A `Label` can be constructed using one of the three constructors as shown in Figure 16.3.

The `graphic` property can be any node such as a shape, an image, or a control. Listing 16.1 gives an example that displays several labels with text and images in the label, as shown in Figure 16.4.

LISTING 16.1 LabelWithGraphic.java

```
1  import javafx.application.Application;
2  import javafx.stage.Stage;
3  import javafx.scene.Scene;
4  import javafx.scene.control.ContentDisplay;
5  import javafx.scene.control.Label;
```

The getter and setter methods for property values and a getter for property itself are provided in the class, but omitted in the UML diagram for brevity.

---

javafx.scene.control.Labeled

-alignment: ObjectProperty\<Pos\>	Specifies the alignment of the text and node in the labeled.
-contentDisplay: ObjectProperty\<ContentDisplay\>	Specifies the position of the node relative to the text using the constants TOP, BOTTOM, LEFT, and RIGHT defined in ContentDisplay.
-graphic: ObjectProperty\<Node\>	A graphic for the labeled.
-graphicTextGap: DoubleProperty	The gap between the graphic and the text.
-textFill: ObjectProperty\<Paint\>	The paint used to fill the text.
-text: StringProperty	A text for the labeled.
-underline: BooleanProperty	Whether text should be underlined.
-wrapText: BooleanProperty	Whether text should be wrapped if the text exceeds the width.

FIGURE 16.2 **Labeled** defines common properties for **Label**, **Button**, **CheckBox**, and **RadioButton**.

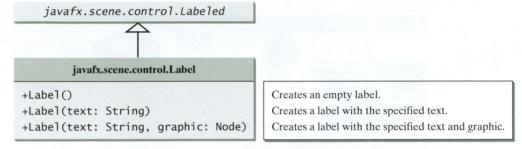

javafx.scene.control.Labeled

△

javafx.scene.control.Label

+Label()	Creates an empty label.
+Label(text: String)	Creates a label with the specified text.
+Label(text: String, graphic: Node)	Creates a label with the specified text and graphic.

FIGURE 16.3 **Label** is created to display a text or a node, or both.

```java
 6  import javafx.scene.image.Image;
 7  import javafx.scene.image.ImageView;
 8  import javafx.scene.layout.HBox;
 9  import javafx.scene.layout.StackPane;
10  import javafx.scene.paint.Color;
11  import javafx.scene.shape.Circle;
12  import javafx.scene.shape.Rectangle;
13  import javafx.scene.shape.Ellipse;
14
15  public class LabelWithGraphic extends Application {
16    @Override // Override the start method in the Application class
17    public void start(Stage primaryStage) {
18      ImageView us = new ImageView(new Image("image/us.gif"));
19      Label lb1 = new Label("US\n50 States", us);          create a label
20      lb1.setStyle("-fx-border-color: green; -fx-border-width: 2");
21      lb1.setContentDisplay(ContentDisplay.BOTTOM);        set node position
22      lb1.setTextFill(Color.RED);
23
24      Label lb2 = new Label("Circle", new Circle(50, 50, 25));   create a label
25      lb2.setContentDisplay(ContentDisplay.TOP);
26      lb2.setTextFill(Color.ORANGE);                       set node position
27
28      Label lb3 = new Label("Retangle", new Rectangle(10, 10, 50, 25));   create a label
29      lb3.setContentDisplay(ContentDisplay.RIGHT);
30
31      Label lb4 = new Label("Ellipse", new Ellipse(50, 50, 50, 25));   create a label
32      lb4.setContentDisplay(ContentDisplay.LEFT);
33
```

```
34        Ellipse ellipse = new Ellipse(50, 50, 50, 25);
35        ellipse.setStroke(Color.GREEN);
36        ellipse.setFill(Color.WHITE);
37        StackPane stackPane = new StackPane();
38        stackPane.getChildren().addAll(ellipse, new Label("JavaFX"));
39        Label lb5 = new Label("A pane inside a label", stackPane);
40        lb5.setContentDisplay(ContentDisplay.BOTTOM);
41
42        HBox pane = new HBox(20);
43        pane.getChildren().addAll(lb1, lb2, lb3, lb4, lb5);
44
45        // Create a scene and place it in the stage
46        Scene scene = new Scene(pane, 450, 150);
47        primaryStage.setTitle("LabelWithGraphic"); // Set the stage title
48        primaryStage.setScene(scene); // Place the scene in the stage
49        primaryStage.show(); // Display the stage
50   }
60 }
```

create a label (line 39)

add labels to pane (line 43)

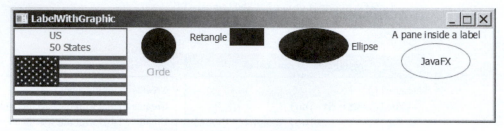

FIGURE 16.4 The program displays labels with texts and nodes.

The program creates a label with a text and an image (line 19). The text is **US\n50 States** so it is displayed in two lines. Line 21 specifies that the image is placed at the bottom of the text.

The program creates a label with a text and a circle (line 24). The circle is placed on top of the text (line 25). The program creates a label with a text and a rectangle (line 28). The rectangle is placed on the right of the text (line 29). The program creates a label with a text and an ellipse (line 31). The ellipse is placed on the left of the text (line 32).

The program creates an ellipse (line 34), places it along with a label to a stack pane (line 38), and creates a label with a text and the stack pane as the node (line 39). As seen from this example, you can place any node in a label.

The program creates an **HBox** (line 42) and places all five labels into the **HBox** (line 43).

Check Point

16.1 How do you create a label with a node without a text?

16.2 How do you place a text on the right of the node in a label?

16.3 Can you display multiple lines of text in a label?

16.4 Can the text in a label be underlined?

16.3 Button

A *button* is a control that triggers an action event when clicked. JavaFX provides regular buttons, toggle buttons, check box buttons, and radio buttons. The common features of these buttons are defined in **ButtonBase** and **Labeled** classes as shown in Figure 16.5.

The **Labeled** class defines the common properties for labels and buttons. A button is just like a label except that the button has the **onAction** property defined in the **ButtonBase** class, which sets a handler for handling a button's action.

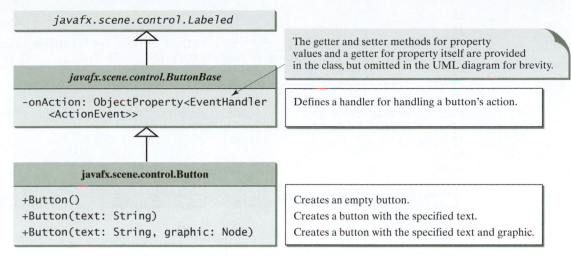

FIGURE 16.5 **ButtonBase** extends **Labeled** and defines common features for all buttons.

Listing 16.2 gives a program that uses the buttons to control the movement of a text, as shown in Figure 16.6.

LISTING 16.2 ButtonDemo.java

```
1   import javafx.application.Application;
2   import javafx.stage.Stage;
3   import javafx.geometry.Pos;
4   import javafx.scene.Scene;
5   import javafx.scene.control.Button;
6   import javafx.scene.image.ImageView;
7   import javafx.scene.layout.BorderPane;
8   import javafx.scene.layout.HBox;
9   import javafx.scene.layout.Pane;
10  import javafx.scene.text.Text;
11
12  public class ButtonDemo extends Application {
13    protected Text text = new Text(50, 50, "JavaFX Programming");
14
15    protected BorderPane getPane() {
16      HBox paneForButtons = new HBox(20);
17      Button btLeft = new Button("Left",                           create a button
18        new ImageView("image/left.gif"));
19      Button btRight = new Button("Right",
20        new ImageView("image/right.gif"));
21      paneForButtons.getChildren().addAll(btLeft, btRight);        add buttons to pane
22      paneForButtons.setAlignment(Pos.CENTER);
23      paneForButtons.setStyle("-fx-border-color: green");
24
25      BorderPane pane = new BorderPane();                          create a border pane
26      pane.setBottom(paneForButtons);                             add buttons to the bottom
27
28      Pane paneForText = new Pane();
29      paneForText.getChildren().add(text);
30      pane.setCenter(paneForText);
31
32      btLeft.setOnAction(e -> text.setX(text.getX() - 10));        add an action handler
33      btRight.setOnAction(e -> text.setX(text.getX() + 10));
34
35      return pane;                                                return a pane
```

```
36      }
37
38      @Override // Override the start method in the Application class
39      public void start(Stage primaryStage) {
40          // Create a scene and place it in the stage
41          Scene scene = new Scene(getPane(), 450, 200);
42          primaryStage.setTitle("ButtonDemo"); // Set the stage title
43          primaryStage.setScene(scene); // Place the scene in the stage
44          primaryStage.show(); // Display the stage
45      }
46  }
```

set pane to scene

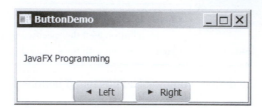 

FIGURE 16.6 The program demonstrates using buttons.

The program creates two buttons **btLeft** and **btRight** with each button containing a text and an image (lines 17–20). The buttons are placed in an **HBox** (line 21) and the **HBox** is placed in the bottom of a border pane (line 26). A text is created in line 13 and is placed in the center of the border pane (line 30). The action handler for **btLeft** moves the text to the left (line 32). The action handler for **btRight** moves the text to the right (line 33).

getPane() protected

The program purposely defines a protected **getPane()** method to return a pane (line 15). This method will be overridden by subclasses in the upcoming examples to add more nodes in the pane. The text is declared protected so that it can be accessed by subclasses (line 13).

Check Point

16.5 How do you create a button with a text and a node? Can you apply all the methods for **Labeled** to **Button**?

16.6 Why is the **getPane()** method protected in Listing 16.2? Why is the data field **text** protected?

16.7 How do you set a handler for processing a button-clicked action?

16.4 CheckBox

A **CheckBox** is used for the user to make a selection. Like **Button**, **CheckBox** inherits all the properties such as **onAction**, **text**, **graphic**, **alignment**, **graphicTextGap**, **textFill**, **contentDisplay** from **ButtonBase** and **Labeled**, as shown in Figure 16.7. Additionally, it provides the **selection** property to indicate whether a check box is selected.

Here is an example of a check box with text **US**, a graphic image, green text color, and black border, and initially selected.

```
CheckBox chkUS = new CheckBox("US");
chkUS.setGraphic(new ImageView("image/usIcon.gif"));
chkUS.setTextFill(Color.GREEN);
chkUS.setContentDisplay(ContentDisplay.LEFT);
chkUS.setStyle("-fx-border-color: black");
chkUS.setSelected(true);
chkUS.setPadding(new Insets(5, 5, 5, 5));
```

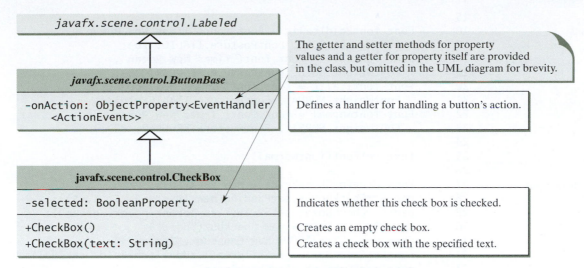

FIGURE 16.7 **CheckBox** contains the properties inherited from **ButtonBase** and **Labeled**.

When a check box is clicked (checked or unchecked), it fires an **ActionEvent**. To see if a check box is selected, use the **isSelected()** method.

We now write a program that adds two check boxes named Bold and Italic to the preceding example to let the user specify whether the message is in bold or italic, as shown in Figure 16.8.

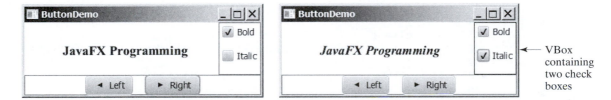

FIGURE 16.8 The program demonstrates check boxes.

There are at least two approaches to writing this program. The first is to revise the preceding **ButtonDemo** class to insert the code for adding the check boxes and processing their events. The second is to define a subclass that extends **ButtonDemo**. Please implement the first approach as an exercise. Listing 16.3 gives the code to implement the second approach.

LISTING 16.3 CheckBoxDemo.java

```
1  import javafx.event.ActionEvent;
2  import javafx.event.EventHandler;
3  import javafx.geometry.Insets;
4  import javafx.scene.control.CheckBox;
5  import javafx.scene.layout.BorderPane;
6  import javafx.scene.layout.VBox;
7  import javafx.scene.text.Font;
8  import javafx.scene.text.FontPosture;
9  import javafx.scene.text.FontWeight;
10
11 public class CheckBoxDemo extends ButtonDemo {
12   @Override // Override the getPane() method in the super class
13   protected BorderPane getPane() {
14     BorderPane pane = super.getPane();
```

override getPane()
invoke super.getPane()

```
15
create fonts              16       Font fontBoldItalic = Font.font("Times New Roman",
                          17         FontWeight.BOLD, FontPosture.ITALIC, 20);
                          18       Font fontBold = Font.font("Times New Roman",
                          19         FontWeight.BOLD, FontPosture.REGULAR, 20);
                          20       Font fontItalic = Font.font("Times New Roman",
                          21         FontWeight.NORMAL, FontPosture.ITALIC, 20);
                          22       Font fontNormal = Font.font("Times New Roman",
                          23         FontWeight.NORMAL, FontPosture.REGULAR, 20);
                          24
                          25       text.setFont(fontNormal);
                          26
pane for check boxes      27       VBox paneForCheckBoxes = new VBox(20);
                          28       paneForCheckBoxes.setPadding(new Insets(5, 5, 5, 5));
                          29       paneForCheckBoxes.setStyle("-fx-border-color: green");
create check boxes        30       CheckBox chkBold = new CheckBox("Bold");
                          31       CheckBox chkItalic = new CheckBox("Italic");
                          32       paneForCheckBoxes.getChildren().addAll(chkBold, chkItalic);
                          33       pane.setRight(paneForCheckBoxes);
                          34
create a handler          35       EventHandler<ActionEvent> handler = e -> {
                          36         if (chkBold.isSelected() && chkItalic.isSelected()) {
                          37           text.setFont(fontBoldItalic); // Both check boxes checked
                          38         }
                          39         else if (chkBold.isSelected()) {
                          40           text.setFont(fontBold); // The Bold check box checked
                          41         }
                          42         else if (chkItalic.isSelected()) {
                          43           text.setFont(fontItalic); // The Italic check box checked
                          44         }
                          45         else {
                          46           text.setFont(fontNormal); // Both check boxes unchecked
                          47         }
                          48       };
                          49
set handler for action    50       chkBold.setOnAction(handler);
                          51       chkItalic.setOnAction(handler);
                          52
return a pane             53       return pane; // Return a new pane
                          54     }
main method omitted       55   }
```

CheckBoxDemo extends **ButtonDemo** and overrides the **getPane()** method (line 13). The new **getPane()** method invokes the **super.getPane()** method from the **ButtonDemo** class to obtain a border pane that contains the buttons and a text (line 14). The check boxes are created and added to **paneForCheckBoxes** (lines 30–32). **paneForCheckBoxes** is added to the border pane (lines 33).

The handler for processing the action event on check boxes is created in lines 35–48. It sets the appropriate font based on the status of the check boxes.

The **start** method for this JavaFX program is defined in **ButtonDemo** and inherited in **CheckBoxDemo**. So when you run **CheckBoxDemo**, the **start** method in **ButtonDemo** is invoked. Since the **getPane()** method is overridden in **CheckBoxDemo**, the method in **CheckBoxDemo** is invoked from line 41 in Listing 16.2, ButtonDemo.java.

16.8 How do you test if a check box is selected?

16.9 Can you apply all the methods for **Labeled** to **CheckBox**?

16.10 Can you set a node for the **graphic** property in a check box?

16.5 RadioButton

Radio buttons, also known as *option buttons*, enable the user to choose a single item from a group of choices. In appearance radio buttons resemble check boxes, but check boxes display a square that is either checked or blank, whereas radio buttons display a circle that is either filled (if selected) or blank (if not selected).

option buttons

RadioButton is a subclass of ToggleButton. The difference between a radio button and a toggle button is that a radio button displays a circle, but a toggle button is rendered similar to a button. The UML diagrams for ToggleButton and RadioButton are shown in Figure 16.9.

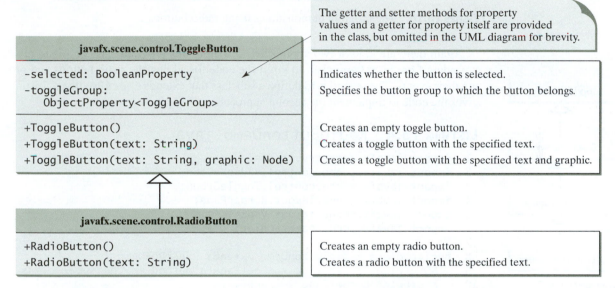

FIGURE 16.9 ToggleButton and RadioButton are specialized buttons for making selections.

Here is an example of a radio button with text US, a graphic image, green text color, and black border, and initially selected.

```
RadioButton rbUS = new RadioButton("US");
rbUS.setGraphic(new ImageView("image/usIcon.gif"));
rbUS.setTextFill(Color.GREEN);
rbUS.setContentDisplay(ContentDisplay.LEFT);
rbUS.setStyle("-fx-border-color: black");
rbUS.setSelected(true);
rbUS.setPadding(new Insets(5, 5, 5,));
```

To group radio buttons, you need to create an instance of ToggleGroup and set a radio button's toggleGroup property to join the group, as follows:

```
ToggleGroup group = new ToggleGroup();
rbRed.setToggleGroup(group);
rbGreen.setToggleGroup(group);
rbBlue.setToggleGroup(group);
```

This code creates a button group for radio buttons rbRed, rbGreen, and rbBlue so that buttons rbRed, rbGreen, and rbBlue are selected mutually exclusively. Without grouping, these buttons would be independent.

When a radio button is changed (selected or deselected), it fires an ActionEvent. To see if a radio button is selected, use the isSelected() method.

We now give a program that adds three radio buttons named Red, Green, and Blue to the preceding example to let the user choose the color of the message, as shown in Figure 16.10.

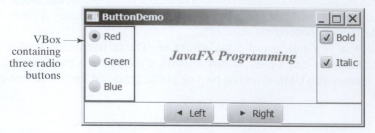

FIGURE 16.10 The program demonstrates using radio buttons.

Again there are at least two approaches to writing this program. The first is to revise the preceding **CheckBoxDemo** class to insert the code for adding the radio buttons and processing their events. The second is to define a subclass that extends **CheckBoxDemo**. Listing 16.4 gives the code to implement the second approach.

LISTING 16.4 RadioButtonDemo.java

```
1  import javafx.geometry.Insets;
2  import javafx.scene.control.RadioButton;
3  import javafx.scene.control.ToggleGroup;
4  import javafx.scene.layout.BorderPane;
5  import javafx.scene.layout.VBox;
6  import javafx.scene.paint.Color;
7
8  public class RadioButtonDemo extends CheckBoxDemo {
9    @Override // Override the getPane() method in the super class
10   protected BorderPane getPane() {
11     BorderPane pane = super.getPane();
12
13     VBox paneForRadioButtons = new VBox(20);
14     paneForRadioButtons.setPadding(new Insets(5, 5, 5, 5));
15     paneForRadioButtons.setStyle("-fx-border-color: green");
16     paneForRadioButtons.setStyle
17       ("-fx-border-width: 2px; -fx-border-color: green");
18     RadioButton rbRed = new RadioButton("Red");
19     RadioButton rbGreen = new RadioButton("Green");
20     RadioButton rbBlue = new RadioButton("Blue");
21     paneForRadioButtons.getChildren().addAll(rbRed, rbGreen, rbBlue);
22     pane.setLeft(paneForRadioButtons);
23
24     ToggleGroup group = new ToggleGroup();
25     rbRed.setToggleGroup(group);
26     rbGreen.setToggleGroup(group);
27     rbBlue.setToggleGroup(group);
28
29     rbRed.setOnAction(e -> {
30       if (rbRed.isSelected()) {
31         text.setFill(Color.RED);
32       }
33     });
34
35     rbGreen.setOnAction(e -> {
36       if (rbGreen.isSelected()) {
37         text.setFill(Color.GREEN);
```

Margin notes:

Application

ButtonDemo

CheckBoxDemo

RadioButtonDemo

override getPane()
invoke super.getPane()

pane for radio buttons

create radio buttons

add to border pane

group radio buttons

handle radio button

```
38          }
39      });
40
41      rbBlue.setOnAction(e -> {
42        if (rbBlue.isSelected()) {
43          text.setFill(Color.BLUE);
44        }
45      });
46
47      return pane;                                    return border pane
48    }
49  }                                                  main method omitted
```

RadioButtonDemo extends **CheckBoxDemo** and overrides the **getPane()** method (line 10). The new **getPane()** method invokes the **getPane()** method from the **CheckBoxDemo** class to create a border pane that contains the check boxes, buttons, and a text (line 11). This border pane is returned from invoking **super.getPane()**. The radio buttons are created and added to **paneForRadioButtons** (lines 18–21). **paneForRadioButtons** is added to the border pane (lines 22).

The radio buttons are grouped together in lines 24–27. The handlers for processing the action event on radio buttons are created in lines 29–45. It sets the appropriate color based on the status of the radio buttons.

The **start** method for this JavaFX program is defined in **ButtonDemo** and inherited in **CheckBoxDemo** and then in **RadioButtonDemo**. So when you run **RadioButtonDemo**, the **start** method in **ButtonDemo** is invoked. Since the **getPane()** method is overridden in **RadioButtonDemo**, the method in **RadioButtonDemo** is invoked from line 41 in Listing 16.2, ButtonDemo.java.

Check Point

16.11 How do you test if a radio button is selected?

16.12 Can you apply all the methods for **Labeled** to **RadioButton**?

16.13 Can you set any node in the **graphic** property in a radio button?

16.14 How do you group radio buttons?

16.6 TextField

A text field can be used to enter or display a string. **TextField** is a subclass of **TextInputControl**. Figure 16.11 lists the properties and constructors in **TextField**.

Here is an example of creating a noneditable text field with red text color, a specified font, and right horizontal alignment:

```
TextField tfMessage = new TextField("T-Strom");
tfMessage.setEditable(false);
tfMessage.setStyle("-fx-text-fill: red");
tfMessage.setFont(Font.font("Times", 20));
tfMessage.setAlignment(Pos.BASELINE_RIGHT);
```

When you move the cursor in the text field and press the Enter key, it fires an **ActionEvent**.

Listing 16.5 gives a program that adds a text field to the preceding example to let the user set a new message, as shown in Figure 16.12.

LISTING 16.5 TextFieldDemo.java

```
1  import javafx.geometry.Insets;
2  import javafx.geometry.Pos;
```

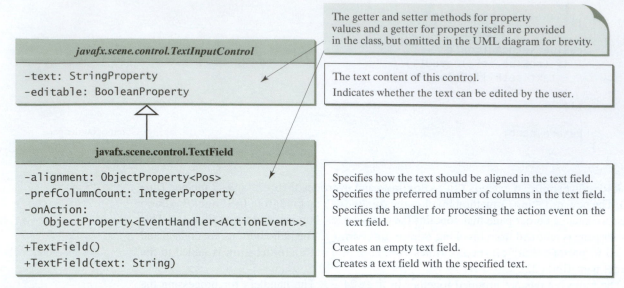

The getter and setter methods for property values and a getter for property itself are provided in the class, but omitted in the UML diagram for brevity.

javafx.scene.control.TextInputControl

-text: StringProperty
-editable: BooleanProperty

The text content of this control.
Indicates whether the text can be edited by the user.

javafx.scene.control.TextField

-alignment: ObjectProperty<Pos>
-prefColumnCount: IntegerProperty
-onAction:
  ObjectProperty<EventHandler<ActionEvent>>

+TextField()
+TextField(text: String)

Specifies how the text should be aligned in the text field.
Specifies the preferred number of columns in the text field.
Specifies the handler for processing the action event on the text field.

Creates an empty text field.
Creates a text field with the specified text.

FIGURE 16.11 `TextField` enables the user to enter or display a string.

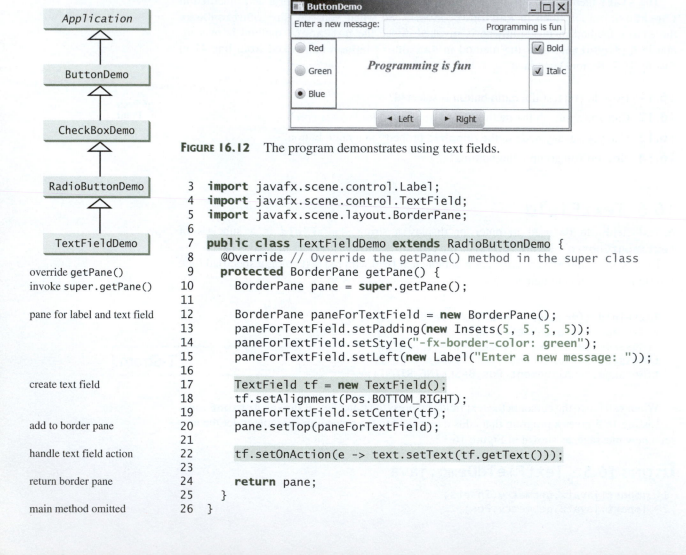

FIGURE 16.12 The program demonstrates using text fields.

```
3    import javafx.scene.control.Label;
4    import javafx.scene.control.TextField;
5    import javafx.scene.layout.BorderPane;
6
7    public class TextFieldDemo extends RadioButtonDemo {
8      @Override // Override the getPane() method in the super class
9      protected BorderPane getPane() {
10       BorderPane pane = super.getPane();
11
12       BorderPane paneForTextField = new BorderPane();
13       paneForTextField.setPadding(new Insets(5, 5, 5, 5));
14       paneForTextField.setStyle("-fx-border-color: green");
15       paneForTextField.setLeft(new Label("Enter a new message: "));
16
17       TextField tf = new TextField();
18       tf.setAlignment(Pos.BOTTOM_RIGHT);
19       paneForTextField.setCenter(tf);
20       pane.setTop(paneForTextField);
21
22       tf.setOnAction(e -> text.setText(tf.getText()));
23
24       return pane;
25     }
26   }
```

override getPane()
invoke super.getPane()

pane for label and text field

create text field

add to border pane

handle text field action

return border pane

main method omitted

TextFieldDemo extends **RadioButtonDemo** (line 7) and adds a label and a text field to let the user enter a new text (lines 12–19). After you set a new text in the text field and press the Enter key, a new message is displayed (line 22). Pressing the Enter key on the text field triggers an action event.

> **Note**
> If a text field is used for entering a password, use **PasswordField** to replace **TextField**. **PasswordField** extends **TextField** and hides the input text with echo characters ✱✱✱✱✱✱.

PasswordField

16.15 Can you disable editing of a text field?

16.16 Can you apply all the methods for **TextInputControl** to **TextField**?

16.17 Can you set a node as the **graphic** property in a text field?

16.18 How do you align the text in a text field to the right?

16.7 TextArea

A **TextArea** *enables the user to enter multiple lines of text.*

If you want to let the user enter multiple lines of text, you may create several instances of **TextField**. A better alternative, however, is to use **TextArea**, which enables the user to enter multiple lines of text. Figure 16.13 lists the properties and constructors in **TextArea**.

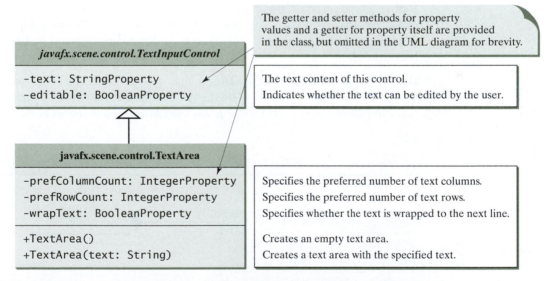

FIGURE 16.13 **TextArea** enables the user to enter or display multiple lines of characters.

Here is an example of creating a text area with **5** rows and **20** columns, wrapped to the next line, **red** text color, and **Courier** font **20** pixels.

```
TextArea taNote = new TextArea("This is a text area");
taNote.setPrefColumnCount(20);
taNote.setPrefRowCount(5);
taNote.setWrapText(true);
taNote.setStyle("-fx-text-fill: red");
taNote.setFont(Font.font("Times", 20));
```

TextArea provides scrolling, but often it is useful to create a **ScrollPane** object to hold an instance of **TextArea** and let **ScrollPane** handle scrolling for **TextArea**, as follows:

```
// Create a scroll pane to hold text area
ScrollPane scrollPane = new ScrollPane(taNote);
```

ScrollPane

Tip
You can place any node in a **ScrollPane**. **ScrollPane** provides vertical and horizontal scrolling automatically if the control is too large to fit in the viewing area.

We now give a program that displays an image and a short text in a label, and a long text in a text area, as shown in Figure 16.14.

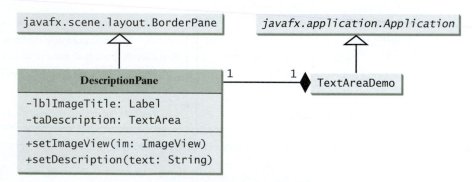

FIGURE 16.14 The program displays an image in a label, a title in a label, and text in the text area.

Here are the major steps in the program:

1. Define a class named **DescriptionPane** that extends **BorderPane**, as shown in Listing 16.6. This class contains a text area inside a scroll pane, and a label for displaying an image icon and a title. The class **DescriptionPane** will be reused in later examples.

2. Define a class named **TextAreaDemo** that extends **Application**, as shown in Listing 16.7. Create an instance of **DescriptionPane** and add it to the scene. The relationship between **DescriptionPane** and **TextAreaDemo** is shown in Figure 16.15.

FIGURE 16.15 **TextAreaDemo** uses **DescriptionPane** to display an image, title, and text description of a national flag.

LISTING 16.6 DescriptionPane.java

```
1  import javafx.geometry.Insets;
2  import javafx.scene.control.Label;
3  import javafx.scene.control.ContentDisplay;
```

```
 4  import javafx.scene.control.ScrollPane;
 5  import javafx.scene.control.TextArea;
 6  import javafx.scene.image.ImageView;
 7  import javafx.scene.layout.BorderPane;
 8  import javafx.scene.text.Font;
 9
10  public class DescriptionPane extends BorderPane {
11    /** Label for displaying an image and a title */
12    private Label lblImageTitle = new Label();               label
13
14    /** Text area for displaying text */
15    private TextArea taDescription = new TextArea();         text area
16
17    public DescriptionPane() {
18      // Center the icon and text and place the text under the icon
19      lblImageTitle.setContentDisplay(ContentDisplay.TOP);   label properties
20      lblImageTitle.setPrefSize(200,  100);
21
22      // Set the font in the label and the text field
23      lblImageTitle.setFont(new Font("SansSerif", 16));
24      taDescription.setFont(new Font("Serif", 14));
25
26      taDescription.setWrapText(true);                       wrap text
27      taDescription.setEditable(false);                      read only
28
29      // Create a scroll pane to hold the text area
30      ScrollPane scrollPane = new ScrollPane(taDescription); scroll pane
31
32      // Place label and scroll pane in the border pane
33      setLeft(lblImageTitle);
34      setCenter(scrollPane);
35      setPadding(new Insets(5, 5, 5, 5));
36    }
37
38    /** Set the title */
39    public void setTitle(String title) {
40      lblImageTitle.setText(title);
41    }
42
43    /** Set the image view */
44    public void setImageView(ImageView icon) {
45      lblImageTitle.setGraphic(icon);
46    }
47
48    /** Set the text description */
49    public void setDescription(String text) {
50      taDescription.setText(text);
51    }
52  }
```

The text area is inside a **ScrollPane** (line 30), which provides scrolling functions for the text area.

The **wrapText** property is set to **true** (line 26) so that the line is automatically wrapped when the text cannot fit in one line. The text area is set as noneditable (line 27), so you cannot edit the description in the text area.

It is not necessary to define a separate class for **DescriptionPane** in this example. However, this class was defined for reuse in the next section, where you will use it to display a description pane for various images.

LISTING 16.7 TextAreaDemo.java

```
1  import javafx.application.Application;
2  import javafx.stage.Stage;
3  import javafx.scene.Scene;
4  import javafx.scene.image.ImageView;
5
6  public class TextAreaDemo extends Application {
7    @Override // Override the start method in the Application class
8    public void start(Stage primaryStage) {
9      // Declare and create a description pane
10     DescriptionPane descriptionPane = new DescriptionPane();
11
12     // Set title, text, and image in the description pane
13     descriptionPane.setTitle("Canada");
14     String description = "The Canadian national flag ...";
15     descriptionPane.setImageView(new ImageView("image/ca.gif"));
16     descriptionPane.setDescription(description);
17
18     // Create a scene and place it in the stage
19     Scene scene = new Scene(descriptionPane, 450, 200);
20     primaryStage.setTitle("TextAreaDemo"); // Set the stage title
21     primaryStage.setScene(scene); // Place the scene in the stage
22     primaryStage.show(); // Display the stage
23   }
24 }
```

create descriptionPane (line 10)

set title (line 13)

set image (line 15)

add descriptionPane to scene (line 19)

The program creates an instance of **DescriptionPane** (line 10), and sets the title (line 13), image (line 15), and text in the description pane (line 16). **DescriptionPane** is a subclass of **Pane**. **DescriptionPane** contains a label for displaying an image and a title, and a text area for displaying a description of the image.

16.19 How do you create a text area with **10** rows and **20** columns?

16.20 How do you obtain the text from a text area?

16.21 Can you disable editing of a text area?

16.22 What method do you use to wrap text to the next line in a text area?

16.8 ComboBox

 A combo box, also known as a choice list or drop-down list, contains a list of items from which the user can choose.

A combo box is useful for limiting a user's range of choices and avoids the cumbersome validation of data input. Figure 16.16 lists several frequently used properties and constructors in **ComboBox**. **ComboBox** is defined as a generic class. The generic type **T** specifies the element type for the elements stored in a combo box.

The following statements create a combo box with four items, red color, and value set to the first item.

```
ComboBox<String> cbo = new ComboBox<>();
cbo.getItems().addAll("Item 1", "Item 2",
  "Item 3", "Item 4");
cbo.setStyle("-fx-color: red");
cbo.setValue("Item 1");
```

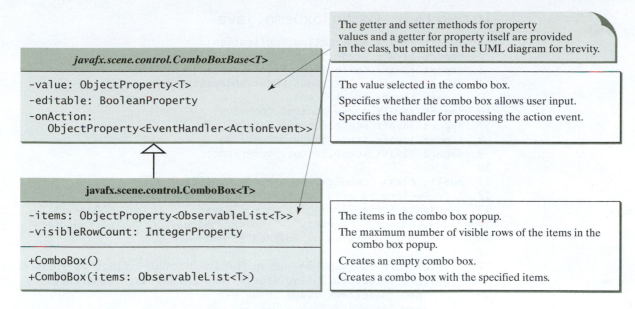

The getter and setter methods for property values and a getter for property itself are provided in the class, but omitted in the UML diagram for brevity.

javafx.scene.control.ComboBoxBase<T>

-value: ObjectProperty<T>
-editable: BooleanProperty
-onAction:
    ObjectProperty<EventHandler<ActionEvent>>

The value selected in the combo box.
Specifies whether the combo box allows user input.
Specifies the handler for processing the action event.

javafx.scene.control.ComboBox<T>

-items: ObjectProperty<ObservableList<T>>
-visibleRowCount: IntegerProperty

+ComboBox()
+ComboBox(items: ObservableList<T>)

The items in the combo box popup.
The maximum number of visible rows of the items in the combo box popup.
Creates an empty combo box.
Creates a combo box with the specified items.

FIGURE 16.16 **ComboBox** enables the user to select an item from a list of items.

ComboBox inherits from **ComboBoxBase**. **ComboBox** can fire an **ActionEvent**. Whenever an item is selected, an **ActionEvent** is fired. **ObservableList** is a subinterface of **java.util.List**. So you can apply all the methods defined in **List** for an **ObservableList**. For convenience, JavaFX provides the static method **FXCollections.observableArrayList(arrayOfElements)** for creating an **ObservableList** from an array of elements.

Listing 16.8 gives a program that lets the user view an image and a description of a country's flag by selecting the country from a combo box, as shown in Figure 16.17.

FIGURE 16.17 Information about a country, including an image and a description of its flag, is displayed when the country is selected in the combo box.

Here are the major steps in the program:

1. Create the user interface.
   Create a combo box with country names as its selection values. Create a **DescriptionPane** object (the **DescriptionPane** class was introduced in the preceding section). Place the combo box at the top of the border pane and the description pane in the center of the border pane.

2. Process the event.
   Create a handler for handling action event from the combo box to set the flag title, image, and text in the description pane for the selected country name.

LISTING 16.8 ComboBoxDemo.java

```
1   import javafx.application.Application;
2   import javafx.stage.Stage;
3   import javafx.collections.FXCollections;
4   import javafx.collections.ObservableList;
5   import javafx.scene.Scene;
6   import javafx.scene.control.ComboBox;
7   import javafx.scene.control.Label;
8   import javafx.scene.image.ImageView;
9   import javafx.scene.layout.BorderPane;
10
11  public class ComboBoxDemo extends Application {
12    // Declare an array of Strings for flag titles
13    private String[] flagTitles = {"Canada", "China", "Denmark",
14        "France", "Germany", "India", "Norway", "United Kingdom",
15        "United States of America"};
16
17    // Declare an ImageView array for the national flags of 9 countries
18    private ImageView[] flagImage = {new ImageView("image/ca.gif"),
19        new ImageView("image/china.gif"),
20        new ImageView("image/denmark.gif"),
21        new ImageView("image/fr.gif"),
22        new ImageView("image/germany.gif"),
23        new ImageView("image/india.gif"),
24        new ImageView("image/norway.gif"),
25        new ImageView("image/uk.gif"), new ImageView("image/us.gif")};
26
27    // Declare an array of strings for flag descriptions
28    private String[] flagDescription = new String[9];
29
30    // Declare and create a description pane
31    private DescriptionPane descriptionPane = new DescriptionPane();
32
33    // Create a combo box for selecting countries
34    private ComboBox<String> cbo = new ComboBox<>(); // flagTitles;
35
36    @Override // Override the start method in the Application class
37    public void start(Stage primaryStage) {
38      // Set text description
39      flagDescription[0] = "The Canadian national flag ...";
40      flagDescription[1] = "Description for China ... ";
41      flagDescription[2] = "Description for Denmark ... ";
42      flagDescription[3] = "Description for France ... ";
43      flagDescription[4] = "Description for Germany ... ";
44      flagDescription[5] = "Description for India ... ";
45      flagDescription[6] = "Description for Norway ... ";
46      flagDescription[7] = "Description for UK ... ";
47      flagDescription[8] = "Description for US ... ";
48
49      // Set the first country (Canada) for display
50      setDisplay(0);
51
52      // Add combo box and description pane to the border pane
53      BorderPane pane = new BorderPane();
54
55      BorderPane paneForComboBox = new BorderPane();
56      paneForComboBox.setLeft(new Label("Select a country: "));
57      paneForComboBox.setCenter(cbo);
58      pane.setTop(paneForComboBox);
```

countries

image views

description

combo box

```
59        cbo.setPrefWidth(400);
60        cbo.setValue("Canada");
61
62        ObservableList<String> items =
63          FXCollections.observableArrayList(flagTitles);
64        cbo.getItems().addAll(items);
65        pane.setCenter(descriptionPane);
66
67        // Display the selected country
68        cbo.setOnAction(e -> setDisplay(items.indexOf(cbo.getValue())));
69
70        // Create a scene and place it in the stage
71        Scene scene = new Scene(pane, 450, 170);
72        primaryStage.setTitle("ComboBoxDemo"); // Set the stage title
73        primaryStage.setScene(scene); // Place the scene in the stage
74        primaryStage.show(); // Display the stage
75      }
76
77      /** Set display information on the description pane */
78      public void setDisplay(int index) {
79        descriptionPane.setTitle(flagTitles[index]);
80        descriptionPane.setImageView(flagImage[index]);
81        descriptionPane.setDescription(flagDescription[index]);
82      }
83    }
```

set combo box value

observable list

add to combo box

The program stores the flag information in three arrays: **flagTitles**, **flagImage**, and **flagDescription** (lines 13–28). The array **flagTitles** contains the names of nine countries, the array **flagImage** contains image views of the nine countries' flags, and the array **flagDescription** contains descriptions of the flags.

The program creates an instance of **DescriptionPane** (line 31), which was presented in Listing 16.6, DescriptionPane.java. The program creates a combo box with values from **flagTitles** (lines 62–63). The **getItems()** method returns a list from the combo box (line 64) and the **addAll** method adds multiple items into the list.

When the user selects an item in the combo box, the action event triggers the execution of the handler. The handler finds the selected index (line 68) and invokes the **setDisplay(int index)** method to set its corresponding flag title, flag image, and flag description on the pane (lines 78–82).

16.23 How do you create a combo box and add three items to it?

16.24 How do you retrieve an item from a combo box? How do you retrieve a selected item from a combo box?

16.25 How do you get the number of items in a combo box? How do you retrieve an item at a specified index in a combo box?

16.26 What events would a **ComboBox** fire upon selecting a new item?

Check Point

16.9 ListView

Key Point

A list view is a control that basically performs the same function as a combo box, but it enables the user to choose a single value or multiple values.

Figure 16.18 lists several frequently used properties and constructors in **ListView**. **ListView** is defined as a generic class. The generic type **T** specifies the element type for the elements stored in a list view.

VideoNote
Use ListView

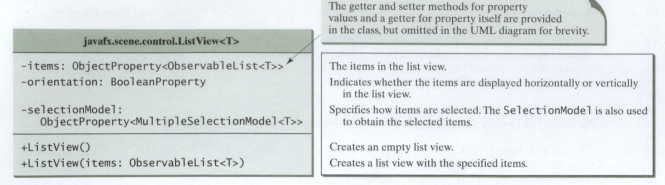

FIGURE 16.18 `ListView` enables the user to select one or multiple items from a list of items.

The `getSelectionModel()` method returns an instance of `SelectionModel`, which contains the methods for setting a selection mode and obtaining selected indices and items. The selection mode is defined in one of the two constants `SelectionMode.MULTIPLE` and `SelectionMode.SINGLE`, which indicates whether a single item or multiple items can be selected. The default value is `SelectionMode.SINGLE`. Figure 16.19a shows a single selection and Figure 16.19b–c show multiple selections.

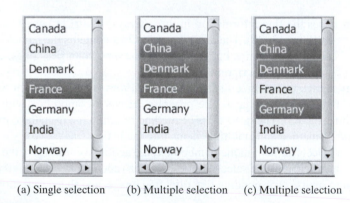

(a) Single selection   (b) Multiple selection   (c) Multiple selection

FIGURE 16.19 `SelecitonMode` has two selection modes: single selection and multiple-interval selection.

The following statements create a list view of six items with multiple selections allowed.

```
ObservableList<String> items =
  FXCollections.observableArrayList("Item 1", "Item 2",
    "Item 3", "Item 4", "Item 5", "Item 6");
ListView<String> lv = new ListView<>(items);
lv.getSelectionModel().setSelectionMode(SelectionMode.MULTIPLE);
```

The selection model in a list view has the `selectedItemProperty` property, which is an instance of `Observable`. As discussed in Section 15.10, you can add a listener to this property for handling the property change as follows:

```
lv.getSelectionModel().selectedItemProperty().addListener(
  new InvalidationListener() {
    public void invalidated(Observable ov) {
      System.out.println("Selected indices: "
        + lv.getSelectionModel().getSelectedIndices());
```

```
          System.out.println("Selected items: "
            + lv.getSelectionModel().getSelectedItems());
        }
      });
```

This anonymous inner class can be simplified using a lambda expression as follows:

```
    lv.getSelectionModel().selectedItemProperty().addListener(ov -> {
      System.out.println("Selected indices: "
        + lv.getSelectionModel().getSelectedIndices());
      System.out.println("Selected items: "
        + lv.getSelectionModel().getSelectedItems());
    });
```

Listing 16.9 gives a program that lets users select the countries in a list view and displays the flags of the selected countries in the image views. Figure 16.20 shows a sample run of the program.

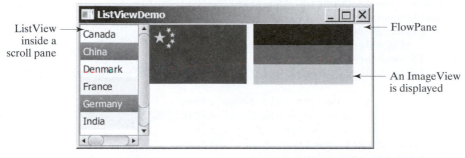

FIGURE 16.20 When the countries in the list view are selected, corresponding images of their flags are displayed in the image views.

Here are the major steps in the program:

1. Create the user interface.
   Create a list view with nine country names as selection values, and place the list view inside a scroll pane. Place the scroll pane on the left of a border pane. Create nine image views to be used to display the countries' flag images. Create a flow pane to hold the image views and place the pane in the center of the border pane.

2. Process the event.
   Create a listener to implement the **invalidated** method in the **InvalidationListener** interface to place the selected countries' flag image views in the pane.

LISTING 16.9 ListViewDemo.java

```
 1  import javafx.application.Application;
 2  import javafx.stage.Stage;
 3  import javafx.collections.FXCollections;
 4  import javafx.scene.Scene;
 5  import javafx.scene.control.ListView;
 6  import javafx.scene.control.ScrollPane;
 7  import javafx.scene.control.SelectionMode;
 8  import javafx.scene.image.ImageView;
 9  import javafx.scene.layout.BorderPane;
10  import javafx.scene.layout.FlowPane;
11
12  public class ListViewDemo extends Application {
```

```
13      // Declare an array of Strings for flag titles
14      private String[] flagTitles = {"Canada", "China", "Denmark",
15        "France", "Germany", "India", "Norway", "United Kingdom",
16        "United States of America"};
17
18      // Declare an ImageView array for the national flags of 9 countries
19      private ImageView[] ImageViews = {
20        new ImageView("image/ca.gif"),
21        new ImageView("image/china.gif"),
22        new ImageView("image/denmark.gif"),
23        new ImageView("image/fr.gif"),
24        new ImageView("image/germany.gif"),
25        new ImageView("image/india.gif"),
26        new ImageView("image/norway.gif"),
27        new ImageView("image/uk.gif"),
28        new ImageView("image/us.gif")
29      };
30
31      @Override // Override the start method in the Application class
32      public void start(Stage primaryStage) {
33        ListView<String> lv = new ListView<>
34          (FXCollections.observableArrayList(flagTitles));
35        lv.setPrefSize(400, 400);
36        lv.getSelectionModel().setSelectionMode(SelectionMode.MULTIPLE);
37
38        // Create a pane to hold image views
39        FlowPane imagePane = new FlowPane(10, 10);
40        BorderPane pane = new BorderPane();
41        pane.setLeft(new ScrollPane(lv));
42        pane.setCenter(imagePane);
43
44        lv.getSelectionModel().selectedItemProperty().addListener(
45          ov -> {
46            imagePane.getChildren().clear();
47            for (Integer i: lv.getSelectionModel().getSelectedIndices()) {
48              imagePane.getChildren().add(ImageViews[i]);
49            }
50        });
51
52        // Create a scene and place it in the stage
53        Scene scene = new Scene(pane, 450, 170);
54        primaryStage.setTitle("ListViewDemo"); // Set the stage title
55        primaryStage.setScene(scene); // Place the scene in the stage
56        primaryStage.show(); // Display the stage
57      }
58    }
```

Margin notes:
- create a list view (line 33)
- set list view properties (lines 35–36)
- place list view in pane (lines 41–42)
- listen to item selected (line 44)
- add image views of selected items (lines 48)

The program creates an array of strings for countries (lines 14–16) and an array of nine image views for displaying flag images for nine countries (lines 19–29) in the same order as in the array of countries. The items in the list view are from the array of countries (line 34). Thus, the index **0** of the image view array corresponds to the first country in the list view.

The list view is placed in a scroll pane (line 41) so that it can be scrolled when the number of items in the list extends beyond the viewing area.

By default, the selection mode of the list view is single. The selection mode for the list view is set to multiple (line 36), which allows the user to select multiple items in the list view. When the user selects countries in the list view, the listener's handler (lines 44–50) is executed, which gets the indices of the selected items and adds their corresponding image views to the flow pane.

16.27 How do you create an observable list with an array of strings?

16.28 How do you set the orientation in a list view?

16.29 What selection modes are available for a list view? What is the default selection mode? How do you set a selection mode?

16.30 How do you obtain the selected items and selected indices?

16.10 **ScrollBar**

ScrollBar is a control that enables the user to select from a range of values.

Figure 16.21 shows a scroll bar. Normally, the user changes the value of a scroll bar by making a gesture with the mouse. For example, the user can drag the scroll bar's thumb, click on the scroll bar track, or the scroll bar's left or right buttons.

Minimal value   Maximal value

Track

Thumb

Left button   Right button

FIGURE 16.21 A scroll bar represents a range of values graphically.

ScrollBar has the following properties, as shown in Figure 16.22.

The getter and setter methods for property values and a getter for property itself are provided in the class, but omitted in the UML diagram for brevity.

javafx.scene.control.ScrollBar	
-blockIncrement: DoubleProperty	The amount to adjust the scroll bar if the track of the bar is clicked (default: 10).
-max: DoubleProperty	The maximum value represented by this scroll bar (default: 100).
-min: DoubleProperty	The minimum value represented by this scroll bar (default: 0).
-unitIncrement: DoubleProperty	The amount to adjust the scroll bar when the **increment()** and **decrement()** methods are called (default: 1).
-value: DoubleProperty	Current value of the scroll bar (default: 0).
-visibleAmount: DoubleProperty	The width of the scroll bar (default: 15).
-orientation: ObjectProperty<Orientation>	Specifies the orientation of the scroll bar (default: HORIZONTAL).
+ScrollBar()	Creates a default horizontal scroll bar.
+increment()	Increments the value of the scroll bar by **unitIncrement**.
+decrement()	Decrements the value of the scroll bar by **unitIncrement**.

FIGURE 16.22 **ScrollBar** enables the user to select from a range of values.

 Note
The width of the scroll bar's track corresponds to **max + visibleAmount**. When a scroll bar is set to its maximum value, the left side of the bubble is at **max**, and the right side is at **max + visibleAmount**.

When the user changes the value of the scroll bar, it notifies the listener of the change. You can register a listener on the scroll bar's **valueProperty** for responding to this change as follows:

```
ScrollBar sb = new ScrollBar();
sb.valueProperty().addListener(ov -> {
   System.out.println("old value: " + oldVal);
   System.out.println("new value: " + newVal);
});
```

Listing 16.10 gives a program that uses horizontal and vertical scroll bars to move a text displayed on a pane. The horizontal scroll bar is used to move the text to the left and the right, and the vertical scroll bar to move it up and down. A sample run of the program is shown in Figure 16.23.

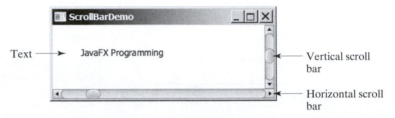

FIGURE 16.23 The scroll bars move the message on a pane horizontally and vertically.

Here are the major steps in the program:

1. Create the user interface.
   Create a **Text** object and place it in the center of the border pane. Create a vertical scroll bar and place it on the right of the border pane. Create a horizontal scroll bar and place it at the bottom of the border pane.

2. Process the event.
   Create listeners to move the text according to the bar movement in the scroll bars upon the change of the **value** property.

LISTING 16.10 ScrollBarDemo.java

```
1   import javafx.application.Application;
2   import javafx.stage.Stage;
3   import javafx.geometry.Orientation;
4   import javafx.scene.Scene;
5   import javafx.scene.control.ScrollBar;
6   import javafx.scene.layout.BorderPane;
7   import javafx.scene.layout.Pane;
8   import javafx.scene.text.Text;
9
10  public class ScrollBarDemo extends Application {
11    @Override // Override the start method in the Application class
12    public void start(Stage primaryStage) {
13      Text text = new Text(20, 20, "JavaFX Programming");
14
15      ScrollBar sbHorizontal = new ScrollBar();
16      ScrollBar sbVertical = new ScrollBar();
17      sbVertical.setOrientation(Orientation.VERTICAL);
18
19      // Create a text in a pane
```

horizontal scroll bar
vertical scroll bar

```
20        Pane paneForText = new Pane();
21        paneForText.getChildren().add(text);
22
23        // Create a border pane to hold text and scroll bars
24        BorderPane pane = new BorderPane();
25        pane.setCenter(paneForText);
26        pane.setBottom(sbHorizontal);
27        pane.setRight(sbVertical);
28
29        // Listener for horizontal scroll bar value change
30        sbHorizontal.valueProperty().addListener(ov ->
31          text.setX(sbHorizontal.getValue() * paneForText.getWidth() /
32            sbHorizontal.getMax()));
33
34        // Listener for vertical scroll bar value change
35        sbVertical.valueProperty().addListener(ov ->
36          text.setY(sbVertical.getValue() * paneForText.getHeight() /
37            sbVertical.getMax()));
38
39        // Create a scene and place it in the stage
40        Scene scene = new Scene(pane, 450, 170);
41        primaryStage.setTitle("ScrollBarDemo"); // Set the stage title
42        primaryStage.setScene(scene); // Place the scene in the stage
43        primaryStage.show(); // Display the stage
44      }
45  }
```

add text to a pane (line 21)

border pane (line 24)

set new location for text (lines 31–32)

set new location for text (lines 36–37)

The program creates a text (line 13) and two scroll bars (**sbHorizontal** and **sbVertical**) (lines 15–16). The text is placed in a pane (line 21) that is then placed in the center of the border pane (line 25). If the text were directly placed in the center of the border pane, the position of the text cannot be changed by resetting its *x* and *y* properties. The **sbHorizontal** and **sbVertical** are placed on the right and at the bottom of the border pane (lines 26–27), respectively.

You can specify the properties of the scroll bar. By default, the property value is **100** for **max**, **0** for **min**, **10** for **blockIncrement**, and **15** for **visibleAmount**.

A listener is registered to listen for the **sbHorizontal value** property change (lines 30–32). When the value of the scroll bar changes, the listener is notified by invoking the handler to set a new *x* value for the text that corresponds to the current value of **sbHorizontal** (lines 31–32).

A listener is registered to listen for the **sbVertical value** property change (lines 35–37). When the value of the scroll bar changes, the listener is notified by invoking the handler to set a new *y* value for the text that corresponds to the current value of **sbVertical** (lines 36–37).

Alternatively, the code in lines 30–37 can be replaced by using binding properties as follows:

```
text.xProperty().bind(sbHorizontal.valueProperty().
  multiply(paneForText.widthProperty()).
  divide(sbHorizontal.maxProperty()));

text.yProperty().bind(sbVertical.valueProperty().multiply(
  paneForText.heightProperty().divide(
  sbVertical.maxProperty())));
```

16.31 How do you create a horizontal scroll bar? How do you create a vertical scroll bar?

16.32 How do you write the code to respond to the **value** property change of a scroll bar?

16.33 How do you get the value from a scroll bar? How do you get the maximum value from a scroll bar?

Check Point

16.11 Slider

Key Point

Slider is similar to ScrollBar, but Slider has more properties and can appear in many forms.

VideoNote

Use Slider

Figure 16.24 shows two sliders. Slider lets the user graphically select a value by sliding a knob within a bounded interval. The slider can show both major tick marks and minor tick marks between them. The number of pixels between the tick marks is specified by the **majorTickUnit** and **minorTickUnit** properties. Sliders can be displayed horizontally or vertically, with or without ticks, and with or without labels.

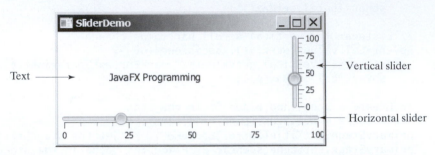

FIGURE 16.24 The sliders move the message on a pane horizontally and vertically.

The frequently used constructors and properties in Slider are shown in Figure 16.25.

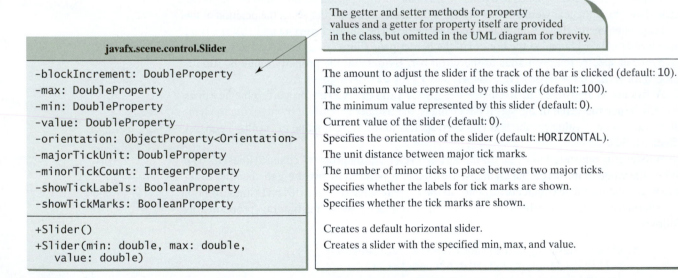

The getter and setter methods for property values and a getter for property itself are provided in the class, but omitted in the UML diagram for brevity.

javafx.scene.control.Slider

-blockIncrement: DoubleProperty	The amount to adjust the slider if the track of the bar is clicked (default: 10).
-max: DoubleProperty	The maximum value represented by this slider (default: 100).
-min: DoubleProperty	The minimum value represented by this slider (default: 0).
-value: DoubleProperty	Current value of the slider (default: 0).
-orientation: ObjectProperty<Orientation>	Specifies the orientation of the slider (default: HORIZONTAL).
-majorTickUnit: DoubleProperty	The unit distance between major tick marks.
-minorTickCount: IntegerProperty	The number of minor ticks to place between two major ticks.
-showTickLabels: BooleanProperty	Specifies whether the labels for tick marks are shown.
-showTickMarks: BooleanProperty	Specifies whether the tick marks are shown.
+Slider()	Creates a default horizontal slider.
+Slider(min: double, max: double, value: double)	Creates a slider with the specified min, max, and value.

FIGURE 16.25 Slider enables the user to select from a range of values.

Note

The values of a vertical scroll bar increase from top to bottom, but the values of a vertical slider decrease from top to bottom.

You can add a listener to listen for the **value** property change in a slider in the same way as in a scroll bar. We now rewrite the program in the preceding section using the sliders to move a text displayed on a pane in Listing 16.11. A sample run of the program is shown in Figure 16.24.

LISTING 16.11 SliderDemo.java

```
1  import javafx.application.Application;
2  import javafx.stage.Stage;
3  import javafx.geometry.Orientation;
4  import javafx.scene.Scene;
5  import javafx.scene.control.Slider;
6  import javafx.scene.layout.BorderPane;
7  import javafx.scene.layout.Pane;
8  import javafx.scene.text.Text;
9
10 public class SliderDemo extends Application {
11   @Override // Override the start method in the Application class
12   public void start(Stage primaryStage) {
13     Text text = new Text(20, 20, "JavaFX Programming");
14
15     Slider slHorizontal = new Slider();                          horizontal slider
16     slHorizontal.setShowTickLabels(true);                        set slider properties
17     slHorizontal.setShowTickMarks(true);
18
19     Slider slVertical = new Slider();                            vertical slider
20     slVertical.setOrientation(Orientation.VERTICAL);             set slider properties
21     slVertical.setShowTickLabels(true);
22     slVertical.setShowTickMarks(true);
23     slVertical.setValue(100);
24
25     // Create a text in a pane
26     Pane paneForText = new Pane();
27     paneForText.getChildren().add(text);                         add text to a pane
28
29     // Create a border pane to hold text and scroll bars
30     BorderPane pane = new BorderPane();                          border pane
31     pane.setCenter(paneForText);
32     pane.setBottom(slHorizontal);
33     pane.setRight(slVertical);
34
35     slHorizontal.valueProperty().addListener(ov ->
36       text.setX(slHorizontal.getValue() * paneForText.getWidth() /    set new location for text
37         slHorizontal.getMax()));
38
39     slVertical.valueProperty().addListener(ov ->
40       text.setY((slVertical.getMax() - slVertical.getValue())        set new location for text
41         * paneForText.getHeight() / slVertical.getMax()));
42
43     // Create a scene and place it in the stage
44     Scene scene = new Scene(pane, 450, 170);
45     primaryStage.setTitle("SliderDemo"); // Set the stage title
46     primaryStage.setScene(scene); // Place the scene in the stage
47     primaryStage.show(); // Display the stage
48   }
49 }
```

Slider is similar to ScrollBar but has more features. As shown in this example, you can specify labels, major ticks, and minor ticks on a Slider (lines 16–17).

A listener is registered to listen for the slHorizontal value property change (lines 35–37) and another one is for the sbVertical value property change (lines 39–41). When the value of the slider changes, the listener is notified by invoking the handler to set a new position for the text (lines 36–37, 40–41). Note that since the value of a vertical slider decreases from top to bottom, the corresponding y value for the text is adjusted accordingly.

The code in lines 35–41 can be replaced by using binding properties as follows:

```
text.xProperty().bind(slHorizontal.valueProperty().
  multiply(paneForText.widthProperty()).
  divide(slHorizontal.maxProperty()));

text.yProperty().bind((slVertical.maxProperty().subtract(
  slVertical.valueProperty()).multiply(
  paneForText.heightProperty().divide(
  slVertical.maxProperty())))));
```

Listing 15.17 gives a program that displays a bouncing ball. You can add a slider to control the speed of the ball movement as shown in Figure 16.26. The new program is given in Listing 16.12.

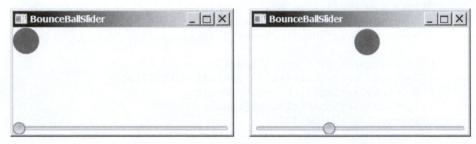

FIGURE 16.26 You can increase or decrease the speed of the ball using a slider.

LISTING 16.12   BounceBallSlider.java

```
 1  import javafx.application.Application;
 2  import javafx.stage.Stage;
 3  import javafx.scene.Scene;
 4  import javafx.scene.control.Slider;
 5  import javafx.scene.layout.BorderPane;
 6
 7  public class BounceBallSlider extends Application {
 8    @Override // Override the start method in the Application class
 9    public void start(Stage primaryStage) {
10      BallPane ballPane = new BallPane();
11      Slider slSpeed = new Slider();
12      slSpeed.setMax(20);
13      ballPane.rateProperty().bind(slSpeed.valueProperty());
14
15      BorderPane pane = new BorderPane();
16      pane.setCenter(ballPane);
17      pane.setBottom(slSpeed);
18
19      // Create a scene and place it in the stage
20      Scene scene = new Scene(pane, 250, 250);
21      primaryStage.setTitle("BounceBallSlider"); // Set the stage title
22      primaryStage.setScene(scene); // Place the scene in the stage
23      primaryStage.show(); // Display the stage
24    }
25  }
```

create a ball pane — 10
create a slider — 11
set max value for slider — 12
bind rate with slider value — 13

create a border pane — 15
add ball pane to center — 16
add slider to the bottom — 17

The **BallPane** class defined in Listing 15.17 animates a ball bouncing in a pane. The **rateProperty()** method in **BallPane** returns a property value for animation rate.

The animation stops if the rate is 0. If the rate is greater than 20, the animation will be too fast. So, we purposely set the rate to a value between 0 and 20. This value is bound to the slider value (line 13). So the slider max value is set to 20 (line 12).

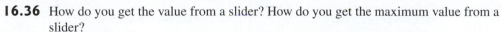

16.34 How do you create a horizontal slider? How do you create a vertical slider?

16.35 How do you add a listener to handle the property value change of a slider?

16.36 How do you get the value from a slider? How do you get the maximum value from a slider?

Check
Point

16.12 Case Study: Developing a Tic-Tac-Toe Game

This section develops a program for playing tic-tac-toe.

**Key
Point**

VideoNote

TicTacToe

From the many examples in this and earlier chapters you have learned about objects, classes, arrays, class inheritance, GUI, and event-driven programming. Now it is time to put what you have learned to work in developing comprehensive projects. In this section, we will develop a JavaFX program with which to play the popular game of tic-tac-toe.

Two players take turns marking an available cell in a 3 × 3 grid with their respective tokens (either X or O). When one player has placed three tokens in a horizontal, vertical, or diagonal row on the grid, the game is over and that player has won. A draw (no winner) occurs when all the cells on the grid have been filled with tokens and neither player has achieved a win. Figure 16.27 shows the representative sample runs of the game.

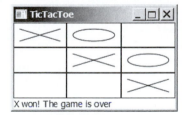
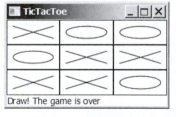
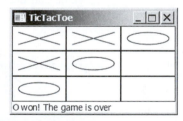

(a) The X player won the game   (b) Draw — no winners   (c) The O player won the game

FIGURE 16.27 Two players play a tic-tac-toe game.

All the examples you have seen so far show simple behaviors that are easy to model with classes. The behavior of the tic-tac-toe game is somewhat more complex. To define classes that model the behavior, you need to study and understand the game.

Assume that all the cells are initially empty, and that the first player takes the X token and the second player the O token. To mark a cell, the player points the mouse to the cell and clicks it. If the cell is empty, the token (X or O) is displayed. If the cell is already filled, the player's action is ignored.

From the preceding description, it is obvious that a cell is a GUI object that handles the mouse-click event and displays tokens. There are many choices for this object. We will use a pane to model a cell and to display a token (X or O). How do you know the state of the cell (empty, X, or O)? You use a property named **token** of the **char** type in the **Cell** class. The **Cell** class is responsible for drawing the token when an empty cell is clicked, so you need to write the code for listening to the mouse-clicked action and for painting the shapes for tokens X and O. The **Cell** class can be defined as shown in Figure 16.28.

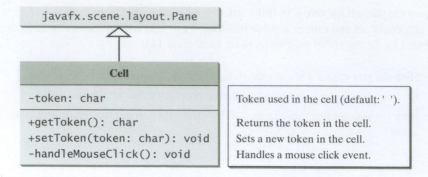

FIGURE 16.28 The `Cell` class displays the token in a cell.

The tic-tac-toe board consists of nine cells, created using `new Cell[3][3]`. To determine which player's turn it is, you can introduce a variable named `whoseTurn` of the `char` type. `whoseTurn` is initially `'X'`, then changes to `'O'`, and subsequently changes between `'X'` and `'O'` whenever a new cell is occupied. When the game is over, set `whoseTurn` to `' '`.

How do you know whether the game is over, whether there is a winner, and who the winner, if any? You can define a method named `isWon(char token)` to check whether a specified token has won and a method named `isFull()` to check whether all the cells are occupied.

Clearly, two classes emerge from the foregoing analysis. One is the `Cell` class, which handles operations for a single cell; the other is the `TicTacToe` class, which plays the whole game and deals with all the cells. The relationship between these two classes is shown in Figure 16.29.

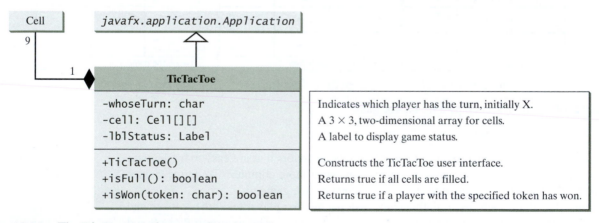

FIGURE 16.29 The `TicTacToe` class contains nine cells.

Since the `Cell` class is only to support the `TicTacToe` class, it can be defined as an inner class in `TicTacToe`. The complete program is given in Listing 16.13.

LISTING 16.13 `TicTacToe.java`

```java
1  import javafx.application.Application;
2  import javafx.stage.Stage;
3  import javafx.scene.Scene;
4  import javafx.scene.control.Label;
5  import javafx.scene.layout.BorderPane;
```

```
 6   import javafx.scene.layout.GridPane;
 7   import javafx.scene.layout.Pane;
 8   import javafx.scene.paint.Color;
 9   import javafx.scene.shape.Line;
10   import javafx.scene.shape.Ellipse;
11
12   public class TicTacToe extends Application {
13     // Indicate which player has a turn, initially it is the X player
14     private char whoseTurn = 'X';
15
16     // Create and initialize cell
17     private Cell[][] cell = new Cell[3][3];
18
19     // Create and initialize a status label
20     private Label lblStatus = new Label("X's turn to play");
21
22     @Override // Override the start method in the Application class
23     public void start(Stage primaryStage) {
24       // Pane to hold cell
25       GridPane pane = new GridPane();
26       for (int i = 0; i < 3; i++)
27         for (int j = 0; j < 3; j++)
28           pane.add(cell[i][j] = new Cell(), j, i);
29
30       BorderPane borderPane = new BorderPane();
31       borderPane.setCenter(pane);
32       borderPane.setBottom(lblStatus);
33
34       // Create a scene and place it in the stage
35       Scene scene = new Scene(borderPane, 450, 170);
36       primaryStage.setTitle("TicTacToe"); // Set the stage title
37       primaryStage.setScene(scene); // Place the scene in the stage
38       primaryStage.show(); // Display the stage
39     }
40
41     /** Determine if the cell are all occupied */
42     public boolean isFull() {
43       for (int i = 0; i < 3; i++)
44         for (int j = 0; j < 3; j++)
45           if (cell[i][j].getToken() == ' ')
46             return false;
47
48       return true;
49     }
50
51     /** Determine if the player with the specified token wins */
52     public boolean isWon(char token) {
53       for (int i = 0; i < 3; i++)
54         if (cell[i][0].getToken() == token
55             && cell[i][1].getToken() == token
56             && cell[i][2].getToken() == token) {
57           return true;
58         }
59
60       for (int j = 0; j < 3; j++)
61         if (cell[0][j].getToken() ==  token
62             && cell[1][j].getToken() == token
63             && cell[2][j].getToken() == token) {
64           return true;
65         }
```

main class TicTacToe

hold nine cells

create a cell

tic-tac-toe cells in center
label at bottom

check isFull

check rows

check columns

```
                        66
check major diagonal    67        if (cell[0][0].getToken() == token
                        68            && cell[1][1].getToken() == token
                        69            && cell[2][2].getToken() == token) {
                        70          return true;
                        71        }
                        72
check subdiagonal       73        if (cell[0][2].getToken() == token
                        74            && cell[1][1].getToken() == token
                        75            && cell[2][0].getToken() == token) {
                        76          return true;
                        77        }
                        78
                        79        return false;
                        80      }
                        81
                        82      // An inner class for a cell
inner class Cell        83      public class Cell extends Pane {
                        84        // Token used for this cell
                        85        private char token = ' ';
                        86
                        87        public Cell() {
                        88          setStyle("-fx-border-color: black");
                        89          this.setPrefSize(2000, 2000);
register listener       90          this.setOnMouseClicked(e -> handleMouseClick());
                        91        }
                        92
                        93        /** Return token */
                        94        public char getToken() {
                        95          return token;
                        96        }
                        97
                        98        /** Set a new token */
                        99        public void setToken(char c) {
                       100          token = c;
                       101
display X              102          if (token == 'X') {
                       103            Line line1 = new Line(10, 10,
                       104              this.getWidth() - 10, this.getHeight() - 10);
                       105            line1.endXProperty().bind(this.widthProperty().subtract(10));
                       106            line1.endYProperty().bind(this.heightProperty().subtract(10));
                       107            Line line2 = new Line(10, this.getHeight() - 10,
                       108              this.getWidth() - 10, 10);
                       109            line2.startYProperty().bind(
                       110              this.heightProperty().subtract(10));
                       111            line2.endXProperty().bind(this.widthProperty().subtract(10));
                       112
                       113            // Add the lines to the pane
                       114            this.getChildren().addAll(line1, line2);
                       115          }
display O              116          else if (token == 'O') {
                       117            Ellipse ellipse = new Ellipse(this.getWidth() / 2,
                       118              this.getHeight() / 2, this.getWidth() / 2 - 10,
                       119              this.getHeight() / 2 - 10);
                       120            ellipse.centerXProperty().bind(
                       121              this.widthProperty().divide(2));
                       122            ellipse.centerYProperty().bind(
                       123              this.heightProperty().divide(2));
                       124            ellipse.radiusXProperty().bind(
                       125              this.widthProperty().divide(2).subtract(10));
```

```
126          ellipse.radiusYProperty().bind(
127            this.heightProperty().divide(2).subtract(10));
128          ellipse.setStroke(Color.BLACK);
129          ellipse.setFill(Color.WHITE);
130
131          getChildren().add(ellipse); // Add the ellipse to the pane
132        }
133      }
134
135      /* Handle a mouse click event */
136      private void handleMouseClick() {                                    handle mouse click
137        // If cell is empty and game is not over
138        if (token == ' ' && whoseTurn != ' ') {
139          setToken(whoseTurn); // Set token in the cell
140
141          // Check game status
142          if (isWon(whoseTurn)) {
143            lblStatus.setText(whoseTurn + " won! The game is over");
144            whoseTurn = ' '; // Game is over
145          }
146          else if (isFull()) {
147            lblStatus.setText("Draw! The game is over");
148            whoseTurn = ' '; // Game is over
149          }
150          else {
151            // Change the turn
152            whoseTurn = (whoseTurn == 'X') ? 'O' : 'X';
153            // Display whose turn
154            lblStatus.setText(whoseTurn + "'s turn");
155          }
156        }
157      }
158    }
159  }
```

The **TicTacToe** class initializes the user interface with nine cells placed in a grid pane (lines 25–28). A label named **lblStatus** is used to show the status of the game (line 20). The variable **whoseTurn** (line 14) is used to track the next type of token to be placed in a cell. The methods **isFull** (lines 42–49) and **isWon** (lines 52–80) are for checking the status of the game.

Since **Cell** is an inner class in **TicTacToe**, the variable (**whoseTurn**) and methods (**isFull** and **isWon**) defined in **TicTacToe** can be referenced from the **Cell** class. The inner class makes programs simple and concise. If **Cell** were not defined as an inner class of **TicTacToe**, you would have to pass an object of **TicTacToe** to **Cell** in order for the variables and methods in **TicTacToe** to be used in **Cell**.

The listener for the mouse-click action is registered for the cell (line 90). If an empty cell is clicked and the game is not over, a token is set in the cell (line 138). If the game is over, **whoseTurn** is set to ' ' (lines 144, 148). Otherwise, **whoseTurn** is alternated to a new turn (line 152).

Tip

Use an incremental approach in developing and testing a Java project of this kind. For   incremental development and
example, this program can be divided into five steps: testing

1. Lay out the user interface and display a fixed token X on a cell.

2. Enable the cell to display a fixed token X upon a mouse click.

3. Coordinate between the two players so as to display tokens X and O alternately.

4. Check whether a player wins, or whether all the cells are occupied without a winner.

5. Implement displaying a message on the label upon each move by a player.

Check Point

16.37 When the game starts, what value is in **whoseTurn**? When the game is over, what value is in **whoseTurn**?

16.38 What happens when the user clicks on an empty cell if the game is not over? What happens when the user clicks on an empty cell if the game is over?

16.39 How does the program check whether a player wins? How does the program check whether all cells are filled?

16.13 Video and Audio

Key Point

*You can use the **Media** class to obtain the source of the media, the **MediaPlayer** class to play and control the media, and the **MediaView** class to display the video.*

VideoNote

Use Media, MediaPlayer, and MediaView

Media (video and audio) is essential in developing rich Internet applications. JavaFX provides the **Media**, **MediaPlayer**, and **MediaView** classes for working with media. Currently, JavaFX supports MP3, AIFF, WAV, and MPEG-4 audio formats and FLV and MPEG-4 video formats.

The **Media** class represents a media source with properties **duration**, **width**, and **height**, as shown in Figure 16.30. You can construct a **Media** object from an Internet URL string.

The getter and setter methods for property values and a getter for property itself are provided in the class, but omitted in the UML diagram for brevity.

javafx.scene.media.Media	
-duration: ReadOnlyObjectProperty <Duration>	The durations in seconds of the source media.
-width: ReadOnlyIntegerProperty	The width in pixels of the source video.
-height: ReadOnlyIntegerProperty	The height in pixels of the source video.
+Media(source: String)	Creates a Media from a URL source.

FIGURE 16.30 **Media** represents a media source such as a video or an audio.

The **MediaPlayer** class plays and controls the media with properties such as **autoPlay**, **currentCount**, **cycleCount**, **mute**, **volume**, and **totalDuration**, as shown in Figure 16.31. You can construct a **MediaPlayer** object from a media and use the **pause()** and **play()** method to pause and resume playing.

The getter and setter methods for property values and a getter for property itself are provided in the class, but omitted in the UML diagram for brevity.

javafx.scene.media.MediaPlayer	
-autoPlay: BooleanProperty	Specifies whether the playing should start automatically.
-currentCount: ReadOnlyIntegerProperty	The number of completed playback cycles.
-cycleCount: IntegerProperty	Specifies the number of time the media will be played.
-mute: BooleanProperty	Specifies whether the audio is muted.
-volume: DoubleProperty	The volume for the audio.
-totalDuration: ReadOnlyObjectProperty<Duration>	The amount of time to play the media from start to finish.
+MediaPlayer(media: Media)	Creates a player for a specified media.
+play(): void	Plays the media.
+pause(): void	Pauses the media.
+seek(): void	Seeks the player to a new playback time.

FIGURE 16.31 **MediaPlayer** plays and controls a media.

The **MediaView** class is a subclass of **Node** that provides a view of the **Media** being played by a **MediaPlayer**. The **MediaView** class provides the properties for viewing the media, as shown in Figure 16.32.

> The getter and setter methods for property values and a getter for property itself are provided in the class, but omitted in the UML diagram for brevity.

javafx.scene.media.MediaView
-x: DoubleProperty
-y: DoubleProperty
-mediaPlayer: ObjectProperty<MediaPlayer>
-fitWidth: DoubleProperty
-fitHeight: DoubleProperty
+MediaView()
+MediaView(mediaPlayer: MediaPlayer)

Specifies the current x-coordinate of the media view.
Specifies the current y-coordinate of the media view.
Specifies a media player for the media view.

Specifies the width of the view for the media to fit.
Specifies the height of the view for the media to fit.

Creates an empty media view.
Creates a media view with the specified media player.

FIGURE 16.32 **MediaView** provides the properties for viewing the media.

Listing 16.14 gives an example that displays a video in a view, as shown in Figure 16.33. You can use the play/pause button to play or pause the video and use the rewind button to restart the video, and use the slider to control the volume of the audio.

FIGURE 16.33 The program controls and plays a video.

LISTING 16.14 MediaDemo.java

```java
1  import javafx.application.Application;
2  import javafx.stage.Stage;
3  import javafx.geometry.Pos;
4  import javafx.scene.Scene;
5  import javafx.scene.control.Button;
6  import javafx.scene.control.Label;
7  import javafx.scene.control.Slider;
8  import javafx.scene.layout.BorderPane;
9  import javafx.scene.layout.HBox;
10 import javafx.scene.layout.Region;
11 import javafx.scene.media.Media;
```

```
12   import javafx.scene.media.MediaPlayer;
13   import javafx.scene.media.MediaView;
14   import javafx.util.Duration;
15
16   public class MediaDemo extends Application {
17     private static final String MEDIA_URL =
18       "http://cs.armstrong.edu/liang/common/sample.mp4";
19
20     @Override // Override the start method in the Application class
21     public void start(Stage primaryStage) {
22       Media media = new Media(MEDIA_URL);
23       MediaPlayer mediaPlayer = new MediaPlayer(media);
24       MediaView mediaView = new MediaView(mediaPlayer);
25
26       Button playButton = new Button(">");
27       playButton.setOnAction(e -> {
28         if (playButton.getText().equals(">")) {
29           mediaPlayer.play();
30           playButton.setText("||");
31         } else {
32           mediaPlayer.pause();
33           playButton.setText(">");
34         }
35       });
36
37       Button rewindButton = new Button("<<");
38       rewindButton.setOnAction(e -> mediaPlayer.seek(Duration.ZERO));
39
40       Slider slVolume = new Slider();
41       slVolume.setPrefWidth(150);
42       slVolume.setMaxWidth(Region.USE_PREF_SIZE);
43       slVolume.setMinWidth(30);
44       slVolume.setValue(50);
45       mediaPlayer.volumeProperty().bind(
46         slVolume.valueProperty().divide(100));
47
48       HBox hBox = new HBox(10);
49       hBox.setAlignment(Pos.CENTER);
50       hBox.getChildren().addAll(playButton, rewindButton,
51         new Label("Volume"), slVolume);
52
53       BorderPane pane = new BorderPane();
54       pane.setCenter(mediaView);
55       pane.setBottom(hBox);
56
57       // Create a scene and place it in the stage
58       Scene scene = new Scene(pane, 650, 500);
59       primaryStage.setTitle("MediaDemo"); // Set the stage title
60       primaryStage.setScene(scene); // Place the scene in the stage
61       primaryStage.show(); // Display the stage
62     }
63   }
```

Margin annotations (left column):
- create a media (line 22)
- create a media player (line 23)
- create a media view (line 24)
- create a play/pause button (line 26)
- add handler for button action (line 27)
- play media (line 29)
- pause media (line 32)
- create a rewind button (line 37)
- create a handler for rewinding (line 38)
- create a slider for volume (line 40)
- set current volume (line 44)
- bind volume with slider (line 45)
- add buttons, slider to hBox (line 50)
- place media view in a pane (line 54)

The source of the media is a URL string defined in lines 17 and 18. The program creates a **Media** object from this URL (line 22), a **MediaPlayer** from the **Media** object (line 23), and a **MediaView** from the **MediaPlayer** object (line 24). The relationship among these three objects is shown in Figure 16.34.

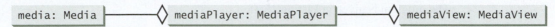

FIGURE 16.34   The media represents the source, the media player controls the playing, and the media view displays the video.

A **Media** object supports live streaming. You can now download a large media file and play it in the same time. A **Media** object can be shared by multiple media players and different views can use the same **MediaPlayer** object.

A play button is created (line 26) to play/pause the media (line 29). The button's text is changed to **||** (line 30) if the button's current text is **>** (line 28). If the button's current text is **||**, it is changed to **>** (line 33) and the player is paused (line 32).

A rewind button is created (line 37) to reset the playback time to the beginning of the media stream by invoking **seek(Duration.ZERO)** (line 38).

A slider is created (line 40) to set the volume. The media player's volume property is bound to the slider (lines 45 and 46).

The buttons and slider are placed in an **HBox** (lines 48–51) and the media view is placed in the center of the border pane (line 54) and the **HBox** is placed at the bottom of the border pane (line 55).

16.40   How do you create a **Media** from a URL? How do you create a **MediaPlayer**? How do you create a **MediaView**?

16.41   If the URL is typed as cs.armstrong.edu/liang/common/sample.mp4 without http:// in front of it, will it work?

16.42   Can you place a **Media** in multiple **MediaPlayer**s? Can you place a **MediaPlayer** in multiple **MediaView**s? Can you place a **MediaView** in multiple **Pane**s?

16.14 Case Study: National Flags and Anthems

This case study presents a program that displays a nation's flag and plays its anthem.

The images for seven national flags, named **flag0.gif**, **flag1.gif**, . . . , **flag6.gif** for Denmark, Germany, China, India, Norway, United Kingdom, and United States are stored under www.cs.armstrong.edu/liang/common/image. The audio consists of national anthems for these seven nations, named **anthem0.mp3**, **anthem1.mp3**, . . . , and **anthem6.mp3**. They are stored under www.cs.armstrong.edu/liang/common/audio.

The program enables the user to select a nation from a combo box and then displays its flag and plays its anthem. The user can suspend the audio by clicking the **||** button and resume it by clicking the **<** button, as shown in Figure 16.35.

FIGURE 16.35   The program displays a national flag and plays its anthem.

The program is given in Listing 16.15.

LISTING 16.15 FlagAnthem.java

VideoNote

Audio and image

```java
 1  import javafx.application.Application;
 2  import javafx.collections.FXCollections;
 3  import javafx.collections.ObservableList;
 4  import javafx.stage.Stage;
 5  import javafx.geometry.Pos;
 6  import javafx.scene.Scene;
 7  import javafx.scene.control.Button;
 8  import javafx.scene.control.ComboBox;
 9  import javafx.scene.control.Label;
10  import javafx.scene.image.Image;
11  import javafx.scene.image.ImageView;
12  import javafx.scene.layout.BorderPane;
13  import javafx.scene.layout.HBox;
14  import javafx.scene.media.Media;
15  import javafx.scene.media.MediaPlayer;
16
17  public class FlagAnthem extends Application {
18    private final static int NUMBER_OF_NATIONS = 7;
19    private final static String URLBase =
20      "http://cs.armstrong.edu/liang/common";
21    private int currentIndex = 0;
22
23    @Override // Override the start method in the Application class
24    public void start(Stage primaryStage) {
25      Image[] images = new Image[NUMBER_OF_NATIONS];
26      MediaPlayer[] mp = new MediaPlayer[NUMBER_OF_NATIONS];
27
28      // Load images and audio
29      for (int i = 0; i < NUMBER_OF_NATIONS; i++) {
30        images[i] = new Image(URLBase + "/image/flag" + i + ".gif");
31        mp[i] = new MediaPlayer(new Media(
32          URLBase + "/audio/anthem/anthem" + i + ".mp3"));
33      }
34
35      Button btPlayPause = new Button(">");
36      btPlayPause.setOnAction(e -> {
37        if (btPlayPause.getText().equals(">")) {
38          btPlayPause.setText("||");
39          mp[currentIndex].pause();
40        } else {
41          btPlayPause.setText(">");
42          mp[currentIndex].play();
43        }
44      });
45
46      ImageView imageView = new ImageView(images[currentIndex]);
47      ComboBox<String> cboNation = new ComboBox<>();
48      ObservableList<String> items = FXCollections.observableArrayList
49        ("Denmark", "Germany", "China", "India", "Norway", "UK", "US");
50      cboNation.getItems().addAll(items);
51      cboNation.setValue(items.get(0));
52      cboNation.setOnAction(e -> {
53        mp[currentIndex].stop();
54        currentIndex = items.indexOf(cboNation.getValue());
55        imageView.setImage(images[currentIndex]);
56        mp[currentIndex].play();
57      });
```

URLBase for image and audio
track current image/audio

image array
media player array

load image
load audio

create play button
handle button action

pause audio

play audio

create image view
create combo box
create observable list

process combo selection

choose a new nation

play audio

```
58
59      HBox hBox = new HBox(10);
60      hBox.getChildren().addAll(btPlayPause,
61        new Label("Select a nation: "), cboNation);
62      hBox.setAlignment(Pos.CENTER);
63
64      // Create a pane to hold nodes
65      BorderPane pane = new BorderPane();
66      pane.setCenter(imageView);
67      pane.setBottom(hBox);
68
69      // Create a scene and place it in the stage
70      Scene scene = new Scene(pane, 350, 270);
71      primaryStage.setTitle("FlagAnthem"); // Set the stage title
72      primaryStage.setScene(scene); // Place the scene in the stage
73      primaryStage.show(); // Display the stage
74    }
75  }
```

The program loads the image and audio from the Internet (lines 29–33). A play/pause button is created to control the playing of the audio (line 35). When the button is clicked, if the button's current text is > (line 37), its text is changed to || (line 38) and the player is paused (line 39); If the button's current text is ||, it is changed to > (line 41) and the player is paused (line 42).

An image view is created to display a flag image (line 46). A combo box is created for selecting a nation (line 47–49). When a new country name in the combo box is selected, the current audio is stopped (line 53) and the newly selected nation's image is displayed (line 55) and the new anthem is played (line 56).

JavaFX also provides the **AudioClip** class for creating auto clips. An **AudioClip** object can be created using **new AudioClip(URL)**. An audio clip stores the audio in memory. **AudioClip** is more efficient for playing a small audio clip in the program than using **MediaPlayer**. **AudioClip** has the similar methods as in the **MediaPlayer** class.

Check Point

16.43 In Listing 16.15, which code sets the initial image icon and which code plays the audio?

16.44 In Listing 16.15, what does the program do when a new nation is selected in the combo box?

CHAPTER SUMMARY

1. The abstract **Labeled** class is the base class for **Label**, **Button**, **CheckBox**, and **RadioButton**. It defines properties **alignment**, **contentDisplay**, **text**, **graphic**, **graphicTextGap**, **textFill**, **underline**, and **wrapText**.

2. The abstract **ButtonBase** class is the base class for **Button**, **CheckBox**, and **RadioButton**. It defines the **onAction** property for specifying a handler for action events.

3. The abstract **TextInputContorl** class is the base class for **TextField** and **TextArea**. It defines the properties **text** and **editable**.

4. A **TextField** fires an action event when clicking the Enter key with the text field focused. A **TextArea** is often used for editing a multiline text.

5. **ComboBox<T>** and **ListView<T>** are generic classes for storing elements of type **T**. The elements in a combo box or a list view are stored in an observable list.

6. A **ComboBox** fires an action event when a new item is selected.

7. You can set a single item or multiple item selection for a **ListView** and add a listener for processing selected items.

8. You can use a **ScrollBar** or **Slider** to select a range of values and add a listener to the **value** property to respond to the change of the value.

9. JavaFX provides the **Media** class for loading a media, the **MediaPlayer** class for controlling a media, and the **MediaView** for displaying a media.

QUIZ

Answer the quiz for this chapter online at www.cs.armstrong.edu/liang/intro10e/quiz.html.

MyProgrammingLab™ **PROGRAMMING EXERCISES**

Sections 16.2–16.5

*16.1 (*Use radio buttons*) Write a GUI program as shown in Figure 16.36a. You can use buttons to move the message to the left and right and use the radio buttons to change the color for the message displayed.

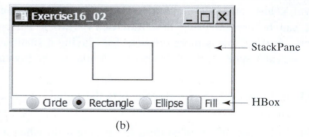

(a)   (b)

FIGURE 16.36   (a) The <= and => buttons move the message, and the radio buttons change the color for the message. (b) The program displays a circle, rectangle, and ellipse when you select a shape type.

*16.2 (*Select geometric figures*) Write a program that draws various figures, as shown in Figure 16.36b. The user selects a figure from a radio button and uses a check box to specify whether it is filled.

**16.3 (*Traffic lights*) Write a program that simulates a traffic light. The program lets the user select one of three lights: red, yellow, or green. When a radio button is selected, the light is turned on. Only one light can be on at a time (see Figure 16.37a). No light is on when the program starts.

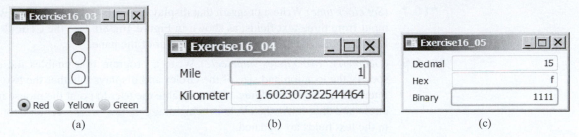

(a)   (b)   (c)

FIGURE 16.37 (a) The radio buttons are grouped to let you turn only one light on at a time. (b) The program converts miles to kilometers, and vice versa. (c) The program converts between decimal, hex, and binary numbers.

*16.4 (*Create a miles/kilometers converter*) Write a program that converts miles and kilometers, as shown in Figure 16.37b. If you enter a value in the Mile text field and press the *Enter* key, the corresponding kilometer measurement is displayed in the Kilometer text field. Likewise, if you enter a value in the Kilometer text field and press the *Enter* key, the corresponding miles is displayed in the Mile text field.

*16.5 (*Convert numbers*) Write a program that converts between decimal, hex, and binary numbers, as shown in Figure 16.37c. When you enter a decimal value in the decimal-value text field and press the *Enter* key, its corresponding hex and binary numbers are displayed in the other two text fields. Likewise, you can enter values in the other fields and convert them accordingly. (Hint: Use the `Integer.parseInt(s, radix)` method to parse a string to a decimal and use `Integer.toHexString(decimal)` and `Integer.toBinaryString(decimal)` to obtain a hex number or a binary number from a decimal.)

*16.6 (*Demonstrate* `TextField` *properties*) Write a program that sets the horizontal-alignment and column-size properties of a text field dynamically, as shown in Figure 16.38a.

VideoNote

Use radio buttons and text fields

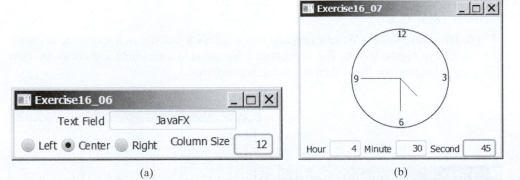

(a)   (b)

FIGURE 16.38 (a) You can set a text field's properties for the horizontal alignment and column size dynamically. (b) The program displays the time specified in the text fields.

*16.7 (*Set clock time*) Write a program that displays a clock and sets the time with the input from three text fields, as shown in Figure 16.38b. Use the **ClockPane** in Listing 14.21. Resize the clock to the center of the pane.

**16.8 (*Geometry: two circles intersect?*) Write a program that enables the user to specify the location and size of the circles and displays whether the two circles intersect, as shown in Figure 16.39a. Enable the user to point the mouse inside a circle and drag it. As the circle is being dragged, the circle's center coordinates in the text fields are updated.

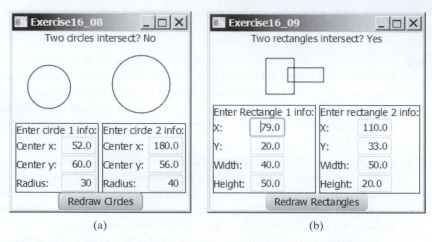

(a)   (b)

FIGURE 16.39 Check whether two circles and two rectangles are overlapping.

**16.9 (*Geometry: two rectangles intersect?*) Write a program that enables the user to specify the location and size of the rectangles and displays whether the two rectangles intersect, as shown in Figure 16.39b. Enable the user to point the mouse inside a rectangle and drag it. As the rectangle is being dragged, the rectangle's center coordinates in the text fields are updated.

Sections 16.6–16.8

**16.10 (*Text viewer*) Write a program that displays a text file in a text area, as shown in Figure 16.40a. The user enters a file name in a text field and clicks the *View* button; the file is then displayed in a text area.

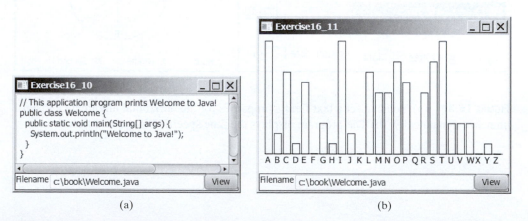

(a)   (b)

FIGURE 16.40 (a) The program displays the text from a file in a text area. (b) The program displays a histogram that shows the occurrences of each letter in the file.

**16.11 (*Create a histogram* for *occurrences of letters*) Write a program that reads a file and displays a histogram to show the occurrences of each letter in the file, as shown in Figure 16.40b. The file name is entered from a text field. Pressing the *Enter* key on the text field causes the program to start to read and process the file and displays the histogram. The histogram is displayed in the center of the window. Define a class named `Histogram` that extends `Pane`. The class contains the property `counts` that is an array of 26 elements. `counts[0]` stores the number of A, `counts[1]` the number of B, and so on. The class also contains a setter method for setting a new `counts` and displaying the histogram for the new `counts`.

*16.12 (*Demonstrate `TextArea` properties*) Write a program that demonstrates the properties of a text area. The program uses a check box to indicate whether the text is wrapped onto next line, as shown in Figure 16.41a.

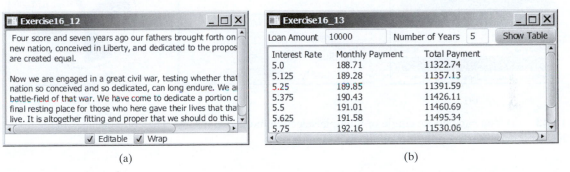

(a)   (b)

FIGURE 16.41 (a) You can set the options to enable text editing and text wrapping. (b) The program displays a table for monthly payments and total payments on a given loan based on various interest rates.

*16.13 (*Compare loans with various interest rates*) Rewrite Programming Exercise 5.21 to create a GUI, as shown in Figure 16.41b. Your program should let the user enter the loan amount and loan period in the number of years from text fields, and it should display the monthly and total payments for each interest rate starting from **5** percent to **8** percent, with increments of one-eighth, in a text area.

16.14 (*Select a font*) Write a program that can dynamically change the font of a text in a label displayed on a stack pane. The text can be displayed in bold and italic at the same time. You can select the font name or font size from combo boxes, as shown in Figure 16.42a. The available font names can be obtained using `Font.getFamilies()`. The combo box for the font size is initialized with numbers from **1 to **100**.

VideoNote

Set fonts

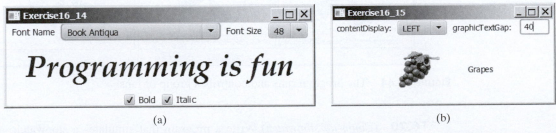

(a)   (b)

FIGURE 16.42 You can dynamically set the font for the message. (b) You can set the alignment and text-position properties of a label dynamically.

**16.15 (*Demonstrate* `Label` *properties*) Write a program to let the user dynamically set the properties `contentDisplay` and `graphicTextGap`, as shown in Figure 16.42b.

*16.16 (*Use* `ComboBox` *and* `ListView`) Write a program that demonstrates selecting items in a list. The program uses a combo box to specify a selection mode, as shown in Figure 16.43a. When you select items, they are displayed in a label below the list.

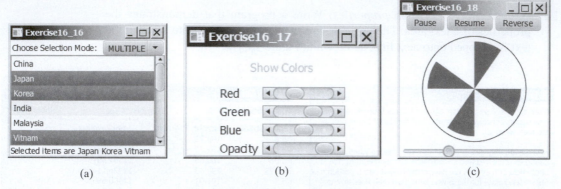

(a)   (b)   (c)

FIGURE 16.43 (a) You can choose single or multiple selection mode in a list. (b) The color changes in the text as you adjust the scroll bars. (c) The program simulates a running fan.

Sections 16.6–16.8

**16.17 (*Use* `ScrollBar` *and* `Slider`) Write a program that uses scroll bars or sliders to select the color for a text, as shown in Figure 16.43b. Four horizontal scroll bars are used for selecting the colors: red, green, blue, and opacity percentages.

**16.18 (*Simulation: a running fan*) Rewrite Programming Exercise 15.28 to add a slider to control the speed of the fan, as shown in Figure 16.43c.

**16.19 (*Control a group of fans*) Write a program that displays three fans in a group, with control buttons to start and stop all of them, as shown in Figure 16.44.

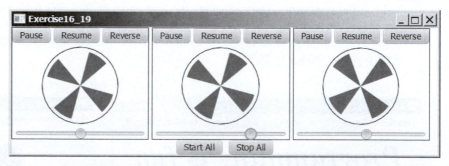

FIGURE 16.44 The program runs and controls a group of fans.

*16.20 (*Count-up stopwatch*) Write a program that simulates a stopwatch, as shown in Figure 16.45a. When the user clicks the *Start* button, the button's label is changed to *Pause*, as shown in Figure 16.45b. When the user clicks the *Pause* button, the button's label is changed to *Resume*, as shown in Figure 16.45c. The *Clear* button resets the count to 0 and resets the button's label to *Start*.

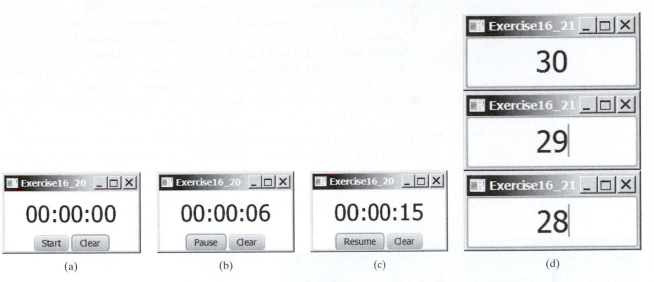

FIGURE 16.45 (a–c) The program counts up the time. (d) The program counts down the time.

*16.21 (*Count-down stopwatch*) Write a program that allows the user to enter time in seconds in the text field and press the *Enter* key to count down the seconds, as shown in Figure 16.45d. The remaining seconds are redisplayed every one second. When the seconds are expired, the program starts to play music continuously.

16.22 (*Play, loop, and stop a sound clip*) Write a program that meets the following requirements:

■ Get an audio file from the class directory using `AudioClip`.
■ Place three buttons labeled *Play*, *Loop*, and *Stop*, as shown in Figure 16.46a.
■ If you click the *Play* button, the audio file is played once. If you click the *Loop* button, the audio file keeps playing repeatedly. If you click the *Stop* button, the playing stops.

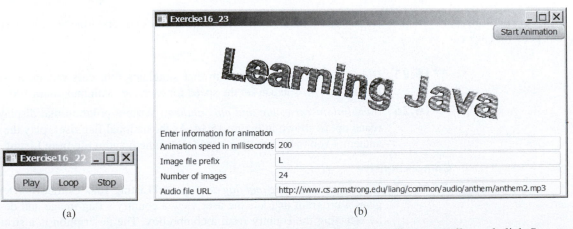

FIGURE 16.46 (a) Click *Play* to play an audio clip once, click *Loop* to play an audio repeatedly, and click *Stop* to terminate playing. (b) The program lets the user specify image files, an audio file, and the animation speed.

**16.23 (*Create an image animator with audio*) Create animation in Figure 16.46b to meet the following requirements:

- Allow the user to specify the animation speed in a text field.
- Get the number of iamges and image's file-name prefix from the user. For example, if the user enters **n** for the number of images and **L** for the image prefix, then the files are **L1.gif**, **L2.gif**, and so on, to **L***n***.gif**. Assume that the images are stored in the **image** directory, a subdirectory of the program's class directory. The animation displays the images one after the other.
- Allow the user to specify an audio file URL. The audio is played while the animation runs.

**16.24 (*Revise Listing 16.14 MediaDemo.java*) Add a slider to enable the user to set the current time for the video and a label to display the current time and the total time for the video. As shown in Figure 16.47a, the total time is 5 minutes and 3 seconds and the current time is 3 minutes and 58 seconds. As the video plays, the slider value and current time are continuously updated.

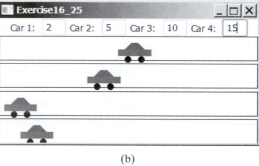

(a)   (b)

FIGURE 16.47 (a) A slider for current video time and a label to show the current time and total time are added. (b) You can set the speed for each car.

**16.25 (*Racing cars*) Write a program that simulates four cars racing, as shown in Figure 16.47b. You can set the speed for each car, with maximum 100.

**16.26 (*Simulation: raise flag and play anthem*) Write a program that displays a flag rising up, as shown in Figure 15.14. As the national flag rises, play the national anthem. (You may use a flag image and anthem audio file from Listing 16.15.)

Comprehensive

16.27 (*Display country flag and flag description*) Listing 16.4, ComboBoxDemo.java, gives a program that lets the user view a country's flag image and description by selecting the country from a combo box. The description is a string coded in the program. Rewrite the program to read the text description from a file. Suppose that the descriptions are stored in the files **description0.txt, . . . , and description8.txt under the **text** directory for the nine countries Canada, China, Denmark, France, Germany, India, Norway, United Kingdom, and United States, in this order.

16.28 (*Slide show*) Programming Exercise 15.30 developed a slide show using images. Rewrite that program to develop a slide show using text files. Suppose ten text files named **slide0.txt, **slide1.txt**, ..., and **slide9.txt** are stored in the **text** directory. Each slide displays the text from one file. Each slide is shown for one second, and the slides are displayed in order. When the last slide finishes, the first slide is redisplayed, and so on. Use a text area to display the slide.

***16.29 (*Display a calendar*) Write a program that displays the calendar for the current month. You can use the *Prior* and *Next* buttons to show the calendar of the previous or next month. Display the dates in the current month in black and display the dates in the previous month and next month in gray, as shown in Figure 16.48.

Exercise16_29						
		January, 2016				
Sunday	Monday	Tuesday	Wednesday	Thursday	Friday	Saturday
27	28	29	30	31	1	2
3	4	5	6	7	8	9
10	11	12	13	14	15	16
17	18	19	20	21	22	23
24	25	26	27	28	29	30
31	1	2	3	4	5	6

Prior   Next

FIGURE 16.48 The program displays the calendar for the current month.

**16.30 (*Pattern recognition: consecutive four equal numbers*) Write a GUI program for Programming Exercise 8.19, as shown in Figure 16.49a–b. Let the user enter the numbers in the text fields in a grid of 6 rows and 7 columns. The user can click the *Solve* button to highlight a sequence of four equal numbers, if it exists. Initially, the values in the text fields are filled with numbers from 0 to 9 randomly.

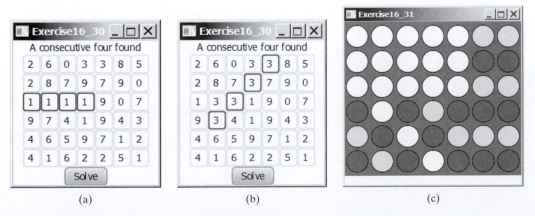

FIGURE 16.49 (a–b) Clicking the *Solve* button highlights the four consecutive numbers in a row, a column, or a diagonal. (c) The program enables two players to play the connect-four game.

***16.31 (*Game: connect four*) Programming Exercise 8.20 enables two players to play the connect-four game on the console. Rewrite a GUI version for the program, as shown in Figure 16.49c. The program enables two players to place red and yellow discs in turn. To place a disk, the player needs to click an available cell. An *available cell* is unoccupied and its downward neighbor is occupied. The program flashes the four winning cells if a player wins and reports no winners if all cells are occupied with no winners.

BINARY I/O

Objectives

- To discover how I/O is processed in Java (§17.2).

- To distinguish between text I/O and binary I/O (§17.3).

- To read and write bytes using `FileInputStream` and `FileOutputStream` (§17.4.1).

- To filter data using the base classes `FilterInputStream` and `FilterOutputStream` (§17.4.2).

- To read and write primitive values and strings using `DataInputStream` and `DataOutputStream` (§17.4.3).

- To improve I/O performance by using `BufferedInputStream` and `BufferedOutputStream` (§17.4.4).

- To write a program that copies a file (§17.5).

- To store and restore objects using `ObjectOutputStream` and `ObjectInputStream` (§17.6).

- To implement the `Serializable` interface to make objects serializable (§17.6.1).

- To serialize arrays (§17.6.2).

- To read and write files using the `RandomAccessFile` class (§17.7).

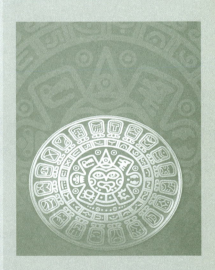

17.1 Introduction

Java provides many classes for performing text I/O and binary I/O.

text file

binary file

Files can be classified as either text or binary. A file that can be processed (read, created, or modified) using a text editor such as Notepad on Windows or vi on UNIX is called a *text file*. All the other files are called *binary files*. You cannot read binary files using a text editor—they are designed to be read by programs. For example, Java source programs are text files and can be read by a text editor, but Java class files are binary files and are read by the JVM.

Although it is not technically precise and correct, you can envision a text file as consisting of a sequence of characters and a binary file as consisting of a sequence of bits. Characters in a text file are encoded using a character encoding scheme such as ASCII or Unicode. For example, the decimal integer **199** is stored as a sequence of three characters **1**, **9**, **9** in a text file, and the same integer is stored as a byte-type value **C7** in a binary file, because decimal

why binary I/O?

199 equals hex **C7** ($199 = 12 \times 16^1 + 7$). The advantage of binary files is that they are more efficient to process than text files.

text I/O

binary I/O

Java offers many classes for performing file input and output. These can be categorized as *text I/O classes* and *binary I/O classes*. In Section 12.11, File Input and Output, you learned how to read and write strings and numeric values from/to a text file using **Scanner** and **PrintWriter**. This chapter introduces the classes for performing binary I/O.

17.2 How Is Text I/O Handled in Java?

*Text data are read using the **Scanner** class and written using the **PrintWriter** class.*

Recall that a **File** object encapsulates the properties of a file or a path but does not contain the methods for reading/writing data from/to a file. In order to perform I/O, you need to create objects using appropriate Java I/O classes. The objects contain the methods for reading/writing data from/to a file. For example, to write text to a file named **temp.txt**, you can create an object using the **PrintWriter** class as follows:

```
PrintWriter output = new PrintWriter("temp.txt");
```

You can now invoke the **print** method on the object to write a string to the file. For example, the following statement writes **Java 101** to the file.

```
output.print("Java 101");
```

The next statement closes the file.

```
output.close();
```

There are many I/O classes for various purposes. In general, these can be classified as input classes and output classes. An *input class* contains the methods to read data, and an *output class* contains the methods to write data. **PrintWriter** is an example of an output class, and **Scanner** is an example of an input class. The following code creates an input object for the file **temp.txt** and reads data from the file.

```
Scanner input = new Scanner(new File("temp.txt"));
System.out.println(input.nextLine());
```

If **temp.txt** contains the text **Java 101**, **input.nextLine()** returns the string **"Java 101"**.

stream

input stream

output stream

Figure 17.1 illustrates Java I/O programming. An input object reads a *stream* of data from a file, and an output object writes a stream of data to a file. An input object is also called an *input stream* and an output object an *output stream*.

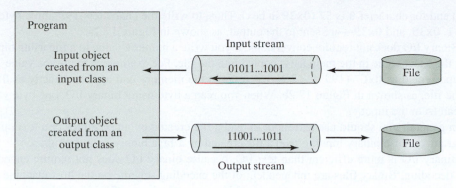

FIGURE 17.1 The program receives data through an input object and sends data through an output object.

17.1 What is a text file and what is a binary file? Can you view a text file or a binary file using a text editor?

17.2 How do you read or write text data in Java? What is a stream?

17.3 Text I/O vs. Binary I/O

Binary I/O does not involve encoding or decoding and thus is more efficient than text I/O.

Computers do not differentiate between binary files and text files. All files are stored in binary format, and thus all files are essentially binary files. Text I/O is built upon binary I/O to provide a level of abstraction for character encoding and decoding, as shown in Figure 17.2a. Encoding and decoding are automatically performed for text I/O. The JVM converts Unicode to a file-specific encoding when writing a character, and it converts a file-specific encoding to Unicode when reading a character. For example, suppose you write the string **"199"** using text I/O to a file, each character is written to the file. Since the Unicode for character **1** is **0x0031**, the Unicode **0x0031** is converted to a code that depends on the encoding scheme for the file. (Note that the prefix **0x** denotes a hex number.) In the United States, the default encoding for text files on Windows is ASCII. The ASCII code for character **1** is 49 (**0x31** in

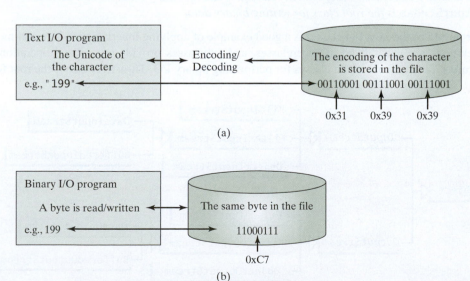

FIGURE 17.2 Text I/O requires encoding and decoding, whereas binary I/O does not.

hex) and for character **9** is **57** (**0x39** in hex). Thus, to write the characters **199**, three bytes—**0x31**, **0x39**, and **0x39**—are sent to the output, as shown in Figure 17.2a.

Binary I/O does not require conversions. If you write a numeric value to a file using binary I/O, the exact value in the memory is copied into the file. For example, a byte-type value **199** is represented as **0xC7** ($199 = 12 \times 16^1 + 7$) in the memory and appears exactly as **0xC7** in the file, as shown in Figure 17.2b. When you read a byte using binary I/O, one byte value is read from the input.

In general, you should use text input to read a file created by a text editor or a text output program, and use binary input to read a file created by a Java binary output program.

Binary I/O is more efficient than text I/O, because binary I/O does not require encoding and decoding. Binary files are independent of the encoding scheme on the host machine and thus are portable. Java programs on any machine can read a binary file created by a Java program. This is why Java class files are binary files. Java class files can run on a JVM on any machine.

.txt and .dat

Note

For consistency, this book uses the extension **.txt** to name text files and **.dat** to name binary files.

17.3 What are the differences between text I/O and binary I/O?

17.4 How is a Java character represented in the memory, and how is a character represented in a text file?

17.5 If you write the string **"ABC"** to an ASCII text file, what values are stored in the file?

17.6 If you write the string **"100"** to an ASCII text file, what values are stored in the file? If you write a numeric byte-type value **100** using binary I/O, what values are stored in the file?

17.7 What is the encoding scheme for representing a character in a Java program? By default, what is the encoding scheme for a text file on Windows?

17.4 Binary I/O Classes

The abstract **InputStream** *is the root class for reading binary data, and the abstract* **OutputStream** *is the root class for writing binary data.*

The design of the Java I/O classes is a good example of applying inheritance, where common operations are generalized in superclasses, and subclasses provide specialized operations. Figure 17.3 lists some of the classes for performing binary I/O. **InputStream** is the root for

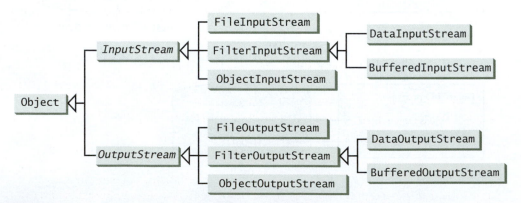

FIGURE 17.3 **InputStream**, **OutputStream**, and their subclasses are for performing binary I/O.

java.io.InputStream	
+*read(): int*	Reads the next byte of data from the input stream. The value byte is returned as an `int` value in the range 0 to 255. If no byte is available because the end of the stream has been reached, the value –1 is returned.
+read(b: byte[]): int	Reads up to `b.length` bytes into array b from the input stream and returns the actual number of bytes read. Returns –1 at the end of the stream.
+read(b: byte[], off: int, len: int): int	Reads bytes from the input stream and stores them in `b[off]`, `b[off+1]`, . . ., `b[off+len-1]`. The actual number of bytes read is returned. Returns –1 at the end of the stream.
+available(): int	Returns an estimate of the number of bytes that can be read from the input stream.
+close(): void	Closes this input stream and releases any system resources occupied by it.
+skip(n: long): long	Skips over and discards n bytes of data from this input stream. The actual number of bytes skipped is returned.
+markSupported(): boolean	Tests whether this input stream supports the `mark` and `reset` methods.
+mark(readlimit: int): void	Marks the current position in this input stream.
+reset(): void	Repositions this stream to the position at the time the `mark` method was last called on this input stream.

FIGURE 17.4 The abstract **InputStream** class defines the methods for the input stream of bytes.

binary input classes, and **OutputStream** is the root for binary output classes. Figures 17.4 and 17.5 list all the methods in the classes **InputStream** and **OutputStream**.

> **Note**
> All the methods in the binary I/O classes are declared to throw **java.io.IOException** or a subclass of **java.io.IOException**.

throws IOException

java.io.OutputStream	
+*write(int b): void*	Writes the specified byte to this output stream. The parameter b is an `int` value. `(byte)b` is written to the output stream.
+write(b: byte[]): void	Writes all the bytes in array b to the output stream.
+write(b: byte[], off: int, len: int): void	Writes `b[off]`, `b[off+1]`,. . ., `b[off+len-1]` into the output stream.
+close(): void	Closes this output stream and releases any system resources occupied by it.
+flush(): void	Flushes this output stream and forces any buffered output bytes to be written out.

FIGURE 17.5 The abstract **OutputStream** class defines the methods for the output stream of bytes.

17.4.1 FileInputStream/FileOutputStream

FileInputStream/**FileOutputStream** is for reading/writing bytes from/to files. All the methods in these classes are inherited from **InputStream** and **OutputStream**. **FileInputStream**/**FileOutputStream** does not introduce new methods. To construct a **FileInputStream**, use the constructors shown in Figure 17.6.

A **java.io.FileNotFoundException** will occur if you attempt to create a **FileInputStream** with a nonexistent file.

FileNotFoundException

To construct a **FileOutputStream**, use the constructors shown in Figure 17.7.

If the file does not exist, a new file will be created. If the file already exists, the first two constructors will delete the current content of the file. To retain the current content and append new data into the file, use the last two constructors and pass **true** to the **append** parameter.

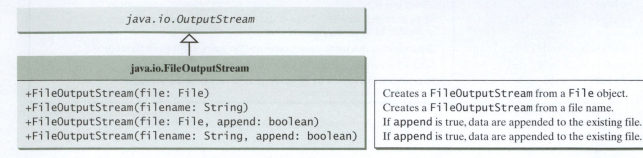

FIGURE 17.6 `FileInputStream` inputs a stream of bytes from a file.

java.io.OutputStream

java.io.FileOutputStream
+FileOutputStream(file: File)
+FileOutputStream(filename: String)
+FileOutputStream(file: File, append: boolean)
+FileOutputStream(filename: String, append: boolean)

Creates a `FileOutputStream` from a `File` object.
Creates a `FileOutputStream` from a file name.
If `append` is true, data are appended to the existing file.
If `append` is true, data are appended to the existing file.

FIGURE 17.7 `FileOutputStream` outputs a stream of bytes to a file.

IOException

Almost all the methods in the I/O classes throw `java.io.IOException`. Therefore, you have to declare to throw `java.io.IOException` in the method or place the code in a try-catch block, as shown below:

Declaring exception in the method

```java
public static void main(String[] args)
    throws IOException {
  // Perform I/O operations
}
```

Using try-catch block

```java
public static void main(String[] args) {
  try {
    // Perform I/O operations
  }
  catch (IOException ex) {
    ex.printStackTrace();
  }
}
```

Listing 17.1 uses binary I/O to write ten byte values from **1** to **10** to a file named **temp.dat** and reads them back from the file.

LISTING 17.1 TestFileStream.java

import

output stream

output

```java
 1  import java.io.*;
 2
 3  public class TestFileStream {
 4    public static void main(String[] args) throws IOException {
 5      try (
 6        // Create an output stream to the file
 7        FileOutputStream output = new FileOutputStream("temp.dat");
 8      ) {
 9        // Output values to the file
10        for (int i = 1; i <= 10; i++)
11          output.write(i);
12      }
13
14      try (
```

```
15          // Create an input stream for the file
16          FileInputStream input = new FileInputStream("temp.dat");
17      ) {
18          // Read values from the file
19          int value;
20          while ((value = input.read()) != -1)
21              System.out.print(value + " ");
22      }
23    }
24  }
```

input stream

input

```
1 2 3 4 5 6 7 8 9 10
```

The program uses the try-with-resources to declare and create input and output streams so that they will be automatically closed after they are used. The **java.io.InputStream** and **java.io.OutputStream** classes implement the **AutoClosable** interface. The **AutoClosable** interface defines the **close()** method that closes a resource. Any object of the **AutoClosable** type can be used with the try-with-resources syntax for automatic closing.

AutoClosable

A **FileOutputStream** is created for the file **temp.dat** in line 7. The **for** loop writes ten byte values into the file (lines 10–11). Invoking **write(i)** is the same as invoking **write((byte)i)**. Line 16 creates a **FileInputStream** for the file **temp.dat**. Values are read from the file and displayed on the console in lines 19–21. The expression **((value = input.read()) != -1)** (line 20) reads a byte from **input.read()**, assigns it to **value**, and checks whether it is −1. The input value of −1 signifies the end of a file.

end of a file

The file **temp.dat** created in this example is a binary file. It can be read from a Java program but not from a text editor, as shown in Figure 17.8.

Binary data →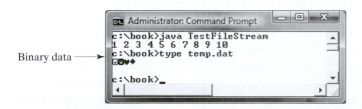

FIGURE 17.8   A binary file cannot be displayed in text mode.

Tip

When a stream is no longer needed, always close it using the **close()** method or automatically close it using a try-with-resource statement. Not closing streams may cause data corruption in the output file, or other programming errors.

close stream

Note

The root directory for the file is the classpath directory. For the example in this book, the root directory is **c:\book**, so the file **temp.dat** is located at **c:\book**. If you wish to place **temp.dat** in a specific directory, replace line 6 with

where is the file?

```
FileOutputStream output =
  new FileOutputStream ("directory/temp.dat");
```

Note

An instance of **FileInputStream** can be used as an argument to construct a **Scanner**, and an instance of **FileOutputStream** can be used as an argument to construct a **PrintWriter**. You can create a **PrintWriter** to append text into a file using

appending to text file

```
new PrintWriter(new FileOutputStream("temp.txt", true));
```

If **temp.txt** does not exist, it is created. If **temp.txt** already exists, new data are appended to the file.

17.4.2 **FilterInputStream/FilterOutputStream**

Filter streams are streams that filter bytes for some purpose. The basic byte input stream provides a **read** method that can be used only for reading bytes. If you want to read integers, doubles, or strings, you need a filter class to wrap the byte input stream. Using a filter class enables you to read integers, doubles, and strings instead of bytes and characters. **FilterInputStream** and **FilterOutputStream** are the base classes for filtering data. When you need to process primitive numeric types, use **DataInputStream** and **DataOutputStream** to filter bytes.

17.4.3 **DataInputStream/DataOutputStream**

DataInputStream reads bytes from the stream and converts them into appropriate primitive-type values or strings. **DataOutputStream** converts primitive-type values or strings into bytes and outputs the bytes to the stream.

   DataInputStream extends **FilterInputStream** and implements the **DataInput** interface, as shown in Figure 17.9. **DataOutputStream** extends **FilterOutputStream** and implements the **DataOutput** interface, as shown in Figure 17.10.

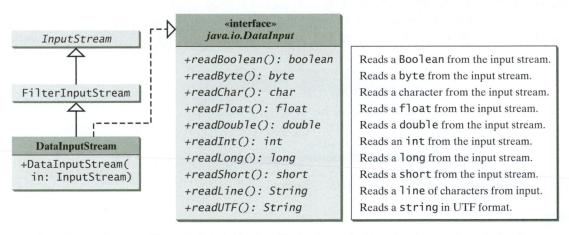

FIGURE 17.9 **DataInputStream** filters an input stream of bytes into primitive data-type values and strings.

   DataInputStream implements the methods defined in the **DataInput** interface to read primitive data-type values and strings. **DataOutputStream** implements the methods defined in the **DataOutput** interface to write primitive data-type values and strings. Primitive values are copied from memory to the output without any conversions. Characters in a string may be written in several ways, as discussed in the next section.

Characters and Strings in Binary I/O

A Unicode character consists of two bytes. The **writeChar(char c)** method writes the Unicode of character **c** to the output. The **writeChars(String s)** method writes the Unicode for each character in the string **s** to the output. The **writeBytes(String s)** method writes the lower byte of the Unicode for each character in the string **s** to the output. The high byte of the Unicode is discarded. The **writeBytes** method is suitable for strings that consist

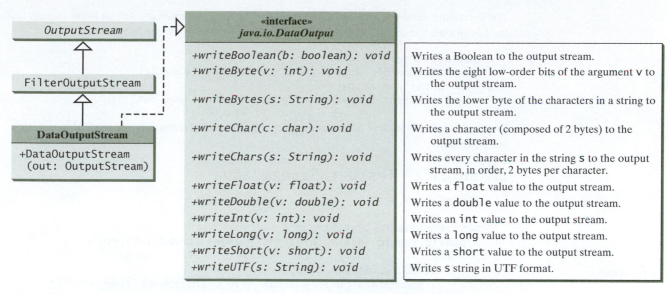

FIGURE 17.10 `DataOutputStream` enables you to write primitive data-type values and strings into an output stream.

of ASCII characters, since an ASCII code is stored only in the lower byte of a Unicode. If a string consists of non-ASCII characters, you have to use the **writeChars** method to write the string.

The **writeUTF(String s)** method writes two bytes of length information to the output stream, followed by the modified UTF-8 representation of every character in the string **s**. UTF-8 is a coding scheme that allows systems to operate with both ASCII and Unicode. Most operating systems use ASCII. Java uses Unicode. The ASCII character set is a subset of the Unicode character set. Since most applications need only the ASCII character set, it is a waste to represent an 8-bit ASCII character as a 16-bit Unicode character. The modified UTF-8 scheme stores a character using one, two, or three bytes. Characters are coded in one byte if their code is less than or equal to **0x7F**, in two bytes if their code is greater than **0x7F** and less than or equal to **0x7FF**, or in three bytes if their code is greater than **0x7FF**.

The initial bits of a UTF-8 character indicate whether a character is stored in one byte, two bytes, or three bytes. If the first bit is **0**, it is a one-byte character. If the first bits are **110**, it is the first byte of a two-byte sequence. If the first bits are **1110**, it is the first byte of a three-byte sequence. The information that indicates the number of characters in a string is stored in the first two bytes preceding the UTF-8 characters. For example, **writeUTF("ABCDEF")** actually writes eight bytes (i.e., **00 06 41 42 43 44 45 46**) to the file, because the first two bytes store the number of characters in the string.

UTF-8 scheme

The **writeUTF(String s)** method converts a string into a series of bytes in the UTF-8 format and writes them into an output stream. The **readUTF()** method reads a string that has been written using the **writeUTF** method.

The UTF-8 format has the advantage of saving a byte for each ASCII character, because a Unicode character takes up two bytes and an ASCII character in UTF-8 only one byte. If most of the characters in a long string are regular ASCII characters, using UTF-8 is more efficient.

Creating **DataInputStream/DataOutputStream**

DataInputStream/DataOutputStream are created using the following constructors (see Figures 17.9 and 17.10):

```
public DataInputStream(InputStream instream)
public DataOutputStream(OutputStream outstream)
```

The following statements create data streams. The first statement creates an input stream for the file **in.dat**; the second statement creates an output stream for the file **out.dat**.

```
DataInputStream input =
  new DataInputStream(new FileInputStream("in.dat"));
DataOutputStream output =
  new DataOutputStream(new FileOutputStream("out.dat"));
```

Listing 17.2 writes student names and scores to a file named **temp.dat** and reads the data back from the file.

LISTING 17.2   TestDataStream.java

```
 1  import java.io.*;
 2
 3  public class TestDataStream {
 4    public static void main(String[] args) throws IOException {
 5      try ( // Create an output stream for file temp.dat
 6        DataOutputStream output =
 7          new DataOutputStream(new FileOutputStream("temp.dat"));
 8      ) {
 9        // Write student test scores to the file
10        output.writeUTF("John");
11        output.writeDouble(85.5);
12        output.writeUTF("Jim");
13        output.writeDouble(185.5);
14        output.writeUTF("George");
15        output.writeDouble(105.25);
16      }
17
18      try ( // Create an input stream for file temp.dat
19        DataInputStream input =
20          new DataInputStream(new FileInputStream("temp.dat"));
21      ) {
22        // Read student test scores from the file
23        System.out.println(input.readUTF() + " " + input.readDouble());
24        System.out.println(input.readUTF() + " " + input.readDouble());
25        System.out.println(input.readUTF() + " " + input.readDouble());
26      }
27    }
28  }
```

Margin notes: output stream (lines 6–7), output (line 10), input stream (lines 19–20), input (line 23)

```
John 85.5
Susan 185.5
Kim 105.25
```

A **DataOutputStream** is created for file **temp.dat** in lines 6 and 7. Student names and scores are written to the file in lines 10–15. A **DataInputStream** is created for the same file in lines 19–20. Student names and scores are read back from the file and displayed on the console in lines 23–25.

DataInputStream and **DataOutputStream** read and write Java primitive-type values and strings in a machine-independent fashion, thereby enabling you to write a data file on one machine and read it on another machine that has a different operating system or file structure. An application uses a data output stream to write data that can later be read by a program using a data input stream.

DataInputStream filters data from an input stream into appropriate primitive-type values or strings. **DataOutputStream** converts primitive-type values or strings into bytes and outputs the bytes to an output stream. You can view **DataInputStream**/**FileInputStream** and **DataOutputStream**/**FileOutputStream** working in a pipe line as shown in Figure 17.11.

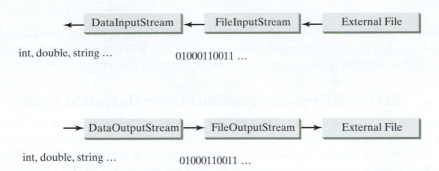

FIGURE 17.11 **DataInputStream** filters an input stream of byte to data and **DataOutputStream** converts data into a stream of bytes.

Caution
You have to read data in the same order and format in which they are stored. For example, since names are written in UTF-8 using **writeUTF**, you must read names using **readUTF**.

Detecting the End of a File

If you keep reading data at the end of an **InputStream**, an **EOFException** will occur. This exception can be used to detect the end of a file, as shown in Listing 17.3.   EOFException

LISTING 17.3 DetectEndOfFile.java

```
 1  import java.io.*;
 2
 3  public class DetectEndOfFile {
 4    public static void main(String[] args) {
 5      try {
 6        try (DataOutputStream output =                            output stream
 7          new DataOutputStream(new FileOutputStream("test.dat"))) {
 8          output.writeDouble(4.5);                                output
 9          output.writeDouble(43.25);
10          output.writeDouble(3.2);
11        }
12
13        try (DataInputStream input =                             input stream
14          new DataInputStream(new FileInputStream("test.dat"))) {
15          while (true)
16            System.out.println(input.readDouble());              input
17        }
18      }
19      catch (EOFException ex) {                                  EOFException
20        System.out.println("All data were read");
21      }
22      catch (IOException ex) {
23        ex.printStackTrace();
24      }
25    }
26  }
```

```
4.5
43.25
3.2
All data were read
```

The program writes three double values to the file using **DataOutputStream** (lines 6–11) and reads the data using **DataInputStream** (lines 13–17). When reading past the end of the file, an **EOFException** is thrown. The exception is caught in line 19.

17.4.4 BufferedInputStream/BufferedOutputStream

BufferedInputStream/BufferedOutputStream can be used to speed up input and output by reducing the number of disk reads and writes. Using **BufferedInputStream**, the whole block of data on the disk is read into the buffer in the memory once. The individual data are then delivered to your program from the buffer, as shown in Figure 17.12a. Using **BufferedOutputStream**, the individual data are first written to the buffer in the memory. When the buffer is full, all data in the buffer are written to the disk once, as shown in Figure 17.12b.

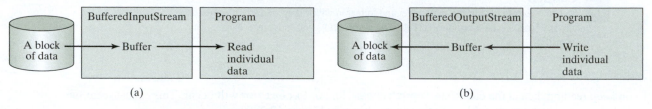

FIGURE 17.12 Buffer I/O places data in a buffer for fast processing.

BufferedInputStream/BufferedOutputStream does not contain new methods. All the methods in **BufferedInputStream/BufferedOutputStream** are inherited from the **InputStream/OutputStream** classes. **BufferedInputStream/BufferedOutputStream** manages a buffer behind the scene and automatically reads/writes data from/to disk on demand.

You can wrap a **BufferedInputStream/BufferedOutputStream** on any **InputStream/OutputStream** using the constructors shown in Figures 17.13 and 17.14.

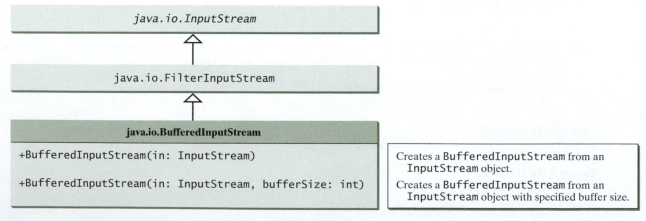

FIGURE 17.13 **BufferedInputStream** buffers an input stream.

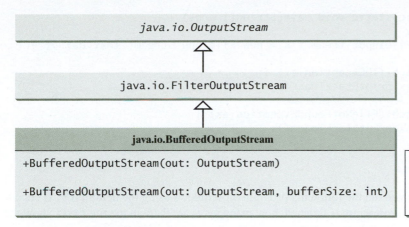

FIGURE 17.14   `BufferedOutputStream` buffers an output stream.

If no buffer size is specified, the default size is `512` bytes. You can improve the performance of the **TestDataStream** program in Listing 17.2 by adding buffers in the stream in lines 6–7 and lines 19–20, as follows:

```
DataOutputStream output = new DataOutputStream(
   new BufferedOutputStream(new FileOutputStream("temp.dat")));
```

```
DataInputStream input = new DataInputStream(
   new BufferedInputStream(new FileInputStream("temp.dat")));
```

Tip

You should always use buffered I/O to speed up input and output. For small files, you may not notice performance improvements. However, for large files—over 100 MB—you will see substantial improvements using buffered I/O.

17.8 Why do you have to declare to throw **IOException** in the method or use a try-catch block to handle **IOException** for Java I/O programs?

17.9 Why should you always close streams? How do you close streams?

17.10 The **read()** method in **InputStream** reads a byte. Why does it return an **int** instead of a **byte**? Find the abstract methods in **InputStream** and **OutputStream**.

17.11 Does **FileInputStream**/**FileOutputStream** introduce any new methods beyond the methods inherited from **InputStream**/**OutputStream**? How do you create a **FileInputStream**/**FileOutputStream**?

17.12 What will happen if you attempt to create an input stream on a nonexistent file? What will happen if you attempt to create an output stream on an existing file? Can you append data to an existing file?

17.13 How do you append data to an existing text file using **java.io.PrintWriter**?

17.14 Suppose a file contains an unspecified number of **double** values that were written to the file using the **writeDouble** method using a **DataOutputStream**, how do you write a program to read all these values? How do you detect the end of a file?

17.15 What is written to a file using **writeByte(91)** on a **FileOutputStream**?

17.16 How do you check the end of a file in an input stream (**FileInputStream**, **DataInputStream**)?

17.17 What is wrong in the following code?

```
import java.io.*;

public class Test {
```

```
    public static void main(String[] args) {
      try (
        FileInputStream fis = new FileInputStream("test.dat"); ) {
      }
      catch (IOException ex) {
        ex.printStackTrace();
      }
      catch (FileNotFoundException ex) {
        ex.printStackTrace();
      }
    }
  }
```

17.18 Suppose you run the following program on Windows using the default ASCII encoding after the program is finished, how many bytes are there in the file **t.txt**? Show the contents of each byte.

```
public class Test {
  public static void main(String[] args)
      throws java.io.IOException {
    try (java.io.PrintWriter output =
        new java.io.PrintWriter("t.txt"); ) {
      output.printf("%s", "1234");
      output.printf("%s", "5678");
      output.close();
    }
  }
}
```

17.19 After the following program is finished, how many bytes are there in the file **t.dat**? Show the contents of each byte.

```
import java.io.*;

public class Test {
  public static void main(String[] args) throws IOException {
    try (DataOutputStream output = new DataOutputStream(
        new FileOutputStream("t.dat")); ) {
      output.writeInt(1234);
      output.writeInt(5678);
      output.close();
    }
  }
}
```

17.20 For each of the following statements on a **DataOutputStream output**, how many bytes are sent to the output?

```
output.writeChar('A');
output.writeChars("BC");
output.writeUTF("DEF");
```

17.21 What are the advantages of using buffered streams? Are the following statements correct?

```
BufferedInputStream input1 =
  new BufferedInputStream(new FileInputStream("t.dat"));

DataInputStream input2 = new DataInputStream(
  new BufferedInputStream(new FileInputStream("t.dat")));

DataOutputStream output = new DataOutputStream(
  new BufferedOutputStream(new FileOutputStream("t.dat")));
```

17.5 Case Study: Copying Files

This section develops a useful utility for copying files.

In this section, you will learn how to write a program that lets users copy files. The user needs to provide a source file and a target file as command-line arguments using the command:

```
java Copy source target
```

The program copies the source file to the target file and displays the number of bytes in the file. The program should alert the user if the source file does not exist or if the target file already exists. A sample run of the program is shown in Figure 17.15.

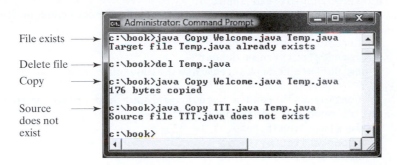

FIGURE 17.15 The program copies a file.

To copy the contents from a source file to a target file, it is appropriate to use an input stream to read bytes from the source file and an output stream to send bytes to the target file, regardless of the file's contents. The source file and the target file are specified from the command line. Create an **InputFileStream** for the source file and an **OutputFileStream** for the target file. Use the **read()** method to read a byte from the input stream, and then use the **write(b)** method to write the byte to the output stream. Use **BufferedInputStream** and **BufferedOutputStream** to improve the performance. Listing 17.4 gives the solution to the problem.

LISTING 17.4 Copy.java

```java
 1  import java.io.*;
 2
 3  public class Copy {
 4    /** Main method
 5       @param args[0] for sourcefile
 6       @param args[1] for target file
 7    */
 8    public static void main(String[] args) throws IOException {
 9      // Check command-line parameter usage
10      if (args.length != 2) {
11        System.out.println(
12          "Usage: java Copy sourceFile targetfile");
13        System.exit(1);
14      }
15
16      // Check if source file exists
17      File sourceFile = new File(args[0]);
18      if (!sourceFile.exists()) {
19        System.out.println("Source file " + args[0]
20          + " does not exist");
```

check usage

source file

```
21              System.exit(2);
22          }
23
24          // Check if target file exists
25          File targetFile = new File(args[1]);
26          if (targetFile.exists()) {
27            System.out.println("Target file " + args[1]
28              + " already exists");
29            System.exit(3);
30          }
31
32          try (
33            // Create an input stream
34            BufferedInputStream input =
35              new BufferedInputStream(new FileInputStream(sourceFile));
36
37            // Create an output stream
38            BufferedOutputStream output =
39              new BufferedOutputStream(new FileOutputStream(targetFile));
40          ) {
41            // Continuously read a byte from input and write it to output
42            int r, numberOfBytesCopied = 0;
43            while ((r = input.read()) != -1) {
44              output.write((byte)r);
45              numberOfBytesCopied++;
46            }
47
48            // Display the file size
49            System.out.println(numberOfBytesCopied + " bytes copied");
50          }
51        }
52      }
```

target file (line 25)

input stream (lines 34–35)

output stream (lines 38–39)

read (line 43)
write (line 44)

The program first checks whether the user has passed the two required arguments from the command line in lines 10–14.

The program uses the **File** class to check whether the source file and target file exist. If the source file does not exist (lines 18–22) or if the target file already exists (lines 25–30), the program ends.

An input stream is created using **BufferedInputStream** wrapped on **FileInputStream** in lines 34 and 35, and an output stream is created using **BufferedOutputStream** wrapped on **FileOutputStream** in lines 38 and 39.

The expression **((r = input.read()) != -1)** (line 43) reads a byte from **input.read()**, assigns it to **r**, and checks whether it is **-1**. The input value of **-1** signifies the end of a file. The program continuously reads bytes from the input stream and sends them to the output stream until all of the bytes have been read.

17.22 How does the program check if a file already exists?

17.23 How does the program detect the end of the file while reading data?

17.24 How does the program count the number of bytes read from the file?

17.6 Object I/O

ObjectInputStream/ObjectOutputStream classes can be used to read/write serializable objects.

DataInputStream/DataOutputStream enables you to perform I/O for primitive-type values and strings. **ObjectInputStream/ObjectOutputStream** enables you to perform I/O

for objects in addition to primitive-type values and strings. Since `ObjectInputStream`/
`ObjectOutputStream` contains all the functions of `DataInputStream`/
`DataOutputStream`, you can replace `DataInputStream`/`DataOutputStream` completely
with `ObjectInputStream`/`ObjectOutputStream`.

VideoNote
Object I/O

   `ObjectInputStream` extends `InputStream` and implements `ObjectInput` and
`ObjectStreamConstants`, as shown in Figure 17.16. `ObjectInput` is a subinterface of
`DataInput` (`DataInput` is shown in Figure 17.9). `ObjectStreamConstants` contains the
constants to support `ObjectInputStream`/`ObjectOutputStream`.

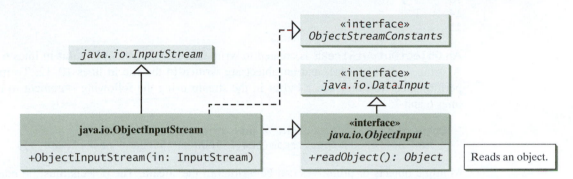

FIGURE 17.16   `ObjectInputStream` can read objects, primitive-type values, and strings.

   `ObjectOutputStream` extends `OutputStream` and implements `ObjectOutput` and
`ObjectStreamConstants`, as shown in Figure 17.17. `ObjectOutput` is a subinterface of
`DataOutput` (`DataOutput` is shown in Figure 17.10).

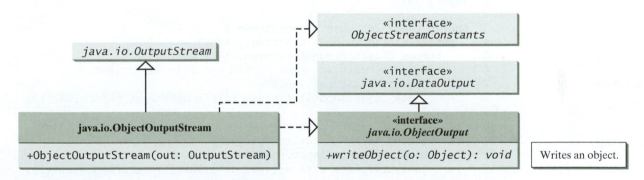

FIGURE 17.17   `ObjectOutputStream` can write objects, primitive-type values, and strings.

You can wrap an `ObjectInputStream`/`ObjectOutputStream` on any `InputStream`/
`OutputStream` using the following constructors:

```
// Create an ObjectInputStream
public ObjectInputStream(InputStream in)

// Create an ObjectOutputStream
public ObjectOutputStream(OutputStream out)
```

Listing 17.5 writes student names, scores, and the current date to a file named **object.dat**.

LISTING 17.5   TestObjectOutputStream.java

```
1  import java.io.*;
2
3  public class TestObjectOutputStream {
```

```
4    public static void main(String[] args) throws IOException {
5      try ( // Create an output stream for file object.dat
6        ObjectOutputStream output =
7          new ObjectOutputStream(new FileOutputStream("object.dat"));
8      ) {
9        // Write a string, double value, and object to the file
10       output.writeUTF("John");
11       output.writeDouble(85.5);
12       output.writeObject(new java.util.Date());
13     }
14   }
15 }
```

output stream (margin note at line 6)
output string (margin note at line 10)
output object (margin note at line 12)

An **ObjectOutputStream** is created to write data into the file **object.dat** in lines 6 and 7. A string, a double value, and an object are written to the file in lines 10–12. To improve performance, you may add a buffer in the stream using the following statement to replace lines 6 and 7:

```
ObjectOutputStream output = new ObjectOutputStream(
  new BufferedOutputStream(new FileOutputStream("object.dat")));
```

Multiple objects or primitives can be written to the stream. The objects must be read back from the corresponding **ObjectInputStream** with the same types and in the same order as they were written. Java's safe casting should be used to get the desired type. Listing 17.6 reads data from **object.dat**.

LISTING 17.6 TestObjectInputStream.java

```
1  import java.io.*;
2
3  public class TestObjectInputStream {
4    public static void main(String[] args)
5        throws ClassNotFoundException, IOException {
6      try ( // Create an input stream for file object.dat
7        ObjectInputStream input =
8          new ObjectInputStream(new FileInputStream("object.dat"));
9      ) {
10       // Read a string, double value, and object from the file
11       String name = input.readUTF();
12       double score = input.readDouble();
13       java.util.Date date = (java.util.Date)(input.readObject());
14       System.out.println(name + " " + score + " " + date);
15     }
16   }
17 }
```

input stream (margin note at line 7)
input string (margin note at line 11)
input object (margin note at line 13)

```
John 85.5 Sun Dec 04 10:35:31 EST 2011
```

ClassNotFoundException (margin note)

The **readObject()** method may throw **java.lang.ClassNotFoundException**, because when the JVM restores an object, it first loads the class for the object if the class has not been loaded. Since **ClassNotFoundException** is a checked exception, the **main** method declares to throw it in line 5. An **ObjectInputStream** is created to read input from **object.dat** in lines 7 and 8. You have to read the data from the file in the same order and format as they were written to the file. A string, a double value, and an object are read in lines 11–13. Since **readObject()** returns an **Object**, it is cast into **Date** and assigned to a **Date** variable in line 13.

17.6.1 The `Serializable` Interface

Not every object can be written to an output stream. Objects that can be so written are said to be *serializable*. A serializable object is an instance of the `java.io.Serializable` interface, so the object's class must implement `Serializable`.

The `Serializable` interface is a marker interface. Since it has no methods, you don't need to add additional code in your class that implements `Serializable`. Implementing this interface enables the Java serialization mechanism to automate the process of storing objects and arrays.

To appreciate this automation feature, consider what you otherwise need to do in order to store an object. Suppose you wish to store an `ArrayList` object. To do this you need to store all the elements in the list. Each element is an object that may contain other objects. As you can see, this would be a very tedious process. Fortunately, you don't have to go through it manually. Java provides a built-in mechanism to automate the process of writing objects. This process is referred as *object serialization*, which is implemented in `ObjectOutputStream`. In contrast, the process of reading objects is referred as *object deserialization*, which is implemented in `ObjectInputStream`.

Many classes in the Java API implement `Serializable`. All the wrapper classes for primitive type values, `java.math.BigInteger`, `java.math.BigDecimal`, `java.lang.String`, `java.lang.StringBuilder`, `java.lang.StringBuffer`, `java.util.Date`, and `java.util.ArrayList` implement `java.io.Serializable`. Attempting to store an object that does not support the `Serializable` interface would cause a `NotSerializableException`.

When a serializable object is stored, the class of the object is encoded; this includes the class name and the signature of the class, the values of the object's instance variables, and the closure of any other objects referenced by the object. The values of the object's static variables are not stored.

Note
Nonserializable fields

If an object is an instance of `Serializable` but contains nonserializable instance data fields, can it be serialized? The answer is no. To enable the object to be serialized, mark these data fields with the `transient` keyword to tell the JVM to ignore them when writing the object to an object stream. Consider the following class:

```java
public class C implements java.io.Serializable {
  private int v1;
  private static double v2;
  private transient A v3 = new A();
}

class A { } // A is not serializable
```

When an object of the `C` class is serialized, only variable `v1` is serialized. Variable `v2` is not serialized because it is a static variable, and variable `v3` is not serialized because it is marked `transient`. If `v3` were not marked `transient`, a `java.io.NotSerializableException` would occur.

Note
Duplicate objects

If an object is written to an object stream more than once, will it be stored in multiple copies? No, it will not. When an object is written for the first time, a serial number is created for it. The JVM writes the complete contents of the object along with the serial number into the object stream. After the first time, only the serial number is stored if the

serializable

serialization
deserialization

NotSerializableException

transient

same object is written again. When the objects are read back, their references are the same since only one object is actually created in the memory.

17.6.2 Serializing Arrays

An array is serializable if all its elements are serializable. An entire array can be saved into a file using **writeObject** and later can be restored using **readObject**. Listing 17.7 stores an array of five **int** values and an array of three strings and reads them back to display on the console.

LISTING 17.7 TestObjectStreamForArray.java

```
1   import java.io.*;
2
3   public class TestObjectStreamForArray {
4     public static void main(String[] args)
5         throws ClassNotFoundException, IOException {
6       int[] numbers = {1, 2, 3, 4, 5};
7       String[] strings = {"John", "Susan", "Kim"};
8
9       try ( // Create an output stream for file array.dat
10        ObjectOutputStream output = new ObjectOutputStream(new
11          FileOutputStream("array.dat", true));
12      ) {
13        // Write arrays to the object output stream
14        output.writeObject(numbers);
15        output.writeObject(strings);
16      }
17
18      try ( // Create an input stream for file array.dat
19        ObjectInputStream input =
20          new ObjectInputStream(new FileInputStream("array.dat"));
21      ) {
22        int[] newNumbers = (int[])(input.readObject());
23        String[] newStrings = (String[])(input.readObject());
24
25        // Display arrays
26        for (int i = 0; i < newNumbers.length; i++)
27          System.out.print(newNumbers[i] + " ");
28        System.out.println();
29
30        for (int i = 0; i < newStrings.length; i++)
31          System.out.print(newStrings[i] + " ");
32      }
33    }
34  }
```

output stream (lines 10–11)

store array (lines 14–15)

input stream (lines 19–20)

restore array (lines 22–23)

```
1 2 3 4 5
John Susan Kim
```

Lines 14 and 15 write two arrays into file **array.dat**. Lines 22 and 23 read two arrays back in the same order they were written. Since **readObject()** returns **Object**, casting is used to cast the objects into **int[]** and **String[]**.

Check Point

17.25 What types of objects can be stored using the **ObjectOutputStream**? What is the method for writing an object? What is the method for reading an object? What is the return type of the method that reads an object from **ObjectInputStream**?

17.26 If you serialize two objects of the same type, will they take the same amount of space? If not, give an example.

17.27 Is it true that any instance of `java.io.Serializable` can be successfully serialized? Are the static variables in an object serialized? How do you mark an instance variable not to be serialized?

17.28 Can you write an array to an `ObjectOutputStream`?

17.29 Is it true that `DataInputStream`/`DataOutputStream` can always be replaced by `ObjectInputStream`/`ObjectOutputStream`?

17.30 What will happen when you attempt to run the following code?

```java
import java.io.*;

public class Test {
  public static void main(String[] args) throws IOException {
    try ( ObjectOutputStream output =
        new ObjectOutputStream(new FileOutputStream("object.dat")); ) {
      output.writeObject(new A());
    }
  }
}

class A implements Serializable {
  B b = new B();
}

class B {
}
```

17.7 Random-Access Files

Key Point

Java provides the RandomAccessFile class to allow data to be read from and written to at any locations in the file.

All of the streams you have used so far are known as *read-only* or *write-only* streams. These streams are called *sequential streams*. A file that is opened using a sequential stream is called a *sequential-access file*. The contents of a sequential-access file cannot be updated. However, it is often necessary to modify files. Java provides the `RandomAccessFile` class to allow data to be read from and written to at any locations in a file. A file that is opened using the `RandomAccessFile` class is known as a *random-access file*.

read-only

write-only

sequential-access file

random-access file

The `RandomAccessFile` class implements the `DataInput` and `DataOutput` interfaces, as shown in Figure 17.18. The `DataInput` interface (see Figure 17.9) defines the methods for reading primitive-type values and strings (e.g., `readInt`, `readDouble`, `readChar`, `readBoolean`, `readUTF`) and the `DataOutput` interface (see Figure 17.10) defines the methods for writing primitive-type values and strings (e.g., `writeInt`, `writeDouble`, `writeChar`, `writeBoolean`, `writeUTF`).

When creating a `RandomAccessFile`, you can specify one of two modes: `r` or `rw`. Mode `r` means that the stream is read-only, and mode `rw` indicates that the stream allows both read and write. For example, the following statement creates a new stream, `raf`, that allows the program to read from and write to the file **test.dat**:

```java
RandomAccessFile raf = new RandomAccessFile("test.dat", "rw");
```

If **test.dat** already exists, `raf` is created to access it; if **test.dat** does not exist, a new file named **test.dat** is created, and `raf` is created to access the new file. The method `raf.length()` returns the number of bytes in **test.dat** at any given time. If you append new data into the file, `raf.length()` increases.

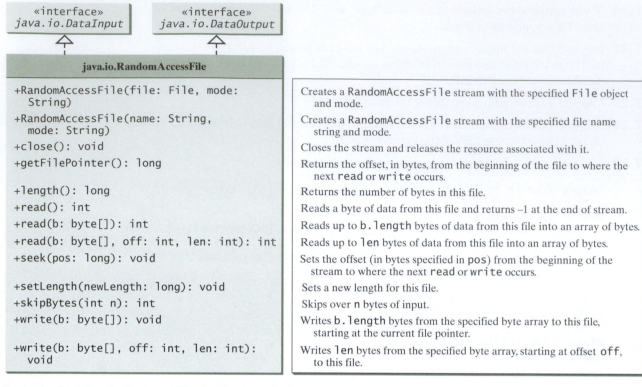

FIGURE 17.18 **RandomAccessFile** implements the **DataInput** and **DataOutput** interfaces with additional methods to support random access.

 Tip
If the file is not intended to be modified, open it with the **r** mode. This prevents unintentional modification of the file.

file pointer

A random-access file consists of a sequence of bytes. A special marker called a *file pointer* is positioned at one of these bytes. A read or write operation takes place at the location of the file pointer. When a file is opened, the file pointer is set at the beginning of the file. When you read or write data to the file, the file pointer moves forward to the next data item. For example, if you read an **int** value using **readInt()**, the JVM reads **4** bytes from the file pointer, and now the file pointer is **4** bytes ahead of the previous location, as shown in Figure 17.19.

For a **RandomAccessFile raf**, you can use the **raf.seek(position)** method to move the file pointer to a specified position. **raf.seek(0)** moves it to the beginning of the file, and **raf.seek(raf.length())** moves it to the end of the file. Listing 17.8 demonstrates

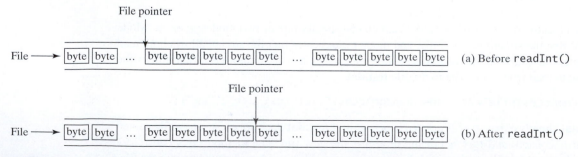

FIGURE 17.19 After an **int** value is read, the file pointer is moved 4 bytes ahead.

RandomAccessFile. A large case study of using **RandomAccessFile** to organize an address book is given in Supplement VI.D.

LISTING 17.8 TestRandomAccessFile.jav

```java
1  import java.io.*;
2
3  public class TestRandomAccessFile {
4    public static void main(String[] args) throws IOException {
5      try ( // Create a random access file
6        RandomAccessFile inout = new RandomAccessFile("inout.dat", "rw");
7      ) {
8        // Clear the file to destroy the old contents if exists
9        inout.setLength(0);
10
11       // Write new integers to the file
12       for (int i = 0; i < 200; i++)
13         inout.writeInt(i);
14
15       // Display the current length of the file
16       System.out.println("Current file length is " + inout.length());
17
18       // Retrieve the first number
19       inout.seek(0); // Move the file pointer to the beginning
20       System.out.println("The first number is " + inout.readInt());
21
22       // Retrieve the second number
23       inout.seek(1 * 4); // Move the file pointer to the second number
24       System.out.println("The second number is " + inout.readInt());
25
26       // Retrieve the tenth number
27       inout.seek(9 * 4); // Move the file pointer to the tenth number
28       System.out.println("The tenth number is " + inout.readInt());
29
30       // Modify the eleventh number
31       inout.writeInt(555);
32
33       // Append a new number
34       inout.seek(inout.length()); // Move the file pointer to the end
35       inout.writeInt(999);
36
37       // Display the new length
38       System.out.println("The new length is " + inout.length());
39
40       // Retrieve the new eleventh number
41       inout.seek(10 * 4); // Move the file pointer to the eleventh number
42       System.out.println("The eleventh number is " + inout.readInt());
43     }
44   }
45 }
```

RandomAccessFile

empty file

write

move pointer
read

```
Current file length is 800
The first number is 0
The second number is 1
The tenth number is 9
The new length is 804
The eleventh number is 555
```

A `RandomAccessFile` is created for the file named **inout.dat** with mode `rw` to allow both read and write operations in line 6.

`inout.setLength(0)` sets the length to 0 in line 9. This, in effect, destroys the old contents of the file.

The `for` loop writes `200 int` values from 0 to 199 into the file in lines 12 and 13. Since each `int` value takes 4 bytes, the total length of the file returned from `inout.length()` is now 800 (line 16), as shown in the sample output.

Invoking `inout.seek(0)` in line 19 sets the file pointer to the beginning of the file. `inout.readInt()` reads the first value in line 20 and moves the file pointer to the next number. The second number is read in line 24.

`inout.seek(9 * 4)` (line 27) moves the file pointer to the tenth number. `inout.readInt()` reads the tenth number and moves the file pointer to the eleventh number in line 28. `inout.write(555)` writes a new eleventh number at the current position (line 31). The previous eleventh number is destroyed.

`inout.seek(inout.length())` moves the file pointer to the end of the file (line 34). `inout.writeInt(999)` writes a 999 to the file (line 35). Now the length of the file is increased by 4, so `inout.length()` returns 804 (line 38).

`inout.seek(10 * 4)` moves the file pointer to the eleventh number in line 41. The new eleventh number, 555, is displayed in line 42.

Check Point

17.31 Can `RandomAccessFile` streams read and write a data file created by `DataOutputStream`? Can `RandomAccessFile` streams read and write objects?

17.32 Create a `RandomAccessFile` stream for the file **address.dat** to allow the updating of student information in the file. Create a `DataOutputStream` for the file **address.dat**. Explain the differences between these two statements.

17.33 What happens if the file **test.dat** does not exist when you attempt to compile and run the following code?

```java
import java.io.*;

public class Test {
  public static void main(String[] args) {
    try ( RandomAccessFile raf =
        new RandomAccessFile("test.dat", "r"); ) {
      int i = raf.readInt();
    }
    catch (IOException ex) {
      System.out.println("IO exception");
    }
  }
}
```

KEY TERMS

binary I/O   678
deserialization   695
file pointer   698
random-access file   697

sequential-access file   697
serialization   695
stream   678
text I/O   678

CHAPTER SUMMARY

1. I/O can be classified into *text I/O* and *binary I/O*. Text I/O interprets data in sequences of characters. Binary I/O interprets data as raw binary values. How text is stored in a file depends on the encoding scheme for the file. Java automatically performs encoding and decoding for text I/O.

2. The `InputStream` and `OutputStream` classes are the roots of all binary I/O classes. `FileInputStream`/`FileOutputStream` associates a file for input/output. `BufferedInputStream`/`BufferedOutputStream` can be used to wrap any binary I/O stream to improve performance. `DataInputStream`/`DataOutputStream` can be used to read/write primitive values and strings.

3. `ObjectInputStream`/`ObjectOutputStream` can be used to read/write objects in addition to primitive values and strings. To enable object *serialization*, the object's defining class must implement the `java.io.Serializable` marker interface.

4. The `RandomAccessFile` class enables you to read and write data to a file. You can open a file with the `r` mode to indicate that it is read-only or with the `rw` mode to indicate that it is updateable. Since the `RandomAccessFile` class implements `DataInput` and `DataOutput` interfaces, many methods in `RandomAccessFile` are the same as those in `DataInputStream` and `DataOutputStream`.

QUIZ

Answer the quiz for this chapter online at www.cs.armstrong.edu/liang/intro10e/quiz.html.

PROGRAMMING EXERCISES

MyProgrammingLab™

Section 17.3

*17.1 (*Create a text file*) Write a program to create a file named **Exercise17_01.txt** if it does not exist. Append new data to it if it already exists. Write 100 integers created randomly into the file using text I/O. Integers are separated by a space.

Section 17.4

*17.2 (*Create a binary data file*) Write a program to create a file named **Exercise17_02.dat** if it does not exist. Append new data to it if it already exists. Write 100 integers created randomly into the file using binary I/O.

*17.3 (*Sum all the integers in a binary data file*) Suppose a binary data file named **Exercise17_03.dat** has been created and its data are created using `writeInt(int)` in `DataOutputStream`. The file contains an unspecified number of integers. Write a program to find the sum of the integers.

*17.4 (*Convert a text file into UTF*) Write a program that reads lines of characters from a text file and writes each line as a UTF-8 string into a binary file. Display the sizes of the text file and the binary file. Use the following command to run the program:

```
java Exercise17_04 Welcome.java Welcome.utf
```

Section 17.6

*17.5 (*Store objects and arrays in a file*) Write a program that stores an array of the five **int** values 1, 2, 3, 4, and 5, a **Date** object for the current time, and the **double** value 5.5 into the file named **Exercise17_05.dat**.

*17.6 (*Store Loan objects*) The **Loan** class in Listing 10.2 does not implement **Serializable**. Rewrite the **Loan** class to implement **Serializable**. Write a program that creates five **Loan** objects and stores them in a file named **Exercise17_06.dat**.

*17.7 (*Restore objects from a file*) Suppose a file named **Exercise17_07.dat** has been created using the **ObjectOutputStream**. The file contains **Loan** objects. The **Loan** class in Listing 10.2 does not implement **Serializable**. Rewrite the **Loan** class to implement **Serializable**. Write a program that reads the **Loan** objects from the file and displays the total loan amount. Suppose you don't know how many **Loan** objects are there in the file, use **EOFException** to end the loop.

Section 17.7

*17.8 (*Update count*) Suppose you wish to track how many times a program has been executed. You can store an **int** to count the file. Increase the count by 1 each time this program is executed. Let the program be **Exercise17_08** and store the count in **Exercise17_08.dat**.

***17.9 (*Address book*) Write a program that stores, retrieves, adds, and updates addresses as shown in Figure 17.20. Use a fixed-length string for storing each attribute in the address. Use random access file for reading and writing an address. Assume that the size of name, street, city, state, and zip is 32, 32, 20, 2, 5 bytes, respectively.

FIGURE 17.20 The application can store, retrieve, and update addresses from a file.

Comprehensive

VideoNote

Split a large file

*17.10 (*Split files*) Suppose you want to back up a huge file (e.g., a 10-GB AVI file) to a CD-R. You can achieve it by splitting the file into smaller pieces and backing up these pieces separately. Write a utility program that splits a large file into smaller ones using the following command:

```
java Exercise17_10 SourceFile numberOfPieces
```

The command creates the files **SourceFile.1**, **SourceFile.2**, . . . , **SourceFile.n**, where **n** is **numberOfPieces** and the output files are about the same size.

**17.11 (*Split files GUI*) Rewrite Exercise 17.10 with a GUI, as shown in Figure 17.21a.

*17.12 (*Combine files*) Write a utility program that combines the files together into a new file using the following command:

```
java Exercise17_12 SourceFile1 . . . SourceFilen TargetFile
```

The command combines SourceFile1, . . . , and SourceFilen into TargetFile.

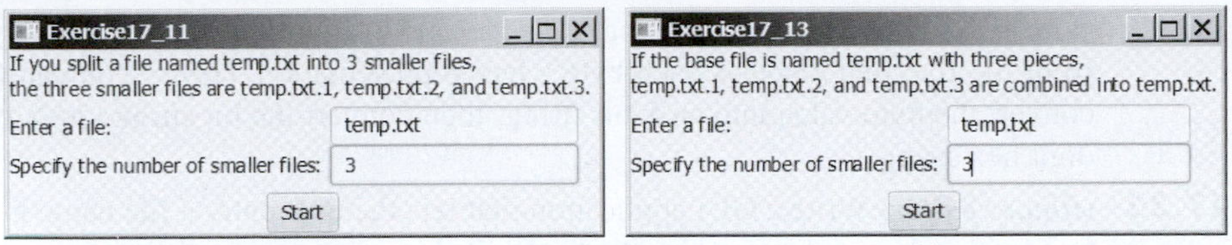

FIGURE 17.21 (a) The program splits a file. (b) The program combines files into a new file.

*17.13 (*Combine files GUI*) Rewrite Exercise 17.12 with a GUI, as shown in Figure 17.21b.

17.14 (*Encrypt files*) Encode the file by adding 5 to every byte in the file. Write a program that prompts the user to enter an input file name and an output file name and saves the encrypted version of the input file to the output file.

17.15 (*Decrypt files*) Suppose a file is encrypted using the scheme in Programming Exercise 17.14. Write a program to decode an encrypted file. Your program should prompt the user to enter an input file name for the encrypted file and an output file name for the unencrypted version of the input file.

17.16 (*Frequency of characters*) Write a program that prompts the user to enter the name of an ASCII text file and displays the frequency of the characters in the file.

17.17 (*BitOutputStream*) Implement a class named `BitOutputStream`, as shown in Figure 17.22, for writing bits to an output stream. The `writeBit(char bit)` method stores the bit in a byte variable. When you create a `BitOutputStream`, the byte is empty. After invoking `writeBit('1')`, the byte becomes `00000001`. After invoking `writeBit("0101")`, the byte becomes `00010101`. The first three bits are not filled yet. When a byte is full, it is sent to the output stream. Now the byte is reset to empty. You must close the stream by invoking the `close()` method. If the byte is neither empty nor full, the `close()` method first fills the zeros to make a full 8 bits in the byte, and then outputs the byte and closes the stream. For a hint, see Programming Exercise 5.44. Write a test program that sends the bits `0100001001000010011011` to the file named **Exercise17_17.dat.

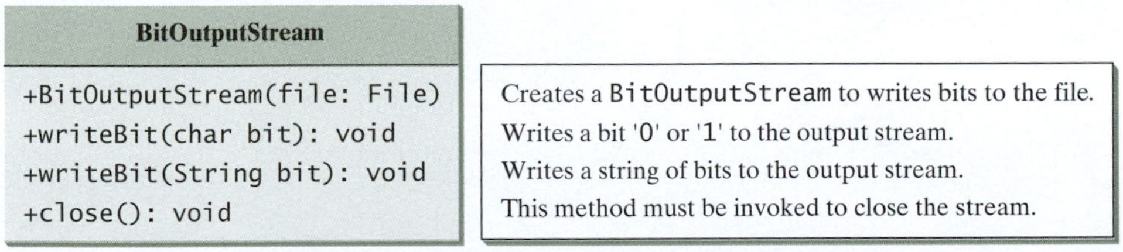

FIGURE 17.22 `BitOutputStream` outputs a stream of bits to a file.

*17.18 (*View bits*) Write the following method that displays the bit representation for the last byte in an integer:

```
public static String getBits(int value)
```

For a hint, see Programming Exercise 5.44. Write a program that prompts the user to enter a file name, reads bytes from the file, and displays each byte's binary representation.

*17.19 (*View hex*) Write a program that prompts the user to enter a file name, reads bytes from the file, and displays each byte's hex representation. (*Hint*: You can first convert the byte value into an 8-bit string, then convert the bit string into a two-digit hex string.)

**17.20 (*Binary editor*) Write a GUI application that lets the user enter a file name in the text field and press the *Enter* key to display its binary representation in a text area. The user can also modify the binary code and save it back to the file, as shown in Figure 17.23a.

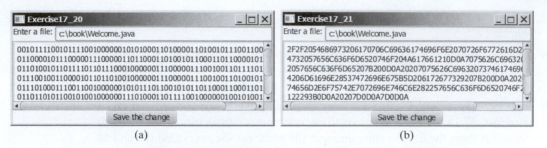

(a)   (b)

FIGURE 17.23 The programs enable the user to manipulate the contents of the file in (a) binary and (b) hex.

**17.21 (*Hex editor*) Write a GUI application that lets the user enter a file name in the text field and press the *Enter* key to display its hex representation in a text area. The user can also modify the hex code and save it back to the file, as shown in Figure 17.23b.

RECURSION

Objectives

- To describe what a recursive method is and the benefits of using recursion (§18.1).

- To develop recursive methods for recursive mathematical functions (§§18.2–18.3).

- To explain how recursive method calls are handled in a call stack (§§18.2–18.3).

- To solve problems using recursion (§18.4).

- To use an overloaded helper method to design a recursive method (§18.5).

- To implement a selection sort using recursion (§18.5.1).

- To implement a binary search using recursion (§18.5.2).

- To get the directory size using recursion (§18.6).

- To solve the Tower of Hanoi problem using recursion (§18.7).

- To draw fractals using recursion (§18.8).

- To discover the relationship and difference between recursion and iteration (§18.9).

- To know tail-recursive methods and why they are desirable (§18.10).

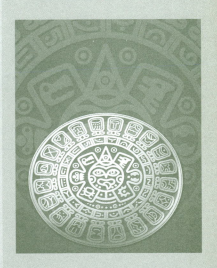

18.1 Introduction

Key Point

Recursion is a technique that leads to elegant solutions to problems that are difficult to program using simple loops.

search word problem

Suppose you want to find all the files under a directory that contain a particular word. How do you solve this problem? There are several ways to do so. An intuitive and effective solution is to use recursion by searching the files in the subdirectories recursively.

H-tree problem

H-trees, depicted in Figure 18.1, are used in a very large-scale integration (VLSI) design as a clock distribution network for routing timing signals to all parts of a chip with equal propagation delays. How do you write a program to display H-trees? A good approach is to use recursion.

(a)

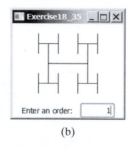
(b)

(c)

(d)

FIGURE 18.1 An H-tree can be displayed using recursion.

recursive method

To use recursion is to program using *recursive methods*—that is, to use methods that invoke themselves. Recursion is a useful programming technique. In some cases, it enables you to develop a natural, straightforward, simple solution to an otherwise difficult problem. This chapter introduces the concepts and techniques of recursive programming and illustrates with examples of how to "think recursively."

18.2 Case Study: Computing Factorials

Key Point

A recursive method is one that invokes itself.

Many mathematical functions are defined using recursion. Let's begin with a simple example. The factorial of a number **n** can be recursively defined as follows:

```
0! = 1;
n! = n × (n - 1)!; n > 0
```

How do you find **n!** for a given **n**? To find **1!** is easy, because you know that **0!** is **1**, and **1!** is **1 × 0!**. Assuming that you know **(n - 1)!**, you can obtain **n!** immediately by using **n × (n - 1)!**. Thus, the problem of computing **n!** is reduced to computing **(n - 1)!**. When computing **(n - 1)!**, you can apply the same idea recursively until **n** is reduced to **0**.

Let **factorial(n)** be the method for computing **n!**. If you call the method with **n = 0**, it immediately returns the result. The method knows how to solve the simplest case, which is referred to as the *base case* or the *stopping condition*. If you call the method with **n > 0**, it reduces the problem into a subproblem for computing the factorial of **n - 1**. The *subproblem* is essentially the same as the original problem, but it is simpler or smaller. Because the subproblem has the same property as the original problem, you can call the method with a different argument, which is referred to as a *recursive call*.

base case or stopping condition

recursive call

The recursive algorithm for computing **factorial(n)** can be simply described as follows:

```
if (n == 0)
    return 1;
```

```
      else
        return n * factorial(n - 1);
```

A recursive call can result in many more recursive calls, because the method keeps on dividing a subproblem into new subproblems. For a recursive method to terminate, the problem must eventually be reduced to a stopping case, at which point the method returns a result to its caller. The caller then performs a computation and returns the result to its own caller. This process continues until the result is passed back to the original caller. The original problem can now be solved by multiplying **n** by the result of **factorial(n - 1)**.

Listing 18.1 gives a complete program that prompts the user to enter a nonnegative integer and displays the factorial for the number.

LISTING 18.1 ComputeFactorial.java

```
 1  import java.util.Scanner;
 2
 3  public class ComputeFactorial {
 4    /** Main method */
 5    public static void main(String[] args) {
 6      // Create a Scanner
 7      Scanner input = new Scanner(System.in);
 8      System.out.print("Enter a nonnegative integer: ");
 9      int n = input.nextInt();
10
11      // Display factorial
12      System.out.println("Factorial of " + n + " is " + factorial(n));
13    }
14
15    /** Return the factorial for the specified number */
16    public static long factorial(int n) {
17      if (n == 0) // Base case                                    base case
18        return 1;
19      else
20        return n * factorial(n - 1); // Recursive call           recursion
21    }
22  }
```

```
Enter a nonnegative integer: 4  ↵Enter
Factorial of 4 is 24
```

```
Enter a nonnegative integer: 10  ↵Enter
Factorial of 10 is 3628800
```

The **factorial** method (lines 16–21) is essentially a direct translation of the recursive mathematical definition for the factorial into Java code. The call to **factorial** is recursive because it calls itself. The parameter passed to **factorial** is decremented until it reaches the base case of **0**.

You see how to write a recursive method. How does recursion work behind the scenes?   how does it work?
Figure 18.2 illustrates the execution of the recursive calls, starting with **n = 4**. The use of stack space for recursive calls is shown in Figure 18.3.

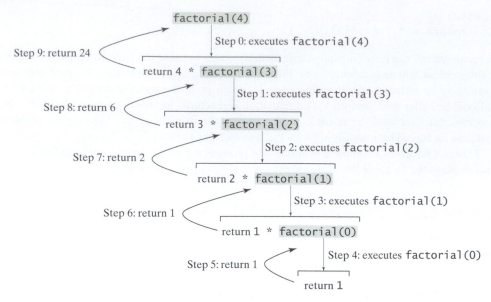

FIGURE 18.2 Invoking `factorial(4)` spawns recursive calls to `factorial`.

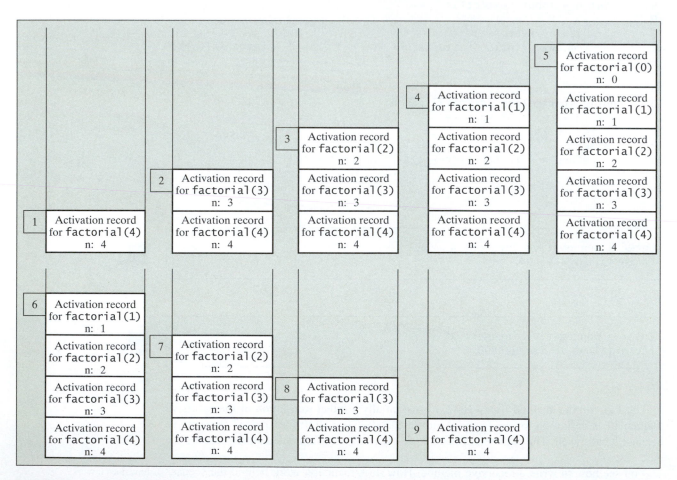

FIGURE 18.3 When `factorial(4)` is being executed, the `factorial` method is called recursively, causing stack space to dynamically change.

Pedagogical Note
It is simpler and more efficient to implement the `factorial` method using a loop. However, we use the recursive `factorial` method here to demonstrate the concept of recursion. Later in this chapter, we will present some problems that are inherently recursive and are difficult to solve without using recursion.

If recursion does not reduce the problem in a manner that allows it to eventually converge into the base case or a base case is not specified, *infinite recursion* can occur. For example, suppose you mistakenly write the `factorial` method as follows:

infinite recursion

```java
public static long factorial(int n) {
  return n * factorial(n - 1);
}
```

The method runs infinitely and causes a `StackOverflowError`.

The example discussed in this section shows a recursive method that invokes itself. This is known as *direct recursion*. It is also possible to create *indirect recursion*. This occurs when method A invokes method B, which in turn invokes method A. There can even be several more methods involved in the recursion. For example, method A invokes method B, which invokes method C, which invokes method A.

direct recursion
indirect recursion

18.1 What is a recursive method? What is an infinite recursion?

18.2 How many times is the `factorial` method in Listing 18.1 invoked for `factorial(6)`?

18.3 Show the output of the following programs and identify base cases and recursive calls.

```java
public class Test {
  public static void main(String[] args) {
    System.out.println(
      "Sum is " + xMethod(5));
  }

  public static int xMethod(int n) {
    if (n == 1)
      return 1;
    else
      return n + xMethod(n - 1);
  }
}
```

```java
public class Test {
  public static void main(String[] args) {
    xMethod(1234567);
  }

  public static void xMethod(int n) {
    if (n > 0) {
      System.out.print(n % 10);
      xMethod(n / 10);
    }
  }
}
```

18.4 Write a recursive mathematical definition for computing 2^n for a positive integer n.

18.5 Write a recursive mathematical definition for computing x^n for a positive integer n and a real number x.

18.6 Write a recursive mathematical definition for computing $1 + 2 + 3 + \ldots + n$ for a positive integer n.

18.3 Case Study: Computing Fibonacci Numbers

In some cases, recursion enables you to create an intuitive, straightforward, simple solution to a problem.

The `factorial` method in the preceding section could easily be rewritten without using recursion. In this section, we show an example for creating an intuitive solution to a problem using recursion. Consider the well-known Fibonacci-series problem:

The series: 0 1 1 2 3 5 8 13 21 34 55 89 ...
indexes: 0 1 2 3 4 5 6 7 8 9 10 11

The Fibonacci series begins with 0 and 1, and each subsequent number is the sum of the preceding two. The series can be recursively defined as:

```
fib(0) = 0;
fib(1) = 1;
fib(index) = fib(index - 2) + fib(index - 1); index >= 2
```

The Fibonacci series was named for Leonardo Fibonacci, a medieval mathematician, who originated it to model the growth of the rabbit population. It can be applied in numeric optimization and in various other areas.

How do you find `fib(index)` for a given `index`? It is easy to find `fib(2)`, because you know `fib(0)` and `fib(1)`. Assuming that you know `fib(index - 2)` and `fib(index - 1)`, you can obtain `fib(index)` immediately. Thus, the problem of computing `fib(index)` is reduced to computing `fib(index - 2)` and `fib(index - 1)`. When doing so, you apply the idea recursively until `index` is reduced to 0 or 1.

The base case is `index = 0` or `index = 1`. If you call the method with `index = 0` or `index = 1`, it immediately returns the result. If you call the method with `index >= 2`, it divides the problem into two subproblems for computing `fib(index - 1)` and `fib(index - 2)` using recursive calls. The recursive algorithm for computing `fib(index)` can be simply described as follows:

```
if (index == 0)
  return 0;
else if (index == 1)
  return 1;
else
  return fib(index - 1) + fib(index - 2);
```

Listing 18.2 gives a complete program that prompts the user to enter an index and computes the Fibonacci number for that index.

LISTING 18.2 ComputeFibonacci.java

```
1  import java.util.Scanner;
2
3  public class ComputeFibonacci {
4    /** Main method */
5    public static void main(String[] args) {
6      // Create a Scanner
7      Scanner input = new Scanner(System.in);
8      System.out.print("Enter an index for a Fibonacci number: ");
9      int index = input.nextInt();
10
11     // Find and display the Fibonacci number
12     System.out.println("The Fibonacci number at index "
13       + index + " is " + fib(index));
14   }
15
16   /** The method for finding the Fibonacci number */
17   public static long fib(long index) {
18     if (index == 0) // Base case
19       return 0;
```

base case

```
20       else if (index == 1) // Base case                    base case
21           return 1;
22       else   // Reduction and recursive calls
23           return fib(index - 1) + fib(index - 2);          recursion
24   }
25 }
```

```
Enter an index for a Fibonacci number: 1 ↵Enter
The Fibonacci number at index 1 is 1
```

```
Enter an index for a Fibonacci number: 6 ↵Enter
The Fibonacci number at index 6 is 8
```

```
Enter an index for a Fibonacci number: 7 ↵Enter
The Fibonacci number at index 7 is 13
```

The program does not show the considerable amount of work done behind the scenes by the computer. Figure 18.4, however, shows the successive recursive calls for evaluating `fib(4)`. The original method, `fib(4)`, makes two recursive calls, `fib(3)` and `fib(2)`, and then returns `fib(3) + fib(2)`. But in what order are these methods called? In Java, operands are evaluated from left to right, so `fib(2)` is called after `fib(3)` is completely evaluated. The labels in Figure 18.4 show the order in which the methods are called.

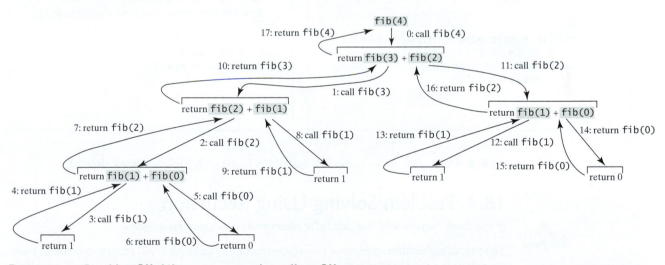

FIGURE 18.4 Invoking `fib(4)` spawns recursive calls to `fib`.

As shown in Figure 18.4, there are many duplicated recursive calls. For instance, `fib(2)` is called twice, `fib(1)` three times, and `fib(0)` twice. In general, computing `fib(index)` requires roughly twice as many recursive calls as does computing `fib(index - 1)`. As you try larger index values, the number of calls substantially increases, as shown in Table 18.1.

TABLE 18.1   Number of Recursive Calls in `fib(index)`

index	2	3	4	10	20	30	40	50
# of calls	3	5	9	177	21891	2,692,537	331,160,281	2,075,316,483

Pedagogical Note

The recursive implementation of the `fib` method is very simple and straightforward, but it isn't efficient, since it requires more time and memory to run recursive methods. See Programming Exercise 18.2 for an efficient solution using loops. Though it is not practical, the recursive `fib` method is a good example of how to write recursive methods.

18.7 Show the output of the following two programs:

```java
public class Test {
  public static void main(String[] args) {
    xMethod(5);
  }

  public static void xMethod(int n) {
    if (n > 0) {
      System.out.print(n + " ");
      xMethod(n - 1);
    }
  }
}
```

```java
public class Test {
  public static void main(String[] args) {
    xMethod(5);
  }

  public static void xMethod(int n) {
    if (n > 0) {
      xMethod(n - 1);
      System.out.print(n + " ");
    }
  }
}
```

18.8 What is wrong in the following method?

```java
public class Test {
  public static void main(String[] args) {
    xMethod(1234567);
  }

  public static void xMethod(double n) {
    if (n != 0) {
      System.out.print(n);
      xMethod(n / 10);
    }
  }
}
```

```java
public class Test {
  public static void main(String[] args) {
    Test test = new Test();
    System.out.println(test.toString());
  }

  public Test() {
    Test test = new Test();
  }
}
```

18.9 How many times is the `fib` method in Listing 18.2 invoked for `fib(6)`?

18.4 Problem Solving Using Recursion

If you think recursively, you can solve many problems using recursion.

The preceding sections presented two classic recursion examples. All recursive methods have

recursion characteristics   the following characteristics:

if-else

- The method is implemented using an `if-else` or a `switch` statement that leads to different cases.

base cases

- One or more base cases (the simplest case) are used to stop recursion.

reduction

- Every recursive call reduces the original problem, bringing it increasingly closer to a base case until it becomes that case.

In general, to solve a problem using recursion, you break it into subproblems. Each subproblem is the same as the original problem but smaller in size. You can apply the same approach to each subproblem to solve it recursively.

Recursion is everywhere. It is fun to *think recursively*. Consider drinking coffee. You may describe the procedure recursively as follows:

think recursively

```java
public static void drinkCoffee(Cup cup) {
  if (!cup.isEmpty()) {
    cup.takeOneSip(); // Take one sip
    drinkCoffee(cup);
  }
}
```

Assume **cup** is an object for a cup of coffee with the instance methods **isEmpty()** and **takeOneSip()**. You can break the problem into two subproblems: one is to drink one sip of coffee and the other is to drink the rest of the coffee in the cup. The second problem is the same as the original problem but smaller in size. The base case for the problem is when the cup is empty.

Consider the problem of printing a message **n** times. You can break the problem into two subproblems: one is to print the message one time and the other is to print it **n - 1** times. The second problem is the same as the original problem but it is smaller in size. The base case for the problem is **n == 0**. You can solve this problem using recursion as follows:

```java
public static void nPrintln(String message, int times) {
  if (times >= 1) {
    System.out.println(message);
    nPrintln(message, times - 1);
  } // The base case is times == 0
}
```

recursive call

Note that the **fib** method in the preceding section returns a value to its caller, but the **drinkCoffee** and **nPrintln** methods are **void** and they do not return a value.

If you *think recursively*, you can use recursion to solve many of the problems presented in earlier chapters of this book. Consider the palindrome problem in Listing 5.14. Recall that a string is a palindrome if it reads the same from the left and from the right. For example, "mom" and "dad" are palindromes, but "uncle" and "aunt" are not. The problem of checking whether a string is a palindrome can be divided into two subproblems:

think recursively

■ Check whether the first character and the last character of the string are equal.

■ Ignore the two end characters and check whether the rest of the substring is a palindrome.

The second subproblem is the same as the original problem but smaller in size. There are two base cases: (1) the two end characters are not the same, and (2) the string size is **0** or **1**. In case 1, the string is not a palindrome; in case 2, the string is a palindrome. The recursive method for this problem can be implemented as shown in Listing 18.3.

LISTING 18.3 RecursivePalindromeUsingSubstring.java

```java
 1  public class RecursivePalindromeUsingSubstring {
 2    public static boolean isPalindrome(String s) {
 3      if (s.length() <= 1) // Base case
 4        return true;
 5      else if (s.charAt(0) != s.charAt(s.length() - 1)) // Base case
 6        return false;
 7      else
 8        return isPalindrome(s.substring(1, s.length() - 1));
 9    }
10
11    public static void main(String[] args) {
12      System.out.println("Is moon a palindrome? "
```

method header
base case

base case

recursive call

```
13              + isPalindrome("moon"));
14          System.out.println("Is noon a palindrome? "
15              + isPalindrome("noon"));
16          System.out.println("Is a a palindrome? " + isPalindrome("a"));
17          System.out.println("Is aba a palindrome? " +
18            isPalindrome("aba"));
19          System.out.println("Is ab a palindrome? " + isPalindrome("ab"));
20      }
21  }
```

```
Is moon a palindrome? false
Is noon a palindrome? true
Is a a palindrome? true
Is aba a palindrome? true
Is ab a palindrome? false
```

The `substring` method in line 8 creates a new string that is the same as the original string except without the first and last characters. Checking whether a string is a palindrome is equivalent to checking whether the substring is a palindrome if the two end characters in the original string are the same.

18.10 Describe the characteristics of recursive methods.

18.11 For the `isPalindrome` method in Listing 18.3, what are the base cases? How many times is this method called when invoking `isPalindrome("abdxcxdba")`?

18.12 Show the call stack for `isPalindrome("abcba")` using the method defined in Listing 18.3.

18.5 Recursive Helper Methods

Sometimes you can find a solution to the original problem by defining a recursive function to a problem similar to the original problem. This new method is called a recursive helper method. The original problem can be solved by invoking the recursive helper method.

The recursive `isPalindrome` method in Listing 18.3 is not efficient, because it creates a new string for every recursive call. To avoid creating new strings, you can use the low and high indices to indicate the range of the substring. These two indices must be passed to the recursive method. Since the original method is `isPalindrome(String s)`, you have to create the new method `isPalindrome(String s, int low, int high)` to accept additional information on the string, as shown in Listing 18.4.

LISTING 18.4 RecursivePalindrome.java

```
1   public class RecursivePalindrome {
2     public static boolean isPalindrome(String s) {
3       return isPalindrome(s, 0, s.length() - 1);
4     }
5
6     private static boolean isPalindrome(String s, int low, int high) {
7       if (high <= low) // Base case
8         return true;
9       else if (s.charAt(low) != s.charAt(high)) // Base case
10        return false;
11      else
12        return isPalindrome(s, low + 1, high - 1);
13    }
```

helper method
base case

base case

```
14
15    public static void main(String[] args) {
16      System.out.println("Is moon a palindrome? "
17        + isPalindrome("moon"));
18      System.out.println("Is noon a palindrome? "
19        + isPalindrome("noon"));
20      System.out.println("Is a a palindrome? " + isPalindrome("a"));
21      System.out.println("Is aba a palindrome? " + isPalindrome("aba"));
22      System.out.println("Is ab a palindrome? " + isPalindrome("ab"));
23    }
24  }
```

Two overloaded **isPalindrome** methods are defined. The first, **isPalindrome(String s)**, checks whether a string is a palindrome, and the second, **isPalindrome(String s, int low, int high)**, checks whether a substring **s(low..high)** is a palindrome. The first method passes the string **s** with **low = 0** and **high = s.length() - 1** to the second method. The second method can be invoked recursively to check a palindrome in an ever-shrinking substring. It is a common design technique in recursive programming to define a second method that receives additional parameters. Such a method is known as a *recursive helper method*.

recursive helper method

Helper methods are very useful in designing recursive solutions for problems involving strings and arrays. The sections that follow give two more examples.

18.5.1 Recursive Selection Sort

Selection sort was introduced in Section 7.11. Recall that it finds the smallest element in the list and swaps it with the first element. It then finds the smallest element remaining and swaps it with the first element in the remaining list, and so on until the remaining list contains only a single element. The problem can be divided into two subproblems:

- Find the smallest element in the list and swap it with the first element.

- Ignore the first element and sort the remaining smaller list recursively.

The base case is that the list contains only one element. Listing 18.5 gives the recursive sort method.

LISTING 18.5 RecursiveSelectionSort.java

```
1  public class RecursiveSelectionSort {
2    public static void sort(double[] list) {
3      sort(list, 0, list.length - 1); // Sort the entire list
4    }
5
6    private static void sort(double[] list, int low, int high) {
7      if (low < high) {
8        // Find the smallest number and its index in list[low .. high]
9        int indexOfMin = low;
10       double min = list[low];
11       for (int i = low + 1; i <= high; i++) {
12         if (list[i] < min) {
13           min = list[i];
14           indexOfMin = i;
15         }
16       }
17
18       // Swap the smallest in list[low .. high] with list[low]
19       list[indexOfMin] = list[low];
20       list[low] = min;
21
```

helper method
base case

recursive call

```
22        // Sort the remaining list[low+1 .. high]
23        sort(list, low + 1, high);
24      }
25    }
26  }
```

Two overloaded **sort** methods are defined. The first method, **sort(double[] list)**, sorts an array in **list[0..list.length - 1]** and the second method, **sort(double[] list, int low, int high)**, sorts an array in **list[low..high]**. The second method can be invoked recursively to sort an ever-shrinking subarray.

VideoNote

Binary search

18.5.2 Recursive Binary Search

Binary search was introduced in Section 7.10.2. For binary search to work, the elements in the array must be in increasing order. The binary search first compares the key with the element in the middle of the array. Consider the following three cases:

- Case 1: If the key is less than the middle element, recursively search for the key in the first half of the array.

- Case 2: If the key is equal to the middle element, the search ends with a match.

- Case 3: If the key is greater than the middle element, recursively search for the key in the second half of the array.

Case 1 and Case 3 reduce the search to a smaller list. Case 2 is a base case when there is a match. Another base case is that the search is exhausted without a match. Listing 18.6 gives a clear, simple solution for the binary search problem using recursion.

LISTING 18.6 Recursive Binary Search Method

```
1  public class RecursiveBinarySearch {
2    public static int recursiveBinarySearch(int[] list, int key) {
3      int low = 0;
4      int high = list.length - 1;
5      return recursiveBinarySearch(list, key, low, high);
6    }
7
8    private static int recursiveBinarySearch(int[] list, int key,
9        int low, int high) {
10     if (low > high) // The list has been exhausted without a match
11       return -low - 1;
12
13     int mid = (low + high) / 2;
14     if (key < list[mid])
15       return recursiveBinarySearch(list, key, low, mid - 1);
16     else if (key == list[mid])
17       return mid;
18     else
19       return recursiveBinarySearch(list, key, mid + 1, high);
20   }
21 }
```

helper method

base case

recursive call

base case

recursive call

The first method finds a key in the whole list. The second method finds a key in the list with index from **low** to **high**.

The first **binarySearch** method passes the initial array with **low = 0** and **high = list.length - 1** to the second **binarySearch** method. The second method is invoked recursively to find the key in an ever-shrinking subarray.

18.13 Show the call stack for `isPalindrome("abcba")` using the method defined in Listing 18.4.

18.14 Show the call stack for `selectionSort(new double[]{2, 3, 5, 1})` using the method defined in Listing 18.5.

18.15 What is a recursive helper method?

Check Point

18.6 Case Study: Finding the Directory Size

Recursive methods are efficient for solving problems with recursive structures.

The preceding examples can easily be solved without using recursion. This section presents a problem that is difficult to solve without using recursion. The problem is to find the size of a directory. The size of a directory is the sum of the sizes of all files in the directory. A directory d may contain subdirectories. Suppose a directory contains files $f_1, f_2, \ldots, f_m$ and subdirectories $d_1, d_2, \ldots, d_n$, as shown in Figure 18.5.

Key Point

VideoNote

Directory size

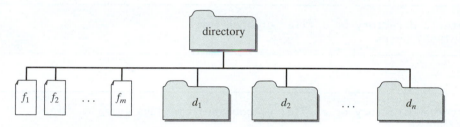

FIGURE 18.5 A directory contains files and subdirectories.

The size of the directory can be defined recursively as follows:

$$size(d) = size(f_1) + size(f_2) + \ldots + size(f_m) + size(d_1) + size(d_2) + \ldots + size(d_n)$$

The **File** class, introduced in Section 12.10, can be used to represent a file or a directory and obtain the properties for files and directories. Two methods in the **File** class are useful for this problem:

- The **length()** method returns the size of a file.

- The **listFiles()** method returns an array of **File** objects under a directory.

Listing 18.7 gives a program that prompts the user to enter a directory or a file and displays its size.

LISTING 18.7 DirectorySize.java

```java
1  import java.io.File;
2  import java.util.Scanner;
3
4  public class DirectorySize {
5    public static void main(String[] args) {
6      // Prompt the user to enter a directory or a file
7      System.out.print("Enter a directory or a file: ");
8      Scanner input = new Scanner(System.in);
9      String directory = input.nextLine();
10
11     // Display the size
12     System.out.println(getSize(new File(directory)) + " bytes");
13   }
```

invoke method

getSize method

is directory?

all subitems

recursive call

base case

```
14
15   public static long getSize(File file) {
16     long size = 0; // Store the total size of all files
17
18     if (file.isDirectory()) {
19       File[] files = file.listFiles(); // All files and subdirectories
20       for (int i = 0; files != null && i < files.length; i++) {
21         size += getSize(files[i]); // Recursive call
22       }
23     }
24     else { // Base case
25       size += file.length();
26     }
27
28     return size;
29   }
30 }
```

```
Enter a directory or a file: c:\book  ↵Enter
48619631 bytes
```

```
Enter a directory or a file: c:\book\Welcome.java  ↵Enter
172 bytes
```

```
Enter a directory or a file: c:\book\NonExistentFile  ↵Enter
0 bytes
```

If the **file** object represents a directory (line 18), each subitem (file or subdirectory) in the directory is recursively invoked to obtain its size (line 21). If the **file** object represents a file (line 24), the file size is obtained and added to the total size (line 25).

What happens if an incorrect or a nonexistent directory is entered? The program will detect that it is not a directory and invoke **file.length()** (line 25), which returns **0**. Thus, in this case, the **getSize** method will return **0**.

testing all cases

Tip
To avoid mistakes, it is a good practice to test all cases. For example, you should test the program for an input of file, an empty directory, a nonexistent directory, and a nonexistent file.

18.16 What is the base case for the **getSize** method?

18.17 How does the program get all files and directories under a given directory?

18.18 How many times will the **getSize** method be invoked for a directory if the directory has three subdirectories and each subdirectory has four files?

18.19 Will the program work if the directory is empty (i.e., it does not contain any files)?

18.20 Will the program work if line 20 is replaced by the following code?

```
for (int i = 0; i < files.length; i++)
```

18.21 Will the program work if lines 20–21 is replaced by the following code?

```
for (File file: files)
  size += getSize(file); // Recursive call
```

18.7 Case Study: Tower of Hanoi

The Tower of Hanoi problem is a classic problem that can be solved easily using recursion, but it is difficult to solve otherwise.

Key Point

The problem involves moving a specified number of disks of distinct sizes from one tower to another while observing the following rules:

- There are *n* disks labeled 1, 2, 3, . . . , *n* and three towers labeled A, B, and C.

- No disk can be on top of a smaller disk at any time.

- All the disks are initially placed on tower A.

- Only one disk can be moved at a time, and it must be the smallest disk on a tower.

The objective of the problem is to move all the disks from A to B with the assistance of C. For example, if you have three disks, the steps to move all of the disks from A to B are shown in Figure 18.6.

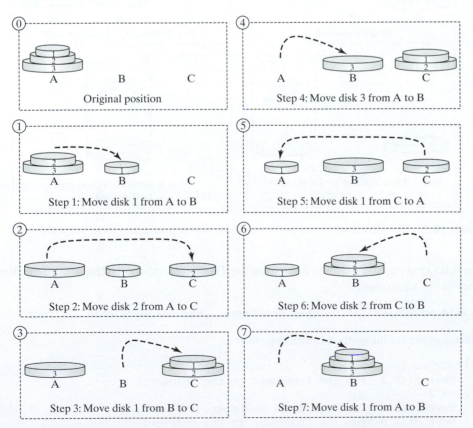

FIGURE 18.6 The goal of the Tower of Hanoi problem is to move disks from tower A to tower B without breaking the rules.

> **Note**
> The Tower of Hanoi is a classic computer-science problem, to which many websites are devoted. One of them worth looking at is www.cut-the-knot.com/recurrence/hanoi.shtml.

In the case of three disks, you can find the solution manually. For a larger number of disks, however—even for four—the problem is quite complex. Fortunately, the problem has an inherently recursive nature, which leads to a straightforward recursive solution.

The base case for the problem is **n = 1**. If **n == 1**, you could simply move the disk from A to B. When **n > 1**, you could split the original problem into the following three subproblems and solve them sequentially.

1. Move the first **n - 1** disks from A to C recursively with the assistance of tower B, as shown in Step 1 in Figure 18.7.

2. Move disk **n** from A to B, as shown in Step 2 in Figure 18.7.

3. Move **n - 1** disks from C to B recursively with the assistance of tower A, as shown in Step 3 in Figure 18.7.

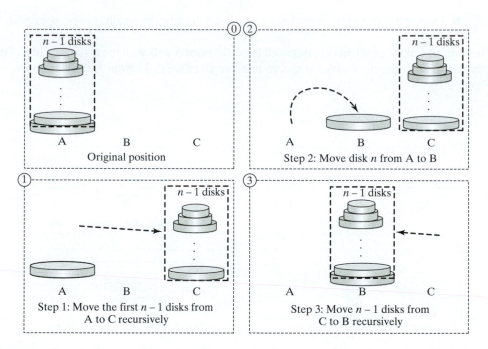

FIGURE 18.7 The Tower of Hanoi problem can be decomposed into three subproblems.

The following method moves *n* disks from the **fromTower** to the **toTower** with the assistance of the **auxTower**:

```
void moveDisks(int n, char fromTower, char toTower, char auxTower)
```

The algorithm for the method can be described as:

```
if (n == 1) // Stopping condition
  Move disk 1 from the fromTower to the toTower;
else {
  moveDisks(n - 1, fromTower, auxTower, toTower);
  Move disk n from the fromTower to the toTower;
  moveDisks(n - 1, auxTower, toTower, fromTower);
}
```

Listing 18.8 gives a program that prompts the user to enter the number of disks and invokes the recursive method **moveDisks** to display the solution for moving the disks.

LISTING 18.8 TowerOfHanoi.java

```java
1  import java.util.Scanner;
2
3  public class TowerOfHanoi {
4    /** Main method */
5    public static void main(String[] args) {
6      // Create a Scanner
7      Scanner input = new Scanner(System.in);
8      System.out.print("Enter number of disks: ");
9      int n = input.nextInt();
10
11     // Find the solution recursively
12     System.out.println("The moves are:");
13     moveDisks(n, 'A', 'B', 'C');
14   }
15
16   /** The method for finding the solution to move n disks
17       from fromTower to toTower with auxTower */
18   public static void moveDisks(int n, char fromTower,
19       char toTower, char auxTower) {
20     if (n == 1) // Stopping condition                          base case
21       System.out.println("Move disk " + n + " from " +
22         fromTower + " to " + toTower);
23     else {
24       moveDisks(n - 1, fromTower, auxTower, toTower);          recursion
25       System.out.println("Move disk " + n + " from " +
26         fromTower + " to " + toTower);
27       moveDisks(n - 1, auxTower, toTower, fromTower);          recursion
28     }
29   }
30 }
```

```
Enter number of disks: 4 ⏎Enter
The moves are:
Move disk 1 from A to C
Move disk 2 from A to B
Move disk 1 from C to B
Move disk 3 from A to C
Move disk 1 from B to A
Move disk 2 from B to C
Move disk 1 from A to C
Move disk 4 from A to B
Move disk 1 from C to B
Move disk 2 from C to A
Move disk 1 from B to A
Move disk 3 from C to B
Move disk 1 from A to C
Move disk 2 from A to B
Move disk 1 from C to B
```

This problem is inherently recursive. Using recursion makes it possible to find a natural, simple solution. It would be difficult to solve the problem without using recursion.

Consider tracing the program for **n** = **3**. The successive recursive calls are shown in Figure 18.8. As you can see, writing the program is easier than tracing the recursive calls. The system uses stacks to manage the calls behind the scenes. To some extent, recursion provides a level of abstraction that hides iterations and other details from the user.

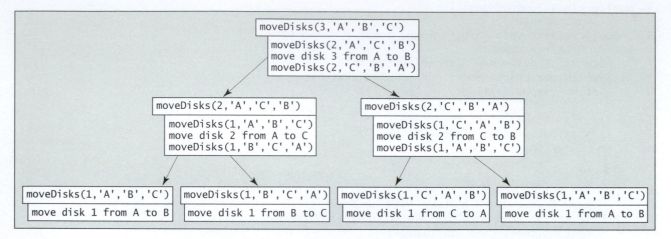

FIGURE 18.8 Invoking **moveDisks(3, 'A', 'B', 'C')** spawns calls to **moveDisks** recursively.

Check
Point

18.22 How many times is the **moveDisks** method in Listing 18.8 invoked for **moveDisks(5, 'A', 'B', 'C')**?

18.8 Case Study: Fractals

Key
Point

Using recursion is ideal for displaying fractals, because fractals are inherently recursive.

VideoNote

Fractal (Sierpinski triangle)

A *fractal* is a geometrical figure, but unlike triangles, circles, and rectangles, fractals can be divided into parts, each of which is a reduced-size copy of the whole. There are many interesting examples of fractals. This section introduces a simple fractal, the *Sierpinski triangle*, named after a famous Polish mathematician.

A Sierpinski triangle is created as follows:

1. Begin with an equilateral triangle, which is considered to be a Sierpinski fractal of order (or level) **0**, as shown in Figure 18.9a.

2. Connect the midpoints of the sides of the triangle of order **0** to create a Sierpinski triangle of order **1** (Figure 18.9b).

3. Leave the center triangle intact. Connect the midpoints of the sides of the three other triangles to create a Sierpinski triangle of order **2** (Figure 18.9c).

4. You can repeat the same process recursively to create a Sierpinski triangle of order **3**, **4**, . . . , and so on (Figure 18.9d).

The problem is inherently recursive. How do you develop a recursive solution for it? Consider the base case when the order is **0**. It is easy to draw a Sierpinski triangle of order **0**. How do you draw a Sierpinski triangle of order **1**? The problem can be reduced to drawing three Sierpinski triangles of order **0**. How do you draw a Sierpinski triangle of order **2**? The problem can be reduced to drawing three Sierpinski triangles of order **1**, so the problem of

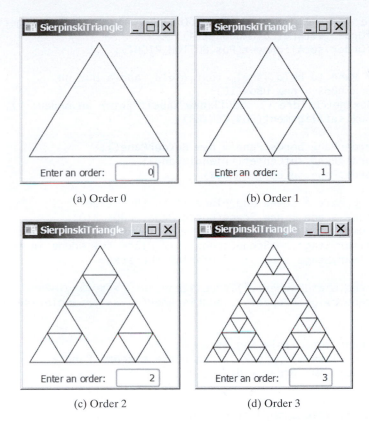

(a) Order 0   (b) Order 1

(c) Order 2   (d) Order 3

FIGURE 18.9 A Sierpinski triangle is a pattern of recursive triangles.

drawing a Sierpinski triangle of order n can be reduced to drawing three Sierpinski triangles of order $n - 1$.

Listing 18.9 gives a program that displays a Sierpinski triangle of any order, as shown in Figure 18.9. You can enter an order in a text field to display a Sierpinski triangle of the specified order.

LISTING 18.9 SierpinskiTriangle.java

```
1  import javafx.application.Application;
2  import javafx.geometry.Point2D;
3  import javafx.geometry.Pos;
4  import javafx.scene.Scene;
5  import javafx.scene.control.Label;
6  import javafx.scene.control.TextField;
7  import javafx.scene.layout.BorderPane;
8  import javafx.scene.layout.HBox;
9  import javafx.scene.layout.Pane;
10 import javafx.scene.paint.Color;
11 import javafx.scene.shape.Polygon;
12 import javafx.stage.Stage;
13
14 public class SierpinskiTriangle extends Application {
15   @Override // Override the start method in the Application class
16   public void start(Stage primaryStage) {
17     SierpinskiTrianglePane trianglePane = new SierpinskiTrianglePane();
18     TextField tfOrder = new TextField();
19     tfOrder.setOnAction(
```

recursive triangle pane

listener for text field

```
20          e -> trianglePane.setOrder(Integer.parseInt(tfOrder.getText()))));
21        tfOrder.setPrefColumnCount(4);
22        tfOrder.setAlignment(Pos.BOTTOM_RIGHT);
23
24        // Pane to hold label, text field, and a button
```

hold label and text field

```
25        HBox hBox = new HBox(10);
26        hBox.getChildren().addAll(new Label("Enter an order: "), tfOrder);
27        hBox.setAlignment(Pos.CENTER);
28
29        BorderPane borderPane = new BorderPane();
30        borderPane.setCenter(trianglePane);
31        borderPane.setBottom(hBox);
32
33        // Create a scene and place it in the stage
34        Scene scene = new Scene(borderPane, 200, 210);
35        primaryStage.setTitle("SierpinskiTriangle"); // Set the stage title
36        primaryStage.setScene(scene); // Place the scene in the stage
37        primaryStage.show(); // Display the stage
38
```

listener for resizing

```
39        scene.widthProperty().addListener(ov -> trianglePane.paint());
40        scene.heightProperty().addListener(ov -> trianglePane.paint());
41      }
42
43      /** Pane for displaying triangles */
44      static class SierpinskiTrianglePane extends Pane {
45        private int order = 0;
46
47        /** Set a new order */
48        public void setOrder(int order) {
49          this.order = order;
50          paint();
51        }
52
53        SierpinskiTrianglePane() {
54        }
55
56        protected void paint() {
57          // Select three points in proportion to the pane size
```

three initial points

```
58          Point2D p1 = new Point2D(getWidth() / 2, 10);
59          Point2D p2 = new Point2D(10, getHeight() - 10);
60          Point2D p3 = new Point2D(getWidth() - 10, getHeight() - 10);
61
```

clear the pane

```
62          this.getChildren().clear(); // Clear the pane before redisplay
63
```

draw a triangle

```
64          displayTriangles(order, p1, p2, p3);
65        }
66
67        private void displayTriangles(int order, Point2D p1,
68            Point2D p2, Point2D p3) {
69          if (order == 0) {
70            // Draw a triangle to connect three points
```

create a triangle

```
71            Polygon triangle = new Polygon();
72            triangle.getPoints().addAll(p1.getX(), p1.getY(), p2.getX(),
73                p2.getY(), p3.getX(), p3.getY());
74            triangle.setStroke(Color.BLACK);
75            triangle.setFill(Color.WHITE);
76
77            this.getChildren().add(triangle);
78          }
79          else {
```

```
80              // Get the midpoint on each edge in the triangle
81              Point2D p12 = p1.midpoint(p2);
82              Point2D p23 = p2.midpoint(p3);
83              Point2D p31 = p3.midpoint(p1);
84
85              // Recursively display three triangles
86              displayTriangles(order - 1, p1, p12, p31);
87              displayTriangles(order - 1, p12, p2, p23);
88              displayTriangles(order - 1, p31, p23, p3);
89          }
90        }
91      }
92    }
```

top subtriangle
left subtriangle
right subtriangle

The initial triangle has three points set in proportion to the pane size (lines 58–60). If **order == 0**, the **displayTriangles(order, p1, p2, p3)** method displays a triangle that connects the three points **p1**, **p2**, and **p3** in lines 71–77, as shown in Figure 18.10a. Otherwise, it performs the following tasks:

displayTriangle method

1. Obtain the midpoint between **p1** and **p2** (line 81), the midpoint between **p2** and **p3** (line 82), and the midpoint between **p3** and **p1** (line 83), as shown in Figure 18.10b.

2. Recursively invoke **displayTriangles** with a reduced order to display three smaller Sierpinski triangles (lines 86–88). Note that each small Sierpinski triangle is structurally identical to the original big Sierpinski triangle except that the order of a small triangle is one less, as shown in Figure 18.10b.

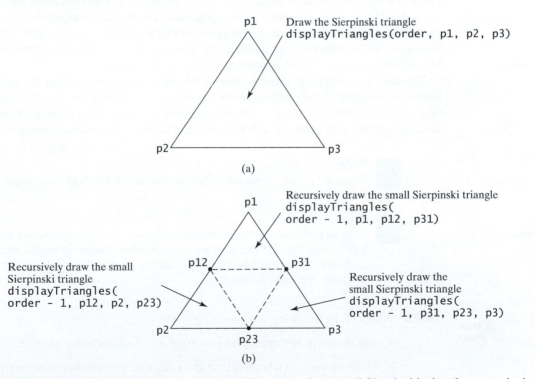

FIGURE 18.10 Drawing a Sierpinski triangle spawns calls to draw three small Sierpinski triangles recursively.

A Sierpinski triangle is displayed in a **SierpinskiTrianglePane**. The **order** property in the inner class **SierpinskiTrianglePane** specifies the order for the Sierpinski triangle. The **Point2D** class, introduced in Section 9.8, The **Point2D** Class, represents a point with *x*- and *y*-coordinates. Invoking **p1.midpoint(p2)** returns a new **Point2D** object that is the midpoint between **p1** and **p2** (lines 81–83).

Check Point

18.23 How do you obtain the midpoint between two points?

18.24 What is the base case for the **displayTriangles** method?

18.25 How many times is the **displayTriangles** method invoked for a Sierpinski triangle of order 0, order 1, order 2, and order n?

18.26 What happens if you enter a negative order? How do you fix this problem in the code?

18.27 Instead of drawing a triangle using a polygon, rewrite the code to draw a triangle by drawing three lines to connect the points in lines 71–77.

18.9 Recursion vs. Iteration

Key Point

Recursion is an alternative form of program control. It is essentially repetition without a loop.

When you use loops, you specify a loop body. The repetition of the loop body is controlled by the loop control structure. In recursion, the method itself is called repeatedly. A selection statement must be used to control whether to call the method recursively or not.

recursion overhead

Recursion bears substantial overhead. Each time the program calls a method, the system must allocate memory for all of the method's local variables and parameters. This can consume considerable memory and requires extra time to manage the memory.

recursion advantages

Any problem that can be solved recursively can be solved nonrecursively with iterations. Recursion has some negative aspects: it uses up too much time and too much memory. Why, then, should you use it? In some cases, using recursion enables you to specify a clear, simple solution for an inherently recursive problem that would otherwise be difficult to obtain. Examples are the directory-size problem, the Tower of Hanoi problem, and the fractal problem, which are rather difficult to solve without using recursion.

recursion or iteration?

The decision whether to use recursion or iteration should be based on the nature of, and your understanding of, the problem you are trying to solve. The rule of thumb is to use whichever approach can best develop an intuitive solution that naturally mirrors the problem. If an iterative solution is obvious, use it. It will generally be more efficient than the recursive option.

StackOverflowError

Note

Recursive programs can run out of memory, causing a **StackOverflowError**.

performance concern

Tip

If you are concerned about your program's performance, avoid using recursion, because it takes more time and consumes more memory than iteration. In general, recursion can be used to solve the inherent recursive problems such as Tower of Hanoi, recursive directories, and Sierpinski triangles.

Check Point

18.28 Which of the following statements are true?

a. Any recursive method can be converted into a nonrecursive method.

b. Recursive methods take more time and memory to execute than nonrecursive methods.

c. Recursive methods are *always* simpler than nonrecursive methods.

d. There is always a selection statement in a recursive method to check whether a base case is reached.

18.29 What is a cause for a stack-overflow exception?

18.10 Tail Recursion

A tail recursive method is efficient for reducing stack size.

Key Point

A recursive method is said to be *tail recursive* if there are no pending operations to be performed on return from a recursive call, as illustrated in Figure 18.11a. However, method **B** in Figure 18.11b is not tail recursive because there are pending operations after a method call is returned.

tail recursion

```
Recursive method A
    . . .
    . . .

    . . .
    Invoke method A recursively
```

```
Recursive method B
    . . .
    . . .
    Invoke method B recursively
    . . .
    . . .
```

       (a) Tail recursion   (b) Nontail recursion

FIGURE 18.11   A tail-recursive method has no pending operations after a recursive call.

For example, the recursive **isPalindrome** method (lines 6–13) in Listing 18.4 is tail recursive because there are no pending operations after recursively invoking **isPalindrome** in line 12. However, the recursive **factorial** method (lines 16–21) in Listing 18.1 is not tail recursive, because there is a pending operation, namely multiplication, to be performed on return from each recursive call.

Tail recursion is desirable: because the method ends when the last recursive call ends, there is no need to store the intermediate calls in the stack. Compilers can optimize tail recursion to reduce stack size.

A nontail-recursive method can often be converted to a tail-recursive method by using auxiliary parameters. These parameters are used to contain the result. The idea is to incorporate the pending operations into the auxiliary parameters in such a way that the recursive call no longer has a pending operation. You can define a new auxiliary recursive method with the auxiliary parameters. This method may overload the original method with the same name but a different signature. For example, the **factorial** method in Listing 18.1 is written in a tail-recursive way in Listing 18.10.

LISTING 18.10 ComputeFactorialTailRecursion.java

```java
 1  public class ComputeFactorialTailRecursion {
 2    /** Return the factorial for a specified number */
 3    public static long factorial(int n) {
 4      return factorial(n, 1); // Call auxiliary method
 5    }
 6
 7    /** Auxiliary tail-recursive method for factorial */
 8    private static long factorial(int n, int result) {
 9      if (n == 0)
10        return result;
11      else
12        return factorial(n - 1, n * result); // Recursive call
13    }
14  }
```

original method
invoke auxiliary method

auxiliary method

recursive call

The first **factorial** method (line 3) simply invokes the second auxiliary method (line 4). The second method contains an auxiliary parameter **result** that stores the result for the factorial of **n**. This method is invoked recursively in line 12. There is no pending operation after a call is returned. The final result is returned in line 10, which is also the return value from invoking `factorial(n, 1)` in line 4.

18.30 Identify tail-recursive methods in this chapter.

18.31 Rewrite the `fib` method in Listing 18.2 using tail recursion.

KEY TERMS

base case   706
direct recursion   709
indirect recursion   709
infinite recursion   709

recursive helper method   715
recursive method   706
stopping condition   706
tail recursion   727

CHAPTER SUMMARY

1. A *recursive method* is one that directly or indirectly invokes itself. For a recursive method to terminate, there must be one or more *base cases*.

2. *Recursion* is an alternative form of program control. It is essentially repetition without a loop control. It can be used to write simple, clear solutions for inherently recursive problems that would otherwise be difficult to solve.

3. Sometimes the original method needs to be modified to receive additional parameters in order to be invoked recursively. A *recursive helper method* can be defined for this purpose.

4. Recursion bears substantial overhead. Each time the program calls a method, the system must allocate memory for all of the method's local variables and parameters. This can consume considerable memory and requires extra time to manage the memory.

5. A recursive method is said to be *tail recursive* if there are no pending operations to be performed on return from a recursive call. Some compilers can optimize tail recursion to reduce stack size.

QUIZ

Answer the quiz for this chapter online at www.cs.armstrong.edu/liang/intro10e/quiz.html.

MyProgrammingLab™ ## PROGRAMMING EXERCISES

Sections 18.2–18.3

*18.1 (*Factorial*) Using the `BigInteger` class introduced in Section 10.9, you can find the factorial for a large number (e.g., `100!`). Implement the `factorial` method using recursion. Write a program that prompts the user to enter an integer and displays its factorial.

*18.2 (*Fibonacci numbers*) Rewrite the `fib` method in Listing 18.2 using iterations.

Hint: To compute `fib(n)` without recursion, you need to obtain `fib(n - 2)` and `fib(n - 1)` first. Let `f0` and `f1` denote the two previous Fibonacci numbers. The current Fibonacci number would then be `f0` + `f1`. The algorithm can be described as follows:

```
f0 = 0; // For fib(0)
f1 = 1; // For fib(1)

for (int i = 1; i <= n; i++) {
  currentFib = f0 + f1;
  f0 = f1;
  f1 = currentFib;
}
// After the loop, currentFib is fib(n)
```

Write a test program that prompts the user to enter an index and displays its Fibonacci number.

*18.3 (*Compute greatest common divisor using recursion*) The `gcd(m, n)` can also be defined recursively as follows:

- If `m % n` is `0`, `gcd(m, n)` is `n`.
- Otherwise, `gcd(m, n)` is `gcd(n, m % n)`.

Write a recursive method to find the GCD. Write a test program that prompts the user to enter two integers and displays their GCD.

18.4 (*Sum series*) Write a recursive method to compute the following series:

$$m(i) = 1 + \frac{1}{2} + \frac{1}{3} + \ldots + \frac{1}{i}$$

Write a test program that displays $m(i)$ for $i = 1, 2, \ldots, 10$.

18.5 (*Sum series*) Write a recursive method to compute the following series:

$$m(i) = \frac{1}{3} + \frac{2}{5} + \frac{3}{7} + \frac{4}{9} + \frac{5}{11} + \frac{6}{13} + \ldots + \frac{i}{2i + 1}$$

Write a test program that displays $m(i)$ for $i = 1, 2, \ldots, 10$.

*18.6 (*Sum series*) Write a recursive method to compute the following series:

$$m(i) = \frac{1}{2} + \frac{2}{3} + \ldots + \frac{i}{i + 1}$$

Write a test program that displays $m(i)$ for $i = 1, 2, \ldots, 10$.

*18.7 (*Fibonacci series*) Modify Listing 18.2, ComputeFibonacci.java, so that the program finds the number of times the `fib` method is called. (*Hint*: Use a static variable and increment it every time the method is called.)

Section 18.4

*18.8 (*Print the digits in an integer reversely*) Write a recursive method that displays an `int` value reversely on the console using the following header:

public static void reverseDisplay(**int** value)

For example, `reverseDisplay(12345)` displays `54321`. Write a test program that prompts the user to enter an integer and displays its reversal.

*18.9 (*Print the characters in a string reversely*) Write a recursive method that displays a string reversely on the console using the following header:

public static void reverseDisplay(**String** value)

For example, `reverseDisplay("abcd")` displays **dcba**. Write a test program that prompts the user to enter a string and displays its reversal.

*18.10 (*Occurrences of a specified character in a string*) Write a recursive method that finds the number of occurrences of a specified letter in a string using the following method header:

```
public static int count(String str, char a)
```

For example, `count("Welcome", 'e')` returns 2. Write a test program that prompts the user to enter a string and a character, and displays the number of occurrences for the character in the string.

*18.11 (*Sum the digits in an integer using recursion*) Write a recursive method that computes the sum of the digits in an integer. Use the following method header:

```
public static int sumDigits(long n)
```

For example, `sumDigits(234)` returns $2 + 3 + 4 = 9$. Write a test program that prompts the user to enter an integer and displays its sum.

Section 18.5

18.12 (*Print the characters in a string reversely*) Rewrite Programming Exercise 18.9 using a helper method to pass the substring **high index to the method. The helper method header is:

```
public static void reverseDisplay(String value, int high)
```

*18.13 (*Find the largest number in an array*) Write a recursive method that returns the largest integer in an array. Write a test program that prompts the user to enter a list of eight integers and displays the largest element.

*18.14 (*Find the number of uppercase letters in a string*) Write a recursive method to return the number of uppercase letters in a string. Write a test program that prompts the user to enter a string and displays the number of uppercase letters in the string.

*18.15 (*Occurrences of a specified character in a string*) Rewrite Programming Exercise 18.10 using a helper method to pass the substring **high** index to the method. The helper method header is:

```
public static int count(String str, char a, int high)
```

*18.16 (*Find the number of uppercase letters in an array*) Write a recursive method to return the number of uppercase letters in an array of characters. You need to define the following two methods. The second one is a recursive helper method.

```
public static int count(char[] chars)
public static int count(char[] chars, int high)
```

Write a test program that prompts the user to enter a list of characters in one line and displays the number of uppercase letters in the list.

*18.17 (*Occurrences of a specified character in an array*) Write a recursive method that finds the number of occurrences of a specified character in an array. You need to define the following two methods. The second one is a recursive helper method.

```
public static int count(char[] chars, char ch)
public static int count(char[] chars, char ch, int high)
```

Write a test program that prompts the user to enter a list of characters in one line, and a character, and displays the number of occurrences of the character in the list.

Sections 18.6–18.10

*18.18 (*Tower of Hanoi*) Modify Listing 18.8, TowerOfHanoi.java, so that the program finds the number of moves needed to move *n* disks from tower A to tower B. (*Hint*: Use a static variable and increment it every time the method is called.)

*18.19 (*Sierpinski triangle*) Revise Listing 18.9 to develop a program that lets the user use the + and – buttons to increase or decrease the current order by **1**, as shown in Figure 18.12a. The initial order is **0**. If the current order is **0**, the *Decrease* button is ignored.

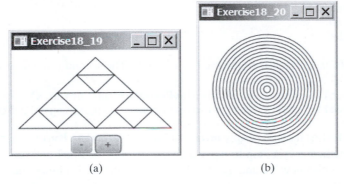

(a)   (b)

Figure 18.12 (a) Programming Exercise 18.19 uses the + and – buttons to increase or decrease the current order by **1**. (b) Programming Exercise 18.20 draws ovals using a recursive method.

*18.20 (*Display circles*) Write a Java program that displays ovals, as shown in Figure 18.12b. The circles are centered in the pane. The gap between two adjacent circles is **10** pixels, and the gap between the border of the pane and the largest circle is also **10**.

*18.21 (*Decimal to binary*) Write a recursive method that converts a decimal number into a binary number as a string. The method header is:

```
public static String dec2Bin(int value)
```

Write a test program that prompts the user to enter a decimal number and displays its binary equivalent.

*18.22 (*Decimal to hex*) Write a recursive method that converts a decimal number into a hex number as a string. The method header is:

```
public static String dec2Hex(int value)
```

Write a test program that prompts the user to enter a decimal number and displays its hex equivalent.

*18.23 (*Binary to decimal*) Write a recursive method that parses a binary number as a string into a decimal integer. The method header is:

```
public static int bin2Dec(String binaryString)
```

Write a test program that prompts the user to enter a binary string and displays its decimal equivalent.

*18.24 (*Hex to decimal*) Write a recursive method that parses a hex number as a string into a decimal integer. The method header is:

```
public static int hex2Dec(String hexString)
```

Write a test program that prompts the user to enter a hex string and displays its decimal equivalent.

18.25 (*String permutation*) Write a recursive method to print all the permutations of a string. For example, for the string **abc, the permuation is

abc
acb
bac
bca
cab
cba

(*Hint*: Define the following two methods. The second is a helper method.)

```
public static void displayPermutation(String s)
public static void displayPermutation(String s1, String s2)
```

The first method simply invokes **displayPermutation(" ", s)**. The second method uses a loop to move a character from **s2** to **s1** and recursively invokes it with a new **s1** and **s2**. The base case is that **s2** is empty and prints **s1** to the console.

Write a test program that prompts the user to enter a string and displays all its permutations.

**18.26 (*Create a maze*) Write a program that will find a path in a maze, as shown in Figure 18.13a. The maze is represented by an 8 × 8 board. The path must meet the following conditions:

■ The path is between the upper-left corner cell and the lower-right corner cell in the maze.

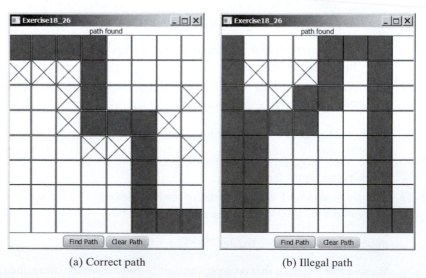

(a) Correct path   (b) Illegal path

FIGURE 18.13 The program finds a path from the upper-left corner to the bottom-right corner.

- The program enables the user to place or remove a mark on a cell. A path consists of adjacent unmarked cells. Two cells are said to be adjacent if they are horizontal or vertical neighbors, but not if they are diagonal neighbors.
- The path does not contain cells that form a square. The path in Figure 18.13b, for example, does not meet this condition. (The condition makes a path easy to identify on the board.)

**18.27 (*Koch snowflake fractal*) The text presented the Sierpinski triangle fractal. In this exercise, you will write a program to display another fractal, called the *Koch snowflake*, named after a famous Swedish mathematician. A Koch snowflake is created as follows:

1. Begin with an equilateral triangle, which is considered to be the Koch fractal of order (or level) **0**, as shown in Figure 18.14a.
2. Divide each line in the shape into three equal line segments and draw an outward equilateral triangle with the middle line segment as the base to create a Koch fractal of order **1**, as shown in Figure 18.14b.
3. Repeat Step 2 to create a Koch fractal of order **2, 3,** . . . , and so on, as shown in Figure 18.14c–d.

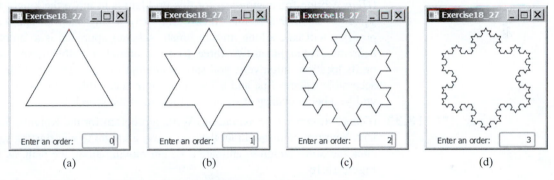

| (a) | (b) | (c) | (d) |

Figure 18.14 A Koch snowflake is a fractal starting with a triangle.

**18.28 (*Nonrecursive directory size*) Rewrite Listing 18.7, DirectorySize.java, without using recursion.

*18.29 (*Number of files in a directory*) Write a program that prompts the user to enter a directory and displays the number of the files in the directory.

**18.30 (*Find words*) Write a program that finds all occurrences of a word in all the files under a directory, recursively. Pass the parameters from the command line as follows:

VideoNote

Search a string in a directory

```
java Exercise18_30 dirName word
```

**18.31 (*Replace words*) Write a program that replaces all occurrences of a word with a new word in all the files under a directory, recursively. Pass the parameters from the command line as follows:

```
java Exercise18_31 dirName oldWord newWord
```

***18.32 (*Game: Knight's Tour*) The Knight's Tour is an ancient puzzle. The objective is to move a knight, starting from any square on a chessboard, to every other square once, as shown in Figure 18.15a. Note that the knight makes only L-shaped moves (two spaces in one direction and one space in a perpendicular direction). As shown in Figure 18.15b, the knight can move to eight squares. Write a program that displays the moves for the knight, as shown in Figure 18.15c. When you click a cell, the knight is placed at the cell. This cell will be starting point for the knight. Clicking the *Solve* button to display the path for a solution.

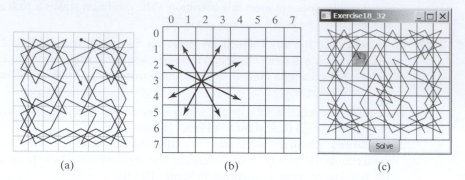

FIGURE 18.15 (a) A knight traverses all squares once. (b) A knight makes an L-shaped move. (c) A program displays a Knight's Tour path.

(*Hint*: A brute-force approach for this problem is to move the knight from one square to another available square arbitrarily. Using such an approach, your program will take a long time to finish. A better approach is to employ some heuristics. A knight has two, three, four, six, or eight possible moves, depending on its location. Intuitively, you should attempt to move the knight to the least accessible squares first and leave those more accessible squares open, so there will be a better chance of success at the end of the search.)

***18.33 (*Game: Knight's Tour animation*) Write a program for the Knight's Tour problem. Your program should let the user move a knight to any starting square and click the *Solve* button to animate a knight moving along the path, as shown in Figure 18.16.

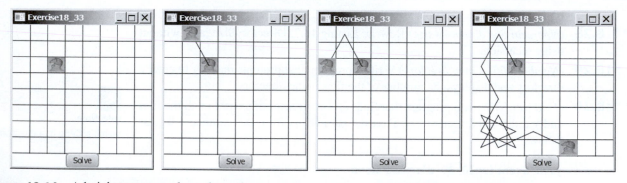

FIGURE 18.16 A knight traverses along the path.

**18.34 (*Game: Eight Queens*) The Eight Queens problem is to find a solution to place a queen in each row on a chessboard such that no two queens can attack each other. Write a program to solve the Eight Queens problem using recursion and display the result as shown in Figure 18.17.

FIGURE 18.17   The program displays a solution to the Eight Queens problem.

**18.35   (*H-tree fractal*) An H-tree (introduced at the beginning of this chapter in Figure 18.1) is a fractal defined as follows:

1. Begin with a letter H. The three lines of the H are of the same length, as shown in Figure 18.1a.
2. The letter H (in its sans-serif form, H) has four endpoints. Draw an H centered at each of the four endpoints to an H-tree of order 1, as shown in Figure 18.1b. These Hs are half the size of the H that contains the four endpoints.
3. Repeat Step 2 to create an H-tree of order 2, 3, . . . , and so on, as shown in Figure 18.1c–d.

Write a program that draws an H-tree, as shown in Figure 18.1.

18.36   (*Sierpinski triangle*) Write a program that lets the user to enter the order and display the filled Sierpinski triangles as shown in Figure 18.18.

  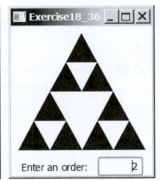 

FIGURE 18.18   A filled Sierpinski triangle is displayed.

**18.37   (*Hilbert curve*) The Hilbert curve, first described by German mathematician David Hilbert in 1891, is a space-filling curve that visits every point in a square grid with a size of $2 \times 2, 4 \times 4, 8 \times 8, 16 \times 16$, or any other power of 2. Write a program that displays a Hilbert curve for the specified order, as shown in Figure 18.19.

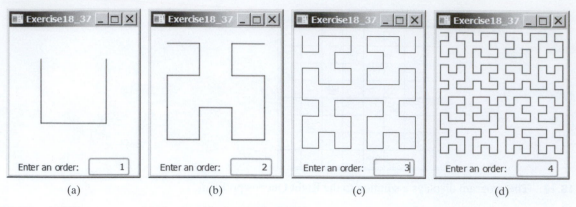

FIGURE 18.19 A Hilbert curve with the specified order is drawn.

VideoNote

Recursive tree

**18.38 (*Recursive tree*) Write a program to display a recursive tree as shown in Figure 18.20.

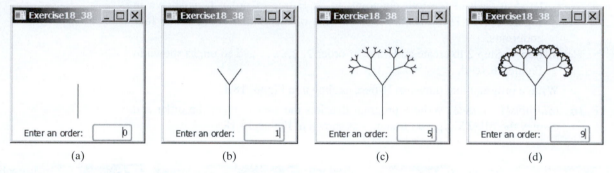

FIGURE 18.20 A recursive tree with the specified depth is drawn.

**18.39 (*Dragging the tree*) Revise Programming Exercise 18.38 to move the tree to where the mouse is dragged.

APPENDIXES

Appendix A
Java Keywords

Appendix B
The ASCII Character Set

Appendix C
Operator Precedence Chart

Appendix D
Java Modifiers

Appendix E
Special Floating-Point Values

Appendix F
Number Systems

Appendix G
Bitwise Operations

Appendix H
Regular Expressions

Appendix I
Enumerated Types

Java Keywords

The following fifty keywords are reserved for use by the Java language:

abstract	double	int	super
assert	else	interface	switch
boolean	enum	long	synchronized
break	extends	native	this
byte	final	new	throw
case	finally	package	throws
catch	float	private	transient
char	for	protected	try
class	goto	public	void
const	if	return	volatile
continue	implements	short	while
default	import	static	
do	instanceof	strictfp*	

The keywords **goto** and **const** are C++ keywords reserved, but not currently used in Java. This enables Java compilers to identify them and to produce better error messages if they appear in Java programs.

The literal values **true**, **false**, and **null** are not keywords, just like literal value **100**. However, you cannot use them as identifiers, just as you cannot use **100** as an identifier.

In the code listing, we use the keyword color for **true**, **false**, and **null** to be consistent with their coloring in Java IDEs.

---

*The **strictfp** keyword is a modifier for a method or class that enables it to use strict floating-point calculations. Floating-point arithmetic can be executed in one of two modes: *strict* or *nonstrict*. The strict mode guarantees that the evaluation result is the same on all Java Virtual Machine implementations. The nonstrict mode allows intermediate results from calculations to be stored in an extended format different from the standard IEEE floating-point number format. The extended format is machine-dependent and enables code to be executed faster. However, when you execute the code using the nonstrict mode on different JVMs, you may not always get precisely the same results. By default, the nonstrict mode is used for floating-point calculations. To use the strict mode in a method or a class, add the **strictfp** keyword in the method or the class declaration. Strict floating-point may give you slightly better precision than nonstrict floating-point, but the distinction will only affect some applications. Strictness is not inherited; that is, the presence of **strictfp** on a class or interface declaration does not cause extended classes or interfaces to be strict.

Appendix B

The ASCII Character Set

Tables B.1 and B.2 show ASCII characters and their respective decimal and hexadecimal codes. The decimal or hexadecimal code of a character is a combination of its row index and column index. For example, in Table B.1, the letter **A** is at row 6 and column 5, so its decimal equivalent is 65; in Table B.2, letter **A** is at row 4 and column 1, so its hexadecimal equivalent is 41.

TABLE B.1 ASCII Character Set in the Decimal Index

	0	1	2	3	4	5	6	7	8	9
0	nul	soh	stx	etx	eot	enq	ack	bel	bs	ht
1	nl	vt	ff	cr	so	si	dle	dc1	dc2	dc3
2	dc4	nak	syn	etb	can	em	sub	esc	fs	gs
3	rs	us	sp	!	"	#	$	%	&	'
4	(	)	*	+	,	-	.	/	0	1
5	2	3	4	5	6	7	8	9	:	;
6	<	=	>	?	@	A	B	C	D	E
7	F	G	H	I	J	K	L	M	N	O
8	P	Q	R	S	T	U	V	W	X	Y
9	Z	[	\	]	^	_	`	a	b	c
10	d	e	f	g	h	i	j	k	l	m
11	n	o	p	q	r	s	t	u	v	w
12	x	y	z	{	|	}	~	del		

TABLE B.2 ASCII Character Set in the Hexadecimal Index

	0	1	2	3	4	5	6	7	8	9	A	B	C	D	E	F
0	nul	soh	stx	etx	eot	enq	ack	bel	bs	ht	nl	vt	ff	cr	so	si
1	dle	dc1	dc2	dc3	dc4	nak	syn	etb	can	em	sub	esc	fs	gs	rs	us
2	sp	!	"	#	$	%	&	'	(	)	*	+	,	-	.	/
3	0	1	2	3	4	5	6	7	8	9	:	;	<	=	>	?
4	@	A	B	C	D	E	F	G	H	I	J	K	L	M	N	O
5	P	Q	R	S	T	U	V	W	X	Y	Z	[	\	]	^	_
6	`	a	b	c	d	e	f	g	h	i	j	k	l	m	n	o
7	p	q	r	s	t	u	v	w	x	y	z	{	|	}	~	del

APPENDIX C

Operator Precedence Chart

The operators are shown in decreasing order of precedence from top to bottom. Operators in the same group have the same precedence, and their associativity is shown in the table.

Operator	Name	Associativity
()	Parentheses	Left to right
()	Function call	Left to right
[]	Array subscript	Left to right
.	Object member access	Left to right
++	Postincrement	Left to right
−−	Postdecrement	Left to right
++	Preincrement	Right to left
−−	Predecrement	Right to left
+	Unary plus	Right to left
−	Unary minus	Right to left
!	Unary logical negation	Right to left
(type)	Unary casting	Right to left
new	Creating object	Right to left
*	Multiplication	Left to right
/	Division	Left to right
%	Remainder	Left to right
+	Addition	Left to right
−	Subtraction	Left to right
<<	Left shift	Left to right
>>	Right shift with sign extension	Left to right
>>>	Right shift with zero extension	Left to right
<	Less than	Left to right
<=	Less than or equal to	Left to right
>	Greater than	Left to right
>=	Greater than or equal to	Left to right
instanceof	Checking object type	Left to right

Operator	Name	Associativity
==	Equal comparison	Left to right
!=	Not equal	Left to right
&	(Unconditional AND)	Left to right
^	(Exclusive OR)	Left to right
|	(Unconditional OR)	Left to right
&&	Conditional AND	Left to right
||	Conditional OR	Left to right
?:	Ternary condition	Right to left
=	Assignment	Right to left
+=	Addition assignment	Right to left
-=	Subtraction assignment	Right to left
*=	Multiplication assignment	Right to left
/=	Division assignment	Right to left
%=	Remainder assignment	Right to left

APPENDIX D

Java Modifiers

Modifiers are used on classes and class members (constructors, methods, data, and class-level blocks), but the `final` modifier can also be used on local variables in a method. A modifier that can be applied to a class is called a *class modifier*. A modifier that can be applied to a method is called a *method modifier*. A modifier that can be applied to a data field is called a *data modifier*. A modifier that can be applied to a class-level block is called a *block modifier*. The following table gives a summary of the Java modifiers.

Modifier	Class	Constructor	Method	Data	Block	Explanation
(default)*	√	√	√	√	√	A class, constructor, method, or data field is visible in this package.
public	√	√	√	√		A class, constructor, method, or data field is visible to all the programs in any package.
private		√	√	√		A constructor, method, or data field is only visible in this class.
protected		√	√	√		A constructor, method, or data field is visible in this package and in subclasses of this class in any package.
static			√	√	√	Define a class method, a class data field, or a static initialization block.
final	√		√	√		A final class cannot be extended. A final method cannot be modified in a subclass. A final data field is a constant.
abstract	√		√			An abstract class must be extended. An abstract method must be implemented in a concrete subclass.
native			√			A native method indicates that the method is implemented using a language other than Java.

*Default access doesn't have a modifier associated with it. For example: `class Test {}`

Modifier	Class	Constructor	Method	Data	Block	Explanation
synchronized			√		√	Only one thread at a time can execute this method.
strictfp	√		√			Use strict floating-point calculations to guarantee that the evaluation result is the same on all JVMs.
transient				√		Mark a nonserializable instance data field.

The modifiers default (no modifier), **public**, **private**, and **protected** are known as *visibility* or *accessibility modifiers* because they specify how classes and class members are accessed.

The modifiers **public**, **private**, **protected**, **static**, **final**, and **abstract** can also be applied to inner classes.

APPENDIX E

Special Floating-Point Values

Dividing an integer by zero is invalid and throws `ArithmeticException`, but dividing a floating-point value by zero does not cause an exception. Floating-point arithmetic can overflow to infinity if the result of the operation is too large for a `double` or a `float`, or underflow to zero if the result is too small for a `double` or a `float`. Java provides the special floating-point values `POSITIVE_INFINITY`, `NEGATIVE_INFINITY`, and `NaN` (Not a Number) to denote these results. These values are defined as special constants in the `Float` class and the `Double` class.

If a positive floating-point number is divided by zero, the result is `POSITIVE_INFINITY`. If a negative floating-point number is divided by zero, the result is `NEGATIVE_INFINITY`. If a floating-point zero is divided by zero, the result is `NaN`, which means that the result is undefined mathematically. The string representations of these three values are `Infinity`, `-Infinity`, and `NaN`. For example,

```
System.out.print(1.0 / 0); // Print Infinity
System.out.print(-1.0 / 0); // Print -Infinity
System.out.print(0.0 / 0); // Print NaN
```

These special values can also be used as operands in computations. For example, a number divided by `POSITIVE_INFINITY` yields a positive zero. Table E.1 summarizes various combinations of the `/`, `*`, `%`, `+`, and `-` operators.

TABLE E.1 Special Floating-Point Values

x	y	x/y	x*y	x%y	x + y	x − y
Finite	± 0.0	± infinity	± 0.0	NaN	Finite	Finite
Finite	± infinity	± 0.0	± 0.0	x	± infinity	infinity
± 0.0	± 0.0	NaN	± 0.0	NaN	± 0.0	± 0.0
± infinity	Finite	± infinity	± 0.0	NaN	± infinity	± infinity
± infinity	± infinity	NaN	± 0.0	NaN	± infinity	infinity
± 0.0	± infinity	± 0.0	NaN	± 0.0	± infinity	± 0.0
NaN	Any	NaN	NaN	NaN	NaN	NaN
Any	NaN	NaN	NaN	NaN	NaN	NaN

Note
If one of the operands is NaN, the result is NaN.

Number Systems

F.1 Introduction

Computers use binary numbers internally, because computers are made naturally to store and process 0s and 1s. The binary number system has two digits, 0 and 1. A number or character is stored as a sequence of 0s and 1s. Each 0 or 1 is called a *bit* (binary digit).

binary numbers

In our daily life we use decimal numbers. When we write a number such as 20 in a program, it is assumed to be a decimal number. Internally, computer software is used to convert decimal numbers into binary numbers, and vice versa.

decimal numbers

We write computer programs using decimal numbers. However, to deal with an operating system, we need to reach down to the "machine level" by using binary numbers. Binary numbers tend to be very long and cumbersome. Often hexadecimal numbers are used to abbreviate them, with each hexadecimal digit representing four binary digits. The hexadecimal number system has 16 digits: 0–9 and A–F. The letters A, B, C, D, E, and F correspond to the decimal numbers 10, 11, 12, 13, 14, and 15.

hexadecimal number

The digits in the decimal number system are 0, 1, 2, 3, 4, 5, 6, 7, 8, and 9. A decimal number is represented by a sequence of one or more of these digits. The value that each digit represents depends on its position, which denotes an integral power of 10. For example, the digits 7, 4, 2, and 3 in decimal number 7423 represent 7000, 400, 20, and 3, respectively, as shown below:

$$\boxed{7 \mid 4 \mid 2 \mid 3} = 7 \times 10^3 + 4 \times 10^2 + 2 \times 10^1 + 3 \times 10^0$$

$$10^3 \ 10^2 \ 10^1 \ 10^0 = 7000 + 400 + 20 + 3 = 7423$$

The decimal number system has ten digits, and the position values are integral powers of 10. We say that 10 is the *base* or *radix* of the decimal number system. Similarly, since the binary number system has two digits, its base is 2, and since the hex number system has 16 digits, its base is 16.

base
radix

If 1101 is a binary number, the digits 1, 1, 0, and 1 represent 1×2^3, 1×2^2, 0×2^1, and 1×2^0, respectively:

$$\boxed{1 \mid 1 \mid 0 \mid 1} = 1 \times 2^3 + 1 \times 2^2 + 0 \times 2^1 + 1 \times 2^0$$

$$2^3 \ 2^2 \ 2^1 \ 2^0 = 8 + 4 + 0 + 1 = 13$$

If 7423 is a hex number, the digits 7, 4, 2, and 3 represent 7×16^3, 4×16^2, 2×16^1, and 3×16^0, respectively:

$$\boxed{7 \mid 4 \mid 2 \mid 3} = 7 \times 16^3 + 4 \times 16^2 + 2 \times 16^1 + 3 \times 16^0$$

$$16^3 \ 16^2 \ 16^1 \ 16^0 = 28672 + 1024 + 32 + 3 = 29731$$

F.2 Conversions Between Binary and Decimal Numbers

Given a binary number $b_nb_{n-1}b_{n-2}\ldots b_2b_1b_0$, the equivalent decimal value is

$$b_n \times 2^n + b_{n-1} \times 2^{n-1} + b_{n-2} \times 2^{n-2} + \ldots + b_2 \times 2^2 + b_1 \times 2^1 + b_0 \times 2^0$$

Here are some examples of converting binary numbers to decimals:

Binary	Conversion Formula	Decimal
10	$1 \times 2^1 + 0 \times 2^0$	2
1000	$1 \times 2^3 + 0 \times 2^2 + 0 \times 2^1 + 0 \times 2^0$	8
10101011	$1 \times 2^7 + 0 \times 2^6 + 1 \times 2^5 + 0 \times 2^4 + 1 \times 2^3 + 0 \times 2^2 +$ $1 \times 2^1 + 1 \times 2^0$	171

To convert a decimal number d to a binary number is to find the bits $b_n, b_{n-1}, b_{n-2}, \ldots, b_2, b_1$ and b_0 such that

$$d = b_n \times 2^n + b_{n-1} \times 2^{n-1} + b_{n-2} \times 2^{n-2} + \ldots + b_2 \times 2^2 + b_1 \times 2^1 + b_0 \times 2^0$$

These bits can be found by successively dividing d by 2 until the quotient is 0. The remainders are $b_0, b_1, b_2, \ldots, b_{n-2}, b_{n-1}$, and b_n.

For example, the decimal number 123 is 1111011 in binary. The conversion is done as follows:

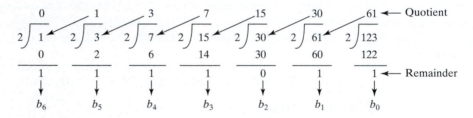

 Tip

The Windows Calculator, as shown in Figure F.1, is a useful tool for performing number conversions. To run it, search for *Calculator* from the *Start* button and launch Calculator, then under *View* select *Scientific*.

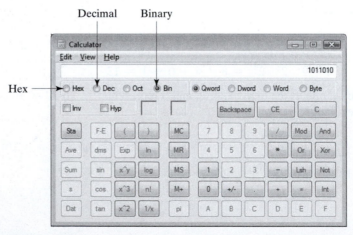

FIGURE F.1   You can perform number conversions using the Windows Calculator.

F.3 Conversions Between Hexadecimal and Decimal Numbers

Given a hexadecimal number $h_n h_{n-1} h_{n-2} \ldots h_2 h_1 h_0$, the equivalent decimal value is

hex to decimal

$$h_n \times 16^n + h_{n-1} \times 16^{n-1} + h_{n-2} \times 16^{n-2} + \ldots + h_2 \times 16^2 + h_1 \times 16^1 + h_0 \times 16^0$$

Here are some examples of converting hexadecimal numbers to decimals:

Hexadecimal	Conversion Formula	Decimal
7F	$7 \times 16^1 + 15 \times 16^0$	127
FFFF	$15 \times 16^3 + 15 \times 16^2 + 15 \times 16^1 + 15 \times 16^0$	65535
431	$4 \times 16^2 + 3 \times 16^1 + 1 \times 16^0$	1073

To convert a decimal number d to a hexadecimal number is to find the hexadecimal digits $h_n, h_{n-1}, h_{n-2}, \ldots, h_2, h_1,$ and h_0 such that

decimal to hex

$$d = h_n \times 16^n + h_{n-1} \times 16^{n-1} + h_{n-2} \times 16^{n-2} + \ldots + h_2 \times 16^2$$
$$+ h_1 \times 16^1 + h_0 \times 16^0$$

These numbers can be found by successively dividing d by 16 until the quotient is 0. The remainders are $h_0, h_1, h_2, \ldots, h_{n-2}, h_{n-1},$ and h_n.

For example, the decimal number 123 is 7B in hexadecimal. The conversion is done as follows:

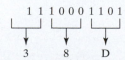

F.4 Conversions Between Binary and Hexadecimal Numbers

To convert a hexadecimal to a binary number, simply convert each digit in the hexadecimal number into a four-digit binary number, using Table F.1.

hex to binary

For example, the hexadecimal number 7B is 1111011, where 7 is 111 in binary, and B is 1011 in binary.

To convert a binary number to a hexadecimal, convert every four binary digits from right to left in the binary number into a hexadecimal number.

binary to hex

For example, the binary number 1110001101 is 38D, since 1101 is D, 1000 is 8, and 11 is 3, as shown below.

```
1 1 1 0 0 0 1 1 0 1
└─┘ └───┘ └───┘
  ↓     ↓     ↓
  3     8     D
```

TABLE F.1 Converting Hexadecimal to Binary		
Hexadecimal	Binary	Decimal
0	0000	0
1	0001	1
2	0010	2
3	0011	3
4	0100	4
5	0101	5
6	0110	6
7	0111	7
8	1000	8
9	1001	9
A	1010	10
B	1011	11
C	1100	12
D	1101	13
E	1110	14
F	1111	15

Note

Octal numbers are also useful. The octal number system has eight digits, 0 to 7. A decimal number 8 is represented in the octal system as 10.

Here are some good online resources for practicing number conversions:

- http://forums.cisco.com/CertCom/game/binary_game_page.htm
- http://people.sinclair.edu/nickreeder/Flash/binDec.htm
- http://people.sinclair.edu/nickreeder/Flash/binHex.htm

Check
Point

F.1 Convert the following decimal numbers into hexadecimal and binary numbers:
100; 4340; 2000

F.2 Convert the following binary numbers into hexadecimal and decimal numbers:
1000011001; 100000000; 100111

F.3 Convert the following hexadecimal numbers into binary and decimal numbers:
FEFA9; 93; 2000

Bitwise Operations

To write programs at the machine-level, often you need to deal with binary numbers directly and perform operations at the bit-level. Java provides the bitwise operators and shift operators defined in Table G.1.

The bit operators apply only to integer types (**byte**, **short**, **int**, and **long**). A character involved in a bit operation is converted to an integer. All bitwise operators can form bitwise assignment operators, such as =, |=, <<=, >>=, and >>>=.

TABLE G.1

Operator	Name	Example (using bytes in the example)	Description
&	Bitwise AND	10101110 **&** 10010010 yields 10000010	The AND of two corresponding bits yields a 1 if both bits are 1.
|	Bitwise inclusive OR	10101110 **|** 10010010 yields 10111110	The OR of two corresponding bits yields a 1 if either bit is 1.
^	Bitwise exclusive OR	10101110 ^ 10010010 yields 00111100	The XOR of two corresponding bits yields a 1 only if two bits are different.
~	One's complement	~10101110 yields 01010001	The operator toggles each bit from 0 to 1 and from 1 to 0.
<<	Left shift	10101110 **<<** 2 yields 10111000	The operator shifts bits in the first operand left by the number of bits specified in the second operand, filling with 0s on the right.
>>	Right shift with sign extension	10101110 **>>** 2 yields 11101011 00101110 **>>** 2 yields 00001011	The operator shifts bit in the first operand right by the number of bits specified in the second operand, filling with the highest (sign) bit on the left.
>>>	Unsigned right shift with zero extension	10101110 **>>>** 2 yields 00101011 00101110 **>>>** 2 yields 00001011	The operator shifts bit in the first operand right by the number of bits specified in the second operand, filling with 0s on the left.

Appendix H

Regular Expressions

Often you need to write the code to validate user input such as to check whether the input is a number, a string with all lowercase letters, or a social security number. How do you write this type of code? A simple and effective way to accomplish this task is to use the regular expression.

regular expression A *regular expression* (abbreviated *regex*) is a string that describes a pattern for matching a set of strings. Regular expression is a powerful tool for string manipulations. You can use regular expressions for matching, replacing, and splitting strings.

H.1 Matching Strings

matches Let us begin with the **matches** method in the **String** class. At first glance, the **matches** method is very similar to the **equals** method. For example, the following two statements both evaluate to **true**.

```
"Java".matches("Java");
"Java".equals("Java");
```

However, the **matches** method is more powerful. It can match not only a fixed string, but also a set of strings that follow a pattern. For example, the following statements all evaluate to **true**.

```
"Java is fun".matches("Java.*")
"Java is cool".matches("Java.*")
"Java is powerful".matches("Java.*")
```

"Java.*" in the preceding statements is a regular expression. It describes a string pattern that begins with Java followed by any zero or more characters. Here, the substring .* matches any zero or more characters.

H.2 Regular Expression Syntax

A regular expression consists of literal characters and special symbols. Table H.1 lists some frequently used syntax for regular expressions.

Note

Backslash is a special character that starts an escape sequence in a string. So you need to use \\d in Java to represent \d.

Note

Recall that a *whitespace character* is ' ', '\t', '\n', '\r', or '\f'. So \s is the same as [\t\n\r\f], and \S is the same as [^ \t\n\r\f].

TABLE H.1   Frequently Used Regular Expressions

Regular Expression	Matches	Example
x	a specified character x	Java matches Java
.	any single character	Java matches J..a
(ab|cd)	ab or cd	ten matches t(en|im)
[abc]	a, b, or c	Java matches Ja[uvwx]a
[^abc]	any character except a, b, or c	Java matches Ja[^ars]a
[a-z]	a through z	Java matches [A-M]av[a-d]
[^a-z]	any character except a through z	Java matches Jav[^b-d]
[a-e[m-p]]	a through e or m through p	Java matches [A-G[I-M]]av[a-d]
[a-e&&[c-p]]	intersection of a-e with c-p	Java matches [A-P&&[I-M]]av[a-d]
\d	a digit, same as [0-9]	Java2 matches "Java[\\d]"
\D	a non-digit	$Java matches "[\\D][\\D]ava"
\w	a word character	Java1 matches "[\\w]ava[\\w]"
\W	a non-word character	$Java matches "[\\W][\\w]ava"
\s	a whitespace character	"Java 2" matches "Java\\s2"
\S	a non-whitespace char	Java matches "[\\S]ava"
p*	zero or more occurrences of pattern p	aaaabb matches "a*bb" ababab matches "(ab)*"
p+	one or more occurrences of pattern p	a matches "a+b*" able matches "(ab)+.*"
p?	zero or one occurrence of pattern p	Java matches "J?Java" Java matches "J?ava"
p{n}	exactly n occurrences of pattern p	Java matches "Ja{1}.*" Java does not match ".{2}"
p{n,}	at least n occurrences of pattern p	aaaa matches "a{1,}" a does not match "a{2,}"
p{n,m}	between n and m occurrences (inclusive)	aaaa matches "a{1,9}" abb does not match "a{2,9}bb"

Note

A word character is any letter, digit, or the underscore character. So \w is the same as [a-z[A-Z][0-9]_] or simply [a-zA-Z0-9_], and \W is the same as [^a-zA-Z0-9_].

Note

The last six entries *, +, ?, {n}, {n,}, and {n, m} in Table H.1 are called *quantifiers* that specify how many times the pattern before a quantifier may repeat. For example, A* matches zero or more A's, A+ matches one or more A's, A? matches zero or one A's, A{3} matches exactly AAA, A{3,} matches at least three A's, and A{3,6} matches between 3 and 6 A's. * is the same as {0,}, + is the same as {1,}, and ? is the same as {0,1}.

quantifier

Caution
Do not use spaces in the repeat quantifiers. For example, `A{3,6}` cannot be written as `A{3, 6}` with a space after the comma.

Note
You may use parentheses to group patterns. For example, `(ab){3}` matches **ababab**, but **ab{3}** matches **abbb**.

Let us use several examples to demonstrate how to construct regular expressions.

Example 1

The pattern for social security numbers is **xxx-xx-xxxx**, where **x** is a digit. A regular expression for social security numbers can be described as

`[\\d]{3}-[\\d]{2}-[\\d]{4}`

For example,

`"111-22-3333".matches("[\\d]{3}-[\\d]{2}-[\\d]{4}")` returns `true`.
`"11-22-3333".matches("[\\d]{3}-[\\d]{2}-[\\d]{4}")` returns `false`.

Example 2

An even number ends with digits **0**, **2**, **4**, **6**, or **8**. The pattern for even numbers can be described as

`[\\d]*[02468]`

For example,

`"123".matches("[\\d]*[02468]")` returns `false`.
`"122".matches("[\\d]*[02468]")` returns `true`.

Example 3

The pattern for telephone numbers is **(xxx) xxx-xxxx**, where **x** is a digit and the first digit cannot be zero. A regular expression for telephone numbers can be described as

`\\([1-9][\\d]{2}\\) [\\d]{3}-[\\d]{4}`

Note that the parentheses symbols **(** and **)** are special characters in a regular expression for grouping patterns. To represent a literal **(** or **)** in a regular expression, you have to use `\\(` and `\\)`.
For example,

`"(912) 921-2728".matches("\\([1-9][\\d]{2}\\) [\\d]{3}-[\\d]{4}")`
returns `true`.
`"921-2728".matches("\\([1-9][\\d]{2}\\) [\\d]{3}-[\\d]{4}")`
returns `false`.

Example 4

Suppose the last name consists of at most 25 letters and the first letter is in uppercase. The pattern for a last name can be described as

`[A-Z][a-zA-Z]{1,24}`

Note that you cannot have arbitrary whitespace in a regular expression. For example, `[A-Z][a-zA-Z]{1, 24}` would be wrong.

For example,

```
"Smith".matches("[A-Z][a-zA-Z]{1,24}") returns true.
"Jones123".matches("[A-Z][a-zA-Z]{1,24}") returns false.
```

Example 5
Java identifiers are defined in Section 2.4, "Identifiers."

- An identifier must start with a letter, an underscore (_), or a dollar sign ($). It cannot start with a digit.

- An identifier is a sequence of characters that consists of letters, digits, underscores (_), and dollar signs ($).

The pattern for identifiers can be described as

```
[a-zA-Z_$][\\w$]*
```

Example 6
What strings are matched by the regular expression `"Welcome to (Java|HTML)"`? The answer is `Welcome to Java` or `Welcome to HTML`.

Example 7
What strings are matched by the regular expression `"A.*"`? The answer is any string that starts with letter A.

H.3 Replacing and Splitting Strings
The `matches` method in the `String` class returns `true` if the string matches the regular expression. The `String` class also contains the `replaceAll`, `replaceFirst`, and `split` methods for replacing and splitting strings, as shown in Figure H.1.

java.lang.String	
+matches(regex: String): boolean	Returns true if this string matches the pattern.
+replaceAll(regex: String, replacement: String): String	Returns a new string that replaces all matching substrings with the replacement.
+replaceFirst(regex: String, replacement: String): String	Returns a new string that replaces the first matching substring with the replacement.
+split(regex: String): String[]	Returns an array of strings consisting of the substrings split by the matches.
+split(regex: String, limit: int): String[]	Same as the preceding split method except that the limit parameter controls the number of times the pattern is applied.

FIGURE H.1 The `String` class contains the methods for matching, replacing, and splitting strings using regular expressions.

The `replaceAll` method replaces all matching substring and the `replaceFirst` method replaces the first matching substring. For example, the following code

```
System.out.println("Java Java Java".replaceAll("v\\w", "wi"));
```

displays

```
Jawi Jawi Jawi
```

The following code

```
System.out.println("Java Java Java".replaceFirst("v\\w", "wi"));
```

displays

```
Jawi Java Java
```

There are two overloaded **split** methods. The **split(regex)** method splits a string into substrings delimited by the matches. For example, the following statement

```
String[] tokens = "Java1HTML2Perl".split("\\d");
```

splits string **"Java1HTML2Perl"** into **Java**, **HTML**, and **Perl** and saved in **tokens[0]**, **tokens[1]**, and **tokens[2]**.

In the **split(regex, limit)** method, the **limit** parameter determines how many times the pattern is matched. If **limit <= 0**, **split(regex, limit)** is same as **split(regex)**. If **limit > 0**, the pattern is matched at most **limit – 1** times. Here are some examples:

```
"Java1HTML2Perl".split("\\d", 0); splits into Java, HTML, Perl
"Java1HTML2Perl".split("\\d", 1); splits into Java1HTML2Perl
"Java1HTML2Perl".split("\\d", 2); splits into Java, HTML2Perl
"Java1HTML2Perl".split("\\d", 3); splits into Java, HTML, Perl
"Java1HTML2Perl".split("\\d", 4); splits into Java, HTML, Perl
"Java1HTML2Perl".split("\\d", 5); splits into Java, HTML, Perl
```

 Note

By default, all the quantifiers are *greedy*. This means that they will match as many occurrences as possible. For example, the following statement displays **JRvaa**, since the first match is **aaa**.

```
System.out.println("Jaaavaa".replaceFirst("a+", "R"));
```

You can change a qualifier's default behavior by appending a question mark (**?**) after it. The quantifier becomes *reluctant*, which means that it will match as few occurrences as possible. For example, the following statement displays **JRaavaa**, since the first match is **a**.

```
System.out.println("Jaaavaa".replaceFirst("a+?", "R"));
```

APPENDIX I

Enumerated Types

I.1 Simple Enumerated Types

An enumerated type defines a list of enumerated values. Each value is an identifier. For example, the following statement declares a type, named MyFavoriteColor, with values RED, BLUE, GREEN, and YELLOW in this order.

```
enum MyFavoriteColor {RED, BLUE, GREEN, YELLOW};
```

A value of an enumerated type is like a constant and so, by convention, is spelled with all uppercase letters. So, the preceding declaration uses RED, not red. By convention, an enumerated type is named like a class with first letter of each word capitalized.

Once a type is defined, you can declare a variable of that type:

```
MyFavoriteColor color;
```

The variable color can hold one of the values defined in the enumerated type MyFavoriteColor or null, but nothing else. Java enumerated type is *type-safe*, meaning that an attempt to assign a value other than one of the enumerated values or null will result in a compile error.

The enumerated values can be accessed using the syntax

```
EnumeratedTypeName.valueName
```

For example, the following statement assigns enumerated value BLUE to variable color:

```
color = MyFavoriteColor.BLUE;
```

Note that you have to use the enumerated type name as a qualifier to reference a value such as BLUE.

As with any other type, you can declare and initialize a variable in one statement:

```
MyFavoriteColor color = MyFavoriteColor.BLUE;
```

An enumerated type is treated as a special class. An enumerated type variable is therefore a reference variable. An enumerated type is a subtype of the Object class and the Comparable interface. Therefore, an enumerated type inherits all the methods in the Object class and the compraeTo method in the Comparable interface. Additionally, you can use the following methods on an enumerated object:

- **public String name();**
  Returns a name of the value for the object.

- **public int ordinal();**
  Returns the ordinal value associated with the enumerated value. The first value in an enumerated type has an ordinal value of 0, the second has an ordinal value of 1, the third one 3, and so on.

Listing I.1 gives a program that demonstrates the use of enumerated types.

LISTING I.1 EnumeratedTypeDemo.java

define an enum type

declare an enum variable

get enum name

get enum ordinal

compare enum values

```java
 1  public class EnumeratedTypeDemo {
 2    static enum Day {SUNDAY, MONDAY, TUESDAY, WEDNESDAY, THURSDAY,
 3      FRIDAY, SATURDAY};
 4
 5    public static void main(String[] args) {
 6      Day day1 = Day.FRIDAY;
 7      Day day2 = Day.THURSDAY;
 8
 9      System.out.println("day1's name is " + day1.name());
10      System.out.println("day2's name is " + day2.name());
11      System.out.println("day1's ordinal is " + day1.ordinal());
12      System.out.println("day2's ordinal is " + day2.ordinal());
13
14      System.out.println("day1.equals(day2) returns " +
15        day1.equals(day2));
16      System.out.println("day1.toString() returns " +
17        day1.toString());
18      System.out.println("day1.compareTo(day2) returns " +
19        day1.compareTo(day2));
20    }
21  }
```

```
day1's name is FRIDAY
day2's name is THURSDAY
day1's ordinal is 5
day2's ordinal is 4
day1.equals(day2) returns false
day1.toString() returns FRIDAY
day1.compareTo(day2) returns 1
```

An enumerated type **Day** is defined in lines 2–3. Variables **day1** and **day2** are declared as the **Day** type and assigned enumerated values in lines 6–7. Since **day1**'s value is **FRIDAY**, its ordinal value is 5 (line 11). Since **day2**'s value is **THURSDAY**, its ordinal value is 4 (line 12).

Since an enumerated type is a subclass of the **Object** class and the **Comparable** interface, you can invoke the methods **equals**, **toString**, and **comareTo** from an enumerated object reference variable (lines 14–19). **day1.equals(day2)** returns true if **day1** and **day2** have the same ordinal value. **day1.compareTo(day2)** returns the difference between **day1**'s ordinal value to **day2**'s.

Alternatively, you can rewrite the code in Listing I.1 into Listing I.2.

LISTING I.2 StandaloneEnumTypeDemo.java

```java
 1  public class StandaloneEnumTypeDemo {
 2    public static void main(String[] args) {
 3      Day day1 = Day.FRIDAY;
 4      Day day2 = Day.THURSDAY;
 5
 6      System.out.println("day1's name is " + day1.name());
 7      System.out.println("day2's name is " + day2.name());
 8      System.out.println("day1's ordinal is " + day1.ordinal());
```

```
 9      System.out.println("day2's ordinal is " + day2.ordinal());
10
11      System.out.println("day1.equals(day2) returns " +
12        day1.equals(day2));
13      System.out.println("day1.toString() returns " +
14        day1.toString());
15      System.out.println("day1.compareTo(day2) returns " +
16        day1.compareTo(day2));
17    }
18 }
19
20 enum Day {SUNDAY, MONDAY, TUESDAY, WEDNESDAY, THURSDAY,
21    FRIDAY, SATURDAY}
```

An enumerated type can be defined inside a class, as shown in lines 2–3 in Listing I.1, or standalone as shown in lines 20–21 Listing I.2. In the former case, the type is treated as an inner class. After the program is compiled, a class named EnumeratedTypeDemo$Day.class is created. In the latter case, the type is treated as a standalone class. After the program is compiled, a class named Day.class is created.

Note

When an enumerated type is declared inside a class, the type must be declared as a member of the class and cannot be declared inside a method. Furthermore, the type is always **static**. For this reason, the **static** keyword in line 2 in Listing I.1 may be omitted. The visibility modifiers on inner class can be also be applied to enumerated types defined inside a class.

Tip

Using enumerated values (e.g., **Day.MONDAY**, **Day.TUESDAY**, and so on) rather than literal integer values (e.g., 0, 1, and so on) can make program easier to read and maintain.

I.2 Using **if** or **switch** Statements with an Enumerated Variable

An enumerated variable holds a value. Often your program needs to perform a specific action depending on the value. For example, if the value is **Day.MONDAY**, play soccer; if the value is **Day.TUESDAY**, take piano lesson, and so on. You can use an **if** statement or a **switch** statement to test the value in the variable, as shown in (a) and (b)

```
if (day.equals(Day.MONDAY)) {
  // process Monday
}
else if (day.equals(Day.TUESDAY)) {
  // process Tuesday
}
else
  ...
```
(a)

Equivalent

```
switch (day) {
  case MONDAY:
    // process Monday
    break;
  case TUESDAY:
    // process Tuesday
    break;
  ...
}
```
(b)

In the **switch** statement in (b), the case label is an unqualified enumerated value (e.g., **MONDAY**, but not **Day.MONDAY**).

I.3 Processing Enumerated Values Using a Foreach Loop

Each enumerated type has a static method **values()** that returns all enumerated values for the type in an array. For example,

```
Day[] days = Day.values();
```

You can use a regular for loop in (a) or a foreach loop in (b) to process all the values in the array.

```
for (int i = 0; i < days.length; i++)
  System.out.println(days[i]);
```
(a)

Equivalent

```
for (Day day: days)
  System.out.println(day);
```
(b)

I.4 Enumerated Types with Data Fields, Constructors, and Methods

The simple enumerated types introduced in the preceding section define a type with a list of enumerated values. You can also define an enumerate type with data fields, constructors, and methods, as shown in Listing I.3.

LISTING I.3 TrafficLight.java

```
1  public enum TrafficLight {
2    RED ("Please stop"), GREEN ("Please go"),
3    YELLOW ("Please caution");
4
5    private String description;
6
7    private TrafficLight(String description) {
8      this.description = description;
9    }
10
11   public String getDescription() {
12     return description;
13   }
14 }
```

The enumerated values are defined in lines 2–3. The value declaration must be the first statement in the type declaration. A data field named **description** is declared in line 5 to describe an enumerated value. The constructor **TrafficLight** is declared in lines 7–9. The constructor is invoked whenever an enumerated value is accessed. The enumerated value's argument is passed to the constructor, which is then assigned to **description**.

Listing I.4 gives a test program to use **TrafficLight**.

LISTING I.4 TestTrafficLight.java

```
1  public class TestTrafficLight {
2    public static void main(String[] args) {
3      TrafficLight light = TrafficLight.RED;
4      System.out.println(light.getDescription());
5    }
6  }
```

An enumerated value `TrafficLight.red` is assigned to variable `light` (line 3). Accessing `TrafficLight.RED` causes the JVM to invoke the constructor with argument "please stop". The methods in enumerated type are invoked in the same way as the methods in a class. `light.getDescription()` returns the description for the enumerated value (line 4).

Note

The Java syntax requires that the constructor for enumerated types be private to prevent it from being invoked directly. The private modifier may be omitted. In this case, it is considered private by default.

INDEX

Symbols

– (decrement operator), 55–56

– (subtraction operator), 46, 50–51

. (dot operator), 330

. (object member access operator), 330, 429

/ (division operator), 46, 50

//, in line comment syntax, 18

/*, in block comment syntax, 18

/**.*/ (Javadoc comment syntax), 18

/= (division assignment operator), 54–55

; (semicolons), common errors, 84

\ (backslash character), as directory separator, 474

\ (escape characters), 126

|| (or logical operator), 93–97

+ (addition operator), 46, 50

+ (string concatenation operator), 38, 131

++ (increment operator), 55–56

+= (addition assignment operator), augmented, 54–55

= (assignment operator), 41–43, 54–55

= (equals operator), 76

–= (subtraction assignment operator), 54–55

== (comparison operator), 76, 432

== (equal to operator), 76

! (not logical operator), 93–97

!= (not equal to comparison operator), 76

$ (dollar sign character), use in source code, 40

% (remainder or modulo operator), 46, 50

%= (remainder assignment operator), 54–55

&& (and logical operator), 93–97

( ) (parentheses), 14, 225

* (multiplication operator), 15, 46, 50

*= (multiplication assignment operator), 54–55

^ (exclusive or logical operator), 93–97

{} (curly braces), 13, 79, 83

< (less than comparison operator), 76

<= (less than or equal to comparison operator), 76

> (greater than comparison operator), 76

>= (greater than or equal to comparison operator), 76

A

abs method, **Math** class, 121–122, 524

Absolute file name, 473

Abstract classes

    case study: abstract number class, 501–503

    case study: **Calendar** and **GregorianCalendar** classes, 503–506

    characteristics of, 500–501

    Circle.java and **Rectangle.java** examples, 498

    compared with interfaces, 517–520

    GeometricObject.java example, 496–498

    InputStream and **OutputStream** classes, 680–681

    interfaces compared to, 506

    key terms, 528–529

    overview of, 366–367, 495–496

    questions and exercises, 528–533

    Rational.java example, 522–524

    reasons for using abstract methods, 498

    summary, 528–529

    TestCalendar.java example, 504–505

    TestGeometricObject.java example, 498–499

    TestRationalClass.java example, 521–522

Abstract data type (ADT), 366

Abstract methods

    characteristics of, 500

    GeometricObject class, 497–498

    implementing in subclasses, 496

    in interfaces, 506

    in **Number** class, 524

    overview of, 225–226

    reasons for using, 498–499

abstract modifier, for denoting abstract methods, 496

Abstract number class

    LargestNumbers.java, 502–503

    overview of, 501–503

Abstract Windows Toolkit. *see* AWT (Abstract Windows Toolkit)

acos method, trigonometry, 120–121

Actions (behaviors), object, 322

ActionEvent, 588–589

Activation records, invoking methods and, 208

Actual parameters, defining methods and, 205

Ada, high-level languages, 8

Addition (+) operator, 46, 50

Addition (+=) assignment operator, augmented assignment operators, 54–55

ADT (abstract data type), 366

Aggregating classes, 374

Aggregating objects, 374

Aggregation relationships, objects, 374–375

AIFF audio files, 662

Algorithms, 34

Ambiguous invocation, of methods, 221

American Standard Code for Information Interchange (ASCII). *see* ASCII (American Standard Code for Information Interchange)

And (&&) logical operator, 93–97

Animation

    ClockAnimation.java, 615–616

    FadeTransition, 612–613

    PathTransition, 609–612

    Timeline, 614–616

Anonymous arrays, 258

Anonymous objects, 331

APIs (Application Program Interfaces), libraries as, 11

Application Program Interfaces (APIs), 11

Apps, developing on Web servers, 11

Arc

    overview, 567

    ShowArc.java, 568–569

Arguments

    defining methods and, 205

    passing by values, 212–215

    receiving string arguments from command line, 272–273

    variable-length argument lists, 264–265

ArithmeticException class, 453

Arithmetic/logic units, CPU components, 3

Array elements, 248

Array initializers, 248–249

arraycopy method, **System** class, 256

ArrayIndexOutOfBoundsException, 251

`ArrayList` class
  case study: custom stack class, 439
  cloning arrays, 514
  creating and adding numbers to array lists, 437–438
  `DistinctNumbers.java` example, 435–438
  storing list of objects in, 432–433
  `TestArrayList.java` example, 433–436
Arrays, multi-dimensional
  case study: daily temperature and humidity, 302–303
  case study: guessing birthdays, 304–305
  overview of, 301–302
  questions and exercises, 305–319
  summary, 305
Arrays, single-dimensional
  accessing elements, 248
  `ArrayList` class, 435–436
  `Arrays` class, 270–272
  case study: analyzing numbers, 253–254
  case study: counting occurrences of letters, 261–264
  case study: deck of cards, 254–256
  constructing strings from, 386
  converting strings to/from, 389–390
  copying, 256–257
  creating, 246–248, 510–512
  declaring, 246
  foreach loops, 251–253
  initializers, 248–249
  key terms, 275
  of objects, 351–353
  overview of, 245–246
  passing to methods, 257–260
  processing, 249–251
  questions and exercises, 276–285
  returning from methods, 260–261
  searching, 265–269
  serializing, 696–697
  size and default values, 248
  sorting, 269–270, 510–512
  summary, 275–276
  treating as objects in Java, 330
  variable-length argument lists, 264–265
Arrays, two-dimensional
  case study: finding closest pair of points, 296–297
  case study: grading multiple-choice test, 294–296
  case study: Sudoku, 298–301
  declaring variables and creating two-dimensional arrays, 288–289
  obtaining length of two-dimensional arrays, 289–290
  overview of, 287–288
  passing to methods to two-dimensional arrays, 293–294
  processing two-dimensional arrays, 291–293
  questions and exercises, 305–319
  ragged arrays, 290–291
  summary, 305
`Arrays` class, 270–271
Arrows keys, on keyboards, 5
ASCII (American Standard Code for Information Interchange)
  character data type (`char`) and, 126
  data input and output streams, 685
  encoding scheme, 3
  text encoding, 678
  text I/O vs. binary I/O, 679
`asin` method, trigonometry, 120–121
Assemblers, 7
Assembly language, 7
Assignment operator (=)
  augmented, 54–55
  overview of, 41–43

Assignment statements (assignment expressions)
  assigning value to variables, 36
  overview of, 41–43
Associativity, of operators, 105
`atan` method, trigonometry, 120–121
Attributes, object, 322
Audio files
  case study: national flags and anthems, 665–667
  `MediaDemo.java`, 663–664
Autoboxing/Autounboxing, 383–384
Average-case analysis, measuring algorithm efficiency, 522
AWT (Abstract Windows Toolkit)
  `Color` class, 546–547
  `Date` class, 334–335, 503–504
  `Error` class, 456, 458
  event classes in, 588
  `EventObject` class, 588–590
  exceptions. *see* `Exception` class
  `File` class, 473–475, 678
  `Font` class, 547–548
  `GeometricObject` class, 496–499
  `GuessDate` class, 304–305
  `IllegalArgumentException` class, 459
  `InputMismatchException` class, 454–455, 479
  `KeyEvent` class, 603
  `MalformedURLException` class, 483
  `MouseEvent` class, 602–603
  `Polygon` class, 569–570
  `String` class, 386
  Swing vs., 536

B

Babylonian method, 239
Backslash character (\), as directory separator, 474
Base cases, in recursion, 712
BASIC, high-level languages, 8
Bean machine game, 280–281, 627
`beginIndex` method, for obtaining substrings from strings, 136
Behaviors (actions), object, 322
Behind the scene evaluation, expressions, 105
`BigDecimal` class, 384–385, 501
Binary
  files, 678
  machine language as binary code, 7
  operators, 47
  searches, 266–269, 716–717
Binary digits (Bits), 3
Binary I/O
  `BufferedInputStream` and `BufferedOutputStream` classes, 719–722
  characters and strings in, 716
  classes, 712–713
  `DataInputStream` and `DataOutputStream` classes, 716–718
  `DetectEndOfFile.java`, 687–688
  `FileInputStream` and `FileOutputStream` classes, 681–682
  `FilterInputStream` and `FilterOutputStream` classes, 684
  overview of, 678
  `TestDataStream.java`, 686–687
  `TestFileStream.java`, 682–683
  vs. text I/O, 679–680
Binary numbers, converting to/from decimal, 731
`binarySearch` method, `Arrays` class, 270–271
Binding properties
  `BindingDemo.java`, 544
  `ShowCircleCentered.java`, 542–543

Bits (binary digits), 3
Block comments, in `Welcome.java`, 12–13
Block style, programming style, 19
Blocks, in `Welcome.java`, 12–13
BMI (Body Mass Index), 89–90, 370–373
Boolean accessor method, 345
`boolean` data type
    `java.util.Random`, 334–335
    overview of, 76–78
Boolean expressions
    case study: determining leap year, 97–98
    conditional expressions, 103–104
    defined, 76
    `if` statements and, 78–79
    `if-else` statements, 80–81
    writing, 86–87
Boolean literals, 77
Boolean values
    defined, 76
    as format specifier, 146
    logical operators and, 93–94
    redundancy in testing, 84
Boolean variables
    assigning, 86
    overview of, 76–77
    redundancy in testing, 84
`BorderPane`
    overview of, 556
    `ShowBorderPane.java`, 557
Bottom-up implementation, 227–229
Boxing, converting wrapper object to primitive value, 383
Braces. *see* Curly braces ({})
`break` statements
    controlling loops, 184–187
    using with `switch` statements, 100
Breakpoints, setting for debugging, 106
Bubble sorts, 279
`BufferedInputStream` and `BufferedOutputStream`
    classes, 688–690
Bugs (logic errors), 21, 106
Bus, function of, 2–3
Button, 632–634
`ButtonBase`, 632–633
Button, `ButtonDemo.java`, 633–634
`byte` type, numeric types, 45
Bytecode
    translating Java source file into, 15
    verifier, 17
Bytes
    defined, 3
    measuring storage capacity in, 4

C

C, high-level languages, 8
C++, high-level languages, 8
Cable modems, 6
`Calendar` class, 503–504
Call stacks
    displaying in debugging, 106
    invoking methods and, 207
Calling
    methods, 206–208
    objects, 331
`canRead` method, `File` class, 474–475
`canWrite` method, `File` class, 474–475
`capacity` method, `StringBuilder` class, 395

Case sensitivity
    identifiers and, 39–40
    in `Welcome.java`, 14
Casting. *see* Type casting
Casting objects
    `CastingDemo.java` example, 428–431
    overview of, 427–428
Catching exceptions. *see also* `try-catch` blocks
    `catch` block omitted when `finally` clause is used, 467
    `CircleWithException.java` example, 463
    `InputMismatchExceptionDemo.java` example, 454–455
    overview of, 459–461
    `QuotientWithException.java` example, 521–522
CDs (compact discs), as storage device, 5
Cells
    in Sudoku grid, 298
    in tic-tac-toe case study, 657–662
Celsius, converting to/from Fahrenheit, 50–51, 236
Chained exceptions, 469–470
`char` data type. *see* Characters (`char` data type)
Characters (`char` data type)
    applying numeric operators to, 223–224
    in binary I/O, 684–685
    case study: counting monetary units, 63–65
    case study: ignoring nonalphanumeric characters when checking
        palindromes, 396–398
    casting to/from numeric types, 127
    comparing, 76
    constructing strings from arrays of, 386
    converting to strings, 389–390
    escape characters, 126
    finding, 136–137
    overview of, 125
    `RandomCharacter.java`, 224
    retrieving in strings, 131–132
    `TestRandomCharacter.java`, 224–225
    Unicode and ASCII and, 125–126
`charAt` (index) method
    retrieving characters in strings, 131–132
    `StringBuilder` class, 395
CheckBox, 634–636
Checked exceptions, 457
`Circle` class, 322
`Circle` and `Ellipse`
    overview, 565
    `ShowEllipse.java`, 566–567
Clarity, class design guidelines, 526
Class diagrams, UML, 323
Class loaders, 17
`ClassCastException`, 428
Classes
    abstract. *see* Abstract classes
    abstraction and encapsulation in, 366–367
    case study: designing class for stacks, 378–380
    case study: designing `Course` class, 376–377
    in `CircleWithPrivateDataFields.java` example, 345–346
    in `CircleWithStaticMembers.java` example, 338–339
    clients of, 325
    commenting, 18–19
    in `ComputeExpression.java`, 14–15
    data field encapsulation for maintaining, 344–345
    defining custom exception classes, 470–473
    defining for objects, 322–324
    design guidelines, 525–528
    identifiers, 39–40
    inner (nested) classes. *see* Inner (nested) classes
    from Java Library, 334

Classes (continued)
  names/naming conventions, 13, 44
  Point2D, 336–337
  preventing extension of, 442–443
  static variables, constants, and methods, 337–338
  in `TestCircleWithPrivateDataFields.java` example, 346–347
  in `TestCircleWithStaticMembers.java` example, 339–342
  in UML diagram, 324
  variable scope and, 337–338
  visibility modifiers, 342–344
  in `Welcome.java`, 12
  in `WelcomeWithThreeMessages.java`, 14
Classes, binary I/O
  `BufferedInputStream` and `BufferedOutputStream` classes, 688–690
  `DataInputStream` and `DataOutputStream` classes, 684–686
  `DetectEndOfFile.java`, 687–688
  `FileInputStream` and `FileOutputStream` classes, 681–683
  `FilterInputStream` and `FilterOutputStream` classes, 684
  overview of, 680–681
  `TestDataStream.java`, 686–687
  `TestFileStream.java`, 682–683
Class's contract, 366
`ClockPane` Class
  `ClockPane.java`, 574–577
  `DisplayClock.java`, 573–574
  `paintClock` method, 576–577
Clock speed, CPUs, 3
`clone` method, shallow and deep copies, 515–516
`Cloneable` interface
  `House.java` example, 514–517
  overview, 513–514
Closest pair problem, two-dimensional array applied to, 296–297
COBOL, high-level languages, 8
Code
  arrays for simplifying, 250–251
  comments and, 101
  incremental development, 161
  programming. *see* Programs/programming
  reuse. *see* Reusable code
  sharing. *see* Sharing code
  in software development process, 61–62
Coherent purpose, class design guidelines, 526
Columns (attributes), creating, 336–337
Combo boxes
  `ComboBoxDemo.java`, 645–646
  overview of, 644–645
Command-line arguments, 272–275
Comments
  code maintainability and, 101
  programming style and, 18
  in `Welcome.java`, 12–13
Common denominator, finding greatest common denominator. *see* Gcd (greatest common denominator)
Communication devices, computers and, 6–7
Compact discs (CDs), as storage device, 4–5
`Comparable` interface
  `ComparableRectangle.java` example, 511–512
  overview of, 509–510
  `Rational` class implementing, 522
  `SortComparableObjects.java` example, 510–511
  `SortRectangles.java` example, 512–513
`compareTo` method
  `Cloneable` interface and, 513
  `Comparable` interface defining, 509–510

`ComparableRectangle.java` example, 511–512
  implementing in `Rational` class, 522
  wrapper classes and, 381
`compareToIgnoreCase` method, strings, Comparing strings, Comparison operators, 76, 432
Compile errors (Syntax errors)
  common errors, 13–14
  debugging, 106
  programming errors, 20
Compilers
  ambiguous invocation and, 221
  reporting syntax errors, 20
  translating Java source file into bytecode file, 15–16
  translating source program into machine code, 8–9
Completeness, class design guidelines, 527
Complex numbers, `Math` class, 531
Components
  `TextFieldDemo.java`, 639–641
  ListView, 647–649
  `ListViewDemo.java`, 649–650, 661–662
  overview of, 629–630
  quiz and exercises, 668–676
  scroll bars, 651–652
  `ScrollBarDemo.java`, 652–653
  `SliderDemo.java`, 655–656
  sliders, 654
  summary, 668
  text area, 641–642
  `TextAreaDemo.java`, 644
Composition relationships
  between `ArrayList` and `MyStack`, 439–440
  aggregation and, 374–375
Compute expression, 14
Computers
  communication devices, 6–7
  CPUs, 3
  input/output devices, 5–6
  memory, 4
  OSs (operating systems), 9–10
  overview of, 2–3
  programming languages, 7–9
  storage devices, 4–5
`concat method`, 131
Concatenate strings, 36, 131
Conditional expressions, 103–104
Connect four game, 313
Consistency, class design guidelines, 526
Consoles
  defined, 12
  formatting output, 145–149
  input, 12
  output, 12
  reading input, 37–39
Constants
  class, 337–338
  declaring, 338
  identifiers, 39–40
  KeyCode constants, 604
  named constants, 43
  naming conventions, 44
  wrapper classes and, 381
Constructor chaining, 417–418
Constructors
  in abstract classes, 498
  for `BMI` class, 372
  calling subclass constructors, 416–417
  creating objects with, 329

creating **Random** objects, 335
for **DataInputStream** and **DataOutputStream**
  classes, 685
for **Date** class, 335
interfaces vs. abstract classes, 517
invoking with **this** reference, 374–375
for **Loan** class, 357–358
object methods and, 322–323
private, 344
in **SimpleCircle** example, 325–326
for **String** class, 386
for **StringBuilder** class, 393
in **TV.java** example, 327
UML diagram of, 324
wrapper classes and, 527
continue statements, for controlling loops, 184–187
Contract, object class as, 322
Control, 539–542
Control units, CPUs, 3
Control variables, in **for** loops, 171–172
Conversion methods, for wrapper classes, 381
Copying
  arrays, 256–257
  files, 691
Core, of CPU, 3
cos method, trigonometry, 120–121
Cosine function, 581
Counter-controlled loops, 159
Coupon collector's problem, 260
Course class, 376
CPUs (central processing units), 3
Curly braces ({ })
  in block syntax, 13
  dangers of omitting, 172
  forgetting to use, 83
currentTimeMillis method, 52
Cursor, mouse, 6

D

.dat files (binary), 680
Data, arrays for referencing, 246
Data fields
  accessing object data, 330–331
  encapsulating, 344–345, 526
  in interfaces, 508
  object state represented by, 322–323
  referencing, 331, 356–357
  in **SimpleCircle** example, 325–326
  in **TV.java** example, 327
  UML diagram of, 324
Data streams. *see* **DataInputStream/DataOutputStream** classes
Data types
  ADT (abstract data type), 366
  boolean, 76–78, 335
  char. *see* Characters (**char** data type)
  double. *see* **double** (double precision), numeric types
  float. *see* Floating-point numbers (**float** data type)
  fundamental. *see* Primitive types
  int. *see* Integers (**int** data type)
  long. *see* **long**, numeric types
  numeric, 44–46, 56–58
  reference types. *see* Reference types
  specifying, 35
  strings, 130
  types of, 41
  using abstract class as, 500

DataInputStream/DataOutputStream classes
  DetectEndOfFile.java, 687
  overview of, 684
  TestDataStream.java, 686
Date class
  case study: **Calendar** and **GregorianCalendar**
    classes, 503–504
  java.util, 334–335
De Morgan's law, 95
Debugging
  benefits of stepwise refinement, 232
  code modularization and, 215
  selections, 106
Decimal numbers
  BigDecimal class, 384–385
  converting to hexadecimals, 182–183, 217–219, 731
  converting to/from binary, 731
  division of, 51
Declaring constants, 43, 337
Declaring exceptions
  CircleWithException.java example, 463–464
  ReadData.java example, 478–479
  TestCircleWithCustomException.java example,
    471–472
  throws keyword for, 458
Declaring methods, static methods, 337
Declaring variables
  array variables, 246
  overview of, 40–41
  specifying data types and, 35–36
  two-dimensional array variables, 288–289
Decrement (--) operator, 55–56
Deep copies, 516
Default field values, for data fields, 331–332
Delete key, on keyboards, 6
Delimiters, token reading methods and, 479
Denominator. *see* Gcd (greatest
    common denominator)
Denominators, in rational numbers, 520
Deployment, in software development process, 60
DescriptionPane class, 642–643
Descriptive names
  benefits of, 40
  for variables, 35
Deserialization, of objects, 695
Design guidelines, classes, 525–528
Dial-up modems, 6
Digital subscriber lines (DSLs), 6
Digital versatile disc (DVDs), 5
Digits, matching, 98
Direct recursion, 709
Directories
  case study: determining directory size, 717
  DirectorySize.java, 717–718
  File class and, 474
  file paths, 473
Disks, as storage device, 5
Display message
  in **Welcome.java**, 12
  in **WelcomeWithThreeMessages.java**, 14
Divide-and-conquer strategy. *see* Stepwise
    refinement
Division (/=) assignment operator, 42
Division operator (/), 46, 50
Documentation, programming and, 18
Dot operator (.), 330
Dot pitch, measuring sharpness of displays, 6

`double` (double precision), numeric types
    converting characters and numeric values to strings, 389
    declaring variables and, 41
    `java.util.Random`, 335
    overview of numeric types, 45
    precision of, 178–179
`do-while` loops
    deciding when to use, 174–175
    overview of, 168–170
Downcasting objects, 427
`drawArc` method, 567–569
Drives, 5
DSLs (digital subscriber lines), 6
DVDs (Digital versatile disc), 5
Dynamic binding, inheritance and, 424–427

E

Eclipse
    built in debugging, 106
    creating/editing Java source code, 15
Eight Queens puzzle
    recursion, 734–735
    single-dimensional arrays, 281
Element type, specifying for arrays, 246
Emirp, 240
Encapsulation
    in `CircleWithPrivateDataFields.java` example, 345–346
    class design guidelines, 525–526
    of classes, 366–367
    of data fields, 344–345
    information hiding with, 225
    of `Rational` class, 525
Encoding schemes
    defined, 3–4
    mapping characters to binary equivalents, 125
End of file exception (`EOFException`), 687
End-of-line style, block styles, 19
Equal (=) operator, for assignment, 76
Equal to (==) operator, for comparison, 76
`equalArea` method, for comparing areas of geometric
    objects, 499
`Equals` method
    `Arrays` class, 271
    `Object` class, 422
`Error` class, 456, 458
Errors, programming. *see* Programming errors
Event delegation, 589
Event handlers/event handling, 587–588, 604, 597–599
Exception class
    exceptions in, 456
    extending, 470
    in `java.lang`, 471
    subclasses of, 456–457
Exception handling. *see also* Programming errors
    catching exceptions, 459–461, 463
    chained exceptions, 469–470
    checked and unchecked, 457
    `CircleWithException.java` example, 463–464
    `ClassCastException`, 428
    declaring exceptions (throws), 458, 463
    defined, 450
    defining custom exception classes, 470–473
    `EOFException`, 687
    in `Exception` class, 456
    `FileNotFoundException`, 681
    `finally` clause in, 466–467

getting information about exceptions, 461–462
in `House.java` example, 515
`InputMismatchExceptionDemo.java` example, 454
`IOException`, 456
key terms, 486
`NotSerializableException`, 695
overview of, 39, 449–450
quiz and exercises, 488–493
`Quotient.java` example, 450
`QuotientWithException.java` example, 452–454
`QuotientWithIf.java` example, 451
`QuotientWithMethod.java` example, 451–452
rethrowing exceptions, 468–469
summary, 487
`TestCircleWithException.java` example, 464–466
`TestException.java` example, 462
throwing exceptions, 458–459, 468
types of exceptions, 455–459
when to use exceptions, 467–468
Exception propagation, 459
Exclusive or (^) logical operator, 93–97
Execution stacks. *see* Call stacks
`exists` method, for checking file instances, 474
Explicit casting, 56–57, 427
Exponent method, `Math` class, 121
Exponent operations, 48
Expressions
    assignment statements and, 41–43
    behind the scene evaluation, 105
    Boolean. *see* Boolean expressions
    evaluating, 50–51
`extends` keyword, interface inheritance and, 518

F

Factorials
    case study: computing factorials, 706–707
    `ComputeFactorial.java`, 707–709
    `ComputeFactorialTailRecusion.java`,
        727–728
    tail recursion and, 727
`FadeTransition`, 612–613
Fahrenheit, converting Celsius to/from, 51, 235
Fall-through behavior, `switch` statements, 101
Feet, converting to/from meters, 236
`fib` method, 710–712
Fibonacci, Leonardo, 710
Fibonacci numbers
    case study: computing, 709–710
    `ComputeFibonacci.java`, 710–712
    computing recursively, 729
`FigurePanel` class
`File` class, 473–475, 678
File I/O. *see* I/O (input/output)
File pointers, random-access files and, 698
`FileInputStream`/`FileOutputStream` classes
    overview of, 681–682
    `TestFileStream.java`, 682–684
Files
    case study: copying files, 691
    case study: replacing text in, 480
    `File` class, 473–475, 678
    input/output, 476
    key terms, 486
    quiz and exercises, 488–493
    reading data from, 478–479
    reading data from Web, 482–484

summary, 487
`TestFileClass.java`, 475
writing data to, 476–477
`FilterInputStream/FilterOutputStream` classes, 684
`final` keyword, for declaring constants, 43
`final` modifier, for preventing classes from being extended, 442–443
`finally` clause, in exception handling, 466–467
`float` data type. *see* Floating-point numbers (`float` data type)
Floating-point literals, 49
Floating-point numbers (`float` data type)
approximation of, 66
converting to integers, 56
`java.util.Random`, 335
minimizing numeric errors related to loops, 178–179
numeric types for, 45
overview of numeric types, 45
specifying data types, 35
specifying precision, 147
Flowcharts
`do-while` loops, 169
`if` statements, 78–79
`if-else` statements, 80
`for` loops, 171
`switch` statements, 100
`while` loops, 158
`FlowLayout` class
`FlowPane`
`HBox` and `VBox`, 558
overview, 552
`ShowFlowPane.java`, 553
Font, `FontDemo.java`, 548
`for` loops
deciding when to use, 175
nesting, 176, 291
overview of, 170–174
processing arrays with, 249
variable scope and, 222–223
foreach (enhanced) loops, overview of, 251–253
Formal parameters. *see* Parameters
Format specifiers, 146–148
FORTRAN, high-level languages, 8
Fractals
case study, 722–723
H-tree fractals, 735
Koch snowflake fractal, 733
`SierpinskiTriangle.java`, 723–725
Frames (windows)
`ScrollBarDemo.java`, 652–653
`SliderDemo.java`, 655–656
Free cells, in Sudoku grid, 298
Function keys, on keyboards, 5
Functions, 205. *see also* Methods
Fundamental types (Primitive types). *see* Primitive types

G

Galton box, 280
Garbage collection, JVM and, 333
GBs (gigabytes), of storage, 4
Gcd (greatest common denominator)
case study: finding greatest common denominator, 179–181
computing recursively, 729
`gcd` method, 216, 424
`Rational` class and, 522
Genome, 367

`GeometricObject` class
`Circle.java` and `Rectangle.java`, 498
overview of, 496
`TestGeometricObject.java`, 498–499
`getAbsolutePath` method, `File` class, 574–575
`getArea` method, `SimpleCircle` example, 325
`getArray` method, 293–294
`getBMI` method, `BMI` class, 372
`getChars` method, converting strings into arrays, 389
`getDateCreated` method, `Date` class, 354
`getIndex` method, `ArrayList` class, 435
`getMinimumSpanningTree` method, `WeightedGraph` class, 107
`getPerimeter` method, `SimpleCircle` example, 325
`getRadius` method, `CircleWithPrivateDataFields.java` example, 346
`getRandomLowerCaseLetter` method, 261, 263
`getSize` method, finding directory size, 440
`getSource` method, events, 588
`getStackTrace` method, for getting information about exceptions, 462
`getStatus` method, `BMI` class, 372
Getter (accessor) methods
`ArrayList` class and, 436
encapsulation of data fields and, 344–347
Gigabytes (GBs), of storage, 4
Gigahertz (GHz), clock speed, 3
GMT (Greenwich Mean Time), 52
Gosling, James, 10
Graphical user interface (GUI), 630
Greater than (>) comparison operator, 76
Greater than or equal to (>=) comparison operator, 76
Greatest common denominator. *see* Gcd (greatest common denominator)
Greenwich Mean Time (GMT), 52
`GregorianCalendar` class
`Cloneable` interface and, 513–514
in `java.util` package, 361
overview of, 503–504
`TestCalendar.java`, 504–506
`GridPane`
overview, 555
`ShowGridPane.java`, 555–556
Grids, representing using two-dimensional array, 298

H

Hand-traces, for debugging, 106
Hangman game, 284, 490, 581
Hard disks, as storage device, 5
Hardware, 2
Has-a relationships
in aggregation models, 374–375
composition and, 440
`HBox` and `VBox`
definition, 560
overview, 558
`ShowHBoxVBox.java`, 559
Heaps, dynamic memory allocation and, 259
Helper methods, recursive
overview of, 714
`RecursivePalindrome.java`, 714–715
Hertz (Hz), clock speed in, 3
Hex integer literals, 49
Hexadecimal numbers, converting to/from decimal, 182–183, 217–219, 731
Hidden data fields, referencing, 356–357
High-level languages, 8–9
Hilbert curve, 736

Horizontal scroll bars, 652
Horizontal sliders, 654, 655
HTML (Hypertext Markup Language), 11
H-trees
    fractals, 735
    recursive approach to, 706
Hz (Hertz), clock speed in, 3

I

Icons. *see* Image icons
Identifiers, 39–40
IDEs (integrated development environments)for creating/editing Java source
        code, 11, 15–16
IEEE (Institute of Electrical and Electronics Engineers), floating point
        standard (IEEE 754), 45
`if` statements
    common errors, 83–87
    in computing body mass index, 89–90
    in computing taxes, 90–93
    conditional operator used with, 104
    nesting, 81
    overview of, 78–80
    `SimpleIfDemo.java` example, 79–80
`if-else` statements
    conditional expressions and, 112
    dangling else ambiguity, 84–85
    multi-way, 81–83
    overview of, 81–83
    recursion and, 712
`IllegalArgumentException` class, 459
`Image` , 549–552
`Image` class, 549
Image icons, 646
Images, `ShowImage.java`, 550–551
`ImageView` , 549–552
Immutable
    `BigInteger` and `BigDecimal` classes, 384–385
    class, 354
    objects, 353–354
    `Rational` class, 525
    `String` object, 386–387
    wrapper classes, 381
Implementation (coding), in software development process,
        61–62
Implementation methods, 229–232
Implicit casting, 127, 427
Importing, types of `import` statements, 38
Increment (++) operator, 55–56
`increment` method, in `Increment.java` example, 212–213
Incremental development
    benefits of stepwise refinement, 232
    coding incrementally, 161
    testing and, 62
Indentation, programming style, 19
Indexed variables Elements, 248
Indexes
    accessing elements in arrays, 246, 248
    finding characters/substrings in a string, 136–137
    string index range, 131
`indexOf` method, 136–137
Indirect recursion, 709
Infinite loops, 160
Infinite recursion, 709
Information
    getting information about exceptions, 461–462
    hiding (encapsulation), 225

Inheritance
    `ArrayList` object, 432–433
    calling subclass constructors, 416–417
    calling superclass methods, 418–419
    case study: custom stack class, 439–440
    casting objects and, 427–428
    `CastingDemo.java` example, 427–431
    `CircleFromGeometricObject.java`
        example, 412–414
    constructor chaining and, 417–418
    `DistinctNumbers.java` example, 436–438
    dynamic binding and, 424–427
    `equals` method of `Object` class, 431–432
    interface inheritance, 506–507, 518
    is-a relationships and, 440
    key terms, 443
    `Object` class and, 422–423
    overriding methods and, 420–422
    overview of, 409–410
    preventing classes from being extended or overridden, 442–443
    `protected` data and methods, 440–442
    questions and exercises, 448–493
    `RectangleFromGeometricObject.java` example, 414–415
    `SimpleGeometricObject.java` example, 411–412
    summary, 443–444
    `TestArrayList.java` example, 433–436
    `TestCircleRectangle.java` example, 415–416
    using `super` keyword, 416
Initializing variables
    AnalyzeNumbers.java, 253–254
    arrays, 249–250
    declaring variables and, 41
    multidimensional arrays, 289
    two-dimensional arrays, 291
Inner (nested) classes
    anonymous, 594–595
    `AnonymousListenerDemo.java`, 595–597
    for defining listener classes, 593–594
    `KeyEventDemo.java`, 604
    `TicTacToe.java`, 658–659
Input. *see also* I/O (input/output)
    reading from console, 37–40
    redirecting using `while` loops, 168–169
    runtime errors, 20–21
    streams. *see* `InputStream` classes
Input, process, output (IPO), 39
`InputMismatchException` class, 454–455, 479
Input/output devices, computers and, 5–6
`InputStream` classes
    `BufferedInputStream`, 688–690
    case study: copying files, 691
    `DataInputStream`, 684–686
    deserialization and, 695
    `DetectEndOfFile.java`, 687–688
    `FileInputStream`, 681–682
    `FilterInputStream`, 684
    `ObjectInputStream`, 692–693
    overview of, 680–681
    `TestDataStream.java`, 686–687
    `TestFileStream.java`, 682–683
    `TestObjectInputStream.java`, 694
Insert key, on keyboards, 6
Instance methods
    accessing object data and methods, 330–331
    in `CircleWithStaticMembers.java`, 338–339
    class design guidelines, 325–328

invoking, 368, 371
   when to use instance methods vs. static, 338–339
Instance variables
   accessing object data and methods, 305
   class design guidelines, 392–393
   static variables compared with, 337–339
   in `TestCircleWithStaticMembers.java`, 339
   when to use instance variables vs. static, 341
Instances. *see also* Objects
   checking file instantiation, 474
   checking object instantiation, 322, 428
Institute of Electrical and Electronics Engineers (IEEE), floating point
   standard (IEEE 754), 45
`int` data type. *see* Integers (`int` data type)
Integer literals, 49
Integers (`int` data type)
   `ArrayList` for, 437
   `BigInteger` class, 387–385
   casting to/from `char` types, 127
   converting characters and numeric values to strings, 389–390
   declaring variables and, 40
   division of, 46, 51, 450–454
   finding larger between two, 205
   floating-point numbers converted to, 56–57
   `java.util.Random`, 335–336
   numeric types for, 44–45
   specifying data types, 35
Integrated development environments (IDEs), 11–12,
   15–16
   for creating/editing Java source code, 15–16
   overview of, 11–12
Intelligent guesses, 161
Interfaces
   abstract classes compared with, 517–520
   benefits of, 512
   case study: `Rational` class, 520–521
   `Cloneable` interface, 513–514
   `Comparable` interface, 509–510
   `ComparableRectangle.java` example, 511–512
   for defining common class behaviors, 560
   `House.java` example, 514–517
   key terms, 528
   overview of, 496
   questions and exercises, 528–533
   `SortComparableObjects.java` example,
   510–512
   `SortRectangles.java` example, 512–513
   summary, 528–529
   `TestEdible.java` example, 506–509
Interned strings, 386–387
Interpreters, translating source program into machine code, 10–11
Invoking methods, 206–207, 331
I/O (input/output)
   binary I/O classes, 680–681
   `BufferedInputStream` and `BufferedOutputStream` classes,
   688–690
   case study: copying files, 391
   case study: replacing text, 580–581
   `Copy.java`, 691–692
   `DataInputStream` and `DataOutputStream` classes, 684–686
   `DetectEndOfFile.java`, 687–688
   `FileInputStream` and `FileOutputStream` classes, 681–682
   `FilterInputStream` and `FilterOutputStream` classes, 684
   handling text I/O in Java, 678–679
   key terms, 700
   object I/O, 692–693
   overview of, 476, 677–678

questions and exercises, 701–704
random-access files, 697–699
reading data from file using `Scanner` class, 478–480
reading data from Web, 482–484
`serializable` interface, 695–696
serializing arrays, 696–697
summary, 701
`TestDataStream.java`, 686–687
`TestFileStream.java`, 682–683
`TestObjectInputStream.java`, 694
`TestObjectOutputStream.java`, 693–694
`TestRandomAccessFile.java`, 699–700
text I/O vs. binary I/O, 679–680
types of I/O devices, 5–6
writing data to file using `PrintWriter` class, 476–477
`IOException`, 681–682
IPO (input, process, output), 39
Is-a relationships
   design guide for when to use interfaces vs. classes, 518
   inheritance and, 440
`isAbsolute` method, `File` class, 474–475
`isDigit` method, `Character` class, 144
`isDirectory` method, `File` class, 474–475
`isFile` method, `File` class, 474–475
`isHidden` method, `File` class, 474–475
Is-kind-of relationships, 518
`isPalindrome` method
   `RecursivePalindrome.java`, 714–715
   as tail-recursive method, 727
`isPrime` method, prime numbers, 217
`isValid` method, applying to grid, 300
Iteration/iterators
   loops and, 158
   recursion compared with, 726

J

`java` command, for executing Java program, 17
Java Development Toolkit (JDK)
   jdb debugger in, 106
   overview of, 11–12
Java EE (Java Enterprise Edition), 12
JavaFX
   `Arc`, 567–569
   binding properties, 542–544
   `BorderPane`, 556–558
   case study: `ClockPane Class`, 572–577
   `Circle` and `Ellipse`, 565–567
   `Color` class, 546–547
   `FlowPane`, 552–554
   `Font` class, 547–549
   `GridPane`, 555–556
   `HBox` and `VBox`, 558–560
   `Image` and `ImageView` Classes, 549–552
   key terms, 577
   Layout panes, 552
   `Line`, 562–563
   nodes, 545–546
   panes, 539–540
   `Polygon` and `Polyline`, 569–572
   quiz and exercises, 578–583
   `Rectangle`, 564–565
   shapes, 560
   structure, 536–539
   summary, 577–578
   `Text`, 560–562
   vs Swing and AWT, 536

JavaFX CSS, 545
JavaFX UI controls
    `BounceBallSlider.java`, 656
    button, 632–634
    `ButtonDemo.java`, 633–634
    case study: developing tic-tac-toe game,
       657–662
    case study: national flags and anthems, 665–667
    `CheckBox`, 634–636
    `CheckBoxDemo.java`, 635–636
    `ComboBox`, 644–647
    `ComboBoxDemo.java`, 646–647
    `DescriptionPane.java`, 642–643
    `Labeled` and `Label`, 630–632
    `LabelWithGraphic.java`, 630–632
    `ListView`, 647–651
    `ListViewDemo.java`, 649–650
    `MediaDemo.java`, 663–665
    programming exercises, 668–676
    quiz, 668
    `RadioButton`, 637–639
    `RadioButtonDemo.java`, 638–639
    `ScrollBar`, 651–653
    `ScrollBarDemo.java`, 652–653
    `Slider`, 654–657
    `SliderDemo.java`, 655
    `TextArea`, 641–644
    `TextAreaDemo.java`, 644
    `Textfield`, 639–641
    `TextFieldDemo.java`, 639–641
    `TicTacToe.java`, 658–661
    video and audio, 662–665
Java language specification, 11–12
Java Library, 334
Java ME (Java Micro Edition), 12
Java programming
    creating, compiling, and executing programs, 15–18
    displaying text in message dialog box, 23
    high-level languages, 8
    introduction to, 11–12
    simple examples, 12–15
Java SE (Java Standard Edition), 12
Java Virtual Machine. *see* JVM (Java Virtual Machine)
`javac` command, for compiling Java program, 17
Javadoc comments (`/**.*/`), 18
`java.io`
    `File` class, 473–475
    `PrintWriter` class, 476–477
    `RandomAccessFile` class, 698
`java.lang`
    `Comparable` interface, 509
    `Exception` class, 471
    `Number` class, 501
    packages, 62
    `Throwable` class, 455–457, 461–462
`java.net`
    `MalformedURLException` class, 483
    `URL` class, 483
`java.util`
    `Arrays` class, 270–272
    `Calandar` class, 503–504
    `Date` class, 334–335, 384
    `EventObject` class, 588–589
    `GregorianCalendar` class, 361, 503–504
    `Random` class, 335–336
    `Scanner` class, 38, 578–480

jdb debugger, 106
JDK (Java Development Toolkit)
    Fork/Join Framework in JDK 7
    jdb debugger in, 106
    overview of, 11–12
JVM (Java Virtual Machine)
    defined, 16
    detecting runtime errors, 450
    garbage collection, 256
    heap as storage area in, 259
    interned string and, 387

K

KBs (kilobytes), 4
Key constants, 604
Keyboards, 5–6
`KeyEvents`
    `ControlCircleWithMouseAndKey.java`, 605–606
    `KeyEventDemo.java`, 604–605
    overview of, 603–604
`KeyListener` interface, 603
Keywords (reserved words)
    `break` and `continue`, 184–187
    `extends`, 518
    `final`, 43
    `super`, 416
    `throw`, 158–459
    `throws`, 458
    `transient`, 295
    in `Welcome.java`, 13
Kilobytes (KBs), 4
Knight's Tour, 733–734
Koch snowflake fractal, 733

L

Label, 630–632
Labeled, 630–632
Labels, `LabelWithGraphic.java`, 630–632
Lambda expression, 597–599
LANs (local area networks), 6
`lastIndexOf` method, strings, 136–137
`lastModified` method, `File` class, 174–175
Latin square, 318–319
Layout panes
    `BorderPane`, 556–558
    `FlowPane`, 552–554
    `GridPane`, 555–556
    `HBox` and `VBox`, 558–560
Length, strings, 130–131, 395
`length` method, `File` class, 474–475
Letters, counting, 263–264
Libraries, APIs as, 11–12
`Line`
    overview, 562
    `ShowLine.java`, 562–563
Line comments, in `Welcome.java`, 13
Line numbers, in `Welcome.java`, 12
Linear searches, arrays, 265–266
Linux OS, 9
Lists, `ListViewDemo.java`, 649–650
`ListView`, 647–651
Literals
    Boolean literals, 77
    character literals, 125

constructing strings from string literal, 386
defined, 48
floating-point literals, 49
integer literals, 49
Loans
    Loan calculator case study, in event-driven programming, 600–602
    `Loan.java` object, 368–370
Local area networks (LANs), 6
Local variables, 222
Locker puzzle, 281
Logic errors (bugs), 21, 106
Logical operators (Boolean operators)
    overview of, 93
    `TestBooleanOperators.java` example, 94–96
    truth tables, 93–94
Long, numeric types
    converting characters and numeric values to strings, 389–390
    integer literals and, 49
    `java.util.Random`, 335–336
    overview of numeric types, 45
Loop body, 158
Loop-continuation-condition
    `do-while` loop, 168–169
    loop design and, 163
    in multiple subtraction quiz, 164
    overview of, 158–159
Loops
    `break` and `continue` keywords as controls in, 184–187
    case study: displaying prime numbers, 188–190
    case study: finding greatest common denominator, 179–181
    case study: guessing numbers, 161–163
    case study: multiple subtraction quiz, 164–165
    case study: predicting future tuition, 181
    creating arrays, 257
    deciding which to use, 174–176
    design strategies, 163
    `do-while` loop, 168–170
    input and output redirections, 167–168
    iteration compared with recursion, 726
    key terms, 190
    `for` loop, 170–174
    minimizing numeric errors related to, 178–179
    nesting, 176–177
    overview of, 158
    quiz and exercises, 191–201
    sentinel-controlled, 165–167
    summary, 191
    `while` loop, 158–161
Low-level languages, 7

M

Mac OS, 9
Machine language
    bytecode compared with, 16
    overview of, 7
    translating source program into, 8–9
Machine stacks. *see* Call stacks
Main class
    defined, 323
    in `TestSimpleCircle.java` example, 324
`main` method
    in `ComputeExpression.java`, 114–15
    invoking, 207
    main class vs., 323

receiving string arguments from command line, 272–273
    in `SimpleCircle.java` example, 326–327
    in `TestSimpleCircle.java` example, 324
    in `TestTV.java` example, 328–329
    in `Welcome.java`, 13
    in `WelcomeWithThreeMessages.java`, 14
Maintenance, in software development process, 60
`MalformedURLException` class, 483
Marker interfaces, 513
Match braces, in `Welcome.java`, 13
`matches` method, strings, 342
`Math` class
    `BigInteger` and `BigDecimal` classes, 384–385
    complex numbers, 531–532
    exponent methods, 121
    invoking object methods, 331
    methods generally, 120
    `pow(a, b)` method, 48
    `random` method, 87–88, 98–99, 122
    rounding methods, 121–122
    service methods, 122
    trigonometric methods, 120–121
Matrices, two-dimensional arrays for storing, 288–289
`max` method
    defining and invoking, 206–208
    overloading, 220
    overview of, 122
`maxRow` variable, for finding largest sum, 292
Mbps (million bits per second), 6
MBs (megabytes), of storage, 4
`Media`, 662–665
`MediaPlayer`, 662–665
`MediaView`, 662–665
Megabytes (MBs), of storage, 4
Megahertz (MHz), clock speed, 3
Memory, computers, 3–4
Mersenne prime, 240
`MessagePanel` class
    `DisplayClock.java`, 573–574
    `ClockPane.java`, 574–576
Meters, converting to/from feet, 236
Method header, 205
Method modifiers, 205
Method signature, 205
Methods
    abstraction and, 225–226
    accessing object methods, 330–331
    calling, 206–208
    case study: converting decimals to hexadecimals, 182–183
    case study: generating random numbers, 223–225
    class, 337–338
    commenting, 18
    defining, 204–206
    identifiers, 39–40
    implementation details, 229–232
    invoking, 206–208, 331
    key terms, 232
    modularizing code, 215–217
    naming conventions, 44
    object actions defined by, 322–323
    overloading, 219–222
    overview of, 203–204
    passing arrays to, 257–260
    passing objects to, 347–351
    passing parameters by values, 212–215

Methods (continued)
passing to two-dimensional arrays, 293–294
quiz and exercises, 234–244
recursive methods, 706
returning arrays from, 260–261
rounding, 121
static. *see* Static methods
stepwise refinement, 225–226, 232
summary, 233
top-down and/or bottom-up implementation, 227–229
top-down design, 226–227
tracing or stepping over as debugging technique, 106
trigonometric, 120–121
variable scope and, 222–223
void method example, 209–211
MHz (Megahertz), clock speed, 3
Microsoft Windows, 9
Million bits per second (Mbps), 6
min method, **Math** class, 122
Mnemonics, in assembly language, 7
Modems (modulator/demodulator), 6
Modifier keys, on keyboards, 5
Modifiers, method modifier, 205
Modularizing code
GreatestCommonDivisorMethod.java, 215–216
overview of, 215
PrimeNumberMethod.java, 216–217
Monitors (displays), 6
Motherboard, 3
Mouse, as I/O device, 6
MouseEvents
ControlCircleWithMouseAndKey.java, 605–606
event-driven programming, 602–603
MouseEvent, 602–603
Multi-dimensional arrays. *see* Arrays, multi-dimensional
Multimedia. *see* JavaFX UI controls
Multiple choice test, 294–296
Multiplication (*=) assignment operator, 54
Multiplication operator (*), 15, 46, 50
Multiplication table, 176
Multiplicities, in object composition, 373
Multiprocessing, 10
Multiprogramming, 10
Multithreading, 10
Multi-way **if-else** statements
in computing taxes, 90–93
overview of, 81–83
Mutator methods. *see* Setter (mutator) methods

N

Named constants. *see* Constants
Naming conventions
class design guidelines, 526
interfaces, 518
programming and, 44
wrapper classes, 380
Naming rules, identifiers, 39–40
N-by-*n* matrix, 238
Negative angles, drawing arcs, 569
Nested classes. *see* Inner (nested) classes
Nested **if** statements
in computing body mass index, 89–90
in computing taxes, 90–93
overview of, 81

Nested loops, 176–177, 291
NetBeans
built in debugging, 106
for creating/editing Java source code, 15
Network interface cards (NICs), 6
new operator
creating arrays, 246–247
creating objects, 329
next method, whitespace characters and, 133
nextLine method, whitespace characters and, 133
Next-line style, block styles, 19
NICs (network interface cards), 6
No-arg constructors
class design guidelines, 526
Loan class, 368
wrapper classes not having, 381
Node, 536–539
Nodes, **JavaFX**, 545–546
Not (**!**) logical operator, 93–97
Not equal to (**!=**) comparison operator, 76
NotSerializableException, 695
null values, objects, 331–332
NullPointerException, as runtime error, 332
Number class
case study: abstract number class, 501
as root class for numeric wrapper classes, 585
Numbers/numeric types
abstract number class, 501–503
binary. *see* Binary numbers
case study: converting hexadecimals to decimals, 217–219
case study: displaying prime numbers, 188–190
case study: generating random numbers, 223–225
case study: guessing numbers, 161–163
casting to/from **char** types, 127
conversion between numeric types, 56–58, 364
converting to/from strings, 389–390
decimal. *see* Decimal numbers
double. *see* **double**
floating-point. *see* Floating-point numbers (**float** data type)
generating random numbers, 87–88
GreatestCommonDivisorMethod.java, 215–216
integers. *see* Integers (**int** data type)
LargestNumbers.java, 502–503
overview of, 44–46
PrimeNumberMethod.java, 216–217
processing large numbers, 384–385
Numerators, in rational numbers, 520
Numeric keypads, on keyboards, 5
Numeric literals, 48–49
Numeric operators
applied to characters, 127
overview of, 46–47

O

Object class, 422–423, 431–432
Object I/O. *see* **ObjectInputStream/ObjectOutputStream** classes
Object member access operator (**.**), 330, 429
Object reference variables, 330
ObjectInputStream/ObjectOutputStream classes
overview of, 692–693
serializable interface, 695–696
Serializing arrays, 696–697
TestObjectInputStream.java, 694
TestObjectOutputStream.java, 693–694
Object-oriented programming (OOP), 322, 330, 370–373

Objects
  accessing data and methods of, 330–331
  accessing via reference variables, 330
  array of, 351–352
  `ArrayList` class, 432–433
  arrays as, 259
  automatic conversion between primitive types and wrapper class types, 383–384
  `BigInteger` and `BigDecimal` classes, 384–385
  cannot be created from abstract classes, 500
  case study: designing class for stacks, 378–380
  case study: designing `Course` class, 376–377
  casting, 427–428
  `CircleWithPrivateDataFields.java` example, 345–346
  `CircleWithStaticMembers.java` example, 338–339
  class abstraction and encapsulation, 366–367
  class design guidelines, 525–527
  classes from Java Library, 334
  comparing primitive variables with reference variables, 332–334
  composing, 374–375
  constructors, 329
  creating, 324–325
  data field encapsulation for maintaining classes, 344–345
  `Date` class, 334–335
  defining classes for, 322–324
  `equals` method of `Object` class, 431–432
  event listener object, 589
  event objects, 588
  immutable, 353–354
  inheritance. *see* inheritance
  key terms, 358, 399
  `Loan.java`, 368–370
  `null` values, 331–332
  `Object` class, 422–423
  object-oriented thinking, 370–373
  overview of, 321–322, 365–366
  passing to methods, 347–351
  polymorphism, 123
  processing primitive data type values as, 380–383
  quiz and exercises, 359–364, 399–408
  `Random` class, 355–356
  reference data fields and, 331
  `SimpleCircle.java` example, 324–325
  static variables, constants, and methods and, 337–338
  summary, 359, 398–399
  `TestCircleWithPrivateDataFields.java` example, 346–347
  `TestCircleWithStaticMembers.java` example, 339–342
  `TestLoanClass.java`, 367–368
  `TestSimpleCircle.java` example, 324–326
  `TestTV.java` example, 328–329
  `this` reference and, 356–358
  `TotalArea.java` example, 352–353
  `TV.java` example, 327–328
  variable scope and, 355–356
  visibility modifiers, 342–344
Octal integer literals, 49
Off-by-one errors
  arrays and, 251
  in loops, 160
OOP (object-oriented programming), 322, 330, 370–373
Operands
  defined, 46
  incompatible, 95
Operators
  assignment operator (=), 41–43
  augmented assignment operators, 54–55
  comparison operators, 76

  increment and decrement operators, 55–56
  numeric operators, 46–47
  precedence and associativity, 104–106
  precedence rules, 50–51
  unary and binary, 47
Option buttons. *See* Radio buttons
Or (`||`) logical operator, 93–97
OSs (operating systems)
  overview of, 9
  tasks of, 9–10
Output. *see also* I/O (input/output)
  redirection, 167–168
  streams, 678–679
`OutputStream` classes
  `BufferedOutputStream`, 688–690
  case study: copying files, 691–692
  `DataOutputStream`, 684–686
  `DetectEndOfFile.java`, 687
  `FileOutputStream`, 681–682
  `FilterOutputStream`, 684
  `ObjectOutputStream`, 692–693
  overview of, 680–681
  serialization and, 695
  `TestDataStream.java`, 686–687
  `TestFileStream.java`, 682–683
  `TestObjectOutputStream.java`, 693–694
Overflows
  `Rational` class, 524
  variables, 45
Overloading methods, 219–222
Overriding methods, 419–422

P

π (pi), estimating, 237
Package-private (package-access) visibility
    modifiers, 342
Packages
  organizing classes in, 343
  organizing programs in, 18
Page Down key, on keyboards, 5
Page Up key, on keyboards, 5
Palindromes
  case study: checking if string is a palindrome, 187–188
  case study: ignoring nonalphanumeric characters when checking palindromes, 396–398
  palindrome integers, 234
  palindromic primes, 240
  `RecursivePalindrome.java`, 714–715
  `RecursivePalindromeUsingSubstring.java`, 713–714
Panels
  `ButtonInPane.java`, 540
  `MessagePanel` class. *see* `MessagePanel` class
Parameters
  actual parameters, 205
  defining methods and, 204–205
  as local variable, 222
  order association, 212
  passing by values, 212–215
  variable-length argument lists, 264–265
Parent, 539
Parentheses (`( )`)
  defining and invoking methods and, 225
  in `Welcome.java`, 14
Parsing methods, 382
Pascal, high-level languages, 8

Pass-by-sharing
  arrays to methods, 258
  objects to methods, 348–349
Pass-by-value
  arrays to methods, 258
  `Increment.java` example, 212–213
  objects to methods, 347–348
  overview of, 212
  `TestPassByValue.java` example, 213–215
`PasswordField`, 641
`PathTransition`, 609–612
Passwords, checking if string is valid password, 238
Pentagonal numbers, 234
Pixels (picture elements)
  measuring resolution in, 6
`Polygon` and `Polyline`
  overview, 569
  `ShowPolygon.java`, 570–571
Polymorphism
  `CastingDemo.java` example, 428–431
  overview of, 423
  `PolymorphismDemo.java` example, 423
Postfix decrement operator, 55–56
Postfix increment operator, 55–56
`pow method`, `Math` class, 48
Precedence, operator, 104–106
Prefix decrement operator, 55–56
Prefix increment operator, 55–56
Prime numbers
  case study: displaying prime numbers, 188–190
  `PrimeNumberMethod.java`, 216–217
  types of, 240
Primitive types (fundamental types)
  automatic conversion between primitive types and wrapper class types, 383–384
  casting, 429
  comparing parameters of primitive type with parameters of reference types, 349
  comparing primitive variables with reference variables, 332–334
  converting wrapper object to/from (boxing/unboxing), 383
  creating arrays of, 351
`print` method, `PrintWriter` class, 38, 476–477
`printf` method, `PrintWriter` class, 476
Printing arrays, 291
`println` method, `PrintWriter` class, 38, 476
`printStackTrace` method, 461
`PrintWriter` class
  case study: replacing text, 480–482
  writing data to file using, 476–477
  for writing text data, 678
`private`
  encapsulation of data fields and, 344–345
  visibility modifier, 343–344, 440–443
Problems
  breaking into subproblems, 190
  creating programs to address, 34
  solving with recursion, 712–713
Procedural paradigm, compared with object-oriented paradigm, 372–373
Procedures, 205. *see also* Methods
Processing arrays, 249–251
Programming errors. *see also* Exception handling
  `ClassCastException`, 428
  debugging, 106
  logic errors, 21–23
  minimizing numeric errors related to loops, 178–179
  runtime errors, 20–21

selections, 83–87
  syntax errors, 14, 20
Programming languages
  assembly language, 7
  high-level languages, 8–9
  Java. *see* Java programming
  machine language, 7
  overview of, 2
Programming style
  block styles, 19
  comments and, 19
  indentation and spacing, 19
  overview of, 18–19
Programs/programming
  assignment statements and expressions, 41–43
  augmented assignment operators, 54–55
  case study: counting monetary units, 63–65
  case study: displaying current time, 52–53
  character data type, 125–130
  coding incrementally, 161
  evaluating expressions and operator precedence rules, 50–51
  exponent operations, 48
  identifiers, 39–40
  increment and decrement operators, 55–56
  introduction to, 34
  with Java language. *see* Java programming
  key terms, 67
  modularizing code, 215–217
  named constants, 43
  naming conventions, 44
  numeric literals, 48–50
  numeric operators, 46–47
  numeric type conversions, 56–58
  numeric types, 44–45
  overview of, 2
  questions and exercises, 68–74
  reading input from console, 37–39
  recursive methods in, 706
  software development process, 59–63
  `string` data type, 130–139
  summary, 67–68
  variables, 40–41
  writing a simple program, 34–37
`protected`
  data and methods, 440–442
  visibility modifier, 343–344, 440–442
Pseudocode, 34
Public classes, 325
`public` method, 346
`public` visibility modifier, 342–344, 440–442
Python, high-level languages, 8

Q

Quincunx, 280
Quotients
  `Quotient.java` example, 450
  `QuotientWithException.java` example, 452–454
  `QuotientWithIf.java` example, 451
  `QuotientWithMethod.java` example, 451–452

R

Radio buttons, `RadioButtonDemo.java`, 638–639
Ragged arrays, 290–291
RAM (random-access memory), 4–5

Random class, **java.util**, 335–336
random method
    case study: generating random numbers, 223–225
    case study: lottery, 98–99
    Math class, 87–88, 122
Random numbers
    case study: generating random numbers, 223–225
    case study: lottery, 98–99
    generating, 87–88
Random-access files
    overview of, 697–699
    TestRandomAccessFile.java, 699–700
Random-access memory (RAM), 4–5
Rational class
    overview of, 520–521
    Rational.java example, 522–525
    TestRationalClass.java example, 521–522
Rational numbers, representing and processing, 520–522
readASolution method, applying to Sudoku grid, 300
Read-only streams, 697
Rectangle
    overview, 564
    ShowRectangle.java, 564–565
Recursion
    binary searches, 716–717
    case study: computing factorials, 706–707
    case study: computing Fibonacci numbers, 709–710
    case study: determining directory size, 717
    case study: fractals, 722–723
    case study: Towers of Hanoi, 719–721
    ComputeFactorial.java, 707–709
    ComputeFactorialTailRecursion.java, 727–728
    ComputeFibonacci.java, 710–712
    DirectorySize.java, 717–719
    helper methods, 714
    iteration compared with, 726–727
    key terms, 728
    overview of, 706
    problem solving by thinking recursively, 712–713
    questions and exercises, 728–736
    RecursivePalindrome.java, 714–715
    RecursivePalindromeUsingSubstring.java,
       713–714
    RecursiveSelectionSort.java, 715–716
    selection sorts, 715
    SierpinskiTriangle.java, 723–724
    summary, 728
    tail recursion, 727
    TowersOfHanoi.java, 721–722
Recursive methods, 706
Reduction, characteristics of recursion, 712
Reference types
    classes as, 330
    comparing parameters of primitive type with parameters of reference
       types, 349
    comparing primitive variables with, 332–334
    reference data fields, 331–332
    string data type as, 130
Reference variables
    accessing objects with, 330
    array of objects as array of, 352
    comparing primitive variables with, 332–334
regionMatches method, strings, 134–135
Register listeners
    ControlCircle.java, 592–593
    ControlCircleWithMouseAndKey.java, 605–606
    KeyEventDemo.java, 604

LoanCalculator.java, 600
    overview of, 589–590
Regular expressions, matching strings with, 388
Relative file names, 473–474
Remainder (%) or modulo operator, 46, 50
Remainder (%=) assignment operator, 54–55
replace method, strings, 388
replaceAll method, strings, 388
replaceFirst method, strings, 388
Requirements specification, in software development process,
    59–60
Reserved words. *see* Keywords (reserved words)
Resources, role of OSs in allocating, 9
Responsibilities, separation as class design principle, 526
return statements, 207
Return value type
    constructors not having, 329
    in defining methods, 205
Reusable code
    benefits of stepwise refinement, 232
    code modularization and, 215
    method enabling, 208
    methods for, 204
reverse method
    returning arrays from methods, 260–261
Rounding methods, **Math** class, 122
Runtime errors
    debugging, 106
    declaring, 457–458
    exception handling and, 39, 450
    NullPointerException as, 332
    programming errors, 21
Runtime stacks. *see* Call stacks

S

Scanner class
    obtaining input with, 67
    for reading console input, 37–39
    reading data from file using, 478–479
    for reading text data, 678
Scanners
    case study: replacing text, 480–481
    creating, 454
Scene, 536–539
Scheduling operations, 10
Scientific notation, of integer literals, 49–50
Scope, of variables, 42, 222–223
Screen resolution, 6
Scroll bars
    overview of, 651
    ScrollBarDemo.java, 652–653
Scroll panes
    DescriptionPanel.java, 643
    overview of, 641
    scrolling lists, 648
Searches
    arrays, 265
    binary searches, 266–269, 716–717
    linear searches, 265–266
    recursive approach to searching for words, 706
Selection sorts
    arrays, 265, 269–270
    RecursiveSelectionSort.java,
       715–716
    using recursion, 715
Selection statements, 76, 78, 724–727

Selections
  `Addition.Quiz.java` example, 77–78
  `boolean` data type, 76–78
  case study: computing Body Mass Index, 89–90
  case study: computing taxes, 90–93
  case study: determining leap year, 97
  case study: guessing birthdays, 139–142
  case study: lottery, 98–99
  common errors, 83–84
  conditional expressions, 103–104
  debugging, 106
  formatting console output, 145–146
  generating random numbers, 87–88
  `if` statements, 78–79
  `if-else` statements, 80–81
  key terms, 107
  logical operators, 93–97
  nested `if` statements and multi-way `if-else` statements, 81–83
  operator precedence and associativity, 104–106
  overview of, 76
  questions and exercises, 108–118
  summary and exercises, 107
  `switch` statements, 100–103
Semicolons (;), common errors, 83
Sentinel-controlled loops, 165–167
Sequential files, input/output streams, 697
Serialization
  of arrays, 696–697
  of objects, 695
`setLength` method, `StringBuilder` class, 395–396
`setRadius` method
  `CircleWithPrivateDataFields.java` example, 346
  `SimpleCircle` example, 325
Setter (mutator) methods
  `ArrayList` class and, 436
  encapsulation of data fields and, 344–347
Shallow copies, `clone` method and, 515–516
Shapes, 539–542
  `Arc`, 567–569
  `Circle` and `Ellipse`, 565–567
  `Line`, 562–563
  `Polygon` and `Polyline`, 569–572
  `Rectangle`, 564–565
  `text`, 560–562
Sharing code, 208
`short`, numeric types, 45
Short-circuited OR operator, 96
Shortest paths, finding with graph, 117
Shuffling arrays, 250–251, 292
Sierpinski triangle
  case study, 722–723
  computing recursively, 729, 735–736
  `SierpinskiTriangle.java`, 723–726
`sin` method, trigonometry, 120–121
Single precision numbers. *see* Floating-point numbers (float data type)
Single-dimensional arrays. *see* Arrays, single-dimensional
Singly linked lists. *see* `LinkedList` class
Sinking sorts, 280
Sliders
  overview of, 654
  `SliderDemo.java`, 655–656
Software
  development process, 59–61
  programs as, 2
`sort` method
  `Arrays` class, 270–271
  `ComparableRectangle.java` example, 511–512

`SortRectangles.java` example, 512–513
  using recursion, 715–716
Sorting arrays
  bubble sorts, 279
  overview of, 269
  selection sorts, 265, 269–270
Source objects, event sources and, 588–589
Source program or source code, 7, 39–40
Spacing, programming style and, 18
Special characters, 14
Specific import, 18
`split` method, strings, 388, 389
`StackOfIntegers` class, 378–379
`StackOverflowError`, recursion causing, 726
Stacks, case study: designing class for stacks, 378–379
`Stage`, 536, 539
State, of objects, 322–323
Statements
  `break` statements, 101
  `continue` statements, 184–185
  executing one at a time, 106
  executing repeatedly (loops), 158
  in high-level languages, 7
  `if`. *see* `if` statements
  `if-else`. *see* `if-else` statements
  `return` statements, 206
  `switch` statements, 100–101
  terminators, 13
Static methods
  in `CircleWithStaticMembers.java`, 338–339
  class design guidelines, 526–527
  declaring, 338
  defined, 338
  when to use instance methods vs. static, 338–339
  wrapper classes and, 382
Static variables
  in `CircleWithStaticMembers.java`, 338–339
  class, 337–338
  class design guidelines, 526–527
  declaring, 338
  instance variables compared with, 337
  in `TestCircleWithStaticMembers.java`, 339
  when to use instance variables vs. static, 340
Stepwise refinement
  benefits of, 232
  implementation details, 229–232
  method abstraction, 225–226
  top-down and/or bottom-up implementation, 227–229
  top-down design, 226–227
Storage devices
  CDs and DVDs, 5
  disks, 5
  overview of, 4–5
  USB flash drives, 5
Storage units, for measuring memory, 3-
`String` class, 386
String concatenation operator (+), 36
String literals, 386
String variables, 386
`StringBuffer` class, 386, 393, 397
`StringBuilder` class
  case study: ignoring nonalphanumeric characters when checking palindromes, 396–397
  modifying strings in, 393–395
  overview of, 338, 393
  `toString`, `capacity`, `length`, `setLength`, and `charAt` methods, 395–396

Strings
    in binary I/O, 684–685
    case study: checking if string is a palindrome, 187–188
    case study: converting hexadecimals to decimals, 188–189
    case study: ignoring nonalphanumeric characters when checking palindromes, 396–397
    `Character` class, 189–190
    command-line arguments, 272–275
    concatenating, 36, 130
    constructing, 386
    converting to/from arrays, 389
    finding characters or substrings in, 388–389
    formatting, 390–392
    immutable and interned, 386–387
    key terms, 275
    matching, replacing, and splitting by patterns, 388–389
    overview of, 386
    questions and exercises, 276–285
    replacing, and splitting, 387
    `string` data type, 130
    `StringBuilder` and `StringBuffer` classes, 393–396
    substrings, 37, 135–136
    summary, 275–276
    in `Welcome.java`, 12–13
Subclasses
    abstract methods and, 496
    abstracting, 500
    constructors, 416–417
    of Exception class, 456–457
    inheritance and, 410–411
    of `RuntimeException` class, 457
Subdirectories, 717
Subinterfaces, 518
`substring` method, 135, 714
Substrings, 135–136
Subtraction (-) operator, 46, 50
Subtraction (-=) assignment operator, 54–55
Sudoku puzzle, 298–301
`sum` method, 293–294
`super` keyword, 416
Superclass methods, 418–419
Superclasses
    of abstract class can be concrete, 500
    classes extending, 517
    inheritance and, 410–411
    subclasses related to, 496
Supplementary characters, Unicode, 125
`swap` method
    swapping elements in an array, 259–260
    in `TestPassByValue.java` example, 213–214
`switch` statements
    `ChineseZodiac.java` example, 102–103
    overview of, 100–101
Syntax errors (compile errors)
    common errors, 14
    debugging, 106–107
    programming errors, 20–21
Syntax rules, in `Welcome.java`, 14
System activities, role of OSs, 9
System analysis, in software development process, 59–60
System design, in software development process, 59, 61
System errors, 456
System resources, allocating, 9
`System.in`, 37
`System.out`, 37, 145–149

T

Tables, storing, 288
Tail recursion
    `ComputeFactorialTailRecusion.java`, 727–728
    overview of, 727
`tan` `method`, trigonometry, 120–121
TBs (terabytes), of storage, 4
Teamwork, facilitated by stepwise refinement, 232
Terabytes (TBs), of storage, 4
Testing
    benefits of stepwise refinement, 232
    in software development process, 60, 62–63
Text
    case study: replacing text, 480–481
    files, 678
    overview, 560
    `ShowText.java`, 561–562
    .txt files (text), 680
    `TextAreaDemo.java`, 644
    `TextFieldDemo.java`, 639–641
    `TextArea`, 641–644
    `TextField`, 639–641
Text I/O
    vs. binary I/O, 679–680
    handling in Java, 678–679
    overview of, 678
TextPad, for creating/editing Java source code, 15
`this` reference
    invoking constructors with, 357–358
    overview of, 356–358
    referencing hidden data fields with, 356–357
Three-dimensional arrays. *see* Arrays, multi-dimensional
`throw` keyword
    chained exceptions, 470
    `throw ex` for rethrowing exceptions, 469
    for throwing exceptions, 459
`Throwable` class
    getting information about exceptions, 461–462
    `java.lang`, 455–456
Throwing exceptions
    `CircleWithException.java` example, 463
    `QuotientWithException.java` example, 453
    rethrowing, 468–469
    `TestCircleWithCustomException.java` example, 471
    `throw` keyword for, 458–459
`throws` keyword
    for declaring exceptions, 458
    `IOException`, 680–681
Tic-tac-toe game, 308
`toCharArray` method, converting strings into arrays, 389
`ToggleButton`, 637
`ToggleGroup`, 637–638
Token reading methods, `Scanner` class, 479–480
Top-down design, 226–227
Top-down implementation, 227–229
`toString` method
    `ArrayList` class, 435
    `Arrays` class, 270–271
    `Date` class, 335
    `Object` class, 431
    `StringBuilder` class, 395–396
`total` variable, for storing sums, 291
Towers of Hanoi problem, computing recursively, 730
Tracing a program, 36
`transient` keyword, serialization and, 695
Transistors, CPUs, 3

`TreeSet` class, `TestTreeSetWithComparator.java` example, 504–506
Trigonometric methods, `Math` class, 120–121
True/false (Boolean) values, 76
Truth tables, 93–94
`try-catch` blocks
  catching exceptions, 457, 459–461
  chained exceptions, 469–470
  `CircleWithException.java` example, 464–465
  `InputMismatchExceptionDemo.java`
    example, 454
  `QuotientWithException.java` example, 452
  rethrowing exceptions, 468–469
  when to use exceptions, 467–468
Twin primes, 240
Two-dimensional arrays. *see* Arrays, two-dimensional
Type casting
  between `char` and numeric types, 127
  loss of precision, 65
  for numeric type conversion, 56–57

U

UML (Unified Modeling Language)
  aggregation shown in, 374
  class diagrams with, 323
  diagram for `Loan` class, 367
  diagram of `StackOfIntegers`, 378
  diagram of static variables and methods, 337–339
Unary operators, 47
Unboxing, 383
Unchecked exceptions, 457
Unconditional AND operator, 104
Underflow, floating point numbers, 66
Unicode
  character data type (`char`) and, 125–129
  data input and output streams, 685
  generating random numbers and, 223
  text encoding, 678
  text I/O vs. binary I/O, 679
Unified Modeling Language. *see* UML
  (Unified Modeling Language)
Uniform Resource Locators. *see* URLs
  (Uniform Resource Locators)
Unique addresses, for each byte of memory, 4
Universal serial bus (USB) flash drives, 5
UNIX epoch, 52
Upcasting objects, 427
`URL` class, `java.net`, 482
URLs (Uniform Resource Locators)
  `ReadFileFromURL.java` example, 483–484
  reading data from Web, 482–483
USB (universal serial bus) flash drives, 5
UTF-8, 685. *see also* Unicode

V

`valueOf` methods
  converting strings into arrays, 389
  wrapper classes and, 382
Value-returning methods
  `return` statements required by, 207
  `TestReturnGradeMethod.java`, 209–211
  `void` method and, 205

Variable-length argument lists, 264–265
Variables
  Boolean variables. *see* Boolean variables
  comparing primitive variables with reference variables, 332–334
  control variables in `for` loops, 171–172
  declaring, 35–36, 41
  declaring array variables, 246
  declaring for two-dimensional arrays, 288–289
  displaying/modifying, 106
  hidden, 355
  identifiers, 39–40
  naming conventions, 44
  overflow, 65
  overview of, 40–41
  reference variables, 330
  scope of, 41, 222–223, 355–356
  static variables, 337–338
Vertical scroll bars, 652
Vertical sliders, 654, 655
Video, `MediaDemo.java`, 663–664
Virtual machines (VMs), 16. *see also* JVM (Java Virtual Machine)
Visibility (accessibility) modifiers
  classes and, 342–343
  `protected`, `public`, and `private`, 440–442
Visual Basic, high-level languages, 8
VLSI (very large-scale integration), 706
VMs (virtual machines), 21. *see also* JVM (Java Virtual Machine)
`void` method
  defined, 205
  defining and invoking, 209
  `TestVoidMethod.java`, 209

W

Web, reading file data from, 482–484
`while` loops
  case study: guessing numbers, 161–163
  case study: multiple subtraction quiz, 164–165
  case study: predicting future tuition, 181
  deciding when to use, 174–176
  design strategies, 163
  `do-while` loop. *see* `do-while` loop
  input and output redirections, 167–168
  overview of, 158–159
  RepeatAdditionQuiz.java example, 160–161
  sentinel-controlled, 165–167
  syntax of, 158
Whitespace
  characters, 133
  as delimiter in token reading methods, 479
Wildcard import, 38
Windows. *see* Frames (windows)
Windows OSs, 9
Wireless networking, 6
Wrapper classes
  automatic conversion between primitive types and wrapper class types, 683–684
  `File` class as, 473
  numeric, 521
  primitive types and, 380–383
Wrapping lines of text or words, 641, 643
Write-only streams, 697. *see also* `OutputStream` class

Java Quick Reference

Console Input

```
Scanner input = new Scanner(System.in);
int intValue = input.nextInt();
long longValue = input.nextLong();
double doubleValue = input.nextDouble();
float floatValue = input.nextFloat();
String string = input.next();
String line = input.nextLine();
```

Console Output

```
System.out.println(anyValue);
```

Conditional Expression

```
boolean-expression ? expression1 :
  expression2

y = (x > 0) ? 1 : -1

System.out.println(number % 2 == 0 ?
  "number is even" : "number is odd");
```

Primitive Data Types

```
byte       8  bits
short      16 bits
int        32 bits
long       64 bits
float      32 bits
double     64 bits
char       16 bits
boolean    true/false
```

Arithmetic Operators

```
+          addition
-          subtraction
*          multiplication
/          division
%          remainder
++var      preincrement
--var      predecrement
var++      postincrement
var--      postdecrement
```

Assignment Operators

```
=          assignment
+=         addition assignment
-=         subtraction assignment
*=         multiplication assignment
/=         division assignment
%=         remainder assignment
```

Relational Operators

```
<          less than
<=         less than or equal to
>          greater than
>=         greater than or equal to
==         equal to
!=         not equal
```

Logical Operators

```
&&         short circuit AND
||         short circuit OR
!          NOT
^          exclusive OR
```

if Statements

```
if (condition) {
  statements;
}

if (condition) {
  statements;
}
else {
  statements;
}

if (condition1) {
  statements;
}
else if (condition2) {
  statements;
}
else {
  statements;
}
```

switch Statements

```
switch (intExpression) {
  case value1:
    statements;
    break;
  ...
  case valuen:
    statements;
    break;
  default:
    statements;
}
```

loop Statements

```
while (condition) {
  statements;
}

do {
  statements;
} while (condition);

for (init; condition;
  adjustment) {
  statements;
}
```

Java Quick Reference

Frequently Used Static Constants/Methods

```
Math.PI
Math.random()
Math.pow(a, b)
Math.abs(a)
Math.max(a, b)
Math.min(a, b)
Math.sqrt(a)
Math.sin(radians)
Math.asin(a)
Math.toRadians(degrees)
Math.toDegress(radians)
System.currentTimeMillis()
Integer.parseInt(string)
Integer.parseInt(string, radix)
Double.parseDouble(string)
Arrays.sort(type[] list)
Arrays.binarySearch(type[] list, type key)
```

Array/Length/Initializer

```
int[] list = new int[10];
list.length;
int[] list = {1, 2, 3, 4};
```

Multidimensional Array/Length/Initializer

```
int[][] list = new int[10][10];
list.length;
list[0].length;
int[][] list = {{1, 2}, {3, 4}};
```

Ragged Array

```
int[][] m = {{1, 2, 3, 4},
             {1, 2, 3},
             {1, 2},
             {1}};
```

Text File Output

```
PrintWriter output =
  new PrintWriter(filename);
output.print(...);
output.println(...);
output.printf(...);
```

Text File Input

```
Scanner input = new Scanner(
  new File(filename));
```

File Class

```
File file =
  new File(filename);
file.exists()
file.renameTo(File)
file.delete()
```

Object Class

```
Object o = new Object();
o.toString();
o.equals(o1);
```

Comparable Interface

```
c.compareTo(Comparable)
c is a Comparable object
```

String Class

```
String s = "Welcome";
String s = new String(char[]);
int length = s.length();
char ch = s.charAt(index);
int d = s.compareTo(s1);
boolean b = s.equals(s1);
boolean b = s.startsWith(s1);
boolean b = s.endsWith(s1);
boolean b = s.contains(s1);
String s1 = s.trim();
String s1 = s.toUpperCase();
String s1 = s.toLowerCase();
int index = s.indexOf(ch);
int index = s.lastIndexOf(ch);
String s1 = s.substring(ch);
String s1 = s.substring(i,j);
char[] chs = s.toCharArray();
boolean b = s.matches(regex);
String s1 = s.replaceAll(regex,repl);
String[] tokens = s.split(regex);
```

ArrayList Class

```
ArrayList<E> list = new ArrayList<>();
list.add(object);
list.add(index, object);
list.clear();
Object o = list.get(index);
boolean b = list.isEmpty();
boolean b = list.contains(object);
int i = list.size();
list.remove(index);
list.set(index, object);
int i = list.indexOf(object);
int i = list.lastIndexOf(object);
```

printf Method

```
System.out.printf("%b %c %d %f %e %s",
  true, 'A', 45, 45.5, 45.5, "Welcome");
System.out.printf("%-5d %10.2f %10.2e %8s",
  45, 45.5, 45.5, "Welcome");
```

Companion Web site: www.pearsonhighered.com/liang